ENCYCLOPEDIA OF EXPLORATION

VOLUME I

The Explorers

ENCYCLOPEDIA OF EXPLORATION
VOLUME I

The Explorers

CARL WALDMAN
AND
ALAN WEXLER

☑®

Facts On File, Inc.

Encyclopedia of Exploration, Volume I: The Explorers

Facts On File, Inc.
132 West 31st Street
New York NY 10001

Library of Congress Cataloging-in-Publication Data

Waldman, Carl.
Encyclopedia of exploration / Carl Waldman and Alan Wexler.
p. cm.
Vol. 2 by Carl Waldman and Jon Cunningham.
Includes bibliographical references and indexes.
ISBN 0-8160-4678-6 (set)
ISBN 0-8160-4676-X (v. 1) — ISBN 0-8160-4677-8 (v. 2)
1. Discoveries in geography—Encyclopedias. 2. Explorers—Biography—
Encyclopedias. 3. Voyages and travels—Encyclopedias. I. Wexler, Alan.
II. Cunningham, Jon. III. Facts On File, Inc. IV. Title.
G80.W33 2004
910'.3—dc22   2004010625

Facts On File books are available at special discounts when purchased in bulk quantities for businesses, associations, institutions, or sales promotions. Please call our Special Sales Department in New York at
(212) 967-8800 or (800) 322-8755.

You can find Facts On File on the World Wide Web at
http://www.factsonfile.com

Text design by Erika K. Arroyo
Cover design by Cathy Rincon

Printed in the United States of America

VB FOF 10 9 8 7 6 5 4 3 2 1

This book is printed on acid-free paper

For John Waldman and Frances LeFevre Waldman
—Carl Waldman

For Nathan Wexler and Minnie Wexler
—Alan Wexler

Note on Photos

Many of the illustrations and photographs used in this book are old, historical images. The quality of the prints is not always up to modern standards because in many cases the originals are from old or poor quality negatives or are damaged. The content of the illustrations, however, made their inclusion important despite problems in reproduction.

Contents

VOLUME II

List of Entries in
Volume I

List of Entries in Volume II

Preface

The term *exploration* comprises the concepts of traveling and seeking. *Discovery*, a term associated with exploration, refers to "finding." But the latter term has often been misused. One cannot "find" or "discover" a land that is already inhabited. But one can "discover" knowledge of that land and take it back to one's place of origin and pass on that knowledge. The history of exploration can therefore be characterized as the record of the diffusion of knowledge. The knowledge most relevant to exploration is geographic; how the world came to be mapped is thus central to chronicling exploration. In exploratory expeditions, information passes back and forth between continents and between cultures, affecting the realities both of the exploring and of the explored.

People have participated in exploration for a variety of reasons over the ages. Two basic human traits—curiosity and the desire for personal accomplishment—must be taken into account in all types of exploration. More specific motives include geographic and scientific inquiry, seeking a new homeland, conquest and/or colonization, commerce and profit, religious zeal, finding others who have gone missing, and searching for new literary or artistic themes. Those who explore come from diverse social and vocational backgrounds, among them, navigators, sailors, soldiers, officials, diplomats, colonists, missionaries, religious scholars, merchants, hunters, fur trappers, whalers, sealers, pirates, guides, interpreters, tribal leaders, cartographers, writers, painters, naturalists, geologists, historians, archaeologists, oceanographers, astronomers, aviators, astronauts, and mountain climbers. Some individuals contributed to exploration by promoting, organizing, and financing expeditions or by making technological breakthroughs, although they themselves may not have ventured far from their homelands.

Explorers lead fascinating, driven lives, and the stories of their expeditions are filled with adventure and danger. Many individuals have died in the pursuit of their dreams. Some have inflicted death, either directly or indirectly, on fellow explorers and especially on indigenous peoples. It can be said that explorers are at the head of the historical curve, the forerunners of good or bad. It also can be said that exploration is the starting point of many historical and cultural themes.

The explorers and the particular expeditions discussed in this work are only part of the story of exploration. Many more individuals have a role in the exploring and charting of the Earth and, in recent decades, outer space.

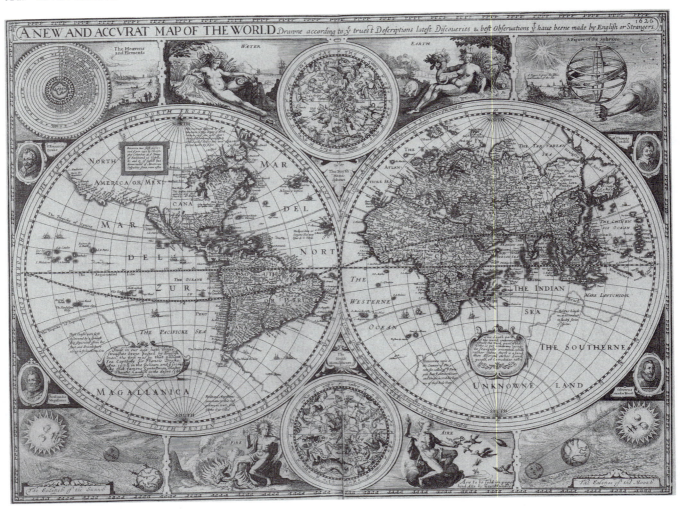

Map of the world by John Speed (1626)   (Library of Congress)

The general topics examined and the terms defined offer some context to the field of exploration, but it is important to remember that the scope of the story of exploration includes the entire historical record, and its sphere of action encompasses the entire world and the solar system. So, in chronicling exploration, particular time periods, cultures, activities, and technologies are given great weight. But one should perceive exploration as a single window into humankind's larger journey through time.

Volume I of the *Encyclopedia of Exploration* presents biographical entries about explorers, organized alphabetically. Volume II, also organized alphabetically, presents various subjects related to exploration: types of exploration, activities relating to exploration, groupings of peoples known for exploration, historical periods, organizations, legends, places, routes, natural phenomena, cartographic terms, oceanographic equipment, navigational tools, and crafts used in transportation.

In the biographical entries of Volume I, expeditions are more likely to be described in detail than in Volume II's entries. At the beginning of each biographical entry can be found the following: alternate names and spellings of names, birth and death dates (when known), nationality (and, if different, the country for whom explorations were carried out), occupations, places of the world explored, and familial relationships to other explorers with entries. After an opening discussion of the individual's background, there follows a description of his or her career in exploration and, if applicable, voyages and routes. Each entry closes with a summary of the person's accomplishments and his or her broader relevance to the history of exploration.

Some of the entries in Volume II provide overviews of historical or geographic information; others are definitions of terms relating to exploration. Geographic terms include continents, regions, islands, capes, oceans, straits, mountain ranges, mountains, mountain passes, deserts, rivers, cities, and routes. In addition to the obvious choices for geographic entries on continents and oceans, which provide overviews, some places have been selected as entries because they generated many expeditions or are central to periods of exploratory history. It should be kept in mind that other such places without their own entries have fascinating stories of exploration attached to them; many such stories can be found in Volume I (see the cumulative index).

Cross-references, indicated by a term set in SMALL CAPITAL letters the first time it appears in an entry, are meant to guide a reader/researcher through the complex material in both volumes. The cross-references run across both volumes; the reader should remember to look for entries on people in Volume I and all other entries in Volume II. A reader should understand that for the sake of convenience, not all terms that are discussed in entries in Volume II are presented as cross-references. For example, the terms *Africa* and *Atlantic Ocean* are mentioned in passing throughout the book, yet their entries appear as "Africa, exploration of" or "Atlantic Ocean, exploration of the" and are not necessarily cross-referenced. It is unlikely that a reader will choose to look up Africa for a general discussion of its geography and exploration every time the term relates peripherally to an entry. But the reader should know that Volume II includes overview entries of every continent, as well as the Arctic region and the Atlantic, Pacific, and Indian Oceans. More-specific places that have their own entries, such as the Himalayas and the Mississippi River, are cross-referenced. Certain terms, such as *colonization,* are not cross-referenced since the heading might appear as "colonization and exploration." A glance at the appendices organized by categories or the List of Entries for Volume II will help clarify questions of organization. Each volume also lists all the entries in both volumes in the "List of Entries" in the front matter.

Appendices in Volume I include a list of explorers with entries organized by region explored (with some names listed more than once, plus a section on cartographers, geographers, and sponsors where relevant); a list of explorers with entries organized chronologically by birth date; a list of explorers with entries organized by sponsoring country, or, when no sponsoring nation can be cited, by nationality or native land; and a list of explorers with entries organized by most relevant occupation. Appendices in Volume II include a chronology based on the explorations of all the individuals in Volume I, a general bibliography, and the already mentioned list of the entries organized by categories. Each volume contains a general index of the material in that volume.

Maps are essential tools in studies of exploration. The photographs of period maps that accompany some of the entries in both volumes offer a glimpse of the evolving cartographic view of the world. Original maps in an appendix in Volume II serve to illustrate the subject matter. A bibliography, in which books are listed by geographic and other general groupings, is provided to encourage and facilitate additional study of the vast and fascinating subject matter.

A to Z
Entries

Abbott, Henry Larcom (1831–1927) *U.S. Army officer in Oregon and Washington*

Henry L. Abbott, born in Beverly, Massachusetts, was educated at the Boston Latin School, then at West Point, graduating in 1854.

As a lieutenant with the U.S. Army Corps of Topographical Engineers, Abbott took part in the Pacific Railroad Surveys conducted under the auspices of Secretary of War Jefferson Davis. In spring 1855, he took command of the final phase of a U.S. Army expedition exploring the region between the Sacramento Valley, California, and Fort Walla Walla, Washington.

With a large military escort, Abbott and his command proceeded northward from the Sacramento Valley to Pit River Canyon in northeastern California, then into the Klamath River Valley. At this point, Abbott led part of the expedition north and east of the Cascade Range, along the Deschutes River to its confluence with the COLUMBIA RIVER. The rest of his command, under Lieutenant R. S. Williamson, continued northward along the western slopes of the Cascades, through the Willamette Valley, to Fort Vancouver on the Columbia River.

Abbott returned to San Francisco south along the west side of the Cascades, through the Willamette, Umpqua, and Rogue River Valleys, a region embroiled in an Indian uprising involving Tututni and Takelma bands under Chief John.

Abbott went on to take part in an engineering survey of the lower MISSISSIPPI RIVER that greatly influenced flood control measures. He served in the Civil War, during which he was brevetted a major-general of volunteers. He retired from the army in 1895 and became a leading consulting engineer in the planning of the Panama Canal 10 years later.

Henry L. Abbott *(Library of Congress)*

1

Henry L. Abbott's 1855 expedition from the Sacramento Valley into Oregon and Washington succeeded in finding two possible railroad routes from northern California into the Pacific Northwest, one east and one west of the Cascades. His official account of the expedition, *Report upon Explorations for a Railroad Route from the Sacramento Valley to the Columbia River,* was included in the U.S. government's publication *Pacific Railroad Reports,* published in 1855–60. The routes he surveyed were ultimately adopted by railroads connecting California with the Snake and Columbia River Valleys. Abbott also commented on the great agricultural potential of the region he surveyed.

Abert, James William (1820–1871) *U.S. Army officer, cartographer, artist in the American West*

Raised in the Washington, D.C., area, James W. Abert was the son of John James Abert, who organized and was the first commander of the U.S. Army's Corps of Topographical Engineers in 1838. Like his father, the younger Abert attended West Point. Soon after his commission of second lieutenant in 1842, James Abert was assigned to the Corps of Topographical Engineers.

While serving, Abert was part of Colonel STEPHEN WATTS KEARNY's expedition, in the spring and summer of 1845, from Fort Leavenworth in what is now northeastern Kansas, south and west to the Santa Fe Trail and New Mexico. Abert led a party of soldiers and topographical engineers westward across present-day Kansas, then followed the Arkansas River into present-day eastern Colorado, reaching Bent's Fort (named for WILLIAM BENT), along the Arkansas River at present-day La Junta, Colorado, on August 2, 1845.

From Bent's Fort, Abert and his men explored southward into what is now western Oklahoma and the Texas Panhandle, the domain of the Kiowa and Comanche Indians. Abert's assignment was to produce charts of the region and provide the government with a report on these tribes. The group then headed westward along the Santa Fe Trail into New Mexico.

While Abert was exploring and charting the Southwest, another detachment of topographical engineers under Kearny's command, led by JOHN CHARLES FRÉMONT, headed westward to explore the central ROCKY MOUNTAINS and the Great Salt Lake Basin.

In 1846–47, Abert undertook several expeditions into central New Mexico, until that time rarely visited by Americans or Europeans. In October 1846, he came upon the Acoma Pueblo of the Keres Indians, located near the headwaters of the Rio de San Jose, west of present-day Albuquerque, New Mexico.

In 1848, the U.S. Congress published Abert's account of his expeditions, entitled *Report of Lieutenant James W. Abert of the Examination of New Mexico in the Years 1846–47.* Abert, an artist as well as cartographer, provided original sketches of early New Mexico scenes along with the text, including life in Kiowa, Comanche, and Pueblo Indian settlements throughout present-day Oklahoma, northern Texas, and New Mexico.

James W. Abert's explorations south and west of the Arkansas River provided some of the earliest accurate maps of the Santa Fe Trail region and proved extremely useful to Kearny and his command the following year, 1846, when Kearny led U.S. troops into New Mexico, soon after the onset of the U.S.-Mexican War of 1846–48.

Abruzzi, Luigi Amedeo di Savoia d' (duca d'Abruzzi, Luigi Amedeo de Savoia, duke of Abruzzi, prince of Savoy) (1873–1933) *Italian mountain climber, explorer in Alaska, the Arctic, Africa, and Asia*

Luigi Amedeo di Savoia d'Abruzzi, was born in Madrid during the last year of the short reign of his father, King Amadeus of Spain. Raised in the rugged Abruzzi region of south-central Italy, near the Gran Sasso d'Italia range of the Apennine Mountains, Abruzzi embarked on a career of MOUNTAIN CLIMBING and exploration.

In 1897, Abruzzi made the first successful ascent of Mount Saint Elias in southeastern Alaska, which, at 18,008 feet above sea level, is one of the highest peaks in North America.

In 1899, Abruzzi commanded an Italian expedition attempting to reach the NORTH POLE. He sailed on the ship *Stella Polare* (polar star) to Franz Josef Land, the icebound archipelago off the Arctic coast of European Russia. From a point north of these islands, his chief assistant, Captain Umberto Cagni, set off across the frozen Arctic Ocean by sledge, and, in April 1900, he reached 86°34' north latitude, slightly farther north than the point reached by Arctic explorer FRIDTJOF NANSEN in 1895 and, up to that time, the closest anyone had been to the North Pole.

In 1906, Abruzzi traveled to East Africa, where he led mountaineering expeditions in the first ascents of the highest peaks in the Ruwenzori Range, associated with the fabled MOUNTAINS OF THE MOON.

In 1909, Abruzzi attempted to climb the 28,251-foot K2, then known as Mount Godwin Austen, in the Karakoram Range of the western HIMALAYAS, the second highest mountain in the world. Although Abruzzi's party did not reach its peak, at 24,600 feet they set a new record for the highest altitude attained to that time.

During World War I, Abruzzi, a high-ranking naval officer, commanded the Italian fleet in the Adriatic Sea. Afterward, in 1919, he returned to East Africa, where he spent the next 10 years exploring and colonizing the Shebeli River (Webi Shebeli) region of what is now Somalia.

Duca d' Abruzzi's accomplishments as a mountaineer and explorer encompassed four continents, from the Arctic

Ocean to the Horn of Africa. His account of his 1899–1900 attempt to reach the North Pole, *On the "Polar Star" in the Arctic Sea,* was published in 1903. Abruzzi's 1909 expedition in the western Himalayas employed photographic mapping techniques to survey a route to the top of K2. His early efforts aided the Italian mountaineering party that made the first successful ascent of K2 in 1954.

Aco, Michel (Michel Accault, Michel Accou)

(fl. 1680s–1690s) *French fur trader, interpreter on the Illinois, Wisconsin, and Mississippi Rivers*

Little is known of Michel Aco's life before he joined the initial phase of RENÉ-ROBERT CAVELIER DE LA SALLE's exploration of the MISSISSIPPI RIVER region in 1679–80. One of the French VOYAGEURS with a wide knowledge of the languages of the Illinois Indians, he became one of La Salle's most trusted lieutenants. In spring 1680, Aco accompanied La Salle from Lake Michigan to Lake Peoria and helped establish Fort Crèvecoeur on the Illinois River.

That same spring, while La Salle returned to Fort Frontenac on the eastern end of Lake Ontario, Aco, Father LOUIS HENNEPIN, and another voyageur were sent to explore the upper Mississippi River and establish a trading post at the mouth of the Wisconsin River. They descended the Illinois River to its outlet into the Mississippi, then followed that river northward to the Wisconsin. According to some sources, Aco and Hennepin were captured by the Sioux (Dakota, Lakota, Nakota) Indians near the Falls of St. Anthony, in the vicinity of what is now St. Paul, Minnesota, which they probably visited in captivity. The Indians held them as prisoners until fall 1680, when they were rescued by DANIEL GREYSOLON DULUTH at Mille Lacs Lake in present-day eastern Minnesota.

Aco settled in the Illinois River region, where he engaged in fur trading with the Indians. In 1693, he reportedly married the daughter of an Illinois chief, but there are no known details of his later life.

Michel Aco's travels with Hennepin northward up the Mississippi River to the Wisconsin River and into Minnesota complemented La Salle's explorations to the south, providing the French with greater understanding of the entire Mississippi Valley.

Acosta, José de (1539–1600) *Spanish missionary, naturalist in Peru and Mexico*

José de Acosta was probably born in Spain. In 1551, he entered the Jesuit order, and, 20 years later, he embarked for the Americas as a missionary priest to Native Americans. Starting in 1571, he spent 15 years ministering to the Inca in Peru and, for one year, to the Aztec in Mexico.

Acosta's academic background included the study of natural history. Throughout his career as a missionary in the Americas, he studied the customs and languages of Indians and made a detailed examination of the wide variety of newly discovered plants and animals.

In 1587, Acosta returned to Europe, and three years later he produced one of the earliest detailed accounts of the natural history of the Western Hemisphere, entitled *The Natural and Moral History of the Indies.* The work provides some of the first accounts of native use of coca leaf, as well as a description of the experience of altitude sickness in the high peaks of the ANDES MOUNTAINS.

José de Acosta was one of the first naturalists to note that many animal species of the Americas were unknown in Europe. His writings sparked interest in the Americas among subsequent European naturalists.

Acuña, Cristóbal de (1597–ca. 1676)

Spanish missionary on the Amazon River

Cristóbal de Acuña was a Spanish Jesuit missionary in the ANDES MOUNTAINS of Ecuador during the first half of the 17th century, serving for a time as the rector of the Jesuit college at Cuenca. When PEDRO DE TEIXEIRA arrived in Quito in 1638, after leading an expedition up the AMAZON RIVER, the Spanish viceroy assigned Acuña and another Jesuit to accompany the Portuguese explorer on his return journey downriver the following February 1639.

With Teixeira's party, Acuña crossed the Andes Mountains to the upper Amazon, then descended the river to its mouth at Para on the northeast coast of Brazil.

Cristóbal de Acuña undertook surveys and kept a record of his journey down the Amazon. His account, *New Discovery of the Great River of the Amazons,* first printed in 1639, was the earliest published description of the Amazon region.

Adair, James (ca. 1720–1783) *British trader, writer in the American Southeast*

Originally from Ireland, James Adair arrived in the North American colonies early in the 1740s. He settled on the South Carolina frontier, where he established himself as a trader to the Cherokee Indians.

In the next years, the South Carolina colonial government sponsored several of Adair's expeditions to the lands of the Choctaw and Chickasaw Indians. He was soon able to establish regular trade routes to these tribes.

Just prior to the outbreak of the American Revolution, Adair returned to London, where he wrote of his travels and experiences. *The History of the American Indians,* first published in 1775, contains observations on the life and customs of Southeast Indians. Adair was particularly impressed by the wide variety and quality of foods that Native Americans gathered from the woodlands and cultivated in their fields.

Unlike most other traders in the region, Adair was well educated, versed in Latin, Greek, and Hebrew, with a wide knowledge of ancient history. In his 1775 book, he presented the fanciful theory that North American Indians were descended from the Ten Lost Tribes of Israel as described in the Bible.

James Adair's descriptions of the South Carolina frontier and the region's tribes were among the earliest to reach British readers, informing them about the largely unexplored region inland from the seaboard settlements.

Adams, Harriet Chalmers (1875–1937)
American traveler in South America

Harriet Chalmers was born in Stockton, California. Her father was an engineer who had emigrated from Scotland and crossed the Great Plains to California in a covered wagon. Her mother was a descendant of a California pioneer family.

Although Chalmers had little in the way of formal schooling, she received a good education from her parents and from private tutors. Her desire to travel was sparked at the age of eight, when she accompanied her father on a tour through the Sierra Nevada on horseback.

In 1899, Chalmers married Franklin Pierce Adams, an electrical engineer from Stockton, who shared his new wife's interest in visiting distant places. They traveled to Mexico in 1900, where Franklin undertook an engineering survey.

In 1903, Adams and her husband began a three-year tour of South America. They visited rubber plantations in the Amazon Basin. In the Bolivian ANDES MOUNTAINS, they visited the ruins of Tiahuanaco, thought to be the oldest native settlement in the Americas. While in Bolivia, they also sailed on Lake Titicaca. In Cuzco, Peru, they visited ancient stone buildings left behind by the Inca civilization. Adams developed a great empathy for Indians of the Andes region, seeing how they had descended into poverty as a result of the Spanish conquest.

In the course of their South American sojourn, Adams and her husband traveled more than 40,000 miles in South America and made four crossings of the Andes.

In the years that followed, Adams lectured on her travels in South America, and produced articles on that region for *National Geographic* and other magazines. She made subsequent journeys to Latin America and also retraced FERDINAND MAGELLAN's epic voyage from Spain to the Philippines. Her observations and studies of Indians of the Americas led her to become one of the earliest proponents of the theory that they had originally come from Asia. In her later travels, she retraced the explorations of the Spanish CONQUISTADORES in the WEST INDIES and in South America, and in so doing visited almost every country in Latin America. She also visited central Asia, including the GOBI DESERT. In 1913, she was elected as a Fellow of the ROYAL GEOGRAPHICAL SOCIETY; in 1925, she became the first president of the Society of Women Geographers.

In a *New York Times* article of 1912, when Harriet Chalmers Adams was questioned on why men had dominated the field of exploration, she commented that in her own travels into uncharted lands she had never faced a difficulty or a danger that she could not surmount just because she was a woman.

Adams, William (Will Adams, Anjin Sama, "Mr. Pilot") (ca. 1564–1620) *English mariner in Japan, in service to Dutch and Japanese*

William Adams was born in Gillingham, Kent, a small seaport on the southeast coast of England. At the age of 12, he embarked on a seafaring career, serving with British merchant ships on voyages to the BARBARY COAST, and later with the Royal Navy.

By 1598, Adams had acquired a substantial knowledge of shipbuilding, mathematics, and navigation. That year, he was engaged as a pilot major by Dutch admiral James Mahu for a trading expedition to the EAST INDIES, the islands that now compose Indonesia and the Moluccas. Adams sailed from Rotterdam with the Dutch fleet of five ships in June 1599. The expedition was beset with hardship. Admiral Mahu died in the Cape Verde Islands off the west coast of Africa. Then the ships were separated in a storm while attempting to reach the Pacific Ocean through the STRAIT OF MAGELLAN at the tip of South America. Adams's ship and two others reached the Mocha Islands off the coast of Chile, where Simon de Cordes, the surviving commander of the expedition, was killed in a clash with local people. Adams and the three remaining ships then headed westward across the Pacific for Japan, intending to trade their cargo there.

Only Adams and his ship, the *Liefde*, managed to reach Japan, arriving in 1600 at Oita on the northeast coast of Kyushu, the southernmost of Japan's main islands. Adams was taken into custody by Japanese military leader Iyeyasu, who compelled him to work for the Japanese in directing maritime affairs, including the construction of ships. Three years later, in 1603, aided by Adams, Iyeyasu became shogun, the military ruler of Japan.

Adams remained in the service of the Japanese for the next 17 years. Although at first not permitted to leave Japan, he eventually rose to prominence as a trusted naval adviser to the shogun. He took part in trading expeditions to the Ryukyu Islands south of Okinawa and traveled to ports in Southeast Asia in present-day Thailand and Vietnam.

In 1613, Adams succeeded in winning a trade concession for the BRITISH EAST INDIA COMPANY, represented by JOHN SARIS. He was subsequently granted a royal title, Anjin Sama (Mr. Pilot), and was rewarded with an estate near Yokosuka. Adams married a Japanese woman and spent the rest of his life in Japan. His logbook was first published in 1850, and his letters in 1916. A street was named after him in Tokyo, where a festival is held in his honor each year.

William Adams was the first Englishman to visit Japan. With his Western expertise as a mariner and shipbuilder, he contributed significantly to the rise of Iyeyasu as shogun and the establishment of a dynasty that ruled Japan for 250 years. Through his influence, the DUTCH EAST INDIA COMPANY was able to maintain a trading foothold in Japan after all other foreign traders were expelled in 1640.

Africanus, Leo   See LEO AFRICANUS.

Agricola, Gnaeus Julius (Cneius Julius Agricola) (ca. 37–93) *Roman general in Britain*

Gnaeus Julius Agricola was born in Forum Julii, a port of the ROMANS on the MEDITERRANEAN SEA, near present-day Frejus and St. Tropez, France. In A.D. 59–61, he served in Britain under SUETONIUS PAULINUS. Agricola returned to the European continent and continued his military career in campaigns in Europe and the Middle East. He rose to the rank of general and served as a magistrate in Roman provinces in Asia Minor. In 74, Agricola was appointed governor of Aquitania in what is now southwestern France. Three years later, he was named governor of Britain.

In 80, Agricola launched a military campaign that pushed Roman conquests northward into Scotland. Under his leadership, the Great North Road—the Romans' main military highway that originated at Ermine Street in present-day London—was extended north of York across the river Tyne to the Tweed in what is now southeastern Scotland.

Beyond the Tweed, troops under Agricola's command built smaller military roads penetrating Scotland above Edinburgh and the Firth of Forth, as far as the Roman outpost at Inchtuthil. From there, Agricola staged his campaign against the Caledonians, culminating in his victory in the Battle of Mons Graupius in 83.

Agricola also directed Roman naval operations in Britain in 77–84. Under his command, the Roman fleet sailed along the east coast of Britain as far north as the Orkney Islands. According to some accounts, the Roman GALLEY ships then proceeded south along the west coast, completing the first recorded circumnavigation of Britain. In 84, Agricola was preparing for a military expedition to Ireland, when he was recalled by Emperor Domitian.

Gnaeus Julius Agricola was immortalized in a biography by his son-in-law, the Roman historian Tacitus. As a military leader and governor, Agricola carried Roman civilization to Britain and pacified most of what is now England, northern Wales, and southern Scotland. He extended the Great North Road well into Scotland. This vital transportation link helped maintain Roman domination of Britain for more than 350 years. Great Britain's present-day north-south highway, the A-1, closely follows the route established by Agricola's army.

Aguirre, Lope de (ca. 1510–1561)
Spanish conquistador in Peru and Venezuela
Lope de Aguirre was probably born in Spain. Arriving in Peru in about 1544, he worked as a horse trainer and later became involved in warfare between rival factions of CONQUISTADORES, during which he developed a reputation for cruelty and unbridled violence.

In 1560, Aguirre joined an expedition led by PEDRO DE URSÚA in search of EL DORADO, a fabled native kingdom of great wealth, which the Spaniards believed lay somewhere in the Amazon Basin. He left Lima with Ursúa's contingent of 300 men in July 1560. After crossing the ANDES MOUNTAINS and following the Huallaga and Marañón Rivers, the expedition reached the AMAZON RIVER. In December 1560, along the Amazon, near the mouth of the Putumayo River, Aguirre incited a mutiny and murdered Ursúa, as well as his second in command, an officer named Don Fernando de Guzmán.

Aguirre led the mutineers down the Amazon, probably crossing to the ORINOCO RIVER by way of the Negro River. They laid waste to several Indian villages along the way. The party eventually reached the Caribbean coast of present-day Venezuela. They captured the island of Margarita above the mouth of the Orinoco, from which Aguirre planned to lead an attack against royal Spanish forces in Panama. Crossing to the mainland, his men were besieged in the northwestern Venezuelan city of Barquisimeto. Before surrendering, Aguirre murdered his own daughter. He was beheaded, and his body was cut in quarters and displayed as a warning to all would-be rebels.

Lope de Aguirre had one of the bloodiest careers of all the conquistadores in South America. His advance in 1561 from the Andes to the Caribbean Sea amounted to the second-known successful crossing of the South American continent, 20 years after FRANCISCO DE ORELLANA's expedition.

Akeley, Carl Ethan (1864–1926)
American naturalist, taxidermist, photographer in East and central Africa, founder of modern taxidermy, husband of Delia Denning Akeley and Mary Kobe Akeley
Born in Clarendon, western New York, south of Lake Ontario, Carl Akeley spent time as a youth in the neighboring woods and was introduced to taxidermy methods. At the age of 19, he became an assistant at Ward's Natural Science Establishment, working there for three years. In 1886–88, he was a self-employed taxidermist in Milwaukee, Wisconsin,

then was hired as the taxidermist for the Milwaukee Public Museum in 1888. In 1895, he switched his focus to natural science, first at the Field Museum of Natural History in Chicago, then at the American Museum of Natural History in New York City in 1909. He also worked in sculpture and photography.

Akeley traveled to Kenya with his first wife, DELIA JULIA DENNING AKELEY, in 1905–06, hunting specimens for the Field Museum. They returned to Africa again in 1909–11, going on safaris in the Belgian Congo (present-day Democratic Republic of the Congo) for the American Museum of Natural History. Akeley designed displays with realistic backdrops, which later became part of the latter museum's Akeley Hall of African Mammals. He returned to Africa in 1921–22. In 1923, he published *In Brightest Africa*. Akeley again traveled to the Belgian Congo with his second wife, MARY LEONORE JOBE AKELEY, in 1926.

In 1926, along with the support of King Albert I of Belgium, Akeley helped found Africa's first wild game preserve, named the Parc National Albert (now the Virunga National Park), as a sanctuary for the area's mountain gorillas and other fauna. Akeley died of tropical fever on this expedition and was buried on Mount Mikeno in the preserve.

Carl Akeley was one of the first Americans to travel extensively in wilderness areas of East Africa and central Africa. He devised new methods of taxidermy—sculpting lifelike bodies around skeletal mounts that consisted of bone, wood, paper, wire, and specially formulated cement—and new types of museum displays depicting habitat based on photography. In addition to 38 tools for taxidermists, he designed a lightweight motion-picture camera for shooting wildlife. Akeley's accomplishments led to a big-game hunting expedition with U.S. president Theodore Roosevelt.

Akeley, Delia Julia Denning (Mickie Akeley)

(1875–1970) *American naturalist in East Africa, wife of Carl Ethan Akeley*

Delia Akeley, née Denning, also known by her nickname, Mickie, grew up in Beaver Dam, Wisconsin. At the age of 13, she ran away from home and never saw her parents again. An aspiring naturalist, she worked as an assistant to the naturalist and taxidermist CARL ETHAN AKELEY, first in Milwaukee, then at the Field Museum of Natural History in Chicago. She married him in 1902.

Three years later, in 1905, the Akeleys set out to Kenya for the purpose of collecting specimens and stayed 18 months. On the safaris, Delia participated in the hunt, becoming skillful with a rifle and shooting an elephant now on display at the Field Museum. Returning to Africa in 1909–11, the Akeleys explored the Belgian Congo (present-day Democratic Republic of the Congo), her husband in the employ of the American Museum of Natural History in

New York at that time. Because Carl was sick for much of this second visit, Akeley oversaw many of the day-to-day responsibilities.

The couple was divorced in 1923. Akeley continued her career in natural science and returned to Africa in 1924–25, collecting for the Brooklyn Museum of Arts and Sciences. She departed from Lamu, Kenya, on the Indian Ocean, crossed Uganda and the Belgian Congo, then traveled along the CONGO RIVER (Zaire River) to Boma, eventually reaching the Atlantic coast. She journeyed by CANOE as well as camel. In the Belgian Congo, she lived among the peoples of the Ituri Forest and studied their hunting and fishing techniques. She visited Africa again in 1929–30.

Delia Akeley, in 1924–25, became the first known non-African woman to cross Africa coast to coast. Her writings about her African experiences include the book *Jungle Por-*

Delia Akeley *(Library of Congress)*

traits (1928). Her study of baboon colonies on her second trip to Africa with Carl Akeley set a precedent among women naturalists of working with primates. She kept a pet monkey late in life.

Akeley, Mary Leonore Jobe (1886–1966)
American naturalist, photographer, geographer in the Canadian Northwest and Africa, wife of Carl Ethan Akeley

Mary Akeley, née Jobe, was born and raised on her parents' farm in Tappan, Ohio. She studied at Bryn Mawr College and Columbia University, then taught history at Hunter College. In 1916, she bought property in Mystic, Connecticut, where she ran a camp for girls, ages eight to 18, which operated from 1916 to 1930.

When in her 20s, Jobe was commissioned by the Canadian government to study the native peoples of the Canadian Northwest. She also charted the headwaters of the Fraser River and parts of the Canadian ROCKY MOUNTAINS and climbed Mount Sir Alexander. For her work in British Columbia, she was elected to the ROYAL GEOGRAPHICAL SOCIETY in 1915.

In 1924, she married the naturalist and taxidermist CARL ETHAN AKELEY after his divorce the year before from DELIA JULIA DENNING AKELEY. With him, in 1926, she traveled to the Belgian Congo (present-day Democratic Republic of the Congo) and helped him hunt specimens and photograph animals and their habitat for the American Museum of Natural History in New York City. Her husband died on this expedition, and Akeley continued their work, exploring in Kenya and Tanganyika (present-day Tanzania). On her return to the United States, she became an adviser for the Akeley Hall of African Mammals, in New York's natural history museum, which opened 10 years later.

Akeley received from King Albert of Belgium the Cross of the Knight, Order of the Crown, for her work in Africa on behalf of the wildlife preserve her husband had helped found. Her books include *Carl Akeley's Africa* (1929); *Lions, Gorillas and Their Neighbors* (1932); and *Congo Eden* (1950). She returned to Africa in 1952, visiting her husband's grave on Mount Mikeno. She died in Mystic, Connecticut, in 1966.

Mary Akeley was one of the earliest women explorers in the Canadian Northwest and parts of Africa. She oversaw some of the last museum taxidermy. In subsequent years after the completion of Akeley Hall, observation of mammals in the field and recording their behavior on film and videotape became the chosen ways of documenting them. The Geographical Board of Canada named Mount Jobe in the Rockies in her honor.

Akkad, Sargon of   See SARGON.

Alarcón, Hernando de (1500–unknown)
Spanish conquistador in the Gulf of California and on the lower Colorado River

In 1540, Hernando de Alarcón was given command of three ships to carry supplies to FRANCISCO VÁSQUEZ DE CORONADO's expedition in the present-day American Southwest. The expedition's organizer, Spanish viceroy ANTONIO DE MENDOZA, also instructed Alarcón to sail northward along the coast in search of the Seven Cities of CIBOLA, the fabled civilization believed to lie north of Mexico at the edge of Asia.

In summer 1540, Alarcón and his fleet sailed from the mouth of the Río Grande de Santiago, near the port city of San Blas on Mexico's Pacific coast, and proceeded into the Gulf of California. At the head of the gulf, he noted the outflow of a river. In 1539, FRANCISCO DE ULLOA had observed the same currents but had not positively identified their source nor explored more than a short distance upstream. Skillfully piloting his ships through the sand bars and shallows, Alarcón entered the stream and recognized that the flow came from a river, which he called the Río de la Buena Guía, meaning "river of the good guide." He navigated what became known as the COLORADO RIVER about 50 miles up river to a point where it became impassable for his ships. From there, he continued his explorations in small boats.

Alarcón soon made contact with the Yuma (Quechan) Indians, with whom he established friendly relations. He made two journeys up the Colorado. On the second one, he reached a point near the mouth of the Gila River. By then, news of Coronado's conquest of Pueblo Indians in western New Mexico had reached Alarcón and the Indians on the lower Colorado. Alarcón attempted to lead his men overland to join Coronado, but they refused to cross the region because of reports of hostile tribes.

Alarcón, believing he would be unable to rendezvous with the main body of Coronado's forces, left a message beneath a stone monument below the mouth of the Gila, at a point where the main Indian trail from the east crossed the Colorado. He then returned to his ships and sailed back to Mexico. Several weeks later, MELCHOR DÍAZ, one of Coronado's lieutenants, reached the Colorado and found Alarcón's message.

Hernando de Alarcón is credited with being the first non-Indian to explore above the mouth of the Colorado River. He traveled 200 miles up the river; the territory beyond would remain unexplored by Europeans for the next 300 years. His expedition in 1540 was one of the first to report that Baja California was not an island, as was commonly thought, but a long peninsula. Yet his finding would not be confirmed until the explorations of Father EUSEBIO FRANCISCO KINO in the early 18th century.

Albanel, Charles (ca. 1613–1696) *French missionary in French Canada*

Charles Albanel was born in Auvergne, France, in either 1613 or 1616. He studied to be a Jesuit priest, entering the order's novitiate in Toulouse in 1633, after which he served in a number of different French villages.

When in his 30s, Albanel traveled to New France. Starting in 1649, he began working with fellow Jesuit Jean de Quen at the Tadoussac mission to Indians (mostly Montagnais) on the Saguenay River north of Quebec City. It is thought that in 1659–60, Albanel accompanied PIERRE-ESPRIT RADISSON and MÉDARD CHOUART DES GROSEILLIERS on an expedition to Lake Superior and the headwaters of the MISSISSIPPI RIVER; after returning to Montreal, he set out with the Indians once again to their homeland. In the mid-1660s, Albanel served as a chaplain to French troops, traveling with them in actions against the Iroquois (Haudenosaunee) Indians around Lake Champlain and helping negotiate peace agreements.

On learning of an English presence in HUDSON BAY, following the founding of the HUDSON'S BAY COMPANY in 1670, French officials dispatched Albanel and fellow Frenchmen Paul Denis de Saint-Simon and Sébastien Provencher to the region. They traveled from Tadoussac westward to Lac Saint Jean in August 1671, where they spent the winter. The following June, by CANOE, with 16 Montagnais Indian guides, they set out northwestward to Lake Mistassini, then westward along Lake Nemiskau and down the Rupert River to James Bay, the southeastern extent of Hudson Bay. At the mouth of the Rupert, they spotted an English ship and two empty buildings—the English presumably on a hunting expedition—and met with Indians living nearby in the hope of preventing their trade with the English. Albanel returned to Tadoussac in August 1672.

In 1673, Albanel, about 60 years old, endured the hardships of another trip to Hudson Bay in response to continuing reports of English presence. On this trip, he was taken prisoner by the English on James Bay and sent to England. After agreeing not to attempt to undermine English trade relations with the Indians of Hudson Bay, Albanel was allowed to return to France. By 1676, he was back in Quebec and was appointed superior of the St. Francis Xavier mission (at present-day De Pere, Wisconsin). He died in 1696 at Sault Sainte Marie in present-day Michigan.

Charles Albanel was among the earliest Europeans to travel the overland route to Hudson Bay. This was the first such expedition, unless Radisson's claimed trip of 1660 to James Bay from Lake Superior did in fact take place.

al-Biruni, Abu ar-Rayhan Muhammad ibn Ahmad   See BIRUNI, ABU AR-RAYHAN MUHAMMAD IBN AHMAD AL-.

Albuquerque, Afonso de (Alphonso d'Albuquerque, Afonso do Albuquerque, Alfonso the Great) (1453–1515) *Portuguese naval officer in the Indian Ocean, India, and Indonesia*

Afonso de Albuquerque was born near Lisbon, Portugal, into a noble Portuguese family. After spending his early years at the court of King Alfonso V the African, he embarked on a naval career, taking part in the Portuguese conflicts with Muslim powers in the MEDITERRANEAN SEA and off the coast of Morocco.

Albuquerque became a leading officer in the Portuguese navy, eventually achieving the rank of admiral. In 1503, he made his first trip around the CAPE OF GOOD HOPE to India, under the sponsorship of the Portuguese monarch Manuel II.

In 1506, with Tristão da Cunha, Albuquerque sailed again for the EAST INDIES. He explored the east coast of Africa, visiting the island of Madagascar, plus the port of Mombasa on the coast of what is now Kenya. Albuquerque assumed command of part of the Portuguese fleet as it approached the Persian Gulf, then launched a military campaign against the Muslim-held island of Hormuz, as well as against the island of Socotra in the Gulf of Aden. In 1507, Albuquerque established the first Portuguese outpost in Asia, on Hormuz. Although forced to abandon Hormuz soon afterward, he ultimately succeeded in retaking this important trading center along the SPICE ROUTE to the Far East by 1515.

In 1509, Albuquerque replaced FRANCISCO DE ALMEIDA as Portuguese viceroy in India, and, in 1510, he led a successful military expedition against Goa and other ports on southwestern India's Malabar Coast. A map provided by a Javanese pilot, detailing the Indian Ocean and the islands of present-day Indonesia, aided Albuquerque in his 1511 conquest of Malacca at the southern end of the Malay Peninsula. This victory wrested from the Muslim powers control of the Strait of Malacca, the main sea route between the Indian Ocean and the South China Sea, providing the Portuguese with direct access to the SPICE ISLANDS (the Moluccas) and the ports of Japan and China.

Portuguese court intrigues led to Albuquerque's removal as viceroy of India in 1515. Although he was restored to this office before long, Albuquerque died of dysentery off the coast of Goa on his way back from his final victory at Hormuz, before he could resume command.

Afonso de Albuquerque's exploits in the Indian Ocean, the Persian Gulf, and the Strait of Malacca expanded Portuguese domination of the sea route from Europe, around the tip of Africa, to China, Japan, and the Spice Islands. His victory at Goa in 1510–11 secured Portuguese control of this Malabar Coast port for the next 450 years. Among the early Portuguese seafarers who ventured around the Cape of Good

Hope to India and Southeast Asia, he was known as "Afonso the Great." In recognition of his military successes, Albuquerque was also dubbed the "Portuguese Mars."

Alexander the Great (Alexander III of Macedonia) (356–323 B.C.) *king of Macedonia, military leader in Asia and North Africa*

Alexander, the son of the Macedonian king Philip II, was born in Pella, the ancient capital of Macedonia (Macedon). His early years were spent under the tutelage of the Greek philosopher Aristotle.

In 336 B.C., Philip was assassinated, and Alexander, then 20 years old, assumed the throne. After consolidating his rule over the Greek states, he undertook, in 334, a military campaign against the Persian Empire to the east.

Alexander's army, about 35,000 strong (although some sources say 65,000), crossed the Hellespont (the Dardanelles) from Greece into what is now Turkey and defeated a Persian force under Darius III at the Granicus River. He proceeded along the east shore of the MEDITERRANEAN SEA, then inland into Asia Minor, conquering all the territory as far as present-day Ankara, Turkey.

Alexander and his army continued southward into present-day Lebanon where he captured the Phoenician city of Tyre. Then, in 332, he headed west along the northern coast of the Sinai Peninsula into Egypt, which he conquered with little resistance. That same year, he established Alexandria on Egypt's northern Mediterranean shore.

In 331, Alexander's army crossed into Syria and soon reached the Tigris and Euphrates Rivers. At the battle of Gaugamela in what is now northern Iraq, he decisively defeated the Persians. Alexander pushed northeastward across present-day Iran in pursuit of the Persian army. South of the Caspian Sea, he crossed the Elburz Mountains by way of a pass known as the Caspian Gates, or the Sirdar Pass. Following the south coast of the Caspian Sea, he led his army across northern Iran to the Gurgan River. From there he headed south and east, entering what is now Afghanistan. En route, he established Alexandria in Ariis (modern Herat, Afghanistan) and Alexandria Arachosia (near modern Kandahar, Afghanistan).

Turning northeast in 329, Alexander and his victorious army entered the Kabul Valley. At the foot of the Hindu Kush range, which he believed to be part of the Caucasus Mountains, he founded the city of Alexandria ad Caucasum. Still in pursuit of the Persians, he crossed the Hindu Kush, probably by way of 11,650-foot-high Khawak Pass, and entered what is now Uzbekistan.

In the southern Russian steppes, Alexander crossed north and east to the Amu Darya, then known as the Oxus River, and conquered the ancient cities of Balkh and Samarkand. He continued northeastward as far as the Syr

Alexander the Great *(Library of Congress)*

Darya River (known in ancient times as the Jaxartes), where he established Alexandria Eschate, the site of what became Leninabad. This settlement was the farthest eastern reach of Alexander's travels.

From Alexandria Eschate, Alexander and his forces moved south across Afghanistan and, in 327, recrossed the Hindu Kush into India, reaching the INDUS RIVER. He led his army across the Indus to the Jhelum River (the ancient Hydaspes) and reached the Beas River (the ancient Hyphasis). Although his army defeated the Indian forces on the Jhelum, his men refused to proceed, fearing the unknown lands to the east. Alexander had planned to conquer the rest of India, as far as the GANGES RIVER, but with his troops on the verge of mutiny, he decided to return west.

After having a fleet of 200 ships built on the Jhelum, Alexander led his army down the river in autumn 325. They reached the Indus and descended to its mouth in the Arabian Sea near present-day Karachi, Pakistan. Alexander sent part of his army aboard 150 ships, under the command of NEARCHUS, on an expedition westward along the coast of the Arabian Sea as far as the mouths of the Tigris and Euphrates Rivers at the head of the Persian Gulf. He led the rest of his army through the desert region of southern Baluchistan back to the Mesopotamian cities of Susa and Babylon. The overland journey was fraught with hardship; it is estimated that Alexander lost thousands of his men to thirst. Moreover, thousands of the camp followers were drowned in desert flash floods.

By 324, Alexander had returned to Persia and undertook explorations of the Tigris River into what is now Iraq. He planned to undertake a seaward exploration around the Arabian Peninsula and may have intended a circumnavigation of Africa. Before he could embark, however, he contracted a fever, probably resulting from malaria, following a 10-day drinking bout, and died in June 323 B.C. Soon afterward, his empire fell into disarray.

Alexander the Great, as he was known after his unprecedented conquest of the Middle East and central Asia, extended European geographic knowledge as far as India. His army traversed 20,000 miles of territory in Europe, Africa, and Asia, including many regions unknown to the Greeks and other Mediterranean civilizations. Traveling with his army were scientists, who sent back to Greece samples of newly discovered plants and animals. In addition, his forces were accompanied by *bematists,* early surveyors who measured his route. Subsequent accounts of Alexander's conquests provided the Hellenistic world with a knowledge of Asia and led to increased contact with India and China. His route across modern Iran, south of the Caspian Sea, became a vital link in the Silk Road, an important trade route in ancient times between China and the eastern Mediterranean.

Alfinger, Ambrosius (Ambrose Alfinger, Ambrosius Dalfinger, Ambrosio Ehinger)

(unknown–1533) *German colonial leader in northern South America*

Ambrosius Alfinger was from the German duchy of Swabia. In 1528, the German banking family of Welser sponsored a colonizing expedition of some 300 settlers to what is now Venezuela in South America, following a land grant to them by Charles I, king of Spain (Holy Roman Emperor Charles V).

It was hoped that expeditions launched from the colony might locate a short route to the Pacific Ocean. Reports about EL DORADO, a fabled land of great riches, provided additional incentive for explorations. After establishing the coastal settlement of Coro in 1529, Alfinger explored the country around Lake Maracaibo. In 1531, he set out from Coro and reached Tamalameque on the Magdalena River in present-day Colombia. He also explored the Sagamoso River. On the return journey in 1533, he was killed in a skirmish with Indians in the Chinácota Valley.

Ambrosius Alfinger, together with fellow Germans NIKOLAUS FEDERMANN and GEORG HOHERMUTH VON SPEYER, who also explored the plains of Venezuela and Colombia, was one of the few northern Europeans to play a part in the exploration of South America.

al-Idrisi, Abu Abd Allah Muhammad ash-Sharif   See IDRISI, ABU ABD ALLAH MUHAMMED ASH-SHARIF AL-.

Allen, Henry Tureman (1859–1930) *U.S. Army officer in Alaska*

Originally from Sharpsburg, Kentucky, Henry T. Allen graduated from West Point in 1882 and was assigned to the Washington Territory under the command of General Nelson A. Miles. Three years later, he was sent on a mission to explore the interior of Alaska. In spring 1885, with a small party of enlisted men and civilian prospectors, Lieutenant Allen undertook an expedition into Alaska's Copper River region. Traveling overland and by CANOE, Allen and his group explored the Copper, Koyukuk, and Yukon Rivers in eastern Alaska, plus their tributaries the Tanana and Chitina Rivers. While exploring the Copper River Basin, the expedition traveled through the Wrangell Mountains northeast of present-day Cordova, Alaska, the site of the present-day Wrangell-St. Elias National Park.

Allen went on to become commander of U.S. forces occupying Germany from 1919 to 1923.

In addition to providing important topographic information and an early survey of the region's natural resources, Henry T. Allen's 1885 expedition resulted in some of the earliest official U.S. government contact with eastern Alaska's natives. The expedition also led to the establishment of a railroad link between Cordova on the Gulf of Alaska and the mineral-rich Copper River Basin.

Allouez, Claude-Jean (1622–1689)
French missionary in the Great Lakes region and the upper Mississippi River

A native of St. Didier, France, Claude-Jean Allouez became a Jesuit at the age of 17. In 1658, he arrived in North America as a missionary priest to Native Americans of the St. Lawrence River region. He spent the next seven years at Trois Rivières and Montreal, and then, as the Jesuit vicar general of the Northwest, he traveled westward to establish a mission to the Algonquian tribes of the western Great Lakes. On the southwestern end of Lake Superior, near present-day Ashland, Wisconsin, he founded the Chequamegon Bay Mission.

In 1665–67, Allouez explored, by CANOE, the south shore of Lake Superior and produced for the Jesuits an early map of this lake, the largest freshwater body of water in the world. From Illinois and Miami Indians, he learned of a large river that ran to the sea. Allouez incorrectly believed that this river's outlet was somewhere on the Virginia coast.

In 1669, Allouez founded the De Père Jesuit mission near present-day Green Bay, Wisconsin where JEAN NICOLET had established a fur-trading post 35 years earlier. That year, Allouez also explored the Fox and Wisconsin Rivers, later speculating they were tributaries of the "Messipi," the great river he had heard about from the Indians. He was the first European to refer to this river by this name, later known as the MISSISSIPPI RIVER.

In 1677, Allouez became head of the Jesuit mission in the Illinois River Indian settlement at Kaskaskia, near Starved Rock, formerly headed by Father JACQUES MARQUETTE. He remained in the upper Mississippi Valley, ministering to area Indians for the remainder of his life. He died on the St. Joseph River, near present-day South Bend, Indiana.

Claude-Jean Allouez's explorations in the western Great Lakes and upper Mississippi River Valley provided a basis for the 1673 Mississippi expedition of LOUIS JOLLIET and Marquette. Allouez is said to have preached to 22 tribes and to have baptized some 10,000 Indians, and has been referred to historically as the "Founder of Christianity in the West." The Wisconsin city of Allouez on the Fox River, at the south end of Green Bay on the west shore of Lake Michigan, was named in his honor.

Almagro, Diego de (ca. 1478–1538)

Spanish conquistador in Peru and Chile

Diego de Almagro was born in the town of Almagro in central Spain. He was of humble origins, having been abandoned as an infant on the steps of a local church.

Little else is known of his life before 1514, the year he accompanied PEDRO ARIAS DE ÁVILA on an expedition to Panama. Almagro became associated with FRANCISCO PIZARRO, with whom he entered into a partnership for the exploration and conquest of what is now Peru. From 1524 to 1528, he explored the northwest coast of South America in conjunction with Pizarro, taking part in military campaigns against Indians. In one encounter in 1525, he was wounded and lost an eye as well as some fingers.

Almagro provided financial support for Pizarro's 1531 expedition against the Inca Indians. In 1533, he took part in the campaign that secured Quito in present-day Ecuador. Later that year, Almagro arrived at Cajamarca, Peru, where he joined Pizarro with a force of 200 men and played an important role in the conquest of the Inca. Although he received no gold for his participation, he was granted governorship of the lands south of Cuzco.

A conflict between Almagro and Pizarro was averted when, in December 1534, Almagro was appointed governor of the newly organized Peruvian province of New Toledo and given permission to lead an expedition of conquest southward.

Almagro, with a force of about 750 Spaniards and thousands of allied Indians, left Cuzco, northwest of Lake Titicaca, in July 1535. Inspired by reports of a civilization rich in gold and other valuables, Almagro led his men southward along the central ANDES MOUNTAINS into what is now Bolivia and northern Argentina. Having set out in the midst of the South American winter season, the Spanish suffered great hardships in the severe cold of the high Andes. At the San Francisco Pass, the expedition turned westward and reached the coastal Copiapó Valley. Almagro and his men continued southward along the coastal plain of present-day Chile into the Central Valley. Along the way, they were repeatedly attacked by Araucanian Indians. One of his lieutenants, Gómez de Alvarado, explored southward to the Itata River, north of what is now the city of Concepcíon. Failing to locate an advanced civilization comparable to the Inca, Almagro decided to head back northward to Peru. The return journey took the Spanish through the Atacama Desert, along the north coast of Chile, where many died of thirst.

By early 1537, Almagro had reached Arequipa in southern Peru, and from there he recrossed the Andes to

Diego de Almagro *(Library of Congress)*

Cuzco. At Cuzco, he found the Inca, under Manco, in open revolt against the Spanish. Almagro succeeded in suppressing the uprising but became embroiled in a conflict with Francisco Pizarro and his brother HERNANDO PIZARRO over who had the right to rule Cuzco and the northern provinces of Peru. Forces under Hernando Pizarro captured Almagro at Cuzco in April 1538. He was put to death by the garrote; his body was then publicly beheaded in the town square. In 1541, Almagro's half-Indian son, Diego, known as "the Lad," led a campaign against the Pizarros and, in revenge for his father's death, killed Francisco Pizarro.

Diego de Almagro's exploration south of Peru into Chile extended Spanish domination along the west coast of South America. On his return journey, he led his men on the first European crossing of the Atacama Desert.

al-Masudi, Abu al-Husan Ali   See MASUDI, ABU AL-HUSAN ALI AL-.

Almeida, Francisco de (1450–1510) *Portuguese admiral in East Africa and India, Portugal's first viceroy of India, father of Lourenço de Almeida*

Born in Lisbon, Portugal, Francisco de Almeida was related to Portuguese royalty. Under Afonso V the African, he served as a soldier and diplomat. In 1492, in conjunction with Spanish forces, he took part in the conquest of the Moorish-held city of Granada.

By 1493, Almeida was a leading admiral in the Portuguese navy. That year, before reaching Spain, CHRISTOPHER COLUMBUS stopped in Lisbon for ship repairs and reported his discoveries to Portugal's King John II. King John, believing that Columbus had reached the outlying islands of Asia, organized his own expedition, under Almeida's command, intended to thwart Spanish encroachment upon Portugal's rich trade with India. Almeida's proposed voyage was canceled, however, when the 1494 Treaty of Tordesillas secured Portugal's interests in Africa and India.

In 1503, Almeida commanded a Portuguese fleet sailing around Africa to India, where he succeeded in gaining a Portuguese trade foothold on the southwest coast, known as the Malabar Coast, by defeating the naval forces of the ruler of Calicut.

Almeida's second voyage to India began in 1505. Under King Manuel I, he commanded a Portuguese fleet of 22 ships that sailed around the CAPE OF GOOD HOPE into the Indian Ocean. His son LOURENÇO DE ALMEIDA accompanied him. Along the east coast of Africa, Almeida established Portuguese forts and trading bases at Sofala, Moçambique, and Kilwa. He then attacked Mombasa, destroying most of that city and establishing Portuguese domination of the route around the Cape of Good Hope from Europe to India. Almeida, who had been appointed Portugal's first viceroy of India, reached Cochin on India's Malabar coast, where he established trade relations.

Over the next years, Almeida defended Arab and Egyptian challenges to the Portuguese presence in India, culminating in a decisive victory in the naval battle at Diu in 1509, off the northwest coast of India, during which Almeida's 19 ships, aided by superior firepower, defeated a combined Muslim fleet of more than 100 vessels.

Later in 1509, Almeida was replaced as viceroy in India by AFONSO DE ALBUQUERQUE. On his return voyage to Portugal, Almeida stopped at Saldanha, just north of the Cape of Good Hope, where he was killed in a clash with native peoples.

Francisco de Almeida established the first Portuguese ports along the Indian Ocean coast of East Africa, thus ensuring his country's control of the Cape of Good Hope route to India. As the first Portuguese viceroy in India, his naval victories ended Arab and Egyptian domination of the sea routes from the Gulf of Aden to the Far East.

Almeida, Lourenço de (unknown–1508) *Portuguese naval commander in the Indian Ocean, son of Francisco de Almeida*

Lourenço de Almeida was the son of Portuguese admiral and viceroy to India FRANCISCO DE ALMEIDA. In 1505, he sailed to India with his father's fleet and took part in naval engagements along the Malabar Coast of southwestern India. He subsequently undertook an expedition to CEYLON (present-day Sri Lanka), where he established a Portuguese trading base at Colombo. From there, he explored southwestward into the Indian Ocean to the Maldive Islands.

In 1506, the younger Almeida defeated naval forces of the king of Calicut, and two years later he was sent by his father to attack MUSLIMs in the RED SEA. In 1508, he was killed in a naval battle with ships under the command of Egyptian admiral Mir Hossein.

Lourenço de Almeida helped Portugal achieve dominance over the important sea route from the Red Sea to the west coast of India. He also expanded Portugal's control over the SPICE TRADE by establishing a base at Colombo, Ceylon, an important source of cinnamon.

al-Rumi, Shihab al-Din Abu Abd Allah Yaqut
See YAQUT AL-RUMI, SHIHAB AL-DIN ABU ABD ALLAH.

Alvarado, Hernando de (fl. 1540s)

Spanish conquistador in the American Southwest

Spanish conquistador Hernando de Alvarado was a lieutenant under FRANCISCO VÁSQUEZ DE CORONADO in his 1540 expedition from Mexico into the American Southwest and took part in the conquest of the Zuni pueblo of Hawikuh near present-day Zuni, New Mexico. From there, in summer 1540, Coronado dispatched exploring parties to the west, north, and east, still hoping to locate an advanced Indian civilization, rich in gold.

On August 29, 1540, Alvarado, in command of a small company of men, led the expedition eastward from Hawikuh across what is now north-central New Mexico. He soon came upon the Keres Indians' Acoma Pueblo, known as "Sky City," perched atop a 350-foot sandstone mesa. Guided by Indians, he headed northeastward from Acoma into the Rio Grande Valley, locating yet another pueblo at Tiguex, just north of present-day Albuquerque, New Mexico.

Alvarado and his men proceeded northward along the upper Rio Grande as far as Taos Pueblo, then headed east and south along the Pecos River. At Cicuye Pueblo, near present-day Pecos, New Mexico, he encountered two Plains Indians, one known as the TURK and the other called Ysopete. They guided Alvarado and his men eastward along the Canadian and Pecos Rivers into the western edge of the southern plains, where they became some of the earliest Europeans to observe vast herds of buffalo.

From the Turk, Alvarado heard news of a fabulously rich Indian kingdom known as QUIVIRA, supposedly situated far to the east and north. He took the Turk back to Coronado, who by then had made his headquarters at Tiguex. In spring 1541, the Turk guided Coronado and his men from Tiguex through present-day Texas and Oklahoma into present-day Kansas, on what proved to be yet another fruitless quest for Indian riches.

Hernando de Alvarado played a significant role in the first major European penetration of the American Southwest. He and his men were the first non-Indians to see Acoma Pueblo, the oldest continuously inhabited site in North America. His introduction of the Turk to Coronado led to one of the most extensive explorations of the southern plains undertaken by the Spanish.

Hernando de Alvarado *(Library of Congress)*

Alvarado, Pedro de (ca. 1485–1541)

Spanish conquistador in Mexico, Guatemala, and Ecuador

Pedro de Alvarado was a native of Badajoz in western Spain's Estremadura region. In 1510, he arrived in Santo Domingo on the Caribbean island of Hispaniola (present-day Haiti and the Dominican Republic). Eight years later, he sailed from Cuba in command of a ship in JUAN DE GRIJALVA's expedition along the coast of the Yucatán Peninsula and the Bay of Campeche, off what is now Mexico.

In April 1519, as a lieutenant under HERNÁN CORTÉS, Alvarado landed near present-day Veracruz, Mexico, and took part in the first Spanish expedition into Aztec Indian territory. By spring 1520, Cortés and his men had established themselves in the Aztec capital at Tenochtitlán. When Cortés left to confront an opposing Spanish force under PÁNFILO DE NARVÁEZ on the Gulf coast, Alvarado was placed in command at Tenochtitlán.

Alvarado soon led the Spaniards in an attack against the Indians, in which thousands of Aztec were slaughtered. Cortés returned to Tenochtitlán to find the Aztec about to rise up against the Spanish. On the night of June 30, 1520 (the "Sorrowful Night"), the Spaniards were forced to flee from Tenochtitlán. At that time, the city was surrounded by the waters of Lake Texcoco and connected to the shore by causeways. The Aztec, in an attempt to trap the Spaniards, had destroyed these bridges. Alvarado reportedly made a daring leap (known later as the "Salto de Alvarado") from the edge of a causeway to safety on the shore of the lake.

In 1521, Alvarado took part in Cortés's counterattack, which resulted in the conquest of the Aztec. In 1523, Cortés sent Alvarado on an expedition southward along the Sierra Madre del Sur range into Mexico's Oaxaca Valley. From there, he continued southward into what is now Guatemala and El Salvador of CENTRAL AMERICA and established Spanish dominion over the region.

In 1527, Alvarado returned to Spain, where he was appointed captain general and governor of Guatemala. Returning to the Americas, he founded new Spanish settlements.

In 1533–34, inspired by FRANCISCO PIZARRO's reports of the great wealth of the Inca Indian civilization, Alvarado undertook an expedition to conquer the Inca province of Quito in present-day Ecuador. He sailed to the northwest coast of South America in command of a force of 500 men. Upon reaching Quito, he found himself opposed by Pizarro's forces under DIEGO DE ALMAGRO and SEBASTIÁN DE BENALCÁZAR, which had already brought Quito under Spanish domination. An open conflict between the CONQUISTADORES was averted when Alvarado, recognizing Pizarro's supremacy, agreed to leave his army and equipment to Pizarro in return for a large payment in gold. He then returned to Guatemala and consolidated his rule.

In 1540, Alvarado organized a seaward expedition to the SPICE ISLANDS (the Moluccas) near present-day Indonesia, which was never realized. His fleet of 13 ships sailed first to the west coast of Mexico. There, the Spanish viceroy ANTONIO DE MENDOZA convinced Alvarado to take part in FRANCISCO VÁSQUEZ DE CORONADO's planned expedition in search of the fabled Seven Cities of CIBOLA, which the Spaniards believed lay somewhere north of Mexico in the American Southwest. Yet the outbreak of an Indian uprising in central Mexico, known as the Mixtón War, delayed his departure. Alvarado led an abortive attack against the Indians at Nochistlán. During the ensuing retreat, he was killed when his horse fell on him.

Following Alvarado's death in the Mixtón War, his widow, Doña Beatriz de la Cueva, succeeded him briefly as governor of Guatemala, the only woman known to have held such a high office during the Spanish colonial period in the Western Hemisphere.

Pedro de Alvarado's career as a conquistador brought him into contact with two advanced Indian civilizations of the Americas, the Aztec and the Inca. He was instrumental in establishing Spanish domination in Central America. After Alvarado's death, the fleet with which he intended to sail to the Spice Islands was placed under the command of JUAN RODRÍGUEZ CABRILLO, who used it in his exploration of the California coast.

Álvares, Francisco (ca. 1490–1540)
Portuguese priest in Ethiopia
Francisco Álvares grew up in the village of Coimbra in central Portugal. In 1515, he was assigned to the Portuguese embassy in Ethiopia under Duarte Galvão. Rui da Lima replaced Galvão as ambassador in 1520.

That same year, Álvares and the new ambassador traveled from Massawa on the RED SEA southward about 500 miles into central Abyssinia (present-day Ethiopia). They visited Mandeley, a Moorish town subject to the negus, the Christian ruler of the region.

In 1527, Álvares left Africa for Italy and reported his travels to the pope. He later wrote an account of his African experiences entitled *The Prester John of the Indies*. It was published the year he died, 1540; in it, he compared Negus Claudius to the legendary Christian ruler PRESTER JOHN. His writing helped bring about a 1541 Portuguese military expedition to Abyssinia headed by Christovão da Gama that defended the negus against an Islamic force.

Francisco Álvares's work is the earliest known written description of Ethiopia. In it, he describes the earlier voyages of the Portuguese diplomat PERO DA COVILHÃ.

Álvarez, Manuel (1794–1856) *American fur trader, trapper in the American West, politician*
Born in Spain's province of León, Manuel Álvarez arrived in the United States in 1823, embarking on a career in the FUR TRADE out of St. Louis. He worked the region between the upper MISSOURI RIVER and the Green and Yellowstone Rivers in what is now western Wyoming. He was also active in the fur trade in the southern ROCKY MOUNTAINS, based at Taos and Santa Fe, New Mexico. He worked as a trapper first for P. D. Papin and Company (also known as the French Company) and later for the AMERICAN FUR COMPANY.

While trapping and trading for furs in 1832–33, Álvarez came upon the geysers of the present-day Yellowstone National Park, becoming one of the earliest non-Indians to see them. At the rendezvous of mountain men on the Green River in summer 1833, he provided an account of these natural wonders.

Álvarez reportedly had three sons by an Indian woman. One of them died while young; the other two were educated in Spain.

After the decline of the Rocky Mountain fur trade in the early 1830s, Álvarez settled in Santa Fe, New Mexico, where he operated a store and trading post. He prospered in the lucrative trade between Missouri and New Mexico during the 1830s. Between 1834 and 1839, he undertook several hazardous trips through Indian country on the southern plains between St. Louis and Santa Fe.

By 1839, Álvarez had achieved considerable stature in New Mexico politics, and, as a result, he was appointed as consul in Santa Fe by the U.S. government, even though he was not at that time an American citizen.

At the outbreak of the U.S.-Mexican War in 1846, Álvarez assisted General STEPHEN WATTS KEARNY in the U.S. military occupation of New Mexico. He subsequently served in the newly organized New Mexico territorial government.

Manuel Álvarez's early travels as a trapper in the Yellowstone region of present-day western Wyoming led to an increased awareness of this unique scenic area, which became America's first national park in 1872. Additionally, his trade expeditions across the southern plains helped open up the Southwest to commercial interests in St. Louis and Independence in present-day Missouri.

Álvarez de Pineda, Alonso (Alonzo Álvarez de Pineda, Alonso de Pineda) (unknown–ca. 1519)
Spanish mariner in the Gulf of Mexico

In late 1518, Alonso Álvarez de Pineda, a Spanish sea captain, was commissioned by Francisco de Garay, the Spanish governor of Jamaica, to explore the shores of the Gulf of Mexico, from Florida to the mouth of the Pánuco River on the east coast of Mexico, in search of a possible strait linking the Gulf of Mexico with the Pacific Ocean.

Álvarez de Pineda was equipped with a fleet of three or four ships and, with the pilot Anton de Alaminos, sailed from Jamaica northward to the southwest coast of Florida. When the Spaniards landed somewhere between what is now Fort Myers and Naples, they were attacked repeatedly by Indians and withdrew to their ships.

Álvarez de Pineda's fleet then followed the Gulf Coast north and west and came upon the mouth of a great river, which they explored upstream for about 20 miles, passing as many as 40 Indian villages along the way. Since it was by then the season of Pentecost, Álvarez de Pineda named the river Río del Espíritu Santo, in honor of the Holy Spirit. On returning to the Gulf of Mexico, the expedition continued westward along the Texas coast, encountering more hostile tribes.

At the Pánuco River's mouth, near present-day Tampico, Mexico, Álvarez de Pineda and his men suffered a decisive defeat by the Aztec Indians. Many of the Spaniards were killed, and all but one of the ships were burned. Álvarez de Pineda, according to one account, was among those killed in battle. The survivors, under the command of Diego de Camargo, escaped on the remaining vessel and sailed southward to Veracruz, where they joined up with HERNÁN CORTÉS and his forces. Back in Jamaica, Francisco de Garay received a grant for the lands explored by Álvarez de Pineda, naming the region Amichel, although his claim on the region was short-lived.

Some sources suggest that the river Alonso Álvarez de Pineda explored may have been the MISSISSIPPI RIVER, making him and not HERNANDO DE SOTO its first European discoverer. Others speculate that Álvarez de Pineda had actually explored the Mobile River and Mobile Bay. According to one account, Álvarez de Pineda survived and returned to Jamaica, where he reportedly told Garay of having located a land rich in gold and inhabited by giants. In any event, as a result of his voyage, the Spanish learned that Florida was not an island, as many had thought, but an extension of the unbroken coastline of a huge continental landmass that lay to the northwest of the known islands of the Caribbean Sea.

Amundsen, Roald Engelbregt Gravning
(1872–1928) *Norwegian polar explorer*

Roald Amundsen was born in Borge, near Oslo, Norway, the son of a shipowner. Inspired by the exploits of SIR JOHN FRANKLIN and FRIDTJOF NANSEN, he decided on a career in polar exploration while still in his teens. At the age of 20, after two years of studying medicine, he went to sea, taking part in Norwegian seal-hunting expeditions in Arctic waters.

In 1897, Amundsen joined Belgian explorer ADRIEN-VICTOR-JOSEPH DE GERLACHE DE GOMERY as first mate on the *Belgica* in an expedition to Antarctica. Following the exploration of Graham's Land, the ship became trapped in ice. Lacking sufficient supplies of fresh food, the crew developed SCURVY. When Gerlache and the ship's captain were stricken, Amundsen was put in command. Aided by the expedition's medical officer, FREDERICK ALBERT COOK, Amundsen managed to save the crew by providing them with fresh meat obtained from frozen seal carcasses found in snowbanks near the ship. He then supervised efforts to break up the ice with dynamite charges and eventually succeeded in clearing a channel. The *Belgica*, icebound for 13 months, was the first vessel to winter in the Antarctic.

Amundsen returned to Norway in 1899. The next year, he was licensed as a sea captain. He soon organized an expedition to locate the NORTH MAGNETIC POLE and negotiate the NORTHWEST PASSAGE from the Atlantic Ocean to the Pacific Ocean. He obtained a small Norwegian fishing boat, the *Gjoa*, and, with a crew of seven, departed Norway in June 1903. He sailed first to Melville Bay on the west coast of GREENLAND, then entered Baffin Bay and Lancaster Sound, threading his way through the islands and straits of the Canadian Arctic. He spent two winters iced in at King William Island, where, in 1904, he discovered the skeletons of two members of the Franklin expedition who had perished a half-century earlier. Also, in 1904, he succeeded in determining the exact location of the North Magnetic Pole at 70°30' north latitude and 95°30' west longitude.

In summer 1905, Amundsen managed to sail the *Gjoa* to the mouth of the Mackenzie River on the western end of Canada's Arctic coast but was once again trapped by ice. Accompanied by the captain of a nearby whaling ship, also icebound, he undertook an overland journey more than 250 miles into the interior of the Yukon and northern Alaska. In February 1906, he reached Fort Egbert, Alaska, then the northernmost U.S. military outpost. He returned to the *Gjoa*, which was freed from the ice in July 1906. Amundsen proceeded along the Arctic mainland of Canada, through the gulf that now bears his name, and reached Point Barrow, Alaska, and the BERING STRAIT, completing the first

Roald Amundsen *(Library of Congress)*

successful navigation of the Northwest Passage. After exploring the coast of the Seward Peninsula and stopping at Nome, Alaska, he sailed down the west coast of North America, reaching San Francisco, California, by October 1906. The *Gjoa,* which Amundsen presented to the city of San Francisco, was subsequently displayed in that city's Golden Gate Park.

Back in Norway in 1908, Amundsen purchased the *Fram,* Fridtjof Nansen's former ship, which he planned to use in an expedition to the Arctic. By mid-1909, news of ROBERT EDWIN PEARY's success in attaining the NORTH POLE had reached Amundsen. He then decided to sail the *Fram* to the Antarctic and make an attempt on the SOUTH POLE. At this time, the British polar explorer, ROBERT FALCON SCOTT, was already en route to the Antarctic on the same mission.

Leaving Norway in June 1910, Amundsen sailed by way of CAPE HORN. He landed on the Antarctic mainland at the Bay of Whales, on the edge of the Ross Ice Shelf, 65 miles closer to the South Pole than Scott's base at McMurdo Sound. There, Amundsen established a base camp known as Framheim, and spent the rest of the Antarctic winter preparing for a trip to the South Pole. During the next year, he and his men made three trips into the interior, establishing food depots.

Amundsen's first attempt to reach the South Pole from Framheim occurred in early September 1911, but severe storms and temperatures of minus 70° F forced him to return to the base camp. He set out again on October 19, 1911, with four men, using four sledges and 52 dogs. By mid-November, they reached the Polar Plateau via the Axel Heiberg Glacier. By early December, he and his companions were at an elevation of over 10,000 feet. Along the way, Amundsen discovered Devil's Glacier.

On December 14, 1911, Amundsen reached the South Pole. His party established an encampment known as Poleheim, then explored within a five-mile radius of the South Pole to confirm navigational findings. After three days, Amundsen and his companions began their return trip to the Bay of Whales, sighting en route the 14,000-foot-high Queen Maud Mountains, which he named after the queen of Norway. At the Pole, Amundsen had left a marker flag, a letter to the king of Norway, a SEXTANT, a spirit level, articles of clothing, a plate with his crew's names, and an envelope addressed to Scott. Scott's party, to their extreme disappointment, found these items on reaching the Pole in mid-January 1912.

After his return to Norway, Amundsen entered the shipping business and wrote and lectured on his experiences in the Arctic and Antarctic. Although most polar exploration had come to a halt with the outbreak of World War I, Amundsen planned another expedition into Arctic waters. On his ship, the *Maud,* he left Norway in July 1918. Despite the danger of German submarines then operating off Norway, he proceeded along the Arctic coasts of Europe and Asia, through the NORTHEAST PASSAGE, finally reaching Nome, Alaska, in spring 1920.

Over the next several years, Amundsen experimented with airplanes as a means for polar exploration. In 1925, with the support of American aviator LINCOLN ELLSWORTH, he obtained two amphibious aircraft. In May of that year, he and Ellsworth took off from Spitsbergen (part of present-day Svalbard), near the Arctic coast of European Russia, in an attempt to fly over the North Pole. One of their planes was forced down just 135 miles from the pole. The other plane made a landing to rescue the rest of the party, but was unable to take off for three weeks until an airstrip could be improvised on the PACK ICE.

In 1926, Amundsen and Ellsworth obtained an AIRSHIP, the *Norge,* from the Italian government. They also engaged the airship's designer, UMBERTO NOBILE, as pilot. They left Spitsbergen on the *Norge* on May 11, 1926, and flew 600 miles, crossing over the North Pole early the next morning. Two days later, they landed at Teller, Alaska. Although RICHARD EVELYN BYRD and Floyd Bennett had reportedly succeeded in making a flight over the North Pole just a few days earlier, Amundsen's dirigible expedition was the first to cross from Europe to North America by that route. (It has been theorized, based on Byrd's diary, that he and Bennett missed the mark.)

In 1928, Amundsen disappeared when his plane was lost in the Arctic during a search for Nobile, whose dirigible the *Italia* had crashed while attempting a second flight over the North Pole.

Roald Amundsen is credited with many significant "firsts" in polar exploration. With the Belgian expedition of 1897–99, he was among the first to winter in the Antarctic. His 1903–06 expedition along the Arctic coasts of Canada and Alaska was the first successful seaward crossing of the Northwest Passage, a feat that European mariners had been attempting for 400 years. Most notably, in 1910–12, he led the first successful expedition to the South Pole. In his subsequent Arctic explorations, he became the first man to negotiate successfully both the Northwest and Northeast Passages, and with his overland and aerial expeditions he became the first man to attain both the Poles: the South Pole by dogsled and the North Pole by airship. His exploits also resulted in such scientific findings as the exact location of the North Magnetic Pole, as well as the discovery that the South Pole was located on a landmass. Amundsen's base at Framheim on the Bay of Whales was later the site of Little America, the first permanent settlement in the Antarctic.

Anabara, Semyon (fl. 1710s) *Russian Cossack fur trader in Siberia*

In 1713–14, Semyon Anabara, a Russian Cossack fur trader, traveling with Ivan Bykov, explored eastern SIBERIA from Yakutsk on the Lena River, to the southeast shore of the Sea of Okhotsk. From there, he crossed to the Shantar Islands. Although sketchy reports of this archipelago had reached Europe as early as 1645, Anabara's trip was the first confirmed visit to these islands. He explored three of them before returning to Yakutsk with furs.

In the years following Semyon Anabara's rediscovery of the Shantar Islands, they became an important fishing base as well as a valuable source of furs and lumber.

Andagoya, Pascual de (ca. 1495–1548) *Spanish naval commander along the Pacific coast of South America*

Basque-born Pascual de Andagoya traveled to what is now Panama with PEDRO ARIAS DE AVILA in 1514. In 1522, soon after HERNÁN CORTÉS's conquest of the Aztec of Mexico, Andagoya commanded the first Spanish maritime exploration of the Pacific coast of South America below Panama. He sailed as far south as Cape Corrientes on the central Pacific shore of present-day Colombia, then returned to Panama with reports of a highly advanced and wealthy Indian kingdom called "Birú," later known as Peru. This civilization turned out to be that of the Inca Indians, and their land was later known to the Spanish as Peru.

Inspired by Pascual de Andagoya's account, FRANCISCO PIZARRO and DIEGO DE ALMAGRO embarked from Panama in 1524 on an expedition that would lead to the Spanish conquest of the Inca Empire 10 years later.

Andrade, Antonio de (Antonio de Andrada) (ca. 1580–1634) *Portuguese or Spanish missionary in Tibet*

Antonio de Andrade, of Portuguese or Spanish origin, was a Jesuit priest in India. In 1624, he set out from Agra in north-central India to investigate reports of Christians living in Tibet. He went northward from Agra to Delhi, then proceeded to the upper GANGES RIVER and reached Srinagar in northern India's Kashmir region. He continued into the HIMALAYAS, crossing that range by way of the 18,000-foot-high Mana Pass.

Andrade entered the kingdom of Tibet, reaching the city of Tsaparang on the upper Sutlej River. Although he found no Christians, he received a friendly reception from the kingdom's Buddhist leaders. Encouraged, he returned to India.

In 1625, Andrade made a second journey to Tibet, during which he established a mission at Tsaparang. He remained there until 1630, when his Jesuit superiors ordered him to the Portuguese colony at Goa on the west coast of India.

Antonio de Andrade was one of the first Europeans to visit Tibet since the journeys of Friar ODORIC OF PORDENONE in the early 1300s. His explorations into the central Himalayas revealed one of the sources of the Ganges River.

Andrée, Salomon August (1854–1897) *Swedish engineer, aviator in the Arctic*

Salomon Andrée was born in Granna, Sweden. Trained in engineering, he went on to become the chief engineer of the Swedish Patent Office. In 1882–83, he took part in Swedish polar expeditions from Spitsbergen, off the Arctic coast of Norway.

Andrée began to experiment with aerial exploration of the Arctic by BALLOON in 1893. He made nine ascents and developed a steering device that enabled him to follow a course not entirely limited by wind direction.

In 1896, with the financial support of the Swedish inventor and industrialist Alfred Nobel and the Swedish monarch Oscar II, Andrée planned an airborne expedition by balloon from Spitsbergen (part of present-day Svalbard) to the NORTH POLE. His first attempt was in June 1896, but unfavorable wind conditions caused him to postpone his expedition until the following summer.

On July 11, 1897, Andrée ascended from Danes Island, Spitsbergen, in his balloon, the *Ornen* (eagle), accompanied by Knut Fraenkel, an engineer, and Nils Strindberg, nephew of Swedish dramatist August Strindberg. The expedition was equipped with sledges, hunting gear, and a collapsible boat. On takeoff, the balloon's steering mechanism failed, causing the *Ornen* to drift uncontrollably northward. After about 400 miles, at about 83° north latitude, an ice sheet formed on the balloon, forcing it down on the frozen polar sea. After a three-month trek across the ice, Andrée and his companions reached White Island near Franz Josef Land, where they survived until mid-October 1897.

Thirty-three years later, in 1930, a Norwegian scientific expedition stopping at White Island discovered the remains of Andrée and his companions. Andrée's written account was found with the final journal entry dated October 17, 1897. A roll of undeveloped film was also recovered, which, upon processing in Sweden, revealed images of the ill-fated expedition's final days. Andrée and the other two men are believed to have died from trichinosis, contracted from eating contaminated polar bear meat. Other scientists have speculated that they died from carbon monoxide fumes given off by their cooking apparatus.

Salomon Andrée was the first to recognize the advantages of aerial exploration in the Arctic. By 1926, with advances in aviation technology, the first successful flights over the North Pole had been accomplished by RICHARD EVELYN BYRD, ROALD ENGELBREGT GRAVNING AMUNDSEN, and UMBERTO NOBILE.

Andreyev, Stepan (fl. 1760s) *Russian army officer on the Arctic coast of eastern Siberia*

Stepan Andreyev was a Russian army officer who explored the Arctic coastal regions of extreme eastern SIBERIA in the early 1760s.

In March 1763, Andreyev set out from Fort Anadyr, the Russian outpost on the Bering Sea coast of the Chukchi Peninsula and headed northwestward to the Arctic coast of eastern Siberia. While exploring the Bear Islands, opposite the mouth of the Kolyma River, he sighted what appeared to be land to the north. Upon his return to Fort Anadyr, his reports led his commanding officer to speculate that Andreyev may have located a new landmass of continental proportions.

In 1764, Andreyev returned to the region to reexamine his earlier finding. In the course of his second investigation of the area, he came upon sledge tracks left by a large unidentified group of people (probably natives). Since he had only a small party under his command, he decided to withdraw without exploring further.

The landmass that Andreyev reported seeing became known as "Andreyev Land." Subsequent attempts to locate it were fruitless, although in 1773, Russian merchant Ivan Lyakhov located the New Siberian Islands in the same general area.

Not until 1951 did a Soviet polar geographic survey determine that what Stepan Andreyev had actually seen from the Arctic coast was New Siberia Island, one of the larger of the New Siberian Islands. As a result, Andreyev is credited with the island group's European discovery.

Anson, George (Baron Anson) (1697–1762)
British admiral in South America and the South Pacific

George Anson was born in Shrugborough Park, Staffordshire, England. He entered the Royal Navy in 1712, becoming a captain 11 years later. From 1724 to 1725, he commanded three expeditions to the coast of South Carolina. During the mid-1730s, he undertook several naval expeditions to America and the west coast of Africa.

In 1740, with the onset of war between Great Britain and Spain, Anson set out on a punitive naval expedition against Spanish possessions on the west coast of South America. His fleet of six ships sailed from England in September 1740, heading for CAPE HORN and the coast of Chile. At Cape Horn, several of the ships were wrecked in rough weather. Anson, aboard the flagship *Centurion*, rounded the tip of South America and explored the Chonos Archipelago, Chiloé Island, and the Juan Fernández Islands along the Pacific coast of Chile. After raiding the Spanish settlement at Paita, Peru, and inflicting damage on the Spanish fleet, he sailed across the Pacific Ocean to China. His was the first British warship to enter Chinese waters. From there, he continued across the Indian Ocean to the CAPE OF GOOD HOPE and back to England, arriving in 1744, having circumnavigated the world.

Anson returned with only one ship of his original fleet of six. About half of the 2,000 men in his expedition died of SCURVY. Nevertheless, with his capture in the Philippines in 1741 of the Spanish galleon *Nuestra Señora de Cobadonga*, laden with a cargo of gold coins and ingots worth £400,000, his expedition was heralded as a great naval triumph.

Upon his return, Anson was promoted to vice admiral. As first lord of the Admiralty in the 1750s, he went on to command the Royal Navy in victorious actions against the French.

George Anson's exploits on his 1740–44 voyage brought back new knowledge about the little-known regions around the southern tip of South America. In addition, the expedition's loss of life from scurvy led the Royal Navy to control this problem by introducing citrus fruits as a dietary supplement for sailors (a measure used with great success during the three voyages of JAMES COOK).

Anville, Jean-Baptiste Bourguignon d'
(1697–1782) *French geographer, cartographer*

Born in Paris, Jean-Baptiste d'Anville engraved his first map at the age of 15. He went on to publish many written works and more than 200 maps. Although he reportedly never left Paris, he used the latest accounts of explorers as source materials and accumulated a library of more than 100,000 maps.

In 1735, d'Anville produced the first relatively accurate map of China. He was also known for his maps of North America, including the 1732 Carte de la Louisiane. His widely read *Géographie Ancienne,* originally published in 1768, included a historical atlas.

Jean-Baptiste d'Anville became the most influential cartographer of his age. U.S. president Thomas Jefferson owned several of his maps.

Anza, Juan Bautista de (1735–1788) *Spanish soldier, governor of New Mexico, founder of San Francisco*

Juan Bautista de Anza was born in northern New Spain, the son of a provincial military leader. Like his father and grandfather before him, he entered the military. By 1759, he had reached the rank of captain, and he was placed in command of the Spanish garrison at Tubac, south of present-day Tucson, Arizona. Over the next 10 years, he took part in major Spanish campaigns against Apache Indians and other tribes of what is now the American Southwest.

In the 1770s, Spanish colonial leaders in Mexico viewed British and Russian encroachment in northern California as a threat to missions, military bases, and agricultural settlements established by JUNÍPERO SERRA and GASPAR DE PORTOLÁ. Spanish settlers along the California coast needed to be resupplied from Mexico, but sending ships up the coast proved unreliable. In 1773–74, Serra lobbied the Spanish colonial government in Mexico City to sponsor an overland expedition that would open a route from the settlement in what is now southern Arizona at Tubac, across the desert and through the Sierra Nevada to San Gabriel Arcangel, near present-day Los Angeles, California.

Commissioned to undertake this task, Anza, leading a company of 35 soldiers and accompanied by the Franciscan missionary FRANCISCO GARCÉS, left Tubac in January 1774, heading westward. The expedition followed the Gila River to the Colorado, which they crossed near the present-day California-Arizona state line. The route west closely paralleled the present U.S.-Mexican border in Arizona.

On crossing the COLORADO RIVER, Anza and his men headed northward along the Sierra Nevada, then crossed into California through the San Carlos Pass. They entered the Cahuilla Valley, reaching the area of present-day Riverside, California. The party arrived at the San Gabriel mission, nine miles from present-day Los Angeles, in March 1774. Anza continued north to Monterey, from where he returned to Tubac.

In November 1775, Anza led a party of 225 colonists, soldiers, and missionaries, including Garcés, from the province of Sonora in northern Mexico to Tubac, and from there, along the trail he had blazed the previous year, to San Gabriel, California. They then went north, via Monterey, to San Francisco Bay, which had been rediscovered by Portolá in 1769. Anza's chief subordinate, Lieutenant José Joaquín Moraga, supervised the establishment of the first permanent settlement on San Francisco Bay, known as San Francisco de Asís. This settlement's garrison later became the site of the U.S. Army's main installation on the central California coast, the Presidio.

Anza returned to New Mexico, where he became governor in 1777. He served in this capacity for 11 years, during which he continued to explore the Southwest. In 1779, he undertook expeditions from Santa Fe, New Mexico, into the Arkansas River region, as well as into the San Luis Valley of New Mexico and Colorado.

The next year, 1780, Anza attempted to establish a direct overland route between Santa Fe and the province of Sonora on the Gulf of California. Although his party reached Sonora, the lack of available water for travelers and their pack animals made this route impractical.

In 1781, the Yuma (Quechan) Indians revolted against Spanish rule, and the route Juan Bautista de Anza had blazed across their Yuma lands in the Colorado Basin to California was closed until after 1821, when Mexico achieved its independence from Spain. The trail then became an important link between Mexican settlements in California and New Mexico. After 1849, Anza's route became an important road for settlers and gold seekers traveling across southern New Mexico and Arizona to central and northern California.

Applegate, Jesse (1811–1888) *American pioneer on the Oregon Trail, settler of Oregon*

Originally from Kentucky, Jesse Applegate moved with his family to the Missouri frontier at the age of 10. He studied surveying at the Rock Springs Seminary in Shiloh, Illinois. From 1828 to 1832, he was employed in the state surveyor general's office in St. Louis, Missouri, where he heard accounts of the frontier regions of the northern plains and ROCKY MOUNTAINS from such MOUNTAIN MEN as WILSON PRICE HUNT, JEDEDIAH STRONG SMITH, and DAVID E. JACKSON.

Applegate was strongly opposed to the spread of slavery; his views brought him into conflict with the powerful proslavery faction in Missouri. In 1843, seeking to settle on new lands free of slavery, Applegate and his family, along with the families of his two brothers, Lindsay and Charles, joined about 1,000 other settlers, among them the missionary MARCUS WHITMAN, in a wagon train migration to Oregon Country. The "Great Migration," led by frontier guide Peter Burnett, was the largest wagon train ever to attempt the westward crossing and included more than 5,000 head of oxen and cattle.

The wagon train left Independence, Missouri, on May 22, 1843, and followed the California and Oregon Trail to Fort Laramie in present-day Wyoming. It then crossed the Continental Divide at the SOUTH PASS of Wyoming's Wind River Range. After stopping for supplies at JAMES BRIDGER's newly opened Fort Bridger on the Green River, the emigrants headed into present-day Idaho and reached Fort Boise on the Snake River.

At Fort Hall in Idaho, the travelers were joined by MARCUS WHITMAN, who helped guide the party on the next leg of the journey. Until that time, the Oregon Trail beyond Fort Hall had been suitable only for pack animals. Applegate's party had to enlarge the route to make it passable for wagon traffic.

Crossing northeastern Oregon's Blue Mountains, Applegate led the migrants along the Umatilla River to its confluence with the COLUMBIA RIVER. They then followed the Columbia River to the HUDSON'S BAY COMPANY trading post at Fort Vancouver, opposite present-day Portland, Oregon. Applegate was received by Hudson's Bay Company director JOHN McLOUGHLIN, who directed the migrants southward to the fertile Willamette Valley, which they reached in November 1843. Applegate and his family settled on Salt Creek, near the present site of The Dalles, Oregon.

In 1846, Applegate, with fellow pioneer Levi Scott and other associates, set out in search of a shorter route from Idaho to Oregon, south of the usual trail along the Snake River. He explored the Humboldt River region and the Black Rock Desert of northwestern Nevada, then traveled northeast to Fort Hall, Idaho.

From Fort Hall, Applegate set out with a party of settlers back to Oregon. Despite repeated raids by Indians, who preyed upon the travelers' cattle, and the hardships wrought by the severe winter weather of 1846–47, Applegate succeeded in leading this party through northern Nevada and northern California into Oregon's Willamette Valley, following a new and shorter route—the Applegate Trail—which traversed the region around Klamath Lake and the Umpqua Valley.

In 1849, Applegate moved his family to the Umpqua Valley, a region suitable for farming, where he founded Yoncalla, one of the earliest settlements in that part of southwestern Oregon.

Applegate was active in territorial and later state politics in Oregon, and he made an unsuccessful bid for governor in 1861. He also served as Oregon's surveyor general and, in 1853, he helped establish a new wagon route into northern California, which became part of the Oregon and California stage road.

Following his initial trek west to Oregon in 1843, Applegate wrote an essay, *A Day with the Cow Column in 1843,* first published in 1868. In it he described the challenges facing the early migrants along the Oregon Trail to the Pacific Northwest.

Jesse Applegate's involvement in the Great Migration of 1843, and subsequent trailblazing efforts in Idaho and Nevada, contributed to the ensuing massive influx of settlers into Oregon during the 1840s and 1850s.

Arago, Jacques (1790–1855) *French artist, writer in the South Pacific*

Jacques Arago was born in the southern French town of Estagel, the younger brother of the physicist and astronomer François Arago.

In September 1817, Arago departed France on the *Uranie* under the command of LOUIS-CLAUDE DE SAULCES DE FREYCINET, as the expedition's artist and journalist. During the next three years, he circled the world and toured the South Pacific Ocean, visiting the Marianas, the Hawaiian Islands, and the British settlements on the southeast coast of Australia. His illustrations of the voyage included watercolors and drawings of native scenes.

Arago returned to France in November 1820. His illustrated, popular account of the voyage, *Journey Around the World,* was published in 1822, several years before the appearance of the official account of the expedition by Freycinet. In the years that followed, Arago was involved in the theater as a writer and director. Although stricken with blindness in 1837, he published an expanded account of the expedition under Freycinet in 1838–40.

In his work as an artist and journalist in the South Pacific, Jacques Arago depicted naturalistic scenes of native life and customs, as well as written and pictorial accounts of meetings between the French and native leaders.

Arculf (fl. 680s) *Frankish pilgrim to the Middle East*

Arculf, of Frankish descent, possibly was the bishop of Périgueux in southwestern France or a monk attached to a mission. The Anglo-Saxon scholar Saint Bede relates in his three-volume *Historia ecclesiastica gentis Anglorum* (Ecclesiastical history of the English people), from about 731, that Arculf landed in a storm on the Scottish island of Iona, where he described his travels to Saint Adamnan, the abbot of the Iona monastery. He claims he had visited holy sites in the Middle East. Adamnan used Arculf's account to write a geography, *De Locis Sanctis* (Concerning the sacred places), which he presented as a gift to Aldfrith, king of Northumbria, in 698.

Arculf, as recorded by Adamnan, gave a detailed account of Jerusalem, Bethlehem, Nazareth, Damascus, and other cities, including their churches. He also describes many geographic sites from the Bible, including the Dead

Sea and the Jordan River. His guide through Palestine was Peter of Burgundy. After leaving Palestine, Arculf visited Alexandria, then crossed the MEDITERRANEAN SEA, sailing past Crete, to Constantinople (present-day Istanbul, Turkey). On the return trip, Arculf describes islands to the east of Sicily, where the third volume of *De Locis Sanctis* ends.

Arculf's trip to the Holy Land was not a unique pilgrimage for his time, yet no similar detailed record exists.

Arias de Ávila, Pedro (Pedro Arias Dávila, Pedrarias Dávila) (ca. 1442–1531)
Spanish conquistador in Central America

Pedro Arias de Ávila, known to his contemporaries as Pedrarias, was born in the Segovia region of Spain, of Spanish-Jewish ancestry. He was well connected to the court of Spanish monarchs Ferdinand and Isabella, and he took part in military campaigns against the North African Moors in 1510.

In July 1513, Arias de Ávila was appointed chief colonial administrator of Darién, the Spanish colony on the Atlantic coast of what is now Panama in CENTRAL AMERICA. Several months later, while Arias de Ávila was still in Spain preparing for his expedition to the Americas, news of VASCO NÚÑEZ DE BALBOA's crossing of the Isthmus of Panama and sighting of the Pacific Ocean reached the Spanish court.

Arias de Ávila arrived in Darién in late June 1514. Among his expedition of about 2,000 men were several Spanish conquistadores who would play significant roles in the conquest and exploration of the Americas, including HERNANDO DE SOTO, SEBASTIÁN DE BENALCÁZAR, DIEGO DE ALMAGRO, and PASCUAL DE ANDAGOYA.

A conflict with Núñez de Balboa developed from the beginning of Arias de Ávila's governorship of Panama, which ultimately led to Núñez de Balboa's arrest and execution on trumped-up charges of treason in 1519. That same year, Arias de Ávila moved the principal settlement from Darién, on the Atlantic coast of Panama, to Panama City, on the Pacific coast. During the next five years, Arias de Ávila organized expeditions that explored to the north and west and that brought the Chiriquí region of western Panama under Spanish domination. In 1524, he supported Almagro and FRANCISCO PIZARRO in their explorations southward along the Pacific coast, which eventually led to the conquest of the Inca in Peru and Ecuador.

In 1526, Arias de Ávila was replaced as governor of Panama. Soon afterward, he undertook an expedition northward into present-day Nicaragua, defeating rival forces under FRANCISCO FERNÁNDEZ DE CÓRDOBA. He remained in control until his death in 1531.

In Spain, Pedro Arias de Ávila had been known as El Galán (the gallant one) for his courtly manner and gallantry, and El Justador (the Jouster) for his military prowess. In Panama, however, his reputation for cruelty and ruthlessness in dealing with both the Indians and his Spanish rivals earned him the title Furor Domini (wrath of God). Panama City, which he founded in 1519, endured as the oldest surviving European settlement on the American mainland.

Arias de Saavedra, Hernando (Hernandarias Saavedra) (1561–1634) *Spanish soldier, colonial leader in Paraguay and Argentina, son-in-law of Juan de Garay*

Hernando Arias de Saavedra, of Spanish ancestry, was born in Asuncíon, in present-day Paraguay. At the age of 15, he participated in an expedition in search of LOS CÉSARES, a fabled city of Indian riches thought to exist in southern South America. At the age of 19, he settled in Buenos Aires, in present-day Argentina, when it was founded for the second time by the conquistador JUAN DE GARAY. He later married Garay's daughter. In his 20s, Arias de Saavedra served in armies sent out against Indians living inland from Buenos Aires.

Arias de Saavedra and his family returned to Asuncíon in 1589, and he served as governor in 1592–94. He was appointed governor of the Río de la Plata colony in 1598 and served through 1609. He served a second term in 1614–18. In 1617, he accomplished the separation of the province of Río de la Plata from the administration of Asuncíon, with Buenos Aires as the seat of the new provincial government.

During his governorships, especially between 1604 and 1608, Arias de Saavedra encouraged further exploration of the interior and launched a series of expeditions, leading some of them himself, ever hopeful of locating Los Césares.

Hernando Arias de Saavedra contributed to Spanish exploration of South America as both a military and political leader.

Armstrong, Neil Alden (1930–   )
American astronaut, first human to walk on the Moon

Neil Armstrong was born in Wapakoneta, Ohio. At the age of 16, he became a student pilot. Earning a navy scholarship, he enrolled at Purdue University in 1947. In 1950–52, he served as a combat pilot in the Korean War. After his tour of duty, he returned to Purdue and in 1955 earned a B.S. degree in aeronautical engineering.

That same year, Armstrong joined the National Advisory Committee for Aeronautics (NACA) at the Lewis Research Center in Ohio, soon transferring to the NACA Flight Research Center at Edwards Air Force Base in California, where he was a test pilot for experimental aircraft. In 1962, he joined the second group of trainees to become ASTRONAUTS of the NATIONAL AERONAUTICS AND SPACE ADMINISTRATION (NASA).

Armstrong's first assignment was as backup to the *Gemini 5* mission, part of the GEMINI PROGRAM. In 1966, he served as command pilot for the *Gemini 8* mission, during which he and David R. Scott performed the first successful docking of two vehicles in space. He then was part of the backup crews for the *Gemini 11* mission and *Apollo 8* mission of the subsequent APOLLO PROGRAM.

In 1968, Armstrong was given command of the *Apollo 11* mission. He, Edwin "Buzz" Aldrin, Jr., and Michael Allen Collins took off from Cape Canaveral, Florida, on July 16, 1969, propelled by the *Saturn V* rocket designed specifically for Apollo craft. They arrived in orbit around the Moon on July 20, and after eight hours of preparation, Armstrong and Aldrin separated from the *Columbia* command module in the *Eagle* lunar module and three hours later landed on the Moon's Mare Tranquilitatis (sea of tranquility).

Armstrong became the first human to walk on the Moon on July 20, 1969, 10:56 P.M., Eastern Daylight Time. For two and a half hours, while Collins orbited the Moon in the command module, he and Aldrin explored the Moon's surface. They planted a U.S. flag, collected 48 pounds of lunar soil and rock, and set up scientific experiments, including an instrument to measure solar wind, a seismometer to detect moonquakes, and a laser reflector to reflect pulses of laser for measurements between the Earth and the Moon. After 21 1/2 hours on the lunar surface, Armstrong and Aldrin lifted off and rejoined Collins in the command module. They returned to Earth on July 24, accomplishing a successful splashdown in the Pacific Ocean about 810 miles southeast of Hawaii.

Armstrong received the Presidential Medal of Freedom and numerous other awards for the *Apollo 11* mission. His activities after his career as an astronaut have included NASA deputy association administrator for aeronautics in the Office of Advanced Research and Technology, professor of engineering, businessman, presidential adviser on space exploration, and media personality.

The expedition to the Moon was the work of a team of scientists, engineers, technicians, and astronauts. But as the first man to walk on the Moon, Neil Armstrong receives special notice in the history of exploration. He is famous for the quote "That's one small step for man, one giant leap for mankind" as he took his first step on the lunar surface, as watched by millions of people around the world. Other missions would follow to the Moon, five of them successful manned landings.

Arthur, Gabriel (fl. 1670s) *English colonist in Virginia and the trans-Appalachian region*

Gabriel Arthur was born in England and arrived in the Virginia colony prior to 1673 as the indentured servant of English military officer and exploration sponsor Major General ABRAHAM WOOD.

In 1673, Arthur and another Virginia colonist, JAMES NEEDHAM, were sent by General Wood to explore the trans-Appalachian frontier lying to the west of the Virginia colony. Arthur and Needham left the Virginia colony's western outpost at Fort Henry, present-day Petersburg, Virginia, in April. Traveling southwestward through North Carolina's Yadkin Valley into what is now eastern Tennessee, they were taken captive by Indians, thought to be a band of Cherokee.

Arthur remained among his captors for more than a year, learning their language and participating in several raids on other tribes. He then traveled southward with them as far as Spanish Florida. Along the way, he explored the Blue Ridge of North Carolina. Returning north with a party of Indians in 1674, he traveled eastward through the CUMBERLAND GAP, becoming one of the first non-Indians to cross the APPALACHIAN MOUNTAINS by this route. He then explored the Kanawha River region of present-day West Virginia. Arthur's companion, Needham, had managed to escape but was later killed by his Indian guide.

Arthur was again taken captive by a raiding party of Shawnee Indians near the mouth of the Scioto River in present-day Ohio. He then traveled with this band into the Scioto River region and explored what is now southeastern Ohio.

After surviving an ambush by Ocaneechi Indians, Arthur convinced the Shawnee that he would be able to open British trade relations with them if they granted his freedom. He returned to Fort Henry some time in 1674.

Gabriel Arthur's travels through what is now West Virginia, southeastern Ohio, eastern Tennessee, the Carolinas, Georgia, and Florida resulted in the first recorded explorations of the trans-Appalachian frontier by an Englishman. His accounts of the Cumberland Gap and the Ohio country to the west provided the impetus for further exploration, including that of DANIEL BOONE a century later.

Ashley, William Henry (ca. 1778–1838)
American fur trader in the West, soldier, politician

William Henry Ashley, a native of Virginia, moved to the Missouri Territory in 1803, the year the United States finalized its acquisition of the Louisiana Territory from France. Settling first in Sainte Geneviève, he later made his home in St. Louis, where he went into business with his friend, the Pennsylvanian ANDREW HENRY. During the War of 1812, Ashley and Henry prospered by selling gunpowder and lead to the U.S. Army. Ashley was also active in the Missouri territorial militia, serving as a major; after the war, he reached the rank of general.

Ashley was prominent in politics, and when Missouri achieved statehood in 1821, he was elected the first lieutenant governor. Because of severe financial reverses resulting from the Panic of 1819, Ashley sought to recoup his losses by initiating the FUR TRADE to the upper MISSOURI RIVER. In partnership with Henry, Ashley recruited MOUNTAIN MEN for an expedition from St. Louis to trade furs with the Mandan and other Indian tribes in present-day North and South Dakota and Wyoming. In the spring of 1822, Ashley and Henry and a small party of trappers and frontiersmen traveled northward from St. Louis via the Missouri River to the mouth of the Yellowstone River, where they established a trading post, Fort Henry (later Fort Union). The venture failed to bring in the necessary profits, and the following year Ashley sponsored a second expedition.

The Arikara Indians, who lived on the Missouri near the present North Dakota-South Dakota state line, and who up to that time had acted as middlemen in the fur trade, felt their interests threatened by the appearance of the trappers. In spring 1823, Ashley's men, heading by KEELBOAT for Fort Henry, stopped at the Arikara settlement along the Missouri to trade for horses. The Indians launched a surprise attack, and Ashley and his men narrowly escaped.

Although a punitive military expedition, headed by Colonel HENRY LEAVENWORTH, soon arrived and dispersed the Arikara to the Mandan Indian villages in North Dakota, Indian attacks made further travel on the upper Missouri into the northern ROCKY MOUNTAINS impractical. To meet this challenge, Ashley instituted the "brigade system," in which parties of trappers were sent westward from Fort Kiowa in present-day South Dakota into the foothills of the Rockies. Taking part in these expeditions were mountain men JAMES PIERSON BECKWOURTH, JAMES BRIDGER, ROBERT CAMPBELL, JAMES CLYMAN, THOMAS FITZPATRICK, HUGH GLASS, DAVID E. JACKSON, EDWARD ROSE, JEDEDIAH STRONG SMITH, and WILLIAM LEWIS SUBLETTE.

In spring 1824, after Andrew Henry had left the fur trade, Ashley assumed complete ownership of what was known as the ROCKY MOUNTAIN FUR COMPANY. In November of that year, Ashley himself led a supply train of pack animals westward along the North Platte and South Platte Rivers over the Wind River Range of what is now southern Wyoming, through the SOUTH PASS to the Green River of what is now northern Utah.

Starting in April 1825, Ashley and his party began to explore the Green River of northern Utah, as well as the Uinta River and the Great Salt Lake region. Using makeshift boats fashioned from buffalo hides stretched over willow sticks, they negotiated the perilous rapids of the Green River as it coursed through what is now northern Utah's Dinosaur National Monument. They explored the river's southern branch to determine whether it was the so-called Buenaventura River, erroneously thought to flow directly to the Pacific Ocean. However, based on reports by French trappers in the area, Ashley correctly concluded that the southern Green River was actually a northern tributary of the COLORADO RIVER. Traveling overland through the Uinta Mountains, Ashley and his mountain men met up with ÉTIENNE PROVOST. The combined party headed northeastward to Henrys Fork on the Green River, where Ashley had arranged to meet with the rest of his trappers in July 1825, the first trappers' annual rendezvous.

After selling supplies to the trappers and purchasing their season's catch of furs, Ashley embarked on an expedition northward through the SOUTH PASS, then explored the Sweetwater, Popo Agie, and Bighorn Rivers. He returned to St. Louis via the Yellowstone and Missouri Rivers.

In summer 1826, Ashley was again at the Green River rendezvous, where he sold his fur interests to David Jackson, Jedediah Smith, and William Sublette.

Ashley returned to St. Louis, his financial condition greatly improved, and he continued to be prominent in Missouri political circles. Although unsuccessful in his bid for election as governor of the state, he was elected to Congress, serving in the House of Representatives from 1831 to 1837.

William Henry Ashley's fur-trading ventures into the Rockies demonstrated that there was a practical overland supply route into the region. His exploits opened the American West to exploration and travel routes not restricted to the rivers. His 1824–25 expedition into the Rockies of southern Wyoming and Utah blazed the trail that would, more than 40 years later, be the basis of the route used by the builders of the Union Pacific Railroad.

Astor, John Jacob (1763–1848) *American fur trader, financier, sponsor of expeditions to the Pacific Northwest*

The son of a butcher, John Jacob Astor was born in Waldorf, near the German university town of Heidelberg. At the age of 16, he moved to England to join his brother's musical instrument business. Five years later, he immigrated to America, arriving first in Baltimore, then settling in New York City.

Through his 1785 marriage to Sarah Todd, whose family was wealthy and politically well-connected, Astor was able to launch a successful business career. Aided by his wife's knowledge of furs, Astor operated a store in New York that developed a thriving trade not only in imported musical instruments, but also in animal pelts from Montreal and the Hudson River Valley. By 1800, he had expanded his business to include real estate development in and around New York City.

Astor also became a leading mercantile force in the trade with China from New York, dealing especially in furs. Still, his profits were limited by fur prices fixed by the

HUDSON'S BAY COMPANY and the NORTH WEST COMPANY based in Montreal. Prompted by the Louisiana Purchase of 1803 and the ensuing explorations of MERIWETHER LEWIS and WILLIAM CLARK in the largely unknown region between the Mississippi River and the Pacific coast, Astor organized a venture to obtain furs from the Pacific Northwest and ship them directly to the lucrative markets in China.

In April 1808, under the aegis of President Thomas Jefferson, Astor chartered the AMERICAN FUR COMPANY. His original plan was to establish a chain of trading forts along the route of the Lewis and Clark Expedition, terminating at the mouth of the COLUMBIA RIVER on the coast of present-day Oregon. He established two subsidiary companies, the Pacific Fur Company in June 1810 and the Southwest Fur Company in June 1811.

The Pacific Fur Company was to establish a settlement called Astoria on the Oregon coast, near the Columbia River site where Lewis and Clark had wintered in 1805. At the same time, Astor entered into an agreement with the Canadian fur companies to supply their Great Lakes operations. He also obtained additional financial backing from the RUSSIAN-AMERICAN COMPANY, agreeing in return to transport supplies to its settlements in Alaska.

Two expeditions were sent to the Oregon coast to establish Astoria. The first, the seaward arm of the enterprise aboard Astor's ship, the *Tonquin*, headed by ROBERT STUART, left New York City in September 1810, rounded CAPE HORN, and reached the Oregon coast in March 1811. After the founding of the Astoria settlement, the *Tonquin* sailed northward along the coast, heading for the Russian posts in southern Alaska. At a stopover in Nootka Sound, where Astor's men intended to trade for sea otter pelts with the Nootka Indians, the ship came under attack. The Nootka killed all hands but one, who, although badly wounded, managed to ignite the ship's powder magazine. The explosion destroyed the ship and killed a number of Nootka.

An overland expedition, led by Astor employee WILSON PRICE HUNT, departed St. Louis in April 1811. The Astorians traveled up the Missouri, then overland into present-day Wyoming and Idaho, where they followed the Bighorn and Snake Rivers to the Columbia River's outlet on the Pacific Ocean at Astoria in February 1812.

Supplying the Astoria enterprise by sea from New York proved difficult. The situation became critical with the outbreak of the War of 1812 and the imposition of British naval blockades. Anticipating the imminent seizure of the Astoria settlement by the British, Astor's agents in Oregon sold the fort to the North West Company in 1813.

After 1815, Astor concentrated his Great Lakes operations out of centers at Green Bay, Wisconsin, and Grand Portage, Minnesota. His South West Company soon dominated most of the trade from Mackinac on Lake Michigan south and west to St. Louis and the ROCKY MOUNTAINS. His American Fur Company proved more efficient than the independent Missouri traders and smaller concerns, such as the ST. LOUIS MISSOURI FUR COMPANY and the ROCKY MOUNTAIN FUR COMPANY, and, by the late 1820s, held a near-monopoly on the FUR TRADE in the trans-Mississippi West, with the exclusion of the Pacific Northwest, which was dominated by the Hudson's Bay Company.

By the 1830s, demand for western beaver pelts by European and American hat manufacturers had declined because silk hats had replaced beaver as the dominant fashion. In addition, the number of beavers throughout the traditional trapping areas of the Great Lakes and eastern Rockies had been depleted. As a result, Astor sold his fur-trading empire to a consortium of St. Louis traders in 1834.

Although John Jacob Astor's expeditions were launched to expand his business empire, they also enabled the earliest organized explorations of large portions of North America, previously known only to Native Americans and a handful of MOUNTAIN MEN. Washington Irving's 1836 book *Astoria* provides a chronicle of the Oregon coast venture, based on Astor's own notes and journals and the accounts of other participants.

Atkinson, Henry (1782–1842) *U.S. Army officer on the Missouri River*

Henry Atkinson was born in North Carolina. In 1808, he joined the U.S. Army, and during the War of 1812, he was promoted to colonel.

On July 4, 1819, Atkinson led 1,100 troops from St. Louis up the MISSOURI RIVER on an expedition in which he hoped to reach the mouth of the Yellowstone River. The steamboats transporting the Yellowstone Expedition broke down, and Atkinson and his command reached only as far as Council Bluffs on the Missouri River in present-day Nebraska. At this point, Atkinson established a log outpost, known as Fort Atkinson.

In summer 1820, Atkinson dispatched military exploring expeditions to the north and west. One group, under Major STEPHEN HARRIMAN LONG, reached as far as Pikes Peak in the ROCKY MOUNTAINS. Another, under Captain Matthew J. Magee, explored northward to the mouth of the Minnesota River.

Five years later, Atkinson led a second Yellowstone Expedition. His command of 476 troops left the Council Bluffs post on May 16, 1825. This time, traveling by hand-cranked, paddle-wheel-driven KEELBOAT, he reached a point on the Yellowstone 100 miles above its mouth and negotiated treaties with Indian tribes of present-day eastern Montana.

Atkinson, who had been promoted to brigadier general in 1820, commanded troops in the Indian wars in Illinois,

Wisconsin, and Minnesota during the late 1820s and early 1830s.

Henry Atkinson's post at Council Bluffs became a focal point for fur traders and MOUNTAIN MEN of the upper Missouri and eastern Rockies. It was also an important starting point for early government explorations of the American West, including the 1827 expedition into present-day Kansas led by Colonel HENRY LEAVENWORTH. Moreover, his 1825 negotiations with the upper Missouri and Yellowstone tribes ended two years of Indian resistance and helped open the northern plains and Rocky Mountains to white trade and exploration.

Atkinson, Lucy (fl. 1820s–1860s) *British traveler, writer in Russia and central Asia, wife of Thomas Wittlam Atkinson*

Few details are known of Lucy Atkinson's origins or early life. She was definitely British by birth, yet her maiden name and place of birth remain unknown.

In about 1840, Atkinson went to live in St. Petersburg, Russia, where she worked as a tutor and governess for a daughter of General Mouravioff, governor general of eastern SIBERIA. It was as a member of Mouravioff's household that she first met English artist and architect THOMAS WITTLAM ATKINSON in 1846. He was about to embark on a sketching trip to SIBERIA and had contacted Mouravioff to obtain travel documents for his journey across Russia and into the regions to the east. Upon Thomas's return to St. Petersburg the following year, he and Lucy became engaged and were married in Moscow soon afterward.

In February 1848, Atkinson left Moscow with her husband, accompanying him on his sketching expedition eastward into Russian Asia. They traveled by horse-drawn sledge southeastward across the Ural Mountains to Barnaul, a goldmining center on the upper Ob River in the Altai Mountains. They crossed the mountains toward the northeastern Mongolia border. At a mountain lake called Altin Kool (golden lake), they were hosted by Kalmuck tribesmen, who accompanied them on a tour of the waters by native CANOE.

After a camel trip across the Kirghiz steppes, Atkinson and her husband reached the town of Kopal in September 1848, near the Russian-Chinese border. Atkinson gave birth to a son there whom the couple named Alatau, after the mountain that rises above Kopal. Six months later, they set out on a return journey to Barnaul, arriving in December 1849.

After a few months at Barnaul, Lucy and Thomas Atkinson resumed their travels, heading eastward into south-central Siberia. For the next several years, while Lucy remained with her infant son at Irkutsk on Lake Baikal, Thomas undertook expeditions into the surrounding country to sketch and make natural history studies.

The Atkinsons returned to England in 1854 in time for young Alatau to begin school. Thomas Atkinson produced an illustrated book of his travels, published in 1857.

After her husband's death in 1861, Lucy Atkinson compiled her own book from letters to her friends, *Recollections of Tartar Steppes and Their Inhabitants* (1863). The work provided the English reading public with details about peoples and lands east of the Ural Mountains.

Atkinson, Thomas Wittlam (1799–1861) *British artist, traveler in Russia and central Asia, husband of Lucy Atkinson*

Thomas Atkinson, an English artist and architect living in the Russian city of St. Petersburg, undertook a sketching trip to Siberia in 1846. Two years later, accompanied by his wife LUCY ATKINSON, he headed eastward across the Ural Mountains. Over the next five years, they journeyed to parts of central Asia rarely visited by western Europeans. Their travels took them from Barnaul, in the Altai Mountains, across the Kirghiz steppes to the Chinese border. He also reportedly visited Mongolia. He and his wife returned to St. Petersburg in 1853, after a journey that had taken them across almost 40,000 miles of Russian territory.

While traveling, Atkinson produced hundreds of watercolor paintings of central Asian scenes. Engravings made from them were used to produce illustrations for his account of his travels, *Oriental and Western Siberia: A Narrative of Seven Years' Explorations and Adventures in Siberia, Mongolia, the Kirghis Steppes, Chinese Tartary, and Part of Central Asia* (1857). The book was well received in both England and the United States, and he became a highly acclaimed lecturer on Russian Asia. He was also elected as a member of the ROYAL GEOGRAPHICAL SOCIETY.

Atlasov, Vladimir Vasilyevich (Vladimir Atlassov) (unknown–1711) *Russian Cossack in eastern Siberia and the Kamchatka Peninsula*

Vladimir Atlasov, a Siberian Cossack, settled in Yakutsk in 1672, where he served as an administrator for the czarist government. In 1695, he took command of Fort Anadyr on the shore of the Bering Sea, then Russia's northeasternmost outpost. From there, in conjunction with fellow Cossack LUKA MOROZKO, Atlasov undertook exploring expeditions into the region south of the Anadyr River that led to Russia's first knowledge and subsequent settlement of the Kamchatka Peninsula.

In 1699, in command of a force of 120 men, Atlasov headed south from Fort Anadyr. Upon reaching the Kamchatka River, he claimed the entire Kamchatka Peninsula for Czar Peter I (Peter the Great). The next year, he founded

Verkhnekamchatsk, the first Russian settlement on the Kamchatka Peninsula.

Atlasov journeyed to Moscow in 1700, where he presented an account of his explorations to Czar Peter. In 1708, he returned to Kamchatka as the region's chief administrator. Five years later, he was killed in a rebellion of his own men.

Vladimir Atlasov is credited with the Russian discovery and conquest of Kamchatka. His exploits helped extend Russia's domination of central Asia to the Pacific Ocean; his explorations revealed that Kamchatka was a peninsula. The Russian settlement of Kamchatka provided the next generation of Russian explorers with a staging point for expeditions across the Sea of Okhotsk to the Kuril Islands of northern Japan, and eastward across the Bering Sea to Alaska and the west coast of North America.

Audubon, John James (1785–1851)

American artist, naturalist in the Ohio and Mississippi Valleys

John James Audubon was born in Les Cayes, Haiti, the son of a French sea captain and a Haitian Creole woman. He was raised in France, studying art under the French artist Jacques-Louis David. In 1803, Audubon settled on his father's Pennsylvania estate, Mill Grove, near Philadelphia. It was there that he first began to study and paint birds.

In 1807, Audubon moved to Louisville, Kentucky, and entered the mercantile business. Three years later, he undertook a trade expedition down the Ohio River to Henderson, Kentucky, and established a general store, as well as a lumber and grist mill. He continued his painting of birds while on hunting expeditions into the largely unsettled Kentucky frontier region. At this time, he became acquainted with frontiersman DANIEL BOONE.

By 1819, Audubon's business had failed, leaving him bankrupt. He moved to Cincinnati and found work as a taxidermist. In 1820, he traveled down the Ohio River and MISSISSIPPI RIVER to New Orleans, where he supported his family by painting portraits and at times taught art. His fortunes improved in 1827, when he went to England and succeeded in winning financial support for the publication of his paintings of birds. This work, *The Birds of North America,* was published serially from 1827 to 1838.

Audubon returned to America in 1831, settling for a time in Charleston, South Carolina. In the 1830s, he undertook expeditions in search of wildlife subjects to paint, traveling over a wide area of North America, including the dunes and lagoons along the Texas coast and the wild regions of Florida, as well as the coast of Labrador.

In his later years, Audubon and his family lived at "Minnielands," their Hudson River estate in what is now New York City.

John James Audubon *(Library of Congress)*

John James Audubon became one of the foremost authorities on North American birds and established an enduring reputation as a painter of wildlife subjects. His painting expeditions through the frontier regions of the United States in the first half of the 19th century resulted in the discovery of 40 previously unknown bird species.

Auribeau, Alexandre Hesmivy d'

(unknown–1794) *French naval officer in the South Pacific and East Indies*

Alexandre Hesmivy d'Auribeau was second in command to ANTOINE-RAYMOND-JOSEPH DE BRUNI, chevalier d'Entrecasteaux, on the French ship *Recherche,* which sailed from Brest, France, in September 1791 in search of JEAN-FRANÇOIS DE GALAUP, comte de La Pérouse, who had become lost in his explorations of the South Pacific Ocean several years earlier.

In July 1793, near the coast of New Guinea, d'Entrecasteaux succumbed to SCURVY, and Auribeau assumed command. Over the next year, his ship sailed through the EAST INDIES, stopping at various Dutch settlements in present-day Indonesia. The French Revolution was then at its height, and Auribeau, a royalist, had to contend with political dissension among his own men as well as the distrust of Dutch authorities, who had become wary of any French presence during this critical time. In August 1794, he died at Semarang on the island of Java. According to some sources, he may have been poisoned, but most scholars believe that he died of dysentery.

Alexandre Hesmivy d'Auribeau played a key role in the first search efforts for the French explorer La Pérouse. Ironically, even in the South Pacific, halfway around the world from France, he was plagued with the political strife of the French Revolution.

Ávila, Pedro Arias de See ARIAS DE ÁVILA, PEDRO.

Avilés, Pedro Menéndez de See MENÉNDEZ DE AVILÉS, PEDRO.

Ayllón, Lucas Vásquez de (ca. 1475–1526)
Spanish colonial official in Santo Domingo, early colonizer on the southeast coast of North America
Few details are known of Lucas Vásquez de Ayllón's life before 1502, the year he first arrived in Santo Domingo, the chief Spanish settlement on the Caribbean island of Hispaniola (present-day Haiti and the Dominican Republic). In Santo Domingo, he served in the colonial government as a magistrate.

In 1520, inspired by the reports of JUAN PONCE DE LEÓN, Ayllón sent out an expedition under Francisco Gordillo that reached the coast of present-day South Carolina. Gordillo returned to Santo Domingo with about 70 Indian captives. The next year, Ayllón took one of these captives, an Indian (probably Shakori) known as Francisco Chicora, to Spain and presented him at the court of Charles I (Holy Roman Emperor Charles V). Chicora related to the Spanish monarch a fabulous account of his homeland, claiming that his native land contained a great wealth of precious stones and gold, that the kings and queens there were giants, and that the people had huge, rigid tails growing out of their posteriors, forcing them to dig holes in the ground in order to sit down.

With the death of Ponce de León in 1521, Ayllón was granted a royal patent to colonize Florida and what is now the southeastern United States. With Chicora, he sailed from Santo Domingo in 1526. His fleet of six ships carried 500 colonists and slaves. On the first landing at the mouth of the Santee River, near present-day Georgetown, South Carolina, Ayllón established the settlement of San Miguel de Guadalupe. He then explored southward along the coast of present-day Georgia, to the mouth of the Savannah River.

Chicora disappeared soon after landing. Over the next few months, the colonists were decimated by swamp fever. Ayllón himself succumbed in the winter of 1526–27. Only 150 of the colonists survived to return to Santo Domingo in 1527.

Lucas Vásquez de Ayllón attempted to establish one of the earliest Spanish settlements on the mainland of the present-day United States. The next major Spanish colonizing effort on the southeast coast of North America did not occur until 40 years later with the founding of St. Augustine, Florida.

Ayolas, Juan de (unknown–ca. 1538)
Spanish conquistador in South America
Juan de Ayolas was a lieutenant in PEDRO DE MENDOZA's 1535 expedition from Spain to the Río de la Plata region of South America.

In 1535–36, encouraged by the reports of SEBASTIAN CABOT, Ayolas explored up the Río de la Plata, from the site of present-day Buenos Aires, Argentina, in search of gold and silver. From the Río de la Plata estuary he reached the Paraná River, which he ascended, and along its banks he founded the settlement of Corpus Cristi. He then explored the Paraguay River in search of a route to Peru. At one point he obtained gold and silver from the Guaraní Indians, but these riches had probably originated among the Inca Indians west of the ANDES MOUNTAINS. He penetrated the interior of South America as far as what is now the Chaco region of Paraguay and northern Argentina, and he may have reached the eastern slopes of the Andes.

Probably in early 1538, Ayolas was killed in a clash with Guaraní near present-day Asunción, Paraguay. Soon afterward, his lieutenant, DOMINGO MARTÍNEZ DE IRALA, succeeded in securing Asunción.

Juan de Ayolas's explorations, along with those of his lieutenant Martínez de Irala, led to the opening of the upper Río de la Plata and its tributaries to extensive Spanish settlement.

Azara, Félix de (1746–1811) *Spanish official, naturalist in South America*
Félix de Azara was born in the Aragon region of Spain. In 1775, while serving as a Spanish army officer against the North African pirates in present-day Algeria, he was wounded and earned a promotion to the rank of brigadier general.

Azara went to the Río de la Plata region of South America in 1781, as a commissioner in a Spanish government survey that determined the boundary between Spanish and Portuguese territory. Over the next 20 years, he undertook extensive explorations along the Paraná and

Félix de Azara *(Library of Congress)*

Paraguay Rivers, during which he made studies of the region's natural history.

Following his return to Spain in 1801, Félix de Azara published a series of scientific and geographic studies of the upper Río de la Plata river system. His works provided Europeans with one of the earliest scientific accounts of the interior of South America, as well as a definitive history of the conquest of the region now comprising Paraguay and northern Argentina.

Azevado, Francisco de (1578–1660)
Portuguese or Spanish missionary in India and Tibet

Francisco de Azevado was a Portuguese or Spanish Jesuit missionary priest in India during the early 1600s. In 1631, he journeyed from Delhi, India, across the HIMALAYAS by way of the Mana Pass, and into Tibet. He succeeded in reestablishing a Jesuit mission and church in Tibet, continuing the work begun several years earlier by missionary priest ANTONIO DE ANDRADE. Azevado's mission in Tibet lasted for only a few years. In 1635, he was forced to abandon it in the face of hostility from Tibetan Buddhist authorities.

Although Francisco de Azevado failed to establish a permanent Christian missionary presence in Tibet, he was one of the first Europeans to journey there since the end of the Middle Ages.

B

Back, Sir George (1796–1878) *British naval officer in the Canadian Arctic*

Born in Stockport, Cheshire, England, George Back entered the Royal Navy in his early teens as a midshipman, serving in the last naval engagements of the Napoleonic Wars.

In 1818, Back served under SIR JOHN FRANKLIN in an unsuccessful attempt to navigate from Spitsbergen (present-day Svalbard), north of Norway, across the Arctic Ocean to the Bering Sea.

The next year, 1819, Back took part in Franklin's overland expedition into the Canadian Arctic. With Franklin, he traveled from York Factory on HUDSON BAY, along the Nelson and Saskatchewan Rivers to Lake Athabasca. From there, he joined Franklin on an exploration northward to Great Slave Lake and the Coppermine River, which they followed to its mouth on the Arctic coast. The expedition then charted the northern coastline of Canada eastward to Point Turnagain. Back spent three years exploring with Franklin, during which the expedition faced extreme hardships due to shortages of food. At one point, Back heroically trekked southward from the Arctic coast to Great Slave Lake in order to obtain food supplies from the Indians for Franklin and his men, covering 250 miles in less than eight weeks. Without adequate food himself, he survived only by eating lichens, a pair of leather trousers, and an old shoe.

Back returned to Arctic Canada with Franklin in 1825. Starting from New York, they journeyed overland to Great Slave Lake and descended the Mackenzie River to its mouth on the Beaufort Sea. They then undertook an exploration westward along the northern coast of Canada, intending to reach British naval vessels waiting for them at Icy Cape, Alaska. Impeded by ice and the rugged coastline, they managed only to reach a point 370 miles west of the Mackenzie's mouth, about half the distance to Icy Cape, Alaska. The expedition returned to England in fall 1827.

In 1833, Back was promoted to the rank of lieutenant in the Royal Navy. That year, he undertook an expedition in search of SIR JOHN ROSS, who, with his nephew SIR JAMES CLARK ROSS, had disappeared while exploring the Arctic coast of Canada by ship. While wintering at Great Slave Lake in 1833–34, Back received news that Ross and his party had safely returned to England and instead set out to explore to the north and east. From the Indians, he heard reports of a stream known as the Great Fish River, which flowed into the Arctic north of Great Slave Lake, several hundred miles east of the Coppermine River. He succeeded in locating the Great Fish River and traveled its 550-mile length to its outlet on Simpson Strait, south of King William Island. Back returned to England in 1835.

In 1836, Back was promoted to captain and embarked on a seaward expedition to the Canadian Arctic in command of the *Terror*. From Hudson Bay, he sailed northward, attempting to negotiate the NORTHWEST PASSAGE. Charting the Arctic coastline, he sailed around Southampton Island but was trapped by the ice in Frozen Strait. The *Terror* was icebound until spring 1837, by which time it had been so severely damaged that Back was forced to head back to England. On the return voyage, the ailing ship was in danger of sinking and had to be beached on the coast of Ireland.

Back returned to regular naval service after 1837. He was awarded a baronetcy for his Arctic explorations, and, in 1857, he was made an admiral.

Sir George Back's exploits in the Canadian Arctic included extensive overland and seaward explorations. His work filled in many gaps in the previously uncharted coastline of northern Canada. The Great Fish River, which he explored during his 1833–35 expedition, was subsequently renamed the Back River in his honor. He recounted his experiences in his books, *Narrative of the Arctic Land Expedition to the Mouth of the Great Fish River* (1836) and *Narrative of Expedition in H.M.S. Terror* (1838).

Baffin, William (ca. 1584–1622) *English mariner in Greenland and the Canadian Arctic*

Little is known of William Baffin's early life except that he was apparently a highly skilled mariner and was self-educated in navigation and mathematics. In April 1612, he sailed as a pilot on the ship *Patience,* captained by JAMES HALL, undertaking an expedition in search of the NORTHWEST PASSAGE, sponsored by London-based COMPANY OF MERCHANTS OF LONDON DISCOVERERS OF THE NORTHWEST PASSAGE.

From the port of Hull, England, Baffin sailed to what is now Godthaab, on the southwest coast of GREENLAND. Baffin and Hall then transferred to the expedition's other ship, the *Heartsease,* and explored northward into Davis Strait along the west coast of Greenland as far as 67° north latitude, then turned south. While ashore at Rommel's Fjord, Greenland, Hall was killed by Inuit. Baffin then returned to England, having made important navigational observations relating to magnetic variations of the COMPASS in high northern latitudes. On this voyage, he also made early calculations of longitude at sea.

In 1613–14, Baffin made two voyages to Spitsbergen (present-day Svalbard) under the sponsorship of the London-based MUSCOVY COMPANY. Baffin returned to the service of the Company of Merchants of London Discoverers of the Northwest Passage in 1615. That year, he sailed as a pilot aboard HENRY HUDSON's former ship, the *Discovery,* under the command of ROBERT BYLOT, a survivor of Hudson's ill-fated final voyage. Baffin navigated the *Discovery* through Hudson Strait and explored the northwest coast of HUDSON BAY, seeking an outlet to the Pacific Ocean. After surveying the coastline northward beyond Southampton Island and into Foxe Basin, Baffin rightfully concluded that Hudson Bay provided no navigable outlet westward to the Pacific, although later explorers would search the region again.

On a second voyage with Bylot in 1616, Baffin sailed northward along the west coast of Greenland and into a large bay that was later named after him. He entered Kane Basin on the extreme northwest coast of Greenland and explored the coast of a large body of land later known as Baffin Island. Proceeding south, he found and named Jones Sound and Lancaster Sound, which flank Devon Island on the north and south. Upon his return to England, he reported that there was little hope in locating a waterway through the islands and frozen straits west of Greenland.

Baffin served next in the BRITISH EAST INDIA COMPANY's fleet, commanding the ship *London.* In 1622, he took part in a military campaign in the Persian Gulf against the Portuguese. He was killed in an assault on the Portuguese-held fortress at Queshm, near the Strait of Hormuz.

William Baffin's geographic findings north and west of Greenland were not confirmed until subsequent British explorations in the early part of the 19th century. His reports slowed down attempts to locate an eastern entrance to the Northwest Passage. On his second voyage with Bylot in 1616, Baffin reached as far north as 77°45' north latitude, a record until SIR GEORGE STRONG NARES's Arctic expedition of 1852. Ironically, Lancaster Sound, which Baffin first charted in 1616, proved to be the eastern entry point for the Northwest Passage, first successfully navigated in the early 20th century.

Baikie, William Balfour (1825–1864)
Scottish naval surgeon, naturalist in West Africa

Born in Scotland, William Baikie became a medical doctor, with a background in the natural sciences. He also developed an interest in the study of foreign languages.

In 1854, he took part in a British government-sponsored expedition to West Africa that attempted to make contact with the German explorer of Africa, HEINRICH BARTH, who had reached the upper NIGER RIVER from the SAHARA DESERT. As a naval surgeon aboard the *Pleiad,* Baikie sailed from England to the Niger Delta, on the west coast of Africa.

Following the death of the ship's captain, Baikie took command of the expedition. Traveling by steamboat, he ascended the Niger to its principal tributary, the Benue, which he followed upstream for several hundred miles. Unable to locate Barth, he returned to England.

Baikie undertook a second exploration into West Africa in 1857. While ascending the Niger, his vessel was wrecked. Nevertheless, he again reached the confluence of the Niger and Benue Rivers, where, in 1859, he established a trading settlement at Lokoja.

Baikie remained on the Niger for the next seven years, during which he studied the region's natural history as well as the various languages and dialects of the native population. He also translated the Bible into Hausa, then the predominant language of West Africa. In 1864, while on his way back to Great Britain, Baikie died on the West African coast in Sierra Leone.

William Baikie's 1854 exploration of the Benue River took him farther upstream than any European had reached to that time. His settlement at Lokoja in what is now south-central Nigeria opened the upper Niger River region to Western commerce. As a scientific explorer, he collected the earliest data on the region's native cultures, languages, and natural history.

Baines, Thomas (1822–1875) *British painter in Africa and Australia*

Born in 1822 in King's Lynn, Norfolk, England, Thomas Baines pursued a career as a painter. He traveled and painted in southern and central Africa and in Australia, some of his work in an official capacity, with assignments from the British government.

In 1848–51, Baines served as artist to the British army in South Africa. In 1855–56, he visited Australia as part of the North Australian Exploring Expedition, led by Augustus Charles Gregory, which traveled along the Victoria River and Sturt Creek in the Northern Territory, before returning overland to Moreton Bay, Queensland.

In 1858–59, back in Africa, Baines accompanied DAVID LIVINGSTONE on his expedition to the ZAMBEZI RIVER and despite frequent personal quarrels with Livingstone, produced valuable work. In 1860–66, he traveled with an expedition headed by James Chapman to Namibia and Victoria Falls. Thereafter he lived in South Africa.

In addition to his sketches made during his travels, from which he painted oils and watercolors, Thomas Baines kept journals in which he recorded his observations on native peoples and wildlife. His paintings were the first views of central and southern Africa seen by Europeans.

Baker, Florence (Florence von Sass Baker, Lady Baker) (ca. 1841–1918) *Hungarian-English explorer in East Africa, wife of Sir Samuel White Baker*

Florence Baker, née von Sass, was the second wife of British explorer SIR SAMUEL WHITE BAKER, whom she met in 1858, while Baker was traveling in the Balkan region of southeastern Europe. The facts of her earlier life are uncertain. She was Hungarian by birth, daughter of Finnicek von Sass, probably 20 years younger than Baker. It is thought that she lost her family during the 1848 revolutions in Europe. She ended up a slave to Turks, and Baker purchased her and liberated her.

In 1861, von Sass accompanied Baker on his first expedition to East Africa, during which he planned to undertake a search for the source of the NILE RIVER. They traveled first to Egypt, then sailed along the Nile to Khartoum in the Sudan, where they remained for 14 months, preparing for the trip into the interior of equatorial East Africa by studying Arabic.

In December 1862, von Sass and Baker left Khartoum and sailed up the Nile to Gondokoro, where they met with the British explorers JAMES AUGUSTUS GRANT and JOHN HANNING SPEKE. They continued up the Nile into the kingdom of Bunyoro, at times traveling with an Arab slave caravan. They encountered some opposition from the brother of the king of Bunyoro, a native chief named M'Gambi. M'Gambi at one point demanded that in order for Baker to continue his explorations, he would have to leave von Sass behind for "his pleasure." Von Sass's indignation led M'Gambi to relent and even provide 300 of his men as an escort.

In March 1863, von Sass and Baker pushed southeastward in search of the uncharted lake known by the local people as Luta N'zige. En route, she suffered an acute case of sunstroke. Although she fell into a coma for a week, she fully recovered.

On March 14, 1864, von Sass and Baker finally reached the lake in what is now western Uganda, which they named Lake Albert (Albert Nyanza). They also located Murchison Falls, a source of the Nile, naming it after the president of the ROYAL GEOGRAPHICAL SOCIETY.

Upon their return to London in 1865, von Sass and Baker were married. While delivering his first lecture to the Royal Geographical Society that year, Baker formally introduced his wife to the English public.

Florence Baker returned to Egypt with her husband in 1869, accompanying the Prince of Wales to the opening ceremonies of the Suez Canal. When her husband was appointed governor general of the equatorial Nile Basin (the White Nile region in south-central Sudan), she accompanied him there, and during the next four years, she assisted in his efforts to eliminate the SLAVE TRADE in the region. They returned to England in 1873, at the conclusion of Baker's term of office.

Florence Baker was one of the few women to play an active role in the history of African exploration and travel into the continent's interior, not as a missionary, but solely for the purpose of exploration. Samuel Baker credited her courage and devotion as essential to his success in exploring East Africa.

Baker, James (Jim Baker) (1818–1898)

American fur trader, guide, interpreter in the American West

James (Jim) Baker left his home in Belleville, Illinois, in the late 1830s, soon embarking on a career in the FUR TRADE in the northern and central ROCKY MOUNTAINS. He was part of the AMERICAN FUR COMPANY's 1838 expedition along the Oregon Trail, led by fur trader THOMAS FITZ-PATRICK. During this trip, Baker left the main party and joined with JAMES BRIDGER to trap in the Green River Valley of what is now eastern Utah and southern Wyoming.

Except for a brief visit to his hometown in Illinois during 1840–41, Baker remained in the northern Rockies, operating as a trapper for Bridger for nearly two decades. During that time, he married a Shoshone Indian woman and became fluent in several Indian languages.

In 1857–58, Baker served as an interpreter and guide to Captain RANDOLPH BARNES MARCY's U.S. Army command, which had been sent to Utah to quell the Mormon uprising. At one point, Baker guided Marcy's troops over more than 600 miles of snow-covered mountain trails—from eastern Utah southwestward to Taos, New Mexico—to obtain supplies for Fort Bridger, which had been cut off during the conflict.

Sometime after 1858, Baker settled on the Green River and operated a store on the Mormon Trail. He then moved to Denver, Colorado, following the Pikes Peak (Colorado) gold rush of 1859.

Starting in 1865, Baker served for several years as a guide and interpreter for the federal government's agency to the Ute Indians. Baker spent his later years in retirement in southern Wyoming near the Colorado border.

As a trader, guide, and interpreter, Jim Baker helped in the opening of the American West to non-Indian settlement.

Baker, Sir Samuel White (1821–1893)

British explorer, writer in East Africa, government official, husband of Florence Baker

Samuel Baker was born in London, the son of a wealthy family with extensive business interests in Great Britain and its overseas empire. He attended private schools in England and Germany, where he was trained as an engineer, with a specialization in railroad construction.

In 1842, following his marriage to the daughter of an English clergyman, Baker traveled to Mauritius, the British island colony in the Indian Ocean, east of Madagascar, where his father owned several sugar plantations. He later moved with his wife to CEYLON (present-day Sri Lanka), off the south coast of India, where he established an agricultural colony as well as a resort at Nuwara Eliya.

Tropical fever in Ceylon caused Baker to return to England in 1855. Soon afterward, on a hunting trip in the Pyrenees, his wife died. He then undertook travels into the Balkan countries of Europe, where he directed the construction of a railroad that connected the Danube River with the Black Sea. During his travels, he met Florence von Sass, a Hungarian woman, who later became his wife (FLORENCE BAKER).

Following travels in Asia Minor (present-day Turkey), Baker and von Sass went to Cairo, Egypt, in 1861, from

Sir Samuel Baker *(Library of Congress)*

where they headed southward into the Sudan, in search of the source of the NILE RIVER. They remained in Khartoum for over a year, studying Arabic and undertaking explorations of the tributaries of the Nile that flowed into the river from Ethiopia. By studying the silt of the Atbara River of northern Ethiopia, they determined that the rich soil of the Nile Delta originated from Ethiopia.

In 1862, Baker and von Sass set out from Khartoum and ascended the Nile southward across the Nubian Desert. By February 1863, they had arrived in Gondokoro and there met up with British African explorers JAMES AUGUSTUS GRANT and JOHN HANNING SPEKE, who informed them they had determined that the source of the Nile was Lake Victoria. Grant and Speke also reported to Baker the existence of an as yet uncharted lake that they believed was also a principal source of the Nile, known by the natives as Luta N'Zige. Baker and von Sass then continued southward to Juba on the White Nile.

Baker and von Sass set out from Juba in March 1863, traveling through the remote East African regions of Latooka and Obbo and making contact with the Dinka people. They were forced to head southward by way of a roundabout route because of problems with porters and hostile local peoples. Heavy rains, and opposition to their expedition by the ruler of the African kingdom of Bunyoro, hampered their progress.

Finally, on March 14, 1864, after two and a half years of exploring along the Nile into unknown regions of East Africa south of the Sudan, Baker and von Sass reached the shores of the Luta N'Zige, in what is now northwestern Uganda. Baker renamed it Lake Albert (Albert Nyanza), in honor of Prince Albert, husband and consort to Queen Victoria, after whom the principal source of the White Nile—Lake Victoria (Victoria Nyanza)—had been named. Over the next two weeks, Baker and von Sass explored Lake Albert in a native CANOE and located the 120-foot-high Murchison Falls, which he named after Sir Roderick Murchison, then president of the ROYAL GEOGRAPHICAL SOCIETY.

Baker and von Sass returned to England in 1865, where they were married. Baker was awarded a gold medal by the Royal Geographical Society. In 1866, he was knighted by Queen Victoria for his achievements in African exploration.

In 1869, the Bakers returned to Egypt for the opening ceremonies of the Suez Canal. Samuel Baker agreed to lead a military expedition into the upper Nile region of the southern Sudan (then still part of Egypt), on behalf of the Ottoman viceroy of Egypt, Ismail Pasha.

With a command of 1,500 men, Baker and his wife again ascended the Nile, reaching as far south as Fatiko. Commissioned to establish Egyptian rule over the region and wipe out the SLAVE TRADE, he established a military outpost. Over the next four years, he ran into conflicts with both Arab slavers and local African rulers. Nevertheless, he did succeed in organizing the government of a new Egyptian province in south-central Sudan, called Equatoria, of which he was appointed governor general.

With the expiration of his term of office in 1873, Baker and his wife returned to England. They settled on his estate in Devonshire but continued to make periodic hunting trips to far-off places, including Japan and the ROCKY MOUNTAINS of the western United States.

Sir Samuel Baker's explorations in East Africa did much to clarify the geography of the region for Europeans. His administration in the southern Sudan helped somewhat to stem the slave trade. In his later years in England, he was considered a foremost authority on Africa. He wrote about his experiences in Ceylon in his book *The Rifle and the Hound in Ceylon* (1854) and recounted his African exploits in *The Albert N'yanza, Great Basin of the Nile, and Explorations of the Nile Sources* (1866) and *The Nile Tributaries of Abyssinia* (1868).

Bakhov, Ivan (unknown–1762) *Russian mariner in the Siberian Arctic*

Ivan Bakhov was a Russian mariner operating out of the Bering Sea port of Anadyr on the Pacific coast of northeastern SIBERIA. In 1748, while on a voyage from Anadyr southward along the coast to the Kamchatka Peninsula, his ship was wrecked on the shores of Bering Island. He survived the winter there, and, the following spring, he improvised a vessel from the wreckage of his ship and sailed it west to Kamchatka.

In 1755, the Russian government authorized Bakhov to explore the Arctic coast of Siberia eastward from the mouth of the Lena River. Bakhov did not begin his expedition until summer 1760. Accompanied by an associate named Nikita Shalaurov, he set out in a small boat from the Lena's outlet into the Laptev Sea; they sailed eastward along the coast to the mouth of the Yana River and wintered there.

Bakhov resumed his eastward exploration in spring 1761. He sailed into the East Siberian Sea, reaching as far as the mouth of the Kolyma River. While encamped the following winter, he succumbed to SCURVY. Shalaurov survived to report the results of the expedition.

In his 1760–62 explorations of the north coast of Siberia, Ivan Bakhov succeeded in navigating through a major Asian portion of the NORTHEAST PASSAGE not previously visited by Europeans.

Balboa, Vasco Núñez de See NÚÑEZ DE BALBOA, VASCO.

Baldaya, Afonso Gonçalves (Alfonso Baldaya)
(fl. 1430s) *Portuguese mariner on the west coast of Africa*

In 1435, Portuguese mariner Afonso Baldaya took part in GIL EANNES's second voyage southward along the West African coast, below Cape Bojador. They were sponsored by HENRY THE NAVIGATOR, prince of Portugal, for whom Baldaya acted as cup bearer.

The next year, Baldaya commanded an expedition of his own that sailed to a point below the TROPIC OF CANCER, to the north of Cape Blanco on the Atlantic coast of the present-day West African nation of Mauritania. He returned to Portugal with a cargo of seal skins, the first time goods from West Africa had been taken directly to Europe without the intervention of Arab middlemen.

Baldaya's 1436 voyage marked the first time a ship from Christian Europe had sailed to a point south of the tropic of Cancer, below the extent of Muslim-controlled territory on the west coast of Africa. With Eannes, he was one of the early pioneers of Prince Henry's program of maritime exploration that eventually led the Portuguese to develop a seaward passage around Africa to India and the Far East.

Balmat, Jacques (1762–1834) *French mountain climber in the Alps*

Jacques Balmat was from Chamonix in Savoy, formerly a duchy and now part of France. Like other men from his village, he became a crystal hunter who climbed into the Alps near his home in search of quartz crystals used in the making of jewelry. In the process, Balmat became an accomplished *montagnard*, the French word for mountaineer.

Back in 1760, Horace Bénédict de Saussure, a Swiss aristocrat and naturalist from Conches, near Geneva, offered a reward to the person who found a route to the top of MONT BLANC, the highest peak in the Alps at 15,771 feet above sea level. Attempts for 25 years, even a number of well-organized expeditions starting in 1775, had failed, but knowledge of possible routes and of mountaineering techniques had been gained. By the time Balmat was in his 20s, he had gained a great deal of experience on the glacier-covered rock of the high Alps. Michel Paccard, a doctor from Chamonix, also had spent time in the Alps seeking the route to Mont Blanc's summit with the help of local guides. While locating a route in advance of their final assault, Balmat became the first known man to spend nights on the upper glaciers. He approached Paccard and told him of his route, and, in a subsequent expedition, the two men reached the summit on August 8, 1786.

Balmat climbed to the summit six more times in his career, one of them in 1787 with a scientific expedition under Saussure, during which he used a barometer to measure Mont Blanc's altitude (his result of 15,626 feet coming close to later readings conducted with more accurate equipment). In one climb late in life, he was accompanied by a local woman, Marie Paradis, in the first female ascent. Balmat's final ascent was in 1817, at the age of 57, although he continued his alpine activities until disappearing in 1834 while searching for gold in the Sixt Valley of the Alps.

Jacques Balmat's efforts, along with those of Paccard and Saussure and other early climbers in the Alps, helped shape what was to become modern MOUNTAIN CLIMBING. Balmat's role in the conquest of Mont Blanc was that of the local guide, beginning a tradition carried on by such other guides as MATTHIAS ZURBRIGGEN and TENZING NORGAY.

Banks, Sir Joseph (1743–1820) *British naturalist in Labrador, Newfoundland, and the South Pacific, sponsor of scientific expeditions*

Born in London, Joseph Banks was the son of an affluent Devonshire doctor. He attended Eton and Harrow, then went on to Oxford University.

Banks's main interest was in NATURAL SCIENCE, especially zoology and botany. On his father's death in 1761, he inherited a fortune, enabling him to devote his life to scientific study. About this time, he initiated the program of plant experimentation and research at London's Kew Gardens.

In 1763, Banks undertook a scientific expedition to Labrador and Newfoundland, seeking specimens of new species of plants and animals.

From 1768 to 1771, Banks circled the world as the chief scientist on JAMES COOK's first voyage to the South Pacific Ocean. Sailing on the *Endeavour,* Banks furnished his own extensive array of scientific equipment and provided his own staff of assistants and servants. His chief assistant was DANIEL CARL SOLANDER.

Banks and his staff collected hundreds of specimens of previously unknown species of plants and animals throughout the voyage. En route to Tahiti, Banks made a landing at Tierra del Fuego and undertook the first scientific studies of the wildlife at the tip of South America. In Tahiti, Banks broadened his research to include the ethnology and language of the native people.

In Australian waters, Banks collected specimens of the life forms found along the Great Barrier Reef. Accompanied by Cook, he made a landing on the eastern Australian coast at a spot subsequently named Botany Bay (modern-day Sydney), after the hundreds of new species of plants that Banks discovered there. Banks collected specimens of Australian marsupials, including the kangaroo, and took the first stuffed specimen of this animal back to Europe.

In 1772, soon after his return to England, Banks led a scientific expedition, including JOHN GORE, to the Hebrides and ICELAND. Six years later, he was elected president of En-

Sir Joseph Banks *(Library of Congress)*

gland's leading scientific organization, the ROYAL SOCIETY. In 1788, Banks helped establish, the Association for Promoting the Discovery of the Interior Parts of Africa, also known as the AFRICAN ASSOCIATION, which under his direction in 1795 sponsored MUNGO PARK's explorations of West Africa.

Sir Joseph Banks, who was knighted and awarded a baronetcy in 1781, became the chief adviser to the British government on scientific matters. Under his influence, government-sponsored exploring expeditions regularly included a scientific staff. The animal and plant specimens that Banks collected on Cook's first voyage formed the basis of the natural history collection of the British Museum.

Baptista, Pedro João (Pedra Baptista)
(fl. early 1800s) *Portuguese colonial official in south-central Africa*

In 1802, Pedro Baptista, of Afro-Portuguese descent, was in the employ of the Portuguese colonial government as a *pombeiros,* a slave agent. He left Cassange on the Atlantic coast of Angola and, accompanied by Amaro José, trekked eastward across south-central Africa. Baptista and José first headed northeastward, then, on reaching the Kasai River, followed it to its headwaters to the south.

Traveling overland, Baptista and José reached the Lualaba River at the settlement of Kolwezi in present-day southern Democratic Republic of Congo. They proceeded eastward to Lake Mweru, then crossed present-day northeastern Zambia to Lake Malawi. From the lake, they traveled into the Tete region of Mozambique and, in 1804, descended the ZAMBEZI RIVER to its outlet on the Indian Ocean at the Mozambique Channel.

Soon after reaching the east coast of Africa, Baptista and José set out on a return journey to Angola, arriving there in 1811. The entire trip, first east to west, then west to east, covered about 4,000 miles.

Pedro Baptista's journey in 1802–04 was the first known European crossing of the African continent, predating the explorations of DAVID LIVINGSTONE by nearly 50 years. His trip established the earliest overland trade links between Angola and Mozambique, at that time Portugal's main colonies in Africa. He also opened up the Kasai River to European commerce. In his 1811 report to Portuguese colonial authorities, he described the interior of south-central Africa as agriculturally well developed, with law and order effectively maintained by a few powerful native rulers.

Baranov, Aleksandr Andreyevich (Alexander Andreyevich Baranov, Alexandr Andreivich Baranof) (1747–1819)
Russian fur trader, administrator of Russian Alaska

Aleksandr Baranov was a native of Kargopol, Russia, a small village near the Arctic Ocean port of Archangel. At the age of 15, he traveled Moscow, where he was employed as a clerk to a German trading firm. In the early 1770s, he moved east to the Siberian city of Irkutsk. From there, he headed to the Anadyr region in the extreme northeastern Siberian Arctic, directly across the BERING STRAIT from Alaska's Seward Peninsula. He attempted to establish a fur-trading enterprise, but his business was destroyed by the Siberian native Chukchi.

Back in Irkutsk, Baranov became acquainted with GRIGORY IVANOVICH SHELIKOV, who was at that time developing the FUR TRADE in Russia's newly acquired North American territory, Alaska. In 1790, Baranov was hired to manage the Shelikov-Golikov Company, then operating on Kodiak Island in the Gulf of Alaska. That year, he sailed for Kodiak from the Siberian port of Okhotsk aboard the *Three Saints.* The ship was wrecked on Unalaska Island in the Aleutian Archipelago, however. In spring 1791, using boats built from skins, Baranov and his men completed the journey to the settlement at Three Saints on Kodiak. Soon afterward, under Baranov's direction, DIMITRY IVANOVICH BOCHAROV, a subordinate, undertook an exploration of the north shores of the Alaska Peninsula. Bocharov's expedition also discovered that the Egegik River provided a shortcut for small boats across the Alaska Peninsula into the Shelikov Strait.

The Shelikov-Golikov enterprise in Alaska flourished. Baranov extended the company's trade operations west and south along the Alaskan coast. In 1791–93, Baranov led explorations around Kodiak Island and the Kenai Peninsula, and into Cook Inlet in the area of present-day Anchorage, Alaska. He also explored islands in Prince William Sound, and, in 1792, he established a shipyard at present-day Seward, Alaska. Three years later, Baranov explored Yakutat Bay and claimed it for Russia. He also expanded the company's operation on what came to be known as Baranof Island, establishing the settlement of Mikhailovsk.

In 1799, the settlement was enlarged to include the city of New Archangel, which developed into a cosmopolitan center with a reputation as the "St. Petersburg of the Pacific." Also that year, Czar Paul I granted Shelikov and Baranov a royal monopoly for trade and exploration of all territory in Russian North America, north of 55° north latitude. In addition, Baranov was granted official status that made him the virtual governor of Russian possessions in North America.

Under Baranov's leadership, the Russians accelerated their exploitation of the fur resources of the Aleutian Islands and Gulf of Alaska region, trapping to near extinction such species as the Alaska blue fox, the Arctic fox, the Alaska seal, and especially the sea otter. Baranov employed native workers in the RUSSIAN-AMERICAN COMPANY enterprise, organizing whole Aleut villages as factories involved in all aspects of production. He was frequently criticized for his harsh treatment of the native peoples, although he was married to an Alaskan Indian woman.

Aleksandr Baranov *(Library of Congress)*

The Tlingit Indians of the panhandle of southeastern Alaska refused to work for Baranov and the Russians; during the 1790s, they came to resent the Russian encroachment on their hunting lands. In 1802, they rose up against the New Archangel settlement, destroying the city. Two years later, with the help of Royal Russian naval forces under explorer and naval officer YURY LISIANSKY, Baranov successfully recaptured New Archangel and rebuilt the city.

In 1804–05, Baranov directed an expedition southward along the North American coast from the Gulf of Alaska to the coast of northern California. He also sponsored an expedition aboard the *Juno* to the mouth of the COLUMBIA RIVER in 1805. Yet the ship was unable to reach the Oregon coast because of storms, instead landing at San Francisco Bay. Had the *Juno* put in to the Columbia, it might have encountered the expedition of MERIWETHER LEWIS and WILLIAM CLARK, then wintering nearby.

The Russian government hoped to maintain exclusive trading rights over its North American interests, but Baranov repeatedly entered into business ventures with foreign commercial interests. He negotiated an arrangement with JOHN JACOB ASTOR's Pacific Fur Company, a subsidiary of the AMERICAN FUR COMPANY, to supply Russian trade centers in Alaska in 1813, but Astor's ship failed to reach Alaska.

From his headquarters at New Archangel, Baranov also attempted to extend Russian influence to California and the South Pacific. In 1812, under Baranov's direction, I. A. Kuskov, an associate of the Russian-American Company, led an expedition south from Alaska to the California coast, and inland to a site on Bodega Bay, 50 miles north of present-day San Francisco, where he established Selenie Ross (later known as Fort Ross) among the Pomo Indians.

In 1815–17, Baranov sought to create a Russian sphere of influence in the HAWAIIAN ISLANDS, under his subordinate Dr. G. A. Schaffer, a venture that was soon abandoned. The Fort Ross settlement also proved unprofitable over subsequent years and, in 1841, was sold to Swiss pioneer John Sutter.

Because of his continued involvement with foreign traders, and amid Russian Orthodox Church criticism of his abusive treatment of the Alaska Natives, Baranov ran afoul of Russian authorities in Moscow. He was recalled as director of the Russian-American Company in 1818. On his voyage home to Russia in 1819, he died at sea in the Indian Ocean, off the coast of the Indonesian island of Batavia.

At the height of his career, Aleksandr Baranov was the chief administrator of a vast trading empire that stretched from Bristol Bay, north of the Aleutian Archipelago, as far south as the Sacramento Valley of California. His life closely paralleled the careers of Canadian and American fur traders, such as DONALD MACKENZIE, JOHN McLOUGHLIN, PETER SKENE OGDEN, and WILLIAM HENRY ASHLEY, who helped open up lands beyond the ROCKY MOUNTAINS to non-Indian development during the same period.

Barents, Willem (Willem Barentzoon, Willem Barentz) (unknown–1597) *Dutch mariner in the European Arctic*

Few details exist of Willem Barents's origins and early life. By 1594, he had established a reputation in the Netherlands as a highly capable mariner and navigator. In June of that year, he commanded the *Gesandte,* one of three ships sent out by the Dutch government in search of the NORTHEAST PASSAGE. Another ship in this fleet was captained by the expedition's principal supporter, JAN HUYGHEN VAN LINSCHOTEN.

From Holland, Barents sailed northward along the coast of Europe, rounded Norway's North Cape, then headed eastward as far as the islands of Novaya Zemlya, off the north coast of eastern European Russia. He navigated northward along the west coast of Novaya Zemlya, reaching its northernmost extremity, which he named Ice Cape. Farther progress eastward beyond this point was blocked by ice.

Barents then turned southward, charting the strait that divides Novaya Zemlya into two large islands. Meanwhile, Linschoten had his ship follow the Russian mainland eastward beyond Novaya Zemlya, sailing in ice-free waters as far as the mouth of the Kara River and the Kara Sea. Barents rejoined Linschoten and the rest of the fleet in an island group west of Novaya Zemlya that he called the Orange Islands in honor of the Dutch ruling family.

Barents returned to Amsterdam after the three-month voyage. His navigational reports were encouraging, and the Dutch government organized another expedition that they hoped would locate an ice-free passage eastward to China and the Far East. In spring 1595, Barents embarked from Holland as the chief pilot of a Dutch fleet of seven ships, commanded by Linschoten. On this expedition, he guided the ships as far as Vaigach Island, lying between the southernmost of the Novaya Zemlya islands and the Russian mainland, before being forced back by ice. Barents returned to Amsterdam with little new geographic or navigational information.

In 1596, Barents undertook his third voyage in search of the Northeast Passage. Backed by a group of Amsterdam merchants, he commanded one of two ships in an expedition that sailed from Holland in June of that year. The other vessel was under the command of Dutch sea captain Jan Cornelizoon Rijp.

In contrast to the first two voyages, which had hugged the northern European coastline, Barents sailed due north this time, from the northern end of Norway toward the NORTH POLE. He followed this northward course to test a theory then held by many European geographers that the waters north of the initial Arctic PACK ICE were freely navigable. North of Norway, Barents and Rijp came upon an island which they called Bear Island, after a violent encounter there with a polar bear. They continued northward and came upon Spitsbergen (present-day Svalbard). Although he made the first European sighting of that region since the days of the VIKINGS, Barents later mistakenly charted these islands as the east coast of GREENLAND.

Finding his way north of Spitsbergen blocked by icebergs, Barents turned eastward, seeking the Northeast Passage by the more conventional route. Following a disagreement, Rijp and his ship turned back to Holland. Barents reached the northern end of Novaya Zemlya, but after rounding Ice Cape again, he found his progress completely blocked and his ship trapped by ice. He made a landing at a bay he called Ice Haven, where his crew of 16 men managed to improvise a shelter from driftwood and parts of the ship. They subsisted on foxes and walruses that they hunted, and were repeatedly troubled by polar bear attacks.

Under Barents's leadership, only one member of the crew died that winter. By June 1597, the ship was still trapped in ice. Barents and his men then set out in two of the ship's small boats. Not far off the coast of Novaya Zemlya, Barents died of SCURVY and was buried at sea. The rest of the crew managed to reach the Russian mainland. With the help of Russian fishermen, they traveled westward more than 1,500 miles to the Kola Peninsula, where they met up with Rijp. From there, they safely reached Holland in November 1597.

In 1871, a Norwegian seal-hunting expedition discovered the house built by Barents and his men at Ice Haven. They also came upon tools and other artifacts of the expedition, including Barents's journal. These items were subsequently acquired by the Dutch government and displayed at a museum in The Hague.

Willem Barents undertook the earliest recorded explorations of the European Arctic regions since the time of the Vikings. His voyages resulted in much new navigational information concerning the Arctic coast of Europe, and his exploits were subsequently followed up by such well-known mariners as HENRY HUDSON and WILLIAM BAFFIN. His exploration of Spitsbergen permanently fixed that region on European charts. While exploring Spitsbergen in 1596, he attained a point farther north than any European on record to that time. Over the ensuing months, he and his men wintered closer to the North Pole than anyone ever had before. The Barents Sea, which stretches eastward from northern Norway and Spitsbergen to the west shores of Novaya Zemlya, was named in his honor.

Baret, Jeanne (Jean Baré) (ca. 1740–ca. 1803)
French traveler in the South Pacific

Jeanne Baret was born in the Burgundy region of France. In 1764, French naturalist JOSEPH-PHILIBERT COMMERSON hired her as a governess to look after his young son. In February 1767, she sailed with Commerson as his scientific assistant from Rochefort, France, aboard the ship *Étoile* as part of LOUIS-ANTOINE DE BOUGAINVILLE's expedition to the South Pacific Ocean.

Baret had boarded the *Étoile* in a man's clothes. None of Bougainville's expedition suspected her deception until they reached Tahiti. There, her true sex was revealed, reportedly detected by the Tahitians, or, according to one account, because of her apparent lack of interest in the uninhibited Tahitian women.

Commerson and Baret left the Bougainville expedition on the island of Mauritius. After Commerson's death in 1773, she married a wealthy colonist there. She is thought to have returned eventually to St. Malo, France.

If she returned to France by a westward route, Jeanne Baret is the first woman known to have completed a CIRCUMNAVIGATION OF THE WORLD.

Barrow, Sir John (1764–1848) *British naval official, founder of the Royal Geographical Society*

John Barrow was born to a family of moderate means in Liverpool, England. He was educated in local schools, studying mathematics, geography, and astronomy.

After working for a brief period at a Liverpool iron foundry, Barrow joined a whaling voyage to GREENLAND. Sailing with a Captain Potts from Liverpool, he made his first voyage into Arctic waters, in the course of which he perfected his skills in mathematics and geography.

Following his return from Greenland, Barrow accepted as appointment as a mathematician at the British Royal

Observatory at Greenwich. He subsequently traveled to China as a staff member of the British diplomatic mission. From there, he went to Cape Town, South Africa, as an aide to the British governor. He returned to England in 1802, when Cape Town reverted to Dutch administration.

In 1804, Barrow became second secretary of the Admiralty, a post he held for 40 years. In 1818, amid reports that previously ice-blocked portions of the Arctic Ocean had become accessible to ships, he initiated a series of exploratory expeditions to survey the Arctic coasts of Greenland and Canada, and to seek a NORTHWEST PASSAGE. Among those who led these explorations were SIR JOHN ROSS, DAVID BUCHAN, SIR WILLIAM EDWARD PARRY, SIR JOHN FRANKLIN, SIR GEORGE BACK, and FREDERICK WILLIAM BEECHEY.

Barrow's geographic interests extended to the then uncharted regions of West Africa, and in the 1820s his influence led to the British government-sponsored expeditions of WALTER OUDNEY and HUGH CLAPPERTON that attempted to explore the NIGER RIVER. At that time, Barrow was among those who mistakenly believed the Niger was a tributary of the NILE RIVER.

In 1830, Barrow helped found the ROYAL GEOGRAPHICAL SOCIETY. As one of its early presidents, he sponsored SIR ROBERT HERMANN SCHOMBURGK's explorations of what is now Guyana in South America in the 1830s and early 1840s.

Awarded a baronetcy and knighted in 1835, Barrow retired from the Admiralty 10 years later.

Under John Barrow's leadership, British naval expeditions into the Arctic in the first half of the 19th century brought back definitive geographic information concerning one of the last uncharted regions of the world. Point Barrow in Alaska and Point Barrow and Cape Barrow in Canada, were named in his honor. Well into the 20th century, Barrow's Royal Geographical Society continued to encourage and support explorations of Africa, Asia and the polar regions.

Bar Sauma, Rabban (ca. 1220–1294) *Turkish monk from China in the Middle East and Europe*

A descendant of Onggud Turks who had allied themselves with the Mongols, Rabban Bar Sauma was born in northern China. He was raised a Nestorian Christian. (The Nestorian Church, also referred to as the Assyrian or East Syrian Church, was one of the most active Christian denominations in Asia.) Pursuing religious studies, he became a Nestorian monk at about age 25.

Sometime before 1278, Bar Sauma, along with his student Markos, who went on to become a Nestorian leader, set out on a pilgrimage to Jerusalem, traveling the southern SILK ROAD below the Takla Makan Desert and arrived in Mongol-held territories in Persia (present-day Iran) two years later. Although Bar Sauma never reached Jerusalem because of reported dangers along the route there, he visited other Nestorian holy sites as well as cities in present-day Armenia and Georgia. He also was appointed as part of a delegation representing the interests of the Mongols that visited Constantinople (present-day Istanbul), Naples, Rome, Genoa, Paris, and Bordeaux. He died in Baghdad in 1294.

Bar Sauma departed China soon after MAFFEO POLO, NICCOLÒ POLO, and MARCO POLO arrived there; his journey crossed some of the same lands in the opposite direction. Their journeys and others in subsequent years led to a sharing of ideas and trade goods between Asia and Europe.

Barth, Heinrich (Henry Barth) (1821–1865)
German scholar, explorer in Africa

Born in Hamburg, Germany, to a wealthy family with extensive commercial interests, Heinrich Barth began his studies at the University of Berlin in 1838, concentrating in history, archaeology, philology, and Arabic. From 1845 to 1847, he made extensive field trips throughout the Middle East and North Africa, and, in 1848, he accepted a professorship at the University of Berlin's department of archaeology.

In 1849, Barth joined a British government-sponsored expedition to West Africa, aimed at suppressing the SLAVE TRADE and promoting legitimate trade contacts. In March 1850, with British antislavery activist JAMES RICHARDSON and German geologist ADOLF OVERWEG, he headed southward across the SAHARA DESERT from Tripoli, Libya. Near Agades, in what is now central Niger, they separated. Barth and Overweg traveled southward into present-day northeastern Nigeria, while Richardson continued south and east toward Lake Chad.

Along the way, disguised as a Muslim scholar, Barth visited the restricted city of Kano. Upon reaching Kukawa, east of Lake Chad, he learned that Richardson had died of fever en route, and he assumed leadership of the expedition.

From late 1851 to mid-1852, Barth Overweg undertook four explorations of Lake Chad. In September 1852, Overweg succumbed to malaria. As the only surviving member of the expedition, Barth continued his explorations of West Africa with a trek to Yola and the upper reaches of the Benue River. In 1853, he headed northwest to TIMBUKTU in the kingdom of Mali, where he remained for more than nine months. By 1854, he was back in Kukawa, from where he began a trip northward across the Sahara, along a route that took him east of the Ahaggar Mountains to the Mediterranean coast at Tripoli.

Barth returned to Europe in 1855 after five years of traveling in West Africa. In 1856, he was awarded a gold medal by the ROYAL GEOGRAPHICAL SOCIETY. Over the next two years, he published a five-volume account of his African experiences, *Travels and Explorations in North and Central Africa*.

In the late 1850s and early 1860s, Barth undertook scientific expeditions throughout Greece and Turkey. In 1863, he was awarded a professorship in geography at the University of Berlin.

Heinrich Barth's five-year exploration of West Africa below the Sahara was one of the first scientific expeditions into the region. His account revealed much about the region's culture and economy. From his explorations of the upper Benue River, he concluded that it had no connection with Lake Chad, as was then believed by European geographers. He was one of the first Europeans to make an extended stay in Timbuktu and live to tell about it.

Bartram, John (1699–1777) *American naturalist in eastern North America, father of William Bartram*

John Bartram was born and raised near Darby, Pennsylvania, where he spent his early years on the farm of an uncle. In 1728, he settled near Philadelphia, establishing a farm of his own on the Schuylkill River.

While in his early 20s, Bartram developed a keen interest in the natural sciences and corresponded with English naturalist Peter Collinson. Soon after settling on the Schuylkill, he established the first botanical garden in North America at Kingsessing, now part of Philadelphia.

Bartram undertook a series of expeditions in search of new plant specimens that took him across a wide area of the North American colonies. In 1743, he traveled northward into what is now New York State to the south shore of Lake Ontario, exploring along the Mohawk Trail. He subsequently went specimen-collecting in the Blue Ridge of the western Carolinas, and, in 1755, with his son WILLIAM BARTRAM, he explored New York's Catskill Mountains and western Pennsylvania.

In 1765, Bartram was appointed the official American botanist for the English king George III. That year, accompanied by his son, he sailed south to eastern Florida and explored northward into Georgia. Among the new species of plants he identified on his expedition was the royal palm.

John Bartram's scientific work and writings became well known in England and throughout Europe, earning him a reputation as one of the foremost botanists of his day. His books also revealed much about life on the North American frontier, including observations on the society and culture of both Indians and non-Indian settlers. In a communication to Benjamin Franklin, he proposed a government-sponsored scientific survey beyond the western limits of non-Indian settlement.

Bartram, William (1739–1823) *American naturalist, writer in the American Southeast, son of John Bartram*

William Bartram was the son of JOHN BARTRAM, who pioneered the study of botany in America. William was born in Kingsessing, Pennsylvania, on the Schuylkill River, in what is now part of the Philadelphia metropolitan area, where, years earlier, his father had established the first botanical garden in North America.

William Bartram, like his father, developed an early interest in botany, especially in drawing the plants and flowers unique to North America. He studied drawing, printing and engraving with Benjamin Franklin in Philadelphia during the early 1750s. In 1757, Bartram began working for a Philadelphia merchant, and, by 1761, he had gone into business as an independent trader on the Cape Fear River in North Carolina.

Four years later, Bartram accompanied his father on an expedition along the St. Johns River of central and northeastern Florida. Although the purpose of this 1765–66 trip was primarily to collect, draw, and study the region's flora and fauna, Bartram also made contact with the Seminole Indians of Florida.

After his return to the Philadelphia area, Bartram's botanical sketches came to the attention of Quaker naturalist Dr. John Fothergill, who subsequently financed a four-year exploration of the Southeast. From 1773 to 1777, Bartram and a small party traveled throughout the Carolinas, Georgia, and Florida, collecting samples and seeds of indigenous plants and making sketches of wildlife.

An account of Bartram's adventures during these years was presented in his 1791 book, *Travels through North and South Carolina, Georgia, East and West Florida, the Cherokee*

William Bartram *(Library of Congress)*

Country, the Extensive Territories of the Muscogulges, or Creek Confederacy, and the Country of the Choctaws. Well received, the work was soon translated into several European languages. Its vivid descriptions of the southeastern frontier landscape soon became a source of imagery for such British Romantic poets as William Wordsworth and Samuel Taylor Coleridge.

Bartram's father died in 1777, after which William helped his older brother John maintain the botanical garden in Kingsessing.

In addition to travel accounts, William Bartram also wrote some of the earliest ethnological studies of the Southeast tribes, including his 1789 work, *Observations on the Creek and Cherokee Indians,* first published in 1853, 30 years after his death.

Basargin, Grigory Gavrilovich (unknown–1853)

Russian naval officer in the Caspian Sea

In 1819, Vice Admiral Grigory Basargin of the Russian navy began his explorations of the Caspian Sea along the west coast of Azerbaijan, acquired by Russia from Persia (present-day Iran) six years earlier.

Under Basargin's command were two ships, the *Kazan,* a warship, and the *Kura,* a transport vessel. During the next two years, he surveyed the Caspian's southwest coast, from Lenkoran to the mouth of the Kura River, compiling geographic data subsequently used to produce the first accurate charts of the region.

Starting in 1823, Basargin charted the northwest coast of the Caspian Sea, around the outlet of the Volga River, a project that took three years.

Grigory Basargin's naval explorations provided the earliest accurate details of the west shores of the Caspian Sea, the world's largest landlocked body of water.

Bashmakov, Pyotr (fl. 1750s) *Russian mariner, trader in the Aleutian Islands*

Pyotr Bashmakov was a Russian seafarer and fur hunter on the Pacific coast of SIBERIA during the mid-1700s. In 1753, he undertook a fur-hunting voyage from the Kamchatka Peninsula eastward into the North Pacific Ocean and Bering Sea. East of Bering Island, Bashmakov's ship, the *Yeremiya,* was wrecked on one of the westernmost of the Aleutian Islands, stranding Bashmakov and his crew there for nearly two years. They eventually managed to construct a small boat from the wreckage and sail back across the Bering Sea to Kamchatka.

In late 1756, Bashmakov sailed again from Kamchatka for the Aleutians. On the ship, *Pyotr i Pavel* (Peter and Paul), he stopped first at Bering Island, and, in spring 1757, he headed as far east as the Aleutian island of Tanaga. His party returned to Kamchatka the next year with a valuable cargo of furs.

Pyotr Bashmakov's fur-hunting expeditions eastward from the Kamchatka Peninsula were among the first commercial ventures to follow up the explorations of the Aleutians undertaken by VITUS JONASSEN BERING in 1740–41.

Basov, Emelyan (Yemelyan Basov)

(ca. 1705–ca. 1765) *Russian Cossack mariner, trader in eastern Siberia and the Bering Sea*

Emelyan Basov was a Russian Cossack who, in 1726, embarked from the eastern Siberian city of Yakutsk and explored northward along the Lena River, in search of a water route to the Pacific ports on the Kamchatka Peninsula.

By 1733, Basov was in command of the port of Okhotsk, and from there he undertook a series of Russian government-authorized explorations of the Sea of Okhotsk.

In 1742–43, Basov organized a fur-trading enterprise and launched his first expedition across the Sea of Okhotsk to the east coast of the Kamchatka Peninsula and the Bering Sea. Using a small wooden boat built without nails, called a *shitik,* he reached Bering Island in 1743. Over the next several years, he extended his fur-hunting expeditions to other parts of the Commander (Komandorski) Islands. He retired from the FUR TRADE after 1748, settling on Kamchatka.

Emelyan Basov helped extend the Russian fur trade from the upper reaches of north-central SIBERIA's Lena River region to the Bering Sea islands off the coast of easternmost Siberia. His development of the Commander Islands as a fur-trading base eventually led to further regional exploration and settlement in the Aleutian Islands and on the Alaskan mainland.

Bass, George (1771–ca. 1805) *British naval surgeon, explorer in Australia and Tasmania*

George Bass was born in Asworthy, Lincolnshire, England. In 1795, after receiving training in medicine, he arrived in Port Jackson (present-day Sydney), Australia, as ship's surgeon on the HMS *Reliance.* Also on that voyage was British naval officer MATTHEW FLINDERS.

Later that year, Bass joined Flinders in an exploration of nearby Botany Bay and the Georges River, which flows into it. Traveling in a small boat called the *Tom Thumb,* Bass and Flinders ascended the Georges River as far as the eastern slopes of the BLUE MOUNTAINS.

In 1796, Bass and Flinders undertook a reconnaissance of the Australian southeast coast below Sydney. They explored what was thought to be the mouth of a river and discovered it was actually a natural harbor, which Bass named Port Hacking after the expedition's pilot.

Bass commanded an exploratory expedition of his own the following year. In December 1797, he sailed with a six-man crew in an open whaleboat from Sydney as far south as Cape Howe, Australia's southeasternmost point. Bass and his party continued around Cape Howe westward along the uncharted south coast of the Australian continent and reached a bay southeast of present-day Melbourne, which Bass named Western Port.

While returning eastward along the coast, Bass rounded Wilson's Promontory and investigated nearby islands. He detected signs of a strong west-flowing ocean current, a discovery that led him to believe he was in an uncharted strait that separated Van Diemen's Land (present-day TASMANIA) and the mainland. Up to that time, Van Diemen's Land was thought to be a southern extension of the Australian continent.

In October 1798, Bass and Flinders undertook another exploration of the Australian south coast. Sailing from Sydney in a sloop called the *Norfolk,* they reached what later became known as Flinders Island, and, starting from there, circumnavigated Tasmania in a counterclockwise direction, firmly establishing that it was indeed an island. Flinders and Bass subsequently explored up the Derwent River, deep into Tasmania's interior.

Little is known of Bass's life after 1799. He is believed to have traveled to South America, where he died between 1803 and 1808.

George Bass, along with Flinders, undertook one of the earliest European penetrations of the Australian interior. His subsequent explorations provided geographers with new information on the south coast of the continent, much of which remained uncharted at the close of the 18th century. The expanse of water that separates Tasmania from the Australian mainland was named Bass Strait in his honor.

Bastidas, Rodrigo de (1460–1526)

Spanish conquistador, colonizer in Central and South America

Rodrigo de Bastidas was born in the town of Triana, near Seville, Spain. He prospered in commerce and served as an official in the Spanish judiciary.

In 1500, Spanish monarchs Ferdinand and Isabella authorized Bastidas to undertake a trading expedition to the region south and west of Trinidad. The venture was inspired by CHRISTOPHER COLUMBUS, who had visited this part of the northeast coast of South America in 1498, returning to Spain with pearls obtained in trade with the Indians.

Bastidas outfitted two ships with trade goods and sailed from Spain in 1501. Accompanying him as pilot was JUAN DE LA COSA, who had sailed to the Caribbean Sea with Columbus on his first two voyages in 1492–93. Also joining Bastidas on the expedition was the young VASCO NÚÑEZ DE BALBOA.

Following Columbus's course, Bastidas's expedition reached Trinidad and the South American mainland. He headed westward along the coast of what is now Venezuela, exploring the Gulf of Maracaibo. He was the first European to visit the Magdalena River, as well as the large natural harbor of Cartagena in present-day Colombia, naming them both.

Bastidas traded with the coastal Indians, obtaining pearls and brazilwood (valued in Europe as a source of red dye and for making musical instruments), in exchange for inexpensive European metal goods. Although the natives did not wear clothes and had no use for sewing implements, Bastidas managed to trade needles for large quantities of pearls after demonstrating how valuable needles could be in removing thorns and in cleaning teeth.

West of Cartagena, the coastline veered sharply southward, leading Bastidas and Cosa to believe they were entering a strait to the Pacific Ocean and Asia. Instead, they came upon the Gulf of Darien at the eastern end of the Isthmus of Panama and explored the Gulf of Urabá. They discovered that the hulls of the ships, infested with wood-eating worms, had begun to leak. They headed eastward for Spain after making temporary repairs on an island near Jamaica. But the ships were in no condition for a transatlantic voyage, and Bastidas was forced to beach the vessels on the island of Hispaniola (present-day Haiti and the Dominican Republic).

Once on Hispaniola, Bastidas and his men carried their cargo of pearls and remaining trade goods overland to the Spanish settlement of Santo Domingo. Along the way, they continued to barter with the local natives, but they were soon arrested for unlicensed trading by the newly appointed governor, Francisco de Bobadilla.

Bastidas remained imprisoned in Santo Domingo until June 1502. He was then sent back to stand trial in Spain aboard one of a fleet of 30 ships. Bobadilla sailed on another of the fleet's ships with a large contingent of native slaves. Soon after embarking, the fleet was struck by a severe hurricane. Only the ship carrying Bastidas and his cargo of pearls managed to reach Spain. Most of the ships, including the one carrying Bobadilla, were lost with all hands.

In Spain, Bastidas was acquitted of all charges against him, and he managed to retain a large portion of the wealth derived from the pearls he had brought back.

In 1524, Bastidas was granted permission from the Spanish Crown to establish a colony on the part of the South American coast he had explored 23 years earlier. In 1526, he founded the settlement of Santa Marta on the coast of what is now Colombia. Bastidas forbade his colonists to exploit or enslave the natives, in contrast to the usual practice in other Spanish colonies. This policy drew resentment among his followers, and they soon rebelled against him. In 1526, suffering from wounds inflicted by the rebels, he withdrew to Cuba, where he died.

Rodrigo de Bastidas was the earliest European to explore and visit the coast of CENTRAL AMERICA, preceding Columbus's 1502 expedition there by one year. He was among the few CONQUISTADORES to treat the natives relatively fairly, and he openly opposed their enslavement. With Cosa, Bastidas explored and charted the coasts of present-day Venezuela, Colombia, and Panama, from the Gulf of Venezuela to the Gulf of Darien. His settlement at Santa Marta became an important port for the Magdalena River. Balboa first learned of Panama while with Bastidas in 1501; 12 years later, he reached the Pacific Ocean.

Batakov, Anton (fl. 1780–1790s) *Russian mariner in northeastern Siberia, the Aleutian Islands, and Alaska*

In 1785, Anton Batakov, a Russian navigator, joined the Russian government's Northeastern Secret Geographical and Astronomical Expedition, a venture organized to locate a sea route from the Kolyma River in northeastern SIBERIA to the BERING STRAIT and the west shores of Alaska.

By 1786, Batakov had traveled eastward across Siberia to Okhotsk. The next year, sailing on a specially constructed vessel, the *Pallas*, he followed the Kolyma northward to its outlet in the East Siberian Sea, from where he explored the Arctic coast of northeastern Siberia.

In 1789, after two years in Okhotsk, Batakov joined the expedition's leader, former British naval officer JOSEPH BILLINGS, in a voyage across the Sea of Okhotsk to the port of Petropavlosk on the Pacific coast of the Kamchatka Peninsula. They sailed across the Bering Sea to Kayak Island in the Gulf of Alaska, arriving in summer 1790.

A year later, Batakov and Billings sailed westward from Kayak Island into the Aleutians, stopping at Unalaska Island, then headed northward into the Bering Strait. After visiting St. Matthew and St. Lawrence Islands, they undertook a reconnaissance of the Alaskan mainland to the east, as well as the coastline of the Chukchi Peninsula on the Asian mainland to the west. They crossed the Chukchi Peninsula, from St. Lawrence Bay eastward to the Kolyma River, traveling on the backs of reindeer.

With the completion of the Northeastern Secret Geographical and Astronomical Expedition in 1793, Batakov returned westward across Siberia, arriving in St. Petersburg in 1794.

Anton Batakov explored the region between northeastern Asia and northwestern North America. His examination of the East Siberian Sea's south shores provided navigational information on the easternmost segment of the NORTHEAST PASSAGE. In addition, he surveyed the Gulf of Alaska, the Aleutian Islands, and the islands in the Bering Strait. Along with Billings, he was one of the earliest Europeans to venture overland across the Chukchi Peninsula.

Bates, Henry Walter (1825–1892)
British naturalist in South America

Henry Bates was born in Leicester, England. He attended local private schools, preparing for a career in business. During his teens, he developed an interest in entomology, the study of insects, making frequent trips into the English countryside to collect butterflies and other specimens.

In 1844, while working as a clerk in a brewery in Burton-upon-Trent, he befriended ALFRED RUSSEL WALLACE, a local schoolteacher who, like Bates, was a naturalist. Inspired by the exploits of CHARLES ROBERT DARWIN and ALEXANDER VON HUMBOLDT, as well as by W. H. Edwards' book *A Voyage Up the River Amazon* (1847), they planned a scientific expedition to South America.

In April 1848, Bates and Wallace sailed to Belém, Brazil, abroad a cargo vessel called the *Mischief*. By late June of that year, they reached the mouth of the Pará River, the southeastern estuary of the AMAZON RIVER. They traveled up the Pará to its principal tributary, the Tocantins, which they explored southward for more than 1,000 miles. Bates and Wallace then returned to the north and, traveling separately, ascended the Amazon across north-central Brazil to Manaus. Meeting up again at Manaus, Bates continued up the Amazon on his own. At the same time, Wallace, who by this time had been joined by his brother Herbert, explored the Negro River flowing into the Amazon at Manaus from the north.

Bates explored westward along the Amazon for almost 400 miles, reaching what is now Tefé, Brazil. He remained there until 1851, when he lost all his money in a robbery and returned to Pará on the Atlantic coast. At Pará, Bates met up with Herbert Wallace, who had contracted yellow fever and would die later that year. Alfred Wallace returned to England in 1852.

Soon afterward, Bates resumed his explorations, traveling up the Amazon to Santarém, halfway between Manaus and the river's mouth at Pará. He remained in the region until 1855, collecting thousands of insect specimens and exploring a great distance southward along the Tapajos River. In 1855, he returned to the western reaches of the upper Amazon, where, over the next three years, he undertook several explorations even farther to the west. On one of his last expeditions, he attempted an overland trek to the ANDES MOUNTAINS but was forced back by illness.

Bates returned to England in 1859. His classic account of his decade of exploring the rivers of northern Brazil, *The Naturalist on the River Amazon*, was first published in 1863. He became assistant secretary of the ROYAL GEOGRAPHICAL SOCIETY.

During his 10 years on the Amazon and its tributaries, Henry Bates collected more than 14,000 insect specimens, including 8,000 newly discovered species. His scientific findings include the earliest observations on the way certain species of butterflies develop natural disguises that put off predators. The idea became known as the Batesian Theory

Henry Bates *(Library of Congress)*

of Mimicry and provided support for some of Darwin's ideas on natural selection.

Batts, Thomas (unknown–1698) *English colonist in Virginia, the Appalachian Mountains, and West Virginia*

In September 1671, Captain Thomas Batts, serving under Virginia colonial military leader Major General ABRAHAM WOOD, set out with ROBERT FALLAM from Fort Henry (present-day Petersburg, Virginia) to explore the Piedmont region in search of new sources of furs.

From the falls of the Appomattox River, Batts and Fallam traveled westward across the Blue Ridge into the Kanawha and New River Valleys of present-day West Virginia through Indian territory. They explored the headwaters of the Kanawha River, then returned to Fort Henry in late October or early November 1671.

With their journey through the Blue Ridge to the New and Kanawha Rivers, Thomas Batts and Fallam became the first Englishmen to cross the APPALACHIAN MOUNTAINS and enter the Ohio Valley watershed region.

Battutah, Abu Abd-Allah Muhammad Ibn

See IBN BATTUTAH, ABU ABD-ALLAH MUHAMMAD.

Baudin, Thomas-Nicolas (1754–1803)
French naval officer in Australia and Tasmania

Nicolas Baudin was born on the Île de Ré, an island in the Bay of Biscay, off the coast of La Rochelle, France. He became an officer in the French navy and a ship's captain by 1793. That year, in command of a scientific expedition for the Museum of Natural History in Paris, he sailed from France to China and India and the islands of present-day Indonesia. He made a successful return trip to France in 1795. During the next two years, Baudin led additional scientific expeditions to the Antilles in the Caribbean, as well as along the coast of South America.

In 1800, Baudin took command of an official French government naval and scientific expedition to Australia. Planned by Napoleon, the project was intended to establish French control over Van Diemen's Land (present-day TASMANIA), as well as the unexplored south coast of Australia. Baudin also had instructions to chart the continent's west and north coasts.

Baudin departed Le Havre, France, in October 1800. He commanded the French warship the *Géographe,* along with the cargo vessel *Naturaliste,* captained by French naval officer Jacques-Felix-Emmanuel Hamelin. A team of 24 scientists, including astronomers, mineralogists, botanists, and zoologists, including zoologist FRANÇOIS PERON, accompanied him. Two other Baudins were among the crew—naval officers Charles Baudin and François-Nicolas Baudin—but they were not related to him. After stopping in the CANARY ISLANDS, Baudin commanded his two ships southward along the coast of Africa, where their progress was slowed by lack of wind. Food and other provisions became short, and many among the crew were stricken with SCURVY. By the time the expedition reached the French Indian Ocean settlement on Île de France (present-day Mauritius), a number had died. Others were too sick to continue and had to be left behind.

From Île de France, Baudin sailed eastward across the Indian Ocean. Still short of provisions, he sailed directly for the west coast of Australia instead of heading to Van Diemen's Land farther to the east. By June 1801, he had reached Cape Leeuwin on the extreme southwest coast of Australia. At a site Baudin named Géographe Bay, he sent a party of scientists ashore to collect samples of wildlife and make contact with the natives.

Soon after heading northward to explore the west coast of Australia, Baudin and the *Géographe* became separated from the *Naturaliste.* He continued up the coast toward the Dutch settlement at Timor, on the way exploring Shark Bay as well as sites along the northwest coast of Australia not visited by Europeans since the voyages of WILLIAM DAMPIER 100 years earlier.

By August 1801, Baudin had reached Timor, where he was joined by the rest of the expedition aboard the *Naturaliste.* At Timor, more men had to be left behind because of scurvy and an outbreak of dysentery. After nearly three months on Timor, Baudin sailed directly southward and eastward around Australia to Van Diemen's Land, reaching it in January 1802. He then undertook a three-month survey of the Tasmanian coast, sending parties inland to study the native Bara-Uru people and collect animal and plant specimens. Proceeding along the coast of Van Diemen's Land, he determined that the supposed small island was actually an extension of the eastern Tasmanian mainland, known today as the Tasman Peninsula.

In April 1802, while exploring along the south coast of Australia, at a site subsequently named Encounter Bay, Baudin met up with British naval captain MATTHEW FLINDERS, who had been mapping the coast from the west. Baudin obtained a copy of Flinders's maps of the newly charted south coastal region, then sailed to the British settlement at Port Jackson, present-day Sydney. From there, the *Naturaliste* sailed for France by way of the Indian Ocean and the CAPE OF GOOD HOPE with a large number of scientific specimens, while Baudin and the *Géographe* returned to the south and explored along the south coast of Australia. They stopped at Kangaroo Island, which Flinders had visited the previous year.

In spring 1803, Baudin retraced his route along the west coast of Australia, then continued along the north coast into the Gulf of Carpentaria. The *Géographe* then started back for France.

That summer, at a stopover at Mauritius, Baudin died from an illness he had contracted on the voyage. Under the command of Pierre Milius, the *Géographe* returned to France in late March 1804.

Nicolas Baudin's 1800–1804 expedition secured for France more than 100,000 samples of animal and plant life from Australia and Tasmania, including many varieties of kangaroos, as well as several hundred live specimens. Following his death in 1803, the French government credited him with mapping much of the Australian and Tasmanian coastlines, although Baudin's reported findings were really those of Flinders (a fact not revealed until Flinders returned to Europe in 1810, after being imprisoned on Mauritius for more than six years by the French).

Bauer, Ferdinand Lucas (1760–1826)
Austrian naturalist, artist in Australia

Born in Feldsberg, Austria, Ferdinand Bauer was the son of artist Lukas Bauer. He also pursued a career in art, becoming known for his drawings of plants. In 1786–87, he accompanied British botanist J. Sibthorp on a scientific expedition to study the flora of the Middle East.

Bauer's work as a botanical illustrator came to the attention of SIR JOSEPH BANKS, on whose recommendation he was appointed as a natural history artist with the English explorer MATTHEW FLINDERS's 1801–03 expedition to Australia aboard the *Investigator*. Along with the expedition's naturalist, ROBERT BROWN, he took part in scientific forays throughout southern Australia, including a specimen-hunting expedition on Kangaroo Island.

Bauer also joined Flinders, Brown, and artist WILLIAM WESTALL in an excursion by small boat up Spencer Gulf, during which they penetrated inland for 200 miles. At the gulf's northern end, they climbed a peak later named Mount Brown in the Flinders Range.

In 1803, Bauer remained with Brown at Port Jackson (Sydney), Australia, while Flinders left to seek a replacement for the *Investigator,* damaged on its passage through the Great Barrier Reef. Over the next 18 months, Bauer and Brown examined the plant life of coastal Australia around Sydney. Bauer undertook an expedition on his own to Norfolk Island in the Pacific Ocean, about 1,000 miles northeast of Sydney. Flinders failed to return by 1805, and Bauer and Brown set out to England on their own.

In England, Bauer prepared illustrations for Sibthorp's multivolume work on the flora of the Middle East. In 1812, he settled at Hietzing, Austria, where he continued his drawing and painting of plants at the Schönbrunn Gardens.

In addition to botanical studies, Ferdinand Bauer assisted Brown in examining the newly discovered animals of Australia, helping to bring back to London the first live specimens of such creatures as the koala and the bare-nostriled wombat.

Baumann, Oskar (1864–1899) *Austrian explorer in Africa*

Oskar Baumann was born in Vienna, Austria. His early career as an explorer took him to present-day Bosnia and Herzegovina and Croatia, where he participated in mountain-climbing expeditions in the southern Dinaric Alps.

In 1885, Baumann was a member of an Austrian expedition to central Africa, which ascended the CONGO RIVER (Zaire River) from its mouth on the Atlantic coast of Angola, to its upper reaches, as far as Stanley Falls in what is now north-central Democratic Republic of the Congo.

The next year, Baumann traveled to West Africa and explored the island of Fernando Po in the Gulf of Guinea, off the coast of present-day Cameroon.

Baumann returned to East Africa in 1888, where he embarked on an expedition to the region around MOUNT KILIMANJARO. In 1890, under the sponsorship of the German East Africa Society, he explored south of Lake Victoria into what is now northern Tanzania, making the European discovery of Lake Manyara and Lake Eyasi.

Two years later, in 1892–93, Baumann led a German expedition to Lake Victoria, from where he undertook the first European investigation of its principal source, the

Kagera River. Baumann spent his last years in East Africa, dying in Zanzibar in 1899.

Oskar Baumann's explorations in Africa revealed that the Kagera River, which drains into Lake Victoria, was the true source of the NILE RIVER.

Beale, Edward Fitzgerald (1822–1893) U.S.
Navy officer, American official, surveyor in the American West
A native of Washington, D.C., Edward Beale was a graduate of the U.S. Naval Academy at Annapolis. In 1845–46, as a lieutenant, he sailed with Commodore Robert Stockton aboard the *Congress* to the California coast. The ship reached San Diego just in time for the outbreak of the California uprising and the U.S.-Mexican War.

Beale went ashore with a party of marines to join U.S. Army forces under STEPHEN WATTS KEARNY at San Pasqual, south of present-day Los Angeles. The Americans were soon surrounded by Mexican troops. With frontiersman CHRISTOPHER HOUSTON CARSON (Kit Carson), Beale managed to pass undetected through the Mexican lines to Commodore Stockton and the American fleet at San Diego, where he brought news of Kearny's besieged forces. A company of marines was soon deployed north to San Pasqual, relieving Kearny's troops.

After the war's end in 1848, Beale made several trips across the North American continent, including one in 1849–50 that carried to the East the earliest news of the 1848 gold strike at Sutter's Mill, near Sacramento, leading to the California gold rush of the following year.

In the early 1850s, Beale was the superintendent of Indian Affairs for California and Nevada. During that time, he came under the patronage of Missouri senator Thomas Hart Benton, who was also the father-in-law of western explorer JOHN CHARLES FRÉMONT. In 1853–54, the federal government enacted legislation sponsoring topographic surveys in preparation for a proposed transcontinental railroad route. Benton, representing Missouri financial interests, backed several privately sponsored railroad surveys and placed Beale in command of an expedition to evaluate a railroad route that would extend from St. Louis, Missouri, along the 38th parallel to California.

Beale succeeded in mapping this route, but sectional differences and the eventual onset of the Civil War delayed construction of the transcontinental railroad for the next 15 years.

In 1857–58, Beale oversaw the famous "Camel Experiment," which employed up to 75 camels as draft animals in the construction of a wagon route from Camp Verde in western Texas near Bandera Pass, across the southern plains and desert to Fort Tejon, California. This road crossed the Colorado River at the western end of the Mojave Desert, later known as Beale's Crossing. While the camels were of great service in the road-building project, their use never caught on in the West among frontier wranglers. The trail itself became an important link for the Butterfield Overland Stage Company's service to California and was a much-traveled route for immigrants to California. It was known first as the Southern Overland Trail and later as the Butterfield Southern Route.

In 1861–65, Beale served as California's surveyor general. In 1876–77, he was the U.S. ambassador to the Austro-Hungarian Empire.

Edward Beale's innovative use of camels failed to endure, but his explorations and road-building projects throughout the 1850s helped paved the way for the construction of the first transcontinental railroad links in the late 1860s.

Beatus of Valcavado (fl. 770s) *Spanish monk, cartographer*
Beatus of Valcavado, a Benedictine monk, lived in Spain during the last half of the eighth century A.D. In 776, he produced a religious work, *Commentary on the Apocalypse,* which included a map of the known world. Unlike modern world maps, Beatus's map depicted Jerusalem and the Middle East at the top, where north usually is, and consequently provided little aid to medieval navigators or geographers. His intention was to symbolically express the importance of Jerusalem as the focus of the Christian world.

Throughout the early medieval period, European mapmakers adopted Beatus's geographic orientation, portraying a view of the world that was considerably more limited than the one held by the ancient Greeks and Romans.

The map by Beatus of Valcavado influenced European geographic knowledge over the next 500 years, until the travels of MARCO POLO in the late 1200s.

Beautemps-Beaupré, Charles-François
(1766–1854) *French cartographer in the South Pacific*
Charles Beautemps-Beaupré was born in the French town of La Neuville-du-Pont, in the Marne region east of Paris. He became a highly skilled cartographer, specializing in the charting of coastlines. In 1785, he took part in a survey of the Baltic Sea, producing scientifically based maps for the French government.

In September 1791, Beautemps-Beaupré sailed from Brest, France, aboard the *Récherche* with ANTOINE-RAYMOND-JOSEPH DE BRUNI, chevalier d'Entrecasteaux's expedition in search of JEAN-FRANÇOIS DE GALAUP, comte de La Pérouse, missing in the South Pacific Ocean since early 1788. As the expedition's chief hydrographer, Beautemps-Beaupré made scientifically based maps of the uncharted coasts of southern Australia and southern TASMANIA. East of

New Guinea, he identified the exact location of New Caledonia, the Solomon Islands, the Santa Cruz Islands, and other island groups in the Melanesian region of the western South Pacific.

As a result of the international crises brought about by the ongoing French Revolution, Dutch authorities on Java detained Beautemps-Beaupré along with the rest of the expedition when it arrived there in fall 1793. In 1796, Beautemps-Beaupré returned to France, sailing there by way of the CAPE OF GOOD HOPE. He went on to direct all of the major navigational and cartographic projects undertaken by the French government in the first half of the 19th century.

Charles Beautemps-Beaupré is considered the "father of hydrography," the technique of mapping coastlines with attention to navigational detail. Although his atlas of the Entrecasteaux expedition to the South Pacific was not published until 1808, British naval authorities captured copies of his charts of Tasmania as early as 1795, making them available to MATTHEW FLINDERS for his 1801–03 explorations. Beautemps-Beaupré was the first cartographer to represent the southeast coast of Tasmania, where the British established the settlement of Hobart in 1803. Moreover, his charts provided the first accurate location of the Solomon Islands, explored by Spanish navigator ÁLVARO DE MENDAÑA in 1567.

Becknell, William (ca. 1790–1865) *American trader in the American Southwest*

Prior to 1821, William Becknell, probably a native of Kentucky, arrived in Franklin, Missouri, where he engaged in trade with Indians of the southern plains. At that time, Spanish provincial authorities had barred American traders from entering their New Mexico province.

In August 1821, Becknell set out with a party of three companions and their pack animals into the southern plains for the purpose of trading horses and mules with the Indians and capturing, according to his own account, "Wild Animals of every description." They left Franklin, Missouri, and headed westward for Fort Osage and the Arkansas River. Becknell's party followed ancient Indian and Spanish trails and reached the mouth of the Purgatoire River in present-day southeastern Colorado by October. From there, they headed southward into the mountains via Raton Pass.

The group soon encountered a detachment of Mexican soldiers, who informed them that Mexico's independence had been declared, and that they would now be able to continue to Santa Fe to sell their much-sought-after trade goods. Becknell and his companions then crossed into northern New Mexico and reached Santa Fe by early November, where they sold their goods at a huge profit.

Becknell returned to his home in Franklin, Missouri, and wasted no time in organizing a second, larger trade expedition. In 1822, he set out with three wagons carrying trade goods and headed across the Kansas plains. Rather than heading southward into New Mexico via Raton Pass, a route that was then nearly impassable to wagon traffic, Becknell and his party blazed a trail across the Cimarron Desert in the region of present-day southwestern Kansas and the Oklahoma Panhandle. This trail, which came to be known as the Cimarron Cutoff, was extremely hazardous because of Comanche and Kiowa Indian attacks and because of lack of water for men and draft animals. Overcoming these obstacles, Becknell and his traders, among them WILLIAM WOLFSKILL and EWING YOUNG, reached Santa Fe and again realized an enormous profit on the goods they had carried from Missouri. Open trade between New Mexico and Missouri soon flourished.

In 1824, Becknell organized a much larger trade caravan, consisting of 24 wagons and 80 men, and again headed from Independence, Missouri, to Santa Fe. Later that year, Becknell took a party of traders northward from Santa Cruz, New Mexico, about 50 miles north of Santa Fe, into the Green River region in what is now northeastern Colorado.

By 1828, Becknell had established a ferry service and trade center on the MISSOURI RIVER at Arrow Rock, near present-day Sibley, Missouri. He went on to serve in the Missouri state legislature, then moved to Texas, where he took part in the Texas Revolution and struggle for independence from Mexico. He eventually settled at Clarksville in northeastern Texas's Red River region.

William Becknell's accomplishments earned him the reputation as the "Father of the Santa Fe Trail." His 1822 expedition to Santa Fe marked the first use of wagons on the route to the New Mexico settlements. Becknell also produced some of the earliest maps of the Santa Fe Trail and provided impetus for the federal government to undertake a topographic survey of this route. His pioneering efforts led the federal government to provide military protection for trade caravans traveling westward to New Mexico across the southern plains. Fur traders soon followed Becknell's route into the southern ROCKY MOUNTAINS.

Beckwith, Edward Griffin (1818–1881)
U.S. Army officer, American topographer in Utah and Nevada

Born in Cazenovia, New York, E. G. Beckwith was an 1842 graduate of West Point. He subsequently took part in several major campaigns in the U.S.-Mexican War of 1846–48.

In 1849, Beckwith served under Major WILLIAM HEMSLEY EMORY in the Mexican Boundary Commission survey of the Gila River region of present-day southern Arizona.

In spring 1853, Beckwith, a lieutenant in the U.S. Army Corps of Topographical Engineers, joined Lieutenant JOHN WILLIAMS GUNNISON in a survey of a proposed transcontinental railroad route along the 38th parallel from Fort Leavenworth, Kansas, to the Pacific coast. After Gunnison and others were killed by Ute Indians in Utah's Sevier River Valley, the expedition was reorganized under Beckwith's command.

In spring 1854, Beckwith led a party of scientists and topographers in a survey along the 41st parallel, westward from Fort Bridger in Wyoming's Green River region to California. He crossed Utah's Wasatch Mountains to Pilot Peak, then followed the Humboldt River to a point north of Pyramid Lake. In the Sierra Nevada, he located two passes, Madeline Pass and Nobles' Pass, that could be used for a rail line to the Sacramento River.

Two years later, in 1856, Beckwith supervised the construction of a military wagon road from Fort Riley, Kansas, into the ROCKY MOUNTAINS to Fort Bridger, Wyoming.

Beckwith went on to serve in the Union army during the Civil War, taking part in campaigns in Virginia and Louisiana.

E. G. Beckwith's route across northern Utah and Nevada in 1854 was eventually adopted by the Union Pacific for the first transcontinental railroad, completed in 1869.

Beckwourth, James Pierson (Jim Beckwith)

(ca. 1800–ca. 1866) *American fur trader, trapper in the American West, army scout*

James (Jim) Beckwourth was born on a plantation in Fredericksburg, Virginia, the son of the Irish aristocrat Sir Jennings Beckwourth and a mixed-race slave woman. In 1810, he moved with his father to the Louisiana Territory, and he later settled in St. Louis, Missouri. On being granted his freedom by his father, Beckwourth set out in the early 1820s for Illinois's Fever River region, where he worked in the lead mines near the town of Galena.

Two years later, Beckwourth was hired by WILLIAM HENRY ASHLEY to take part in his 1824–25 expedition up the MISSOURI RIVER from St. Louis. The purpose of this trip was to take supplies and trade goods to Ashley's fur trappers and traders in the Green River region of present-day Wyoming and Utah. Beckwourth, serving as a blacksmith and personal assistant to Ashley, attended the first annual fur traders' rendezvous at Henrys Fork, a branch of the Green River, in summer 1825. Soon afterward, Beckwourth himself became a trapper, and he spent the winter of 1825–26 with mountain man JEDEDIAH STRONG SMITH in the Cache Valley of what is now northern Utah.

In 1828, Beckwourth trapped the ROCKY MOUNTAINS of Utah and southern Wyoming with ROBERT CAMPBELL, narrowly escaping death when Campbell's party was attacked by Blackfeet Indians in the "Fight in the Willows." Reportedly, it was Beckwourth who saved his companions by breaking through the line of attacking Indians and summoning the help of another party of MOUNTAIN MEN.

Later in 1828, fellow mountain man CALEB GREENWOOD convinced the Crow Indian chief, Big Bowl, that Beckwourth, with his Indian-like mixed-race features, was actually the chief's long-lost son, who had been kidnapped as a child by marauding Cheyenne Indians. Welcomed into the tribe, Beckwourth soon rose to prominence among the Crow as a warrior and chief. At this time, both Greenwood and Beckwourth were associated with KENNETH MCKENZIE and the AMERICAN FUR COMPANY, and, during the next six years, Beckwourth used his influential position among the Crow to advance his and Greenwood's trade activities in the northern and central Rockies.

Leaving the Rocky Mountain FUR TRADE in 1837, Beckwourth traveled to Florida, where he took part in the Second Seminole War of 1835–42, as a muleteer for U.S. Army troops.

Returning to the West in 1838, Beckwourth traveled to the southern plains, where he undertook trading expeditions with LOUIS VASQUEZ and Andrew Sublette along the Santa Fe Trail. In the early 1840s, Beckwourth lived for a time in Pueblo, Colorado. At the outbreak of the U.S.-Mexican War in 1846, he was in California and took an active part in the Bear Flag Republic's revolt against Mexican rule.

Beckwourth settled in Santa Fe after the war, where he operated a saloon for a short time before returning to California with the gold rush of 1849. In 1851, he was involved in building wagon roads to supply miners in the Sierra Nevada.

The Pikes Peak (Colorado) gold rush of 1859 took Beckwourth to Colorado, where he was two years later, at the onset of the Civil War. He served as an army scout and interpreter for Colorado militia forces under Colonel John Chivington in the 1864 campaign against the Cheyenne.

In 1866, Colonel Henry B. Carrington hired Beckwourth as a peace emissary to his former adoptive tribe, the Crow. While on this mission, Beckwourth was reportedly killed by tribal members, who may have poisoned him because they believed he had brought an earlier smallpox epidemic to their people. Other reports indicate Beckwourth may have died in Denver the following year.

Jim Beckwourth's early career as a fur trapper and mountain man during the 1820s and early 1830s took him to parts of the middle and northern Rockies then known only to other trappers and Indians. He accompanied some of the men who undertook the earliest significant explorations of that region. His subsequent experiences on the old Santa Fe Trail and in the Sierra Nevada took him to uncharted territory. He is sometimes confused with ED-WARD ROSE, another mountain man of African descent.

Beebe, Charles William (1877–1962)
American naturalist, oceanographer

Charles William Beebe was born in Brooklyn, New York, and attended Columbia University. In 1899, he became curator of the New York Zoological Society and started a collection of living birds in the New York Zoological Park in the Bronx. In 1916, he became the director of tropical research and as such, led scientific expeditions in North America, CENTRAL AMERICA, South America, the Caribbean region, and Asia. He became increasingly interested in oceanographic research, and in 1923 he conducted studies in the waters off Bermuda and the Galapagos Islands.

With American engineer Otis Barton, Beebe developed the BATHYSPHERE, a type of SUBMERSIBLE. On August 15, 1934, after a series of dives beginning in 1930, each progressively deeper, Beebe and Barton made a descent of 3,028 feet, a record at that time.

Beebe wrote about the bathysphere expeditions in *Half Mile Down* (1934). Among his many other books are *Galapagos* (1923), *Jungle Days* (1925), *Beneath Tropic Seas* (1928), *Book of Bays* (1942), *High Jungle* (1949), and *Unseen Life in New York* (1953). He also edited *Book of Naturalists* (1944).

William Beebe was one of the pioneers of underwater exploration. His design for the bathysphere was later incorporated into that of the BATHYSCAPH, developed by AU-GUSTE PICCARD and first used in 1947.

Beechey, Frederick William (1796–1856)
British naval officer in the Pacific Ocean and Arctic regions

Frederick Beechey was born in London, England. The son of portrait artist Sir William Beechey, he had a background in art and natural history. He entered the Royal Navy in his early teens, taking part in naval engagements throughout the Napoleonic Wars, and he served aboard a British warship at the Battle of New Orleans in January 1815, part of the War of 1812.

Promoted to lieutenant, Beechey joined SIR JOHN FRANKLIN in his 1818 naval expedition north of Spitsbergen (present-day Svalbard). In 1819–20, with SIR WILLIAM ED-WARD PARRY, he explored the Arctic coast of Canada. Beechey produced drawings of Arctic scenes on these polar expeditions.

In 1821–22, Beechey, accompanied by his brother Henry Beechey, undertook a coastal survey of North Africa east of Tripoli, Libya.

In 1825, at the rank of commander, Beechey embarked on a three-year expedition to the Pacific Ocean. His main objective was to reach the north Alaskan coast and there meet up with Franklin, who was at that time exploring Arctic Canada from the east. In command of the *Blossom,* he sailed from Spithead, England, in May 1825, and reached the Pacific coast of South America by the following autumn. A scientific team with the expedition made several inland investigations into the coastal regions of Chile and Peru.

From South America, Beechey headed westward across the Pacific, stopping at Easter Island, then continued to Pitcairn Island, where he met with the last surviving member of the *Bounty* mutineers.

Beechey headed eastward from Pitcairn Island to Tahiti and made the European discovery of islands in the Gambier archipelago. From Tahiti, he sailed northward to Oahu in the HAWAIIAN ISLANDS, then proceeded northwestward to the Kamchatka Peninsula, extending from the Pacific coast of SIBERIA.

From Petropavlovsk on Kamchatka, Beechey and the *Blossom* sailed to the islands of the BERING STRAIT and the west coast of Alaska. He reached Kotzebue Sound on the northwest Alaskan coast in late July 1826. An exploring party in a small boat reached as far north as a small peninsula that Beechey named Point Barrow in honor of second secretary of the Admiralty SIR JOHN BARROW. It proved to be Alaska's northernmost point. Beechey's men were unable, however, to reach Franklin and his expedition, who were then at a point 146 miles to the west. With PACK ICE becoming a problem, Beechey commanded his ship southward toward the Spanish settlements on the California coast.

In spring 1827, after repairs to the ship, Beechey sailed from California to the Bonin Islands, an archipelago south of Japan not visited by Europeans since 1639. He then headed back to Kamchatka and the Bering Strait and reexplored the Alaskan coast, making the European discovery of Port Clarence. Expeditions sent out in small boats this time reached as far north as Icy Cape, but were again unable to locate Franklin.

Beechey then headed southward along the coasts of North and South America, rounded CAPE HORN, and arrived in England in mid-October 1828. Less than three weeks earlier, Franklin had also safely returned.

Over the next two decades, Beechey directed maritime surveys of South America and Ireland for the British government. In 1854, he was appointed a rear admiral; the next year, he was elected president of the ROYAL GEOGRAPHICAL SOCIETY.

Frederick Beechey's 1825–28 explorations took him farther north along the coast of North America than any European had been up to that time. Members of that expedition visited and named Point Barrow, Alaska's northernmost extremity. He completed the first comprehensive exploration of the west coasts of both North and South

America. In the western Pacific Ocean, he located islands only briefly explored by the Spanish two centuries earlier. His account of his Arctic and Pacific explorations, *Narrative of a Voyage to the Pacific and Bering's Strait,* was first published in 1831.

Begichev, Nikifor Alekseyevich (1874–1927)
Russian mariner, fur trader in the Siberian Arctic

Russian seafarer Nikifor Begichev participated in BARON EDUARD VON TOLL's 1900–1902 attempt to negotiate the NORTHEAST PASSAGE across the top of Asia. With Toll, he sailed around Cape Chelyuskin, Asia's northernmost point, and explored the New Siberian Islands of the Laptev Sea. Following Toll's disappearance in the Siberian Arctic in 1902, Begichev took part in search operations the next year. Traveling overland from the mouth of the Yana River to Bennett Island in the New Siberian chain, he came upon letters indicating that Toll and his entire party had perished.

In 1904, Begichev took part in the Russo-Japanese War, serving in the defense of Port Arthur on the Pacific coast of SIBERIA. He subsequently entered the northern Siberian FUR TRADE, operating around the Taymyr Peninsula on the Arctic coast of central Siberia. In 1908, he located an island in a region previously thought to be a peninsula and named it Bolshoy Begichev. While revisiting the area in 1915, he took part in the rescue of crewmembers of a fleet of Russian icebreakers.

In 1921–22, while engaged in fur trapping on the Taymyr Peninsula, Begichev aided in the search for members of ROALD ENGELBREGT GRAVNING AMUNDSEN's expedition, who had become separated from the *Maude* on its voyage through the Northeast Passage. Begichev was with the Soviet scientific expedition that found the remains of Amundsen's men on the west coast of the Taymyr Peninsula in 1922.

In 1926, Begichev undertook a fur-trapping expedition down the Pyasina River to its mouth on the eastern shore of the Kara Sea, where he remained until his death from SCURVY in 1927.

Nikifor Begichev explored the northernmost reaches of the central Siberian Arctic, a region still largely uncharted as late as the 1920s. His exploits in support of Toll and Amundsen contributed to the opening of the Northeast Passage as a trade route.

Behaim, Martin (Martin Boeheim, Martin Behem, Martin of Bohemia) (ca. 1436–ca. 1506)
German cartographer, mariner, in service to Portugal

Martin Behaim was born in the German city of Nuremberg. There are conflicting reports regarding his birth date: either 1436 or 1459. His early education included the study of astronomy and mathematics. He became involved in textile manufacturing in what is now Belgium.

By the late 1470s, Behaim's scientific curiosity was aroused by the explorations of Portuguese navigators. He traveled to Lisbon, where he became acquainted with CHRISTOPHER COLUMBUS and supported his ideas on the feasibility of a westward passage to India.

Behaim's interest in mathematics and astronomy broadened to the applied science of navigation. In 1485–86, he may have served as cosmographer on the expedition of DIOGO CÃO, which explored the west coast of Africa as far south as the mouth of the CONGO RIVER (Zaire River).

Behaim became active in Portuguese navigational research under King John II, taking part in the development of an improved version of the ASTROLABE, an important navigational instrument of the 15th and 16th centuries. In 1484, the Portuguese monarch knighted him for this accomplishment.

In 1486, Behaim was instrumental in establishing an early Flemish settlement on Fayal in the AZORES.

By 1490, Behaim had returned to Nuremberg, where, in 1492, he completed an early GLOBE of the known world. He made several diplomatic trips between Portugal and the Low Countries before settling permanently in Portugal.

Martin Behaim's 1492 globe, still in existence, depicts a large island, west of the Azores, thought by some historians to indicate a knowledge of Brazil and the South American mainland that predated Columbus's return from his first voyage. In addition, FERDINAND MAGELLAN used a copy of Behaim's globe to gain Spanish sponsorship for his 1519–22 voyage to the SPICE ISLANDS (the Moluccas), which also accomplished the first CIRCUMNAVIGATION OF THE WORLD.

Beketov, Pyotr (fl. 1620–1660s) *Russian Cossack leader in Siberia*

Pyotr Beketov was a Russian Cossack leader who in 1628 initiated a campaign of conquest that brought much of southeastern SIBERIA under Russian domination. From the central Yenisey River, he led a force of Cossacks south and east into the upper Tunguska River region and established a fur-trading settlement at the mouth of the Oka River.

Three years later, in 1631, Beketov pushed eastward across central Siberia, from the Yenisey to the Lena River, and from there headed southwestward toward Lake Baikal. The next year, he headed northward along the Lena, and on its banks established a settlement that later developed into the Siberian city of Yakutsk. Starting in 1633, he expanded Cossack and Russian influence into the Aldan River region to the east.

In the 1640s, Beketov commanded important central Siberian outposts, including Bratsk. From there, in 1652, he undertook a military expedition into the region southeast of Lake Baikal. In 1654, he traveled up the Amur River. The next year, his force succeeded in defending against a Manchu invasion from the south.

By 1660, Beketov had consolidated Russian control over territory as far south as the Amur River. He later returned to the Yenisey River to the north, having opened up the fur resources of southeastern Siberia to European Russian traders.

Pyotr Beketov was one of the Cossack leaders who contributed to the Russian exploration and conquest of the region east and south of the Yenisey River, as far as the Lena River to the east and as far as the Amur River to the south. His settlement at Yakutsk on the Lena developed into an important center of the FUR TRADE for all of eastern Siberia.

Bekovich-Cherkassky, Aleksandr (Alexandr Bekovich-Cherkassky) (unknown–ca. 1717) *Russian mariner, military leader in the eastern Caspian Sea region*

Aleksandr Bekovich-Cherkassky was born to a noble family in Kabardia, a Circassian Muslim principality between the Black and Caspian Seas. In his early years, he went to live in European Russia, where Czar Peter I (Peter the Great) took charge of his education, sending him to western Europe in 1707 to study navigational techniques.

By 1715, Bekovich-Cherkassky was an accomplished navigator and military officer. At that time, Czar Peter was seeking to expand Russian interests south and east into central Asia, and he believed that the Amu Darya River (the Oxus of ALEXANDER THE GREAT's time) could provide an access route from the southern Caspian Sea to its headwaters in the Hindu Kush, north of India. Accordingly, in 1715, he dispatched Bekovich-Cherkassky on an exploratory expedition in search of the mouth of the north-flowing Amu Darya.

Bekovich returned to Czar Peter with reports from native tribesmen that the Amu Darya River flowed into the southern Aral Sea, east of the Caspian, after being diverted by the Uzbek people of Khiva. Plans were then made to redirect the Amu Darya to its original course.

In 1716, Bekovich led a 3,000-man military expedition by ship from the mouth of the Volga River, along the north coast of the Caspian Sea, to the mouth of the Ural River. He then proceeded southward overland across the Ust-Urt Plateau, toward Khiva.

Bekovich and his Russian forces defeated the Khivans in preliminary engagements. The Khivan monarch, known as the Khan, pretended to sue for peace and convinced Bekovich to divide his forces. On entering the city of Khiva, each Russian contingent was attacked and defeated. Most were killed, and the few survivors were enslaved. Bekovich himself never returned from the campaign and is presumed to have died in about 1717.

Aleksandr Bekovich-Cherkassky's expedition into the eastern Caspian region was the last Russian attempt to take the area until the middle of the 19th century. The Aral Sea, which Bekovich-Cherkassky had heard about in 1715, was not identified by Europeans until 1844.

Belcher, Sir Edward (1799–1877) *British naval officer in the Pacific Ocean and Arctic regions*

Born in Halifax, Nova Scotia, Edward Belcher entered the Royal Navy in 1812. As a midshipman, he served in naval engagements off the coast of North Africa in 1816.

In 1818, at the rank of lieutenant commander, Belcher took part in a British naval expedition to the North Pacific Ocean. Trained in chartmaking as well as navigation, he subsequently undertook a hydrographic survey of the coasts of North and West Africa, producing official maps of these regions for the Royal Navy.

Belcher sailed with FREDERICK WILLIAM BEECHEY on the *Blossom* in his 1825–28 expedition to the South Pacific and North American Arctic, serving as the principal hydrographer. Part of the expedition's objective was to make contact with SIR JOHN FRANKLIN, then exploring overland in the Canadian Arctic.

On the second visit to the northwest coast of Alaska in summer 1827, Belcher led an exploring party northward from Kotzebue Sound as far as Icy Cape. Unable to contact Franklin, he attempted a return, but his small boat was wrecked in heavy seas near Chamisso Island. Although four of his party drowned, Belcher and the survivors managed to reach an island, where they were soon rescued by Beechey and the *Blossom*.

In 1837, Belcher, by then a captain, traveled to the west coast of Panama and there took command of the *Sulphur*, relieving the ailing Beechey, who had become ill during his explorations along the west coast of South America.

Over the next year, Belcher sailed along the coasts of the Americas, undertaking inland exploring expeditions in Nicaragua and El Salvador. He ranged as far north as Alaska's Prince William Sound and visited the Russian settlement at Sitka. In addition, on this voyage he charted the Sacramento and Columbia Rivers, making a stop at the HUDSON'S BAY COMPANY post, Fort Vancouver, near present-day Portland, Oregon.

Belcher and the *Sulphur* headed west across the Pacific in late 1839. While visiting the Fiji Islands, he met up with the American exploring expedition commanded by CHARLES WILKES. At Singapore, Belcher was ordered to sail to the southeast coast of China to take part in the naval operations of what later became known as the Opium War of 1839–42. In October 1840, Belcher commanded the *Sulphur* in a naval battle against Chinese forces that ended with the British capture of Hong Kong.

In November 1840, Belcher's ship was damaged in a typhoon and he was compelled to sail back to England. The homeward course took the ship along the east coast of

Africa. Belcher explored the Mozambique Channel between Madagascar and the African mainland before rounding the CAPE OF GOOD HOPE.

Belcher reached England in July 1842. Soon afterward, he was knighted for his efforts in the Opium War. The next year, he was appointed commander of the *Samarang* and undertook a three-year expedition to present-day Indonesia and the South China Sea.

In 1852, Belcher took command of the Royal Navy's last official effort to locate Franklin, missing in the Canadian Arctic since 1845. SIR FRANCIS LEOPOLD McCLINTOCK served under him. Once again in command of the *Blossom*, he sailed into the islands of the Canadian Arctic from the east, passing through Lancaster Sound, then headed northward along the west coast of Devon Island into Wellington Strait.

In 1854, with his fleet of five ships icebound near Dealy Island, Belcher ordered his men to abandon the vessels, fearing their destruction. They managed to reach supply ships anchored off Beechey Island, on which they then returned to England. One of the abandoned ships, the *Resolute,* was recovered by American whalers in Davis Strait almost a year later. It was taken to Connecticut, restored to seaworthiness, and presented by the United States to Queen Victoria as a gift.

After Belcher's return to England, the Admiralty denied him further naval commands because it was felt he had exercised poor judgment in abandoning his ships in the Canadian Arctic. Yet he remained in the navy for the rest of his life, reaching the rank of full admiral in 1872.

Sir Edward Belcher was a naturalist as well as a navigator and undertook natural history studies in North America, South America, and CENTRAL AMERICA. Although his 1852–54 search for Franklin was fruitless, it did result in additional knowledge of the geography of the maze of straits and islands of the polar regions of northern Canada.

Bell, Gertrude Margaret Lowthian

(1868–1926) *British archaeologist, mountain climber, traveler, writer in the Middle East*

Born in England, Gertrude Bell attended Oxford University in 1883–87, graduating with honors in history. In the late 1880s, she engaged in MOUNTAIN-CLIMBING expeditions in Europe in which she set several alpine records.

In 1892, Bell traveled extensively in Persia (present-day Iran), studying its ancient heritage. Starting in 1901, she toured throughout the Middle East, visiting present-day Israel, Turkey, Syria, and Iraq, while undertaking archaeological studies.

In 1913–14, Bell traveled with a native trade caravan from Damascus southward into the Arabian Desert, planning to reach Riyadh. Forced to turn back by Muslim opposition at the northern Arabian city of Ha'il, she followed a different route to Damascus by way of Palmyra, covering areas of the Middle East not usually visited by Europeans.

Bell was fluent in both Farsi and Arabic, skills she put to use at the outbreak of World War I, when she went to work for the British intelligence service, operating out of Cairo, Egypt.

Soon after the war's end in 1918, Bell was assigned as an assistant political officer with the British government's Arab Bureau in what was then Mesopotamia. Working alongside the British Middle East explorer and scholar THOMAS EDWARD LAWRENCE (Lawrence of Arabia), she played an important role in the organization of the modern nation of Iraq by supporting the selection of King Faisal I as the nation's first ruler.

Bell went on to establish the Iraqi state museum for antiquities in Baghdad, serving as its first director. From 1897 until her death by suicide in 1926, she published a prolific body of writings about her experiences in the Middle East and her archaeological discoveries, including *Poems from the Divan of Hafiz* (1897), *The Desert and the Sown* (1907), *Amurath to Amurath* (1911), *Palace and Mosque at Ukaidir* (1914), *The Arab of Mesopotamia* (1917), and her first book, *Persian Pictures,* issued posthumously in 1928. She was the first woman to receive a medal from the ROYAL GEOGRAPHICAL SOCIETY, in 1918.

Gertrude Bell was one of the first European women to travel extensively in the Arabian Desert, and was one of the earliest female archaeologists to undertake field research in the Middle East.

Bellingshausen, Fabian Gottlieb Benjamin von (Baron von Bellingshausen, Thaddeus Bellingshausen, Faddey Faddeyevich Bellingsgauzen)

(1778–1852) *German-born naval officer in Antarctica and the South Pacific, in service to Russia*

Fabian Gottlieb von Bellingshausen was born on the Baltic island of Saaremaa, into a noble Estonian family of German descent. In his youth, he entered the Russian navy; in 1803–06, he circumnavigated the world as a midshipman with ADAM IVAN RITTER VON KRUSENSTERN's expedition.

In 1819, at the rank of captain, Bellingshausen took command of a Russian naval expedition to the Antarctic seas south of the known latitudes. He sailed from the port of Kronstadt, near present-day St. Petersburg, in July 1819. Accompanying his ship, the *Vostok* (east), was the *Mirny* (peaceful), captained by MIKHAIL PETROVICH LAZAREV.

Bellingshausen and his expedition headed into the South Atlantic Ocean, touching first at Rio de Janeiro before reaching South Georgia Island. From there, he headed east and south, commanding the first ships to sail below the ANTARCTIC CIRCLE since the voyages of JAMES COOK in the 1770s. On January 27, he came within 20 miles of Princess

Martha Coast of Greater (East) Antarctica and sighted the edge of the ice sheet, which some claim constitutes the first sighting of the continent (before the Englishman EDWARD BRANSFIELD).

With the onset of the antarctic winter season, Bellingshausen and his ships headed northward into the central South Pacific Ocean. Over the next few months, he located a number of uncharted islands in the Fiji Islands and the Tuamotu Archipelago. The expedition also visited Tahiti, explored the coast of TASMANIA, and reprovisioned at Sydney, Australia.

In December 1820, Bellingshausen returned to the Antarctic. At 69° south latitude, he sighted and named Peter I island. Soon afterward, he located a larger body of land that he named Alexander I Land, known today as Alexander I Island.

On his return northward, in February 1821, Bellingshausen and his men encountered American whaling captain NATHANIEL BROWN PALMER at South Shetland Island.

During his travels, Bellingshausen conducted studies in the natural sciences. The expedition brought back many species of birds from the Southern Hemisphere, including the first specimen of the emperor penguin. He also undertook observations of ocean currents and studied the Sargasso Sea. He went on to a distinguished career in the Russian navy, including service against the Turks in the eastern MEDITERRANEAN SEA. He was appointed an admiral in 1843, after which he commanded the port of Kronstadt.

Baron von Bellingshausen's circumnavigation of Antarctica resulted in an early sighting of land below the Antarctic Circle (some claim his as the first sighting of the Antarctic continent). The Bellingshausen Sea is named in his honor.

Beltrami, Giacomo Costantino (1779–1855)
Italian traveler in northwestern Minnesota

Giacomo Beltrami was born in the northern Italian town of Bergamo, near Milan, and grew up to hold judicial offices in the Venetian government. In 1821, he was exiled from Venice after being implicated in a plot against the Austrian-backed government.

In his first year of exile, Beltrami toured the European continent, covering a wide area between Livorno in Italy and Brussels in Belgium, visiting major cities as well as rural areas in France and what is now Germany. He then crossed to England, spending time in London, Windsor, and Oxford and, in mid-1822, sailed from Liverpool for the United States. After landing in Philadelphia, he traveled to Baltimore and Washington, D.C., where he was received by President James Monroe.

From Washington, Beltrami set out westward on a tour across the APPALACHIAN MOUNTAINS and into the Ohio Valley. As he traveled by stagecoach and hired wagon

Giacomo Beltrami *(Library of Congress)*

through Kentucky, he recorded his impressions of the region and its inhabitants. He eventually reached Pittsburgh, from where he headed southwestward, toward the MISSISSIPPI RIVER.

Beltrami had originally planned to travel southward to New Orleans and Mexico, but, upon reaching the confluence of the Ohio and Mississippi Rivers, near what is now Cairo, Illinois, he decided instead to head northward into the upper reaches of the Mississippi. He began his journey up the Mississippi from St. Louis aboard the steamboat *Virginia,* on a voyage that marked the first successful attempt by a steam-powered vessel to travel upstream as far as Fort St. Anthony (near present-day Minneapolis, Minnesota). He was accompanied on this trip by the newly appointed Indian agent to the Chippewa (Ojibway) and Sioux (Dakota, Lakota, Nakota), Major Lawrence Taliaferro.

From Fort St. Anthony, Beltrami traveled up the Minnesota River with a U.S. Army expedition commanded by Major STEPHEN HARRIMAN LONG. Long had been assigned to survey the border between the United States and Canada, from the Red River of the North eastward to Lake Superior. Near Pembina, in what is now northeastern North Dakota, Beltrami left Long and his soldiers and traveled southeastward up the Red Lake River by CANOE, in search of the source of the Mississippi River.

In mid-August 1823, following an attack by Sioux, Beltrami's Chippewa guides abandoned him. Unskilled at paddling, he waded upstream, towing the canoe behind him. He entered Red Lake, and there obtained new Indian guides. Soon afterward, he came upon an as yet unnamed lake, which he christened Lake Julia. A stream he observed flowing southward out of this body of water he wrongly concluded was the source of the Mississippi. (The true source is Lake Itasca as determined by HENRY ROWE SCHOOLCRAFT in 1832.)

By mid-October 1823, Beltrami was back in St. Louis, then continued southward to New Orleans. Over the next two years, he wrote and published an account of his exploration and supposed discovery of the Mississippi's source.

Beltrami traveled into Mexico before returning to Europe in 1826. In 1849, he was permitted to return to Italy, where he spent his remaining years.

Giacomo Beltrami's claim that he had located the source of the Mississippi was rejected by most geographers of his day. Nonetheless, in 1866, the Minnesota state government named a newly organized section of northwestern Minnesota, Beltrami County, in recognition of his explorations. It contains Red Lake and the upper Red Lake River, which he explored in 1823.

Benalcázar, Sebastián de (Sebastián de Belalcázar, Sebastián Moyano) (ca. 1479–1551)
Spanish conquistador in Peru, Ecuador, and Colombia

Sebastián de Benalcázar was born in Belalcázar, a village in south-central Spain. Little is known of his origins, or early life, except that he was of a humble family; his original surname was Moyano.

In 1498, Benalcázar accompanied CHRISTOPHER COLUMBUS on his third expedition, which explored the coasts of present-day Trinidad and northeastern South America. He remained in the WEST INDIES, settling first on Hispaniola (present-day Haiti and the Dominican Republic), then moving to the Spanish settlement of Darién on the mainland of CENTRAL AMERICA in what is now Panama. By 1522, he had established himself as a military and colonial leader, participating in the Spanish conquest of Nicaragua.

In 1531, Benalcázar joined forces with FRANCISCO PIZARRO in his third attempt to conquer the Inca Empire of Peru, taking part in the Spanish victory at Cajamarca in 1532. In 1534, he launched his own expedition of conquest. He pushed into what is now Ecuador, and, with the support of local Canari Indians, he occupied the Inca Indian provincial capital of Quito. In 1535, he established the port city of Guayaquil.

In 1536, Benalcázar undertook another expedition farther north, penetrating the interior of what is now Colombia. Along the way, he established settlements at Popayán and Cali. An Indian captured the previous year had told Benalcázar of a fabulous kingdom to the east, rich in gold and precious stones, ruled by the "Gilded One," an Indian monarch covered by gold dust in sacred ceremonies.

Benalcázar continued to search for the land he dubbed EL DORADO for the next few years. In 1539, he went eastward across Colombia's central mountains, the Cordillera, reaching the upper Magdalena River Valley, near present-day Bogotá. There, he met up with GONZALO JIMÉNEZ DE QUESADA as well as NIKOLAUS FEDERMANN, both of whom had been exploring the region from the east. Subsequently, the three conquistadores traveled to Spain to resolve their conflicting claims. In Spain, Benalcázar was named governor of the Popayán in what is now southwestern Colombia.

During the 1540s, Benalcázar became embroiled in the civil wars generated by GONZALO PIZARRO and DIEGO DE ALMAGRO. He ordered the execution of a rival without authorization and was himself condemned to death. In 1551, in Cartagena, while en route to Spain to appeal this sentence, he died of fever.

Sebastián de Benalcázar expanded the Spanish conquest of the Inca northward into what is now Ecuador and Colombia. He founded the first important seaports on the northwest coast of South America and led the first European explorations across what is now Colombia. He is credited with introducing the legend of El Dorado, an idea that continued to generate explorations into the South American interior until the early 1600s.

Benavides, Alonzo de (Alonso de Benavides) (fl. 1620s) *Spanish missionary in New Mexico*

Alonzo de Benavides was born in the AZORES off Portugal, on the island of São Miguel. He traveled to the Americas in about 1600, settling in Mexico City, where he studied for the priesthood and entered the Franciscan order three years later. He subsequently became director of the novices at the Franciscan monastery in Puebla in east-central Mexico.

With the beginning of organized Spanish colonization of New Mexico in 1621, Benavides was appointed as father custodian of that province, in charge of all Franciscan missionary activities, including the construction of missions, schools, and churches.

In 1622, Benavides traveled with a party of some 30 Franciscan friars to New Mexico, where he undertook expeditions into the lands of the Apache Indians of the upper Gila River Valley of present-day southwestern New Mexico. In 1626, at Santa Fe, he established the Chapel of San Miguel, one of the earliest Catholic chapels in the United States.

From Santa Fe, Benavides and his missionary staff embarked on a series of expeditions along the Rio Grande and Pecos River, seeking to convert the Indians. Their missionary work took them into the lands of the Navajo (Dineh) and Hopi Indians, as well as the Rio Grande Pueblo Indians. Benavides established a mission at the Acoma Pueblo of Keres Indians in 1629. That same year, he founded a missionary settlement, Santa Clara de Capoo, on the edge of Apache country. Santa Clara de Capoo developed into a base for further missionary forays into the lands of the Apache.

From 1622 to 1629, Benavides succeeded in converting as many as 16,000 Indians to Christianity and provided a strong cultural base for Spanish domination of the region's native population.

In 1630, Benavides was relieved of his duties as father custodian of New Mexico. He then returned to Spain, via Mexico City, where he presented a detailed report of his activities to King Philip IV, hoping to gain increased support for his missionary pursuits in New Spain. This report, known as the *Memorial*, includes extensive physical descriptions of the territory that Benavides explored during his years among the Indians of the American Southwest.

During the early 1630s, Benavides again traveled to the Americas and revisited the missions he had established in New Mexico. In 1634, he left for Goa, the Portuguese colony on the east coast of India, where he eventually became archbishop.

Through his missionary work, Alonzo de Benavides helped open the American Southwest to Spanish colonization.

Benjamin of Tudela (Rabbi Benjamin of Tudela)

(unknown–1173) *Spanish rabbi in the Middle East and central Asia*

A Spanish Jew, Rabbi Benjamin was born at Tudela in northeastern Spain. In 1159, he set out from Saragossa for the Mediterranean coast near Barcelona. He then embarked from the port of Marseilles on an eastward journey in which he planned to visit Jewish communities.

Benjamin of Tudela first sailed to Italy, then traveled into Greece, Anatolia (Turkey), and Syria and visited Jerusalem and the Holy Land. He crossed into Mesopotamia (present-day Iraq), where he met with the caliph of Baghdad. After traveling in Arabia and Persia (present-day Iran), according to his own later account, he reached China's western frontier before going on to India and Ceylon (present-day Sri Lanka).

In 1173, Rabbi Benjamin of Tudela returned to Spain by way of Egypt and Sicily. He died later that same year. His account, *Massoth Schel Rabbi Benjamin*, originally written in Hebrew, was soon translated into Latin and other languages and became one of the first widely circulated travel books in medieval Europe. An English edition, *The Itinerary of Rabbi Benjamin of Tudela* (also known as *Book of Travels*

and *The Travels of Rabbi Benjamin*), first appeared in the 1840s. He was the first medieval explorer of the Orient and is thought to be the first European to have reached China.

Bent, Charles (1799–1847) *American trader, first U.S. territorial governor of New Mexico, brother of William Bent*

Charles Bent was born in the Virginia town of Charleston, part of present-day West Virginia. In 1806, his family moved to the Louisiana Territory and settled in St. Louis, where his father, Silas Bent, was appointed first deputy surveyor and then a justice of the supreme court of the Missouri Territory.

Starting in 1822, Bent embarked on a career in the FUR TRADE on the upper MISSOURI RIVER. He worked for JOSHUA PILCHER's ST. LOUIS MISSOURI FUR COMPANY for three years, eventually becoming Pilcher's partner. By the late 1820s, however, competition by JOHN JACOB ASTOR's larger AMERICAN FUR COMPANY, coupled with the decline in the demand for beaver pelts brought on by a change in fashion to hats made of silk, led Bent to leave the fur trade and concentrate on the commercial opportunities presented by the newly reopened Santa Fe Trail.

Starting in about 1826, Bent became active in the trade in furs and buffalo hides on the upper Arkansas River, near present-day La Junta, Colorado. In 1829, he organized and led a trade caravan westward from Westport, Missouri (near present-day Kansas City), and followed the Santa Fe Trail across the southern plains. Accompanying him on this trip was WILLIAM BENT, one of six brothers who, at various times, participated in frontier trade. This 1829 trade expedition was one of the earliest to use oxen to pull wagons along the Santa Fe Trail. Near the present Colorado–New Mexico stateline, Bent led his trade caravan through the Cimarron Cutoff established by WILLIAM BECKNELL. They eventually reached Santa Fe, where they sold their trade goods at a considerable profit.

By 1833, Bent was in partnership with frontier entrepreneur CÉRAN DE HAULT DE LASSUS DE ST. VRAIN. That year, he founded Bent's Fort on the Arkansas River, just above the mouth of the Purgatoire in what is now southeastern Colorado. Bent's Fort soon became an important base for traders and settlers headed westward from Kansas and western Missouri. Bent himself began to reside in Taos at about this time, and placed his brother William in charge of the operations at Bent's Fort.

In 1837, Bent and St. Vrain established a second trading post in Colorado: Fort St. Vrain, on the South Platte River, north of Pikes Peak. With supplies from the American Fur Company and the HUDSON'S BAY COMPANY, Bent and St. Vrain's enterprise dominated the Indian trade south of the Black Hills.

In 1835, Bent married Maria Ignacio Jaramillo, the daughter of a prominent Taos family. Her sister, Josephine, later married frontiersman CHRISTOPHER HOUSTON CARSON (Kit Carson), a hunter at Bent's Fort.

In 1842, Bent entered into a peace agreement with the Comanche Indians that enabled him to expand his trade operation into the Canadian River region of northern Texas.

Colonel STEPHEN WATTS KEARNY's military expedition from Kansas used Bent's Fort as a staging area for the 1846 invasion of New Mexico. With the successful occupation of Santa Fe and the surrounding area, Kearny named Bent as the first governor of the provisional U.S. Territory of New Mexico.

In January 1847, the Mexicans and Tiwa Indians of Taos rose in rebellion against the American occupation. While in Taos that month, Bent was killed and scalped by warriors, who then paraded his body through the streets of that town. American forces under Sterling Price soon put down the revolt.

Charles Bent's trade enterprise along the Santa Fe Trail and his forts on the Arkansas and Platte Rivers contributed to the non-Indian settlement of southern Colorado. By developing the Santa Fe Trail as a regular route from the Missouri frontier, Bent also paved the way for future settlers headed across the southern plains to Arizona and California. Bent's Fort itself provided an important stopover point for the subsequent explorations of JOHN CHARLES FRÉMONT, JAMES WILLIAM ABERT, JOHN WILLIAMS GUNNISON, EDWARD FITZGERALD BEALE, and others to the ROCKY MOUNTAINS and Far West.

Bent, James Theodore (1852–1897)
British archaeologist in Africa and the Middle East
Born in England, James Theodore Bent studied archaeology at Oxford University, graduating in 1875.

In 1885–87, Bent studied the native customs in the Aegean Sea islands; in 1889–90, he undertook a study of antiquities in what is now Turkey, as well as in Bahrain in the Persian Gulf.

Bent's next studies, in 1891, involved the ancient burial grounds in present-day Zimbabwe in southern Africa. He described his work in the 1892 book *The Ruined Cities of Mashonaland.*

Accompanying Bent on many of his expeditions was his wife, Mabel Bent. Starting in 1893, the Bents began four years of study and travel in Arabia, during which James produced one of the earliest European maps of the Hadhramaut region of what is now Saudi Arabia.

James Theodore Bent's archaeological studies led to travel and exploration of islands in the MEDITERRANEAN SEA, and in Africa and the Near East, increasing European knowledge of those regions.

Bent, William (1809–1869)
American trader, trapper, scout, Indian agent in the West, brother of Charles Bent
William Bent, one of CHARLES BENT's six brothers, was born in St. Louis. At the age of 15, he traveled up the Arkansas River to trap for furs in what is now southeastern Colorado. In 1830, he joined his brother Charles and CÉRAN DE HAULT DE LASSUS DE ST. VRAIN in the FUR TRADE. In 1833, they established Bent's Fort on the Arkansas River, about 12 miles above the mouth of the Purgatoire River, near present-day La Junta, Colorado.

While Charles Bent directed the company's operations from Taos and Santa Fe, New Mexico, William Bent remained at the upper Arkansas River site, where he supervised the construction of Bent's Fort, completed in 1833. William remained as the manager of this post and directed operations there over the next 16 years.

In 1846, Colonel STEPHEN WATTS KEARNY arrived at Bent's Fort in command of U.S. forces on their way to invade New Mexico and northern Mexico at the outbreak of the U.S.-Mexican War. Bent was commissioned by Kearny as an army scout to lead his troops along the remaining stretch of the Santa Fe Trail into New Mexico. In New Mexico, he also served as a scout for Sterling Price in the suppression of the Mexican and Pueblo revolt in Taos in early 1847, during which his brother Charles was killed.

With Céran St. Vrain's retirement in 1849, William Bent assumed sole control of Bent, St. Vrain & Co. Also in 1849, the federal government tended an offer to buy Bent's Fort for use as a military base. Rather than accept the government's low price, Bent blew up the fort. In 1853, he established a new trading post 40 miles downstream on the Arkansas at the mouth of the Purgatoire River. Bent's New Fort, as it came to be known, served as an important stopover point and trading center on the Santa Fe Trail, as well as a base for government surveys of the West. American settlers were attracted to the lands around the post and it became the first permanent Anglo-American settlement in present-day Colorado.

The Pikes Peak (Colorado) gold rush of 1859 brought about a great influx of non-Indian fortune-seekers and settlers into eastern Colorado, increasing tensions with the Cheyenne Indians. Bent, a respected figure among tribes of the southern plains because of his years of fair dealing with them and his three marriages to local Indian women, was given the position of Indian agent, which he held for several years.

In 1860, Bent leased Bent's New Fort to the U.S. Army. Soon afterward, it was destroyed by a flood. A new army post, Fort Lyon, was later built on the site.

Bent spent his retirement years in Westport, Missouri, which had been the starting point of the Santa Fe Trail. Among his neighbors was CHRISTOPHER HOUSTON CARSON (Kit Carson), who had worked for Bent as a hunter at the upper Arkansas River post in the 1830s, as well as LOUIS VASQUEZ and other fur traders who operated in the southern ROCKY MOUNTAINS during the 1820s and 1830s.

From his early days as a fur trapper on the upper Arkansas River, through his career in the Santa Fe Trail trade on the southern plains, William Bent played a key role in the exploration and settlement of the region. He served as an intermediary between the Indians, the settlers, and U.S. Army forces that began to arrive in southeastern Colorado during the years before and shortly after the Civil War. In addition, both government and commercial expeditions exploring the region north and south of the Santa Fe Trail made use of trading posts managed by him.

Bering, Vitus Jonassen (1681–1741) *Danish mariner in Siberia and Alaska, in service to Russia*

Vitus Bering was born in Horsens, Denmark. In the early 1700s, he embarked on a seafaring career that began with a trip to the EAST INDIES aboard a Dutch ship. Returning to Europe in 1703, he entered the service of the Royal Russian Navy as a sub-lieutenant, reaching the rank of captain in 1724.

In 1725, Czar Peter the Great commissioned Bering to undertake an exploration of SIBERIA's Pacific coast to determine if there were a land connection between Asiatic Russia and the extreme northwestern part of North America. Czar Peter I and other Russian leaders were also interested in establishing an Arctic route to open trade connections with China and India.

That year, in what became known as the First Kamchatka Expedition, Bering traveled overland across Russia and Siberia to the mouth of Kamchatka River on the Siberian peninsula of the same name. Here, he directed the construction of a ship, the *St. Gabriel*. In 1728, he sailed from Kamchatka northeast along the Siberian coast to the Gulf of Anadyr. During this leg of the expedition, he explored Krest Sound and Preobrazheniya Bay.

Bering continued northward through what later became known as the BERING STRAIT, as far as 67°18' north latitude, making the European discovery of St. Lawrence Island and the Diomede Islands along the way. Because of heavy fog, he failed to sight the coast of Alaska. Determining to his satisfaction that there was no land connecting Siberia and North America, he sailed south and west back to Kamchatka.

Bering returned to St. Petersburg in 1730, where Empress Anna had come to the Russian throne. Although the Russian admiralty deemed the results of his initial explorations to be inconclusive, Empress Anna appointed Bering to lead a much larger exploration of eastern Siberia and the unknown seas to the east. In 1733, Bering again headed eastward across Russia and Siberia in command of what came to be known as the Great Northern Expedition, which also included the Second Kamchatka Expedition. This venture was organized on a large scale, involving 13 ships and as many as 600 men.

Over the next six years, with Martin Spanberg and ALEKSEY ILYICH CHIRIKOV serving as Bering's chief lieutenants, explorations were undertaken from the Pacific port of Okhotsk into the Lake Baikal region and the Amur Basin. Seaward expeditions were also made along the Arctic and Pacific coasts of Siberia, and southward to the Kuril Islands, north of Japan.

Bering resumed his seaward explorations to the east in 1740. Sailing on the *St. Peter,* which had been constructed at Okhotsk, he rounded the southern end of the Kamchatka Peninsula to the newly established settlement of Petropavlovsk on the Pacific coast. There, he joined Chirikov, who had directed the construction of another vessel, the *St. Paul.* (The settlement's name had been derived from the Russian names for these two ships.)

On June 5, 1741, the two ships sailed from Petropavlovsk and headed eastward. Accompanying Bering was German naturalist GEORG WILHELM STELLER, who had been sent by the Russian Academy of Science to study the flora and fauna of Siberia and regions to the east. They explored Avacha Bay and searched in vain for the fabled Gama Land, a non-existent landmass that was believed to lie in the mid-Pacific. The two ships were soon separated, and Bering continued eastward. On July 16, 1741, he sighted Mount St. Elias on the Alaskan mainland and, soon afterward, he landed on Kayak Island in the northeastern corner of the Gulf of Alaska. Chirikov's contingent had also sighted the Alaskan coast farther to the south.

Bering went on to explore Kodiak Island. On his return journey toward Siberia, he charted the Kenai Peninsula of Alaska and the Aleutian Islands. In early November 1741, near one of the Commander (Komandorski) Islands off the coast of the Siberian Kamchatka Peninsula (later called Bering Island), Bering's ship ran aground.

Although Bering and his crew survived the shipwreck, they were stricken with SCURVY while stranded. Bering, along with 18 of his crew, died. The survivors were able to build small boats from the wreckage of the *St. Peter* and eventually reached the Siberian mainland.

Chirikov and Spanberg returned to St. Petersburg in 1743, with navigational reports indicating conclusively that Siberia and North America were separated by the Bering Strait. They also brought back samples of sea otter pelts, which soon inspired the expansion of the Russian FUR TRADE eastward from Siberia to the Aleutians and into the Gulf of Alaska.

Reports of the Bering Strait had been made as early as the mid-16th century, considered by some to be the western outlet to the fabled STRAIT OF ANIAN, a mythical NORTHWEST PASSAGE through North America to the Atlantic. Cossack seafarer and explorer SEMYON IVANOVICH DESHNEV, based on his explorations of the Gulf of Anadyr during the 1650s, had also suspected that Siberia did not extend into the North American continent. Vitus Bering's expeditions were the first to base this finding on modern navigational methods. His explorations provided the basis for Russia's colonization of the Aleutians over the next 100 years, as well as the coastal islands and the mainland of Alaska.

Berlandier, Jean-Louis (ca. 1805–1851)
French naturalist in Texas

Jean-Louis Berlandier was born in the French town of Fort de l'Ecluse, not far from Geneva, Switzerland. He was largely self-educated, studying Latin and Greek on his own while working as an apprentice to a pharmaceutical company in Geneva.

The young Berlandier studied under Swiss botanist Auguste-Pryame de Candolle and accompanied him on field trips in France and Switzerland. Berlandier's talent as a naturalist came to the attention of Mexico's foreign minister, Lucas Alemán, one of Candolle's former students. In 1825, the Mexican government was organizing a scientific expedition to explore Texas and establish the boundary between Mexico and the United States. Alemán enlisted Berlandier to take part in this expedition, and the young Frenchman journeyed to Mexico City in 1827.

Berlandier left Mexico City with the Mexican Comisión de Límites on November 10, 1827. The group under General Manuel de Mier y Terán headed northward into Texas, reaching the Rio Grande at present-day Laredo on February 2, 1828. They then continued toward the settlement of San Fernando de Bexar (present-day San Antonio), arriving on March 1, 1828.

During the following spring and summer, Berlandier made an extensive exploration of the region northwest of San Antonio including a detailed study of the area's flora. In fall 1828, he was invited to take part in a buffalo and bear hunt with a group of Comanche Indians. A detachment of Mexican soldiers and civilians also took part in this hunt, commanded by Colonel José Francisco Ruiz, who was well acquainted with the Comanche.

In early November 1828, Berlandier traveled with the Comanche and Mexican hunting party into the largely unexplored area northwest of San Antonio. After the Comanche had left the Mexican soldiers and civilians at the Guadalupe River in late November, the group continued on and explored northward as far as the Pedernales River, then headed southward through Frio Canyon before returning to San Antonio on December 18, 1828.

Following his service with the Mexican scientific expedition into Texas, Berlandier settled in Matamoros, Mexico, across the Rio Grande from present-day Brownsville, Texas. He established himself as a medical doctor and married a Mexican woman. He died in a drowning accident while attempting to cross the San Fernando River, south of Matamoros, in 1851.

Jean-Louis Berlandier's account of his experiences with the Comanche hunting party, entitled "Caza del oso y cibolo en el noroeste de Tejas" ("Hunting bear and bison in northwestern Texas"), first appeared in a Mexican scientific journal in 1844. An artist as well as a naturalist, he illustrated his writings with field sketches, landscapes, and some of the earliest scientifically drawn maps of the interior of Texas. Berlandier's observations on the topography of the Texas interior and on the ethnology of its native people provide an accurate depiction of this area in the years prior to the extensive non-Indian settlement of the 1830s and 1840s.

Bernier, Joseph Elzéar (1852–1934)
Canadian mariner in the Arctic

Born in L'Islet, Quebec, J. E. Bernier followed family tradition and pursued a career as a mariner. At the age of 14, he started as a cabin boy and, after three years, became captain of the first of 105 ships that he would command during his lifetime. He also served as a dockmaster at Lauzon, managed an ice company, and served as governor of a prison.

Bernier developed an interest in Arctic navigation. He also came to the conclusion that Canadian Arctic holdings were being violated by foreign whaling ships: He believed that any country adjacent to the Arctic had rights to any islands within a triangle from the north shore of its mainland to the apex at the NORTH POLE. To assert Canadian sovereignty over Arctic islands, he first proposed an expedition to the Canadian government in 1902. In the years to come, from 1904 to 1911, he carried out Arctic expeditions on behalf of Canada, during which he left documentation declaring sovereignty on most islands up to the 80th parallel.

In 1912–17, Bernier led several private expeditions to the Arctic archipelago, prompted by rumors of gold on Baffin Island. In 1922–25, he again sailed for the Canadian government, charting islands in the eastern Arctic. He came out of retirement at the age of 75 for one last expedition, seeking an Arctic route for grain ships to and from Churchill on HUDSON BAY.

J. E. Bernier's 12 Arctic expeditions helped establish the dominant presence of Canada in the use of islands to its north. They also provided a body of knowledge concerning the geography of the Canadian Arctic and the navigation of Arctic waters.

Berrío, Antonio de (Antonio de Berreo)
(ca. 1520–1597) *Spanish mariner in South America*

Little is known of Antonio de Berrío's early life, except that he was probably born in Spain and was a seafarer. He married a niece of GONZALO JIMÉNEZ DE QUESADA, Spanish colonial governor of what is now eastern Colombia, becoming his heir.

Starting in 1584, Berrío initiated a series of thorough explorations of the ORINOCO RIVER, seeking the fabled land of EL DORADO. Over the next 10 years, he expanded his search to include the Guiana (present-day Guyana) region of northeastern South America. His son, Fernando de Berrío, explored the southern tributaries of the Orinoco.

In 1595, Berrío was taken prisoner at Trinidad by English explorer SIR WALTER RALEIGH. He was soon released at the port settlement of Cumana in present-day Venezuela. With information provided by Berrío, Raleigh himself set out in search of El Dorado. Berrío died in the Americas in 1597.

Antonio de Berrío's efforts to find mythical, gold-laden Indian lands led to increased knowledge among both the Spanish and the English of the Orinoco River system.

Beutler, August (fl. 1750s) *Dutch pioneer in South Africa*

August Beutler was an 18th-century Dutch settler in southern Africa's Cape Town colony. In 1752, Beutler organized and led a group of colonists in an overland expedition eastward from Cape Town, along the south coast of Africa, beyond Algoa Bay, and into the present-day Transkei region.

August Beutler's expedition was one of the earliest efforts to expand European settlement in southern Africa beyond the region around the CAPE OF GOOD HOPE.

Bienville, sieur de   See LE MOYNE, JEAN-BAPTISTE.

Billardière, Jacques-Julien Houtou de la
See LA BILLARDIÈRE, JACQUES-JULIEN HOUTOU DE.

Billings, Joseph (ca. 1758–1806) *British navigator, astronomer in the Siberian Arctic and Alaska, in service to Great Britain and Russia*

Joseph Billings was born in Furnham Green, England, near London. He embarked on a naval career, becoming skilled in navigation and astronomy. Serving on the *Discovery* as an astronomer on JAMES COOK's expedition of 1776–80, he made his first journey into Arctic waters, to the north of the BERING STRAIT.

In 1783, Billings entered the Russian navy. Two years later, at the rank of captain lieutenant, he took command of Russia's Northeastern Secret Geographical and Astronomical Expedition, which was dispatched to locate a NORTHEAST PASSAGE from the extreme northeast coast of SIBERIA into the Bering Strait.

With Cook, Billings had reached as far as Cape Shmidta on the central coast of the East Siberian Sea. For the Russians, he planned to explore from the mouth of the Kolyma River eastward to Alaska. Yet, in 1786–87, he only succeeded in reaching the western end of the East Siberian Sea, hundreds of miles west of Cape Shmidta and Bering Strait. With the onset of winter, he settled at Yakutsk for almost a year, engaging in the central Siberian FUR TRADE.

Starting in 1789, Billings, along with ANTON BATAKOV and NIKOLAY DAURKIN directed a seaward attempt to pass through Bering Strait and reach northeastern Siberia. Sailing from Okhotsk on the east coast of Siberia, he failed in an attempt to find an ice-free passage northwestward.

In 1790, in command of the ship *Slava Rossy,* with Batakov and GAVRIIL ANDREYEVICH SARYCHEV, Billings explored the Aleutian Islands, as well as the Gulf of Alaska as far east as Mount Saint Elias. The next year, he made an overland crossing of the Chukchi Peninsula, traveling by reindeer westward to the Kolyma River region. By 1793, Billings was in Irkutsk, and from there he returned to St. Petersburg.

Joseph Billings spent nearly 10 years exploring the northern reaches of eastern Siberia. His work revealed geographic information on the relationship between North America and Asia and resulted in some of the first accurate maps of the Chukchi Peninsula and the Sea of Okhotsk, as well as the Aleutian Islands and Prince William Sound of Alaska.

Binger, Louis-Gustave (1856–1936) *French explorer, colonial official in West Africa*

Louis-Gustave Binger was a native of Strasbourg, France. His first visit to Africa was with the French military. He returned to the coast of Senegal in 1887, from where he began a three-year exploration of the interior. The expedition was supported in part by the French government, which at the time was interested in establishing a colonial presence in West Africa.

Binger ascended the Senegal River. Heading southeastward across present-day Mali, he reached Bamako on the upper NIGER RIVER. From that point, he examined the region south of the great bend of the Niger River to the headwaters of the Volta. By late 1889, he had reached the Comoe River, which he descended to its mouth on the Gulf of Guinea. For this achievement, Britain's ROYAL GEOGRAPHICAL SOCIETY later awarded him its Founder's Medal.

In 1892, Binger surveyed the boundary between the Ivory Coast and the Gold Coast (present-day Ghana). In carrying out this work, he ascended the Volta River northward to its confluence with the Comoe.

In 1893, Binger became French colonial governor of the Ivory Coast, and in 1897, he was appointed director of African Affairs for the French colonial office.

As a result of the explorations of Louis-Gustave Binger, the region north of the Ivory Coast, which now comprises much of Mali and Guinea, came under French control as French West Africa. Binger was known as one of the creators of France's one-time colonial empire in West Africa. An Ivory Coast city near the mouth of the Comoe River is known today as Bingerville.

Bingham, Hiram (1875–1956) *American historian in South America, explorer of Inca sites in the Andes*

Born in Honolulu, Hawaii, Hiram Bingham was the grandson of the American missionary of the same name who founded the first Protestant mission in Hawaii. He studied at Yale and Harvard Universities and at the University of California and in the course of his academic career, specializing in Latin American history, taught at Yale, Harvard, and Princeton.

In 1906–07, Bingham explored Venezuelan general Simón Bolívar's route across Venezuela and Colombia a century earlier. In 1908–09, Bingham explored an old Spanish trade route from Buenos Aires, Argentina, to Lima, Peru. In 1911, as director of the Yale Peruvian Expedition, Bingham explored the Urubamba Valley in the ANDES MOUNTAINS in search of the Inca sites of Vilcabamba and Vitcos, men-

Hiram Bingham *(Library of Congress)*

tioned in Spanish texts. He located instead the ruins of the ancient Inca city of Machu Picchu, located on a peak rising up above the valley about 50 miles northwest of Cuzco, Peru. Archaeological evidence indicates that Machu Picchu was a country retreat for Inca emperors, with temples, shrines, and baths. Bingham subsequently located the ruins of Espíritu Pampa (plain of ghosts), now believed to be Vilcabamba, the last Inca capital, which fell to the Spanish in 1572. In the years to come, Bingham carried out additional fieldwork of Inca sites. The National Geographic Society sponsored some of his work.

In World War I, Bingham directed an Aviation Instruction Center at Issoudun, France. In 1923–24, he served as lieutenant governor of Connecticut, then as governor for one year before becoming a U.S. (Republican) senator from Connecticut for eight years.

Hiram Bingham's expeditions, which he wrote about in *Inca Land* (1922), *Machu Picchu* (1930), and *Lost City of the Incas* (1948), increased knowledge of the Inca and the Spanish conquest. The road to Machu Picchu is known as the Hiram Bingham Highway in his honor.

Biruni, Abu ar-Rayhan Muhammad ibn Ahmad al- (Abu Raihan Muhammad al-Biruni, al-Ustadh) (973–1048) *Arab scholar in India*

Al-Biruni was born in Kath, formerly considered part of the Persian Empire and presently part of Karakalpak in Uzbekistan. Of Arab ancestry, he was associated with the court of Sultan Mahmud and later Sultan Mawdud—probably originally as a captive, then as an adviser as well as a tutor—in the city of Ghazna (present-day Ghazni, near Kabul, Afghanistan). He became one of the most renowned scholars among Muslims, mastering the Arabic, Persian, Turkish, Sanskrit, and Hebrew languages and writing about mathematics, astronomy, physics, botany, geography, geology, mineralogy, and history in 113 works.

In 1017 or 1018, al-Biruni traveled to India for the first time, accompanying Mahmud's military force. While there, he studied Indian customs, languages, science, and geography, which he wrote about in one of his best-known books, *India.* Al-Biruni explored parts of the GANGES RIVER and theorized that the sea had once covered the INDUS RIVER. Among his observations in other writings were a computation of the Earth's circumference close to modern values and different ways to determine north and south and LATITUDE AND LONGITUDE.

Al-Biruni, known as al-Ustadh (the master), influenced his contemporaries as well as Islamic and Hindu scholars for generations. Although most of his works were lost, and surviving works were not translated into European languages until the 20th century, some historians refer to the period of intellectual activity during his lifetime as "the age of al-Biruni."

Biscoe, John (1794–1843) *British mariner, seal hunter in Antarctica*

Born in Enfield in Middlesex, England, John Biscoe joined the Royal Navy in 1812. Starting in 1830, he commanded seal-hunting expeditions on ships owned by the Enderby brothers of England. Charles Enderby, a fellow of the ROYAL GEOGRAPHICAL SOCIETY, encouraged Biscoe and his other captains to explore for new lands during their voyages in the Southern Hemisphere.

In 1831, Biscoe sailed from TASMANIA southward in search of signs of land in the portion of the Antarctic adjacent to the Indian Ocean. He circumnavigated Antarctica, reaching as far as 69° south latitude by late January. He came upon what he took to be a part of the mainland, naming it Adelaide Land. Less than a month later, while exploring the Antarctic south of the Indian Ocean, Biscoe sighted ice cliffs, which he determined were actually exposed parts of a landmass covered with ice from the sea. He named the region Enderby Land, after his employers.

John Biscoe was one of the first mariners to chart large areas of the world's last known continent. Enderby Land was not explored again until SIR DOUGLAS MAWSON's expedition of 1929–31. In 1908–10, French polar explorer JEAN-BAPTISTE-ÉTIENNE-AUGUSTE CHARCOT showed that Adelaide Land, which Biscoe also sighted and named, was really an island. Biscoe Bay, near the Bay of Whales, as well as Biscoe Island off Graham Land, are named in recognition of his Antarctic explorations.

Bishop, Isabella Lucy Bird (1831–1904)
British world traveler, writer

Isabella Bishop, née Bird, was originally from Yorkshire, England, where her father was a clergyman. She suffered from a variety of maladies, including insomnia, severe headaches, and a chronic spinal problem. At the age of 21, partly to regain her health, she embarked on a life of travel.

In 1854–55, Bird traveled widely in the United States and Canada. She set off again in 1872, visiting Australia and NEW ZEALAND. From there she went to the HAWAIIAN ISLANDS, where she climbed Mauna Loa, the 13,675-foot volcanic mountain.

From Hawaii, Bird went to San Francisco, California, and after resting for a few months at a sanatorium, she set out by train for the Sierra Nevada in fall 1873. At Truckee, Nevada, she left the train and over the next four months, traveled 800 miles on horseback into the ROCKY MOUNTAINS. At Fort Collins, Colorado, she lived for a short time with a family of settlers.

In 1878, Bird journeyed to the Far East. She visited the remote regions of northern Japan, where she lived among the aboriginal Ainu people. From Japan, she traveled to Hong Kong, then to the Malay Peninsula.

Bird married Dr. John Bishop in 1881, settling in Edinburgh, Scotland. Her husband died five years later. In 1888, Bishop resumed her life of travel, visiting India, Persia (present-day Iran), Syria, and the Kurdistan region of present-day Iraq.

In 1894, Bird traveled to Korea. She proceeded to China in 1896, traveling in a small boat to the farthest navigable point of the YANGTZE RIVER (Chang). By sampan, she reached as far as the Tibet border. Soon afterward, she made a final visit to Morocco.

In her 50 years of travels, Isabella Bishop circled the globe three times, journeying to places in the American West, the Pacific, and Asia seldom visited by Europeans, especially European women. She authored a number of books detailing her exploits as a world traveler, including *Englishwoman in America* (1856), *The Hawaiian Archipelago* (1875), *A Lady's Life in the Rocky Mountains* (1879), *Unbeaten Tracks in Japan* (1880), *Journeys in Persia and Kurdistan* (1891), and *Korea and Her Neighbors* (1898). In 1892, she was elected as the first woman member of the ROYAL GEOGRAPHICAL SOCIETY.

Bjarni Herjulfsson   See HERJULFSSON, BJARNI.

Black Beaver (1806–1880) *Lenni Lenape (Delaware) Indian guide, U.S. Army scout, interpreter, fur trapper, trader in the American West*

Black Beaver, a member of the Lenni Lenape (Delaware) Indian tribe, was born in Illinois. As a young man, he moved to the West and took part in the FUR TRADE in the ROCKY MOUNTAINS during the 1820s–30s.

In 1834–35, Black Beaver joined General HENRY LEAVENWORTH and Colonel HENRY DODGE in their exploration of the southern plains. The purpose of these expeditions was twofold: to convince Comanche, Kiowa, and Pawnee Indians to accept the resettlement of Southeast tribes into the Indian Territory, and to explore and chart the little-known regions lying to the west and south of what is now eastern Oklahoma.

Along with the part-Cherokee Indian JESSE CHISHOLM, Black Beaver traveled with the Dodge-Leavenworth expedition westward from Fort Gibson in present-day eastern Oklahoma, southwestward along the Arkansas River, and across the southern plains into the Washita Mountains and Red River region of present-day western Oklahoma and northern Texas. This first expedition of 1834 penetrated the lands of Osage and Kiowa Indians. Black Beaver served as the interpreter in the ensuing negotiations between the army and tribal leaders.

Over the next year, several other expeditions from Fort Leavenworth, Kansas, onto the southern plains were undertaken by Leavenworth's command, with Black Beaver as guide and interpreter. He participated in the exploration of the Cross Timbers region, a 30-mile-wide belt of forested land lying between the Arkansas River and COLORADO River, where contact was made with the Comanche. Black Beaver helped guide Leavenworth's men as far as the eastern Rockies of what is now Colorado.

During the U.S.-Mexican War of 1846–48, Black Beaver was an army scout for U.S. forces under General William Selby Harney in his campaign on Mexico's east coast.

In 1849, following the discovery of gold in California, the flow of migrants across the southwestern desert to the Pacific coast increased dramatically. That year, Black Beaver assisted Captain RANDOLPH BARNES MARCY in leading a wagon train of 500 settlers westward across Texas and New Mexico. On the return journey, Black Beaver blazed a new trail from the Brazos River, in northwest Texas, eastward to Fort Smith, Arkansas, then the gateway to the southwestern frontier.

Black Beaver worked as a trader and trapper in the Southwest throughout the 1850s, and, with the outbreak of the Civil War in 1861, he served as a scout for Union forces in the New Mexico and western Texas campaigns. At the war's close in 1865, Black Beaver served as an interpreter for the U.S. Army at the Little Arkansas Council, an important diplomatic conference with tribes of the southern plains.

In his later years, Black Beaver settled on Lenni Lenape lands along the Washita River near Anadarko in the Indian Territory (present-day Oklahoma). He became a leader and spokesperson for the Lenni Lenape in their dealings with the army and the Bureau of Indian Affairs.

Black Beaver was one of many Native American guides, interpreters, and trailblazers essential to the non-Indian exploration of North America.

Blaeu, Willem Janzoon (Guillielmus Blaeu)

(1571–1638) *Dutch geographer, cartographer, publisher*
A native of the Netherlands, Willem Blaeu studied geography and astronomy under the 16th-century Danish astronomer Tycho Brahe. In the early 1600s, Blaeu established

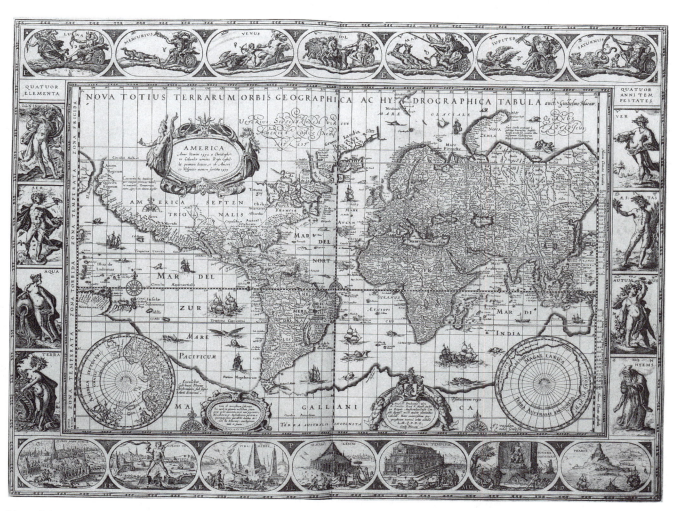

Map of the world by Willem Blaeu (1610) *(Library of Congress)*

a printing business in Amsterdam, which became one of the foremost publishers of maps and atlases.

Blaeu's earliest works were mainly celestial and terrestrial globes. He published a large atlas in 1630, the first such work to appear since ABRAHAM ORTELIUS's annual atlas of 1570–98. Blaeu's atlas included the first detailed maps of both North and South America, plus recently discovered geographic information. It was one of the first maps to show accurately that Tierra del Fuego was not connected to a GREAT SOUTHERN CONTINENT, but was an island off the tip of South America.

Over the next 42 years, the Blaeu atlas appeared in new editions, eventually encompassing 11 volumes, with information on all the known continents. Blaeu compiled geographic data for his maps from the works of English mapmaker John Speed, and also drew from the maps of the Flemish cartographers Ortelius and GERARDUS MERCATOR. After his death, Blaeu's sons Cornelius and Johann carried on the business until 1672.

Throughout the 1600s, Willem Blaeu's maps and atlases reflected the latest geographic findings. Although his maps were among the first to be mass-produced, they gained a reputation throughout Europe for high quality and accuracy, largely due to Blaeu's development and use of specially designed printing presses.

Blaxland, Gregory (1778–1853) *Australian pioneer in the Blue Mountains*

Born in Kent, England, Gregory Blaxland was among the first generation of colonists in what is now New South Wales, Australia. As a farmer near the coastal settlement of present-day Sydney, he faced financial ruin because of severe drought conditions in 1810.

In search of new pasture lands and a new source of water, Blaxland traveled up the Warragamba River, hoping to find a route through the high cliffs and deep canyons of the BLUE MOUNTAINS, less than 50 miles west of Sydney. From his two forays up the Warragamba, Blaxland determined that a route through the Blue Mountains could be found by following interconnected ridges rather than attempting any direct ascents.

In May 1813, accompanied by fellow landowner WILLIAM CHARLES WENTWORTH, surveyor William Lawson, and aboriginal guide James Burnes, as well as several convict servants, Blaxland set out from his farm at South Creek. The party, equipped with pack-horses, followed the high ridges without making descents into the canyons. They eventually reached a peak affording a view of the Bathurst Plains, a large fertile region to the west, naturally irrigated by the abundant waters of the Lett River.

Later that year, an expedition sponsored by the British colonial governor, Lachlan Macquarie, followed Blaxland's route, continued beyond his westernmost point, and, on crossing the GREAT DIVIDING RANGE, located the Fish River.

Less than two years after Blaxland's 1813 trek into the Blue Mountains, convict laborers constructed a road along his route that connected Sydney with the newly established inland settlement of Bathurst. In 1815, Blaxland himself settled at Bathurst, the first British settlement west of the Blue Mountains.

By blazing a trail through the Blue Mountains, Gregory Blaxland opened up eastern Australia to the rapid exploration and settlement that took place over the next 75 years. The peak from which he first saw the region west of the Blue Mountains is known today as Mount Blaxland.

Bligh, William (1754–1817) *British naval officer in the Pacific*

William Bligh was born and raised in Tyntan, near the port city of Plymouth, England. He began his naval career in his early teens, and then, in 1776–80, he served as sailing master on the *Resolution* during JAMES COOK's third Pacific expedition. On this voyage, Bligh first visited Tahiti; explored Prince William Sound, Alaska; and, in January 1779, undertook a reconnaissance of Kealakekua Bay on the newly explored island of Hawaii.

Upon his return to England in 1780, Bligh was promoted to lieutenant. He took part in hydrographic surveys, as well as naval engagements at Dogger Bank in the North Sea and at Gibraltar.

In December 1787, Bligh took command of the *Bounty* in an expedition aimed at obtaining breadfruit trees in Tahiti and introducing them as a food source for slaves in the WEST INDIES. After a 10-month journey, the *Bounty* reached Tahiti in late October 1788. Six months later, Bligh set out for the WEST INDIES with a cargo of living breadfruit trees. On April 28, 1789, while off the Friendly Islands, members of the crew, led by Fletcher Christian, rose up in mutiny. Along with 18 loyal crew members, Bligh was set adrift in a 23-foot-long open boat, with a minimal supply of food and water.

Using only basic navigational instruments and no charts, Bligh sailed the open boat across nearly 4,000 miles of the western Pacific. After three months, he safely brought his men to Timor, a Dutch colonial port in what is now Indonesia. Some of the mutineers were later captured, tried, and executed. Others, including Christian, founded a community on Pitcairn Island, where their descendants still live.

Bligh returned to England in spring 1790. Soon afterward, he was given command of the *Providence*, and in 1791–93, he undertook another voyage to Tahiti, succeeding in transporting more than 300 live breadfruit trees to Jamaica.

In the late 1790s and early 1800s, Bligh distinguished himself in naval actions against the French. In 1801, he was commended by Admiral Horatio Nelson for his service in the victory at Copenhagen.

William Bligh *(Library of Congress)*

In 1613, Block returned to New York Bay as commander of one of five ships in a fleet sent out by the Dutch government to trade for furs with the Indians of the Hudson River Valley. His ship, the *Tiger,* ascended the Hudson River and spent the winter in contact with Native Americans near present-day Albany, New York. In early 1614, the *Tiger* was destroyed by fire. Block then directed his crew in the construction of a new ship, the *Unrest.*

From Albany, Block sailed down the Hudson to Manhattan, then navigated the treacherous currents of a narrow channel of the East River between present-day Wards Island and Astoria, Queens. With its passage through what he named *Hellegat* or Hell Gate, Block's *Unrest* became the first European ship to enter Long Island Sound from the west. While exploring along the south coast of present-day Connecticut, Block became the first European to discover the Housatonic and Connecticut Rivers. He sailed up the Connecticut River for a distance of about 50 miles, to the site of present-day Hartford, before returning south to Long Island Sound. Then, sailing eastward, he came upon a large island, which became known as Block Island.

Block next explored what is now Rhode Island and the Massachusetts coast, rounding Cape Cod and reaching as far north as Nahant Bay, just north of present-day Boston. Leaving the *Unrest* at Cape Cod, he joined the rest of the Dutch fleet on a return trip to the Netherlands.

Adriaen Block led the first Dutch expedition to follow up Henry Hudson's explorations of the east coast of North America. Soon after his return to Amsterdam in 1614, he produced an early map of New Netherland, which clearly showed Long Island as separate from Manhattan. The *Unrest,* which his men built on the Hudson, was one of the first European ships to be constructed in what is now the United States.

Bligh was appointed governor of New South Wales, Australia, in 1805. His attempts to stem alcohol consumption led to the so-called Rum Rebellion, in which the officers under his command mutinied and imprisoned him in 1808. Released in 1810, Bligh returned to England, where he was appointed rear admiral in 1811, then vice admiral in 1814.

William Bligh's naval career is most associated with the 1789 *Bounty* mutiny, and his reputation as an overly harsh disciplinarian often obscures his maritime accomplishments. Yet, as a sailing master, he played a significant role in Cook's explorations of the Gulf of Alaska, where Prince William Sound's Bligh Reef was named in his honor. Moreover, his 1789 open-boat voyage following the *Bounty* mutiny was a remarkable navigational endeavor. Although Bligh succeeded in his second attempt to transport live Tahitian breadfruit plants to Jamaica and the British West Indies, his efforts had limited practical results. The native laborers of the West Indies did not take to breadfruit as a staple food, continuing to prefer bananas and plantains.

Block, Adriaen (Adriaen Blok) (fl. 1610s)
Dutch navigator on the east coast of North America
Dutch seafarer Adriaen Block first explored the waters off the coast of present-day New York and New England with HENRY HUDSON in 1609.

Blunt, Anne Isabella (Lady Anne Blunt, Baroness Wentworth) (1837–1917) *British traveler in the Middle East, writer, wife of Wilfrid Scawen Blunt*
Born Anne Isabella Noel, Lady Anne Blunt was the daughter of William, earl of Lovelace, and Augusta Ada Byron; granddaughter of Lord Byron the poet; and great-great-granddaughter of the British naval officer and explorer JOHN BYRON. She had become an accomplished artist by the time of her marriage in 1869 to British diplomat and later poet WILFRID SCAWEN BLUNT.

Lady Anne accompanied her husband on his many travels into North Africa and the Middle East. In 1877–79, she joined him in an expedition into the heart of the Arabian Peninsula, including present-day Iraq. Although she and Blunt wore native clothes, they made no attempt to disguise themselves as Muslims.

Lady Anne Blunt's 1881 book, *A Pilgrimage to Nejd,* is an account of her experiences as the first European woman to travel openly in present-day Saudi Arabia.

Blunt, Wilfrid Scawen (1840–1922) *British traveler in the Middle East, writer, husband of Anne Isabella Blunt*

Wilfrid Blunt served briefly in the British diplomatic service before embarking on a career as a poet and political activist with strong anti-imperialist convictions. With his wife, ANNE ISABELLA BLUNT, he traveled widely in North Africa and the Middle East.

Blunt was a breeder of Arabian horses. In 1877, he planned a trip deep into the Arabian Peninsula to buy breeding stock for his stud farm. Blunt and his wife started from Iskenderun on the Mediterranean coast of southeastern Turkey and traveled down the Euphrates River to Baghdad. From Baghdad, they followed the Tigris River northward, touring the region that once comprised ancient Mesopotamia (present-day Iraq), then returned to Damascus and the coast of the MEDITERRANEAN SEA.

The Blunts returned to Damascus in 1879. They befriended an influential Arab sheik and, under his protection, traveled southward from Damascus into the Nefud (Nejd) region of present-day central Saudi Arabia. They studied the life and culture of the bedouin and Shammar people, then headed northward to Baghdad. They eventually reached the Persian Gulf port of Bushehr, where they obtained passage back to Europe.

Wilfrid Blunt and Lady Anne Blunt were among the first Europeans to travel into the interior of Arabia openly as Christians. Blunt's outspoken sentiments on behalf of the rights of Muslims in the face of European colonialism probably aided in his travels through regions not usually hospitable to non-Muslims.

Bocharov, Dmitry Ivanovich (fl. 1770s–1790s)
Russian mariner in southern Alaska

Dmitry Bocharov was a Russian mariner along the Pacific coast of SIBERIA. In 1771, along with GERASIM ALEKSEYE-VICH IZMAILOV, he became involved in a mutiny on the Kamchatka Peninsula and was forced to travel southward through the Kuril Islands and the islands of northern Japan to Canton in southern China. He made his way to Europe aboard a French vessel. Back in Russia, he was jailed briefly but was soon cleared of complicity in the mutiny.

By the early 1780s, Bocharov had returned to seafaring around Kamchatka and the Sea of Okhotsk. He entered the service of Russian fur entrepreneur GRIGORY IVANOVICH SHELIKOV, taking part in the 1783–84 voyages establishing the first Russian fur-trading settlements at the eastern end of the Gulf of Alaska.

In 1786, Bocharov, sailing in an open boat, surveyed the Aleutian Islands southwest of Kodiak. Two years later, again with Izmailov, he explored a wide stretch of the north coast of the Gulf of Alaska, from the Kenai Peninsula eastward to Yakutat Bay.

Bocharov commanded the *Three Saints* in 1790, when it took ALEKSANDR ANDREYEVICH BARANOV from eastern Siberia to Alaskan waters. On that voyage, the ship was wrecked on Unalaska Island, but under Bocharov's direction, the passengers and crew constructed small open boats on which they were able to reach Kodiak.

In 1791, Bocharov explored the eastern end of the Alaska Peninsula and succeeded in finding a water route between Bristol Bay to the north and the Gulf of Alaska to the south.

Dmitry Bocharov's explorations led to an expansion of the Russian FUR TRADE in southern Alaska. By discovering a passage through the Alaska Peninsula, he provided an important shipping link between the trading settlements north of the Aleutians and the principal Russian settlements on the Gulf of Alaska.

Bodega y Quadra, Juan Francisco de la (Juan Francisco de la Bodega y Quadra Mollineda, Juan Francisco Bodega y Cuadra) (1744–1794) *Spanish naval officer in Alaska and the Pacific Northwest*

Juan Francisco de la Bodega was born in Lima, Peru. His father was a Spanish diplomat at Cuzco, and his mother, a descendant of a leading Peruvian family. In 1762, Bodega joined the Spanish navy's marine guard, and, over the next 12 years, he rose in rank to ship's lieutenant while serving on Spanish warships.

In 1774, Bodega traveled to San Blas, the main port of the Spanish navy's North Pacific Fleet, on the central west coast of Mexico. The following year, with an expedition headed by BRUNO HECETA, he commanded the schooner *Sonora* along the Pacific coast of North America, and explored what is now known as Grays Harbor in Washington. Accompanied by JUAN JOSEF PÉREZ HERNÁNDEZ, Bodega followed the coast of what is now British Columbia and the southern Alaskan panhandle, reaching 58°30' north latitude. En route, he explored Prince of Wales Island; on its western side, he located and named Bucareli Sound. Also on this voyage, Bodega sailed into Sitka Sound and sighted Mount Edgecombe. Heceta meanwhile had been forced to turn back off Vancouver Island in present-day British Columbia.

In 1776, Bodega returned to Peru, where he obtained a new ship for Spanish exploration in the Pacific Northwest. In command of the *Favorita,* he again sailed to Alaskan waters as part of Lieutenant Ignacio de Arteaga's expedition of 1779. The Spanish government had sent the fleet to investigate the extent of Russian colonization in Alaska and to intercept the ships in JAMES COOK's expedition that were then exploring the BERING STRAIT for a northern passage across Asia or North America.

Bodega again reached Prince of Wales Island and undertook an extensive survey of Bucareli Sound. He then continued northward into the eastern Gulf of Alaska, sighting Mount Saint Elias and Kayak Island. He took part in the official ceremonies at Nuchek Bay and on the Kenai Peninsula, in which Arteaga officially claimed southern Alaska for Spain. Bodega reached as far west as Kodiak Island but did not venture beyond that point, and was thus unable to meet up with Cook's expedition, at that time commanded by CHARLES CLERKE.

Throughout the 1780s, Bodega held high positions in the Spanish navy in Havana, Cuba, and in Cádiz, Spain. He returned to San Blas in 1789. In 1792, he took command of the Spanish naval base at Nootka Sound on the west shore of Vancouver Island. His appointment came in the wake of the Nootka Sound Crisis of 1789, which had brought Great Britain, Spain, and the United States to the brink of war.

At Nootka in 1792–93, Bodega supervised the administration of the diplomatic settlement of the crisis. There he met with American sea captain ROBERT GRAY and British naval officer GEORGE VANCOUVER, providing both with navigational information about the Pacific coast. Bodega directed further Spanish exploration around Vancouver Island, especially the Strait of Juan de Fuca. He also established a Spanish naval installation at what is now Neah Bay, Washington. Ships under his command explored northward from Nootka into the fjords of British Columbia and southeastern Alaska, making one of the final searches for the NORTHWEST PASSAGE undertaken by a European power. After a year in command at Nootka, Bodega returned to San Blas. Before long, he died of a seizure in Mexico City.

In the early 1790s, under the leadership of Juan Francisco de la Bodega, Spanish influence in the Pacific Northwest reached its highest point. Bodega's explorations along the northwest coast of North America resulted in accurate navigational data, which aided in the subsequent findings of Vancouver and Gray. While seeking to carry out the terms of the diplomatic settlement at Nootka, Bodega directed one of Spain's last great official explorations of North America.

Bodmer, Karl (Carl Bodmer) (1809–1893)

Swiss artist on the upper Missouri River

Karl Bodmer was born in Riesbach, Switzerland. He first studied art with his uncle, Swiss draftsman Johann Jakob Mayer, then went to art school in Paris.

While on a sketching trip in Germany in 1832, Bodmer was engaged by ALEXANDER PHILIPP MAXIMILIAN to accompany him on an expedition to the American West and provide drawings and pictures of Indians and frontier

scenes. In May of that year, he traveled with Maximilian and the prince's servant to Boston, New York, and St. Louis. From there, they traveled on a fur company steamboat up the MISSOURI RIVER to the frontier trading posts in what is now Nebraska, South and North Dakota, and Montana.

Bodmer produced pictures of the Sioux (Dakota, Lakota, Nakota) Indians who came to trade at Fort Pierre in present-day South Dakota. Farther up the river at Fort Clark (now Bismarck, North Dakota), he painted portraits of the Mandan Indians and scenes of their daily life.

Bodmer and Maximilian went on to Fort Union at the mouth of the Yellowstone River. They continued by KEELBOAT into present-day Montana as far as the mouth of the Marias River, where they spent a few weeks at Fort McKenzie.

At Fort McKenzie, Bodmer painted portraits of Blackfeet Indians and produced landscapes of the distant ROCKY MOUNTAINS. He witnessed a surprise attack by Assiniboine and Cree Indians against the Blackfeet encamped outside the fort, recording the incident in a painting.

Bodmer and Maximilian returned in fall 1833 to Fort Clark, where they spent the winter. Over the next several

Karl Bodmer *(Library of Congress)*

months, Bodmer made pictures of Mandan life around the post. He also painted Arikara and Hidatsa Indians.

Bodmer returned to St. Louis with Maximilian in spring 1834. The two traveled back to New York, then sailed for Europe.

In Paris, Bodmer worked at turning his pictures into engravings that served as illustrations for Maximilian's 1839 account of the expedition: *Travels in the Interior of North America*. Although the book was published in a limited edition, Bodmer's pictures were well received and gained him widespread recognition.

In his later career, Bodmer became part of the art colony at Barbizon and developed a long association with the artist Jean-François Millet. He continued to execute scenes of early American frontier life, including depictions of the exploits of frontiersman DANIEL BOONE.

Karl Bodmer took part in one of the earliest expeditions to the upper Missouri whose aims were cultural and scientific, rather than commercial and political. His pictures preserve the images of the vanished Mandan, who were all but wiped out by a smallpox epidemic just three years after his visit.

Bogle, George (1746–1781) *British official in Tibet*

George Bogle was born near Haddington in southern Scotland to a fairly prominent family. After his early education at Haddington and Glasgow, he attended the University of Edinburgh, then studied at a private school until 1764. That year, he began to work for his older brother's banking business, but he left in 1769 and entered the service of the BRITISH EAST INDIA COMPANY.

By 1774, Bogle had become a judicial official in India, serving on behalf of the British East India Company and its governor general, Warren Hastings. That year, Hastings commissioned Bogle to undertake a diplomatic mission across the HIMALAYAS into Tibet. With Alexander Hamilton and a small party of other East India Company men, along with several natives, Bogle traveled northward from Calcutta through Bhutan, crossed the Tsangpo River, and reached Shigatse in southern Tibet. He established friendly relations with the Dalai Lama of Tibet, then returned to India.

From 1776 to 1779, Bogle continued to hold high positions as a colonial administrator in northeastern India. He planned a second expedition to Tibet but died before he could carry it out. Soon after his death in 1781, the rulers of Tibet forbade further visits by Europeans, and no trade connections were made.

George Bogle was the first European to visit Tibet since Jesuit missionaries earlier in the 18th century. In 1876, nearly a century after his death, British geographer Clement R. Markham published an account of the journey, based upon private papers and journals provided by Bogle's family.

Boller, Henry A. (1836–1902) *American fur trader on the upper Missouri River*

Henry Boller was born in Philadelphia, Pennsylvania, the son of a fairly successful merchant. As a boy, he developed an interest in the western frontier, especially the life of the Indians. He was particularly influenced by frontier artist GEORGE CATLIN's illustrations of Indian life on the upper MISSOURI RIVER.

Although Boller entered the University of Pennsylvania in 1852, he left short of graduation, soon seeking his father's support for a voyage to India or China. Instead of sending his son to the Far East, the elder Boller accompanied Henry on a trip to St. Louis, Missouri, in spring 1857, where they investigated the possibility of entering the upper Missouri FUR TRADE. Henry again traveled to St. Louis the next year and found a job with the independent fur-trading outfit Clark, Primeau & Company.

Boller was hired as a clerk and was assigned to the company's fur-trading post near Fort Berthold, on the north bank of the Missouri, not far from present-day Stanton, North Dakota. At this post, he dealt extensively with Mandan and Gros Ventre (Atsina) Indians.

Boller's tenure at the Knife River trading post ended in spring 1860, when Clark, Primeau & Company was acquired by the AMERICAN FUR COMPANY. He returned to St. Louis and entered into a business partnership with the veteran frontier fur trader CHARLES LARPENTEUR.

Because of the American Fur Company's domination of the upper Missouri fur trade, Boller and Larpenteur were unable to arrange steamboat service to carry their goods to the Dakotas and points west. As a result, in August of that year, they shipped their goods north via the Mississippi River to the port of St. Paul, Minnesota. From St. Paul, Boller, Larpenteur, and their men carried their goods overland by wagon train to Pembina on the Red River of the North in present-day northeastern North Dakota. As planned, the wagon caravan broke into two groups at Pembina. Larpenteur led one party westward to the mouth of the Yellowstone River, into the lands of the Assiniboine Indians. Several miles above the mouth of the Yellowstone, he established his trading post, Fort Stuart. Meanwhile, Boller accompanied the rest of the wagons and men in a journey across what is now central North Dakota to Fort Berthold, on the Missouri, where he had started in the fur trade three years earlier.

Boller, along with another partner, trapper Jeff Smith, spent the next summer, fall, and winter trading for furs in the Fort Berthold region, operating out of a makeshift trading station they had converted from an Indian earth lodge. In March 1861, Boller and Smith traveled up the Missouri and Yellowstone Rivers to join Larpenteur and the rest of the trading expedition at Fort Stuart.

Boller and Smith arrived at Fort Stuart just as the winter fur-trapping season was coming to a close. Since at that time there were no steamboats servicing the independent fur traders that far up the Missouri, they suggested to Larpenteur that they transport the winter's fur harvest back along the overland route to Pembina and St. Paul for shipment down the Mississippi River to St. Louis. Larpenteur disagreed with this idea; he prevailed in his plan to ship the furs down the Missouri by boat directly to St. Louis. A 65-foot flat-bottomed craft, known as a Mackinaw boat, was constructed for the trip; after Boller and Smith had gone on ahead, Larpenteur traveled downriver with the furs. In this way, Boller and his partners were able to ship their goods directly to St. Louis by the easier and cheaper downriver route, thereby avoiding the costly and time-consuming overland trek to St. Paul.

In St. Louis that summer, Boller received his share of the profits, then left the firm and returned to Philadelphia. There he soon became engaged to marry Mary Parsons, a journalist. In 1863–64, he lived in Montana, taking part in the gold rush around Bannack and Virginia City. He also spent time in the Salt Lake region of Utah.

In 1864, Boller briefly returned to Philadelphia, but he soon set out again for Montana. In 1866, he traveled to California, purchased a herd of horses, and drove them back to Montana to sell at a considerable profit. He then returned to Philadelphia to marry Mary Parsons.

Boller's wife was an accomplished journalist, and with her encouragement, he wrote of his career on the upper Missouri River and the Montana frontier in the book *Among the Indians: Eight Years in the Far West, 1858–1867* (1867). The work includes detailed descriptions of steamboat travel on the upper Missouri and everyday life of Native Americans.

In 1868, Boller and his wife settled in Junction City, Kansas, where he became involved in the cattle business. In about 1878, he moved with his family to Denver, Colorado, finding work first in insurance and then in the real estate business. Boller had plans to revise his book, but he died before its completion.

Henry Boller witnessed the last years of the fur trade on the upper Missouri. His travels and those of earlier mountain men helped open the American west to non-Indian settlement.

Bombay, Sidi (unknown–1889) *African guide, interpreter in East and central Africa*

Sidi Bombay was a Yao tribesman from the interior of what is now Tanzania. Little is known of his origins or early life except that he had been a slave owned by a man from Bombay, India, and that he had adopted that city's name as his own. After gaining his freedom, he served as a soldier with the forces of the sultan of Zanzibar.

In summer 1857, Bombay, who was fluent in Hindustani, Arabic, and East African languages, was hired by SIR RICHARD FRANCIS BURTON and JOHN HANNING SPEKE as guide and interpreter for their expedition into the interior of East Africa in search of the source of the NILE RIVER. Soon after the explorers set out from the coastal settlement of Bagamoyo in August, Bombay was given the additional responsibility of managing the supply caravan. In August 1858, while Burton remained behind at Tabora to recover from illness, Bombay accompanied Speke on a journey northward to Lake Victoria.

Bombay, who proved essential to the success of the expedition, was again engaged by Speke on his return to East Africa in 1860 to follow up his earlier investigations of Lake Victoria, this time with JAMES AUGUSTUS GRANT. Bombay's duties included recruiting additional porters as well as serving as Speke's second in command when Grant was incapacitated by a leg injury. Although many of the native bearers eventually deserted, Bombay and his men remained loyal to Speke and Grant throughout the expedition.

Bombay was employed by SIR HENRY MORTON STANLEY in 1871, when he set out in search of Dr. DAVID LIVINGSTONE in East Africa's lake region. Two years later, he accompanied English explorer VERNEY LOVETT CAMERON in his east-to-west trek across the African continent.

Bombay served for a short period as a missionary. He then retired to a farm in Zanzibar purchased for him by Speke and lived on a pension granted to him by the ROYAL GEOGRAPHICAL SOCIETY in recognition of his contributions to European exploration in Africa. He died on his farm in 1885.

Sidi Bombay, like other native guides and interpreters, proved indispensable to the European exploration and discovery of the interior of Africa. His geographic knowledge, linguistic abilities, and administrative skill helped Burton, Speke, Cameron, and Stanley in their travels throughout hazardous regions of the African continent.

Boncourt, Louis-Charles-Adélaïde Chamisso de   See CHAMISSO DE BONCOURT, LOUIS-CHARLES-ADÉLAÏDE.

Bonin, Charles (1865–1929) *French traveler in Asia*

In 1893, Frenchman Charles Bonin traveled into Southeast Asia, visiting Malaya (present-day Malaysia) and Laos. He then went to China, and over the next seven years, he traveled widely throughout Mongolia and Tibet and into SIBERIA. Bonin subsequently served in the French Ministry of Foreign Affairs as director of archives.

In the course of his travels in China, Charles Bonin charted the YANGTZE RIVER (Chang) and YELLOW RIVER (Huang He) using modern scientific methods. In 1898, he made the first European foray into the lands of the Lolo people.

Bonneville, Benjamin Louis Eulalie de

(1796–1878) *U.S. Army officer, American fur trader in the American West*

Benjamin de Bonneville was born near Paris, France, as the French Revolution was giving way to the rise of Napoléon Bonaparte. His family was prominent in radical politics and among family friends were many revolutionary sympathizers, including Marie-Joseph de Lafayette and the American political writer Thomas Paine.

When Bonneville was seven, his family chose to leave France rather than live under the Bonaparte autocracy. In 1803, with the help of Paine, they moved to the United States, where Bonneville was raised and educated. He attended West Point, receiving a commission as second lieutenant in 1815.

Bonneville's first army assignments took him to garrisons in New England. He also saw service supervising the construction of a military road in Mississippi. In 1821, he was sent to what was then the western frontier post of Fort Smith in present-day Arkansas, and subsequently he was stationed at posts in present-day Oklahoma and Missouri. During his military service on the western frontier in the 1820s, he was in close contact with fur traders working the ROCKY MOUNTAINS in present-day Colorado, Utah, and Wyoming.

In 1825, Bonneville accompanied Lafayette on a tour of the Mississippi River Valley. The next year, Bonneville was promoted to the rank of captain and assigned to the frontier garrison at Fort Gibson in present-day Oklahoma.

In 1830–31, Bonneville organized his own fur-trading venture. In New York City, he obtained the financial support of veteran fur entrepreneur JOHN JACOB ASTOR. Soon afterward, he applied to the army for a two-year leave of absence. In addition to developing business interests, Bonneville intended to provide the army with topographic data on the regions west of the Rocky Mountains and north of Mexico.

On May 1, 1832, Bonneville led a wagon caravan of 110 men from Fort Osage on the Missouri River in western Missouri, northwest toward the Green River region of what is now northeastern Utah and southwestern Wyoming. His expedition crossed the Continental Divide by traveling through the SOUTH PASS in Wyoming's Wind River Range, one of the early successful crossings westward through the Rockies with loaded wagons.

From the South Pass, Bonneville led his men westward along the Oregon Trail. Along the way, they passed by the rock formations known as Red Buttes. Then, entering the Green River Basin, high in the Rockies, they traveled into the Bear Lake region of present-day northeastern Utah.

The expedition arrived in time for the fur trappers' rendezvous in summer 1832, held that year at Pierre's Hole on the western slopes of the Teton Mountains. Soon afterward, Bonneville directed the construction of Fort Bonneville along the Green River, north of Pierre's Hole—a site that provided a commanding presence over the passes through the Rockies. Over the next three years, Bonneville led two expeditions from this installation north and west into the COLUMBIA RIVER region of Oregon.

In 1833, Bonneville dispatched one of his mountain men, JOSEPH REDDEFORD WALKER, along with 40 others, to explore the region westward, across the Sierra Nevada to the California coast. That same year, he sent an application to his superiors in Washington, D.C., to extend his leave, but this communication never reached its destination.

Veteran fur traders tended to bypass Fort Bonneville in favor of the more lucrative prices available from the HUDSON'S BAY COMPANY's posts on the Columbia River and from the other posts on the MISSOURI RIVER and Yellowstone River. With his business losing money, Bonneville headed back East in 1835. At Independence, Missouri, he learned that the army had never received his application for an extension of his leave. Believing he had overstayed his leave for two years without authorization, his superiors cashiered him from the service.

Bonneville journeyed to Washington, D.C., where he remained throughout 1836 seeking reinstatement. During this time, he contacted author Washington Irving, selling him a firsthand account of his experiences in the FUR TRADE. Irving edited Bonneville's narrative and published this work the following year as *The Adventures of Captain Bonneville.*

Bonneville's reinstatement in the military was accomplished in 1836 through the direct intercession of President Andrew Jackson. Historians have speculated, based on the ease with which he obtained his leave and his subsequent reinstatement, that Bonneville's leave from the army may actually have been a cover for intelligence-gathering activities concerning the Mexicans in California, the British in Oregon, and Indian tribes. Moreover, Bonneville's main competition in the fur trade was from Astor's own AMERICAN FUR COMPANY forts, which seems paradoxical considering that it was Astor who provided much of Bonneville's financial backing. In any event, after 1836, Bonneville was once again an officer in the U.S. Army.

Bonneville remained in the army for the next 29 years. He fought in the U.S.-Mexican War of 1846–48, and, during the 1850s, commanded U.S. garrisons in Oregon. In 1857, as a colonel in command of U.S. forces in the New Mexico territory, he led a military expedition, comprised of U.S. Army troops and Pueblo Indian auxiliaries, from Albuquerque into the Gila River region of what is now south-central Arizona. The Gila River Expedition of 1857 was intended as a punitive military strike against the Apache Indians. In meeting this objective, Bonneville also led his command into the little-known region of the recently acquired Gadsden Purchase of 1853, undertaking one of the earliest official U.S. explorations of this area.

During the Civil War, Bonneville directed recruiting operations for the Union army, retiring from the service in 1865, at the rank of brevet brigadier general. He settled at Fort Smith, Arkansas, where he lived until his death in 1878.

Benjamin de Bonneville's explorations of the Rocky Mountains and the Columbia River region provided the government with important geographic and military data that was useful in the subsequent U.S. takeover of the Oregon Country in 1846. In addition, Bonneville's expedition under Joseph Walker blazed an important route for emigrants across Utah, northern Nevada, and the Sierra Nevada into California, which later became the well-traveled California Trail. In addition to Irving's account of Bonneville's explorations, Bonneville himself prepared one of the earliest scientifically based maps of the river system of the central Rockies and Pacific Northwest. Bonneville Lake and Bonneville Dam in southern Oregon were named after him, as well as the Bonneville Salt Flats on the western edge of northwestern Utah's Great Salt Lake Desert.

Boone, Daniel (1734–1820) *American frontier hunter, soldier, guide in Kentucky*

Daniel Boone was born to a family of English Quakers near Reading, Pennsylvania. In 1749, he moved south with his family to the Yadkin Valley in the frontier region of northwestern North Carolina.

With the outbreak of the French and Indian War in 1754, Boone became a wagoneer for British troops and colonial militia forces in western Pennsylvania. He survived General Edward Braddock's disastrous 1755 offensive against the French and Shawnee Indian allies at Fort Duquesne (present-day Pittsburgh). The next year, he married his neighbor Rebecca Bryan. In 1758, he again took part in an assault on Fort Duquesne, which resulted in a British victory under General John Forbes.

In 1763, following the conclusion of the French and Indian War, Boone traveled south to East Florida, which had then become a British possession. He explored the St. Johns River of northeastern Florida, with plans to settle there. But his wife refused to move from North Carolina, and Boone remained in the Yadkin Valley for the next several years. In 1767–68, he made a hunting expedition into the APPALACHIAN MOUNTAINS but failed to reach Kentucky.

Boone had become acquainted with frontiersman JOHN FINLEY during his service in the French and Indian War.

On their reunion in 1768, Finley told Boone about the territory of eastern Kentucky. Later that year, Boone set out on a hunting expedition. A hunter by profession, he periodically went on extended forays into the wilderness to hunt for deer, whose hides provided an important cash supplement to his farming income. Because of threatened resistance from Cherokee Indians, who resented Boone's encroachment on their lands in defiance of the Proclamation Line of 1763, Boone was forced to return to his North Carolina home without reaching his intended destination, the Blue Grass country of Kentucky.

Accompanied by his brother Squire Boone, his brother-in-law John Stuart, Finley, and several other frontier companions, Daniel Boone set out on another hunt in 1769, sponsored in part by North Carolina land developer Judge Richard Henderson. Henderson and his Transylvania Company sought to develop the lands beyond the Proclamation Line and engaged Boone and his small party, who, as hunters, would be less likely to arouse the suspicions of British authorities concerning settlement plans.

The group passed through the CUMBERLAND GAP of southwestern Virginia, then followed an ancient Cherokee Indian trail known as the Warriors' Trace. Boone and part of his company then traveled by way of the South Fork of the Kentucky River to the site of present-day Irvine,

Daniel Boone *(New York State Library, Albany)*

Kentucky. From there, they explored the Kentucky and Red Rivers as far as the Eskippikithiki region. By December 1769, Boone had traveled throughout much of central Kentucky, including the Blue Grass region. That same month, Stuart and Boone were captured by a Shawnee Indian war party, but they soon escaped.

Stuart disappeared over the winter of 1769–70, while hunting on his own (his body was found five years later—he had apparently been killed by Indians). That spring, Boone's brother Squire returned east to North Carolina for additional supplies. Left alone, Boone explored the Licking and Kentucky River Valleys of northeastern Kentucky. He reached the Ohio River and followed it as far as the Falls of the Ohio in the vicinity of present-day Louisville, Kentucky.

Boone was rejoined by his brother in late July 1770 at an encampment on the Red River and spent the rest of that year hunting for deer in the Green and Cumberland Valleys. With a substantial quantity of valuable hides and furs, the brothers set out on the return journey to North Carolina in March 1771. Near the Cumberland Gap, however, they were waylaid by Cherokee. The Indians confiscated all of the Boones' furs, hides, horses, and mules and warned the frontiersmen against trespassing on their reserved lands in the future. Boone and his brother returned safely to the Yadkin Valley soon afterward.

In 1773, in defiance of the Indians, Boone undertook a colonizing expedition into the Cumberland Gap region. In addition to his own family, Boone led seven other families of frontier settlers into eastern Kentucky from North Carolina. They had hardly penetrated the Cumberland Gap when they were ambushed by Cherokee. Boone's 17-year-old son James was killed in the attack, and the party fled back to North Carolina.

Boone's colonizing efforts into the trans-Appalachian region were interrupted by the outbreak of Lord Dunmore's War of 1774 against the Shawnee. In this conflict, Boone served as courier for colonial troops and surveyors operating around the headwaters of the Ohio River near present-day Louisville, Kentucky.

In 1775, Boone undertook another colonizing expedition through the Cumberland Gap, sponsored again by Judge Richard Henderson and his Transylvania Company. With an advance party of about 30 frontiersman, he blazed a route from the Shenandoah Valley through the Cumberland Gap as far as the southern reaches of the Kentucky River, south of present-day Lexington, Kentucky. He established a permanent settlement, known as Boonesborough (or Boonesboro). Settlers from east of the Appalachians soon arrived, and the area was annexed as a county of Virginia.

With the onset of the American Revolution, Boonesborough was subject to attacks by the British-allied Shawnee. Boone himself was captured by a war party in 1778, but he was adopted into the tribe by a chief known as Blackfish. He managed to escape after a few months of captivity and provided military intelligence to the American forces concerning British and Shawnee strategy.

In 1779, Boone established a settlement at Boone's Station, near present-day Athens, Kentucky. Financial reverses precipitated by legal problems concerning his land claims led Boone to take his family to the area of present-day Mayesville, West Virginia, where he operated a tavern.

In 1796, Boone attempted to win the government contract to develop his Wilderness Road into a wagon route, but the project was granted to another party. Meanwhile, one of his sons, Nathan Boone, had migrated westward to the Louisiana country, at that time a Spanish possession. Three years later, Boone also traveled westward; he was granted a land claim by the Spanish government in the Femme Osage region of what is now Missouri. He lost title to these lands following the acquisition of the Louisiana Territory by the United States in 1803. A special act of Congress eventually reinstated Boone's claim to his Spanish land grant.

Boone lived on the Missouri frontier at the settlement of St. Charles near St. Louis for the remainder of his life. From about 1800 to 1818, he continued to make expeditions into the western wilderness, hunting and exploring. He entered the Platte River region, perhaps as far west as the eastern ROCKY MOUNTAINS, before his death in 1820.

Daniel Boone's hunting and colonizing expeditions into eastern and central Kentucky helped to bring about the non-Indian settlement of that region after the American Revolution. The Wilderness Road, established by Boone in the mid-1770s, encouraged migration into the trans-Appalachian country of Kentucky and Tennessee, providing the basis for regular travel between the original settlements in the East and the newly established frontier regions extending west to the Mississippi and Missouri Rivers. Boone's exploits were popularized in John Filson's 1784 book, *Discovery, Settlement, and Present State of Kentucky.* His reputation in the popular culture as a frontiersman and explorer only deepened in 1824, when his character was immortalized in verse as part of British Romantic poet Lord Byron's work *Don Juan.*

Borchgrevink, Carsten Egeberg (1864–1934)
Norwegian explorer in the Antarctic

Born in Norway, Carsten E. Borchgrevink settled in Australia in 1888. His first trip to the Antarctic region was in 1894–95, aboard the Norwegian whaling ship *Antarctica.* On January 23, 1895, he was among the crewmembers who went ashore on Victoria Land, becoming one of the first men to set foot on the Antarctic continent.

Borchgrevink was in England in the late 1890s, where he succeeded in obtaining support for a scientific expedition to Antarctica from British newspaper publisher Sir George Newnes. After a stopover in NEW ZEALAND, his expedition sailed to Antarctica on the *Southern Cross* in August 1898, reaching the coast at Cape Adare in mid-February 1899 during the Antarctic summer. The ship soon returned to New Zealand, leaving Borchgrevink and the nine others in his party for the Antarctica winter.

Over the next year, Borchgrevink made several expeditions overland on skis and dogsleds into the interior of Antarctica. On one expedition from the Cape Adare base, he reached 78° 50' south latitude, which up to that time was the most extreme southern point ever reached.

Borchgrevink and his expedition were picked up by the *Southern Cross* when it returned in early February 1900. Before leaving the Antarctic, he made a navigational study of the Ross Ice Shelf, revealing that it had moved southward almost 30 miles since its first sighting by SIR JAMES CLARK ROSS in the early 1840s.

Carsten E. Borchgrevink was a pioneer in Antarctic exploration. His 1899–1900 expedition was the first to winter on the Antarctic continent and undertake extensive exploration into the interior. His account of his exploits, *First on the Antarctic Continent,* was published in 1901.

Borough, Stephen (Stephen Burrough)

(1525–1584) *English mariner in Russia and the European Arctic, brother of William Borough*

Stephen Borough was born in Northam, Devonshire, England. Embarking on a career as a seafarer, he became an accomplished sea captain and navigator. In 1553, he commanded the *Edward Bonaventure* in a three-ship trading expedition to Russia, sponsored by SEBASTIAN CABOT and headed by SIR HUGH WILLOUGHBY. The pilot general on the voyage was RICHARD CHANCELLOR.

Following the west coast of Norway northward, Borough and Chancellor located and named North Cape, then rounded it and entered the White Sea. They soon reached the Russian port of Archangel.

In 1556, Borough again sailed to the Arctic coast of European Russia, supported by Cabot and his newly formed MUSCOVY COMPANY. In command of the *Searchthrift,* Borough went even farther east on this voyage, locating a strait between Vaigach Island and Novaya Zemlya providing an entrance to the Kara Sea.

Borough had planned to travel as far as the mouth of the Ob River, east of Novaya Zemlya, but was forced back by ice. He wintered at Archangel and in the spring, he undertook a search for Sir Hugh Willoughby and his ships, missing since 1554. From a Dutch vessel, he learned that Willoughby's fleet had been wrecked and all hands lost. Before returning to England in 1557, Borough explored the coasts of the Kola Peninsula, Finland, and Lapland.

In 1561, Borough commanded the *Swallow* for the Muscovy Company in a voyage to Russia, taking the company's chief factor, ANTHONY JENKINSON, on the first leg of his trade mission to the Caspian Sea and central Asia.

In 1563, Borough entered the naval service of Queen Elizabeth I and, for the next 20 years, he served as chief pilot for her fleet of ships on the Medway River in southeastern England. His brother, WILLIAM BOROUGH, was also a seafarer and served with Stephen in his voyages to Russia in 1553 and 1556.

Stephen Borough's voyages not only opened up Russia to English commerce, but also provided the earliest navigational information for subsequent maritime expeditions in search of a NORTHEAST PASSAGE between Europe and the Far East.

Borough, William (William Burrough)

(1536–1599) *English mariner in Russia and the European Arctic, brother of Stephen Borough*

Born in Northam, Devonshire, England, William Borough was the younger brother of STEPHEN BOROUGH. Starting at the age of 16, he sailed as an ordinary seaman on his brother's voyages to Russia.

Over the next 20 years, William Borough continued to make regular trips from England to Russia as a captain for the London-based MUSCOVY COMPANY's trading fleet. In 1568, he helped organize an expedition attempting to find a NORTHEAST PASSAGE in the eastern reaches of the Barents Sea. Over the next six years, he traveled widely in the region between the ports on the White Sea and Moscow. He helped plan and organize MARTIN FROBISHER's 1576 exploration of GREENLAND.

In about 1579, Borough entered the English navy and commanded warships in campaigns against pirates in the Baltic Sea. In 1581, he published a major work on navigation, *A Discourse of the Variation of the Compass, or Magnetical Needle.* He served under SIR FRANCIS DRAKE in a naval campaign against the Spanish at Cádiz in 1587, and, the next year, he commanded a warship in the English victory over the Spanish Armada.

William Borough produced written accounts of his travels and observations in Russia during his years there for the Muscovy Company. He also drew up new navigational charts based on the latest explorations of the Russian Arctic coast. In his 1581 *Discourse* he was one of the earliest navigators to cite the errors in maps by GERARDUS MERCATOR and other cartographers, caused by their not taking into account variations in COMPASS readings in high northern latitudes.

Bougainville, Hyacinthe-Yves-Philippe Potentien de (baron de Bougainville)

(1782–1846) *French naval officer in the South Pacific, son of Louis-Antoine de Bougainville*

Hyacinthe de Bougainville was the eldest son of French naval officer and explorer LOUIS-ANTOINE DE BOUGAINVILLE. He was born in Nantes, France, and following his early education at the École Polytechnic in 1798–1800, he entered the French navy.

In 1800, Bougainville sailed to the South Pacific with NICOLAS BAUDIN as a midshipman on the *Géographe,* then returned from Australia in 1803 on the expedition's other ship, the *Naturaliste.* He held numerous naval assignments in the Napoleonic Wars of 1803–14.

In 1817–19, Bougainville was a lieutenant commander in a French naval expedition to Southeast Asia and the Moluccas. He commanded the *Thetis* and *Espérance* in a CIRCUMNAVIGATION OF THE WORLD in 1824–26. In 1838, he was made a rear admiral.

In the first half of the 19th century, Hyacinthe, baron de Bougainville, carried on the tradition of French maritime exploration in the Pacific begun by his father in the 1760s. His account of his 1824–26 voyage, *Journal of a Circumnavigation of the World,* along with an atlas, was published in 1827.

Bougainville, Louis-Antoine de (comte de Bougainville) (1729–1811) *French naval officer in the Atlantic and Pacific, father of Hyacinthe-Yves-Philippe Potentien de Bougainville*

Louis-Antoine de Bougainville was born in Paris, the son of a prominent lawyer in the court of Louis XV. He first embarked on a legal career but then undertook the study of mathematics under French mathematician Jean le Rond d'Alembert. By 1756, he had published a major work on integral calculus, *Traité du calcul integral,* for which he was elected to Great Britain's prestigious ROYAL SOCIETY.

Bougainville entered the French army in 1753. He served in French Canada as aide-de-camp to General Montcalm in the French and Indian War of 1754–63, taking part in engagements on Lake Champlain and negotiating the French surrender at Quebec.

Back in France in 1763, Bougainville launched a campaign to reestablish a French overseas colonial empire. With financial backing of relatives and merchants of the port of St. Malo, he succeeded in organizing a colonizing enterprise on the Falkland Islands in the South Atlantic Ocean (known by the French as the Malouines and by the Argentines as the Malvinas), for the resettlement of Acadians displaced from Canada by the British. The French government supported Bougainville's plan, hoping that it would provide France with control of the main sea route to the Pacific Ocean, one of the last regions where the British had not yet established a strong naval presence.

From 1764 to 1766, Bougainville headed three expeditions to the Falklands and established a small Acadian colony called Fort St. Louis. In this period, he also explored Tierra del Fuego and Patagonia. His chief maritime adviser, PIERRE-NICOLAS DUCLOS-GUYOT, undertook a navigational survey of the eastern approach to the Strait of Magellan.

In 1766, when France was compelled by international circumstances to sell the Falklands to Spain, Bougainville was sent to oversee the transfer of the islands. To compensate him for the loss of his colony, France offered him the governorship of the French Indian Ocean colonies on Île de France (present-day Mauritius) and Bourbon (present-day Réunion). Instead, Bougainville chose to undertake a government-sponsored CIRCUMNAVIGATION OF THE WORLD.

Bougainville sailed from Brest, France, in December 1766, commanding the frigate *Boudeuse.* Two months later, the expedition's other vessel, the *Étoile,* sailed from the French port of Rochefort, joining up with Bougainville and the *Boudeuse* at Rio de Janeiro in June 1767. On reaching the Falklands, Bougainville negotiated the Spanish takeover of the islands, then sailed to Tierra del Fuego. Hampered by rough seas and bad weather, his ships took 52 days to make the westward passage through the STRAIT OF MAGELLAN, during which a detailed study of the strait was made, including the charting of a bay that now bears his name. Bougainville also studied the inhabitants of Patagonia and Tierra del Fuego, disproving earlier reports that these natives were giants.

One of the intended aims of Bougainville's world voyage was to search for Terra Australis, the elusive GREAT SOUTHERN CONTINENT. Upon entering the Pacific, he first headed northward to the TROPIC OF CAPRICORN, then sailed due west. The expedition soon came upon the Tuamotu Islands. Unable to make a landing because of outlying reefs, Bougainville named them the Dangerous Archipelago. Continuing westward, he reached Tahiti in April 1768. Although British navigator SAMUEL WALLIS had visited Tahiti eight months earlier, Bougainville claimed the island for France, calling it New Cythera. The French were well received by the Tahitians; Ahutoru, the chief's son, was allowed to join the expedition.

Still seeking the fabled Great Southern Continent, as well as the east coast of New Holland (which turned out to be Australia), Bougainville sailed westward from Tahiti to the islands of Samoa, which he named the Navigator Archipelago. He also charted the Solomon Islands, which originally had been visited by Spanish navigator ÁLVARO DE MENDAÑA in 1568, but had been lost to navigation because of inaccurate charting.

At one point, Bougainville and his ships were less than 250 miles off the coast of northeastern Australia, but they were prevented from reaching the mainland by the Great Barrier Reef, a portion of which is now known as Bougainville Reef.

Short on provisions, Bougainville was forced to head his expedition northward in search of a passage to the SPICE IS- LANDS (the Moluccas) where he planned to obtain live spice plants for transplanting on Île de France. His explorations around the New Hebrides revealed that they were islands, and not part of a great landmass as previously thought. Landing on New Britain, he came upon a plaque left by British explorer PHILIP CARTERET on his visit there a few months earlier.

In summer 1768, Bougainville reached the Dutch set- tlement of Batavia in what is now Indonesia. Outbreaks of scurvy forced him to abandon plans to obtain spice plants in the Moluccas. After obtaining fresh provisions from the Dutch, he sailed back to France by way of Île de France and the CAPE OF GOOD HOPE, arriving at St. Malo in March 1769.

In 1771, Bougainville published his account of the trip, *A Voyage Around the World.* The next year, he tried un- successfully to gain support for a French expedition to the NORTH POLE. Appointed a commodore in the French fleet, he took part in 1779 in naval operations against the British in the American Revolution. In 1782, following his defeat by the British at Martinique in the Caribbean Sea, he retired from the navy. He returned to active service under the French revolutionary government after 1790. He was made a count of the empire by Napoléon I in 1808.

Louis-Antoine, comte de Bougainville commanded the first official French expedition to circumnavigate the world. His explorations in 1766–69 confirmed the existence of many islands unknown to Europeans since the Spaniards had explored the western Pacific Ocean in the 16th century. His voyage resulted in the European discovery of straits in the Solomons and in the New Hebrides that now bear his name. Bougainville Island, the largest of the Solomons, was also named in his honor. The Louisiade Archipelago and New Cyclades reappeared on maps as a result of Bou- gainville's Pacific expedition. The expedition's naturalist, JOSEPH-PHILIBERT COMMERSON, sent back thousands of new species of plants and animals during the voyage. Among them was the tropical flowering vine known as the bougainvillea, named after Bougainville. Observations on the culture of the Tahitians influenced French Enlighten- ment authors Jean-Jacques Rousseau and Denis Diderot in their concept of the noble savage. Bougainville's eldest son, HYACINTHE-YVES-PHILIPPE POTENTIEN DE BOUGAINVILLE, also embarked on a naval career that took him around the world.

Bourgmont, Étienne-Veniard de (sieur de Bourgmont, Étienne de Bourgmond)

(1680–ca. 1730) *French soldier, fur trader on the Missouri River and Great Plains*

Étienne de Bourgmont was born in the Normandy region of France, the son of a doctor. In about 1700, he immigrated to French Canada, where he worked as one of the VOYA- GEURS in the FUR TRADE on the eastern Great Lakes.

Within a few years, Bourgmont entered the French mil- itary, serving as an ensign under HENRI DE TONTI at the French fur-trading settlement at Detroit. When Tonti re- tired in 1705, Bourgmont temporarily took command at Detroit. An Indian uprising erupted the following year, and in 1707, Bourgmont deserted, fleeing to an island in Lake Erie with other army defectors. He was soon joined there by Madame Tichenet, known as La Chenette, a woman with whom he was romantically linked.

In about 1712, Bourgmont and the other deserters were apprehended by French authorities. He soon became friendly with French colonial governor ANTOINE LAUMET DE LA MOTHE, who allowed Bourgmont to escape south- ward into the French Louisiana country. Eventually Bourgmont settled among the Indians of the central MIS- SOURI RIVER region.

Over the next five years, Bourgmont established friendly relations with the Oto, Omaha, Pawnee, and other tribes of the Missouri River and its tributaries. He also un- dertook explorations up the Missouri, reaching as far as the mouth of the Platte River in present-day eastern Nebraska.

In 1717, Bourgmont wrote an account of his travels on the Missouri, *La Description,* describing the region as far to the north as the Arikara Indian villages in what is now cen- tral South Dakota, although it is not certain he traveled there himself.

In 1719, the French colonial governor of Louisiana, JEAN-BAPTISTE LE MOYNE, appointed Bourgmont a captain in recognition of his efforts in establishing peaceful relations with the Indians of the upper Louisiana country. Bourgmont subsequently took part in the French victory over the Spanish in western Florida. Soon afterward, he re- turned to France and reported his findings on the upper Missouri to the French government.

In 1723, the Company of the Indies, the French trading monopoly in Louisiana, concerned over Spanish encroach- ment from the west, commissioned Bourgmont to return to North America and establish a French outpost in what is now north-central Missouri. Bourgmont founded Fort Or- leans at the mouth of the Grand River. In 1724, he set out with a small detachment of French soldiers to the west to make peace with the Comanche Indians. He ascended the Missouri to the mouth of the Kansas River. After following that stream briefly, he set out overland. In present-day west- ern Kansas, where almost 200 years earlier FRANCISCO

VÁSQUEZ DE CORONADO had fruitlessly sought Indian riches, Bourgmont met with Comanche chiefs and succeeded in gaining their allegiance to the French.

Not long after his return to Fort Orleans, Bourgmont convinced several Plains Indian chiefs to accompany him to Paris, where they were received with great acclaim by the French royal court. Bourgmont married a wealthy widow and remained in France. For his efforts in securing an alliance with the Missouri River tribes, the French government granted him a title of nobility.

Although he did not ascertain the actual source of the Missouri, Étienne de Bourgmont's explorations took him to a point on the river farther north than any known European had been to that time. His 1724 expedition across the Kansas plains into Comanche country was the deepest French penetration into the territory west of the MISSISSIPPI RIVER to date.

Bouvet de Lozier, Jean-Baptiste-Charles

(1704–1786) *French naval officer in the South Atlantic*
An orphan at the age of seven, Jean-Baptiste Bouvet studied for a time in Paris before working in the shipyards of St. Malo. He decided to pursue a career in navigation and by 1731 had reached the rank of lieutenant in the FRENCH EAST INDIA COMPANY.

In 1733, Bouvet proposed a plan to locate the GREAT SOUTHERN CONTINENT, or Terra Australis, in the South Pacific Ocean—perhaps the same land reportedly located by Binot Paulmier de Gonneville in 1504 and known as GONNEVILLE'S LAND—where ships might stop over on journeys to the Far East. His proposal was finally accepted, and in July 1738, Bouvet departed Lorient, France, with two ships, the *Aigle* and *Marie*. The following October, the expedition arrived at Santa Catarina Island off the coast of Brazil and continued southward the next month.

On January 1, 1739, in the South Atlantic Ocean, east of the South Sandwich Islands, southwest of Africa's CAPE OF GOOD HOPE, and north of the ANTARCTIC CIRCLE, Bouvet and his expedition encountered a landmass covered in glaciers that they thought to be a promontory of Antarctica; Bouvet named it the Cape of Circumcision. Bouvet waited for 12 days, hoping to land, but finally gave up because of perpetual fog. Avoiding DRIFT ICE, the expedition headed eastward in search of other lands. With supplies dwindling and the crew suffering from cold and SCURVY, Bouvet directed his ships northward on January 24 for the Cape of Good Hope. The expedition returned to France in late February.

Because Jean-Baptiste Bouvet did not correctly chart the location of what turned out to be a 22-square-mile island, neither JAMES COOK nor SIR JAMES CLARK ROSS could locate it. It was not until 1808 that British whalers rediscovered it. In 1822, the American sealer Benjamin Morrell managed the first landing and named it Bouvet Island in honor of the French discoverer. Great Britain claimed the island in 1825, calling it Liverpool Island. Norway occupied it in 1924, however, and, the next year, Great Britain relinquished its claim. In 1971, Bouvet Island and adjacent waters were designated a nature reserve, and in 1977, Norway established an automated meteorological station on the island.

Boyd, Louise Arner (1887–1972) *American explorer in the Arctic*

Louise Arner Boyd was born in San Rafael, California, near San Francisco, into a family with a fortune made by her maternal great-grandfather in the California gold rush of 1849. A 1907 debutante, she became socially active in wealthy circles. In 1910, she joined her parents in a year-long tour of Europe and Egypt.

By 1920, both of her parents had died, and Boyd inherited her family's considerable wealth. She made another trip to Europe soon afterward. In 1924, she first ventured into the Arctic regions as a passenger on a Norwegian cruise ship.

In 1926, Boyd embarked on her first Arctic exploring expedition. In Norway, she chartered the ship *Hobby* and, along with a few friends, sailed northward into the Arctic Ocean to Franz Josef Land. This was primarily a recreational cruise in which Boyd and her companions hunted polar bears and seals, recording the trip with both motion pictures and photographs.

Boyd's next expedition to the Arctic was in summer 1928. Again sailing from Norway on the *Hobby,* she assisted the Norwegian government in its search efforts for ROALD ENGLEBREGT GRAVNING AMUNDSEN, who had disappeared on a rescue mission on behalf of Italian Arctic explorer UMBERTO NOBILE and his expedition. During the next few months, Boyd and her companions on the *Hobby* explored eastward and westward from Spitsbergen (present-day Svalbard), covering more than 10,000 miles between Franz Josef Land and the Greenland Sea. Although the search for Amundsen was fruitless, the Norwegian government awarded Boyd the Chevalier Cross of the Order of St. Olav for her efforts. She was the first non-Norwegian woman to be so honored. In addition, she received from the French government the Cross of the Legion of Honor.

In 1931, Boyd undertook a scientifically oriented exploration of the Arctic, aimed at collecting geographic and geological data as well as making a photographic study of Arctic animals and plants. She engaged the ship the *Veslekari* and sailed to the east coast of GREENLAND. Among her party were a botanist, a big game hunter, and the writer Winifred Menzies. Boyd and her expedition stopped at an Inuit settlement near Scoresby Sound, where she made a study of their life and culture; she later reported the experience in a series of articles published in *The Christian Science Monitor* in 1932. In her surveys of Greenland's east coast, she reached the uncharted De Geer Glacier. The region between De Geer Glacier and the Jaette Glacier was later named Louise Boyd Land, in her honor.

In summer 1933, Boyd undertook her third Arctic expedition, under the sponsorship of the AMERICAN GEOGRAPHICAL SOCIETY. Again sailing on the *Veslekari,* a vessel that she used on all her subsequent Arctic explorations, Boyd and her scientific team studied the glacial features along Greenland's east coast. They explored north of Scoresby Sound, examining Franz Josef Fjord and King Oscar Fjord. A sonic depth finder was used on this expedition to study subsurface coastal features. Boyd recounted her experiences on this expedition in her book, *The Fiord Region of East Greenland,* published in 1935.

In 1937 and 1938, Boyd explored the Arctic seas north and east of Norway, between Bear Island and Jan Mayen Island. These two expeditions used ultrasonic depth research to determine the existence of a submarine ridge between

these Arctic islands. Boyd's book about this expedition was to be published in 1940. However, with the onset of World War II in Europe, she was advised by the U.S. government that the information included in it, especially her photographs, could be of a strategic value to the Germans. The work, *The Coast of Northeast Greenland,* was finally published in 1948.

In 1941, in connection with preparations for the impending war, the National Bureau of Standards commissioned Boyd to undertake an expedition to the Arctic region to study the effects of polar magnetic phenomenon on radio communications. After America's entry into the war later that year, she became a technical adviser to the War Department on matters dealing with strategic planning in the Arctic. In recognition of her services, the U.S. Army awarded Boyd a Certificate of Appreciation in 1949, citing her valuable contributions of Arctic geographic knowledge to the war effort.

Boyd's next and last Arctic exploit took place in 1955 when, at the age of 68, she chartered an airplane and became the first woman to fly over the NORTH POLE. She spent her last years in San Francisco, where she died at the age of 85.

Louise Arner Boyd's Arctic explorations resulted in new geographic information about Greenland's east coast and revealed significant features about the floor of the Greenland Sea. She was the first woman to play a leading role in the history of modern Arctic exploration.

Louise Arner Boyd *(Library of Congress)*

Bozeman, John Merin (1835–1867) *American pioneer in Colorado and Montana*

John Bozeman, originally from Georgia, headed westward to Colorado in 1861 to try his luck as a prospector. With new gold strikes in southwestern Montana, he relocated to Virginia City and Bannack.

At that time, to reach Montana from the east, non-Indians traveled to the headwaters of the MISSOURI RIVER by way of Fort Benton, or westward along the Oregon Trail, northward through the SOUTH PASS of Wyoming's Wind River Range, then along the Overland Trail through Idaho via Fort Hall. Both the Missouri River route and the overland routes were circuitous. Travelers along the Oregon and Overland Trail were forced to cross the Continental Divide twice. The direct route northward from Colorado crossed through the heart of hunting lands that the government had reserved for the Sioux (Dakota, Lakota, Nakota) and Northern Cheyenne Indians, east of the Bighorn Mountains of north-central Wyoming.

In the winter 1862–63, Bozeman and a companion, the trapper John Jacobs, with Jacobs's mixed-blood daughter, departed Bannack, Montana, heading eastward across the Bighorn Mountains of Wyoming, then southward, accomplishing a more direct route to Colorado.

The following spring, 1863, Bozeman led a wagon train out of Julesburg, Colorado, a settlement on the South Platte River in northeastern Colorado, and followed the river and the Overland Trail along the first leg of the usual route to the Montana goldfields at Bannack and Virginia City. When warned by Indian war parties to stay off lands reserved by treaty, the majority of emigrants remained on the long route west of the Bighorns. Bozeman and a small party left the wagon train, however, and, traveling mostly at night, headed northward along the east side of the Bighorn Mountains. When they reached the Yellowstone River, they crossed the Belt Mountains through what later came to be known as the Bozeman Pass, and arrived in the Montana gold country, having avoided the usual roundabout route along the Overland Trail to Fort Bridger in Wyoming and to Fort Hall in Idaho. In spring 1864, Bozeman led a second, larger wagon train the entire distance of his new route, the first such crossing.

Indian attacks against travelers on the new trail were common. Yet the U.S. government wanted to encourage gold mining in Montana, mainly because the U.S. Treasury was short of gold in 1865, following the conclusion of the Civil War. As a result, starting about 1865, the army began constructing forts to protect the travelers heading northward from Colorado into southwestern Montana. Among these were Fort Phil Kearny, Fort C. F. Smith, and Fort Reno. Soon regular wagon traffic was following the Bozeman Trail.

Meanwhile, Bozeman had begun to prosper as a result of his new trade route into Montana, and, in 1864, he had established the town of Bozeman in Montana's Gallatin Valley. The Bozeman Trail attracted cattlemen, who saw a great opportunity to bring much needed beef cattle north from Texas into the Montana mining country around Bannack and Virginia City. The first cattle drive from Texas to Montana was undertaken in 1866.

The increased number of travelers passing through Sioux lands, coupled with the devastating effects on hunting lands inflicted by the cattle drives, led to increased Indian raids. By the end of 1866, a full-scale conflict was underway, known as Red Cloud's War or the War for the Bozeman Trail, under the Oglala Sioux Red Cloud and younger war chiefs, such as Crazy Horse and Hump.

Bozeman himself was killed on the trail by Blackfeet Indians in 1867. The next year, that portion of the Bozeman Trail between Fort Reno and Fort Phil Kearny in north-central Wyoming, and Fort C. F. Smith on the Bighorn River in southern Montana, was closed by the government in accordance with the Fort Laramie Treaty of 1868, ending Red Cloud's War. The Bozeman remained closed for nearly 10 years, until the final defeat of the allied Sioux, Northern Cheyenne, and Northern Arapaho under Sitting Bull in the wars for the Black Hills in 1876–77. The road was then re-opened and served as the main trade and cattle route into Montana.

John Bozeman's journey in 1863 blazed a much-needed cut-off from the Oregon Trail east of the Bighorn Mountains into the Montana goldfields. His endeavors opened the northern plains to commerce from Colorado and Texas and helped bring about U.S. military action against the Plains tribes and their subsequent displacement by non-Indian settlers.

Brackenridge, Henry Marie (1786–1871)
American traveler, writer on the Missouri River, envoy to South America

Born in Pittsburgh, Pennsylvania, Henry Marie Brackenridge, starting at the age of two, was tutored by his father, the writer and scholar Hugh Henry Brackenridge. When seven years old, he was sent by his father to St. Genevieve on the MISSISSIPPI RIVER near St. Louis, a port city at that time under Spanish dominion. From 1793 to 1796, the young Brackenridge learned French at St. Genevieve; he then returned home to continue his education, studying the classics with his father and attending the Pittsburgh Academy. He went on to study law and was admitted to the Pennsylvania Bar in 1806.

Brackenridge first settled in Baltimore, Maryland, intending to establish a practice in admiralty law. Unable to build a clientele, he returned to the MISSOURI RIVER frontier about 1810, settling in St. Louis. Because of his interest in exploration, he joined MANUEL LISA's fur-trading expedition up the Missouri, which departed St. Louis in April 1811. Traveling by KEELBOAT with Lisa's ST. LOUIS MISSOURI FUR COMPANY contingent, Brackenridge journeyed through the lands of the Sioux (Dakota, Lakota, Nakota) Indians and reached the Mandan and Arikara villages in present-day South and North Dakota in June. After spending some time among the fur traders and trappers on the upper Missouri, as well as with the naturalist JOHN BRADBURY, he returned downriver to St. Louis in August. Brackenridge's account of his journey was later incorporated into Washington Irving's 1836 work on the upper Missouri and western FUR TRADE, *Astoria*.

Between 1811 and 1814, Brackenridge practiced law in St. Louis and New Orleans. During this period, he learned the Spanish language and studied the principles of Spanish law and helped formulate the code of laws that would become the legal system of Louisiana. He also served as a territorial deputy attorney general as well as a judge. In 1814, Brackenridge's account of his travels and observations on the lower Mississippi, *Views of Louisiana*, was first published.

Brackenridge's knowledge of Spanish and Spanish law came to the attention of President James Madison, and in 1817, he was appointed as a secretary to the U.S. State Department's commission that traveled to South America to report on the newly established independent republics. His subsequent report provided a basis for the Monroe Doctrine. His account of his experiences on that tour, *Voyage to South America,* appeared in 1819.

In 1821, Brackenridge was sent to Florida, where he served first as a secretary to Florida territorial governor Andrew Jackson, then as a federal judge. He was on the bench in Florida until his removal in 1832, following a dispute with Jackson, who had become president.

Brackenridge spent his remaining days on his estate near Pittsburgh, where he founded the community of Tarentum. In 1834, he published an account of his frontier experiences, *Recollections of Persons and Places of the West.*

Since most of the exploration of the upper Missouri in the first decades of the 19th century was undertaken by commercial interests, especially unlettered mountain men and frontier trappers, Henry Marie Brackenridge's account serves as a rare record of the region as seen through the eyes of an educated person. His writings include a description of travel by keelboat on the Missouri River in the years before the introduction of the steamboat.

Bradbury, John (1768–1823) *Scottish naturalist in North America*

John Bradbury, a native of Scotland, was educated in England, concentrating in botany and zoology. In 1809, the Botanical Society of Liverpool sent him to the United States for a scientific study of the plant life of the American frontier. Upon his arrival, he was welcomed by former president and fellow naturalist Thomas Jefferson. At that time, St. Louis was the gateway to the frontier regions to the west, and Jefferson arranged for Bradbury to travel to that city and use it as a base for his scientific expeditions.

Over the following year, Bradbury undertook numerous excursions into the region surrounding St. Louis, up to a distance of 300 miles from the city.

In spring 1811, Bradbury joined WILSON PRICE HUNT's fur-trading expedition up the MISSOURI RIVER, the overland contingent of JOHN JACOB ASTOR's venture to the Oregon coast. Bradbury remained with the Astorians until June 1811, when they reached one of Astor's trading forts on the Missouri in what is now southern South Dakota. He joined fellow writer HENRY MARIE BRACKENRIDGE, who was touring the upper Missouri with MANUEL LISA's expedition, and traveled farther up the Missouri into what is now North Dakota, spending time among the Mandan and Arikara Indians, before returning to St. Louis in August.

The outbreak of hostilities between the United States and England in the War of 1812 prevented Bradbury's return to England, and he undertook an extensive tour of the Ohio Valley.

Returning to England in 1815, John Bradbury published an account of his travels on the American frontier. His book, entitled *Travels in the Interior of North America in the Years 1809, 1810, and 1811,* includes information on the geographic features of the upper Missouri region, as well as detailed studies of its flora and fauna. Noteworthy among his wildlife descriptions is the account of the massive herds of buffalo on the banks of the Missouri in the Dakotas, extending for miles and numbering in the many thousands. In addition, Bradbury describes the lives of Indian peoples and of Missouri River boatmen.

Bransfield, Edward (ca. 1785–1851) *British naval officer in the Antarctic*

Irish-born Edward Bransfield was serving on the British ship *Andromache,* based in Valparaíso, Chile, in 1819, when he heard reports from whalers and sealers of land sightings to the south in uncharted seas. He commandeered the brig *Williams,* under Captain William Smith, for an exploratory expedition on behalf of the British navy.

Heading southward, Bransfield reached and charted the South Shetland Islands, landing on King George Island. On January 30, 1820, farther to the south, he spotted snow-covered mountains on an expanse of land that would later be charted as the northwest coast of the Antarctic Peninsula. At about the same time, FABIAN GOTTLIEB VON BELLINGSHAUSEN, sailing for Russia, was also south of the ANTARCTIC CIRCLE.

With its energy and resources directed toward the discovery of the NORTHWEST PASSAGE, the British Admiralty showed little interest in Edward Bransfield's discovery. In November of that same year, 1820, the American mariner NATHANIEL BROWN PALMER sighted the southern Antarctic Peninsula and, for a time, received credit for the first sighting of Antarctica. Bransfield had originally named the peninsula Trinity Land. It later became known as Palmer Land. With newfound interest in the region, Great Britain renamed the peninsula Graham Land, after R. G. Graham, Lord of the Admiralty. In 1965, the United States and Great Britain agreed on the name Antarctic Peninsula. Bransfield Island, Bransfield Strait, and Mount Bransfield are named after the British explorer.

Brazza, Pierre-Paul-François-Camille Savorgnan de (Pietro Paolo Savorgnan di Brazza) (1852–1905) *Italian-born French naval officer, official in West Africa*

Born in Rome, Pietro di Brazza attended the French naval academy, a position arranged by his father, an Italian count. In 1874, as a young officer, Brazza traveled to the French colony of Gabon in West Africa. After returning to Europe, he became a naturalized French citizen and adopted the French form of his name, Pierre Savorgnan de Brazza.

In 1875–77, Brazza, on behalf of French interests in the region, explored Africa's Ogowe River as well as the Alima, a tributary of the CONGO RIVER (Zaire River). In 1879–82, in the employ of the French National Committee of the International Association, which sought to counter SIR HENRY MORTON STANLEY's efforts to annex the Congo basin on behalf of King Leopold II of Belgium, Brazza explored and developed the upper Congo region. In 1880, he founded Franceville in what is now Gabon and Brazzaville in what is now Congo. Brazza's treaties with tribal leader Makoko that same year provided the basis for France to assume control of the French Congo, an area of 193,000 square miles north and west of the Congo, which was declared a French protectorate in 1891 and became part of French Equatorial Africa (modern-day Gabon and Republic of the Congo) in 1910. Belgium's Congo Free State came to be known as Zaire and is now the Democratic Republic of the Congo.

Starting in 1883, Brazza served as a French colonial official. During his tenure, he continued to carry out expeditions in the region. In 1886–98, he was commissioner general of the French Congo. In 1905, he again traveled there on behalf of the French government to investigate reports of forced labor and cruelty on French-run rubber plantations, but he died of dysentery during the trip.

Pierre Savorgnan de Brazza helped open up the Congo River to French interests and helped France secure a foothold in West Africa.

Brébeuf, Jean de (Saint Jean de Brébeuf)
(1593–1649) *French missionary in the eastern*
Great Lakes region
Jean de Brébeuf was born in the Normandy region of France to a noble family. Starting in 1617, he studied under the Jesuits, becoming a priest five years later.

In 1625, Brébeuf traveled to North America and began his missionary work among the Montagnais Indians of Quebec. The next year, accompanied by Indian guides, Brébeuf undertook a CANOE voyage westward to the Georgian Bay region of Lake Huron, where he soon established a Jesuit mission to the Huron (Wyandot) Indians. When French Canada was threatened by a British invasion in 1628, he was recalled to Quebec. He returned to France the next year.

With French control of Quebec reestablished in 1633, Brébeuf returned to Canada and resumed work among the Huron. He was the author of the 1635 and 1636 editions of the *Jesuit Relations* about the Huron missions. In 1640, Brébeuf and other Jesuit missionaries were forced to flee from the Georgian Bay settlements following an outbreak of smallpox, which the Huron blamed on them. They went south to live among the Neutral (Attiwandaronk) Indians in present-day southeastern Ontario between Lake Ontario and Lake Erie.

Brébeuf's efforts among the Neutral were hampered by the Indians' belief that he was a sorcerer and he left in 1641. By 1644 he was again at work among the Huron.

In 1649, the Iroquois (Haudenosaunee) invaded Huron territory. Brébeuf, GABRIEL LALEMENT, and several other Jesuit missionaries were captured and tortured, then burned to death. In 1930, Brébeuf, along with Lalement, was declared one of the Jesuit Martyrs of North America and canonized by Pope Pius XI.

Jean de Brébeuf's work among the Indians of Georgian Bay and the Straits of Mackinac established some of the earliest non-Indian settlements in that part of French Canada. He developed the St. Ignace missionary settlement on Mackinac Island, which served as a base for the MISSISSIPPI RIVER explorations of JACQUES MARQUETTE and LOUIS JOLLIET.

Bréhant de Galinée, René de (ca. 1645–1678)
French missionary in the eastern Great Lakes region
René de Bréhant was born at Rennes in northwestern France, a descendant of a French noble family that traced its lineage back to the CRUSADES. He attended the Sorbonne in Paris, studying astronomy and mathematics in addition to preparing for the priesthood. Soon after receiving a degree in theology, he entered the Sepulcian Order, and in 1668, he arrived in French Canada as a missionary priest.

Bréhant spent a year at the Sepulcian headquarters near Montreal, learning the Algonquian language in preparation for a planned evangelical mission to the Potawatomi Indians of the upper Mississippi Valley.

In early July 1669, Bréhant left Montreal with a group of missionaries led by FRANÇOIS DOLLIER DE CASSON. The missionaries were accompanied by a number of VOYAGEURS, including RENÉ-ROBERT CAVELIER DE LA SALLE as interpreter. They followed the St. Lawrence River to Lake Ontario, then proceeded along its south shore to the Niagara River. After crossing the Niagara River, near what is now Hamilton, Ontario, Bréhant and his missionary companions parted company with La Salle, whose abilities as an interpreter proved limited.

Bréhant, Dollier, and the other missionaries explored westward for some distance, then encamped for the winter on the north shore of Lake Erie. In late March, they set out again for Potawatomi territory, but they were forced to change their plans when the CANOE carrying their religious items, including a portable altar, was lost in a storm. Without proper equipment to carry out their evangelical work, the missionaries decided to head back toward Montreal.

Not wanting the expedition to be a total failure, Bréhant and the others decided to explore the Great Lakes by following a northern route back to Montreal. From Lake Erie, they followed the Detroit River into Lake St. Clair and Lake Huron. After a visit to the mission in the Straits of Mackinac, they headed eastward into Georgian Bay and Lake Nipissing. On the last leg of the journey, they traveled up the Ottawa and St. Lawrence Rivers, arriving back in Montreal on June 18, 1670.

Upon his return to Montreal, Bréhant became ill. During his convalescence over the next few months, he wrote an account of his journey, producing a map of the route followed to and from the Great Lakes. The map, one of the first ever drawn of the eastern Great Lakes, was presented to the colonial governor of New France, Jean-Baptiste Talon.

Bréhant returned to France in 1671. He died seven years later while en route to Rome.

René de Bréhant's travels with Dollier into the Great Lakes covered much territory already known at that time to the French. Nevertheless, his map clearly showed for the first time that Lakes Ontario, Erie, and Huron were connected.

Brendan, Saint (Saint Brendan the Navigator, Brandan, Brandon, Brendon, Brendan of Clonfert, Brendan the Voyager) (ca. 484–ca. 578)
Irish monk, legendary explorer of the North Atlantic

Born in or near Tralee on the southwest coast of Ireland, Brendan was ordained a priest in A.D. 512. He established monasteries in Ireland at Ardfert and Clonfert and under-

took evangelical missions to the Shetland Islands, Brittany, Cornwall, and Wales.

As reported in the early-10th-century Irish geographic works *The Book of Lismore* and *Navigatio Sancti Brendani* (also known as *The Voyage of St. Brendan*), Brendan reportedly went on a pilgrimage across the Atlantic Ocean. Sea pilgrimages in an open boat made of ox-hides stretched over a wooden frame, known as a CURRAGH, were a common practice.

According to the *Navigatio,* Brendan and a party of 17 Irish monks sailed westward from the southwest coast of Ireland and visited several islands in the Atlantic. Along the way, they came upon fabulous creatures, including giant sheep, pygmies, and sea-cats. Some historians have speculated that Brendan may have reached the Faeroe Islands between ICELAND and northern Scotland. The pygmies may have been Inuit (Eskimo) encountered off the coast of GREENLAND, and the sea-cats could have been walruses. In addition, as the story is told, a friendly whale named Jasconius is described as visiting the monks each Easter; the monks reportedly celebrated Easter Sunday mass on its back.

After five years of wandering among the islands of the North Atlantic, Brendan and his companions supposedly arrived in a land of continental dimensions, which they identified as "The Land Promised to the Saints." After exploring the interior for weeks, they reached a large river, where an

The legend of Saint Brendan *(Library of Congress)*

angel reportedly appeared to tell them that this land was reserved for others to missionize at some point in the future. As instructed, they returned to Ireland.

In his later years, Brendan was associated with St. Columba at the monastery on the island of Iona, off the west coast of Scotland.

Although there is little historical evidence on where Brendan actually went on his voyage to the west, some historians have theorized that between 566 and 573, he may have reached Iceland, the CANARY ISLANDS, the AZORES, or the Madeira Islands. A popular speculation is that the Irish monk reached the Western Hemisphere and made a landing on Bermuda or the North American mainland.

St. Brendan's legendary explorations inspired medieval cartographers to include a ST. BRENDAN'S ISLE on their maps, lying west of Africa, near the conjectured islands of "Antillia" and "High Brassil." On his 1492 globe of the world, MARTIN BEHAIM indicated a "St. Brendan's Island" west of the Canary Islands, near the EQUATOR. Throughout the later Middle Ages, the story of St. Brendan's voyage preserved hopes that unknown lands lay waiting to be discovered westward across the Atlantic. Coupled with the sagas of the VIKINGS, the legend of St. Brendan influenced the voyages of CHRISTOPHER COLUMBUS and other European explorers of the late 15th and early 16th centuries.

Bressani, Francesco-Gioseppe (Father Francis Joseph Bressani) (1612–1672) *Italian missionary in French Canada*

Francesco-Gioseppe Bressani was born in Rome. He joined the Jesuit order at the age of 15 and subsequently embarked on an academic career, becoming a professor of mathematics, philosophy, and literature.

In 1642, Bressani traveled to French Canada, where he ministered to French colonists and Huron (Wyandot) Indians near Quebec. In 1644, he left the Jesuit settlement at Trois Rivières on the St. Lawrence River, and, accompanied by a party of Christianized Huron, he headed westward up the river for the Jesuit mission on the shores of Lake Huron's Georgian Bay. Soon after starting out, Bressani and his Huron companions were attacked by an Iroquois (Haudenosaunee) Indian war party near present-day Sorel, Quebec. The priest was taken captive and held for four months. During a trip to the upper Hudson River region, Bressani won his release when he was ransomed by Dutch fur traders. He then made his way to the Dutch colony of New Amsterdam (present-day New York City), from where he sailed to France.

In July 1645, Bressani returned to Quebec and again traveled westward to the Lake Huron region for missionary work among the Huron. In 1648, with the outbreak of a full-scale war between the Iroquois and the Huron, Bressani set out for Quebec with a group of Huron refugees. En route, he was wounded in an Iroquois attack, but he managed to reach Quebec, where he remained for the next year. On his way back to the Lake Huron mission, he learned that it had been destroyed by Iroquois. Soon afterward, he returned to Europe, and he lived his remaining years in Florence, Italy.

Francesco-Gioseppe Bressani's account of his years as a missionary in French Canada, entitled *Brève Relation,* was published in Macerata, Italy, in 1653. His experience as a captive of the Iroquois illustrates the resentment the Iroquois maintained against the French and the Jesuits that stemmed from SAMUEL DE CHAMPLAIN's initial military alliance with the Huron in 1609.

Bridger, James (Jim Bridger) (1804–1881)
American fur trapper, scout, guide in American West

Born in Richmond, Virginia, James (Jim) Bridger moved with his family to Missouri, settling near St. Louis. By the time he was 13, he was orphaned and working as a blacksmith in the St. Louis area.

In 1822, Bridger answered WILLIAM HENRY ASHLEY's call for fur trappers to take part in his first expedition up the MISSOURI RIVER to the Dakotas and northern ROCKY MOUNTAINS. He was with Ashley's original contingent of men who trapped for furs during the winter of 1822–23, based around the newly established Fort Henry at the mouth of the Yellowstone River.

The following winter of 1823–24, Bridger trapped under Ashley's partner ANDREW HENRY, along with fellow mountain men John Fitzgerald and HUGH GLASS, exploring the Green River region of present-day southern Wyoming and northern Utah.

The next winter, 1824–25, Bridger trapped northwestern Utah's Rocky Mountains, and, in late 1824 or early 1825, he reached the Great Salt Lake, becoming one of the first non-Indians to explore it. Noting that the water was salty rather than fresh, Bridger speculated that he had come across an arm of the Pacific Ocean. JAMES CLYMAN, HENRY FRAEB, LOUIS VASQUEZ, and other trappers determined the lake was landlocked in 1826.

From 1826 to 1834, Bridger continued to trap for Ashley's various successors in the FUR TRADE, including JEDEDIAH STRONG SMITH and WILLIAM LEWIS SUBLETTE of the ROCKY MOUNTAIN FUR COMPANY. In 1835, he attended the Green River fur traders' rendezvous with CHRISTOPHER HOUSTON CARSON (Kit Carson). From 1838 to 1843, he was associated with JOHN JACOB ASTOR's AMERICAN FUR COMPANY and worked the Rocky Mountains in search of beaver pelts.

By the late 1830s, fur trappers had seriously depleted the supply of beaver in the Rockies. Meanwhile, demand for the pelts declined as silk became more fashionable among eastern and European hatmakers. In 1843, with his trapping partner Louis Vasquez, Bridger established a trading post, Fort Bridger, on the Oregon Trail, at the Green River's Black Fork, near the present-day town of Green River, Wyoming. Bridger and Vasquez traded for buffalo hides with Indian and non-Indian hunters and provided supplies and accommodations for travelers along the Oregon Trail headed for the Pacific Northwest and northern California.

In its first year of operation, Bridger's post was host to a large Oregon-bound wagon train, led by JESSE APPLEGATE. In 1847, BRIGHAM YOUNG, leading the first Mormon wagon train westward into the what is now Utah, stopped at Fort Bridger, where Bridger provided supplies and helpful information about the route south and west into the Great Salt Lake Basin. JOHN CHARLES FRÉMONT, during his expeditions of the 1840s into the Rockies, also stopped at Fort Bridger, where he received trail information and supplies from the mountain man.

In 1849–50, Bridger was a guide for Captain HOWARD STANSBURY's expedition seeking a route through Utah's Wasatch Mountains. During this venture, Bridger explored the route known as Cheyenne Pass, as well as what later became known as Bridger's Pass. The latter, in years to come,

Jim Bridger (drawing by Frederic Remington) *(Library of Congress)*

served as an important route for overland stages and for the Union Pacific Railroad.

In 1853, the Mormons in Utah and southern Wyoming, suspecting that Bridger was supplying firearms and ammunition to the Ute Indians, forced Bridger to sell his interest in the trading post.

In 1855–56, Bridger served as guide for Irish big-game hunter Sir George Gore on a hunting expedition into the Yellowstone Valley of present-day northwestern Wyoming. This expedition brought back oral accounts of scenic wonders, spurring interest in the region among easterners.

When Mormon settlers in northern Utah openly resisted federal authority during the Mormon War of 1857–58, federal troops under Colonel Albert Sidney Johnston were sent to put down the uprising, with Bridger as guide.

In 1859–60, Bridger was a guide to Captain WILLIAM FRANKLIN RAYNOLDS's expedition from Fort Pierre and Fort Union in the Dakota Territory through Wyoming and Montana. In the course of this government-sponsored enterprise, Bridger helped locate a suitable wagon route connecting the Oregon Trail with the Walla Walla Valley of present-day eastern Washington.

In 1861, Bridger helped lead the Berthoud party through the Rockies from Denver in an attempt to find a shorter wagon route to the Great Salt Lake.

In about 1864, Bridger blazed a trail northward from Denver to the gold mining country around Bannack and Virginia City, Montana. Unlike the Bozeman Trail, established about the same time, Bridger's route ran west of Wyoming's Bighorn Mountains, thus circumventing the sacred hunting grounds of the Sioux (Dakota, Lakota, Nakota) and Cheyenne Indians. Although Bridger's trail northward from Colorado may have been safer for travelers to Montana, as well as less antagonistic to the Indians, it was longer and less traveled than JOHN MERIN BOZEMAN's route. The inevitable conflict with the Sioux led to the government's Powder River Expedition of 1865, during which Bridger again served as a scout for federal troops, this time commanded by General Patrick Edward Connor.

Although Bridger was troubled by failing eyesight, he continued to act as a guide and scout for the U.S. government and railroad interests. In 1866, he led a survey party measuring the length of the Bozeman Trail and conducted an expedition surveying the route across Wyoming and Utah for Grenville Mellon Dodge's Union Pacific Railroad project.

By 1868, Bridger's health had forced him into retirement. He settled near his old trading partner, Louis Vasquez, at Westport, Missouri, where he spent the remainder of his life.

Jim Bridger's career as a fur trapper in the 1820s and 1830s, and his later adventures as a trader and guide for explorers, military men, and settlers, spanned nearly the entire period of exploration and settlement of the northern plains and northern Rockies. The trails he helped blaze later became routes for wagon trains and railroads. Moreover, his explorations of the Yellowstone Valley of northwestern Wyoming contributed to the eventual preservation of this wilderness area as the nation's first national park in 1872.

Brosses, Charles de (1709–1777) *French geographer*

Charles de Brosses was born at Dijon in the Burgundy region of France. He became one of the leading scholars of his time, contributing to Diderot's *Encyclopedia* of 1751–72. Also prominent in politics, he was president of Burgundy's local governing body.

De Brosses had a keen interest in geography, and, in 1756, he published his *Histoire de la navigation aux terres australes* (History of navigation to southern lands), a study of explorations into the world's southern latitudes. Among the exploits he chronicled were those of French navigator Binot Palmier de Gonneville who sailed the southern seas in 1504, where he reportedly reached a large landmass, later known as the legendary GONNEVILLE'S LAND. Based on this and other accounts, de Brosses promoted the idea of a GREAT SOUTHERN CONTINENT, maintaining that such a landmass had to exist in the Southern Hemisphere in order to counterbalance the continents of the Northern Hemisphere.

De Brosses found further evidence to support his idea of geographic equilibrium in French sea captain JEAN-BAPTISTE-CHARLES BOUVET DE LOZIER's voyage of 1738–39, in which he reached land at 54° south latitude, farther south than any lands then charted in the Southern Hemisphere. He named it Cape Circumcision, after the feast day (January 1, 1739) on which he reached it, and concluded that it was the northern tip of a huge continent that extended to the south, the fabled Gonneville's Land. In his 1756 book, de Brosses held the cape as proof of the existence of the Great Southern Continent. Subsequent explorations would reveal that what Bouvet had found was actually only a small island, 1,100 miles off the Atlantic coast of Antarctica, known today as Bouvet Island.

In his *History of Navigation,* de Brosses first coined the term *Australasia* to refer to the Great Southern Continent. He also originated the term *Polynesia* as a reference to the many island groups in the South Pacific. Many of his geographic notions were erroneous. He contended that large stretches of open sea could not freeze, and that icebergs originated from freshwater rivers, their existence in southern latitudes underscoring the existence of a large southern landmass with an extensive inland river system that flowed to the sea.

De Brosses's geographic work influenced the French and British navigators who, following the conclusion of the Seven Years War in 1763, set out to explore the great uncharted regions of the Southern Hemisphere. South Pacific explorers JOHN BYRON, LOUIS-ANTOINE DE BOUGAINVILLE, and JAMES COOK were both familiar with his work when they searched for the Great Southern Continent during the 1760s.

Charles de Brosses promoted the idea that the aim of exploration into uncharted lands should be to advance scientific knowledge and to elevate the cultures of primitive peoples encountered, rather than merely for national gain by conquest. He was one of the first to propose that newly located lands could be used as places where European criminals could be sent for resettlement and rehabilitation, an idea that was eventually realized with the establishment of the first penal colony in New South Wales in Australia, in 1788.

Broughton, William Robert (1762–1821)
British naval officer on the Pacific coasts of North America and Asia

Few details exist of William Broughton's early life. After entering the British navy as a midshipman in his early teens, he took part in naval operations against the French on the Atlantic coast of North America and off the coast of India in 1778–83, during the American Revolution.

In 1791, as a naval lieutenant, Broughton took command of the brig *Chatham,* accompanying GEORGE VANCOUVER and the *Discovery* on an expedition to the northwest coast of North America. They first sailed to the Pacific Ocean by way of the CAPE OF GOOD HOPE and Australia. The two ships separated. Broughton headed across the Pacific toward Tahiti, locating an island group about 400 miles east of NEW ZEALAND, which he named the Chatham Islands after his ship.

In late May 1792, on North America's Pacific Northwest Coast, Broughton, guided by American merchant captain ROBERT GRAY's reports, located and entered the mouth of the COLUMBIA RIVER and undertook the first exploration by non-Indians up that river from the Pacific. His party reached a point 119 miles upstream, near what is now Washougal, Washington, east of the Willamette River's mouth at present-day Portland, Oregon.

Broughton subsequently sailed with Vancouver to Monterey, California, and, after traveling overland across Mexico to Vera Cruz, he returned to England in 1793.

In 1796, Broughton, in command of the *Providence,* returned to the northwest coast of North America. Arriving too late to rejoin Vancouver, he sailed westward across the Pacific, then surveyed Asia's Pacific coast from the Kamchatka Peninsula southward to Korea and Japan. On May

16, 1797, the *Providence* was wrecked when it struck a reef off the coast of Formosa (present-day Taiwan). Nevertheless, all of the crew survived, and Broughton carried out the rest of the Asian coast survey aboard a sloop that had been accompanying his ship. In May 1798, he arrived at Macao, the Portuguese colony off the southeast coast of China, from where he returned to England.

Broughton went on to serve in British naval campaigns in the Napoleonic Wars of the early 1800s. In 1810, he participated in the British campaign against the French colony on the Indian Ocean island of Mauritius, and, the next year, he took part in the attack on the Dutch colony on Java. After 1812, he returned to England, later settling in Florence, Italy.

In 1804, Broughton published an account of his expedition along the Asian coast, entitled *A Voyage of Discovery to the North Pacific Ocean*. He also left journals describing his exploration of the northwest coast of North America and his journey across Mexico.

Although Robert Gray is generally credited with the non-Indian discovery of the Columbia River, it was William Broughton who first charted it in 1792. Great Britain later claimed sovereignty over the Oregon Country partly on the basis of Broughton's investigations of the lower Columbia River Basin. In 1805, WILLIAM CLARK and MERIWETHER LEWIS relied on Broughton's charts of the lower Columbia River during their overland expedition to the Pacific.

Brown, Robert (1773–1858) *Scottish naturalist in Australia and Tasmania*

Robert Brown was born in Montrose, Scotland, the son of an Episcopal clergyman. He attended the Montrose grammar school, where he befriended James Mill, who later became a leading British philosopher. After studying philosophy at Marichal College in Aberdeen, Brown entered the University of Edinburgh in 1789. By that time, he had developed a keen interest in natural history, especially botany, and had become a member of the Natural History Society of Edinburgh. In 1791, he prepared a comprehensive collection and study of the flora of Scotland.

In 1795, Brown was commissioned as an officer and assistant surgeon in a Scottish regiment of the British army. After his service with the army in the north of Ireland, he was sent to London on recruiting duty in 1798, where he met British naturalist SIR JOSEPH BANKS. Banks recognized Brown's potential as a scientist and secured his appointment as the official naturalist on MATTHEW FLINDERS's expedition to Australia in 1801.

Brown sailed from Portsmouth with Flinders on the *Investigator* in July 1801, reaching the west coast of Australia that December. Over the next few months, he made numerous landings on the Australian coast. Accompanied by natural history artist FERDINAND LUCAS BAUER, he undertook an extensive study of the region's wildlife. In addition to thousands of plant specimens, Brown collected animals unique to Australia, including kangaroos, emus, and certain varieties of lizards and cockatoos.

In February 1802, the *Investigator* sailed 148 miles up Spencer Gulf on Australia's south coast. Near its head, Flinders sighted a peak he named Mount Brown, in honor of the Scottish naturalist. Two months later, at Encounter Bay, Brown served as Flinders's interpreter in his meeting with the French maritime explorer THOMAS-NICOLAS BAUDIN.

Following a stop at Port Jackson (present-day Sydney), Brown continued with the Flinders expedition in an exploration of the east and north coasts of Australia. He examined the flora and fauna along the shores of the York Peninsula, and the coast of the Gulf of Carpentaria, and encountered several aborigines.

In August 1803, Brown and the rest of the scientific staff remained behind at Port Jackson; Flinders continued to explore in ships borrowed from the BRITISH EAST INDIA COMPANY while the *Investigator* underwent repairs. Flinders had instructed the scientists to seek their own return passage if he did not return after 18 months. Brown took part in studies of plant life around Sydney, including an investigation of the reproductive features of orchids.

Brown then sailed to the newly established British colony on TASMANIA, where he spent 10 months examining the island's plants and animals. Among the species he studied was the Tasmanian wolf, found only on that island.

Brown returned to Port Jackson in early 1805, but Flinders failed to arrive within the arranged time, having been taken prisoner by the French at Île de France (present-day Mauritius) in late 1803. Soon afterward, Brown and the other scientists sailed back to England on the refurbished *Investigator*. On the return voyage, they made a stopover at Cape Town, South Africa, where Brown collected additional plant specimens. He arrived back in England in October 1805, with a total of almost 4,000 specimens of plants, 1,700 of which were new to science. He also brought back various live animals, including the bare-nostriled wombat.

Over the next five years, Brown compiled a comprehensive catalogue and study of the plants he had collected in Australia and Tasmania, published in 1810 as *Prodromus Florae Novae Hollandiae*. In addition, he contributed scientific material to Flinders's account of the expedition, published in 1814. In classifying the new plants he had discovered, Brown had to establish 14 new genera.

Brown went on to a long and distinguished career as one of England's foremost natural scientists. He developed a close association with Joseph Banks, and upon Banks's death in 1820 Brown inherited his house, library, and natural history collection. He was made a fellow of the ROYAL SOCIETY in 1811, and, in 1827, he became curator of the British Museum's botanical collection. That same year, he published the scientific findings for which he is best known, the phenomenon known as Brownian Movement, which substantiated the kinetic molecular theory of matter. In 1831, he discovered the nucleus of the plant cell.

With his work as a naturalist in Australia and Tasmania, Robert Brown carried on the tradition of British scientific exploration and inquiry in the South Pacific begun in the late 1760s with the voyages of JAMES COOK.

Bruce, James (Laird of Kinnaird) (1730–1794)
Scottish explorer in East Africa

James Bruce was born on his family's estate, Kinnaird, in Sterlingshire, Scotland. Following his early education at Harrow, he went on to Edinburgh University in 1747. In about 1750, forced to curtail his studies for health reasons, he went to London and worked for a wine merchant's firm, marrying the owner's daughter in 1753. Nine months after his marriage, his wife died, and Bruce sought solace in travel to exotic places.

Starting in 1755, Bruce journeyed along the southern shore of the MEDITERRANEAN SEA, visiting sites of Roman ruins from Tunis to Tripoli. He also sailed to Crete, Rhodes, and the Mediterranean coast of present-day Turkey.

In 1763, Bruce was appointed Great Britain's consul general at Algiers. Commissioned also to continue his study of classical ruins in North Africa, he hired Italian artist Luigi Balugani to make drawings and serve as his assistant. He remained in the diplomatic service for two years.

In 1768, Bruce resolved to undertake an expedition into the interior of East Africa in search of the source of the NILE RIVER. An accomplished linguist, he readied himself for his journey by becoming fluent in Spanish, Portuguese, Arabic, and Amharic, the principal language of Ethiopia. Accompanied by Balugani, he traveled to Alexandria, Egypt, where he drew on earlier medical training to practice as a doctor. With his reputation as a medical man, he obtained diplomatic letters that aided in his subsequent travels to Arabia and Ethiopia.

In mid-1768, Bruce and Balugani ascended the Nile from Alexandria, reaching as far upriver as Aswan. Because of hostile tribes, Bruce and his assistant headed eastward across the desert to the RED SEA coast. They crossed over to Jidda on the Arabian Peninsula, then headed southward, recrossing the Red Sea to the Eritrean port of Massawa, which they reached in September 1769. From Massawa, they journeyed into the Ethiopian interior, arriving at the capital city of Gondar in February 1770.

In Gondar, Bruce was received by the Ethiopian king, Tecla Haimanot, and by the regent and real power behind the throne, Ras Michael of Tigre. He won the favor of the Ethiopian rulers by instituting sanitary measures that stemmed an outbreak of smallpox in the royal palace. At that time, a civil war was raging in the country, and Bruce took part in several military campaigns on behalf of the monarchy. Following his appointment as a provincial governor, he explored the region around Lake Tana, visiting Tissiat Falls. On November 14, 1770, at the nearby Springs of Geesh, he found what he (mistakenly) took to be the source of the Nile emanating from underground streams. These he named the Fountains of the Nile. Actually, he had located the source of the Blue Nile, a principal tributary of the main course of the Nile.

Bruce remained in Gondar until late 1771. Earlier that year, his artist assistant Balugani had died. From Gondar, Bruce descended the Blue Nile to its confluence with the White Nile at the site of present-day Khartoum. Although the White Nile appeared to be the greater stream at that junction, Bruce still concluded the Blue Nile to be the main course of the river.

Bruce left the river at Berber and undertook an arduous 18-day overland trek northward across 400 miles of the Nubian Desert. Upon reaching Aswan, he traveled down the Nile to Cairo, from where he sailed to Europe, returning to England in June 1774.

Bruce presented the results of his explorations in an interview with King George III; he was subsequently elected a fellow of the ROYAL SOCIETY. Nonetheless, his account of his African exploits was met with much skepticism by London's intelligentsia, including the renowned man of letters Dr. Samuel Johnson.

Soon after his return, Bruce retired to his family estate in Scotland and wrote a multivolume work on his explorations in Africa, *Travels to Discover the Source of the Nile*, first published in 1790. Four years later, he was fatally injured in a fall down the main staircase at Kinnaird as he descended to assist a lady into a carriage.

James Bruce's explorations rekindled European interest in the uncharted interior of Africa, especially with regard to the elusive source of the Nile, and helped lead to the founding of the AFRICAN ASSOCIATION. He was not the first European to locate the source of the Blue Nile in Ethiopia, having been preceded by Portuguese missionaries PEDRO PAEZ and JERONIMO LOBO by about 150 years. Bruce's mistaken conclusion that the Blue Nile was the main branch of the river was not revealed until the explorations of SIR RICHARD BURTON and JOHN HANNING SPEKE in the late 1850s. Nevertheless, he was the first European to undertake an expedition aimed specifically at finding the Nile's source, and was one of the earliest explorers to report the connection between the White Nile and the Blue Nile at Khartoum.

Bruce, William Spiers (1867–1921)
Scottish physician, polar explorer

William S. Bruce was born in London of Scottish parentage. Trained in medicine at Edinburgh University, he also studied natural sciences, especially oceanography. In 1892–93, he made his first voyage to the polar regions as ship's surgeon on the Scottish whaler *Baleena*, sailing from Dundee to the Antarctic.

In the late 1890s, Bruce continued his polar explorations in Franz Josef Land, the Arctic archipelago north and east of Scandinavia. He returned to the South Polar region in command of the Scottish National Antarctic Expedition of 1902–04. Aboard the ship *Scotia*, he surveyed the shore of the Weddell Sea, along the Atlantic portion of Antarctica. He observed a range of 150-foot cliffs on the coast and determined that although covered with ice, they were part of an Antarctic landmass. He named this region Coats Land, after his chief sponsor, Scottish industrialist Andrew Coats. No landing was possible at this time because of ice conditions.

Between 1906 and 1920, Bruce turned his attention back to the Arctic, making seven voyages to Spitsbergen (present-day Svalbard), where he continued his oceanographic studies. During these years, he also edited the multivolume report of the 1902–04 Scottish National Antarctic Expedition, and he recounted his experiences in the Arctic and Antarctic in the book *Polar Explorations* (1911).

The Scottish National Antarctic Expedition led by Dr. William S. Bruce took place at the same time as the British expedition under ROBERT FALCON SCOTT, as well as those sponsored by France and Sweden. Bruce also helped initiate Argentina's annual expeditions to the Antarctic when he arranged for that country to take over the Laurie Island weather station, in recognition of Argentine rescue efforts of explorers from other countries.

Brûlé, Étienne (ca. 1592–1633) *French explorer in four of the five Great Lakes*

Étienne Brûlé first traveled to North America in 1608, as a protege to French explorer and colonizer SAMUEL DE CHAMPLAIN. He remained at the newly founded Quebec settlement for the next two years, and, in 1610, he was sent to live among the Algonquian-speaking Indians of the St. Lawrence River Valley to learn their language and customs.

The next year, Champlain, before returning to France, sent Brûlé to live among the Huron (Wyandot) Indians. Brûlé became familiar with the Iroquoian language and culture and was accepted as a friend by tribal leaders.

In 1611–12, Brûlé traveled westward along the St. Lawrence River with the Huron, visiting the lands of other tribes, including the Montagnais and Nipissing. He traveled by birchbark CANOE to the western extent of the St. Lawrence River, then along the Ottawa River, part of the present-day boundary between Quebec and Ontario, Canada. Crossing along the south shore of Lake Nipissing, he entered the French River and followed it to its outlet at the northern end of Georgian Bay, becoming the first European to see Lake Huron.

From the Huron settlements on Georgian Bay, Brûlé, traveling by canoe with intermittent overland portages, headed southward and reached the northwestern end of Lake Ontario. He then journeyed back to Montreal and Quebec, rejoining Champlain, who had returned from France.

In 1615, Brûlé joined Champlain on an expedition to gain Huron support for an attack on the Iroquois (Haudenosaunee) Indians in what is now central New York State. Brûlé served as Champlain's interpreter, and the two Frenchmen, with a small party of Huron, retraced Brûlé's previous route to Georgian Bay. After traveling southward, they parted at Lake Simcoe: Champlain headed for the Iroquois settlements on Lake Oneida near present-day Syracuse, New York, and Brûlé continued with his own party of Indians across Lake Ontario and into the Niagara River. He crossed the narrow strip south of Niagara Falls and came upon Lake Erie. After recruiting a force of Erie Indians for the campaign against the Iroquois, he headed southwestward to join Champlain.

Brûlé and his Indian allies arrived too late to be of any service to Champlain at Lake Oneida. Champlain then sent Brûlé farther south to gain the support of the Susquehannock Indians. He reached Otsego Lake near present-day Cooperstown, New York, and entered the Susquehanna River, following it for 440 miles to its outlet into the Atlantic Ocean at Chesapeake Bay, through parts of the present-day states of New York, Pennsylvania, Maryland, and Virginia. In spring 1616, while returning to Montreal, Brûlé was captured by the Iroquois, but eventually managed to escape.

In 1621, Brûlé embarked on yet another expedition to the Great Lakes. He headed westward from the St. Lawrence and, following his earlier route along the Ottawa River, Lake Nipissing, and the French River, entered Georgian Bay. This time, he continued westward along the north shore of Lake Huron. With him traveled another Frenchman, named Grenolle. In the Manitoulin Island area, Brûlé came across valuable copper deposits. Although he missed the entrance to Lake Michigan at the Straits of Mackinac, he proceeded through Sault Sainte Marie and the St. Marys River, thus becoming the first European to enter Lake Superior. His accounts are sketchy, but it is thought he continued along the south shore of Lake Superior as far west as present-day Duluth, Minnesota.

Throughout the 1620s, Brûlé remained among his Huron friends, with intervening visits to Montreal and

Quebec. In 1628, when the British Kirke brothers succeeded in wresting control of the St. Lawrence Valley from the French, Brûlé offered his services to them. He reportedly was aboard the vessel that captured his former mentor, Champlain, in 1629. French control of Quebec was restored in 1632. The next year, a disagreement with his Huron hosts led to Brûlé's death at their hands.

During his 25 years in French Canada, Étienne Brûlé's explorations took him to four of the five Great Lakes: Lake Ontario, Lake Erie, Lake Huron, and Lake Superior. Moreover, his 1615–16 journey from Otsego Lake, in New York, down the Susquehanna to Chesapeake Bay revealed the existence of a canoe-and-portage route linking the Great Lakes to the Atlantic coast. His expedition to the western end of Lake Superior in 1621 took him about 1,200 miles into the interior of North America.

Brunel, Olivier (Oliver Brunel) (ca. 1540–1585)
Dutch mariner in Russia and the European Arctic
Olivier Brunel, born in Brussels or Louvain, was of Flemish ancestry. He pursued a career in navigation and hoped to make a fortune in trade with the Orient by discovering the NORTHEAST PASSAGE.

Brunel carried out his first known voyage in about 1565, sponsored by the White Sea Trading Company, rounding the North Cape of Norway into the Barents Sea and onto its inlet, the White Sea. He was taken prisoner by Russian authorities, accused of being a spy by the MUSCOVY COMPANY of London, and held at Yaroslavl, north of Moscow, until 1570. The Stroganovs, an influential Russian merchant family, lobbied for his release and hired him to develop trade relations between Russia and the Netherlands. During this period, he reportedly became the first European to make the overland journey from Moscow to the Ob River to the west. It was this journey that prompted him to plan a sea journey through the Kara Sea to the mouth of the Ob River for a proposed route to the empire of Cathay (China). He reportedly first spoke of his plans for this voyage as early as 1581 and perhaps made a failed attempt that summer.

In 1583, under the sponsorship of Frederick II of Denmark and Norway, Brunel, together with a Norwegian business partner, Arent Meyer, undertook a voyage of exploration to GREENLAND from Bergen, Norway. DRIFT ICE and fog off Greenland caused them to abandon the mission.

In 1584, backed by a Dutch consortium and again in partnership with Meyer, Brunel pursued his dream of a sea route to Cathay but made it only as far as the west coast of Novaya Zemlya before being blocked by ice. The next year, he made another attempt to reach the Ob River, entering the Kara Sea by way of the Yugor Strait. With passage again blocked by ice, he decided instead to make a landing at Pe-

chora Bay and trade his cargo with the native Samoyeds, an undertaking that proved successful. The landing boat capsized on the return to the ship, however, and Brunel was drowned.

Olivier Brunel's sea and land voyages helped further trade contacts between European nations and expand knowledge of the European Arctic, as started by the Britons SIR HUGH WILLOUGHBY, RICHARD CHANCELLOR, and STEPHEN BOROUGH and continued by fellow Dutchman WILLEM BARENTS.

Bruni, Antoine-Raymond-Joseph de (chevalier d'Entrecasteaux) (1737–1793)
French naval officer in the South Pacific
Antoine-Raymond-Joseph de Bruni, chevalier d'Entrecasteaux, was born at his family's chateau in the Provence region of southern France. He was of noble descent, and his father served as a high government official in Provence.

After entering the Marine Guard in 1754, d'Entrecasteaux went on to serve with distinction in the Battle of Minorca of 1756, a French naval victory over the British in the western MEDITERRANEAN SEA. By 1770, he had been promoted to lieutenant commander, and, over the next several years, he directed the operations of ports and arsenals in France.

In 1785, d'Entrecasteaux was made commander of French naval forces in the Indian Ocean and the Far East. Two years later, he was named governor of the French colony on Île de France (present-day Mauritius) in the Indian Ocean.

Promoted to rear admiral in 1791, d'Entrecasteaux took command of an expedition commissioned to search for JEAN-FRANÇOIS DE GALAUP, comte de La Pérouse, who had been missing with his two ships since 1788. In command of the *Recherche*, d'Entrecasteaux was accompanied by another vessel, the *Espérance*, captained by JEAN-MICHEL HUON DE KERMADEC. In addition to seeking the lost La Pérouse expedition, he had been instructed to survey the coasts of New Holland (present-day Australia), Van Diemen's Land (TASMANIA), and New Caledonia. From New Caledonia, Entrecasteaux planned to follow La Pérouse's assumed course to the northeast coast of New Guinea. They departed from Brest on September 29, 1791.

Upon arriving in Cape Town in January 1792, d'Entrecasteaux received secondhand reports that traces of the La Pérouse expedition might have been sighted in the Admiralty Islands. With this news, he changed his plans: instead of going to Australia, he headed directly for the Admiralty Islands by way of the SPICE ISLANDS (the Moluccas). Unfavorable sailing conditions held back the ships' progress across the Indian Ocean. Running low on food and water, the expedition was compelled to head south and east to southern Tasmania.

By April, d'Entrecasteaux had reached the southeast coast of Tasmania. Upon reconnaissance of the shoreline, he learned that Adventure Bay was not part of the mainland, but was actually part of one of two islands in an uncharted bay.

From Tasmania, d'Entrecasteaux sailed northeastward to New Caledonia, where he undertook the first survey of that island's west coast. He then continued into the Bismarck Archipelago, stopping at Baku and New Ireland. After failing to find a trace of La Pérouse's expedition in the Admiralty Islands, d'Entrecasteaux explored around the Solomon Islands, a group that had been incorrectly indicated on maps since their initial European discovery by Spanish navigator ÁLVARO DE MENDAÑA in 1568.

By the time d'Entrecasteaux and his expedition arrived at the Dutch settlement on Amboina in September 1793, the Reign of Terror had begun in France. Class tensions developed among the men under his command. Although the Netherlands was on the verge of war with France, the Dutch provided help. A month later, d'Entrecasteaux sailed back toward the west coast of Australia, then made an extensive cruise along the Great Australian Bight, making the European discovery of the Recherche Archipelago. Meanwhile, Jean-Michel Huon de Kermedec made the European discovery of Esperance Bay. The expedition returned to the southern Tasmanian coast, coming into contact with native peoples. After cruising along the coast of NEW ZEALAND, where the French engaged in some trading with the native Maori, they again explored New Caledonia and visited the Santa Cruz Islands. D'Entrecasteaux then directed the course westward to the Solomon Islands. He soon located a new island group now known as D'Entrecasteaux Islands.

D'Entrecasteaux next expanded his search for La Pérouse to the eastern end of New Guinea. By chance he explored Vanikoro Island, unaware that it was on that very island's reefs that La Pérouse's ships had been wrecked.

The French government had allowed only three years for d'Entrecasteaux's expedition. By July 1793, he decided to return to France. He became ill with SCURVY and dysentery en route to the Dutch East Indian port of Batavia and died at sea. Command of the expedition went to ALEXANDRE HESMIVY D'AURIBEAU, who was soon faced with political problems with the Dutch and with his own crew.

Much of the geographic and scientific data obtained by chevalier d'Entrecasteaux fell into the hands of the British, inspiring them to establish present-day Hobart, Tasmania. The islands south of Hobart are named North and South Bruny (Bruni) after the French explorer, as is D'Entrecasteaux Channel, which separates them from the mainland. D'Entrecasteaux is credited with finally establishing the correct position of the Solomons, which had been mistakenly charted by Mendaña in 1568, PHILIP CARTERET in 1767, and LOUIS-ANTOINE DE BOUGAINVILLE in 1768.

Brunner, Thomas (1821–1874) *British explorer in New Zealand*

Thomas Brunner immigrated to NEW ZEALAND from England as a 19-year-old assistant surveyor with the New Zealand Company. Starting in 1843, he undertook the first penetration by Europeans into the interior of New Zealand's South Island. He headed southward from the site of present-day Motueka on the west shore of Tasman Bay, reaching as far as the Richmond Range.

In 1845, Brunner set out again, guided by a Maori named Ekuhu and accompanied by Charles Heaphy and William Fox. On this expedition, Brunner and his party traveled southward from the eastern side of Tasman Bay into what is now known as New Zealand's Hot Springs District, where they explored the region around Lake Rotoroa.

Brunner continued his explorations of South Island the next year, in an expedition from Golden Bay on the island's northwestern corner. Again guided by Ekuhu and accompanied by Heaphy, he followed the west coast of South Island to the Grey River, then headed eastward into the interior and explored the Taramakau River.

Later in 1846, Brunner began his most extensive exploration of South Island. With Ekuhu as his guide, he headed southward from Tasman Bay to the upper reaches of the Buller River, then descended that stream westward to its mouth at Cape Foulwind, on the Tasman Sea. He proceeded southward along the west coast of South Island to the Grey River. Following the Grey River north and east into the interior, he traversed the Southern Alps to the slopes of the Paparoa Range.

After exploring the Taramakau River, Brunner returned to the west coast of South Island, exploring as far south as Mount Cook and Titihira Head.

Thomas Brunner's explorations revealed much about the major rivers and mountain ranges of South Island, New Zealand, a region that had been until that time known only from earlier coastal surveys. The Lake Rotoroa area that he visited, with its natural hot springs, subsequently became a major New Zealand health resort region. In the course of his 1846–48 expedition, Brunner became the first European to visit the lake in the northern part of New Zealand's South Island that now bears his name. His book, *Journal of an Expedition to Explore the Interior of the Middle Island of New Zealand,* was published in 1851, the same year he received a medal from the ROYAL GEOGRAPHICAL SOCIETY.

Bruyas, Jacques (1635–1712) *French missionary in North America*

Jacques Bruyas was originally from Lyon, France. Ordained a Jesuit missionary priest, he crossed the Atlantic Ocean to New France, arriving in Quebec in early August 1666. The following summer, he began his missionary work among the Iroquois (Haudenosaunee) tribes who then dominated what is now central and western New York State. He journeyed to the lands of the Mohawk, Oneida, and Onondaga part of the Iroquois League, remaining among them a few years, then was transferred to Sault St. Louis mission among the Huron (Wyandot), the main Jesuit settlement in the St. Lawrence Valley.

Bruyas served as superior to all the Jesuit missions in French Canada from 1693 to 1699. He was subsequently named Jesuit envoy to the Onondaga.

While traveling throughout the lands of the Iroquois, Bruyas, a philologist, made a study of their language, subsequently producing a Mohawk dictionary.

As with other French Jesuits of the 1600s, Father Jacques Bruyas's work among the Native Americans led to the exploration of uncharted regions of northeastern North America.

Brydges, Harford Jones (1774–1829)
British diplomat in central and southwest Asia

Harford Brydges was a diplomatic officer for the British government in the first decade of the 19th century. At that time, mounting concerns over Russia's expansion of its sphere of influence in the Middle East led the British government to seek stronger ties with Persia (present-day Iran) and its neighboring countries. To this end, Brydges was commissioned to lead a diplomatic mission to Persia in 1807.

Sailing westward from Bombay, India, Brydges and his party entered the Persian Gulf and disembarked at the port of Bushehr in what is now Iran. He then undertook a tour of the kingdom of Persia, visiting such major cities as Esfahan, Qazvin, and Teheran.

Brydges remained in Persia for four years, during which he traveled extensively throughout the coastal Baluchistan region on the Arabian Sea coast, as well as the south shore of the Caspian Sea. He also explored parts of Afghanistan and the Caucasus Mountains to the north. His journeys took him across much of the same territory covered 2,100 years earlier by ALEXANDER THE GREAT and his army.

Harford Brydges's reports provided the British government with new information about parts of central and southwest Asia that had rarely been visited by Europeans.

Buchan, David (1790–1845) *British naval officer in the Arctic Ocean*

As an officer in the British navy, David Buchan served in the Napoleonic Wars of 1803–15. By 1818, he had reached the rank of captain. That year, under the direction of SIR JOHN BARROW, second secretary of the Admiralty, he was commissioned to lead a seaward expedition across the Arctic Ocean to the Pacific Ocean, passing as close as possible to the NORTH POLE.

In April 1818, Buchan, in command of the *Dorothea,* accompanied by then-lieutenant SIR JOHN FRANKLIN in command of the *Trent,* sailed from London to Spitsbergen (present-day Svalbard), north of Norway. At that time, it was believed that the Arctic PACK ICE did not extend northward beyond a point between GREENLAND and Spitsbergen, and that an open, ice-free polar sea existed around the North Pole. Two other ships, commanded by SIR JOHN ROSS and SIR WILLIAM EDWARD PARRY, also took part in the Royal Navy's 1818 Arctic expedition. Buchan and Franklin were to sail from Spitsbergen due north to the BERING STRAIT, while Ross and Parry sailed westward through Davis Strait, west of Greenland. The four ships then were to rendezvous in Bering Strait.

Buchan and Franklin reached the northwest coast of Spitsbergen, where their ships were trapped by ice for more than a month. At one point, icebergs nearly crushed Buchan's vessel. His expedition reached as far north as 80°34' north latitude before the impregnable, southward-drifting pack ice forced him to abandon the expedition. The ships returned to England in October 1818.

The notion of an open polar sea as pursued by David Buchan died hard. The North Pole would be reached early the next century using sledges.

Bukhgolts, Ivan Dmitryevich (fl. 1700s)
Russian army officer in central Asia

Ivan Bukhgolts, a high-ranking army officer in the service of Russian czar Peter the Great, was commissioned in 1715 to lead a gold-prospecting expedition south from the Irtysh River settlement of Tobolsk to the Yarkand River region of Chinese Turkestan. In command of a force of 2,000 men, Bukhgolts ascended the Irtysh in boats.

In the western Altai Mountains, Bukhgolts's party was attacked by a force of Kalmyk tribesmen. Although outnumbered five to one, they managed to hold off the Kalmyks for three months. They then retreated down the Irtysh River to its confluence with the Om, where they constructed fortifications the following year.

Although Ivan Bukhgolts did not realize his objective of penetrating the Yarkand River region of Chinese Turkestan, his post at the junction of the Om and Irtysh Rivers endured as an important permanent Russian foothold in central Asia, becoming the present-day city of Omsk.

Burchell, William John (ca. 1782–1863)
British naturalist in South Africa and Brazil

William J. Burchell was born in Fulham, near London, England, where his father operated a plant nursery. In 1805, he traveled to the South Atlantic Ocean island of St. Helena, for work as a schoolmaster and botanist in the employ of the BRITISH EAST INDIA COMPANY. While on St. Helena, he contacted Dutch colonial authorities in Cape Town, South Africa, and obtained permission to undertake a scientific exploration of the region.

Burchell arrived in Cape Town in November 1810, and he set out for the interior the following June. Traveling in a frontier wagon, and accompanied only by a small party of native tribesmen, he crossed the Karroo Desert, east of Cape Town. From the Orange River, he traveled into Bechuanaland (present-day Botswana) and also visited the region around the settlement of Griqualand, southwest of present-day Kimberly. In the course of his explorations, Burchell collected over 63,000 specimens of plant and animal life, undertook astronomical studies, and made weather observations.

After five years in Africa, Burchell returned to England. His account of his explorations, *Travels in the Interior of Southern Africa,* was first published in 1822 and included panoramic views of Africa produced by a process known as scenographic projection, a precursor to photographic techniques. Burchell also presented 43 African animal specimens to the British Museum.

In 1825, Burchell sailed to Rio de Janeiro, from where he conducted a scientific expedition into the interior of Brazil, studying the Brazilian rainforest in the Minas Gerais region. He became the first European to venture into the Goias region near present-day Brasilia. In 1829, he headed northward to Belem, from where he returned to England with thousands of flora and fauna specimens.

In recognition of his scientific contributions, William J. Burchell received an honorary degree from Oxford University in 1834. Moreover, many of the new botanical and zoological species he brought back from Africa and South America were named after him.

Burckhardt, Johann Ludwig (Jean-Louis Burckhardt, John Lewis Burckhardt, Ibrahim ibn Abdullah) (1784–1817) *Swiss scholar, explorer in Syria, Egypt, and Arabia*

Johann Ludwig Burckhardt was born in Lausanne, Switzerland, the son of a wealthy German-Swiss family. He attended universities in Leipzig and Göttingen, Germany, studying Arabic and the culture and history of the Middle East.

In 1806, Burckhardt arrived in London, where a professor at Göttingen had arranged for him to meet with SIR JOSEPH BANKS, then an influential member of the AFRICAN ASSOCIATION, which hoped to send an explorer across the SAHARA DESERT from the NILE RIVER and reach TIMBUKTU on the NIGER RIVER. With his background in Arabic, Burckhardt succeeded in winning this commission in 1808.

In spring 1809, Burckhardt traveled from England to Aleppo, Syria. He expanded his knowledge of Arabic and immersed himself in a study of Islam in preparation for the proposed trip across the Sahara with a caravan of Muslim pilgrims returning from Mecca. While in Syria, he assumed the Arabic name Ibrahim ibn Abdullah. Burckhardt remained in Syria for more than two years, during which he lived with the nomadic tribes of northern Arabia and made several trips into the interior from Aleppo, visiting the site of the ancient city of Palmyra north of the Syrian Desert.

In June 1812, Burckhardt set out for Cairo, the first leg of his intended journey to the Niger River. Traveling southward through the valley of the Jordan River, he reached the site of the ancient tomb of Khaznet Firaun, then entered the forgotten city of Petra. Carved into the rock cliffs above the Wadi Musa in what is now Jordan, Petra had been settled since the days of the Old Testament and had eventually become a thriving Roman city. Burckhardt was the first European to visit Petra since the CRUSADES in the Middle Ages.

By September 1812, Burckhardt was in Cairo, where he attempted, without success, to arrange for passage with a caravan westward across the Sahara into the Fezzan region of present-day Libya. He then undertook two years of exploration into Egypt, the Sudan, and Arabia. Starting from the town of Isna, he ascended the Nile as far as Tinareh. En route back to Isna in March 1813, he located the ancient Egyptian temple at Abu Simbel, with its 60-foot-high statues of Pharaoh Ramses II.

Still unable to find a westward-heading caravan, Burckhardt, in early 1814, decided to explore the Nubian Desert, then cross the RED SEA to Arabia. Once in Arabia, he planned to make a pilgrimage to Mecca, believing it would give him credibility as a Muslim. He reached Shendi in the northeastern Sudan, then headed eastward to the Red Sea port of Suakin. From Suakin, he sailed to Jidda on the Arabian Peninsula. Proceeding toward Mecca, he was aided by letters from the viceroy of Egypt that vouched for him as a faithful Muslim. Burckhardt entered Mecca, then visited the other Islamic holy city, Medina, the first European to do so.

Following Arabia's Red Sea coast northward, Burckhardt reached the Sinai Peninsula, which he explored before returning to Cairo in late June 1815. In Cairo, he continued his search for a westward caravan that would take him to Libya and the southern Sahara, and also set about preparing a written account of his journeys.

In 1817, Burckhardt developed a severe case of dysentery and died. Soon afterward, the African Association began to publish his works on the Middle East.

Johann Ludwig Burckhardt did not succeed in his initial objective of reaching the Niger from North Africa. Nonetheless, the surviving accounts of his journeys in Egypt, the Sudan, and Arabia provided much new information for Europeans. His reports on the Wahhabi in Arabia, the reformist religious movement that took control of that region in 1811, were the first to reach Europe. In addition, he is credited with rediscovering the city of Petra in what is now Jordan. His descriptions of Medina and Mecca later inspired the subsequent explorations of SIR RICHARD FRANCIS BURTON.

Burke, Robert O'Hara (ca. 1821–1861)
Irish colonist in Australia

Robert O'Hara Burke was a native of St. Clerans in County Galway, Ireland. Educated in Belgium, he embarked on a military career with the army of the Austrian Empire in 1840. Eight years later, he returned to Ireland and served with the Irish Mounted Constabulary.

In 1853, Burke immigrated to Victoria, Australia, and continued his career with the colony's police force. By 1860, he had reached the rank of police inspector. At that time, an overland telegraph route was sought that would connect the settled southern region of Australia with the north, thereby providing a link with shipping from British India. In 1860, the colonial government of Victoria, spurred on by South Australia's offer of a prize of £2,000 to anyone who could make the first south-to-north crossing of the Australian continent, organized the Great Northern Exploration Expedition and appointed Burke to lead it.

Equipped with camels and horses, Burke, with WILLIAM JOHN WILLS as second in command, and a company of 18 men, left Melbourne in late August 1860. In late September, upon reaching Menindee in western New South Wales, Burke decided to push on with a small advance party, leaving the bulk of his command to await his return.

From Menindee, Burke, Wills, Charles Gray, and several others pushed north and east to the Bulloo River. They crossed the northern section of the Sturt Desert and reached Cooper's Creek, where Burke planned to rendezvous later with the rest of the expedition. On December 16, 1860, Burke, accompanied by Wills, Gray, and camel driver John King, left the Cooper's Creek encampment and set out for a final push to the coast. After nearly three months of trekking across the deserts and plains of northern Australia, they reached the tidal basin of the Flinders River. With their progress hampered by coastal swamps, they could not reach the seacoast, but they were close enough to hear the surf breaking on the shores of the Gulf of Carpentaria.

The very next day, Burke, Wills, Gray, and King set out on the return journey southward. By that time, they were critically short of food. Yet they pushed on, hoping to reach the supply depot at Cooper's Creek. Gray died along the way, although Burke, Wills, and King managed to reach Cooper's Creek on April 21, missing a relief party by only hours. Two days later, they set out down Strzelecki Creek, hoping to reach JOHN MCDOUALL STUART's outpost at

Mount Hopeless, 150 miles distant. The rest of the journey proved disastrous; they were forced to kill their remaining camels for food, and in their weakened state, had inadvertently wandered in a circle back to Cooper's Creek, where they arrived again on May 28. Earlier that day, the relief party had also returned to Cooper's Creek, but, seeing no sign of Burke and his companions, had left again.

By this time, Wills was too weak to continue, so Burke and King left him behind and went in search of aid. Two days later, Burke died of starvation, and when King returned to Wills in early July, he found him dead as well. For the next few months, King managed to survive on food provided by a local group of Aborigines and was finally rescued by a relief expedition on September 15.

Robert O'Hara Burke's 1860–61 expedition suffered from poor planning and wavering leadership on his part. Despite the tragic outcome, he nonetheless succeeded in making a south-to-north crossing of the Australian continent. Stuart, however, gained official recognition for accomplishing the deed first.

Burnes, Sir Alexander (1805–1841)
British diplomat in central Asia

Alexander Burnes was born in Montrose, Scotland. At the age of 17, he entered the service of the BRITISH EAST INDIA COMPANY, serving as an officer with its armed forces at Surat, on the west coast of India north of Bombay. He studied Indian languages there, becoming an interpreter for the company.

In 1826, Burnes was sent to the Kutch region of western India, where he developed an interest in the geography of central Asia. His explorations into central Asia began in 1831, when he ascended the INDUS RIVER into what is now northern Pakistan on a diplomatic mission to the Maharajan Ranjit Singh of Lahore.

The next year, Burnes left Lahore dressed as an Afghani native. Traveling northward through Peshawar, he crossed the Hindu Kush and entered Afghanistan. After visiting the Afghani cities of Kabul and Balkh, he continued northwestward to Bukhara in what is now Uzbekistan. He visited the eastern Caspian Sea region, then headed southward for Teheran and the Persian Gulf port of Bushehr, from where he sailed to England.

Back in England, Burnes wrote an account of his experiences in south-central Asia, *Travels into Bokhara,* first published in 1834.

In 1839, Burnes returned to Afghanistan as Great Britain's diplomatic representative to that country's unpopular ruler, Shah Shujah. Two years later, Burnes was killed by an assassin in Kabul.

Sir Alexander Burnes's travels into Afghanistan and central Asia provided the British government with firsthand information on the geography and culture of the territory north of the Indian subcontinent, a region that during the 1830s and 1840s had great strategic bearing on the competing expansionist policies of Great Britain and Russia.

Burney, James (1750–1821) *British naval officer in the Pacific, writer*

James Burney was born in London, the eldest son of English composer and musical historian Charles Burney. At the age of 10, he entered the Royal Navy as a cabin boy. At 20, he sailed to Bombay, India, as a seaman.

In 1772–74, Burney served as a lieutenant on the *Adventure* in JAMES COOK's second voyage to the Pacific Ocean. In December 1773, he led a party of marines ashore on the coast of NEW ZEALAND, in search of some missing crew members. His discovery of their grisly remains revealed that the indigenous peoples there were hostile and cannibalistic, a finding that warned Cook and other mariners to be cautious on later visits to New Zealand.

Returning to England on the *Adventure* with Burney in summer 1774 was a Tahitian native named Omai. With the help of Burney's sister, novelist Fanny Burney, Omai was presented to London society and was received with great celebrity.

Burney joined Cook on his third voyage to the Pacific in 1776–80, serving as first lieutenant on the *Discovery*. On this expedition, he led a party that explored the island of Atiu in the Cook Island group, where he established friendly relations with the natives.

Burney was promoted to captain in 1782. He left active sea duty two years later. Starting in 1804, and continuing for 12 years, he published a comprehensive record of explorations in the Pacific, entitled *Chronological History of the Voyages and Discoveries in the South Sea or Pacific Ocean*. His history of buccaneers in the Americas was published in 1816 and was followed three years later by a book on Russian explorations in eastern SIBERIA. He was appointed a rear admiral in 1821 and died in London later that same year.

Known for his writings, James Burney was an eyewitness to many of the maritime voyages of exploration detailed in his works.

Burton, Sir Richard Francis (Mirza Abdullah)
(1821–1890) *British soldier, writer, linguist, explorer in India, Arabia, Africa, and South America*

Richard Burton was born in Torquay on the south coast of England. His father, an Irishman, was a colonel in the British army. Following his early education at schools on the European continent, Burton entered Oxford University, where he began his study of Arabic. He remained at Oxford for only about a year, being expelled in 1840 for dueling.

In 1842, Burton enlisted in the BRITISH EAST INDIA COMPANY's armed forces in western India, the Bombay Native Infantry, serving as an officer in the lower Indus Valley's Sind region for the next seven years. He traveled widely throughout what is now Pakistan, studying native languages, including Persian, Afghani, and Hindustani, and perfecting his command of Arabic. Burton became the official interpreter for his regiment. He also undertook an undercover mission that involved spying on his fellow soldiers at all-male brothels in Karachi. His reports aroused a great deal of controversy, and Burton was transferred from India back to England in 1849.

In 1853, Burton obtained a year's leave of absence to continue his studies of Arabic and travel in Arabia. That year, he sailed to Suez, from where he undertook a journey to the Muslim holy cities of Mecca and Medina. Disguised in native dress as an Afghani physician, he traveled under the name of Mirza Abdullah. To ensure that his non-Muslim identity would not be detected, Burton had himself circumcised before embarking on his trip into Arabia. He reached Mecca in late January 1854, then proceeded to Medina. He made sketches of the holy shrines of Islam, including the Kaaba, the cube-shaped building containing Islam's most sacred object: the Black Stone. Although Burton had planned to travel across the Arabian Peninsula and explore the Rub' al-Khali (the EMPTY QUARTER) in the southeast, illness forced him to return by steamer to Egypt. From there, he reached Bombay.

In 1854, Burton was commissioned by the Indian army to undertake an exploration of Somaliland, present-day Somalia, the region of East Africa around the Horn of Africa. Along with a small number of other officers, including JOHN HANNING SPEKE, G. E. Herne, and William Stroyan, Burton organized the expedition at Aden. Before the main party set out, Burton journeyed to the slave-trading center of Harar in northwestern Ethiopia. Again disguised in native dress, he succeeded in entering the city, which until that time had never been visited by a non-Muslim, and managed to meet the region's ruler. After 10 days, he returned to Aden, making a harrowing journey across the desert by himself.

Burton's subsequent expedition into Somalia with Speke and the other officers met with less success. They had not yet begun to explore the interior when they were attacked by natives at the coastal city of Berbera. Stroyan was killed, and both Burton and Speke were wounded.

Burton recovered and went on to serve with the British army in the Crimean War of 1854–56. In 1855, reports by German missionaries JOHANN LUDWIG KRAPF and JOHANN REBMANN suggested that a large inland sea, comparable in size to the Caspian, lay deep in the interior of East Africa, and might prove to be the long-sought-after source of the NILE RIVER. In 1856, with backing from both the ROYAL

GEOGRAPHICAL SOCIETY and the British Foreign Office, Burton organized an expedition to find this body of water and solve the mystery of the Nile's source. Accompanying him to Africa again was John Hanning Speke.

In August 1857, Burton and Speke set out from Bagamoyo on the Indian Ocean coast of present-day Tanzania, opposite Zanzibar. Unlike earlier expeditions in search of the Nile's source, which usually began from the Nile's delta in Egypt, Burton planned to reach the headwaters of the river by penetrating the continent from the east. The expedition included 130 porters and 30 pack animals, carrying supplies to last two years. The sultan of Zanzibar provided guides and a caravan leader; one guide in particular, SIDI BOMBAY, proved to be of invaluable service.

Following the route of Arab slave caravans, Burton and Speke reached Tabora (then called Kezeh), about 500 miles inland. From Arab traders at Tabora, they learned that the great inland sea was actually three separate large lakes. Continuing westward, they followed the Malagarasi River to its mouth, and, on February 13, 1858, reached the shores of Lake Tanganyika (the second largest lake in Africa) at Ujiji, becoming the first Europeans to see it. Both explorers were by this time stricken with malaria and other tropical ailments. Burton was nearly paralyzed and suffered from an infected jaw; Speke was practically blind from fever. They spent some time recovering among the Arab traders at Ujiji. Speke then undertook an exploration by dugout CANOE of Lake Tanganyika. Burton at that time was convinced that this immense inland body of water was the source of the Nile. Yet Speke, after partially surveying the lake, returned to Ujiji without any conclusive proof that the great White Nile flowed from it.

Burton and Speke, running low on supplies and not fully recovered, headed back to the coast from Ujiji in summer 1858. Returning to Tabora, Speke decided to explore northward on his own, upon hearing reports of an even larger lake. Burton, too ill to continue, instead recuperated at Tabora and undertook an ethnological study of the natives. Six weeks later, Speke returned, claiming he had located the source of the Nile at Lake Victoria, 200 miles to the north. Burton still held to his belief that the Nile flowed from Lake Tanganyika, and the issue became a serious point of contention between them.

On the homeward trip, Burton remained in Aden while Speke continued on to England, arriving two weeks ahead of Burton. Despite a pledge not to reveal his findings until Burton had returned, Speke appeared before the Royal Geographical Society. By the time Burton arrived in England, Speke had received most of the glory and credit for the African expedition. Over the next few years, Burton hotly contested Speke's claim that Lake Victoria was the principal source of the Nile. Their dispute ended in September 1864, when Speke died in an apparent hunting accident on the eve of a public debate with Burton on this issue.

Soon after returning from Africa, Burton married Isabel Arundell. In 1860–61, he visited North America, traveling to Salt Lake City, Utah, where he made a study of the Mormon community, the subject of his 1861 book, *City of the Saints.*

Burton returned to Africa in 1861, beginning four years of service as British consul in the Gulf of Guinea regions of Benin, Dahomey, and Biafra, in what is now Nigeria. In his first year in West Africa, he succeeded in making the first known ascent of Mount Cameroon.

In 1865, Burton was appointed British consul in São Paulo, Brazil. His South American travels included a crossing of the continent.

Burton returned to the Middle East in 1869, serving as a diplomat in Damascus. Starting in 1872, he assumed a similar post at Trieste, then a part of Austria.

In 1877–78, Burton took part in a gold-seeking expedition to Arabia. In 1881–82, he joined VERNEY LOVETT CAMERON in search of gold in what is now Ghana.

In 1886, Burton was knighted by Queen Victoria. He died in Trieste four years later.

Sir Richard Burton *(Library of Congress)*

Sir Richard Burton's efforts to find the source of the Nile ended in controversy. As it turned out, in 1874, HENRY MORTON STANLEY confirmed Speke's claim that Lake Victoria was the principal source of the Nile, although it was subsequently revealed that the Kagera River, which flows into Lake Victoria, is technically the ultimate source. Burton nonetheless played a major role in the exploration of central Africa, undertaking one of the first expeditions to reach the interior from the Indian Ocean coast. He was the first Englishman to visit Mecca, and the first European to travel to Harar, Ethiopia, and live to tell about it. Burton was also an accomplished linguist, having mastered 29 languages and 11 dialects. Furthermore, he was a major literary figure of the 19th century; he published numerous works about the places he explored, as well as a multivolume translation of the *Arabian Nights*.

Button, Sir Thomas (unknown–1634)
English naval officer, explorer in Hudson Bay

Thomas Button was an English naval captain in 1611, when HENRY HUDSON's ship the *Discovery* returned to England following an unsuccessful expedition sponsored by the MUSCOVY COMPANY in search of the NORTHWEST PASSAGE, the fabled all-water route westward across the top of North America to the Pacific Ocean and the Orient. Hudson's men had mutinied and abandoned him to die of exposure in the bay that now bears his name. The mutineers had then brought back to England news of Hudson Strait and the great body of water to the west, actually HUDSON BAY. They reported the existence of tides coming from the western side of the bay, which led many of Hudson's sponsors to believe that the outlet to the fabled Northwest Passage could be found there.

Some of Hudson's former backers then reorganized as the COMPANY OF MERCHANTS OF LONDON DISCOVERERS OF THE NORTHWEST PASSAGE, and hired Button and another captain, by the name of Ingram, to undertake a voyage and retrace Hudson's route. The company was chartered by England's King James I and underwritten in part by geographer RICHARD HAKLUYT. It was hoped that this expedition might find the Northwest Passage and possibly rescue Hudson, whose fate at that time was unknown. Also along on this expedition was ROBERT BYLOT.

Button, in command of the *Resolution*, and Ingram, on Hudson's old ship, the *Discovery*, sailed westward through Hudson Strait, hoping to determine that it led into the Pacific. But the ensuing westward voyage brought them to the northwest shore of Hudson Bay, forcing a course southward.

Button and his men spent the winter of 1612–13 near the mouth of the Nelson River, named in honor of one of the ship's officers who had died on the voyage. This point on the southwestern edge of Hudson Bay in present-day northeastern Manitoba, Canada, would become the site of the important HUDSON'S BAY COMPANY post—York Factory—in 1684.

In spring 1613, Button sailed the *Resolution* northward along the west coast of Hudson Bay, but he soon surmised that it provided no outlet to a western ocean. He explored as far north as Southampton Island at the extreme northwestern corner of Hudson Bay, then set sail for England.

Thomas Button's 1612–13 exploration, and the subsequent expeditions of WILLIAM BAFFIN, JENS MUNK, LUKE FOXE, and THOMAS JAMES, eventually led geographers to conclude that Hudson Bay had no access to the Pacific Ocean. Although Button's voyage yielded neither the Northwest Passage, nor any trace of Henry Hudson, his reports added to the navigational knowledge of Hudson Bay and laid the basis for subsequent voyages.

Bylot, Robert (fl. early 1600s) *English mariner in the Canadian Arctic*

Robert Bylot, an English seafarer of the early 17th century, first appears in history as a crewmember on HENRY HUDSON's last voyage to North America on the *Discovery* in 1610–11, in which HUDSON BAY was explored. After the mutiny and marooning of Hudson and several others in June 1611, Bylot commanded the *Discovery* on its return voyage across the Atlantic Ocean, landing first on the southwest coast of Ireland, then continuing to England. Along with the seven other survivors of the ill-fated voyage, Bylot was subsequently acquitted of any wrongdoing.

Bylot returned to Hudson Bay the following year in another attempt to locate the NORTHWEST PASSAGE, sailing with SIR THOMAS BUTTON on the *Resolution* and spending the winter of 1612–13 on the west shore of Hudson Bay, at the mouth of the Nelson River.

In 1614, Bylot sailed again to the North American coast on the *Discovery*, serving as mate under Captain William Gibbons. During that voyage, the ship reached no farther than a bay on the coast of Labrador. Beset by bad weather there, the expedition was forced to return to England without having undertaken any additional explorations.

In 1615, Bylot commanded the *Discovery* in yet another expedition in search of the Northwest Passage. His pilot and navigator was WILLIAM BAFFIN. In exploring the northern part of Hudson Bay, they attempted to negotiate Frozen Strait near Southampton Island. Unable to find a clear passage, they concluded that the bay did not provide a western outlet with enough sea-room for large sailing ships.

The last recorded voyage undertaken by Bylot was in 1616. Sailing with Baffin on the *Discovery*, he took part in the European discovery of Baffin Bay and Lancaster Sound.

Robert Bylot, along with RICHARD HAKLUYT, was a member of the COMPANY OF MERCHANTS OF LONDON DISCOVERERS OF THE NORTHWEST PASSAGE. As an early Arctic explorer of North America, he took part in five major expeditions in search of the Northwest Passage. Although Bylot and Baffin were unable to navigate Lancaster Sound on their 1616 voyage, it proved, two centuries later, to be the entrance to a seaward route to the BERING STRAIT—the long-sought Northwest Passage.

Byrd, Richard Evelyn (1888–1957) *American naval officer, aviator, polar explorer*

A native of Winchester, Virginia, Richard E. Byrd was the son of one of that state's most prominent families. He attended the Virginia Military Institute, then went on to the United States Naval Academy, graduating as an ensign in 1912.

Byrd briefly left the navy in 1916 due to an ankle injury but returned as a training officer in World War I. In 1917, he underwent training as a naval aviator in Pensacola, Florida.

In the years following World War I, Byrd took an active role in the development of naval aviation. For the proposed navy transatlantic flight of 1919, he prepared fueling stations in Nova Scotia. He subsequently was a liaison between the navy's newly formed Bureau of Aeronautics and the U.S. Congress, and was briefly assigned to duty in England in 1921, where he took part in AIRSHIP test flights.

Byrd's first venture into the polar regions was in 1924–25, when he commanded an airborne squadron attached to Donald MacMillan's expedition to GREENLAND. From the camp established at Etah, Greenland, Byrd navigated an aircraft piloted by American aviator Floyd Bennett in a series of flights over the Greenland ice cap, resulting in the charting of some 30,000 square miles of territory.

The next year, Byrd organized a flight over the NORTH POLE. By this time, he had been promoted to the rank of commander in the U.S. Navy and had become a leading figure in aeronautical exploration of the Arctic. With the financial backing of American auto manufacturer Edsel Ford, Byrd obtained a Fokker monoplane and arrived in Spitsbergen (present-day Svalbard), north of Norway, in April 1926. His ship, the *Chantier,* put in to the harbor at Spitsbergen at the same time that ROALD ENGELBREGT GRAVNING AMUNDSEN, LINCOLN ELLSWORTH, and UMBERTO NOBILE were making preparations for their own flight, by airship, over the North Pole. The presence of the two teams of explorers in Spitsbergen at the same time led to much public speculation about a race to the Pole.

On May 9, 1926, with Bennett as pilot and Byrd in command and navigating, their plane, dubbed the *Josephine,* took off from Spitsbergen. When engine trouble developed en route, Byrd refused to make an emergency landing, and

the mechanical problem resolved itself. After a seven-hour flight, Byrd and Bennett flew over the North Pole, the first men ever to do so. While circling over the top of the world, Byrd threw down the medal worn by ROBERT EDWIN PEARY on his 1909 overland trek to the North Pole. (There is some indication, based on Byrd's diary, that they may have missed the mark, however, making Amundsen, Ellsworth, and Nobile, who passed over the Pole three days later on May 12, the first men to do so.)

In June 1927, shortly after Charles Lindbergh's historic transatlantic aeronautical achievement, Byrd was a crew member on the trimotor *America* in its successful New York–to–Paris flight.

Byrd undertook his first Antarctic exploration in 1928. Traveling by way of NEW ZEALAND, his expedition of 75 men and four aircraft arrived at the Bay of Whales in December of that year. Byrd established Little America, a large base camp not far from where Amundsen had established his Framheim base 18 years earlier. During the next several months, Byrd undertook preliminary explorations from the air, resulting in the mapping of the Rockefeller Mountains. In addition, a geological expedition undertook a survey of the Transantarctic Mountains.

On November 28, 1929, in the late Antarctic spring, Byrd and his flight crew took off from Little America aboard the trimotor aircraft the *Floyd Bennett* (named after Byrd's former partner, who had died in the course of an Arctic search-and-rescue mission in 1928). Byrd was again navigator on this flight; his pilot was Bernt Balchen, who formerly had served with Amundsen in the Arctic. Aerial photographer Ashley McKinley was also on board. From the Bay of Whales, they flew over the Queen Maud Range, seeking a pass southward to the Polar Plateau. To clear the peaks, they were forced to jettison more than 250 pounds of emergency food and survival gear. At 1:15 A.M. on November 29, 1929, Byrd and his crew flew over the SOUTH POLE. With this flight, Byrd became the first man to have flown over both the North and South Poles. What was known as the First Byrd Antarctic Expedition headed back to New York in February 1930. Upon his return, Byrd was promoted to the rank of rear admiral.

During the next three years, Byrd raised financial backing for another assault on the South Polar region. By January 1934, he was back in Little America, where he established a larger base camp. His equipment this time included six tractors and several early snowmobile-type vehicles. There were also four aircraft. This party of 120 men, one of the largest expeditions ever to visit the Antarctic, intended to undertake scientific studies involving physics, biology, geology, and meteorology.

Byrd established a scientific research station in a small hut situated 125 miles inland from Little America. Traveling overland with a convoy of three light Citroën trucks that had been fitted out for the roadless Antarctic interior with

Richard E. Byrd *(New York State Library, Albany)*

caterpillar-type tractor tracks, Byrd arrived at the site on March 28, 1934. Left there alone, Byrd was able to contact the main base of Little America by radio. However, a rescue expedition, if needed, could not reach him until the end of the Antarctic winter season (August in the Northern Hemisphere). After only two months alone at the advance base, Byrd began to suffer from the effects of carbon monoxide poisoning from fumes emitted from a faulty generator. He was in an extremely weakened state when a relief party arrived by tractor on August 10, 1934. Another two months elapsed before he was well enough to be flown back to Little America on the coast.

The Second Byrd Antarctic Expedition yielded much new geographic knowledge, including the location of the Edsel Ford Mountains and Marie Byrd Land. Byrd's aerial explorations of the Ross Ice Shelf revealed for the first time the continental proportions of Antarctica. At the beginning of February 1935, Byrd and his team left Antarctica for the United States.

In 1939, Byrd commanded the United States Antarctic Service Expedition, a large, government-sponsored undertaking initiated to counter German encroachments on Antarctic territory previously claimed by Norway. This was the first U.S. government venture into the Antarctic since CHARLES WILKES's voyage in the late 1830s. Byrd established

two new bases, one at Stonington Island off the Antarctic Peninsula and another near Little America. The expedition was brought to an end in summer 1941 with the U.S. entry into World War II.

Byrd took part in the war in the Pacific, surveying sites for air strips and establishing transpacific air routes that were adopted in the postwar years.

In 1946, Byrd was placed in command of Operation High Jump, which was the largest polar expedition to that time, involving 4,500 men, 19 aircraft, four helicopters, and a naval task force of 13 ships. Extensive aerial reconnaissance of Antarctica was undertaken in 1947–48. Byrd made another flight to the South Pole, passing over previously unexplored regions. A helicopter survey discovered the Bunger Oasis, a series of uncharted lakes.

In preparation for the INTERNATIONAL GEOPHYSICAL YEAR of 1957–58, Byrd was senior adviser to the U.S. Navy's large-scale 1956 expedition to Antarctica: Operation Deep Freeze. In January of that year, he made his third and final flight over the South Pole. He had campaigned for an international treaty of cooperation in regard to Antarctic research and exploration, and his hopes for such an agreement were realized before his death in 1957.

Admiral Richard E. Byrd modernized polar exploration and pioneered American leadership in the exploration of the Antarctic in the 20th century. He has a prominent place in the history of aviation aerial exploration as the first man to fly over both the North and South Poles. As the first man to spend a winter alone in the interior of the Antarctic continent, he is one of the pioneers of modern polar exploration. Byrd's organized aerial exploration of Antarctica conclusively showed that the South Polar landmass was indeed a continent, and not a series of island chains, as had been previously speculated.

Byron, John (1723–1786) *British naval officer in the South Atlantic Ocean and South Pacific Ocean*

John Byron, the son of an aristocratic and titled family, was born on his family's baronial estate, Newstead Abbey, in Nottinghamshire, England. He reportedly first went to sea as a cabin boy in the Royal Navy at the age of eight or nine. In 1740, he sailed as a midshipman on the *Wager* in Commodore GEORGE ANSON's voyage to South America.

Shipwrecked off the coast of Patagonia the following year, the young Byron was held under brutal conditions by Native Americans, who eventually turned him over to Spanish authorities in Chile. Byron was imprisoned briefly by the Spanish, who were at war with Great Britain, then was sent back to Europe on a French vessel. He did not reach England until 1745. His account of his ordeal in South America was published in 1746 and proved an immediate literary success.

Promoted to captain, Byron took part in naval actions in the last years of the War of the Austrian Succession (1740–48). In 1760, during the Seven Years War (1756–63), he commanded British naval vessels in engagements against the French off the coast of New Brunswick and Cape Breton Island, Canada.

By the war's end in 1763, Byron had reached the rank of commodore. In 1764, he was placed in command of a naval expedition assigned to seek out uncharted lands between the CAPE OF GOOD HOPE and CAPE HORN. The onset of a period of international peace provided the British Admiralty with an opportunity to explore the southern reaches of the Atlantic Ocean and Pacific Ocean for Terra Australis, the fabled GREAT SOUTHERN CONTINENT. Geographers at that time speculated that this undiscovered land existed around the southernmost Southern Hemisphere as a counterbalance to the great known landmasses of the Northern Hemisphere. Finding this unknown land was to be Byron's primary objective.

Byron's ship, the *Dolphin,* sailed from Plymouth in June 1764. It was one of the earliest vessels to have a hull sheathed in copper. Accompanying the *Dolphin* was the sloop *Tamar.*

After sailing to Rio de Janeiro by way of Madeira and the Cape Verde Islands, Byron's expedition continued southward to the coast of Patagonia. In the STRAIT OF MAGELLAN, Byron located Port Famine, and, in late 1764, he encountered LOUIS-ANTOINE DE BOUGAINVILLE's ship on its way back from the Falkland Islands. Unaware of the French colony on the Falklands, Byron laid claim to this island group for Great Britain on his subsequent survey of the South Atlantic in January 1765.

By April 1765, Byron and his ships had entered the Pacific Ocean. He sailed westward along a latitude that would have taken him to the east coast of Australia had he not been forced by weather conditions to head northwestward. He sighted several uncharted islands in the Tuamotu Archipelago, including Napuka and Tepoto, bestowing on them the name Disappointment Islands, after he was unable to find a suitable anchorage there. Farther westward, in the Gilbert Islands, he sighted Nukunau, which he named Byron Island. He also explored previously uncharted islands in the Marshall and Mariana chains.

Byron then came upon an archipelago he called the King George Islands. While ashore on one of them, Takaroa, in search of fresh coconuts and scurvy grass, he came upon a portion of a boat left there in 1722 by the Dutch explorer JAKOB ROGGEVEEN in his CIRCUMNAVIGATION OF THE WORLD. Byron eventually reached Formosa (present-day Taiwan) and from there, continued around the world by way of Batavia (present-day Jakarta) and Cape Town, South Africa, reaching England in May 1766.

In 1769, Byron began three years of service as the colonial governor of Newfoundland. He returned to active naval duty in 1775 as a rear admiral. Promoted to vice admiral in 1778, he took part in naval battles against the French in the American Revolution. In 1779, Byron earned the nickname "Foul-Weather Jack," when a convoy under his command, carrying British troops to North America, was beset by the worst Atlantic storms in British naval history. Later that year, he commanded the British fleet in a costly but indecisive naval battle against the French near Grenada in the Caribbean Sea. After that action, he held no other major commands.

Byron was the grandfather of English romantic poet George Gordon, Lord Byron, and the great-great-grandfather of the travel writer Lady ANNE BLUNT. The elder Byron's 1746 book, *Narrative of Great Distresses on the Shores of Patagonia,* was an inspiration for the shipwreck scenes in his grandson's verse work *Don Juan.*

John Byron's 1764–66 voyage was the first purely scientific expedition undertaken by the British navy. His *Account of a Voyage round the World in the Years 1764, 1765, and 1766* was first published in 1767. Great Britain's claim over the Falkland Islands dates back to Byron's explorations. Although he succeeded in adding several islands to the charts of the South Pacific, Byron provided no conclusive proof for the existence or nonexistence of Terra Australis. Over the next 10 years, the Admiralty sent out additional exploring expeditions, including those led by SAMUEL WALLIS, PHILIP CARTERET, and JAMES COOK.

Cabeza de Vaca, Álvar Núñez

(ca. 1490–ca. 1564) *Spanish soldier in the American Southeast and Southwest*

Álvar Núñez Cabeza de Vaca was born to a noble family at Jerez de Frontera in Andalusia, Spain. Early in his life, he embarked on a career in the military, serving in campaigns in Navarre and Italy. In 1513, he entered the service of the duke of Medina Sidonia.

In 1527, Cabeza de Vaca was appointed treasurer of PÁNFILO DE NARVÁEZ's expedition to Florida. In April 1528, the expedition landed at Tampa Bay. Despite Cabeza de Vaca's objections, Narváez sent his fleet northward up Florida's Gulf Coast, planning to rendezvous with them later. Cabeza de Vaca then traveled with Narváez and his 300 men through the Florida Panhandle in a vain search for Indian gold and riches. After several months, they tried to meet up with the ships near Apalachee Bay but failed to find them.

Cabeza de Vaca then supervised the construction of five makeshift barges on which Narváez and his men planned to follow the Gulf Coast to Panuco (present-day Tampico), Mexico. By late 1528, the barges were south of the Mississippi Delta, where they were swept out to sea by the river's current and separated in a storm. Cabeza de Vaca, in command of one of the barges, managed to reach the shore of what was probably Galveston Island, Texas, along with a number of his men. They were joined by other survivors, including two officers of the expedition, Alonso del Castillo

Maldonado and Andrés Dorantes de Carranza, plus Dorantes's Moorish slave ESTEVANICO.

Without food on the island, some of the men resorted to cannibalism. Cabeza de Vaca, stricken with fever, was forced to remain behind when Castillo and Dorantes took the remaining survivors to the Texas mainland. Eventually he regained his strength and followed them. Unable to contact the other Spaniards, he wandered through northeast Texas for the next four years, subsisting through trade with the Indians.

In 1533, Cabeza de Vaca met up with Castillo, Dorantes, and Estevanico at a point on the Colorado River of Texas about 100 miles north of present-day San Antonio, where the Indians gathered annually to feast on the region's harvest of wild pecans. He learned that all of the other members of the Narváez expedition were either dead or enslaved by Indians. The four present were at that time involuntary guests of the Indians, unable to travel freely. Nonetheless, they agreed to meet at the same spot the following summer and attempt to reach a Spanish settlement in Mexico.

In summer 1534, Cabeza de Vaca rejoined the other men as planned. A year later, led by Indian guides, they headed north and west across Texas into present-day New Mexico. Cabeza de Vaca gained a wide reputation as a healer among the tribes of the Southwest by performing Catholic rites over the sick, with some success.

The four men reached the Rio Grande at what is now Rincon, New Mexico, about 60 miles north of present-day

Las Cruces. They crossed the river at this point and turned south into Chihuahua, Mexico. It is thought they entered the desert region of southeastern California before wandering through Sonora, Mexico. They reached the Gulf of California, passed through the Sierra Madre, and finally met up with a Spanish slave-hunting party in north-central Mexico. After a month's rest at Culiacán, Cabeza de Vaca went on to Mexico City, arriving in July 1536.

Cabeza de Vaca reported to Mexico's royal governor, ANTONIO DE MENDOZA, that he had heard reports of Indian cities located north of the region through which he had wandered, prompting the later search for the Seven Cities of CIBOLA. Back in Spain in 1538, he contributed to the official report on the fate of the Narváez expedition. He was asked to join HERNANDO DE SOTO's expedition to Florida, but declined, refusing to be second in command.

In 1540, Cabeza de Vaca was appointed governor of the Río de la Plata colony, present-day Paraguay. In late 1541, he arrived at Santa Catarina, an island off the coast of Brazil, where he obtained additional supplies. Crossing to the South American mainland, he set out for the colonial capital at Asunción, 600 miles inland. He followed northeastern Argentina's Paraná River from its mouth to its confluence with the Iguaçu, where he and his party became the first Europeans to see the spectacular Iguaçu Falls, higher and wider than Niagara Falls. The inland journey to Asunción took over four months. Without Indian trails to follow, his 250-man expedition had to hack their way into the South American interior, as well as construct bridges to cross the numerous bends in the river.

Arriving in Asunción in March 1542, Cabeza de Vaca discovered that the colonists were short on supplies and oppressed by corrupt royal officials. He immediately instituted reforms, which led the officials to conspire against him.

In September 1542, Cabeza de Vaca led 400 Spanish soldiers and about 800 Guaraní Indians in an exploration up the Paraguay River as far as Puerto de los Reyes, were they were forced to turn back, unable to penetrate the dense rainforest.

On returning to Asunción in April 1543, Cabeza de Vaca was imprisoned by his political enemies. Two years later, he was sent back to Spain in chains to face charges of malfeasance in office. Nevertheless, his allies in Asunción managed to smuggle back documents that eventually cleared him of any wrongdoing. He remained in Spain for the rest of his life, serving as a royal magistrate in Seville.

Álvar Núñez Cabeza de Vaca's account of his adventures in North America, entitled *Naufragios* (Shipwrecks), was published in 1542. His eight-year sojourn from Florida to the Gulf of California constituted the first known crossing of the North American continent, predating SIR ALEXANDER MACKENZIE's voyages and the MERIWETHER LEWIS and WILLIAM CLARK expedition by more than 250 years. His re-

ports gave impetus to the subsequent expeditions of Hernando de Soto and FRANCISCO VÁSQUEZ DE CORONADO. In South America, Cabeza de Vaca's explorations increased geographic knowledge about the headwaters of the Río de la Plata.

Cabot, John (Giovanni Caboto)

(ca. 1450–ca. 1499) *Italian spice trader, mariner in North America, in service to England, father of Sebastian Cabot*
John Cabot is believed to have been born Giovanni Caboto in Genoa, Italy, about the middle of the 15th century. By 1461, he had moved with his family to Venice and had become an accomplished navigator, sailing for Venetians in the SPICE TRADE. In this capacity, he made voyages throughout the eastern MEDITERRANEAN SEA and to trade centers in what is now Lebanon, and may have visited Mecca in present-day Saudi Arabia.

The Venetian merchants in the spice trade obtained pepper, nutmeg, and cloves—items essential in Europe for the preservation of meat—from caravans that traveled across Asia. Cabot claimed that while in Mecca he learned that the spices originated in eastern Asia. He theorized that if a direct route to Asia could be found, higher profits could be realized by circumventing Arab middlemen.

By 1476, Cabot had become a naturalized Venetian citizen. During this period, CLAUDIUS PTOLEMY's *Geographia* was translated into Latin and published in Europe, reviving the theory that the world was round and that Asia could be reached on a westward crossing of the Atlantic Ocean. During the 1480s, Cabot tried to obtain backing for an expedition across the Atlantic Ocean to China, then known as Cathay, in order to establish a direct all-water route to the markets of the Far East. He first went to Valencia, where he attempted to gain the support of Spanish king Ferdinand at the same time CHRISTOPHER COLUMBUS was seeking sponsorship for a similar enterprise. Cabot is thought to have been in Barcelona in 1493, when Columbus made his triumphant return with news of his reaching what was then believed to be the outlying islands of the Indies.

Cabot journeyed to England in 1494 to seek the support of King Henry VII. Also in 1494, sovereignty over the newly explored lands in the Western Hemisphere was divided between Spain and Portugal under the terms of the Treaty of Tordesillas, following the bull of Pope Alexander VI in 1493. King Henry VII of England, in defiance of this proclamation, granted Cabot royal patents to explore westward across the Atlantic, as well as a trade monopoly on any new lands or routes to Asia that he might locate.

Cabot had at this time settled in Bristol, one of England's principal seaports, whose merchants had for years been involved with the trade in fish between Iceland and the Iberian Peninsula. Bristol merchants were forced to pay the highest prices for spices, which they obtained through mid-dlemen in the Middle East and Venice. Seeking to circumvent the Scandinavians in the fish trade and the Venetians in the spice trade, a syndicate of merchants provided financing for Cabot's proposed expedition across the Atlantic, presumably to Asia.

On May 20, 1497, John Cabot set sail aboard the ship the *Mathew* with a crew of 18 men, probably including one of his three sons, SEBASTIAN CABOT. They put in first at Dorsey Island on the southwest coast of Ireland, then sailed westward, maintaining a course between latitudes 50 and 51 degrees, the approximate latitude of Bristol. Cabot successfully navigated due west across the Atlantic, reaching the coast of North America on June 24, 1497.

The precise location of Cabot's landfall is uncertain. If he did in fact follow a course due west from Bristol, it is likely that he reached the shores of either northern Newfoundland or Cape Breton Island in what is now Nova Scotia. During his brief visit ashore, he encountered no people, but did see tools, fishing nets, and the remains of a settlement. He may have also explored southwestern GREENLAND.

Cabot sailed the *Mathew* around the east coast of Newfoundland, possibly as far south as present-day Maine. He soon headed back to England, with a brief stopover in Brittany, France. He reached Bristol in early August, with the news that he had reached China and the lands of the Great Khan. Later that month, he met with King Henry VII, who rewarded him with a sum of money and an annuity for his accomplishments. A second, larger expedition across the Atlantic was soon planned.

With five ships and 200 men, Cabot again sailed from Bristol in May 1498. His objective on this journey was to reach the island of "CIPANGU," presumably present-day Japan, where Cabot believed the spices originated. One of the ships developed trouble and was forced to put in on the west coast of Ireland; the four remaining ships sailed westward with Cabot. Nothing is known for certain of the results of this voyage. Some accounts say that Cabot and his crew were lost at sea; others relate that he reached the North American mainland and explored as far south as Chesapeake Bay, then returned to England, and, having failed to establish a new route to Asia, died in obscurity.

In any event, John Cabot's voyages, along with those of Christopher Columbus in the WEST INDIES and PEDRO ÁLVARS CABRAL in South America, enabled 16th-century geographers to understand that a large continent lay between Europe and Asia and contributed to the first published maps of the Americas, produced by JUAN DE LA COSA, AMERIGO VESPUCCI, and MARTIN WALDSEEMÜLLER. America, considered to have been named in honor of Amerigo Vespucci, may actually have been named after one of Cabot's original Bristol backers, a merchant named Richard Amerike. Al-though Cabot returned from his first voyage with no treasures from the Orient, he did bring back a quantity of cod, which he reported to be in abundance in the waters off the islands of northeastern North America. His report brought about soon afterward an influx of European fishing fleets to the Grand Banks region off the Canadian coast. Cabot's explorations also inspired attempts to find the fabled NORTHWEST PASSAGE across the top of North America to Asia. The voyages of GASPAR CÔRTE-REAL and MIGUEL CÔRTE-REAL to Labrador followed in the early 1500s. One of them took back to Europe Beothuk Indians in possession of a gold sword and other items made in Venice and believed to have been left behind by Cabot's crew. The body of water lying between Cape Breton Island and Newfoundland, although never explored by Cabot, was later named Cabot Strait in his honor. His son Sebastian went on to undertake numerous expeditions to both North and South America.

Cabot, Sebastian (ca. 1475–1557) *Italian mariner in the Americas in service to England and Spain, cartographer, merchant, sponsor of expeditions in search of Northeast Passage, son of John Cabot*

Sebastian Cabot was born in Venice, the son of explorer and navigator JOHN CABOT. He may have accompanied his father on at least one of his two voyages to North America in 1497–98. In 1500, the younger Cabot reportedly undertook a voyage of exploration from the English port of Bristol to the coast of what is now Nova Scotia.

In 1509, Cabot, with the sponsorship of Bristol merchants, again sailed the Atlantic Ocean to the northeast coast of North America. By that time, the explorations of his father, as well as those of CHRISTOPHER COLUMBUS, had been documented in maps published by MARTIN WALDSEEMÜLLER, indicating a large continuous landmass between Europe and the Far East. Cabot's 1509 voyage westward from Bristol was an attempt to find a water route north of the newly explored continent, one of the earliest attempts to seek the fabled NORTHWEST PASSAGE.

During the expedition, Cabot, sailing along the coast, may have entered Hudson Strait and the eastern portion of HUDSON BAY. According to his own account, he believed this arm of the Atlantic Ocean to be the Pacific Ocean, but he was forced to turn around because of a threatened mutiny. On the return voyage, Cabot first sailed southward along the coast and reported sighting Newfoundland, Nova Scotia, and Long Island.

In 1512, Cabot was appointed chief cartographer to the court of Henry VIII of England. After several more years in England, he sought sponsorship from the Spanish Crown for additional exploring expeditions. In about 1518, he was named chief pilot to the court of Charles I, king of Spain and emperor of the Holy Roman Empire (as Charles V).

By 1522, the news of the successful CIRCUMNAVIGATION OF THE WORLD by FERDINAND MAGELLAN had reached Spain, and it was now firmly established that the Orient could be reached via an all-water route around the tip of South America. In 1525, Cabot was commissioned captain general of a large Spanish expedition to the EAST INDIES. He was to travel to the SPICE ISLANDS (the Moluccas) of present-day Indonesia and seek the legendary land of OPHIR; he was also assigned to make astronomical observations and undertake a geographic survey of the South American coast.

In April 1526, Cabot sailed with a fleet of four ships, carrying 200 soldiers and colonists, from the Spanish port of Sanlúcar de Barrameda, south of Seville. He headed southward to the Cape Verde Islands off the west coast of Africa. From there, his ships turned southwestward and reached the port of Recife, Brazil, in September 1526. While exploring the southeast coast of Brazil, he located the island of Santa Catarina, which he named in honor of his wife.

Cabot also landed in the estuary of the Río de la Plata near present-day Buenos Aires, where he encountered sur-

John Cabot and Sebastian Cabot in North America *(Library of Congress)*

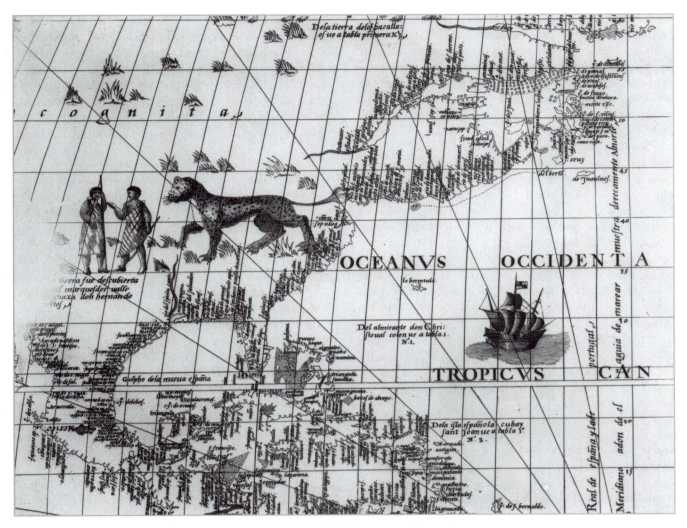

Detail of map of eastern North America by Sebastian Cabot (1544) *(Library of Congress)*

vivors of the JUAN DÍAZ DE SOLÍS expedition of 1515–16, who had heard reports of a "White King" with a domain rich with gold and silver. (ALEJO GARCÍA was the individual most associated with the reports.) Cabot had been directed by the Spanish Crown to survey the boundary line between Spanish and Portuguese territory in South America established by the 1494 Treaty of Tordesillas, then proceed southward around CAPE HORN to the East Indies. The lure of riches in the interior of South America led Cabot to abandon his plans to go to the Orient. Instead, he spent the next three years exploring the inland waterways of the Paraguay and Barmejo Rivers of present-day Argentina, Uruguay, Paraguay, and Brazil. He found little gold but explored the Paraná River to the Apipe Rapids, and possibly as far as the site of Asunción, Paraguay.

In 1528–29, one of Cabot's lieutenants, Francisco César, led an advance expedition deep into the interior and reached the foothills of the ANDES MOUNTAINS. He re-turned with samples of gold, probably from the kingdom of the Inca, further inspiring Cabot to search for a fabled wealthy kingdom. The city of LOS CÉSARES, named after César, became a persistent legend from this time. The concept of EL DORADO also grew out of such reports. During this period, Cabot established the colony of San Espíritu on the Paraná River. Soon after his departure for Spain in 1529, however, the settlement, which was peopled by colonists originally headed for the Moluccas, was wiped out by Timbu tribesmen.

Cabot returned to Spain in 1530, resuming his duties as chief pilot, a position previously held by AMERIGO VESPUCCI and Díaz de Sólis. He remained in service to Spain until the late 1540s, at which time he returned to England. He now sought the backing of London merchants for trade expeditions to northern Russia. He also intended to locate a NORTHEAST PASSAGE to the Orient across the top of Europe and Asia.

In 1551, Cabot was appointed first governor of the London-based MUSCOVY COMPANY. Between 1553 and 1556, he organized and financed expeditions into regions northeast of Scandinavia. Explorers such as SIR HUGH WILLOUGHBY and RICHARD CHANCELLOR sailed under his sponsorship. In 1556, well into his eighties, Sebastian Cabot sponsored STEPHEN BOROUGH's expedition from England to the White Sea on the Arctic coast of European Russia.

Sebastian Cabot's reputation as an explorer was for a time tarnished with accusations that he attempted to claim for himself the accomplishments of his father. Yet his own explorations in both North and South America provided Europeans with their first clear idea of the extent of the new lands. His early expeditions initiated a search for the Northwest Passage that would persist for more than 400 years, into the age of nuclear-powered icebreakers and submarines. In South America, Cabot's explorations of the inland waterways of the Río de la Plata and other rivers led to the rapid colonization of these regions by Spain and Portugal. His later efforts to find a Northeast Passage led to increased trade to the northern ports of Russia and broke the trade monopoly of the North Sea and Baltic Sea cities of the HANSEATIC LEAGUE. Along with HENRY HUDSON, he was one of the few early explorers to seek both the Northwest and the Northeast Passage.

Cabral, Gonçalo Velho (ca. 1386–ca. 1447)
Portuguese colonist in the Azores

Gonçalo Cabral, a Portuguese nobleman, was an associate of HENRY THE NAVIGATOR, prince of Portugal, working at his navigational study center at Sagres in southwestern Portugal. In the early 15th century, the Isles of SAINT BRENDAN appeared as real places on Catalan maps used by Henry and other geographers at Sagres. In 1431, Cabral was sent by the Portuguese prince to investigate these islands, which were believed to lie several hundred miles southwest of Portugal.

On his first attempt, in 1431, Cabral reached as far as the Formigas Rocks in the Atlantic Ocean, only about 25 miles east of his destination. In the course of a voyage the next year, he located and named Santa Maria; on a subsequent voyage, he came upon a second island, Sao Miguel. Soon afterward, he reached a third island, Terceira. It was Prince Henry who named the island group, giving them the Portuguese designation Ilhas dos Acores ("Isles of the Hawks"), known in English as the AZORES.

Given dominion over the Azores, Cabral undertook to colonize them, bringing in settlers from Portugal as well as Flemings from the Low Countries. Over the next century, the Azores became an agricultural center, as well as an important stopover point for early Atlantic crossings.

Although the Azores had been known to Portuguese mariners as early as 1427, Gonçalo Cabral is generally rec-

ognized as having made the first accurate sighting of them, and it was his voyages that led to their initial colonization. In the decades that followed, most Portuguese exploration concentrated on following the African coastline to India. Nevertheless, Cabral's reports of the Azores instilled in the minds of Portuguese and other European explorers the idea that additional new and fertile lands lay west of Europe across the Atlantic.

Cabral, João (1599–1669) *Portuguese missionary in India and Tibet*

João Cabral was a Portuguese Jesuit who arrived at the Ganges Delta, near the site of present-day Calcutta, India, in 1626, along with fellow Jesuit ESTEVÃO CACELLA. The purpose of their intended journey was to introduce Christianity to Tibet.

Cabral and Cacella traveled northeastward into the Brahmaputra River region and headed westward to Cooch Behar. From there, they headed northward into Bhutan and traversed the HIMALAYAS and entered into Tibet. At the Tibetan town of Shigatse, they established a Christian mission.

Soon after founding the Shigatse mission, Cacella undertook a trip along the Himalayas in an attempt to visit another mission at Tsaparang, while Cabral headed back to India for supplies. Cabral followed a route that took him through Katmandu in Nepal, then traveled eastward back to Cooch Behar. There, he met up with Cacella, who had been unable to reach his destination.

Cabral was back at the Shigatse mission in 1631, but he remained for only a year before being transferred back to India. Cacella died in Tibet after contracting an illness.

João Cabral was among the handful of Jesuit missionaries who kept alive links with remote Tibet during the 17th century. His work, along with that of fellow Jesuits ANTONIO DE ANDRADE and FRANCISCO DE AZEVADO, carried on a tradition of Western religious contacts with Tibetan Buddhists.

Cabral, Pedro Álvars (Pedro Álvares Cabral, Pedralvarez Cabral, Pedro Álvarez de Cabral)
(ca. 1467–ca. 1520) *Portuguese mariner in Brazil and India*

Pedro Cabral was a native of Belmonte in east-central Portugal. His family's close ties to the Portuguese monarchy led, in 1483, to his appointment as a page to the court of King John II.

After 1495, Cabral continued his career at court under Manuel I. In 1499, soon after VASCO DA GAMA's return from his successful voyage around the CAPE OF GOOD HOPE, Manuel chose Cabral to command a large trading fleet in a follow-up voyage to India. Cabral had been appointed an admiral, although more for his diplomatic and commercial ability than for his nautical experience. In charge of part of the fleet was BARTOLOMEU DIAS, the Portuguese navigator who, in 1487, had determined Africa's southernmost point and rounded the Cape of Good Hope.

Cabral's 13 ships sailed from Lisbon in March 1500, carrying more than 1,200 men, including merchants, soldiers, and Franciscan missionaries, as well as a number of convicts. Sailing southward from Portugal, they stopped at the CANARY ISLANDS, then proceeded toward the Cape Verde Islands. Although earlier Portuguese navigators, including Dias, had closely followed the coastline of Africa in their search for a route to India, Cabral acted on da Gama's advice to sail due south from the Cape Verdes, away from the African continent, thus avoiding unfavorable winds in the Gulf of Guinea. He planned on taking advantage of strong westerly winds at a point south and west of the African mainland to carry his fleet around the Cape of Good Hope and into the Indian Ocean.

Sailing farther southwest than any other European navigator had yet ventured, Cabral's fleet neared the coast of Brazil and, on April 22, 1500, sighted the South American mainland at about 17° south latitude. They anchored off the coast of present-day Caravelas, within sight of Mount Pascoal, about midway between Salvador to the north and pre-

sent-day Rio de Janeiro to the south. Four days later, at Port Seguro, Cabral went ashore and took formal possession of the new land for Portugal, calling it Terra da Vera Cruz (land of the true cross), despite his uncertainty concerning whether he had discovered an island or a continent.

Cabral's men undertook a brief exploration inland, coming into contact with the region's Tupinanba Indians. News of his accomplishment was immediately sent back to Portugal on one of the ships. Two of the convicts were left on the Brazilian mainland, with instructions to learn what they could about the land; it is believed that they fell victim to cannibalistic natives soon after Cabral's departure on May 2, 1500.

Ten days after setting out from Brazil, the Portuguese sighted a comet that many took as an omen of troubles yet to come. Approaching the Cape of Good Hope from the west, the ships were caught in a severe storm. Four of them went down with all hands, Dias among them. Another ship was lost and did not rejoin the fleet until the following year. With his few remaining vessels, Cabral made his way around the Cape of Good Hope and northward along the east coast of Africa, stopping at Kilwa and Malindi, before heading northeastward across the Arabian Sea to India's Malabar Coast.

At the Indian port city of Calicut, Cabral attempted to establish a Portuguese trading post. Arab traders, resentful of any European encroachment, incited an attack on Cabral's settlement. In response, Cabral attacked and destroyed 10 Arab trading vessels, massacred their crews, and bombarded the city of Calicut. He then headed 120 miles southward along the Malabar Coast to the friendlier port of Cochin, where he became the first European to purchase spices and other valuable items directly from Eastern merchants.

On the return voyage to Portugal, at the Cape Verde Islands, Cabral met up with AMERIGO VESPUCCI's expedition, which had set out to investigate Cabral's earlier claims on Brazil. He was also rejoined by the ship separated in the storms off the cape. Commanded by Diogo Dias, brother of Bartolomeu Dias, it had returned from a visit to Madagascar.

Cabral returned to Portugal in July 1501. In the course of the voyage to India, he had lost more than half of his ships and nearly 900 of his original 1,200 men. Nevertheless, the profitable cargo he brought back from India, in addition to the news of his exploration of Brazil, soon earned him command of Portugal's next major trading venture. Before he could set out, however, the king replaced him with da Gama.

Cabral is not known to have taken part in any subsequent voyages. He settled at Santarém, Portugal, marrying the well-connected and wealthy Dona Isabel da Castro in 1503.

Pedro Cabral's Terra da Vera Cruz became known to later geographers as Brazil, after a type of wood found

Pedro Cabral (Library of Congress)

there, much valued as a source of red dye. Brazil had also been the name of a fabled mid-Atlantic island which had appeared in medieval maps since the days of SAINT BRENDAN. Although he is generally considered the European discoverer of Brazil, Cabral was not the first explorer to sight the Brazilian mainland, having been preceded by less than a year by Spanish mariners, including ALONSO DE OJEDA and VICENTE YÁÑEZ PINZÓN. Nevertheless, Cabral had sailed into an area where no land had been anticipated, while his predecessors had explored the extensions of known coastlines. As the European discoverer of Brazil, Cabral provided Portugal with its only significant territorial claim in the Western Hemisphere, an outcome of the division of the New World agreed to by Spain and Portugal under the terms of the Treaty of Tordesillas of 1494. Cabral also achieved the main objective of his 1500–1501 voyage by establishing trade with India and breaking the monopoly on the European SPICE TRADE with the Orient exercised by the Arabs and the Venetians in the eastern Mediterranean. Cabral's reports of new lands west of Africa led to the 1501–02 voyage of Vespucci, who ultimately determined that the Americas were in fact continents and not part of the Far East.

Cabrillo, Juan Rodríguez (João Rodrigues Cabrilho) (ca. 1500–1543) *Portuguese mariner on the California coast, in service to Spain*

Juan Cabrillo, originally from Portugal, entered the service of Spain sometime before 1520. That year, he took part in the Spanish conquest of the Aztec in Mexico under the command of PÁNFILO DE NARVÁEZ. Three years later, he served under PEDRO DE ALVARADO in the conquest of what is now Guatemala and El Salvador.

Cabrillo remained in Guatemala as an assistant to Alvarado, who had been named the colony's captain general. In 1540, Alvarado was commissioned to lead an expedition to the SPICE ISLANDS (the Moluccas), a key source of spices in what is now Indonesia. His fleet of 13 ships landed at Navidad, a port on the central Pacific coast of Mexico south of present-day Guadalajara, in 1540. Because of reports of the fabled Seven Cities of CIBOLA from explorers MARCOS DE NIZA and ÁLVAR NÚÑEZ CABEZA DE VACA, however, ANTONIO DE MENDOZA, the Mexican governor, directed Alvarado to undertake a side exploration of the coast north of Baja California, in the hope of finding a seaward route to Cibola and the riches it promised. He also was to search for the fabled STRAIT OF ANIAN, which was thought to lead from the Pacific Ocean to the Atlantic Ocean. Alvarado was diverted from the expedition because of an Indian uprising—the Mixtón War—in the vicinity of Guadalajara. After Alvarado's death during a retreat, Cabrillo was placed in command of the expedition northward.

Cabrillo sailed from Navidad on June 27, 1542, in command of two ships, the *San Salvador* and the *Victoria*. He headed along the west coast of Mexico, rounded the tip of Baja California, then continued along the coast beyond Cabo del Engaño (Cape Deceit). An earlier expedition, led by FRANCISCO DE ULLOA, had attempted to explore beyond this point in 1539–40, but had never returned to Mexico.

After about a week at sea, Cabrillo and his men sighted the mainland of what is now southern California and, in September 1542, they became the first Europeans to explore San Diego Bay, which Cabrillo originally named San Miguel. Cabrillo sent a small party ashore to explore inland. The Spaniards managed to survey some of the territory around present-day San Diego despite an Indian attack.

Cabrillo directed his ships along the California coast, visiting Santa Monica and San Pedro Bays, as well as Santa Catalina and San Miguel Islands. In his account, Cabrillo noted the dense Indian population along the coast; the number of campfires sighted on the shore near San Pedro Bay led him to name it Bahía de los Fumos (Bay of Fires). The expedition made landings to explore the inland regions, encountering Native Americans of various tribes, all of them friendly. The expedition continued to Monterey Bay and in November 1542, eventually reached Point Reyes and explored what came to be known as Drake's Bay.

Severe weather forced Cabrillo's return southward to Monterey Bay. The expedition then landed at San Miguel Island for the winter; Cabrillo suffered a fall and developed a fatal infection, dying on January 3, 1543.

Command was assumed by Cabrillo's chief pilot, BARTOLOMÉ FERRELO. The expedition departed San Miguel in February 1543, again sailing northward along the California coast. Ferrelo is thought to have reached the coast of present-day Oregon near the mouth of the Rogue River, or possibly even the COLUMBIA RIVER, before returning to Mexico in April.

Juan Cabrillo's voyage was the first European exploration along the California coast.

Cacella, Estevão (1585–1630) *Portuguese missionary in India and Tibet*

Estevão Cacella was a Portuguese Jesuit who traveled to India as a missionary in 1626 with JOÃO CABRAL. The two priests traveled from Cooch Behar, near what is now Calcutta, up the GANGES RIVER and into Bhutan, then crossed the HIMALAYAS, and entered Tibet.

After establishing a mission at Shigatse, Cacella undertook a journey along the northern side of the Himalayas to the mission at Tsaparang, which had been established in 1625 by ANTONIO DE ANDRADE. Cabral had meanwhile returned to India for additional supplies.

Severe snowstorms led Cacella to abandon his attempt to negotiate the northern slopes of the Himalayas. He made his way south to India, rejoining Cabral at the village of Cooch Behar.

Cacella returned to Tibet in February 1630. Having become seriously ill in the course of the seven-month journey, he soon died.

Estevão Cacella, with other Jesuit missionaries of the 16th and 17th centuries, helped maintain what little contact there was between Europe and Tibet.

Cadamosto, Alvise da (Alvise Ca'da Mosto, Luigi da Cadamosto, Luigi da Cada Mosto) (1432–1488)
Italian mariner along coastal Africa, in service to Portugal
Alvise da Cadamosto, from a Venetian noble family, embarked on a seafaring career. By the early 1450s, he was engaged in the maritime trade between Italy and the Flemish ports on the coast of what is now Belgium.

In 1454, a storm drove Cadamosto's ship ashore on the coast of Portugal. News of the arrival of the experienced Venetian mariner reached HENRY THE NAVIGATOR, prince of Portugal, who had been sponsoring explorations in search of a sea route to the Orient. Henry soon met with Cadamosto and persuaded him to undertake a series of voyages along the west coast of Africa in order to establish trade contacts with tribes of the sub-Saharan region, beyond the control of the Muslim nations to the north.

Cadamosto, equipped by Henry with a ship, crew, and supplies, sailed on his first voyage under the Portuguese flag in 1455. He had been instructed to learn what he could about the inland trade between TIMBUKTU and the African coast, especially in regard to spices, gold, and slaves. Accompanying Cadamosto was Portuguese seafarer Vincent Dias. After stops at the CANARY ISLANDS and Madeira, they headed for Cape Blanco and the coast of Mauritania, where Cadamosto investigated the trade practices of the natives, later reporting on the commerce in salt and gold between the coastal peoples and inland peoples.

Cadamosto continued southward along Africa's west coast, reaching as far as the continent's westernmost point, Cape Verde, then explored up the Senegal River about 60 miles. There he met with the local ruler, an African Muslim named Budomel, staying on as a guest for a month. On his return to the mouth of the Senegal River, he was joined by another Italian navigator in service to Portugal, Antoniotto Usodimare, of Genoa. With Usodimare, Cadamosto sailed to the mouth of the Gambia River.

Having reached about 13° south latitude, farther south than any European mariner had been to that time, he noted how low the NORTH STAR was over the horizon, an indication that he was approaching the EQUATOR. He soon became the first known European to observe and identify the Southern Cross, a constellation visible only near or south of the equator. While attempting to explore up the Gambia River, Cadamosto's ship was attacked by native warriors in canoes and forced to withdraw to the open sea. Soon afterward, he sailed back to Portugal.

The next year, 1456, Cadamosto embarked on his second expedition for Prince Henry. Again joined by Usodimare, he commanded a fleet of three ships. After sailing southward to Cape Verde, they proceeded westward. Relying on basic navigational instruments, they sailed 320 miles out of sight of land until they came upon a group of uncharted islands. Cadamosto named them the Cape Verde Islands and claimed them for Portugal. On the return trip to Portugal, he explored the coast of what is now Guinea-Bissau, where he made the European discovery of the Bijagos Islands.

Alvise da Cadamosto returned to his native Venice in 1463. Although the Portuguese were highly secretive about their geographic discoveries, he produced an eyewitness account of early European exploration of Africa. Published posthumously in Italy in 1507, it provided details of tribal customs, as well as descriptions of animal and plant life Cadamosto observed in his travels, including the earliest account of the hippopotamus. Sailing in sturdy lateen-rigged CARAVEL ships, he made some of the earliest extended voyages out of sight of land, preceding the later expeditions of Italian-born explorers CHRISTOPHER COLUMBUS, JOHN CABOT, and AMERIGO VESPUCCI. Like Cadamosto, they also carried out explorations in the service of a country other than their own.

Cadillac, Sieur de   See LA MOTHE, ANTOINE LAUMET.

Caesar, Gaius Julius (100–44 B.C.) *Roman general, statesman in northern Europe*
Julius Caesar was born into one of the Roman Republic's most prominent patrician families. Through family connections and his marriage to the daughter of the powerful Lucius Cornelius Cinna, he rose politically in Roman society and achieved a position as one of Rome's chief military leaders.

Caesar led an invasion into Gaul (present-day France and Belgium) in 58–56 B.C., extending Roman influence northward from the MEDITERRANEAN SEA. He remained active in the region over the next years, leading to Roman domination of the Gallic tribes and extensive road building.

To link Italy with newly acquired Gaul, Caesar established a route through the Alps by way of the 8,000-foot-high Great St. Bernard Pass, providing northern Italy with overland access to the Upper Rhone Valley and the Lake Geneva region of present-day Switzerland.

Caesar also undertook an invasion of the island of Britain, landing with two Roman legions at present-day Dover in 55. The next year, he landed five more legions from Rome. While the Roman subjugation of Britain was not completed until the next century, Caesar's campaign was the first recorded contact between Mediterranean peoples and those of the British Isles since PYTHEAS in the fourth century B.C. In his brief sojourn there, Caesar undertook astronomical studies on the length of days in the higher latitudes. He subsequently reported on Britain's geographic location relative to the rest of the Roman provinces, erroneously placing it east of the known region of Spain.

Caesar returned to Italy in 49. He became embroiled in a power struggle with Roman leader Pompey, but achieved victory in the ensuing civil war. A group of senators, fearful of his influence and power over the Roman people, assassinated Caesar in the senate building in Rome on March 15, 44 B.C.

Julius Caesar extended the scope of classical civilization as far as the Atlantic coasts of present-day France and England, providing the Romans with the first accurate accounts of those regions.

Caillié, René-Auguste (René-Auguste Caillé)

(1799–1838) *French explorer in West Africa*

René-Auguste Caillié was a native of Mauze in western France's Deux-Sévres region. Coming from a family of modest means, he had little formal education. While he was still very young, his family fell into disgrace when his father, the village baker, was jailed for larceny.

By his mid-teens, Caillié had been drawn to the idea of exploring Africa, his interest reportedly sparked by the great expanses of territory marked "unknown" on contemporary maps of that continent. In 1816, at the age of 17, he ran away to the nearby port of Rochefort and signed on as a cabin boy on a ship headed for the African west coast. Caillié jumped ship in Senegal, where he joined a British expedition, led by a Major Gray, in search of news of MUNGO PARK, who had disappeared 10 years earlier along the NIGER RIVER. On his first venture to Africa, Caillié made several trips between the Senegalese coastal settlements of Dakar and St. Louis, and explored along the lower Senegal River. After less than a year, he was stricken with tropical fever, becoming so ill that he had to return to France.

Caillié remained in France for the next seven years, saving his money and preparing for another trip to Africa. He had determined that posing as an Arab traveler was the only effective way to explore the interior.

In 1824, Caillié returned to Senegal. He traveled to the desert region of Mauritania and lived for a year among the Braknas tribe, who taught him the Arabic language and Islamic ritual.

In 1825, having been refused financial support by the French colonial governor of Senegal for a proposed expedition to the Niger River and TIMBUKTU, Caillié traveled to the British colony in Sierra Leone, where he found employment as superintendent of an indigo plantation. Learning that the Geographical Society of Paris was offering a prize of 10,000 francs to anyone who could reach Timbuktu and return to Europe with a description of the fabled metropolis in the desert, he organized an expedition.

In March 1827, Caillié embarked from Freetown, Sierra Leone, and, after a short voyage along the coast, reached Conakry in present-day Guinea. He headed inland, traveling alone across the desert to the foothills of the Fouta Djallon Range and the upper reaches of the Senegal River. Arriving at Tieme in August 1827, he was stricken with SCURVY, which laid him up for four months. He resumed his journey in January 1828, reaching the upper Niger River Valley at Kouroussa. Pretending to be an Egyptian Arab returning to his homeland from France, Caillié descended the Niger River on a large trading CANOE. He arrived at Kabara, the port of Timbuktu, in late April 1828.

In Timbuktu, Caillié was struck by how the actual city, an austere trading settlement in the desert, differed from the fabled magnificence described by the 16th-century historian LEO AFRICANUS and other early travelers. Caillié remained there for two weeks, during which he learned that another European, the Scotsman ALEXANDER GORDON LAING, had reached the city in 1826, but had been murdered by his Muslim guide soon after their departure. On May 4, 1828, Caillié left Timbuktu, traveling northward across the SAHARA DESERT with a slave caravan. He crossed the Great Atlas Mountains, reaching the MEDITERRANEAN SEA at Tangier, where he secured passage back to France.

The Geographical Society of Paris awarded Caillié the cash prize; he was further honored with admission to the Legion of Honor. Nevertheless, some critics, especially those in England, doubted Caillié's claim of having reached Timbuktu, principally because his realistic descriptions did not live up to the expectations fueled by earlier legendary accounts. Granted a pension by the French government, Caillié retired in France. While in Africa, he had developed tuberculosis, and he succumbed to this illness in 1838.

Although René-Auguste Caillié brought back no new geographic information concerning the course of the Niger River, a mystery that puzzled European geographers until the middle of the 19th century, his three-volume account, published in 1830, provided the first accurate description of Timbuktu. His last journey in Africa had taken him across 4,500 miles of territory, most of which at that time was unknown to Europeans. Doubts about his accomplishments were put to rest in the 1850s after German explorer HEINRICH BARTH's expedition to Timbuktu confirmed Caillie's findings.

Cam, Diego See CÃO, DIOGO.

Cameron, Verney Lovett (1844–1894)
British naval officer in central Africa

Verney Lovett Cameron, the son of a clergyman, was born in Radipole, Dorsetshire, on England's south coast. At the age of 13, he entered the British navy as a midshipman, and, over the next 10 years, he saw active service in the Indian Ocean, taking part in British efforts to stem the SLAVE TRADE. In 1868, he participated in a British military expedition against Ethiopia.

Promoted to lieutenant by 1870, Cameron returned to England, where he was stationed at the naval base at Sheerness, off the coast of Kent. That year, he offered his services to the ROYAL GEOGRAPHICAL SOCIETY, proposing to lead an expedition into East Africa in search of the missing missionary and explorer, DAVID LIVINGSTONE.

Cameron's initial offer was turned down; soon afterward, in 1871, American journalist SIR HENRY MORTON STANLEY succeeded in locating Livingstone. Nonetheless, the following year, the Royal Geographical Society organized an expedition to take supplies to Livingstone, who had remained in Africa, and appointed Cameron to lead it, directing him also to undertake an exploration of the region around Lake Tanganyika.

Cameron, in command of the Livingstone East Coast Expedition, headed into the interior of what is now Tanzania in late March 1873. Starting out from Bagamoyo, an Indian Ocean port city opposite Zanzibar, he traveled with W. E. Dillon, a British naval surgeon; Lieutenant Cecil Murphy, a British army artillery officer; and Robert Moffat, Livingstone's nephew.

After a 500-mile trek inland, Cameron and his party reached Tabora. In late October 1873, they received word that Livingstone had died; a few days later, Livingstone's body was brought to Tabora. Moffat by then had died, and Dillon and Murphy decided to head back to England.

Undaunted, Cameron stayed on to explore Africa. Proceeding farther westward, he reached Ujiji on Lake Tanganyika. He undertook an extensive exploration of this vast inland body of water, Africa's second largest lake, and subsequently produced the first detailed map of it. His survey revealed that 96 rivers flowed into the lake. He also made the European discovery of the Lukuga River, the only river flowing out of it.

In Ujiji, Cameron arranged to have Livingstone's personal belongings and journals shipped back to England, then headed into the region east of Lake Tanganyika. He soon reached Nyangwe, a slave trading center on the Lualaba River. He determined that the Lualaba could not be a tributary of the NILE RIVER, as many geographers believed at that time. Using a barometer to determine altitude, he concluded that this river, at a much lower elevation than the Nile to the north, and with a much greater volume of water than was found in the upper Nile, was more likely a tributary to Africa's other great river, the CONGO RIVER, now known as the Zaire.

Hostile Arab slavers made it impossible for Cameron to hire canoes and native bearers to explore the Lualaba northward and find out if it did indeed join the Congo as he believed. Instead, he set out on a southwestward journey across the watershed between the Congo and the ZAMBEZI RIVER. Traveling overland by way of Kabambare, he crossed present-day Zaire and reached the Atlantic coast of Africa in northern Angola, arriving on November 7, 1875.

Upon his return to England the following April, Cameron was proclaimed the first European to have traversed tropical Africa from the Indian Ocean to the Atlantic coast and was awarded the Founder's Medal by the Royal Geographical Society. He recounted his experience in his 1877 book *Across Africa.*

In the early 1880s, Cameron returned to Africa, joining SIR RICHARD FRANCIS BURTON in an expedition to present-day Ghana, in search of mineral wealth. With Burton, he coauthored an account of this adventure, *To the Gold Coast for Gold,* first published in 1883. That year, Cameron left the navy, but he continued in government service as a diplomat in Africa, aiding in Britain's campaign against the SLAVE TRADE. During the late 1880s, he was active in promoting a railroad link between Cape Town, South Africa, and Cairo, Egypt. In 1894, while in southern England, he was killed in a horseback riding accident.

Verney Lovett Cameron's speculation that the Lualaba River flowed northward to the Congo River was shown to be true with the subsequent explorations of Henry Morton Stanley and JOSEPH THOMSON. Moreover, Cameron's 1873–75 expedition into central Africa brought back the first detailed information on the region east of Lake Tanganyika, and the first report of the Lukuga River. Although unable to undertake an exploration of the Congo River itself, he traversed its entire watershed with the Zambezi, and, in so doing, became the first European to make an east-to-west crossing of the African continent below the SAHARA DESERT.

Campbell, John (1766–ca. 1840) *Scottish missionary in South Africa*

John Campbell was born in Edinburgh, Scotland, where, in his early years, he was a schoolmate of author Sir Walter Scott. He excelled in business and went on to become a philanthropist, using his financial resources to sponsor religious causes.

In 1812, soon after Great Britain gained control of the Dutch colony around the CAPE OF GOOD HOPE, the

London Missionary Society requested that Campbell go to South Africa to inspect its missions.

After sailing to Cape Town that year, Campbell journeyed eastward along the coast into the largely unsettled region around what is now Port Elizabeth. At Algoa Bay, he headed inland, traveling northward across the open grasslands known as the highveld. Eventually he entered the land of the Botswanas, at Kuruman, on the southern edge of the Kalahari Desert. From there, he followed the course of the Hartz River eastward to the Vaal River, which took him to the west-flowing Orange River and the Atlantic coast of Namaqualand, in present-day southern Namibia. From there, he returned to Cape Town in 1814, where he lived for the next several years.

Campbell undertook a second journey into the interior of South Africa in 1819–21. He traveled northward into the Kalahari region and penetrated the northern part of the present-day Transvaal region, where he located the source of the 1,000-mile-long Limpopo River. He returned to London after 1821, having covered more than 2,000 miles of remote inland territory. He continued to work on behalf of African missions for the next 20 years. He also authored several books recounting his African experiences.

John Campbell's explorations beyond the frontier region of early-19th-century South Africa preceded by more than two decades the mass migrations of the Boers into what later became the Orange Free State and the Transvaal.

Campbell, Robert (1804–1879) *American trapper, merchant on the Missouri River and in the Rocky Mountains*

Robert Campbell was born near the town of Omagh in what is now Northern Ireland. He came from a fairly affluent family and received a good education before immigrating to America in his late teens.

By 1824, Campbell was in St. Louis, Missouri, at that time the hub of the burgeoning FUR TRADE to the upper MISSOURI RIVER and northern ROCKY MOUNTAINS. Troubled by chronic lung disease, Campbell sought to recover his health with a trip into the unspoiled wilderness and joined WILLIAM HENRY ASHLEY's 1824–25 expedition to take supplies to the fur traders and trappers in the Uinta Mountains in what is now northeastern Utah.

Campbell, with Ashley's party, including THOMAS FITZPATRICK, traveled up the Missouri to the North Platte River at Fort Atkinson, near present-day Omaha, Nebraska. Following the North Platte westward across the plains, the group explored present-day western Nebraska and the eastern Colorado Rockies. They proceeded southward, reached the South Fork of the Platte River, then headed westward to the Green River. They traveled down the Green on makeshift boats into the Uinta Mountains, east of the Great Salt Lake. Along the way, Campbell traveled through the

Green River's Flaming Gorge, a narrow waterway that passed between 2,500-foot-high overhanging cliffs. He was among the first non-Indians to explore Browns Hole and the rapids of the Green River in what is now northeastern Utah's Dinosaur National Monument.

At a point below Browns Hole, the group encountered French-Canadian explorer and trapper ÉTIENNE PROVOST and his party, and the leaders of the two expeditions conferred on what each had learned en route.

Campbell then explored with the combined Ashley-Provost expedition into the Uinta Mountains, and, in July 1825, he attended the first annual trappers' rendezvous at Henrys Fork of the Green River, at the south end of what is now known as the Flaming Gorge Reservoir on the Utah-Wyoming boundary line.

Campbell remained active in the Rocky Mountain fur trade. On his way to the trappers' rendezvous of 1828, his party, including JAMES PIERSON BECKWOURTH, was attacked by Blackfeet warriors, but they successfully fought off the Indians in a battle that later came to be known as the "Fight in the Willows." During the 1829 trapping season, he explored Crow Indian lands between the Powder and Bighorn Rivers in what is now north-central Wyoming. Following this expedition, Campbell visited his Irish homeland in 1830–31.

Back in the Rockies in 1832, Campbell and WILLIAM LEWIS SUBLETTE trapped the western slopes of the Teton Mountains, south of what is now Yellowstone National Park. During this expedition, the mountain men survived an attack by Gros Ventre (Atsina) Indians in a skirmish at Pierre's Hole.

Campbell and Sublette remained partners in the fur trade for the next 10 years. From St. Louis, they operated a thriving supply business to the fur trappers on the upper Missouri, northern plains, and northern Rockies. In 1833, they established Fort William, a large trading fort at the mouth of the Yellowstone River (near the American Fur Company's main fur-trading center at Fort Union), in what is now northwestern North Dakota. Campbell himself managed this trade center in 1833–34. CHARLES LARPENTEUR sometimes worked with him.

In 1834, Campbell and Sublette founded Fort Laramie in southeastern Wyoming, a settlement that became an important stopover point for travelers on the Oregon Trail.

Campbell ended his partnership with Sublette in 1842. Campbell went on to establish a prosperous mercantile business in St. Louis, specializing in supplying the fur trade and buying beaver pelts for shipment to the East.

In 1851, Campbell returned to his old post at Fort Laramie, which had since been sold to the U.S. Army. There he assisted his old trapping friend, Thomas Fitzpatrick, in negotiating a peace treaty with Sioux (Dakota, Lakota, Nakota) Indians.

Campbell's business dealings in St. Louis made him a wealthy man. He expanded his enterprises into commercial banking and real estate. Yet he never broke his ties with the frontier, and during the post–Civil War years, he served as a peace commissioner for President Ulysses S. Grant's Peace Policy to the Indians.

Robert Campbell, like the other traders and trappers of the 1820s and 1830s, explored uncharted lands and helped open the American West to non-Indian settlement.

Campbell, Robert (1808–1894) *Scottish fur trader in western and northwestern Canada and Alaska*

At the age of 22, Scottish-born Robert Campbell immigrated to North America to work for the HUDSON'S BAY COMPANY at its fur-trading posts on the Canadian frontier. Starting in 1834, he began a series of annual explorations of the Mackenzie and Yukon Rivers.

During his explorations of the Mackenzie River, Campbell became the first known non-Indian man to see the Pelly River. In 1843, he returned to the Pelly and followed it northwestward to the Lewes and Yukon Rivers, thus determining the headwaters of eastern Alaska's interior river system, which eventually flowed into the Bering Sea. In 1848, at the confluence of the Lewes and Yukon, he established the northwesternmost post for the Hudson's Bay Company at that time, Fort Selkirk, which abutted the region controlled by the RUSSIAN-AMERICAN COMPANY.

In 1850–51, Campbell continued his explorations of the Yukon River, reaching its confluence with the Porcupine River in northeastern Alaska. Soon afterward, Fort Yukon was established there as another post for the Hudson's Bay Company.

In 1852, Campbell traveled to London, where he helped prepare maps of the interior river system of northeastern Alaska and what is now the western Yukon Territory. He soon returned to the Canadian West, where he was the Hudson's Bay Company's chief factor for Saskatchewan until his retirement in 1871. He spent his later years on his Manitoba ranch.

Robert Campbell's account of his penetrations into the Canadian northwest, *The Discovery and Exploration of the Pelly River,* was first published in 1883. His explorations of the rivers to the north and west of the Great Slave Lake provided geographers with important data on the then-uncharted areas of Canada's northern regions, as well as the previously uncharted area of northern Alaska.

Cano, Juan Sebastián del (Juan Sebastián de Elcano, Juan Sebastián Delcano) (ca. 1476–1526) *Spanish mariner in first circumnavigation of the world*

Juan Sebastián del Cano, of Basque ancestry, was born in northern Spain. By 1519, he had become an experienced seafarer and navigator and was appointed captain of the *Concepción,* one of five ships that set out from Spain for the EAST INDIES under the command of FERDINAND MAGELLAN.

Six months into the voyage, while wintering on the Atlantic coast of Patagonia, Cano took part in a mutiny by some of Magellan's officers and men who wanted to abandon the expedition and return to Spain. Magellan prevailed, however, and subsequently sent Cano, still in command of the *Concepción,* along with another vessel, the *San Antonio,* in search of a passage westward to the Pacific Ocean. In October 1520, following a violent storm, Cano returned to Magellan, having located the entrance to what later became known as the STRAIT OF MAGELLAN.

The expedition, following up Cano's report, sailed into the strait and entered the Pacific. In April 1521, Magellan was fatally wounded in the Philippines. That September, Cano was elected to command the expedition, then reduced to only three ships, the *Concepción,* the *Trinidad,* and the *Victoria.* With less than half of the original 237 men in the expedition surviving, there were too few crew members to man all three ships; as a result, Cano ordered the *Concepción* burned.

By late November 1521, Cano, in command of the *Victoria* and accompanied by the *Trinidad,* finally reached Magellan's intended destination, the SPICE ISLANDS (Moluccas), in what is now Indonesia. After obtaining a valuable cargo of spices, the two ships set sail in January 1522. The *Trinidad* was not seaworthy enough to attempt a passage around the CAPE OF GOOD HOPE, and instead sailed eastward in the hope of reaching a Spanish port in Panama. But it was soon captured by the Portuguese. Cano avoided capture by entering the Indian Ocean by way of Banda Strait and Timor, then sailed directly across the Indian Ocean and around the Cape of Good Hope, not making a landfall until he reached the Portuguese-held Cape Verde Islands off the coast of West Africa. There, he tried to persuade the Portuguese that he had just returned from the Americas, not the restricted East Indies. The Portuguese did not believe him, however, and took 13 of his men prisoner.

In September 1522, Cano reached Spain. Of the 237 men and five ships that had started out with Magellan, only 18 men and one ship returned. Nevertheless, the spices that Cano brought back from the Moluccas more than paid the cost of the enterprise. Spanish monarch Charles I (Holy Roman Emperor Charles V) honored Cano for completing the first CIRCUMNAVIGATION OF THE WORLD, and his participation in the mutiny in Patagonia was forgiven.

In 1525, Cano again sailed for the Moluccas in an expedition that planned to claim that rich source of spices for Spain. The next year, while retracing Magellan's route across the Pacific, he died of SCURVY.

Juan Sebastián del Cano initially received most of the credit for undertaking the first circumnavigation of the world. Magellan's role as the expedition's originator and leader was not recognized until years later. In any event, CHRISTOPHER COLUMBUS's idea of reaching the Orient by sailing westward was first realized by Cano, who also played a key role in locating the eastern entrance to the Strait of Magellan.

Cão, Diogo (Diego Cam) (ca. 1450–1486)
Portuguese mariner on the Atlantic coast of Africa
Diogo Cão, or Diego Cam, was probably born in Trás or Montes, Portugal. While still young, he served as a squire at the court of HENRY THE NAVIGATOR, prince of Portugal, at Sagres, where he was exposed to work being done by geographers and navigators at Henry's school of navigation.

By 1480, Cão had become an accomplished seafarer and navigator, serving as admiral with the Portuguese navy. That year, he undertook his first recorded voyage to the west coast of Africa, and, while visiting ports on the Gulf of Guinea, he may have met CHRISTOPHER COLUMBUS.

Soon after coming to the throne in 1481, King John II of Portugal commissioned Cão to continue the exploration of Africa that had begun under Prince Henry. Cão left Portugal in June 1482, and, sailing southward along the west coast of Africa, went beyond what is now Santa Catarina in Gabon, the southernmost point previously reached by European navigators.

In August 1482, Cão came upon the mouth of a great river. On its north bank, he erected a 13-foot-high limestone pillar known as a *PADRÃO*, proclaiming Portuguese sovereignty over the region, with inscriptions in Portuguese, Latin, and Arabic. From local natives, Cão learned that the river was called the Kongo (or CONGO RIVER, now known as the Zaire River), after the powerful monarch, Mani Kongo, who controlled the region from Mbanzu farther upriver. Four members of Cão's crew set out to explore the Congo and contact the king, as well as seek out the legendary white ruler known as PRESTER JOHN. Meanwhile, Cão continued his exploration southward.

In late August 1483, at what is now Cape St. Mary, Angola, about 500 miles south of the mouth of the Congo, Cão erected a *padrão*, then headed back northward. He stopped at the Congo's mouth to pick up the men he had left there; not finding them, he took four native potentates back to Portugal, as hostages.

Cão reached Lisbon on April 8, 1484, where King John honored him with a knighthood. The next year, Cão embarked on a second voyage. He reached the mouth of the Congo, where he was joined by the four Portuguese left behind in 1483. The four native princes were returned to their homeland as well, having been well treated in Portugal. Cão

then sailed his ship up the Congo for a distance of about 100 miles. A record of his visit still exists as graffiti carved into the face of the cliffs overhanging the river at the Yellala Falls.

From the Congo, Cão sailed farther southward along the coast of what is now Angola and erected a *padrão* at Cabo Negro. He had hoped to find an end to the African continent and a passage eastward to India. His supplies running low, he set up another *padrão* at Cape Cross, on the Atlantic coast of what is now Namibia, and headed back to Portugal, having explored an additional 1,500 miles of African coastline with no southern end of the continent in sight.

By 1486, Cão was in Portugal. He may have taken with him the African prince known as Cacuto, who returned to west-central Africa in the early 1490s and aided the Portuguese in winning control of the region. Cão also took back a large shipment of black pepper, which, although it had a disastrous effect on the Portuguese spice market, nonetheless made the voyage highly profitable. Cão may have again explored the coast of West Africa. He reportedly died south of Cape Cross, Namibia, later that same year, 1486.

Diogo Cão's explorations revealed that the African continent extended much farther southward than had been speculated. His charting of the Congo River provided Portugal with access to trade with the interior of central Africa. The pillars he set up along the African coast endured for hundreds of years, and several of them were recovered and deposited in museums in Europe. In reaching the coast of Namibia at Walvis Bay, he was the first European to sail almost as far south as the TROPIC OF CAPRICORN. His explorations along the coast of Africa soon led to the first European voyage around the CAPE OF GOOD HOPE, accomplished by Portuguese navigator BARTOLOMEU DIAS in 1487. German cartographer MARTIN BEHAIM accompanied Cão on at least one of his voyages.

Cárdenas, García López de See LÓPEZ DE CÁRDENAS, GARCÍA.

Carpini, Giovanni da Pian del (John de Piano de Carpini, John of Pian de Carpini, John de Plano Carpini, John of Plano, John of Piano Carpini)
(1182–1252) *Italian friar, early traveler in central Asia*
Giovanni del Carpini was born in the north-central Italian city of Perugia, near Assisi. A disciple of St. Francis of Assisi, he entered the religious order established by his companion.

In 1245, Carpini headed the Franciscan order in Cologne. That year, he was summoned to Lyons by Pope Innocent IV. The eastern frontier of Europe had undergone a siege by the Mongol tribes from the steppes of central Asia, who had advanced as far west as Kiev and Hungary by 1240. Soon afterward, there was a lull in their aggression, and rumors began to circulate in the West that the Mongols were sympathetic to the Christians and might be persuaded to ally themselves with the European powers in an attack against the Muslim Turks, then occupying the Holy Land and also threatening Europe.

In Lyons, Carpini was designated envoy to the Mongols. With a letter from the pope, entreating the current Mongol khan (ruler), Ogadei, a descendant of GENGHIS KHAN, to desist from the further slaughter of Christians and to embrace Christianity, Carpini departed Lyons on April 16, 1245. He first traveled to Bohemia, where he met with King Wenceslaus, who had had some contact with the Mongols during their most recent onslaught on his eastern frontier. In Poland, Carpini was joined by another Franciscan, Friar Benedict, who acted as his interpreter. They proceeded eastward across the Ukraine by horseback, stopping at Kiev before continuing to the Dnieper and Don Rivers, north of the Black Sea.

In February 1246, Carpini and his party reached the Volga River, where they encountered a large encampment of Mongols, headed by Batu. From Batu, they obtained the horses necessary to cross the barren steppes of central Asia, and, with a letter of safe conduct, they continued their journey, traveling north of the Caspian and Aral Seas into the northern reaches of the GOBI DESERT.

Carpini arrived at the Mongol Imperial Encampment near Karakorum on July 22, 1246. Since leaving Lyons 15 months earlier, he had traveled across 3,000 miles of eastern Europe and central Asia. At that time, more than 2,000 Asian princes and their respective entourages had assembled at Karakorum to witness the coronation of the new khan, Kuyuk, uncle of Batu. Carpini learned then that the former khan, Ogadei, had died in 1241, and he realized that Ogadei's death was the reason for the sudden lull in Mongol aggression against Europe.

Carpini presented his papal letters to Kuyuk. In turn the khan gave Carpini letters for the pope in which he curtly communicated that he would not become a Christian, and that he could not accept the overtures for peace unless they were presented personally by the pope and the princes of Christendom. He then offered to send his own emissaries back to the pope with Carpini, but the Franciscan declined the suggestion, fearing the Mongols would learn how disunified the European powers actually were.

On November 13, 1246, Carpini and Friar Benedict were allowed to leave Karakorum. Over the next 10 months, they made a harrowing winter crossing of central Asia, reaching Kiev in June 1247.

On his return to western Europe, Carpini presented his account to the pope in Lyons. He was subsequently appointed archbishop of Antivari on the Dalmatian coast, in what is now Yugoslavia, and served as a papal diplomat to the court of Louis IX of France.

Giovanni del Carpini wrote a detailed account of his journey into Mongolia, entitled *The Book of the Tartars,* which provided Europeans with one of the first descriptions of the life and customs of the native peoples of central Asia. Carpini initiated the first dialogue between the East and West in medieval times, setting a precedent for the subsequent diplomatic missions of WILLIAM OF RUBROUCK and André de Longjumeau, as well as for the commercial travels of MARCO POLO.

Carson, Christopher Houston (Kit Carson)
(1809–1868) *American frontiersman, guide in the American West*

Christopher (Kit) Carson was born near Richmond, Kentucky. In 1811, his family took him to the Missouri frontier. In 1826, he left Old Franklin, Missouri, where he had been apprenticed to a saddle-maker, and traveled with a trade caravan along the Santa Fe Trail to Taos, New Mexico.

Over the next several years, Carson operated out of Taos as a trapper, trader, and hunter. In 1829, he accompanied EWING YOUNG on an expedition from Taos across the Mojave Desert to California's San Joaquin Valley.

Carson returned to Taos with Young in 1831. That year, he explored the Old Spanish Trail with fur trader Richard Bland Lee and crossed the southern ROCKY MOUNTAINS into what is now central Utah to ANTOINE ROBIDOUX's post at Fort Uinta.

In about 1832, fur trader THOMAS FITZPATRICK recruited Carson in Taos. Over the next decade, Carson trapped beaver throughout the Rockies and Far West, gaining much knowledge of little-known passes, rivers, deserts, and mountain ranges. In 1835, he attended the Green River fur traders' rendezvous with trapper JAMES BRIDGER.

With the decline in the beaver trade after 1838, Carson turned to other pursuits. In 1840–42, he worked as a hunter and guide out of Bent's Fort in present-day eastern Colorado. In 1842, while traveling back from St. Louis by riverboat, Carson met explorer JOHN CHARLES FRÉMONT, who hired him as a guide for his expedition to the northern Rockies.

Carson guided Frémont's 1842, 1843, and 1845 expeditions into the Rockies, the Great Basin, and the Far West. His explorations with Frémont took him from the northern plains to the Snake River and COLUMBIA RIVER and across the Sierra Nevada into California.

While in California with Frémont in 1845–46, Carson became active in the California revolt and the subsequent U.S.-Mexican War of 1846–48. In fall 1846, Carson was sent eastward from California with military dispatches reporting the progress of the war there. En route, in the valley of the upper Rio Grande, south of Albuquerque, New Mexico, he encountered General STEPHEN WATTS KEARNY and his forces traveling westward across the desert toward San

Kit Carson *(Library of Congress)*

Diego. Carson informed Kearny of the rough terrain over which he had just come, prompting Kearny to leave his wagons behind and proceed westward with only a column of mounted soldiers. The general was so impressed by Carson's knowledge of the territory to the west, that he drafted the frontiersman into service as his chief guide. Carson led Kearny's men westward along a route that, after skirting the southern end of the Rockies, followed the Gila River, then crossed the southern Sierra Nevada to reach San Diego on the Pacific coast.

In 1849, Carson completed an overland trip from California to Washington, D.C., in which he brought to the East one of the earliest reports that gold had been discovered at Sutter's Fort.

After the U.S.-Mexican War, Carson settled in Taos. In 1853, he joined other former mountain men in driving 135,000 head of sheep from Taos to the booming market in central California. During the 1850s and the Civil War years, Carson took part in military campaigns against Kiowa, Comanche, Ute, Apache, and Navajo (Dineh) Indians. He was a federal Indian agent for the Moache Ute and Jicarilla Apache and took part in treaty negotiations with them and other Southwest and southern plains bands.

Kit Carson applied the skills he learned as a fur trapper and mountain man to the exploration of the American West. Through the reports of Frémont, he achieved a reputation as the foremost frontiersman and western guide of his day. The trail through the Sierra Nevada that he and Frémont pioneered in 1844 was later named Carson Pass in his honor. It soon became an important route for settlers and gold seekers headed into California from Nevada.

Carteret, Philip (ca. 1733–1796) *British naval officer in the South Pacific*

Philip Carteret was born at Trinity Manor on England's island of Jersey. Descended from a long line of distinguished seafarers, he entered the British navy as a midshipman in his early teens. During the Seven Years War of 1756–63, he took part in naval engagements in the MEDITERRANEAN SEA, and, in August 1758, he was promoted to the rank of second lieutenant.

In 1764, Carteret served as first lieutenant on the *Dolphin,* under the command of JOHN BYRON, with whom he circumnavigated the world, returning to England in May 1766.

Just three months after returning from his voyage with Byron, Carteret again sailed from Plymouth on another British naval exploring expedition, in command of the sloop *Swallow,* accompanying the expedition's commander, SAMUEL WALLIS, on the *Dolphin.* After crossing the Atlantic Ocean, the ships reached the entrance to the STRAIT OF MAGELLAN in December 1766, then spent the next four months negotiating a passage to the Pacific Ocean. In April 1767, as both ships entered the Pacific, they were driven apart by strong winds and currents. Each then continued on alone, with Wallis and the *Dolphin* sailing westward across the Pacific, while Carteret and the *Swallow* followed a northward course along the west coast of South America. Off the coast of central Chile, he headed westward. After several months at sea, he located an island, which he named Pitcairn, after the marine on board who had first sighted it. He then came upon an archipelago, which he called the Admiralty Islands, and he subsequently charted the Santa Cruz Islands, which had not been visited since the voyage of ÁLVARO DE MENDAÑA in 1595.

Carteret sailed north of New Guinea, made a stop at Mindanao in the Philippines, and also charted some islands in the Solomons. Approaching the coast of Australia, he detected a southward current, which led him to conclude that NEW ZEALAND and Australia were separated by a channel. He also explored New Britain in the Melanesian archipelago, where he left a plaque that was found a few months later by French explorer LOUIS-ANTOINE DE BOUGAINVILLE. Soon afterward, Carteret located and named nearby New Ireland; Carteret Harbor there is named in his honor.

In November 1767, Carteret reached the Dutch colony of Makasar on the Indonesian island of Celebes, where he was forced to remain for four months while his crew recovered from sickness and his ship underwent extensive repairs.

Carteret sailed from Makasar in spring 1768, and, after long stopovers in Batavia (present-day Jakarta, Indonesia) and Cape Town, South Africa, he returned to England in March 1769. His voyage around the world had taken 31 months, during which he had lost half of his original crew. Carteret remained in the British navy, reaching the rank of vice admiral in 1794.

Philip Carteret's CIRCUMNAVIGATION OF THE WORLD was remarkable in that he completed the voyage in the face of severe problems with both his ship and the health of his crew. Pitcairn Island, charted in the course of Carteret's 1766–69 voyage, served as a refuge for the *Bounty* mutineers in 1789.

Cartier, Jacques (1491–1557) *French mariner, fur trader in eastern Canada*

Jacques Cartier was born in Saint-Malo, a seaport in France's Brittany region. A member of a prominent family, he became an accomplished master pilot and navigator and, by 1520, had married the daughter of a high city official. He is thought to have accompanied explorer GIOVANNI DA VERRAZANO on his 1524 voyage to the mid-Atlantic coast of North America; he may also have been with Verrazano on his 1527 expedition to the coast of Brazil.

In 1532, King Francis I of France paid a visit to the Abbey of Mont-St.-Michel, not far from St.-Malo. The abbey's treasurer, a relative of Cartier, introduced Cartier to the king. With Spain and Portugal dividing up newly explored lands in the Americas, Francis I was eager to initiate a French transatlantic expedition and accepted Cartier's proposal to undertake a voyage in search of a NORTHWEST PASSAGE to the Far East. Francis I provided some backing for this expedition, with the rest coming from commercial interests in Brittany.

With two ships and about 120 men, Cartier set sail from St.-Malo on April 20, 1534. Following a course due west, he landed at Cape Bonavista on the east coast of Newfoundland on May 10, 1534. Although the islands and peninsulas of the present-day Canadian Maritime Provinces had been visited by French fishing fleets for some years prior to Cartier's arrival, his was the first organized French expedition to this part of North America.

Seeking the Northwest Passage, Cartier sailed around the coast of Newfoundland, which had not yet been determined to be an island. He passed through the Strait of Belle Isle, separating Newfoundland from southern Labrador, and entered the Gulf of St. Lawrence. He charted the coast of southern Labrador and visited numerous islands in the gulf, including Anticosti Island, the Magdalen Islands (Îsles de la Madeleine), and Prince Edward Island. At Dog Island he set up a large cross.

The expedition reached the coast of the Gaspé Peninsula and visited Chaleur Bay, where Cartier's men had contacts with the Micmac Indians, trading European manufactured goods for furs. In July 1534, Cartier went ashore at Gaspé Bay and officially claimed the land for the king of France. Cartier's men befriended a party of Huron (Wyandot) Indians under Chief DONNACONNA, who had journeyed from their home on the St. Lawrence River to hunt seals. Cartier convinced the Huron chief to allow his two sons to accompany the expedition as guides, promising to return the boys within a year.

By early August 1534, Cartier had explored the Atlantic shoreline of what is now Quebec province. Although he had failed to locate the Northwest Passage, he had heard from the Indians of the land of SAGUENAY, a country reportedly rich in gold and valuable minerals. The expedition soon set sail for France, reaching St.-Malo on September 5, 1534.

By the next spring, Cartier had received a commission to sail beyond the known coast of Newfoundland, continue

Jacques Cartier *(Library of Congress)*

his search for the Northwest Passage to China, and locate Saguenay. With three ships and a company of 112 men, Cartier set sail from St.-Malo on May 19, 1535. After a voyage of 50 days, he sighted Funk Island, off the northeast coast of Newfoundland. Cartier's ships then rounded the northern tip of Newfoundland and sailed southwestward through the Strait of Belle Isle into the Gulf of St. Lawrence. On August 10, 1535, he put in at a natural harbor on the mainland, north of Anticosti Island, naming the site "La Baye sainct Laurins" (the Bay of St. Lawrence) in honor of the saint whose feast day falls on that date. In the years that followed, the name was used to identify both the great gulf and the river flowing into it, whose wide estuary Cartier soon reached.

On August 29, 1535, Cartier began his explorations up the St. Lawrence River (which he called "La Grande Rivière" and later "Rivière de Hochelaga," after the Indian settlement he was to find on its banks). A week later, he arrived at the Huron village of Stadacona, Donnaconna's home village at the site of present-day Quebec City. Donnaconna was reunited with his sons, who had traveled to France with Cartier the previous fall and had returned with Cartier on

this voyage. On being informed of another, larger Huron settlement farther up the St. Lawrence, Cartier led a small French party in longboats 150 miles farther upriver, reaching Hochelaga on the site of present-day Montreal, on October 2, 1535.

At Hochelaga, Cartier climbed the mountain that he called Montreal (Mount Royal) and from the top saw that rapids would make further exploration west on the St. Lawrence difficult. At this point, he had penetrated the Canadian mainland to a distance of 1,000 miles from the open sea.

Cartier returned to Stadacona, where his men built a fort in which to spend the winter. Over the next months, the French were beset with SCURVY. More than one-third died; others survived by drinking a Huron tea made from the bark of evergreen trees, a source of vitamin C unknown to them.

In late May 1536, Cartier set sail for France with only two of the ships because of the loss of crew; the smallest of the three vessels was presented to the Huron as a gift, which the Indians stripped for its iron. Chief Donnaconna was cajoled into accompanying the French on this return voyage. Along the way, they explored Cape Breton Island, the Cape

Jacques Cartier at the Huron village of Hochelaga (present-day Montreal) *(Library of Congress)*

of St. Lawrence, and the Magdalen Islands. Cartier also explored Cabot Strait and determined that Newfoundland was an island. By mid-July 1536, Cartier and his expedition arrived back in St.-Malo. Donnaconna and other Huron accompanying him contracted European diseases and died abroad.

War with Spain delayed preparations for a third expedition to Canada. In spring 1541, French nobleman JEAN-FRANÇOIS DE LA ROCQUE DE ROBERVAL, the king's lieutenant general, was directed to establish a colony in Canada. Cartier departed St.-Malo that May; Roberval was to follow later. Five ships with more than 1,000 crew and colonists, many drawn from France's prisons, made this crossing.

Cartier reached the mouth of the St. Lawrence River in early summer, then sailed upriver to Cap Rouge, just above Stadacona. After founding a settlement, Cartier continued his explorations. He had all but given up his search for the Northwest Passage to the north of Stadacona, seeking instead the fabled land of Saguenay. A branch of the St. Lawrence River—later named the Saguenay—led Cartier to a region where he found what he thought was gold and precious stones. After obtaining mineral samples, the expedition sailed for France in June 1542.

En route, Cartier put in at St. John's, Newfoundland, where he encountered Roberval and his ships. Although ordered by Roberval to return to the St. Lawrence and Cap Rouge, Cartier and his men left under cover of darkness, heading for home. They arrived in St.-Malo in mid-October 1542. The minerals from Canada turned out to be pyrite, or FOOL'S GOLD, and quartz, both without cash value.

Cartier may have been sent on a fourth voyage to the St. Lawrence River region in 1543 to bring Roberval and his beleaguered colonists home to France, but no conclusive proof of this journey exists.

In any case, after 1543, Cartier remained in France for the rest of his life. He wrote an account of his Canadian adventures, commonly known as *Bref récit,* first published in Paris in 1545, then translated into Italian and published in Venice in 1556. In London, in 1580, RICHARD HAKLUYT published an English translation of the Italian edition as *A Short and Briefe Narration.*

Jacques Cartier's expeditions provided the foundation for France's claim to Canada. His explorations along the St. Lawrence River Valley had additional significance in that, unlike other early-16th-century voyages, they made use of small boats, among them the native CANOE, to investigate inland waterways that would have been unnavigable by larger vessels. He also initiated the practice of trading European manufactured goods with Indians for furs, a practice that would have great commercial impact in the coming centuries, with the development of the FUR TRADE. France realized that, despite the fact that the Northwest Passage to China had not been discovered, North America itself had natural resources to exploit. Nevertheless, full-scale French settlement of Canada was delayed for over 60 years after Cartier's last voyage because of the religious wars that persisted in Europe throughout the 16th century. French explorations of the region resumed again in the early 1600s under SAMUEL DE CHAMPLAIN.

Carver, Jonathan (1710–1780) *British colonist, soldier in the western Great Lakes and on the upper Mississippi River*

Jonathan Carver was born in the town of Weymouth, Massachusetts, south of Boston. He was raised in Connecticut, where he became a shoemaker. From 1746 to 1763, he served with the colonial militia in the last two phases of the French and Indian Wars.

In 1766, the British sent famed Indian fighter Major ROBERT ROGERS to assume command over their garrison on Mackinac Island at the northern entrance to Lake Michigan. Rogers had long dreamed of discovering a NORTHWEST PASSAGE from the Great Lakes that would provide a water route to the Pacific Ocean. Carver, who may have known Rogers from his militia days, was hired by Rogers to undertake an expedition from Mackinac, exploring the rivers in the lands beyond the west shores of Lake Michigan, a precursor to a planned expedition to locate a river route to the Pacific.

In spring or summer 1766, Carver and a small party, starting from Mackinac Island, traveled along the north and west coasts of Lake Michigan to Green Bay. From there, they followed the Fox River, then traveled overland to the Wisconsin River, which they followed to its outlet on the MISSISSIPPI RIVER near present-day Prairie du Chien, Wisconsin. En route, Carver explored much of what is now southern and western Wisconsin.

Carver and his group then ascended the Mississippi River as far as present-day Minneapolis-St. Paul. At this point on the upper Mississippi, they came upon the Falls of St. Anthony, which had been visited by French explorer LOUIS HENNEPIN in 1680.

Carver continued to explore the Minnesota River beyond the Falls of St. Anthony, then wintered among the Sioux (Dakota, Lakota, Nakota) Indians. In spring 1767, he returned to the Mississippi, descending it back to Prairie du Chien. He joined up with a second party, led by Captain James Tute, which had been sent into the field by Rogers in search of the Northwest Passage.

The intended route up the Mississippi and westward was not passable at this time due to a war between the Sioux and Chippewa (Ojibway) Indians. Carver was forced to follow the Minnesota River until it turned northwestward. From the Minnesota River, the expedition entered the

Jonathan Carver *(Library of Congress)*

Chippewa River and followed that stream into what is now southwestern and central Minnesota.

Carver continued eastward via rivers and overland portages, until he reached the northeastern extent of Lake Superior. He crossed this section of the lake and stopped at Grand Portage in the extreme northeastern region of present-day Minnesota, near the outlet of the Pigeon River. Rogers had promised to provide supplies to the expedition at this point, but they had not yet arrived. After a period of waiting, Carver abandoned the planned expedition to the Pacific, heading back to Massachusetts sometime in 1768.

Over the next two years, Carver tried without success to receive payment from Rogers for his efforts in exploring the Minnesota and Wisconsin frontiers. In 1769, he sailed for England, where he wrote a book about his journeys, entitled *Travels Through the Interior Parts of North America in the Years 1766, 1767, and 1768,* which was not published until 1778. He died, impoverished, two years later.

Jonathan Carver's book was the first English-language account of the upper Mississippi and western Great Lakes areas, a region previously explored for the most part by the French. It had success in both Europe and North America, generating interest in the region and bringing sufficient funds to Carver's estate to raise his family from poverty. According to the publisher of a later edition of Carver's book, the Sioux had granted Carver more than 10,000 square miles of Minnesota territory while he lived among them in 1766–67. This led to claims by Carver's descendants, as well as by assignees of these claims, which persisted well into the 20th century.

Casson, François Dollier de   See DOLLIER DE CASSON, FRANÇOIS.

Catesby, Mark   (ca. 1679–1749)   *British naturalist, traveler in the American Southeast, Bermuda, Jamaica, and the Bahamas*

Mark Catesby was born in Sudbury, Suffolk, England. He had an interest in the natural sciences from an early age, and after his initial scientific training in London, he raised funds for a trip to America, where he planned to investigate new species of plants and animals.

In 1712, Catesby traveled to Virginia, where some of his relatives had settled, and began a seven-year study of the fauna and flora of North America, collecting specimens while traveling through a wide area of the mid-Atlantic and southern region of the American colonies. He went inland as far as the Blue Ridge, and also traveled to the Caribbean Sea, undertaking plant and animal studies in Bermuda and Jamaica.

Throughout his travels in colonial America, Catesby sent back seed and plant specimens to scientists in England; by the time he returned to England in 1719, he had earned a reputation as one of the foremost collectors of American wildlife.

Catesby's work had come to the attention of prominent British naturalist Sir Hans Sloane, and with Sloane's support as well as assistance from South Carolina colonial governor Francis Nicholson, Catesby undertook a second scientific expedition to America. He arrived in Charleston, South Carolina, in May 1722, and after exploring the interior of the Carolinas, he lived among the Indians at Fort Moore on Georgia's Savannah River. He also undertook field trips into Florida and made a study of plant and animal life in the Bahamas.

Catesby settled in London in 1726, where he produced his two-volume illustrated scientific study, *The Natural History of Carolina, Florida, and the Bahama Islands,* published serially from 1731 to 1743. In 1733, he won official recognition for his scientific work with admission to the ROYAL SOCIETY.

Mark Catesby's published work includes color illustrations depicting both plants and animals in a single setting, a technique later adopted by JOHN JAMES AUDUBON. He went on to produce scientific work on the migratory patterns of birds, basing these findings on his ornithological studies in South Carolina. He was among the earliest naturalists to refute the theory that birds hibernated underwater over the winter months, correctly theorizing that they actually migrated to warmer climates. Catesby's plant specimens later formed the basis for the British Museum's initial botanical collections. His 1731 *Natural History,* reportedly used by Thomas Jefferson and MERIWETHER LEWIS, included a new map of the Carolinas and other regions he had visited, providing new insights into the geography as well as the wildlife of the little-known interior of the American Southeast. Largely as a result of his work, many plants originally found only in North America were first introduced and cultivated in Europe. A Caribbean plant, the catesbea, was named in his honor.

Catlin, George (1796–1872) *American artist in North and South America*

George Catlin was born and raised on his family's farm near Wilkes-Barre, Pennsylvania. He went on to study law at Litchfield, Connecticut, eventually passing the Pennsylvania bar and opening a law practice near his hometown in Luzerne County, Pennsylvania.

Losing interest in his law career, Catlin studied art in Philadelphia and New York and soon managed to earn a living as a portrait painter. In 1824, he happened to see a delegation of western Indian chiefs at Charles Willson Peale's natural history museum in Philadelphia. Regarding these Native Americans as the remnants of a doomed race, whose images would be lost to history unless preserved by art, he resolved to undertake this task. During the rest of the 1820s, he made numerous painting trips to Indian reservations in the East and also painted delegations of Indians visiting Washington, D.C.

In 1830, Catlin traveled to St. Louis, where, with the help of the former explorer WILLIAM CLARK, who was serving as superintendent of Indian affairs, he spent the next two years painting upper MISSOURI RIVER Indians visiting the frontier settlement.

Clark helped Catlin make arrangements to travel up the Missouri by riverboat. The artist departed St. Louis on March 26, 1832, aboard the steamer *Yellowstone,* on its maiden voyage for JOHN JACOB ASTOR's AMERICAN FUR COMPANY, and reached Fort Union at the confluence of the Yellowstone and Missouri Rivers in present-day northeastern North Dakota on June 26, 1832. Throughout the summer, Catlin painted portraits of Indians who came to trade at the

Painting by George Catlin (the artist being chased by buffalo in the American West) *(Library of Congress)*

post. That fall, he returned to St. Louis by CANOE, accompanied by two trappers.

The following spring, 1833, Catlin again set out for the frontier, journeying into what is now southeastern Wyoming along what came to be known as the Oregon Trail. Over the next months, Catlin's painting expeditions took him westward across the northern plains and into the ROCKY MOUNTAINS, as far as Utah's Great Salt Lake.

In winter 1833–34, Catlin traveled along the Gulf Coast, between Pensacola, Florida, and New Orleans, Louisiana. In spring 1834, he left New Orleans and traveled up the MISSISSIPPI RIVER by boat to Fort Gibson on the Arkansas River in what is now Oklahoma.

From Fort Gibson, Catlin traveled along the Santa Fe Trail with the U.S. First Regiment of Mounted Dragoons, commanded by General HENRY LEAVENWORTH and Colonel HENRY DODGE. The expedition passed through the lands of the Comanche, Wichita, and other Indians of the southern plains. Catlin produced portraits of tribal leaders, as well as scenes of everyday life. He observed and painted a buffalo hunt, as well as ritualistic practices such as the Sun Dance. The expedition reached the Red River region of what was then Mexican-held Texas. Catlin, like Leavenworth and many other members of the Dragoon Regiment, was stricken with fever. Leavenworth soon died. Catlin remained in a Comanche village and, though sick, continued to paint. Recovering after a few weeks, he returned to St. Louis.

In 1835–36, Catlin traveled northward into the frontier regions of Minnesota and Wisconsin. In addition to painting the indigenous tribes, he explored uncharted parts of Minnesota. The Indians took him to their pipestone quarry in southwestern Minnesota near the present South Dakota state line, where they obtained the mineral they used in making ceremonial pipes and ornaments. Catlin was one of the first non-Indians to visit this site; the mineral, unique to this region, was subsequently named catlinite in his honor.

For two years, starting in 1837, Catlin toured the major cities of the eastern United States with his paintings. During the 1840s, he was in Europe, where his works were met with critical acclaim. By 1851, however, he was beset by financial difficulties and was forced to sell most of his paintings to satisfy creditors. He returned to the United States in about 1852, but he soon left to paint the Indians of Central and South America. From 1852 to 1857, he traveled throughout Central America and South America, including the ANDES MOUNTAINS. He also continued his journeys in North America during the 1850s and 1860s, traveling to the Pacific Northwest and Alaska. In 1870, he settled in Jersey City, New Jersey, where he died two years later.

Catlin published several illustrated books of his travels, including *Manners, Customs, and Condition of the North American Indians* (1841); *Catlin's North American Indian Portfolio* (1844); and *Last Rambles Amongst the Indians of the Rocky Mountains and the Andes* (1868).

Like fellow frontier painters KARL BODMER, PAUL KANE, and RUDOLPH FRIEDERICH KURZ, George Catlin provided images of the vanishing Indian way of life. His far-reaching painting expeditions throughout the Americas also provided visual perspectives of lands as they appeared prior to non-Indian settlement.

Cermenho, Sebastián Meléndez Rodríguez (Sebastião Rodriques Cermenho, Rodríguez Cermeño, Cermeñón) (fl. 1590s) *Portuguese mariner along the California coast, in service to Spain*

Sebastián Rodríguez Cermenho was born in Portugal. As a young man, he found work as a navigator on Spanish ships out of Manila in the Philippines.

In 1595, Cermenho sailed from Manila aboard the *San Agustín* to explore North America's Pacific coastline and locate an inlet where Spanish ships could find shelter from British privateers and be refitted. On November 30, the ship ran aground near Point Reyes, north of present-day San Francisco, a region explored more than 50 years earlier by JUAN RODRÍGUEZ CABRILLO. Cermenho named the bay to the south San Francisco, but it later came to be known as Drake's Bay after SIR FRANCIS DRAKE. The expedition built a smaller boat from the wreckage, the *San Buenaventura*. Sailing southward, the Spanish made a sighting of another bay on December 10, which Cermenho named San Pedro. SEBASTIÁN VISCAÍNO would make a landing here seven years later and rename it Monterey Bay. Cermenho's expedition continued south, charting the coastline and eventually reaching Acapulco, Mexico.

Although Cabrillo's and Viscaíno's explorations are better known, Sebastián Rodríguez Cermenho contributed to Spanish knowledge of California's coastline and can be credited with the European discovery of Monterey Bay.

Céron, Álvaro de Saavedra   See SAAVEDRA CÉRON, ÁLVARO DE.

Chaillé-Long, Charles (1842–1917)
American explorer in central Africa, in service to Great Britain and Egypt

Charles Chaillé-Long was born in Princess Anne on Maryland's east shore, a descendant of a French-Huguenot family that had settled there in about 1685. His great-grandfather had been one of the signers of the U.S. Constitution in 1787.

Chaillé-Long attended Washington Academy in Maryland. Upon completion of his studies in 1860, he entered the Union army, serving in the Maryland Infantry throughout the Civil War, during which he was promoted to captain.

Mustered out of the service at war's end, Chaillé-Long undertook literary studies on his own until 1869, when he resumed his military career with an appointment as a lieutenant colonel in the Egyptian army, which was under British control. In Cairo, he became chief of staff to the general in chief and taught French at a military school. In 1874, he was appointed chief of staff to British general Charles "Chinese" Gordon, governor general of Egypt's southernmost province in equatorial Africa.

In April 1874, Chaillé-Long embarked on a secret diplomatic mission into the kingdom of Buganda (present-day Uganda), where he succeeded in negotiating a treaty with King Mutesa that led to Egypt's annexation of the upper Nile Basin. While in that region, he undertook an investigation of the headwaters of the White Nile River and, in so doing, became the first European to come upon Lake Ibrahim (now known as Lake Kioga) in what is now central Uganda. Chaillé-Long subsequently traveled along a stretch of the NILE RIVER that JOHN HANNING SPEKE had been unable to explore in 1862, and he determined that Lake Kioga was one of the principal sources of the White Nile. At Mooli on the White Nile, he was wounded in an attack. Returning to northern Egypt, he was promoted to colonel and made an honorary nobleman by the khedive of Egypt.

In January 1875, Chaillé-Long led a military expedition from Gondokoro in the Sudan into the Niam Niam region west of the Nile and succeeded in bringing the area under Anglo-Egyptian control. He also explored the natural divide between the CONGO RIVER (Zaire River) and Nile River, examining the upper Bahr el Ghazal River and its tributaries and completing the geographic investigation of the region undertaken by GEORG AUGUST SCHWEINFURTH five years earlier. He returned to Cairo with an adult Akka Pygmy, one of the first of the pygmy people to travel outside their rainforest habitat.

Chaillé-Long's next expedition took him to the east coastal region around the Horn of Africa. In September 1875, he led an Anglo-Egyptian force into what is now Somalia. After occupying the city of Kismayu, he explored Somalia's Giuba River. He returned to Egypt in early 1876, when the military expedition was recalled by the British.

In August 1877, Chaillé-Long left the Egyptian military and returned to the United States. He settled in New York City and received an appointment as chief clerk of the city's police court. Attending Columbia University's school of law, he graduated and was admitted to the bar in 1880. The next year, he returned to Egypt to practice international law in Alexandria.

In 1882, an insurrection broke out in Alexandria against the ruling khedive, and Chaillé-Long took charge of American diplomatic affairs after the regular consular staff fled the city. As provisional U.S. consul general in Alexandria, he helped rescue hundreds of foreign refugees and, with the help of U.S. naval forces in the harbor, managed to restore order following a British counterattack. For his bravery in the face of grave danger, the Egyptian government offered him a commission as a brigadier general, which he did not accept.

In August 1887, U.S. president Grover Cleveland appointed Chaillé-Long ambassador to Korea. The next year, while in Korea, he took part in a scientific expedition to Cheju (then known as Quelpart), an island formed from an extinct volcano in the East China Sea. He subsequently served as the U.S. delegate to a number of major international conferences in Europe.

Charles Chaillé-Long received the Charles P. Daly Gold Medal from the AMERICAN GEOGRAPHICAL SOCIETY in 1910, in recognition of his contributions to geographic knowledge of Africa, especially for identifying one of the principal sources of the White Nile. He recorded his experiences in Uganda and the southern Sudan in his book, *Central Africa: Naked Truths of Naked People,* first published in 1876.

Charles Chaillé-Long *(Library of Congress)*

Chamisso de Boncourt, Louis-Charles-Adélaïde (Adelbert von Chamisso) (1781–1836)

French-born German naturalist, poet in South America, the Pacific, Alaska, and northeastern Siberia

Louis Chamisso de Boncourt was born at his family's estate in the Champagne region of northeastern France. In 1792, with the onset of the Reign of Terror during the French Revolution, he departed France with his family, settling first in Holland, then in the German city of Würzburg. In his mid-teens, Chamisso served as a page in the Prussian royal court at Berlin, and in 1798, he entered the Prussian army as an ensign.

Although his family was able to return to France in 1803, Chamisso remained in Prussia. Having left the army in 1808, he embarked on a literary career, achieving great fame in France and Germany as a lyric poet. From about 1810 to 1812, he joined Madame de Staël (Germaine de Staël) and her literary associates in Paris and at her estate on Lake Geneva, Switzerland.

In 1812, Chamisso returned to Prussia to study botany, zoology, and anatomy at the University of Berlin. In 1815, he accepted an appointment as naturalist on a Russian-sponsored maritime expedition to the Pacific Ocean, and, in August of that year, he boarded the *Rurik* at Copenhagen, commanded by OTTO VON KOTZEBUE. Also engaged as a naturalist on this voyage was the German physician and scientist JOHANN FRIEDRICH ESCHSCHOLTZ. LOUIS CHORIS sailed with the expedition as a draftsman.

During the next three years, Chamisso sailed around the world aboard the *Rurik*. Traveling first to the coast of Brazil, he made a study of animal and plant life. He discovered a new type of palm tree, which he called *Cocos romansoffiana,* after the expedition's chief Russian supporter, Nicholas Petrovitch Romanzof. He also studied the marine life of the South Atlantic Ocean, especially jellyfish and mollusks.

After rounding CAPE HORN and visiting the coast of Chile, the *Rurik* stopped at Easter Island, then sailed westward across the Pacific to the Marshalls and Gilberts before heading northward for the Russian port of Petropavlovsk on northeastern SIBERIA's Kamchatka Peninsula.

By summer 1816, the *Rurik* had reached the west coast of Alaska, where Chamisso undertook studies of animal and plant life around Kotzebue Sound. From there, the expedition sailed to the Asian side of the BERING STRAIT. Chamisso studied the Chukchi people of eastern SIBERIA, comparing them to the Inuit (Eskimo) he had observed in Alaska. With the onset of winter, the *Rurik* returned to southern waters, stopping first at the Spanish missions on the California coast.

Chamisso made observations on the mission society in San Francisco, especially its impact on the Native American population of coastal California. He also conducted a study of marine life around San Francisco Bay, with special attention to a creature he identified as the California eared seal, more commonly known as the California sea lion.

In November 1816, the expedition reached the HAWAIIAN ISLANDS. Chamisso participated in native ceremonies and rituals and observed the Hawaiian festive dance, the hula. From Hawaii, the expedition sailed to Guam in the Marianas, then went on to the Philippines. Chamisso made a study of insects around Manila Bay.

In spring 1817, Kotzebue sailed the *Rurik* back to Bering Strait, but, because of ill health, decided to end the expedition and return to Europe by way of the CAPE OF GOOD HOPE. On a stopover in England, Chamisso made a journey to London and conferred with veteran naturalists of the South Pacific, SIR JOSEPH BANKS, ROBERT BROWN, and JAMES BURNEY.

The *Rurik* returned to in St. Petersburg in August 1818. Chamisso returned to Berlin, where he was named conservator and chief horticulturalist for the royal botanical gardens. He continued to flourish as a poet and prose writer in Europe. In 1821, he published an account of his CIRCUMNAVIGATION OF THE WORLD with Kotzebue, as well as an expanded version, entitled *Voyage Journal,* which first appeared in 1835.

Louis Chamisso de Boncourt was known in Germany as Adelbert von Chamisso. His accomplishments as a botanical scientist in the Pacific and in Brazil are less well known than his literary endeavors; his work as a naturalist was honored, however, in the naming of Chamisso Island in Alaska's Kotzebue Sound. Chamisso's published account maintains that the Indians of South America had never become a seafaring people, an idea widely accepted in Europe and not seriously challenged until the voyage of THOR HEYERDAHL in 1947.

Champlain, Samuel de (1567–1635) *French mariner, soldier, fur trader, cartographer in northeastern North America*

Samuel de Champlain was born in Brouage, France, on the Bay of Biscay. Descended from a long line of seafaring men, he carried on the family tradition, embarking on a career in the French navy. He became a skilled geographer and cartographer as well as a navigator. He also served in the French army in the wars with Spain of the 1590s and developed skills as a surveyor.

Following the Treaty of Vervins in 1598, which ended the French Wars of Religion and led to the removal of Spanish troops from France, Champlain traveled to Spain, where his uncle held some influence. In 1599, with his uncle's help, Champlain traveled with a Spanish fleet to colonies in Cuba, Mexico, Puerto Rico, the Antilles, and Panama. Upon his return in 1601, he wrote an account of his travels, entitled *Bref Discours* (Brief discourse), which included one of the earliest proposals for the construction of a canal route across the Isthmus of Panama.

At the beginning of the 17th century, France, under King Henry IV, was facing severe financial problems following nearly a century of warfare with Spain. Once the military situation had been resolved in 1598, the king sought ways to bring needed commerce and money into the country. With the Spanish and Portuguese developing prosperous colonies in the Americas, he wanted France to do the same and solicited the financial backing and military expertise of his former officers to initiate voyages of exploration and settlement into Canada. Among them were Aymar de Chastes, governor of Dieppe and vice admiral of France; François Grave, sieur de Pontgrave; and Pierre de Gua, sieur de Monts. In exchange for a monopoly on the FUR TRADE over an area stretching from the Gulf of St. Lawrence to the shores of what is now southern New Jersey, de Chastes agreed to head an expedition to the coast of Canada in 1603. As royal geographer, Champlain was assigned to the expedition to prepare maps and seek a NORTHWEST PASSAGE through the North American continent to China and the Far East.

In summer 1603, Champlain and de Chastes sailed from the port of Honfleur in Normandy. The expedition passed through the Strait of Belle Isle and entered the Gulf of St. Lawrence. This region had been visited by French and Portuguese fishermen and early fur traders throughout the 16th century, since before JACQUES CARTIER's voyages of the 1530s and 1540s.

Champlain and de Chastes reached Tadoussac at the mouth of the Saguenay River, about 400 miles from the Atlantic outlet of the St. Lawrence River. Earlier French colonists had attempted to establish a settlement there, but it had been abandoned by 1601. From the Indians at Tadoussac, Champlain learned of water routes and portages north, south, and east.

After exploring northward up the Saguenay River for a distance of 40 miles, Champlain returned to the St. Lawrence and visited the Huron (Wyandot) village at Hochelaga (present-day Montreal). At this point, he encountered the same obstacle that had blocked Cartier's explorations 60 years earlier: the Lachine Rapids, barely navigable by CANOE and impassable by ship or longboat. The expedition returned to France in the fall of 1603, with glowing reports of the potential for the fur trade in the St. Lawrence River and Gulf of St. Lawrence region. Champlain also wrote an account of observations on the Indians he had encountered, entitled *Des Sauvages*.

Despite de Chastes's death in France in 1603, a second and larger expedition was planned. In June 1604, two ships sailed from France under the command of Champlain and de Gua. While part of the expedition returned to Tadoussac, Champlain's party remained in the Bay of Fundy and explored Cape Breton Island, the south coast of Nova Scotia,

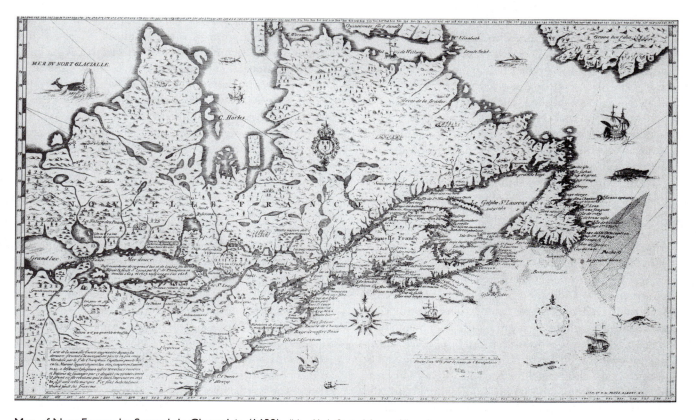

Map of New France by Samuel de Champlain (1632) *(New York State Library, Albany)*

and Passamaquoddy Bay on the coast of what is now northern Maine. Locating the Atlantic outlet of the St. Croix River, the border between present-day Maine and New Brunswick, Champlain traveled 10 miles upriver and established the Acadia colony of about 80 men on Dochet Island to exploit the fur trade of the southern Laurentian Mountains.

About half the colonists died during the winter of 1604–05 as a result of food shortages and an outbreak of SCURVY. In spring 1605, Champlain and the Sieur de Monts moved the colony to a better location on the Annapolis Basin of southeastern Nova Scotia. The settlement, Port Royal, later became Annapolis-Royal, Nova Scotia.

Over the next two years, Champlain used Port Royal as a base for his explorations of the east coast of Canada and the present northeastern United States. In 1605–07, he sailed and charted southward to Cape Breton Island, Maine, Boston Bay, Plymouth Harbor, Cape Cod, Narragansett Bay, Nantucket, and Martha's Vineyard. He reached and named Mount Desert Island off the Maine coast and traveled up the Penobscot River as far as present-day Bangor, Maine. In his continuing search for a Northwest Passage to the Pacific Ocean, he also explored Maine's Kennebec and Dead Rivers, the Chaudière River of Quebec, and the Charles River in Massachusetts. Champlain was also seeking "Norumbega," a fabled Indian land of riches, first reported by GIOVANNI DA VERRAZANO nearly a century earlier. De Gua lost his fur monopoly in 1607, and Champlain and the Port Royal colonists returned to France.

In 1608, Champlain departed France on another expedition, sailing for the upper St. Lawrence River. At the Huron village of Stadacona, located at the narrows of the St. Lawrence, he established Quebec (present-day Quebec City), the first permanent French colony on the North American mainland. Champlain soon made trade and military alliances with the Huron, Algonkin, and Montagnais tribes.

Champlain again returned to France in 1608–09, where he married Helen Boulle, the daughter of a royal official. Although she was only 12 years old and Champlain 40, her substantial dowry enabled him to proceed in his efforts at colonization and exploration in New France.

In return for French military support in their perpetual wars against the Iroquois (Haudenosaunee) Indians to the south, the Huron and various Algonquian-speaking tribes agreed to take Champlain on explorations into the rivers and uncharted wilderness south of the St. Lawrence. In spring 1609, he left Quebec with a party of French and Indians and journeyed by birch-bark canoe along the St. Lawrence to the entrance of the Richelieu River. They traveled south along the Richelieu until they entered the valley lying between the Adirondacks and the Green Mountains. The river led them into a large freshwater body extending

south for 107 miles. At present-day Chimney Point, Vermont, Champlain named the lake after himself. At the same time, HENRY HUDSON was less than 150 miles away exploring what is now the Hudson River.

A confrontation with the Iroquois soon ensued at the southern end of Lake Champlain at present-day Crown Point, New York. Although his party was outnumbered by the Iroquois (probably Mohawk), the French were able to rout the attackers by firing guns as they charged. The Indians fled, never having seen firearms.

After a brief period in France, where Champlain consolidated his trade monopoly over the St. Lawrence region, he returned to Canada in 1611. Traveling to the upper St. Lawrence, he established a summer outpost above the Lachine Rapids—Sault Saint Louis—which developed into the city of Montreal.

Two years later, in 1613, Champlain and a company of French and Indians successfully negotiated the rapids of the upper St. Lawrence in birch-bark canoes and reached the Ottawa River. Exploration to the south was blocked because of the Iroquois, but Champlain was confident that the Ottawa would lead him to the great body of water to the west, which he believed to be the Pacific Ocean, based on the reports of another French explorer, Nicolas de Vignau. Champlain and his party traveled as far as Allumette Island in what is now southwestern Quebec before returning to Montreal.

Champlain made a second attempt to reach the body of water at the western end of the Ottawa River in 1615, accompanied by his protégé, ÉTIENNE BRÛLÉ. Together they traveled beyond Allumette Island, portaged to Lake Nipissing, then canoed along the French River to its outlet into Georgian Bay on the northeast shore of Lake Huron, which was one of the Great Lakes, and not the Pacific Ocean as they had believed.

From the Georgian Bay Huron, Champlain and Brule recruited a large force of warriors, then headed southward to attack the Onondaga tribe of the Iroquois confederacy at their stronghold on Onondaga Lake near present-day Syracuse, New York. Champlain left Brûlé and his group at Lake Simcoe and proceeded southward along the eastern end of Lake Ontario to Oneida Lake. Champlain was wounded in the attack against the Onondaga, which proved to be less than a military success. Instead of returning to Montreal, however, he traveled again to Georgian Bay with the Huron, where he spent the winter. He sent Brûlé to follow the course of the Susquehanna River.

In spring 1616, Champlain was back in Montreal, where he continued to administer New France for the next 19 years. Although he did not undertake any major explorations of his own after 1615, he directed trade and exploration expeditions by a group that came to be known as "Champlain's Young Men," including Brûlé, who traveled as far west as Lake Superior and as far south as Chesapeake

Bay, and JEAN NICOLET, who visited Lake Michigan and Green Bay.

In the early 1620s, the administration of New France came under the direction of Cardinal Richelieu. Champlain was appointed as Richelieu's chief representative and was a leader of the Company of 100 Associates overseeing the French fur monopoly in Canada. In 1627, Quebec and Montreal were besieged by the British, and in 1629, Champlain was taken prisoner and sent to England, where he worked on a third edition of his book, *Voyages de la Nouvelle France.*

French control of Canada was restored in 1632, and Champlain returned to administer the colonial empire in 1633. He died in Montreal two years later.

Called the "Father of New France," Samuel de Champlain did much to open up the western frontier of Canada for France. His explorations, along with those of his "Young Men," penetrated the interior of Canada west and south of the St. Lawrence region, deep into the central part of the North American continent. Unlike the British colonists on the Eastern Seaboard, who were blocked from westward expansion by the Iroquois tribes and the APPALACHIAN MOUNTAINS, the French, under Champlain, exploited the network of inland rivers and portages to expand their trade interests as far as the west shores of Lake Superior and Lake Michigan. Champlain, cartographer and geographer, also produced the first accurate maps of eastern Canada. His pro-Algonquian ties incurred the wrath of the Iroquois, affecting French-Iroquois relations throughout the French and Indian Wars, from 1689 to 1763.

Chancellor, Richard (ca. 1520–1556)

English mariner in the Russian Arctic

Little is known of Richard Chancellor's origins or early life. By the early 1550s, he had gained a reputation in England as an accomplished navigator. At that time, English commercial interests were seeking an alternative to the southern sea routes to India and the Far East then dominated by Portugal and Spain. In 1551, veteran explorer SEBASTIAN CABOT and London merchants organized a joint stock company, the MUSCOVY COMPANY, for the purpose of establishing a northern sea route to the Orient by way of the NORTHEAST PASSAGE.

Chancellor was named pilot general of a three-ship expedition sponsored by Cabot and his company and headed by SIR HUGH WILLOUGHBY. He sailed on the ship *Edward Bonaventure* with STEPHEN BOROUGH as captain. Willoughby sailed on the flagship *Bona Esperanza.* Cornelius Durforth was the captain of the third ship, the *Bona Confidentia.*

Chancellor and Borough sailed from the Thames River port of Gravesend in May 1553. They planned to join up with the other two ships off the coast of northern Norway. Just east of North Cape, at Varangerfjord, the ships were separated in a storm. Willoughby and Durforth's ships temporarily found safe harbor on the coast of the Kola Peninsula (Lapland), but the crews perished in the Arctic winter. Chancellor and Borough meanwhile reportedly crossed the Barents Sea and reached the west coast of the Novaya Zemlya islands in their search for the Northeast Passage.

Driven back by ice, Chancellor and Borough sailed the *Edward Bonaventure* westward into the White Sea and made a landing at the mouth of the Northern Dvina River, where they established an English trading post. They soon learned they had arrived in Russia, and, upon invitation of the Russian government, traveled about 1,000 miles by sled to the court of Czar Ivan IV (Ivan the Terrible) in Moscow.

The English were warmly welcomed by Ivan, and, after establishing trade contacts with the Russian monarch, returned to their ship on the White Sea. Instead of continuing their search for the Northeast Passage, Chancellor and Borough sailed back to England, arriving in summer 1554. Although the voyage had not revealed any new geographic knowledge in regard to a northern sea route to the Far East, his visit to Russia provided a new market for English goods and was greeted in London with great enthusiasm. Cabot's merchant company became known as the Muscovy Company and concentrated its efforts on the development of Anglo-Russian trade.

In 1555, Chancellor made his second voyage to Russia for Cabot's company, again sailing to the White Sea and traveling overland to Moscow, where he learned the fate of Willoughby and the rest of the previous expedition. He recovered Willoughby's journal and set off for England in summer 1556 with a formal trade agreement from the Russian government. Chancellor's wife accompanied him on his second voyage to Russia. Returning to London with him was the first Russian ambassador to the English court. On the return voyage, the *Edward Bonaventure* was wrecked off the coast of Scotland. Chancellor and his wife were drowned, although the Russian ambassador survived and eventually reached London.

Richard Chancellor was a pioneer of modern British Arctic exploration. The ships used in his voyages were the first to be specially outfitted and reinforced for heavy ice conditions in the Arctic seas. A highly skilled navigator, Chancellor was one of the first mariners to use a navigational instrument known as the arbalest, a predecessor of the SEXTANT, which enabled him to determine latitude by measuring the altitude of the sun above the horizon. Although his 1553 voyage to the Arctic coast of Russia fell far short of locating the Northeast Passage, the trading post he established on the White Sea developed into the port of Archangel and opened up trade in Russian furs and English woolen cloth. ANTHONY JENKINSON, who succeeded Chancellor as chief

English trade agent in Russia, subsequently extended the Muscovy Company's trade to the Caspian Sea.

Chang Ch'ien (Zhang Qian, Chang K'ien)

(unknown–114 B.C.) *Chinese diplomat in central Asia*
Originally from Hangchung, west of present-day Beijing, Chang Ch'ien was an officer in service to the Chinese emperor Wu-ti (Wudi) in the latter part of the second century B.C. China, at that time ruled by the Han dynasty, was threatened by the nomadic Hsiung-nu (Xiongnu) people from northern Asia, known in the West as the Huns.

In 138 B.C., Chang was sent on a diplomatic mission from China westward to the land of the Yue-chi (Yuezhi, also known as the Tocharians), a nomadic people who had been driven across the Hindu Kush mountain range into the region now comprising Afghanistan. His party of 100 Chinese envoys and soldiers was soon attacked by the Hsiung-nu, and Chang, taken prisoner, was taken to the Hsiung-nu's stronghold in the Altai Mountains of central Asia. He remained a captive for 10 years, during which time he married a Hsiung-nu woman by whom he had a child.

Chang managed to escape from the Hsiung-nu in about 128. He continued westward to the upper reaches of the Jaxartes River (the present-day Syr Darya River, near Tashkent in what is now Uzbekistan). From there, he traveled into Bactria and Fergana (present-day northern Afghanistan). He noted that bamboo and cloth produced in southern China were traded in the region, having been shipped there from India, a land all but unknown to the Chinese. He also received reports of other civilizations to the west, including Persia (present-day Iran), Mesopotamia (present-day Iraq), and the Eastern Roman Empire in Asia Minor.

Unable to negotiate an alliance with the Yue-chi, he set out for China by way of Tibet. Along the way, he was again taken prisoner by the Hsiung-nu, but he escaped this time after only a year of captivity and returned home.

In 115, the Han emperor again sent Chang on a diplomatic mission, this time to seek an alliance with the Wusan (Wusan) people, a nomadic tribe of the Issyk Kul region that had settled in Sinkiang in western China. He set out in command of an expedition of 300 mounted men, carrying a large shipment of gold and silk.

Although Chang did not succeed in creating an alliance with the Wu-san tribe, he did send out envoys laden with gifts of silk and gold to Persia and the eastern Roman provinces, opening up trade links between China and the Hellenistic world of the eastern MEDITERRANEAN SEA. He is thought to have returned to China by 109 B.C.

Chang Ch'ien was the earliest known Chinese explorer. His two diplomatic missions brought back geographic information that ultimately affected the Chinese view of the world, leading China to become aware of civilizations beyond its borders to the west and south, including Mesopotamia, Rome, India, and Burma (present-day Myanmar). One tangible result of his travels was the establishment of the SILK ROAD, which opened up trade with the Roman Empire far to the west and provided the main communication link between the East and the West for the next 1,300 years.

Ch'ang-ch'un (Chang Chun, Chen-jen)

(1148–1227) *Chinese priest in central Asia, in service to the Mongols*
Ch'ang-ch'un was a Taoist (Daoist) sage, well respected among his fellow Chinese. In 1219, he was ordered by GENGHIS KHAN, ruler of the Mongols, to embark on a trip of reconnaissance through central Asia and visit the ruler on his expedition of conquest.

That same year, at age 69, Ch'ang-ch'un departed Laichou (Laizhou), near present-day Yantai on the Gulf of Chihli (Bo Hai), and set out toward Genghis Khan's court at Yen-King (present-day Beijing). Two years later, in May 1221, with a Mongol escort and 19 disciples, he traveled northward to the Kerulen River in Mongolia, then westward through the steppelands and across the Altai and Tian Shan mountain ranges to Tashkent and Samarkand in present-day Uzbekistan. Next, he crossed the Hindu Kush, arriving in Perwali, south of present-day Kabul, Afghanistan, after 14 months. There, he met up with Genghis Khan and reported on the peoples and politics of the steppelands.

Accompanying Ch'ang-ch'un on his journey was Li Chih-chang, who wrote a narrative of the journey, providing an early account of the geography and peoples of central Asia.

Charbonneau, Jean-Baptiste (Pomp)

(1805–1866) *Shoshone-French Canadian guide, trapper in the American West, son of Toussaint Charbonneau and Sacajawea*
Jean-Baptiste Charbonneau was born in a Mandan Indian village by Mandan the upper MISSOURI RIVER, near the site of present-day Bismarck, North Dakota. He was the son of French-Canadian trapper TOUSSAINT CHARBONNEAU and the Shoshone Indian SACAJAWEA (Sacagawea).

At the time of his birth in February 1805, the Lewis and Clark Expedition was encamped at its nearby winter headquarters, Fort Mandan, preparing to continue its expedition across the northern plains and ROCKY MOUNTAINS to the Pacific coast. Toussaint Charbonneau and Sacajawea were hired as guides and interpreters for the expedition, and the infant, referred to as Pomp in the journals of MERIWETHER LEWIS and WILLIAM CLARK, was carried on a cradleboard by his mother to the Pacific coast in present-day

Oregon and back. In the years after the expedition, young Charbonneau lived with Clark in St. Louis and there received his early education at a Catholic-run day school.

By the age of 17, Charbonneau had returned to the Great Plains and was employed at a trading settlement on the Kansas River. In 1823, he met Prince Paul Wilhelm of Württemberg (a former state of Germany), who was gathering scientific data west of the Missouri River. The prince was so impressed by Charbonneau's intelligence, as well as his skills as a frontiersman, that he offered to take the young man with him to Europe.

From 1823 to 1829, Charbonneau lived with Prince Paul Wilhelm at his castle near Stuttgart, Germany, where he studied French, German, and Spanish. He also took part in hunting expeditions in the nearby Black Forest and traveled throughout Europe and North Africa.

In 1829, Charbonneau returned to the United States with the prince for an expedition into the upper Missouri River regions of present-day North Dakota and Montana. He remained on the Great Plains following the prince's return to Europe.

In the early 1830s, Charbonneau was a trapper for the AMERICAN FUR COMPANY, working with ANTOINE ROBIDOUX in present-day northern Utah and southern Idaho. He was present at the fur trappers' rendezvous on the Green River in summer 1833. As a trapper in the central and northern Rocky Mountains, Charbonneau became friends with such mountain men as JOSEPH L. MEEK, JAMES BECKWOURTH, and JAMES BRIDGER.

By the end of the 1830s, the trade in beaver pelts had declined, and Charbonneau turned to guiding parties of emigrants and other travelers into the Rockies and Great Plains.

In 1839, Charbonneau worked with frontier traders LOUIS VASQUEZ and Andrew Sublette (WILLIAM LEWIS SUBLETTE's brother), helping establish Fort Vasquez on the South Platte River, located near the site where Denver, Colorado, would develop 20 years later. In 1840, Charbonneau transported one of the earliest shipments of buffalo robes and dried buffalo tongues down the South Platte to St. Louis.

Sir William Drummond, a hunter and sportsman from Scotland, hired Charbonneau as a guide for his 1843 hunting trip into the northern Rockies. Charbonneau guided the party through the SOUTH PASS of Wyoming's Wind River Range into the Green River region of northern Utah, then northward into the area of present-day Yellowstone National Park. After the expedition, Charbonneau continued to hunt buffalo and antelope for Drummond, sending the meat back to his patron's castle in Scotland.

In August 1845, Charbonneau was a guide for Lieutenant JAMES WILLIAM ABERT and a detachment of the U.S. Corps of Topographical Engineers in their expedition to the Canadian River region of the Texas Panhandle and present-day western Oklahoma.

The next year, 1846, saw the outbreak of the U.S.-Mexican War. Starting in October, Charbonneau served as a guide for Colonel Philip St. George Cooke's Mormon Battalion in its expedition across the southwestern desert, from Santa Fe, New Mexico, to San Diego, California. Along the way, he helped blaze a wagon road through northern Mexico and present-day southern Arizona. Charbonneau led the expedition west and north to the Gila and Colorado Rivers, then to the Pacific coast at San Diego by January 1847.

Following the war, Charbonneau was drawn to the California goldfields in 1849. He lived in the American River region near Sacramento for the next decade and a half, where he was joined by his former trapping companion, Jim Beckwourth.

In 1866, Charbonneau left California and traveled eastward to join the gold rush in southwestern Montana. On the way, he contracted a fever and died on the Owyhee River near the present Idaho-Nevada border.

During his career as a trapper, hunter, and guide, Jean-Baptiste Charbonneau helped open a vast area of North America to non-Indian travel and settlement. This territory stretched west from St. Louis and the upper Missouri to the Pacific coast and from the rivers and mountains of present-day Utah and Wyoming to the southwestern deserts of present-day New Mexico, Arizona, and southern California.

Charbonneau, Toussaint (ca. 1758–ca. 1840)

French Canadian guide, interpreter in the American West, husband of Sacajawea, father of Jean-Baptiste Charbonneau

Details of Toussaint Charbonneau's early life are obscure. He was probably born in Montreal while Canada was still under the control of the French. In the 1790s, he worked for the NORTH WEST COMPANY, a Montreal-based fur trading enterprise, as one of their VOYAGEURS. He trapped and traded for furs with the Indians of the upper MISSOURI RIVER region, becoming familiar with their language and customs. He had married as many as three Indian women by 1804.

In fall 1804, Charbonneau was operating around the Mandan Indian villages near what is now Bismarck, North Dakota. At that time, he was married to the Shoshone Indian woman SACAJAWEA (Sacagawea). In early November, he met with MERIWETHER LEWIS and WILLIAM CLARK at their winter headquarters among the Mandan and, along with Sacajawea, was hired as a guide and interpreter. With their newborn son, JEAN-BAPTISTE CHARBONNEAU, Charbonneau and Sacajawea set out with the expedition in April 1805.

Although Charbonneau probably provided valuable service as an interpreter in dealing with the northern plains tribes, most of the references to him in the journals of Lewis and Clark refer to his ineptitude as a guide in contrast to his wife's abilities. In early May 1805, Charbonneau's

CANOE was nearly swamped, and it was only the forbearance of Sacajawea that saved the craft from capsizing. Charbonneau was described as responding to this incident by crying out in terror. A few weeks later, in early June 1805, Charbonneau was chased by a large grizzly bear that had been shot by some of the expedition members near the Marias River in the vicinity of present-day Loma, Montana. On the return trip, in late April 1806, Charbonneau's horse threw him and his load. For his services to the Corps of Discovery, Charbonneau was paid $500.33.

After the expedition, Charbonneau settled briefly in the St. Louis area. He eventually left his young son in the care of Clark in St. Louis and returned to the life of a fur trader on the upper Missouri. Among his employers during this period were MANUEL LISA and JOHN JACOB ASTOR's AMERICAN FUR COMPANY.

During the War of 1812, Charbonneau helped prevent the upper Missouri tribes from siding with the British. After the war, he was employed from time to time as a guide to various expeditions to the West, including early forays by American traders on the Santa Fe Trail to Taos, New Mexico. These expeditions took him into unexplored regions of the southern and central ROCKY MOUNTAINS, as far west as the Great Salt Lake.

In 1820, Charbonneau was an interpreter and guide for Colonel STEPHEN HARRIMAN LONG's expedition to the Great Plains region of Kansas. Three years later, Charbonneau provided his services to Prince Paul Wilhelm of Württemberg on his tour of the Great Plains. Soon afterward, Prince Paul Wilhelm took Charbonneau's son Jean-Baptiste to Europe to be educated.

In the early 1830s, Charbonneau, although in his seventies, worked as a fur trader and trapper for WILLIAM SUBLETTE and ROBERT CAMPBELL. In 1833–34, he was hired as an interpreter by ALEXANDER PHILIPP MAXIMILIAN and the artist KARL BODMER for a tour of upper Missouri.

In about 1839, Charbonneau made a trip to St. Louis to claim back pay owed by the federal government for his diplomatic services among the Indians, then returned to the Mandan lands in present-day North Dakota, where he died soon afterward.

Toussaint Charbonneau left behind a less than heroic image as a frontiersman and explorer of the Great Plains and Far West. Yet his contributions as an interpreter with many important expeditions have earned him a place in the history of exploration of the American West.

Charcot, Jean-Baptiste-Étienne-Auguste

(1867–1936) *French physician, oceanographer, polar explorer*

Jean-Baptiste Charcot was born in the Paris suburb of Neuilly-sur-Seine, the son of the noted French neurologist

Jean-Baptiste Charcot *(Library of Congress)*

Jean-Martin Charcot. The younger Charcot became a doctor of medicine and also pursued his interest in the natural sciences, especially oceanography.

In 1902, Charcot raised funds for a French expedition to the Antarctic. At that time, German, Swedish, English, and Scottish teams were actively engaged in exploration of the continent. Although Charcot had planned to relieve the Swedish expedition under NILS OTTO GUSTAF NORDENSKJÖLD, which was stranded on the Antarctic Peninsula, by the time he arrived there in 1903, the Swedes had already been rescued by an Argentine vessel. Charcot then set about exploring and mapping the west coast of the peninsula.

In the Antarctic summer of 1904–05, Charcot led survey expeditions to Alexander I Island. He sighted and named the Loubet coast after then-president of France Émile-François Loubet. Although his vessel, the *Français,* was damaged when it struck a rock, he proceeded with his exploration of western Antarctica's coastline, then sailed to Patagonia, where he sold the ship to the Argentine government. Two years later, the *Français* was lost in a wreck in the Río de la Plata.

Back in France, Charcot planned a second French Antarctic expedition. In August 1908, he sailed from Le Havre, France, on the *Pourquoi-Pas?* (the "Why Not?"), a ship specially designed for polar exploration. His expedition reached western Antarctica by way of the STRAIT OF MAGELLAN. First stopping at Wiencke Island, the expedition explored the Palmer Archipelago, where again the ship was damaged on a rock. Despite this setback, Charcot continued to explore and map the Antarctic shoreline, determining that the Loubet Coast was identical with the land identified as Adelaide Land by JOHN BISCOE in 1831, and determined that it was actually an island. Charcot also located and named the Fallières Coast. An island off the coast of Graham Land was subsequently named Charcot Island. In 1910, Charcot concluded his second Antarctic expedition and returned to France.

Over the next 25 years, Charcot undertook oceanographic studies in the Atlantic and Arctic Oceans. In 1921, he led a scientific expedition to Rockall off the west coast of Scotland. Some of his later expeditions attempted to trace the voyages of such ancient explorers as PYTHEAS and SAINT BRENDAN. On one such venture in 1936, the *Pourquoi-Pas?* went down off the coast of ICELAND, and Charcot and 38 members of his expedition died.

Dr. Jean-Baptiste Charcot contributed much to the geographic knowledge of Antarctica. The charts he produced of the Antarctic coastline were the only accurate ones available as late as 1935.

Charlevoix, Pierre-François-Xavier de

(1682–1761) *French historian on the Great Lakes and Mississippi River*

Born in France, Pierre-François de Charlevoix entered the Jesuit order as a young man. After studying at the College Louis le Grand in Paris, he sailed to New France, probably arriving in 1705. For the next four years, he taught rhetoric at Quebec's Jesuit college. In 1709, he returned to Paris and served as a professor at the College Louis le Grand, eventually receiving an appointment as the school's prefect.

In 1720, Charlevoix made another trip to New France, during which he traveled westward along the St. Lawrence

Pierre-François-Xavier de Charlevoix *(Library of Congress)*

River into the Great Lakes. From the southern end of Lake Michigan, he explored the Illinois River in the vicinity of present-day Peoria, Illinois, then proceeded to the MISSISSIPPI RIVER. He traveled the entire length of the Mississippi to New Orleans and the Gulf of Mexico.

Charlevoix survived a shipwreck in the gulf on his return trip to France. He eventually arrived in Paris and resumed teaching.

Pierre-François de Charlevoix's six-volume *History of New France,* first published in 1744, contains a detailed account of his 1720 journey through the Great Lakes and down the Mississippi to New Orleans. This narrative provides a view of the central and lower Mississippi River region, including descriptions of Native American tribes, only a few decades after RENÉ-ROBERT CAVELIER DE LA SALLE and his followers explored the area in the late 17th century.

Chatillon, Henri (1816–1875) *American trader, trapper, guide in the American West*

While a young man, Henri Chatillon was a mountain man and fur trapper throughout the Great Plains and ROCKY MOUNTAINS. As such, he was among the earliest non-Indians to use little-traveled mountain trails.

In 1846, while in St. Louis, Missouri, in the employ of the frontier trading concern of PIERRE CHOUTEAU, JR., Chatillon was hired as a guide by the historian Francis Parkman. He led Parkman's party on an expedition west from Independence, Missouri, to Fort Leavenworth in present-day Kansas. They then headed up the Platte River to Fort Laramie in present-day Wyoming. The expedition turned south and visited Bent's Fort on the Arkansas River in southeastern Colorado, then returned eastward to Missouri via the Santa Fe Trail.

Chatillon was married to Bear Robe, the daughter of a Sioux (Dakota, Lakota, Nakota) chief. After his Indian wife died, he married a non-Indian woman and settled in St. Louis.

Like other MOUNTAIN MEN of his day, Henri Chatillon used his knowledge of Indian trails to earn a living as a guide following the decline of the FUR TRADE. He is depicted in Parkman's account of his 1846 western journey, *The California and Oregon Trail,* which first appeared in 1849.

Cheadle, Walter Butler (1835–1919)

British physician, explorer in the Canadian West

In 1862, Walter Cheadle, a British pediatrician and medical researcher, and WILLIAM-WENTWORTH FITZWILLIAM MILTON (Viscount Milton), a young British nobleman, left Quebec, Canada, on the first leg of a journey in search of an overland NORTHWEST PASSAGE across western Canada. Two years earlier, gold had been discovered in the Cariboo district of eastern British Columbia, and finding a direct route to these goldfields from central Manitoba was the expedition's main objective.

From Quebec, Cheadle and Milton traveled by boat and train westward through the Great Lakes region by way of Toronto, Detroit, and Chicago. From St. Paul, Minnesota, they headed overland by stagecoach to eastern North Dakota and the Red River of the North. Progressing up the Red River by CANOE, they reached Fort Garry—present-day Winnipeg, Manitoba—in late August 1862. After equipping themselves with horses and supplies for the journey across Canada's northern plains, they set out for Carlton House, a fur-trading post on the North Saskatchewan River in what is now northwestern Saskatchewan.

Cheadle and Milton wintered at Witchekan Lake. In spring 1863, they continued along the North Saskatchewan River toward the ROCKY MOUNTAINS. In the eastern foothills of the Canadian Rockies, at Jasper, Alberta, they hired an Iroquois (Haudenosaunee) guide to lead them through the Yellowhead Pass, a route at that time little known to non-Indian travelers. Before embarking on the trek through the Rocky Mountains, Cheadle and Milton had been joined by a fur trader named Louis Battenotte and his wife and child, as well as another adventurer identified only as a Mr. O'B. After leading Cheadle and his companions through the Yellowhead Pass to the Fraser River west of the Continental Divide, the Iroquois guide left the expedition before it reached the Cariboo district.

Cheadle and his party wandered through what is now eastern British Columbia's Mt. Robson Provincial Park and, unable to locate an overland trail north to the goldfields, were compelled to follow the North Thompson River southward. By the time they had reached Kamloops, they were short on supplies and suffering from exhaustion and starvation. They found aid at the nearby HUDSON'S BAY COMPANY post and among the Shuswap Indians.

Cheadle and Milton took the usual route to the Fraser River, which they followed to Victoria, British Columbia, on the Pacific coast, where they recovered from their ordeal. They then completed their journey to the Cariboo goldfields by following the Fraser River northward from Yale.

After returning to England, Dr. Walter Cheadle and Viscount Milton published, in 1865, an account of their travels in the Canadian West, with the self-explanatory title *The North-West Passage by Land, Being the Narrative of an Expedition from the Atlantic to the Pacific, Undertaken with the View of Exploring a Route across the Continent to British Columbia through British Territory, by One of the Northern Passes in the Rocky Mountains.* In later published articles, as well as in lecture appearances in England, they urged the development of more direct east-west routes through the Rockies to the interior of eastern British Columbia. In 1865, soon after the completion of their trans-Canada expedition,

the Canadian government completed the Cariboo Wagon Road, which ran from the head of navigation on the Fraser at Yale, 400 miles northward into the Cariboo district. Several decades passed before a more direct route into the Cariboo district was established.

Chelyuskin, Simeon (fl. 1740s) *Russian mariner in the Siberian Arctic*

There are few available details of 18th-century Russian navigator Simeon Chelyuskin's origins or early life. He was a captain in VITUS JONASSEN BERING's second expedition beginning in 1733 and lasting until 1743, carried on by others after Bering's death in 1741.

In 1742–43, in the course of that expedition, Chelyuskin was assigned to explore the Arctic coast of northern SIBERIA. Sailing from the White Sea, he headed eastward and explored Novaya Zemlya, then continued to the Ob River estuary.

Beyond the Ob River, Chelyuskin followed the Arctic coast of Siberia to the east shore of the Kara Sea. His ship was stopped by ice as he approached the northern end of the Taymyr Peninsula, at which point he resorted to sledges. Traveling over the frozen sea, Chelyuskin and his party rounded the Taymyr Peninsula, the northernmost point of Asia, becoming the first Europeans ever to do so. They entered the Laptev Sea, completing a survey of the Arctic coast of Siberia begun almost 20 years earlier.

The point of the Taymyr Peninsula around which Simeon Chelyuskin traveled in 1743 was subsequently called Cape Chelyuskin in honor of his accomplishment. Cape Chelyuskin is the northernmost point of the Asian continent and of any continental landmass.

Cheng Ho (Zheng He, Zheng Ho) (1371–ca. 1434) *Chinese admiral in the Indian Ocean and East Africa*

Cheng Ho was born in Kunyang, a town in China's southern Yunan province, the son of Chinese Muslims. In 1381, at the age of 10, he entered the service of the Ming rulers as a eunuch. Over the next 10 years, under the command of the emperor's uncle, Chu Ti, he served with distinction in military campaigns against the Mongols.

In 1402, when Chu Ti usurped the throne and came to power as the Ming emperor Yung-lo (Yongle), Cheng Ho was commissioned to mount a series of naval expeditions in search of the deposed former ruler, Chu Yun-wen, who was believed to have fled overseas. As it turned out, Chu Yun-wen was never found. Although some sources suggest he was actually killed in the rebellion in 1402, legend has it that he managed to elude capture and lived as an itinerant monk until his death in 1440.

Appointed an admiral by the new emperor, Cheng Ho departed the estuary of the YANGTZE RIVER (Chang), near Shanghai, in 1405. His fleet, consisting of 62 large ships, plus 225 smaller vessels—varying designs of the JUNK—carried a combined crew of more than 27,000 men. This first expedition sailed southward to the South China Sea and, after stopovers on the coast of what is now Vietnam, continued on to Sumatra. There it defeated the fleet of the Chinese pirate Chen-Tsu-i. The pirate leader, taken captive, was escorted to the Ming capital at Nanking (Nanjing), where he was executed.

In 1407, Cheng Ho's fleet sailed westward across the Indian Ocean and reached Calicut on the Malabar Coast of India, where trade contacts were established. On the homeward journey, his ships visited Siam (present-day Thailand) and the island of Java in the Indonesian archipelago.

Cheng Ho's third expedition left China in 1409. After another voyage to India, his ships visited Ceylon (present-day Sri Lanka), Malacca, and Sumatra. A fourth expedition, undertaken from 1413 to 1415, extended Chinese trading contacts as far as Hormuz at the entrance to the Persian Gulf. The Chinese fleet also visited ports on the south coast of Arabia and in Aden.

Starting in 1417, under Cheng Ho's command, Chinese vessels began trading along the east coast of Africa, establishing commercial contacts with African ports along the Indian Ocean from Mogadishu southward to Mombasa and Zanzibar.

Cheng Ho's maritime ventures were stalled with the death of Emperor Yung-lo in 1424. He commanded one more large-scale expedition in 1433. On the way to East Africa, with a stopover at Calicut, India, in 1434–35, he died. His body was taken back to Nanking for burial.

Cheng Ho's accomplishments earned him the nickname "The Three-Jeweled Eunuch." His seven voyages opened up most of the coastal regions of the Indian Ocean to Chinese trade. Careful records were kept, including nautical charts, detailing extensive Chinese geographic knowledge extending from Southeast Asia to India, the Persian Gulf, and East Africa. China established trade and diplomatic contacts with more than 35 countries. Among the many items brought back to the Ming emperor from Cheng Ho's explorations were exotic animals, including a giraffe, which arrived from the African kingdom of Malindi in 1415. During the years immediately following Cheng Ho's death, China reverted to its traditional isolationism, and the SPICE TRADE between the Far East and Europe came under the control of the Muslim powers of the Persian Gulf and western India. Although many of the records of Cheng Ho's expeditions were destroyed by his political rivals after his death, some endured and provide evidence of Chinese contacts with southern Asia and East Africa just prior to the be-

ginning of the EUROPEAN AGE OF EXPLORATION in the 1400s.

Chen-jen   See CH'ANG-CH'UN.

Chesnard de la Giraudais, François   (fl. 1760s)
French naval officer in the South Atlantic and South Pacific

François Chesnard was born in the French seaport of Saint-Malo. He embarked on a seafaring career at a very early age, and went on to command French naval vessels in the Seven Years War of 1756–63.

In 1759, Chesnard captained one of the ships in the French naval convoy that carried LOUIS-ANTOINE DE BOUGAINVILLE to Canada. At the war's end in 1763, Bougainville appointed Chesnard to command the *Sphinx* in his colonizing expedition to the Falkland Islands.

Chesnard subsequently commanded the supply ship *Étoile* in Bougainville's exploring expedition to the Pacific Ocean. Sailing from the French port of Rochefort in February 1767, Chesnard headed for the Falkland Islands to join Bougainville. The *Étoile,* in need of repairs, was forced to put in at Rio de Janeiro; Bougainville, commanding the expedition's other vessel, the *Boudeuse,* met Chesnard there in late June.

Now sailing with the *Boudeuse,* Chesnard directed the *Étoile* to the Spanish port of Montevideo, Uruguay. In November 1767, with the onset of the Southern Hemisphere's summer season, Chesnard and Bougainville sailed southward to the STRAIT OF MAGELLAN. The difficult passage through the strait to the Pacific Ocean took 52 days. Continuing across the Pacific, the *Étoile* and the *Boudeuse* visited Tahiti and other recently explored island groups, as well as the Dutch colonies in present-day Indonesia. After a stopover at the French colony on what is now the island of Mauritius in the Indian Ocean, Chesnard and Bougainville continued westward to Europe by way of the CAPE OF GOOD HOPE. Chesnard returned to Rochefort in April 1769, a month after Bougainville had reached Saint-Malo.

François Chesnard's skill as a seafarer and navigator contributed greatly to the success of Bougainville's scientific expedition to the Pacific, an early French CIRCUMNAVIGATION OF THE WORLD.

Ch'ien, Chang   See CHANG CHIEN.

Chirikov, Aleksey Ilyich (Aleksei or Alexei Ilich Chirikov)   (1703–1748)   *Russian naval officer in Alaska*

Russian-born Aleksey Chirikov began his naval career at the age of 12, when he entered the Moscow School of

Navigation. He went on to the St. Petersburg Naval Academy, graduating in 1721.

From 1725 to 1730, Chirikov was a lieutenant and scientist in VITUS JONASSEN BERING's First Kamchatka Expedition. Bering had been commissioned by Czar Peter I to explore eastern SIBERIA and determine if a land connection existed between Asiatic Russia and the North American continent.

In 1728, Chirikov was aboard the *St. Gabriel* with Bering and took part in the exploration to the north and east of the Siberian coast, leading to exploration of the Gulf of Anadyr, the Chukchi Peninsula, Krest Sound, St. Lawrence Island, and the two Diomede Islands.

In spring 1741, Chirikov commanded the ship *St. Paul* in Bering's second expedition eastward from Kamchatka across the North Pacific Ocean. His orders were to continue the search for an isthmus between North America and Russia. Chirikov was also looking for the fabled Gama Land, a large island that Russian geographers believed was in the northern Pacific to the east of Siberia. Chirikov lost sight of Bering's ship but continued sailing eastward. On July 15, he made the first sighting of Alaskan land at Prince of Wales Island. The next day, Bering independently sighted Alaskan land at Kayak Island. On his return trip to Kamchatcka, Chirikov sighted Alaska's Kenai Peninsula, as well as a number of the Aleutian Islands, one of them later named in his honor.

In 1742, Chirikov again sailed from the Siberian port of Okhotsk and explored the Pacific coast of Kamchatka as well as the Commander Islands.

Aleksey Chirikov, along with Bering, helped clarify the geography of the region between Siberia and Alaska. Their reports of an abundance of fur-bearing animals in the islands of the Gulf of Alaska spurred the later development of the RUSSIAN-AMERICAN COMPANY's FUR TRADE.

Chisholm, Jesse (ca. 1805–1868) *American guide, interpreter, trader on the southern plains*

Born in Tennessee, Jesse Chisholm was the son of a frontier trader of Scottish descent and a Cherokee Indian woman. In about 1817, he moved with his family to the vicinity of Fort Smith in what is now western Arkansas. At that time, this post on the Arkansas River was a gateway to the southern plains.

Chisholm's Indian heritage was an advantage in his subsequent career as a trader to the Native Americans of present-day Oklahoma, northern Texas, and southern Kansas. He was said to be able to converse in at least a dozen Native American languages in addition to Cherokee.

After the opening of the Santa Fe Trail in 1821, federal military expeditions were sent out to survey the route westward and to negotiate treaties with the region's Indians. During the 1820s, Chisholm worked as a guide and interpreter for several of these military forays onto the southern plains.

In 1834–35, Chisholm helped blaze a trail for the U.S. First Dragoon Regiment, led by General HENRY LEAVENWORTH and Colonel HENRY DODGE, into the territory south and west of Fort Gibson. The expedition explored Comanche and Kiowa Indian lands of present-day southwestern Oklahoma and the Red River region of northern Texas, as far west as Pikes Peak in the eastern Colorado Rocky Mountains.

In the ensuing years, Chisholm established frontier trading posts in the Indian Territory, including one at Camp Holmes, which later developed into the south-central Oklahoma city of Lexington, and one at Left Hand Spring, near present-day Oklahoma City, Oklahoma.

At the outbreak of the Civil War in 1861, Chisholm acted as an intermediary between the tribes of western Oklahoma and the Confederate government. But as the war persisted, he left the Indian Territory and settled among the neutral Indian tribes of southern Kansas. In 1864, he founded a trading post among the Wichita Indians at the confluence of the Arkansas and Little Arkansas Rivers.

At the war's end in 1865, Chisholm undertook a trade expedition south from his Kansas post across the Indian Territory into northern Texas and the Red River region. He took trade goods to the Kiowa and Comanche, exchanging them for a shipment of buffalo hides. His return journey by wagon led him across the Colorado River of Texas, the Brazos River, and the Washita River. His wagon was so loaded down that it created deep ruts in the trail on his way back north, forming the beginnings of a permanent route between Texas and Kansas. Chisholm continued to trade with the Indians until his death at Left Hand Spring (now Geary, Oklahoma) in 1868.

In fall 1867, cattle and meat entrepreneur Joseph McCoy developed Jesse Chisholm's route as a cattle trail from San Antonio, Texas, northward through the Indian Territory into Kansas. Because it had few settlements, forests, hills, or other obstacles for cattle drovers, the trail was ideal for the overland transportation of cattle. It passed through Chisholm's settlement on the Little Arkansas River, which soon developed into the city of Wichita, Kansas. From there, the trail continued to the small community of Abilene and connected with the Kansas Pacific Railroad. For the next 10 years, until the late 1870s, this route, which became known as the Chisholm Trail, provided passage for millions of head of cattle to the meat markets of St. Louis and Chicago. Abilene and Wichita, because of their strategic location at the northern terminus of the Chisholm Trail, were rapidly transformed into booming "cow towns." The Chisholm Trail fell into disuse with the expansion of the Santa Fe Railroad in the late 1870s. Part of Chisholm's original route was adopted by the Santa Fe Railroad through central Kansas.

Choris, Louis (1795–1828) *German-Russian painter in Brazil and the North and South Pacific*

Louis Choris was born in Iekaterinoslav, the son of German parents who had settled in Russia. His ability as a painter of natural subjects gained early recognition, and, in 1813, at the age of 18, he served as the official artist in a scientific expedition to the Caucasus Mountains.

In 1815, Choris joined OTTO VON KOTZEBUE's Russian expedition to the Pacific Ocean, as a draftsman. Sailing on the *Rurik* from the Russian port of Kronstadt, near present-day St. Petersburg, he spent the next three years traveling around the world. En route, he took part in inland investigations of plant and animal life in Brazil, Polynesia, Alaska, the Aleutian Islands, the HAWAIIAN ISLANDS, and northeastern SIBERIA.

Choris returned to Europe in 1818. Settling in Paris, he undertook a study of lithography. From 1823 to 1826, he published his *Picturesque Journey Around the World 1815–18,* including his own lithographs, which were based on the paintings and drawings he had made on Kotzebue's expedition. Much of the flora and fauna depicted had been collected and identified by the expedition's naturalist, LOUIS-CHARLES-ADÉLAÏDE CHAMISSO DE BONCOURT.

Choris traveled to the United States in 1827, living briefly in New Orleans. He then went to Veracruz, Mexico, from where he planned to embark on an expedition into the Mexican interior. Shortly after he began his journey inland in March 1828, he was killed, probably in an attack by bandits.

Among the artists who had accompanied the late-18th-century and early-19th-century scientific expeditions to the Pacific, Louis Choris was one of the few whose drawings not only detailed plant and animal life, but also depicted the life and culture of native peoples. His skill as a lithographer enabled him to mass-produce his illustrations and make them widely available in Europe.

Chouart des Groseilliers, Médard (Sieur des Groseilliers) (1618–ca. 1697) *French-Canadian trader in the western Great Lakes and Hudson Bay regions, brother-in-law of Pierre-Esprit Radisson*

Médard Chouart, a native of the Marne region of north-central France, was known as the Sieur des Groseilliers after his St. Lawrence River estate. He migrated to French Canada in the early 1640s, where he first worked as a lay assistant at a Jesuit mission to the Huron (Wyandot) Indians on Georgian Bay in Lake Huron. He returned to Quebec following the Iroquois (Haudenosaunee) invasion of Huron country, whereupon he entered the FUR TRADE.

In August 1654, Groseilliers traveled to the western Great Lakes with a group of unlicensed fur traders, the COUREURS DE BOIS. After heading westward on the upper St. Lawrence, they reached the Ottawa River, then followed the portage route to Lake Nipissing and the French River to Georgian Bay. From Lake Huron, they passed through Mackinac Strait and then into Lake Michigan, which they crossed to Green Bay.

Groseilliers established himself in the region as a trader to such tribes as the Chippewa (Ojibway), Potawatomi, and Menominee. During his two-year stay, he explored parts of present-day Illinois, Michigan, and Wisconsin, including the Fox and Wisconsin Rivers. He also visited the upper reaches of the MISSISSIPPI RIVER. From the Indians, he heard reports of Lake Winnipeg to the northwest.

Groseilliers returned to Quebec in August 1656 with 250 Huron and a large shipment of furs. He embarked on his second fur-trading expedition to the western Great Lakes in spring 1659, accompanied by his brother-in-law PIERRE-ESPRIT RADISSON. From Georgian Bay, they passed through Sault Sainte Marie and traveled the length of Lake Superior to Chequamegon Bay, where they established a fur-trading post. The Indians told them of a north-flowing river that drained into a great sea, probably HUDSON BAY or James Bay. Groseilliers believed the "great sea" might lead to the much-sought-after NORTHWEST PASSAGE to China and the Orient.

Upon their return to Montreal in August 1660, Groseilliers and Radisson were arrested by French authorities for unlicensed fur trading, and most of their furs were confiscated. As a result, over the next years, they attempted to elicit British support for a trading enterprise to Hudson Bay. They first went to Boston, where they generated enough interest for some New England merchants to sponsor a 1663 seaward expedition, which was turned back by ice in Hudson Strait.

In London, in 1665–67, Groseilliers and Radisson gained the support of a merchant group for an expedition to Hudson Bay. Groseilliers, aboard the *Nonsuch,* sailed from London in spring 1668, reaching James Bay about two months later. Sailing from London on the *Eaglet,* Radisson was forced to turn back off Ireland. At the mouth of the same river where HENRY HUDSON had wintered more than 50 years earlier, Groseilliers and his men constructed a trading post, Charles Fort (Rupert Post), the first permanent non-Indian settlement on Hudson Bay. They named the river the Rupert, in honor of the expedition's chief sponsor, Prince Rupert, a cousin of King Charles II.

In August 1669, Groseilliers returned to London with a cargo of furs. In May 1670, Groseilliers and his backers received a charter for the HUDSON'S BAY COMPANY from King Charles II, granting them a royal trade monopoly over all the lands whose rivers drain into Hudson Bay. The area of one and a half million square miles comprised almost half of present-day Canada, as well as large portions of what is now Minnesota and North Dakota.

Groseilliers subsequently worked for the French-owned Compagnie du Nord fur-trading enterprise, retiring in 1684.

Sieur des Groseilliers's explorations of Lake Michigan and Lake Superior firmly established the location and extent of the western Great Lakes for future traders and settlers. His exploits in Hudson Bay led to the formation of the Hudson's Bay Company, one of the oldest continually operating business enterprises in history and a key force in the exploration of the Canadian West for the next two centuries.

Chouteau, Auguste Pierre (1786–1838)

American fur trader, guide on the Santa Fe Trail and southern plains, son of Jean Pierre Chouteau, brother of Pierre Chouteau, nephew of René Auguste Chouteau

August Pierre Chouteau was the eldest son of early Missouri frontier trader JEAN PIERRE CHOUTEAU. He attended West Point, graduating in 1806. He soon resigned from the army, however, to join his family's business and, in 1809, helped found the ST. LOUIS MISSOURI FUR COMPANY. In 1809–11, he took part in several of the company's fur-trading expeditions to the upper MISSOURI RIVER and northern ROCKY MOUNTAINS, along with MANUEL LISA and ANDREW HENRY.

Chouteau returned to military service for the War of 1812. After the war's end, he undertook trade expeditions from St. Louis westward across the southern plains into the lands of Arapaho, Comanche, and Kiowa Indians.

In 1817, Chouteau, with Jules de Mun, ventured into New Mexico, which was then held by Spain. The two were arrested and detained at Santa Fe by the Spanish. Chouteau was soon released, but Spanish officials confiscated his $30,000 worth of trade goods intended for sale to the fur traders of the southern Rockies.

In the 1820s and 1830s, Chouteau extended his business to Indian tribes of present-day Oklahoma and Kansas. He expanded his family's Arkansas River trading business at Salina, in what is now northeastern Oklahoma, and established additional trading posts throughout the Indian Territory, as far west as the Wichita Mountains in what is now southwestern Oklahoma.

In 1832, Chouteau guided author Washington Irving on a journey across the Great Plains from St. Louis to the Arkansas River trading post at Salina. Irving published an account of this trip in his 1835 book, *Tour of the Prairies.*

Chouteau supplied guides and other assistance to the 1834 expedition under HENRY LEAVENWORTH and HENRY DODGE into the Wichita Mountains and Canadian River Valley.

Participating in the FUR TRADE with Manuel Lisa, Auguste Pierre Chouteau played an important role in the early exploration of the upper Missouri and northern Rockies. He also was an early American pioneer trader and explorer of the Santa Fe Trail west from St. Louis.

Chouteau, Jean Pierre (Pierre Chouteau, Sr.)

(1758–1849) *American fur trader on the Mississippi River and in Oklahoma, half brother of René Auguste Chouteau, father of Auguste Pierre Chouteau and Pierre Chouteau*

Born in New Orleans, Jean Pierre Chouteau, also known as Pierre Chouteau, Sr., settled in St. Louis, which was founded in 1764 by his half brother RENÉ AUGUSTE CHOUTEAU. Entering the family's trading concern, he dealt with the Osage Indians of the southeastern plains under a monopoly issued by Spain.

In 1796, Chouteau journeyed to the future site of Salina, Oklahoma, north of the Arkansas River where, six years later, he established a trading post.

In 1809, Chouteau was commissioned by the federal government to escort Mandan Indian chief Shahaka back to his tribal home near present-day Bismarck, North Dakota. The chief had visited President Thomas Jefferson in Washington, D.C., on the invitation of MERIWETHER LEWIS and WILLIAM CLARK.

Later in 1809, Chouteau, along with his eldest son AUGUSTE PIERRE CHOUTEAU, became a partner with MANUEL LISA, ANDREW HENRY, PIERRE MENARD, and other St. Louis merchants in the ST. LOUIS MISSOURI FUR COMPANY. Chouteau provided Lisa with trade goods and supplies for

Jean Pierre Chouteau *(Library of Congress)*

his expeditions to the upper MISSOURI RIVER and northern ROCKY MOUNTAINS.

In the following years, Chouteau continued in the FUR TRADE as an independent trader with his son Auguste Pierre. He operated trading posts on the lower Missouri until his retirement in 1820. Like his brother, René Auguste, Chouteau was an original trustee of St. Louis and served in the Missouri territorial legislature. Both were among St. Louis's most prominent citizens.

The trading fort established by Jean Pierre Chouteau north of the Arkansas River in 1802 played an important role in the settlement of the Indian Territory and served as a starting point for government expeditions into what is now Oklahoma and northern Texas.

Chouteau, Pierre (Pierre Chouteau, Jr.)

(1789–1865) *American fur trader in the American West, son of Jean Pierre Chouteau, brother of Auguste Pierre Chouteau, nephew of René Auguste Chouteau*

Pierre Chouteau, Jr., son of frontier trader JEAN PIERRE CHOUTEAU, was born in St. Louis, Missouri, when it was still Spanish territory. At the age of 16, he joined his family's St. Louis fur-trading concern. Over the next years, he accompanied his father and MANUEL LISA on several expeditions to the upper MISSOURI RIVER for furs.

In 1813, Chouteau went into partnership with Bartholomew Berthold and traded for furs with the Indian tribes of the upper Missouri River. They were later joined by Bernard Pratte. Their company, known as Berthold, Chouteau & Pratte, grew to dominate the upper Missouri FUR TRADE.

By 1833, Chouteau had become the managing partner of the AMERICAN FUR COMPANY's western division, and, the next year, he purchased the division from JOHN JACOB ASTOR. Also in 1833, he journeyed up the Missouri to the mouth of Teton River on the company's steamship, the *Yellowstone*, accompanying ALEXANDER PHILIPP MAXIMILIAN and artist KARL BODMER. Chouteau visited the company's trading post, Fort Pierre, named in his honor, at the site of present-day Pierre, South Dakota.

Chouteau's company was reorganized in 1838 as Pierre Chouteau, Jr. & Co. Until 1864, this company dominated commercial activity over a vast region of the West, stretching from the MISSISSIPPI RIVER to the Rockies, and from Texas to Minnesota.

In his later years, Chouteau settled in New York City, where he became a leading railroad financier.

As the youngest member of a family of traders, Pierre Chouteau, Jr., participated in the early exploration of trade routes. His business empire grew with the FUR TRADE on the upper Missouri and northern Rockies and was one of the earliest beneficiaries of the exploration of the American West.

Chouteau, René Auguste (1749–1829)

American fur trader on the Mississippi River, founder of St. Louis, Missouri, half brother of Jean Pierre Chouteau, uncle of Auguste Pierre Chouteau and Pierre Chouteau

René Auguste Chouteau was born in New Orleans. In August 1763, he joined his stepfather, PIERRE LIGUESTE LACLEDE, on a fur-trading expedition up the MISSISSIPPI RIVER to the Illinois River.

In early November 1763, Chouteau and Laclede arrived at Kaskaskia in present-day Illinois and crossed the Mississippi in search of a suitable site for a trading post on the west bank. They decided on a rocky bluff a few miles south of the mouth of the MISSOURI RIVER.

Chouteau returned to the site in February 1764 and, on the instructions of his stepfather, established the fur-trading settlement that became St. Louis, Missouri

In 1768, Chouteau became his stepfather's partner in a trading concern. Laclede died 10 years later, and Chouteau and his half brother, JEAN PIERRE CHOUTEAU, assumed control of the company.

Chouteau's business spread to the Osage Indians. His profits increased dramatically when he started shipping his goods directly to Montreal via the Mississippi and Great Lakes, thus eliminating middlemen in New Orleans.

René Auguste Chouteau *(Library of Congress)*

In 1794, the Spanish governor of Louisiana granted Chouteau a monopoly over trade with the Osage Indians. That year, he established Fort Carondelet on the Osage River in present-day western Missouri. After the Louisiana Purchase of 1803, he was appointed U.S. commissioner to the Osage. He came to be the wealthiest landowner in St. Louis and served as a judge, a territorial legislator, and a trustee of the city.

René Auguste Chouteau played a key role in the St. Louis FUR TRADE, thus contributing to the exploration of the upper Missouri, Great Plains, and ROCKY MOUNTAINS. Fort Carondelet, Chouteau's post on the Missouri frontier, was an important base for the 1806–07 explorations of ZE-BULON MONTGOMERY PIKE. St. Louis, which Chouteau founded, blossomed into the gateway to the West and was the starting point for the western explorations of MERI-WETHER LEWIS and WILLIAM CLARK, as well as JOHN CHARLES FRÉMONT.

Christie, Charles (unknown–1812) *British army officer, surveyor in Pakistan, Persia, and Afghanistan*

Captain Charles Christie, a British officer and surveyor, served with Sir John Malcolm in several diplomatic missions to Persia (present-day Iran) in the early 1800s.

In 1810, accompanied by SIR HENRY POTTINGER, Christie sailed northward along India's west coast from Bombay to Karachi, then set out to explore inland into Baluchistan. Disguised as native traders, Christie and Pot-tinger reached Nushki in present-day northern Pakistan. From there, Christie traveled on his own, heading north and west across the Dasht-e Margow, a sunken desert region in southern Afghanistan. He continued northward across cen-tral Afghanistan to the city of Herat, then returned to Persia, and, traveling east-to-west, he rejoined Pottinger at Esfahan. They visited Teheran, then Qazvin, south of the Caspian Sea. Christie traveled on his own to Tabriz in what is now Iranian Azerbaijan, and finally to Baku, a port on the west coast of the Caspian Sea.

Charles Christie's explorations into what is now Pak-istan, Iran, and Afghanistan provided the British Foreign Office with information about the interior of western Asia, a region that remained strategically important throughout the 19th century in the international rivalry between Great Britain and Russia.

Chu Ssu-pen (Chu-Ssu-Pen, Zhu Siben)
(1273–1337) *Chinese cartographer*

Chu Ssu-pen studied under Daoist teachers Chang Jen-ching and Wu Chhlian-chieh. He became a renowned car-tographer of the Mongol Yuan dynasty (1260–1368) in China. He drew on the work of earlier scholars, going back as far as the astronomer Chang Heng, of the second cen-tury and the cartographer P'ei Hsiu of the third century, and gathered new information from his own travels and those of contemporary Persian and Arab traders and European explorers such as MAFFEO POLO, NICCOLÒ POLO, and MARCO POLO.

Between 1311 and 1320, using principles of geometry, Chu Ssu-pen created a seven-foot-long roll-map of China known as Yü T'u Yuditu, or "Earth map." The original map has been lost, but it was revised by the Ming scholar Lo Hung-hsien and published as an atlas, *Kuang Yü T'u*, in about 1555.

Chu Ssu-pen's work influenced cartography among the Chinese and other peoples for generations, until more sci-entific methods began to be applied in the early 19th cen-tury. The Italian missionary MATTEO RICCI's 1602 world map obviously drew on information from Lo Hung-hsien's derivative atlas, which presented fairly accurate geographic information of Africa, including its triangular shape and the location of the NILE RIVER and CONGO RIVER (Zaire River), the East and South China Seas, and Asian and In-dian Ocean island groups.

Clapperton, Hugh (1788–1827) *British naval officer, explorer in North and West Africa*

Hugh Clapperton was born in Annan on the southwest coast of Scotland, the son of a surgeon. While still very young, he embarked on a seafaring career, serving first as a cabin boy on a merchant ship, then eventually entering the British navy.

By 1820, Clapperton was a naval lieutenant, having served in the Great Lakes region of Canada as well as in the East Indies. That year, he was selected to take part in a British government-sponsored expedition into West Africa. Known as the Bornu Mission, one of its major objectives was to trace the course of the NIGER RIVER.

In October 1821, Clapperton and the expedition's leader, WALTER OUDNEY, a British botanist and naval sur-geon, traveled to Tripoli in present-day Libya, where they were joined by the rest of the expedition, including British army officer DIXON DENHAM.

From Tripoli, Clapperton and the others headed south-ward across the SAHARA DESERT, arriving at Murzuk in southwestern Libya in April 1822. Although they were de-layed at Murzuk for several months by the local ruler, the bey of Murzuk, the expedition was soon permitted to leave. South of the Fezzan region, they headed eastward at Ghat, Libya, and explored the Ahaggar Mountains in present-day southern Algeria.

Clapperton, Oudney, and Denham continued their trek toward the upper Niger River, traveling southward through what is now the West African nation of Niger, and entered

Hugh Clapperton *(Library of Congress)*

the kingdom of Bornu in present-day northeastern Nigeria. They reached Lake Chad on February 4, 1823, becoming the first Europeans ever to penetrate that far into the interior of West Africa.

In December 1823, from Kuka, the capital of the Bornu kingdom (present-day Kukawa, Nigeria), Clapperton and Oudney set out for the Nupe region to the southwest, while Denham went to explore around Lake Chad on his own. Seeking to determine the true course of the Niger, Clapperton and Oudney intended to test the theory that the river flowed southward into the Gulf of Guinea, and was not a western tributary of the NILE RIVER, as many geographers mistakenly believed.

Clapperton and Oudney traveled westward across northern Nigeria's Hausa region, reaching Kano, an important city on the caravan route to the coast, in early January 1824. Oudney, stricken with tropical fever, died before long, and Clapperton continued by himself, reaching the city of Sokoto, north of the Niger.

Clapperton was unable to proceed beyond Sokoto to the Niger due to opposition from local Muslim rulers, who were wary of any British presence north of the Gulf of Guinea as a threat to the West African SLAVE TRADE. Forced to turn back to Kuka without learning anything new about

the Niger, he returned to Tripoli with Denham, and from there went on to London, arriving in June 1825.

In London, Clapperton reported his findings to British government officials as well as to the AFRICAN ASSOCIATION. The association's members were still hoping to receive word of the German explorer FRIEDRICH CONRAD HORNEMANN, who had disappeared in West Africa more than 20 years earlier. Clapperton, promoted to the rank of commander, immediately organized another expedition to West Africa.

In August 1825, Clapperton sailed for the Gulf of Guinea. He planned to explore the interior of West Africa from the south and establish the true course of the Niger, as well as visit TIMBUKTU. Among the members of his expedition were RICHARD LEMON LANDER and the Hausa guide WILLIAM PASCOE.

Landing at Badagri, near Lagos, in November 1825, Clapperton and his expedition proceeded northward into the former Youraba kingdom of present-day southeastern Nigeria. They traveled inland from the Bight of Benin, an area rife with insect-borne tropical diseases. Most of the European members of the expedition were soon stricken; only Clapperton and Lander managed to reach the Youraba capital at Katunga in late January 1826. Within two more months, they had arrived at Bussa on the Niger River.

After crossing the Niger at Komie, Clapperton and Lander made their way to Sokoto, where Clapperton had been turned back on his earlier expedition from the north. They remained at Sokoto for over a year, trying without success to find guides for their proposed trip to Timbuktu and exploration of the Niger. They had planned, on reaching Timbuktu, to follow the Niger downstream to its mouth and resolve the question of its true course. Yet Clapperton became ill in Sokoto and died there in 1827, reportedly succumbing to dysentery. Lander made his way to Kano and the Gulf of Guinea, eventually returning to England with Clapperton's notes and journals.

Clapperton's accounts of his two expeditions into West Africa were published posthumously in England. His *Narrative of Travels and Discoveries in Northern and Central Africa* first appeared in 1828. The next year, the record of his expedition from the south, *Journal of a Second Expedition into the Interior of Africa,* was published.

Hugh Clapperton's explorations did not conclusively settle the question of the course of the Niger. Nevertheless, he did contribute significantly to European geographic knowledge of Africa. He was among the first Europeans to see Lake Chad, and his own expeditions into West Africa, taken together, constitute the first north-to-south crossing of the western part of Africa. His written accounts of his travels in northern Nigeria provide the earliest European descriptions of the regions's Hausa people. Richard Lander returned to west Africa in the early 1830s and finally proved that Clapperton had been correct in theorizing that the Niger flowed into the Gulf of Guinea, and was not connected to the Nile.

Clark, William (1770–1838) *U.S. Army officer, coleader of Lewis and Clark Expedition in the American West, territorial governor, Indian superintendent*

William Clark, younger brother of Revolutionary War Indian fighter George Rogers Clark, was born in Caroline County, Virginia. In about 1784, his family settled on the Kentucky frontier near the Falls of the Ohio. As he was growing up, he developed skills as a frontiersman. A self-taught naturalist, he studied plants and wildlife and became familiar with the customs of various Indian tribes.

In 1789, Clark joined the local militia, taking part in campaigns against Indians. Three years later, he was commissioned a lieutenant of artillery in the regular army. In 1793, while serving with General "Mad" Anthony Wayne in the war against the allied tribes of the Old Northwest under the Miami chief Little Turtle, he first met MERIWETHER LEWIS.

Leaving the army in 1796, Clark returned to his Kentucky plantation. In 1802, he accepted Lewis's offer to colead a government-sponsored expedition across the ROCKY MOUNTAINS to the Pacific Ocean. Although com-

missioned a lieutenant, Clark, at Lewis's request, would serve as an honorary captain.

With his African-American servant York, Clark joined Lewis at Louisville in the late summer of 1803. They traveled on a KEELBOAT down the Ohio River to the MISSISSIPPI RIVER, to a site opposite St. Louis called Camp Wood River. In winter 1803–04, Clark played a major role in recruiting and training the men who would take part in the trip to the Pacific. Clark's responsibilities as second in command of the Corps of Discovery, as the Lewis and Clark Expedition was known, would also include making charts and establishing peaceful contacts with Native Americans encountered on the way.

On May 14, 1804, Clark and a party of about 45 soldiers, traders, and trappers departed St. Louis up the MISSOURI RIVER. In addition to the keelboat, the group traveled by PIROGUE. Their first stop was the Missouri River settlement of St. Charles, where they were soon joined by Lewis, who had traveled there overland after finishing up his affairs in St. Louis.

The expedition continued to the Mandan Indian villages near present-day Bismarck, North Dakota. During the winter stopover, 1804–05, Clark interviewed Indians and traders, seeking data on the lands lying beyond the headwaters of the Missouri. Clark recommended to Lewis the hiring of the trader TOUSSAINT CHARBONNEAU and his

William Clark and his men building huts, as shown in an 1810 publication of the journals of Patrick Gass, a member of the Corps of Discovery *(Library of Congress)*

Shoshone wife SACAJAWEA (Sacagawea) as interpreters and guides. Clark's servant York generated interest among Native Americans as the first black man they had ever seen. His popularity would persist among the women of the more than 50 tribes the expedition encountered.

In spring 1805, after traveling 1,200 miles beyond the Mandan villages in the Dakotas, Clark explored the main branch of the Missouri, while Lewis examined the course of the Marias River. He rejoined Lewis at the Great Falls of the Missouri. From there, they continued westward to the Oregon coast, reaching the mouth of the COLUMBIA RIVER on November 15, 1805.

On the return journey from the Oregon coast in spring 1806, Clark led part of the group overland from the Bitterroot Valley, across present-day Yellowstone National Park, to the Yellowstone River. He soon rejoined Lewis and the rest of the expedition on the Missouri River, a few miles below the mouth of the Yellowstone.

Clark and Lewis returned to St. Louis in September 1806, then traveled to Washington, D.C., to report their findings to President Thomas Jefferson.

In 1807, Clark was appointed principal Indian agent to the tribes of the Louisiana Territory and brigadier general in the territorial militia. He was back in St. Louis in 1808.

In August 1808, Clark led an overland expedition westward from St. Charles to the mouth of the Kansas River, where he established Fort Osage, near what is now Kansas City. His guide for this trip was Nathan Boone, son of frontier explorer DANIEL BOONE. The post, designed to prevent Spanish and British encroachment into the newly acquired Louisiana Territory, became an important starting point for trade and military expeditions onto the Great Plains.

In 1809, with MANUEL LISA, ANDREW HENRY, ANTOINE PIERRE MENARD, JEAN PIERRE CHOUTEAU, and others, he founded the ST. LOUIS MISSOURI FUR COMPANY.

In 1810, the AMERICAN FUR COMPANY's WILSON PRICE HUNT arrived in St. Louis and conferred with Clark in preparation for his own overland expedition to establish a fur-trading post on the Pacific coast for New York financier JOHN JACOB ASTOR.

During the War of 1812, Clark was charged with maintaining the neutrality of the upper Missouri and northern plains tribes, especially the Sioux (Dakota, Lakota, Nakota). To this end, in 1814, he led a military expedition up the Mississippi and established an outpost at Prairie du Chien, in what is now Wisconsin, which became an important site for peace treaty conferences with the region's Indian tribes.

In 1813, Clark was appointed territorial governor of Missouri. When Missouri was admitted to the Union as a state in 1821, Clark failed in his bid for election as the state's first governor. At that time, he received an appointment as superintendent of Indian affairs at St. Louis, serving for the rest of his life. In his later years, he took part in military campaigns in the Winnebago Uprising of 1827 and the Black Hawk War of 1832.

William Clark's expertise in dealing with Native Americans, aided by his friendship with the Shoshone Sacajawea, played a vital role in the success of the Lewis and Clark Expedition. His skills as a naturalist and mapmaker contributed much to the final report of the expedition, published in 1814. Clark's account of his 1808 expedition provided the first description of what is now the western part of the state of Missouri. With Lewis he was also the first to apply the descriptive name Great Plains to the region between the Missouri River and the Rocky Mountains.

Clavijo, Ruy González de (unknown–1412)
Spanish diplomat in central Asia

Ruy González de Clavijo was born in Madrid to a prominent Spanish family. In the early 1400s, he served as a nobleman at the court of Henry III, king of Castile. At that time, diplomatic contacts with the Mongol Empire east of the Black Sea had declined. The Mongol emperor Tamerlane had recently consolidated his power over much of present-day Georgia, and he ruled an empire that extended across much of central Asia and the Middle East.

In an attempt to reopen diplomatic and commercial ties with the Mongols, Henry III sent Clavijo on a diplomatic mission to meet with Tamerlane at his capital in Samarkand, then the leading cultural center of central Asia. Clavijo embarked from the southern Spanish port of Cádiz in May 1403, heading eastward across the MEDITERRANEAN SEA. He traversed Persia (present-day Iran), visiting the cities of Tabriz, Teheran, and Meshed.

In Samarkand by late summer 1404, Clavijo was welcomed by Tamerlane, who at that time was preparing for an invasion into China. Clavijo conferred with the Mongol ruler, then left for Spain in 1405, reaching Madrid the following year.

The results of Ruy González de Clavijo's diplomatic mission were probably negligible since Tamerlane died in 1405, while the Spanish envoy was on his homeward journey. Yet back in Spain, Clavijo wrote an influential account of his travels across what is now Iran and Uzbekistan. Entitled *Embassy to Tamerlane*, it was first published in Seville in 1582, and it provided Europe with an updated view of Persia and central Asia.

Clerke, Charles (1741–1779) *British naval officer in the Pacific*

Charles Clerke was born at Weathersfield Hall, in Essex, England, northeast of London, where his father was a local magistrate. At the age of 12, he joined the British navy, serving throughout the Seven Years War of 1756–63.

In 1764–66, Clerke sailed as a midshipman with JOHN BYRON's voyage around the world. After his return from this expedition, he wrote an account describing giants he reportedly observed while exploring Patagonia. It was published in the official journal of the ROYAL SOCIETY in 1768, as *An Account of the very tall men seen near the Streights of Magellan in the year 1764 . . .*, but it was subsequently exposed as a good-natured hoax on Clerke's part.

Starting in 1768, Clerke began more than 10 years of service under the command of JAMES COOK, taking part in all three of Cook's voyages of exploration.

On Cook's first voyage to the Pacific Ocean and around the world (1768–71), Clerke was a midshipman on the *Endeavor,* and, toward the end of that expedition, in May 1771, he was promoted to lieutenant.

On Cook's second voyage (1772–75), Clerke was second lieutenant on the *Resolution.* In fall 1774, on a newly explored island in the South Pacific near New Caledonia, he assisted the expedition's astronomer, William Wales, in an observation of a solar eclipse, in which they made the first use of an astronomical instrument known as Hadley's QUADRANT.

Soon after his return to England in 1775, Clerke was held in a debtor's prison, where he contracted tuberculosis. Upon his release in 1776, he sailed on Cook's third and final expedition (1776–80), as captain of the *Discovery.* In 1778, he made a study of the natural history of the Pacific coast of what is now British Columbia and Alaska. In April 1778, he joined Cook in a visit to a Nootka Indian village near present-day Vancouver, British Columbia.

Following Cook's death in the HAWAIIAN ISLANDS in February 1779, Clerke assumed command of the expedition on the flagship, the *Resolution.* Although suffering from advanced tuberculosis, he sailed northward to BERING STRAIT to complete Cook's assignment to survey the coast of Alaska and search for an entrance to the NORTHWEST PASSAGE. In summer 1779, the *Resolution* reached Icy Cape, Alaska, near 70°33' north latitude, at which point further progress was blocked by ice.

Clerke correctly concluded that no practical Northwest Passage could be found at that latitude, and he returned to the Asian side of the Bering Sea. In August 1779, en route to the Russian port of Avacha Bay on the Kamchatka Peninsula, he finally succumbed to tuberculosis. Command of the expedition then passed to JOHN GORE.

Charles Clerke was one of Captain Cook's most loyal officers. He returned to the cold and fog of the North Pacific to complete Cook's explorations for the Northwest Passage, despite the jeopardy to his own health, and helped prove that no viable sea route existed around the north coast of North America.

Clyman, James (Jim Clyman) (1792–1881)

American fur trader, trapper, guide in the American West

James (Jim) Clyman was born in central Virginia's Blue Ridge, where his family farmed on lands leased from George Washington. In 1811, Clyman and his family moved west to Ohio, where they established a farm. With the onset of the War of 1812, Clyman applied the skills learned on the frontier as a scout in the Ohio state militia campaigning against British-backed Shawnee Indians.

Soon after the war's end, Clyman moved farther west, settling first in Indiana, then Illinois. In Illinois, while employed as a surveyor, he explored the Sangamon River in the region between present-day Springfield and Decatur.

In early 1823, Clyman journeyed to St. Louis, where he was hired by fur trader WILLIAM HENRY ASHLEY to organize and accompany a fur-trapping expedition up the MISSOURI RIVER into the Yellowstone region of the Dakotas and present-day eastern Montana. He became the clerk for one company of Ashley's trappers and commanded a KEELBOAT. He departed from St. Louis that spring. When his party reached the Arikara Indian villages on the upper Missouri in present-day South Dakota, a war party attacked, killing 15. Clyman narrowly escaped, making his way downriver to Fort Atkinson near Council Bluffs, Nebraska.

Three months later, Clyman returned to the upper Missouri as part of Colonel HENRY LEAVENWORTH's punitive military expedition against the Arikara.

Jim Clyman *(Library of Congress)*

Ashley's objective for his 1823 fur-trading expedition was the Green River region of what is now northeastern Utah and southern Idaho and Wyoming. With the river route through the northern plains and ROCKY MOUNTAINS blocked by Indians, he decided to send an overland expedition from Fort Kiowa, a post on the Missouri more than 300 miles south of the mouth of the Yellowstone River, due west across the northern plains and into the Rockies. Clyman was part of this party, along with THOMAS FITZPATRICK, JEDEDIAH STRONG SMITH, and WILLIAM LEWIS SUBLETTE.

Setting out on horseback from Fort Kiowa in September 1823, the group headed westward across the Black Hills of South Dakota for the Wind River Range in what is now western Wyoming. In early February 1824, they reached the mountains' eastern slopes and attempted to proceed through Union Pass. Severe winter storms drove them back, but friendly Crow Indians directed Clyman and Smith to a pass farther south. This proved to be the SOUTH PASS of the Wind River Range, which had been used a decade earlier by WILSON PRICE HUNT but had not been charted at that time. Following the Sweetwater Creek into the South Pass, Clyman and the others crossed the Continental Divide and reached the Green River in late March 1824.

Fitzpatrick soon returned to St. Louis with a bountiful harvest of pelts. In June 1824, Clyman and Smith, setting out on their return trip, attempted to negotiate the Sweetwater by makeshift CANOE after their horses had been stolen by Indians. Clyman was soon separated from the rest of the party and walked more than 700 miles through the eastern ranges of the Rockies, and across the Great Plains, to Fort Atkinson, near Council Bluffs.

The 1823–24 explorations of Clyman and Smith had revealed that the Sweetwater could be reached by following the Platte River, a tributary of the Missouri. This route enabled fur traders to enter the Green River region, avoiding Indian attacks along the Yellowstone.

Clyman returned to the upper Green River for the 1824–25 trapping season. He later attended Ashley's first trappers' rendezvous at Henrys Fork of the Green River in summer 1825.

During the next two years, Clyman explored the region around Utah's Great Salt Lake. In 1826, with Moses "Black" Harris, HENRY FRAEB, and LOUIS VASQUEZ, Clyman circumnavigated the large body of water, proving that it was not an arm of the Pacific Ocean.

Clyman and Sublette continued to trap in the Rockies. In 1827, Clyman led a party of trappers, with their annual catch, back to St. Louis, then returned to Illinois. While living in Danville, he served in military campaigns in the Black Hawk War of 1832, as part of the same company of volunteer militia as Abraham Lincoln.

In 1834, Clyman moved north to a settlement on the west shore of Lake Michigan near present-day Milwaukee, Wisconsin. He opened a sawmill and profited from the booming lumber trade.

In spring 1844, Clyman joined a wagon train from Independence, Missouri, to Oregon, led by Moses "Black" Harris. The group traveled through the South Pass, which had become an integral part of the Oregon Trail. He spent the winter of 1844–45 with HUDSON'S BAY COMPANY factor JOHN McLOUGHLIN at Fort Vancouver on the COLUMBIA RIVER opposite present-day Portland, Oregon.

In spring 1845, Clyman led a party of emigrants southward through Oregon's Umpqua Valley into northern California. Once there, he joined up with an eastbound party led by CALEB GREENWOOD. This expedition attempted a more southerly route, rather than northward through present-day Idaho; it crossed the Sierra Nevada, then proceeded through the desert regions south and west of the Great Salt Lake and Utah's Wasatch Mountains, following the much touted but what proved to be harrowing Hastings Cutoff. On reaching Fort Laramie in June 1846, Clyman and Greenwood reportedly tried to warn the Donner Party against using the southern route from Fort Bridger. Their advice went unheeded, and the Donner Party went on to face disaster in the snows of the Sierra Nevada later that fall.

Clyman was back in Wisconsin by 1848, remaining only long enough to organize a wagon train westward to California. He took the conventional route through South Pass, which he had explored 25 years earlier. Clyman then guided the party southwestward along the Humboldt River, to the Truckee River, and into the fertile valleys north of San Francisco Bay. He married a member of this wagon train, a woman named Hannah McCombs, and settled permanently in California's Napa Valley.

Jim Clyman's explorations west of the Missouri as one of the MOUNTAIN MEN and a guide contributed to America's westward expansion. Although he had no formal education, he recorded his frontier experiences in diaries. His accounts include vivid descriptions of the 1844 crossing to Oregon. They were first published in 1928, in Charles L. Camp's *James Clyman, American Frontiersman, 1792–1881.*

Cnidus, Ctesias of   See CTESIAS OF CNIDUS.

Cocking, Matthew (Mathew Cochin, Mathew Cockan, Mathew Cockings) (1743–1799)
British fur trader, traveler in the Canadian West
Matthew Cocking was a tailor's son from York, England. Little is known of his early life or education. In 1765, he joined the HUDSON'S BAY COMPANY and traveled to its post at York Factory on HUDSON BAY. His first job was that of "writer," and, over the next few years, he worked at transcribing journals and correspondence and recording accounts.

By 1770, Cocking was second in command at York Factory. At that time, the Hudson's Bay Company did not have outposts at any distance from the south coast of Hudson Bay, but obtained furs from the Indians who traveled annually to York Factory from the inland regions. Independent traders from Montreal were beginning to encroach into the Hudson's Bay Company's vast territory, which extended from what is now eastern Manitoba to western Saskatchewan. To counter this competition, the company needed information on native peoples and geography to the west of Hudson Bay. Although traders and agents had been sent out, their reports were less than clear or literate. In 1772, Cocking offered to explore west of Hudson Bay himself, and Andrew Graham, director at York Factory, arranged for him to journey westward with a band of Indians returning to their homeland on the Canadian prairies.

Cocking and his Indian companions left York Factory on June 27, 1772. They traveled from Hudson Bay by CANOE, following the Fox, Hayes, and Minago Rivers to the North Saskatchewan River, which took them into what is now the western Saskatchewan province. At Peonan Creek, they disposed of the canoes and, traveling overland, headed southward onto the prairies south of present-day North Battleford, Saskatchewan. Along the way, Cocking explored the Eagle Hills and the region to the south as far as the South Saskatchewan River.

Cocking wintered among the Indians, taking part in buffalo hunts and roundups and establishing friendly contacts with the Assiniboine, Cree, and Blackfeet, western tribes then unknown to the British. In spring 1773, Cocking and the Indians made their way back to the North Saskatchewan River for the annual fur-trading journey to York Factory. In new canoes, they returned along the same route they had followed the previous year, arriving at the Hudson Bay post on June 18, 1773.

In his report to the company, Cocking described the territory he had visited and recommended that the competition from the independent traders could be met by hiring more men who could handle canoes for the trade inland. He also suggested to the company's directors in London that trading posts be immediately established in the West.

In 1774, Cocking set off for Cumberland House in eastern Saskatchewan, the company's first inland trading post, where he planned to join SAMUEL HEARNE. While traveling westward by way of Lake Winnipeg, he encountered two of the company's traders who had been abandoned by their Indian guides.

At that point, Cocking's own Indian companions deserted him. He engaged other native guides who agreed to take him and the two traders westward, but to Lake Winnipegosis and not Cumberland House. From Lake Winnipegosis, he then explored the Red Deer River region south of Cumberland House. After a winter at Good Spirit Lake, he made his way back to York Factory, arriving there in late June 1775. Although he had been unable to reach Cumberland House that season, the experience underscored for him the necessity of relying less on Indians for guides.

Later in 1775, Cocking reached Cumberland House. He served there for a few years, then directed operations at Severn House in present-day Ontario. In 1781, he served briefly as director at York Factory. He returned to York, England, the following year, where he retired on a pension from the Hudson's Bay Company.

During his years in Canada, Cocking had fathered three mixed-blood daughters, who remained at York Factory. In his will, he provided a legacy for them.

Matthew Cocking's vivid and accurate accounts of the regions west of Hudson Bay are preserved at the company's archives in Winnipeg. Largely because of his efforts, the Hudson's Bay Company expanded its field operations and was able to compete in the FUR TRADE with the independent traders from Montreal at a time when the Montrealers were about to consolidate into the formidable NORTH WEST COMPANY.

Colenso, William (1811–1899) *British colonist on New Zealand's North Island*

William Colenso was an early colonist on NEW ZEALAND's North Island. In 1838, he landed at Poverty Bay, on the island's east coast. Three years later, he undertook the first of three expeditions into the interior.

In 1841, Colenso went westward from Poverty Bay as far as Lake Waikaremoana, then explored the territory to the northwest, visiting the region around Lake Rotorua. He went northward, beyond present-day Auckland, and explored the island's northern peninsula as far as the Bay of Islands.

Colenso next set out to explore the southern part of North Island. In 1843, he explored southward along the east coast, reaching its southernmost point, near Wellington. His return trip to the north took him inland around Hawke Bay, and once again to Lake Waikaremoana. Colenso visited the interior of North Island again in 1847, exploring the region around Lake Taupo, the island's largest lake, and making one of the earliest crossings of the Ruahine Range to the south.

Taken together, William Colenso's three expeditions, between 1841 and 1847, amounted to the first comprehensive investigation into the interior of the North Island of New Zealand.

Collinson, Sir Richard (1811–1883) *British naval officer in the Canadian Arctic*

Born in Gateshead in northern England, Richard Collinson entered the British navy as a midshipman at the age of 12.

From 1828 to 1831, he served in maritime survey expeditions in the South Atlantic Ocean and in the seas around Antarctica. During the 1830s, he took part in SIR EDWARD BELCHER's survey of the coast of South America.

During the Opium War in 1839, Collinson undertook surveys for British naval operations in Chinese waters. By the time he returned to England in 1846, he had been promoted to captain, and he was subsequently named commander.

In 1850, Collinson was appointed to command a rescue expedition in search of SIR JOHN FRANKLIN and his men, who had been missing in the Canadian Arctic since 1845. The expedition's two ships, the *Enterprise,* commanded by Collinson, and the *Investigator,* captained by ROBERT McCLURE, departed England on January 31, 1850. They planned to search for Franklin in the Canadian Arctic from the Pacific Ocean, starting from BERING STRAIT and proceeding eastward along the north coast of Alaska.

Collinson's ship separated from the *Investigator* in the voyage around CAPE HORN. McClure, who had reached Bering Strait first, sailed northward into the Arctic Ocean; he eventually became icebound at Melville Island in September 1850. By the time Collinson had arrived at Bering Strait in late 1850, PACK ICE prevented him from continuing until spring 1851.

In July 1851, the ice cleared, and Collinson managed to sail the *Enterprise* around Alaska to Coronation Gulf on the Arctic coast of Canada. When the ice cleared again the following spring, he continued his eastward course, navigating through Dease Strait to Cambridge Bay on Victoria Island, where he spent the winter of 1852–53. While there, Collinson met some Inuit who gave him pieces of iron, which may have come from the auxiliary engine of one of Franklin's ships. Although these fragments could very well have been the first tangible relics recovered from that ill-fated expedition, without Inuit interpreters, Collinson was unable to obtain further information to confirm this.

In spring 1853, Collinson led a sledge party in an exploration of the east coast of Victoria Island, a region that was subsequently named the Collinson Peninsula in his honor.

Collinson and the *Enterprise* crew spent the winter of 1853–54 on the Arctic coast of Alaska. In the spring, they turned back westward for the homeward voyage. After a southward passage through Bering Strait, they reentered the North Pacific and sailed back to England, arriving there in May 1855. Collinson learned that most of the Canadian Arctic he had charted had previously been visited by McClure. McClure, after his ship had become icebound, had made his way eastward by sledge to Sir Edward Belcher's fleet near Melville Island, and, in so doing, he had made the first crossing of the NORTHWEST PASSAGE.

Collinson retired from active naval service in 1855, and in 1875 he was awarded a knighthood for his accomplishments as a naval surveyor and Arctic explorer. In 1889, an account of his exploits in the Canadian Arctic, entitled *Journal of H.M.S. Enterprise on the Expedition in Search of Sir John Franklin's Ships by Behring Strait, 1850–55,* was published.

Although Sir Richard Collinson failed to find the Northwest Passage, one of the objectives of his expedition, he did unwittingly come closer than any of the other rescue expeditions to the actual site of Franklin's final end in Victoria Strait. Furthermore, his navigation through the polar seas covered more degrees of longitude above the ARCTIC CIRCLE than any other expedition until that time, a record not matched until 1878 and the NORTHEAST PASSAGE expedition of the Swedish Arctic explorer NILS ADOLF ERIK NORDENSKJÖLD. Collinson's navigational charts and descriptions of Coronation Gulf and Dease Strait were later cited as extremely accurate and helpful by ROALD ENGELBREGT GRAVNING AMUNDSEN following his seaward navigation of the Northwest Passage in 1903–06.

Colter, John (ca. 1775–1813) *American fur trapper, guide in the American West*

John Colter was born at the outbreak of the American Revolution near Staunton, Virginia, on the eastern slopes of the Shenandoah Mountains. When about 28 years old, he enlisted as a private in the Corps of Discovery, better known as the Lewis and Clark Expedition.

In early May 1804, MERIWETHER LEWIS sent Colter and another expedition member, Moses Reed, up the MISSOURI RIVER from St. Louis to meet up with the rest of the party, camped at St. Charles, Missouri. Colter delivered letters from Lewis, as well as a quantity of tallow for the expedition.

After the expedition reached the Oregon coast in November 1805, Clark dispatched Colter to survey a site for a winter encampment. Later that month, Colter explored around Cape Disappointment near the mouth of the COLUMBIA RIVER with WILLIAM CLARK and eight other expedition members.

On the return journey through the northern Rocky Mountains in mid-June 1806, Clark noted in his journal that Colter and his horse fell into a stream known as Hungry Creek, but Colter managed to survive without injury and without losing his gun.

In mid-August 1806, while the expedition was approaching the Mandan villages on the upper Missouri near present-day Bismarck, North Dakota, Colter was given permission by Lewis and Clark to return to the Yellowstone River region with two trappers from Illinois, Joseph Dickson and Forest Hancock. Little is known of this group's exploits; they may have traveled westward into what is now northwestern Wyoming and the area of present-day Yellowstone National Park.

Colter was returning to St. Louis via the Missouri in 1807, when he met the outward-bound party of MANUEL LISA at the mouth of the Platte River in present-day eastern Nebraska. Colter decided to travel with Lisa's trappers to the Yellowstone, following that stream to the mouth of the Bighorn River. Near present-day Custer, Montana, he helped Lisa and his men, including GEORGE DROUILLARD, construct a fur-trading post, Fort Raymond.

Lisa then sent Colter into the country of the Crow Indians to solicit their cooperation in the collection of beaver pelts. Colter spent the next months wandering through parts of present-day Wyoming and Idaho. He traveled from Pryor's Fork across the Pryor Mountains into the Bighorn Basin. Although his exact route is unclear, he probably headed southward into Wyoming's Wind River Mountains and may have crossed the Continental Divide by traveling westward through Union Pass. He continued westward toward the Teton Mountains and is believed to have been the first non-Indian to cross through Teton Pass. He then headed northward across the Madison River, then eastward back to Fort Raymond at the mouth of the Bighorn River. During his wanderings, he came upon gas vents in the ground spewing forth sulphurous fumes, as well as geysers and hot springs. This region of thermal activity, near present-day Cody, Wyoming, along the North Fork of the Shoshone River, became known as "Colter's Hell."

In 1808, Colter again set out from Fort Raymond for the beaver country of the Gallatin River, this time accompanied by about 500 Flathead Indians. While traveling northward toward what later became known as Bozeman Pass (named after JOHN MERIN BOZEMAN), the group was attacked by a force of about 1,500 Blackfeet Indians. Although Colter was wounded in the leg during the battle, he managed to kill one of the attackers and was later rescued by Crow Indians. He made his way back to Fort Raymond, where he soon recovered from his wounds.

In fall 1808, Colter again set out from Fort Raymond, joined by another Lewis and Clark Expedition veteran working for Manuel Lisa, a man named John Potts. The two trappers headed westward toward the Three Forks of the Missouri. Near the Jefferson River, Colter and Potts were attacked by another party of Blackfeet. Potts was killed and scalped by the Indians, and Colter was taken captive. His captors stripped him naked and, after giving him a brief head start, made him run through the wilderness and set out in pursuit. One of them caught up with him, but Colter managed to wrest his attacker's spear from him and kill him with it. He then ran to the Jefferson River and dove in. Finding a log jam and an air pocket, he hid until dark, then

waded six miles downstream. He reached the safety of Fort Raymond 10 days later.

In 1810, at Fort Mandan in present-day North Dakota, Colter met up with fur traders PIERRE MENARD, ANDREW HENRY, and George Drouillard. He guided this party to the Three Forks of the Missouri region of present-day Montana. The group suffered from snow blindness crossing the mountains via the Bozeman Pass, as well as repeated attacks by Blackfeet.

Colter left the upper Missouri FUR TRADE in late 1810, traveling 2,000 miles down the Missouri alone in a dugout CANOE. On reaching St. Louis, he conferred with William Clark, providing him with important data about the newly explored regions around the Bighorn and Yellowstone Rivers, including such features as the passes through the Wind River Mountains and Teton Mountains of Wyoming. Information gleaned from Colter later appeared in Nicholas Biddle's 1814 publication of the Lewis and Clark journals. His tales of thermal activity in Wyoming also appeared in Washington Irving's 1837 book *The Adventures of Captain Bonneville.* Colter spent his remaining years farming in Missouri.

Although no definite record of his travels in the northern Rockies exists, John Colter is believed to have been the first non-Indian to explore west of the Continental Divide into the regions that now comprise Yellowstone National Park and Grand Teton National Park. As a guide to fur traders, he participated in the earliest commercial applications of the geographic data from the Lewis and Clark Expedition.

Columbus, Christopher (Cristoforo Colombo, Cristóbal Colón, Cristovão Colombo)

(1451–1506) *Italian mariner in the West Indies, South America, and Central America, in service to Spain*

Christopher Columbus was born in the northwestern Italian seaport city of Genoa into a family of weavers and cloth merchants. His father also operated a wineshop and sold cheeses. Columbus may have studied mathematics, astronomy, and natural sciences at the University of Pavia. More likely, starting in 1474, after serving an apprenticeship in the weaving trade, he began to sail the MEDITERRANEAN SEA on commercial voyages for his father. In 1476, he sailed with a merchant fleet bound for Lisbon and England. Shipwrecked off the south coast of Portugal after an attack by French naval forces, Columbus managed to reach the Portuguese shore, near Lagos, then went on to Lisbon, where he joined his brother, Bartholomew, a cartographer.

Columbus settled in Lisbon, where he and his brother became known as leading map dealers. In 1477, Columbus may have taken part in a voyage to ICELAND, where he could have heard traditional accounts of the VIKINGS of lands to the west.

Christopher Columbus *(Library of Congress, Prints and Photographs Division [LC-USZ62-103980])*

Christopher Columbus's flagship, the *Santa María* (replica) *(Library of Congress)*

In 1479, Columbus married Dona Filipa Perestrello e Moniz, daughter of a prominent Portuguese settler on the Atlantic island of Madeira. Soon afterward, he moved with his wife to Madeira, where he worked as a buyer of sugar for Genoese merchants. He made several voyages along the coast of West Africa, possibly for the Portuguese–West African SLAVE TRADE, as far south as the Portuguese settlement of Elmina on the coast of present-day Ghana, the southernmost point then known to Europeans. There, he heard reports from mariners of evidence of land lying westward across the Atlantic Ocean.

By the early 1480s, Columbus had developed a plan to sail to Japan or China. His idea, known as "Enterprise of the Indies," had been influenced by his reading of PTOLEMY, MARCO POLO, and the geographic works of the Florentine cosmographer Paolo Toscanelli.

From his interpretation of Ptolemy's ideas on LATITUDE AND LONGITUDE, Columbus believed the Earth to be smaller than was commonly believed at that time. Based on his readings of Marco Polo, Columbus also theorized that eastern Asia extended closer to western Europe than had been depicted by geographers. Moreover, to Columbus, Polo's description of an island, known as CIPANGU, lying 1,500 miles offshore from Asia, made a westward crossing to that land seem even more feasible.

Toscanelli, with whom Columbus corresponded, provided him with a map of the Atlantic, known then as the Ocean Sea and not distinguished from the rest of the world's oceans. On this chart appeared the fabled island— ST. BRENDAN'S ISLE—supposedly discovered by the medieval Irish monk SAINT BRENDAN, as well as the legendary island of "Antillia."

Columbus also relied on religious writings to back up his assertion. In his studies of the book of the prophet Esdras in the Apocrypha, he had read that the Earth was six parts land and only one part ocean. This view, taken together with an overestimation of the size of Asia, led him to conclude that the east coast of Asia was less than 3,000 miles from the CANARY ISLANDS, a distance the ships of his day were regularly sailing in voyages to and from Africa.

When, in 1484, Columbus presented his plan to John II of Portugal, the king's geographers determined that what he proposed was impossible. They correctly estimated the westward distance across the Atlantic between Europe and eastern Asia to be more than 10,000 miles, far too great for a seaward expedition to be practical. The next year, Columbus's wife died, and soon afterward, still seeking support for his project, he left Portugal for Spain, taking with him his five-year-old son, Diego.

Columbus reached the tiny port town of Palos, where he left his son in the care of monks at a nearby monastery. He then traveled to Cordoba and presented his plan to the court of King Ferdinand II and Queen Isabella I. The Spanish monarchs also rejected his plan, although he had the support at court of the duke of Medina Celi. Columbus briefly returned to Portugal in 1488, where King John again showed interest in his proposal. Yet, that year, BARTOLOMEU DIAS returned to Lisbon and reported his finding of the CAPE OF GOOD HOPE and a possible sea route around Africa to India, making Columbus's plan seem unnecessary.

Back in Spain in early 1492, Columbus sent his brother Bartholomew to France to seek the support of King Charles VIII and to England to seek that of King Henry VII. Meanwhile, the Spanish finance minister, Luis de Santangel, advised Queen Isabella that Columbus's venture was worth backing since the possible returns were immense compared to the relatively small initial investment. At that time, there was a shortage of gold in Europe, providing commercial incentive for continued voyages of exploration. Moreover, Turkish MUSLIMS had closed off the overland SPICE ROUTE to the Far East. Isabella was also concerned with finding new converts to Christianity.

In April 1492, an agreement between Columbus and the Spanish Crown was reached, under the terms of which Columbus was to become governor of any uncharted islands he should locate; to receive 10 percent of any profit from the enterprise; and to be granted the title of admiral of the Ocean Sea. Additional backing for the expedition came from the Genoese merchant community in Seville.

Columbus had befriended the Pinzóns, a family of seafarers and shipowners from Palos de Moguer. With their help, he obtained the *Santa María* and two smaller vessels, the *Niña* and the *Pinta*. About 90 men were recruited from among the local mariners, with MARTÍN ALONZO PINZÓN in command of the *Pinta* and his brother VICENTE YÁÑEZ PINZÓN as captain of the *Niña*. Columbus, as captain general, sailed on his flagship, the *Santa Maria,* with JUAN DE LA COSA as the expedition's chief pilot.

Columbus and his small fleet sailed from Palos de Frontera on August 3, 1492. He headed directly for the Canaries, where he stopped for repairs to one of the ships. Taking advantage of the prevailing northeast TRADE WINDS, he set out across the Atlantic on September 6. Although the next three weeks of sailing were uneventful, the fact that he was sailing westward into unknown seas alarmed many of his men, and, by the first week of October 1492, the crew of the *Santa María* was on the brink of mutiny, demanding that Columbus turn back. Meanwhile, Martín Alonzo Pinzón advised Columbus that land might be encountered if they turned more to the southwest, which they did. On October 12, 1492, at two o'clock in the morning, a shoreline was sighted under a moonlit sky.

Columbus landed on what he called San Salvador, naming it in gratitude to the Savior. This was one of the Bahamas, afterward known as Watling Island and called Guanahani by the Arawak (Taino) people (although some scholars theorize that Columbus first touched soil at Samana Cay, 65 miles to the southeast). Believing he had come upon one of the outlying islands of the EAST INDIES, Columbus concluded that the Arawak were "Indians," a name that came to be used for the indigenous peoples of the Western Hemisphere. From the Arawak he learned that islands with more gold lay to the south and west.

Taking some of the local people as guides, Columbus sailed southward, sighting and naming the islands of Ferdinanda (now Long Island) and Isabella (now Crooked Island) in the Bahamas. He came upon what he took to be the mainland of Asia, which in fact was the north coast of Cuba. While exploring eastward, Columbus lost contact with Martín Alonzo Pinzón, who had sailed off on the *Pinta* in search of gold. On Cuba, Columbus sent an exploring party inland, led by his interpreter, a Spanish Jew named Luiz de Torres, in the hope of making contact with the Chinese ruler, the Great Khan. On returning, the party reported contacts with more tribal peoples; Columbus therefore decided to sail onward in search of the civilizations of China, Japan, and India.

On December 5, 1492, after crossing the Windward Passage, Columbus reached the eastern end of a large island he believed to be part of Japan, and which he named Española (later known as Hispaniola, now comprising Haiti and the Dominican Republic). On Christmas Eve, 1492, while anchored off the north coast of the island, the *Santa María* was wrecked when it was swept aground. Columbus

and his crew received aid in unloading the vessel from the Arawak leader GUANCANAGARI and his people and soon established a small fort with the wreckage of the ship. Called Navidad, Spanish for "Christmas," in honor of its being founded on that day, it was the first attempted European settlement in the Western Hemisphere since the explorations of the Vikings about 500 years earlier.

With only one ship remaining, Columbus decided to leave 40 men behind to establish a colony, planning to return for them on his next voyage. He set out for Spain on January 4, 1493, and soon encountered Martín Alonzo Pinzón and the *Pinta*. The ships were separated again in a storm near the AZORES. Columbus was compelled to put in at Lisbon for repairs before continuing to Palos de Frontera, which he reached on March 15, 1493. Although Martín Alonzo Pinzón had arrived earlier at a northern Spanish port, by royal order he had to await the return of Columbus before he was permitted to disembark and report his findings.

Columbus was given a triumphant welcome by King Ferdinand and Queen Isabella. He presented the Spanish

The landing of Christopher Columbus in the Americas (painting by John Vanderlyn) *(Library of Congress)*

monarchs with gifts of gold, parrots, and a number of Native Americans and reported that he had reached the outlying islands of Asia. Although he had sailed farther westward than any European had until that time, he was unaware that the lands he had found were part of an uncharted continent.

Less than six months later, Columbus embarked on his second voyage, in command of a fleet of 17 ships, among them the *Niña,* carrying an expedition of 1,200 soldiers and colonists, including artisans and farmers, with livestock, tools, and seeds. Departing from Cádiz on September 25, 1493, Columbus first sailed to the Canaries, then took a more southerly route across the Atlantic, arriving on November 3, 1493, at an island he called Dominica in the Windward Islands, where he encountered the Carib Indians, a warlike people.

Columbus then made his way northward through the Lesser Antilles, sighting and naming many islands, including Mariagalante and Guadeloupe, as well as St. Thomas and St. Croix in the Virgin Islands. He came upon the coast of another large island, Puerto Rico, then sailed for Hispaniola and his settlement at Navidad, which he reached on November 28, 1493. The fort, however, had been burned to the ground and its men had been killed by the Arawak. From Guancanagari, Columbus learned that, in the course of the past year, the colonists had repeatedly abused the native peoples, leading them to retaliate.

Columbus then founded a new, larger settlement, farther to the east, which he named Isabella. Exploring parties were sent inland in search of gold. Leaving another of his brothers, Diego, in charge of the new colony, Columbus then returned to reconnoiter Cuba's south coast. He sailed almost to Cuba's western end at Cape San Antonio, where he erroneously surmised that the coastline continued westward and that Cuba was a peninsula of the Asian mainland. He then sailed back to Hispaniola, making the European discovery of Jamaica along the way.

From the settlement of Isabella, Columbus sent ALONSO DE OJEDA to explore the interior and subdue the Indians, who had become hostile in response to brutal treatment by the Spanish. Not finding an easy source of gold on Hispaniola, Columbus, in 1495, turned to enslaving the Native Americans, sending back 500 native women to Spain that year. This practice led to the sickness and death of many of the captives as well as the introduction into Europe of a particularly virulent strain of syphilis. Soon after the arrival of Bartholomew Columbus in 1496, who assumed command of the colony, Columbus left for Spain, leaving instructions to establish a city on the south shore of Hispaniola. This city became present-day Santo Domingo, the oldest inhabited city in the Americas.

After Columbus arrived back in Cádiz in June 1496, he had to wait two years before he could begin his next voyage. The delay, due in part to international problems in Europe, also stemmed from Queen Isabella's disapproval of his treatment of the Indians, whom she considered her subjects as well as candidates for conversion to Christianity.

Columbus embarked on his third voyage on May 30, 1498, sailing with six ships from Seville. In the Canaries, he sent half his fleet directly to Hispaniola, and, with the other three ships, sailed southward to the Cape Verde Islands, then southwestward across the South Atlantic. On July 31, 1498, he sighted an island he named Trinidad in honor of the Holy Trinity. From there, he continued southward into the Gulf of Pará, where he traded for pearls with the natives. Although he at first thought he had found another island, which he named the Island of Zeta, he soon decided, from the great volume of freshwater emptying into the sea off the Orinoco Delta, that he had come upon a mainland. After examining the Venezuelan coast westward, he sailed back to Hispaniola, arriving at Santo Domingo in September 1498, where he found the colony to be in revolt against his brother Bartholomew.

Because of continuing abuse and exploitation of the Indians, a new governor was appointed for Hispaniola, Francisco de Bobadilla, in 1500. On his arrival in Santo Domingo, he ordered Columbus and his brother arrested for their misconduct in administering the colony, sending them back to Spain in chains. Although he was not prosecuted, Columbus was never reinstated to his former office. Yet he was placed in command of a fourth voyage in 1502, the aim of which was to continue the search for gold and to push westward beyond Cuba in the hope of locating a passage to the Far East.

Columbus sailed from Cádiz on May 11, 1502, with a fleet of four ships and 140 men. On his return to the Caribbean, he first landed on the island of Martinique, then proceeded to Hispaniola, where he was forbidden to land. He headed westward and soon came upon the Islas de la Bahía (Bay Islands), an island group off the coast of Honduras. Soon afterward, he reached the mainland of CENTRAL AMERICA near present-day Trujillo, Honduras, where he encountered Maya Indians from the Yucatán. Exploring southward along the coasts of present-day Nicaragua and Costa Rica, he made contact with more Indians, from whom he received gold. By October 1502, he was off the coast of Panama. The Indians informed him that it was an isthmus, leading Columbus to believe he was sailing along the Malay Peninsula. He continued southward, in the hope of finding a strait to Malacca.

Columbus attempted to establish a colony on the coast of Panama at Santa María de Belén. By February 1503, however, he had lost one of his ships in a wreck and some of his men to Indian attacks and disease, and he decided to sail back to Hispaniola. Unfavorable winds drove him to St. Ann's Bay on the north coast of Jamaica. His ships in disrepair, Columbus and his men were forced to remain there a year, until a rescue vessel arrived from Santo Domingo.

Columbus made no more voyages after his return to Seville in September 1504. Although he had become wealthy from his exploits, he spent his last years in disfavor with the Spanish court and in obscurity. He died at Valladolid on May 20, 1506. Some years later, his remains were moved to Santo Domingo.

In addition to the economic inducements for his voyages, Columbus's expeditions were in effect experiments, to prove or disprove his hypothesis about world geography— the distance of Asia and the size of the world. Along with most educated people of his time, he knew that the world was a GLOBE (albeit a pear-shaped globe in his view), and not flat; he did not set out to prove that the world was round as is commonly believed. Yet he wrongly maintained until his death that he had reached Asia, not realizing the far greater ramifications of his landings. At the heart of his contribution to the history of exploration was his idea to sail westward across the ocean.

Columbus's voyages had the immediate effect of inspiring many more expeditions, especially those of seafarers who had sailed with him, including Juan de la Cosa, Alonso de Ojeda, and Vicente Yáñez Pinzón. For the native peoples of the WEST INDIES, the sudden European contact brought about by Columbus's voyages soon wrought catastrophic results. Through disease, military conquest, forced labor, and the slave trade, the Indians of the Caribbean were virtually exterminated by the middle of the 16th century. There followed in the years to come massive displacement and cultural dispossession of native peoples in other parts of the Americas.

Christopher Columbus of course did not "discover" America. The Indians of the Americas had arrived from Asia thousands of years before. And the Vikings had crossed from Europe five centuries earlier, thus making the first known "discovery" of the Americas by a European people. Yet Columbus was the first to reveal the existence of the Americas to all of Europe, and, in so doing, drastically altered Europeans' view of the world. He had sailed hoping to prove that the world was smaller than it was, and, after 10 years of exploring, his findings revealed just the opposite, that the world was considerably larger, containing vast uncharted lands and seas. In addition to new geographic awareness, Columbus's expeditions brought back to Europe new crops, such as sweet potatoes, corn, and tobacco; and new technologies, such as the Arawak use of the hammock, which was adopted by Europeans in their ships, improving sleeping conditions for crews. His exploits spurred on the EUROPEAN AGE OF EXPLORATION and redirected the course of world events, making 1492 one of the most widely known dates in history and Columbus the most famous explorer.

Commerson, Joseph-Philibert (Philibert de Commerçon) (1727–1773) *French physician and naturalist in the Pacific and Indian Oceans*

Joseph-Philibert Commerson was born in Châtillon-les-Dombes, near Bourg, in eastern France. His father was a lawyer. He studied medicine at Montpellier in the south of France, becoming a physician in 1747.

During the next eight years, Commerson pursued his interest in natural history, especially botany, studying under the direction of French botanist Bernard de Jussieu and the Swedish botanist Carolus Linnaeus (Karl von Linne). In 1755, he was commissioned by the Swedish government to undertake a study of marine life in the MEDITERRANEAN SEA.

By 1767, he had become prominent in French scientific and philosophical circles; that year, he was appointed royal naturalist and botanist and he accepted a position as doctor and naturalist with LOUIS-ANTOINE DE BOUGAINVILLE's expedition around the world. He sailed on the expedition's supply vessel *Étoile,* which left Rochefort in February 1767.

Commerson's first scientific work on this expedition was undertaken in the Falkland Islands, where he found several previously unknown species of sea birds. He also studied the king penguin and attempted, without success, to bring a living specimen back to Europe. Near Montevideo in present-day Uruguay, he studied a popular tropical plant, bestowing upon it the name Bougainvillea after the expedition's leader. A marine mammal he observed off the South American coast was subsequently named by French marine zoologists as Commerson's dolphin.

In the STRAIT OF MAGELLAN, Commerson studied many species of plants then unknown to science; he also observed an animal known as a colpeo or Magellan's wolf.

Commersons's wife of two years had died in childbirth in 1762, and he had hired JEANNE BARET as governess for his young son. Commerson had brought Baret on the voyage as his scientific assistant, having left the boy in France in the care of a relative. Disguised as a man, she managed to conceal her true gender from the crew until the truth was discovered on Tahiti.

At Batavia, present-day Jakarta, Indonesia, Commerson discovered and named a plant known as the hortensia. He left the expedition at Île de France (present-day Mauritius) in the Indian Ocean in December 1768. In 1770, he sailed to Madagascar, where he undertook an extensive study of that island's flora and fauna. After six months on Madagascar, he returned to Île de France and worked at organizing his botanical collection. Developing pleurisy, he died there in March 1773.

Joseph-Philibert Commerson was one of the first scientists to circumnavigate the world. He sent back to France a collection that included thousands of specimens of plants and animals, the majority of which were unknown to science. Ironically, Commerson had written a *Martyrology of*

Botany, which recounted the lives of naturalists who had died in their pursuit of scientific knowledge. Published after his death by fellow French scientist Joseph Lalande, it was updated to include a chapter on Commerson himself.

Condamine, Charles-Marie de la   See LA CONDAMINE, CHARLES-MARIE DE.

Conti, Niccolò di   (ca. 1395–1469) *Italian traveler in southern Asia*

Niccolò di Conti was born in Chioggia, an Italian fishing port on the Adriatic near Venice. He grew up to be a Venetian merchant.

In about 1419, Conti traveled to Damascus in present-day Syria, where he spent several years learning Arabic. From there, he traveled southward to Baghdad, then proceeded to the southern end of the Persian Gulf at Hormuz. After making a study of the life and culture of peoples along coastal Persia (present-day Iran), as well as learning the Persian language, he continued eastward across the Arabian Sea to India and eventually reached the Bay of Cambay north of Bombay.

In his subsequent journey across the Indian subcontinent, Conti visited the Malabar Coast, where he saw the shrine of St. Thomas; and, in the Madras region of southeastern India, he visited the ancient city of Vijayanagar. He then traveled north and east to the GANGES RIVER, and, from there, continued eastward to the Irrawaddy River region of Burma (present-day Myanmar). Crossing into the Malay Peninsula, he sailed to ports on the Indonesian islands of Java and Sumatra.

Conti's return to Italy was mostly by sea, during which he visited ports in Southeast Asia and stopped at Ceylon (present-day Sri Lanka). From Calicut on the Malabar Coast of India, he sailed to the island of Socotra, south of the Arabian Peninsula. After reaching Aden, he traveled up the RED SEA along the Arabian coast to Jidda.

In the course of his travels in Asia, Conti had been compelled to embrace Islam. He also had married an East Indian woman, who bore him four children. Upon reaching Cairo, on his way back to Italy, two of his children, as well as his wife, died of the plague.

In 1444, after 25 years in southern Asia, Conti finally returned to Venice. He converted back to Catholicism and reestablished himself as a merchant. His account of his travels in Asia was recorded by Giovanni Francesco Poggio Bracciolini, papal secretary to Pope Eugenius IV.

Niccolò di Conti was one of the few Europeans to visit India and the Far East since 1368, at which time Christian missionaries had been expelled from China. The story of his travels, as recorded by Poggio Bracciolini, provided Eu-

ropeans with updated information of life and culture in Asia in the later Middle Ages, and inspired the expeditions by Portuguese mariners, who began sailing from Europe to India at the close of the 15th century.

Cook, Frederick Albert   (1865–1940)
American physician, polar explorer

Frederick Cook was born near Callicoon in southeastern New York State, the son of a doctor who had emigrated from Germany. When he was five, his father died, and he moved with his family to Brooklyn, New York. Cook went on to study medicine at Columbia University and continued his medical training at New York University, which awarded him an M.D. in 1890.

In 1891, Cook took part in his first polar expedition, accompanying ROBERT EDWIN PEARY to GREENLAND's Inglefield Gulf. Serving as the expedition's ethnologist and surgeon, he made a study of the Greenland Inuit, concentrating on their hunting and survival skills. His medical ability was called upon during this expedition when he treated Peary for a broken leg, resulting from a shipboard accident.

After taking part in two more expeditions to Greenland, Cook joined the Belgian Antarctic expedition under the command of ADRIEN-VICTOR-JOSEPH DE GERLACHE DE GOMERY. He sailed to Tierra del Fuego with Gerlache on the *Belgica* in 1897. Accompanying him was the Norwegian polar explorer ROALD ENGELBREGT GRAVNING AMUNDSEN. The *Belgica* was trapped in the Antarctic ice for more than 13 months, and the crew was stricken with SCURVY. Largely through the resourcefulness of Amundsen and Cook, the ship was finally freed and the crew members nursed back to health. Cook and the others on this expedition were among the first men to winter south of the ANTARCTIC CIRCLE.

In 1906, Cook led an expedition to Alaska, where he made an attempt at scaling MOUNT MCKINLEY. After most of the other members of his party turned back, Cook persisted in his efforts with only one other man. In September 1906, he reportedly reached the summit, becoming the first man to climb to the top of North America's highest peak.

Cook's next polar exploit was an attempt to reach the NORTH POLE itself. With the financial support of the Explorers Club, he sailed from Gloucester, Massachusetts, in July 1907 on a yacht belonging to his friend John R. Bradley. At a point on the northwest coast of Greenland called Anoatok, not far from Etah, where Peary later established his base camp, Cook set out with a party of Inuit and crossed Kane Basin to Ellesmere Island. From the northern end of Ellesmere Island, he reached Cape Stallworthy, the northernmost point of Axel Heiberg Island. On March 17, 1908, accompanied by only four Inuit, Cook embarked on the last leg of the trek to the Pole. Two of the Inuit soon turned back. Cook continued northward and, as he later

Frederick Cook *(Library of Congress)*

with settling the question, was unable to prove conclusively whether Cook had preceded Peary there.

The debate over who had first reached the North Pole raged on. Peary alleged not only that had Cook failed to reach the Pole, but also that his prior accomplishment on Mount McKinley was a fraud as well. Noted explorers of the day were split on the issue. Lacking evidence, Cook's claim was discredited. He was accused of falsifying records that supported his claim, and he was expelled from the Explorers Club.

In the years that followed, Cook traveled to Europe and Argentina. Upon his return to the United States, he appeared in vaudeville shows as an acrobat and mime. Despite the doubts cast on his North Pole expedition, his 1911 book, *My Attainment of the Pole,* became a bestseller.

In the early 1920s, Cook was implicated in an illegal financial scheme involving oil leases in Texas. He was found guilty by a federal court of mail fraud in 1925 and was sentenced to 14 years in prison. After serving five years at the federal penitentiary in Leavenworth, Kansas, he was released on parole, and in 1940, shortly before his death, he was pardoned by President Franklin Roosevelt.

Dr. Frederick Cook is one of the most controversial figures in the history of exploration. Whether he reached the North Pole is still a subject of contention.

claimed, he reached the North Pole on April 21, 1908. En route, he reportedly sighted a landmass that he called Bradley Land, although a subsequent aerial reconnaissance of the North Pole was unable to verify this finding. Ice conditions forced Cook and his two Inuit companions to winter on Cape Sparbo on Devon Island. He then made his way back to Anoatok, Greenland, arriving there in early April 1909.

During Cook's return to Greenland, Peary had set out on his own journey to the North Pole. At Anoatok, Cook encountered Peary's ship. Aboard was American financier and sportsman Harry Payne Whitney, husband of American heiress and artist Gertrude Vanderbilt Whitney. Entrusting his scientific data to Whitney, Cook headed overland to an ice-free port on the Greenland coast, from where he sailed to Copenhagen, Denmark. Five days later, Peary returned from his successful trek to the Pole and immediately cast doubt on Cook's claimed achievement.

In Denmark, and later in New York City, Cook was hailed as the first man to reach the North Pole. However, soon after Peary returned to the United States, a controversy erupted over whether Cook had actually accomplished the journey. Peary had not permitted Whitney to bring Cook's scientific data back to the United States, and its whereabouts has never been revealed. Although Peary's astronomical and navigational observations indicated that he had been at the Pole, the University of Copenhagen, charged

Cook, James (Captain James Cook) (1728–1779)
British naval officer in the Atlantic and Pacific

James Cook was born in Marton-in-Cleveland, an agricultural village in Yorkshire, England, where his parents were farm workers. At the age of 16, he was apprenticed to a dry goods merchant in the fishing village of Staithes. About two years later, Cook moved to Whitby, the English seaport on Yorkshire's North Sea coast, where he began his seafaring career as shipwright and later as a ship's boy on the *Freelove,* which carried coal down the coast from Whitby to London. Over the next few years, Cook studied mathematics and astronomy on his own and developed his skills as a navigator.

In 1755, at the beginning of the Seven Years War between England and France, Cook enlisted in the Royal Navy as an able-bodied seaman, serving on the HMS *Eagle* under Sir Hugh Palliser. Palliser recognized Cook's talent for navigation and seamanship and helped to advance his naval career.

In 1759, Cook undertook a detailed navigational survey of the St. Lawrence River and its estuary. His charts were invaluable in the British landing and victory at Quebec that September.

Cook's expertise as a navigator and hydrographer became well known in 1760, with the publication of his *New Chart of the River St. Lawrence.* After Great Britain gained control of Canada in 1760, Palliser was appointed governor of Newfoundland, and Cook continued to conduct coastal surveys of Newfoundland. He charted the northern approach to the Gulf of St. Lawrence through the Strait of Belle Isle, as well as the southern route through Cabot Strait. In spring 1764, Cook was given his first Royal Navy command, the schooner *Grenville.* Two years later, in July 1766, he took the *Grenville* to the Newfoundland coast to observe a solar eclipse. In 1768, the findings of this expedition were published by the ROYAL SOCIETY.

At this time, Great Britain had political and commercial, as well as scientific, motives to explore the Pacific Ocean. The BRITISH EAST INDIA COMPANY had achieved a dominant commercial and political position in the Bengal region of India by 1765. With the military situation in North America stabilized, the British turned their attention to seeking new trade routes to Asia. France, Britain's longtime military and commercial rival, was sending out expeditions to the South Pacific, providing further impetus for British exploration.

In early 1768, the Royal Society in conjunction with the Royal Navy, organized an expedition to Tahiti in the South Pacific. The official purpose of this mission was to observe an astronomical event, the Transit of Venus, on June 3, 1769, and thereby to calculate the distance between the Earth and the Sun and obtain data for accurate determinations of longitude. A second scientific motive, later revealed, was to locate what was thought to be the GREAT SOUTHERN CONTINENT, also known as Terra Australis. Geographers based their belief in its existence on the theory that the great continents of the Northern Hemisphere had to be counterbalanced with corresponding landmasses in the Southern Hemisphere. Earlier Dutch and Portuguese explorations of Australia and the EAST INDIES had been inconclusive in determining whether or not such a landmass existed, and newly developed navigational techniques had not yet been employed in the higher latitudes of the Southern Hemisphere.

Originally, Alexander Dalrymple, a fellow of the Royal Society, who later became the hydrographer for the British East India Company, had planned to lead the Tahiti expedition. Because he was not a seafarer, however, British naval authorities declined to grant him official command, leading to his withdrawal from the project and Cook's appointment instead.

A former coal ship from Cook's home port of Whitby, the *Endeavour,* was refitted for the voyage. With a crew of 94 men, including sailors, marines, and scientists, the *Endeavour* departed Plymouth on August 26, 1768, sailing southwestward to the east coast of South America and putting in at Rio de Janeiro. The expedition then proceeded southward along the coast to Tierra del Fuego and CAPE HORN.

Among the scientists aboard the *Endeavour* during Cook's first Pacific expedition were naturalists SIR JOSEPH BANKS and DANIEL CARL SOLANDER. Cook joined Banks and Solander and their assistants in periodic sojourns into the South American coastal regions, including a study of Tierra del Fuego and its native peoples.

By April 1769, Cook had reached the central Pacific and put in at Tahiti. Good relations with the Tahitians were established, although there were periodic clashes, usually stemming from theft by the natives of the expedition's supplies and equipment. The islanders also stole nails from the underside of the hull for iron.

A temporary observatory was set up on Tahiti, called Fort Venus. The observation of the Transit of Venus, the passage of that planet across the face of the sun, was successfully completed in early June 1769, and Cook sailed southward from Tahiti, naming the island group of which it was a part the Society Islands, perhaps in honor of the Royal Society. Other accounts report that Cook named this chain the Society Islands because, as he wrote in his journal, "they lay contiguous to one another."

Having followed a southwestward course in search of the Great Southern Continent, Cook, on October 7, 1769, reached the east coast of NEW ZEALAND's North Island. He explored northward, rounded the island's northern tip at

James Cook *(Library of Congress)*

North Cape, then headed along the west coast. By the last week of January, after several anchorings near shore, the expedition came upon Queen Charlotte Sound, which had been thought to be a bay, according to earlier reports by Dutch navigators. On January 23, after surveying the area from a hilltop, Cook determined that it was actually a strait dividing New Zealand into two large islands, dispelling earlier Dutch reports that New Zealand was the western edge of a larger landmass. Sir Joseph Banks soon dubbed the passage Cook Strait in the captain's honor, and, on January 31, 1770, Cook officially claimed both islands in the name of the British Crown.

By the end of March 1770, Cook had completed his circumnavigations of both of New Zealand's main islands, during which his officers had made detailed charts of more than 2,400 miles of coastline. Although the Great Southern Continent remained elusive, Cook decided to sail for home. He had considered carrying on the search for Terra Australis along the way, but that would have required sailing southward into the high southern latitudes during the approaching Southern Hemisphere winter months. Moreover, the *Endeavour*, after two years at sea, was in no condition to withstand the storms so prevalent around Cape Horn at that time of year. Accordingly, Cook decided on a westward course back to England, by way of the Indian Ocean and the CAPE OF GOOD HOPE. On March 31, 1770, the *Endeavour* embarked from its anchorage in Cook Strait (near present-day Wellington, New Zealand) and sailed westward into the Tasman Sea.

Cook planned to sail first to Van Diemen's Land (present-day TASMANIA) and from there try to locate the north coast of New Holland and follow it westward into the Indian Ocean. Using copies of charts originally made by Dutch navigator ABEL JANSZOON TASMAN nearly 130 years earlier, he also hoped to determine if Van Diemen's Land was connected to New Holland, as was then thought, or was actually a separate island. As it turned out, gale-force winds from the south drove the *Endeavour* northward, and instead of reaching Van Diemen's Land, on April 19, 1770, Cook came in sight of the mainland of southeast New Holland (Australia) at Cape Everard on the coast of what is now Victoria.

Cook then followed the coastline northward, discovering, on April 28, 1770, a large natural harbor. At first, Cook named it "Stingray Bay," when a reconnaissance revealed it was shaped like that marine creature. Moreover, during their stay the crew managed to catch and eat more than a few large stingrays, which the bay seemed to contain in abundance. Within a short time, however, Cook decided to change the name to Botany Bay when his scientists reported finding a wide variety of new plants there.

After a week at Botany Bay, Cook and the *Endeavour* continued northward. Fifteen miles up the coast they came upon another bay, which they did not explore, although Cook named it Port Jackson, after the then-current secretary of the Admiralty. Also known as Sydney Harbor, the settlement of Sydney was founded on its shores in 1788. One of the earliest penal colonies in Australia, its name had been adopted from Cook's patron, British nobleman Viscount Sydney.

Cook's northward course took him into the waters between the Australian mainland and the Great Barrier Reef, a 1,250-mile-long coral formation that parallels Australia's northeast coast. On June 11, 1770, off Cape Tribulation in present-day Queensland, the *Endeavour* became stuck on the reef. Although the hull had been punctured, the protruding coral spike broke off from the reef, partially plugging the hole.

The *Endeavour* was still leaking badly, however, and it took two days for the crew to free the vessel from the reef. Nine days later, they reached a suitable anchorage at the mouth of a river that Cook named the Endeavour River after his ship. They remained there for the next six weeks to make extensive repairs to the vessel's underside.

When the voyage resumed, Cook cautiously continued northward, mindful of the hazards of the reef. On August 21, 1770, he reached Cape York, the northernmost point of the Cape York Peninsula. Before rounding it to the west, he went ashore on August 23, 1770, and took possession of the newly located east coast of New Holland in the name of King George III, naming the region New South Wales.

Cook then left Australian waters and headed for Torres Strait, which separates Australia from New Guinea and the Indonesian Archipelago. The *Endeavour* anchored for additional repairs at Batavia, present-day Jakarta, on Java, then headed across the Indian Ocean. In spring 1771 the *Endeavour* reached the Cape of Good Hope, where additional crewmen were obtained to replace those who had died of disease contracted in Batavia. After stopping at the island of St. Helena in the South Atlantic Ocean, the *Endeavour* sailed northward along the west coast of Africa, reaching England in July 1771.

Cook's first expedition to the South Pacific had taken nearly three years and had carried out a CIRCUMNAVIGATION OF THE WORLD. In addition to acquiring important astronomical data, its participants had learned much concerning the geography of New Zealand and Australia. Cook recorded observations on the life and customs of the South Pacific people he had encountered, including the Polynesians of Tahiti, the Maori of New Zealand, and the Aborigines of Australia. Banks, Solander, and their staff also brought back a wealth of scientific data about plant and animal species then unknown to Europeans, including the first specimens of kangaroo and other marsupials from Australia. The voyage also proved that a strict dietary regimen of fresh fruits and vegetables, as well as sauerkraut, a preservable food high in vitamin C, prevented outbreaks of SCURVY among the crew.

Still believing that Terra Australis might exist, the Royal Society and Royal Navy organized a second expedition to the South Pacific under Cook. On July 11, 1772, two ships, the *Resolution,* commanded by Cook, and the *Adventure,* captained by TOBIAS FURNEAUX, departed Plymouth. Cook planned to head for Antarctic regions by way of the Cape of Good Hope and circumnavigate the world in the high southern latitudes, a route that could not help but bring him in contact with the Great Southern Continent.

After stopping at the AZORES and the Cape Verde Islands off Africa's west coast, Cook and his ships sailed southward, reaching Cape Town in November 1772. German naturalist JOHANN REINHOLD FORSTER and his son, JOHANN GEORG ADAM FORSTER, led the scientific contingent of the expedition. They made a brief investigation of the plant and animal life around Cape Town. The ships then sailed southward toward the Antarctic Ocean later in November, crossing the ANTARCTIC CIRCLE on January 17, 1773, the first such penetration in recorded history.

By late January 1773, Cook had decided that further exploration toward the Pole would be too hazardous because of the mammoth icebergs and the impassable frozen Antarctic waters. About this time, Cook's ship, the *Resolution,* lost sight of the *Adventure.* A rendezvous in New Zealand's Cook Strait had been prearranged in anticipation of such an occurrence. Cook sailed the *Resolution* north and reached southern New Zealand in March 1773, catching up with the *Adventure* about six weeks later at Cook Strait. In the meantime, Furneaux had explored Tasmania and made the European discovery of Adventure Bay.

The two ships sailed eastward across the Pacific to spend the rest of the season exploring the Pacific islands lying between New Zealand and the southern tip of South America. Proceeding northeastward, Cook and his ships reached Tahiti in August 1773, where he was welcomed by native leaders he had met on his first expedition. From Tahiti, Cook headed westward and came upon Tonga in an archipelago he named the Friendly Islands. From there, the ships returned to New Zealand. In late October 1773, the *Resolution* and *Adventure* were again separated, this time by a storm off the coast of New Zealand. The *Adventure* missed Cook by six days at a rendezvous point at Cook Strait and returned to England. With only the *Resolution,* Cook again headed into Antarctic waters in late November 1773. Blocked by ice, he was forced to head northward in February 1774, after reaching the southernmost point at 71°11" south latitude and unknowingly completing a circumnavigation of Antarctica.

In 1774, Cook relocated and correctly charted many South Pacific Islands that had not been visited since Portuguese, Dutch, and Spanish explorations of the previous two centuries. Among these were Easter Island, the Marquesas, the New Hebrides, and other islands in the Polynesian and Melanesian archipelagoes. The expedition returned to Tahiti in April, then headed westward across the Pacific to New Zealand. He also made the European discovery of New Caledonia. In November 1774, Cook made his final exploration toward Antarctic regions, but was once again turned back by the ice. Sailing for Tierra del Fuego at the tip of South America, Cook was in the South Atlantic by early 1775 and soon made the European discovery of South Georgia Island and the South Sandwich Islands. He then headed back to Cape Town, then northward to England, arriving at Spithead on July 30, 1775.

With his circumnavigation of Antarctica, Cook brought back proof that there was no large habitable Great Southern Continent. In addition, he had added considerably to the geographic knowledge of the South Pacific. Longitudinal measurements were made with greater accuracy with the aid of the newly developed chronometer, designed by John Harrison, which kept a record of Greenwich Mean Time.

Both the British Admiralty and the Royal Society were pleased with the results of Cook's second voyage. He was received by King George III, promoted to the rank of ship's captain, and admitted as a member of the Royal Society. He was also granted the position as director of Greenwich Hospital, a post requiring little responsibility but with a substantial salary.

At the urging of the HUDSON'S BAY COMPANY, an expedition was arranged in search of an all-water route across the top of the North American continent, the long-sought NORTHWEST PASSAGE. In July 1776, Cook left England aboard the *Resolution,* on which he had sailed on his second voyage to the Pacific. The master of the ship for this journey was WILLIAM BLIGH, who would later gain notoriety as the captain of the HMS *Bounty.* CHARLES CLERKE also accompanied the expedition in command of the *Discovery.*

The expedition headed for the Pacific via the Cape of Good Hope, reaching the coast of Tasmania in late January 1776. Following a stopover at New Zealand, Cook headed eastward across the South Pacific. Along the way, he charted an archipelago now known as the Cook Islands. He also revisited the Friendly Islands and Tahiti.

In early 1778, Cook came upon the Sandwich Islands, known today as the HAWAIIAN ISLANDS. His scientific team made a study of the native peoples, as well as the plants and animals in the region. Heading north and east, the ships were off the west coast of Canada at Vancouver Island's Nootka Sound by early March 1778. The crew had contact with the Nootka Indians and learned that an abundance of valuable sea otter pelts were available for trade. The expedition headed northward to the Gulf of Alaska and explored Prince William Sound, then reached Unalaska Island in the Aleutian Islands in early July 1778. Cook pushed northward through the BERING STRAIT, stopping for a time on Siberia's Chukchi Peninsula. After reaching the northernmost latitude of 70° 44' north, where ice prevented further advance, he decided to head southward for the Sandwich Islands to spend the winter.

In January 1779, Cook and his expedition were back in Hawaiian waters. He undertook further explorations of the islands, including Maui and the largest island, Hawaii. On February 14, 1779, he was killed in a skirmish with native peoples at Kealakekua Bay on Hawaii.

Clerke assumed command of the expedition and returned northward to the North American coast to search for the Northwest Passage. Although no such route was found, the expedition's crew were able to trade with the Nootka for pelts, which they then took to China and sold at a spectacular profit. When Clerke died that same year, JOHN GORE assumed command. The *Resolution* and *Discovery* headed home by way of the Indian Ocean and the Cape of Good Hope, reaching England on August 23, 1780.

James Cook's three voyages of exploration had not only determined that there was no Great Southern Continent other than Antarctica but also cast doubts on the existence of a practical Northwest Passage across North America. Moreover, his travels had led to a variety of scientific discoveries in navigation and natural history. His explorations of Australia and New Zealand provided the basis for Great Britain's claim to these lands, where settlement would occur at a rapid rate in the years to come.

Cooper, Thomas Thornville (1839–1878)

British trader, traveler in China

In 1868, Thomas Cooper attempted to establish a trade route linking Shanghai, China, with northern Burma and India. That year, with two Chinese companions, he traveled from Shanghai to the south-central Chinese city of Batang. From there, he made his way to the upper course of the YANGTZE RIVER (Chang) then traveled southward along the upper Yangtze toward the Burmese border, but he was unable to go beyond the city of Atuntze, north of the present border with Vietnam.

Thomas Cooper was among the first Europeans to visit the interior of China following the loosening of the Chinese government's travel restrictions on foreigners in 1860. Although he did not reach his intended destination, he left an account of his adventures that described then little-known geographic features of southern China.

Coronado, Francisco Vásquez de
(Francisco Vázquez de Coronado) (ca. 1510–1554)

Spanish conquistador in the American Southwest

Francisco de Coronado was born in Salamanca, Spain, a university town in the western province of León. At the age of 25, he was appointed to the staff of ANTONIO DE MENDOZA, Spain's first viceroy to the newly conquered Mexico, and he traveled to Mexico City with Mendoza in 1535. By 1539, after his marriage to Beatriz de Estrada, the daughter of a wealthy Spanish colonial family, Coronado was governor of the newly organized province of Nueva Galicia on the west coast of Mexico.

In 1536, ÁLVAR NÚÑEZ CABEZA DE VACA and the slave ESTEVANICO returned to Mexico City from their eight years of wandering in the American Southwest, with tales of cities of great wealth to the north. Their accounts of CIBOLA seemed to coincide with the stories of the Seven Cities of Antillia, which, according to legend, had been established in the eighth century by seven Portuguese bishops who had somehow crossed the Atlantic Ocean. Three years later, under the sponsorship of Mendoza and Coronado, the Franciscan friar MARCOS DE NIZA and Estevanico were dispatched northward to locate this fabled land of wealth. In 1539, the expedition explored present-day southern Arizona. Estevanico was killed by the Indians, but Niza returned to Coronado in Nueva Galicia with reports that he had indeed seen a golden city.

Mendoza soon mounted a massive military expedition to claim these riches for Spain under Coronado's leadership. In February 1540, Coronado led a force of more than 300 Spanish CONQUISTADORES, 800 allied Indians, and nearly 1,000 African and Indian slaves northward from the Nueva Galician town of Compostela on the west coast of Mexico, north of Puerto Vallarta. The force reached the port of Culiacán inland from the mouth of the Gulf of California. A seaward expedition, commanded by HERNANDO DE ALARCÓN, left the nearby port of Altata with three ships and sailed northward into the gulf, hoping to reach Cibola via the mouth of the COLORADO RIVER.

In April 1540, Coronado led an advance party of about 100 soldiers and Indians from Culiacán along the Sierra Madre into the Sonora region of northwestern Mexico. This group crossed into the present-day United States, near the site of present-day Bisbee, Arizona, in early summer 1540.

On July 7, 1540, Coronado and his army came upon the Zuni pueblo of Hawikuh in what is now western New Mexico, the settlement espied by Niza on his earlier expedition. Hawikuh, soon captured by the Spaniards, proved to have no gold or other riches. Niza accompanied one of Coronado's lieutenants, MELCHOR DÍAZ, back to Mexico with instructions that the rest of the expedition proceed northward.

Díaz reached the main part of the Spanish force at Ures in Sonora, Mexico, then headed westward to make contact with Alarcón and his ships on the Colorado River. Díaz and his party reached the confluence of the Gila and Colorado Rivers but were unable to find the Spanish fleet. They soon found a message from Alarcón informing them that the naval force, after sailing up the Colorado River for a distance of 50 miles, had been unable to meet up with Coronado and had returned to Mexico. Díaz then crossed the Colorado River and explored the plateau regions north of the Gulf of California. He was injured en route in an accident with a Spanish lance and soon died.

Coronado had meanwhile set up his headquarters at Hawikuh. On July 15, 1540, he sent out an expedition to the northwest under PEDRO DE TOVAR, accompanied by Friar JUAN DE PADILLA, to search for another of the fabled cities, still hoping to find gold. Tovar came upon the Hopi Indian settlement of Awatovi, in what is now eastern Arizona. After

Francisco Vásquez de Coronado's march through the American Southwest (painting by Frederic Remington)   *(Library of Congress)*

conquering the pueblo, he learned from the subjugated inhabitants of a great river to the west, probably the Colorado.

Coronado dispatched another officer, GARCÍA LÓPEZ DE CÁRDENAS, with a small force to the north and west. In mid-September 1540, López de Cárdenas and his men reached the rim of the Grand Canyon, the first Europeans to see this natural wonder.

At about the same time, another of Coronado's men, HERNANDO DE ALVARADO, reached the Acoma Pueblo of the Keres Indians, west of present-day Albuquerque, New Mexico. Alvarado and his party subdued its people, then headed eastward to the Indian pueblos of the upper Pecos River, near present-day Las Vegas, New Mexico. At the Pecos pueblo, Alvarado encountered two Plains Indians held captive, Ysopete and the TURK. The Turk informed Alvarado of a tribe of Indians far to the north and east who lived in towns resplendent with gold and jewels. Although Ysopete revealed the Turk's tales as lies, Alvarado took both of them back to Coronado in the hope that they would lead the Spaniards to this wealthy Indian civilization, identified as QUIVIRA.

In winter 1540–41, Coronado had moved his headquarters east to the Indian settlement of Tiguex on the Rio Grande, just north of what is now Albuquerque. Because of the Turk's reports, Coronado, in spring 1541, led his expedition eastward into the northern panhandle of present-day Texas. He followed the Red and Canadian Rivers across the Staked Plains, making the European discovery of the Palo Duro and Tule Canyons. In the course of this journey, Coronado and his men became the first Europeans to encounter the vast buffalo herds of the Great Plains and witness how the Plains Indians hunted them.

Near Palo Duro Canyon, Texas, Coronado and an advance party of about 42 men turned northward through the western part of present-day Oklahoma, entering present-day Kansas. They crossed the Arkansas River, somewhere near present-day Dodge City, and came upon what is thought to have been Wichita Indian villages. After exploring the plains as far as present-day Lindsborg in central Kansas, Coronado decided he had been deceived by the Turk. It is theorized that the guide had used the Spaniards as a means to reach his home. Other sources suggest that the Turk had misunderstood the Spaniards, believing they would be interested in visiting the Pawnee, a people of the southern plains known to other tribes for the power of their medicine. Coronado had the Turk strangled for his apparent deception and an alleged attempt to incite the Pawnee against the Spanish, and began the long trek back to Tiguex.

The conquistadores spent the winter of 1541–42 at the Tiguex pueblo near present-day Albuquerque. In December 1541, Coronado suffered an injury when he fell from his horse. Weakened by this mishap, he led the expedition southward to the east shore of the Gulf of California, then proceeded to Compostela. He arrived in spring 1542, in time to take part in suppressing an Indian rebellion in Nueva Galicia known as the Mixtón War.

Charges of official misconduct were lodged against Coronado, stemming from his summary execution of the Turk and his failure to claim and occupy all the regions he had explored, although some of the priests in his party did remain behind to proselytize among the Pueblo Indians. In 1544, Coronado was dismissed from his post as governor of Nueva Galicia. Following an official inquiry, he was acquitted of any wrongdoing, and he spent the remainder of his life as a colonial administrator in Mexico City.

Although Francisco de Coronado's two-year expedition yielded no golden cities for Spain, his explorations brought back much information concerning the extent of the lands north of Mexico. His men were the first known Europeans to see the Grand Canyon, which was not visited again by Spaniards until the explorations of FRANCISCO TOMÁS HERMENEGILDO GARCÉS in 1776. The tribes of the Southwest also had their first contact with Europeans as a result of Coronado's quest. Horses that escaped from the Spanish were captured and used by the Native Americans, beginning the transformation of Plains Indian culture. In addition, the naval arm of the expedition, under Hernando de Alarcón, determined that Baja California was not an island but actually a peninsula. At the same time Coronado was seeking Quivira in Oklahoma and Kansas in spring 1541, another Spanish explorer, HERNANDO DE SOTO, was exploring the lower MISSISSIPPI RIVER region of present-day Arkansas less than 500 miles away.

Côrte-Real, Gaspar (Gaspar Côrte Real, Gaspar Côrtereal, Gaspar Côrterreal)

(ca. 1450–ca. 1501) *Portuguese mariner in the northern coastal regions of North America, brother of Miguel Côrte-Real* Gaspar Côrte-Real was born in the Algarve region of southern Portugal, the youngest son of João Vaz Côrte-Real. According to some sources, his father may have been a member of a joint Portuguese-Danish expedition to GREENLAND and Newfoundland as early as 1472, supposedly sponsored by Alfonso V of Portugal and Christian I of Denmark. Documentation of this pre-Columbian voyage across the North Atlantic Ocean dates back only to the mid-1520s and cannot be authenticated. Nevertheless, as early as 1474, João Vaz Côrte-Real was named by the Portuguese crown as Discoverer of La Terra do Bacalhao (land of the codfish), which suggests that he may have explored as far as the fishing grounds between Greenland and Newfoundland.

In 1474, Gaspar's father was appointed military leader of Terceira, one of the AZORES, about 900 miles west of Portugal. As a branch of the aristocratic da Costa family, the Côrte-Reals were well connected, and, during the 1490s, Gaspar became a gentleman of the Portuguese court and a friend of King Manuel I. Following his father's death, he assumed the office of deputy captain of Terceira in 1497.

In 1499, Gaspar Côrte-Real may have undertaken a transatlantic expedition at his own expense. During this undocumented voyage, he supposedly located the fabled STRAIT OF ANIAN, the long-sought-after route through the North American continent to the Orient. Scholars have speculated that Côrte-Real's 1499 voyage took him along the North American coast, from the Gulf of St. Lawrence to the Gulf of Mexico.

By May 1500, Côrte-Real had moved to Lisbon, where he was given official sanction by Manuel I to undertake a voyage of exploration across the Atlantic, probably because of reports of newly explored lands brought back by JOHN CABOT and SEBASTIAN CABOT. There is some evidence to suggest that the same syndicate of merchants in Bristol, England, who sponsored the Cabots may have also provided financing for Côrte-Real's expedition.

Sailing from Lisbon, Portugal, in May 1500, Côrte-Real took his ship northward to ICELAND. He navigated through the Denmark Strait but was turned back by icebergs. The expedition then headed southward and rounded Cape Farewell at the southern tip of Greenland. Sailing northward along Greenland's southwest coast, the Portuguese encountered the remnants of a Norse colony. Côrte-Real continued north along the west coast of Greenland into the Davis Strait, near or beyond the ARCTIC CIRCLE, near the present-day settlement of Godthaab. But floating ice proved too much of an obstacle, and the expedition turned back southward, arriving in Lisbon in fall 1500. JOÃO FERNANDES also may have explored for Portugal, reaching Greenland and possibly even Newfoundland in 1500.

Côrte-Real believed he had reached the northeast coast of Asia, the riches and spices of the Orient lying to the south of this frozen region. He organized a second expedition, consisting of three ships, one of them commanded by his older brother MIGUEL CÔRTE-REAL, according to some sources. Departing Lisbon in May 1501, they sailed to the coast of what is now Labrador and headed southward. Although the Côrte-Reals spotted the Strait of Belle Isle leading into the Gulf of St. Lawrence, they declined to explore it, believing it would lead them inland only a few miles. Instead, they put in at Newfoundland, where they captured more than 50 Indians, probably Beothuk, with plans to take them back to Portugal as proof that they had reached Asia.

Miguel and two of the ships returned to Portugal with the Indians, while Gaspar and his ship continued to explore southward, confident that he would soon reach the coast of

China. The two ships under Miguel reached Lisbon in fall 1501, but Gaspar and his ship failed to appear.

In spring 1502, Miguel sailed again from Lisbon with two ships to search for his long overdue brother. But Miguel and his ship also disappeared somewhere off North America, and only one ship returned. No conclusive trace of either of the Côrte-Real brothers was ever found. An inscription on a rock at the mouth of the Taunton River, near present-day Dighton, Massachusetts, has been variously attributed to one or both of them.

The voyages of the Côrte-Reals were possible because of the use of a type of ship known as the CARAVEL, which was developed during the 15th century. The additional lateen sails allowed these vessels to take advantage of the northeast trade winds.

Some Portuguese historians still attribute the European discovery of the Americas to the Côrte-Reals rather than to CHRISTOPHER COLUMBUS. Gaspar Côrte-Real reportedly claimed the lands he visited for Portugal, calling them Terra Verde. Some European maps of the 1520s show the coastal regions of Labrador and Newfoundland as the "Land of the Côrtereals." Even though no European settlements developed from the explorations of Gaspar Côrte-Real, Portuguese fishermen continued to visit the Labrador and Newfoundland coasts for generations afterward to take back to European markets the region's abundant codfish.

Côrte-Real, Miguel (Miguel Côrte Real, Miguel Côrtereal, Miguel Côrterreal) (ca. 1450–ca. 1502)
Portuguese mariner in North America, brother of Gaspar Côrte-Real

Miguel Côrte-Real was the son of Portuguese mariner João Vaz Côrte-Real, related to Portugal's prominent da Costa family. Born in southern Portugal's Algarve region, he was raised in the AZORES, where his father was captain of the island of Terceira.

Following his father's death in 1496, Côrte-Real moved to Lisbon, where he joined his brother GASPAR CÔRTE-REAL; both of them became friendly with the king of Portugal, Manuel I. Miguel provided financial support for Gaspar's voyage to ICELAND and GREENLAND in 1500. According to some sources, Miguel played an active role in Gaspar's second voyage of exploration to North America in 1501. On that expedition, Miguel may have commanded one of the three ships that reached the coast of Labrador in June 1501, and explored around Newfoundland and the entrance to the Strait of Belle Isle and the Gulf of St. Lawrence. Other sources indicate that although Miguel had invested in the second voyage, he had taken part in a naval campaign against the Turks in the eastern MEDITERRANEAN SEA while his brother sailed to North America.

In any event, Gaspar failed to return from the 1501 voyage, and in January 1502, Miguel received permission from King Manuel to undertake an expedition in search of him. On June 24, 1502, Miguel and his ships arrived off the coast of present-day St. John's in southern Newfoundland. The three vessels separated at that point, planning to reunite there in late August.

After Côrte-Real sailed southward to search for his brother, he was never seen again. When he failed to arrive at the rendezvous two months later, the two remaining ships returned to Lisbon. A third brother, Vasco Annes Côrte-Real, sent out another expedition in search of Gaspar and Miguel, but no trace of them was found.

Some historians and archaeologists have speculated that Miguel may have reached the coast of New England, where he became the leader of an Indian tribe, living until at least 1511. This theory is based on an interpretation of an inscription found on the "Dighton Rock," at the mouth of the Taunton River in Massachusetts.

Miguel Côrte-Real, with his brother Gaspar, undertook some of the first voyages across the North Atlantic since the days of the VIKINGS. His family's claim to Newfoundland was upheld by the Portuguese Crown until his last male heir, Manuel Côrte-Real, died in 1578.

Cortés, Hernán (Hernando Cortés, Hernando Cortez) (1485–1547) *Spanish conquistador in Mexico and Central America*

Hernán Cortés was born in Medillín, a town in central Spain's Estremadura region. His father had been a captain in the Spanish army, and his family, although of the nobility, was of modest means. At the age of 14, Cortés went to Salamanca, where he embarked on a study of law, but he returned home after two years.

Entering the army in 1501, Cortés took part in Spanish campaigns in Italy. In 1502, he planned to sail to the WEST INDIES with CHRISTOPHER COLUMBUS's fourth voyage. Just prior to departure, however, he broke his leg while climbing the wall of a prestigious boarding school for girls in Madrid following an amorous escapade.

In 1504, Cortés finally sailed to the Americas and became a minor government official at Azua in what is now the Dominican Republic. In 1511, he served with DIEGO VELÁSQUEZ in the conquest of Cuba, and he was later granted lands near Santiago and appointed a treasury official in Velásquez's colonial government.

In 1518, Velásquez commissioned Cortés to lead a large expedition to the Yucatán Peninsula. FRANCISCO FERNÁNDEZ DE CÓRDOBA and JUAN DE GRIJALVA had recently undertaken voyages westward from Cuba to the Yucatán coast and had explored northward, returning to Santiago with reports of an advanced Indian civilization, rich in gold. Cortés had been instructed to follow up these reports and establish a small settlement on the mainland.

Hernán Cortés *(Library of Congress)*

Although Velásquez had dismissed Cortés as the expedition's commander following a disagreement between the two, Cortés defied his superior and sailed out of Cuba's Santiago Harbor. His fleet of 11 ships carried more than 500 soldiers and 16 horses and was equipped with cannons. He put in at Havana for additional supplies, then, on February 19, 1519, sailed westward to the island of Cozumel, off the coast of Yucatán. There he met Jerónimo de Aguilar, a priest who had been shipwrecked eight years earlier. Aguilar, who was fluent in the Mayan language of the region's Indians, joined Cortés as an interpreter.

At Tabasco at the mouth of the Grijalva River, Cortés landed and made contact with Maya Indians. The Indians paddled by CANOE to Cortés's flagship, the *Capitana,* and presented the Spanish commander with gifts of gold, cotton goods, and 20 female slaves. Among them was an Aztec princess, MALINCHE, who was later baptized as Doña Marina. She was fluent in both the Nahuatl language of the Aztec and Mayan, and together with Aguilar, who spoke Mayan and Spanish, provided Cortés with a direct means of communicating with the Aztec.

From Malinche, Cortés learned of the great wealth of the Aztec, whose capital city, Tenochtitlán (present-day Mexico City), was 560 miles inland. His fleet sailed farther up the Mexican coast, and, at present-day Veracruz, Cortés and his men established a small settlement in April 1519. When Cortés made plans to lead an expedition overland to the Aztec capital, some of his men objected, claiming that he was overstepping Velásquez's orders. To prevent them from deserting, Cortés had the ships burned, sparing only one vessel with which to send the gold he had taken from Indians to King Charles I in Spain.

Guided by Totonac and other Indians who allied themselves with him against the Aztec, Cortés began his march to Tenochtitlán in August 1519. Along the way, he defeated the Indians at the city of Tlaxcala, who then joined his march to the Aztec capital. He reached the city of Cholula, the site of sacred Aztec shrines, where he defeated an Aztec force. Although the Spaniards were greatly outnumbered by the Aztec, they were able to gain the support of as many as 6,000 subjects of the Aztec Empire.

By the time Cortés had neared Tenochtitlán in early November 1519, the Aztec leaders were seeking a peaceful way to rid themselves of the Spanish threat. But the great quantities of gold sent to the invaders as gifts only encouraged the Spaniards in their campaign of conquest. Cortés and his men entered Tenochtitlán on November 8, 1519. He was greeted by the Aztec emperor, Montezuma (Moctezuma). Taking him hostage, Cortés claimed all of Mexico in the name of Spain and established an uneasy peace with the Aztec as he and his men continued to obtain gold from them.

In spring 1520, Cortés learned that Spanish forces under PÁNFILO DE NARVÁEZ had landed at Veracruz with orders to arrest him for having left in defiance of the Cuban governor's orders. With PEDRO DE ALVARADO in command at Tenochtitlán, Cortés took half his men back to the coast, where he defeated and imprisoned Narváez, then enlisted Narváez's forces against the Aztec.

In May 1520, Cortés and his augmented forces returned to Tenochtitlán. Alvarado had meanwhile incited a revolt by the Aztec on reacting violently to their ritualistic human sacrifices. Montezuma attempted to quell the uprising, but his people stoned him to death. On June 30, 1520, Cortés and his forces fled the Aztec capital, losing about half their numbers in the retreat. The defeat subsequently became known as Noche Triste (Sorrowful Night), because Cortés reportedly wept outside the city afterward.

Cortés and his men withdrew to Tlaxcala, and in spring 1521 he launched a counterattack against the Aztec. He had ships transported to Lake Texcoco, on which Tenochtitlán had been built, and, with the support of other Indians, recaptured the Aztec capital by late summer. The rapid ravages of a smallpox epidemic among the Aztec aided Cortés in his victory.

On October 15, 1522, Cortés was named Captain General of New Spain, as Mexico was called. Soon afterward, he sent out expeditions to the west and south to seek a route to the Pacific coast. In 1523, Alvarado led one group into

Oaxaca and subjugated Guatemala. In 1525, Cortés himself led an expedition into what is now Honduras. In 1527, he sponsored a voyage by ÁLVARO DE SAAVEDRA CÉRON that sailed westward from Mexico, across the Pacific Ocean, to New Guinea and the SPICE ISLANDS (the Moluccas).

In 1528, Cortés returned to Spain, where King Charles I named him Marquis of Oaxaca and granted him extensive lands in central Mexico. Cortés also obtained permission to explore the west coast of Mexico. Back in New Spain by 1530, he sent his cousin, Diego Hurtado de Mendoza, on an expedition that explored as far as La Paz Bay in the Gulf of California in 1532. In April 1535, Cortés sailed from the Pacific coast of Mexico to the east coast of Baja California, where he established a small settlement called Santa Cruz.

Cortés returned to Mexico City, the former Tenochtitlán, in 1536. Three years later, he sent out FRANCISCO DE ULLOA on a voyage northward along the Pacific coast that may have reached present-day California.

In 1540, Cortés returned to Spain to protest the challenge to his authority from the king's viceroy, ANTONIO DE MENDOZA. He also felt rebuffed at having been passed over for an expedition to the north, the leadership of that venture going to FRANCISCO VÁSQUEZ DE CORONADO. Although Cortés supported the king in his efforts against the Moors in Algeria, he did not succeed in regaining his former position. He settled on his estate near Seville, where he died in 1547.

Hernán Cortés's conquest of the Aztec Empire was the first large-scale confrontation between the native peoples of the Americas and the Europeans. The great riches obtained from the Aztec subsequently inspired the expeditions of other CONQUISTADORES, including Pánfilo de Nárvaez and HERNANDO DE SOTO in North America's Southeast, Francisco Coronado in the Southwest, and FRANCISCO PIZARRO in Peru.

Cosa, Juan de la (ca. 1460–1510) *Spanish navigator and cartographer in the Caribbean, Central America, and South America*

Juan de la Cosa was born in Spain. Sources vary on the exact place of his birth, some indicating he was from Orduña in the Basque region, while others make him a native of Santa María near Cádiz in the south.

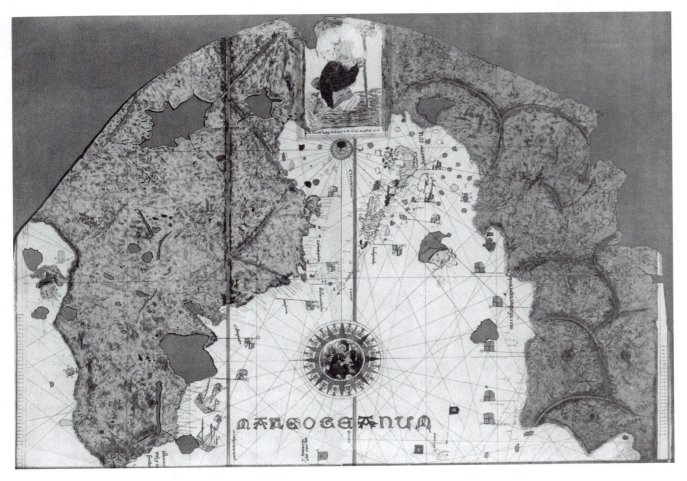

Detail of map of the world by Juan de la Cosa (1500) *(Library of Congress)*

By 1492, Cosa had become a highly skilled navigator and cartographer. He owned the ship the *Santa María,* on which he sailed in 1492 as CHRISTOPHER COLUMBUS's pilot on his first voyage to the Americas. Columbus reportedly relied on Cosa's maps in his historic expedition across the Atlantic Ocean. The next year, Cosa again sailed with Columbus on his second voyage.

In 1499, Cosa explored the north coast of South America with ALONSO DE OJEDA and AMERIGO VESPUCCI. In 1501, he took part in RODRIGO DE BASTIDAS's voyage to the coast of Central America.

Back in Spain in 1503, Queen Isabella granted Cosa a license to enslave the Indians along the coast of South America, from Cabo de Vela, in present-day Venezuela, to the Gulf of Uraba, on the Caribbean coast of present-day Colombia. Again with Ojeda, Cosa left Spain in September 1504, reaching the island of Margarita off the coast of Venezuela. After obtaining gold, pearls, and brazilwood from the natives, he explored north and west to the coast of Darién (present-day Panama), where he encountered the remnants of an expedition led by another Spanish adventurer, Luis Guerra.

Problems with his ships caused Cosa to remain on the coast of Darién for almost a year. He then managed to sail with his men in small boats to Hispaniola (present-day Haiti and the Dominican Republic), eventually returning to Spain with a fortune in gold and pearls.

In 1509–10, Cosa joined Ojeda in an expedition to the north coast of South America. After landing near present-day Cartagena, Colombia, he marched inland with Ojeda's men on a slave-hunting expedition, and he was killed in an attack by Indians.

Juan de la Cosa played an important role in the early exploration of South and Central America in the years immediately following the first two voyages of Columbus. He also produced the earliest maps to show the explorations of JOHN CABOT and SEBASTIAN CABOT and VASCO DA GAMA, as well as Christopher Columbus. His map of the world, produced in 1500, was one of the first to cast doubt on Columbus's claim that he had reached the coast of Asia. The newly visited lands were shown on Cosa's map as receding off to the west, with no clear indication that they were part of the Asian continent. Cosa also showed Cuba to be an island on this early map (contrary to Columbus's claim that it was part of the Asian mainland), a fact not established by navigators until 1508.

Courtauld, Augustine (1904–1959) *British explorer in Greenland*

In the late 1920s, Augustine Courtauld attended England's Cambridge University, where he was a classmate of GINO WATKINS. Under Watkins's leadership, Courtauld took part in the 1930–32 British Arctic Air Route Expedition, which sought to determine the feasibility of an air route between Europe and North America by way of ICELAND and GREENLAND.

Courtauld arrived on the east coast of Greenland with Watkins and subsequently took part in establishing a base at Angmagssalik. An inland weather station was then set up on the Greenland ice cap, and Courtauld volunteered to man this isolated post alone and make meteorological observations throughout five months of the Arctic winter.

From December 1930 to May 1931, Courtauld lived in a tent buried in the snow on the ice cap, making an extensive study of weather conditions and their effects on proposed polar air routes.

Augustine Courtauld's winter alone in Arctic Greenland was the first such solo scientific endeavor of its kind. It preceded Admiral RICHARD EVELYN BYRD's solo Antarctic winter by three years.

Cousteau, Jacques-Yves (1910–1997)
French oceanographer

Jacques Cousteau was born in Saint André de Cubzac, France. He attended the French Naval Academy in Brest and became a gunnery officer. After serving in the Far East in 1934–35, he trained to be a navy pilot but was injured in an automobile accident. Swimming was part of his rehabilitation, during which he became interested in diving.

In 1943, during World War II, Cousteau and French engineer Émile Gagnan developed the aqualung, a breathing apparatus, to enable divers to stay underwater for several hours. It consists of a cylinder of compressed air connected through a pressure-regulating valve to a face mask.

In 1950, Cousteau purchased *The Calypso,* a U.S. World War II minesweeper, and converted it into a research vessel for oceanographic studies. In it, he began traveling the world's oceans and investigating marine life, geology, and archaeology. He also invented a watertight camera case and developed underwater filming techniques. In 1959, Cousteau designed the *Diving Saucer,* a two-man SUBMERSIBLE capable of diving to a depth of 1,000 feet. Later in life, he experimented with underwater houses in which divers lived for up to a month.

Cousteau wrote or cowrote more than 100 books, among them *The Living Sea* (1963) and *World Without Sun* (1965). He also produced documentaries, including the Academy Award–winning *The Silent World* (1956) and *World Without Sun* (1966), as well as *Voyage to the End of the World* (1975). He also created several television series; the best known, *The Undersea World of Jacques Cousteau,* ran from 1968 to 1976. Cousteau won numerous awards over the course of his life, including his induction into the Académie Française in 1989.

Jacques Cousteau, in addition to expanding the frontiers of oceanography through his inventions, helped make

Jacques Cousteau *(Library of Congress)*

the public aware of the world's ecosystems through his writings and films. He founded the Cousteau Society in 1973, which has carried on his work and is now run by his wife, Francine Cousteau.

Covilhã, Pero da (Pedro de Covilham, Pêro da Cavilhão, Pedro de Covilhão, Pedro de Cavilhã)

(ca. 1450–ca. 1530) *Portuguese diplomat in the Middle East, India, and East Africa*

Pero da Covilhã, a native of Portugal, served in the army in his country's wars with Spain. A spy, he spent some years living as a guest of the duke of Medina-Sidonia in Andalusia. He was fluent in both Spanish and Arabic and undertook several missions to North Africa.

In 1486, while Covilhã was serving in the royal bodyguard of King John II of Portugal, the Portuguese government received news from the west coast of Africa of a great Christian king, who ruled a powerful kingdom somewhere in the interior of East Africa. King John suspected that this African ruler was the legendary PRESTER JOHN and hoped that his Christian kingdom could serve as a buffer against the Arab powers in the Middle East, as well as provide an important link in the overland trade route to India. At that

time, Portuguese navigators were attempting to round the coast of Africa, although it was not known for certain whether a sea route existed between the Atlantic and Indian Oceans. To resolve the rumors about Prester John, as well as to obtain vital geographic information about the southeast coast of Africa, King John commissioned Covilhã to undertake a journey eastward to Africa and India.

In May 1487, Covilhã left Portugal, along with an Arabic-speaking native of the CANARY ISLANDS named Afonso de Paiva, and traveled to the island of Rhodes in the eastern MEDITERRANEAN SEA. Several months later, Portuguese navigator BARTOLOMEU DIAS embarked on the first voyage around the CAPE OF GOOD HOPE.

Upon reaching Rhodes, Covilhã and Paiva disguised themselves as Arab traders and sailed to Alexandria, arriving there with a shipment of honey. They both became ill at Alexandria, but they soon recovered and continued the journey, traveling first to Cairo, then to Sinai and the RED SEA. They sailed down the Red Sea in an Arab trading vessel, stopping at the Sudanese port of Suakin before arriving two months later at Aden. They then separated; Paiva headed into the interior of Ethiopia in search of Prester John, while Covilhã sailed across the Arabian Sea to the southwest coast of India.

Covilhã first visited the port of Cannanore on the Malabar Coast, then went on to Calicut and Goa, making a detailed study of the kinds of exotic products that were traded by Arab and Oriental merchants at these Indian commercial centers. He then sailed back across the Arabian Sea, stopping in Hormuz at the mouth of the Persian Gulf. From Hormuz, he sailed on an Arab trading ship southward along the east coast of Africa, as far as Sofala on the African mainland opposite the island of Madagascar, arriving there in 1490. During his stay, he was informed by Arab traders that there was a sea route around the tip of Africa. Covilhã then headed northward along the coast for Cairo to rejoin Paiva, visiting the East African ports of Kilwa, Mombasa, and Malindi.

At Cairo, Covilhã learned that Paiva had died. He was met there by two of King John's representatives, who told him that he could either return to Portugal or complete Paiva's mission in East Africa. Covilhã elected to continue the search for Prester John in Africa.

After sending a detailed report of his travels to King John in Portugal, Covilhã escorted one of the king's representatives to Hormuz, then sailed to the Red Sea port of Jidda on the Arabian Peninsula, which he reached in 1492. Soon afterward, disguised as a Muslim pilgrim, he entered the holy city of Mecca.

In 1493, Covilhã reached the kingdom of Abyssinia (Ethiopia), where he was well received by the Christian emperor, known as the Negus. Either he was not permitted to leave, however, or stayed by choice. He married an Ethiopian woman and spent the remaining years of his life as a trusted adviser to the Negus, living a life of privilege and relative affluence, according to a Portuguese ambassador who visited him there 27 years later.

Pero da Covilhã's reports on the east coast of Africa provided important geographic information to VASCO DA GAMA in his 1497 voyage around the Cape of Good Hope to India. In addition, Covilhã sent back to Europe the earliest knowledge of the island of Madagascar, and his 1492 sojourn into Mecca may have been the first such visit to that holy city by a non-Muslim. His influence in the Ethiopian government helped Portugal become a dominant European power in East Africa.

Cresap, Thomas (ca. 1702–ca. 1790) *British soldier and frontiersman in the Ohio Valley*

Born in Skipton in Yorkshire, England, Thomas Cresap immigrated to colonial Maryland in 1717. In 1727, he settled near the present site of Wrightsville in south-central Pennsylvania. The Pennsylvania and Maryland colonies both claimed this territory, and an armed conflict between territorial militias erupted. Cresap, a captain with the Maryland militia, departed soon after the Pennsylvanians triumphed.

In 1740, Cresap established a trading fort on Maryland's westernmost frontier along a route frequently used by Iroquois (Haudenosaunee) Indian raiding parties in their attacks against the Cherokee Indians to the south. In time, Cresap established peaceful relations with Native Americans, serving often as a government representative in official dealings with both groups.

In about 1753, as one of the organizers of the Ohio Company, Cresap explored the Redstone Creek and Monongahela River of western Pennsylvania, accompanied by his friend, the Lenni Lenape (Delaware) Indian Nemacolin. Together they extended and improved the trail previously blazed into the Ohio Valley by CHRISTOPHER GIST, a route that later became famous as Braddock's Road.

Thomas Cresap helped open routes into the APPALACHIAN MOUNTAINS. On 18th-century maps of the northern Ohio Valley, Cresap's fort was indicated as one of the few stopover points for westward journeys from Maryland, Virginia, and Pennsylvania.

Cresques, Abraham (Cresques le Juif) (fl. 1370s) *Spanish cartographer*

Abraham Cresques, a Spanish Jew, lived in Palma on the Mediterranean island of Majorca. He was a highly skilled cartographer, and, in about 1375, he produced a large map of the world based on the most recent reports from MARCO POLO and ODORIC OF PORDENONE.

Commissioned by King Peter IV of Aragon, Cresques's world map became known as the *Catalan Atlas*. On a series of 12 panels, Cresques depicted the region to the east of Europe as far as the Pacific Ocean. His map concentrated on those parts of the world recently visited by Europeans and did not detail northern Europe, northern Asia, or southern portions of Africa.

Cresques was one of the earliest cartographers to indicate caravan routes across the SAHARA DESERT, extending northward from the NIGER RIVER and Senegal River. He obtained new geographic information from Arabian seamen and Jewish merchants who, unlike most Europeans, could travel freely throughout much of the Islamic world of North Africa and the Middle East. His map was the first to show the Indian subcontinent as a peninsula, and to indicate clearly the AZORES in the Atlantic Ocean.

Abraham Cresques's *Catalan Atlas* was a milestone in the history of modern cartography. It was the first time that an image of the world was depicted based on the experience of travelers and reports from distant lands. Up to that time, most maps relied on traditional but unfounded concepts of world geography, with erroneous representations from myths and legendary accounts. Cresques also produced a copy of the *Catalan Atlas* for King Charles V of France. Abraham Cresques's son, Judah Cresques, eventually settled in Portugal and converted to Christianity. He continued his father's work as a cartographer in the service of HENRY THE NAVIGATOR, prince of Portugal, at his navigational school at Sagres. Known in Portugal as Jaume Ribes, the younger Cresques was Prince Henry's geographic adviser and produced many of the maps that detailed discoveries of Portuguese explorers along the west coast of Africa during the early 1400s.

Crevaux, Jules-Nicolas (1847–1882) *French physician, explorer in South America*

Jules-Nicolas Crevaux was born and raised in the Lorraine region of northeastern France. Trained as a physician, he served with French forces in the Franco-Prussian War of 1870. In 1871, he became a naval surgeon.

In 1876, Crevaux began a series of explorations into the interior of South America. He traveled to Cayenne on the coast of French Guiana, from where he undertook a survey of the Maroni River. From the headwaters of the Maroni, he continued southward into parts of French Guiana that had not yet been visited by Europeans. He crossed the Tumuc-Humac Mountains and reached the Jari River, which he followed to its confluence with the AMAZON RIVER in northeastern Brazil.

In 1878, Crevaux embarked on his second expedition into French Guiana. From Cayenne, he headed south and west to the upper Amazon, following it to its junction with the Ica. He also explored the Japurá and Putumayo Rivers, following them deep into the eastern slopes of the ANDES MOUNTAINS. In the Andes, he discovered relics of the Inca Indian civilization.

The next year, Crevaux undertook an exploration of the interior of what is now Colombia as well as Venezuela. He traveled along the Magdalena and Guaviare Rivers, eventually descending the ORINOCO RIVER back to the coast.

After a time in France, Crevaux, in 1882, sailed to Buenos Aires, from where he undertook what turned out to be his final exploration of South America. He had planned to complement his exploration of the Amazon Basin in the northern part of South America with a study of the Paraná River and its tributaries in the south. He also intended to visit the Indian tribes of the Gran Chaco region. It was while exploring the Pilcomayo River region in the Gran Chaco that Crevaux and 18 members of his expedition were attacked and killed by Toba Indians. Two Bolivian members of the expedition escaped and reported what had happened.

Jules-Nicolas Crevaux was the first European to cross the Tumuc-Humac Mountains of South America. His explorations of the Amazon and its northern tributaries provided significant new geographic information. Soon after his death, an updated atlas of the rivers of South America was published and was dedicated to him by the Geographical Society of Paris. Crevaux's own account of his travels, *Voyages dans l'Amérique du Sud* (Voyages in South America), was published in 1883.

Croghan, George (unknown–1782) *Irish-American frontier trader in the Ohio Valley, Indian agent*

George Croghan was born in Ireland and immigrated to Philadelphia, Pennsylvania, in about 1740. The next year, he undertook a trading expedition to the Indians of the Susquehanna Valley. He traveled west from Philadelphia, crossed the Blue Mountains, and reached the Susquehanna River near present-day Harrisburg, Pennsylvania.

By the late 1740s, Croghan had established a string of Indian trading centers in the Forks of the Ohio region, near present-day Pittsburgh. These included outposts at Pine Creek, Beaver Creek, and Logstown. He used these posts as bases for additional trading expeditions into the Ohio Valley. In 1748, he established a center at Pickawillany on the Maumee River in western Ohio. From there, Croghan explored as far west as the Wabash and Illinois Rivers, establishing trade contacts with Indian bands of the region.

In 1750, Croghan accompanied CHRISTOPHER GIST in his trans-Appalachian exploration.

Six years later, during the French and Indian War, as deputy to Indian superintendent Sir William Johnson, Croghan traveled throughout the Ohio Valley and negotiated neutrality agreements with the Shawnee and other Indians.

In May 1765, Croghan led an expedition from Fort Pitt westward into the Ohio Valley in order to assert British authority over former French settlements in the Ohio Valley and to establish trade with the Indians. Croghan and his party were captured by Kickapoo Indians at the mouth of the Wabash River, but were released. Soon afterward, he accepted the surrender of the Ottawa chief Pontiac, who had led a rebellion of allied tribes in 1763.

In 1766, Croghan organized a large-scale trading expedition, known as the Grand Illinois Venture, to the Indians of the Wabash River, Illinois River, and MISSISSIPPI RIVER. He took 65 barges of trade goods, manned by 350 men, down the Ohio River from Fort Pitt and reached Indian settlements at Vincennes, Kaskaskia, Cahokia, and Fort de Chartres.

During the late 1760s, Croghan became involved in the land speculations of the Illinois Company and the Indiana Company. Business reversals, legal problems, and the outbreak of the American Revolution caused him to lose most of his large landholdings in 1775 around Fort Pitt. He returned to Philadelphia, where he died in 1782.

George Croghan pioneered trade routes west of the Allegheny Mountains into the Ohio Valley. His familiarity with the Ohio and Pennsylvania frontiers greatly assisted British and colonial forces in the French and Indian War of 1756–63. The Grand Illinois Venture of 1766 was the largest trade enterprise to the west during the American colonial period.

Crozier, Francis Rawdon Moira (1796–1848) *British naval officer, polar explorer*

Francis Crozier was born in Ireland. At about the age of 14, he entered the British navy as a midshipman.

In 1821, Crozier was a lieutenant with SIR WILLIAM EDWARD PARRY's second expedition to the Canadian Arctic. Three years later, he returned to the Arctic with Parry's third expedition, which explored Lancaster Sound and Prince Regent Inlet. Then, in 1827, he took part in Parry's unsuccessful attempt to reach the NORTH POLE from Spitsbergen (present-day Svalbard).

Crozier served on British naval vessels off the coast of Portugal in the early 1830s, and, in 1835, he participated in a voyage into Baffin Bay.

In 1839, Crozier was appointed captain of the *Terror,* and, in September of that year, accompanied by the *Erebus,* he sailed to TASMANIA from London on the first leg of SIR JAMES CLARK ROSS's four-year exploration of the Antarctic. After sailing to Hobart, in Tasmania, where they arrived in August 1840, the expedition headed southward, crossing the ANTARCTIC CIRCLE in early January 1841. Soon afterward, Crozier joined Ross in a landing at Victoria Land on the Antarctic continent, and he subsequently explored the Ross Sea, Ross Ice Shelf, and the coast of Graham Land. In the following Antarctic summer, after wintering in NEW ZEALAND, Crozier again sailed to Antarctica with Ross and set a record for the southernmost point reached to that time.

In 1845, Crozier served as second in command to SIR JOHN FRANKLIN in his final attempt to find the Northwest

Passage. Again commanding the *Terror,* Crozier sailed to the Canadian Arctic with Franklin and the *Erebus.* The ships were ultimately trapped in the ice north of King William Island. Following Franklin's death in 1847, Crozier assumed command of the expedition. In spring 1848, he led 105 of the survivors southward from Prince William Island over the ice in a sledge journey for the HUDSON'S BAY COMPANY outpost, Fort Resolution, at the mouth of the Back River. Crozier and the remaining members of the expedition managed to reach land at Point Victory, but all soon died of SCURVY or starvation. The details of the fate of Crozier and the last members of the Franklin expedition were left in a canister on King William Island, but the canister was not discovered until 1859 by a search expedition commanded by SIR FRANCIS LEOPOLD McCLINTOCK.

Francis Crozier played a leading role in British naval expeditions to both polar regions. On Ross Island in the Antarctic, and on King William Island in the Canadian Arctic, there are points of land each named Cape Crozier in recognition of his exploits.

Ctesias of Cnidus (fl. 420s–410s B.C.)
Greek physician, writer, traveler in Persia and India

Ctesias was a native of the Greek city of Cnidus in Asia Minor, now part of Turkey. He was trained in medicine, and, from about 420 to 400 B.C., he served as court physician to Darius II and Artaxerxes Mnemon of Persia (present-day Iran). He traveled throughout the Persian Empire, as well as in India, and, upon his return to Greece, wrote about his experiences. In two historical and geographic works, known as *Indicus* and *Persicus,* he attempted to discredit earlier accounts of the regions east of Greece put forth by HERODOTUS.

Although Ctesias included descriptions of fabulous creatures, including men with giant feet, others with dog-like faces, and giant worms in the GANGES RIVER, fed on camels and oxen (a possible description of crocodiles), some of his reports were accurate. He was among the first to report correctly on the course of the Oxus River (now known as the Amu Darya).

Ctesius's *Indicus* and *Persicus* survive only as fragments in other ancient writings. Written in about 398 B.C., they may have served, along with the works of Herodotus, as an inspiration and guide for the subsequent expeditions of conquest undertaken by ALEXANDER THE GREAT less than 100 years later.

Cunningham, Allan (1791–1839) *British naturalist in New South Wales and Queensland, Australia*

Allan Cunningham was born in Wimbledon in Surrey, England, near London. He was educated in the London suburb of Putney; at the age of 18, he went to work as a botanist at the Royal Botanic Gardens in Surrey, commonly known as Kew Gardens.

Cunningham's skill as a naturalist came to the attention of SIR JOSEPH BANKS. In about 1813, under Banks's sponsorship, Cunningham took part in a two-year scientific expedition to Brazil in which he collected specimens of South American plants for the botanical collection at Kew.

Cunningham next went to New South Wales, Australia. Arriving there in 1816, he was attached as a botanist to several government-sponsored expeditions that explored the region north and west of Sydney, beyond the BLUE MOUNTAINS. In 1817, he joined the surveyor general of New South Wales, JOHN JOSEPH WILLIAM MOLESWORTH OXLEY, in an exploration of the Lachlan River.

In 1817–22, Cunningham made a study of Australia's coastal plant life with PHILIP PARKER KING. In 1823, he explored inland again, this time blazing a trail from the Hunter Valley northward through Pandora's Pass. This route enabled settlers from Bathurst to reach the fertile region north of Sydney known as the Liverpool Plains.

Cunningham's next expedition set out from Bathurst in May 1827. He reached the upper Hunter River at Segenhoe and crossed the Liverpool Range. Soon afterward, he became the first European to visit the Namoi, Gwydir, Dumaresq, and Macintyre Rivers. On June 8, 1827, he caught sight of a large tract of open country, ideal for settlement by sheep farmers. He named the region the Darling Downs, after the colonial governor of New South Wales, Sir Charles H. Darling. The next year, Cunningham succeeded in finding a direct route from the Pacific coast to that region.

Cunningham carried out a scientific expedition to Norfolk Island off the east coast of Australia, soon after which he returned to England. He served at Kew Gardens for several years, then was offered the position of official botanist of New South Wales in 1837. His career as the colony's botanist was cut short after only two years, when he developed tuberculosis following a voyage to NEW ZEALAND. He died near Sydney in 1839.

Allan Cunningham's explorations of New South Wales and Queensland uncovered new expanses of fertile lands that enabled sheep farming in Australia to expand and prosper. The route he established through the GREAT DIVIDING RANGE, linking the grazing country of the Darling Downs with the Pacific coast, is named Cunningham's Gap.

Da Gama, Vasco See GAMA, VASCO DA.

Dallman, Eduard (1830–1896) *German mariner in the Antarctic, Siberia, and New Guinea*
Born near the German seaport of Bremen, Eduard Dallman first went to sea at the age of 15. He found work on both freighters and whalers, and by 1859, he captained his own ship on a voyage to the Pacific Ocean.

In 1873, Dallman sailed on a whaling expedition to the waters off the Antarctic Peninsula. In addition to hunting whales, Dallman recorded geographic and scientific information. In 1877–83, he attempted to establish a sea route from Germany to SIBERIA, in particular to the estuaries of the Ob and Yenisei Rivers. In 1884, in the employ of the New Guinea Company, he explored the coastline of New Guinea.

Eduard Dallman is credited with the first German expedition to Antarctica.

Dampier, William (ca. 1651–1715) *English writer, mariner in western Australia, New Guinea, and the South Pacific*
William Dampier was probably born in England, although few details are known of his early life. He went to sea at the age of 16, serving in the British navy in actions against the Dutch. He settled in Jamaica for a few years, where he man-aged a plantation, then moved to Honduras in about 1675, engaging in the logging business until 1678.

In 1679, Dampier joined a party of buccaneers with whom he crossed the Isthmus of Panama to the Pacific Ocean and carried out raids on Spanish shipping along the coast of Peru.

Dampier sailed from the coast of Virginia in 1683 as part of a fleet of PRIVATEERS under the command of a Captain Swan. He participated in raids against Spanish shipping on the west coast of Africa as well as on the north coast of South America and in the Caribbean Sea. He then sailed into the Pacific by way of CAPE HORN and, with his buccaneer companions, continued to raid Spanish possessions on the west coast of South America. From the Gulf of California, he sailed westward on one of the privateer vessels to the Philippines and the SPICE ISLANDS (the Moluccas), where he led attacks on Dutch and Spanish ships.

According to one source, Dampier captained a ship in 1687 in a pirating expedition along the coast of Chile, visiting the Galapagos and making an early sighting of Easter Island.

In 1688, Dampier and his crew spent five weeks exploring the northwest coast of Australia, between King Sound and Bathurst Island, a region largely unknown to European geographers at that time. He was subsequently marooned on the Nicobar Islands in the Bay of Bengal, but he managed to make his way back to England by 1691, having completed a CIRCUMNAVIGATION OF THE WORLD.

William Dampier *(Library of Congress)*

Dampier was unusual among the seafaring adventurers of his day in that he was well educated, with a background in the natural sciences. He wrote an account of his travels, published in 1697 as *A New Voyage Round the World.* An immediate popular success in England, it brought him to the attention of the British Admiralty. Commissioned an officer in the Royal Navy, Dampier was placed in command of a government-sponsored scientific expedition with plans to proceed to the east coast of Australia, a region relatively unexplored at that time.

Dampier, in command of the *Roebuck,* attempted to sail to eastern Australia by way of Cape Horn and the Pacific, but because of severe storms, he instead traveled to western Australia by way of the CAPE OF GOOD HOPE and the Indian Ocean. His first landing was at Shark Bay. He further explored and charted the northwest coast of Australia, locating an island group that later came to be known as the Dampier Archipelago. At the northern end of what is now known as Western Australia's Eighty Mile Beach, he explored a peninsula later named Dampier Land. From there, he sailed northward to Timor.

Dampier's subsequent exploration of the east coast of New Guinea revealed a strait, later known as Dampier Strait, which separates that large island from the smaller island of New Britain. (The narrow channel between northwestern New Guinea and the island of Waigeo is also named Dampier Strait.)

Dampier attempted to sail the *Roebuck* back to England by way of the Atlantic Ocean, but, on the return voyage, the ship became unseaworthy and had to be left at Ascension Island in the South Atlantic. A British naval vessel eventually carried Dampier and his expedition to England by 1701.

Dampier wrote an account of his voyage to Australia, *A Voyage to New Holland,* the first volume of which was published in 1703 and the second in 1709. In 1703, he embarked on another privateering expedition to the Pacific coast of South America. On this trip, a mutiny on one of the pirate vessels resulted in the marooning of several crew members in the Juan Fernandez Islands off the coast of Chile. Only one among them survived, a mariner named ALEXANDER SELKIRK, who was later rescued in 1709 by an expedition under Captain Woodes Rogers with Dampier serving as pilot. Selkirk's real-life adventure served as the inspiration for Daniel Defoe's 1719 novel *Robinson Crusoe.*

William Dampier and his crew were the first Englishmen to set foot on Australian soil and see kangaroos. In his scientific work, *Discourse of Trade Winds* (part of *Voyages and Descriptions*), published in 1699, Dampier speculated that the Australian continent was actually a group of large islands, separated by straits, an idea that was pursued by PHILLIP PARKER KING as late as 1817. Some early-19th-century explorers of Australia believed an inland passage into these straits could be found around the Dampier Archipelago. Along with his depiction of coastal Australia, Dampier provided some of the earliest descriptions of the region's Aborigines. Generally, he depicted Australia in less than favorable terms, and his account helped dissuade British settlement until the last decades of the 18th century. Among his geographic discoveries was the determination that New Britain was separate from New Guinea. Dampier's voyages marked the beginning of British scientific exploration of the Pacific, setting a precedent for the voyages of JOHN BYRON, SAMUEL WALLIS, PHILLIP CARTERET, and JAMES COOK.

Dana, James Dwight (1813–1895)
American naturalist in Australia and the Pacific

James D. Dana was born in Utica, New York, the descendant of an early New England family. He began his education at Charles Bartlett's Academy in Utica, where he developed a strong interest in the natural sciences.

In 1830, Dana entered Yale College, but he left three years later to become an instructor in the navy. Part of his service included a tour of the MEDITERRANEAN SEA aboard the *Delaware.* He returned to Yale in 1836, serving briefly as an assistant to natural history professor Benjamin Silliman. Dana soon accepted an appointment as geologist and mineralogist for an expedition under the command of Lieutenant CHARLES WILKES that toured the world in 1838–42.

Dana remained with the rest of the scientific team in Sydney, Australia, from January to the end of March 1840, while Wilkes and his ships explored Antarctic waters. Wilkes had dismissed the expedition's marine biologist in Sydney, and Dana assumed the responsibility of studying marine animal life in addition to his geological work.

Dana had started out on the *Peacock,* surviving the wreck of that vessel off the coast of Oregon in July 1841. From the site of the wreck near the mouth of the COLUMBIA RIVER, he traveled overland to San Francisco, where he boarded another of the expedition's ships.

Dana returned to New York by way of the CAPE OF GOOD HOPE in June 1842, having collected hundreds of specimens of zoophytes and mollusks new to science. Over the next 14 years, he wrote the volumes on geology, crustaceans, zoophytes, mollusks, and coral formations for the U.S. government's 20-volume report of the expedition. In 1849, he took over Silliman's position as professor of natural history at Yale.

James D. Dana went on to become the leading American naturalist of his day, his reputation based largely on the scientific work he accomplished on the Wilkes expedition. During his career at Yale, where he remained on staff the rest of his life, he produced a number of widely used standard texts on geology and mineralogy. He received many honorary degrees and awards for his scientific work.

Darwin, Charles Robert (1809–1882)
British naturalist in South America and the South Pacific, cousin of Sir Francis Galton

Charles Darwin was born in Shrewsbury, England, the son of a doctor. His maternal grandfather was the famous potter Josiah Wedgwood, and his paternal grandfather was the botanist and poet Erasmus Darwin. He was a cousin of SIR FRANCIS GALTON.

As a boy in the Shropshire countryside, the young Darwin collected butterflies, minerals, and shells. In 1825, he entered the University of Edinburgh, where he began three years of medical study. By 1827, Darwin had decided against a career as a doctor, reportedly because he could not stand the sight of blood. Consequently, in 1828, he began to study theology at Cambridge University, intending to become a minister.

While at Cambridge, Darwin's ability as a naturalist came to the attention of John S. Henslow, a professor of geology and botany. In 1831, on Henslow's recommendation, Darwin was appointed official naturalist for a British government-sponsored scientific expedition to the coast of South America.

On December 27, 1831, Darwin sailed from the naval base at Devonport, near Plymouth, aboard the British naval vessel HMS *Beagle,* captained by ROBERT FITZROY. The ex-

pedition's first stop was in the Cape Verde Islands off the west coast of Africa, where Darwin undertook a geological study of a volcanic island. From there, he sailed to Bahia, Brazil, and explored inland, collecting specimens of animal and plant life in the Brazilian rainforest. In April 1832, Darwin accompanied an Irish planter to his coffee plantation about 100 miles north of Rio de Janeiro, adding more specimens to his collection.

Darwin rejoined the *Beagle* for its southward cruise along the coast of South America. While Fitzroy and the rest of the expedition undertook an offshore hydrographic survey, Darwin explored up the Río de la Plata. While in Uruguay, Darwin discovered the fossilized bones of extinct animals, which appeared to be related to existing animals on the South American continent, a find that helped in the formulation of his later theory of evolution.

At Tierra del Fuego, Darwin made an early anthropological study of the natives, including observations on the experiences of three Indians who had been returned to Tierra del Fuego after three years in England. From the Patagonian coast of Argentina, he made a journey along the Santa Cruz River to within sight of the ANDES MOUNTAINS. The expedition then visited the Falkland Islands before making a passage through the STRAIT OF MAGELLAN and around CAPE HORN.

Darwin made several scientific forays into the interior of Chile in 1834. Traveling with a small party on horseback from Valparaíso, he crossed the Andes by way of Santiago and the Portillo Pass, reaching the Argentine town of Mendoza, then returned to the Pacific coast through the Uspallata Pass.

While in southern Chile in February 1835, Darwin experienced a severe earthquake and witnessed the eruption of the Osorno volcano. Soon afterward, the *Beagle* arrived at Concepción, where Darwin and the rest of the expedition observed the devastation the great earthquake had wrought on that seaport.

Later in 1835, Darwin did field work on the Galapagos Islands, 600 miles off the coast of Ecuador, studying animal and plant life, especially the giant tortoises and several varieties of iguanas.

The *Beagle* sailed westward across the Pacific Ocean from the Galapagos. After stopovers at Tahiti, NEW ZEALAND, Australia, and TASMANIA, the expedition entered the Indian Ocean and put in at Mauritius, where Darwin studied the natural process behind the formation of coral reefs and atolls.

Darwin and the *Beagle* returned to the Atlantic Ocean by way of the CAPE OF GOOD HOPE. On Ascension Island in the South Atlantic, he made a geological study of volcanic rocks.

Darwin arrived back in England in early October 1836. His voyage around the world had taken almost five years.

Throughout the trip, he had sent back reports and specimens to Henslow in England, and, by the time of his return, he had earned a reputation as one of the nation's foremost naturalists.

Over the next several years, Darwin was occupied in organizing and studying the specimens he had collected. He married his cousin Emma Wedgwood in 1839, and that same year, he published his first major scientific work, *Journal of Researches into the Natural History and Geology of the Countries Visited During the Voyage of the H.M.S. Beagle.*

In 1858, Darwin received a scientific paper by ALFRED RUSSEL WALLACE, who had also done extensive scientific research in South America. Darwin combined his own observations and correlations with those of Wallace to produce his epoch-making work, *On the Origin of Species by Means of Natural Selection* (1859), in which he first put forth his ideas on evolution. He subsequently formulated a theory on natural selection.

Charles Darwin's voyage on the *Beagle* from 1831 to 1836 laid the basis for the scientific work he produced throughout the rest of his life. He never went abroad again, having been a victim of acute seasickness during his time on the *Beagle.* For years after his return from that voyage, he suffered from ill health, which some have speculated was caused by Chagas disease, contracted from insect bites in the Andes. Darwin's work in the natural sciences had a profound impact, not only on the fields of biology and geology, but also on philosophy and theology. His theories on evolution and natural selection created an uproar in their challenge to the accepted belief that all species had been individually created and were generally immutable. As an explorer, Darwin added no new geographic knowledge, yet his scientific findings profoundly changed the way scientists perceived the Earth and its wildlife.

Daurkin, Nikolay (fl. 1760s–1790s) *Native explorer, interpreter in northeastern Siberia*

Nikolay Daurkin was a member of the nomadic Chukchi tribe of northeastern SIBERIA. In about 1760, he became a Cossack and served at the Russian military outpost at Anadyr on the Bering Sea. That year, he undertook an exploration on behalf of the Russian government into the Chukchi Peninsula. From natives on the Gulf of Anadyr, he learned of a huge landmass east of the Bering Sea. This was Alaska, known to the Chukchi as the "Great Land."

In late 1763, Daurkin explored Ratmanova Island in the BERING STRAIT, which he reached from the mainland, traveling over the ice by reindeer. His findings on this expedition were subsequently used in an official Russian map of the region. Daurkin explored the Chukchi Peninsula again in 1774, and, in the late 1780s and early 1790s, he served

as an interpreter in JOSEPH BILLINGS's expedition to northeastern Siberia and the islands of the Bering Strait.

Nikolay Daurkin was one of the few natives of eastern Siberia to take an active part in the Russian exploration of his homeland, most of which was undertaken by European Russians and others from western Europe.

David-Néel, Alexandra (1868–1969)
French traveler, writer in China, India, and Tibet

Alexandra David-Néel, née David, was born in Paris, where her father, a teacher and political activist, was an associate of Victor Hugo. From her reading of such authors as James Fenimore Cooper and Jules Verne, she was inspired to travel to distant places. In her late teens, she ran away from home several times, once walking as far as the Italian Alps before being sent back to her parents in Paris. As a student in Paris, she undertook a study of comparative religion, developing an interest in Buddhism and Far Eastern cultures.

In about 1889, a small inheritance allowed David to make her first trip to Asia. She traveled by ship from France to CEYLON (present-day Sri Lanka) and, after touring that land, crossed the Gulf of Mannar to India. By train, she traveled throughout India, eventually returning to France for lack of funds.

David then embarked on a career as a singer with several touring opera companies. As a performer during the 1890s, she traveled to Greece and Tunis, as well as to Hanoi and Haiphong in French Indochina. In 1904, she settled for a time in Tunis, where she married Frenchman Philippe-François Néel, although, soon after the marriage, she and her new husband embarked on separate lives. She traveled and studied in Europe for the next seven years.

In 1911, David-Néel left Paris for India. From Calcutta, she headed northward to the principality of Sikkim in the foothills of the HIMALAYAS. In Darjeeling, she became the first European woman to obtain an audience with the Dalai Lama of Tibetan Buddhists, then in exile from Tibet. Her published interview established her reputation as a journalist and authority on central Asia.

In 1912, David-Néel went to Nepal, then settled in Benares, India, where she studied Hindu philosophy. Back in Sikkim by 1913, she lived in a cave with a Tibetan holy man and learned the Tibetan language. The next year, she obtained the services of a young Sikkimese named Yongden, who would become her assistant and traveling companion for the next 40 years. In 1916, she left India and traveled in Burma (present-day Myanmar), Japan, and Korea, reaching Peking (Beijing) in October 1917. She continued to western China, where she remained for three years, staying at Buddhist monasteries.

In 1921–22, David-Néel visited the Lake Koko Nor region of western China, traveled into Szechwan (Sichuan) province, and attempted to enter Tibet, but was turned back by Chinese soldiers. In 1923, she entered Mongolia and traveled into the GOBI DESERT and the upper Mekong River region. Disguising herself as a native beggar and traveling with the Japanese philosopher and monk Ekai Kawagachi, she crossed into Tibet through the Dokar Pass of the Kha Karpo range, a route, at an elevation of 21,000 feet, never previously traveled by a European. In February 1924, still in disguise, she became the first European woman to enter the Tibetan holy city of LHASA and remained there two months.

David-Néel returned to British India in August 1924, traveling southward through the Himalayan passes into Sikkim. Soon afterward, she returned to Europe and settled in the south of France, where she wrote articles and books about her travels in the Far East, including her 1927 book *My Journey to Lhasa.*

In 1936, David-Néel again set out for the Orient, traveling across Russia on the Trans-Siberian Railroad to Vladivostok. From there, she went to Manchuria, crossed western China, then returned to Tibet. She lived in the mountains along the Tibetan-Chinese border during most of World War II. In 1944, she returned to France, resuming her career as a journalist. She died at her home in the south of France in 1969, at the age of 101.

Alexandra David-Néel spent more than a half-century traveling and living in central Asia. In addition to being the first European woman to enter the forbidden city of Lhasa in Tibet, she also traveled along unmapped portions of western China. She was considered one of the foremost authorities on Tibetan Buddhism. In recognition of her accomplishments, she was admitted to the French Legion of Honor in 1964.

Dávila, Pedrarias   See ARIAS DE ÁVILA, PEDRO.

Davion, Albert (unknown–1726) *French missionary on the lower Mississippi River*

Albert Davion was born in the northern French town of Saint-Omer, near the port of Calais. He was ordained a Jesuit priest, and in 1690, he arrived in Quebec to serve in the parish located on the Île d'Orléans in the St. Lawrence River.

In 1698, Davion was selected by the Catholic bishop of Quebec, Jean-Baptiste de la Croix Saint-Vallier, to join a missionary expedition to the lower MISSISSIPPI RIVER region, then known as Louisiana. In early July 1698, he embarked from Lachine, near Montreal, with another priest, Jean-François Buisson de Saint-Cosmé, along with a company of 12 VOYAGEURS. Traveling by CANOE, they reached the Great Lakes by way of the Ottawa River in early September. From Fort Michilimackinac, at the northern end of Lake Michigan, they were guided down the portage route to the MISSISSIPPI RIVER by HENRI DE TONTI.

By late December 1698, Davion and his party had descended the Mississippi as far south as present-day Arkansas. He then explored the Yazoo River in what is now west-central Mississippi and established a mission to the Tunica Indians. Soon afterward, he traveled southward to Biloxi Bay and Mobile Bay, then returned to his mission on the Yazoo.

Over the next 20 years, Davion ministered to the Tunica and traveled frequently to the French settlements to the south on the Gulf Coast of present-day Mississippi and Alabama. In 1722, he retired from missionary service and settled in New Orleans before returning to his hometown in northern France three years later.

Albert Davion established one of the first settlements in the lower Mississippi less than 10 years after the explorations of RENÉ-ROBERT CAVELIER DE LA SALLE. His mission on the Yazoo provided JEAN-BAPTISTE LE MOYNE, sieur de Bienville, and PIERRE LE MOYNE, sieur d'Iberville, with a northern outpost for their subsequent settlements on the Gulf of Mexico.

Davis, John (John Davys) (ca. 1550–1605)
English mariner in the Arctic and South Atlantic

John Davis was born near Dartmouth in Devon, England, the son of a farmer. Educated at Totnes, he was a boyhood friend of John Gilbert and SIR HUMPHREY GILBERT, and probably knew their kinsman SIR WALTER RALEIGH. By the time he had embarked on a seafaring career at the age of 16, he had acquired extensive knowledge of navigation, and, by 1579, he had earned a reputation as one of England's foremost navigators and hydrographers.

In 1584, Davis organized an expedition to seek a NORTHWEST PASSAGE to the Far East from England. Among his supporters, known collectively as the North-West Company, were his Devon neighbors, the Gilberts; mathematician John Dee; Sir Frances Walsingham, a leading minister to Queen Elizabeth; and merchant William Sanderson, who provided financial backing for the venture.

In spring 1585, Davis sailed from Dartmouth with two ships, the *Moonshine* and the *Sunshine*. He reached the southern tip of GREENLAND, which he named Cape Farewell, rounded it and explored along the island's southwest coast, which he dubbed the Coast of Desolation. At a fjord he named Gilbert Sound, later the site of Godthaab, he sailed westward across what later became known as Davis Strait, to the east coast of Baffin Island.

On the southeastern portion of Baffin Island, Davis located and named Cumberland Sound, which he hoped would provide the much-sought-after Northwest Passage to the Orient. The onset of winter conditions forced him to sail back to England, where he arrived at the end of September 1585.

In 1586, Davis undertook his second expedition into Arctic waters west of Greenland. In addition to the two vessels from his earlier voyage, he had with him two more ships, the *Mermaid* and the *North Star.* While he returned to Godthaab on the southwest coast of Greenland on the *Moonshine,* he sent two of his ships to seek a passage between Greenland and ICELAND.

At Godthaab, Davis and his men kidnapped an Inuit who guided them farther northward along the west coast of Greenland, as far as what is now Sukkertoppen. The expedition again crossed Davis Strait to Baffin Island, this time exploring Exeter Sound in the hope that it would prove to be an ice-free passage to the Orient. When his progress was blocked by icebergs, Davis headed southward and reexplored Cumberland Sound, then returned to England, arriving at Ratcliffe on the Thames River in October 1586.

Davis's final expedition in search of a Northwest Passage west of Greenland departed England in spring 1587. With three ships under his command—the *Sunshine,* the *Elizabeth* and the *Ellen*—he sailed again to the southeast coast of Baffin Island, where he made the first sighting of a peak he named Mount Raleigh. He then sailed northeastward across Davis Strait to Greenland's west coast. He reached a point near present-day Upernavik, which he named Sanderson's Hope. At 72°46', it was the northernmost point anyone had yet reached. Davis attempted to penetrate the region to the west, but heavy ice conditions forced him southward. He explored southward beyond the southern end of Baffin Island and crossed the eastern entrance to what would later be known as Hudson Strait. Davis then reached the northern tip of Labrador, which he named Cape Chidley. Having explored both sides of Davis Strait, he sailed back to England.

Undaunted by his failure to find a navigable Northwest Passage in the waters west of Greenland, Davis next sought to find the western entrance to the Northwest Passage in the Pacific Ocean. To this end, he sailed in 1591 with an expedition under Thomas Cavendish that planned to circumnavigate the world, east-to-west. Yet the fleet was unable to negotiate a westward passage through the STRAIT OF MAGELLAN. In 1592, Davis, on the *Desire,* became separated from the other vessels near the strait's eastern entrance; after losing his sails in a storm, he drifted across the South Atlantic Ocean and came upon the Falkland Islands. He returned to Britain in 1593.

Starting in 1598, Davis piloted three English maritime expeditions to the EAST INDIES. He took part in the BRITISH EAST INDIA COMPANY's first trading expedition to the Orient in 1601, during which he sailed around the CAPE OF GOOD HOPE and visited Madagascar, as well as other Indian Ocean island groups, including the Chagos Archipelago and the Nicobar Islands. He also reached the SPICE ISLANDS (the Moluccas) in the far western Pacific.

Davis's final voyage to the East Indies was in 1605, during which he was killed in a battle with Japanese pirates off the coast of present-day Singapore.

John Davis was a pioneer in British Arctic exploration. His three expeditions west of Greenland provided the basis for the subsequent voyages of HENRY HUDSON and ROBERT BYLOT and the exploration of HUDSON BAY in the first part of the 17th century. Although he did not succeed in finding a navigable Northwest Passage, a feat not accomplished until the early 20th century, Davis provided new geographic information about the region west of Greenland. His reports on these voyages included some of the earliest English accounts of contacts with Greenland Inuit. In addition to his exploits as an explorer, Davis invented an improved navigational instrument that enabled mariners to determine their position in high latitudes. Known as the Davis QUADRANT, it was widely used until the development of the SEXTANT in the early 1700s. Davis wrote about the Northwest Passage in his 1595 book, *Worldes Hydrographical Discription,* and authored a 1599 handbook for mariners entitled *The Seaman's Secrets.*

Davydov, Gavriil Ivanovich (1784–1809)
Russian naval officer in Alaska and the North Pacific

In 1802, just after completing his training as a naval officer with Russia's Naval Cadet Corps, Gavriil Davydov joined the RUSSIAN-AMERICAN COMPANY. Accompanied by a friend, Nikolay Alexandrovich Khvostov, he traveled from St. Petersburg eastward across the breadth of Russia and SIBERIA to the port of Okhotsk on the Pacific coast. He then sailed to the Russian-American Company's trading factories in the Aleutian Islands and Alaska, where he remained for over a year, returning to European Russia in early January 1804.

In 1805, after making a second journey to the Pacific coast of Siberia, Davydov and Khvostov sailed from a port on the Kamchatka Peninsula to the Russian fur-trading settlement at Sitka, at the eastern end of the Gulf of Alaska. Accompanying Davydov on this trip was the German naturalist and world traveler, GEORG HEINRICH VON LANGSDORFF, and N. P. Rezanov, a founder of the Russian-American Company.

In 1807, Davydov was back at Okhotsk, with the rank of lieutenant in the Russian navy. That year, he commanded the ship the *Avos* in a cruise southward across the Sea of Okhotsk to the Kuril Islands and the southern region of Sakhalin Island, north of Japan. Khvostov sailed in command of the *Juno.* In the course of this expedition, they attacked trading settlements on the northern Japanese island of Hokkaido, an action that led to their arrest when they returned to Okhotsk. Davydov and Khvostov managed to escape from the authorities and made their way westward across Siberia and European Russia to St. Petersburg, where they were cleared of any wrongdoing in their raid on Japanese territory.

In 1808, Davydov served in Russian naval actions against Sweden, then settled in St. Petersburg. He was at work on an account of his travels in Siberia and Alaska when, in 1809, he and Khvostov both drowned in the Neva River, following a night out with friends in St. Petersburg. His book was finished by his friend Admiral A. S. Shishkov and published in Russian in 1810–12.

Gavriil Davydov's naval career in the North Pacific and North America coincided with the consolidation of Russian maritime and commercial dominance in eastern Siberia and Alaska. His account of his travels in Siberia and Alaska was published in a German edition in 1816, providing Europeans with a description of Russia's settlements in North America.

Dease, Peter Warren (1788–1863) *Canadian fur trader, surveyor in the Canadian Arctic and Alaska*

Raised in Montreal, Peter Dease entered the FUR TRADE at the age of 13. He served in the XY Company, then the NORTH WEST COMPANY, and in 1821, he became chief trader for the HUDSON'S BAY COMPANY.

In 1825–27, Dease was part of SIR JOHN FRANKLIN's second Arctic expedition from the mouth of the Mackenzie River in Canada's Northwest Territories to Prudhoe Bay on Alaska's North Slope. In 1837–39, in a series of three expeditions, Dease, along with THOMAS SIMPSON, completed the survey of the coast, which had been begun by Franklin, from the mouth of the Mackenzie River westward to Point Barrow and eastward to the south shore of Victoria Island (which he and Simpson named after Queen Victoria) and King William Island and the west coast of the Boothia Peninsula. Dease retired from the fur trade in 1843, settling near Montreal.

Peter Dease was essential to the mapping of the Canadian Arctic. The geographic details he helped provide led to the British navy's attempts to navigate the NORTHWEST PASSAGE.

De Haven, Edwin Jesse (1816–1865) *U.S. naval officer, American polar explorer*

Born in Philadelphia, Edwin J. De Haven entered the United States Navy as a midshipman at the age of 13. He served on naval vessels in the Caribbean Sea and in the South Atlantic Ocean from 1829 to 1835, and, in 1837, he was in the Pacific Ocean.

At Callao, Peru, in 1839, De Haven joined the crew of the *Vincennes,* the flagship of a U.S. government expedition under the command of CHARLES WILKES. Over the next three years, he sailed with the expedition in its explorations in the Antarctic, the South Pacific, and along the northwest coast of North America. In July 1841, off the Oregon coast, De Haven acted heroically in saving some of the crew when one of the expedition's ships, the *Peacock,* was wrecked near the mouth of the COLUMBIA RIVER. Soon afterward, he was commissioned a lieutenant.

De Haven saw naval action in the U.S.-Mexican War of 1846–48, after which he was assigned to the U.S. Naval Observatory in Washington, D.C., where he took part in meteorological research.

In 1850, De Haven, because of his background in polar exploration and in science, was selected to command an expedition in search of SIR JOHN FRANKLIN and his men, who had been missing in the Canadian Arctic since 1845. New York shipping magnate Henry Grinnell financed this rescue mission, during which scientific studies would also be undertaken. Two ships were outfitted for the expedition, the *Advance* and the *Rescue.*

De Haven, in command of the two vessels, sailed from New York City on May 22, 1850. By the end of July, he was in Baffin Bay west of GREENLAND. In September 1850, his ships were trapped in the ice in Wellington Channel, northeast of Baffin Island. Unable to navigate freely, the expedition drifted with the PACK ICE northward for the next nine months, covering a distance of more than 1,000 miles. During this ordeal, De Haven charted land on the northern end of Devon Island, which he called Grinnell Land, after the expedition's sponsor.

By late May 1851, De Haven's ships were freed from the ice, and, without having found any trace of Franklin's expedition, they returned to New York the following September.

De Haven took part in a coastal survey along the southeastern United States from 1853 to 1857. With deteriorating health and failing eyesight, he retired from the navy in 1862.

Edwin J. De Haven was one of the first U.S. naval officers to take part in polar exploration in both the Arctic and Antarctic. He led the first American effort to find Franklin, and, although the rescue mission did not succeed, he added new geographic information about the Canadian Arctic north of Lancaster Sound.

del Cano, Juan Sebastián   See CANO, JUAN SEBASTIÁN DEL.

de León, Juan Ponce   See PONCE DE LEÓN, JUAN.

De Long, George Washington (1844–1881)

U.S. naval officer, American explorer in the Siberian Arctic

George W. De Long was born in New York City. He attended public schools in Brooklyn until 1861, then entered the U.S. naval academy at Annapolis, Maryland. Soon after graduating in 1865, he was commissioned an ensign and began serving with naval forces off the coast of Europe and in the South Atlantic Ocean. By 1869, he had been promoted to lieutenant.

In 1871, during a break from active duty in the North Atlantic, De Long was married to Emma J. Wotton aboard an American vessel off Le Havre, France. In summer 1873, De Long, aboard the *Juanita,* commanded by Captain D. L. Braine, took part in the search for CHARLES FRANCIS HALL and his expedition, missing in the region north of GREENLAND on the Arctic steamer *Polaris.* At Upernavik, south of western Greenland's Melville Bay, De Long and a fellow officer, Lieutenant Charles W. Chipp, along with seven others, continued the search northward along the ice-choked coast in a small steam launch. They cruised along the shore of Melville Bay, almost crossing it from south to north. Ten miles south of Cape York, just below the northwestern corner of Greenland, they were forced to turn back when their small craft was caught in a gale.

In fall 1873, De Long returned to New York City, where he took up duties as the executive officer of the school ship *St. Mary's,* anchored in New York Harbor. He served in that capacity for the next five years.

In 1879, De Long was appointed to lead an expedition planning to reach the NORTH POLE by way of the BERING STRAIT, as well as make an east-to-west crossing of the NORTHEAST PASSAGE. James Gordon Bennett, Jr., publisher of the *New York Herald,* had outfitted a ship for this purpose, the *Jeannette* (which had previously seen service in the Arctic as the *Pandora,* under the command of British polar explorer Sir Allen Young). By special act of Congress, the U.S. government assumed authority over the project while Bennett, who, 10 years earlier, had sponsored HENRY MORTON STANLEY's search for DAVID LIVINGSTONE in Central Africa, provided the financing.

De Long and a crew of 33 embarked from San Francisco, California, on the *Jeannette* on July 8, 1879. Among the five naval officers aboard was Lieutenant Chipp, who had accompanied De Long on his previous exploration of Melville Bay in Greenland. Stopping first at Unalaska Island, the *Jeannette* headed northward into the Bering Strait. De Long had planned to meet up with NILS ADOLF ERIK NORDENSKJÖLD, who was engaged in his west-to-east voyage through the Northeast Passage, but he arrived at Cape Serdze Kamen on the northern Siberian coast after Nordenskjöld had left for the Far East.

De Long had planned to make for Wrangel Island after passing through the Bering Strait, and use it as a jumping-off point for a dash to the North Pole, using sledges and small boats. Wrangel Island, then known as Wrangel Land, was believed by some leading geographers to be the south coast of a large landmass, extending across the top of the world from the Arctic coast of SIBERIA to Greenland. But, on September 5, 1879, the *Jeannette* became trapped in the PACK ICE off the north coast of Wrangel Island. The ship drifted northwestward for the next 17 months. Passing around Wrangel Island, De Long realized that it was not part of a large landmass. Finally, on June 13, 1881, after being carried 600 miles north and west, to a point 150 miles north of the New Siberian Islands, the *Jeannette* was crushed and sank.

De Long and his expedition then headed by whale boats and sledges across the frozen East Siberian Sea, planning to reach the Asian mainland, 300 miles to the south. En route they came upon the northernmost New Siberian Islands, which they named Bennett, Henrietta, and Jeanette Islands. From there, they headed southward across the ice-free sea in several small boats. One boat, with eight crewmen under the command of Lieutenant Chipp, was lost in a gale with all hands, near the Delta of the Lena River. Another group, under the command of the engineering officer, George W. Melville, managed to reach the eastern mouths of the Lena and found aid in a small village.

De Long and 14 others entered the main mouth of the Lena on September 17, 1881, and attempted to travel up the frozen river. By early October, however, they were too weakened by exposure and starvation to continue. De Long sent two men ahead, who managed to reach the safety of a Russian settlement 25 miles away. Severe weather prevented them from returning for De Long, and he perished with 12 of his party sometime after October 30, 1881. The surviving members of the De Long expedition were reunited at Bulun on the lower Lena in late October 1881. In March 1882, Melville went back to the Lena Delta, where he located the bodies of De Long and the others, and recovered his commander's notes, journals, and scientific data.

In 1884, the U.S. government arranged to have De Long's remains, along with those of the others who had perished, returned to New York City. Emma Wotton De Long edited her husband's journals, and, in 1883, they were published as *The Voyage of the Jeannette.* George W. Melville's account of his rescue attempt, *In the Lena Delta,* was published in 1885.

Although George W. De Long's attempt to reach the North Pole ended in tragedy, his expedition led to several important findings about the Arctic Ocean. In addition to charting the ocean's 50,000 square miles, he determined the true dimensions of Wrangel Island, disproving the notion that it was part of a landmass extending to Greenland. When debris from the wrecked *Jeannette* began to appear off the coast of Greenland in 1884, it indicated the extent of the westward drift of the Arctic Sea, and inspired FRIDTJOF NANSEN to undertake an intentional drift across the frozen Arctic Ocean 10 years later. The New Siberian Islands located by De Long now bear his name.

Denham, Dixon (1786–1828) *British army officer in North and West Africa*

Dixon Denham was born in London and, while still in his teens, entered the British army. He served in the Napoleonic Wars of 1798–1815, seeing action in the Peninsular Campaign in Spain as well as at the Battle of Waterloo in 1815.

In 1821, the British Foreign Office selected Denham, by then a major, to accompany HUGH CLAPPERTON and WALTER OUDNEY in an expedition into the Bornu kingdom of West Africa to trace the course of the NIGER RIVER. By the end of that year, Denham joined Oudney and Clapperton at Tripoli in present-day Libya.

Denham, Clapperton, and Oudney made a southward crossing of the SAHARA DESERT and, in February 1823, they became the first Europeans to see Lake Chad. While Clapperton went south and west in an attempt to reach TIMBUKTU, Denham explored to the southeast, examining the Chari River, the principal source of Lake Chad. After exploring the Waube and Logone Rivers as well, Denham rejoined Clapperton at a settlement south of Lake Chad, and the two made their way northward back to Tripoli. Oudney, in the meantime, had died of tropical fever.

Denham was back in England in 1825, where he was appointed superintendent of liberated slaves in West Africa. He was also named lieutenant governor of the British colony of Sierra Leone. He arrived in Sierra Leone in 1827; he died of fever there the following year.

Dixon Denham, with Clapperton and Oudney, undertook some of the earliest official British explorations into the interior of West Africa. Although the expedition did not settle the question of the course of the Niger, it did provide new information on the caravan routes between that river and Lake Chad. His account of his African explorations, entitled *Narrative of Travels and Discoveries in Northern and Central Africa*, was published in 1826.

Desideri, Ippolito (1684–1733) *Italian missionary in India and Tibet*

Ippolito Desideri was born in the town of Pistoia, in northern Italy's Tuscany region. At the age of 16, he began to study with the Jesuits, and he was ordained a priest in 1712.

One year after his ordination, Desideri sailed from Lisbon, Portugal, to the Portuguese colony of Goa on the southwest coast of India. At Goa, he studied some of India's native languages in preparation for missionary work. In 1714, Desideri journeyed inland to Delhi, where he was joined by a Portuguese Jesuit named Emmanuel Freyre. The two missionaries traveled northward to Lahore, on the first leg of a journey to Tibet, where Desideri intended to reestablish a Jesuit mission at LHASA, the Tibetan capital.

From Lahore, Desideri and Freyre traveled into the Himalayas, crossing that range by way of the 11,758-foot-high pass of Zoji La. They reached Leh, the capital of the kingdom of Ladakh. Because Father Freyre had become ill, they decided to return to India. Instead of recrossing the mountains, they traveled by way of a southeastward route along the upper INDUS RIVER. They crossed Kashmir and visited the cities of Srinagar and Gartok. Their journey took them around Lake Mansarowar, which Desideri mistook for the source of the GANGES RIVER.

Desideri and Freyre made the final part of the journey with a military convoy taking a Tartar princess to Tibet and entered Lhasa in March 1716. Soon afterward, Freyre made his way back to India via Nepal; Desideri remained in Lhasa and studied the Tibetan language and Buddhism. The Mongol ruler of Tibet allowed him to preach Christianity. In 1720, Desideri witnessed the Tartar invasion of Tibet and the subsequent annexation of the kingdom by China. In 1721, when the Capuchin order was granted the exclusive right to maintain a mission in Tibet, Desideri was ordered by his superiors in Rome to return to India.

Desideri remained in Agra and Delhi for the next five years. In 1727, he sailed back to Europe by way of the CAPE OF GOOD HOPE, arriving in Port-Louis on the north coast of France in August of that year. He settled in Rome and wrote an account of his experiences in Tibet. Not translated until 1904, it was published in 1931 as *An Account of Tibet: The Travels of Ippolito Desideri*.

Ippolito Desideri was the last Christian missionary allowed to preach in Tibet until the early years of the 20th century. With Emmanuel Freyre, he entered Tibet along a route that would not be traveled by Europeans until the expedition of SIR FRANCIS EDWARD YOUNGHUSBAND in the early 1900s.

De Smet, Pierre-Jean (1801–1873)
Belgian missionary, guide in the Pacific Northwest

Pierre-Jean De Smet was born in Belgium. At the age of 20, he arrived in Florissant, Missouri, near St. Louis, where he studied at the Jesuit St. Stanislau Seminary. Ordained a priest in 1827, he returned to Europe and spent the next 10 years raising funds and recruiting personnel to establish Jesuit missions to the northern plains and the Pacific Northwest.

In 1838, De Smet returned to St. Louis, and he soon journeyed up the Missouri to found a Jesuit mission among the Potawatomi Indians at present-day Council Bluffs, Iowa. Over the next two years, he made a series of trips up and down the MISSOURI RIVER, visiting the Sioux (Dakota, Lakota, Nakota) tribes of what is now South Dakota. In 1839, he traveled aboard an AMERICAN FUR COMPANY steamboat farther upriver to present-day Sioux City, Iowa, for a peace council between the Potawatomi and the Sioux. He returned several weeks later by CANOE.

In 1840, De Smet traveled with an American Fur Company caravan overland to the Bitterroot Valley region of western Montana inhabited by the Flathead Indians. At present-day Stevensville, Montana, he established the St. Mary's mission. The next year, he was back in St. Louis to obtain additional supplies and personnel for the mission.

On his return trip to Montana, De Smet was accompanied by fur trader and mountain man THOMAS FITZPATRICK. In May 1841, at Sapling Grove in eastern Kansas, De Smet and Fitzpatrick met up with the first organized wagon train of emigrants headed for the rich farmlands of California, a group organized by settlers from Platte County, Missouri, under the name of the Western Emigration Society. The emigrants lacked the knowledge and experience to cross the Great Plains and the ROCKY MOUNTAINS, and De Smet and Fitzpatrick agreed to guide them.

Departing eastern Kansas in May 1841, De Smet and Fitzpatrick led the wagon train along the Platte River Valley of present-day Nebraska of southern Wyoming. After a stopover at Fort Laramie, the group headed westward to the Sweetwater River. They cut through the Rockies via the SOUTH PASS of Wyoming's Wind River Range, thus crossing the Continental Divide. From the western slopes of the Wind River mountains, they followed the Green River Valley northward into Soda Springs in what is now southeastern Idaho.

Near what is now Pocatello, Idaho, the wagon train divided. De Smet and Fitzpatrick led 32 of the pioneers to the COLUMBIA RIVER, which they followed to Fort Vancouver near present-day Portland, Oregon, then proceeded southward into northern California. The rest of the emigrants headed west and south from Pocatello, following the Humboldt River into the deserts of north-ern Nevada, and across the Sierra Nevada into central California.

From 1840 to 1846, De Smet established six interconnected missions—the Rocky Mountain missions—administering to such tribes as the Flathead, Kalispel, Coeur d'Alene, Blackfeet, Nez Perce, Cayuse, and Sioux. He became an important intermediary between Indians and the increasing number of non-Indian settlers in the Bitterroot

Detail of map of the American West by Pierre-Jean De Smet (1851) *(Library of Congress)*

Pierre-Jean De Smet *(Library of Congress)*

Valley of present-day Montana and eastern Idaho. In order to obtain additional support for his work, he made frequent trips across the Rockies and Great Plains to St. Louis. In the 1850s, he served as a government peace commissioner to the Yakama and Coeur d'Alene under Kamiakin, and, in the 1860s, to the Lakota Sioux under Red Cloud.

Pierre-Jean De Smet contributed to U.S. exploration and settlement by helping guide the first wagon train westward. The route he and Fitzpatrick followed became the primary route for thousands of emigrants heading for California via the Oregon and California Trails. Moreover, his missions provided important links for the construction of the Mullan Wagon Road, built by the U.S. Army in 1859, which connected Fort Benton, Montana, the westernmost navigable point of the Missouri River, with Fort Walla Walla, Washington. De Smet wrote prolifically about his work and experiences in the Far West, including the 1847 book, *Oregon Missions and Travels.*

de Solís, Juan Díaz   See DÍAZ DE SOLÍS, JUAN.

de Soto, Hernando   See SOTO, HERNANDO DE.

de Vaca, Alvar Núñez Cabeza   See CABEZA DE VACA, ALVAR NÚÑEZ.

Dezhnev, Semyon Ivanovich (Semeon Dezhnyov, Semen Ivanov Deshnef, Simon Dezhnev) (ca. 1605–1672) *Russian Cossack leader in northeastern Siberia*

Semyon Dezhnev, a Russian Cossack, lived in frontier settlements in eastern and northern SIBERIA in the 1630s, including Tobolsk, Yeniseysk, and, after 1638, Yakutsk. In 1640–41, he took part in fur-trading expeditions to the Yana River, and the next year, he went farther eastward to the upper Indigirka River.

In 1644, Dezhnev accompanied a band of Cossacks descending the Indigirka River to its mouth on the East Siberian Sea, an arm of the Arctic Ocean. With Cossack leader MIKHAIL STADUKHIN, he was part of an expedition traveling in small boats along the Arctic coast of Siberia eastward from the mouth of the Indigirka to the Alazeya River's outlet on the East Siberian Sea. From there, he traveled with the Cossacks overland to the mouth of the Kolyma River, farther to the east.

Under the command of FYODOT ALEKSEYEV POPOV, Dezhnev and other Cossacks, in 1647, attempted to travel eastward from the mouth of the Kolyma River in search of a region supposed to be teeming with walruses, and thus a great potential source of ivory. The Cossacks were unable to proceed around the Chukchi Peninsula that year, but in 1648, Dezhnev led a party of 90 Cossacks in small boats and succeeded in circumnavigating the Chukchi Peninsula. Having advanced more than 1,000 miles eastward from the Kolyma's mouth, he sailed south of Wrangel Island. He rounded a cape at the Chukchi Peninsula's northeastern end and headed southward along the eastern Siberian coast, reportedly passing through what later came to be known as BERING STRAIT. Along the way, some of the boats were wrecked. Temporarily stranded, Dezhnev and only a handful of his men survived the winter on the Siberian coast.

Dezhnev may have made a landing on the northern portion of the Kamchatka Peninsula in 1648. In any event, he led his men inland from the mouth of the Anadyr River, of which he made the European discovery, and established the settlement of Anadyrsk.

In 1652, Dezhnev explored the Gulf of Anadyr. The region proved rich in walruses and provided a supply of furs and ivory for years. In 1662, after 10 years in the Gulf of Anadyr region, Dezhnev returned overland to Yakutsk. In 1664, he journeyed to Moscow with the proceeds of his trading exploits in eastern Siberia. He was made an Atman, or Cossack leader. He lived in Yakutsk until 1671, then spent his remaining years in Moscow.

Semyon Dezhnev's voyage around the Chukchi Peninsula demonstrated that the north coast of Russia and Siberia did not dip southward (as many hopeful seekers of the NORTHEAST PASSAGE had incorrectly speculated), but extended north of the ARCTIC CIRCLE as far as the Pacific coast. His sighting of the channel between Siberia and Alaska preceded the explorations of VITUS JONASSEN BERING by almost a century. Yet Dezhnev's explorations were never officially documented, and, although the strait he discovered appeared on early maps, it took Bering's expeditions to confirm the eastern limits of the Asian continent. The point of land east of the East Siberian Sea, at the northern end of Bering Strait, was named Cape Dezhnev. Also known as East Cape, it is the northeasternmost point of Asia.

Dias, Bartolomeu (Bartholomew Diaz, Bartholomeo Díaz de Novaes, Bartolomé Díaz)

(ca. 1450–1500) *Portuguese mariner on the west coast of Africa*

Few details exist of Bartolomeu Dias's early life or origins. Some sources suggest he was related to DINÍS DIAS, the Portuguese navigator who made the European discovery of Cape Verde, and João Dias, who first rounded Cape Bojador on the Atlantic coast of West Africa.

Dias first appears in official Portuguese records of 1478, indicating he was then involved in the ivory trade on the west coast of Africa. In 1481, John II (John the Perfect) became king of Portugal and immediately set about renewing Portuguese efforts to find a sea route around Africa to India—efforts that had been initiated earlier in the century by HENRY THE NAVIGATOR, prince of Portugal. That year, Dias, who was prominent at the court of King John and an accomplished mariner and navigator, commanded a vessel in a fleet under Diogo d'Azambiya on a trading expedition along West Africa to the Gold Coast (present-day Ghana) on the Gulf of Guinea. Dias was back in Lisbon in 1486, where he served as superintendent of the royal warehouses.

In 1487, Dias was placed in command of a follow-up expedition to DIOGO CÃO's voyage of 1485. Cão had reached as far south along the African coast as Cape Cross, part of present-day Namibia. It was not then known to Europeans how far south the African continent extended, or whether there was a passage into the Indian Ocean. While Dias was assigned to seek the southernmost extent of Africa by sea and possibly a route to India, PERO DA COVILHÃ was dispatched by King John on an overland journey to Africa and India.

Dias sailed from Lisbon in August 1487. His fleet of three ships consisted of two of the CARAVEL type and a supply vessel. Earlier voyages of exploration along the African coast had been limited in their range because of shortages of food and other supplies. It was hoped that a separate ship to carry stores would provide adequate support to circumnavigate the continent. King John also wanted to make contact with PRESTER JOHN, a fabled Christian monarch whose kingdom was believed to lie in the interior of East Africa. It was hoped that an alliance with Prester John would help overcome Muslim domination of the trade route to India, as

well as provide safe havens for the Portuguese in their sea voyages around Africa.

At various points along the west coast of Africa, Dias put ashore six African natives, who had been taken to Lisbon several years earlier by Cão. He gave them gold, silver, and spices as samples of what the Portuguese were seeking in trade, hoping at least one of them would eventually reach Prester John.

By December 1487, Dias had arrived in Luderitz Bay on the coast of present-day Namibia, several hundred miles beyond the farthest point reached by Cão. He set up a *PADRÃO* (pillar) declaring possession of the region for Portugal, and, leaving his supply ship with a party of nine men, he headed southward along the coast. But contrary winds and a north-flowing current led him to sail out to sea about 500 miles north of the CAPE OF GOOD HOPE. A subsequent storm blew the two vessels southward.

After almost two weeks of sailing out of sight of land, Dias picked up westerly winds. Expecting to reach the African coast, he found he could approach the mainland only by sailing northward, indicating that he had rounded the southern end of Africa. After a landing at Mossel Bay (which Dias named Cowherd Bay after the cattle he saw grazing there), he headed several hundred miles eastward along the south coast of Africa to a point where it appeared to angle to the northeast. He made a brief landing and had a hostile encounter with native Hottentot, killing one. At the mouth of the Great Fish River, which he dubbed Rio do Iffante in honor of Prince Henry, his crew compelled him to return to the supply ship they had left on the southwest coast of Africa. On the return voyage, he caught sight of Africa's southernmost point, Cape Agulhas, and, soon afterward, he sighted and perhaps named the Cape of Good Hope.

When Dias returned to Luderitz Bay, he discovered that only three of the nine men he had left had survived. The supply ship had become rotten with worms, and Dias had it burned. Following the coast, Dias sailed to the Gulf of Guinea, where on the island of Principe he rescued Portuguese navigator and soldier DUARTE PACHECO and several shipwrecked companions. Dias returned to Lisbon in December 1488.

In 1494, Dias was named to a high post in a trading syndicate on the Gulf of Guinea. Ten years passed after his epoch-making exploration of the southern limits of Africa until a voyage was undertaken, commanded by VASCO DA GAMA. In 1497, Dias, who had supervised the construction of the expedition's ships, accompanied da Gama as far as the Cape Verde Islands, from where he traveled to the West African coast and prospered in the ivory trade.

In 1500, Dias commanded several of the ships in PEDRO CABRAL's India fleet, intending to travel with the expedition as far as Sofala on the East African mainland, opposite Madagascar, with a royal charter to establish a Portuguese trading post. Following Dias's advice, Cabral sailed westward, away from the West African coast, and made the first European sighting of the southeast coast of Brazil. Shortly after leaving Brazil, Dias and all hands on his ship were lost, along with four other vessels, in a storm off the Cape of Good Hope. A ship captained by his brother was separated from Cabral's fleet in that storm; it went on to explore Madagascar and the Gulf of Aden before rejoining Cabral's ship in the Cape Verde Islands on the homeward voyage.

Bartolomeu Dias's determination of the southern extent of Africa proved to European geographers that the Indian Ocean was not landlocked and could be entered from the Atlantic Ocean. When Dias returned to Lisbon with this momentous news in 1488, CHRISTOPHER COLUMBUS was attempting to win King John's support for his proposed westward voyage to India. With Dias's findings, the Portuguese felt Columbus's project was unnecessary and rejected it. European knowledge of the coast of Africa had been extended 1,260 miles by Dias; an Atlantic entrance to the Indian Ocean provided the basis for a da Gama's historic voyage to India in 1497–99. In addition, Dias's 1487–88 voyage demonstrated that Africa was not connected to the hypothetical GREAT SOUTHERN CONTINENT. Some sources suggest that Dias originally named the point of land he saw on his return voyage around Africa the Cape of Storms, and it was King John II who later gave it the more optimistic name Cape of Good Hope.

Dias, Dinís (Diniz Díaz) (fl. 1440s) *Portuguese mariner on the west coast of Africa*

Dinís Dias was a squire serving under HENRY THE NAVIGATOR, prince of Portugal, at Sagres, Portugal. In 1444, he was commissioned to explore southward along the west coast of Africa, beyond the Senegal River. It was to be a follow-up to NUÑO TRISTÃO's exploration of the Senegal River one year earlier.

By early 1445, Dias had descended the African coast south of the delta of the Senegal River and had reached a point of land that he named Cape Verde (green cape), after a green wooded peninsula he spotted there. It was the first greenery he had seen after sailing down 800 miles of desolate desert coastline. Sailing beyond Cape Verde, he noted that the coast of Africa began to extend eastward, and his subsequent reports inspired false hopes that he had rounded Africa. Near Cape Verde, he left a record of his voyage on a palm tree before returning to Portugal.

Soon afterward, Dias undertook a second voyage to the delta of the Senegal River and beyond, on behalf of a group of Portuguese merchants. This effort met with little success because of hostility by the natives.

Although Dinís Dias did not realize it at the time, Cape Verde is the westernmost point of the African continent. In any case, he significantly advanced the geographic knowledge of Africa with his reports on the eastward curve of the African coast south of Cape Verde. (An island group to the west of the cape, discovered by ALVISE DA CADAMOSTO in 1456, is also called Cape Verde.)

Díaz, Melchor (Melchior Díaz) (unknown–1540) *Spanish conquistador in Mexico and the American Southwest*

In 1536, Melchor Díaz, a professional soldier with Spanish forces in Mexico, was the local colonial administrator, or *alcalde,* of Culiacán, then a frontier garrison on the Pacific coast. Early in 1536, ÁLVAR NÚÑEZ CABEZA DE VACA and ESTEVANICO, after five years of wandering in the American Southwest, arrived in Culiacán, where they were welcomed by Díaz.

Three years later, in 1539, the Spanish viceroy of Mexico, ANTONIO DE MENDOZA, sent Díaz with a cavalry detachment northward from Culiacán to reconnoiter the region visited by Friar MARCOS DE NIZA, who, with Estevanico, had traveled there to investigate reports of the fabled Seven Cities of Cibola. The next year, Díaz and Niza took part in FRANCISCO VÁSQUEZ DE CORONADO's expedition into what is now New Mexico. Following the capture of the Hawikuh pueblo of the Zuni Indians, near present-day Zuni, New Mexico, Díaz escorted Niza back to Sonora in what is now northern Mexico.

At Ures in Sonora, Díaz met up with Coronado's additional forces and directed them to join the expedition's leader in the north. In September 1540, he set out from Ures with a small company of soldiers and headed westward toward the Gulf of California, where he planned to join the expedition's fleet, under HERNANDO DE ALARCÓN.

Díaz followed a route along the present Arizona-Mexico border. He reached the COLORADO RIVER at its confluence with the Gila River by following an ancient Indian trail. Near the Yuma (Quechan) Indian settlements on the Colorado, he came upon a stone monument that had been erected by Alarcón's men, and beneath it he found a message left by Alarcón informing him that the ships had sailed for Mexico.

Díaz then led his men across the Colorado River and explored the northern region of the Baja California peninsula. In late 1540, he was injured with a lance, dying after three weeks. His men then headed northeastward to rejoin Coronado in New Mexico.

As one of Coronado's lieutenants, Melchor Díaz traveled into the territory southwest of the main Spanish penetration of western New Mexico and Arizona, leading the first European exploration of northern Baja California. When he came upon the Colorado River, he named it the Tizon, which means "firebrand" in Spanish, after the torches he saw carried by the Yuma downstream. He correctly surmised in his report that the river was the same one previously sighted from the rim of the Grand Canyon farther upstream by GARCÍA LÓPEZ DE CÁRDENAS. In his account, Díaz also described the starkly barren and inhospitable terrain around the northern end of the Gulf of California, an image that discouraged subsequent Spanish exploration into Baja California until the travels of Father EUSEBIO FRANCISCO KINO more than 150 years later.

Díaz del Castillo, Bernal (Bernal Díaz)

(ca. 1492–ca. 1584) *Spanish conquistador in Panama and Mexico*

Bernal Díaz del Castillo was born in Medina del Campo, Spain. By the age of 22, he had joined the ranks of the CONQUISTADORES in the Americas, and after settling in Cuba, he took part in the colonization of Panama under PEDRO ARIAS DE ÁVILA.

In 1518, Díaz del Castillo enlisted in HERNÁN CORTÉS's expedition to Mexico; over the next three years, he took part in the campaign against the Aztec Indians. For his efforts in support of Cortés, he was granted a large estate in what is now Guatemala, where he remained for the next 60 years as a landed squire and magistrate.

In the 1570s, Díaz del Castillo read with great dissatisfaction Francisco López de Gómara's history of Cortés's campaign, and in response he wrote his own account based on his eyewitness experience, entitled *Crónica verdadera de la conquista de la Nueva España* (The true history of the conquest of New Spain).

Bernal Díaz del Castillo's account was not published until 1632, long after his death. Although it has been criticized for exaggerating some of his own exploits in the campaign, it provides details of the campaign not revealed in the work of Gomara, who had never left Spain. It was the first major historical work of the Spanish conquest written by a participant and was among the earliest accounts to describe the Aztec point of view, relating how they believed that the arrival of the Europeans was the fulfillment of a divine prophecy.

Díaz de Solís, Juan (ca. 1470–1516)

Spanish mariner in the Caribbean and South America

Juan Díaz de Solís was born at Lebrija in southwestern Spain, near the ports of Sanlúcar de Barrameda and Cádiz. He became a seafarer in service to Portugal, taking part in voyages around the CAPE OF GOOD HOPE to India and developing a reputation as an accomplished pilot and navigator.

In the late 1490s, Díaz de Solís reportedly killed his wife in Portugal. To escape the consequences, he fled back to his native Spain. He became associated with VICENTE YÁÑEZ PINZÓN, a veteran of CHRISTOPHER COLUMBUS's first voyage.

In 1506, at the request of King Ferdinand II of Spain, Díaz de Solís produced the first marine chart of the South American coast. That year, he and Pinzón jointly commanded a Spanish expedition in search of a transoceanic strait through the Americas. After following the route taken by Columbus in his fourth voyage of 1502–04, they circumnavigated Cuba and established with certainty that it was an island. In their exploration along the mainland, they examined the Yucatán and the Bay of Campeche, which they named the Gulf of the Nativity, then sailed southward into the Gulf of Honduras, returning to Spain by 1507.

In 1508, King Ferdinand commissioned Díaz de Solís to undertake another search for a southwest passage. On June 29, 1508, he sailed from the Spanish port of Sanlúcar de Barrameda with two ships, the *Isabeleta* and the *Magdalena,* again joined by Pinzón as co-commander. Having determined on their earlier voyage that no strait was to be found along the mainland of CENTRAL AMERICA, they explored southward along the Atlantic coast of South America. At 41° south latitude, they came upon the mouth of the Río Negro, flowing into the sea at a point on what is now the central Atlantic coast of Argentina. Díaz de Solís and Pinzón disagreed on how the rest of the voyage should be conducted, and they sailed back to Spain in 1509, where King Ferdinand had Díaz de Solís imprisoned for bringing the voyage to an abrupt conclusion. Yet he was released after two years, and, in 1512, he was named as Spain's "pilot major," succeeding AMERIGO VESPUCCI.

In late November 1514, the king commissioned Díaz de Solís to explore the coast of South America once again in an attempt to find a strait into the South Sea (the Pacific Ocean). This voyage had been given greater impetus by VASCO NÚÑEZ DE BALBOA's sighting of the Pacific Ocean the previous year, news that had rekindled hopes that a passage through the Americas, if found, would provide Spain with an all-water western sea route to the SPICE ISLANDS (the Moluccas) and the riches of the EAST INDIES.

In command of three ships, Díaz de Solís sailed from Spain on October 8, 1515. He reached the South American coast near present-day Rio de Janeiro, then proceeded southward, taking possession for Spain of much of what is now Uruguay and coming upon La Plata and Lobos Islands. In mid-February 1516, he reached what he at first thought was the entrance to the southwest passage. Díaz de Solís named it El Mar Dulce (the freshwater sea), the same name that Pinzón in 1500 had given to what later became known as the AMAZON RIVER.

Exploring upstream, Díaz de Solís soon determined that he had in fact reached the outlet of a river, not a passage to the Pacific, and renamed the estuary the Río Solís. He sailed a short distance up one of its chief tributaries, the Uruguay, and at Martín García Island, near present-day Buenos Aires, he went ashore with a landing party, intending to kidnap some natives to take to Spain. Although they appeared friendly, they were actually the fierce and cannibalistic Charrua, and they suddenly attacked Díaz de Solís and the men with him. The men aboard his ship watched helplessly as the natives hacked Díaz de Solís and the others to death, roasted the remains, and ate them.

After Díaz de Solís's death, command of the expedition went to his brother-in-law, Francisco de Torres. Torres took on a cargo of brazilwood, highly prized in Europe as a source of textile dye, and headed back to Spain, arriving in September 1516. On the homeward voyage, one of the ships was wrecked on the island of Santa Catarina off the Brazilian coast, and some of the survivors remained there until they were rescued by SEBASTIAN CABOT 10 years later. Cabot heard reports from the castaways of an Indian kingdom rich in silver thought to exist beyond the point on the river where Díaz de Solís had died and to have been discovered by ALEJO GARCIA. He then explored the estuary himself, renaming it the Río de la Plata (river of silver).

Juan Díaz de Solís made the European discovery of the Río de la Plata, the estuary of South America's second largest river system. In Spain, FERDINAND MAGELLAN heard from survivors of Díaz de Solís's last expedition that the coastline of South America appeared to extend southwestward. The news supported his idea that a westward passage to the Pacific existed in Spanish territory and helped him gain the backing of the Spanish government for his historic voyage of 1519–21.

Dietrich, Koncordie Amalie Nelle (1821–1891)
German naturalist in Australia

Amalie Dietrich, née Nelle, was born in the German state of Saxony. Growing up in a small village, she gained an understanding of plants and natural science through her mother's work as an herbal healer.

At the age of 24, she married an apothecary named Wilhelm Dietrich. They decided to supplement his income by gathering plants for scientists and collectors. When her husband was otherwise busy, Dietrich wandered throughout the countryside with her daughter and a cart pulled by a dog, in search of rare plant specimens as well as insects and rocks. Divorced at the age of 40, she applied for work as a naturalist with Johann Godeffroy, the owner of a Hamburg shipping firm, who was stocking his private museum. A letter of introduction from a collector helped her get hired, but at only half the pay as a male naturalist.

In 1863, Dietrich departed Hamburg on one of Godeffroy's boats, sailing around Africa's CAPE OF GOOD HOPE for Australia. Over the next 10 years, she traveled throughout the Queensland outback on collecting forays. In addition to flora, she gathered mammals, fish, and insects. She eventually settled in the coastal town of Bowen, where she maintained a zoo of animals that she intended to take back to Germany.

When she returned to Germany, Dietrich settled in Hamburg; there she cataloged her collections. Godeffroy later went bankrupt, and his museum was sold. Having lost her job and without help from her now-married daughter, she spent the rest of her life in a Hamburg home for the elderly.

Amalie Dietrich amassed an enormous collection of flora and fauna, among the largest ever gathered by a woman. Some of her samples and much of her written work were lost in the fire bombings of Hamburg during World War II, but records exist of the species she gathered. Six different species have been named for her, including the *Acacia dietrichiana* plant, the *Cephrenes amalia* butterfly, and the *Nortonia amaliae* wasp.

Diogenes (Diogenes the Greek) (fl. A.D. 40s–50s)
Greek merchant in East Africa

Diogenes the Greek was a mariner and merchant during the reign of the Roman emperor Claudius, A.D. 41–54. He plied his trade between India and the MEDITERRANEAN SEA, crossing the Arabian Sea and the Indian Ocean. On a return voyage from India, his ship was blown off course in the Gulf of Aden and was forced around the Horn of Africa (northeast tip of present-day Somalia), then southward down the continent's east coast.

Near Dar es Salaam, on the coast of what is now Tanzania, Diogenes managed to land at an ancient port known as Rhapta. From there, he traveled inland, reportedly reaching two large bodies of fresh water that might have been Lake Victoria and Lake Albert. He also reported seeing a range of snow-capped mountains. According to Diogenes, it was the runoff from the mountains' melting snow that formed the great lakes, which in turn were the source of the NILE RIVER.

Diogenes the Greek is one of the earliest known explorers of central Africa. After his return to the Mediterranean region, news of his travels began circulating among ancient scholars. In the second century, PTOLEMY wrote about the source of the Nile and the fabled MOUNTAINS OF THE MOON, thought to be the Ruwenzori Range or possibly MOUNT KILIMANJARO and Mount Kenya. The geography of the region was not determined until the mid-19th century and the explorations of SIR RICHARD BURTON, JOHN HANNING SPEKE, and SIR SAMUEL WHITE BAKER, among others.

Dodge, Henry (1782–1867) *U.S. Army officer in the American West*

Henry Dodge was born in Vincennes in present-day Indiana, then a frontier settlement on the Wabash River. When still in his teens, he moved with his family to the Missouri country, which was at that time under Spanish control.

In about 1806, Dodge took part in an independent military expedition down the MISSISSIPPI RIVER in support of Aaron Burr's plan to create a separate colony in the Spanish-held Southwest. Burr was arrested for treason, but Dodge returned to Missouri, never officially implicated in the conspiracy.

During the early 1800s, Dodge was a territorial sheriff and marshal in the newly organized Missouri Territory. With the outbreak of the War of 1812, he became a major of mounted troops in the Missouri territorial militia.

In 1827, Dodge moved to the Wisconsin Territory, where he founded the lead-mining settlement of Dodgeville. That year, he took part in suppressing a Winnebego Indian uprising under Red Bird. In 1832, he was made a colonel of a mounted Michigan militia unit as well as a major in the regular army, and he fought in the principal battles of the Black Hawk War involving Sac and Fox (Mesquaki) Indian bands.

In 1833, Dodge organized the First Dragoon Regiment, the precursor of the cavalry, which was sent to Fort Gibson in the Indian Territory (present-day Oklahoma). In 1834, under General HENRY LEAVENWORTH, Dodge set out from Fort Gibson and explored western Oklahoma's Wichita Mountains. Dodge's contingent also explored the Red River region of Mexican-held Texas and made diplomatic contacts with the area's Comanche, Kiowa, and Wichita Indian bands. The Lenni Lenape (Delaware) Indian BLACK BEAVER and part-Cherokee JESSE CHISHOLM served as guides with the expedition, and GEORGE CATLIN, the painter, traveled with it. The troops were afflicted with malaria, and one-third of the men died, including General Leavenworth.

The next year, 1835, Dodge led a large dragoon expedition that explored the ROCKY MOUNTAINS and the easternmost segment of the Oregon Trail. He and his men returned to Fort Gibson by way of the Santa Fe Trail and Bent's Fort, after covering 1,600 miles of territory. Also in 1835, Dodge established Camp Holmes on the Arkansas River and explored the Cross Timbers region of west Texas.

After 1836, Dodge returned to Wisconsin, where he served as Wisconsin territorial governor and later as the territory's representative in Congress. When Wisconsin achieved statehood in 1848, Dodge was one of its first two U.S. senators.

The official account of Dodge's spring 1834 expedition was written by Lieutenant Thomas B. Wheelock and submitted to the U.S. Congress as *Journal of the Campaign of the Regiment of Dragoons under Col. Henry Dodge from Fort Gibson to the Rocky Mountains in 1834.*

As a leader of early military exploration of the southern plains, Henry Dodge helped increase the U.S. government's knowledge of the region and open it to the relocation of the Southeast tribes, as well as to later non-Indian settlement. He was also a leading pioneer on the Wisconsin frontier, playing a key role in the development of Wisconsin as a state.

Dollier de Casson, François (1636–1701)
French missionary in Canada and the Great Lakes

François Dollier was born in the city of Nantes on the west coast of France. His family was of the bourgeois class, with connections to both the nobility and the military. He served for three years in the army under the command of French general Henri de Turenne, during which he reached the rank of captain of cavalry in campaigns against Spanish and Austrian forces in the European wars of the late 1650s.

Following his military service, Dollier entered the Sepulcian order, completing his studies at a seminary in Paris. Ordained a priest by 1666, he left that year for French Canada to take up duties as a missionary. Immediately upon his arrival in Quebec in September 1666, he was attached as a chaplain to a French regiment in a military expedition against the Mohawk Indians. He was soon sent on a similar mission to a garrison at Fort Sainte-Anne on Lamothe Island in Lake Champlain, in present-day northeastern New York State. He remained there almost a year, during which he helped the troops recover from an outbreak of SCURVY.

In summer 1667, Dollier was back at Montreal. He was sent to serve as a parish priest at the French settlement of Trois Rivières on the St. Lawrence River. After a year there, he made a journey to the Lake Nipissing region to study Indian languages. At that time, he learned of the Ottawa and Potawatomi Indians who dwelled in the upper Mississippi Valley to the south. Planning to expand his missionary work to these tribes, Dollier set about organizing an evangelical expedition.

Dollier and a number of Sepulcian priests departed Montreal in early July 1669, accompanied by a crew of *voyageurs*. Included in the party was fur-trader and explorer RENÉ-ROBERT CAVELIER DE LA SALLE, who was to serve as interpreter. Among the priests was RENÉ DE BRÉHANT DE GALINÉE, who had some geographic knowledge of the Great Lakes region to the west.

Leaving La Salle on the south shore of Lake Ontario, Dollier and the other priests continued westward to the Niagara River, guided by a friendly Iroquois (Haudenosaunee). Near what is now Hamilton, Ontario, they met up with Adrien Jolliet, brother of LOUIS JOLLIET, who provided them with directions on the best route to the upper MISSISSIPPI RIVER region and information on the region's tribes.

Dollier and his companions wintered on the north shore of Lake Erie. On March 23, 1670, Dollier erected a cross, claiming the region for Louis XIV of France. Before long, the CANOE carrying Dollier's portable altar was lost. Without the necessary equipment to carry out his missionary work among the upper Mississippi tribes, Dollier decided to return to Montreal. Nevertheless, instead of traveling back to the St. Lawrence along the same route as the outbound journey, he led the party along the Niagara River into Lake Erie as far as the Detroit River and Lake St. Clair. The party then headed northward into Lake Huron, visiting the Sepulcian mission at Michilimackinac at the northern entrance to Lake Michigan. From there, they headed eastward to Georgian Bay, and made their way back to Montreal by way of Lake Nipissing and the Ottawa River, arriving in June 1670.

The outbreak of a new Iroquois-Huron (Wyandot) conflict later that year brought an end to Dollier's missionary work among the Indians. He did undertake a peace mission to Lake Ontario in summer 1670, returning to Montreal in mid-August. Soon afterward, he was named superior of the Sepulcian mission at Montreal, and he subsequently became vicar general of the diocese of Quebec. He remained in Montreal for the rest of his life, except for one brief visit to France in the mid-1670s. Dollier played a leading role in the development of the city of Montreal, including the laying out of the settlement's first streets and the construction of its first public buildings and churches. Toward the end of his life, he was involved in several projects to build canals around Montreal. He also wrote an early history of the city.

In the 1669–70 expedition, François Dollier and his companions became the first Europeans to enter the Niagara River from Lake Ontario. His explorations showed conclusively that the Great Lakes were interconnected and provided the basis for French claims to what is now southern Ontario. Dollier wrote an account of the journey, but he later destroyed it in favor of a superior work by Bréhant.

Domínguez, Francisco Atanasio (ca. 1740–1805)
Spanish missionary in the American Southwest
A native of Mexico City, Francisco Domínguez was ordained a Franciscan priest. In 1776, he was sent to New Mexico in a supervisory role, inspecting the missions at Santa Fe and Taos. He also was assigned the task of helping to organize and lead an expedition overland to the missionary outposts on the California coast along with fellow friar FRANCISCO SILVESTRE VÉLEZ DE ESCALANTE.

The Escalante-Domínguez expedition departed Santa Fe on July 29, 1776, and, until its return on January 2, 1777, covered a total of nearly 1,500 miles in present-day Colorado, Utah, and Arizona. A journal of the expedition kept by Escalante was also signed by Domínguez. The cartographer Don Bernardo Miera y Pacheco drew a detailed map of the lands visited.

Upon his return to Santa Fe and Mexico City, Francisco Domínguez submitted to his Franciscan superiors a report that was highly critical of the administration of the New Mexico missions. His negative views caused him to fall out of favor with the Franciscan hierarchy, leading to his assignment to an obscure missionary post in northern Mexico. Although the Escalante-Domínguez expedition failed to reach California, it brought back knowledge of uncharted lands of present-day Utah.

Donnaconna (ca. 1490–ca. 1539) *Huron chief in the St. Lawrence River region of Canada*
In summer 1534, Huron (Wyandot) chief Donnaconna led about 200 of his people from their village near the site of present-day Quebec City on the St. Lawrence River to the northeast shores of the Gaspé Peninsula to fish for mackerel. On July 16, 1534, the Huron encountered French explorer JACQUES CARTIER and his fleet, which was then exploring the Gulf of St. Lawrence as part of Cartier's first voyage of exploration to Canada.

Members of Donnaconna's Huron band first paddled out to Cartier's ships by CANOE, and then Cartier and a party of Frenchmen rowed ashore. Eight days later, on July 24, 1534, the French erected a large cross on the shores of Gaspé Harbor, formally claiming the land for France. Donnaconna then visited Cartier's vessel to explain that he was the chief of this region and to protest against the French taking possession of his domain. The French presented him with numerous trade goods and convinced him of their peaceful intentions. Donnaconna subsequently allowed two of his teenage sons, Domagaya and Taignoagny, to sail with the expedition to Europe.

While in France, Donnaconna's sons learned the French language and helped Cartier win backing for his second expedition to North America.

Cartier returned to Canada in summer 1535 with his second expedition, along with Donnaconna's sons, as promised. This time, Cartier's fleet sailed into the St. Lawrence River after exploring, with the help of the Huron, the bays, islands, and straits of the Gulf of St. Lawrence. The French ships then traveled up the St. Lawrence River, reaching the Huron settlement of Stadacona (present-day Quebec City) that September.

Despite Donnaconna's protests, Cartier and some of his crew proceeded up the St. Lawrence, guided by the chief's son Domagaya, to the larger Huron settlement of Hochelaga (present-day Montreal). The expedition then returned to Stadacona, where they spent the winter.

Donnaconna informed Cartier of a legendary land, rich in jewels and precious metals, that could be reached via the Ottawa or Saguenay Rivers. The Huron chief claimed to have visited this land himself. He told of its strange inhabitants who were white. Donnaconna also claimed to know of lands of one-legged people and pygmies. Cartier, hoping to gain backing for another expedition, decided to kidnap the chief and take him to Europe. Although Donnaconna was originally held against his will by Cartier, and his warriors paddled out to the ships to rescue him, he reportedly agreed to go to France voluntarily with nine other Huron.

As they left Canada in spring 1536, Donnaconna shared his geographic knowledge with the French in the exploration of Cape Breton Island, the Cape of St. Lawrence, the Magdalen Islands (Îles de la Madeleine), and Renewse Harbor on Newfoundland. From there, the expedition sailed for France in June 1536, arriving in St.-Malo on July 15, 1536.

Donnaconna was well received in France. He met personally with King Francis I and became something of a celebrity of the royal court before dying, probably in 1539, from a European disease.

Donnaconna and his sons contributed to the French exploration of North America with accurate geographic information. Huron legends of Saguenay helped inspire backing for Cartier's third expedition to the St. Lawrence region in 1541. More than 60 years later, French explorer SAMUEL DE CHAMPLAIN retraced Cartier's route to Stadacona. At that time, no trace of Donnaconna's band could be found. The Huron had possibly been driven west by invading Iroquois (Haudenosaunee).

D'Orbigny, Alcide-Charles-Victor Dessalines   See ORBIGNY, ALCIDE-CHARLES-VICTOR DESSALINES D'.

Dorion, Marie (Marie Aoie, Marie of the Iowas, Dorion Woman) (1786–ca. 1853) *Ioway Indian guide and interpreter for Astorians in the Pacific Northwest, wife of Pierre Dorion, Jr.*

Marie Dorion was an Ioway Indian. She was living in the Red River region of what is now southwestern Arkansas, when, in about 1806, she married the part-Sioux (Dakota, Lakota, Nakota) fur trader and mountain man PIERRE DORION, JR. His father, PIERRE DORION, SR., was also a frontier trader and trapper.

Pierre Dorion, Jr., was active in the FUR TRADE on the upper Missouri River, working for a time for MANUEL LISA'S ST. LOUIS MISSOURI FUR COMPANY. In winter 1810–11, while in St. Louis, he signed up with JOHN JACOB ASTOR'S expedition, headed by WILSON PRICE HUNT, up the MISSOURI RIVER, then westward to the Oregon coast and the Pacific Fur Company (a subsidiary of the AMERICAN FUR COMPANY) outpost at Astoria. Dorion also arranged to have his wife and two small children accompany the Astorians.

The group set out from St. Louis in spring 1811. Although Hunt had voiced objections to having Marie Dorion and her children along, she proved to be valuable to the expedition. She helped guide the Astorians on their way westward from the Dakota region, across the northern plains to the Snake River, the COLUMBIA RIVER, and the Pacific coast. Dorion's linguistic ability also helped Hunt's party deal peaceably with the numerous Indian tribes.

Pregnant with her third child on the journey, Dorion gave birth to a son in December 1811. The infant survived only about eight days, however. The Astorians reached the mouth of the Columbia and Astoria the following February.

Dorion and her family remained at Astoria a year and a half, until fall 1813, when Astor's agents sold the Oregon outpost to the NORTH WEST COMPANY, anticipating its seizure by the British in the War of 1812. The Dorions were part of a group of trappers journeying eastward to the Snake River of what is now western Idaho to contact one of the Astorian trapping parties before returning to St. Louis. Along the way, they suffered from repeated Indian attacks. Her husband and the other trappers were killed, leaving Dorion and her two small children as the only survivors.

Dorion continued eastward to join Hunt's party. She managed to cross the Snake River, but heavy winter snows made the trail through the Blue Mountains of what is now northeastern Oregon and southeastern Washington impassable. She had to kill the remaining horses, drying their meat to preserve as food. For shelter, she fashioned a makeshift tent out of the hides of the slaughtered animals.

With the coming of spring, Dorion and her children turned back westward, making their way across 250 miles of wilderness to the land of Walla Walla Indians at the confluence of the Snake and upper Columbia Rivers in present-day southeastern Washington. She eventually met up with the rest of the Astorians, on their way back to St. Louis. She opted to stay in the West, however, heading northward to the Okanogan Mountains near the present-day Washington–British Columbia border.

Dorion settled at Fort Okanogan, marrying a trapper by the name of Venier. Within three years, however, Venier either had died or deserted her. By 1823, Dorion was living at Fort Walla Walla to the south, married to her third husband, Jean Baptiste Toupin, the post's interpreter. In the early 1840s, Dorion and Toupin migrated southwestward to the Willamette Valley, near what is now Salem, Oregon, where she spent her remaining years.

Dorion's eldest son, Baptiste Dorion, went on to work as an interpreter for the HUDSON'S BAY COMPANY in the Columbia River region. He subsequently worked in the upper Missouri River and Yellowstone region; one of his assignments was as interpreter for ALEXANDER PHILIPP MAXIMILIAN and KARL BODMER in spring 1833.

Like the Shoshone woman SACAJAWEA (Sacagawea), who traveled with the expedition of MERIWETHER LEWIS and WILLIAM CLARK, Marie Dorion played an important role in one of the early overland journeys by non-Indians to the Far West.

Dorion, Pierre, Jr. (unknown–1814) *American trader, guide, interpreter on the upper Missouri River, son of Pierre Dorion, Sr., husband of Marie Dorion*

Pierre Dorion, Jr., born along the MISSOURI RIVER, was the son of PIERRE DORION, SR., and his Sioux (Dakota, Lakota, Nakota) Indian wife. He grew up learning many of the frontier skills of his father and of his mother's people.

By 1804, the younger Dorion was representing the CHOUTEAU family of St. Louis in the FUR TRADE with the Sioux. In June of that year, his father had been engaged as an interpreter to the Sioux for the Lewis and Clark Expedition. On August 31, 1804, Dorion joined his father, MERIWETHER LEWIS, and WILLIAM CLARK in a conference with Yankton Sioux leaders near the confluence of the James and Missouri Rivers in present-day South Dakota. At this meeting, he persuaded the Indians to deal with American traders from St. Louis, rather than with British traders operating out of Canada. Soon afterward, Dorion, with his father, accompanied a delegation of Sioux to Washington, D.C., where they were received by President Thomas Jefferson and other federal officials.

In about 1806, Dorion married the Ioway Indian woman Marie Aioe, who became known as MARIE DORION. Until 1810, he took part in St. Louis fur trader MANUEL LISA's expeditions to the upper Missouri.

In 1811–12, Dorion and his wife, acting as interpreters and guides, accompanied WILSON PRICE HUNT and his party of Astorians from St. Louis up the Missouri, across the northern plains and ROCKY MOUNTAINS, to the Oregon Coast. This was the overland contingent of JOHN JACOB ASTOR's fur-trading enterprise to the mouth of the COLUMBIA RIVER on the Pacific coast. Three years later, in January 1814, near the confluence of the Boise and Snake Rivers along the present-day Idaho-Oregon border, Dorion was killed by Indians.

Pierre Dorion, Jr., took part in the initial American penetration of the upper Missouri with Lewis and Clark; with Lisa and Hunt, he was a member of the first two major overland commercial expeditions westward from St. Louis.

Dorion, Pierre, Sr. (ca. 1750–ca. 1820) *French-Canadian interpreter, trader, guide along the Missouri River, father of Pierre Dorion, Jr.*

A native of Quebec, Pierre Dorion, Sr., was a member of a prominent French-Canadian family. Sometime before 1780, he moved to the frontier region of the upper MISSOURI RIVER, where he developed extensive contacts with the Sioux (Dakota, Lakota, Nakota) Indians of what is now South Dakota and mastered several Siouan dialects.

In early June 1804, Dorion met MERIWETHER LEWIS and WILLIAM CLARK as they traveled up the Missouri out of St. Louis. Because of his knowledge of Indian languages and customs, he was hired as an interpreter to the Sioux tribes. He also aided the Corps of Discovery with his knowledge of the region's geography. That August, he served as the interpreter at a conference between the Americans and several prominent Sioux chiefs. He also traveled with a delegation of Sioux leaders to visit Washington, D.C., and meet with President Thomas Jefferson.

In 1805–06, Dorion was hired by federal officials to transport a shipment of presents to the Arikara Indians north of Council Bluffs, as reparations for an Arikara chief who had become ill and died on a visit to the nations's capital. He was accompanied on this journey up the Missouri River by RENÉ JUSSEAUME.

Dorion was married, at various times, to several Sioux women. One of his mixed-blood children, PIERRE DORION, JR., would later serve as guide and interpreter for WILSON PRICE HUNT during his expedition from St. Louis to Astoria on the Oregon coast.

Dorion settled permanently on the Missouri River among the Sioux, near a fur-trading post that developed into the modern city of Pierre, South Dakota.

Frontiersmen such as Pierre Dorion, Sr., with their knowledge of Indian country, customs, and languages, were essential to the non-Indian exploration of North America.

D'Orville, Albert   See ORVILLE, ALBERT D'.

Doudart de Lagrée, Ernest-Marc-Louis de Gonzague (1823–1868) *French naval officer, diplomat in Southeast Asia*

Ernest Doudart de Lagrée was born in St. Vincent de Mercure, in southeastern France's Isère region. In 1845, he embarked on a career as a French naval officer, later taking part in the Crimean War of 1854.

After commanding troops in French military actions in Southeast Asia in 1862, Doudart de Lagrée was named as his nation's ambassador to the king of Cambodia. Through his diplomatic efforts, the French were soon able to establish a colonial presence in Cambodia and neighboring Vietnam.

In 1866, Doudart de Lagrée, by then a commander in the French navy, was commissioned to lead the French government-sponsored Mekong Expedition. Inspired and promoted by French colonial official MARIE-JOSEPH-FRANÇOIS GARNIER, the purpose of the expedition was to explore the upper reaches of the Mekong River to determine whether it could be used as a trade route into China. In June of that year, Doudart de Lagrée led a party of 21 men, including Garnier as second in command, up the Mekong River from Saigon (present-day Ho Chi Minh City), Vietnam.

Members of Doudart de Lagrée's party, led by Garnier, conducted a scientific survey of Cambodia's Angkor ruins. On coming upon the Sambor Rapids and the Khone Falls near the Cambodia-Laos border, Doudart de Lagrée and Garnier concluded that the Mekong would not provide a usable commercial water route from the Southeast Asian coast into China. They then set about making a scientific survey of the largely unknown region east of the Mekong, the Bolevens Plateau in southern Laos.

Although weakened by tropical fever contracted in southern Laos, Doudart de Lagrée continued toward southeastern China. By the time the expedition had entered China in August 1867, he was further afflicted with amoebic dysentery. He managed to reach Yunnan province, where he died the following March. Garnier took command, leading the expedition back to Saigon two months later.

Ernest Doudart de Lagrée's geographic expedition revealed much about the territory around the upper Mekong River. His notes and journals, published by Garnier, provided a detailed account of a region of Southeast Asia, which, at that time, had seldom been visited by Europeans. With Garnier, he was the first European to report on the unnavigability of the upper Mekong, a factor that led French colonial interests to concentrate their efforts on the region around the Gulf of Tonkin.

Charles Montagu Doughty *(Library of Congress)*

Doughty, Charles Montagu (1843–1926)
British writer and traveler in Arabia

Born in England to a well-off family, Charles Montagu Doughty studied geology at Cambridge University, graduating in 1865. Soon afterward, he traveled to Norway for field work on glaciers, then lived for a time in Scotland, studying philology.

During the late 1860s and early 1870s, Doughty continued his scientific and classical education at Oxford as well as at universities in Germany, Denmark, and France.

In 1875, Doughty left England for the Middle East, arriving in what is now Israel, from where he traveled into the Sinai region and the Jordan River Valley. By November 1876, he was in Damascus, Syria, and joined a caravan of Muslim pilgrims headed across the Arabian desert to the holy cities of Mecca and Medina. Unlike his predecessors JOHANN LUDWIG BURCKHARDT and SIR RICHARD FRANCIS BURTON, Doughty refrained from pretending to be a Muslim, although he did adopt native dress. As a self-professed Christian in Arabia, he did suffer occasional bad treatment. At the ruins of the ancient city of Petra (Wadi Musa), Doughty studied stone inscriptions. He also found writings at Mada' in Salih. From there, he went on his own into western and central Arabia, traveling with different bands of nomadic bedouins. At Tayma, he located an inscription on an ancient wall that corresponded with the biblical story of Job. His journey with the bedouins took him through the Najd Desert, from Buraida to Jidda on the coast of the RED SEA, along a route that followed the mountain fringe of the central Arabian deserts. He left from Jidda for England in 1878.

Upon his return, Doughty wrote a long account of his experiences, entitled *Travels in Arabia Deserta,* first published in 1888. This work, known for its eccentric style, reminiscent of Elizabethan prose and the type of language found in the Bible, provided Victorian England with one of the most personal and detailed accounts of Arabian life and culture up to that time. THOMAS EDWARD LAWRENCE (Lawrence of Arabia) cited Doughty's *Arabia Deserta* as having had a profound influence on his own travels and writings.

Along with Burton and Burckhardt, Charles Montagu Doughty is considered one of the greatest explorers of Arabia. His archaeological observations in Arabia increased historical knowledge about the pre-Islamic Nabataean civilization. He also provided European geographers with the earliest accounts of the lava beds, known as Harras, at the western edges of the Nafud and Najd Deserts. He is also well known for several volumes of poetry published in the early 1900s.

Drake, Sir Francis (ca. 1540–1596) *English mariner, privateer in the Americas and the Pacific Ocean, cousin of Sir John Hawkins*

Francis Drake was born in Tavistock in Devonshire, England, the eldest of 12 children of a farm worker. His parents were early converts to Puritanism, and his father, who had become a lay preacher, fled to Kent in the face of religious persecution. Raised on the southeast coast of England near Dover, the young Drake embarked on a seafaring career in his early teens.

Although Drake had only a rudimentary education, he acquired a practical knowledge of navigation and ship-handling during years of cruising the North Sea and the Bay of Biscay. A relative of SIR JOHN HAWKINS and his family of shipowners in Plymouth, Drake went to work with them.

In 1567–68, Drake commanded the *Judith* in an expedition to the north coast of South America and the Gulf of Mexico. With Hawkins, he eluded capture by the Spanish off the coast of Veracruz, Mexico. On his return to England, Drake's exploits came to the attention of Queen Elizabeth I and her secretary of state, Sir William Cecil. The queen commissioned Drake to undertake privateering expeditions against Spanish shipping in the WEST INDIES.

Starting in 1570, Drake regularly sailed to the Caribbean and the SPANISH MAIN for attacks on both Spanish ships and colonial settlements. In 1572, he made his most successful series of raids, in which he attacked and looted Nombre de Dios, Panama, and Cartagena in what is now Colombia. He then led his forces inland across the Isthmus of Panama, capturing a gold-laden mule train on its way to the royal treasury at Nombre de Dios. While in Panama in 1572, he climbed a mountain and from its peak gazed upon the Pacific Ocean, the first English sea captain to do so. He later claimed that the experience inspired him to sail the first English ship into the Pacific.

In 1573, Drake returned to England with a fortune in gold, silver, jewels, and other valuable cargo from his raids on Spanish ships and ports in the Americas. He then commanded English naval forces against rebels in Ireland. Meanwhile, English merchants and government officials had become interested in finding Terra Australis, the GREAT SOUTHERN CONTINENT of ABRAHAM ORTELIUS's 1570 atlas of the world. With the backing of both Queen Elizabeth and merchants, an expedition was organized to locate the fabled land and, if possible, find the Pacific entrance to the STRAIT OF ANIAN, a NORTHWEST PASSAGE believed to exist through North America. Shortly before embarking in December 1577, Drake was secretly instructed by Elizabeth and her chief foreign minister, Sir Francis Walsingham, to sail through the STRAIT OF MAGELLAN and raid Spanish colonial settlements and ships on the Pacific coast of South America.

Drake's fleet of five ships sailed from Plymouth on December 13, 1577. Along with his flagship, the *Pelican* (renamed the *Golden Hind* during the voyage), were the *Elizabeth,* the *Marigold,* the *Swan,* and the *Christopher.* After leaving two of the ships at the mouth of the Rio de la Plata, off the coast of northern Argentina, Drake remained on the coast of Patagonia for about two months, during which he suppressed a mutiny on one of his vessels, executing Thomas Doughty, the leading conspirator. In August 1578, Drake and his three ships entered the Strait of Magellan, then passed into the Pacific 17 days later. Soon afterward, a series of storms struck, scattering Drake's fleet and driving his own ship, the *Golden Hind,* south and east of CAPE HORN. The *Marigold* went down with all hands, and the *Elizabeth,* blown back into the Strait of Magellan, sailed for England.

Drake, on the *Golden Hind,* determined that he had reached a latitude south of the Strait of Magellan, finding open sea beyond Tierra del Fuego, which at that time was believed by geographers to be the northern tip of the Great Southern Continent. This stretch of ocean between Cape Horn and the South Shetland Islands has since been named Drake Passage. Drake then proceeded westward past the southern end of Tierra del Fuego, proving it was an island and putting to rest rumors that prevailing winds and currents would make a westward passage south of the strait impossible.

On having found open ocean south of Tierra del Fuego, Drake abandoned his search for Terra Australis and headed northward along the coast of Chile and Peru. En route, he raided Valparaíso and captured the Spanish treasure ship *Cacafuego* off Callao. In addition to gold and silver, Drake also captured secret Spanish charts that guided him on his subsequent explorations of the west coast of the Americas and the Pacific.

Drake's search for the Pacific entrance to the Northwest Passage took him as far north as Vancouver Island near the present United States–Canada border. At that point, the coastline extended to the northwest, and Drake abandoned the quest, heading back southward along the Oregon and California coast. At Point Reyes, California, north of San Francisco, he put in at a natural harbor later known as Drake's Bay. While the *Golden Hind* underwent repairs on the beach, a small party of Drake's men explored about 30 miles inland from the coast. Drake took possession of the region in the name of Queen Elizabeth, calling it Nova Albion, the ancient name for England, because the coast at

Sir Francis Drake *(New York State Library, Albany)*

Drake's Bay reminded him of the White Cliffs of Dover near his home in Kent. The exact location of their landing has never been determined—either California or Oregon.

Drake and the *Golden Hind* left the California coast in July 1579, failing to sight the Golden Gate and San Francisco Bay because of heavy fog. Sailing westward, he stopped briefly at the Farallon Islands, several miles off the coast of San Francisco, where the crew stocked up on supplies of seal meat. Drake's voyage across the Pacific took him within sight of the Mariana Islands. In the Philippines, he again wreaked havoc on Spanish ships. At that time, no English maritime forces had entered the Pacific, and the Spanish were taken off-guard by Drake's attacks. Some sources suggest that Drake intended to return to England through the Strait of Magellan, but with Spanish warships pursuing him from the south, and his own ship heavily laden with loot, he decided a westward course back to England would be more prudent.

By October 1579, Drake was in the SPICE ISLANDS (the Moluccas). In early January 1580, the *Golden Hind* was nearly lost when it ran upon a reef off the coast of the Indonesian island of Celebes. Drake demonstrated his great skill as a mariner when he saved his ship by maneuvering it off the reef without serious damage. At Ternate in the Moluccas, he entered into a trade agreement with the sultan, then sailed back to England by way of the Indian Ocean and the CAPE OF GOOD HOPE.

Having circled the world, Drake arrived back in Plymouth on September 26, 1580. Although he had not located the Great Southern Continent, Drake had brought back plundered riches showing a 5,000 percent profit on his backers' investment. The *Golden Hind,* the first English vessel to circumnavigate the world, was put on display at Deptford near London, although it fell into disrepair and had to be dismantled in the late 1600s. In November 1580, at Deptford, Queen Elizabeth went aboard and knighted Drake for his achievement. He was made mayor of Plymouth and appointed to a high naval position.

In 1585, Drake commanded English naval forces in raids on Vigo, Spain, and São Tiago in the Cape Verde Islands. He then sailed to the West Indies, where he captured Santo Domingo on Hispaniola (present-day Haiti and Dominican Republic), held Cartagena for ransom, and destroyed the Spanish settlement of St. Augustine on the east coast of Florida. In June 1586, he arrived at Roanoke, SIR WALTER RALEIGH's colony on the Carolina coast, and rescued the surviving colonists under Ralph Lane. Along with the colonists, Drake brought back two New World plants that would have a great influence on European life and culture: tobacco and the potato.

In 1587, Drake made a daring raid on the Spanish fleet at Cádiz. The next year, as a vice admiral, he played a commanding role in England's defeat of the Spanish Armada.

Drake undertook his final privateering expedition to the West Indies in 1595. With Hawkins, he attempted to attack Puerto Rico but was driven off by Spanish warships. The next year, stricken with dysentery, he died off the coast of Portobelo, Panama, and was buried at sea.

Sir Francis Drake commanded the first English circumnavigation of the world and the second such voyage, after that of FERDINAND MAGELLAN in 1519–22. His exploration of Drake Passage revised European geographic ideas about the Great Southern Continent. The chaplain on Drake's 1577–80 voyage, Francis Fletcher, wrote an account of the trip, *The World Encompass'd,* which included the earliest descriptions of what is now coastal California. In reaction to Drake's sudden appearance in the Pacific, the Spanish set about securing their position on the west coast of the Americas, and these efforts led to the seaward explorations of SEBASTIÁN VISCAÍNO to Monterey Bay, as well as the overland colonizing expedition of JUAN DE OÑATE into the American Southwest.

Drouillard, George (George Drewyer)

(ca. 1770–1810) *French-Canadian trader, guide, interpreter on the upper Missouri*

George Drouillard grew up on the frontier of the Great Lakes region. His mother was a Pawnee Indian woman, his French-Canadian father an interpreter for the British army at Detroit.

In late 1803, Drouillard joined the Corps of Discovery at its encampment at Fort Massac on the Ohio River in southern Illinois. He had been appointed on the recommendation of George Rogers Clark, the older brother of WILLIAM CLARK, coleader of the expedition with MERIWETHER LEWIS.

Drouillard, a skilled hunter and marksman, shot much of the wild game consumed during the Lewis and Clark Expedition. He also helped maintain good relations with the many tribes the expedition encountered, trading with them for food. On the return journey in spring 1806, he negotiated with the Nez Perce Indians of the Clearwater River region for the return of the horses left in their care the previous fall.

In 1807, Drouillard was part of fur trader MANUEL LISA's expedition to the mouth of the Bighorn River, during which he helped establish Fort Raymond, the first non-Indian settlement in what is now Montana. Mountain man JOHN COLTER was also part of this expedition. While in Montana, Drouillard explored the Yellowstone River country and the Absaroka Mountains. He also made fur-trading expeditions to the Rosebud and Tongue River region.

Drouillard returned to St. Louis in fall 1808, where he conferred with William Clark. From information provided by Drouillard, Clark produced the first map of the Bighorn River.

In March 1810, Drouillard made his last trip up the MISSOURI RIVER from St. Louis, traveling through Bozeman Pass to the Three Forks of the Missouri in southwestern Montana with ANDREW HENRY, PIERRE MENARD, EDWARD

ROSE, and John Colter. About two months later, near the mouth of the Jefferson River, Drouillard was killed in an ambush by Blackfeet warriors.

Drouillard's diligence as a hunter and a diplomat to the Indians contributed to the success of the Lewis and Clark Expedition. His explorations with Manuel Lisa and Andrew Henry expanded geographic knowledge of what is now central Montana and opened up the region to the St. Louis FUR TRADE.

Drygalski, Erich Dagobert von (1865–1949)
German geographer, geophysicist in Greenland and the Antarctic

Erich von Drygalski was born in Königsberg, a former German city on the Baltic, now Kaliningrad, Russia. He was educated in the earth sciences, with a special concentration in geophysics and marine studies.

In 1891, Drygalski led his first expedition to GREENLAND; the following year, he headed a scientific team that wintered in western Greenland. In 1901, Drygalski, as a leading German geophysicist and experienced polar explorer, was commissioned by his government to lead the German Antarctic Expedition. The project's aim was to study terrestrial magnetism around the South Polar region and explore unknown portions of the continent's Indian Ocean coastline.

Drygalski sailed from Kiel, Germany, on the *Gauss,* a vessel specially fitted out for polar exploration. In the southern Indian Ocean, the expedition made stops at the remote Kerguelen and Heard Islands, then headed due south for the Antarctic continent.

Drygalski and his party on the *Gauss* approached Antarctica from about 90° east longitude, along that part of the continent adjacent to the Indian Ocean. In February 1902, while still 40 miles from the Antarctic mainland, they became trapped in the PACK ICE. Over the next 12 months, Drygalski sent out exploring parties on sledges to survey a newly located strip of land he named Kaiser Wilhelm II Land, now known as Wilhelm II Coast. A captive BALLOON was employed by Drygalski and his team to make aerial observations of the interior. They also sighted the black cone of an extinct volcano on Wilhelm II Coast, which they named Gaussberg, or Mount Gauss, after their ship.

The *Gauss* remained trapped in the ice until February 1903, when under Drygalski's direction, the crew managed to free it by laying out ashes that drew enough radiated heat from the sun to melt a trench. The ship sailed through the trench into open water and back to Germany.

Drygalski wrote an account of his Antarctic experiences, *Zum Kontinent des Eisegens Sudens* (To the continent of the southern ice), published in 1904. The next year, he set to work editing the 18 volumes of the scientific reports from

Erich von Drygalski *(Library of Congress)*

the expedition, including three atlases. The task was not completed until 1931. In that time, he also held a professorship in geography at the University of Munich.

Erich von Drygalski's 1901–03 German Antarctic Expedition coincided with Scottish, Swedish, British, and French explorations in the Antarctic, all inspired by the Sixth International Geophysical Conference, which had convened in London in 1895. In recognition of his contributions to Antarctic exploration and research, a fjord on South Georgia Island and an island in Antarctica were named in his honor.

Dubuque, Julien (Julian Dubuque, Little Cloud)
(1762–1810) *French-Canadian trader, pioneer in the upper Mississippi Valley*

Julien Dubuque was born in St. Pierre les Brecquets in what is now southern Quebec, Canada. When in his early 20s, he headed westward into the upper Mississippi frontier to seek his fortune, and, in 1785, he arrived in Prairie du Chien on the upper MISSISSIPPI RIVER.

Upon exploring the region along the west shore of the Mississippi, Dubuque found lead deposits on the lands of the Fox (Mesquaki) Indians. He soon secured exclusive rights from that tribe to mine the lead on what is now the Iowa side of the Mississippi. He also established a fur-trading post there. Over the next 20 years, he made regular journeys down the Mississippi to St. Louis to trade his furs.

His lead-mining enterprise expanded to include a smelting furnace.

Dubuque originally named his settlement "The Mines of Spain," and the governor of Spanish Louisiana, Francisco Luis Hector, baron de Carondelet, granted him official title to his holdings. In 1805, Dubuque's mining operation was visited by American military explorer ZEBULON MONTGOMERY PIKE.

Julien Dubuque is credited with establishing the first non-Indian settlement in what is now Iowa. Twenty-seven years after his death, the city of Dubuque, named in his honor, was established near the site of his original settlement. He was highly regarded by the Fox Indians, who conferred upon him the name Little Cloud. When he died in 1810, he was buried with the honors of a Fox chief. His grave is located on a bluff overlooking the city that now bears his name.

Du Chaillu, Paul Belloni (ca. 1831–1903)
French-American traveler, writer in central Africa
Paul B. Du Chaillu probably was born in Paris, France. He was raised in the former colony of French Equatorial Africa (present-day Gabon on the west coast of central Africa), where his father was a trader. Educated by missionaries in his early years, he also taught himself native languages.

During the early 1850s, Du Chaillu's accounts of his hunting expeditions into the interior of equatorial Africa began to appear in American newspapers. He moved to the United States in 1852, eventually becoming an American citizen.

Starting in 1855, with the support of the Philadelphia Academy of Natural Sciences, Du Chaillu undertook a four-year exploration into uncharted regions of the lower Gabon and Ogowe Rivers. He also collected specimens of rare birds and animals, many new to science. On this expedition, while exploring the N'tem Highlands, Du Chaillu encountered a gorilla, becoming the first non-African known to have seen one. He attempted to bring two young gorillas back, but the creatures died before they reached the United States.

Du Chaillu's account of his expedition, *Explorations and Adventures in Equatorial Africa,* was published in 1861, two years after his return from Africa. His geographic reports, having no scientific data to back them up, were called into question by critics, as was his description of gorillas in the wild.

Resolving to make another exploration of the Gabon and Ogowe river regions, Du Chaillu acquired a practical knowledge of navigation to better document his explorations. From 1863 to 1865, he again explored equatorial Africa, this time verifying his findings with accurate navigational data. He also made the first known non-native contact with area tribes, confirming the existence of the Pygmy people in the lower Congo River Valley. Du Chaillu returned from this expedition with scientific data proving his earlier charts, as well as the first gorillas ever to be seen in the United States. His account of his second expedition into equatorial Africa. *A Journey into Ashango-Land,* was published in 1867.

Du Chaillu continued to produce works on Africa, including *Stories of the Gorilla Country* (1867), *Wild Life Under the Equator* (1868), and *The Country of the Dwarfs* (1871). In 1871, he began seven years of extensive travel in Scandinavia, which he wrote about in his later books. He died in 1903 while on a visit to Russia.

Although his assertions were met with skepticism among his peers, Paul B. Du Chaillu's geographic findings in west-central Africa were proven accurate in later explorations. His accounts of gorillas in the African wild were also confirmed.

Duclos-Guyot, Pierre-Nicolas (1722–1794)
French naval officer in the South Atlantic and South Pacific
A native of the northwestern French seaport of Saint-Malo, Pierre Duclos-Guyot went to sea when he was 13, serving his apprenticeship on merchant ships until 1742. That year, he entered the service of the BRITISH EAST INDIA COMPANY's fleet as an ensign, and soon afterward he was commissioned a lieutenant.

In 1759, during the Seven Years War, Duclos-Guyot accompanied LOUIS-ANTOINE DE BOUGAINVILLE in a French naval expedition to Quebec. After the war in 1764, he commanded the *Aigle* in Bougainville's colonizing efforts in the Falkland Islands. In 1765, he commanded the *Lion* in a voyage from the Falklands to the Pacific coast of South America. On his return trip, he located South Georgia Island in the South Atlantic Ocean.

Duclos-Guyot was second in command on the *Boudeuse* in Bougainville's 1766–69 CIRCUMNAVIGATION OF THE WORLD. In 1777, he became captain of the port of Île de France, on present-day Mauritius in the Indian Ocean, serving in that post until health problems caused him to leave active naval service in 1784. Back in France, he returned to the navy with the outbreak of the French Revolutionary Wars in 1792. He died near Saint-Malo two years later.

Pierre Duclos-Guyot made the second recorded sighting of South Georgia Island in 1765, the first having been made by Anglo-French merchant-captain Antoine de la Roche in 1675. In 1775, JAMES COOK charted the island, named it, and claimed it for Great Britain. In the ensuing years, South Georgia Island became strategically important in explorations of Antarctica. Duclos-Guyot also played a significant role in the first official French circumnavigation of the world.

Duluth, Daniel Greysolon (sieur Duluth, sieur Dulhut, sieur Du Luth, sieur Du Lhut)

(1636–1710) *French fur trader and soldier in Great Lakes, cousin of Henri de Tonti*

Daniel Greysolon, sieur Duluth was born in the French city of Saint-Germain-en-Laye, just west of Paris. He fought for France in the Dutch Wars of the 1670s, taking part in the 1674 French victory at Seneffe, Belgium.

Shortly afterward, Duluth traveled to Montreal, Canada, along with his younger brother, Claude Greysolon, sieur de la Tourette. Meanwhile, his cousin HENRI DE TONTI was in the employ of RENÉ-ROBERT CAVELIER DE LA SALLE.

In 1678, Duluth was sent by French officials westward from Montreal to negotiate a peace between the warring Sioux (Dakota, Lakota, Nakota) and Chippewa (Ojibway) tribes in the western Great Lakes region of present-day Michigan, Wisconsin, and Minnesota. Additionally, Duluth was commissioned to further the search for a route to the Pacific Ocean, which many geographers then thought was not far to the west of the Great Lakes. For this expedition, he commanded a party of COUREURS DE BOIS, fur traders whose quasi-legal status would later cause Duluth difficulties with the French colonial authorities.

Traveling along the usual CANOE and portage routes from Montreal, Duluth and his men reached Lake Huron, then spent the winter of 1678–79 at Sault Sainte Marie. In spring 1679, he headed northwestward into Lake Superior and followed its south shore to its eastern terminus, near the site of the present-day city of Duluth, Minnesota. Duluth and his party continued westward into the interior of present-day Minnesota to the Sioux settlements at Mille Lacs Lake.

There, in 1679, Duluth secured a peace agreement that ended hostilities between the Sioux and Chippewa Indians, thus opening up the region's FUR TRADE to the French. That same year, at the Sioux village of Izatys, Duluth claimed the region around western Lake Superior for France.

Duluth also dispatched an advance party to explore westward. This group may have reached the region of present-day eastern North Dakota. Duluth's men later returned with reports of Sioux who had obtained salt from a body of water some three weeks' journey to the west. Hearing this, Duluth speculated that the salt had come from the shores of an outlet to the Great Western Sea and concluded that the Pacific Ocean, and the riches of China and the Orient, could easily be reached from the western Great Lakes. Some historians have speculated that the Sioux had meant the Great Salt Lake of Utah, but others doubt that the Minnesota and North Dakota Sioux ranged that far west. It has also been conjectured that the Indians actually obtained their salt from deposits along the Red River of the North in northeastern North Dakota.

To further stabilize the fur trade, Duluth had to arrange a peace settlement between the Sioux and Assiniboine. In search of other Indian bands, he headed northeastward along the shore of Lake Superior, wintering at the mouth of the Kaministikwia River, the site of present-day Fort William, Ontario. In summer 1680, Duluth set out in search of a route to the Western Sea. Traveling southwestward, then south along the St. Croix River, along part of what is now the Wisconsin-Minnesota boundary, he reached the MISSISSIPPI RIVER near present-day Prescott, Wisconsin. At one point in his explorations, confident that he was nearing the Pacific, he reported that the Sioux he encountered spoke with Chinese accents.

In the course of his travels, Duluth learned that several members of La Salle's expedition were held captive by the Sioux. He returned to Mille Lacs Lake to obtain the release of MICHEL ACO, La Salle's lieutenant, and LOUIS HENNEPIN, a Belgian priest and, like Duluth, a veteran of the Battle of Seneffe. Duluth then escorted Aco and Hennepin to Mackinac, where they spent the winter of 1680–81. In spring 1681, Duluth was recalled to France amid charges of illegal fur trading with his band of coureurs de bois.

Acquitted of any wrongdoing, Duluth returned to Lake Superior in 1683. He established a trading fort at the mouth of the Kaministikwia River on Lake Superior's northwest shore. In 1683–84, Duluth assisted his brother Claude in establishing a second trading post in the area, Fort Tourette on the northeast shore of Lake Nipigon in present-day Ontario.

At the outbreak of fighting between the French and the Iroquois (Haudenosaunee) Indians in 1683, Duluth was sent to take charge of a company of soldiers in the St. Clair River region, the water link between Lake Huron and Lake Erie. He established Fort St. Joseph on the St. Clair River in 1686 and subsequently commanded Fort Frontenac at the eastern end of Lake Ontario.

In 1688, Duluth and his fur-trading associates returned to western Lake Superior and established a trading post at Rainy Lake. This site, 200 miles east of present-day Winnipeg, was at that time the westernmost extent of French settlement into the interior of Canada. Seven years later, in 1695, Duluth was forced to retire to Montreal because of failing health.

Through his voyages of diplomacy, trade, and exploration, sieur Duluth advanced knowledge of the western frontier to French interests. His ability to negotiate peace among warring tribes of the western Great Lakes enabled the rapid commercial development of the region.

Dumont d'Urville, Jules-Sébastien-César

(1790–1842) *French naval officer in the Pacific and Antarctica*

A native of France's Normandy region, Jules Dumont d'Urville was born in Condé-sur-Noireau, Calvados, to a noble family of modest means. His father died when he was seven, and his early education was under the direction of his uncle, a priest.

After attending school at Caen, Dumont d'Urville entered the French navy in 1807 as a cadet. While at the naval academy at Toulon, he studied botany and entomology, becoming an accomplished naturalist as well as a midshipman. Graduating in 1810, he reached the rank of ensign two years later.

In 1819, Dumont d'Urville sailed on the *Chevrette* to the eastern MEDITERRANEAN SEA where he charted the Dardanelles and the Black Sea. While cruising the Aegean Sea in 1820, he secured for France an ancient statue of Venus that had recently been discovered on the Greek island of Milos. The Venus de Milo was subsequently presented to the Louvre in Paris; for his efforts in this regard, Dumont d'Urville was inducted into the Legion of Honor in 1821.

Commissioned a lieutenant commander, Dumont d'Urville continued his naturalist studies at the Museum of Natural History in Paris. In 1822, he sailed on the *Coquille* as second in command under LOUIS-ISADORE DUPERREY in a voyage around the world. Throughout the expedition, which included stops at the Gilbert and Caroline archipelagoes in the Pacific Ocean as well as the Falklands and other islands in the South Atlantic, Dumont d'Urville collected thousands of plant and insect specimens, many of which were new to science.

Following his return from his voyage on the *Coquille* in spring 1825, Dumont d'Urville submitted a plan to the French navy for another expedition to study a limited area of the far western Pacific. His expedition won approval a few months later, and, at the rank of captain, he was given command of the *Coquille*. In addition to producing maps and studying flora, fauna, and native languages, Dumont d'Urville was directed to search for traces of the lost expedition of JEAN-FRANÇOIS DE GALAUP, comte de La Pérouse, missing in the Pacific since 1788.

In April 1826, Dumont d'Urville embarked from Toulon aboard the *Coquille,* renamed the *Astrolabe* after one of the vessels in La Pérouse's expedition. He first surveyed the entire southern coast of Australia, then explored an uncharted inlet, Jervis Bay, near Sydney. The naturalists and ethnologists with the expedition made a study of the Aborigines. While visiting Parramatta, also near Sydney, Dumont d'Urville met with British missionary SAMUEL MARSDEN, who provided him with information on NEW ZEALAND.

Dumont d'Urville sailed next to Cook Strait between the North Island and South Island of New Zealand. He had some contact with the region's Maori natives and undertook a study of New Zealand wildlife. In New Zealand, he was the first European to observe the kiwi bird in its native habitat. An island off the north coast of New Zealand's South Island was subsequently named after him.

From New Zealand, Dumont d'Urville's expedition sailed to the Fiji archipelago, where he charted more than 120 islands. He then visited the Laughlan Islands and located and named the great Astrolabe Reef off Vatulele.

After exploring the Loyalty Islands and New Ireland off the coast of New Guinea, Dumont d'Urville stopped at Hobart, Tasmania, where he learned from an English sea captain that natives on Vanikoro, north of the New Hebrides, had been seen with items that may have come from the La Pérouse expedition. Upon reaching Vanikoro, his men sighted wreckage from La Pérouse's ships on offshore reefs. Dumont d'Urville raised a monument there in memory of La Pérouse and the original *Astrolabe,* then sailed to Guam in the Marianas. From there, he returned to France, arriving in Marseilles in late February 1829.

Although his expedition had brought back much new scientific information on the western Pacific, Dumont d'Urville did not receive the recognition of the French Academy of Sciences as he had hoped. In 1830, he commanded the ship that took deposed French monarch Charles X and his family to England.

In 1832–34, Dumont d'Urville published his *Picturesque Journey Around the World,* which summarized European voyages around the world since FERDINAND

Jules Dumont d'Urville *(Library of Congress)*

MAGELLAN's journey for Spain. The popular success of this work led to Dumont d'Urville's next assignment, that of exploring the southern latitudes and locating the SOUTH MAGNETIC POLE. Sailing from Toulon in September 1837, the expedition included the *Astrolabe* as well as a corvette, the *Zélée.* The ships reached Tierra del Fuego at the tip of South America and attempted to penetrate the Antarctic ice pack. In early February 1838, the ships were trapped for five days in the ice at about 63° south latitude. During this period, the crew sighted land on the Antarctic coast. Dumont d'Urville named one section of the coastline Louis-Phillipe Land, after the reigning French king, and another part of the mainland Joinville Land, after the king's son, the Prince of Joinville. These sections of the Antarctic mainland were actually uncharted sections of Graham Land on the Antarctic Peninsula.

From the Antarctic, Dumont d'Urville took his ships to the South Orkney and South Shetland Islands and conducted meteorological studies and readings of deep-sea temperature. He proceeded up the Pacific coast of South America to Valparaíso, Chile, and, after a stopover of several months, sailed westward across the Pacific to Tahiti and the Tonga Islands. In the Fiji Islands, Dumont d'Urville directed a punitive action against a native village for the murder of a French naval officer on an earlier expedition. He then cruised throughout the Solomon and Caroline Islands, visited several Dutch colonial ports in present-day Indonesia, and arrived at Hobart, TASMANIA, in December 1839.

In Hobart, Dumont d'Urville conferred with the governor of Tasmania, SIR JOHN FRANKLIN, and with English seal-hunter JOHN BISCOE, who had sailed into the Antarctic some years earlier. With a large portion of his crew ill with dysentery and SCURVY, Dumont d'Urville left the *Zélée* at Hobart and undertook a search for the South Magnetic Pole with only the *Astrolabe.* He crossed the ANTARCTIC CIRCLE, reaching a latitude of 73° south, and sighted a portion of the mainland he named Adélie Land (now the Adélie Coast) after his wife. He also determined that the South Magnetic Pole was situated nearby. Soon afterward, he sighted an American vessel, the *Porpoise,* one of the ships in Lieutenant CHARLES WILKES's expedition. Neither ship acknowledged the other, and the incident was the cause of controversy over the European discovery of that portion of the Antarctic continent.

Dumont d'Urville returned to Hobart. With both ships, he undertook additional explorations of the Loyalty Islands and the Louisiade Archipelago off the coast of New Guinea, before returning to France by way of the Indian Ocean and the CAPE OF GOOD HOPE.

Dumont d'Urville reached Toulon, France, in early November 1840. He was soon promoted to the rank of rear admiral, awarded a medal by the Geographical Society of Paris and commissioned to write an account of his voyage to the Antarctic. In May 1842, he was killed along with his wife and son in a railroad accident near Versailles. His *Voyage to the South Pole and Oceania,* a 23-volume work with seven atlases, was published between 1841 and 1854.

Jules Dumont d'Urville's voyage to the Pacific in 1826–29 brought back much new scientific and geographic data and also shed light on the fate of the earlier La Pérouse expedition. Geographers identified Melanesia, Micronesia, and Polynesia (*see* OCEANIA) as the major divisions of the island groups of the Pacific as a result of his explorations. Moreover, he led the first French expedition to the Antarctic in 1837–40. Near the Adélie Coast, not far from the South Magnetic Pole, which he located, the French subsequently established a permanent scientific base in 1950, named Dumont d'Urville Station in his honor.

Dunbar, Sir William (1749–1810) *Scottish scientist, surveyor in the lower Mississippi Valley*

The son of a nobleman, William Dunbar was born on his family's estate near Elgin, in Morayshire, Scotland. Following his early education in Glasgow, he studied astronomy and mathematics in London.

In 1771, Dunbar moved to North America for health reasons, settling for a brief time at Fort Pitt, present-day Pittsburgh, Pennsylvania. Two years later, he went into partnership with another native of Scotland, Philadelphia merchant John Ross. Together they established a plantation near Baton Rouge in the present state of Louisiana, then part of British-held West Florida.

Dunbar and his partner suffered financial reverses in 1775, losing much of the plantation's labor force in a slave uprising. The outbreak of the American Revolution brought additional losses. Continental troops sacked their plantation in 1778, and soon afterward, marauding Spanish forces further depleted their holdings.

Dunbar and Ross founded a new plantation in 1792, near present-day Natchez, Mississippi. With his background in science, Dunbar instituted such innovations as an improved cotton gin and a technique to pack cotton in bales by means of a screw-press. He was also instrumental in promoting the manufacture of cottonseed oil. These advancements helped him recover his earlier losses; he eventually bought out his partner and became the sole proprietor of the Natchez plantation, which he called "The Forest."

In 1798, Dunbar took part in a boundary survey to determine the demarcation line between Spanish and U.S. territory along the lower MISSISSIPPI RIVER. Although he acted as the Spanish representative, his findings resulted in Natchez becoming part of the newly established U.S. territory of Mississippi. He soon became a U.S. citizen and was appointed surveyor general of Mississippi. In addition to operating his plantation, Dunbar continued his scientific research, and in 1799, he made the first meteorological observations in the Mississippi Valley.

Dunbar's scientific work came to the attention of Thomas Jefferson, under whose sponsorship he was elected to the American Philosophical Society. With the acquisition of the Louisiana Territory in 1803, Jefferson commissioned Dunbar to undertake a survey of its southwestern boundary and explore the Red River to its source. Accompanied by chemist George Hunter and a detachment of 17 men, Dunbar set out from Natchez in October 1804 and explored the Red River in what is now Arkansas and Louisiana. Near the border of Spanish-held Texas, they received word that their expedition would be unwelcome to the Spanish, so they turned their attention to the Ouachita River. On that river, Hunter examined natural mineral springs, where he made the first extensive chemical analysis of the phenomenon. The site—present-day Hot Springs, Arkansas—later became a national park and health resort. Dunbar submitted a report of his explorations, entitled *Documents Relating to the Purchase and Explorations of Louisiana*. It was published in 1904, to commemorate the centennial of the Louisiana Purchase.

Dunbar continued to undertake scientific studies at his Natchez plantation, including work on the Mississippi Delta and an examination of fossil bones he uncovered in Louisiana. In his time, he was considered the leading scientist in the lower Mississippi region, and many of his scientific papers were published by the American Philosophical Society. He also later served in the Mississippi territorial legislature. Significant to the history of exploration was a technique he developed that enabled him to single-handedly determine longitude without the aid of a timepiece. He was known as Sir William Dunbar by virtue of a hereditary title.

Sir William Dunbar undertook one of the earliest U.S. government–sponsored explorations into the frontier regions acquired in the Louisiana Purchase of 1803. Other expeditions into the new territory during the same period included one led by MERIWETHER LEWIS and WILLIAM CLARK and another led by ZEBULON MONTGOMERY PIKE.

Duperrey, Louis-Isadore (1786–1865) *French naval officer, scientist in the Pacific, the South Atlantic, and South America*

Born in Paris, Louis-Isadore Duperrey entered the French navy when he was 17. In 1809, he took part in a French naval cruise along the coast of Italy, during which he produced charts of the waters between Tuscany and the island of Corsica.

Promoted to second lieutenant in 1817, Duperrey sailed the Pacific Ocean on the *Uranie* under the command of LOUIS-CLAUDE DE SAULCES DE FREYCINET. Following the wreck of that vessel in the Falklands in February 1820, he returned to France.

In 1821, Duperrey cruised the eastern MEDITERRANEAN SEA with JULES-SÉBASTIEN-CÉSAR DUMONT D'URVILLE. Later that year, he presented the French government with a plan for an expedition around the world to complete the work left incomplete by Freycinet's 1817–20 voyage.

Duperrey won approval for his expedition directly from French monarch Louis XVIII. Promoted to lieutenant commander, he departed Toulon on August 11, 1822. His second in command was Dumont d'Urville. After stopping at the CANARY ISLANDS, Duperrey sailed westward across the Atlantic Ocean to the island of Santa Catarina, off the coast of Brazil, arriving just in time to witness a popular uprising against Portuguese rule. The expedition then visited the Falkland Islands, viewing the wreckage of the *Uranie*. On East Falkland Island, the expedition's naturalists made a study of birds.

Duperrey then returned to the South American mainland, sailing southward along the coast of Patagonia to Tierra del Fuego. After rounding CAPE HORN, he headed up the Pacific coast of Chile, putting in at Concepción, where a military coup was under way. With some other scientists, he made several expeditions into the interior to make a study of the Araucanian Indians. The *Coquille* then continued on to Peru, visiting the ports of Callao and Paita. Situated on the north coast of Peru, Paita was the site of Duperrey's scientific observations relating to terrestrial magnetism near the EQUATOR.

From Peru, Duperrey and the *Coquille* sailed across the Pacific, stopping first in the Tuamotu Archipelago, where he charted several islands. He and his crew were the first Frenchmen to visit Tahiti since LOUIS-ANTOINE DE BOUGAINVILLE in the late 1760s. Duperrey's subsequent report revealed that Tahitian social mores had become more conservative after 40 years of British missionary influence. While in the Society Islands, he charted the region around Bora Bora, correcting the errors of previous navigators and cartographers.

In the western Pacific, Duperrey explored around the north coast of New Guinea, reconnoitering the volcanic island of Waigeo, one of the Moluccas.

After a visit to the British colony at Sydney, Duperrey sailed northward into the Carolines, where he located and named the island of Ualan. He then returned to France by way of Java, Mauritius, and the CAPE OF GOOD HOPE.

Duperrey and the *Coquille* arrived in Marseilles on March 24, 1825. His account of the voyage, as well as the published reports of the expedition's scientists, began to appear the following year.

In the years following his voyage on the *Coquille*, Duperrey turned his attention to producing scientific works on physics and geography. He was made an officer of the Legion of Honor and went on to become president of the French Academy.

One of the most notable discoveries of the 1822–25 expedition was made by Louis-Isadore Duperrey himself. By observing the variations in the movements of a pendulum at different latitudes, he was able to determine that the surface of the Earth flattened near the NORTH POLE and SOUTH POLE. His later published works included a map of the movements of OCEAN CURRENTS throughout the world. He was the first to show how the Atlantic Ocean current, resulting from the outflow of South America's Río de la Plata, was divided into two distinct streams; and he identified the source of the Humboldt Current, which caused low ocean temperatures in the coastal waters of Peru.

Dupetit-Thouars, Abel-Aubert (1793–1864)
French naval officer in the South Pacific
Abel-Aubert Dupetit-Thouars was born in La Fessardier, in the Loire Valley of France, near the town of Saumur, the son of a French naval captain. His uncle was the botanist and plant physiologist Charles-Marie Dupetit-Thouars.

In his early teens, Dupetit-Thouars entered the French navy as a midshipman, sailing with the fleet based at Boulogne. In 1829–30, he took part in the French conquest of Algeria.

By 1830, Dupetit-Thouars was commanding French warships; that year, as captain of the *Griffon,* he cruised the west coast of South America. The expedition's goals, unlike those of earlier French naval forays into the Pacific Ocean, were less scientific than political. At Callao, Peru, he met with the nation's leaders, to whom he voiced his country's concern over possible British encroachment in that newly independent nation.

In 1836, Dupetit-Thouars commanded the *Venus* in a three-year French naval expedition around the world. On this voyage, while stopping in Tahiti in September 1838, he was joined by fellow French navigator JULES-SÉBASTIEN-CÉSAR DUMONT D'URVILLE and his expedition. In an audience with Pomare, queen of Tahiti, Dupetit-Thouars and Dumont D'Urville expressed the French government's displeasure over her having recently expelled two French Catholic missionary priests, which, as it turned out, had been done at the urging of rival Protestant missionaries on the island.

Dupetit-Thouars was made a rear admiral in 1841; the following year, in command of the *Reine Blanche,* he led an expedition to Tahiti and the Marquesas that brought those islands under French domination. Appointed a vice admiral in 1849, he went on to serve as a representative in the French legislature.

Starting in 1840, and continuing for the next 24 years, Abel-Aubert Dupetit-Thouars wrote and published an 11-volume account of his CIRCUMNAVIGATION OF THE WORLD. His diplomatic efforts in 1842–43 were vital in establishing France's colonial presence in Tahiti and the south-central Pacific, and marked the culmination of French exploration in the Pacific begun by LOUIS-ANTOINE DE BOUGAINVILLE in the 1760s.

Dupuis, Jean (1829–1912) *French trader in China and Southeast Asia*
A native of France, Jean Dupuis traveled to China in the early 1850s to make his fortune. He soon established himself as a trader at Shanghai; he expanded his operations to include Hankow (now part of Wuhan) after 1862, with the opening of that inland YANGTZE RIVER (Chang) port to foreigners.

Dupuis dealt mainly in armaments, and his contacts in the Chinese civil government and the military provided him with extensive knowledge of the vast country's interior. In the 1860s, French colonial interests were seeking a navigable water route from the coast of Southeast Asia into southeastern China's Yunnan province. One expedition, led by ERNEST DOUDART DE LAGRÉE and MARIE-JOSEPH-FRANÇOIS GARNIER, had attempted, without success, to find such a route by ascending the Mekong River. Dupuis had met with that party when it stopped at Hankow in 1868.

In 1871, Dupuis, in an attempt to establish the route on his own, traveled down the Red River from Yunnan province and reached the coast of northern Vietnam. His subsequent written account included the earliest descriptions by a European of that part of Southeast Asia.

Two years later, Jean Dupuis attempted to repeat his earlier exploit in reverse; his efforts met with resistance from Vietnamese officials. His arrest and detention at Hanoi provided French colonial leaders with a motive to mount an invasion of northern Vietnam and extend their colonial influence throughout the entire country.

Jean Dupuis's trading and exploring expeditions laid the foundation for French colonial influence in that part of Southeast Asia.

Duveyrier, Henri (1840–1892) *French explorer in North Africa*
Henri Duveyrier was born in Paris, the son of noble parents from the Languedoc region of southern France. His father, a follower of the French philosopher Claude Saint-Simon, was an active supporter of socialism.

At the age of 14, Duveyrier was sent to a school in southern Germany's Allgau region, where he studied medieval dialects of France and Germany. After a year, he went on to a business college at Leipzig. He continued his independent studies of languages, in particular Arabic and the Berber dialects of North Africa.

Duveyrier was only 17 in 1857 when he made his first trip to North Africa. He traveled a short distance southward into the SAHARA DESERT from Algiers, as far as the northernmost oasis, where he befriended Ikhenouken of the Tuareg tribe, a nomadic Berber people who roamed the south-central desert regions of Algeria.

During his brief visit, Duveyrier was invited to visit the Tuareg homelands, but his plans precluded such an expedition. Later in 1857, after his return to Europe, his dictionary of the Berber language, published by the Oriental Society of Berlin, came to the attention of the German explorer of Africa HEINRICH BARTH. Duveyrier met with Barth at his home in London and became the veteran explorer's protégé. Back in France, Duveyrier perfected his knowledge of Arabic and Berber, studied the principles of ethnology, and learned how to establish his geographic position with navigational instruments.

In 1859, Duveyrier set out on his second expedition into North Africa. Traveling by camel, he left Biskra, southeast of Algiers, and headed southwestward into the Grand Erg Occidental Desert. He visited the Arab city of Ghardia, then went on to the El Golela Oasis. He had planned to continue his journey southward to the Touat Oases in south-central Algeria, but hostile treatment by Muslims forced his sudden departure and return to Algiers.

Duveyrier set out across the Sahara again in 1860, starting from the southwestern Libyan cities of Ghat and Ghadames. He headed westward and entered the homeland of the northern Tuareg. Adopted by one band, he traveled with them for over a year, crossing the Ahaggar Mountains and entering the Tassili region, territory that had not yet been visited by Europeans. Duveyrier's expedition was directly supported by Napoleon III, who hoped that the young explorer would establish friendly relations with the warlike Tuaregs and advance French colonial interests in the isolated regions of south-central Algeria.

Upon his return to France in 1861, Duveyrier was awarded a gold medal by the Geographical Society of Paris and was inducted into the Legion of Honor. As a result of his efforts, Tuareg leader Ikhenouken visited Paris and was royally received by Napoleon III.

Soon after his return from Africa in 1861, Duveyrier was stricken with typhus and suffered a temporary memory loss. Nevertheless, he recovered sufficiently to write an account of his explorations in the Sahara, known in English as *The Tuareg of the North,* which was published in 1864.

Duveyrier became a professor at the Sorbonne. He later served as a captain of the French army in the Franco-Prussian War of 1870, during which he was taken prisoner at the Battle of Sedan.

Duveyrier made several more trips to North Africa, including one in 1884 in which he accompanied the sultan of Morocco on a journey from Tangier to Meknes and explored the Er Rif Mountains of Morocco. He also traveled extensively in Tunisia.

In his later years, Duveyrier became increasingly disillusioned by French colonial policies in North Africa. His despondency over the ensuing conflicts between the French and the Berbers may have led to his suicide in the Bois de Boulogne outside Paris in 1892.

Henri Duveyrier was recognized as the foremost authority on the people, vegetation, and geographic conditions of the Saharan regions beyond the Atlas Mountains, and his geographic reports aided in the establishment of the first modern travel routes into the interior of Algeria. His studies of the culture and language of the Tuareg complemented Barth's earlier work. Through his efforts, the French were able to establish a vast colonial empire that encompassed most of the Sahara by the end of the 19th century.

E

Eannes, Gil (Gil Eanes) (ca. 1395–ca. 1445)
Portuguese explorer on the west coast of Africa

Gil Eannes was a wealthy Portuguese courtier under HENRY THE NAVIGATOR, prince of Portugal. Few details exist of his origins or early life. In the early 1430s, he held the title of Shield Bearer in Prince Henry's retinue.

Although not an experienced mariner or navigator, Eannes was commissioned by Prince Henry to command a seaward expedition to sail around Cape Bojador on the west coast of Africa. In the early 15th century, Cape Bojador (bulging cape), located just south of the CANARY ISLANDS and the jutting African coastline, was considered the farthest limit of navigation along that continent. Superstitious sailors believed that beyond it the sea became boiling hot and white men were turned black by the extreme temperatures. Less fanciful theories held that the prevailing winds and currents would make a return from south of the cape impossible.

Eannes sailed to Tenerife in the Canary Islands in 1433. After the sighting of Cape Bojador, the crew, fearing certain death from what appeared to be the fabled boiling waters, demanded that he return to Portugal. Prince Henry was not pleased with Eannes's hasty retreat and admonished him for abandoning the enterprise so close to the cape. Henry also explained to the inexperienced mariner that the appearance of the boiling sea was actually surf running over coastal shoals at ebb tide.

Eager to redeem himself in the eyes of the prince, Eannes sailed again from Portugal in 1434 with a different crew. Although apprehensive about the waters beyond Cape Bojador, he nevertheless rounded it and explored the coast below for a few miles. He soon discovered there was no truth to the legendary terrors associated with Cape Bojador, and that the much feared current was not strong enough to prevent his ship from returning northward. After briefly exploring the shore, Eannes returned to Portugal with a type of flower from the African coast that became known as St. Mary's Rose.

Well rewarded for his achievement, Eannes undertook a third voyage in 1435, accompanied by the prince's Cup Bearer, AFONSO GONÇALVES BALDAYA. With the purpose of extending trade contacts to African people beyond Muslim domination, the expedition sailed along the West African coast to a point beyond Cape Bojador, north of the TROPIC OF CANCER, and reached a bay Eannes named Angra dos Rivos. Although he saw no human inhabitants, he sighted footprints of people and camels.

Eannes later commanded expeditions sponsored by the merchants of Lagos, Portugal, exploring as far south as the mouth of the Rio de Oro.

Gil Eannes was the first European to sail around Cape Bojador and return to describe it. His 1434 voyage dispelled the superstitions concerning exploration of the African coast and inspired subsequent Portuguese expeditions. Encouraged by Eannes's reports of signs of human inhabitants near Angra dos Rivos, Prince Henry soon sent Baldaya on an expedition exploring still farther southward along the west coast of Africa. Portuguese exploration along that route culminated in VASCO DA GAMA's voyage around Africa to India in 1497–99.

Eberhardt, Isabelle (Si Mahmoud Essadi)

(1877–1904) *Swiss traveler, writer in North Africa*

Isabelle Eberhardt was born in Geneva, Switzerland. Her Russian-born father, a former Russian Orthodox priest, was a political activist and convert to Islam, and he encouraged his daughter's Arab language studies. Her mother, from an aristocratic German family, converted to Islam at the same time that Eberhardt did—on a trip to North Africa when Eberhardt was 20. After the death of her mother, she made her home in northern Algeria.

For the next seven years, Eberhardt traveled widely in North Africa, including expeditions on horseback to the SAHARA DESERT. In order to gain access to Arab society, including the secret Sufi brotherhood known as Qadriya, Eberhardt regularly dressed as a man and went by the name of Si Mahmoud Essadi. In 1901, she married an Algerian, Slimane Ehnni. She died in a flashflood at Aïn Sefra, Algeria, three years later.

In her books, written in French, including *Nouvelles algériennes* (Algerian news, 1905), *Dans l'ombre chaude de l'Islam* (In the hot shadow of Islam, 1906), and *Les journaliers* (The day laborers, 1922), Isabelle Eberhardt described places and situations forbidden to both Europeans and women.

Egede, Hans (1686–1758) *Norwegian missionary in Greenland*

Hans Egede was born in Harstad on the Atlantic coast of Norway, north of the ARCTIC CIRCLE. In 1707, he became a pastor in the Lutheran Church, and, over the next seven years, he served at Drontheim and Vaagen.

In 1717, Egede gave up his post at Vaagen and sought backing from merchants in Bergen, Norway, for a missionary expedition to GREENLAND. At that time, it was thought that Norse settlers were still living in Greenland as Roman Catholics, and Egede intended to convert them to Lutheranism. Finding little interest for his project in Bergen, Egede went on to the Danish capital at Copenhagen. At that time, Denmark ruled Norway, and it was Danish monarch Frederick IV who finally agreed to organize a trading company to support Egede's proposed expedition.

Egede and a party of 46 colonists sailed on the *Haabet* in May 1721, landing two months later at the site of present-day Nuuk (also known as Godthaab) in southwestern Greenland. Although he was welcomed by the Inuit, he saw no European descendants of the early Norse settlers as he had expected. After establishing a settlement with a church, Egede ministered to the Inuit for several years, winning many converts and learning their language. In 1724, he preached his first sermon in the Inuit language.

Additional settlers from Denmark arrived at Egede's Greenland colony in 1728, and, within several years, Egede was joined by more missionaries. In 1736, two years after his wife's death in Greenland, he returned to Copenhagen with her remains. He established a seminary in Denmark for future missionaries to Greenland, and, in 1740, he was named a bishop and superintendent of the Greenland Mission, headquartered in Copenhagen. In 1741, his authoritative account, *A Description of Greenland,* was first published. After his retirement in 1747, Egede spent his remaining years on the island of Falster near Copenhagen. His son, Paul Egede, followed his father into the ministry and also served as a missionary in Greenland, producing the first edition of the New Testament in the Inuit language.

Known as the "Apostle of Greenland," Hans Egede established the first European settlement in Greenland since the days of the VIKINGS. Some sources suggest that he may have come into contact with the descendants of Norse settlers who had intermarried with the Inuit. Yet most historians believe the last original Norse colonists of Greenland died out 200 years before Egede's arrival.

Eiríksdottir, Freydis (fl. early 1000s) *Norse colonist in North America, daughter of Eric the Red, half sister of Leif Ericsson and Thorvald Ericsson*

As related in the traditional Norse sagas, Freydis Eiríksdottir was the illegitimate daughter of ERIC THE RED, and presumably was born and raised near Brattahlid, his home on the southwest coast of GREENLAND.

In about 1010, Freydis joined her husband, Thorvard, in THORFINN KARLSEFNI's colonizing expedition to the shores of VINLAND, a land that had been visited several years earlier by her half brother LEIF ERICSSON, and believed to be what is now Newfoundland. After wintering at a landlocked bay called Hop, the Norse colonists established trading contacts with the Inuit or Indians, whom they called the Skraelings. At one point, a bull that had been brought from Greenland broke loose, and the Skraelings, never having seen such an animal, fled in terror. About a month later, the native people responded by attacking the Norse settlement with bows and arrows. Freydis, enraged by her male companions' hesitation in launching a counterattack, recovered a sword from a fallen Viking and, although at that time pregnant, slapped it against her bared breasts and screamed at the attackers, driving them off. In about 1013, following another winter in Vinland, she returned to Greenland with Karlsefni's colonists.

Soon afterward, Freydis reportedly took part in another Norse expedition to Vinland. In about 1014, she convinced two brothers, Helgi and Finnbogi, recently arrived from Norway with their own ship, to join her in a voyage to Vinland, hoping to return with a cargo of wild grapes, wheat, and other goods. Leif Ericsson granted permission for them to use a house he had built on what may have been the northeast coast of Newfoundland at a site later known as L'Anse aux Meadows.

Freydis, with her husband, Thorvard, and a party of colonists on one ship, and the brothers Helgi and Finnbogi on their own ship with additional colonists, sailed from Brattahlid, Greenland, to Vinland, arriving in summer 1014. Conflicts soon developed between Freydis and the brothers. She would not permit them the use of Leif's house and eventually caused an open dispute when she accused them of making improper advances upon her. Her husband became incensed and, with his companions, killed the brothers and their colonists in a surprise raid. Freydis reportedly took part in the attack, slaughtering the female members of the brothers' party herself. She and Thorvard then appropriated the murdered brothers' ship and sailed back to Greenland with a load of foodstuffs.

Freydis had attempted to cover up the murders by saying that the brothers and their colonists had opted to remain on Vinland. Nevertheless, Leif soon learned what had really happened. Although outraged, he was unable to bring himself to punish his half sister and her husband, although he did denounce them and put a curse on their offspring. No record exists of Freydis's later life.

The Vinland expedition undertaken by Freydis, Thorvard, and the other Greenlanders in about 1014 marked the end of early European explorations of North America, as depicted in the Norse sagas. In the context of the traditional accounts contained in the sagas, Freydis was one of the few women to play a significant role in the voyages of the Vikings to North America.

Elias, Ney (1844–1897) *British official in central Asia*
British-born Ney Elias was of Jewish ancestry. He pursued a career as a civil servant and found work in a foreign office in China.

In September 1872, with plans to return to England, Elias set out across the GOBI DESERT from Kuei Hua Cheng in China, accompanied by a Chinese servant, an interpreter, and a camel driver, plus camels and ponies. Two months later, he reached the frontier post of Uliastay in Mongolia. Continuing northwestward along the river Dzavhan Gol, he crossed the frozen lake Har Us Nuur and reached the village of Hovd. From there, he crossed the Altai Mountains into SIBERIA, reaching Biysk on the Ob River. His wintertime journey across Siberia was by way of horse-drawn sled. Elias crossed the Ural Mountains and finally reached Nizniy Novgorod east of Moscow. He continued westward through Europe, now by train, eventually reaching England after a total of some 4,800 miles.

Elias was later hired by India and sent on diplomatic missions throughout central Asia. He also explored the passes in the Pamirs. In 1885–86, he became the first Englishman to cross this range.

Ney Elias carried out eight expeditions throughout central Asia in the course of his career, thus becoming one of the greatest British explorers of the region in that period. In 1873, he received the Founder's Medal of the ROYAL GEOGRAPHICAL SOCIETY for his first trek across central Asia.

Ellsworth, Lincoln (1880–1951) *American aviator, polar explorer*
Lincoln Ellsworth was born in Chicago into an affluent family. After attending Columbia and Yale Universities, he left school to work as a surveyor and engineer in the construction of a transcontinental railroad in Canada. He later engaged in prospecting and worked as a mining engineer in northwestern Canada. In World War I, he was trained as an aviator, although illness kept him from overseas service.

In 1924, Ellsworth organized and led a scientific expedition to Peru for Johns Hopkins University, in which he made a geological survey of the ANDES MOUNTAINS from the Pacific coast to the headwaters of the AMAZON RIVER.

In 1925, Ellsworth contacted Norwegian polar explorer ROALD ENGELBREGT GRAVNING AMUNDSEN during his lecture tour in the United States, offering to provide financing for a proposed airplane flight over the NORTH POLE. Amundsen soon agreed to a joint expedition with Ellsworth, who, with $85,000 of his own money, acquired two German Dornier "Whale" seaplanes, equipped with Rolls-Royce engines.

As navigator on one of the planes, Ellsworth took off from Spitsbergen (present-day Svalbard) in May 1925. Mechanical problems forced one of the planes down, and the other landed to rescue the passengers. The expedition had reached as far as 87°43' north latitude, which, although short of the North Pole, was a new record for air travel in0 the Arctic.

The next year, 1926, Ellsworth purchased an Italian AIRSHIP and renamed it the *Norge*. Ellsworth and Amundsen, along with Italian aviator UMBERTO NOBILE as pilot, used it for the first transpolar flight. They set out across the Arctic Ocean from Spitsbergen, passed over the North Pole, and landed at Teller, Alaska. (RICHARD EVELYN BYRD had succeeded in crossing over the Pole in an airplane several days before.)

In 1931, Ellsworth was an official observer on the German airship *Graf Zeppelin* in flights over Franz Josef Land and Northern Land. Also in the early 1930s, he provided

Lincoln Ellsworth *(Library of Congress)*

backing for SIR GEORGE HUBERT WILKINS's early attempts at exploration of the Arctic by SUBMARINE.

Starting in 1933, Ellsworth began the first of a series of expeditions aimed at making the first flight across the Antarctic continent. Planning to fly from the Ross Sea to the Weddell Sea, Ellsworth, Sir Hubert Wilkins, and Bernt Balchen arrived at the Bay of Whales on the icebreaker *Wyatt Earp.* The aircraft intended for the project was damaged while being unloaded from the ship, however, and the expedition had to be delayed until the following year. In fall 1934, Ellsworth established a base at Deception Island in the Weddell Sea region, planning for a flight across Antarctica to the Ross Sea, but, before he could set out, he was again delayed a year because of engine problems.

Finally, on November 20, 1935, Ellsworth took off from Dundee Island in the Weddell Sea. His aircraft, the *Polar Star,* was piloted by Herbert Hollick-Kenyon. Ellsworth planned to survey the region between the Weddell and Ross Seas and determine whether Antarctica was a single landmass or two large islands. He also wanted to learn if the mountain ranges of central Antarctica was a continuation of the ANDES MOUNTAINS, extending southward from South America.

Ellsworth's plane was forced down four times by bad weather, including one severe blizzard. With their fuel supply gone, Ellsworth and Hollick-Kenyon made a landing about 15 miles from the abandoned American base, Little America, near the Bay of Whales on the Ross Sea, which they soon reached by foot. The *Wyatt Earp* arrived three weeks later and picked up the two men.

Ellsworth's 2,200-mile flight across Antarctica yielded much new geographic information. He charted the Sentinel Range, which included the highest peaks in Antarctica, and named one Mount Mary Louise Ulmer, after his wife. He also sighted a mountain range that appeared to be a continuation of Graham Land. He called these mountains the Eternity Range and named three of its peaks Mount Hope, Mount Faith, and Mount Charity. His aerial survey included 400,000 square miles of previously unexplored territory between Hearst Land and Marie Byrd Land, which he claimed for the United States and named James W. Ellsworth Land after his father.

In 1939, Ellsworth undertook further aerial reconnaissance of Antarctica, this time approaching the continent from its Indian Ocean side, surveying an additional 81,000 square miles of previously unknown territory east of the Ross Sea.

Lincoln Ellsworth's early aerial explorations yielded much new geographic information, providing the earliest accounts of large and previously unknown areas of the Arctic Ocean. With Amundsen, he authored *Our Polar Flight* (1925) and *First Crossing of the Polar Sea* (1927). During his 1935 flight, he not only made the first crossing of the Antarctic continent, but also demonstrated that a plane could safely land and take off again in remote parts of the Antarctic interior.

Emin Pasha, Mehmed (Dr. Eduard Schnitzer)
(1840–1892)   *German physician, government official in East Africa*

The man later known as Mehmed Emin Pasha was born Eduard Schnitzer in the city of Oppeln (Opole) in what is now central Poland, the son of German-Jewish parents. He studied medicine in addition to natural sciences, becoming a practicing physician. In 1865, he became a physician with the Turkish army. Five years later, he was appointed governor of northern Albania, which at that time was a province of the Ottoman Empire. Over the next several years, he adopted a Turkish way of life.

In 1876, Emin Pasha, as he chose to be known, journeyed into the Sudan region south of Egypt, where he became a physician with Anglo-Egyptian armed forces at Khartoum, under the command of British general Charles "Chinese" Gordon. Two years later, he was appointed governor of the Egyptian province of Equatoria, which included much of what is now Uganda and the southern Sudan.

Emin Pasha took up his post at Lado on the White Nile River. From there, he undertook explorations into the former Unyoro region of present-day Uganda and made botanical and ornithological studies, periodically sending collections of rare central African plants and birds back to scientists in Europe. His travels during the late 1870s took him into the region northwest of Juba in the Sudan, as well as southwest into the watershed region between the NILE RIVER and the CONGO RIVER (Zaire River). He also explored south of Juba to the north shore of Lake Victoria.

With the outbreak of the revolt of the Mahdi in 1881, Emin Pasha found himself isolated from the support of the besieged Anglo-Egyptian forces to the north. In 1883, he withdrew up the Nile with his garrison of 10,000 men, women, and children, settling in at a remote position on Lake Albert, northwest of Lake Victoria. Following the massacre of General Gordon and his troops at Khartoum in 1885, Emin Pasha commanded the last stronghold against the Egyptian rebel forces.

An expedition to relieve Emin Pasha and his garrison was organized in 1887 under SIR HENRY MORTON STANLEY. After an arduous journey from the mouth of the Congo, Stanley arrived at Emin Pasha's outpost and succeeded in evacuating the Lake Albert garrison back to Bagamoyo on the Indian coast of present-day Tanzania, opposite Zanzibar.

In Bagamoyo, in what was then German East Africa, Emin Pasha entered the service of the German government in 1890, as the leader of an official expedition that sought to explore the many lakes in the region and claim the source of the Nile for Germany. On reaching Tabora in what is now central Tanzania, he raised a German flag. After leading his expedition to Lake Albert, he pushed westward into what is now northeastern Democratic Republic of the Congo. In October 1892, at Kinena, about 100 miles south of Stanley Falls, he was murdered in his encampment by Arab slave traders, probably in retaliation for his previous efforts to stamp out the SLAVE TRADE during his British service in the Sudan. His journals were later recovered by Belgian authorities and sent back to Europe.

Emin Pasha's explorations in the Sudan and in East Africa resulted in new geographic and scientific knowledge of the Congo and upper Nile region. On his trek with Stanley from Lake Albert to the Indian Ocean coast in 1889, he was among the first Europeans to sight the Ruwenzori Range, the fabled MOUNTAINS OF THE MOON, and also joined Stanley in his exploration of the Semliki River connecting Lake Edward with Lake Albert.

Emmons, George Foster (1811–1884) *U.S. Navy officer in the Pacific Northwest*
Born in Clarendon, Vermont, George F. Emmons entered the U.S. Navy as a midshipman in 1828. Following his maritime training at the New York Naval School, he cruised the MEDITERRANEAN SEA from 1830 to 1833. In 1836, he took part in a hydrographic survey.

In 1838, Emmons joined the U.S. South Seas Surveying Expedition under the command of CHARLES WILKES. He served on the *Porpoise,* one of the main ships of the expedition, from mid-August 1838 until July 1841, when the vessel was wrecked off the mouth of the COLUMBIA RIVER on the Oregon coast. He then led an exploring expedition inland investigating the region south of the Columbia River to the headwaters of the Sacramento River in northern California. The scientists and topographers, including JAMES DWIGHT DANA, obtained a great deal of new data on the natural history and geography of the Pacific Northwest. After a visit to Sutter's Fort, Emmons led his party to San Francisco and rejoined Wilkes's fleet. The expedition sailed for the South Pacific Ocean, exploring until August 1842.

Emmons's next assignment was with U.S. naval forces off the coast of Brazil. In the U.S.-Mexican War of 1846–48, he took part in actions on the California coast, including several forays into the Sierra Nevada. After the war, he served in Washington, D.C., in several administrative naval posts. In 1850–53, he wrote a definitive, ship-by-ship history of the U.S. Navy, entitled *The Navy of the United States, from the Commencement, 1775 to 1853, with a Brief History of Each Vessel's Service and Fate* (1853).

In the Civil War, Emmons commanded U.S. warships in the Gulf of Mexico, capturing a number of Confederate blockade-runners. He also commanded the ship that took American and Russian officials to Alaska in 1867, when the sale of that region to the United States was finalized. Promoted to commodore on his return, he was subsequently named commander of the navy's hydrographic office. Emmons retired from the navy in 1873, at the rank of rear admiral.

The information acquired by George F. Emmons and his scientific team in their 1841 explorations of what is now western Oregon and northern California was of great assistance to the U.S. government in its subsequent negotiations with England over the Oregon Country.

Emory, William Hemsley (1811–1887)
U.S. Army officer, topographical engineer in the American Southwest
William H. Emory was born in Queen Annes County, Maryland, to a prominent family descended from Maryland's colonial founders. He entered West Point in 1827; among his classmates were Jefferson Davis and Henry Clay, Jr., who nicknamed him Bold Emory. He graduated four years later as a second lieutenant in the artillery. He left the army in 1836, and, two years later, he married Matilda Wilkins Bache, a great-granddaughter of Benjamin Franklin.

In 1838, Emory returned to active duty as a first lieutenant in the U.S. Army Corps of Topographical Engineers.

In 1844, he took part in the Northeastern Boundary Survey along the U.S.-Canadian border. He also produced a map of Texas, marking its claims as far as the Rio Grande.

At the outbreak of the U.S.-Mexican War in 1846, Emory was attached to General STEPHEN WATTS KEARNY's forces. Starting from Fort Leavenworth, Kansas, he surveyed the army's route through the Arkansas River Valley to Bent's Fort, Colorado, along the Santa Fe Trail, and across Arizona's Gila River region. He made thousands of astronomical observations determining the route's exact location in terms of LATITUDE AND LONGITUDE. In addition, through hundreds of barometric readings, he accurately determined elevations. Based on the information, he created the first scientific map of the region to the west of the American Southwest, from the Gulf of Mexico to the Pacific Ocean.

While traveling through the Southwest with Kearny's forces, Emory and his party came upon the ruins of Casa Grande Pueblo, as well as other Indian ruins that had not been visited by non-Indians since Father FRANCISCO TOMÁS HERMENEGILDO GARCÉS explored the region in 1776. He also determined the exact location of the junction of the Gila River and COLORADO RIVER through astronomical sightings.

Emory was brevetted a major in the California campaign. After the war's conclusion, from 1849 to 1855, he commanded the 1,500-mile survey of the U.S.-Mexican Border for the Mexican Boundary Commission. During this project, he was one of the leading proponents for the Gadsden Purchase of 1853, citing the region as feasible for a proposed transcontinental railroad's southwestern link.

After 1855, Emory was attached to the Second Cavalry regiment and supervised the construction of wagon roads in New Mexico and present-day Arizona.

At the onset of the Civil War in 1861, Emory was in command of U.S. forces in the Indian Territory (present-day Oklahoma). By successfully withdrawing his troops to Fort Leavenworth, Kansas, he was credited with preventing Missouri from joining the Confederacy.

Emory retired from the army in 1876 as a brigadier general after 45 years of service.

William H. Emory's report on his 1846 topographic expedition across the Southwest, *Notes of a Military Reconnaissance from Fort Leavenworth in Missouri, to San Diego in California, Including Parts of the Arkansas, Del Norte, and Gila Rivers,* was published by the government in 1849. His description of the Southwest as unsuitable for slave-based agriculture had bearing on the sectional disputes that resulted in the Compromise of 1850. The report included a map of the Southwest detailing trails that had previously been known only to Indian peoples and fur trappers.

William H. Emory *(Library of Congress)*

Entrecasteaux, chevalier d'   See BRUNI, ANTOINE-RAYMOND-JOSEPH DE.

Eratosthenes (Eratosthenes of Cyrene, Beta, Pentathlos) (ca. 276–ca. 195 B.C.) *Greek mathematician, astronomer, geographer*

Born in Cyrene, in present-day Libya, Eratosthenes studied under well-known scholars of his age, including the philosopher Ariston and poet-critic Callimachus. After living in Athens, Greece, he became head of the library at Alexandria, in North Africa, in about 240 B.C.

Eratosthenes's interests were wide ranging. He wrote poetry and works about literature, theater, and philosophy, as well as about history, producing a chronology of events since the siege of Troy by the Greeks. He also pursued the sciences, including mathematics and astronomy. He measured the circumference and tilt of the Earth and the sizes and distances from the Earth of both the Sun and Moon. He is also said to have created a catalog of 675 fixed stars.

Eratosthenes also made major contributions to the field of geography. He drew a map of the world, the first known map to use a grid pattern, and wrote a treatise on geography. The route he presented of the NILE RIVER to

Khartoum, showing two Ethiopian tributaries, was fairly accurate. He also suggested that lakes were the source of the Nile and that heavy rainfall near the source created flooding downriver.

Eratosthenes is said to have committed suicide by starvation after becoming blind. Because of his many accomplishments he was given the nickname Beta, in reference to being second only to Alpha (that is, second only to the gods). Another nickname was Pentathlos, in reference to an athlete who consistently takes second prize. He is considered the first systematic geographer.

Erauso, Catalina de (Alonso Díaz Ramírez, Antonio de Erauso) (1585–1650) *Spanish woman soldier in South America*

Catalina de Erauso was born into a noble Basque family of San Sebastián in the Spanish province of Guipúzcoa. At age four, she was placed in a convent by her parents. Often at odds with the nuns, she determined to escape and did so at the age of 15, on the night before she was to take her vows. She managed to avoid capture by cutting her hair and wearing boy's clothing—transgressions punishable by death. Her deception worked, and she supported herself with odd jobs, such as tending horses.

In 1603, at the age of 18, Erauso, still hiding her womanhood and using the name Alonso Díaz Ramírez, worked as a cabin boy on a ship bound for South America. In Peru, she trained in the use of a sword and enlisted as a soldier in the Spanish army. She served for 13 years, stationed near the present border between Peru and Chile, seeing action against the Araucanian Indians of the region. She later spent time in mining towns in northern Chile and Argentina but reenlisted in 1620. One day, when taking refuge in a church after a sword fight, Erauso decided to confess. Rather than being punished, she was celebrated by many of her fellow soldiers and was granted a pension by the army. She returned to Spain four years later.

Deciding to make a pilgrimage to Rome, Erauso traveled through France, where she was held for a time as a spy. She finally was allowed to proceed on her travels and gained an audience with the pope. She returned to the Americas in 1630, where she spent the rest of her life as a tradesperson and mule driver under the name Antonio de Erauso.

Catalina de Erauso wrote about her escape from the nunnery and her experiences in South America in a memoir, which has been translated into several languages; a recent volume in English is entitled *Lieutenant Nun* (1996). Her story of adventure and exploration, that of a woman disguised as a man, is unique in regard to the Spanish conquest of South America.

Ericsson, Leif (Leifr Eiríksson, Leif Eriksson, Leif Erikson, Leif Ericson, Leif the Lucky)

(ca. 975–ca. 1020) *Norse mariner in North America, son of Eric the Red, brother of Thorvald Ericsson, half brother of Freydis Eiríksdottir*

Leif Ericsson was the son of Viking leader ERIC THE RED. Ericsson was probably born in ICELAND, but it is possible he was born in GREENLAND. In any case, in about A.D. 981, his father was exiled from Iceland for three years for killing a neighbor. He and his family explored to the south and west of Iceland, reaching the coast of Greenland.

In about 985, after his return to Iceland, Eric the Red led a group of Norse colonists to the southwest coast of Greenland, where he established a colony at Brattahlid. Also about this time, BJARNI HERJULFSSON, another Norse seaman, sailed still farther to the west and south, returning with reports of lands unknown in Europe, possibly the coast of what is now Labrador or Baffin Island.

According to Norse folk tradition, contained in *Eiríks saga,* or the *Saga of Eric the Red,* Leif Ericsson, in 999, sailed from Greenland for Norway with his wife, Thorgunna. On the way, their ship was blown off course, and the couple landed in the Hebrides, the island chain off the northwest coast of Scotland. After spending some time there, they finally reached Norway and the court of King Olaf I.

King Olaf commissioned Ericsson to introduce Christianity to the Norse colonists on Greenland. In about the year 1000, Ericsson supposedly sailed westward from Norway, intending to reach Greenland, but was blown off course to the coast of North America. The party went ashore at a site on the eastern seaboard, probably somewhere between Nova Scotia and Chesapeake Bay. After wintering there, they returned to Greenland in the spring with samples of wheat and grapes. On the return journey, Ericsson reportedly rescued some Norse seamen who had been shipwrecked on the North American coast. For this, he earned the nickname Leif the Lucky.

Ericsson's adventures in North America are described differently in another Norse folk narrative, *Groenlendinga,* or the *Saga of the Greenlanders.* According to this source, Ericsson was in contact with Herjulfsson, who told him of the wooded lands he had found 15 years earlier across the Davis Strait, west of the Greenland settlement. At that time, timber for building and fuel was scarce in the North Greenland settlement. Ericsson purchased Herjulfsson's ship, intending to use it to bring back much needed timber from these lands to the west.

Also according to the *Saga of the Greenlanders,* in about 1001, Ericsson and a crew of 35 Norsemen sailed westward from what is now Godthaab on the southwest coast of Greenland and soon reached the coast of possibly either southern Baffin Island or Labrador. He may also have explored the Ungava Bay region of what is now extreme northern Quebec.

Ericsson named this northernmost region Helluland, meaning "land of flat rocks," after its rugged terrain. He then followed the coastline southward to present-day eastern Labrador and named the region Markland, which in Norse means "land of woods." Continuing southward, Ericsson and his men came to a region rich in self-sowing wheat. He made a landing there and sent a reconnaissance party to explore inland, led by a German named Tyrkir. When Tyrkir returned to the coast, he brought back samples of wild grapes. The region was later dubbed VINLAND, for "wineland" or, more likely, "meadowlands."

The *Saga of the Greenlanders* goes on to relate how Ericsson and his crew built shelters and continued their explorations, at one point traveling up a river. At the end of winter, probably in 1002, they returned to Greenland with a cargo of wood, as well as samples of the region's plants.

Several years later, Leif's brother, THORVALD ERICSSON, led a colonizing expedition to Vinland. The settlement met with resistance from native North Americans, possibly Beothuk, Micmac, or Inuit (Eskimo), called Skraelingar or Skraelings by the Norse. In one encounter, Thorvald was killed. Soon afterward, the Norse settlers abandoned their colony and returned to Greenland.

Ericsson did not return to North America. He inherited his father's landholdings in Greenland, remaining there until his death in about 1020.

Archaeological investigations at L'Anse aux Meadows in northern Newfoundland indicate actual Norse settlements existed about the time of Ericsson's reported voyage, believed by many historians to be the site where he wintered in about 1001. The Norse sagas also mention subsequent colonizing attempts in Vinland by THORFINN KARLSEFNI in about 1010 and Ericsson's half sister, FREYDIS EIRÍKSDOTTIR, in 1014–15.

Several hundred years after Ericsson's voyage, the Norse colony on Greenland disappeared, its remaining members possibly intermarrying with Inuit.

No recorded information about Leif Ericsson's explorations of North America exist other than what is contained in the Norse sagas, which were not written down until the 13th and 14th centuries. Nevertheless, by the early 1400s, English fishermen from Bristol were regularly visiting Iceland and may have brought back reports of lands west of Greenland that may have influenced JOHN CABOT. During the 1470s, CHRISTOPHER COLUMBUS reportedly visited Iceland, where he too may have obtained knowledge of lands across the Atlantic Ocean.

Ericsson, Thorvald (Thorvald Eiríksson, Thorwald Ericksson, Thorvaldr Erikson, Torvald Ericson) (unknown–ca. 1007) *Norse mariner in North America, son of Eric the Red, brother of Leif Ericsson, half brother of Freydis Eiríksdottir*

Thorvald Ericsson, a son of ERIC THE RED, was possibly born at his family's homestead, Brattahlid, on the southwest coast of GREENLAND; other sources indicate he was born in ICELAND.

According to one account in the Norse sagas, in about 1005, Thorvald undertook a voyage westward from Greenland to VINLAND, a land his brother, LEIF ERICSSON, had reached several years earlier. With a group of about 50 Vikings, he arrived on the shore of Vinland, somewhere between Labrador and New England, and located Leif's former settlement, where they spent the winter. The following summer, they explored southward and may have reached Long Island Sound. The next year, while exploring to the east, Thorvald encountered a group of about eight natives, either Indians or Inuit (Eskimo) referred to in Norse writings as Skraelingar or Skraeling. A conflict arose in which the Vikings killed all but one of the native people. Soon afterward, the natives counterattacked, and Thorvald was fatally wounded by an arrow. His men buried him on the coast of Vinland, then returned to Greenland.

A different account of Thorvald's exploits in Vinland appears in another of the sagas. In that version, he accompanied THORFINN KARLSEFNI and his half sister FREYDIS EIRÍKSDOTTIR on an expedition of 1010 to Vinland, also encountered natives, and was subsequently killed in an attack by a one-legged, human-like creature.

The traditional Norse literature about Thorvald Ericsson's exploits in Vinland depicts the first known contacts between European, and Native Americans.

Eric the Red (Erik the Red, Eirík Thorvaldsson) (ca. 950–1010) *Norse mariner and colonizer in Greenland, father of Leif Ericsson, Thorvald Ericsson, and Freydis Eiríksdottir*

Eric the Red (his nickname derived from the color of his hair) was born in Jaeren in southwestern Norway, the son of a Viking nobleman named Thorvald Aswaldsson. In about A.D. 950, his father, having been exiled from Norway for killing a man, took Eric and the rest of his family to ICELAND, settling on the island's northwest coast.

Growing up in that part of Iceland, the young Eric may have heard accounts of new lands to the west, known as Gunnbjorn's Skerries, that had been sighted years earlier by a Norse mariner named Bjarni Gunnbjorn. From the heights of local mountaintops in northwestern Iceland, he may have also caught sight of GREENLAND 120 miles across the Denmark Strait.

In about 981, Eric killed one of his neighbors in a feud and was banished for three years from Iceland. The next year, he sailed with his family from Bredifjord on the west coast of Iceland, planning to spend his exile exploring the lands reported by Gunnbjorn. In addition to his wife and children, Eric brought several neighboring families, as well as livestock and other essentials for a farming settlement.

Eric and his party soon reached the southeast coast of Greenland, near what is now Angmagssalik, and made a landing at a site they called Blaserk ("Blue Shirt"). The coast here was choked with ice. Seeking a region more suitable for settlement, they headed southward along the coast and rounded Cape Farewell, although some sources suggest they passed around the southern end of Greenland by way of Prins Christian Sound, north of Cape Farewell. On the southwest coast, Eric and his party made a landing at what is now Julianehaab, at an inlet he called Ericsfjord.

Eric and his companions established a small farming settlement at Ericsfjord. Over the next two years, they explored northward along Greenland's west coast as far as Disko Island.

In about 985, Eric, having completed his sentence of exile, returned to Iceland, and he soon organized a colonizing expedition to what he called Greenland. According to the Norse *Eiríks saga,* or the *Saga of Eric the Red,* he hoped that people would be drawn there if the land had an attractive name.

Eric's colonists, numbering over 1,500 men, women, and children, sailed from Iceland in 985 or 986, on 25 vessels. Eleven of the ships were lost or returned to Iceland. The remaining 14 ships, with about 500 colonists, arrived on the southwest coast of Greenland and soon established a settlement around Eric's homestead, called Brattahlid. In the following years, Norse mariners explored westward from the colony, known as the Western Settlement, and they may have sailed across the Davis Strait to the south coast of Baffin Island.

Between 1000 and 1015, Eric's sons, LEIF ERICSSON and THORVALD ERICSSON, and his daughter, FREYDIS EIRÍKSDOTTIR, sailed westward from the Greenland settlements and reached the coasts of North America.

Eric the Red made the first reported European sighting of Greenland, the world's largest island. His colony on the southwest coast of Greenland endured until the early 1400s, when the outbreak of the bubonic plague in Europe cut off communication with Norway. Soon afterward, the last European settlers died out. Some historians speculate that a "mini ice age" or of conflicts with Inuit in Greenland contributed to the decline of the Norse settlement. Eric's journey led to the establishment of the first regular sea routes from Europe, across the North Atlantic, to waters west of Iceland. His exploits, preserved in the Norse sagas, may have influenced CHRISTOPHER COLUMBUS.

Ermak See YERMAK.

Escalante, Francisco Silvestre Vélez de

(ca. 1745–1780) *Spanish missionary in the American Southwest*

Originally from Spain, Francisco de Escalante arrived in Mexico City in 1768. He had studied for the priesthood and was ordained a Franciscan missionary at Mexico City's Convent of San Francisco in early 1769. Escalante was assigned to northern Mexico's Sonora province to proselytize to the Indians, then to New Mexico, where he worked among the Zuni and other Pueblo Indians.

In 1775, Spanish colonial authorities were seeking an overland route to supply the newly established missions on the California coast between San Diego and Monterey. They feared encroachment from the north by Russian and British trade interests. Supplying these California coastal settlements by sea had proved impractical. In February 1775, Escalante, who had by this time become prominent among the Zuni, was ordered to locate an overland route between Sonora and California by way of New Mexico.

On June 22, 1775, Escalante, accompanied by Mayor Cisneros and about 20 Christianized Indians, departed Zuni Pueblo in what is now western New Mexico, passed through the lands of the Hopi Indians, and attempted to trace a route across the COLORADO RIVER in the Grand Canyon region of present-day north-central Arizona.

Despite two weeks of searching, the expedition was unable to find a crossing of the Colorado River's wide canyons, and they returned east. Later that year, Escalante submitted a report and a map of his explorations of northern Arizona to Governor Mendinueta, the chief Spanish colonial administrator of New Mexico.

Escalante was then assigned to establish an overland route from the Spanish settlements north of Santa Fe to the mission at Monterey, California. He also was to make contact with the Indians north and west of the Colorado River and convert them to Christianity.

Escalante's second expedition left Santa Fe on July 29, 1776. Earlier that year, Franciscan missionary FRANCISCO TOMÁS HEMENEGILDO GARCÉS had explored in present-day western Arizona, also seeking an overland route from the California coast to Sonora and Santa Fe. Escalante's party included Father FRANCISCO ATANASIO DOMÍNGUEZ, his superior in the Franciscan order, as well as eight soldiers and about 20 Mission Indians. Also part of this expedition was the multi-talented Don Bernardo Miera y Pacheco, who served as the expedition's cartographer, artist, and engineer. Miera was adept at determining latitude by the use of a COMPASS and helped in the preparation of a detailed map of the expedition.

Traveling northwest from Santa Fe, the Escalante-Domínguez expedition traveled to Abiquiu and followed the western slopes of the San Juan Mountains part of the ROCKY MOUNTAINS. They traveled through western Colorado along the Dolores River, a tributary of the Colorado River. At the edge of the Uncompahgre Plateau, their Indian guides lost the trail westward. Escalante and Domínguez then decided to head eastward to find more knowledgeable guides among the Ute Indians.

A Ute guide known as Silvestre led them north to the Colorado River, which they were able to cross near the site of the modern city of Collbran, Colorado. They continued northwestward, crossing into the Uinta Basin of northeastern Utah, becoming the first Europeans to enter that region. Heading westward, they crossed the Green River, then continued to Utah Lake and Utah Valley, just south of the Great Salt Lake. Although the Spanish heard reports from the Indians about the lake, they did not see it. Instead, near what is now Provo, Utah, they headed southward into the Sevier Desert, traveling along the western edge of the Wasatch Mountains. Crossing the Great Basin of western Utah from north to south, they entered a region of southwestern Utah known today as the Escalante Desert. Their Indian guides led them along a difficult route rather than the more easily traversed ridges because of Comanche Indian war parties in the region.

By early October 1776, the Escalante-Domínguez expedition believed it had reached the latitude of Monterey. But a severe snowstorm held them back. After drawing lots, they decided not to attempt to cross the snow-covered passes of the Sierra Nevada to the west, instead heading eastward back to Santa Fe. They traveled southeastward into what is now northern Arizona. Near present-day Lees Ferry on the Utah-Arizona border, they searched for a place to cross the wide Colorado River. At a site later named the Crossing of the Fathers, they forded the river and ascended the high canyon walls by chiseling steps into the rocky buttes. The steps, carved into a cliff that came to be known as Domínquez Butte, were visible for nearly two centuries until the building of Glen Canyon Dam and the creation of Lake Powell Reservoir.

For the next three months, Escalante and Domínguez made their way across what is now northeastern Arizona to lands of the Zuni in western New Mexico. They arrived back in Santa Fe on January 2, 1777.

Afterward, Escalante was assigned to the mission of San Ildefonso, north of present-day Los Alamos, New Mexico. He died while on a journey in 1780.

Although the Escalante-Domínguez expedition failed to find an overland route to California, it explored lands in Utah previously unknown to non-Indians and produced a fairly accurate map of the region of central Utah, which remained in use through the mid-1800s. Moreover, with Father Domínguez, Francisco de Escalante kept a detailed diary of their travels. The expedition's route northwestward from Santa Fe into the Green River region of Utah—known as the Escalante Trail—came to be used by fur traders in the early 1820s.

Escandón, José de (1700–1770) *Spanish colonial governor, colonizer in southeastern Texas*

In 1746, José de Escandón, a veteran Indian fighter in Mexico, was appointed Spanish governor of Nuevo Santander province, which had been established that year in the Seno Mexicano, a sparsely inhabited region stretching northward from the mouth of the Panuco River at Tampico, along the Gulf Coast, to Matagorda Bay, Texas.

Escandón had been instructed to colonize the new province and establish a series of missions and presidios (military posts) in the region as a buffer against French encroachment along the northeastern frontier of New Spain.

Setting out from Querétaro in south-central Mexico in December 1748, Escandón led 2,500 settlers and 750 soldiers along the eastern slopes of the Sierra Gorda Mountains, establishing ranches and missions as well as several garrisons. Among the settlements he founded was Laredo, which straddled the Rio Grande at the present U.S. border with Mexico. In all, 23 new towns, along with 15 new missions, were founded over the next several years throughout the Lower Rio Grande Valley.

In addition to serving as governor until his death in 1770, Escandón was given the title Count of Sierra Gorda, in recognition of his efforts in southeastern Texas, particularly for establishing peaceful relations with the region's Native Americans.

José de Escandón extended Spanish colonial influence northeastward from Mexico into Texas, checking French encroachment onto the southern plains from New Orleans and St. Louis. In 1763, the transfer of French Louisiana to Spain ended the threat to New Spain's northeast frontier, and the settlement of Texas became less strategically important.

Eschscholtz, Johann Friedrich (J. F. von Eschscholtz) (1793–1831) *Estonian physician and naturalist in the Pacific*

Johann Friedrich Eschscholtz was born in the Estonian city of Dorpat (now Tartu). His family was of German descent. Trained in medicine at Dorpat, he joined OTTO VON KOTZEBUE's Russian-sponsored expedition to the South Pacific Ocean and BERING STRAIT in 1815, serving on the *Rurik* as naturalist and doctor.

Over the next three years, with fellow naturalist LOUIS-CHARLES-ADÉLAÏDE CHAMISSO DE BONCOURT, Eschscholtz made studies of marine animal life, including a survey of jellyfish. While exploring Chamisso Island on the west coast of Alaska, he discovered tusks and teeth of mammoths. In California, near San Francisco Bay, he undertook a study of the region's salamanders, identifying three new species.

In 1823–26, Eshscholtz sailed again with Kotzebue on his second expedition to the Pacific and Alaska, aboard the *Predpriyatiye*. On this voyage, he collected several new species of birds; in his second scientific investigation of the Alaskan coast, he concentrated on marine life, especially mollusks and jellyfish.

On his return to Russia in 1826, Johann Friedrich Eschscholtz began work on his *Zoological Atlas,* the last volumes of which appeared posthumously in 1833, two years after his death at the age of 38. The California poppy, a wildflower found on the West Coast of the United States, is also known as *Eschscholtzia californica* in honor of his early scientific work in California. Eschscholtz Bay in Alaska's Kotzebue Sound was named after him.

Espejo, Antonio Estevan de (fl. 1580s)
Spanish merchant, prospector, explorer in New Mexico and Arizona

Antonio de Espejo was reportedly born in Córdoba, Spain, although some sources suggest he may have been born in London, England. Few details of his early life are known.

By 1582, Espejo had achieved some degree of wealth as a merchant. That year, he was engaged in prospecting in the San Bartolomé Valley of north-central Mexico. One year earlier, a Franciscan missionary expedition, led by Friar Agustín Rodríguez, had set out from San Bartolomé for the north and soon had disappeared in the lands of the Pueblo Indians in present-day New Mexico. Espejo, at his own expense, organized an expedition to find them, including 15 mounted soldiers and another Franciscan priest, Friar Bernardino Beltrán. Diego Perez de Luxán chronicled the expedition.

Espejo led his party down the Conchos River to the Rio Grande into what is now southern New Mexico. On learning from the Indians that Friar Rodríguez and his companions had been killed, Beltrán and the soldiers returned to Mexico, while Espejo continued exploring and prospecting in the regions to the east and north. Over the next nine months, he traveled throughout much of New Mexico, visiting regions as far north as the Sangre de Cristo Mountains around Taos and venturing into the plains to the east. In addition to some of the more remote pueblos, he visited Acoma, a pueblo of the Keres Indians, and Hawikuh, a pueblo of the Zuni in western New Mexico. At Hawikuh, he encountered several Spaniards who had remained there since FRANCISCO VÁSQUEZ DE CORONADO's expedition of 1540.

Espejo also explored westward across what is now Arizona, becoming the first European to visit the Little Colorado River. Near what is now known as the Bill Williams River, he discovered rich deposits of valuable mineral ores.

While returning to Mexico, Espejo came upon a stream he named the Río de las Vacas (river of cows) after the cattle he saw along its banks. Traveling by way of the Pecos River, he reached its confluence with the Rio Grande, then returned to San Bartolomé by ascending the Conchos, arriving there on September 20, 1583. He brought with him more than 4,000 cotton blankets he had obtained from the Hopi Indians.

Antonio de Espejo's reports of mineral wealth in the region north of Mexico led to an influx of prospectors and other settlers, culminating in the colonizing efforts of JUAN DE OÑATE, starting in 1598. Although the region now comprising Arizona and New Mexico had been visited by Coronado and his army of CONQUISTADORES in 1540–41, it was Espejo's later explorations that provided the Spanish with the first detailed information concerning the region's geographic features and indigenous peoples. His written account of his explorations of 1582–83, *Relación del viaje al Nuevo Mexico* (An account of travels in New Mexico), was published in 1636.

Estevanico (Estebanico, Estevanito, Estevan, Esteban, Black Stephen, Stephen the Moor)
(ca. 1500–1539) *North African traveler in the American Southeast and Southwest, guide*

Estevanico was a slave held by the Spanish. Some scholars have theorized that he was Moorish, but he was probably a black from North Africa who had been owned by Moors there. During the 1520s, he came into the service of the Spaniard Andrés Dorantes. With Dorantes, he left Spain in 1527, as part of PÁNFILO DE NARVÁEZ's abortive expedition to Florida.

When the expedition was shipwrecked in the Gulf of Mexico in 1528, Estevanico and Dorantes were among the few survivors to reach the coast of southern Texas. They were enslaved by Indians, with whom they traveled throughout central Texas. In spring or summer 1533, they met up with another survivor of the expedition, ÁLVAR NÚÑEZ CABEZA DE VACA. The following summer, Estevanico, Dorantes, Cabeza de Vaca, and another expedition member named Alonso del Castillo Maldonado met at a site near present-day San Antonio, Texas, and attempted to reach the safety of Spanish settlements in Mexico. They wandered through what is now New Mexico, Arizona, and possibly southeastern California for the next two years. In early 1536, Estevanico and the others reached Culiacán in the northern Mexican province of Sonora, where they were rescued by a party of Spaniards slave-hunting among the Indians.

With Cabeza de Vaca, Estevánico arrived in Mexico City in July 1536. Spanish colonial governor ANTONIO DE MENDOZA, hearing tales from the travelers of gold-laden Indian settlements to the north—the fabled Seven Cities of CIBOLA—organized an expedition under Franciscan missionary, Father MARCOS DE NIZA. Estevanico was purchased by Mendoza and sent along as a guide.

Estevanico, Niza, and a small party of soldiers set out northward from Culiacán in March 1539 and soon crossed into the present-day United States somewhere near the modern town of Lochiel, Arizona. Niza sent Estevanico ahead with an advance party of Mission Indians in search of Indian cities.

In May 1539, Estevanico reached the Zuni pueblos of what is now western New Mexico. He was undoubtedly the first black man the Indians had ever seen, and his unique appearance led many of the natives to believe he was the incarnation of a god. The Indians gave him gifts of turquoise and other semi-precious stones; Estevanico used them to decorate his clothing, along with bells and multicolored ribbons.

At one Zuni pueblo, either Hawikuh or Kiakima, Estevanico is thought to have offended the ruling chiefs and medicine men because of his overbearing manner and his popularity with the women. He also reportedly brandished a medicine rattle he had obtained several years earlier from enemies of the Zuni. Zuni warriors took him captive and killed him.

On learning of Estevanico's death, Niza retreated to Mexico. He had espied Hawikuh from a distance and, believing the reflection of the sun on the adobe walls to be gold, he carried this misinformation back to Spanish colonial authorities. His reports inspired the later expedition of FRANCISCO VÁSQUEZ DE CORONADO.

Estevanico's striking appearance and the Indian response to it is thought to have played a major part in the survival of some from the Narváez expedition. His not-so-successful relations with the Zuni Indians delayed Marcos de Niza's search for the Seven Cities of Cibola and indirectly led to Coronado's expedition.

Etholén, Arvid Adolf (Adolf Karlovich Etolin)

(1799–1876) *Finnish-born naval officer in Alaska, in service to Russia*
Arvid Adolf Etholén was born in Finland to a family of Swedish descent. In 1817, soon after he had entered the Russian maritime service, he sailed from St. Petersburg, halfway around the world, to the RUSSIAN-AMERICAN COMPANY's colonies in Alaska.

Etholén arrived in Alaskan waters in 1818. During this voyage, he participated in a coastal survey of the American coast of the BERING STRAIT.

In 1821, accompanied by another employee of the Russian-American Company, Etholén explored the west coast of Alaska, including Hagemeister Strait and Hagemeister Island, Good News Bay, and the mouth of the Nushagak River in Bristol Bay, north of the Alaska Peninsula. To the north, they traveled part way up the Kuskokwim River. Their subsequent reports to the Russian-American Company included geographic data as well as observations on the natives.

Etholén rose to prominence in the Russian-American Company; by 1840, he had been appointed chief manager of the firm's fur-trading posts in Alaska. During the next five years, he undertook several explorations along the coast of the Gulf of Anadyr on the Siberian side of the Bering Sea. He left the maritime service of the Russian-American Com-

pany at the rank of rear admiral. Following his return to St. Petersburg in 1847, he was appointed to a high administrative post in the company's headquarters in that city.

Arvid Adolf Etholén traveled to Alaska soon after the Russian-American Company began sailing its ships directly to Alaska, avoiding the costly overland journey across SIBERIA. His survey of the Alaskan coast of Bering Strait provided the Russians with knowledge of the region north of their original settlements on the Alaskan Peninsula and the Gulf of Alaska.

Eudoxus (Eudoxus of Cyzicus) (fl. 120s–110s B.C.)

Greek mariner in coastal Africa and India, in service to Egypt
Eudoxus was born in the Greek city of Cyzicus, on the Sea of Marmara, in what is now northwestern Turkey. Becoming a skilled navigator in the eastern MEDITERRANEAN SEA and RED SEA, he entered the maritime service of the Egyptian king Ptolemy Euergetes II.

In about 120 B.C., the king commissioned Eudoxus to undertake a voyage across the Arabian Sea to India. Guided by an Indian mariner who had been shipwrecked on the Red Sea, Eudoxus succeeded in making one of the earliest direct voyages from Egypt to India. He soon returned to Egypt with a cargo of gems and spices.

Soon afterward, Eudoxus made a second voyage to India. On the return trip, he was blown far to the south and east by monsoon winds. He eventually made a landing on the coast of East Africa, where he established friendly relations with some natives and made a study of their language. He also found the front end of a ship, which the natives told him was from the west.

With the coming of favorable winds, Eudoxus sailed back to Egypt with the remains of the wrecked ship. In Egypt, he learned the vessel was the type that usually sailed along the West African coast from the western Mediterranean. His discovery of a western European ship on the east coast of Africa led Eudoxus to speculate that a circumnavigation of the African continent was possible.

To test his theory, Eudoxus traveled to the port of Gades (Cádiz), on the southwest coast of Spain. From there, he set out to sail around Africa. The voyage ended when his ship ran aground on the coast of Morocco. On a subsequent attempt, Eudoxus and his vessel disappeared, and it is not known how far southward he may have sailed along the coast of West Africa.

As recorded in the writings of the first-century A.D. geographer STRABO, Eudoxus made one of the earliest known sea voyages from Egypt to India, establishing direct coastal trade links between India and the cities of Greece, Asia Minor, and Egypt. His voyages from Spain were the first attempts to circumnavigate Africa from western Europe. Some sources suggest that Eudoxus actually succeeded in sailing around Africa in an east-to-west voyage, which began in the

Red Sea and ended with his arrival at Gades on the Spanish coast.

Everest, Sir George (1790–1866) *British surveyor in India*

British-born George Everest, ranked a lieutenant though only 16, began serving with the BRITISH EAST INDIA COMPANY and saw action in India. In 1814, he carried out a survey of the island of Java. In 1816–17, he oversaw the clearing of navigational obstacles along the lower GANGES RIVER and tributaries.

The Great Trigonometrical Survey of India—as it came to be known under the direction of the British government, which assumed control of it from the British East India Company—had, since 1802, the purpose of triangulating the Indian subcontinent on a gridiron plan. In 1819, Everest led his first surveying mission as assistant to Colonel William Lambton, mapping about 70 miles between Hyderabad in south-central India and the Godaavari River. Both men worked under Colin Mackenzie, surveyor general of India. Everest became superintendent of the survey in 1823, applying a new level of efficiency to the project, planning a series of trigonometrical triangulations on a grid covering the subcontinent, and building observation towers to accomplish this.

Everest was elected to the ROYAL SOCIETY in 1827. Three years later, he became surveyor general of India. In 1841, he conducted surveys in the HIMALAYAS. He retired in 1843. Four years later, he published *An Account of the Measurement of Two Sections of the Meridional Arc of India*. He was knighted in 1861.

In 1856, George Everest's former assistant, Andrew Waugh, surveying in the Himalayas, named its highest peak—and highest peak in the world—MOUNT EVEREST after his predecessor. Work continued on the Great Trigonometrical Survey in the subsequent decades, involving Indian explorers—the PUNDITS—such as NAIN SINGH, KISHEN SINGH, and KINTUP.

Evliya, Çelebi (Evliya ibn-Dervis Mehmed Zilli, Ewliya Efendi) (1611–1684) *Turkish traveler, writer in the Ottoman Empire*

Çelebi Evliya was born into a wealthy Turkish family with close ties to the sultan of the Ottoman Empire. His early education included training in calligraphy, music, and art. He also wrote poetry.

Starting in 1640, Evliya began a career of travel into the far reaches of the Ottoman Empire, which at that time stretched from Hungary in the north to Egypt and the Sudan in the south. Over the next 40 years, he visited much of eastern Europe and the Balkans, as well as the Middle East and North Africa.

Çelebi Evliya wrote a 10-volume account of his journeys, *Seyahatname* (travel book), in which he described the diverse regions of the Ottoman Empire, as well as the cultures of the many different subject peoples living within it. Writing in a style that conformed to contemporary Turkish, his work had great popular appeal among 17th-century Turkish readers, enlightening many about the diverse lands and people then under Turkish rule.

Eyre, Edward John (1815–1901) *British sheep farmer, explorer in Australia, colonial administrator*

John Edward Eyre was born in Whipsnade, in Bedfordshire, England, the son of a clergyman. In 1833, after attending school at Louth, Lincolnshire, he applied for a commission in the British army but was turned down. That same year, at the age of 18, Eyre immigrated to Australia.

In his first years in Australia, Eyre engaged in sheep farming around present-day Canberra near the east coast, south of Sydney. He also worked as an "overlander," taking part in cattle drives out of Sydney southwestward to the newly established settlements around Adelaide on the south coast.

By 1838, Eyre had established a sheep ranch 150 miles north of Adelaide. Soon afterward, he was appointed a magistrate for the Murray River region and was also named "Protector of Aborigines." In search of new grazing lands, he began to explore northward into the Flinders Range. In May 1839, he followed the Flinders Range eastward as far as Mount Arden, which he climbed, and from its peak he became the first non-Aborigine to see Lake Torrens, a large shallow body of saltwater north of the head of Spencer Gulf.

Eyre attempted to circle north and west around Lake Torrens, but the harsh desert conditions, and lack of water and other supplies, forced him to turn southward for the coast. He crossed what later became known as the Eyre Peninsula and reached Port Lincoln, west of Adelaide. In August 1839, Eyre left Port Lincoln to explore along the coast of the Great Australian Bight, reaching as far as Streaky Bay. On the way, he sighted and named Mount Deception and Mount Hopeless.

In 1840, Eyre took part in a cattle drive from Albany, on Australia's southwest coast, northwestward to settlements at Swan River, near Perth. Later that year, he organized an expedition to make a south-to-north crossing of the Australian continent, from Adelaide to Port Essington.

In June 1840, Eyre and his assistant, John Baxter, and a number of Aborigines headed northwestward from Adelaide in an effort to travel around Lake Torrens. From a high peak in the Flinders Range, he sighted what he took to be a northern extension of Lake Torrens, which led him to wrongly conclude that Lake Torrens was a large horseshoe-shaped lake, running east to west, blocking any direct route into the center of Australia. Eyre did not realize then that he had actually seen an entirely different lake to the north of Lake Torrens; this lake later was named Lake Eyre.

With progress to the north blocked by the salt lakes, Eyre headed back to the coast, arriving at Fowlers Bay, several hundred miles west of Adelaide. Although he was met there by a ship with word from the Australian governor requesting that he return to Adelaide, Eyre nevertheless decided to continue his explorations by making an attempt at an east-to-west crossing of the continent, along the coast of the Great Australian Bight.

Accompanied by Baxter and three Aborigines, Eyre set out from Fowlers Bay in February 1841. Heading westward, they were forced to travel between the coast and the edge of the completely arid Nullarbor Plain. The livestock he took along to test the viability of the route for future cattle drives soon died. In late April, two of the Aborigines killed Baxter and made off with most of the supplies of food and water. With the remaining Aborigine, a boy named Wylie, Eyre struggled on, pushing westward along the inhospitable coast of the Great Australian Bight. In early June, Eyre met up with a French whaling ship, the *Mississippi*, at a place he named Rossiter Bay after the ship's captain, an Englishman named Rossiter.

After Eyre and Wylie recuperated on the *Mississippi* for 12 days, they completed the journey to Albany on King George Sound, arriving there on July 7, 1841, after a four-month trek of more than 750 miles. From Albany, they crossed the southwesternmost corner of Australia to Fremantle, south of Perth.

Eyre returned to England in 1845, accompanied by two native boys, whom he presented to Queen Victoria. Later that year, he published an account of his expeditions, *Discoveries in Central Australia.*

In 1846, Eyre began a career as colonial administrator, serving first in NEW ZEALAND as lieutenant governor until 1853. In 1854, he was appointed governor of the island of St. Vincent in the Caribbean Sea, a post he held until 1860. Following a short visit to England, he became acting governor of Jamaica in 1861, and, in 1864, he was named governor. In 1865, a rebellion broke out in Morant Bay, Jamaica, which Eyre put down with great severity. Among the rebel leaders he ordered executed was a prominent Jamaican mulatto and member of the colonial legislature, George William Gordon. Amid popular outcry against his brutality in suppressing the insurrection, the British government recalled Eyre from Jamaica in 1866. Over the next few years, he was the center of a great controversy when a group known as the "Jamaica Committee" attempted to prosecute him for murder. Cleared of any wrongdoing in the affair, he retired on his government pension to an estate in Devon, England.

Edward John Eyre succeeded in completing the first east-to-west crossing of Australia, an accomplishment for which he was awarded a medal by the ROYAL GEOGRAPHICAL SOCIETY in 1843. The reports from his explorations north of Spencer Gulf led geographers to characterize the fertile region near Adelaide as surrounded by a vast inland desert. He also popularized the idea that further attempts to explore into the interior of Australia would be blocked by the presence of numerous shallow lakes and salt plains. Lake Eyre, of which he made the European discovery in 1840, is Australia's largest lake.

F

Fadlan, Ahmad ibn   See IBN FADLAN, AHMAD.

Fa-hsien (Faxian, Fa Hsien, Fu-hsien, Fa-hien)
(319–414) *Chinese Buddhist monk, traveler in central Asia and northern India*
Fa-hsien was originally from the city of Ch'angan (present-day Xi'an) in east-central China. By A.D. 399, he had become a Buddhist monk and scholar. That year, accompanied by three other monks, he set out for India in search of Buddhist texts in the original Sanskrit, from which he planned to make accurate Chinese translations.

Traveling westward across China, Fa-hsien followed the ancient SPICE ROAD across central Asia. He visited the ancient lands of Tartary and crossed the Takla Makan desert to the Pamirs in what is now Tajikistan. After crossing the HIMALAYAS into what is now Afghanistan, he followed the Kabul River into the Punjab region of present-day northern Pakistan. He reached the upper INDUS RIVER then made his way eastward across northern India to the present-day city of Patna, where he spent three years copying and translating Buddhist texts.

While in India, Fa-hsien visited many Buddhist shrines and sites where important events in Buddha's life had taken place. After two more years at a seaport near present-day Calcutta, he sailed to the island of CEYLON (present-day Sri Lanka) and continued his Buddhist studies for two more years.

In about 413, Fa-hsien began his journey back to China by sea. On a course eastward from Ceylon across the Indian Ocean, his ship went aground near the south coast of Java. Then, while heading for Canton (Guangzhou), the ship was lost at sea for 70 days. It eventually reached Shantung on the coast of China. Fa-hsien traveled from there to Nanking (Nanjing), arriving in 414, after 15 years of travels.

Fa-hsien settled at the Buddhist monastery in Nanking, where he completed his Chinese translations of the Sanskrit texts. He also wrote an account of his experiences in central Asia and India entitled *Fo kuo chi* (Memoirs of the Buddha realms). He was the first Chinese known to have traveled from north-central China into southern Asia, then to have returned to China by sea.

Fallam, Robert (fl. 1670s) *English colonist in Virginia, the Appalachian Mountains, and West Virginia*
In September 1671, Robert Fallam joined Captain THOMAS BATTS in an expedition westward. They were sponsored by Major General ABRAHAM WOOD, a leading Virginia colonist, who hoped to locate new sources of furs west of the Piedmont region.

Batts and Fallam left Fort Henry, now the site of Petersburg, Virginia, and followed the Roanoke River into the Blue Ridge. Crossing the mountains, they reached the Kanawha and New River Valleys of present-day West Virginia, then returned to the English post.

Fallam kept a journal of the expedition, which was the first recorded English crossing of the APPALACHIAN MOUNTAINS to the watershed of the Ohio River.

Fanning, Edmund (1769–1841) *American mariner in the South Pacific*

Edmund Fanning was born in Stonington, Connecticut. After several years of schooling, he embarked on a seafaring career, shipping out as a 14-year-old cabin boy on a coastal trading vessel. By 1790, he was a ship's officer; that year, he married Sarah Sheffield, also of Stonington.

In 1792, Fanning made his first voyage to the South Atlantic on a sealing expedition to the vicinity of CAPE HORN. The next year, he took command of his own ship and undertook a number of commercial voyages to and from the WEST INDIES.

Fanning began his first CIRCUMNAVIGATION OF THE WORLD out of New York in 1797. He rounded CAPE HORN and stopped at the Juan Fernández Islands on the coast of Chile, where he obtained a large cargo of sealskins from Native Americans in exchange for inexpensive trinkets and cheap trade-goods. Heading westward across the Pacific Ocean, he visited the Marquesas Islands.

On June 11, 1798, Fanning reached a previously uncharted island, 1,200 miles south of the HAWAIIAN ISLANDS, known today as Fanning Island, and, several days later, he came upon two other islands to the northwest, which he named Palmyra and Washington Islands. This group became known as Fanning's Islands.

At the port of Canton (Guangzhou), China, Fanning traded the sealskins for a valuable shipment of tea, silk, and other Oriental commodities. Upon his return to New York by way of the Indian Ocean and the CAPE OF GOOD HOPE, Fanning and his investors sold the Chinese merchandise for more than $120,000, yielding an astounding net profit, considering that they outfitted the ship for about $8,000.

Fanning settled in New York. During the next 30 years, he organized and promoted American trading expeditions to the South Pacific and the Far East. In addition to obtaining sealskins in the southernmost islands of the Atlantic, Pacific, and Indian Oceans, his ships also engaged in trading with the South Sea islanders for pearls, tortoise shells, and sandalwood, items that also brought a handsome profit in China.

In 1804, Fanning organized an expedition captained by his brother Henry Fanning, during which the Crozet Islands were charted in the southern Indian Ocean to the south of Madagascar. They provided a rich source of seals.

In addition to the 1797–98 voyage during which he visited Fanning's Islands, Edmund Fanning sponsored more than 70 expeditions to the South Pacific, personally sailing on some of them. He made a study of modern navigational techniques and employed the most updated nautical designs in his ships. Moreover, he studied the older charts of Dutch mariners in an attempt to clarify the true geography of the Pacific. Some of his expeditions included naturalists who made some of the first American scientific studies in the Pacific. He was one of the sponsors of NATHANIEL BROWN PALMER's 1829 voyage to the Antarctic waters south of Cape Horn. In 1833, Fanning published *Voyages Around the World,* an account of his seafaring career, which was widely read. His book reportedly influenced the U.S. government to allocate funds for its first official naval exploring expedition, which was commanded by CHARLES WILKES in 1838–42.

Fawcett, Percy Harrison (1867–ca. 1925) *British army officer, surveyor in South America*

Percy Fawcett was born at Torquay in Devon, England. In his early teens, he embarked on a military career at the Royal Military Academy at Woolwich near London, graduating as an officer in the artillery with a background in surveying and cartography in 1886.

Over the next 20 years, Fawcett served with the British army in assignments in CEYLON (present-day Sri Lanka), Malta, and Ireland. In 1906, on extended leave from the military, he was engaged by the Bolivian government to undertake a boundary survey of that country's borders with Brazil.

Landing on the Peruvian coast at Mollendo in 1906, Fawcett traveled inland into the ANDES MOUNTAINS to Lake Titicaca. In northern Bolivia, he surveyed along the Alto Acre and Abunã Rivers, the sources of the Madeira River, which were seldom visited by non-Indians. On Bolivia's eastern border with Brazil, he explored the Río Verde to its source in the Sierra de Huanchaca, and he penetrated the remote Mato Grosso region of southwestern Brazil.

In 1908, Fawcett explored the interior of South America from Buenos Aires on the east coast. He ascended the Paraná and Paraguay Rivers to the Chapada dos Parecis, a watershed region that drains into both the AMAZON RIVER and Paraguay River, on the frontier between Brazil and Bolivia. Two years later, he traveled again to Lake Titicaca in the Peruvian Andes, where he surveyed the mountains southeastward to La Paz, Bolivia.

Fawcett returned to England in 1914 to serve in World War I. After the war, he retired from the military at the rank of colonel.

In 1920, Fawcett began a search in South America for a fabled lost city. During his earlier explorations, he had reportedly come across documentary evidence indicating that, in 1753, before their disappearance in the Amazon Basin, a group of Portuguese explorers had come upon an Indian civilization with cities containing buildings and statues made of quartz. Fawcett also claimed to have encountered what he

Percy Fawcett and an exploration party in Brazil *(Library of Congress)*

described as "white Indians," natives with red hair and blue eyes. From this evidence, he speculated that a continent across the South Atlantic Ocean had once connected South America with Europe and Africa, and he believed the Inca and other, yet-to-be-determined tribes had been in contact with non-Indians since pre-Columbian times.

In 1920, Fawcett traveled westward into Paraguay from Rio de Janeiro, then headed northward into the interior of Brazil, by way of the Cuibabá River. The next year, he explored the region of northern Brazil, inland from Salvador and Vitoria da Conquista.

Four years later, with the backing of a U.S. newspaper syndicate, Fawcett made another attempt to find the lost civilization in the interior of Brazil. Accompanied by his son John and his son's friend Raleigh Rimell, Fawcett set out from Cuiabá, in the Brazilian state of Mato Grosso in late April 1925, and headed northward toward the Paranatinga River. He planned to descend that 1,200-mile stream by CANOE to the Amazon Delta, then explore the Tocantins and Araguaia Rivers, and eventually reach the São Francisco River.

Fawcett, his son, and Rimell reached Dead Horse Camp, at about 10° south latitude, near the headwaters of the Xingu River in central Brazil, after which nothing more was heard of them. They became the subject of international search expeditions, including one led by George Dycott in 1928 and another in 1933. It is assumed they were killed by native tribesmen.

Percy Fawcett's experiences in South America were recounted in his posthumously published book, *Exploration Fawcett* (1968). One of the first 20th-century explorers of the Amazon Basin and the central Andes, his exploits mirrored those of Spanish and Portuguese explorers who, 300 years earlier, had sought the fabled city of EL DORADO.

Fedchenko, Aleksey Pavlovich (1844–1873)
Russian naturalist in central Asia, husband of Olga Fedchenko

Aleksey Fedchenko was educated at Moscow University, where he studied anthropology and zoology. Starting in 1868, he led a series of scientific expeditions into central

Asia, exploring the Pamirs, a mountainous region in what is now Tajikistan.

Fedchenko's explorations into the Pamir coincided with the Russian military conquest of the region. In 1871, while exploring the Altai and Turkestan Mountains, he became the first European to locate a previously uncharted range, the Trans-Altai (Zaalai). He named its highest peak Mount Kaufman after the commander of Russia's forces in central Asia, Konstantin Petrovich Kaufman. Subsequently renamed Lenin Peak, at 23,377 feet it is the second highest mountain in the Pamirs.

Fedchenko's wife, OLGA FEDCHENKO, a botanist, accompanied him in his explorations of the Pamir. Fedchenko was killed in 1873 in a climbing accident on a glacier near Mount Blanc in the Alps.

Aleksey Fedchenko contributed to the geographic and scientific knowledge of the Pamirs, where a large glacier was named in honor of his work.

Fedchenko, Olga (1845–1921) *Russian botanist in central Asia, wife of Aleksey Pavlovich Fedchenko*

Olga Fedchenko, a Russian botanist, joined her husband, ALEKSEY PAVLOVICH FEDCHENKO, in his explorations of the Pamir region in south-central Asia from 1868 to 1871.

Following her husband's death in 1873, Fedchenko supervised the publication of his scientific findings in the Pamirs and organized his collections of animal and plant specimens from the region.

In the 1890s and early 1900s, Fedchenko continued her botanical fieldwork with subsequent expeditions of her own into the Pamirs. She also explored the region around the Caspian Sea, including the Crimea, the Caucasus Mountains, and the Ural Mountains.

Olga Fedchenko was one of the few early female botanists to work in uncharted regions of the world.

Federmann, Nikolaus (Nicolás Federman)

(1501–1542) *German official in northern South America*

Nikolaus Federmann was born in Ulm, in the southern German principality of Württemberg. In his early 20s, he went to work for the banking business of the Welser family in the Bavarian city of Augsburg.

In 1530, the Welsers sent Federmann to the north coast of South America to help administer their newly acquired colony in what is now Venezuela. Two years earlier, Charles I, king of Spain (Holy Roman Emperor Charles V), had granted most of present-day Venezuela to the Welsers as repayment for loans that he was unable to repay in cash and they had sent out a colonizing expedition under AMBROSIUS ALFINGER.

Federmann landed at Coro as acting governor of the colony. Soon after his arrival, he led one of the earliest explorations into the interior of Venezuela, seeking the legendary riches of the fabled land of EL DORADO.

Following a brief visit to Europe, Federmann returned to Venezuela in 1533. Soon afterward, he undertook another search for El Dorado, reaching as far southward as the foothills of the Colombian ANDES MOUNTAINS, and the next year he explored the prairie region of the eastern Colombian llanos (plains).

Federmann and his party of CONQUISTADORES and Indians wandered for three years in southern Venezuela and eastern Colombia. Near present-day Bogotá, Federmann encountered two different armies of Spanish conquistadores, one under the command of SEBASTIÁN DE BENALCÁZAR and the other led by GONZALO JIMÉNEZ DE QUESADA. Federmann and the leaders of the other two armies agreed to a truce until the matter of who had a rightful claim to the newly explored region of what is now Colombia could be resolved. Meanwhile, GEORG HOHERMUTH VON SPEYER, who had superseded Federmann as governor of the colony, also sought El Dorado in an expedition in 1535–38.

Some sources suggest that Quesada may have paid Federmann a large sum of money to drop any claim the Germans had on the region. In any case, Federmann, Benalcázar, and Jiménez de Quesada sailed to Spain in 1539 or 1540, where the Council of the Indies ultimately granted New Granada to Alonso Luis de Lugo since he had inherited the governorship of nearby Santa Marta upon his father's death.

Federmann remained in Madrid, where the Welser family initiated a legal proceeding against him, charging that he had given up their claim to New Granada without authorization. Federmann in turn accused the Welsers of defrauding the emperor, Charles V, an accusation that he later recanted shortly before his death in Madrid in 1542.

Nikolaus Federmann was one of the few northern Europeans to play a decisive role in the early exploration of northern South America. His expeditions in what is now southern Venezuela and eastern Colombia yielded much new geographic information on the upper ORINOCO RIVER and the Colombian Highlands. His second journey southward from Coro in 1536 took him across the Arauca and Meta Rivers and, by way of passes 13,000 feet high, across the Andes, making him the first European to cross the mountains from east to west.

Fernandes, Álvaro (fl. 1440s) *Portuguese navigator on the west coast of Africa*

Álvaro Fernandes was a nephew of João Gonçalves Zarco, a seafarer and captain of the island of Madeira, who, in 1441, established the Portuguese SLAVE TRADE on the coast of West Africa.

By 1445, Fernandes was an accomplished navigator and sea captain. That year, he commanded a ship in a Portuguese fleet on a punitive naval expedition against the Moorish-held island of Tider. Instead of returning to Portuguese waters after the attack, Fernandes sailed his vessel southward along the coast of West Africa, reaching a point several hundred miles beyond Cape Verde. On a strip of land there, he sighted palm trees on the shore as tall as a ship's mast, and called it the Cape of Masts.

In 1446, Fernandes was commissioned by HENRY THE NAVIGATOR, prince of Portugal, to lead another expedition along the coast of West Africa. He was urged by Zarco to push even farther southward along the coast during this endeavor, and not be deterred by lure of the slave trade. On this voyage, he explored part way up the Gambia River, but he was forced back when natives attacked his men with poisoned arrows. Before returning to Portugal in 1447, Fernandes had progressed as far south as Conakry on the coast of Guinea, just north of present-day Freetown, Sierra Leone.

Álvaro Fernandes's voyages along the coast of West Africa in the mid-1440s were important stages in Prince Henry's plan to learn the true geography of the African continent and expand Portuguese trade beyond the barriers imposed by the Muslims in North Africa and the Middle East. The Cape of Masts, which he sighted in 1445, became an important landmark for Portuguese navigators sailing southward along the African coast.

Fernandes, João (unknown–ca. 1501)
Portuguese mariner in Greenland and possibly Newfoundland
Portuguese-born João Fernandes lived on the island of Terceira in the AZORES. Little is known of his life other than that he was a landowner (*lavrador*) and that in 1499, he received a royal patent to explore islands in the Atlantic Ocean to the west of Europe. Portuguese interest in this region to the west had been prompted by Spanish expeditions to the Americas by CHRISTOPHER COLUMBUS and British expeditions by JOHN CABOT in the 1490s. The Portuguese had already carried out numerous expeditions around Africa to Asia in the 15th century. Some scholars, however, theorize that Portuguese mariners reached Newfoundland before Cabot did.

The exact number of Fernandes's expeditions is not known, nor is it known whether he even reached North America, but it is believed that in association with two other Portuguese living in the Azores, Francisco Fernandes and João Gonçalves, Fernandes undertook a voyage to the west in 1500, reaching at least as far as GREENLAND, which he called Tiera del Lavrador. The name later came to be applied to Labrador in North America. Afterward, Fernandes joined a commercial syndicate operating out of Bristol, England, and he is thought to have died at sea on a subsequent voyage to the Americas in 1501.

João Fernandes sought to develop Portuguese interests in North America at the same time as GASPAR CÔRTE-REAL and MIGUEL CÔRTE-REAL. His peers, Francisco Fernandes and João Gonçalves, made a series of subsequent voyages in 1502–05, with the purpose of exploring the Newfoundland fishery.

Fernández de Córdoba, Francisco (Francisco Hernández de Córdoba, Francisco Hernandes de Cordova) (unknown–1518)
Spanish conquistador on the Yucatán Peninsula
Francisco Fernández de Córdoba was among the first Spanish settlers on Cuba, arriving soon after the Spanish conquest in 1511. He was an hidalgo, a member of the landed gentry, having received one of the original land grants on the island.

On February 8, 1517, Fernández de Córdoba sailed from Cuba in command of three ships, commissioned by Cuba's colonial governor, DIEGO VELÁSQUEZ, to undertake a slave-hunting expedition to the nearby Bahama Islands to the northeast. On encountering heavy gales, his ships were driven far to the west. After three weeks, the expedition landed on the northeasternmost corner of the Yucatán Peninsula, at what is now Cape Catoche.

In the course of their explorations inland, Fernández de Córdoba and his men encountered Mayan-speaking Indians. These Maya had dwellings constructed of stone and masonry materials, unlike the reed huts of the Caribbean island natives. Their agriculture also was more advanced than that of the Arawak (Taino) and Carib Indians, and they wore clothes of woven cotton. Their gold ornaments were the first indication the Spanish had of the Aztec civilization inland. At one point, the Indians asked Fernández de Córdoba if he and his men had come from the east, indicating that news of the Spanish arrival in the WEST INDIES had reached the mainland by 1517.

The Spaniards explored westward along the northern Yucatán coast. The Maya proved more warlike than their island counterparts and launched repeated attacks. In one skirmish, Fernández de Córdoba himself was wounded 12 times. By the time the Spanish had reached the east shore of the Bay of Campeche and departed for Cuba, half the expedition members had been killed and all the survivors had been wounded.

Upon reaching Cuba, Fernández de Córdoba reported his findings to Governor Velásquez, who immediately organized a follow-up expedition. Two Indians Fernández de Córdoba had taken to Cuba to train as interpreters related the fabulous wealth to be found in the Yucatán, fueling Spanish enthusiasm to explore these lands to the south and west.

Soon after his return, Fernández de Córdoba died of his wounds. Velásquez's nephew JUAN DE GRIJALVA was appointed to command a second expedition, which reached Cozumel Island and the Mexican mainland in the spring of 1518.

Francisco Fernández de Córdoba's explorations provided the Spanish with the first reports of the Aztec civilization and ultimately led to the 1519 expedition of HERNÁN CORTÉS and the subsequent conquest of Mexico. He is also credited with naming the peninsula he explored. According to some accounts, when Fernández de Córdoba asked some Indians what they called their country, they replied, "*Tectetan*," meaning "I do not understand you." This was misinterpreted to denote their name for the region and evolved into *Yucatán*.

Fernández de Córdoba, Francisco
(Francisco Hernández de Córdoba, Francisco Hernándes de Cordova) (ca. 1475–ca. 1526)
Spanish conquistador in Panama and Nicaragua

Francisco Fernández de Córdoba took part in the consolidation of Spanish rule in Panama, arriving there in 1514 with Spanish forces under the command of PEDRO ARIAS DE ÁVILA.

In 1522, Arias de Ávila put Córdoba in command of a seaward expedition to occupy Nicaragua in CENTRAL AMERICA. A few years earlier, a rival conquistador, Gil González de Ávila, had reached the Lake Nicaragua region and had claimed the country for himself before withdrawing in the face of Indian hostility.

Fernández de Córdoba sailed from Panama northward along the Pacific coast of Central America to the Gulf of Nicoya, in what is now northwestern Costa Rica. He then led his expedition inland into Nicaragua, exploring the regions around Lake Managua and Lake Nicaragua. In 1523, he established León near Lake Managua, and Granada along Lake Nicaragua.

In 1524, Fernández de Córdoba suffered a military defeat at the hands of troops under González de Ávila, who had returned from Hispaniola (present-day Haiti and the Dominican Republic) in command of a military expedition to reassert his claims on Nicaragua. Córdoba retained control of the region around León, renouncing his allegiance to Arias de Ávila and attempting to establish his own colonial domain. In response, Arias de Ávila led his forces into Nicaragua. After a year of fighting, he forced Fernández de Córdoba to surrender at León. Soon afterward, Fernández de Córdoba was put to death on the orders of his former leader, who then installed himself as governor of Nicaragua.

Although Francisco Fernández de Córdoba's efforts to colonize Nicaragua were short-lived, he nonetheless founded León and Granada, which endured as the first permanent European settlements in Nicaragua. Both settlements eventually became important centers of political power and commerce.

Fernández de Oviedo y Valdez, Gonzalo
(1478–1557) *Spanish colonial official, historian, naturalist in Panama and the West Indies*

Gonzalo Fernández de Oviedo was born in Madrid, Spain. As a youth, he served as a page in the court of Prince John, son of Spanish rulers Queen Isabella I and King Ferdinand II, and, as part of the royal household, he took part in the final victory over the Moors at Granada in 1492.

With Prince John's death in 1497, Fernández de Oviedo entered the service of Frederic of Aragon, ruler of the southern Italian kingdom of Naples. In 1513, Fernández de Oviedo was appointed as warden of the gold mines of Castilla de Oro on the Isthmus of Panama, and the following year, he sailed with PEDRO ARIAS DE ÁVILA to the newly established Spanish settlement of La Antigua on the Atlantic coast of Panama.

In Panama, Fernández de Oviedo supervised the smelting and shipment of gold back to Spain and also served on the colony's ruling council. He began his comprehensive history of the Spanish exploration and colonization of the Americas in 1515, returning to Spain that same year to report on economic and political conditions in the colony.

Fernández de Oviedo returned to Panama as governor of La Antigua and nearby Cartagena in 1526. By 1532, he was back in Spain, and King Charles I (Holy Roman Emperor Charles V) made him the official historian of the Americas. Three years later, he sailed to Hispaniola (present-day Haiti and the Dominican Republic), having been named governor of the island's chief settlement at Santo Domingo.

In 1535, the first volumes of Fernández de Oviedo's *Historia general y natural de las Indias Occidentales* (General and natural history of the West Indies) were published in Seville. He remained in Santo Domingo until 1545, at which time he returned to Spain to complete his history of Spanish exploration in the Americas. His work was completed in 1548, and publication continued until his death in 1557.

The publication of Gonzalo Fernández de Oviedo's *Historia* was not resumed until 1851, nearly 300 years after his death, under the sponsorship of the Spanish government's Royal Academy of History. Partial editions did appear from 1550 to 1577, from which translations were made into Italian and English. His work is considered to be the earliest historical account of Spanish exploration in the Western Hemisphere, and it included one of the first descriptions of the natural history of the Americas, illustrated with Fernández de Oviedo's own drawings.

Ferreira, Alexandre Rodrigues (1756–1815)
Brazilian naturalist on the Amazon River

Born in Bahia, Brazil, Alexandre Rodrigues Ferreira studied at the University of Coimbra in Portugal and became a teacher there. In 1778, he began working at the Real Museu da Ajuda in Lisbon, cataloging its collection, and was later elected to the Academy of Sciences.

Ferreira was commissioned by the Portuguese government to undertake a journey of scientific exploration into the interior of Brazil and returned to his homeland in 1783. For the next nine years, he studied its natural history, first on the island of Marajó, then in the coastal region of Pará and along the AMAZON RIVER and its tributaries, among them the Tocantins, Negro, Içana, Uaupés, Branco, Tacutu, Surumu, Uraricoera, Araça, Solimões, Madeira, Guaporé, Cuiabá, Paraguay, and Jauru. The artists José Joachim Freire and Joaquim José Codina worked with him, producing 912 drawings and prints of fauna and flora. Ferreira also conducted studies of Brazil's native peoples.

After his return to Lisbon in 1793, Alexandre Rodrigues Ferreira continued his relationship with the Museo da Ajuda and was also appointed director of the Gabinete de Historia Natural and of the Jardim Botânico. His work helped in the classification of wildlife of the Brazilian rain forest and in determining the topography of the Amazon watershed. He has been referred to as the Brazilian ALEXANDER VON HUMBOLDT.

Ferrelo, Bartolomé (Bartolomé Ferrer)
(1499–1548) *Spanish mariner on the Pacific coast of Mexico, California, and Oregon*

Bartolomé Ferrelo was born in Bilbao, Spain. He became a skilled mariner and navigator, and in 1542, he served as a pilot in JUAN RODRÍGUEZ CABRILLO's voyage northward along the Pacific coast of Mexico and California. The expedition planned to search for the fabled STRAIT OF ANIAN, which it was thought would provide a seaward route through North America from the Pacific Ocean to the Atlantic Ocean.

Cabrillo's two ships embarked from Navidad, near Manzanillo, Mexico, on June 27, 1542, in an expedition that had been organized by Mexican governor ANTONIO DE MENDOZA. In early January 1543, Ferrelo assumed command of the expedition following Cabrillo's death on an island in the Santa Barbara Channel. He continued the search for the Strait of Anian, reaching as far as Cape Blanco on the Pacific coast of Oregon, which he sighted and named. Problems with the ships, food shortages, and severe weather led Ferrelo to end his explorations and head back to Mexico. While sailing southward along the coast of what is now northern California, he sighted a strip of land, which he named Cape Mendocino in honor of Mendoza. Ferrelo and the expedition arrived back at Navidad, Mexico, on April 14, 1543.

The eleven-month cruise, begun by Cabrillo and completed by Bartolomé Ferrelo, demonstrated to Spanish geographers and navigators that the coastline from Mexico to California was unbroken. Although Ferrelo brought no news about the Strait of Anian, he had gone farther north along the Pacific coast of North America than any other European had up to that time, making the first recorded sighting of the Oregon coast.

Ferris, Warren Angus (1810–1873)
American fur trapper, cartographer, writer in the West

Warren Ferris was originally from Glens Falls, New York. His family, who were Quakers, later moved to Erie, Pennsylvania, before settling in Buffalo, New York.

Following his early education, Ferris studied civil engineering. At the age of 19, he made his way westward, arriving in St. Louis, Missouri, in 1829. He soon joined an AMERICAN FUR COMPANY expedition from St. Louis to the upper MISSOURI RIVER and the northern ROCKY MOUNTAINS. While working under Joseph Robidoux, brother of ANTOINE ROBIDOUX, Ferris became acquainted with some of the best-known fur trappers and MOUNTAIN MEN of that time, including JOSEPH REDDEFORD WALKER, JAMES BRIDGER, and THOMAS FITZPATRICK.

In about 1835, Ferris left the FUR TRADE on the Missouri and headed southward for Texas. Along with his brother, Charles, he took part in the Texas War of Independence of 1836, then settled in the east Texas county of Nacogdoches, serving as county surveyor. He later settled with his family in Dallas, where his wife and all his children died of disease. Ferris eventually moved on to Reinhardt, Texas, where he started a second family.

In 1836, Warren Ferris produced his "Map of the Northwest Fur Country," depicting most of what is now Oregon, Idaho, Montana, and Washington. Six years later, he published an account of his career in the fur trade, *Life in the Rocky Mountains*. His map and his written memoirs both provide some of the earliest published accounts of the Yellowstone region, identifying locations and natural features with the original names used by fur traders of the 1820s and 1830s.

Fiennes, Celia (1662–1741) *English writer, traveler in England*

Celia Fiennes was born in Newton Toney in Salisbury, England. Her grandfather William Fiennes, first viscount Saye and Sele, an English nobleman, served in the House of Lords and was active in the Puritan cause against the monarchy from 1628 to 1642.

In 1685, Fiennes began to travel throughout England with her servants, partly as a way of regaining her health through exercise and exposure to fresh air. Her first travels, through 1696, were in southern England. She embarked on what she called a "northern journey" in 1697. The next year, she made forays into Scotland and Wales. In 1701–03, she explored London environs. Fiennes kept a journal of her experiences, entitled *Through England on a Side-Saddle* (another title *The Journeys of Celia Fiennes, 1685–c. 1712*). First published in 1888, it provides descriptions of many different aspects of contemporary life in the places she visited, from narrow wilderness lanes to the great estates to mines and quarries and manufacturing centers.

Celia Fiennes was one of the first women known to have traveled for the express purpose of seeing and experiencing new places at a time when most overland journeys were difficult, with public transportation being rare or nonexistent, and the means of transport having to be provided by the traveler.

Filchner, Wilhelm (1877–1957) *German army officer, geophysicist in central Asia and the Antarctic*

Wilhelm Filchner was born in Munich, Germany. Following his education as a geophysicist, he entered the German army as an officer.

Filchner made several explorations into the Balkans and Russia. Then, in 1900, he made a crossing by horseback of the Pamirs, the mountainous region of central Asia in what is now Tajikistan. Three years later, in 1903, accompanied by his wife and Albert Tafel, he undertook a two-year survey of eastern Tibet and southern China, exploring the upper YELLOW RIVER (Huang He) and visiting the Szechwan (Sichuan) region to the south, including Shensi, Shansi, Langchow, and Kansu. On this expedition, he conducted his first studies of terrestrial magnetism in Asia.

Filchner led the Second German Antarctic Expedition of 1910–12. His ship, the *Deutschland,* reached Coats Land on the Weddell Sea coast about the same time that ROBERT FALCON SCOTT and ROALD ENGELBREGT GRAVNING AMUNDSEN were involved in separate attempts to reach the SOUTH POLE from the Ross Sea on the opposite side of the continent. Filchner's main scientific purpose was to learn whether the Weddell Sea and the Ross Sea were connected, and determine whether two distinct landmasses made up the continent. Filchner and his team on the *Deutschland* penetrated farther into the Weddell Sea than had any previous explorers. His progress was eventually stopped by an ice barrier, similar to the Ross Ice Shelf, in which his ship became icebound in March 1912. After establishing a base camp on the ice, his men explored the region and came upon a new strip of Antarctic mainland adjacent to Coats Land, which

Wilhelm Filchner *(Library of Congress)*

Filchner named Luitpold Land (now the Luitpold Coast), after the prince regent of Bavaria. The ship survived the Antarctic winter without being crushed in the PACK ICE and, after drifting northward several hundred miles, managed to break free in November 1912.

Filchner returned to central Asia as the head of German scientific surveys during 1925–28. On these expeditions, he mapped the terrain and established a series of stations to study terrestrial magnetism. In 1939–40, he undertook a magnetic survey in Nepal.

Wilhelm Filchner's Antarctic explorations of 1910–12 helped scientists develop a true geographic image of the ice-shrouded continent. The ice barrier at the head of the Weddell Sea that Filchner located was named the Filchner Ice Shelf in his honor. In the course of the INTERNATIONAL GEOPHYSICAL YEAR of 1957–58, scientific bases were established between the Ross Ice Shelf and the Filchner Ice Shelf, enabling seismologists to determine that the Ross Sea and the Weddell Sea were actually closer to each other than previously thought, separated by an isthmus less than 700 miles wide. From this finding, Antarctica was henceforth depicted as composing two major regions: Greater Antarctica and Lesser Antarctica.

Finley, John (John Findley) (1722–ca. 1769)
American frontiersman in Kentucky

Born in northern Ireland, John Finley immigrated with his family to Pennsylvania when in his early 20s. In 1744, he was granted a license to trade with the Indians on the upper Ohio River, and in the following years, he ranged throughout present-day eastern Kentucky and southern Ohio.

In 1752, Finley was taken captive by Shawnee Indians near the Falls of the Ohio. He was taken to the Indian villages in the Kentucky lowlands, where he was one of the first non-Indians to see the fertile forests and prairies that later became known as the Bluegrass country of Kentucky. Although he was at first unsure of where he was in relation to the settled regions to the east, Finley soon learned from other itinerant traders that the region was readily accessible from western North Carolina and what is now eastern Tennessee, by way of the CUMBERLAND GAP.

Within a short time, the Shawnee released Finley, and he made his way back to the settlements on the Pennsylvania frontier. Although there was a growing demand for new lands to settle, his reports of the Bluegrass country were not followed up due to the outbreak of the French and Indian War in 1754. In that conflict, Finley served as a wagon driver in General Edward Braddock's unsuccessful 1755 campaign against Fort Duquesne, near present-day Pittsburgh. In that campaign, Finley befriended frontiersman DANIEL BOONE.

After the war's end in 1763, Finley became a peddler of wares to frontier housewives. In 1768, he arrived in western North Carolina's Yadkin Valley, where Boone had settled. While wintering with Boone in 1768–69, Finley related accounts of a possible route north and west from the Yadkin Valley into the fertile Kentucky lands he had visited in 1752. By spring 1769, Boone had organized a small expedition to explore westward from the Yadkin Valley, hoping to locate new lands to settle west of the APPALACHIAN MOUNTAINS.

Accompanied by Boone and three of his hunting companions, and equipped by frontier land developer Judge Richard Henderson, Finley set out from the Yadkin Valley settlement on May 1, 1769. Traveling on horseback, Finley, Boone, and the others traveled into the valleys of the upper Tennessee River, then down the Watauga and Holston Rivers into a region known as the Clinch. From there, they reached Powell's Valley, then found an ancient north-south route used by the Cherokee Indians, known as the Warriors' Trace. Following the Warriors' Trace, they passed through the Cumberland Gap and, having crossed the Cumberland River, arrived in the rich country Finley had reached 18 years earlier from the Ohio River.

While the other members of the party set out on their own to hunt, Finley explored the region with Boone. In December 1769, the two frontiersmen were captured by Shawnee but managed to escape. Soon afterward, Boone and his companions returned to North Carolina and the Yadkin Valley, where Boone soon organized a colonizing expedition through the Cumberland Gap into what is now Kentucky. Finley subsequently returned to his life as a frontier trader, but he died in the wilderness not long after his 1769 explorations with Boone.

John Finley was one of the first non-Indians to travel into the trans-Appalachian frontier in the years prior to the French and Indian War of 1756–63. His trip through the Cumberland Gap with Boone in 1769 helped establish a regular route for the subsequent wave of emigrants who began to settle on the Kentucky frontier in the 1770s.

Fitch, Ralph (ca. 1550–1611) *English merchant, traveler in India and the Far East*

Ralph Fitch was a merchant in London in the final decades of the 16th century. In 1583, he took part in a commercial expedition that planned to establish trade contacts with India and China by means of an overland route from the eastern MEDITERRANEAN SEA.

On February 12, 1583, Fitch sailed from London on the ship the *Tiger*, part of a group of six merchants from the London-based LEVANT COMPANY. Along with JOHN NEWBERRY, who had only recently completed a trip to Persia (present-day Iran), the other travelers included William Leeds, a jeweler; J. Story, a painter; and J. Eldred, a merchant. In May 1583, after landing at the port of Tripolis (present-day Tripoli, Lebanon), the English merchants traveled inland to Aleppo in present-day Syria, where they joined a camel caravan across the desert to Bir on the Euphrates River. They purchased a boat there and sailed down the Euphrates to Felujah, then made their way overland to Baghdad. From Baghdad, they descended the Tigris River in a flat-bottomed boat, to Basra at the head of the Persian Gulf, where Eldred remained to trade.

In Hormuz, at the entrance to the Persian Gulf, Fitch and his companions were arrested by Portuguese authorities on the instigation of Venetian commercial interests, who feared English encroachment into their trading domain. Taken in custody to Goa, the Portuguese colony on the southwest coast of India, they were held as prisoners until late December 1583, when their release was secured with the help of an English Jesuit in India, THOMAS STEVENS.

From Goa, Fitch decided to head inland for the capital of the Mogul empire at Agra in north-central India. Newberry headed back to England by way of Lahore, but he vanished soon afterward in the Punjab in what is now northern Pakistan, probably murdered by bandits. Fitch made his way across the Deccan Plateau to the newly established Mogul capital, Fatehpur Sikri, near Agra, where he met with the Mogul emperor, Akbar, to whom he presented diplomatic letters from Queen Elizabeth I.

While no commercial treaty was established between India and England, Fitch did initiate the earliest diplomatic ties between the two countries. William Leeds, the jeweler, remained in service to the court of Akbar, and J. Story returned to Goa, where he married an Indian woman and settled down as a foreign trader. Fitch, meanwhile, resolved to reach China in order to establish diplomatic and commercial contacts with that country.

From Agra, Fitch went by boat along the Jumna River to Allahabad, then traveled along the GANGES RIVER. He visited Benares and soon entered what is now Bangladesh. He headed northward to Cooch Behar, seeking a route into China. Failing to find one, he headed back southward down the Ganges to the ancient city of Sunargon. In November 1586, he traveled to Burma (present-day Myanmar) by ship, then ascended the Irrawaddy River to Rangoon and the ancient Burmese capital at Pegu. From Burma, he traveled into what is now Thailand, Vietnam, and Cambodia. In January 1588, he sailed from Pegu in what is now southern Burma, to Malacca at the tip of the Malay Peninsula.

Fitch was unable to book passage into China as he had hoped, and, in 1590–91, he made his way back to London by way of the southwest coast of India, the Persian Gulf, the Euphrates, and the Mediterranean, returning on April 29, 1591, after a journey of more than eight years.

Ralph Fitch was among the first Englishmen to reach India by way of an overland route. The main purpose of the expedition—to develop an overland trade route to India that would favorably compete with the long seaward passage around the CAPE OF GOOD HOPE—proved to be impractical. Nonetheless, Fitch gained invaluable experience in his travels. He later played an active part in the organization of the BRITISH EAST INDIA COMPANY, serving as a consultant in the preparation of its first voyage to India in 1601. In 1598, RICHARD HAKLUYT published an account of Fitch's journey to India and the Far East.

Fitzpatrick, Thomas (ca. 1799–1854) *Irish fur trader, trapper, guide in the American West*

Thomas Fitzpatrick, a native of County Cavan in north-central Ireland, first traveled to the American West in spring 1823, when he joined WILLIAM HENRY ASHLEY's fur-trading expedition to the upper MISSOURI RIVER, out of St. Louis. Following a raid by the Arikara Indians on Ashley's supply boats about 200 miles north of Fort Kiowa in north-central South Dakota, Fitzpatrick joined Colonel HENRY LEAVENWORTH's men in a counterattack.

With continuing Indian attacks threatening the FUR TRADE on the upper Missouri, Ashley decided to send a party of his trappers westward across the plains to explore for new sources of beaver pelts in the region west of the Continental Divide, beyond the Wind River Mountains of present-day Wyoming. Fitzpatrick, JEDEDIAH STRONG SMITH, JAMES CLYMAN, WILLIAM LEWIS SUBLETTE, and others made up this expedition, which departed Fort Kiowa on the Missouri in fall 1823.

Snowstorms prevented Fitzpatrick and his party from crossing the ROCKY MOUNTAINS through Union Pass. They wintered with the Crow Indians and, in February 1824, they headed southward for the Sweetwater River. Following this stream into the Rockies, they made their way across the Continental Divide via the SOUTH PASS, a 50-mile-wide plateau through the Wyoming Rockies, to the upper reaches of the Green River by March. They found beaver in great abundance and soon had amassed a small fortune in furs.

Fitzpatrick hoped to navigate the Sweetwater and reach St. Louis by way of the Missouri, but his boats sank. After hiding his furs, he walked 500 miles across the plains to Fort Atkinson on the Missouri near present-day Omaha, Nebraska. Before returning with horses to retrieve his cache by way of the Platte River, he wrote to Ashley in St. Louis to report his finding of a land rich in beaver on the western slopes of the Wind River Mountains, just west of the South Pass.

In fall 1824, Fitzpatrick accompanied Ashley's expedition, which included ROBERT CAMPBELL, from Fort Atkinson up the Platte River across the Laramie, Medicine Bow, and Front Mountains, a route later approximated by the Union Pacific Railroad. The Ashley party traveled along the edge of south-central Wyoming's Red Desert, then headed southward to the North Platte. They reached the South Pass and finally the Green River. In June 1825, Fitzpatrick attended the first annual trappers' rendezvous at Henrys Fork of the Green River in present-day northeastern Utah.

During the late 1820s and early 1830s, Fitzpatrick was among the most successful fur traders of the upper Missouri. He eventually became a principal of the ROCKY MOUNTAIN FUR COMPANY.

In 1831, Fitzpatrick joined a trade caravan from St. Louis, Missouri, to Santa Fe, New Mexico, then still part of Mexico. On reaching Santa Fe, he organized a group of trappers to head northward into the Rockies, thus expanding the geography of the fur trade. Among the Santa Fe personnel was frontiersman CHRISTOPHER HOUSTON CARSON (Kit Carson).

During the 1830s, Fitzpatrick's fur-trading activities took him all over the West, from Santa Fe across the Great Basin to what is now Idaho and eastern Oregon. In 1835, he purchased Fort Laramie from William Sublette and Robert Campbell. In 1836, he used the knowledge gained from his years as a mountain man to guide the Presbyterian missionary MARCUS WHITMAN across the plains to the Oregon Country. In 1838, accompanied by JAMES BAKER, Fitzpatrick led an AMERICAN FUR COMPANY expedition along the Oregon Trail. By the late 1830s, the fur trade had declined, and Fitzpatrick sold out his shares in the business to the American Fur Company.

In 1841, along with the Jesuit missionary PIERRE-JEAN DE SMET, Fitzpatrick served as a guide for the Western Emigration Society, the first large wagon-train migration across the Rockies. The Bidwell-Bartleson wagon train traveled from Independence, Missouri, westward through what is now Topeka, Kansas, along the Platte River to Fort Laramie. After passing Independence Rock, the emigrants followed the Sweetwater River, through the South Pass, to the Green River Valley, then headed northward to Soda Springs, near present-day Pocatello, Idaho. At a point north of the Great Salt Lake on the Bear River, Fitzpatrick led part of the wagon train northwestward, while the rest of the party opted to head south and west across Nevada's Humboldt Desert. He left his group at Fort Hall, Idaho, from where they safely traveled to Oregon. The next year, he guided a wagon train to Oregon for Methodist missionary Elijah White.

In 1843–44, Fitzpatrick, along with Kit Carson, served as a guide for JOHN CHARLES FRÉMONT's second expedition across the Rockies, from Westport, Missouri, up the Arkansas River. Frémont dispatched Fitzpatrick to lead an advance party to the South Pass, while he sought a more southerly route through the eastern Rockies. Fitzpatrick led his contingent westward across the Green River Valley to Fort Hall in what is now southwestern Idaho, where he rejoined Frémont.

Starting in 1845, Fitzpatrick served as the Indian agent to tribes living between the Arkansas and Platte Rivers, with his headquarters at Bent's New Fort in what is now southeastern Colorado.

In 1845–46, Fitzpatrick served as a guide for both STEPHEN WATTS KEARNY and JAMES WILLIAM ABERT in military explorations of the Canadian River and Arkansas River regions of what is now northern Texas and southern Oklahoma. Soon afterward, he was a guide for Kearny and his invasion force as it crossed the southern plains from Kansas into New Mexico at the outbreak of the U.S.-Mexican War of 1846–48. Kearny subsequently sent Fitzpatrick to Washington, D.C., with military dispatches.

In 1851, at Fort Laramie in present-day Wyoming, Fitzpatrick participated in a peace conference with tribal leaders of the northern plains. In 1853, he held a subsequent conference with tribal leaders of the southern plains near present-day Dodge City, Kansas. The next year, on a trip to Washington, D.C., to oversee the implementation of the resulting Indian treaties, he became ill and died.

Thomas Fitzpatrick's early expeditions in the fur trade during the 1820s led to the first westward crossing of the Rockies through the South Pass. His pioneering a route to the Green River widely expanded the fur trade. As a guide to the earliest wagon trains, Fitzpatrick established the overland route that led to settlement of Oregon and California. His efforts as a guide for the government-sponsored explorations of the 1840s helped in charting the wide region that the United States was to acquire in Oregon in 1846, as well as in the Southwest and Far West with the Mexican Cession of 1848.

Fitzroy, Robert (1805–1865) *British naval officer, meteorologist in South America, the Pacific, and the Indian Ocean*

Robert Fitzroy was born at Ampton Hall in Suffolk, England. A direct descendant of Charles II and his mistress Barbara Villiers, he was the son of a lord, the grandson of a duke, and the nephew of Robert Stewart, Viscount Castlereagh, the British foreign minister at the close of the Napoleonic Wars.

In 1819, Fitzroy entered the Royal Naval College, eventually joining the British navy. By 1824, he had reached the rank of lieutenant. In 1826, after serving in the MEDITERRANEAN SEA, he accompanied Commander PHILLIP PARKER KING, aboard the *Adventure,* on a four-year hydrographic survey of the coasts of South America. In 1828, Fitzroy was given command of the expedition's other ship, the *Beagle,* when Captain Pringle Stokes committed suicide.

In 1831, Fitzroy, at the rank of lieutenant commander, was again given charge of the *Beagle* for a scientific expedition to continue the coastal survey of South America and to make a series of chronometric measurements at various points around the globe in order to establish meridians of longitude. CHARLES ROBERT DARWIN accompanied the expedition as naturalist.

Fitzroy sailed from Portsmouth, England, in December 1831. He cruised along the coast of Brazil and Uruguay, putting in at Buenos Aires in September 1832. He sailed to the Falkland Islands, then surveyed the coast of Patagonia, south to Tierra del Fuego. On his earlier voyage with King, Fitzroy had taken three native Patagonians back to England, where he had paid for their education. The two men, Jemmy Button and York Minster, and a woman, Fuegia Basket, returned to Tierra del Fuego with Fitzroy on the *Beagle* in January 1833. They went ashore at Ponsonby Sound, along with a missionary named Mathews. Their arrival in European garb was met with some hostility by other natives; the missionary, fearing for his life, soon returned to the ship. Despite some difficulties, the three decided to remain in their homeland.

Fitzroy carried on the survey of the Atlantic and Pacific coasts of the southern part of South America for most of 1833, while Darwin undertook scientific expeditions into the interior of Chile and Argentina. In April 1834, Fitzroy and Darwin ascended the Santa Cruz River of southern Argentina in whaleboats, reaching a point 60 miles from the Pacific coast of South America, before heading back to the *Beagle* in the Atlantic.

Fitzroy navigated through the STRAIT OF MAGELLAN, then visited Chiloé Island off the coast of southern Chile. After a month in the Galapagos, the expedition headed across the Pacific, reaching Tahiti in September 1835. From there, Fitzroy went to NEW ZEALAND, then to Sydney, Australia, and finally to TASMANIA. Throughout the voyage across the Pacific, Fitzroy made chronometric observations at various points and succeeded in establishing accurate readings of longitude. After a stopover at the western Australian settlement at King George Sound, the *Beagle* headed into the Indian Ocean. Off the Cocos Islands, in the mid-Indian Ocean, Fitzroy and Darwin explored coral atoll formations. From Cape Town, Fitzroy sailed northwestward to Ascension Island and on to the Brazilian coast, where he continued his chronometric measurements. He reached England in October 1836.

Fitzroy spent the next few years preparing an account, with Darwin, of his 10 years of world explorations. It was first published in 1839 with the self-explanatory title, *Narrative of the Surveying Voyages of H. M. Ships Adventure and Beagle between the years 1826 and 1836, describing their Examination of the Southern Shores of South America, and the Beagle's Circumnavigation of the Globe.* The ROYAL GEOGRAPHICAL SOCIETY awarded Fitzroy a gold medal in 1837.

Fitzroy was elected to the House of Commons in 1841, serving until 1843, when he accepted an appointment as governor of New Zealand. Because he sided with the native Maori in a dispute with colonists involving land claims, he was recalled to England in 1845.

In 1854, Fitzroy became head of the Meteorological Department of the British Board of Trade. In this capacity, he introduced many innovations, including a system of storm warnings that developed into daily weather forecasts. He also wrote and published a classic treatise on meteorology, *The Weather Book* (1861), and developed a new and inexpensive type of barometer that came to be known as the Fitzroy Barometer. Promoted to rear admiral in 1857, he was made a vice admiral in 1863.

Fitzroy was prone to mental instability; he reportedly had informed Darwin during the *Beagle* voyage of 1831–35 that insanity ran in his family. In April 1865, he committed suicide in Surrey, England, by cutting his throat.

Robert Fitzroy's 1831–36 scientific expedition on the *Beagle,* through Darwin's subsequent theoretical conclusions, changed the course of scientific and social thought worldwide. Ironically, he was one of the first to criticize Darwin's findings on religious grounds. In 1832, Fitzroy, who was an adherent of literal interpretation of Scripture, challenged Darwin's speculations about the age of fossils uncovered in Patagonia because the naturalist's views seemed to contradict the biblical account of the Great Flood.

Fitzwilliam, William   See MILTON, VISCOUNT.

Flatters, Paul-Xavier (1832–1881) *French army officer in North Africa*

A colonel in the French army, Paul-Xavier Flatters was directed, in 1879, to organize and lead a survey for a proposed railroad route from the coast of Algeria on the MEDITERRANEAN SEA southward to a point on the southern edge of the SAHARA DESERT, between Lake Chad and the NIGER RIVER. At that time, France was developing its colonial empire in North Africa, and, fearful of German encroachment into its sphere of influence, hoped to use the railroad to link its colonies in West Africa with the Mediterranean ports of Algeria and Tunisia.

In command of a small party of soldiers, Flatters set out from the Algerian coastal town of Skikda, between Tunis and Algiers, in 1880. He headed southward to the oasis at Biskra, then advanced another 400 miles beyond Ouargla, to a point northeast of the Tassili n' Ajjer Mountains. Flatters's expedition had not been intended as a military operation, and he had been instructed to avoid conflict with the Tuareg tribes who ranged across the Ahaggar, the high desert plateau region of southeastern Algeria. Nevertheless, on the northern edge of the Ahaggar, Flatters and his men encountered open opposition from the Tuareg and were forced to withdraw northward to the Mediterranean coast.

In 1880–81, Flatters again attempted to survey southward for a railroad route across the Sahara. He started out from Algiers with a group of soldiers that included a Lieutenant Dianous as second in command. The expedition reached Ouargla, then penetrated the Ahaggar as far as the TROPIC OF CANCER. Soon afterward, Flatters and some of his men were killed in a Tuareg ambush at a desert waterhole. Lieutenant Dianous led the surviving members of the expedition back to a French military post in the Grand Erg Oriental to the north.

For 30 years after the ill-fated expeditions in 1880–81 of Paul-Xavier Flatters, subsequent official French expeditions into the Sahara were usually military operations, aimed at bringing the Tuareg tribes of the Ahaggar region under control.

Fleuriot de Langlé, Paul-Antoine-Marie (1744–1787) *French naval officer in the South Pacific*

Paul Fleuriot de Langlé was a native of Quimper-Guezennec, in the Lower Brittany region of northwestern France. His early maritime career took him to Santo Domingo in the WEST INDIES. In 1778, he took part in the naval battle against the British off the island of Ushant, on the French coast.

In 1782, Fleuriot de Langlé commanded the French warship *Astrée* in JEAN-FRANÇOIS DE GALAUP, comte de La Pérouse's attack on the British in HUDSON BAY.

Fleuriot de Langlé was named director of the Royal Naval Academy in 1783. Two years later, he joined La

Pérouse on his voyage of exploration to the South Pacific. In command of the *Astrolabe,* he left Brest on August 1, 1785, with the *Boussole* under La Pérouse. While exploring Sakhalin Island in June 1787, La Pérouse sighted a bay that he named after Fleuriot de Langlé.

In December 1787, the expedition arrived in the eastern Samoa islands. On one of them known as Tutuila, Fleuriot de Langlé led a party ashore to replenish his ship's water supply. A group of natives, massed on the beach, suddenly turned hostile and attacked Fleuriot de Langlé and the 61 men with him. Fleuriot de Langlé and 11 other men were killed, and 20 were wounded. Three months later, La Pérouse and both of his ships vanished after leaving Botany Bay, Australia, en route to the Friendly Islands.

News of the violent incident in which Paul Fleuriot de Langlé and the other Frenchmen lost their lives reached France by way of reports sent by La Pérouse from Australia. The site on the Samoan island of Tutuila where the event occurred has since become known as Massacre Bay.

Flinders, Matthew (Mathew Flinders)

(1774–1814) *British naval officer in Australia and Tasmania, cousin of Sir John Franklin*

Born in Donington, in Lincolnshire, England, Matthew Flinders was the son of a doctor. He attended Donington Free School and Horbling Grammar School. Inspired to embark on a life of travel and adventure from his reading of *Robinson Crusoe,* he entered the British navy as a 15-year-old midshipman in 1789.

Flinders served under Captain WILLIAM BLIGH on the *Providence* in a 1791–93 voyage that succeeded in taking live breadfruit trees from Tahiti in the South Pacific Ocean, to Jamaica in the WEST INDIES.

In 1794, serving under Admiral Richard "Black Dick" Howe on the *Bellerophon,* Flinders took part in the British naval victory over the French at Brest. The next year, he sailed to Port Jackson (part of present-day Sydney), Australia, on the *Reliance.* Also aboard was the newly appointed governor of New South Wales, Captain John Hunter, and the ship's surgeon, GEORGE BASS.

During the next three years, with Hunter's support, Flinders and Bass undertook explorations along the Australian coast south of Port Jackson. They investigated the Georges River at the head of Botany Bay, just south of Port Jackson; farther south they located another bay, which they named Port Hacking. In late 1798, Flinders and Bass sailed the sloop *Norfolk* westward around the southeastern corner of Australia. They then circumnavigated TASMANIA, conclusively showing that it was an island separated from the mainland by a strait, which Flinders named Bass Strait.

Matthew Flinders *(Library of Congress)*

Back in England in 1800, Flinders sought SIR JOSEPH BANKS's support for his plan to explore the uncharted portions of the Australian coasts. Banks, president of the Royal Society, used his influence to win the approval of the British Admiralty. At that time, the British government was alarmed over possible French designs on Tasmania and Australia, as indicated by the expedition of THOMAS-NICOLAS BAUDIN, which sailed in October 1800.

Flinders, at the rank of frigate captain, was given command of the *Investigator.* Among the crew of officers, seamen, scientists and artists was a 15-year-old midshipman and cousin of Flinders, the future polar explorer SIR JOHN FRANKLIN.

Although on the brink of war with Great Britain in 1801, Napoleon granted the British a written promise of safe conduct for Flinders and the *Investigator,* in exchange for a similar British pledge in regard to the ongoing Baudin expedition. The *Investigator* embarked from the British naval port at Spithead on July 18, 1801, and navigated around the tip of Africa and through the Indian Ocean. By late November, Flinders sighted the west coast of Australia at Dirk Hartogs Island. Sailing southward, he rounded Cape Leeuwin at the southwestern corner of the continent, then sailed eastward along the uncharted coastline of the Great Australian Bight.

When the coast angled sharply northward, Flinders thought he had reached the entrance to either a strait that led through the continent to the north coast, or the outlet of a great sea in the interior of Australia. Upon further exploration, he learned that it was a gulf leading 200 miles into the continent. Exploring in a small boat with FERDINAND LUCAS BAUER, ROBERT BROWN, and artist WILLIAM WESTALL, Flinders made a landing at present-day Port Augusta at the head of what he named Spencer Gulf (after the first lord of the Admiralty), and climbed Mount Brown in what came to be known as the Flinders Range.

Proceeding eastward on his survey of Australia's south coast, Flinders soon came upon another, smaller gulf, Gulf St. Vincent, around which the city of Adelaide later developed. At the mouth of Gulf St. Vincent, across what came to be known as Investigator Strait, a large island was sighted. Upon landing there, Flinders and his crew discovered it to be teeming with seals and kangaroos. The kangaroos, unfamiliar with humans, were easy prey for the British and provided the expedition with an ample supply of fresh meat. Flinders later named the place Kangaroo Island.

On April 8, 1802, soon after the stop at Kangaroo Island, at a place later known as Encounter Bay, Flinders met up with the French expedition under Nicolas Baudin on the *Géographe*. At a friendly meeting aboard the French ship, Flinders related to Baudin the details of his explorations along the south coast of Australia, providing the French commander with a copy of a map of his recent survey.

Leaving the French at Encounter Bay, Flinders decided to put in at Port Jackson, his crew then beginning to suffer from SCURVY. By the time he had reached Port Jackson in May 1802, he had completed his examination of the entire south coast of Australia and determined that the coastline was continuous, thus indicating that Australia was of continental proportions, and not a group of large islands, as some geographers then believed. In addition, Flinders and his party had some contact with Aborigines of the south coast, and noted that their language was different from that spoken by the Aborigines indigenous to New South Wales on the southeast coast.

Flinders resupplied his expedition at Port Jackson, then sailed northward along the east coast of Australia. While negotiating a passage through the northern end of the Great Barrier Reef, he made some of the earliest correct observations on the origins of these coral formations. Beyond Cape York, the *Investigator* sailed through Torres Strait, where Flinders found a new entrance into the Gulf of Carpentaria by way of Prince of Wales Strait.

From November 1802 to March 1803, Flinders charted the entire length of the Gulf of Carpentaria, from Cape York on the east to Cape Arnhem on the west. This survey determined that the Gulf was closed, with neither a transcontinental strait nor an inland sea opening up in that part of Australia's north coast.

By March 1803, the only segment of the Australian shore that remained for Flinders to chart was the north-

western Indian Ocean coastline. However, more signs of scurvy, and the deteriorating condition of the less than seaworthy *Investigator,* led Flinders to call an end to his survey and head for the Dutch settlement on Timor. Contrary winds compelled him to return to Port Jackson from Timor by sailing counterclockwise around Australia, thus completing a circumnavigation of the continent.

In Port Jackson, Flinders obtained three vessels from the BRITISH EAST INDIA COMPANY fleet to take his expedition back to England, where he hoped to find a replacement for the *Investigator* and complete his explorations of the Australian coastline. Sailing on the *Porpoise,* he left Port Jackson on August 10, 1803. A week later, the *Porpoise* went aground on a sandbar off the Great Barrier Reef. Flinders then commanded a 14-man party in one of the ship's small open boats and returned to Port Jackson, covering the 700 miles in less than two weeks.

Flinders soon sailed again from Port Jackson on the *Cumberland,* accompanied by two other ships that picked up the crew of the *Porpoise* at what later became known as Wreck Reef Bank.

Flinders, in command of the *Cumberland,* sailed northward to Timor, then headed across the Indian Ocean for England. Near the French-held island of Île de France (present-day Mauritius), it became apparent to Flinders that the ship was in no condition to make the voyage around the CAPE OF GOOD HOPE. With supplies of food running low, he made for Port Louis on Île de France, where he was arrested by the French governor, Charles Decaen.

Although Flinders presented Napoleon's letter of protection, the French governor held that it only applied to the *Investigator.* Not long before Flinders had arrived on Île de France, war had been declared between France and England, and Decaen strongly suspected Flinders of being a spy.

Flinders was held prisoner on Île de France for the next six and a half years. His captivity was protested by many leading figures, both French and British, and became a cause célèbre, known in France as "L'Affaire Flinders." Finally, in June 1810, following a British naval blockade of Île de France, Flinders was released. He arrived back in England in October 1810, where he began to work on an account of his expedition.

While Flinders had been detained on Île de France, the French had published the reputed findings of Baudin's expedition to Australia, giving him credit for Flinders's actual accomplishments in exploration. These false claims were exposed by the publication of Flinders's *A Voyage to Terra Australis* in 1814. Flinders had lost his health during the years of imprisonment and he died in 1814 at the age of 40, reportedly on the very day his book appeared. Although his work was not a big seller, it popularized the name "Australia" for the continent.

The explorations undertaken by Matthew Flinders from 1795 to 1803 established the true outlines of Australia and

Tasmania, putting to rest some erroneous notions. Flinders Island off the coast of Tasmania, Flinders Bay at the southwestern tip of Australia, and the Flinders River on the Gulf of Carpentaria were all named in recognition of his efforts in the exploration of Australia.

Fontenelle, Lucien (ca. 1800–ca. 1840)
American fur trader on the Missouri and Platte Rivers

Lucien Fontenelle was born on his family's plantation in southern Louisiana. Orphaned at an early age when both his parents were killed in a hurricane, he was taken in by an aunt. In rebellion against her strictness, he eventually ran away from home. Arriving in St. Louis, he embarked on a career as a fur trader.

Fontenelle went on to become a brigade leader on fur-trading expeditions to the upper MISSOURI RIVER region and into the ROCKY MOUNTAINS of present-day Colorado, Wyoming, Idaho, and Montana. In the late 1820s, he established a trading post at Bellevue on the Missouri River, south of what is now Omaha, Nebraska, and north of the mouth of the Platte River.

In 1830, Fontenelle became a subcontractor for JOHN JACOB ASTOR'S AMERICAN FUR COMPANY, organizing and leading fur-trading expeditions into the Rockies and northern plains.

Fontenelle's post at Bellevue on the Missouri served as the staging area for MARCUS WHITMAN and Samuel Parker in their missionary expedition to the Oregon Country in 1836. That same year, he went into partnership with THOMAS FITZPATRICK, JAMES BRIDGER, and Milton Sublette, starting a firm known as Fontenelle, Fitzpatrick & Co. Soon afterward, Fontenelle and his associates expanded their operations westward up the Platte River and purchased Fort Laramie in what is now southeastern Wyoming.

Fontenelle had an Indian wife, the daughter of an Omaha chief, who bore him four children. He died in 1839 or 1840 at Fort Laramie under circumstances that are still not clear, possibly from natural causes, although some sources suggest he committed suicide while drunk.

Lucien Fontenelle was a leading figure in the Rocky Mountain FUR TRADE during its peak years in the 1820s and 1830s. Around his post at Bellevue developed the earliest non-Indian settlement in what later became the state of Nebraska. After 1835, Fort Laramie, an important way station for emigrants traveling along the Oregon Trail, was also known as Fort Lucien.

Forbes, Edward (1815–1854) *British naturalist, marine biologist on the British Isles and in the Mediterranean Sea*

Edward Forbes was born on the Isle of Man in the Irish Sea between England and Ireland. He attended the University of Edinburgh in Scotland, during which time he studied the flora and fauna of the waters around the Isle of Man and off Norway. He also spent time in Paris, taking classes at the Jardin des Plantes.

In 1841–42, Forbes served as naturalist on a surveying expedition to the MEDITERRANEAN SEA on the *Beacon,* under the command of Captain Graves. He then ran the botany department at King's College, part of the University of Cambridge. He was elected to the Linnean Society in 1843 and to the ROYAL SOCIETY in 1845. He also served as secretary and curator of the Geological Society and professor of natural history at the University of Edinburgh.

In the course of his studies, Forbes collected samples from the deep seabed of the Irish and Aegean Seas. He determined that the amount of marine life varied the greater the depth and defined eight, what he called, "zones of abundance." He mistakenly concluded, however, that all aquatic life ceased below 300 fathoms. He also drafted a geological and paleontological map of the British Isles.

Edward Forbes's pioneering work in marine biology set the stage for later studies in the field, as well as for oceanographic work. He has been referred to as the father of marine biology.

Forrest, Alexander (1849–1901) *Australian explorer in Western Australia and Northern Territory, brother of John Forrest*

Born in Perth, on the west coast of Australia, Alexander Forrest was a younger brother of Australian explorer JOHN FORREST.

In 1871, Forrest explored up the Swan River from Perth into the interior of Western Australia and as far as the GREAT VICTORIA DESERT. On the return journey, he followed Australia's south coast back to Perth. Forrest joined his brother John in his historic west-to-east crossing of Western Australia in 1874, from Perth to Adelaide.

In 1879, Forrest turned his attention to the northwestern region of Australia. In February of that year, he sailed northward from Perth and landed at the mouth of the De Grey River. His expedition then headed inland, northeastward across Dampier Land, to the Fitzroy River. After an unsuccessful attempt to traverse the King Leopold Range, Forrest returned to the Fitzroy River and explored the southwestern part of the Kimberley Plateau. In July 1879, Forrest decided to leave the Fitzroy and travel overland eastward to the Daly River in Australia's Northern Territory. He soon came upon the Central Overland Telegraph Line, which led him to a settlement on the north coast of present-day Darwin.

Alexander Forrest's 1879 explorations of northwestern Australia resulted in the opening of land for grazing in the upper Fitzroy River region, south of the King Leopold Range. His journey from the Fitzroy River to the Daly River and the coast was one of the earliest non-Aborigine crossings of a large area of northern Australia, west of the Gulf of Carpentaria.

Forrest, John (Baron of Bunbury) (1847–1918)
Australian surveyor in interior Australia, statesman, brother of Alexander Forrest

John Forrest was born in Bunbury, Western Australia, and educated at Bishop's School in Perth. At the age of 18, he joined Western Australia's Survey Department.

Three years later, in 1869, Forrest led an expedition eastward into the interior of Western Australia from Perth, in search of traces of the German FRIEDRICH WILHELM LUDWIG LEICHHARDT, who had disappeared with his party 20 years earlier during an attempt to cross the continent from east to west. From Perth, Forrest traveled northeastward to Lake Moore, then continued eastward beyond the northern end of Lake Barlee to Lake Raeside. No sign of Leichhardt or his expedition was found. The skeletal remains discovered by Aborigines, which had prompted the search, were identified as those of stray horses from an 1854 expedition. Nevertheless, Forrest continued his explorations, surveying new pastoral lands as far as Mount Weld, on the western edge of the Great Victoria Desert. The expedition covered 2,000 miles, revealing much new territory suitable for raising livestock.

In 1870, Forrest commanded a coastal survey expedition eastward along the Great Australian Bight to Adelaide. His west-to-east journey to the Spencer Gulf and the Yorke Peninsula covered in reverse the territory explored by SIR EDWARD JOHN EYRE in 1841.

Forrest's next expedition started out from Perth in March 1874. He sailed 250 miles northward along the west coast of Australia, landing at Geraldton. From there, with four others, including his brother ALEXANDER FORREST, and equipped with 18 pack horses, he set out northwestward to explore the headwaters of the Murchison River. The group then went eastward to Weld Spring and Fort Mueller. After traversing the Gibson Desert, they explored southward into the Petermann Ranges of southwestern Northern Territory, and into the Tomkinson Ranges of northwestern South Australia. They followed the Alberga River to Lake Eyre, then traced the Central Overland Telegraph line southward to Adelaide, arriving in early November 1874.

With his arrival in Adelaide, Forrest had completed the first west-to-east crossing of the interior of Western Australia, and had traversed much of the continent's largely unexplored central region as well. The journey had been extremely difficult, with much hardship caused by shortages of food and water and the loss of all but four horses. For his efforts, Forrest was rewarded with a land grant of 5,000 acres, and, in 1876, he was made deputy surveyor general of Western Australia.

In 1878, Forrest led an expedition to the region around Western Australia's Ashburton River, and, in 1882, he surveyed the Fitzroy River region to the north. The next year, he was named surveyor general of Western Australia.

Forrest went on to become one of Western Australia's leading statesmen. He was elected its first premier in 1890, and, after 1901, he represented the newly organized state in the Australian federal parliament. In 1918, he was made the first baron of Bunbury, the first native-born Australian to be admitted to the British nobility. He died later that year while returning from England.

John Forrest recounted his exploits in his 1875 book *Explorations in Australia* and the 1884 work *Western Australia*. In addition to completing the first west-to-east crossing of the state of Western Australia in 1874, he created maps used to plot the first overland telegraph lines between Perth and the settlements of New South Wales, Victoria, and Queensland.

Forster, Johann Georg Adam (Georg Forster)
(1754–1794) *German naturalist in the South Pacific, in service to Great Britain, son of Johann Reinhold Forster*

Born in the East Prussian town of Nassenhuben, near present-day Gdańsk, Poland, Georg Forster was the son of German naturalist JOHANN REINHOLD FORSTER. At the age of 10, he accompanied the elder Forster on a botanical and zoological expedition to Russia as his assistant. After attending school in St. Petersburg, Russia, he moved to England with his family, where he continued his education.

Forster and his father served as the naturalists on JAMES COOK's second voyage of 1772–75. Sailing on the *Resolution* to the islands of the South Pacific Ocean, they collected specimens of plants and animals in NEW ZEALAND, Tahiti, and newly explored Norfolk Island, between New Zealand and New Caledonia.

When the expedition returned to England in July 1775, Forster set to work on his account of the voyage. Although Forster's father lost out to Cook in his bid to write the official account of the voyage, the British Admiralty did allow the publication of the younger Forster's unofficial account, *A Voyage Round the World*, published in 1777, which presented scientific information in the form of a popular travel narrative.

In 1778, Forster accepted an appointment as professor of natural history at Kassel in present-day Germany, where he remained for the next six years. In 1784, he moved to Vilnius, in what is now Lithuania, where he taught natural history and obtained a degree as doctor of medicine.

Catherine the Great of Russia invited Forster to take part in a proposed Russian voyage of exploration in the late 1780s, but plans for the expedition were abandoned with the outbreak of war with Turkey.

Forster then accepted the post as librarian to the Elector of Mainz in present-day Germany in 1788. Two years later, he accompanied the young ALEXANDER VON HUMBOLDT on a three-month expedition down the Rhine River through Belgium and Holland.

In 1792, when French forces occupied Mainz, Forster, who had rallied to the cause of the French Revolution, won an appointment as the city's official representative to the National Convention, the French revolutionary government in Paris. He traveled to the French capital in March 1793, hoping to secure the annexation of Mainz into the newly established French Republic. Not only were his efforts unsuccessful, but also he soon found himself without adequate means of support. His poverty led to malnutrition, and, in January 1794, he died in Paris of scorbutic fever, a disease with SCURVY-like symptoms.

Georg Forster, along with his father, carried on the scientific work in the South Pacific begun by SIR JOSEPH BANKS and greatly inspired the subsequent explorations of Alexander von Humboldt.

Forster, Johann Reinhold (1729–1798)
German naturalist in the South Pacific, in service to
Great Britain, father of Johann Georg Adam Forster
Johann Reinhold Forster was born at Dirschau in what is now northern Poland, the descendant of a Yorkshire family that had left England and settled in Prussia soon after the overthrow of Charles I in 1649. Although his primary interest was in natural history, he became a minister of the Reformed Church at his father's behest, heading a congregation at Nassenhuben, south of present-day Gdańsk.

In 1765, Forster went to St. Petersburg, where he took part in a Russian scientific expedition. The next year, he moved with his family to England; at Warrington, near Liverpool, he taught French, German, and the natural sciences.

With the help of geographer Alexander Dalrymple, Forster tried, without success, to secure an appointment with the BRITISH EAST INDIA COMPANY in 1770. In London over the next two years, he translated into English LOUIS-ANTOINE DE BOUGAINVILLE's account of his recent CIRCUMNAVIGATION OF THE WORLD.

In 1772, Forster sailed on the *Resolution* as the naturalist on JAMES COOK's second voyage of exploration to the South Pacific Ocean. Serving as his assistant on the expedition was his son JOHANN GEORG ADAM FORSTER. While en route to the Pacific, the elder Forster made a study of antelopes and seals around Cape Town, South Africa. Over the next three years, he collected specimens of plants and birds in NEW ZEALAND. Tahiti, and other South Pacific islands visited by Cook. In Australia, Forster made the earliest identification of the Australian sea lion; on Norfolk Island, between New Zealand and New Caledonia, he cataloged a previously unknown variety of palm tree. In the waters around Antarctica, Forster collected specimens of the region's birds, among them the snow petrel and the king and emperor penguins.

By the time the expedition had returned to England in 1775, differences had developed between Forster and Cook over who would write the official account of the voyage. The British Admiralty interceded on Cook's behalf and forbade Forster from publishing such a work in England, although his son published an account, using some of his manuscripts. Forster soon returned to Germany and, at Göttingen, wrote an account in Latin of his scientific work while on Cook's second voyage. In 1778, Forster's *Observations Made During a Voyage Round the World* was published in England.

In 1780, Forster accepted an appointment from Prussian king Frederick II to become director of the botanical gardens at Halle and teach natural history at that city's university. His book covering the history of exploration in the Northern Hemisphere was published in 1787.

While with Cook on the 1772–75 voyage, Johann Reinhold Forster, in addition to his studies of wildlife, undertook some of the earliest oceanographic studies. In his experiments at sea, he revealed the disparity between surface and subsurface ocean temperatures and conducted deep-sea soundings in which he collected blue mud from the floor of the Pacific at depths of 4,200 feet. Forster also undertook some of the earliest research in comparative anthropology, becoming one of the pioneers of that discipline. He made studies on the various racial types of the South Pacific islanders, noting the differences between natives of Polynesia and Melanesia in both their physical traits as well as their cultures.

Foureau, Fernand (1850–1914) *French engineer*
in North and central Africa
Fernand Foureau was born in Barbant, a town in west-central France. Trained as an engineer, he traveled to Algeria to take part in well-drilling projects in the SAHARA DESERT.

Starting in 1888, Foureau began to explore into the Algerian interior. On his eighth such expedition in 1895–96, he explored the desert region south of Biskra known as the Grand Erg Oriental. The next year, he went to Paris and succeeded in getting some support from the French government in the form of a military escort for a proposed railroad survey expedition from the Mediterranean coast of Algeria to Lake Chad on the northern edge of central Africa.

Known as the Sahara Mission, Foureau and his party, accompanied by a French military unit under a Major L. Lamy, left Ouargla, Algeria, in 1900 and made a north-to-south crossing of the Sahara, threading their way between the Tassili n' Ajjer and Ahaggar Mountains of southern Algeria, into present-day Niger. At Zinder, they went eastward to Lake Chad. At Kousseri, south of Lake Chad, the expedition was attacked by Bornu tribesmen. Although the French drove off the attackers, Lamy was killed in the battle.

Before long, Foureau joined up with two other ongoing French expeditions, the Congo-Chad Mission and the Central African Mission. He then proceeded overland southward to the Hari and Ubangi Rivers, ultimately reaching the CONGO RIVER (Zaire River), which he followed to the Atlantic Ocean.

Fernand Foureau went on to become governor of Mayotte and the nearby Comoro Islands in the Indian Ocean, west of Madagascar. His 1900–01 expedition succeeded in traversing the Sahara, establishing direct overland communications links between French colonies in North and central Africa, and completing the mission begun by PAUL-XAVIER FLATTERS 20 years earlier.

Fowler, Jacob (Major Fowler) (1765–1850)

American fur trader, trapper, guide on the southern plains and in southern Rocky Mountains

Originally from New York, Jacob Fowler moved to the northeastern Kentucky frontier while in his early twenties, settling in Covington, just south of what is now Cincinnati, Ohio. Known as Major Fowler, he was an accomplished surveyor, and, in the years immediately before and after the War of 1812, he took part in U.S. government survey expeditions to the Great Plains and the foothills of the ROCKY MOUNTAINS, accompanied at times by his wife Esther.

Fowler, together with Cincinnati trader Hugh Glenn, undertook several supply expeditions to army posts in the Old Northwest, the upper Mississippi Valley, and the eastern edge of the southern plains. By 1821, Glenn had established a trading post near Fort Gibson in what is now northeastern Oklahoma, and, that year, he organized a fur-trapping and hunting expedition into the southern Rockies.

In September 1821, with Fowler as guide, Glenn and a party of 18 trappers and hunters set out from what later became Fort Smith, Arkansas. The Fowler-Glenn Expedition, as the venture was later known, followed the Verdigris River northward into present-day Kansas and, at the site of what is now Wichita, they headed westward along the Arkansas River across the Kansas plains, and into eastern Colorado. By November 13, they had reached the mouth of the Purgatory River, where one member of the party, Lewis Dawson, was killed in an attack by a grizzly bear. Soon afterward, they reached the Arapaho and Kiowa Indian settlements near what is now Pueblo, Colorado, where they planned to spend the winter.

At the end of December 1821, a group of Mexican traders visited the Fowler-Glenn encampment. They informed the Americans that, with Mexican independence declared earlier that year, they were now free to go southward

into the Taos region to pursue the FUR TRADE. Soon afterward, Fowler led the trappers through the Sangre de Cristo Mountains to Taos. Following a brief stay there, he and the group explored and trapped northward into the San Juan Mountains and the upper Rio Grande, as far as what is now Del Norte, Colorado.

Fowler and Glenn set out on their return trek across the southern plains in spring 1822. In Santa Fe, they joined up with another party of American traders under Thomas James, and the combined expedition headed eastward, south of the Arkansas River and the Santa Fe Trail, through the Chico Rico Mesa of eastern Colorado and along Two Butte Creek, reaching the Arkansas River on the present-day Colorado-Kansas stateline. In their eastward trek across Kansas, they made for the Whitewater and Verdigris Rivers, reaching the Missouri River at Fort Osage, near present-day Kansas City. The expedition arrived in St. Louis on July 17, 1822, having completed one of the first American fur-trapping forays into what was then Mexican territory.

The Fowler-Glenn Expedition of 1821–22 pioneered the route into Taos, New Mexico, through the Sangre de Cristo Mountains of southern Colorado, a pathway that came to be known as the Old Taos Trail. On the return journey, the expedition did not follow the Santa Fe Trail, but instead took a more direct route to the Arkansas River between the Cimarron Cutoff and Raton Pass. Along with WILLIAM BECKNELL and Thomas James, Jacob Fowler was one of the first American traders to enter the Mexican province of New Mexico in 1822, soon after it was opened to American trade. He led the first expedition known to have reached Pueblo, in present-day eastern Colorado, by way of the Verdigris and Arkansas Rivers, and also was one of the earliest Americans to explore the upper Rio Grande. The Old Taos Trail, which Jacob Fowler pioneered southward from Pueblo into Taos, did not become popular among trappers and traders until the 1840s. His account of the expedition into the southern Rockies was published in 1898 as *The Journal of Jacob Fowler*.

Foxe, Luke (Luke Fox) (1586–1635)

English mariner in Hudson Bay and the Canadian Arctic

Luke Foxe was born in Hull, a seaport on the northeastern coast of England. The son of a master mariner, he was largely self-educated, developing an early interest in the history of explorations into the Arctic regions.

Foxe became an accomplished seaman and coastal pilot, taking part in voyages between England and France. As early as 1606, he had become interested in the possibility of a NORTHWEST PASSAGE to the Orient. In 1629, with the help of SIR THOMAS ROE and a group of London merchants known as Trinity House, Foxe won the support of King Charles I for a proposed voyage to HUDSON BAY in search of the Northwest Passage.

On May 5, 1631, Foxe's expedition left Deptford on the *Charles,* carrying a crew of 23 men and provisioned for an 18-month voyage. Anticipating that he would find a route to the Far East by sailing northwestward, he carried a letter from King Charles for the emperor of Japan. After sailing along the east coast of England, he arrived at the Orkney Islands, then headed westward across the North Atlantic Ocean, reaching Hudson Strait on June 22, 1631.

In his quest for the Northwest Passage, Foxe sailed along the west coast of Southampton Island, exploring a channel he dubbed Sir Thomas Roe's Welcome Sound, then headed southward along the west shore of Hudson Bay. In late August, at the entrance to James Bay, he encountered a rival expedition from Bristol, England, under the command of THOMAS JAMES. He conferred with James off Cape Henrietta Maria, then headed northward to complete his explorations. He entered the strait east of Southampton Island, later known as Foxe Channel, and surveyed the southeasternmost coast of Baffin Island, which he named "Fox His Farthest" (known later as the Foxe Peninsula). He explored north of Southampton Island into the Foxe Basin, almost as far north as the ARCTIC CIRCLE.

Although he was equipped with enough supplies to spend the winter in Hudson Bay, Foxe decided to head back to England when his progress northward was blocked by DRIFT ICE and his crew began to show early signs of SCURVY.

Foxe returned to England at the end of October 1631, after a voyage of six months, and without the loss of a single crew member. Nevertheless, some of his backers were less than pleased with the short duration of his expedition; in response, Foxe set down his findings in his account *Northwest Fox, or Fox from the Northwest-Passage,* published in 1635. The work summarized all known Arctic explorations up to that time and detailed the survey of the west shore of Hudson Bay, stating that no outlet suggested a passage to the Pacific. Considered a classic account of Arctic exploration, it includes observations on the northern lights, ice formations, and Arctic flora and fauna. It also reports on tides around Southampton Island, which indicated that a westward passage might exist north of Hudson Bay. The book also includes a circumpolar map by Foxe.

Luke Foxe's voyage of 1631, along with that of Thomas James that same year, confirmed that the west shore of Hudson Bay was continuous and did not provide an outlet to the west, a finding that discouraged further British maritime exploration of the Canadian Arctic over the next two centuries. Foxe is additionally credited with being the first mariner known to have used in his navigations the newly devised logarithmic tables of one of his patrons, English mathematician Henry Briggs.

Fraeb, Henry (Old Frapp) (unknown–1841)
American fur trader, mountain man in the Rocky Mountains
There are few details of Henry Fraeb's origins or life prior to 1826, except that he was probably a German or Dutch emigrant. That year, he was exploring and trapping the Great Salt Lake region of present-day Utah with JAMES CLYMAN.

In 1830, Fraeb entered into a partnership with THOMAS FITZPATRICK, JAMES BRIDGER, Milton Sublette, and Jean B. Gervais to purchase the ROCKY MOUNTAIN FUR COMPANY from JEDEDIAH STRONG SMITH and his associates. Over the next four years, he led the company's fur-trapping brigades into the ROCKY MOUNTAINS, ranging across a wide area of the West, from northwestern Idaho to northern Arizona.

Competition from JOHN JACOB ASTOR'S AMERICAN FUR COMPANY, as well as problems in obtaining supplies, led Fraeb and his partners to sell the company to WILLIAM LEWIS SUBLETTE at the 1834 fur traders' rendezvous at Hams Fork of the Green River in present-day southwestern Wyoming.

In 1837, Fraeb founded a fur-trading post on the South Platte in eastern Colorado known as Fort Jackson, which he sold the following year to CHARLES BENT and CÉRAN DE HAULT DE LASSUS ST. VRAIN. He joined with James Bridger, again in 1840, in a fur-trading enterprise into the Green River region of western Wyoming. The two mountain men founded a fur-trading fort on the west branch of the Green River. In summer 1841, while leading a brigade of his trappers southeast of the fort, Fraeb was killed in an attack by Cheyenne, Arapaho, and Sioux (Dakota, Lakota, Nakota) Indians.

Henry Fraeb, known by his contemporaries as "Old Frapp," worked alongside some of the most famous fur traders and MOUNTAIN MEN of the 1820s and 1830s. His own career as a mountain man and trapper in the Rockies coincided with the heyday of the fur trade in the West, and the trading posts he established in present-day Colorado and Wyoming went on to serve as important way stations for emigrant parties headed for California and Oregon.

Franchère, Gabriel (1786–1863) *Canadian fur trader in the Pacific Northwest*
Gabriel Franchère was a native of Montreal, Canada, and spent his early adulthood involved with his father's mercantile business. In 1810, he joined JOHN JACOB ASTOR's fur-trading expedition to the Pacific Northwest.

Franchère and a party of nine VOYAGEURS, left Montreal in a birch-bark CANOE on the first leg of their voyage to the West. From the St. Lawrence River, they paddled and portaged southward by way of the Richelieu River, Lake Champlain, and the Hudson River, to Brooklyn and the port of New York. On September 6, 1810, Franchère and his companions embarked from New York on Astor's ship, the *Tonquin,* and, after a seven-month voyage by way of the CAPE HORN route, along with ROBERT STUART, arrived on the Oregon coast in February 1811.

Franchère soon became one of the directors at Astoria, the fur-trading fort he helped establish near the mouth of the COLUMBIA RIVER. He acquired a knowledge of Indian languages and, after the post was sold to the British-owned NORTH WEST COMPANY in October 1813, he remained there for another five months, serving the new owners as an interpreter. Franchère left for the East in April 1814, traveling overland with a brigade of trappers. By the following September, he was back in Montreal.

Over the next 20 years, Franchère was the Montreal agent for the AMERICAN FUR COMPANY. In 1834, he was Astor's agent at Sault Sainte Marie in northern Michigan. Franchère lost his position when the American Fur Company went out of business in 1842. He then joined PIERRE CHOUTEAU, JR.'s firm in New York and took over that company in 1857.

Gabriel Franchère's account of his adventures in the Oregon fur trade, entitled *Narrative of a Voyage to the Northwest Coast of America in the Years 1811, 1812, 1813, and 1814 or the First American Settlement on the Pacific,* was originally published in French in 1820. In 1846, U.S. senator Thomas Hart Benton used translated passages from it to buttress his arguments for an American takeover of the Oregon Country. The English version of Franchère's book was published in 1854.

Francis Xavier   See XAVIER, FRANCIS.

Franklin, Jane (Lady Franklin, Jane Griffin)

(1792–1875) *British world traveler, sponsor of expeditions to the Canadian Arctic, wife of Sir John Franklin*

Lady Jane Franklin was born Jane Griffin, the daughter of John Griffin of London, England. In the years before her marriage, she traveled widely with her father on trips throughout England and Europe.

She married British polar explorer SIR JOHN FRANKLIN on November 5, 1828. It was her first marriage and his second; his first wife, the poet Eleanor Anne Porden, had died three years earlier.

In the first years of her marriage, Lady Franklin traveled throughout Syria, Asia Minor (present-day Turkey), and Egypt, regularly joining up with Sir John, who was then in command of a British navy frigate in the eastern MEDITERRANEAN SEA. Starting in 1837, she resided for six years in Van Diemen's Land (present-day TASMANIA), while her husband served as the colony's governor. She campaigned for improved conditions for women convicts consigned to the

island's penal colonies. She also traveled to Australia and NEW ZEALAND.

In 1848, three years after Sir John had disappeared on his final polar expedition in search of the NORTHWEST PASSAGE, Lady Franklin offered a reward of £2,000 sterling for his rescue or for information about his fate. She also began to raise support for privately funded search expeditions, undertaken at times in conjunction with the British navy's relief efforts.

Lady Franklin gained the support of Henry Grinnell, a New York City businessman, who sent out an American search expedition commanded by EDWIN JESSE DE HAVEN in 1850.

Later, with her own funds, Lady Franklin organized a search expedition on the steam schooner *Isabel.* She had planned to send the *Isabel* into the Arctic by way of the BERING STRAIT but was unable to engage a crew for such a long and hazardous mission. In July 1852, the *Isabel,* under Captain Edward Augustus Inglefield, sailed to Greenland and Baffin Island, seeking traces of Franklin and his men and taking supplies to SIR EDWARD BELCHER's expedition, which was then involved in the British navy's search efforts in the Canadian Arctic. Inglefield and his crew searched the west coast of GREENLAND because of rumors that Franklin's expedition had been massacred by Inuit there. They explored Baffin Island, then entered Lancaster Sound in the Canadian Arctic, where they met up with Belcher. The expedition returned to England later in 1852 with little encouraging news about Franklin, although it had made some geographic findings in Smith Sound. She sponsored other expeditions as well during these years.

In 1854, when traces of the Franklin expedition were recovered by JOHN RAE of the HUDSON'S BAY COMPANY during an exploration of the Boothia Peninsula, Rae also heard reports from Inuit of their death. Yet Lady Franklin mounted another search effort for her husband. She outfitted the *Fox,* which sailed for the Canadian Arctic in 1857 under the command of SIR FRANCIS LEOPOLD McCLINTOCK. After two icebound winters, McClintock and his command located places on King William Island and Beechey Island where the Franklin expedition had been more than 10 years earlier and found written accounts of what had happened to its members. He learned that Sir John Franklin had died in June 1847, and the other members of the expedition had most likely perished on their attempted southward trek to the Back River the following year.

For her efforts in support of polar exploration, and her commitment to discovering what had happened to her husband in the Canadian Arctic, Lady Jane Franklin was awarded the ROYAL GEOGRAPHICAL SOCIETY's Founder's Medal in 1860, the first woman ever to be so honored. Moreover, based on evidence recovered by McClintock, she established that before his death, her husband had proved

Lady Jane Franklin *(Library of Congress)*

the existence of a Northwest Passage between Bering Strait and Victoria Strait. In the 1850s, when the search efforts for her husband were at their peak, she continued to travel, visiting such widely diverse parts of the world as Japan and the American West. Along with the official search expeditions, those supported by Lady Franklin also made important discoveries regarding the geography of the islands and channels of the Canadian Arctic. The voyage of the steam schooner *Isabel,* which she financed in 1852, demonstrated the advantages of steam-powered navigation in the ice-choked waters of the Arctic Ocean.

Franklin, Sir John (1786–1847) *British naval officer in the Canadian Arctic, husband of Lady Jane Franklin, cousin of Matthew Flinders*

Sir John Franklin was born in Spilsby in Lincolnshire, England. He entered the Royal Navy at the age of 14, soon serving aboard the *Polyphemus* at the Battle of Copenhagen in April 1801.

Three months later, in July 1801, Franklin sailed from England as a midshipman on the *Investigator* under the command of his cousin, Captain MATTHEW FLINDERS. Over the next three years, he took part in the exploration of the western Australian coastline. On the continent's south coast, he traveled with Flinders and a small party to the head of Spencer Gulf, where he officially claimed a large portion of what is now South Australia for Great Britain.

In August 1803, on the return voyage, Franklin was among the crewmen left on Wreck Reef Bank off the northeast coast of Australia. They were picked up by one of the relief vessels sent from Port Jackson, Australia; Franklin and most of the expedition reached England one year later. In late 1804, he returned to sea in Britain's naval war against Napoleon. He took part in the Battle of Trafalgar on the *Bellerophon* in October 1805. While serving on the *Bedford* off the coast of South America in 1808, Franklin was promoted to lieutenant. He also served aboard that warship in the Battle of New Orleans in January 1815.

In spring 1818, Franklin began his career as an Arctic explorer in a British navy expedition that attempted to sail from Spitsbergen (in Svalbard), across the Arctic Ocean, to the BERING STRAIT. In command of the *Trent,* Franklin sailed to Magdalenefjorden, on the northwest coast of Spitsbergen, accompanied by Captain DAVID BUCHAN, commanding the *Dorothea.* Both vessels were nearly crushed by PACK ICE. They became icebound, breaking free and returning to England after a voyage of only a few months. FREDERICK WILLIAM BEECHEY served as official painter on this expedition.

In 1819, the British navy put Franklin in command of an overland expedition to the Canadian Arctic to chart the north coast of North America in conjunction with a seaward search for the NORTHWEST PASSAGE. On May 23, 1819, he sailed from England on a HUDSON'S BAY COMPANY supply ship to York Factory on the southwest shore of HUDSON BAY. Joining him were midshipmen GEORGE BACK and ROBERT HOOD, along with naturalist SIR JOHN RICHARDSON. Franklin followed the overland fur traders' route to Great Slave Lake. North of Great Slave Lake, he established a base camp, Fort Enterprise, from which he set out in July 1821 to descend the Coppermine River. Traveling by CANOE and guided by Copper Indians under Chief Akaitcho, he came upon Bloody Falls, the site of an attack on Inuit by Chipewyan Indians under MATONABBEE, as recorded by SAMUEL HEARNE. They reached the Arctic Ocean, and, after determining the correct geographic coordinates of the mouth of the Coppermine River, set out to explore eastward, hoping to meet up with ships under SIR WILLIAM EDWARD PARRY and SIR JAMES CLARK ROSS, then on a planned voyage westward from Lancaster Sound.

Franklin and his expedition, which included about 20 VOYAGEURS hired from the NORTH WEST COMPANY and the Hudson's Bay Company, managed to explore the entire coastline of Coronation Gulf, as far as Bathurst Inlet. By the time they had reached Turnagain Point on the Kent Peninsula, supplies of food were running dangerously low. In addition, the canoes had become so damaged from traveling along the rough coast that they had to be abandoned.

With the approach of winter, and with no sign of Parry or Ross, whose ships had become icebound, Franklin was forced to head back overland across the Barren Grounds to Fort Enterprise. The return trek was fraught with hardships. Nearly half of the voyageurs died of starvation, and Franklin had one of them executed for killing Midshipman Hood, a crime in which cannibalism was suspected as a motive.

After wintering in the Great Slave Lake region, Franklin returned to Hudson Bay, then headed for England, arriving in fall 1822. He was promoted to the rank of captain and made a member of the ROYAL SOCIETY for his maps of unknown coastline in Arctic Canada. In August 1823, he married the poet Eleanor Anne Porden.

Franklin's second expedition to the Canadian Arctic set out from New York in spring 1825. Traveling overland, and accompanied by British naval personnel, as well as the fur trader PETER WARREN DEASE, he reached Great Bear Lake, on which he established Fort Franklin. In June 1826, again with Back and Richardson, Franklin descended the Mackenzie River to its delta on the Beaufort Sea. While Richardson led part of the group eastward to the mouth of the Coppermine River, Franklin and Back explored westward along the coast, hoping to meet up with a supply vessel under Captain Frederick William Beechey at Icy Cape on the north coast of Alaska. In the trek along Alaska's North Slope, fog and ice hampered progress. At Return Reef, after sighting and naming Prudhoe Bay, Franklin turned back. Meanwhile, Beechey and his ship were unable to proceed beyond Point Barrow, about 200 miles west of Prudhoe Bay.

Franklin, Back, and Richardson returned to England in September 1827. In his expeditions of 1819 and 1825, Franklin had charted most of the Arctic coast of the Canadian mainland. He recounted these exploits in his books *Narrative of a Journey to the Shores of the Polar Sea* (1823) and *Narrative of a Second Expedition to the Shores of the Polar Sea* (1828). In April 1828, Franklin was honored with a knighthood. In November of that year, he married his second wife, JANE FRANKLIN. He also received the gold medal of the Geographical Society of Paris that year.

Franklin returned to sea duty in command of the *Rainbow*, serving in the eastern Mediterranean from 1830 to 1834. In 1836, he was appointed governor of Van Diemen's Land (present-day TASMANIA), a post he held until 1843.

Back in England in 1844, Franklin accepted the British Admiralty's commission to lead a seaward expedition through the Canadian Arctic archipelago, and, by way of the Northwest Passage, to reach the Bering Strait. In command of the *Erebus*, he was joined by Lieutenant FRANCIS RAWDON MOIRA CROZIER on the *Terror*. They sailed from London on May 29, 1845. The ships were reported last seen in late July 1845, by a Scottish whaling vessel in upper Baffin Bay, west of GREENLAND, and near the approach to Lancaster Sound.

Concern began to mount in 1847, when no word of Franklin or his ships had been received in England. Search efforts were undertaken by the British navy: Ships were dispatched into the Canadian Arctic from the east and west, and overland expeditions were undertaken from the south. Over the next decades, numerous of ships and nearly 2,000 men took part in the search. Among those involved were such leading figures of Arctic exploration as Sir John Richardson, Sir James Clark Ross, SIR JOHN ROSS, SIR RICHARD COLLINSON, SIR ROBERT McCLURE, EDWIN JESSE DE HAVEN, SIR EDWARD BELCHER, ELISHA KENT KANE, CHARLES FRANCIS HALL, and FREDERICK SCHWATKA.

In 1854, JOHN RAE of the Hudson's Bay Company, while exploring the Boothia Peninsula, recovered relics of the Franklin expedition from local Inuit, including silver dinnerware bearing Franklin's crest. In 1859, an expedition sponsored by Lady Jane Franklin and led by SIR FRANCIS LEOPOLD McCLINTOCK found notes on King William Island and the mainland relating that Franklin had died on June 11, 1847, of natural causes, probably heart failure, aboard the *Erebus* while icebound in Victoria Strait.

Sir John Franklin *(Library of Congress)*

Before Franklin's death, his ships had succeeded in navigating westward through Lancaster Sound, but progress in that direction had been blocked by ice in Barrow Strait. After a turn to the north into Wellington Channel, he had circumnavigated Cornwallis Island. He then had made his way southward through Peel Sound and what is now known as Franklin Strait, heading for the Boothia Peninsula and a possible ice-free channel to the west along the mainland. Late in 1846, the ships had become trapped in ice floes off the coast of King William Island in Victoria Strait. The notes also revealed that 23 other members of the expedition had succumbed to starvation and SCURVY by April 1848, and the surviving 105 crewmen had abandoned the ships and attempted to reach the mainland. All had subsequently perished, according to Inuit eyewitnesses, dying where they fell in their abortive attempt to reach the Hudson's Bay Company post, Fort Resolution, on the Back River. Skeletal remains of some of the crew were recovered on the Boothia Peninsula, with indications that the men had resorted to cannibalism in their last, desperate days.

Historians have speculated that the tragic end of Franklin's last Arctic expedition may have been caused in part by his mistaken belief that King William Island was a peninsula, as it was erroneously depicted on Sir John Ross's 1829 map of the Canadian Arctic. Ironically, the only ice-free channel around King William Island was to the south and east. Franklin, unaware that the strait existed, attempted to pass along the ice-choked west coast of the island, where his ship became trapped. The ensuing search for Franklin and his expedition resulted in major findings in the Canadian Arctic, including the successful negotiation of the Northwest Passage by Robert McClure in 1853–54. Nonetheless, based on evidence recovered by McClintock, Lady Franklin subsequently established that in entering Victoria Strait from the north and east, her husband had been the first to demonstrate the true location of the Northwest Passage. Arctic explorers continued to search for more clues to the fate of the Franklin expedition for decades, including aerial surveys of the King William Island and Victoria Strait region in the 1930s.

The British navy posthumously promoted Sir John Franklin to the rank of rear admiral in 1854, shortly after the end of the last official search effort. Franklin Island, a volcanic island in the Antarctic, was located and named in his honor by Sir James Clark Ross in 1841. At Prudhoe Bay, Alaska, which Franklin had first sighted in 1826, the largest reserve of petroleum in North America was discovered in 1968. Prior to Franklin's expeditions of 1819–22 and 1825–27, the only two charted points on the Arctic coast of North America were the mouths of the Mackenzie and Coppermine Rivers. Franklin's explorations resulted in new geographic knowledge of territory between Hudson Bay and Point Barrow.

Fraser, Simon (1776–1862)

American-born Canadian trader in western Canada

Originally from Bennington, Vermont, Simon Fraser moved with his Loyalist family to Cornwall, Ontario, shortly after the American Revolution. In about 1793, he began working as a clerk for the British-owned fur-trading concern, the NORTH WEST COMPANY, and, by 1801, he had become one of the company's partners.

In 1805, Fraser traveled to Fort Chipewyan on Lake Athabasca, the North West Company's outpost in what is now northeastern Alberta. He was commissioned to establish fur-trading posts west of the ROCKY MOUNTAINS and to seek a river route to the Pacific Ocean.

Fraser followed the route of SIR ALEXANDER MACKENZIE and explored the upper reaches of the Peace and Parsnip Rivers into what is now western British Columbia. He crossed the Rockies and the Continental Divide and established settlements at present-day Hudson Hope, Fort St. James, and Stuart Lake. He became the first non-Indian to visit McLeod Lake; he also established the first non-Indian settlement west of the Canadian Rockies, Fort McLeod.

In 1808, Fraser explored from the Peace River to its confluence with the Parsnip River at the southern end of Williston Lake. He followed the Parsnip to what is now Prince George, British Columbia.

From Prince George, Fraser continued along a river he mistakenly believed was a tributary of the COLUMBIA RIVER, traveling south, then west. On July 2, 1808, he and his party of about 20 fur traders and VOYAGEURS reached the river's Pacific outlet at the Strait of Georgia near present-day Vancouver, British Columbia.

The Fraser River, as it came to be known (despite the fact that it was explored by Mackenzie in 1792–93), flows southward through British Columbia and is unnavigable until a point about 80 miles upriver from Vancouver. At one point, it cuts through a gorge whose rock walls are more than 3,000 feet high. Fraser called the region of central British Columbia "New Caledonia," because it resembled the lands of northern Scotland where his ancestors had lived.

After 1811, Fraser was assigned to the North West Company's trading posts near the Red River in southern Manitoba. In 1816, he was implicated in an attack on the HUDSON'S BAY COMPANY's post, Seven Oaks. Although acquitted of any wrongdoing, he retired from the FUR TRADE in 1820, spending the rest of his life in Ontario.

Fraser's explorations west of the Rockies opened British Columbia to the fur trade and to non-Indian settlement. Although he failed to find a route to the Columbia, he located a previously uncharted outlet to the Pacific. The Fraser River became an important conduit for furs from the interior of British Columbia to the Pacific coast. In the mid-19th century, the Queen's Highway was built along the Fraser River Gorge to provide a wagon route to the goldfields of eastern British Columbia's Cariboo Mountains.

Freeman, Thomas (unknown–1821) *Irish surveyor, engineer in the American Southwest*

Born in Ireland, Thomas Freeman arrived in the United States in 1784. Although details of his early life and education are few, he apparently received extensive training as a topographical engineer and astronomer.

In March 1794, Freeman joined the federal survey team assigned to plot the boundaries of the newly established U.S. capital. By June 1795, he had completed a survey of the northern limits of Washington, D.C., establishing its boundary with Maryland. He next initiated the first topographic survey of the District of Columbia, leaving that project in July 1796 when appointed to survey the U.S. border with the Spanish-held territory to the west.

Joining Freeman in the project, and apparently in charge, was Andrew Ellicoot, with whom he left Washington, D.C., in mid-September 1796. They traveled down the MISSISSIPPI RIVER to Natchez, at that time part of Spanish territory, arriving in late February 1797. Disagreements developed between the two men during the downriver boat trip, reportedly stemming from Freeman's objections to a female companion Ellicoot had brought along on the expedition. Freeman also criticized Ellicoot's slow progress in getting the survey under way. Ellicoot, responding with accusations of his own, dismissed Freeman from the project.

Cleared of the charges lodged against him, Freeman returned to government survey work in 1804. That year, President Thomas Jefferson appointed him to lead an expedition to chart the Red River to its source and explore the headwaters of the Arkansas River. The United States had just purchased the Louisiana Territory from France, and the United States' border with Spanish territory to the west was in dispute, with Spain maintaining that it was determined by the Red River and the United States claiming all the territory up to the Rio Grande.

Reports of Spanish opposition to any American encroachment into territory west of the Red River delayed the start of Freeman's expedition until April 1806. He then set out from Fort Adams, in what is now southwestern Mississippi, with a party that included naturalist Peter Custis and a contingent of 34 soldiers under the command of Captain Enoch Humphreys. Freeman and his expedition traveled up the Red River in two flatboats, establishing diplomatic contacts with several Indian tribes. By mid-July 1806, they had reached a point near what is now Texarkana, Texas,

about 600 miles upriver from Fort Adams, where they were met by a large Spanish army from Texas. Unable to persuade the Spanish commander to allow them to continue, and outnumbered, Freeman withdrew, returning down the Red River to Fort Adams.

Freeman continued his survey work on the southern frontier in an 1807 expedition that mapped out the boundary between Alabama and Tennessee. The next year, he led an investigation of land speculators who were unlawfully encroaching on U.S. lands in the Southeast, and, in 1811, he accepted a federal appointment as surveyor of public lands south of Tennessee, headquartered at Washington, Mississippi, near Natchez. He held that post until November 1821, when he died suddenly while on government business in Huntsville, Alabama.

Thomas Freeman's 1806 expedition up the Red River coincided with other federally funded explorations then being undertaken in the North and West by MERIWETHER LEWIS and WILLIAM CLARK, as well as by ZEBULON MONTGOMERY PIKE. It was also the second attempt organized by President Jefferson to explore the newly established southwestern U.S. frontier along the Red River, an earlier expedition under SIR WILLIAM DUNBAR having also been turned back by Spanish forces. Although Freeman was unable to reach the source of the Red River, his explorations in 1806 yielded the first accurate map of the river's lower course, a region previously known only through the accounts of Spanish and French traders.

Frémont, John Charles (The Pathfinder)

(1813–1890) *U.S. Army officer, American surveyor, explorer in the American West, senator, territorial governor*

Born in Savannah, Georgia, John C. Frémont was the son of French-royalist émigré Charles Frémon and Virginia socialite Ann Beverly Whiting (the *t* was added to his last name by the late 1830s). After his father's death in 1818, he and his mother settled in Charleston, South Carolina. In 1829–31, Frémont studied science at the College of Charleston; because of a reported amorous escapade, he was expelled before his graduation.

In 1833, Frémont taught mathematics to naval cadets aboard the U.S. warship *Natchez*. In 1836, he engaged in a survey for the proposed Charleston & Cincinnati Railroad. During the same period, he also undertook a survey of Cherokee Indian lands in the western Carolinas.

In 1838, Frémont won an appointment as second lieutenant in the army's Corps of Topographical Engineers through the help of a family friend, U.S. congressman Joel Poinsett. He was assigned that same year as assistant to scientist JOSEPH NICOLAS NICOLLET. Nicollet's party started from Fort Snelling at the junction of the MISSISSIPPI RIVER and Minnesota River near present-day Minneapolis,

Minnesota. Traveling southwestward, they followed the Minnesota River to Red Pipestone Quarry in what is now southwestern Minnesota.

The next year, 1839, Frémont accompanied Nicollet on a topographic and scientific survey of the upper MISSOURI RIVER, from present-day Pierre, South Dakota, north to the Canadian border, then east to Lac Qui Parle, Minnesota, and back to the Mississippi. Nicollet's expeditions yielded the first accurate maps of the upper Mississippi and Missouri regions.

In 1841, Frémont commanded a detachment of the Corps of Topographical Engineers on an expedition that charted the course of the lower Des Moines River, flowing through what is now southeastern Iowa to the Mississippi. Frémont was in Washington, D.C., in October of that year and eloped with the daughter of Thomas Hart Benton, the influential Missouri senator with expansionist sentiments.

Through Benton's influence, Frémont, instead of Nicollet, was placed in command of a government-sponsored scientific and surveying expedition to the northern ROCKY MOUNTAINS in 1842. The objective of Frémont's first western expedition was to explore the region between the Missouri River and the Rockies and determine the exact longitude of the SOUTH PASS through the range along the Oregon Trail in what is now southwestern Wyoming. Frémont was also to survey the best sites for military posts. An expansionist faction in Washington, headed by Benton, also hoped to generate American settlement in the Oregon Country, which at that time was jointly held by the United States and Great Britain, by demonstrating an overland route to the Pacific Northwest.

Frémont and his party of about 21 Creoles and French-Canadian VOYAGEURS, plus the cartographer and artist Charles Preuss, left Westport, Missouri, on June 1, 1842. While traveling up the Missouri, Frémont met frontiersman CHRISTOPHER HOUSTON CARSON (Kit Carson) and hired him as a guide. The expedition reached the Kansas River, followed it for a distance, then crossed over to the Platte. In early July 1842, at the forks of the Platte near present-day North Platte, Nebraska, Frémont divided his men into two groups. Carson led most of the party up the North Platte River to Fort Laramie in what is now southeastern Wyoming. Frémont and four others explored the South Platte as far as Fort St. Vrain, not far from the site of present-day Denver, Colorado. Along the way, they sighted Longs Peak in the Colorado Rockies. He then headed northward to meet Carson and the rest of the men at Fort Laramie.

Despite reports of raids by Sioux (Dakota, Lakota, Nakota), Cheyenne, and Blackfeet war parties, Frémont led his expedition toward South Pass in August 1842. He reached the pass, then explored the headwaters of the Green River in what is now western Wyoming. Frémont turned eastward to explore the Wind River Mountains and climbed one of that range's highest mountains, Frémont Peak, on August 15, 1842. Soon afterward, he began the return journey eastward by way of the Platte River to its outlet into the Missouri at Omaha. He reached Westport, Missouri, on October 1, 1842, then headed to Washington, D.C., where he and Preuss submitted their reports and maps of their expedition.

Frémont's mission on his next government-backed survey in the West was to complement the findings of CHARLES WILKES's 1838–42 explorations of the Pacific coast. He was also to penetrate into northern California and evaluate the status of American settlers living under Mexican rule, perhaps in anticipation of a planned move by the United States to acquire California from Mexico.

Frémont's party of 39 voyageurs, MOUNTAIN MEN, cartographers, and scientists left Westport in early May 1843. THOMAS FITZPATRICK was the chief guide for this expedition. The party traveled northwestward across Nebraska toward the Oregon Trail. Frémont wanted to find a route through the Rockies that was more southerly than the South Pass. Accordingly, he headed southward from the Oregon Trail to the Arkansas River, followed it for a time, then crossed over to Fort St. Vrain, which he reached in early July 1843.

Heading westward to Pikes Peak, Frémont encountered Christopher "Kit" Carson and again hired him as a guide.

John C. Frémont (Library of Congress)

Near Pueblo, Colorado, he sent Carson and some of his men to Bent's Fort for supplies. Fitzpatrick and another group headed northward to the South Pass, while Frémont went southward to explore for a new southern route through the mountains. This mission led him into the Medicine Bow Mountains of south-central Wyoming.

Frémont, unable to locate a pass through the Rockies, headed northward to rejoin Fitzpatrick and the others at South Pass. The group divided again at Soda Springs, Idaho. Frémont and his men proceeded southward to the Great Basin and the Great Salt Lake, which he explored in a rubber boat.

Frémont also explored the Uinta and Wasatch Ranges of Utah, then headed northward into what is now Idaho, rejoining Fitzpatrick and the rest of his party at Fort Hall. He followed the Snake River to the Columbia, then on to Fort Vancouver, opposite the site of present-day Portland, Oregon, where he obtained a map of the Great Basin from the HUDSON'S BAY COMPANY'S JOHN MCLOUGHLIN.

Frémont's party proceeded southward along the eastern slopes of the Cascade Mountains and entered northwestern Nevada, reaching Pyramid Lake on January 10, 1844. They camped near the site of present-day Reno, Nevada, then followed the Truckee River through the Sierra Nevada, crossing into California during severe snowstorms. Washo

Indian guides led them into the Sacramento Valley to Sutter's Fort on the American River.

In March 1844, Frémont led his men southward into California's San Joaquin Valley, then crossed the southern Sierra Nevada via the Tehachapi Pass. He followed the Old Spanish Trail across Nevada and the Great Basin region of western Utah, exploring Utah Lake and the Wasatch Mountains. On this leg of the journey, he located the Muddy Pass through the Rockies. He then headed southward around Pikes Peak to present-day Pueblo, Colorado, and followed the Arkansas River to Bent's Fort in southeastern Colorado, reaching it in July 1844. From there, he went to the Missouri River and returned to the East.

Frémont's third western expedition started out from Fort Leavenworth, Kansas, in summer 1845. It was part of Colonel STEPHEN WATTS KEARNY's military expedition to the southern plains. Frémont's contingent consisted of 62 men, including Kit Carson, artist EDWARD MEYER KERN, and mountain man JOSEPH REDDEFORD WALKER.

From Bent's Fort, Frémont traveled northward to the South Pass, then entered the Great Basin, reaching the Great Salt Lake. He used the Hastings Cutoff from Fort Bridger to Walker Lake in the eastern Sierra Nevada. Frémont and part of the group traveled northward to Pyramid Lake, crossed into California, and arrived at Monterey in fall 1845.

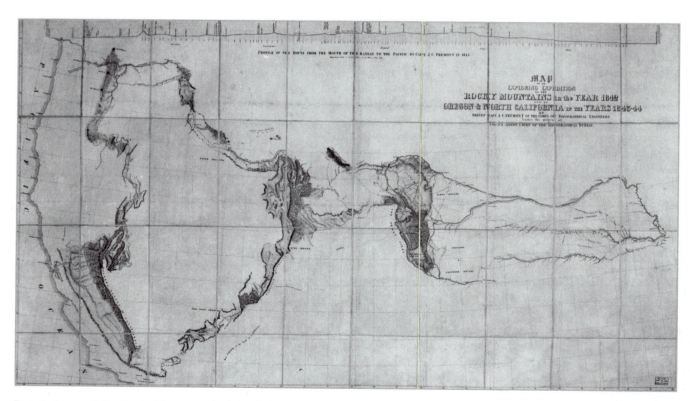

Detail of map of the Rocky Mountains by John C. Frémont (1842–44) *(Library of Congress)*

The Mexican authorities, suspicious of Frémont's presence, granted him permission to winter in the mountains above Salinas, but, in spring 1846, they ordered him to leave California. After a brief standoff with the Mexican army, Frémont headed northward into southern Oregon's Klamath Lake region. While there, he received orders from Washington, D.C., through an official messenger, Marine Lieutenant Archibald Gillespie, to return to California to oversee a possible revolt by American settlers.

In summer 1846, Frémont and his men played an active role in the Bear Flag revolt in northern California; they also became involved in securing California for the United States in the U.S.-Mexican War of 1846–48.

In January 1848, Frémont was court-martialed for disobeying orders while embroiled in a power struggle between Kearny and Commodore Robert Stockton in California. He was found guilty, but he was reinstated on orders of President James Polk.

Frémont resigned from the army in protest against the guilty verdict. He soon resumed his explorations of the West with private funding from Senator Benton and several St. Louis businessmen, who hoped to promote a central route for a proposed transcontinental railroad.

In October 1848, Frémont and a party of 35 men set out from Westport Landing (now in Kansas City, Missouri) to survey a route along the 38th parallel for the planned railroad from St. Louis to San Francisco. Accompanying the expedition were Edward Meyer Kern and his brothers, BENJAMIN JORDAN KERN and RICHARD HOVENDON KERN, who served as topographers, artists, and naturalists. Frémont and his party traveled westward along the Kansas River, then crossed southward to the Arkansas River, which they followed upstream into the Colorado Rockies.

By December 1848, Frémont had led his expedition as far westward as Pueblo in what is now central Colorado. From there, they traveled southwestward through the Sangre de Cristo Mountains by way of the Robidoux Pass, and entered the San Luis Valley, near the headwaters of the Rio Grande. He then pushed westward in search of a year-round pass through the San Juan Mountains. In order to find out if the route ahead through Wagon Wheel pass remained open even in the severest weather, he now intended to attempt a winter crossing of the mountains.

Frémont's guide was frontiersman WILLIAM SHERLEY WILLIAMS, who reportedly was familiar with the largely uncharted San Juan Mountains. While ascending the eastern slopes of the mountains, the expedition encountered a blinding snowstorm and became lost among the range's towering ridges. Unable to find shelter from the storm's hurricane-force winds, Frémont and his men were forced to turn back down the mountains and head southward to Taos. The retreat was disorganized, with Frémont reportedly leaving his men behind to find their own way to safety. Eleven of them, one-third of the expedition, died in the extreme cold, high winds, and blizzard conditions on the trip down from the mountains. Eventually the survivors straggled into Taos in small groups a few days behind Frémont.

Among the survivors were the Kern brothers who, when they reached Taos, accused Frémont of abandoning them in the mountain snowstorm, and quit the expedition. The following March, Benjamin Kern and William Sherley Williams returned to the mountains to retrieve some papers and other items that had been left behind in December. En route, they were killed by a Ute war party.

Meanwhile, Frémont and his expedition, blocked by winter weather from continuing westward along the central route, traveled southward part way down the Rio Grande before heading westward again along a more southerly route. They followed the Gila River across present-day southern Arizona to the lower COLORADO RIVER, then continued across the Sierra Nevada to Los Angeles. Frémont then traveled back East to report to Benton that his expedition was a success, despite the disastrous outcome of his abortive attempt at a winter crossing of the San Juan Mountains. Benton would later cite Frémont's findings to support his call for the construction of a railroad through the southern Rockies.

In 1850–51, Frémont served as one of the first two U.S. senators from California. He conducted his fifth and final western exploring expedition in 1853. Again commissioned by Benton and his associates, he undertook another survey in support of the proposed western railroad route. From Kansas City, Missouri, he went westward to the Green River and Wasatch Mountains of present-day northern Utah. He then headed southwestward to Parowan in southwestern Utah, where he turned westward and, after traveling across the Great Basin of what is now central Nevada, crossed the Sierra Nevada into central California.

Frémont unsuccessfully ran for president in the election of 1856 as the first Republican Party candidate. In the early Civil War, he was commissioned a general and served as military commander in Missouri, also participating in the Virginia campaign. He left the army in 1862. In the ensuing years, he became involved in railroad and mining ventures in California. From 1878 to 1883, he served as territorial governor of Arizona. He died of ptomaine poisoning in 1890, while on a trip to New York.

John C. Frémont's western expeditions earned him the popular name the Pathfinder, even though, for the most part, he followed trails long established by Indians, Spanish missionaries, and mountain men. He contributed to the history of exploration through his extensive reports on geography as well as wildlife. He is credited with dispelling the notion that the Great Plains stretching from the Missouri River to the Rockies were a "Great American Desert," as reported earlier by STEPHEN HARRIMAN LONG. His report on the fertile regions of present-day Nebraska, Kansas, and Oklahoma helped open that area to future agricultural settlement. Frémont also publicized an accessible route to California and Oregon, thus helping inspire the Great Migration of the early 1840s. His survey of Utah's Great Salt Lake region in 1843 came to the attention of Mormon leader BRIGHAM YOUNG, whose efforts prompted the settlement there of tens of thousands of Mormons after the U.S.-Mexican War of 1846–48. Frémont's wife, Jessica Benton Frémont, became a literary figure in the late 19th century. She is credited with editing Frémont's reports of his first two expeditions, published in 1845 by the U.S. government, entitled *Report of the Exploring Expedition to the Rocky Mountains in the year 1842, and to Oregon and Northern California in the Years 1843–44.*

Freycinet, Louis-Claude de Saulces de
(Louis-Claude Desaulses de Freycinet)

(1779–1842) *French naval officer in the South Pacific*

Louis-Claude de Freycinet was born at Montelimar in southeastern France. In 1794, at the age of 15, he entered the French navy as a midshipman, serving with his older brother Louis-Henri de Saulces, baron de Freycinet, aboard the *Hepreaux;* he subsequently took part in engagements in the MEDITERRANEAN SEA in the course of the French Revolutionary Wars of 1792–1802.

Promoted to ensign in 1800, Freycinet sailed on the *Naturaliste* in NICOLAS BAUDIN's 1800–04 expedition to the coasts of Australia and TASMANIA. He was present at Dirk Hartogs Island on the west coast of Australia when a plaque left in 1697 by the Dutch navigator Willem de Vlamingh was discovered. In Sydney, Freycinet, having been appointed lieutenant commander, was put in charge of the *Casuarina,* a schooner, which he sailed to Kangaroo Island on the south coast of Australia, then to Île de France (present-day Mauritius).

Upon his return to France in 1804, Freycinet was given command of the *Voltigeur,* on which he served for a year before being transferred to the French navy's map and chart department. In 1811, soon after the death of FRANÇOIS PÉRON, he assumed the task of completing the naturalist's account of the Baudin voyage, which he completed in 1816 and published as *Journey to the Southern Lands.*

In August 1816, Freycinet first proposed his plan for a scientific voyage around the world to the minister of the navy. He planned to conduct experiments with an invariable pendulum at various locations around the globe to determine accurately the shape of the Earth. Studies of the flora and fauna of the South Pacific islands, as well as anthropological studies of the people of the South Pacific Ocean, were also planned. Within a few months, Freycinet won the approval of the newly installed French monarch, Louis XVIII,

who was eager to reestablish French prestige overseas in the wake of the 1815 defeat of Napoléon and the loss of most French colonial possessions.

In command of the *Uranie,* named in honor of the muse of music, astronomy, and geometry, Freycinet sailed from Toulon on September 17, 1817. Members of the scientific team included the artist and writer JACQUES ARAGO, hydrographer LOUIS-ISADORE DUPERREY, and naturalists JOSEPH-PAUL GAIMARD, CHARLES GAUDICHAUD-BEAUPRÉ, and JEAN-RENÉ-CONSTANT QUOY. Freycinet's wife, Rose Pinon de Freycinet, also was aboard, despite regulations to the contrary, having boarded the *Uranie* disguised as an ordinary sailor.

After stopping first at the CANARY ISLANDS and Rio de Janeiro, Freycinet reached Cape Town, where he met with the Russian expedition on the *Rurik* under the command of OTTO VON KOTZEBUE. He then headed eastward across the Indian Ocean, reaching the west coast of Australia at Shark Bay in September 1818. Some contact was made with the region's Aborigines. At Dirk Hartogs Island, Freycinet recovered the Dutch plaque he had located 15 years earlier with Baudin, intending to take it to France.

From Australia's west coast, Freycinet sailed northward to Timor and the Moluccas. En route, the expedition had a threatening encounter with Malay pirates, who were persuaded to withdraw without a violent confrontation. After exploring around the northern end of Timor, he sailed out into the Pacific, visiting the Carolines and Guam in the Marianas. In August 1819, the expedition reached the HAWAIIAN ISLANDS, where the Hawaiian king's prime minister, Kalanimoku, was baptized as a Christian, with Freycinet acting as godfather in the ceremony aboard the *Uranie.*

While sailing from Hawaii to southeastern Australia, Freycinet came across a previously uncharted island in the Navigators' Islands, which he named Rose Island in honor of his wife. It is now part of the territory of American Samoa.

In November 1819, Freycinet reached the port of Sydney, where expedition members set up an observatory; over the next three months, the scientific team conducted experiments in atmospheric refraction and terrestrial magnetism. The *Uranie* set sail for the homeward voyage in February 1820. Less than two months later, the ship encountered a hurricane as it approached Tierra del Fuego, and, driven into the Atlantic Ocean, it ran aground on a reef off the Falkland Islands. With the ship damaged beyond repair, Freycinet and his expedition were stranded near Penguin Island until picked up by a passing American vessel, the *Mercury,* two months later.

The *Mercury* took Freycinet and his party to Montevideo, where he purchased the ship from its captain, renamed it the *Physicienne,* and sailed with the expedition to France, arriving at Le Havre in November 1820, completing a CIR-CUMNAVIGATION OF THE WORLD.

Promoted to captain soon after his return, Freycinet set to work on what turned out to be a 13-volume account of his voyage plus four atlases. It was published over the next 24 years, the final volumes appearing posthumously in 1844.

Freycinet was a founding member of the Geographical Society of Paris in 1821; five years later, he was inducted into the French Academy of Sciences. He retired from the service in 1832 as director of the French navy's department of maps and charts.

Louis-Claude de Freycinet's 1817–20 expedition to the South Pacific was one of the great scientific voyages of the French Restoration era, as were the voyages of Duper-rey and JULES-SÉBASTIEN-CÉSAR DUMONT D'URVILLE. Among the many new species discovered by his scientific team was a freshwater fish with bulging eyes that slithered in the mud, which they named "Freycinet's mudskipper" in his honor. The plaque left by the Dutch navigator Vlamingh, which Freycinet took back to France in 1820, was returned to a museum in Perth, Western Australia, in the years after World War II. Rose de Pinon de Freycinet wrote her own account of the 1817–20 voyage around the world, first published in 1927.

Freydis   See EIRÍKSDOTTIR, FREYDIS.

Fritz, Samuel (ca. 1659–1725) *Bohemian missionary in the upper Amazon Basin of Ecuador, Peru, and Brazil*
Samuel Fritz was born in the former kingdom of Bohemia, in what is now western Czech Republic. In 1685, having been educated by the Jesuits and ordained a priest, he traveled to Quito, then part of Peru, where he embarked on a career as a missionary to the Indians of the upper AMAZON RIVER.

Fritz spent a year studying at the Jesuit college at Quito, and, in 1686, he made an eastward crossing of the ANDES MOUNTAINS into the Napo River region of northeastern Peru. During the next three years, he explored down the Napo to its junction with the Amazon, making contacts and winning converts among upper Amazon tribes. In the region inhabited by the Omagua, he established the San Joachim mission, and then he founded another mission farther down the Amazon among the Jurimaguas.

Among the native peoples, Fritz earned a reputation as a champion of their welfare in his efforts against Portuguese slave hunters. In 1689, his health failed, and for medical attention he was taken 3,000 miles downriver to the mouth of the Amazon at Pará, arriving at the Portuguese settlement on September 11, 1689. Portuguese colonial officials in Pará,

suspicious of any travelers entering from the Spanish-held territory to the west, believed Fritz was a Spanish spy and held him prisoner for the next two years.

Released from custody in July 1691 on direct orders from the king of Portugal in Lisbon, Fritz was escorted back up the Amazon to his mission at San Joachim. In 1692, he set out to report on his Amazon explorations to Spanish colonial officials in Lima, Peru. After ascending the Huallaga and Parapura tributaries of the Amazon, he reached Caja-marca, then headed southwestward to Lima on the Pacific coast.

Fritz presented an account of travels in the upper Amazon to the Spanish viceroy at Lima, relating how the Portuguese were steadily encroaching up the Amazon into Spanish territory, beyond the boundary line established by the Treaty of Tordesillas in 1494. He returned to his missionary work on the Napo River in 1693, traveling widely on the Pongo, Jaen, and other Amazon tributaries, expanding his contacts with the Indians and acquiring knowledge of parts of the upper Amazon that had not yet been explored by non-Indians.

In the early 1700s, Fritz became the superior general for all the Jesuit missionaries on the upper Amazon. Over the next 10 years, he made frequent journeys between Quito and northeastern Peru. He became an accomplished carpenter and architect and directed the construction of church and mission buildings. Fritz also developed his skills as an artist, using his own religious pictures to decorate the churches he founded.

Starting in 1714, Fritz ventured into the lands of the Jívaro Indians of the Marañón River region of northern Peru, a tribe notorious for their raids on distant villages and their practice of ritualistic head-shrinking.

Father Samuel Fritz ended his work among the Jívaro in 1724. In his more than 40 years among the Indians of the upper Amazon and its tributaries, Fritz traveled through many regions largely unknown to the Spanish in Peru or the Portuguese in Brazil. His large-scale map of the Amazon River system, depicting for the first time the entire course of the great river, was reproduced at Quito in 1707. In 1743, 15 years after Fritz's death, French explorer CHARLES-MARIE DE LA CONDAMINE consulted this map while in Quito for his scientific voyage down the length of the Amazon.

Frobisher, Sir Martin (ca. 1535–1594)
English mariner in the Canadian Arctic
Martin Frobisher was born in Doncaster, near Wakefield, in Yorkshire, England, into a well-off country family. While he was still very young, his father died, and his mother sent him to be raised by his uncle, Sir John York, a London merchant who promoted trading voyages to the coast of Africa.

In 1553, through his uncle's influence, the young Frobisher joined a trading expedition to the coast of West Africa under the command of Thomas Wyndham. Frobisher was among the few survivors to return to England from the Gulf of Guinea, two-thirds of the men, including the commander, having succumbed to tropical fever.

In 1562, Frobisher served on another English voyage to West Africa, in which he was taken captive by Africans and turned over to the Portuguese. He eventually made his way back to England, where he became one of England's PRIVATEERS, preying on Spanish and French shipping. On one privateering voyage, he mistakenly attacked a ship carrying a cargo of wine to London, leading to a brief imprisonment in England.

In about 1570, while serving on blockade duty off the Irish coast, Frobisher befriended SIR HUMPHREY GILBERT, who had by then developed a theory regarding the NORTH-WEST PASSAGE. Gilbert had concluded that North America was actually an island, which could be circumnavigated. He reasoned that the STRAIT OF MAGELLAN at the southern tip of South America had as its counterpart the STRAIT OF ANIAN across the top of North America, a passage that led to China, then known as Cathay. Gilbert, along with other geographers of the day, speculated that the Asian mainland extended eastward toward northernmost North America, and a Northwest Passage would therefore provide a far shorter route to Asia than either the CAPE OF GOOD HOPE or the Strait of Magellan.

Frobisher, with Gilbert's support and connections, including London merchant Michael Lok, organized an expedition to find the Northwest Passage. In the spring of 1576, Frobisher sailed from London for the Shetland Islands, in command of two small vessels, the *Gabriel* and the *Michael,* both equipped with the latest navigational instruments. A small sailboat known as a pinnace, also part of the expedition, was soon lost in heavy seas in the Shetlands. Frobisher on the *Gabriel,* accompanied by the *Michael,* then sailed north by northwest, to the east coast of GREENLAND. The captain of the *Michael* began to have doubts about the project, however, and slipped back to England.

Left with only the *Gabriel* and a crew of 18, Frobisher pushed on to the west, rounding the tip of Greenland, and came upon what he called Queen Elizabeth's Foreland, now known as Resolution Island, off the southeastern-most cape of Baffin Island. He headed northwestward, entering what he took to be a westward-leading strait and sailed northwestward through it. Frobisher was convinced that he had found the Strait of Anian, believing that the continent on his right was Asia, and the land on his left was North America.

Frobisher explored as far as Butcher's Island, about 180 miles above the mouth of what was later called Frobisher

Sir Martin Frobisher *(New York State Library, Albany)*

Bay, before he was turned back by ice floes. He encountered Inuit (Eskimo), with whom he traded. When five of his men went ashore and failed to return, Frobisher believed them kidnapped. He took an Inuit man hostage to force the return of the missing men, but without success. Severely shorthanded, he sailed back to England.

Frobisher reached London in October 1576. During the expedition, a landing party on an island at the mouth of Frobisher Bay had collected a small rock that seemed to be heavy enough to be a valuable metal, possibly gold. The ore sample was examined by assayers, and although it was actually pyrite, or FOOL'S GOLD, they erroneously identified it as gold. This announcement generated great support for Frobisher's second expedition the following year. In addition, the Asian appearance of the kidnapped man, who created a sensation before his death from illness, encouraged hopes that Frobisher had found a route to the Orient. A joint-stock company was formed called the CATHAY COMPANY, with an official charter from Queen Elizabeth I. The Queen, a major investor herself, provided a large naval vessel, the *Aid,* to accompany the *Gabriel* and the *Michael.* Frobisher was appointed as high admiral of the expedition, with a commission to govern all the uncharted lands he might locate in the name of the Crown.

In May 1577, from Blackwall near London, Frobisher and his fleet sailed northward to the Orkney Islands off the coast of Scotland, then headed westward for Greenland. Among the crew were miners recruited in Cornwall to recover the ore from the newly explored land, named Meta Incognita (destination unknown) by Queen Elizabeth. Frobisher's primary objective was to obtain a large amount of ore to bring back to England for refining, the search for the Northwest Passage now being of secondary importance.

Frobisher's second expedition landed in Baffin Island's Frobisher Bay. In summer 1577, 200 tons of ore were loaded onto the *Aid*. He explored the islands at the mouth of the bay, claiming them for England and the queen. Three more captured Inuit were taken back to London in the fall—a man, a woman, and her infant child. In London, they demonstrated their skills, but all three died of European diseases within less than two months of their arrival.

A third expedition was planned for the following year, in which Frobisher was instructed to undertake some limited exploration for the Northwest Passage and establish a colony, as well as continue mining operations. Along with the three vessels of the 1577 voyage, he was given command of 12 other ships. Sailing on his flagship, the *Aid*, Frobisher and his fleet embarked from Harwich on the east coast of England in spring 1578. Heading westward from the north of Ireland, they made a landing on Greenland's south coast in late June 1578, where Frobisher formally took possession of the region in the name of the queen, calling the land "West England." Although no subsequent English claim over southern Greenland was ever exercised, Frobisher's visit there was the first one known to have been made by Europeans since the days of the Vikings.

On reaching the entrance to Frobisher Bay, he found his way blocked by ice. The fleet, struck by gale-force winds, separated. Frobisher and the *Aid* were blown south and west into what is now Hudson Strait, which he subsequently explored westward during a period of three weeks. Reaching a point 200 miles west of the entrance to Hudson Strait, and just missing HUDSON BAY, Frobisher decided to head back to resume mining operations. He later called Hudson Strait, the passage he had been unable to explore thoroughly, the "Mistaken Strait."

By late July, Frobisher and the fleet had regrouped at the mouth of Frobisher Bay. The digging of the ore began, with over 1,300 tons being loaded on the ships and taken to England. One of his ships made a landing to the south, at the northern tip of Quebec's Ungave Peninsula. Winterlike weather arrived in late summer, and the bay started to freeze over. Frobisher abandoned the plans for establishing a colony when a ship carrying housing material and equipment for the proposed settlement struck an iceberg and sank. With the early onset of severe weather, Frobisher decided to call an end to the mining operations and return to England.

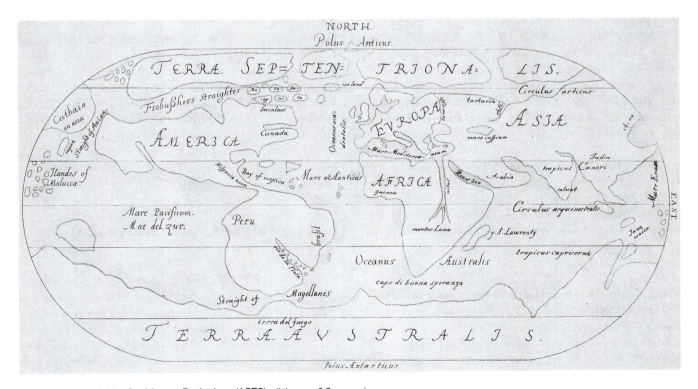

Map of the world by Sir Martin Frobisher (1578) *(Library of Congress)*

It was finally determined that the ore that Frobisher brought back from Baffin Island was pyrite with trace amounts of gold. Michael Lok, depending on the anticipated mineral wealth to cover his investment, was financially ruined and thrown into debtors' prison when the subscribers to the venture refused to honor their pledged support. The ore from Frobisher Bay was discarded in Bristol and later was used as paving stones.

Frobisher returned to privateering, joining SIR FRANCIS DRAKE in 1585 in raids on Spanish ships and ports in the WEST INDIES and on the north coast of South America. He took part in the battle against the Spanish Armada in the English Channel in 1588, for which he was honored with a knighthood. In 1592, he accompanied SIR WALTER RALEIGH in a raid on the coast of Spain. Two years later, while attacking the port of Brest, France, he suffered a wound in the leg, which became infected on the homeward voyage, causing his death soon after his arrival in Plymouth.

Sir Martin Frobisher undertook the first English voyage of exploration in search of the Northwest Passage. Although the gold rush he instigated led to financial disaster for many of his backers, his findings in the waters west of Greenland inspired the subsequent Northwest Passage expeditions of JOHN DAVIS and HENRY HUDSON. For the next three centuries Frobisher Bay was identified on Arctic maps as Frobisher Strait, bisecting the southeastern part of Baffin Island. Its true extent as a closed bay was determined in 1860 by American polar explorer CHARLES FRANCIS HALL, while searching for traces of SIR JOHN FRANKLIN's expedition. Hall also may have learned the fate of the five sailors kidnapped from Frobisher's 1576 expedition. From an old Inuit woman at Frobisher Bay, he was told a traditional story about the five whites who had been held captive until Frobisher had departed. They attempted to improvise a boat and sail away, but all froze to death before they could embark. George Best, who served as an officer on all three of Frobisher's Arctic expeditions, published his account, *The Three Voyages of Martin Frobisher,* in 1578. English artist JOHN WHITE, who subsequently took part in Raleigh's colonizing venture in Virginia in the 1580s, was with Frobisher on his second voyage in 1578, during which he produced the first European paintings of Inuit.

Fuca, Juan de (Apostolos Valerianos, Phokus Valerianatos) (1536–1602) *Greek mariner on the west coast of North America, in service to Spain*

Juan de Fuca was born in Valeriano, a village on the Ionian island of Cephalonia, off the west coast of Greece. Few details of his life are known before 1556, when, by his own account, he entered the service of Spain as a navigator and pilot. For the next 40 years, he sailed the coastal waters of the Spanish possessions in the Americas.

Fuca claimed that he was directed by the Spanish viceroy of Mexico to undertake a voyage northward along the coast of California in an attempt to locate the STRAIT OF ANIAN, the fabled waterway that geographers believed provided a connection through the North American continent between the Atlantic and Pacific Oceans. In 1592, he followed the west coast of North America to a point lying between 47° and 48° north latitude, near the entrance to Puget Sound that now bears his name, where he reportedly located an eastward passage into the continent. He explored eastward into the strait until he reached what he identified as the "North Sea" (denoting either the Arctic Ocean or the North Atlantic), then headed back to the Pacific and returned to Mexico.

In 1596, Fuca's claims came to the attention of London merchant Michael Lok, who, 20 years earlier, had been one of the principal sponsors of SIR MARTIN FROBISHER's expeditions in search of the Northwest Passage. According to an account by 17th-century travel historian Samuel Purchas, Lok was in direct contact with Fuca in 1596 and believed that Fuca had explored the western outlet to the NORTHWEST PASSAGE sought by Frobisher in the late 1570s. He tried, without success, to raise English sponsorship for the Greek mariner to undertake additional explorations for the Strait of Anian. Fuca instead returned to his Greek homeland, where he spent his remaining years.

Juan de Fuca's explorations of the Pacific coast of North America are without documentation other than his own statements to Lok. Nevertheless, they inspired Spanish and English expeditions over the next two centuries, from SEBASTIÁN VISCAÍNO in the early 17th century, to JAMES COOK and GEORGE VANCOUVER in the latter part of the 18th century. In 1787, a Captain Charles William Barkley, while exploring along the coast of Vancouver Island, found a southern entrance to Puget Sound at the approximate location where Fuca had also reported an entrance in 1592, and named it the Strait of Juan de Fuca, by which it is known today.

Fuchs, Sir Vivian Ernest (Bunny Fuchs) (1908–1999) *British geologist, explorer in Greenland, Africa, and the Antarctic*

Vivian "Bunny" Fuchs, born on the Isle of Wight, was the son of Ernest Fuchs, who had emigrated from Germany as a child, become a successful farmer, and married an Englishwoman, Violet Watson. He studied at the University of Cambridge, earning an M.A. degree in 1929. That same year, Fuchs served as geologist with the Cambridge East Greenland Expedition, headed by Sir James Wordie, who had accompanied SIR ERNEST HENRY SHACKLETON on the

Imperial Trans-Antarctic Expedition of 1914–16, when the ship *Endurance* was stranded in the Weddell Sea.

In 1930–32, Fuchs participated in Cambridge expeditions conducting survey, geological, and archaeological work in East Africa. In 1933, he headed an expedition to Lake Rudolf (Kenya). In 1935, he completed his doctoral thesis on the geology of the Rift Valley. The next year, he returned to Africa to study the geology of Lake Rukwa (Tanzania).

Fuchs was commissioned a second lieutenant in the British army in World War II and rose to the rank of major, serving in West Africa and northwestern Europe. In 1947, Fuchs directed the Falkland Islands Dependencies Survey, which included surveying Antarctica. In 1961, the project became known as the British Antarctic Survey, which he headed until his retirement in the 1970s.

Fuchs, as director of the survey, decided to revive Shackleton's plan of a crossing of the Antarctic continent and organized the Commonwealth Trans-Antarctic Expedition to be carried out in 1957 in connection with the INTERNATIONAL GEOPHYSICAL YEAR. In November of that year, after extensive training, Fuchs led a 12-member team, equipped with dogsleds and snow tractors, from Shackleton Base on the Weddell Sea. Meanwhile, SIR EDMUND PERCIVAL HILLARY headed a five-man team of New Zealanders who set up supply bases, traveling in the other direction from Scott Base on the Ross Sea. The two teams met at the U.S. station at the SOUTH POLE, Fuchs's group arriving on January 19, 1958, 15 days after Hillary's group. They then crossed to the Ross Sea together, arriving in March 1958. Fuchs's journey of 2,158 miles had taken 99 days. These were the first overland trips to the South Pole since the expeditions of ROALD ENGLEBREGT GRAVNING AMUNDSEN and ROBERT FALCON SCOTT in 1910–12.

Fuchs earned a knighthood in 1958. He also served in the International Glaciological Society, the ROYAL GEOGRAPHICAL SOCIETY, the British Association for the Advancement of Science, and the ROYAL SOCIETY. The Royal Geographical Society, which he headed in 1982–84, awarded him a Special Gold Medal for the trans-Antarctic journey. Fuchs's books include *The Crossing of Antarctica* (1960), which he wrote with Hillary; *Of Ice and Men* (1982), about the work of the British Antarctic Survey; and *A Time to Speak* (1985), his autobiography.

Fuchs's first wife, Joyce Connell, accompanied him on some of his expeditions to East Africa. In 1991, after her death the previous year, Fuchs married Eleanor Honnywill.

Sir Vivian Fuchs's trans-Antarctic crossing has been referred to as "the last great journey in the world." In addition to the expeditionary feat of traveling under extreme conditions, it contributed to knowledge of Antarctica through its scientific studies, which included experiments in seismology and gravity.

Furneaux, Tobias (1735–1781) *British naval officer in the South Pacific and Antarctic*

Tobias Furneaux was born at Swilly in Devon, England, not far from the port of Plymouth. In his early maritime career, he served in ships on the coasts of France and Africa and saw naval service in the WEST INDIES in 1760–63.

In 1766–68, Furneaux served on the *Dolphin* under the command of his cousin, Captain SAMUEL WALLIS, traveling to the South Pacific Ocean and around the world. As a second lieutenant on the expedition, Furneaux was the highest ranking officer fit enough to make an official landing on Tahiti on June 24, 1767, since Wallis and the other ranking officers were too ill to take part. He claimed Tahiti for Great Britain, naming it King George Island.

Back in England in 1771, Furneaux was promoted to commander, and, the next year, he sailed with JAMES COOK's second expedition to the South Pacific as captain of the *Adventure*. In January 1773, along with Cook on the *Resolution*, he made the first crossing of the ANTARCTIC CIRCLE. Soon afterward, Furneaux's ship was separated from Cook in the Antarctic ice and fog. Having arranged to meet up with Cook at Queen Charlotte Sound (Cook Strait) in NEW ZEALAND, he headed northward, touching first at TASMANIA.

Furneaux's visit was the first European visit to Tasmania, then known as Van Diemen's Land, since the island's European discovery by Dutch navigator ABEL JASZOON TASMAN in 1642. Furneaux explored its south coast and reached Adventure Bay, naming it after his ship. Sailing northward, he attempted to determine if Tasmania were separated from the Australian mainland, incorrectly concluding that it was not.

Furneaux and the *Adventure* met up with Cook and the *Resolution* in Queen Charlotte Sound, New Zealand, in May 1773. The two ships then made for Tahiti, where Furneaux took aboard a Tahitian man named Omai, who wanted to visit England. After sailing to numerous South Pacific islands, the ships returned to New Zealand. In Queen Charlotte Sound, a storm drove them apart once again. Furneaux, after searching in vain for Cook's ship, decided to sail back to England. Before embarking, he sent a 10-man landing party ashore on New Zealand to gather edible plants. When they failed to return, he sent out a search party, who discovered that the men had been killed and eaten by the Maori.

Furneaux arrived back in England in July 1774, a year before Cook returned. He turned Omai over to the care of SIR JOSEPH BANKS; the young man subsequently made a sensation in London society, being the first South Pacific Islander to visit England.

Promoted to captain in 1775, Furneaux took part in the British attack on the French at New Orleans two years later. He later returned to his home in Swilly, where he died in 1781.

Tobias Furneaux took part in the earliest British voyages to Tahiti. From his explorations of southern Tasmania in 1773, he produced the first charts of that part of the island and is credited with the European discovery of Adventure Bay. His mistaken conclusion that Tasmania was part of Australia was not rectified until the explorations of GEORGE BASS and MATTHEW FLINDERS in 1798. While cruising the various island groups of the South Pacific, Furneaux had some success in his attempts to introduce domestic animals and European vegetables, especially potatoes, to the islands. On his third voyage of 1776–80, Captain Cook named the islands off the northeast coast of Tasmania the Furneaux Islands, in honor of the former captain of the *Adventure*. Cook also named a series of coral islets in the Low Archipelago after Furneaux.

G

Gagarin, Yury Alekseyevich (Yuri Alexeyevich Gagarin) (1934–1968) *Soviet cosmonaut, first human in space*

Yury Gagarin, the son of a Russian carpenter, was born in the Smolensk region west of Moscow in the former Union of Soviet Socialist Republics (USSR, or Soviet Union). He grew up on a collective farm, then studied at a manufacturing trade school in Lyubertsy and an industrial technical school in Saratov. While in Saratov, he joined a flying club and learned to pilot airplanes. Upon the recommendation of his flight instructor, he was recruited by the Soviet air force. In 1955–57, he attended the air force's cadet training school at Chkalov (present-day Orenburg), in Russia. Proving himself as a fighter and test pilot, he was selected to train as one of the first Soviet cosmonauts (*see* ASTRONAUTS).

Gagarin was selected for the VOSTOK PROGRAM's first mission just four days before the scheduled launch and was promoted to the rank of major. At 9:07 A.M., on April 12, 1961, with a shout of *"Poyekhali!"* ("Let's go!"), he took off from the Baikonur Cosmodrome and became the first human in space. After separation from the rocket, the capsule, controlled from Earth, circled the planet at an average altitude of about 150 miles in an elliptical orbit. The flight, consisting of one orbit, lasted 108 minutes. The capsule landed in a field near Saratov. Since the breakup of the Soviet Union, released documents indicate that Gagarin bailed out of the capsule at an altitude of about four miles and descended separately by parachute.

After the mission, Gagarin was appointed a deputy of the Supreme Soviet, awarded the Order of Lenin, and named Hero of the Soviet Union. In the ensuing years, he

Yury Gagarin *(Library of Congress)*

helped train other cosmonauts, including the first woman in space, VALENTINA VLADIMIROVNA TERESHKOVA. He eventually reached the rank of colonel. Gagarin served on the backup crew for the *Soyuz 1* mission of the SOYUZ PROGRAM and was a candidate for a planned lunar landing. He was killed in a MiG-15 plane crash near Moscow in 1968. The town of Gzhatsk, his birthplace, is now known as Gagarin; Gagarin Crater on the far side of the Moon and the Gagarin Cosmonaut Training Center at Star City also commemorate him.

Yury Gagarin's mission began the modern era of space flight with human participation. That and a subsequent Soviet mission in 1961, in which Gherman Titov remained in space for more than 24 hours, spurred the U.S. manned space program. Later in 1961, the Americans ALAN BARTLETT SHEPARD, JR., and Virgil Grissom each accomplished suborbital space flights, and in 1962, JOHN HERSCHELL GLENN, JR., became the first American to orbit the Earth.

Gaimard, Joseph-Paul (1796–1858) *French naval surgeon, zoologist in the South Pacific*

Joseph-Paul Gaimard was born in St. Zacharie, in the Provence region of southeastern France. He entered the French navy's medical service and served as assistant surgeon and zoologist in LOUIS-CLAUDE DE SAULCES DE FREYCINET's scientific voyage on the *Uranie*, sailing around the world in 1817–20.

On this expedition, Gaimard worked along with naturalist JEAN-RENÉ-CONSTANT QUOY in the study of marine and land animals. En route to Cape Town from Toulon, France, Gaimard obtained several giant albatrosses that had been following the ship, and, from his examination of the carcasses, determined what type of marine life they ate. At Shark Bay on the west coast of Australia, he collected several rare species of marsupials, including a kangaroo rat and a bandicoot. On Dorre and Bernier Islands at the mouth of Shark Bay, Gaimard and Quoy captured a striped kangaroo and several types of parakeets. Later in the voyage, while exploring Boni in the Moluccas and on Tinian in the Mariana Islands, Gaimard came upon a variety of chicken previously unknown to science, which he called megapodes. His work on the voyage also included a study of the birds in the HAWAIIAN ISLANDS. CHARLES GAUDICHAUD-BEAUPRÉ served as pharmacist and zoologist on this expedition.

Back in Europe in the early 1820s, Gaimard visited naval scientific teams in Holland and England. In 1826, he embarked on a second French scientific expedition to the South Pacific Ocean, as surgeon and naturalist on the *Astrolabe* under the command of JULES-SÉBASTIEN-CÉSAR DUMONT D'URVILLE, working again with Quoy. Among the places visited on the three-year voyage was New Guinea,

where he obtained an Aru scrub wallaby, a type of kangaroo. In NEW ZEALAND, he made a study of marine animal life, including mollusks, and identified a type of dolphin unique to that region. He also collected birds in New Zealand, including a quail native to the islands as well as a new type of plover.

In November 1828, while the *Astrolabe* headed back across the Indian Ocean on its homeward voyage to France, Gaimard became ill with SCURVY and had to be left on the French island of Bourbon. After several weeks, he regained his health and secured passage to Marseilles on a French vessel, arriving in March 1829.

Gaimard concentrated on medical matters during the early 1830s. He took part in the French Academy of Sciences' study of an 1831–32 cholera epidemic in Central and Eastern Europe. He returned to other scientific work in an 1835–36 voyage to GREENLAND aboard the *Recherche*. In 1836, Gaimard was named president of the Scientific Commission of Iceland, and, over the next several years, he took part in scientific voyages to Scandinavia. He became a leading member of a French commission that promoted exploration of the Arctic and Antarctic regions in 1839. His published accounts of his scientific work and travels in Iceland, Sweden, and Spitsbergen (present-day Svalbard) first appeared in 1844 and 1847.

Joseph-Paul Gaimard took part in two of the major scientific expeditions undertaken by the French navy in the first part of the 19th century. The zoological work he undertook with Quoy on Dumont d'Urville's 1826–28 voyage brought back the largest collection of animal specimens from the South Pacific to reach France until that time.

Galaup, Jean-François de (comte de La Pérouse) (1741–ca. 1788) *French mariner on the coasts of Alaska and northeastern Asia and in the South Pacific*

Jean-François de Galaup, comte de La Pérouse, was born at his family's chateau near the southern French city of Albi. In 1756, at the age of 15, he became a marine with the French navy. Soon afterward, he took part in campaigns in the Seven Years War of 1756–63 on the east coast of North America. He was promoted to ensign in 1767; three years later, he was given command of his own ship. In the early 1770s, he served in the Indian Ocean in French naval operations off the east coast of India as well as in the waters off China.

La Pérouse took part in French naval actions against the British in the American Revolution. In August 1782, he commanded a small French fleet in HUDSON BAY, which captured and destroyed the HUDSON'S BAY COMPANY's Fort Prince of Wales and York Factory. The governor of Fort Prince of Wales, SAMUEL HEARNE, was taken prisoner and transported to France; it was at La Pérouse's insistence that

Hearne's journal of his explorations in northwestern Canada was finally published.

In 1783, La Pérouse married Louise-Eleonore Broudou a Creole woman he had met while stationed at Île de France (present-day Mauritius) in the Indian Ocean eight years earlier.

By 1785, La Pérouse was recognized as one of the foremost naval commanders and navigators in France. That year, he was selected by King Louis XVI to lead a French scientific expedition to the Pacific Ocean. Louis, well acquainted with the voyages of JAMES COOK, wanted La Pérouse to complete the British navigator's work by exploring the western Pacific and continuing the search for the NORTHWEST PASSAGE on the coast of Alaska. He also directed La Pérouse to investigate the extent of Russian colonization on the northwest coast of North America, with the idea of expanding French fur-trading interests into the region.

La Pérouse's expedition was equipped with two former French naval storeships recommissioned as frigates: the *Astrolabe,* commanded by PAUL-ANTOINE-MARIE FLEURIOT DE LANGLÉ, and the *Boussole,* captained by La Pérouse. Among the crew was a complete scientific staff planning to undertake studies of geography, physics, and natural history. The British Admiralty provided La Pérouse with scientific equipment to measure variations in magnetic compass readings, and with the latest instruments for determining longitude.

Jean-François de Galaup, comte de La Pérouse *(Library of Congress)*

La Pérouse and his ships sailed from the port of Brest on August 1, 1785. After stopovers in the CANARY ISLANDS and on the island of Santa Catarina off the coast of Brazil, the expedition rounded CAPE HORN and entered the Pacific in April 1786. The ships visited Concepción, Chile, then sailed to Easter Island, where some of the scientific team made measurements of the island's mysterious ancient monuments. From there, the expedition headed northward across the Pacific, visiting Maui in the Hawaiian Islands.

La Pérouse then directed the ships for the coast of the Gulf of Alaska, reaching a point near Mount St. Elias on June 23, 1786. Sailing eastward along the coast, he located a previously uncharted inlet that he named Port des Français (present-day Lituya Bay). Although some effort was made to find a Northwest Passage linking the Pacific with Hudson Bay or the Atlantic Ocean, La Pérouse soon came to the same conclusion that Cook had in the previous decade, that no such waterway existed in those latitudes. The scientific team undertook studies on the formations of icebergs and made studies of marine life, especially whales. From Alaska, the expedition sailed southward along the North American coast to the Spanish settlement at Monterey Bay, California, arriving on September 14, 1786.

La Pérouse and his men remained in California for 10 days, then set sail across the Pacific. They reached the Portuguese colony of Macao, near Hong Kong, on January 2, 1787, where they sold a quantity of furs acquired in trade with Alaskan Natives. They also sent back some exceptionally fine pelts to the queen of France, along with geographic data and an account of the voyage to that point.

The expedition then embarked on an exploration of the western rim of the Pacific, sailing first to Manila in the Philippines, then to Formosa (present-day Taiwan) and the Ryukyu Islands, south of Japan. In the strait between Korea and Japan, La Pérouse verified the existence of Cheju Island, then explored Sakhalin Island, north of the Japanese island of Hokkaido. From accounts of the natives, he learned that Sakhalin was actually separated from the northernmost Japanese island and located a strait between them.

After visiting the Kuril Islands, La Pérouse entered the Sea of Okhotsk and sailed to the eastern Siberian port of Petropavlovsk on the Kamchatka Peninsula, arriving on September 6, 1787. An updated record of the voyage was sent back to France overland across SIBERIA with the expedition's interpreter, JEAN-BAPTISTE-BARTHÉLEMY DE LESSEPS, who reached Paris in mid-October 1788. While in Petropavlovsk, La Pérouse received word from France directing him to investigate a newly established British colony on the southeast coast of Australia.

From Kamchatka, La Pérouse continued his explorations into the western Pacific, attempting to locate the Solomon Islands, an archipelago that had been incorrectly charted by Spanish mariner ÁLVARO DE MENDAÑA in 1568 and misidentified by Dutch, French, and English navigators over the next two centuries. A landing was made at Tutuila in what is now American Samoa, where 12 of the crew were killed in a native attack. Among those killed were the commander of the *Astrolabe*, Fleuriot de Langlé, and one of the naturalists, Robert de Paul, chevalier de Lamanon.

La Pérouse made for Botany Bay, part of present-day Sydney, Australia, which he reached on January 26, 1788, just as the British were in the process of setting up their penal colony. While anchored in the harbor, several of the recently transported British convicts escaped and tried to seek refuge on La Pérouse's ships, but the French commander returned them to their jailers. Records of his voyage from Kamchatka to Australia were carried back to France aboard a British vessel.

La Pérouse sailed from Botany Bay on March 10, 1788, planning to explore the north coast of Australia around the Gulf of Carpentaria, and perhaps claim some of the island continent for France. It took years to find out what happened to the La Pérouse expedition after that date. In 1791, two years after his ships had failed to arrive in France in 1789 as planned, a search expedition, led by ANTOINE-RAYMOND-JOSEPH DE BRUNI, chevalier d'Entrecasteaux, was sent to the Pacific but found no sign of the vanished expedition. It was not until 1828 that another French expedition, under JULES-SÉBASTIEN-CÉSAR DUMONT D'URVILLE succeeded in locating relics of the *Astrolabe* near the Melanesian island of Vanikoro in the Santa Cruz group. It is believed that La Pérouse's ships were wrecked on the island's reefs, after which the survivors may have attempted to sail for Australia on a boat made from the wreckage, although no trace of La Pérouse or any of his men was ever found.

Comte de La Pérouse attempted to complete the extensive scientific exploration of the Pacific Ocean originally undertaken by James Cook. Because he sent back navigational and scientific data before the expedition disappeared, some of the results did manage to reach geographers in Europe. Among these was his finding that Sakhalin Island was separated from the northern Japanese island of Hokkaido; the channel between them was subsequently named La Pérouse Strait in his honor. His disappearance inspired a series of French search expeditions, which led to extensive exploration of the South Pacific. One small irony of history is that among the cadets who applied to join the voyage in 1785, but were rejected by La Pérouse, was a 16-year-old student of a Paris military academy named Napoléon Bonaparte.

See also SEARCHES FOR MISSING EXPLORERS.

Galinée, René de Brehant de   See BREHANT DE GALINÉE, RENÉ DE.

Gallus, Gaius Aelius (fl. 20s B.C.) *Roman army officer in Egypt and Arabia*

Gaius Aelius Gallus was a Roman officer in Egypt soon after it was annexed by Rome under the emperor Augustus.

In about 25 B.C., Gallus left Cleopatris, a port on the site of present-day Suez at the northern end of the RED SEA, in command of an expedition to the land of Saba and its principal city, Marib, on the southwestern corner of the Arabian Peninsula.

The Sabaeans were the descendants of the people ruled in biblical times by the queen of Sheba. During the first century B.C., they were a major commercial power, acting as intermediaries in the spice and incense trade between India and Egypt. Geographically insulated on the Arabian Peninsula, they had never come under the influence of the Persian Empire to the east or the Roman Empire to the west. With the incorporation of Egypt into the Roman Empire, Roman domination of the Sabaeans became a prerequisite for the opening of direct trade contacts with the Orient.

Gallus led his expedition along the eastern bank of the Red Sea and, near the present northern border of the Yemen Arab Republic, headed inland to the Sabaean trade center at Marib.

Although unsuccessful in his attempt to subjugate the Sabaeans, Gaius Aelius Gallus managed to return to Roman Egypt with some new geographic knowledge about the territory east and south of the Red Sea, a region then largely unknown to the Romans.

Galton, Sir Francis (1822–1911) *British geographer, scientist in southwestern Africa, cousin of Charles Robert Darwin*

Francis Galton was born in Sparkbrook, near Birmingham, England. He was a cousin of CHARLES ROBERT DARWIN. He studied medicine at General Hospital in Birmingham and at King's College in London, and mathematics at Cambridge University. On inheriting his father's estate, he was able to live the life of a country gentleman and travel casually in Europe, the Middle East, and North Africa as a tourist and hunter. In 1850, he decided to undertake an exploration to southwestern Africa and pursue geography in a scientific manner.

In 1850, Galton, accompanied by amateur naturalist Karell Johan Andersson, landed at Walvis Bay in present-day Namibia. His original intention had been to follow DAVID LIVINGSTONE's route of the previous year north from Cape Town in the Cape Colony to Lake Ngami, but, because of unrest between Boer settlers and Bantu, he decided to approach from the west along the Swakop River. Galton and Andersson had contact with the Khoikhoi (called the Hottentots by European settlers) and at Otjimbingwe negotiated a peace with the chief Jan Jonker Afrikaner, preventing further Khoikhoi raiding against European missions. Instead of continuing westward to Lake Ngami, they traveled from the region known as Damaraland northward into Ovamboland, mostly unexplored by Europeans, in the hope of reaching the Cunene River, which they failed to do. Galton returned to England in 1852, while Andersson stayed in Damaraland, operating a store at Otjimbingwe and continuing his studies in natural science. (He carried out later expeditions through the Kalahari Desert to Lake Ngami and to the Kubango River in Bechuanaland.)

Following a written report to the ROYAL GEOGRAPHICAL SOCIETY, Galton published an account of his trip for the general public entitled *Narrative of an Explorer in Tropical South Africa* (1853), which was widely read. The society awarded him a gold medal for African exploration. He also wrote *The Art of Travel, or Shifts and Contrivances Available in Wild Countries* (1855), a handbook for explorers. Galton later worked in a variety of disciplines: meteorology, statistics, psychology, fingerprint identification, and heredity, including a discipline he invented, eugenics. He was knighted in 1909.

Sir Francis Galton's contributions to the field of exploration include, in addition to his geographic studies in Africa and his book *The Art of Travel*, the pioneering use of weather maps based on the charting of air pressure data.

Gama, Vasco da (ca. 1460–1524) *Portuguese naval officer in the Indian Ocean*

Vasco da Gama was a native of Sines, a small seaport on the coast of southern Portugal; his father, Estevão da Gama, was the provincial governor. The younger da Gama went to sea at an early age and, while serving in the Portuguese navy, acquired a knowledge of mathematics and navigation.

Soon after BARTOLOMEU DIAS had rounded the CAPE OF GOOD HOPE in 1487, da Gama's father was chosen by King John II of Portugal to command a follow-up expedition to India. Portugal's internal political problems, along with conflicts with Spain, delayed the start of the voyage for almost a decade. News of CHRISTOPHER COLUMBUS's explorations of 1492–93, and the Treaty of Tordesillas of 1494, giving Portugal dominion over an eastern sea route to India, rekindled interest in the enterprise. In 1495, Manuel I became king of Portugal. With the death of the elder da Gama two years later, command of the expedition went to his son, by then a high-ranking naval officer and a member of the new king's personal staff.

Da Gama's fleet of four ships was constructed and outfitted under the supervision of Dias. Along with the flagship, the *St. Gabriel*, the expedition included the *St. Raphael*, captained by da Gama's brother Paolo; the *Berrío*, under the command of Nicola Coelha; and a supply vessel. Da Gama's chief pilot was Pedro de Alemquer, a veteran of Dias's voyage of 1487. The combined crews totaled about 170 men, including a number of convicts who were taken along for deployment in especially hazardous situations.

Da Gama, at the rank of captain major, sailed with his fleet from Lisbon on July 8, 1497. After a stopover in the CANARY ISLANDS, he continued to the Cape Verde Islands. Dias served as his pilot for this initial leg of the voyage. Following instructions from Dias, da Gama sailed south and west from the Cape Verde Islands in order to avoid the DOLDRUMS in the Gulf of Guinea. His course took him within 600 miles of the coast of Brazil, where he picked up favorable winds. They carried him to the south coast of Africa at St. Helena Bay, about 125 miles north of the Cape of Good Hope.

In late November 1497, da Gama and his expedition rounded the Cape of Good Hope, landing on the south coast of Africa at Mossel Bay, where they claimed the territory for Portugal by erecting the traditional *PADRÃO*, or stone pillar. (He would erect four more on the expedition.) There his men made the earliest European contacts with the southern African people later identified by the Dutch as the Khoikhoi (Hottentot). At Mossel Bay, the supply ship's stores were distributed among the fleet, after which that vessel was dismantled.

By mid-December 1497, da Gama's expedition was sailing northward along the east coast of present-day South Africa, beyond the farthest point Dias had reached 10 years earlier. On Christmas Day 1497, da Gama sighted and named Natal.

In early March 1498, after exploring a river he called the Rio Cobre (the "copper river," after the copper ornaments worn by the region's natives), da Gama reached Mozambique, at that time the southernmost point of Muslim influence on the east coast of Africa. There he met armed opposition from Muslim rulers, who feared Portuguese intrusion into their trading empire. His men fought off attacks at Mombasa as well.

At Malindi on the coast of what is now Kenya, da Gama was well received by the local Muslim ruler, who hoped to forge an alliance against his enemies to the south. In Malindi, da Gama engaged one of the foremost navigators of the Indian Ocean at that time, an Arab seafarer named Ahmed ibn Majid. In just 23 days, Ibn Majid piloted da Gama's fleet across the Arabian Sea to southwestern India's Malabar Coast by way of the Laccadives Islands.

On May 20, 1498, da Gama arrived at the Indian port of Calicut. He attempted to establish relations with the local Hindu ruler, known as the Zamorin, but met opposition from Arab merchants who dominated the Malabar Coast cities. In addition, da Gama had taken mostly cheap trade goods to India, suitable for dealing only with the less sophisticated people of the west coast of Africa, and his attempt to do business in Calicut was met with derision. Nevertheless, after three months, he managed to obtain a modest shipment of pepper.

Vasco da Gama *(Library of Congress)*

Da Gama's return voyage from India to the coast of Africa took three times longer than the outward trip because of unfavorable winds. So many of his crew had succumbed to SCURVY by the time the expedition reached Malindi that da Gama decided to reduce the fleet and burned the *St. Raphael.* The expedition rounded the Cape of Good Hope again in late March 1499, then followed the coastline of West Africa for the remaining voyage to Portugal. Coelho and the *Berrío* arrived in Lisbon in July 1499. Da Gama meanwhile had sailed to the AZORES, seeking care for his brother Paolo, who had become ill on the homeward voyage. His brother soon died on Terceira. Da Gama reached Lisbon in early September 1499, where he was named admiral of the Indian Sea in recognition of his successful navigation of the sea route to India.

In 1502, following PEDRO CABRAL's 1500–01 voyage, Da Gama commanded Portugal's third major expedition to India. His new fleet numbered 20 ships, including squadrons under his uncle and nephew. He raided Muslim trading centers along the east African coast and undertook a campaign against Muslim shipping off the southwest coast of India. In one attack, the Portuguese captured and burned a Muslim ship, the *Meri,* killing more than 400 men, women, and children, mostly pilgrims returning from Mecca. After attacking Calicut with artillery, da Gama went

on to Cochin and brought that port under Portuguese control. On the return voyage along the east African coast, da Gama established Portuguese trading settlements at Sofala and Mozambique.

Back in Portugal by September 1503, da Gama was richly rewarded by the Portuguese government. In 1519, he was named Count of Vidigueira; five years later, he was appointed Portuguese viceroy of India. He sailed again to Cochin, but he died there soon after his arrival in December 1524. His body was sent back to Lisbon. His son, Cristoval da Gama, subsequently participated in Portuguese campaigns in East Africa, supporting the Ethiopian Christians against the Muslims.

Vasco da Gama commanded the first European expedition to reach India by sea, the successful realization of a plan initiated more than 70 years earlier by HENRY THE NAVIGATOR, prince of Portugal. He also pioneered the sea route to the Orient by sailing far to the west before rounding the Cape of Good Hope. On that leg of the voyage, the expedition was out of sight of land for more than 13 weeks, much longer than Columbus had been on his first voyage, and probably the longest stretch of open-sea sailing undertaken by Europeans until that time. The lack of adequate fresh food supplies also led to an outbreak of scurvy at sea. By rounding southern Africa, da Gama showed that the Indian Ocean, with an outlet to the Atlantic Ocean, was not a landlocked sea as many European geographers believed. Da Gama's first voyage of 1497–99, which covered 24,000 miles, took the first European ships into the Indian Ocean. On his second expedition to India, he left behind the first permanent European naval force in Asian waters. Commercially, da Gama's expeditions had a profound impact in Europe. Lisbon became a center of the SPICE TRADE, especially in pepper, becoming more important than Venice. In the years that followed, Portugal established an overseas empire that dominated trade in East Africa, the southwestern ports of India, and present-day Indonesia. Da Gama's first voyage was the subject of the Portuguese epic poem, *Os Lusiadas (The Lusiads),* by Luíz Vaz de Camões, published in 1572.

Gamboa, Pedro Sarmiento de   See SARMIENTO DE GAMBOA, PEDRO.

Garay, Juan de   (ca. 1528–1583) *Spanish conquistador, colonial leader in Peru, Bolivia, Paraguay, and Argentina, father-in-law of Hernando Arias de Saavedra*

Juan de Garay traveled to Peru in 1544, as a teenager, accompanying the royal viceroy Blasco Núñez Vela and helped repress the colonial revolt led by GONZALO PIZARRO, which lasted until 1548.

In the early 1560s, Garay helped found Santa Cruz de la Sierra in Upper Peru (present-day Bolivia). Threats from the indigenous population and lack of food supplies prompted Garay to lead Spanish settlers to Asunción, in present-day Paraguay, in 1568. Five years later, he sought a route from there through the Paraná Valley to the Pacific Ocean.

In the 1570s–80s, Garay served as lieutenant governor of the provinces of the Río de la Plata. In 1573, he founded the settlement of Santa Fe, in present-day Argentina, and, in 1580, he founded Buenos Aires for the second time (the original settlement of 1536 had been abandoned in 1541). That same year, Garay explored the coast around Mar del Plata to the south of Buenos Aires in the hope of finding the fabled native city of LOS CÉSARES, rumored to contain precious metals and jewels. Three years later, he was killed by Indians at the confluence of the Carcarañá and Coronada Rivers.

Juan de Garay, as a military leader and colonizer, helped open up central South America to Spanish settlement. His son-in-law, HERNANDO ARIAS DE SAAVEDRA, continued his efforts and reorganized and expanded the Spanish colonies.

Garcés, Francisco Tomás Hermenegildo   (1738–1781) *Spanish missionary in the American Southwest*

Francisco Garcés was born in Villa Morata del Conde in the Aragon region of northeastern Spain. At the age of 16, he entered the Franciscan order, and nine years later, in 1763, he was ordained a priest. That year, he traveled to Mexico to study at the College of Santa Cruz de Querétaro.

In 1768, soon after the Jesuits were expelled from New Spain, Father Garcés began his missionary work among the Indians at the mission of San Xavier del Bac, near present-day Tucson, Arizona. Later that year, he set out on a series of explorations along the Gila River and COLORADO RIVER to the lands of the Pima (Akimel O'odham) Indians. In 1771, he traveled westward to the Yuma Indian villages on the COLORADO RIVER. From there, he explored the northernmost mountains of Baja California, then traversed the deserts of what is now southern California, as far as the San Jacinto Mountains, near present-day Palm Springs, California.

In 1774, Garcés and Friar Juan Díaz joined JUAN BAUTISTA DE ANZA, commander of the Spanish garrison at nearby Tubac, in an expedition intending to establish an overland route to the Spanish settlements in California. They set out from Tubac on January 8, 1774, accompanied by a small military escort. They crossed the Colorado near its junction with the Gila River, and, continuing westward, made the European discovery of the Cocopas Mountains, which they crossed. On March 22, 1774, Anza, Garcés, and the others arrived at the San Gabriel mission, not far from present-day Los Angeles.

The next year, Garcés accompanied Anza on his large-scale colonizing expedition from Tubac. At the confluence of the Gila and Colorado Rivers, he separated from the main party. Exploring on his own, he descended the Colorado River to its mouth, then traversed the Mojave Desert and the San Bernardino Mountains to the San Gabriel mission. From there, he attempted to blaze a trail overland to Monterey on the Pacific coast. After passing through present-day Bakersfield, California, he reached as far as Tulare Lake, where he decided to head back eastward to the Colorado, hoping to win converts among the Hopi Indians of what is now northern Arizona.

Garcés established initial contacts with the Hopi Indians, then returned to the San Xavier del Bac mission by way of the Colorado and Gila Rivers. In 1776, he set out again for the land of the Hopi, this time planning to reach the region from the west. He ascended the Colorado River to the Mojave Indian villages near present-day Needles, California, where he engaged several Indian guides, who led him eastward across what is now northern Arizona, until he came upon Cataract Canyon, not far from the Grand Canyon. Following a narrow trail that appeared to be carved into the canyon's wall, he made a dangerous descent to the floor of the canyon, and there came upon the Havasupai Indians, a tribe unknown to the Spanish. Garcés stayed with the Havasupai for five days, after which the Indians guided him out of Cataract Canyon by a less hazardous route, leading him to a point near the southern rim of the Grand Canyon. Soon afterward, he saw the Grand Canyon itself, then headed eastward into the country of the Hopi in the Little Colorado River region.

In 1780, Garcés returned to the Yuma villages on the Colorado, near the site of the future Fort Yuma, California, where he established the mission of La Purísima Concepción on the California side of the river. Relations with the Yuma began to deteriorate when presents, which Garcés had promised, failed to arrive. In spring 1781, Spanish settlers began coming to the mission, which also included a garrison, as well as provisions for a settlement, or pueblo. The influx of the settlers further antagonized the Indians, who, on July 17, 1781, rose up against Garcés, his church people, and the military detachment. Garcés was clubbed to death. The Indian uprising effectively shut down direct overland communication between Spanish settlements in California and those in present-day Arizona, New Mexico, and northern Mexico for the next 40 years.

Father Francisco Garcés was the first European to cross the San Bernardino Mountains of southern California. On his 1776 explorations into what is now Arizona, he was the first non-Indian to see the Grand Canyon since 1540, when GARCÍA LÓPEZ DE CÁRDENAS and his men had come upon it in conjunction with the expedition of FRANCISCO VÁSQUEZ DE CORONADO. After Garcés, the next recorded sighting of the Grand Canyon was in 1857–58, when it was explored by JOSEPH CHRISTMAS IVES of the U.S. Army Corps of Topographical Engineers. Garcés's journals of his travels and experiences in the American Southwest were edited by Elliot Couse and published in 1900 as *On the Trail of a Spanish Pioneer*.

García, Alejo (Aleixo García) (unknown–ca. 1526)
Portuguese castaway, explorer along the Paraguay River in South America

Portuguese-born Alejo García is thought to have been a member of the 1515–16 expedition of JUAN DÍAZ DE SOLÍS and one of the castaways following a shipwreck along the Brazilian coast on or near the island of Santa Catarina. He married a native woman and had a child by her.

At some point between 1522 and 1526, García reportedly made a journey inland in search of a "White King" who ruled over mountains of silver. With other Spanish castaways and a force of Indians, he reached the Paraguay River north of present-day Asunción, in Paraguay, and followed it as far as the foothills of the ANDES MOUNTAINS in what is now Bolivia, the domain of the Inca Indians. There, from unknown peoples, the Spaniards plundered a small amount of silver. García was killed on the return journey or soon after his arrival back on the coast. SEBASTIAN CABOT, who had landed on the estuary of the Río de la Plata in 1526, heard reports of García's exploits and obtained some of the booty. As a result, he abandoned his plans to continue from South America to the Orient and spent three years looking for the legendary White King.

Alejo García's adventure, along with that of one of Cabot's lieutenants, Francisco César, contributed to growing myths of wealthy native kingdoms in South America, such as LOS CÉSARES, prompting further explorations of the Río de la Plata and the Paraguay and Paraná Rivers. The similar legend of EL DORADO also inspired expeditions into the next century.

Gardar Svarsson   See SVARSSON, GARDAR.

Garnier, Marie-Joseph-François (Francis Garnier) (1839–1873) *French naval officer, colonial officer in Southeast Asia*

Francis Garnier was born in St.-Étienne, in the upper Loire Valley of southeastern France, the son of an army officer. He joined the French navy and, as a young officer in 1861, took part in the French conquest of what is now southern Vietnam. The next year, he was named governor of Saigon, present-day Ho Chi Minh City.

While serving in the French colonial administration of what was then Cochin China, Garnier sought government backing for an expedition to explore up the Mekong River to determine if it could be used as a trade route into the southwestern Chinese province of Yunnan to the north. The French colonial office agreed to his proposal and appointed Garnier as the expedition's inspector of indigenous affairs and second in command under ERNEST-MARC-LOUIS DE GONZAGUE DOUDART DE LAGRÉE, a veteran explorer of the Mekong River and Cambodia.

Garnier embarked upriver from Saigon with the Mekong Expedition in June 1866. While Doudart de Lagrée and the rest of the party proceeded into Cambodia and Laos, Garnier, accompanied only by one other French member of the expedition, explored separately into northeastern Cambodia, descending the Mekong's rapids in that region, then traveling overland 500 miles to the site of the ancient Khmer ruins at Angkor in western Cambodia.

Garnier returned to Laos, subsequently rejoining Doudart de Lagrée and the rest of the expedition farther up the Mekong in southwestern China's Yunnan province in late 1867. By this time, Doudart de Lagrée had fallen seriously ill with amoebic dysentery. Garnier meanwhile explored the upper Red River to see if it could be used as a commercial route southward to Hanoi.

Garnier assumed command of the Mekong Expedition when Doudart de Lagrée died at Tungchwan in March 1868. Instead of returning by the route they had come, he led the party from the upper YANGTZE RIVER (Chang), known in Yunnan as the Kinsa, downriver and eastward across southwestern China to the port of Shanghai, from where they returned to Saigon in June 1868.

Garnier was back in Europe in 1870. That year, Great Britain's ROYAL GEOGRAPHICAL SOCIETY awarded him a medal in recognition of his explorations, which had yielded detailed geographic information about 3,100 miles of previously uncharted territory along the Mekong, Yangtze, and Red Rivers. He subsequently served in the Franco-Prussian War of 1870–71, taking part in the defense of Paris.

At the war's end, Garnier returned to the Far East, where he traveled into the interior of China in search of the source of the tea and silk trade, as well as a possible river route between Tibet and China. In 1873, in conjunction with JEAN DUPUIS's unauthorized Red River expedition, he took part in a military campaign against the kingdom of Tonkin in what is now northern Vietnam. He commanded French colonial forces in an action that temporarily brought the Red River delta near Hanoi under French control. After battling Chinese pirates in the Gulf of Tonkin, Garnier was killed in a skirmish outside Hanoi in December 1873. His account of the Mekong Expedition of 1866–68 was published in Paris in 1885 as *Voyage d'exploration en Indo-Chine* ("Journey of Exploration in Indo-China").

Francis Garnier's explorations with Doudart de Lagrée on the Mekong River in 1866–68 took him into remote parts of Southeast Asia seldom visited by Europeans. On the return journey, he charted portions of the upper Yangtze River that had not been visited by Europeans since the 13th-century travels of MARCO POLO.

Gaudichaud-Beaupré, Charles (1789–1854)
French naturalist in Australia, the South Pacific, and South America

Charles Gaudichaud-Beaupré was born in the city of Angoulême in western France. After studying botany at the Museum of Natural History in Paris, he joined the French navy's medical service, serving as a pharmacist at Antwerp from 1811 to 1814.

In 1817, Gaudichaud-Beaupré was recruited by LOUIS-CLAUDE DE SAULCES DE FREYCINET to serve as the pharmacist and botanist on a scientific voyage to the South Pacific Ocean aboard the *Uranie*. JOSEPH-PAUL GAIMARD served as assistant surgeon and zoologist. During the next three years, he collected thousands of live plants and a large number of dried plant specimens from a wide area of the Pacific, ranging from the west coast of Australia to the HAWAIIAN ISLANDS. On Dorre and Bernier Islands at the mouth of Western Australia's Shark Bay, he discovered a previously uncataloged type of shrub, which he named the Keraudren, after a French naval medical officer who had assisted in organizing the expedition.

In October 1818, while examining the flora on Timor in what is now Indonesia, Gaudichaud-Beaupré found a climbing species of the screw pine shrub unknown to science, which he named the freycinetia, after the expedition's commander. In his subsequent botanical investigations in the Hawaiian Islands the following August, he found a type of sandalwood tree, new to science, which he also named in honor of Freycinet, dubbing it *Santalum freycinetiana*.

On the homeward voyage, the *Uranie* stopped at Sydney, Australia, where Gaudichaud-Beaupré had the opportunity to explore the BLUE MOUNTAINS for botanical species. When the ship was subsequently wrecked in the Falkland Islands in February 1820, he managed to save most of his collection of dried plants. Before the party was rescued by a passing American ship two months later, he undertook a survey of the plant life of the Falklands, collecting several hundred species. In 1825, Gaudichaud-Beaupré published his botanical study of this South Atlantic Ocean island group, entitled "Flora des îles Malouines" (Flora of the Falkland Islands).

Gaudichaud-Beaupré's published account of his botanical work on the *Uranie* voyage appeared in 1826. After his appointment as a correspondent for the French Academy of Sciences in 1828, Gaudichaud-Beaupré took part in another French scientific expedition in 1830–32. As pharmacist and botanist on the *Herminie*, he sailed to South America, where he made a study of the flora of Brazil, Chile, and Peru. While the ship stopped at Rio, he traveled inland to the Mato Grosso region and explored the interior of Brazil's São Paulo province and collected more than 3,000 plants for the Museum of Natural History in Paris. In 1836–37, he accompanied the zoologist Fortuné Eydoux on the *Bonité*, under the command of Auguste-Nicolas Vaillant, and undertook additional botanical studies in the South Pacific.

Soon after his return from the *Bonité* voyage, Charles Gaudichaud-Beaupré was made a member of the French Academy of Sciences. In his voyages, he had amassed more than 10,000 plant specimens, more than 1,200 of which were wholly new to science. A red flowering grevillea plant he had discovered on the west coast of Australia in 1818 was named the *Grevillea gaudichaudi* in recognition of his contributions to botanical science.

Genghis Khan (Jenghiz Khan, Chingis Khan)
(ca. 1162–1227) *Mongol conqueror of central Asia*

Named Temuchin (or Temujin), which means "the finest steel" in the Mongol language, Genghis Khan (really a title, not a name) was the son of Yekusai, a chieftain of the nomadic Yakka Mongols who ranged across the northern GOBI DESERT from Lake Baikal in the west to Manchuria in the east. His mother was named Houlun, a woman captured from a neighboring tribe.

When Temuchin was 13, his father was murdered by tribal rivals, and the young man became chieftain of the Yakka clan. Although his leadership was challenged for a number of years, he eventually triumphed over his enemies, a confederation of Mongol tribes, completing the conquest of what is now Mongolia by 1206. On the advice of a sooth-sayer, he assumed the title Genghis Khan, which has been interpreted to mean "World Encompassing" or "Emperor of All Men." In the northern Gobi, he established a military capital at Karakorum.

Over the next two decades, Genghis Khan led his highly mobile cavalry armies across the steppes of central Asia in a campaign of conquest that resulted in the creation of the largest empire ever the exist in human history. In 1215, he conquered the Jin Empire of what is now northern China, occupying its capital, Yen-King or Yenching (present-day Beijing), Genghis Khan subsequently led his Golden Horde, as his forces came to be known, westward across central Asia, bringing Turkistan, Transoxiana, Afghanistan, Persia (present-day Iran), and much of southern Russia under his domination. In 1221, Genghis Khan sent out Taoist sage CH'ANG-CH'UN on a voyage of exploration through central Asia.

At his death in 1227, Genghis Khan's empire stretched from the Caspian Sea to the Pacific coast of China. In the two decades after his death, his successors pushed west-ward into Europe, extending the Mongol conquest into present-day Hungary and threatening to invade the rest of Christian Europe. It was these developments that prompted Pope Innocent IV in 1245 to dispatch Father GIOVANNI DA PIAN DEL CARPINI on a diplomatic mission to the Mongols, hoping to establish peaceful relations. The Italian priest also sought to investigate the possibility of forming an alliance with the Mongols against the Islamic Turks, who then controlled the trade routes through the Middle East.

Genghis Khan had a far-reaching influence on the his-tory of European exploration. For centuries before his con-quests, European culture had little direct contact with the East. Yet his rapid push westward across central Asia forcibly brought the East to Europe's doorstep. The tight monopoly exercised over the SILK ROAD to and from the Far East by the Muslims was broken by his conquests. The perceived threat of future Mongol encroachment shocked western Europe out of its insularity and led to the first organized travels into uncharted lands undertaken by Europeans since the days of the Vikings. In addition to the diplomatic mission of Carpini, there was the journey of WILLIAM OF RUBROUCK in 1253–55. Traders followed, including MARCO POLO and his father and uncle in the late 1200s. News of the Far East began to filter back to Europe, and interest in direct trade with the Orient became a prime goal of Italian and Por-tuguese commercial interests.

Gerlache de Gomery, Adrien-Victor-Joseph de (comte de Gerlache) (1866–1934) *Belgian naval officer, polar explorer*

Adrien de Gerlache was born to a noble family in the town of Hasselt, in the eastern Belgian province of Limbourg. His educational background included the science of oceanogra-phy, a specialty that he put to use in his subsequent career as naval officer and polar explorer.

In 1895, Gerlache conducted a scientific expedition to remote Jan Mayen Island, which lies in the Greenland Sea midway between Norway and GREENLAND. He also undertook studies on the mainland of eastern Greenland.

In 1897, Gerlache commanded the Belgica Expedi-tion, named for the *Belgica*, a former Norwegian sealer converted for scientific exploration in polar regions. Among his crew of 18 departing Antwerp that year were the first mate, ROALD ENGELBREGT GRAVNING AMUND-SEN, and the expedition's medical officer, FREDERICK AL-BERT COOK.

One of the objects of Gerlache's scientific mission was to seek the SOUTH MAGNETIC POLE. Delays in getting under way caused Gerlache and his expedition to arrive in the Antarctic late in the summer season of 1897–98. He had planned to land a party on the Antarctic mainland to spend the winter while the ship withdrew northward to a temper-ate climate. The *Belgica* approached the coast of the Antarc-tic Peninsula, off Palmer Land, where a landing party went ashore in January 1898. By March 1898, the ship had be-come icebound, and it remained trapped for the next 13 months, drifting from Alexander Island along the coast of the Antarctic Peninsula to Peter I Island through 600 miles of frozen sea.

Over the next year, Gerlache and most of his crew were stricken with SCURVY. Command of the expedition then went to Amundsen, who, with Cook, helped the crew re-cover by providing them with fresh seal meat. Dynamite charges were used to free the ship in spring 1899, and the expedition then sailed back to Belgium.

In 1905, Gerlache returned to his study of Greenland, this time exploring its northeastern region. Two years later, he led an oceanographic research team into the Barents and Kara Seas north of Scandinavia and eastern European Russia. In 1909, he undertook additional oceanographic work in the Greenland Sea. Gerlache went on to play a role in the planning stages of ERNEST HENRY SHACKLETON's abortive British Imperial Trans-Antarctic Expedition of 1914–17.

Comte de Gerlache's ship, the *Belgica*, was the first to winter in the Antarctic. His 1897–99 expedition, the first scientific expedition to visit the Antarctic since that of SIR JAMES CLARK ROSS in 1841, marked the beginning of the re-vival of formal exploration there.

Gibault, Pierre (1737–1804) *French-Canadian missionary in the Mississippi Valley*

Pierre Gibault was born in Montreal; his family had originally emigrated from France to French Canada in the mid-1600s. Educated at the Seminary of Quebec, he was ordained a Catholic priest and served at the Cathedral of Quebec.

In 1768, Gibault was sent as a missionary to the frontier region of the central Mississippi Valley. Accompanied by his mother and sister, he traveled to the former French settlement at Kaskaskia on the MISSISSIPPI RIVER, in what is now southwestern Illinois, where his parish extended upriver to include Ste. Genevieve and St. Louis. The next year, he journeyed eastward to the Wabash River, where he extended his missionary work to the settlement at Vincennes in present-day southwestern Indiana.

In the American Revolution of 1775–83, Gibault was instrumental in gaining the support of the residents of Kaskaskia for the American cause, when the settlement was captured by Virginia militia forces under George Rogers Clark in July 1778. Soon afterward, he traveled from Kaskaskia to Vincennes, and, aided by French trader Francis Vigo, he again succeeded in winning the allegiance of the French settlers against the British at that strategic settlement on the Wabash.

In 1780, British officials in Quebec alleged that Gibault had committed treason for providing aid to the American forces in the Illinois country, although no steps were taken to prosecute him for this charge.

Gibault settled in Vincennes in 1785. Four years later, he again headed westward to the Mississippi River. He first attempted to establish a seminary at Cahokia in present-day Illinois. After failing to obtain a land grant from the territorial government, he crossed the Mississippi into Spanish territory, where he became a parish priest at New Madrid in what is now southeastern Missouri.

In 1804, the year of Father Pierre Gibault's death, the United States expanded across the Mississippi into the vast Louisiana Territory. His missionary career had spanned the years between the initial exploration of the central Mississippi Valley by the French and the subsequent forays westward into the continent made in the St. Louis–based FUR TRADE of the early 19th century.

Gilbert, Sir Humphrey (Sir Humfry Gilbert) (ca. 1539–1583) *English geographer, colonizer in North America, half brother of Sir Walter Raleigh*

Humphrey Gilbert was born to a wealthy family at Greenway House, near Dartmouth, in Devon, England. His father died when he was eight years old, and his mother married the elder Walter Raleigh, by whom she had a son, Gilbert's half brother, the future SIR WALTER RALEIGH.

After attending Eton, Gilbert went on to study at Oxford University. He then obtained an appointment to the staff of Princess Elizabeth, continuing to serve her after her ascent to the English throne in 1558 as Queen Elizabeth I. In the early 1560s, Gilbert embarked on a military career, serving first in northern France on behalf of the Protestant Huguenots, and later in campaigns in Ireland under the command of Sir Henry Sidney. While serving in Ireland, Gilbert first became acquainted with English navigator SIR MARTIN FROBISHER.

Gilbert had become interested in geography while at Oxford, especially in the possibility of finding a NORTHWEST PASSAGE to the Far East. In 1565–66, he debated with the MUSCOVY COMPANY's ANTHONY JENKINSON before Queen Elizabeth, on the feasibility of finding such a water route. Jenkinson maintained that, during his travels in Russia, he had heard reports from sailors on the Kara Sea that a NORTHEAST PASSAGE across the top of Asia was possible. Gilbert, on the other hand, argued that a Northwest Passage across the top of North America was far more practical. He held that the coast of North America ran southward west of Labrador, and was therefore likely to be free of ice. In addition, Gilbert declared that the Northwest Passage to the Far East was a much shorter route than the one proposed eastward around Europe and Asia. For authority, he cited the first-century A.D. Roman naturalist PLINY THE ELDER who had reported the appearance of East Asian Indians on the coast of Germany in classical times. Since there was no account of their journey across Europe in that period, Gilbert asserted that they could only have come across the sea by way of the Northwest Passage.

Gilbert buttressed his arguments with an account of a large inland sea north of Mexico as reported by David Ingram, a sailor left on the Gulf Coast of Mexico by SIR JOHN HAWKINS in 1567, who had later returned to England after traveling overland across North America to the shores of what is now Maine. Gilbert further theorized that North America was actually the lost island of ATLANTIS, and that a strait ran across its northern end, complementing the STRAIT OF MAGELLAN at the tip of South America. He firmly believed in the existence of the STRAIT OF ANIAN, a supposed water route that led from the Pacific Ocean into the Atlantic Ocean. Although most of the ideas put forth in his written work on the subject, *A Discourse of a Discoverie for a New Passage to Cataia,* were based more on fable than on fact, he was the first geographer to speculate correctly that a Continental Divide existed within the interior of North America.

In recognition of his military exploits in Ireland, Gilbert was knighted in 1570. He went on to aid the Dutch in their revolt again Spain in 1572. Although he had written his *Discourse* in 1566, it was not published until 1576, when it was used to help promote financial support for Frobisher's expeditions to find the Northwest Passage, of which Gilbert was a principal backer.

In 1578, Gilbert obtained a royal patent from Queen Elizabeth to explore and colonize new lands for the Crown. Soon afterward, he undertook two expeditions, one with his half brother Walter Raleigh. On both occasions his ships were driven back by storms off the coast of Ireland. Other misadventures soon followed, and the enterprise was abandoned.

Undaunted, Gilbert tried again in 1583, this time planning to establish a colony in North America to which to send England's undesirables, as well as to provide a way station for ships en route to China and Japan through the Northwest Passage, the imminent discovery of which he was certain. He assembled a fleet of five ships and, with about 260 colonists, sailed westward from Plymouth, England, on June 11, 1583. Soon after the departure, one of the ships deserted and returned to England. The rest reached the coast of Newfoundland on July 30, 1583. On August 5, at what is now St. John's Bay, Gilbert took formal possession of Newfoundland in the name of the queen. At that time, Newfoundland was well known to European fishermen, and, when Gilbert arrived there, he found several dozen fleets of fishing vessels and their crews from Portugal, Spain, France, and England, who accepted Gilbert as their new governor.

Over the next two weeks, Gilbert and his party explored the interior of Newfoundland, undertaking a survey for valuable minerals. He then sailed to the south and west, searching the coastline for the entrance to the Northwest Passage. Off Sable Island, near present-day Nova Scotia, Gilbert's largest ship and supply vessel, the *Delight,* was wrecked on a reef, with the loss of many of its crew. Earlier, another of his ships had been sent back to England with some members of the expedition who had fallen ill. Left with only two vessels, and short on food and other essentials, Gilbert decided to sail back to England at the end of August 1583.

Gilbert himself was aboard the smallest vessel of his fleet, the *Squirrel,* on the eastward crossing, accompanied by the other remaining ship, the *Golden Hind.* North of the AZORES in the mid-Atlantic, the ships ran into storms and heavy seas. The *Squirrel* disappeared in a heavy swell and was lost with all hands. The *Golden Hind* managed to return safely to England with the news of Gilbert's death.

The year after Gilbert's expedition to Newfoundland, his commission to explore and colonize was granted to Sir Walter Raleigh, who subsequently undertook three settlement attempts on the Virginia coast.

Sir Humphrey Gilbert was a major promoter of English explorations for the Northwest Passage, his geographic speculations giving impetus to the later voyages of JOHN DAVIS and HENRY HUDSON. Moreover, he was one of the first proponents of a permanent English colony in the New World.

Giles, Ernest (1835–1897) *British explorer in Western Australia*

Ernest Giles was a native of Bristol, England. He was schooled at Christ's Hospital in London and, in his 15th year, immigrated to Adelaide, South Australia, where his parents had settled earlier.

Giles worked for a time as a clerk in the goldfields of Victoria in southeastern Australia. From 1861 to 1865, he undertook a series of expeditions into the territory around the Darling River and its tributaries, seeking new grazing lands for Australia's rapidly expanding sheep-raising industry.

In 1872, a group of wealthy Victoria-based sheep farmers and other businessmen commissioned Giles to explore west of the recently completed Central Overland Telegraph Line traversing the continent from Adelaide in the south to Darwin on the north coast. In addition to seeking new pasture lands, Giles hoped to make the first east-to-west inland crossing of Australia.

Leaving Charlotte Waters, a frontier settlement on the Finke River in the south-central Northern Territory in August 1872, Giles followed the river westward to the Macdonnell Ranges, and into the desert region beyond. He proceeded as far as Lake Amadeus on the edge of desert country, where he was forced to turn back when it became apparent that some special means of transport was necessary to make any headway across the vast waterless tract.

Giles made another attempt at a westward crossing of Australia in 1873. On this expedition, he set out from Lake Eyre, several hundred miles south of his starting point the previous year. Accompanied by an assistant, Alfred Gibson, he headed northwestward across the Alberga River, then traveled around the Musgrave Mountains in an attempt to avoid the GREAT VICTORIA DESERT. Nevertheless, he soon came upon a greater expanse of desert as he entered Western Australia from the east. Gibson became lost, and Giles, unable to find him, was forced to abandon the attempt because of lack of water, returning to South Australia alone.

In 1875, Giles decided to undertake the crossing of the central Australian deserts with camels. In May of that year, he obtained 24 of the animals and set out from Port Augusta, near the head of South Australia's Spencer Gulf. After skirting Lake Torrens, he ventured once again into the Great Victoria Desert. With his camels able to carry reserves of water, and the animals themselves able to cover great distances with minimal amounts, he succeeded in crossing the desert. On one leg of the journey, he covered some 325 miles of territory devoid of any trace of water at all. After traveling for five months across 2,500 miles, he arrived at Perth on the west coast of Australia, having completed the first successful inland east-to-west crossing of the Australian continent.

After a two-month rest in Perth, Giles and his camels began the return trip, taking a more northerly route from the headwaters of the Gascoyne and Fortescue rivers of northwestern Australia. Traveling eastward, just south of the TROPIC OF CAPRICORN, he traversed the same desert region where Alfred Gibson had disappeared two years earlier. Giles searched the region for some trace of his missing companion but found nothing. After traveling southward into the Northern Territory, he reached Lake Amadeus and the Finke River settlements, from where he returned to Adelaide in August 1876.

Giles took part in explorations of southwestern Australia in 1882. He then settled in the goldmining regions around Coolgardie in Western Australia, where he spent his remaining years employed as a clerk.

Ernest Giles's 1875 crossing of Australia demonstrated that camels were indispensable for the exploration of the continent's central desert regions. He personally gained little from his explorations, having failed to locate the new pasture lands that his sponsors hoped for in the interior of Western Australia. His record as an accomplished desert explorer persists indirectly in the name of the great arid region of Western Australia, which Giles called the Gibson Desert, in honor of his lost assistant.

Giraudais, François Chesnard de la
See CHESNARD DE LA GIRAUDAIS, FRANÇOIS.

Gist, Christopher (ca. 1706–1759) *Colonial American trader, surveyor, guide in the trans-Appalachian region*
By 1745, Christopher Gist, a native of Baltimore County, Maryland, had moved with his wife and children to the Yadkin Valley of central North Carolina, where he was a trader to the Indians.

Gist was hired by the Ohio Company to explore and survey the region of what is now western Pennsylvania, southern Ohio, and northern Kentucky. The Ohio Company had been granted a half-million acres of land in a region bounded by the Ohio and Kanawha Rivers, west of the Allegheny Mountains, part of the APPALACHIAN MOUNTAINS. Gist was assigned to select lands there suitable for agricultural settlement.

In 1750, Gist explored the Ohio watershed as far west as the Falls of the Ohio, near the site of present-day Louisville, Kentucky. He also investigated the lands as far west as present-day Dayton, Ohio, near what is now the southeastern Indiana state line. That November, he reached the trading post at Logstown, on the Ohio River, about 30 miles above the Forks of the Ohio. Accompanied by the trader GEORGE CROGHAN, he headed westward to the Great Miami River and visited lands then inhabited by the Shawnee Indians. Along the way, he explored the regions of the Great Miami and Scioto Rivers in what is now southwestern Ohio. On the western banks of the Ohio River, as he later reported, he saw herds of buffalo.

On the return journey, Gist traveled eastward across parts of present-day Kentucky and West Virginia. While traveling back along the Ohio River, he visited a site where there was a large number of mammoth bones. He headed southward to the Yadkin Valley, from where he went to Williamsburg, Virginia, and submitted his report and maps to the officials of the Ohio Company.

Gist's findings included a description of the fertile Great Meadows region between the western slopes of the Allegheny Mountains and the Monongahela River, across the mountains from the CUMBERLAND GAP.

In 1752–53, Gist blazed a trail from the Potomac River in western Maryland, through the Alleghenies, to the region west of the mountains at the mouth of Redstone Creek, a tributary of the Monongahela River, where he constructed a small settlement for the Ohio Company. THOMAS CRESAP later extended the trail.

In 1753–54, he was the guide for George Washington's expedition to the French post at the Forks of the Ohio, Fort Duquesne (present-day Pittsburgh). The purpose of this mission was to warn the French against further encroachment in western Pennsylvania. The ensuing skirmishes with the French led to the outbreak of the French and the Indian War of 1754–63.

In 1755, Gist was a guide for General Edward Braddock's abortive campaign against Fort Duquesne. He continued to serve as a scout and Indian diplomat for the British. In 1759, he was sent to the western Carolinas to gain the support of the Cherokee Indians against the French. While there, he contracted smallpox and died.

Christopher Gist's explorations of the trans-Appalachian frontier and his reports of potentially rich agricultural lands inspired many frontier farmers and hunters to travel westward across the Alleghenies, among them DANIEL BOONE, who led settlers into Kentucky in the 1770s.

Glass, Hugh (ca. 1780–1833) *American fur trader, trapper in the northern Rocky Mountains and on the southern plains*
Details of Hugh Glass's origins and early life are sketchy. He reportedly claimed to have been held captive first by Jean Lafitte and his Gulf Coast pirates, then by Pawnee Indians in present-day Nebraska.

In spring 1823, Glass went to work for WILLIAM HENRY ASHLEY and ANDREW HENRY in their fur-trading expedition to the upper MISSOURI RIVER region. While traveling up the Missouri in what is now central South Dakota, he was wounded in the leg when Arikara Indians ambushed the traders.

Glass soon recovered and joined Andrew Henry in an expedition to Fort Henry at the junction of the Missouri and Yellowstone Rivers in present-day North Dakota. Indian hostilities farther up the Missouri necessitated an overland journey. In August 1823, while traveling along the Grand River in what is now South Dakota, Glass was attacked by a grizzly bear and severely injured. Henry left two of his men, JAMES BRIDGER and John Fitzgerald, to stay with him. Soon after Henry's departure, Bridger and Fitzgerald, believing Glass would soon die, abandoned him on the Grand River.

Glass survived, however, and, over the next month, managed to crawl more than 100 miles back to Fort Kiowa on the Missouri. He then traveled upriver with another party of trappers and reached Fort Henry. By this time, Ashley and Henry had abandoned their Yellowstone River post, so Glass set out westward to the company's new post in the Bighorn region of what is now Montana. Unable to reach that trading fort, he turned back down the Missouri. At Fort Atkinson near present-day Council Bluffs, Nebraska, he met up with Bridger and Fitzgerald, and despite his ordeal in the wilderness, he reportedly was reconciled with them.

During the mid-1820s, Glass took part in the trade caravans along the Santa Fe Trail between St. Louis and New Mexico.

In 1828, Glass returned to the upper Missouri FUR TRADE. That year, he was involved in a battle with the Indians at Bear Lake in the Green River region of what is now northern Utah and was wounded a third time.

In 1829, Glass attempted to involve the AMERICAN FUR COMPANY in the annual fur trappers' rendezvous at Pierre's Hole. In the following years, he worked out of the company's post on the Yellowstone River, Fort Union. During the 1832–33 trapping season, he was killed in an attack by Arikara Indians.

Although many of Hugh Glass's adventures are undocumented, his exploits in the fur trade of the 1820s indicate the perilous nature of the work undertaken by the mountain men, who were among the first non-Indians to explore west of the Missouri River into the ROCKY MOUNTAINS. Glass's remarkable survival after he was attacked by a bear on the Grand River inspired poet John G. Niehardt to write the 1915 epic poem, *The Song of Hugh Glass.*

Glazunov, Andrey (Andrei Glasunof)

(fl. 1830s–1840s) *Russian-American fur trader in western Alaska*

Andrey Glazunov was born in Alaska soon after the first Russian settlements were established there at the close of the 18th century.

In the 1830s, Glazunov, having entered the service of the RUSSIAN-AMERICAN COMPANY, the great Russian fur-trading enterprise in Alaska, was commissioned by the company's director (and Russian colonial governor of Alaska), Baron Ferdinand Petrovich von Wrangel, to explore inland along the west coast of Alaska, along the lower Yukon and Kuskokwim Rivers. Traveling by kayak, he surveyed the lower course of the Yukon River in 1834, charting the river's delta, south of Norton Sound. The next year, he undertook an exploration of the territory between the two rivers, resulting in the first charts of the inland regions to the north and east of Kuskokwim Bay.

Andrey Glazunov went on to establish a new Russian fur trading post at Ikogmiut in 1842. His explorations provided the Russians, and later the Americans, with the first detailed descriptions of the coast of western Alaska south of Norton Sound and north of the earlier Russian settlements on Bristol Bay and the Alaska Peninsula. He was among the first Alaskan-born explorers of Russian America.

Glenn, John Herschell, Jr. (1921–)

American astronaut, first American to orbit Earth, politician

John Glenn, born in Cambridge, Ohio, attended Muskingum College in New Concord, Ohio, starting in 1939. With World War II, he left his junior year to join the Naval Aviation Cadet Program and became a pilot in the U.S. Marine Corps. He flew combat missions in both World War II and the Korean War. After service in Korea, Glenn became a test pilot. In 1957, he made the first supersonic flight from Los Angeles to New York City, setting a speed record.

In 1959, Glenn was selected as an ASTRONAUT, one of the original seven selected by the NATIONAL AERONAUTICS AND SPACE ADMINISTRATION (NASA). He was also selected for the third manned spaceflight in the MERCURY PROGRAM, following the 1961 suborbital flights of ALAN BARTLETT SHEPARD, JR., and Virgil Grissom. On February 20, 1962, taking off from Cape Canaveral, Florida, Glenn reached an altitude of approximately 162 miles in the *Friendship 7* capsule. Traveling at a maximum orbital velocity of 17,545 miles per hour, he became the first American to orbit Earth, doing so three times, for a total of about 81,000 miles. (The Russian YURY ALEKSEYEVICH GAGARIN had orbited Earth once in the first manned spaceflight in 1961, and another Russian, Gherman Titov, had become the second man to do so that same year.) Technical problems forced Glenn to pilot the capsule manually during the second and third orbits and during reentry. The mission lasted four hours, 55 minutes, and 23 seconds, from launch to splashdown in the Atlantic Ocean.

Because of Glenn's fame and popularity following his first mission, NASA officials chose to use him for public relations rather than for additional spaceflights. Frustrated, he retired from NASA and the Marine Corps in 1965 and

John Glenn *(Library of Congress)*

in 1727. After an appointment to a professorship four years later, he joined the scientific team of the Second Kamchatka Expedition in 1733, under the general command of VITUS JONASSEN BERING.

From St. Petersburg, Gmelin, accompanied by STEPAN PETROVICH KRASHENINNIKOV, traveled eastward across European and Central Asiatic Russia, arriving at Yakutsk sometime in 1735. Along the way, he made an extensive study of the plant and animal life of the central Asian steppes, from the Ural Mountains to Lake Baikal. During the next two years, he undertook a scientific survey in the heart of SIBERIA, exploring along the Tunguska River and descending the Angara River to the settlement at Yeniseysk. He spent winter 1737–38 there, meeting up with another member of the expedition's scientific staff, fellow German naturalist GEORG WILHELM STELLER.

In spring and summer 1738, Gmelin followed the Yenisey River northward almost as far as the ARCTIC CIRCLE. In subsequent explorations of Siberia, he went as far east as the Lena River, before beginning the homeward journey to European Russia in 1741. Along the way, he undertook studies of the flora and fauna of the steppe region between the Yenisey and Ob Rivers, as well as the territory around the Caspian Sea.

Gmelin returned to St. Petersburg early in 1743, following nearly 10 years of scientific work in Siberia. In 1749, he was back in Germany, where he spent his remaining years as a professor of natural history at the University of Tübingen in the principality of Württemberg.

In his published account of his scientific work in Siberia, *Flora Sibirica* (1747–69), Johann Georg Gmelin described more than 1,100 plant species and provided nearly 300 illustrations. In addition to his botanical work, he undertook geological studies in which he attempted to ascertain the depth limits of the permafrost in eastern Siberia. His observations on the Caspian Sea revealed that its level was lower than both the MEDITERRANEAN SEA and Black Sea. Although most geographers had traditionally regarded the Ural Mountains as the boundary between Europe and Asia, Gmelin's observations determined that the Yenisey River provided a natural demarcation between the two regions because of the distinct differences in the animal and plant life to the east and west of it.

pursued a career in business. He did, however, continue to act as a consultant for NASA. He entered politics and was elected U.S. (Democratic) senator from Ohio, serving four terms from 1974 to 1998. He was a member of the Special Intelligence Committee, the Governmental Affairs Committee, and the Armed Services Committee. In 1984, he unsuccessfully sought the Democratic presidential nomination.

Glenn lobbied NASA for another spaceflight, which was finally granted to him as part of the SPACE SHUTTLE program. In October 1998, at the age of 77, after extensive training, Glenn became the oldest person to fly in space. The nine-day mission, aboard the *Discovery,* included a study of the effects of space travel on aging.

In the course of his career as a navy pilot, astronaut, and politician, John Glenn received many awards. In addition to his accomplishments as the first American to orbit Earth and the oldest human in space, he helped put a human face on the U.S. space program.

Gmelin, Johann Georg (1709–1755)
German naturalist in Siberia, in service to Russia
Johann Georg Gmelin, a German-born botanist, entered the service of the Russian Academy of Sciences at St. Petersburg

Godin des Odanais, Isabela
(Isabel Grandmaison y Bruno) (1729–1792)
Peruvian traveler on the Amazon River
Isabela Godin des Odanais, née Grandmaison y Bruno, was the daughter of a prominent citizen of Riobamba in what is now Ecuador. In 1743, although only 13 at the time, she married Jean Godin des Odanais, who was the assistant of the French scientific team, led by CHARLES-MARIE DE LA CONDAMINE, that was then undertaking a geodesic survey

in the Peruvian ANDES MOUNTAINS and the upper Amazon Basin.

At the end of the equatorial survey in 1743, Jean Godin had planned to join La Condamine in a descent of the AMAZON RIVER from Peru to the Atlantic coast at Pará. His departure was delayed by his wife's four pregnancies over the next six years. Finally, in March 1749, he set out from Riobamba alone and made his way to Lagunas in northeastern Peru, the head of navigation of the western tributaries of the Amazon. After a year of traveling, he finally reached Pará, from where he went to the port of Cayenne on the coast of French Guiana.

Once at Cayenne, Godin attempted to obtain the assistance of the Portuguese colonial government of Brazil for a trip up the Amazon to bring his wife to Pará, then sail to France. Yet permission for his upriver voyage was long in coming from the Portuguese due to international rivalries among France, the Spanish government in Upper Peru (now Ecuador), and Portugal. He waited at Cayenne for 15 years, petitioning La Condamine and the French government for help. Meanwhile, news of the Godins had reached France, and Isabela's long separation from her husband had made her a heroic figure in French intellectual circles.

Finally, in April 1765, a Portuguese riverboat and a crew arrived at Cayenne with instructions to take Godin back up the Amazon to Lagunas, where he could meet his wife and family, then return with them to Pará. He was suspicious of the motives of the Portuguese, however, fearing they had learned of his secret letters to the French government in which he had suggested the feasibility of a French takeover of the Amazon as a route through the Americas to the Pacific Ocean. He suspected that the Portuguese would arrest him once he was in Brazilian territory. Instead of returning upriver himself on the Portuguese vessel, he sent a trusted friend with letters to his wife, instructing her to travel from Riobamba to meet the boat at Lagunas, then travel down the Amazon and join him at Cayenne.

Finally, in 1769, Isabela Godin received word of the travel plans. By that time, all four of her children had died of tropical diseases, including her youngest, then aged 19, born soon after Jean Godin had left in 1749.

The journey proved to be a nightmarish experience for Isabela. Her father, Pedro Grandmaison y Bruno, had gone on ahead to arrange for local Indians to convey his daughter overland and by CANOE to Lagunas. She left Riobamba in late 1769, accompanied by her two brothers, a nephew, about 30 Indians, and several French travelers. Mishaps, coupled with disease, eventually claimed the lives of everyone in the party but Isabela. Left alone in the upper Amazon rainforest, she wandered for nine days along the Bobonaza River before she was rescued by local Indians, who took her safely to Lagunas and the waiting Portuguese riverboat.

The rest of Isabela Godin's journey down the Amazon was relatively uneventful. She was reunited with her husband at Cayenne in spring 1770. They remained in the French Guiana colony for another three years, then sailed to France, settling in Godin's ancestral home at Saint-Amand, Montrand, south of Paris.

Isabela Godin was the first woman known to have descended the entire length of the Amazon River. In May 1988, the people of Saint-Amand dedicated a statue of her near the Godin home in recognition of her forbearance in her long separation from her husband, her heroic solo trek through the jungle, and her pioneer Amazon journey.

Gões, Bento de (Benedict de Goes)

(1562–1607) *Portuguese missionary in India and China*

Bento de Gões was a lay brother at the Portuguese Jesuit mission at Agra in north-central India during the early 1600s.

In 1603, Gões set out northward from Agra, intending to reach China by way of an overland route from the west. Although Portuguese mariners had been regularly voyaging to the Pacific coast of China, European geographers were still not certain whether this was the same land identified as Cathay by MARCO POLO and other medieval travelers more than 300 years earlier. Gões hoped to resolve this question by reaching Peking (Beijing) and making contact with Jesuit missionary MATTEO RICCI, who, several years earlier, had established himself in that city after arrival by sea.

From Agra, Gões traveled to Lahore in what is now Pakistan, then entered Afghanistan, visiting Kabul before passing through the Hindu Kush range and crossing the Pamirs into the westernmost provinces of present-day China. By 1605, he was in Yarkand on the western edge of the Takla Makan desert. After making a visit to the jade mines at Khotan, at the southern end of the desert, he arranged to continue his travels with a caravan heading eastward.

Over the next year, Gões traversed the entire width of northern China. In 1605, he reached Suchow, about 500 miles south of Peking and 200 miles inland from the Yellow Sea. Although government officials in Suchow barred him from traveling to Peking to join Father Ricci, he was permitted to contact the Jesuit missionary by messenger.

It was not until April 1607 that Gões finally received direct word from Ricci in Peking. Gões died at Suchow several days later. Ricci sent the news back to Europe by sea that Gões had succeeded in making the overland journey from India to China, and, by doing so, had demonstrated that the land identified as Cathay in medieval times, and the China known to 17th-century European sea voyagers, were one and the same.

Bento de Gões's journey was the first overland trip made by a European into China since the early 1300s. Traveling alone and following a circuitous route northward around the HIMALAYAS, he had solved one of the great geographic puzzles of the Middle Ages. On his grave at Suchow, the following epitaph was inscribed: "Seeking Cathay he had found heaven."

Golovnin, Vasily Mikhailovich (Vasili Golovnin)

(1776–1831) *Russian naval officer in Alaska and the North Pacific*

Vasily M. Golovnin began his maritime career as a midshipman in the Russian navy, serving on warships in the North Sea from 1795 to 1800. He was promoted to lieutenant by 1801, then was attached to the British navy for five years, sailing the MEDITERRANEAN SEA, Atlantic Ocean, and Caribbean Sea.

Golovnin returned to Russian naval service in 1807. In command of the sloop *Diana,* he left the Baltic port of Kronstadt, planning on rounding CAPE HORN and sailing on to Kamchatka, on the Pacific coast of SIBERIA. As he approached the tip of South America, unfavorable winds caused him to alter his course and attempt to reach the Pacific by way of the CAPE OF GOOD HOPE around Africa. British authorities detained him and his expedition at Cape Town. After spending a year at the South African port of Simonstown, Golovnin, under cover of darkness, eluded the British fleet guarding the harbor.

Golovnin reached Kamchatka by late 1809. The next year, he explored the coast of Alaska, then known as Russian America. In 1811, he sailed south to survey the Kuril Islands, north of Japan. On Kunashiri, an island just northeast of the northernmost Japanese island of Hokkaido, he made a landing with a small party. Taken prisoner by the Japanese, he was held for more than two years. In 1813, Golovnin's shipmates on the *Diana* managed to secure his release. Golovnin sailed back to Kamchatka, then set out for St. Petersburg in an overland journey westward across Siberia and European Russia.

In 1817, Golovnin embarked on a CIRCUMNAVIGATION OF THE WORLD in command of the sloop *Kamchatka.* Over the next two years, he undertook additional explorations along the coasts of Alaska and Kamchatka.

Golovnin was promoted to the rank of vice admiral in the Russian navy in 1830. The following year, he was stricken with cholera and died in St. Petersburg.

Vasily M. Golovnin's account of his experiences as a prisoner was published in 1816 as *Narrative of My Captivity in Japan, 1811–1813.* In addition, he left published accounts of his 1807–10 voyage to Kamchatka, as well as a narrative of his 1817–19 voyage in which he circumnavigated the world. He also wrote an account of famous shipwrecks.

Gomery, Adrien-Victor-Joseph, Gerlache de

See GERLACHE DE GOMERY, ADRIEN-VICTOR-JOSEPH DE.

Gomes, Diogo (Diego Gomez)

(ca. 1440–ca. 1482) *Portuguese mariner on the coast of West Africa*

In the late 1450s, Portuguese navigator Diogo Gomes undertook the last voyages of exploration along the coast of West Africa sponsored by HENRY THE NAVIGATOR, prince of Portugal.

From 1458 to 1460, the year of Prince Henry's death, Gomes explored the African coast as far south as Cape Palmas, the westernmost point on the Gulf of Guinea on the coast of present-day Liberia. At times he was accompanied by Venetian explorer ALVISE DA CADAMOSTO. In 1458, Gomes explored up the Gambia River, where he made friendly contacts with a native king named Nomi-Mansa, whose interest in becoming a baptized Christian inspired the first Portuguese missionaries to venture into West Africa. Gomes returned from the lower Gambia River region with a quantity of gold, as well as reports of gold mines beyond the Sierra Leone Mountains, prompting subsequent Portuguese expeditions to West Africa in search of commercial gain as well as geographic knowledge.

In 1462, Gomes sailed again to Africa, and, after landing at Cape Verde, headed westward and made the European discovery of Sao Tiago in the Cape Verde Islands. He also visited the AZORES.

Diogo Gomes's findings on the coast of West Africa were later incorporated into MARTIN BEHAIM's 1492 world globe. In addition, Gomes was the first European to bring back reports of a great inland city in Africa—TIMBUKTU—a place that attracted European explorers to West Africa well into the 19th century.

Gomes, Estevão (Esteban Gómez, Stephen Gomez)

(ca. 1474–ca. 1538) *Portuguese or Spanish mariner on the east coast of North America and in the Río de la Plata and Gran Chaco region of South America*

Some sources indicate that Estevão Gomes was born in Oporto, Portugal, in 1474, or as late as 1483, while others state that he was born in Cádiz, Spain, in 1478. He became a seaman, serving with Portuguese ships sailing to India and the EAST INDIES.

In 1518, with a reputation as a skilled navigator and pilot, Gomes entered the service of Spain and the next year sailed as a pilot on the *San Antonio* with FERDINAND MAGELLAN's expedition. On this voyage, in January 1520, he was among those who openly rebelled against Magellan's authority along the coast of South America. Magellan managed to quell the uprising, putting to death some of the rebels but sparing Gomes because of his much-needed skills as a navigator. Nonetheless, Gomes soon incited another mutiny on the *San Antonio,* while the fleet was exploring what came to be known as the STRAIT OF MAGELLAN. He was instrumental in leading the crew of that vessel to desert the expedition, returning to Spain in March 1521.

On his arrival in Spain, Gomes was imprisoned for his role in the mutiny, but he was soon released. In 1523, he was a member of a council of pilots that attempted to settle disputes between Portugal and Spain over conflicting claims to the newly explored possessions in the Western Hemisphere as well as the new sea routes to India and the Far East. That year, he won the support of Spanish king Charles I (Holy Roman Emperor Charles V) for his plan to resolve the conflict by finding a westward passage for Spain somewhere along the east coast of North America between Florida and Newfoundland. Gomes believed that the new route would be far shorter than the one established on Magellan's 1519–22 expedition.

For Gomes's expedition, a CARAVEL-type ship, *La Anunciada,* was built at Bilbao. On September 24, 1524, he sailed from the port of La Coruna in northwestern Spain with a crew of 29 men. His first stop was the port of Santiago in Cuba, from where he headed northward to the Florida coast, which he sighted in January 1525. Sailing northward along the east coast of North America, he made an extensive survey of all bays and inlets sighted, hoping to find the one that might provide a passage to the Far East. According to his navigational records, he explored what is now Chesapeake Bay, then continued along the coast as far as Cape Race, Newfoundland. He then returned southward. Not wanting the expedition to be a total loss, he captured about 60 Indians along the coast of Maine or Nova Scotia for the SLAVE TRADE in Spain.

After a voyage of almost a year, Gomes returned to Spain, reaching Coruna in August 1525. King Charles was not pleased with the enslavement of Indians, whom he soon freed. Many died of disease, however.

Gomes won the support of Spanish merchants for another voyage in search of a low-latitude NORTHWEST PASSAGE in 1530. Equipped with two ships, he sailed from Spain that year, and, according to some accounts, he was never heard of again, although some sources indicate that he died in Toledo, Spain, in 1534.

Varying accounts of Gomes's life relate that he sailed to the Rio de La Plata region of South America as chief pilot under the command of PEDRO DE MENDOZA in 1535. In February 1537, he reportedly accompanied JUAN DE AYOLAS and a party of Spaniards on an exploration of South America's Gran Chaco region in search of gold and silver. When the group returned to the Paraguay River, Gomes, Ayolas, and the others were killed by Indians, probably in 1538.

In the decades after the initial explorations of the Spanish and Portuguese in the Americas, Estevão Gomes was among the first navigators to seek a low-latitude Northwest Passage to the Far East. With the Portuguese monopoly on the trade route around Africa, and, with the Spanish in control of the sea lanes into the Pacific from the Strait of Magellan, interest in a northern passage to the Far East continued only among the Dutch, English, and French. Gomes's diary of his 1524–25 expedition was published in Spain in 1529. It included a map that depicted the coastline of what is now New England and Nova Scotia as the "Land of Esteban Gómez, discovered by him in 1525, by order of his Majesty; abundance of trees, game, salmon, turbot, and soles, but no gold is found." After his 1524–25 voyage, Spanish maps of North America showed a continuous coastline extending from Florida to Newfoundland.

Gomes, Fernão (Ferdinand Gomes) (fl. 1470s)
Portuguese merchant, trader on the coast of West Africa
Fernão Gomes, a wealthy Lisbon merchant, was one of the first to take part in the trade along the newly explored regions of the coast of West Africa. In 1469, he entered into a commercial agreement with King Alfonso V of Portugal and was granted exclusive trading rights on all lands beyond Cape Verde. In return, Gomes agreed to give the king a percentage of his profits and committed himself to exploring at least 100 leagues (about 400 miles) per year beyond Cape Palmas, the farthest point reached by previous navigators under Alfonso's uncle, HENRY THE NAVIGATOR, prince of Portugal.

By 1475, Gomes's expeditions had revealed most of the south coast of the great bulge of West Africa, reaching as far as the Bight of Benin, Point St. Catherine, and the shores of present-day Nigeria. He also located the island of Fernando Po at the eastern end of the Gulf of Guinea.

Although Gomes had fulfilled his contract, the agreement was not renewed. Instead, the monopoly on exploration and trading rights along the Guinea Coast went to King Alfonso's son, Prince John, who, in the 1480s, as King John II of Portugal, sponsored the expeditions of DIOGO CÃO and BARTOLOMEU DIAS. Their voyages resulted in the determination of the southernmost extent of the African continent.

Fernão Gomes's voyages marked the resumption of the program of organized exploration along the coast of West Africa begun by Prince Henry in 1430, which had come to a halt with his death in 1460. During his contract of 1469–75, Gomes discovered as much of the African coast as had Prince Henry's navigators between 1430 and 1460.

González de Clavijo, Ruy See CLAVIJO, RUY GONZÁLEZ DE.

Gordon, Robert (fl. 1770s) *Scottish explorer in South Africa*
Originally from Scotland, Robert Gordon arrived in Cape Town, South Africa, in about 1770. He undertook some of the first explorations beyond the settled areas along the south coast.

In 1777, Gordon and a small party explored inland along a route eastward from Cape Town to Algoa Bay, near present-day Port Elizabeth. He then traveled northward, penetrating the interior as far as the grasslands of the 6,000-foot-high plateau region known as the High Veld, reaching the confluence of the Groote and Vaal Rivers before returning southward to Cape Town.

Gordon set out again in 1779 with a small Dutch and British group, including Scottish botanist William Paterson, exploring northward from Cape Town, along South Africa's Atlantic coast into Namaqualand, just below present-day Namibia. Locating the Groote River at its mouth, he ascended it eastward across most of what is now South Africa into the High Veld country of what later became the Orange Free State. Along the way, Gordon and his party explored the lands north of the Groote, which he subsequently renamed the Orange River.

Robert Gordon's explorations into both the western and eastern regions of South Africa revealed much about the previously uncharted territory north of the Cape Town settlement. He was one of the first Europeans to trace the course of the Orange River, and, in so doing, almost completed the first west-to-east crossing of the African continent south of the SAHARA DESERT. The reports he brought back of lands suitable for grazing in the interior north and east of Cape Town inspired the Boer migration into the region and the establishment of the Orange Free State in the years following the British takeover of the Cape Colony in 1806.

Gore, John (1730–1790) *British naval officer in the Pacific*

John Gore was born in the British North American colonies. Entering the British navy in 1755, he went on to serve as an assistant master on the *Dolphin* in a 1764–66 expedition, under the command of Commodore JOHN BYRON, which explored the South Pacific Ocean and completed a CIRCUMNAVIGATION OF THE WORLD.

Three months after his return to England in 1766, Gore sailed to the South Pacific Ocean on the *Dolphin* again, as midshipman under the command of SAMUEL WALLIS. On the voyage with Wallis, he was among the first Englishmen to visit Tahiti.

Gore returned to England from his second voyage to the South Pacific in May 1768. The next August, he sailed from Plymouth as a lieutenant on the *Endeavour* on JAMES COOK's first voyage. During this expedition, he revisited Tahiti. On the east coast of Australia, he shot a kangaroo, a creature then unknown to most European zoologists. The expedition's naturalist, SIR JOSEPH BANKS, had the creature stuffed and took it back to Great Britain.

Gore did not sail with Cook on his second voyage in 1772. Instead, he sailed with Banks on a scientific expedition to ICELAND that year.

On Cook's final voyage of 1776–80, Gore was a first lieutenant aboard the *Resolution*. In the south-central Pacific archipelago that came to be known as the Cook Islands, he was among the party that explored Atiu Island and Hervey Island. When the expedition was sailing along the coast of southeastern Alaska in spring and summer 1778, Gore briefly explored Prince William Sound. He suggested to Cook that a river emptying into Prince William Sound could actually be the NORTHWEST PASSAGE, leading into Baffin or HUDSON BAY. Convinced he could reach England by this route in only three months, Gore offered to lead an expedition of 20 crew members up the supposed passage in two of the ship's open boats, a proposal that Cook prudently declined.

With Cook's death in the HAWAIIAN ISLANDS in February 1779, command of the expedition went to CHARLES CLERKE, and when Clerke died in the North Pacific the following August, command went to Gore. He sailed to Petropavlovsk on the Kamchatka Peninsula of eastern SIBERIA, then headed southward to the Kuril Islands and Japan. He followed the Asian coast, stopping at Macao and what is now Vietnam, then entered the Indian Ocean by way of Sunda Strait between Java and Sumatra. He returned to the British Isles by way of the CAPE OF GOOD HOPE, although he first landed in the Orkneys, off the coast of Scotland, having been blown northward by gale-force winds. Gore and the expedition finally reached London on October 4, 1780, after a voyage of more than four years.

Back in England, Gore assumed Cook's former position as captain of Greenwich Hospital, a post he held until his death in 1790.

During his naval career, in which he circled the world three times in 16 years, John Gore participated in the first British scientific expeditions to the South Pacific. In the Bering Sea in 1778, Cook sighted an island, which he named Gore Island, after his first lieutenant. Unknown to him, it was actually the island of St. Matthew, visited over 30 years earlier by Russian navigators sailing to North America.

Gosnold, Bartholomew (ca. 1572–1607)
English mariner in New England, colonizer of Virginia

Bartholomew Gosnold attended Cambridge University before going to sea in the late 1590s. By 1602, he had become an accomplished sea captain and navigator. That year, fellow Cambridge graduate Henry Wriothesley, the third earl of Southampton and chief patron of William Shakespeare, sponsored Gosnold to lead an expedition to the coast of North America to obtain sassafras bark, which was selling in London at premium prices.

After the 1588 British victory over the Spanish Armada, English maritime endeavors regained their momentum. Also by that time, syphilis had become widespread throughout Europe. There was great demand for a medicine made from sassafras bark. Expeditions sponsored by SIR WALTER RALEIGH to North America in the 1580s had reported sassafras to be growing in abundance.

In command of a small vessel, the *Concord,* Gosnold sailed westward from England in 1602, crossed the North Atlantic Ocean, and reached the coast of what is now southeastern Maine. Accompanying Gosnold on this trip was Bartholomew Gilbert, son of Raleigh's half brother, explorer SIR HUMPHREY GILBERT. Earlier maritime expeditions by Portuguese, English, and French explorers had reached New England only after stopping along the east coast of Canada to the north, or the Chesapeake Bay region to the south. Gosnold's 1602 expedition marked the first direct transatlantic crossing to what became known as New England.

The English anchored off the Maine coast and received some Native Americans who visited the ship in a small sailboat. Gosnold reported that their boat appeared to be of European origin, a "French shalop." The Indians, according to Gosnold's account, also wore some European garments and could speak a few words of either French or English, indicating that Gosnold and his crew were not the first Europeans they had met.

Gosnold sailed the *Concord* southward along the Maine coast to Cape Cod, a name he chose because of the great number of codfish caught by his men. Gosnold and a party put ashore there, thus making the first recorded European landing in present-day Massachusetts. After trading for sassafras with Indians, the English sailed around Cape Cod and explored islands off the southeast coast of Massachusetts, including Martha's Vineyard, which Gosnold named in honor of his eldest daughter as well as for the abundant grapevines. In his official report, Gosnold also reported seeing large numbers of "penguins," actually giant auks, then flourishing on islands off Massachusetts.

Gosnold next headed eastward into the mouth of Buzzards Bay and made the European discovery of Cuttyhunk Island, where he established a small military post. He also explored Narragansett Bay and traded with some other New England coastal Indians, probably Wampanoag or Narragansett. The expedition returned to England that same year, with a cargo of lumber, furs, and sassafras.

Through the Earl of Southampton's influence, Gosnold was appointed vice admiral, with CHRISTOPHER NEWPORT as admiral, of the newly charted VIRGINIA COMPANY's merchant fleet in 1606. The Virginia Company had been sanctioned by King James I to reassert English sovereignty over North America.

Three of the company's ships, the *Susan Constant,* the *Discovery,* and the *Godspeed,* the last commanded by Gosnold, set sail from London in December 1606 to establish a colony on the Virginia coast. JOHN SMITH was military commander of this colonizing expedition.

On April 25, 1607, Gosnold and the fleet reached Chesapeake Bay and made a brief landing at Cape Henry at the north end of present-day Virginia Beach, Virginia. In early May, the English traveled about 30 miles up the James River, where they established James Forte, later known as Jamestown. Gosnold objected to this site because, although it was on a defendable position on a peninsula in the river, it was swampy and mosquito-infested, thus conducive to fever. Less than four months later, in August 1607, Gosnold was afflicted with malaria and died.

Bartholomew Gosnold's 1602 voyage was not only the first direct European crossing of the Atlantic to New England, but also one of the earliest expeditions to the Americas with a specific commercial motive. Eighteen years later, the Pilgrims retraced Gosnold's route when they established Plymouth Colony. Additionally, Gosnold played a key role in establishing Jamestown, the first permanent English settlement in North America.

Gosse, William Christie (1842–1881)

Australian surveyor, explorer in Australia's Northern Territory

In the early 1870s, William Gosse, a surveyor for the government of South Australia, was commissioned to attempt the first east-to-west crossing of Australia from the center of the continent.

In July 1873, Gosse, equipped with horses, set out from Alice Springs and headed southwestward across the Macdonnell Ranges, intending to reach Perth, 1,500 miles distant on the Indian Ocean coast. Beyond the Macdonnell Ranges, he became the first non-Aborigine to see Ayers Rock, a single block of sandstone towering 2,845 feet above the surrounding flat country.

Gosse was unable to bypass the Musgrave Mountains, which form a natural east-to-west barrier at the northwestern corner of South Australia. The rugged terrain and thorny vegetation all but crippled his horses, forcing him to abandon the expedition and turn back to Alice Springs.

William Gosse undertook one of three separate expeditions that attempted to cross Australia westward from the Central Overland Telegraph line in 1873. The others were led by ERNEST GILES and Colonel PETER EGERTON WARBURTON, who did reach the west coast after almost dying in the attempt. Although Gosse's expedition failed in its primary goal, he brought back news of Ayers Rock, one of Australia's most spectacular natural wonders.

Grant, James Augustus (1827–1892) *British army officer in East Africa*

James Grant was born in Nairn on the north coast of Scotland. Entering the British army at the age of 19, he served in India as an officer, where he took part in the Sikh War of

1848–49. While in India, Grant became friends with fellow British officer JOHN HANNING SPEKE, with whom he traveled into the Himalayas on hunting expeditions.

Wounded in the siege of Lucknow in the Sepoy Mutiny of 1857–58, Grant returned to England. In 1860, he was recruited by Speke to participate in his second attempt to find the source of the NILE RIVER.

Sailing from England at the end of April 1860, Grant and Speke arrived in Zanzibar the following October, after stopping in Cape Town to recruit porters and armed escorts for the expedition. They proceeded westward across what is now Tanzania, reaching the capital of the native kingdom of Karagwe on the southwest shore of Lake Victoria, in November 1861. While Speke went on to explore Lake Victoria, which he had reached several years earlier while in East Africa with SIR RICHARD FRANCIS BURTON, Grant was compelled to remain behind at Karagwe, incapacitated by his old leg wound.

Grant rejoined Speke on August 19, 1862, near Urondogani at the northern end of Lake Victoria, where, less than a month earlier, Speke had reached Ripon Falls emptying from Lake Victoria into what he firmly believed was the Nile. The two then headed northward into what is now Uganda, intending to descend the river into the Sudan and Egypt and thereby establish for certain that it was indeed the Nile, and that Lake Victoria was its ultimate source. Tribal warfare and problems with native chieftains in Bunyoro delayed their journey and forced them to leave the river at times. In February 1863, between Juba and Gondokoro on the White Nile River, in what is now southern Sudan, they met up with SIR SAMUEL WHITE BAKER and FLORENCE BAKER. Reprovisioned by the Bakers, they traveled downriver to Khartoum, and from there returned to England, arriving in June 1863.

With Speke's death in a shooting accident in September 1864, Grant became the principal supporter of his late partner's conviction that Lake Victoria was the true source of the Nile. Recording his experiences in East Africa in his 1864 book *A Walk Across Africa,* he came to be regarded as one of Great Britain's leading authorities on Africa. In 1868, he returned to Africa as an intelligence officer with the British Abyssinian Expedition, and he represented Great Britain at an international conference on African exploration convened by King Leopold of Belgium in the mid-1870s. Grant was also a member of an expedition sent to relieve MEHMED EMIN PASHA, under siege in the southern Sudan during the late 1880s.

Grant retired from the British army at the rank of lieutenant colonel and spent his last years at his home in Scotland. He was a talented painter, as well as a zoologist and botanist, and his volume of the botanical collection acquired in his 1860–63 exploration of East Africa, illustrated with his own watercolors, was published by the Linnean Society in 1872. He also wrote an account of the southern Sudan region, entitled *Khartoum As I Saw It in 1863,* published in 1885.

In his explorations with Speke, James Grant was among the first Europeans to enter what is now Uganda. Although not present when Speke explored Lake Victoria's Ripon Falls, he played a vital supporting role in the expedition that determined that Lake Victoria was a principal source of the Nile, a finding verified with the explorations of SIR HENRY MORTON STANLEY in the 1870s.

Gray, Robert (1755–1806) *American mariner, fur trader in circumnavigation of world, explorer of mouth of Columbia River*

Robert Gray, a native of Tiverton, Rhode Island, spent his early seafaring career with the Continental Navy during the American Revolution of 1775–83.

In 1787, Gray was commissioned by a group of Boston, Salem, and New York merchants to undertake a voyage from Boston to Nootka Sound, on the Pacific coast of what is now British Columbia, to trade for sea otter pelts. Two ships were used in this expedition, the *Columbia Rediviva,* commanded by American sea captain John Kendrick, and the smaller sloop, the *Lady Washington,* commanded by Gray.

The ships sailed from Boston and headed first for the Cape Verde Islands off western Africa. They then headed southward, rounded CAPE HORN, and sailed northward up the coast of the Americas, arriving at Nootka Sound in September 1788. Unable to obtain sea otter pelts at that time of year, they spent the winter of 1788–89 anchored off Vancouver Island. During this time, Gray and his command witnessed the confrontation between the Spanish and British that gave rise to the Nootka Sound controversy of 1789.

The Americans exchanged trade goods for sea otter pelts with the Nootka Indians in spring and summer 1789. Gray was then placed in charge of the larger ship, the *Columbia,* and sent across the Pacific Ocean to trade the furs for a cargo of tea in Canton, China, while Kendrick remained on the Northwest Coast with the *Lady Washington.*

Gray sailed westward across the Pacific, stopping at the HAWAIIAN ISLANDS, then continuing to Canton. After selling the furs and obtaining tea, he sailed south and west into the Indian Ocean. He rounded the CAPE OF GOOD HOPE and returned to Boston on August 10, 1790. He was greeted with great celebration, having completed the first CIRCUMNAVIGATION OF THE WORLD aboard an American vessel. The trip had taken more than three years and had covered over 49,000 miles.

Gray soon sailed from Boston on the *Columbia* for a second voyage around CAPE HORN to the Pacific Northwest, reaching his destination in spring 1791. To the south of

Nootka Sound, at Clayoquot Sound, he constructed a temporary settlement, Fort Defense, where he wintered in 1791–92. While at Fort Defense, he had his men construct a small sloop, the *Adventure*.

In spring 1792, Gray sent the *Adventure* northward up the coast to trade for sea otter pelts at the southern tip of Alaska. Gray himself headed southward along what is now the coast of Washington and Oregon. On the way, he noticed breakers and a strong current coming from the mainland. He attempted to cross the breakers to investigate this phenomenon, believing that it indicated a river flowing westward into the Pacific. Since the early 1770s, fur traders in the Great Lakes region had reported Indian accounts of a great western river, known as the Oregon. Geographers at the time speculated that such a river would connect the upper Missouri with the Pacific.

In late April 1792, Gray decided not to cross the sand bar beyond the breakers into what was referred to as Deception Bay. Soon afterward, he conferred at sea with the British naval officer GEORGE VANCOUVER. He headed northward to the Strait of Juan de Fuca, south of present-day Vancouver Island.

Gray and the *Columbia* soon returned southward, and on May 11, 1792, he crossed the sand bar and entered Deception Bay. It turned out to be the estuary of a great river. Gray sailed the *Columbia* up the river about 36 miles, then returned to its outlet to the Pacific. He named the river Columbia's River, after his ship. It subsequently became known simply as the COLUMBIA RIVER. At this time, he also explored and named Grays Harbor on the central coast of what is now the state of Washington.

Gray sailed from the mouth of the Columbia to China, again traded for tea, and returned to Boston on July 31, 1793, having completed his second circumnavigation of the globe.

Gray continued as a merchant captain until his death in Charleston, South Carolina, in 1806.

Robert Gray's circumnavigation of the world inspired other U.S. seafaring voyages of exploration. His exploration of the Columbia River provided the basis for U.S. claims to the Oregon Country, which would be challenged by Britain and Spain for the next 40 years, and gave impetus to the overland expedition of MERIWETHER LEWIS and WILLIAM CLARK to the Pacific Ocean in 1804–06. Moreover, Gray's successful fur-trading enterprise influenced JOHN JACOB ASTOR's decision to develop direct trade between the Pacific Northwest and China and sponsor expeditions to the region in 1810–11.

Greely, Adolphus Washington (1844–1935)
U.S. Army officer in the Canadian Arctic

Adolphus W. Greely was born in Newburyport, Massachusetts, the descendant of a family that had settled in New England in the first half of the 17th century. Upon his graduation from Newburyport's Brown High School in 1860, he enlisted in a Massachusetts volunteer regiment, serving in the American Civil War alongside future Supreme Court justice Oliver Wendell Holmes. Greely was wounded three times, including twice at the Battle of Antietam in 1862. Rising rapidly through the ranks, he was a brevet major of volunteers by the war's end.

Greely remained in the military after the war, reverting to the rank of lieutenant in the regular army. He took part in actions against Indians on the northern and southern plains in the late 1860s. Then, during the 1870s, he went on to serve in the U.S. Army Signal Corps. In 1876–79, he supervised the construction of more than 2,000 miles of telegraph lines in Texas, the Dakota Territory, and Montana.

In 1881, Greely was commissioned to lead the U.S. Army's Lady Franklin Bay Expedition in conjunction with the proposed International Polar Year of 1882–83. At an international geographic conference held in Hamburg in 1879, 13 circumpolar scientific observation stations were proposed to study various natural phenomena around the Arctic regions of the world, and the northernmost of these bases, the Lady Franklin Bay station, was assigned to the United States.

Greely and his team of 24 army officers and enlisted men (later joined by American physician OCTAVE PAVY) sailed from St. John's, Newfoundland, on July 7, 1881, aboard the *Proteus,* a sealing ship specially equipped for the Arctic. They reached Lady Franklin Bay on the northeast coast of Ellesmere Island, above Smith Sound, on August 12. Greely and his men established Fort Conger at nearby Discovery Harbor. The *Proteus* returned to Newfoundland, leaving Greely and his men with a portable house, scientific equipment, and enough supplies to last for the next 27 months. Although relief expeditions were planned for the following two years, Greely had been directed to start back on his own if no relief vessel arrived by the end of summer 1883.

Throughout the winter season of 1881–82, Greely and his expedition undertook hundreds of weather observations as well as studies of gravity and tides. Exploring expeditions were also sent out. On May 15, 1882, a small party led by Lieutenant J. B. Lockwood and Sergeant D. L. Brainard explored the north coast of GREENLAND, reaching 83°24' north latitude, thereby setting a new record for the northernmost point reached until that time. Several weeks later, Greely himself proceeded by sledge and on foot westward across Ellesmere Island, exploring 60-mile long Hazen Lake, which he named after the commander of the U.S. Army Signal Corps, General William B. Hazen. In May 1883, he traversed the northern end of Ellesmere Island to a long inlet on its west coast, which was named Greely Fjord in his honor. In addition, he sighted a mountain range in the interior of northern Ellesmere Island, naming

Adolphus W. Greely *(Library of Congress)*

its highest peak Mount Arthur, after President Chester A. Arthur.

Relief vessels were dispatched in spring 1882 but were unable to break through the ice of Smith Sound and reach Greely's base. Over the next winter at Fort Conger, rations were cut back, and the expedition supplemented its food supply by hunting polar bears and seals and fishing for shrimp. By summer 1883, it became apparent to Greely that ice conditions to the south would again prevent the supply vessel from arriving. In mid-August 1883, the expedition headed southward into Smith Sound, traveling in small boats and a small steam launch. They managed to reach as far as Cape Sabine, where progress southward was blocked by DRIFT ICE. They set up a temporary base, Camp Clay.

Conditions at the new base soon became critical for Greely and his men. SCURVY broke out, and the men began to die of starvation. Greely was forced to take drastic measures to conserve what rations remained, and even ordered the death by shooting of a Private Henry, who had been caught repeatedly stealing food. By spring 1884, expedition members had been reduced to eating their sealskin clothing and leather shoes, in addition to the shrimp they

managed to catch and the lichens they found growing on rocks.

On June 22, 1884, a relief ship, the *Thetis,* under the command of Captain Winfield Scott Schley, arrived at their encampment at Cape Sabine. By that time, only Greely and six others remained alive; on the homeward voyage, at a stopover at Godhavn, Greenland, one of them died.

On his return to the United States, allegations were made against Greely for his mismanagement of the expedition. However, the army commended Greely for leading the survivors through their ordeal. In 1885, both the ROYAL GEOGRAPHICAL SOCIETY and the Geographical Society of Paris honored Greely with gold medals. The next year, he was promoted to captain. In 1888, he was one of the principal founders of the NATIONAL GEOGRAPHIC SOCIETY in Washington, D.C. Greely was named commander of the U.S. Army Signal Corps in 1887 by President Grover Cleveland, and was made a brigadier general.

From 1898 to 1902, Greely directed the construction of telegraph lines in Puerto Rico, Cuba, the Philippines, and China. In Alaska in 1904, he supervised the construction of 3,900 miles of telegraph and ocean cable and established the first regular commercial wireless radio service, with stations at Nome and St. Michael.

Toward the end of his military career, Greely suppressed an uprising of the Ute Indians without resorting to armed force. That same year, he directed relief operations in the aftermath of the great San Francisco earthquake. He retired from the army in 1908 at the rank of major general.

Greely became embroiled in the controversy surrounding FREDERICK COOK's claim of having been the first man to reach the NORTH POLE, resigning from the Explorers Club in 1909 when that organization refused to recognize Cook's achievement.

Subsequent reports about General Adolphus W. Greely's 1881–84 expedition to the Arctic regions of Ellesmere Island and northwestern Greenland revealed the extent of the hardships he and his men faced, including evidence that in the last months before the rescue, they had resorted to cannibalism. Nevertheless, Greely retained his stature as one of the greatest American explorers of the Arctic. He was honored with the National Geographic Society's Charles P. Daly Medal in 1923 for having undertaken observations on the earth's gravity at a point closer to the North Pole than ever before, as well as for his copious meteorological and glacial studies on Ellesmere Island. In 1935, at the age of 91, Greely was awarded the Congressional Medal of Honor by special act of Congress. He died later that year in Washington, D.C., the first volunteer private of the Civil War to have reached the rank of major general. His own account of the Lady Franklin Bay Expedition, *Three Years of Arctic Service,* was published in 1886. He also wrote many articles on the Arctic for *National Geographic* magazine and published other books, including *Handbook of Alaska* (1925) and *The Polar Regions in the Twentieth Century* (1928).

Greenwood, Caleb (1763–1850) *American fur trader, trapper, hunter, guide in the American West*

Although details of Caleb Greenwood's early life are sketchy, it is known that in 1810–11 he worked as a hunter for JOHN JACOB ASTOR's fur-trading enterprise in the northern ROCKY MOUNTAINS. The next year, he hunted for MANUEL LISA's operation on the upper MISSOURI RIVER and Yellowstone River. In 1823, he joined WILLIAM HENRY ASHLEY's fur-trading expedition into the Arikara Indian lands in present-day South Dakota, and, in 1825, he attended the first fur trappers' rendezvous on the Green River, at Henrys Fork, near the present Wyoming-Utah state border. He was later associated with KENNETH MCKENZIE of the AMERICAN FUR COMPANY and worked with JAMES PIERSON BECKWOURTH.

In 1826, at the age of 63, Greenwood married the mixed-blood daughter of a French trader and an Indian woman, who bore him five children. At the age of 81, he worked as a guide, leading the first wagon train across the Sierra Nevada into California in 1844. Three years later, he took part in the rescue of the survivors of the Donner Pass party. A few years before his death in 1850, he went to California to prospect for gold.

Although Caleb Greenwood was unable to read or write, his adventures as a mountain man in the American West were well documented in the journals and reports of those who knew him. Few MOUNTAIN MEN of his day covered as much territory. What is even more noteworthy is the duration of his career, which spanned the entire pre-Civil War era of westward expansion in the United States, from the opening of the Appalachian frontier in the 1770s, to the American settlement of California in the late 1840s. By the time he was working for Ashley in the 1820s, he was already in his sixties, and he was known by his contemporaries even then as "Old Greenwood."

Gregory, Sir Augustus Charles (1819–1905) *British surveyor, government official in Australia, brother of Francis Thomas Gregory*

Augustus Gregory was born in Farnsfield in Nottinghamshire, England, the elder brother of FRANCIS THOMAS GREGORY. When he was 10, he moved to Western Australia with his family, where his father, a former British army officer, had been granted a tract of land upon his retirement.

In 1841, Gregory entered the service of the Western Australia government as a surveyor. Five years later, he joined his brothers Francis and Henry in an attempt to cross the Australian continent. The three set out from Perth and traveled northeastward to the Irwin River, where they located coal deposits. Progress eastward was blocked by a large salt lake, and they headed back to Perth along a route that took them southward and closer to the west coast of Australia.

Gregory was in command of the Settlers' Expedition when it headed northward from Perth in 1848, in search of new grazing lands inland from Shark Bay. Upon reaching the Murchison River, about 350 miles north of Perth, he discovered traces of more mineral resources, this time evidence of minable quantities of lead ore. His explorations in the region east of Shark Bay also revealed additional grazing land for Australia's sheep and cattle industry.

In 1855, both the British government and the ROYAL GEOGRAPHICAL SOCIETY commissioned Gregory to undertake his most ambitious exploration of Australia's interior. The government was eager to find new lands in what is now the Northern Territory suitable for more agricultural development; the Royal Geographical Society also hoped to find some trace of the explorer FRIEDRICH WILHELM LUDWIG LEICHHARDT, who had vanished during his expedition of 1848.

Gregory traveled by sea to the mouth of the Victoria River, on the northwest coast of Australia, at the easternmost corner of Joseph Bonaparte Gulf. From there, he first went south and west, soon locating Sturt Creek. Following its course, he came upon Gregory Lake, a seasonal lake at the eastern edge of the Great Sandy Desert. At this point, he retraced his route eastward back to the Victoria, then followed that river's course into the region south of Arnhem Land.

Gregory continued along a route that approximated the one taken by Leichhardt in his expedition of 1844–45 across northern Australia, although in the opposite direction. Along the way, he charted thousands of square miles of new lands suitable for grazing.

Having traveled eastward along the entire southern end of the Gulf of Carpentaria, Gregory reached the Gilbert River at its southeastern corner and followed that stream eastward across the southern portion of the Cape York Peninsula. He eventually found the Burdekin and Belyando Rivers, which he followed as far south as the TROPIC OF CAPRICORN. Traveling eastward, he crossed the Mackenzie and Dawson Rivers, made his way through the GREAT DIVIDING RANGE, and reached the Pacific coast of what is now Queensland at Bustard Head, near the present-day city of Rockhampton.

Gregory next undertook an expedition into the central region of the Australian continent. Leaving Brisbane on Moreton Bay in 1858, he made a westward crossing of the Great Dividing Range and explored the upper Dawson River and Warrego River region, where he found some relics of Leichhardt's ill-fated expedition of 10 years earlier. His examination of the Barcoo River revealed that it was the same stream as Cooper's Creek, which CHARLES STURT had explored in 1845. The extremely harsh conditions of the Sturt Desert forced Gregory to abandon his search for further traces of Leichhardt. Instead, he headed southward around Lake Eyre to Lake Frome and the Flinders Range, continuing onward to Adelaide on the south coast.

In 1859, about a year after making his epic crossing from northeastern Australia to the south coast, Gregory was appointed surveyor general of Queensland, which had been established as a British colony. He settled in Brisbane, where he went on to hold additional government positions and continued to undertake explorations into western Queensland. In 1903, Gregory was knighted for his contributions to the knowledge of the geographic and geological characteristics of the interior of Australia.

Sir Augustus Gregory's explorations resulted in the charting of more than 5,000 square miles of territory in northern and central Australia. He also located much new usable land north of Perth in Western Australia as well as in the regions south and west of the Gulf of Carpentaria, and in the interior of Queensland. His 1858 expedition from Brisbane southwestward took him across a largely unexplored region north of Lake Eyre, conclusively demonstrating that central Australia did not contain a large horseshoe-shaped lake that barred colonial expansion northward from Adelaide, as had been believed. It also revealed that many of the rivers of south-central Australia drained into Lake Eyre.

Gregory, Francis Thomas (Frank Gregory)

(1821–1888) *British surveyor in Western Australia, brother of Sir Augustus Charles Gregory*
Born in Nottinghamshire, England, Frank Gregory, the younger brother of SIR AUGUSTUS CHARLES GREGORY, moved to Western Australia with his family when he was eight years old. Both brothers became surveyors for the government of Western Australia.

At times accompanied by Augustus and another brother, Henry, Frank Gregory took part in a number of explorations in the territory north of Perth. In addition to attempting the west-to-east crossing of the continent with his brothers in 1846, he explored the Lake Moore region northeast of Perth that same year.

In 1857, Gregory investigated the course of the Murchison River as far as Impey. He then crossed the Macadam Plains to the Gascoyne River, following it downstream to its mouth in Shark Bay. The next year, he surveyed the territory around Mount Augustus westward to the Gascoyne and Lyons Rivers.

In 1861, Gregory undertook a series of explorations in search of new grazing lands around the Nickol Bay region in the northern portion of Western Australia. He ascended the Fortescue River to its upper reaches, then crossed the Hamersley Range and explored inland, undertaking surveys of the Yule, Ashburton, Shaw, De Grey, and Oakover Rivers before returning to the coast at Nickol Bay.

Although Frank Gregory's explorations were not continental in scope, as were those of his brother Augustus, by locating the region's few areas of arable land, his survey work had a great impact on Western Australia's subsequent inland settlement.

Grenfell, George (1849–1906) *British missionary in central Africa*

George Grenfell was born in Sancreed, a small town near Penzance, in Cornwall, England. In 1874, after completing his education in Birmingham, he entered the service of the Baptist Missionary Society, which sent him to the Cameroons on the west coast of central Africa.

At the time of Grenfell's arrival in the Cameroons in 1874, Germany and Belgium were beginning to assert their colonial presence in the Congo region. In his first years in central Africa, Grenfell surveyed the river systems of the Cameroons. In 1884–87, when King Leopold II of Belgium was consolidating his rule over the newly established Congo Free State, Grenfell undertook a series of expeditions along the lower course of the CONGO RIVER (now known as the Zaire River), exploring southward as far as the EQUATOR.

Grenfell's travels in the Congo brought him into contact with colonial as well as tribal leaders, to whom he became a familiar and trusted figure. In 1891, his influence in central Africa earned him an appointment as the Belgian government's representative in negotiations over the Congo River border between the Portuguese colony of Angola and the Congo Free State.

Grenfell settled near Basoko in what is now north-central Zaire, from where he extended his explorations into the northeastern Congo, exploring the Aruwimi River and the region between Lake Albert and the Congo River in 1900–02.

Along with SIR HENRY MORTON STANLEY, George Grenfell was among the first Europeans to venture into the interior of central Africa, one of the last regions of the continent to be explored by Europeans.

Grenville, Sir Richard (1540–1591) *English naval officer, colonizer on the Carolina coast of North America, cousin of Sir Walter Raleigh*

Sir Richard Grenville was born at Buckland Abbey, in Cornwall, England, the son of a poet and former courtier to the court of Henry VIII. A cousin of SIR WALTER RALEIGH, he was a member of the House of Commons, as well as a military leader, taking part in battles against the Turks in Hungary in 1566–67, and, the next year, in the suppression of a peasant revolt at Munster, Ireland. In 1573–75, he sought sponsorship from Queen Elizabeth I for a CIRCUMNAVIGATION OF THE WORLD, a plan later carried out by SIR FRANCIS DRAKE in 1577–80.

Grenville commanded the British warship the *Tiger* in naval actions against the Spanish in the Caribbean in the early 1580s. In 1585, he sailed the *Tiger* with six other ships to the Carolina Coast, transporting a group of 108 settlers for Raleigh's first colonizing venture to Roanoke Island. Upon approaching the mainland, the fleet rode out a storm and was nearly wrecked in the shoals off a point of land, which Grenville, in consequence, dubbed Cape Fear. With the colony established on Roanoke Island, he explored the Carolina coast, including Pamlico Sound, visiting Indian villages at Secoton and Aquascogoc. At Aquascogoc, when an Indian stole a silver cup from the explorers' party, Grenville retaliated by having the Indian village and all its crops destroyed.

After eight days, Grenville sailed from Roanoke. Upon his return the following year, he found the Roanoke settlers gone and from a captured Indian learned that the colonists had departed a few weeks earlier with Drake, who had stopped by while engaged in privateering along the southeast coast of North America. Leaving a small contingent of his crew to maintain English possession of the colony, Grenville sailed back to England, intending to return with additional colonists, but the English were subsequently killed by the Indians, possibly in retaliation for Grenville's earlier harsh treatment. A second colony on Roanoke was founded in 1587, but it had disappeared when relief vessels under JOHN WHITE finally arrived in 1590, becoming known as the LOST COLONY.

In 1591, while serving as a vice admiral in command of the *Revenge,* Grenville was involved in a prolonged sea battle with the Spanish fleet off the AZORES. His ship was sunk in the engagement, and Grenville was gravely wounded and was taken prisoner. He died three years later.

Sir Richard Grenville was one of the first English navigators to explore the southeast coast of North America, and his colonizing efforts along the Carolina coast laid the basis for the first attempted permanent English settlement in what is now the United States.

Grey, Sir George (1812–1898) *British colonial administrator in Australia and New Zealand*

Born in England, George Grey embarked on a military career in his late teens, and, by 1836, he was a captain in the British army. That year, he sailed to Perth, the newly established colony on the west coast of Australia, and over the next few years, he explored the interior regions to the north.

In 1837, accompanied by a Lieutenant Lushington, Grey sailed northward along the coast from Perth, rounding North West Cape. He landed at Brunswick Bay, then traveled inland and explored the King Leopold Range. Although Grey had planned an overland trek southward to Perth, a distance of 1,200 miles, he instead returned to the settlement by ship.

Grey followed the course of the Swan River northeastward from Perth in 1838, and the next year, he undertook a second expedition. He sailed to Shark Bay and, during his survey of the territory to the north and east, made the European discovery of the Gascoyne River. On the return voyage to Perth, the ship was wrecked off the mouth of the Murchison River, and Grey was compelled to lead his expedition on a southward march along the coast.

Grey went on to a long career as a British colonial administrator, serving as governor of South Australia from 1841 to 1845 and governor of NEW ZEALAND from 1845 to 1854. In 1854, he moved to South Africa, where he was governor of the Cape Colony until 1860, and he then returned to his former post in New Zealand, where he remained until 1868. After a brief stay in England, he returned to New Zealand, and in 1877–79, he served as premier.

Sir George Grey's explorations of Western Australia in the late 1830s were notable for, in addition to the European discovery of the Gascoyne River, one of the most interesting archaeological finds on the continent. In the King Leopold Range, he discovered a series of cave paintings of human figures, one of them depicting a man 10 feet high and dressed in a red robe. Although first thought to have been left by early visitors from the Malay Peninsula, archaeologists later determined that they had been painted by Aborigines, probably members of the Wondjina people, who lived in the nearby Kimberley Ranges. According to Aborigine legend, the images, known as the Wondjina Figures, were impressions left in the rocks by the spirits of departed members of the tribe. Grey, a student of Pacific anthropology as well as an explorer, wrote *Polynesian Mythologies,* published in 1855.

Grijalva, Juan de (Juan de Grijalba)

(ca. 1489–1527) *Spanish conquistador in Cuba, Mexico, and Nicaragua, nephew of Diego Velásquez*

Born in the town of Cuellar, in what is now the Spanish province of Segovia, Juan de Grijalva was a member of a noble family, well connected to the royal government of Castile. He arrived in Cuba soon after its conquest in 1511, joining his uncle, DIEGO VELÁSQUEZ, Cuba's first colonial governor, at Santiago.

In 1518, Grijalva was commissioned by his uncle to further investigate FRANCISCO FERNÁNDEZ DE CÓRDOBA's reports of gold and an advanced Indian civilization in the lands west of the newly explored Yucatán Peninsula. Sailing from Santiago de Cuba on May 1, 1518, in command of a fleet of four ships with 200 soldiers and crew, he initially followed the north coast of Cuba westward, then crossed the Yucatán Channel, making his first landing on the island of Cozumel, off the northeasternmost tip of the Yucatán Peninsula.

Grijalva and his fleet soon reached the mainland and, sailing eastward along the north coast of the Yucatán, passed into Campeche Bay. He frequently made landings along the shore, coming upon the river that now bears his name, where he encountered Maya Indian chieftains who presented him with gold plates fashioned into armor. Although he met some armed resistance from the Indians on the mainland, he was better equipped than the earlier Fernández de Córdoba expedition and sustained only minimal losses.

All along the coast, Grijalva saw evidence of the advanced architecture of the Maya, by then a subject people of the Aztec Indians. The huge stone crosses that the Indians had erected for religious purposes reminded Grijalva of his homeland, and he was the first to apply the name "New Spain" to the Mexican mainland.

Proceeding northward along Campeche Bay, Grijalva came upon the mouth of another river, which he dubbed the Río de las Banderas (river of banners) after the many colored pennants displayed by a delegation of Aztec he found on its banks. He established friendly contacts with the Aztec emissaries, trading some inexpensive European trinkets for a fortune in gold and jewels. Although his men urged him to establish a colony in order to continue bartering with the natives, Grijalva declined, having been ordered by his uncle, Velásquez, only to trade and explore. Instead, he dispatched PEDRO DE ALVARADO to sail one of the vessels back to Cuba and report what he had found.

Grijalva then continued his exploration northward along the Mexican coast, reaching as far as present-day Tuxpán, south of the Pánuco River. Along the way, he made the European discovery of the island of San Juan de Ulúa, off present-day Veracruz. A second island he located he called the Isla de los Sacrificios (island of sacrifices) after the large quantity of human remains he found in temples there (the first evidence that the native religion included the practice of human sacrifice).

Without receiving further instructions from his uncle, he decided to sail back to Cuba. Upon his arrival at Santiago, he found that Velásquez was already outfitting an even larger expedition to search for him and establish a permanent Spanish presence in Mexico. Although Grijalva had more than fulfilled his mission by confirming Fernández de Córdoba's findings and returning with a treasure of gold and jewels acquired in trade with the Indians, Velásquez nonetheless rebuked his nephew for not founding a colony on the Mexican mainland while he was there.

Grijalva returned to Mexico in 1523, following the conquest of the Aztec under HERNÁN CORTÉS. He subsequently took part in the Spanish conquest of Nicaragua, where, in 1527, he was killed in an Indian attack along with 19 other conquistadores.

Juan de Grijalva's expedition of 1518 led directly to the Spanish conquest of Mexico, which was launched almost as soon as he returned to Cuba. He and his men were the first Europeans to venture into the territory of the Aztec Empire and the first to have direct contact with the Aztec and learn of their ruler, Montezuma. Many members of his expedition sailed with Cortés in 1518, including Pedro de Alvarado and BERNAL DÍAZ DEL CASTILLO, who both played critical roles in the conquest of Mexico.

Groseilliers, sieur de   See CHOUART DES GROSEILLIERS, MÉDARD.

Grueber, Johann (John Grueber) (1623–1680)
Austrian missionary in China, Tibet, and India

Johann Grueber was born in Linz, an Austrian city on the Danube River. Educated as a mathematician, he entered the Jesuit order as a missionary priest.

In 1656, Grueber left Rome for the Far East, accompanied by Father Bernard Diestel. They traveled through the eastern MEDITERRANEAN SEA and made their way to Hormuz, at the mouth of the Persian Gulf. From there, they sailed to Surat on the west coast of India, north of Bombay. They continued their journey aboard an English ship that took them to the Portuguese colony of Macao, off the coast of China.

At that time, Portuguese shipping from Macao was being preyed upon by Dutch privateers from Batavia (present-day Jakarta, Indonesia), and, in order to circumvent this threat, Portuguese colonial officials encouraged Grueber to seek a westward overland route back to India and Europe.

After arriving at Peking (Beijing) in 1658, Grueber undertook missionary work. In Peking, he was met by a Flemish Jesuit priest, Father ALBERT D'ORVILLE, who was studying geography and surveying while in the Chinese capital.

In search of a westward overland route back to India, Grueber and Orville left Peking in April 1661, traveling westward to the Yellow River (Chang) and the city of Hsining (Xining), at that time the western limit of the Chinese Empire. They continued across the Ordos desert to Koko Nor, the great salt lake in northeastern Tsing-Hai (Qinghai) province. After skirting the rim of the desolate salt swamps of the Tsaidam region, they crossed the Burkan,

Buddha, and Shuga Mountains, at elevations sometimes exceeding 15,000 feet, and entered Tibet. They reached its capital city, LHASA, in October 1661.

Grueber and Orville remained in Lhasa for a month, where they were the first Europeans to observe the use of prayer wheels and other practices unique to Tibetan Buddhism.

In November 1661, Grueber and his companion continued their trek to India, crossing the HIMALAYAS into Nepal, where they visited Katmandu. From there they traveled across the plain of the upper GANGES RIVER. They arrived in Agra in north-central India in March 1662, nearly a year after they had started out from Peking. Orville soon died in Agra, and Grueber continued alone. He went first to Delhi, then crossed into what is now Pakistan. From Lahore, he descended the INDUS RIVER to its mouth on the Arabian Sea, then made an arduous trek westward across Baluchistan and the Makran desert country into Persia (present-day Iran).

From Hormuz, Grueber sailed to the head of the Persian Gulf, then followed the Tigris and Euphrates Rivers northward through what is now Iraq and Syria, to the Mediterranean coast. He arrived back in Rome in February 1664.

In his later years, Grueber served as a chaplain with the Austrian army in Transylvania. He later settled at Tyrnau (present-day Trnava, Slovakia), where he died in 1680. (Some accounts relate that he died in Italy or Hungary in 1665.) An account in Latin of Grueber's journey from China was written by the German Jesuit archaeologist and orientalist Athanasius Kircher, and was first published in Amsterdam in 1667.

Johann Grueber and Albert d'Orville were the first Europeans to visit Lhasa. The next European to do so was IPPOLITO DESIDERI in 1716. In addition to a wealth of updated information about central Asia, and his reports about the little-known religion and culture of the Tibetans, Grueber returned to Europe with the first sketch of Lhasa's Potala palace and monastery, a focal point of Tibetan Buddhism.

Guancanagari (fl. 1490s) *Arawak tribal leader in the Caribbean*

Guancanagari was an Arawak (Taino) Indian chieftain, one of five kings, or caciques, who ruled the native people of Hispaniola (present-day Haiti and the Dominican Republic), when CHRISTOPHER COLUMBUS arrived on the island on December 5, 1492, in the course of his first voyage.

Guancanagari's people gave Columbus and his men a friendly reception when his ships landed at Puerto de San Nicolás on the eastern end of the island, and the Arawak leader soon invited Columbus to visit him at his village, where he received the admiral and his officers at his court.

From Guancanagari, Columbus learned that the island he had named Española (Hispaniola) was known to the natives as Haiti. The Spaniards also obtained gold from the interior of the island, a region the Arawak called Cibao. Columbus interpreted this as a reference to Cipangu, the name by which Japan was then known to Europeans; he was thus encouraged in his belief that he was near the mainland of Asia.

In late December 1492, Guancanagari helped Columbus salvage what he could from his flagship, the *Santa María,* after the vessel had become grounded on an offshore reef while the crew had been celebrating Christmas. The Arawak leader sent his men by CANOE to carry its contents ashore. Afterward, Guancanagari invited Columbus to reside at his home while the Spanish established their settlement, Villa de Navidad, near present-day Limonade, Haiti, on the island's north coast.

After Columbus had departed for Europe in mid-January 1493, Guancanagari attempted in vain to help defend the small Spanish garrison left at Navidad against an attack led by rival native rulers. All 43 of Columbus's officers and men were killed, and Guancanagari, who had been wounded in the battle, was forced to retreat with his people into the mountains.

Guancanagari greeted Columbus when he returned to Hispaniola in late November 1493, in command of a large-scale colonizing expedition. Over the next year, the other Arawak tribes united under the leadership of Caonabo and Manicaotex, who conspired to rise up against the European invaders and exterminate them. Guancanagari refused to lead his people in the planned uprising, instead warning Columbus of the impending attack. In March 1495, he allied himself with the Spanish in a military campaign against Manicaotex's faction in the Vega Real region of central Hispaniola.

Guancanagari's actions incurred the animosity of all the tribes on the island, forcing him to once more take refuge in the mountains, where he lived out the rest of his life in exile, stripped of his former status and authority.

Guancanagari was among the earliest native leaders of the Western Hemisphere to be known by name to Europeans and to help in their explorations. His efforts to gain the friendship of Columbus and the early Spanish settlers on Hispaniola led not only to his own downfall, but also to the eventual enslavement and extermination of his people, foreshadowing the dire impact that the process of European discovery was ultimately to have on Native Americans.

Gunnison, John Williams (1812–1853) *U.S. Army officer, American topographical engineer in the American West*

John W. Gunnison was a native of Goshen, New Hampshire, and received his early education at New Hampshire's Hopkinton Academy. He attended West Point from 1833 to 1837, graduating with honors as a second lieutenant in the artillery.

From 1837 to 1840, Gunnison served in Florida in the campaign against the Seminole Indians and assisted in the relocation of the Cherokee Indians, from Georgia to the Indian Territory (present-day Oklahoma). In 1838, he transferred to the U.S. Army Corps of Topographical Engineers.

During the 1840s, Gunnison took part in surveys in the Pacific Northwest, resulting in the region's first scientifically based maps. In 1849–50, he joined Captain HOWARD STANSBURY's expedition into present-day Utah's Great Basin and explored the country around the Great Salt Lake in search of a central route for a proposed transcontinental railroad.

On June 23, 1853, Gunnison led a company of topographical engineers in an expedition westward from Fort Leavenworth in what is now Kansas to explore and survey a possible route for a transcontinental railroad along the 38th parallel. Gunnison and his party went first to Bent's Fort, Colorado, via the Arkansas River Valley, then followed the Huerfano River into the Sangre de Cristo Mountains. He then dispatched part of his command southward to establish a road to Taos.

With the rest of his party, Gunnison headed north and west through Cochetopa Pass, across the Grand and Green Rivers, and found a little-known pass across the Wasatch Mountains that took him into Utah's Great Basin near Utah Lake.

On October 23, 1853, along the Sevier River south of Utah Lake, Gunnison and nine other members of his party, including artist-topographer RICHARD HOVENDON KERN, were killed in an attack by Ute Indians. Government officials suspected that Mormon settlers had incited the Ute to attack the party, but these allegations were never proven. Gunnison's survey in Utah was resumed the following spring under the command of Lieutenant EDWARD GRIFFIN BECKWITH.

Gunnison made a study of the Mormons while wintering in Salt Lake City in 1849–50. It was published in 1852 as *The Mormons, or Latter-Day Saints, in the Valley of the Great Salt Lake,* and was hailed at that time as one of the most comprehensive works on the subject.

Although Gunnison did not live to complete the survey of the 38th parallel, his explorations determined that a rail line through that part of Utah would require too many bridges and tunnels to be financially feasible. He also provided preliminary reports that led to the construction of military roads into Utah from the west and south.

Gutiérrez, Diego   (unknown–1554)
Spanish cartographer
Diego Gutiérrez was a cartographer for Spain's House of Trade for the Indies (Casa de la Contratacion de las Indias), the Spanish government's office that licensed mariners and maintained updated maps of the world. In 1562, Gutiérrez produced the first map of South America detailing the continent's interior. Incorporating information gleaned from the explorations up the Río de la Plata undertaken by SEBASTIAN CABOT in 1526–30, as well as from FRANCISCO DE ORELLANA's journey down the AMAZON RIVER in 1542, his chart was the first to depict the extent of the river systems within South America.

By 1540, European mariners had revealed the outline of South America in their voyages. Diego Gutiérrez was the first to include information from inland explorations to show details of the interior of the continent. In contrast, it was not until the early 1800s that the North American interior was known to such an extent.

Guzmán, Nuño Beltrán de (Nuño de Guzmán; Núñez Beltrán de Guzmán)
(unknown–1544) *Spanish conquistador in Mexico*
Nuño de Guzmán was born in the city of Guadalajara, in the New Castile region of central Spain. Guzmán was one of the first Spanish magistrates to serve on the island of Hispaniola (present-day Haiti and the Dominican Republic) in the 1520s. In 1528, he was appointed as governor of the Mexican province of Pánuco on the central Gulf Coast region, near present-day Tampico. Soon after assuming office in May 1528, he began a program of exploitation of the Indians, enslaving many of them and transporting them to Hispaniola in exchange for livestock.

In December 1528, Guzmán was selected to succeed HERNÁN CORTÉS as head of the Spanish colonial administration of Mexico, known as the *audiencia*. He persisted in his cruel treatment of the native population while in that office, incurring the severe criticism of Catholic Church authorities, most notably Bishop Zumárraga.

Guzmán and an army of 500 Spaniards, along with as many as 10,000 Indian allies, marched from Mexico City in November 1529 and headed westward into the Jalisco region. He then launched a military campaign, which succeeded in subjugating the Tarascan, a tribe not under the domination of the Aztec. He soon extended his rule to the northwest with an expedition he sent out under the command of Cristobál de Oñate, which conquered much of what is now Sinaloa and Sonora on Mexico's northwest coast. He organized the new territory as the province of Nueva Galicia, and, on December 3, 1530, he founded its capital, which he named Guadalajara, after his hometown in Spain. Before long, he also established the city of Culiacán, as well as Tepic and Lagos.

By 1531, Guzmán had been replaced as head of the colonial government of Mexico, and the new governor sent an armed force into Nueva Galicia to arrest him on charges stemming from his previous abuses against the Indians.

During the next two years, he resisted efforts to capture him. As governor of Nueva Galicia, he also took steps that hampered Cortés's efforts at seaward exploration along Mexico's Pacific coast in 1532–33.

By 1536, Guzmán's political support had weakened, and he was compelled to surrender himself to the Spanish viceroy in Mexico City, ANTONIO DE MENDOZA. Although he was well received by the viceroy, a special commission for his prosecution ordered his arrest. He was held in a dungeon for more than a year and was sent back to Spain in 1538, where he spent his remaining years in obscurity and poverty.

Nuño de Guzmán was a leading figure in the second stage of the Spanish conquest of Mexico, following the destruction of the Aztec Empire. Because of his abuses in dealing with the Indians, he is usually regarded as one of the cruelest of the Spanish CONQUISTADORES. His exploits extended Spanish influence into western Mexico. Culiacán, which he established in the early 1530s, became the staging point for the explorations into the American Southwest undertaken by FRANCISCO VÁSQUEZ DE CORONADO, Guzmán's successor as governor of Nueva Galicia.

Hakluyt, Richard (ca. 1552–1616)

English geographer

Richard Hakluyt was born in Herefordshire, north of London. His family was of Welsh origin, with considerable wealth and influential ties to the English government.

Orphaned at an early age, the young Hakluyt was raised by an uncle, a lawyer whose name was also Richard Hakluyt, and whose client was the London-based MUSCOVY COMPANY. As the legal representative for the firm that had sponsored numerous voyages in search of both the NORTHEAST PASSAGE and NORTHWEST PASSAGE, the elder Hakluyt had a keen interest in geography and recent explorations, which he passed on to his nephew.

After attending Westminster School, Hakluyt entered Oxford University's Christ Church College in 1570, earning his baccalaureate degree four years later and his master's degree in 1577. That same year, he became a teacher at Oxford, and, in 1580, he became the university's first professor of modern geography.

In 1582, Hakluyt published his first major geographic work, *Divers Voyages Touching the Discovery of America and the Islands Adjacent,* which included accounts of the voyages and explorations of JOHN CABOT and SEBASTIAN CABOT and of GIOVANNI DA VERRAZANO. At the request of SIR WALTER RALEIGH, he wrote another work two years later, *A Discourse Concerning Western Planting,* promoting English overseas colonization in North America. Hakluyt argued that, in addition to countering Spanish commercial and naval competition, English colonial expansion in North America would provide bases for the eventual discovery of the Northwest Passage. To support his position, he cited the explorations of Verrazano and JACQUES CARTIER 50 years earlier. Hakluyt went on to suggest that these colonies could be settled by the nation's unemployed and ultimately provide England with an exclusive overseas market. The work was privately circulated among Queen Elizabeth I and high government officials; a published edition did not appear until 1877.

In 1583, soon after his ordination as a priest in the Church of England, Hakluyt traveled to Paris, where he served for the next five years as chaplain to England's ambassador to the French court. During this time, Hakluyt had the opportunity to gather additional accounts of explorations undertaken by European navigators.

Hakluyt was largely responsible for the publication of JOHN WHITE's drawings and paintings of the Roanoke colony. On his recommendation, they appeared in German engraver Theodore de Bry's translations of THOMAS HARRIOT's *Briefe and True Report of the New Found Land of Virginia,* first published in Frankfort in 1589.

On his return to England in 1589, Hakluyt published the first edition of his *Principal Navigations, Voyages, Traffics, and Discoveries of the English Nation.* This work was widely read and provided a basic source of geographic knowledge in England. An expanded version was published in three volumes from 1598 to 1600.

During the early 1600s, Hakluyt was a principal shareholder in the VIRGINIA COMPANY of London, which established the Jamestown colony in 1607, the first permanent English settlement in the present-day United States. In 1609, Hakluyt published *Virginia Richly Valued,* which detailed the explorations of HERNANDO DE SOTO in the 1540s and which fueled enthusiasm for English exploration and settlement in North America. He was also a member of the COMPANY OF MERCHANT ADVENTURERS DISCOVERERS OF THE NORTHWEST PASSAGE, founded in 1612.

Richard Hakluyt died in London in 1616. He played no active role in any voyage of exploration, and, in fact, traveled only a few hundred miles from his birthplace during his entire lifetime. Nevertheless, his writings helped raise support for many important English expeditions of the Elizabethan age, including those undertaken by JOHN DAVIS, SIR HUMPHREY GILBERT, and SIR RICHARD GRENVILLE. He was a financial backer of the English company that initiated the colonization of Virginia and New England. In contrast to the Portuguese and Spanish policy of secrecy in regard to geographic discoveries, Hakluyt made geographic knowledge widely available. His work had a great influence on subsequent explorations and illustrates how the rise of printing and book publishing in the 16th century accelerated all aspects of human endeavor, especially exploration. Since 1846, the HAKLUYT SOCIETY, established in his honor, has carried on his work, with the publication of firsthand accounts of exploration.

Hall, Charles Francis (1821–1871)

American journalist, explorer in northern Greenland and the Canadian Arctic

Charles Francis Hall was born in Rochester, New Hampshire, the son of a blacksmith. As a young man, he briefly took up his father's trade, then moved west to Cincinnati, Ohio, where he worked in the newspaper business, first as an engraver, then as a journalist.

Hall's interest in Arctic exploration was sparked in 1848 by the first reports of the disappearance of SIR JOHN FRANKLIN's expedition and the efforts undertaken by the British navy to find him. He resolved to take part in the search; in 1850, he tried, without success, to join EDWIN JESSE DE HAVEN's expedition. Nine years later, he was also turned down when he applied for a position with SIR FRANCIS LEOPOLD MCCLINTOCK's search expedition on JANE FRANKLIN's ship, the *Fox.*

Finally, in 1860, Hall won the support of Henry Grinnell, a New York merchant who had previously sponsored search expeditions under De Haven and ELISHA KENT KANE. Hall speculated that, if any of the Franklin party were still alive after more than 10 years in the Canadian Arctic, they could only have survived by adopting the Inuit way of life. He therefore decided to travel to the southeast coast of Baffin Island and learn the Inuit language and their survival techniques. He planned to attempt a passage through Frobisher Bay (thought to be a strait) into Foxe Basin, and continue across the Melville Peninsula to the Boothia Peninsula and finally King William Island, where traces of Franklin's expedition had already been found.

Hall received free transport to Baffin Island aboard a New London-based whaling vessel, the *George Henry,* on which he sailed in May 1860. Outfitted by the ship's owners with sledges, a boat, and provisions, he spent the next two years exploring around Frobisher Bay among the Inuit. From them he heard a traditional story about earlier white visitors and realized it was a reference to SIR MARTIN FROBISHER's expeditions of the late 1570s. He learned that the five men who had disappeared from the expedition in 1576 had later perished when they attempted to sail back to England in a makeshift boat.

By summer 1862, Hall had learned Inuit language and survival skills. In his subsequent attempt to reach Foxe Basin, he discovered that what had been thought of as Frobisher Strait was actually a bay. At its closed western end, he named an island Frobisher's Farthest. He later located the remains of the house erected by Frobisher and his men in 1578.

With his route westward through Frobisher Bay to the Canadian Arctic blocked by impassable mountains and an icefield, Hall returned to lower Baffin Island. From there, he set out for the United States, arriving in August 1862.

With the Civil War raging, Hall volunteered to lead a naval expedition against Confederate coastal PRIVATEERS preying on Union shipping, an offer declined by President Abraham Lincoln. Hall then resumed his efforts to find the Franklin expedition, sailing in June 1864 to the north shores of HUDSON BAY aboard the whaling vessel *Monticello.* It took him nearly five years before he managed to reach Boothia Peninsula and King William Island. There, he heard Inuit accounts of how, 20 years earlier, the 79 survivors of the Franklin Expedition had died of exhaustion and starvation after abandoning the remaining vessel in Victoria Strait. From Inuit he obtained silverware and other relics of the expedition; he also managed to recover a skeleton of one of Franklin's men.

In his final expedition, Hall attempted to reach the NORTH POLE. In this project, funded by an act of Congress, he was provided with the *Polaris,* a vessel specially designed to withstand Arctic ice conditions. He sailed from New London, Connecticut, on July 3, 1871, and headed for Smith Sound, the narrow channel between Ellesmere Island and northwestern GREENLAND, the northernmost stretch of open water then known. The ship managed to negotiate the ice floes and passed north of Smith Sound into what was later called Hall Basin in his honor. In fall 1871, Hall explored farther to the north by sledge, reaching the north coast of Ellesmere Island and the entrance to the Lincoln

Sea. According to a geographic theory popular at that time, it was thought that an open, ice-free polar sea existed north of Greenland, providing access to the North Pole. The Smith Sound passage had been pioneered by Elisha Kent Kane and ISAAC ISRAEL HAYES. Upon reaching the northern limit of Ellesmere Island, however, Hall could see that seaward progress was blocked by ice. He returned to his expedition's winter quarters at Thank God Harbor, where he died of a stroke on November 8, 1871. The rest of the expedition continued explorations until 1873.

Hall's northernmost record endured only until 1876, when a British expedition led by SIR GEORGE STRONG NARES exceeded it. Officers from the Nares party visited Hall's grave at what had been named Polaris Peninsula after his ship, where they raised an American flag and left a commemorative plaque.

Charles Francis Hall helped facilitate subsequent Arctic exploration through his adaptation of Inuit survival techniques. His 1871 expedition revealed that both Ellesmere Island and Greenland extended much farther north than anyone had thought and helped put to rest the erroneous idea of an open polar sea. His earlier expedition to Prince William Island and the Boothia Peninsula provided more details of the final outcome of the ill-fated Franklin expedition and added significant information to geographic knowledge of the Canadian Arctic. His account of his 1860–62 expedition to eastern Baffin Island and Frobisher Bay, entitled *Researches and Life Among the Eskimaux,* was published in 1864.

Hall, James (unknown–1612) *English mariner in western Greenland, in service to Denmark and England*

James Hall was born in Hull, England, a seaport on the North Sea. Little is known of his early life, other than that he grew up to be an accomplished mariner and pilot.

In 1605, Hall joined an expedition organized by King Christian IV of Denmark to explore the west coast of GREENLAND. Encouraged by reports of the explorations of the 16th-century English navigator JOHN DAVIS, the Danish monarch hoped to reestablish contact, after a lapse of 200 years, with the Greenland colonies founded by Vikings. Like Hall, most of the officers with the Danish expedition were English, including its commander, John Cunningham.

Serving as pilot and first mate on one of the expedition's three ships, Hall sailed around the southern tip of Greenland into Davis Strait, then along Greenland's southwest coast, where the small fleet made landings at King Christian Fjord and other points. The expedition failed to locate European colonists; five Inuit (Eskimo) were captured and taken to Denmark, along with some rocks believed to contain traces of silver ore.

King Christian, encouraged by the possibility of mineral wealth on Greenland, sent out a second and larger ex-

pedition in 1606, with Hall serving as the pilot on the flagship of the five-vessel fleet. Upon reaching Davis Strait, ice conditions forced the ships westward, away from the Greenland shore. Although a sighting was made of land to the west, known later as Baffin Island, a landing was not attempted. Instead, the expedition continued northward as far as 66° north latitude and reached the Greenland coast. More Inuit were kidnapped and more rock samples gathered. The expedition then returned to Denmark.

Hall took part in a third expedition, sponsored by the Danish king in 1607, which failed to reach Greenland because of severe ice conditions. Danish interest in Greenland soon diminished when it was learned that the ore from the first two voyages contained no silver but only quartz, feldspar, and mica.

Soon after his 1607 voyage, Hall returned to England and succeeded in raising support among London commercial interests, led by Sir William Cockayne and Richard Bell, for his own expedition to Greenland in 1612. In command of two ships, the *Heartsease* and the *Patience,* he sailed from the port of Hull in April 1612. Accompanying Hall on the voyage as pilot was WILLIAM BAFFIN. After rounding Greenland's Cape Farewell, Hall sailed northward along the coast, exploring as far as a point just above the ARCTIC CIRCLE.

Turning southward, Hall anchored off present-day Holsteinborg, Greenland, known then as Rommel's Fjord, the very site where the Inuit had been abducted by Cunningham's men seven years before. On landing with some of the crew, Hall was recognized by a group of Inuit for his earlier complicity. One of the natives approached him and stabbed the Englishman with a harpoon. He died the following day and was buried on a nearby island. The expedition then returned to England.

James Hall's voyages to Greenland prompted other English explorations into Davis Strait, including those undertaken by William Baffin and ROBERT BYLOT in their search for the NORTHWEST PASSAGE. Soon after the 1605 voyage, James Hall prepared a report of the expedition for King Christian, which included the first charts of the west coast of Greenland.

Hamilton, William Thomas (Wildcat Bill)

(1822–1908) *American fur trader, trapper, guide in the American West*

Born in England, William Hamilton was brought to the United States as an infant by his parents in 1824. The family settled in St. Louis, Missouri, then the hub of the FUR TRADE on the MISSOURI RIVER and in the ROCKY MOUNTAINS.

As a youth in St. Louis, Hamilton had been plagued by health problems, probably respiratory in nature. His father, believing a long sojourn in the mountains would help in his son's recovery, provided financing for mountain man

WILLIAM SHERLEY WILLIAMS's fur-trading expedition into the Rockies on the condition that he take the younger Hamilton along.

Hamilton set out from St. Louis with Williams in 1842. During the next three years, they roamed the region between the Green River and the North Platte River in what is now southwestern Wyoming and northern Utah.

In 1849, Hamilton headed for California with the gold rush. From the northern California goldfields, he moved on to the Oregon Country, where he embarked on a career as an Indian fighter, taking part in the Rogue River War of 1855 and the Modoc War of 1856. He developed a reputation as a fierce and skilled opponent in these conflicts, becoming known as "Wildcat Bill."

Hamilton returned to the northern Rockies in 1857, where he assisted the U.S. Army in its efforts to subdue the Nez Perce, Blackfeet, and Crow Indians. In 1858, he established a trading post near the confluence of the Bitterroot and Clark Fork Rivers, and, in 1864, he moved his business to the upper Missouri settlement at Fort Benton in present-day Montana. While at Fort Benton, he became sheriff of surrounding Chouteau County.

With the outbreak of a major conflict with the Sioux (Dakota, Lakota, Nakota) and Cheyenne Indians on the northern plains in 1876, Hamilton returned to his former career as an Indian fighter. As a scout for General George Crook, he took part in the Battle of the Rosebud in June 1876.

In the late 1870s, Hamilton settled at Columbia, Montana, where he served as a guide for scientific expeditions into the Rockies. He spent his last years in Billings, Montana.

William Hamilton related his experiences on the frontier in his 1905 book, *My Sixty Years on the Plains, Trapping, Trading, and Fighting Indians*. The city of Missoula, Montana, developed around the post he had established in 1858 at the Bitterroot's junction with the Clark Fork.

Hanno (Hanno the Carthaginian) (fl. 470s B.C.)

Carthaginian admiral, colonizer on the coast of West Africa, possibly brother of Himilco

Hanno was a leading statesman and admiral of Carthage, the Phoenician city on the coast of North Africa, near the site of present-day Tunis. Some scholars believe he was the son of the Carthaginian military leader Hamilcar and brother of HIMILCO, the Carthaginian explorer of western Europe. In about 470 B.C., soon after the Carthaginians were defeated in their efforts to subjugate the Greek colony on neighboring Sicily, Hanno undertook a large-scale expedition of exploration and colonization along the northwest coast of Africa.

According to a Greek translation of Hanno's own report of the voyage (*see* PERIPLUS), he embarked from Carthage in command of a fleet of 60 oared GALLEYS, carrying as many as 30,000 men and women colonists, equipped with all essentials for establishing cities. After passing through the STRAIT OF GIBRALTAR, Hanno continued southwestward along the African coast. He established the first colony, Thymiaterium, on the site of present-day Mehdia, Morocco. He then continued along the coast, founding the Phoenician cities of Agadir and Mogador on what is now the central Atlantic shore of Morocco.

After establishing six new colonies on the northwest coast of Africa, Hanno and his remaining ships and crew continued exploring southward along the coast of West Africa. He established an outpost on the island of Herne, known in ancient times as Cerne, at the mouth of the Senegal River. He reportedly continued southward to Cape Verde and the Gambia River, although some sources suggest he may have reached as far as the Gulf of Guinea.

Hanno recounted that, on what may have been one of the Bijagos Islands off the coast of the present-day West African nation of Guinea-Bissau, his men encountered small, hairy creatures—probably chimpanzees—and tried to capture some females. When the animals resisted, they were killed and taken back to Carthage, where their skins were displayed. This was the first contact the Mediterranean world had with these animals.

Hanno also reported that he sighted large portions of the shore ablaze in a region he named "Chariot of the Gods," probably a reference to the seasonal grass fires common to coastal Sierra Leone. He also described a mountain with fire spewing from it, suggesting that he had seen the active volcano Mount Cameroon on the south coast of the Gulf of Guinea.

Shortages of food and problems in making headway into contrary winds forced Hanno to sail back northward to the MEDITERRANEAN SEA and Carthage. On his return, he wrote his account on stone tablets and deposited them in the temple to the Phoenician god Melkarth.

Hanno is considered the first person known to have undertaken a voyage the primary objective of which was exploration and the expansion of geographic knowledge. His voyage was among those chronicled by RICHARD HAKLUYT in the late 16th century. Although the extent of Hanno's travels along the coast of West Africa is not certain, it is believed he reached at least as far as the shores of present-day Sierra Leone. Even if Cape Verde were his southern limit, Hanno reached within 15 degrees of latitude of the EQUATOR and covered a 3,000-mile stretch of the coast of West Africa. In contrast, Portuguese navigators of the 1400s would require nearly half a century of exploration to travel the same distance.

Hannu (Hennu) (fl. ca. 2450s B.C.) *Egyptian mariner on the Red Sea*

Hannu, also referred to as Hennu, the name of a sacred boat in Egyptian mythology, was an Egyptian mariner during the Fifth Dynasty.

Based on hieroglyphics of the Egyptians, in about 2450 B.C. (although some sources indicate three decades earlier), Hannu and a force of some 3,000, sent by the pharaoh Sahure, traveled southward by way of the NILE RIVER, then overland, reaching the land of PUNT—possibly parts of what is now Sudan, Eritrea, Ethiopia, and Somalia—and the Arabian Peninsula. He reportedly returned to Egypt by the RED SEA with precious metals and spices, including gold and silver, as well as ebony and myrrh.

Hannu's journey is the first recorded expedition for the purpose of exploration.

Harpe, Bernard de la   See LA HARPE, JEAN-BAPTISTE BÉNARD.

Harriot, Thomas (Thomas Hariot) (1560–1621) *English mathematician, naturalist on the Carolina coast of North America*

Thomas Harriot was born in Oxford, England, where he went on to study at St. Mary's Hall, receiving his baccalaureate degree in early 1580. He then entered the service of SIR WALTER RALEIGH as a tutor of mathematics.

In 1585, Harriot was appointed geographer, surveyor, and naturalist for Raleigh's first colonizing expedition to North America. On his arrival with the other colonists on the coast of what is now North Carolina, he accompanied the expedition's commander, SIR RICHARD GRENVILLE, and a small party in an exploration of Pamlico Sound and helped in locating a site for the colony on Roanoke Island.

In summer 1585, Harriot conducted studies of the plants and animals around the colony, identifying more than 86 species of birds as well as many varieties of plants, trees, and shrubs then unknown to European naturalists. He also designed the fort erected by the colonists at the northern end of Roanoke Island and undertook a study of the Indians.

Harriot returned to England with the colonists aboard one of SIR FRANCIS DRAKE's ships in June 1586. He wrote an account of his observations of North America, entitled *A Briefe and True Report of the New Found Land of Virginia* and first published in 1588. He also wrote the text that accompanied JOHN WHITE's illustrated account of the Roanoke colony and environs, published in 1590.

In about 1600, Harriot won the support and patronage of Henry Percy, Earl of Northumberland, who provided him with the financial means with which to carry on his scientific work. Harriot's later mathematical studies resulted in innovations in algebraic notations as well as several basic discoveries concerning equations. He also undertook astronomical observations with a telescope; in 1784, almost two centuries after his death, it was revealed that he had made discoveries of sunspots and studies of planetary orbits about the same time as those made by Galileo. He also corresponded with German scientist Johannes Kepler in connection with his study of optics.

Thomas Harriot's 1588 report on the Roanoke colony was the first critical study of North American flora and fauna undertaken by an Englishman. The work also contained observations on the Indians' reaction to the Europeans, citing that they regarded the English as supernatural beings. Also in regard to Indians, Harriot described their food crops and social customs and related how diseases such as measles and smallpox, first introduced by the English colonists in 1585, soon decimated the native population. Harriot's book, translated by German engraver Theodor de Bry into French, Latin, and German, became a principal source of scientific knowledge of North America for Europeans until the early 1700s.

Hartog, Dirk (Dirck Hartogszoon, Dirke-Hertoge) (fl. early 1600s) *Dutch mariner in Australia*

Dirk Hartog was a sea captain and navigator for the DUTCH EAST INDIA COMPANY. In 1616, he sailed from Amsterdam on a voyage to the Dutch EAST INDIES (present-day Indonesia) by way of the CAPE OF GOOD HOPE.

Hartog was instructed to round the tip of Africa, then to follow a course eastward, between 40° and 50° south latitude, across the southern Indian Ocean. Several years earlier, Dutch mariners had discovered that the constant, nearly gale-force westerly winds that blew along these latitudes, known as the "Roaring Forties," sailed their ships eastward in less than half the time it took them to travel along the more conventional northern route to the East Indies by way of Mauritius.

Sailing the *Eendracht* eastward beyond southern Africa and along the Roaring Forties, Hartog was driven southward. On October 25, 1616, the crew sighted an island lying off an unknown coastline, at the mouth of what later came to be known as Shark Bay. Hartog went ashore with a small party, claiming the island for the Dutch and naming it Dirk Hartogs Island. He commemorated the landing by leaving behind an inscribed pewter plate at the island's northern end, later known as Cape Inscription.

Hartog then followed the coastline northward, naming it Eendrachtland, after his ship, and eventually reached Batavia, the Dutch colony on Java.

Unknown to Dirk Hartog at the time, he and his crew were the first Europeans to sight and land on the west coast of Australia. Other Dutch navigators followed, and the western Australian mainland became known as New Holland. The next European to land on Dirk Hartogs Island was Captain Willem de Vlamingh in 1697, also a Dutchman. Vlamingh found Hartog's plate and replaced it with another, which was inscribed with details of both his and Hartog's landfalls. In 1801, French naval officer LOUIS-CLAUDE DE SAULCES DE FREYCINET landed on Dirk Hartogs Island while exploring Australia's west coast with THOMAS-NICOLAS BAUDIN's expedition. He found Vlamingh's plate and took it back to Europe, where it eventually found its way to the States Museum in Amsterdam.

Hatshepsut (Queen Hatshepsut, Hatchepsut, Hatshopsiti, Hatasu, Hashopsitu, Hatshopsiti, Hashepsowe) (1501–1479 B.C.) *Egyptian queen, organizer of trading expeditions to the coast of East Africa*

Hatshepsut was the daughter of Thutmose I, a pharaoh of the 18th Dynasty. She married her half brother, Thutmose II, who seized the throne from his ailing father. Hatshepsut, who had a claim to the throne by birth, shared the Egyptian monarchy with her husband/half brother until his death in 1504 B.C. She then assumed all power as pharaoh of Egypt, even going as far as wearing the traditional garb of a ruling male monarch.

As ruler of Egypt, Hatshepsut set about reviving the building program around the holy cities of Luxor, Karnak, and Thebes. To obtain the most luxurious materials for this project, she dispatched expeditions to distant places. On one of the first, she sent a party of EGYPTIANS up the NILE RIVER from the city of Memphis, near present-day Cairo, to the granite quarries at the First Cataract, near what is now the Aswan High Dam, to obtain a 350-ton stone obelisk.

In about 1492, Hatshepsut initiated her most ambitious trade expedition. She commissioned her lieutenant, Nehsi, to undertake an expedition of five ships down the RED SEA to PUNT, an ancient kingdom to the south, in the region of the Gulf of Aden, including parts of East Africa and possibly the Arabian Peninsula. The main object of the voyage was to acquire myrrh, cinnamon, frankincense, gold, ivory, and other items needed for Hatshepsut's grand temple of Deir al-Bahri, then under construction near Thebes. Both myrrh and cinnamon were essential for embalming and for use as incense in religious ceremonies, and Hatshepsut needed the gold to pay for the temple's lavish appointments.

Hatshepsut's enterprise to Punt was apparently a great success. Details of the voyage were later depicted on the walls of the temple of Deir al-Bahri, showing the Egyptians' arrival and the surprised reaction of the natives, who had lost contact with the people north of the Gulf of Aden. In hieroglyphics and colored reliefs, her men are depicted returning with myrrh trees in tubs, with gold and silver, with ebony and ivory, and with live animals, including baboons, a panther, and dogs.

Upon Hatshepsut's death in 1479, her stepson, Thutmose III, became king, and he soon embarked on a great campaign of national conquest, extending the Egyptian empire into the Euphrates Valley. Yet the program of exploration by sea that she had initiated came to a halt, and Egyptian maritime enterprise did not resume for another 1,000 years.

Queen Hatshepsut's overseas trading ventures restored the flow of riches into Egypt and led to the first recorded, long sea journey in history. In addition, the pictorial representations of the expedition to Punt, which adorned the walls of her temple of Deir al-Bahri, constitute the earliest known illustrated account of travel and exploration. The hieroglyphic inscriptions also relate how the people of Punt, unable to understand that there was a place of which they had no knowledge, believed the visiting Egyptians were supernatural beings who had come from the sky.

Haven, Edwin Jesse de   See DE HAVEN, EDWIN JESSE.

Hawkins, Sir John (1532–1595) *English mariner, slave trader in South America, the Caribbean, and Florida, cousin of Sir Francis Drake*

John Hawkins was born in Plymouth, England, into a family of prominent ship owners and seafarers. His father, William Hawkins, had been involved in trading expeditions between the east coast of Africa and Brazil.

In October 1562, Hawkins embarked from Plymouth with three or four ships and sailed to Sierra Leone, Africa, where he obtained a cargo of slaves from Portuguese traders. He then sailed his fleet to the Caribbean island of Hispaniola (present-day Haiti and the Dominican Republic), where he sold the slaves to Spanish colonists. He returned to England in 1563 with a cargo of WEST INDIES goods, including hides and sugar.

The financial success of Hawkins's first expedition led to the sponsorship of a more ambitious trade endeavor. Among his backers were Queen Elizabeth I and officials of the Royal Navy. On October 18, 1564, Hawkins left Plymouth in command of a fleet of four ships, including the queen's own vessel, the *Jesus of Lubeck,* as well as three ships owned by Hawkins's family, the *Solomon,* the *Tiger,* and the *Swallow.*

After obtaining slaves, gold, and ivory from Portuguese traders in Sierra Leone, Hawkins sailed to the island of

Trinidad in the Caribbean, using it as a base for trade with the Spanish colonies on the northeast coast of South America, known then as the SPANISH MAIN.

In summer 1565, Hawkins headed for England by way of the coast of Florida. That July, his fleet stopped at Fort Caroline, the French Huguenot colony at the mouth of Florida's St. Johns River under the command of RENÉ GOULAINE DE LAUDONNIÈRE. Hawkins sold supplies to the French, then returned to England, arriving in September.

In October 1567, Hawkins undertook a third slave-trading expedition to Africa and the Americas. With him on this trip, as on earlier voyages, was his younger cousin SIR FRANCIS DRAKE. At Sierra Leone, he took part in an intertribal war and obtained a shipment of slaves as a reward for his services. Hawkins then sailed for the Caribbean Sea and the Spanish Main, where he sold all the slaves as well as a cargo of English goods. His main vessel, the *Jesus of Lubeck*, suffered severe damage in stormy weather off the coast of Mexico, forcing repairs at San Juan de Ulúa, near present-day Veracruz, Mexico, in September 1568. While in port, the English were attacked by a Spanish squadron in an attempt to seize their ships for unauthorized trading in the Americas and for piracy in the Caribbean.

Hawkins managed to escape with one vessel, the *Minon*, and reached England in January 1569. Short of food supplies, he was forced to leave about 100 of his men on the Mexican coast near Tampico. Most either fell prey to the Indians or were captured and enslaved by the Spanish. Three of those left behind—David Ingram, Richard Browne, and Richard Twide—reportedly marched northward, eventually reaching Cape Breton, Nova Scotia, and obtained passage back to Europe aboard a French ship.

Back in England, Hawkins became a member of Parliament in 1572 and subsequently received an appointment as treasurer and comptroller of the Royal Navy. He was knighted for his efforts in the defeat of the Spanish Armada in 1588. In 1595, with Drake, he undertook a naval expedition against the Spanish in the Caribbean, but he died off the coast of Puerto Rico that November.

Sir John Hawkins, one of the first Englishmen to enter the lucrative SLAVE TRADE between Africa and the Spanish possessions in the Western Hemisphere, established the pattern of triangular trade between England, Africa, and the Americas. The accounts of his voyages to the Caribbean, South America, and Florida were published in Richard Hakluyt's *Principal Navigations* (1589). They relate early English impressions of Native American life, as well as a description of the short-lived French colony in Florida. An account by David Ingram, one of the three crew members who reportedly reached Nova Scotia, is also included in this work.

Hawqal, Abu al Qasim ibn Ali al-Nasibi ibn

See IBN HAWQAL, ABU AL QASIM IBN ALI AL-NASIBI.

Hayden, Ferdinand Vandeveer (1829–1887)

American geologist in the American West, physician

Ferdinand V. Hayden, a native of Westfield, Massachusetts, spent his early years in Rochester, New York. He attended Oberlin College in Ohio and received his M.D. degree from Albany Medical School in 1853.

Hayden, who was also an accomplished geologist and paleontologist, explored the Badlands of what is now southwestern South Dakota in 1853, while on a fossil-collecting field trip for the Smithsonian Institution.

In 1859, as a geologist with the WILLIAM FRANKLIN RAYNOLDS expedition, Hayden explored the upper Yellowstone River, as well as the Bighorn, Cheyenne, upper Platte, and Powder Rivers of present-day North Dakota, Montana, and Wyoming. Based on the geological investigations he undertook, he produced one of the first stratigraphical maps of the region comprising Montana, Idaho, and the Dakotas. He also wrote in 1860 his *Geological Report of the Yellowstone and Missouri Rivers*, one of the earliest scientific studies of the region between the MISSOURI RIVER and the ROCKY MOUNTAINS.

In 1867, following Civil War service as an army surgeon, Hayden was appointed head of the geological survey of Nebraska. In 1869, the project was expanded into the U.S. Geological and Geographical Survey of the Territories, sponsored by the Department of the Interior, including geological and ethnological studies of much of the Great Plains and Rocky Mountain region. In 1871–72, he conducted most of his work in what is now northwestern Wyoming, including what is now Yellowstone National Park.

In 1872–76, Hayden explored Colorado, sighting Mount of the Holy Cross in the west-central part of that state. This peak, designated a national monument in 1929, features snow-filled crevasses that form a large cross. Hayden also located ancient Indian cliff dwellings in Colorado.

In 1877, the Department of the Interior gave Hayden instructions to continue work on geographic and geological information. JOHN WESLEY POWELL, head of the simultaneous U.S. Geographical and Geological Survey of the Territories, was to specialize in ethnological and geological research. In 1879, the two surveys, plus two other surveys sponsored by the War Department under CLARENCE KING and GEORGE WHEELER, were organized into the U.S. Geological Survey. Hayden continued to collect specimens for the government until his death.

Ferdinand V. Hayden's published reports on the Yellowstone country brought the natural beauty of the area to national attention, eventually leading to the establishment of Yellowstone National Park in 1872.

Ferdinand V. Hayden (Library of Congress)

Hayes, Isaac Israel (1832–1881) American physician, Arctic explorer

Isaac Hayes was born in Chester County, Pennsylvania, just west of Philadelphia. Following his early education at West-town Academy, he studied medicine at the University of Pennsylvania, graduating as a medical doctor in 1853.

Hayes joined ELISHA KENT KANE in his search for SIR JOHN FRANKLIN, as the expedition's surgeon. In spring 1853, the party sailed to the coast of northwestern GREEN-LAND aboard the *Advance*. After spending the first winter at the expedition's base at Van Rensselaer Harbor, on the Greenland side of Smith Sound, Hayes crossed over to Ellesmere Island in May 1854 and explored on his own from Dobbin Bay northward along the coast to Cape Frazier. Be-cause of a broken sledge and a case of snow blindness, he ended his journey and returned to the ship at Van Rensselaer Harbor.

In August 1854, Hayes was among the expedition members who opted to leave Kane and the rest of the party on the *Advance* when the ship, becoming entrapped by DRIFT ICE, was unable to embark for home. Hayes, three other civilians, and five sailors tried to reach the Danish out-post at Upernavik, some 700 miles southward, taking with them a small boat and sledges. The attempt nearly cost them their lives. Beyond Littleton Island, they were stalled by storms. They broke up the wooden boat for fuel and con-structed a makeshift hut. With their supplies running low,

they had to rely on the help of local Inuit, who provided them with food and guided them back to the ship. They reached it at the beginning of December 1854, after three months of trekking along the Arctic coast of northwestern Greenland.

Hayes returned with the expedition to New York in 1855. Despite his ordeal of the previous year, including the loss of several toes to frostbite, he was still enthusiastic about Arctic exploration. He was a strong proponent of the the-ory that there existed an open polar sea north of Ellesmere Island and Greenland, across which a passage could be made to the NORTH POLE. Over the next few years, he held lec-tures and made personal appearances to raise support for his own Arctic expedition. He also wrote an account of his earlier experience, entitled *An Arctic Boat Journey,* published in 1860.

With the financial backing of Henry Grinnell, the AMERICAN GEOGRAPHICAL SOCIETY, and others, Hayes was able to launch his attempt on the North Pole in 1860. He acquired a schooner, the *United States,* and, with a 14-man crew, sailed from Boston on July 9, 1860, heading for Baffin Bay and the Greenland coast. He recruited Inuit as hunters and dogsled handlers at Upernavik, then continued north-ward, hoping to reach Kane Basin and Smith Sound for a push to the polar sea before ice blocked his way. By the time he reached Hartstene Bay, however, it became apparent that further progress by ship would not be possible until the fol-lowing spring. He put in at a harbor he called Port Foulke after one of his backers, and established winter headquarters.

Hayes and some of his party undertook inland explo-rations of the Greenland ice cap, examining a region that at one point proved to be at least 5,000 feet thick. Over the winter, disease killed most of the dogs. During an attempt to reach an Inuit village near what is now Thule Air Force Base for more dogs, two of his party perished, including the ex-pedition's astronomer.

Despite the setbacks, Hayes set out with three other men in April 1861, in an attempt to reach a point above Kane Basin, where he was convinced he could find an entrance to the open polar sea. Equipped with dog sledges and a portable metal boat, the small party proceeded northward along the coast of Ellesmere Island and entered the southern end of Kennedy Channel, where the apparent southward drift of ice indicated an outflow of the polar sea. Hayes climbed a peak at Cape Josiah Good. He believed he could see open water far in the distance, but he probably saw the sky appearing to meet the frozen expanse to the north. He then continued up Kennedy Channel and, in May 1861, he reached a large inlet, which he called Lady Franklin Bay, after Franklin's widow JANE FRANKLIN. Because of the PACK ICE, the route north-ward was blocked. Although Hayes calculated this location to be 81°35' north latitude, he was unable to make an accu-rate determination because of the death of his astronomer the previous winter. Subsequent explorers put his farthest point north at 80°14' north latitude, not quite the record for that time as Hayes's own reading indicated.

Hayes and his expedition left on the homeward voyage on July 14, 1861, surveying en route the west shore of Smith Sound around Cape Isabella. The party then headed southward into Baffin Bay. Following a stopover at Halifax, Nova Scotia, for repairs, Hayes arrived back in Boston in October 1861.

With the Civil War under way, Hayes donated his ship to the government and enlisted in the Union army as a surgeon, serving at a military hospital in Philadelphia. He reached the rank of brevet colonel by the war's end. Convinced that he had reached the edge of the polar sea, he set down his convictions in his 1867 book *The Open Polar Sea.*

Hayes undertook another Arctic trip in 1869; he accompanied the artist William Bradford on a voyage to Greenland, an experience Hayes described in his book *Land of Desolation,* published in 1871.

Passed over for command of the *Polaris* expedition in 1870 in favor of CHARLES FRANCIS HALL, Hayes settled in New York City. He later served in the New York State legislature, becoming an active proponent of the first Hudson River tunnel project.

Isaac Hayes's ideas about an open polar sea were proven erroneous when ROBERT EDWIN PEARY trekked across the frozen Arctic Ocean to reach the North Pole in 1909. Yet his techniques of establishing base camps and using Inuit hunters in order to survive several consecutive Arctic seasons were adopted by Peary and other explorers.

Hearne, Samuel (1745–1792) *British fur trader, explorer in northern Canada*

Born in London, England, Samuel Hearne entered the Royal Navy when he was just 11 years old and participated in the Seven Years War of 1756–63. In 1766, he joined the HUDSON'S BAY COMPANY and sailed to the company's post, Fort Prince of Wales (present-day Fort Churchill), on the southwest shore of HUDSON BAY.

In November 1769, Hearne led an expedition north from Fort Prince of Wales in search of a river that, according to Indian reports, emptied into the ocean. Indians of the region also described the area around the river as rich in copper deposits. Hudson's Bay Company officials hoped that the Coppermine River was the NORTHWEST PASSAGE through North America and would provide a shipping route to the Pacific Ocean.

Hearne abandoned his first attempt after three weeks because of problems with supplies and Indian guides. His second Coppermine expedition set out from Fort Prince of Wales in February 1770. Exploring northward from the Churchill River, Hearne and his party reached Dubawnt Lake but were forced to return to Fort Prince of Wales after Hearne's navigational instrument was damaged.

Hearne's third attempt to find the Northwest Passage began in December 1770. Guided by the Chipewyan chief MATONABBEE, Hearne traveled northwestward from Fort Prince of Wales. He explored the Barren Grounds north of the lake and reached the Coppermine River. Following the Coppermine as it flowed northward, the expedition reached its outlet at Coronation Gulf on the Arctic Ocean on July 18, 1771. After claiming the coast for the Hudson's Bay Company, Hearne briefly surveyed the region around the river's mouth for copper, but found no significant deposits. The expedition returned southward along a different route, reaching Great Slave Lake in December 1771. Hearne became the first non-Indian to see this body of water. He reached Fort Prince of Wales on June 30, 1772.

In 1774, Hearne went westward from York Factory along the Saskatchewan River and established Cumberland House, the Hudson's Bay Company's first inland trading fort.

Hearne commanded Fort Prince of Wales from 1775 until 1782, when he was captured by the French under JEAN-FRANÇOIS DE LA GALAUP, comte de La Pérouse. After his release in Europe, he returned to the post, staying until 1787.

Samuel Hearne *(Library of Congress)*

Samuel Hearne's 1770–72 expedition traversed more than 3,500 miles of northern Canada's Barren Grounds. He was the first European to cross Canada overland from Hudson Bay to the Arctic Ocean; his explorations proved there was no short Northwest Passage west of Hudson Bay. Hearne's account of his expedition, *Journey from Prince of Wales Fort on Hudson's Bay to the Northern Ocean,* was posthumously published in 1795.

Hearsey, Hyder Jung (1782–1840) *British army officer in northern India, Nepal, and Tibet*

Hyder Jung Hearsey's father was an Englishman, and his mother a native of India. He entered the British army in India and, as a young officer, took part in the Great Trigonometrical Survey that had begun in 1802.

Hearsey first ventured into the western HIMALAYAS in 1808 on an expedition to the region north of Delhi and east of Dehra Dun. On the return journey, he explored the western frontier of Nepal, then headed southward and visited the city of Bareilly, east of Delhi.

In 1812, Hearsey accompanied British engineer WILLIAM MOORCROFT in an expedition that attempted to trace the GANGES RIVER to its source. They ascended the Ramganga River, a western tributary of the Ganges, and followed it northward to Dehra Dun. Disguised as wandering holy men, or *fakir,* they managed to enter Tibet through the 16,628-foot-high Niti Pass near Mount Kamet. Skirting the northern slopes of the Himalayas, they reached Lake Manasarowar and determined that it was not the source of the Ganges River, as European geographers then thought. On the return journey, Hearsey and Moorcroft were held captive in Nepal, but they were soon released and made their way back to Delhi.

Hyder Jung Hearsey's explorations of the western Himalayas and what is now northern Pakistan yielded much new geographic data for the British, who were then competing against Russian expansion southward into the Indian subcontinent. In their 1812 survey of Lake Manasarowar, Hearsey and Moorcroft became the first Europeans to explore that part of Tibet since IPPOLITO DESIDERI's visit nearly a century earlier.

Hecataeus of Miletus (Hekataios)

(fl. 520s–490s B.C.) *Ionian Greek author, traveler in the eastern Mediterranean and Egypt*

Hecataeus was a citizen of the ancient Ionian Greek seaport of Miletus on the mainland of present-day Turkey. He became known in his day as a historian and travel writer.

Some of Hecataeus's work was based on his own travels in the eastern MEDITERRANEAN SEA. In the sixth century B.C., he made a visit to Egypt in which he ascended the NILE RIVER as far as Thebes. Based on this trip, he later put forth one of the earliest speculations about the source of the Nile, theorizing that it flowed from the great Ocean Stream, which the Greeks believed encircled the Earth.

With information from merchants and mariners, Hecataeus learned details about the Greek colonies of the western Mediterranean, as well as the neighboring regions in Spain and North Africa as far as the STRAIT OF GIBRALTAR. His geographic knowledge of the territory east of Asia Minor extended to the Caucasus Mountains and the Caspian Sea.

During the 490s, Hecataeus was one of a minority of Ionian Greeks aware of the great range and power of the Persian Empire to the east. In his geographic work *Periegesis* (translated as *Tour Round the World*), he attempted to warn his countrymen of the futility of rebellion against the Persians, who then dominated the Ionians; he also introduced into a European language the terms *India* and *Indus* as a reference to these far-off eastern lands recently conquered by the Persians.

With the defeat of the rebellion in 494, Hecataeus served as the Ionian ambassador and negotiated peace terms with the victorious Persian forces. Although Hecataeus's *Tour Round the World* has survived only in fragments, it was known to many ancient writers, including HERODOTUS, and is considered to be the earliest systematic description of the known world.

Heceta, Bruno (Bruno de Heceta, Bruno de Hezeta) (1751–1807) *Spanish naval officer on the northwest coast of North America*

Spanish naval officer Bruno Heceta commanded two ships in an expedition that explored the California coast north of San Francisco Bay in summer 1775. His mission had a two-fold purpose: to investigate how far southward Russian encroachment from Alaska had reached, and to seek the western entrance to the NORTHWEST PASSAGE, which had reportedly been discovered on the Oregon coast by JUAN DE FUCA in his 1596 voyage.

Heceta, sailing on the corvette *Santiago,* was accompanied on this expedition by JUAN FRANCISCO DE LA BODEGA Y QUADRA, who commanded the other vessel, the schooner *Sonora.* Upon reaching the latitude where Fuca had reportedly located the entrance to an inland passage leading to the Great Lakes, they found only a bay. Soon afterward, on July 14, 1775, they made a landing on the coast of what is now Washington State, at a point north of what later came to be called Grays Harbor, the first time Europeans had set foot on the shores of what is now the state of Washington. Once ashore, seven of Heceta's men were killed in an attack by Indians. Heceta claimed the region for Spain, naming the spot Point of the Martyrs (Punta de los Martires) in honor of the men he had lost. It was later renamed Point Grenville by British navigator GEORGE VANCOUVER.

Although Heceta and his expedition made other landings along the coast, they were deterred from exploring inland by Indian hostility and decided to continue the coastal reconnaissance northward by sea. While Bodega y Quadra managed to reach as far as the Gulf of Alaska, Heceta was forced to turn back off Vancouver Island, when his ship started to take on water and his crew was stricken with SCURVY. On the voyage southward, heavy fog hindered a close examination of the shoreline. On August 17, 1775, Heceta reached a large inlet at 46°17' north latitude, which he called Assumption Bay. By that time, his crew had become so weakened by scurvy that he dared not drop anchor, fearing they would not have the strength to raise it. He did remain in the bay long enough to detect strong currents, leading him to believe that he was opposite the mouth of a great river or passage to another great body of water. He named the points at the entrance to the bay Cape San Roque and Cape Frondoso (now known as Cape Disappointment and Cape Adams). The currents soon drove Heceta's ship out to sea, from where he headed southward to Mexico.

Bruno Heceta turned out to be correct in his speculations about the currents. What he had unwittingly detected was the mouth of what later came to be known as the COLUMBIA RIVER, the location of which was not confirmed until the explorations of ROBERT GRAY and WILLIAM ROBERT BROUGHTON in 1792.

Hedin, Sven Anders (Sven Anders von Hedin)

(1865–1952)   *Swedish explorer in central Asia*

Sven Hedin was born in Stockholm, Sweden. In 1879, at the age of 14, he was inspired to dedicate his life to exploration, reportedly on witnessing the triumphant return of NILS ADOLF ERIK NORDENSKJÖLD to Stockholm after the completion of the first successful voyage through the NORTHEAST PASSAGE.

Soon after his graduation from a Stockholm secondary school in 1885, Hedin made his first trip to central Asia, traveling to Baku, on the west shore of the Caspian Sea, where he had been engaged as a tutor for the son of a Swedish engineer working in the region's oilfields. The next year, he embarked on a series of overland journeys across Persia (present-day Iran), traveling by horseback southward from Teheran to the Persian Gulf, then heading northward to Baghdad before returning to Teheran and finally Europe the following year.

Hedin attended the University of Uppsala in Sweden, then completed his formal education in Berlin, studying under the German explorer of Asia FERDINAND PAUL WILHELM VON RICHTHOFEN. In addition to the geography, geology, and ethnology of central Asia, Hedin also studied central Asian archaeology. He became conversant in the Persian language, an ability that, in 1890, led to an appointment as interpreter for the Swedish diplomatic delegation to the court of the shah of Persia in Teheran.

Hedin remained with the Swedish embassy in Teheran for less than a year. In 1891, he embarked on a reconnaissance to the east, traveling across northern Persian into Russian Turkestan. He visited the ancient city of Samarkand and eventually reached the caravan trade center at Kashgar on the western edge of Chinese Turkestan. His journey also took him across the Kara-Kum desert to the city of Bukhara.

Hedin returned to Sweden in spring 1891. He soon organized his first scientific expedition into central Asia. He traveled across Russia to Tashkent, and, in winter 1893–94, he crossed the Pamir region. Along the way, he made several unsuccessful attempts to climb Mount Muztagh Ata. Returning to Kashgar in western Chinese Turkestan, he explored the Tarim Basin, then made a harrowing crossing of the Taklimakan desert, during which some of his guides died of thirst. On this expedition, he also came upon ruins of ancient settlements that had lined the old SILK ROAD. Hedin next explored Lop Nor, a large shallow lake in western China, its shifting location long a puzzle to European geographers. He went on to Peking (Beijing), then returned to Europe.

On his next scientific expedition into central Asia in 1899, Hedin descended the Tarim River to its outlet at Lop Nor, producing the first accurate charts of its course. On this journey, he determined that the lake had no fixed site, but shifted periodically as the course of its river sources moved from year to year. At the northern end of Lop Nor, he located the ruins of the ancient caravan way station at Loulan. He headed southward into Tibet but was turned back by Tibetan authorities as he approached the capital city of LHASA. He then headed westward and explored the Tibetan Plateau, becoming the first known European to sight the mountain range rimming its northern edge, which he named the Transhimalaya. Hedin's journey westward took him across these mountains eight times. He again traversed the Taklimakan and finally reached Kashgar. He then returned to Tibet and made an eastward crossing of northern India, descending the GANGES RIVER to Calcutta.

On his third expedition to central Asia in 1905, because of increasing international tensions, Hedin was unable to obtain permission to enter Tibet from British-held territory in northern India. He nonetheless proceeded with his venture, crossing the deserts of eastern Persia. He accurately recorded the LATITUDE AND LONGITUDE of his route, thus making the first geodetic survey of that region. He managed to reach Tibet from the northwest, through Ladakh, and made the first maps of the Transhimalaya region. On this expedition, he was able to locate with certainty the source of the INDUS RIVER, as well as that of the Brahmaputra and Sutlej Rivers. While in Tibet, he visited the Monastery of the Living Dead, produced maps, and made sketches depicting the panoramas of the Tibetan HI-

MALAYAS. He also collected a large number of geological and botanical specimens. In 1908, after three years in central Asia, Hedin returned to Sweden.

Hedin's explorations resumed after World War I with a 1923 expedition into western China's GOBI DESERT. In 1926, Lufthansa, the German airline, commissioned him to undertake a survey of western China in preparation for a proposed air route between Berlin and Peking. On this expedition, a meteorological team accompanying him established weather stations at regular intervals, including one alongside a previously uncharted river, which Hedin named the Edsingol.

From 1928 to 1933, Hedin was in charge of the Sino-Swedish Scientific Expedition. He led a large contingent of Swedish and Chinese scientists, including archaeologists, ethnographers, geologists, botanists, astronomers, and paleontologists, across a wide area of seldom-visited northwestern China. Their findings were published in a 50-volume work not completed until the 1970s. His last exploit in China was on behalf of the Chinese government, in which he attempted to survey an automobile route from Peking to the province of Sinkiang (Xinjiang) in the west in 1933–35.

Back in Sweden in the late 1930s, Hedin became a supporter of Nazism, notwithstanding his partial Jewish ancestry, and accepted an invitation to Munich in 1944, where he received an honorary doctorate. He continued to travel until his last years, undertaking a trip around the world when he was 82.

Sven Hedin's journeys in central Asia took him across a distance equal to that between the NORTH POLE and SOUTH POLE. He mapped more than 6,500 miles of previously uncharted territory, a total that approaches one-quarter of the earth's circumference. His archaeological findings in western China revealed much about the Silk Road, the caravan route that had linked China with the Mediterranean civilizations from ancient times until the early 20th century. Among his many books about his experiences in central Asia were *Transhimalaya* (1909–12), *Southern Tibet* (1917–22), and *The Silk Road* (1938).

Henday, Anthony (Anthony Hendry, Anthony Hendey) (fl. 1750s–1760s) *British fur trader in central Canada*

Anthony Henday, a former smuggler from England's Isle of Wight, went to work for the HUDSON'S BAY COMPANY as a net mender in 1750. In June 1754, the company sent Henday westward from the York Factory post to search for the NORTHWEST PASSAGE and generate more trade with the Indians of central Canada. Traveling with a band of Cree Indians, Henday followed the Nelson and Hayes Rivers southwestward to Lake Winnipeg.

Henday crossed Lake Winnipeg and explored the region between the north and south branches of the Saskatchewan River. He traversed the prairies of Canada's midwest to a point within 40 miles of the eastern slopes of the ROCKY MOUNTAINS (although he did not mention seeing the peaks in his journals). He returned to York Factory in June 1755.

In 1759, Henday undertook a second expedition from York Factory and explored what is now northern Manitoba and Saskatchewan. Three years later, Henday left the Hudson's Bay Company and returned to England.

Anthony Henday explored the Canadian prairies and the Saskatchewan River system, increasing knowledge of the region west of HUDSON BAY to the Rockies. He also brought back the first reports of the buffalo-hunting Blackfeet Indians.

Hennepin, Louis (Jean-Louis Hennepin)
(ca. 1626–ca. 1705) *French missionary, explorer of the upper Mississippi Valley*

Louis Hennepin, a native of Ath (in present-day Belgium), was born in 1626, although some accounts give his birth date as 1640. Little is known about his early life other than that he studied at Ghent and later became a Franciscan missionary priest, passing his novitiate at the Récollet Monastery in Béthune in present-day France. In 1675, he sailed to French Canada as chaplain to RENÉ-ROBERT CAVELIER DE LA SALLE's expedition to the Great Lakes.

In 1676–77, Hennepin served as chaplain at La Salle's headquarters on the eastern end of Lake Ontario, Fort Frontenac. In 1678, he took part in La Salle's expedition to the western Great Lakes. Along the way, he made the earliest recorded European visit to Niagara Falls.

In 1679, Hennepin sailed on the *Griffon*, from the Niagara River, across Lake Erie and Lake Huron to Green Bay, on the west shore of Lake Michigan. On the passage between Lake Erie and Lake Huron, he sailed across and named Lake St. Clair.

Hennepin traveled with the La Salle expedition into the upper Mississippi Valley in 1680. That spring, from Fort Crèvecoeur (present-day Peoria, Illinois), La Salle sent Hennepin and MICHEL ACO to search for the source of the MISSISSIPPI RIVER. They also planned to establish a trading post at the mouth of the Wisconsin River. Hennepin and Aco descended the Illinois to the Mississippi, then followed that river into the Minnesota River, exploring parts of present-day Wisconsin and Minnesota.

While seeking the source of the Mississippi, Hennepin and Aco were captured by Sioux (Dakota, Lakota, Nakota) Indians. During his captivity, Hennepin visited the region of present-day Minneapolis, Minnesota, and named the Falls of St. Anthony.

In fall 1680, Hennepin and Aco were rescued by French explorer DANIEL GREYSOLON DULUTH at Mille Lacs Lake, Minnesota. From eastern Minnesota, they traveled with Duluth to Mackinac, where they spent the winter. In 1682, Hennepin returned to France. He died sometime after 1701.

Hennepin's 1683 book *Description de la Louisiane* includes the first written description of Niagara Falls. In his later literary efforts, Hennepin erroneously stated that he, and not La Salle, led the first successful expedition to the mouth of the Mississippi River. His writings, despite their inaccuracies and exaggerations, stimulated further European interest in the exploration of the upper Mississippi region.

Henry, Alexander (the elder) (1739–1824)
British-American fur trader in Canada, uncle of Alexander Henry (the younger)

Alexander Henry was a native of New Brunswick, New Jersey. He served under General Jeffrey Amherst in the French and Indian War of 1754–63. In 1761, he traveled to northern Lake Michigan to assume control of the former French fur-trading posts at Mackinac.

In 1763, during the rebellion of Great Lakes tribes under the Ottawa chief Pontiac, Henry was taken prisoner following an attack on Fort Michilimackinac. After a six-month captivity, he managed to escape and took part in the British battle against Pontiac's warriors at Detroit.

In 1775, Henry left the Great Lakes to pursue the FUR TRADE on the Saskatchewan River to the north. At Lake Winnipeg, he joined with fur traders PETER POND and Thomas and Joseph Frobisher. Henry and the Frobisher brothers traveled throughout the region between the Saskatchewan and Churchill Rivers via Portage du Traite, reaching Île-a-la-Crosse Lake in what is now northwestern Saskatchewan.

At Lake Île-a-la-Crosse, Henry heard reports from Athapascan Indians about the Peace River, the ROCKY MOUNTAINS, and another river that flowed north from Lake Athabasca into the sea.

Henry and Joseph Frobisher departed Lake Île-a-la-Crosse eastward in July 1776. They followed the Saskatchewan River to Lake Winnipeg and crossed to the Lake of the Woods. In October 1776, they reached Grand Portage on the northwest shore of Lake Superior. On returning to Montreal, they sold their year's catch of furs.

Henry continued in the fur trade at Montreal during the 1780s. He helped found the NORTH WEST COMPANY, one of the first collections of traders to challenge the monopoly of the HUDSON'S BAY COMPANY. His nephew ALEXANDER HENRY acquired his shares of that company in 1791.

Henry wrote about his life in the fur trade in his 1809 book *Travels and Adventures in Canada and the Indian Territories.*

Earlier, in 1781, Alexander Henry had contacted British scientist SIR JOSEPH BANKS, a veteran of JAMES COOK's first voyage, presenting Banks with a proposal for an overland expedition from Lake Athabasca to the Pacific coast of southern Alaska, which then was the focus of the lucrative trade in sea otter pelts. Although Banks is not known to have supported Henry's plan, he later encouraged JOHN LEDYARD to attempt to reach Alaska via an overland crossing of SIBERIA. Henry's speculations on the geography of northwestern Canada prompted SIR ALEXANDER MACKENZIE and other North West Company men to explore the river system of what is now British Columbia.

Henry, Alexander (the younger)
(unknown–1814) *American fur trader in the American West, nephew of Alexander Henry (the elder)*

Alexander Henry was a nephew of the fur trader ALEXANDER HENRY. Little is known of his early life.

In 1791, Henry acquired his uncle's shares in the NORTH WEST COMPANY. Over the next 23 years, he established several fur-trading posts in the Red River region of present-day northeastern North Dakota.

The younger Henry eventually managed North West Company posts from Lake Superior to the Pacific Ocean. He drowned while visiting Fort George (formerly Astoria) on the Oregon coast in 1814.

In 1897, Alexander Henry's journal was published with that of DAVID THOMPSON, as *New Light on the Early History of the Greater Northwest.* It contains descriptions of daily life at the Red River trading posts, as well as accounts of life among the Cree, Mandan, and Chippewa (Ojibway) Indians.

Henry, Andrew (Major Henry) (ca. 1775–1833)
American fur trader on the upper Missouri and in the Rocky Mountains

Andrew Henry was born and raised in York County, Pennsylvania. He settled for a time at Nashville, Tennessee, before moving to Ste. Genevieve, Missouri, where he operated a lead-mining business.

In March 1809, he became a partner in the ST. LOUIS MISSOURI FUR COMPANY. Along with MANUEL LISA, he departed St. Louis to the upper MISSOURI RIVER in June 1809. At the site of what is now Bismarck, North Dakota, he established Fort Mandan.

Henry embarked upriver from Fort Mandan in March 1810, accompanied by JOHN COLTER, GEORGE DROUILLARD, PIERRE MENARD, and EDWARD ROSE. At the Three Forks of the Missouri, Henry and his men constructed a stockade, but they were driven away by Indian attacks. They headed southward to the Madison River, ascending it in June and July 1810, then crossed the Continental Divide along the valley of the Snake River into present-day Idaho. At the mouth of a tributary of the Snake River, known as Henrys Fork of the Snake, the party established a trading post.

Limited success in trapping beaver and repeated attacks by Blackfeet Indians made the venture unprofitable and dangerous. Henry left the Snake River and returned to St. Louis in spring 1811. During the War of 1812, he went into business with WILLIAM HENRY ASHLEY, supplying gunpowder to U.S. troops. Henry himself served in the Missouri militia as a major, becoming known as Major Henry.

In 1822, Henry and Ashley founded the ROCKY MOUNTAIN FUR COMPANY and undertook an expedition out of St. Louis up the Missouri. Henry established a post at the mouth of the Yellowstone, known as Fort Henry, where he spent the winter. In spring 1823, he headed farther upriver to the Great Falls of the Missouri with a party of trappers, JEDEDIAH STRONG SMITH among them.

In summer 1823, Henry headed down the river to aid Ashley, whose party had been attacked by the Arikara Indians. He then returned to his fort at the mouth of the Yellowstone. When that region's Indians declined to trade, he headed westward from Fort Henry to the mouth of the Bighorn River in present-day western Montana.

In spring 1824, Henry followed Jedediah Smith and another trapper, THOMAS FITZPATRICK, through the ROCKY MOUNTAINS via the SOUTH PASS, and supervised his company's trapping operations in the Green River Valley to the west in present-day Wyoming.

Henry returned to St. Louis with a load of furs in late summer 1824, whereupon he gave up the FUR TRADE to concentrate on his lead-mining interests at Ste. Genevieve, Missouri.

Andrew Henry played a key role in the first two major fur-trading enterprises to the upper Missouri River and Rocky Mountains. His exploits took him into uncharted parts of what is now western Montana and southern Idaho. His 1810–11 expedition to the Snake River resulted in the first fur-trading operation west of the Rockies undertaken by Americans.

Henry the Navigator (Henry the Navigator, prince of Portugal; Prince Henry the Navigator; Infante Dom Henrique) (1394–1460) *Portuguese sponsor of voyages of exploration*

Prince Henry was born in Oporto (Porto), the seaport on the northwest coast of Portugal. His father was King John I of Portugal and his mother was Philippa of Lancaster, the daughter of the English duke of Lancaster, John of Gaunt.

Henry's early education gave him a background in science, mathematics, and astronomy. In August 1415, he joined with his father and brothers in a crusade against the Moors on the North African coast, taking part in the Portuguese victory at Ceuta, the Muslim stronghold in present-day Morocco, opposite Gibraltar.

Appointed as military governor of the city soon afterward, Henry learned from its Arab inhabitants that it was the terminus for caravans laden with gold, spices, and other valuable commodities then being traded in Europe. By that time, the revival of commercial enterprise in Europe had given rise to a great demand for gold, and Henry saw an opportunity to advance Portugal's prestige and influence by seizing the source of the North African gold trade. The inhabitants of Ceuta told him that the gold originated in the region south of the SAHARA DESERT, along the upper Senegal River. Realizing that his Portuguese forces were not large enough to launch a successful military campaign of conquest southward beyond North Africa's Atlas Mountains, he resolved instead to circumvent the Arab monopoly on the African gold trade with a program of seaward exploration to the regions south of the Sahara along the coast of West Africa.

As a further reward for his valor in the victory at Ceuta, Henry was made a knight, granted the title Duke of Covilhā, and made governor of the Algarve, Portugal's southernmost province. In 1416, he established a naval depot at Sagres near Cape St. Vincent, Europe's southwesternmost point, and began sending out voyages of exploration to the west and south from the nearby port of Lagos. At Sagres, he also founded an observatory and a school of navigation and brought together astronomers, chartmakers, and highly skilled mariners. Among them was the Spanish-Jewish cartographer Judah Cresques, son of ABRAHAM CRESQUES of Majorca.

In one of the first expeditions organized by Henry, two of his mariners, João Gonçalves Zarco and Tristão Vaz Teixeira, discovered the island of Porto Santo in 1418, in the Atlantic Ocean about 700 miles southwest of Portugal. The next year, Zarco and Bartolomeu Perestrelo reached nearby Madeira Island. Portuguese colonization of the Madeira Island soon followed, providing bases for future explorations.

In addition to reaching the sources of the African gold trade, Henry wished to make contact with PRESTER JOHN, a fabled Christian king with a large and wealthy domain in the interior of Africa. It was the hope of many Christian monarchs that an alliance with Prester John would enable them to drive the infidels from the Holy Land, as well as eliminate the Arab middlemen in the eastern MEDITERRANEAN SEA, who then dominated trade with India and the Far East.

At Sagres, Henry's work included the development of improved navigational instruments, such as the ASTROLABE and CROSS-STAFF, along with the necessary mathematical tables. One of the most important developments he helped foster was a program of shipbuilding, which produced the CARAVEL, a type of vessel ideally suited for long sea voyages.

In 1420, the pope appointed Henry as grand master of the Order of Christ, a post that gave him access to great revenues, which he could use to carry on his explorations for the ostensible purpose of extending Christianity. Starting in 1431, GONÇALO VELHO CABRAL and other mariners under Henry's sponsorship, located and colonized the AZORES, making the first recorded long voyages out of sight of land. Henry's program of exploration along the coast of West Africa was initially delayed by the fears many European sailors had about going beyond Cape Bojador (the "bulging cape"), the southernmost limit of the African coast known by Europeans. After 15 expeditions, Cape Bojador was finally rounded by GIL EANNES in 1434. A subsequent attempt to conquer the nearby CANARY ISLANDS ended in 1436, when the pope recognized Spain's claim to them.

Under Henry's sponsorship, AFONSO GONÇALVES BALDAYA also sailed beyond Cape Bojador in 1435–36, reaching Cape Blanco. The next year, Henry suffered a military defeat in a failed campaign against Tangier in which his brother Ferdinand was taken prisoner and died in Arab captivity. Henry then returned to Sagres, where he dedicated the rest of his life to his program of exploration.

In 1441, Antão Gonçalves, who was part of an expedition with NUÑO TRISTÃO, returned from a point near Cape Blanco with a number of black African slaves. They were presented to Henry along with a quantity of gold in return for his freeing of several Moorish captives. This event marked the beginning of Portugal's entry into the SLAVE TRADE, and a slave-trading depot was soon established on the island of Arguin, along the north coast of what is now Mauritania.

In 1444–45, DINIZ DIAS reached the mouth of the Senegal River and Cape Verde, Africa's westernmost point. An exploring party was sent up the Senegal, in accordance with Henry's desire to make contact with Prester John, marking the first European penetration of the African interior below the Sahara.

In 1455, Henry forbade the kidnapping of black Africans as slaves and restricted his mariners to buying slaves from Arab and native dealers. That same year, ALVISE DA CADAMOSTO explored the Gambia River, and the next year, he reached the Cape Verde Islands.

The last voyages undertaken with Henry's support were made shortly before his death in 1460. In 1458, DIOGO GOMES sailed beyond Cape Verde, and in 1460, Pedro de Sintra went as far as the coast of Sierra Leone, which he named after the roaring sound of thunderstorms he encountered there, as well as the "lionlike" appearance of the mountains. Soon afterward, Cape Palmas, on the coast of

what is now Liberia, was reached, the farthest point explored by Henry's sailors. In 1469, Henry's nephew, King Alfonso V, continued his uncle's work by engaging FERNÃO GOMES to explore the coast of West Africa; during this expedition, a point well into the Gulf of Guinea was attained.

Prince Henry's efforts mark the beginning of the great EUROPEAN AGE OF EXPLORATION. He was not known as "Henry the Navigator" until 1868, when the title was bestowed upon him by his British biographer, Richard Henry Major. Known also as "the explorer who stayed home," he was a progressive thinker who emerged from the shadows of medieval dogmatic belief to apply science and practical techniques to the advancement of knowledge about the world around him. The explorations he financed and encouraged had far-reaching results. Not only did his efforts initiate the slave trade, with its great impact on Africa and eventually in the Americas, but his work gave rise to the Portuguese overseas empire that developed after the voyages of VASCO DA GAMA. The advances in ship design and navigational techniques he fostered contributed to the success of CHRISTOPHER COLUMBUS in his 1492 voyage to the Americas.

Henson, Matthew Alexander (1866–1955)
American explorer in the Arctic

Matthew Henson was born in Charles County, Maryland, the son of a farmer. His family moved to Washington, D.C., when he was still very young, and there he attended elementary school. He then worked for a time in a restaurant, and, in 1878, at the age of 12, he embarked on a career as a merchant seaman.

Aboard the *Katie Hines,* Henson served first as a cabin boy, then went on to become a seaman. He sailed throughout the world, visiting ports in China, Japan, the Philippines, North Africa, and Europe.

Henson returned to Washington, D.C., after six years at sea. He held a variety of jobs, including one as a clerk in a Washington hat store. In 1887, he met ROBERT EDWIN PEARY, then a U.S. naval lieutenant and civil engineer. Peary soon hired Henson as his valet.

Henson accompanied Peary on his travels for the next 22 years, including a surveying expedition to Nicaragua, as well as several Arctic explorations. In 1908, he sailed to Greenland with Peary and took part in a trek across the frozen Arctic Ocean that brought him, Peary, and four Inuit (Eskimo) to the NORTH POLE on April 6, 1909.

Because he was an African American, racial prejudices led the public to overlook Henson's contributions to the first expedition to reach the North Pole. Nonetheless, he eventually won some recognition through the efforts of his supporters, and, in 1913, he was granted a position as clerk at the U.S. Customs House in New York City upon the direct recommendation of President William Howard Taft.

Matthew Henson *(Library of Congress)*

Henson retired from his civil service job in 1933. In his 88th year, he finally received full recognition for his polar exploits with honorary degrees from Morgan State College and Howard University. The Explorers Club made him a member shortly afterward, and, in 1944, Congress included him in a joint medal granted to Peary's Arctic team. He was honored by President Harry S. Truman in 1950 and was received at the White House by President Dwight D. Eisenhower in 1954.

Within five years of his death in 1955, some historians began to suggest that Matthew Henson had played a larger role in attaining the North Pole in 1909 than had previously been thought, some even proposing that he had arrived there as much as an hour before Peary. Others have shed doubts on this speculation, maintaining that Henson had no knowledge of navigation and that only Peary was equipped to determine the exact location of the North Pole. Henson's account of the expedition, *A Negro Explorer at the North*

Pole, was first published in 1912. A later work, *Dark Companion*, written by Henson with Bradley Robinson, first appeared in 1947.

Herbert, Thomas (fl. 1620s) *English traveler, writer in Persia*

In 1627, Englishman Thomas Herbert undertook a journey to Persia (present-day Iran) accompanied by England's ambassador to the shah, Sir Dodmore Cotton, and the shah's own ambassador to England, Robert Sherley, an Englishman in Persian service and younger brother of SIR ANTHONY SHERLEY. Five years earlier, a combined English and Persian force had driven the Portuguese from the port of Hormuz. With increased English commercial interest in India in the early 17th century, Persia, with its strategic position midway between lands of the eastern MEDITERRANEAN SEA and India, was becoming a center of interest for English traders and diplomats.

Both of Herbert's English traveling companions died at Qazvin in northwestern Persia, soon after their arrival in the country. Yet Herbert continued on by himself, traveling throughout Persia, from Bandar Abbas, near Hormuz, to the capital city at Esfahan in the center of the country.

Thomas Herbert's travels in Persia took him across large expanses of territory unknown to Europeans. He remained in Persia until 1629, and upon his return to England he recounted his experiences in the book *Description of the Persian Monarchy* (also known as *A Relation of Some Years Travaile*). First published in 1634, it was widely read and became a basic sourcebook for information on Persia.

Herjulfsson, Bjarni (Bjarni Herjolfsson, Bjarne Herjolfsson) (fl. 980s) *Norse mariner in Iceland, Greenland, and North America*

Bjarni Herjulfsson was the son of Herjulf, who with ERIC THE RED was one of the original Norse settlers on the southwest coast of GREENLAND.

According to Norse oral tradition, as written down in *Groenlendinga*, or the *Saga of the Greenlanders*, Herjulfsson set out from southwestern ICELAND in the summer of A.D. 985 or 986 to visit his father at his farm, known as Herjolfsnes, at the Greenland settlement. Sailing southwestward, his ship became enveloped in fog and was driven off course to the south and west, probably carried by the Greenland and Labrador currents.

Once out of the fog, Herjulfsson determined his latitude by solar observations, and, realizing that he had reached a point far south of Greenland, sailed northward. To the west, he reportedly sighted three distinct coastlines. The first of these appeared to be flat and wooded, the second was also wooded but with hills, and the third he later described as mountainous and capped by a glacier. This last he determined to be an island. Although he had come close enough to make these observations, he made no landings. He subsequently sailed northward to what is now Frobisher Bay on southern Baffin Island, then crossed Davis Strait, reached southern Greenland, and rounded its southern tip, returning to Iceland.

Herjulfsson next appears in the Norse sagas in connection with the voyages of LEIF ERICSSON. Although there is no written record, he may have described to Leif Ericsson the western lands he had reached on his earlier voyage. It is recorded that Ericsson purchased Herjulfsson's ship and, in 1001–02, he used it to sail to the shores of what he later identified as VINLAND, Markland, and Helluland.

Historians have speculated that Bjarni Herjulfsson may have sailed along the coast of northeastern North America, and that the lands he sighted were present-day Long Island, Nova Scotia, Newfoundland, and Labrador. In the context of the Norse sagas, he was the first of the VIKINGS, and the first European, to see the North American continent.

Herkhuf (Harkhuf, Harkhaf) (fl. 2270s B.C.) *Provincial governor in ancient Egypt*

Herkhuf held the position as governor of one of ancient Egypt's southernmost provinces during the reign of the pharoah Mernera of the Sixth Dynasty. In about 2270 B.C., Herkhuf undertook a trading expedition up the Nile into equatorial East Africa, which brought back a cargo of ebony, ivory, and frankincense, the latter commodity being highly valued for embalming and for use in religious ceremonies.

Under Herkhuf's command, additional expeditions ventured into the regions south of Egypt, returning with more valuable items from the tropics. He also reportedly brought a native captive from the upper Congo River (Zaire River) region.

Herkhuf's trading enterprises constitute some of the first long voyages to be undertaken by EGYPTIANS and provide an early record of the earliest known contacts between the ancient civilizations of the eastern MEDITERRANEAN SEA and those in the interior of Africa.

Hernandez, Juan Josef Pérez   See PEREZ HERNANDEZ, JUAN JOSEF.

Herodotus (Herodotus of Halicarnassus) (ca. 490–420 B.C.) *Greek historian, geographer in the Mediterranean region*

Herodotus was a native of the Greek city of Halicarnassus on the east coast of Asia Minor, now the site of Bodrum, Turkey. Starting in about 457 B.C., Herodotus began his travels around the MEDITERRANEAN SEA, heading northward along the coast of Asia Minor to the Greek colonies on the shores of the Black Sea. He also traveled into the western parts of Scythia in eastern Europe and western Asia, as well as Syria, Palestine, and Egypt. In Egypt, he ascended the NILE RIVER as far as the First Cataract and visited Memphis, Heliopolis, and Thebes.

In about 447, he went to Athens. In 443, Herodotus traveled westward to the southern part of the Italian peninsula, where he took part in establishing with other Greeks the colony of Thurii on the Gulf of Taranto.

Settling permanently at Thurii, Herodotus undertook the writing of his great *History* (the Greek word for "inquiry"), chronicling the wars between Persia (present-day Iran) and Greece of 500–479. As a background to historical events, he described the geography and culture of the Mediterranean and surrounding regions, based on his own travels, reports from traders, and information from the writings of HECATAEUS OF MILETUS.

Herodotus wrote in detail about the great Persian Empire to the east, stretching as far as the INDUS RIVER. He described the great interior highway system, the Persian Royal Road, which connected the cities of the empire. The lands beyond the INDUS RIVER, he believed, were not inhabited by people, but by giant animals and birds. Herodotus also related accounts of Persian explorations, including one of a voyage made by SCYLAX, a Greek mariner in the service of Persian ruler Darius I, who descended the Indus and sailed along the coast of the Persian Gulf and Arabian Sea to the mouth of the RED SEA.

Concerning Africa, Herodotus told the story of five North African Berber princes who journeyed southward across the SAHARA DESERT and came upon a great eastward-flowing river, probably the NIGER RIVER, although Herodotus wrote that it was the source of the Nile in the region around Lake Chad. Herodotus also related that, in about 600, NECHO II, pharaoh of Egypt, had commissioned Phoenicians to undertake a voyage from the Red Sea, southward around Africa. After three years, they had returned to Egypt by way of the STRAIT OF GIBRALTAR, thus completing a circumnavigation of the continent. Herodotus also wrote of another voyage undertaken by a Persian prince who, after passing westward through the Strait of Gibraltar, explored the coast of West Africa and returned with reports of the trade in gold among the natives south of the Sahara.

Among other peoples, Herodotus identified the Scythians, the early nomadic dwellers of the central Asian steppes, and may have made one of the earliest Western references to the Chinese beyond. He also correctly identified the Caspian Sea as a landlocked lake.

Herodotus's writings had a great influence on classical thinking. A century after his death, his *History* helped inspire ALEXANDER THE GREAT's campaign of conquest eastward across Persia and western India. With only limited sources, Herodotus presented a remarkably accurate view of the world. He correctly put forth the idea that the Earth was a sphere, rather than a flat disk, as many of his contemporaries believed. He also correctly surmised that there was a southern limit to Africa. He is sometimes referred to as the "father of history."

Heyerdahl, Thor (1914–2002)

Norwegian anthropologist, zoologist in the Pacific and Atlantic

Thor Heyerdahl was born in Larvik, Norway. At the University of Oslo, he specialized in zoology and geography.

In 1937–38, while studying marine life and its transoceanic origins in Polynesia, specifically on Tahiti and Fatu Hiva of the Marquesas Islands, Heyerdahl became interested in the origins of the Polynesians. Because of easterly OCEAN CURRENTS and winds, he became convinced that the islands' inhabitants had arrived from North America, like the flora and fauna, as opposed to paddling against the current from Southeast Asia to the west. In 1940–41, he spent time in British Columbia and studied Native Americans of the Pacific coast. He developed his theory that the South Pacific islands had been reached by two waves of peoples: The first had arrived at Polynesia from Peru via Easter Island by balsa RAFT; the second, centuries later, had arrived at the HAWAIIAN ISLANDS by large double-CANOE from British Columbia.

Heyerdahl's studies were interrupted by World War II in which he served with the Free Norwegian forces as a parachutist. Afterward, along with five companions, he built the balsa raft *Kon-Tiki,* based on an ancient South American design and in 1947, sailed across 4,300 miles of the Pacific Ocean from Callao, Peru, to the Tuamotu Archipelago of Polynesia in 101 days. In 1954, Heyerdahl led the Norwegian Archaeological Expedition to the Galapagos Islands and examined Inca and pre-Inca Indian artifacts. In 1955–56, he led an archaeological expedition to Easter Island, further developing his eastern migration theory.

Continuing his study of ancient navigation, Heyerdahl also developed the theory that ancient Egyptians traveled across the Atlantic Ocean to South America and perhaps founded cultures there or passed on knowledge. He built a papyrus boat made of reeds based on an ancient Egyptian design. In 1969, in an attempt to follow currents from North Africa to the Americas, the *Ra I* broke up and sank after 2,000 miles. In 1970, Heyerdahl and a crew of six aboard the *Ra II* set out from Safi, Morocco, and reached the island of Barbados in 57 days.

In the late 1970s, Heyerdahl began a 6,200-mile journey from Iraq to the Indian Ocean in a reed boat, the *Tigris,* to demonstrate a possible route used by the Sumerians of Mesopotamia (making up parts of present-day Iraq and

Thor Heyerdahl *(Library of Congress)*

Syria) some 5,000 years ago, but warfare in Ethiopia prevented him from passing the port of Massawa. He participated in an expedition to the Tigris River in the Middle East in 1977, as well as three expeditions to the Maldive Islands in the 1980s.

Heyerdahl's books include *American Indians in the Pacific* (1952), *Kon-Tiki* (1948), *Aku-Aku, the Secret of Easter Island* (1957), *Sea Routes to Polynesia* (1967), and *The Ra Expeditions* (1967). His documentary film of the *Kon-Tiki* voyage won an Academy Award in 1951.

Thor Heyerdahl's theories on Pacific migrations are now supported by many scholars. Moreover, his *Ra* expeditions proved that vessels built in ancient times, long before the EUROPEAN AGE OF EXPLORATION, could have made Atlantic crossings.

Hillary, Sir Edmund Percival (1919–   )
New Zealander mountain climber on Mount Everest in the Himalayas, explorer in the Antarctic

Born and raised in Auckland, NEW ZEALAND, Edmund Hillary served in the Royal New Zealand Air Force during World War II. A beekeeper by profession, he pursued MOUNTAIN CLIMBING as a hobby in New Zealand's Southern Alps. He also climbed peaks in the Alps of Europe.

In 1951 and 1952, Hillary participated in two British reconnaissance expeditions to the HIMALAYAS. Afterward, Colonel John Hunt invited him to join the British Mount Everest Expedition, sponsored by the Joint Himalayan Committee of the Alpine Club of Great Britain and the ROYAL GEOGRAPHICAL SOCIETY, as one of the chief climbers. On May 29, 1953, Hillary and the Nepalese mountaineer TENZING NORGAY, with the help of teammates, became the first men to reach the summit of MOUNT EVEREST, the highest peak in the world at 29,028 feet above sea level. They reached the top via the southeast. The climb back down the peak was as treacherous as the ascent. Hillary and Hunt earned knighthoods that same year for their accomplishment; Tenzing received a commendation, the highest possible citation for a non-British national.

In 1955, Hillary was appointed leader of the New Zealand party of the Commonwealth Trans-Antarctic Expedition, headed by the Englishman SIR VIVIAN ERNEST FUCHS. In 1957, he led a five-man team from the Ross Sea across Antarctica by dogsled and snow tractors and reached the SOUTH POLE on January 4, 1958, 15 days before Fuchs's team, which was traveling from the Weddell Sea. These were the first overland journeys to the South Pole since the simultaneous expeditions of ROALD ENGELBREGT GRAVNING AMUNDSEN and ROBERT FALCON SCOTT in 1910–12. Hillary and Fuchs's teams crossed to the Ross Sea together, arriving in March 1958.

Hillary returned to the Himalayas for other expeditions. He climbed Mount Herschel at 10,941 feet in 1967. Ten years later, he led an expedition up the GANGES RIVER to find its source in the Himalayas. His books include *High Adventure* (1955); *The Crossing of Antarctica* (with Vivian Fuchs, 1959); *No Latitude for Error* (1961); *High in the Thin Cold Air* (with Desmond Doig, 1962); and *Nothing Venture, Nothing Win* (1975). In May 2003, Hillary traveled to Katmandu, Nepal, to participate in the 50th anniversary of his Everest climb with Tenzing, choosing to do so there instead of in London with Queen Elizabeth II. The Nepalese royal family sponsored parades, parties, exhibitions, and a symposium on the Himalayan environment and mountaineering. Hillary, who was granted honorary citizenship for his services to the Sherpa community, and Jamling Norgay—the son of Tenzing and also an Everest summiteer—spoke out against the desecration of Mount Everest as a result of commercialized mountaineering.

Sir Edmund Hillary is assured his place in the history of world exploration as one of the two men first to reach the top of Mount Everest, as well as for his overland journey to the South Pole. He is also known for his work on behalf of the Nepalese people and the protection of Nepalese lands.

Edmund Hillary *(Library of Congress)*

Himilco (fl. 450s B.C.) *Carthaginian mariner on the Atlantic coast of western Europe, possibly brother of Hanno* Himilco was a Carthaginian seafarer and, according to some sources, the son of Hamilcar, who invaded Sicily, and the brother of HANNO, who explored the coast of West Africa. In about 450 B.C., the same period as Hanno's voyage, Himilco commanded a fleet that sailed westward in the MEDITERRANEAN SEA from Carthage, near present-day Tunis on the coast of North Africa, then passed through the STRAIT OF GIBRALTAR to the Carthaginian colony at Gades (Cádiz) in southernmost Spain.

Himilco sailed northward in the Atlantic Ocean along the Spanish and French coasts seeking to obtain tin, which was then mined in northwestern Spain and in southwestern Britain. While some scholars believe he reached only as far as Cape Finisterre, the northwestern tip of the Iberian Peninsula, others speculate that he made landings on the Brittany coast of northern France and visited Britain and Ireland.

Himilco returned to Carthage after a voyage of four months. While no contemporary account of the expedition survived, the details of it were later incorporated by the Roman poet Avienus in his *Ora Maritime,* written in about A.D. 400. According to Avienus, the Carthaginians traveled through becalmed waters thick with seaweed, leading some scholars to suggest that Himilco had traveled as far as the Sargasso Sea, south of the AZORES. The Roman poet goes on to describe Himilco's encounters with sea monsters, which many believe were actually whales sighted in the Bay of Biscay. At that time, the Carthaginians maintained a monopoly on trade beyond the Strait of Gibraltar, and, in order to discourage Greek shipping from entering the Atlantic Ocean, circulated tales about monsters and other imaginary dangers west of Gibraltar. These fanciful accounts, surviving into the Middle Ages, may have contributed to the fears most European sailors had about sailing into the Atlantic until the end of the 1400s.

Himilco is thought to have pioneered the overseas trade routes between the western MEDITERRANEAN SEA and the British Isles centuries before the Romans invaded Britain and is credited with having made the first recorded sea exploration into the North Atlantic.

Hind, Henry Youle (1823–1908) *Canadian geologist in central and eastern Canada* Henry Hind was born in Nottingham, England. He studied geology and natural sciences in Germany and France, as well as at Cambridge University in England, before arriving in North America in 1846.

Following a tour of Mexico and the southeastern United States, Hind settled near Toronto, Canada. He taught at a provincial school in Toronto, where he also attended nearby Trinity College, receiving his master's degree in 1851. He joined Trinity's faculty as a professor of chemistry in 1853.

In 1857, Hind served as a geologist with the British government's Red River Exploring Expedition. The party, which included Simon Dawson, who was assigned the task of studying transportation possibilities, surveyed the CANOE and portage route between Lake Superior and the Red River Settlement, on the site of present-day Winnipeg, Manitoba.

The next year, Hind led the Assiniboine and Saskatchewan Exploring Expedition. His party first explored the region around the Assiniboine and Qu'Appelle Rivers. The group then ascended the South Saskatchewan River to its junction with the North Saskatchewan and explored Lake Winnipegosis as well as the Souris and Assiniboine Rivers, investigating reports of the discovery of coal deposits. A simultaneous expedition under JOHN PALLISER also studied the region.

Hind next sought additional government funding for an exploration of the passes in the Canadian ROCKY MOUNTAINS. Failing to gain support for that project, he undertook an investigation of Labrador's inland river network in 1861, accompanied by his brother, the artist William G. Hind.

In 1864, Hind became professor of chemistry and natural history at Nova Scotia's King's College. That year, he undertook a geological survey of New Brunswick. Five years later, he embarked on two years of mineralogical research in eastern Canada, first in the goldfields of Nova Scotia, then in northeastern Labrador. While in Labrador, he located previously unknown cod fisheries. In 1890, he became president of a newly organized secondary school at Edgehill, Nova Scotia.

Henry Hind's comprehensive multivolume reports on his exploration and geological surveys of Labrador and central Canada were published by the government in 1860–63. In 1860, he was elected as a member of the ROYAL GEOGRAPHICAL SOCIETY.

Hippalus (fl. A.D. 40s) *Greek mariner in the Indian Ocean, in service to Egypt*

Hippalus was a Greek seafarer and pilot in service to the rulers of Egypt, then under Roman domination, in the early years of the first century A.D. At that time, Egypt and the rest of the Mediterranean world carried on trade with India either through the Sabaean people of the southwestern Arabian Peninsula, or by long and perilous sea voyages along the coast of Persia (present-day Iran) and the Arabian Sea.

Hippalus had knowledge that India was a peninsula jutting southward into the Indian Ocean, and, with favorable wind conditions, could be reached by ship in a direct voyage eastward across the Arabian Sea, although out of sight of land. In about A.D. 45, he determined that the wind blowing across the Arabian sea, known as the monsoon, changed direction seasonally: southwestward from May to October, and northeastward from November to March. Putting this finding to use, he sailed directly from the mouth of the RED SEA to the Indus Delta and southward to the Indian ports on the Malabar Coast. The spring and summer monsoons then carried his ship back to Egypt, laden with a valuable cargo of exotic goods.

Hippalus's journey was chronicled in the anonymous first century A.D. geographic account, the *Periplus of the Erythrean Sea* (see PERIPLUS), and also by PLINY THE ELDER. His route across the Arabian Sea enabled merchants to circumvent the middlemen of the Arabian Peninsula and the coastal points in between, revolutionizing commercial ties between the Roman Empire and India. The southwestern monsoon that carried ships from the Red Sea to India came to be called the "Hippalus," after him. Centuries later, knowledge of these regularly changing winds became critical in the voyages of VASCO DA GAMA and other early European seafarers who ventured around Africa and into the Indian Ocean on their way to southwestern India.

Hipparchus (Hipparchus of Bithynia, Hipparchus of Nicaea, Hipparchus of Rhodes)

(ca. 190–ca. 120 B.C.) *Greek astronomer, mathematician*
Little is know of Hipparchus's early life other than that he was born in Nicaea, Bithynia (an ancient country on the south shore of the Black Sea), now Iznik, Turkey. He became an influential mathematician and astronomer. He made celestial observations from the city of Alexandria in Egypt in 146 B.C. and from the island of Rhodes in about 127–126. The hellenized Egyptian PTOLEMY, who worked out of Alexandria in the second century A.D., was greatly influenced by Hipparchus and preserved much of his research. The only surviving writings attributed directly to Hipparchus are commentaries on Eudoxus of Cnidus, an astronomer of the fifth century B.C., and Aratus, a Greek poet of the third century B.C.

Among his many accomplishments, Hipparchus, according to Ptolemy, determined the distance of the Earth from the Moon, the size and paths of the Sun and the Moon, the length of the year, and the precession of the equinoxes (see TROPIC OF CANCER and TROPIC OF CAPRICORN); created a chart of about 1,000 stars and organized them by magnitude; and devised an early system of LATITUDE AND LONGITUDE. He was also one of the earliest mathematicians to use trigonometry. According to some texts, he invented the ASTROLABE.

Although Hipparchus believed in an Earth-centered solar system, his mathematical procedures resulted in remarkable accuracy in his astronomical observations. His discoveries were important in both navigation and cartography.

Hoehnel, Ludwig von (Baron Hoehnel, Ludwig von Höhnel) (1857–after 1905) *Hungarian explorer in East Africa*

A member of a noble Hungarian family, Ludwig von Hoehnel was born at Bratislava on the Danube River in what is now Slovakia. His early professional career was as a naval officer.

Inspired by the expeditions of HENRY MORTON STANLEY and the interest in African exploration generated by the international geographic conference convened by Belgian king Leopold II at Brussels in 1876, Hoehnel undertook a series of explorations into the regions above the lake country of present-day Uganda and Tanzania. From 1886 to 1889, he and fellow Hungarian nobleman Count SAMUEL TELEKI traveled into what is now northwestern Kenya, where they made the European discovery of Lake Rudolf, a 200-mile-long lake surrounded by volcanic mountains. They also explored the Orno River. In nearby southern Ethiopia, they became the first Europeans to visit Lake Stefanie.

Hoehnel continued his African explorations with American William A. Chanler; they made a south-to-north crossing of Kenya from Zanzibar and Mombasa in 1892–93. In 1905, Hoehnel traveled to Australia and the Far East, subsequently settling in NEW ZEALAND.

Baron Ludwig von Hoehnel's explorations penetrated the African continent north of the usual route from Zanzibar, revealing much about the geography of northern Kenya's Great Rift Valley region.

Hohermuth von Speyer, Georg (Jorge Hohermuth, Jorge de Espira) (unknown–1540) *German official in northern South America*

German-born Georg Hohermuth was chosen by the Welser banking family as governor of the colony of Coro on the coast of present-day Venezuela, land that had been granted to the Welsers by Charles V, king of Spain and Holy Roman Emperor. Soon after his arrival in 1534, Hohermuth organized an expedition to the region of Los Llanos (the plains) to the south in search of the legendary land of EL DORADO and its supposed riches.

Hohermuth's party of 400 men departed Coro in May 1535 and proceeded southward. He explored the tributaries of the Río Meta on the plains of modern-day Colombia. In August 1537, the expedition reached as far south as the site where San Juan de los Llanos would be founded near the Ariari River. From Native Americans, Hohermuth had heard reports of riches in the highlands to the west, part of the ANDES MOUNTAINS. Not finding a route of ascent and facing the hostility of the Choque Indians, he led the expedition back to Coro, arriving in 1538. Of the 400 men, only 90 had survived the trip, and Hohermuth lost the backing of the Welsers and lived out his life in disgrace. The man whom Hohermuth had replaced as leader of the colony, NIKOLAUS FEDERMANN, carried out a simultaneous expedition for the Welsers and managed to cross the Andes from east to west.

Georg Hohermuth, like fellow Germans Federmann and AMBROSIUS ALFINGER, was one of the few northern Europeans to play a part in the exploration of South America and provided Europeans with geographic knowledge of the plains and rivers to the east of the Andes. He is part of the story of the search for the legendary land of El Dorado and the resulting journeys of exploration.

Holywood, John (John of Holywod, John of Halifax, Johannes de Sacrobosco) (ca. 1200–ca. 1250) *English mathematician, astronomer*

Originally from Yorkshire, England, John Holywood was a mathematician and, after 1221, a professor in Paris. Known professionally as Johannes de Sacrobosco, Holywood was among the first medieval European scholars to study the mathematical works of MUSLIMS. In 1230, he produced *De sphaera* (*Treatise on the Sphere*), in which he applied Arabic mathematics to a study of astronomy. His account of the movement of the planets and the perceived movement of the stars presupposed an idea of the Earth as a GLOBE and challenged the traditional medieval view that the world was flat.

John Holywood's theories on celestial movement and the spherical shape of the world provided a basis for the principles of modern navigation and geography that developed in Europe during the RENAISSANCE.

Hood, Robert (ca. 1800–1821) *British naval officer in the Canadian Arctic*

Robert Hood, a midshipman in the British navy, served under SIR JOHN FRANKLIN in his first overland expedition into the Canadian Arctic. In 1819, under Franklin's command, Hood, along with fellow midshipman GEORGE BACK, naturalist SIR JOHN RICHARDSON, and a team of VOYAGEURS hired from the ranks of the HUDSON'S BAY COMPANY and NORTH WEST COMPANY, traveled westward across Canada from York Factory to Great Slave Lake.

In summer 1821, Hood accompanied Franklin and the rest of the party in a journey down the Coppermine River to the Arctic coast of Canada along Coronation Gulf. On the trip back to Great Slave Lake, supplies of food ran out, and one of the voyageurs, driven to cannibalism, murdered Hood. Franklin had the man executed soon afterward.

An account of Robert Hood's experiences in the Canadian Arctic survives in his book, published posthumously,

Narrative of the Proceedings of an Expedition of Discovery in North America. Hood was also an artist, and his paintings of northern Canada's native peoples and wildlife were taken back to England by Franklin in 1822.

Hooker, Sir Joseph Dalton (1817–1911)
British botanist in New Zealand, Tasmania, Antarctica, the Himalayas, and the Rocky Mountains

Joseph Dalton Hooker was born in Halesworth, in Suffolk, England, the son of botanist Sir William Jackson Hooker. He studied medicine, and, by the late 1830s, he had established himself as a medical doctor in Glasgow. He was a friend of CHARLES ROBERT DARWIN, whose views on evolution he later supported.

Hooker shared his father's passion for botany; in 1839, he accepted an appointment as botanist and assistant surgeon with SIR JAMES CLARK ROSS's expedition to the waters around Antarctica. In the course of his four years on the *Erebus,* Hooker conducted botanical research over a wide area of the southwestern Pacific Ocean. On the outward voyage, he visited the Kerguelen Islands in the southern Indian Ocean, midway between South Africa and Australia, where he studied giant sea algae, some measuring over 150 feet long.

Stopping over at NEW ZEALAND's Bay of Islands, Hooker collected 1,700 plant specimens, and, on a subsequent visit to TASMANIA, he made a comprehensive inventory of the island's plant life, collecting more than 1,200 species and greatly supplementing the earlier work of naturalist ROBERT BROWN. One of Hooker's more notable discoveries on Tasmania was a unique species of eucalyptus tree. Hooker also made observations on the vegetation of islands in southern waters, and, one year after his return to England in 1843, he began to publish a comprehensive multivolume scientific report, *Flora Antarctica* (1844–47).

Hooker went on to a long scientific career that took him all over the world. In 1846–47, he was the botanist for the Geological Survey of Great Britain. He was elected as a member of the ROYAL SOCIETY in 1847. In 1847–51, he undertook a botanical expedition into the HIMALAYAS of eastern Nepal, as well as similar research in the eastern Bengal region of India, now Bangladesh.

From 1853 to 1860, Hooker published botanical studies based on his work in Tasmania and New Zealand. In 1855, he became assistant director of Kew Gardens, for which he undertook a scientific expedition to the Middle East in 1860. He succeeded his father as director of Kew Gardens in 1865, and, in 1873, he became president of the Royal Society. His exploration of the Atlas Mountains of Morocco in 1874 was followed by an 1877 expedition to the United States, where he toured the ROCKY MOUNTAINS in search of botanical specimens.

Sir Joseph Dalton Hooker retired in 1885, spending his remaining years at Sunningdale in Berkshire, England. A close associate of Darwin, he applied data drawn from his explorations to support his colleague's conclusions about the origins of species.

Hornemann, Friedrich Conrad (1772–1801)
German explorer in North and West Africa

Friedrich Hornemann was born in the north German town of Hildesheim, near Hanover, the son of a minister. His interest in traveling to uncharted lands had begun in his early teens through reading about the exploits of the French, Spanish, and English explorers of the Americas.

In 1791, Hornemann entered the University of Göttingen, where he studied theology, intending to carry on his father's work as a minister. However, in 1795, just before he was to complete his degree, he asked his professor of natural history, Dr. Johann Friedrich Blumenbach, to recommend him to his colleague in London, SIR JOSEPH BANKS, hoping that Banks could use his influence with the AFRICAN ASSOCIATION to gain support for Hornemann's plan to explore Africa.

Hornemann met with Banks in London, and, by summer 1797, he had succeeded in winning the sponsorship of the African Association for an expedition across the SAHARA DESERT from Cairo to determine the source and ascertain the flow of the NIGER RIVER. He hoped also to locate TIMBUKTU, the fabled trading center of West Africa.

While Hornemann was making preparations for his departure from Cairo, MUNGO PARK, who had also been exploring on behalf of the African Association, was about to leave West Africa for London, having completed his first expedition in search of the Niger and Timbuktu.

In September 1797, soon after Hornemann had arrived in Cairo, an outbreak of plague led to the city being quarantined for almost a year. Unable to leave, he studied Arabic and became acquainted with another German, Joseph Frendenburgh, who had converted to Islam and settled in Egypt. Frendenburgh, who spoke fluent Arabic, agreed to accompany Hornemann as his interpreter.

Although the quarantine on Cairo had been lifted by September 1798, Hornemann's departure was further hampered when, due to the French invasion of Egypt, he was unable to draw funds on his British letter of credit from the local French bank. Finally, with the help of the leader of the French forces, Napoleon Bonaparte, Hornemann was able to leave Cairo in December 1798.

Disguised as Muslim merchants, Hornemann and Frendenburgh traveled westward from Cairo to the Siwa Oasis, at the northwestern edge of the Great Sand Sea straddling the present-day border between Egypt and Libya. They eventually reached the caravan trade center at Murzuq in the Fezzan region of southwestern Libya, where Frendenburgh died of fever.

Instead of setting out immediately southward in search of the Niger in the Bornu region below the Sahara, Hornemann traveled northward to the Libyan port of Tripoli, which he reached in August 1799. From there, he sent back a report to London detailing his progress. After four months, he set out southward with a caravan across the Sahara, and he was never seen again.

Subsequent African Association expeditions established that Hornemann had entered the land of the Hausa in present-day Niger, and had possibly sighted Lake Chad. He had then followed the Kano River northwest to Katsina, and, in 1801, at Bokani in the Nupe region of what is now Nigeria, he had died of dysentery, just short of reaching his ultimate goal, the Niger.

Although he did not live to tell about it, Friedrich Hornemann was probably the first European to see Lake Chad, and, in any event, was the first European to complete a crossing of the Sahara since the time of the Romans. He had made his journey under the mistaken notion that the distance to the Niger River from Cairo was about the same as from Tripoli. It soon became apparent to later explorers that Tripoli, and not Cairo, was the closer and more feasible starting point for an expedition across the Sahara to the source of the Niger and Timbuktu. Hornemann's diary was later recovered and published in Europe. His journeys of 1799–1801 constituted one of the earliest scientific explorations of northeastern Africa.

Houghton, Daniel (ca. 1740–1791) *British army officer in West Africa*

In 1790, Daniel Houghton, a major in the British army, was engaged by SIR JOSEPH BANKS and his London-based AFRICAN ASSOCIATION to undertake an exploration into West Africa to locate the source of the NIGER RIVER and determine in which direction it flowed.

Houghton sailed from England to the mouth of the Gambia River on the coast of West Africa. He arrived at the British trading post at Pisania, on the Gambia, where he made contact with John Laidley, a British doctor who ran the post and who subsequently relayed Houghton's reports from the interior back to England.

Houghton ascended the Gambia River from Pisania. In order to facilitate his relations with the natives, he traveled with a quantity of trade goods. He had also become conversant in the region's principal native language, Mandingo.

Upon reaching Medina, the capital of the Woolli kingdom, Houghton lost a large part of his equipment when a fire struck the city. Nevertheless, he pushed onward to the Senegal River, into the kingdom of Bondou, where he was robbed of more of his possessions by the local rulers. Despite these setbacks, he sent back word to England in September 1791, by way of Laidley at Pisania, that he was near the Niger and had heard reports that it flowed from west to east.

He also learned that the Niger was navigable and soon made plans to travel by ship along it to TIMBUKTU.

North of Bambouk, Houghton joined up with a Moorish trade caravan with which he planned to reach the Niger. The traders soon stole his remaining possessions and abandoned him in the desert region of what is now southwestern Mali, east of the upper course of the NILE RIVER.

In 1795, MUNGO PARK, who had also been sent by the African Association on a similar mission, learned from the natives that Houghton had died near Nioro in western Mali, less than 200 miles from the Niger.

Daniel Houghton was the first European to report accurately on the flow of the Niger River in modern times. The looping nature of the river's course through West Africa had long puzzled European geographers, leading many to believe erroneously that it flowed from east to west.

Houtman, Cornelius (Cornelis de Houtman) (ca. 1540–1599) *Dutch mariner, trader in the East Indies, brother of Frederik Houtman*

Cornelius Houtman was born in Gouda in the western Netherlands. He was the older brother of FREDERIK HOUTMAN.

In 1592, the Houtman brothers were commissioned by a group of nine Amsterdam merchants to journey to Portugal and learn what they could about the newly developed sea routes to the EAST INDIES. Because the ports of the Iberian Peninsula, notably Lisbon, had been closed to Dutch trade after the declaration of Dutch independence from Spain in 1584, the merchants of Amsterdam needed to find a new and direct way of obtaining spices from the East Indies.

In Lisbon that year, Houtman and his brother attempted to acquire classified Portuguese navigational charts detailing the sailing routes to the Indies. They were arrested and briefly held in a Portuguese jail when they were caught trying to smuggle the charts back to Holland.

By 1595, a Dutch trading concern, the Vierre Company, had been organized to trade directly with India and the SPICE ISLANDS (the Moluccas). Its first expedition, consisting of four vessels, was commanded by Houtman, who sailed later that year with his brother from the Dutch port of Texel, having acquired the necessary sailing instructions from Dutch navigator JAN HUYGHEN VAN LINSCHOTEN.

In 1596, Houtman and his fleet arrived at Bantam, on the island of Java, where they succeeded in establishing trade relations with the local ruler. He founded Dutch trading posts on Sumatra and Bali before returning to the Netherlands. On the homeward voyage in 1596–97, Houtman pioneered a new sea route that followed the north coast of Java eastward into the Bali Strait. The expedition was costly with regard to human life, however, with two-thirds of the crew succumbing to SCURVY.

Houtman led a second Dutch trading expedition to the East Indies in 1598. On the way, he stopped in Madagascar and in Cochin China (present-day Vietnam), where he was able to establish additional Dutch overseas bases for foreign trade.

In Sumatra in 1599, Houtman ran afoul of a local ruler, the sultan of Atjeh, and was killed in an attack by his Malay subjects. His brother Frederik was taken prisoner.

Cornelius Houtman opened the East Indies to Dutch trade, laying the foundation for the great Dutch overseas empire that supplanted the Portuguese in the southwestern Pacific Ocean by the beginning of the 17th century. His imprisonment in 1592 for attempting to acquire navigational data is indicative of how secretive the Portuguese were about their geographic information long after the voyages of VASCO DA GAMA, FRANCISCO DE ALMEIDA, and AFONSO D'ALBUQUERQUE.

Houtman, Frederik (Frederik de Houtman)

(1571–1627) *Dutch mariner, colonial administrator in East Indies and coastal Australia, brother of Cornelius Houtman*
Born in Gouda, the Netherlands, Frederik Houtman was the younger brother of CORNELIUS HOUTMAN, the founder of the Dutch overseas trading empire in the EAST INDIES. Houtman joined his brother on a visit to Lisbon in 1592, where their attempts to acquire classified navigational information concerning the sea routes to the Far East landed them in a Portuguese jail. In 1595 and 1599, he accompanied Cornelius on the first two Dutch trading voyages to Java, Sumatra, and Bali.

In 1599, his brother Cornelius was killed in a conflict with the Malayan sultan of Atjeh on Sumatra. Frederik was one of eight Dutchmen taken prisoner whom the sultan did not have beheaded. He was held for two years, during which he studied astronomy and the Malayan language. On his release in 1601, he returned to Holland, and, in 1603, he published the first known dictionary of that language.

Houtman returned to the East Indies in 1605, where he served for the next six years as the first Dutch governor on the island of Amboina in the SPICE ISLANDS (the Moluccas). He later served as colonial administrator for all Dutch settlements in the Moluccas from 1621 to 1623.

In addition to his administrative work in the East Indies, Houtman undertook explorations south of the Moluccas. In a 1619 voyage, in command of two ships, the *Dordrecht* and the *Amsterdam,* he made one of the earliest sightings of the coast of western Australia near what is now the city of Perth. Afterward, while following the coast northward, he encountered a group of hazardous rocks lying about 50 miles offshore, subsequently named Houtman's Abrolhos in his honor.

Frederik Houtman spent his final years at Alkmaar in the Netherlands. Along with his brother Cornelius, he was one of the founders of the Dutch colonial presence in the southwestern Pacific Ocean, which endured until the years after World War II and the establishment of the nation of Indonesia.

Hovell, William Hilton (1786–1875)

British explorer of southeastern Australia
English-born William Hovell was a sea captain. In the early 1820s, he gave up his career and moved to Australia, settling near Sydney.

In October 1824, Hovell traveled southward from Sydney to Lake George, northeast of the present-day Australian capital city of Canberra, where he joined HAMILTON HUME, a native-born New South Wales settler, in an exploration of the region to the south in search of new grazing lands.

Hovell and Hume, accompanied by six convict laborers, headed southwestward from Lake George in a covered wagon. They soon reached the Murrumbidgee River, which they crossed by improvising a raft from the wagon, then continued to the upper reaches of the Murray River. South of that point, they made the European discovery of the Australian Alps, the continent's highest mountain range. They continued along its inland slopes to the Goulburn and Murray Rivers, where they found large tracts of usable grazing lands. Beyond the Goulburn River, they had to trek through rough and wet country, infested with leeches, before reaching the southeast coast at Geelong on Port Phillip Bay, near present-day Melbourne.

William Hovell returned to Lake George in January 1825, where he announced his findings of country suitable for settlement on the southeast coast. Although skilled as a navigator, he erred in determining the exact location of Geelong, mistakenly citing its geographic coordinates as those of Western Port, which is just east of Port Phillip Bay. When the colonial government of New South Wales sent settlers into the region around Western Port, they found not the fertile lands described by Hovell, but a region totally unsuitable for agricultural development. As a result, the settlement of what later became the state of Victoria was put off for a number of years. Furthermore, Hovell expressed support for the idea that the rivers of southeastern Australia drained into a large inland lake or sea in the interior of the continent, a concept that was not dispelled until after the 1850s.

Hsüan-tsang (Hsüan Tsang, Hsüan-chuang, Hiouentang, Yuan Chang, Xuanzang, Tripitaka, Master of the Law) (ca. 600–664) *Chinese Buddhist monk in central Asia*

Hsüan-tsang was native to the eastern Chinese city of Luoyang. Educated in Confucianism and Daoism, he converted to Buddhism and was ordained as a monk in A.D. 620, becoming a well-respected philosopher and religious thinker among the Chinese, known as "The Master of the Law."

As a Buddhist monk, Hsüan-tsang was aware of the need for accurate Buddhist texts from India to settle doctrinal disputes and fill in gaps in religious knowledge; he planned a journey to obtain them. More than two centuries earlier, another Chinese monk, FA-HSIEN, had traveled great distances with the same purpose. In 629, Hsüan-tsang requested permission to travel to India from the Tang emperor but, in keeping with a general ban on travel outside of China, his request was denied. Yet he set out secretly from Lanzhou, at the western end of the Great Wall of China, and headed westward across the GOBI DESERT. Abandoned by his guide, Hsüan-tsang followed a trail of animal bones across the desert. Weakened by thirst, he was saved when his horse scented water and carried him to an oasis. Turfan tribesmen then escorted him into the Sinkiang (Xinjiang) province of western China.

Hsüan-tsang crossed the Tian Shan mountain range and followed the south shore of Issyk Kul, the high mountain lake in the Kirghiz region of central Asia, into the lands of the western Turks, north of Kashgar, where he was welcomed by the Great Khan. He proceeded to Tashkent and Samarkand, into the lands southeast of the Aral Sea, where he crossed the Oxus (Amu Darya) River, then made his way through the Hindu Kush mountain range into Afghanistan.

For the next two years, Hsüan-tsang remained at a monastery near Balkh in Afghanistan, studying sacred Buddhist texts and making copies and translations into Chinese. He then headed southward, entering northern India by way of the KHYBER PASS and the Swat Valley, arriving at Peshawar in present-day northern Pakistan. He traveled across the plains of northern India, and, following the valley of the upper GANGES RIVER to Patna and Benares, he reached the Nalanda, the Buddhist university in Baragaon, where he devoted the next five years to studying more Buddhist texts and acquiring sacred relics, including a hair from Buddha's head, one of his fingernails, and his begging bowl.

Hsüan-tsang next traveled to the mouth of the Ganges and along the east coast of India to Madras. He intended to visit Buddhist shrines on the island of CEYLON (present-day Sri Lanka), but political turmoil led him to change his plans. Traveling inland, he reached the Deccan table land of southwestern India, where he visited sites sacred to Buddhism. In 642, he arrived at Kannauj, the capital of the northern Indian principality ruled by Emperor Harsha, who welcomed Hsüan-tsang as a great religious scholar. He presented the Buddhist monk with many additional sacred texts, as well as an elephant with which to make his homeward journey to China.

On his return, Hsüan-tsang followed the valley of the INDUS RIVER northward into the Pamirs, then traveled with a trade caravan to Kashgar and Khotan. En route, in the foothills of the Pamirs, the party was attacked by bandits, and his elephant hurled itself into a river, resulting in the loss of about 50 sacred texts. Hsüan-tsang had to wait two months for additional copies to be made. Afterward, he followed the southern edge of the Taklimakan desert to the southern rim of the Tarim Basin; he reached the Tang capital of Chang'an (Xi'an) in 645.

Although Hsüan-tsang had defied the official ban against foreign travel, the Chinese emperor T'ai-tsung (Taizong) warmly welcomed him, regaling his 16-year pilgrimage as a heroic accomplishment. He was given a private residence at the Hung-Fu monastery where, over the next 20 years, he translated the Buddhist scriptures he had brought back from India and prepared an account of his great journey, later known as *Memoirs of Western Countries*. He died in 664 from the effects of a bad fall.

Hsüan-tsang's epic journey took him through more than 40,000 miles of central Asian territory. He became known in his later years as Tripitaka, or "Three Bags Full," in recognition of the wealth of religious, cultural, and geographic knowledge he brought back to China. His travel experiences and contacts with the non-Chinese people to the west and south were later chronicled by his disciples, and his adventures became the subject of a classic 16th-century Chinese novel *Hsi Yu Chi*, known in the West as *Monkey*. His efforts also laid the basis for the spread of Buddhism in China and Japan after that religion's decline in India during the early Middle Ages.

Huc, Évariste-Régis (Abbé Huc) (1813–1860)

French missionary in Mongolia and Tibet

Évariste-Régis Huc was born in Caylus, near Toulouse, in southeastern France. In 1836, he entered the Lazarist (also known as Vincentian) order, and he was ordained a priest three years later.

In 1839, soon after his ordination, Huc embarked on a career as a missionary, sailing to the Portuguese colony of Macao on the south coast of China. He then traveled across China to Mongolia, where he spent the next five years ministering to the native Tartar people and learning their language.

Accompanied by a fellow Lazarist missionary, Joseph Gabet, Huc traveled from Mongolia with a diplomatic caravan in early 1845, and, journeying westward along the Great Wall of China, crossed the Ordos desert and the swamps of the Tsaidam region to the western Chinese lake known as Koko Nor.

Huc and Gabet remained at the Kun Bum monastery near Koko Nor for eight months, studying the Tibetan language while waiting to continue their journey. Their opportunity came when a large caravan transporting Tibetan ambassadors on their way back from Peking (Beijing) arrived at the monastery in October 1845, and the two missionaries, disguised as Tibetan monks, or lamas, joined it for the final leg of the trip into Tibet. They reached the capital city of LHASA on January 29, 1846, and, despite the ban on foreign visitors, were at first permitted to stay. After two months, however, the Chinese ambassador, fearing that Huc and Gabet would begin preaching, had them expelled. On their return trip eastward through southern China, they crossed the headwaters of the Mekong and other major rivers of Southeast Asia, and, by the end of 1846, they had reached Macao. Huc was compelled by poor health to return to Europe in 1852, and he left the Lazarist order the following year.

Évariste-Régis Huc was one of the few Europeans to visit Lhasa during the 18th and 19th centuries. His account of his experiences, *Travels in Tartary, Thibet and China, 1844–46,* was first published in 1850.

Hudson, Henry (ca. 1550–ca. 1611) *English mariner in Greenland, the European Arctic, and eastern North America, in service to England and the Netherlands*

There are no records of Henry Hudson's origins or early life other than that he was English and probably from London. By the early 1600s, he was known in England as an accomplished mariner and navigator.

In 1607, a group of London merchants, the MUSCOVY COMPANY, hired Hudson to lead an expedition in search of a NORTHEAST PASSAGE to the Orient. Hudson, commanding the *Hopewell*, sailed from London to the Shetland Is-

Henry Hudson *(New York State Library, Albany)*

Discovery of the Hudson River by Henry Hudson *(Library of Congress)*

lands, then west to ICELAND. He explored the east coast of GREENLAND and made the European discovery of Jan Mayen Island. Sailing eastward from Greenland, Hudson reached Spitsbergen (in Svalbard), north of Norway. Icebergs prevented further exploration to the east, and Hudson and the *Hopewell* returned to England.

The next year, 1608, Hudson embarked on a second expedition in search of the Northeast Passage. He sailed northward and rounded North Cape at the northern end of Norway, then entered the Arctic Ocean and explored the Novaya Zemlya archipelago. Again, progress eastward was blocked by ice, and Hudson returned to England.

The DUTCH EAST INDIA COMPANY soon commissioned Hudson to lead another expedition in search of the Northeast Passage. In the ship, the *Half Moon,* he left Amsterdam on March 25, 1609, sailing northward along the coast of Norway and rounding North Cape.

Near Novaya Zemlya, ice threatened to strand the *Half Moon* in the Arctic Ocean. To quell a possible mutiny, Hudson changed course and sailed southwestward into the Atlantic Ocean. He decided instead to locate a NORTHWEST PASSAGE through North America to the Pacific Ocean, which his friend JOHN SMITH had described in a letter and map.

Hudson reached the coast of Newfoundland and headed southward along North America's east coast as far as Chesapeake Bay. He explored both Chesapeake Bay and Delaware Bay, vainly searching for an inland water route to Asia.

On September 11, 1609, Hudson sailed into what is now New York Bay. He explored the bay and entered the south-flowing river that now bears his name. He continued upstream as far as present-day Albany, where he determined that the river would not provide a navigable route through North America.

After three weeks of exploring the Hudson Valley and trading with the Algonquian-speaking Indian tribes, Hudson sailed the *Half Moon* back to Europe. He stopped at Dartmouth, England, planning to continue to the Netherlands, but was barred from doing so by English officials. Nonetheless, his findings reached his backers in Amsterdam, who established a Dutch colony in the Hudson Valley the next year.

In 1610, Hudson was still in England, where he again obtained the support of London merchants. He was placed in command of the *Discovery* and was commissioned to seek a Northwest Passage somewhere beyond Greenland and the Davis Strait.

Hudson and the *Discovery* left England in April 1610. He sailed beyond Greenland, and, on June 25, 1610, he explored Hudson Strait. Sailing through the strait, he entered a large inland sea now known as HUDSON BAY.

Hudson explored southward along the east coast of the bay, reaching what is now James Bay, where he and the *Discovery* crew spent the winter of 1610–11. The crew mutinied on learning that Hudson had been hoarding scarce supplies of food. On June 23, 1611, Hudson, his young son John and some ailing crew members were set adrift in a small boat. They were never seen again. The *Discovery* now navigated by his second in command ROBERT BYLOT, whom Hudson had demoted, sailed back to England with news of Hudson Strait and Hudson Bay, which the expedition's sponsors believed for a time was the Northwest Passage to the Pacific. The mutineers were imprisoned. Bylot, however, went on to participate in subsequent expeditions, which also failed to locate the Northwest Passage.

Hudson's explorations of Spitsbergen and the Russian Arctic soon took English whaling operations there. His exploration of the Hudson River region led to the establishment of the Dutch New Netherland colony. Moreover,

English claims to the entire Hudson Bay region were based on Hudson's 1610–11 voyage.

Humboldt, Alexander von (Baron Friedrich Wilhelm Karl Heinrich Alexander von Humboldt)

(1769–1859) *German naturalist, geographer in South America, Cuba, Mexico, and central Asia*

Alexander von Humboldt was born in Berlin, the son of a Prussian army officer. From an early age, he had a keen interest in natural sciences, collecting specimens of plants and rocks around his family's home. He was educated at universities in Frankfurt, Berlin, Jena, Hamburg, Freiburg, and Göttingen, concentrating on languages, biology, astronomy, and geology. It was at Göttingen that he became acquainted with naturalist JOHANN GEORG ADAM FORSTER, who had sailed with JAMES COOK on his second voyage in 1772–75. Forster inspired the young Humboldt to undertake scientific explorations into little-known parts of the world.

Following his formal education, Humboldt worked for the Prussian government as an assessor of mines in the Bayreuth region near Freiburg. In 1796, he came into an inheritance that provided him with the financial means to pursue his scientific interests in distant places.

While in Paris, Humboldt became acquainted with the French botanist Aimé Bonpland, and together they planned to journey to Egypt. They were about to embark from Marseilles in 1798, when news of Napoléon's invasion of Egypt caused them to cancel the trip. Instead, they traveled to Spain, where Humboldt undertook a geological survey of the country's central plateau region. Humboldt's family connections led to a meeting with the Spanish king Charles IV, who granted Humboldt and Bonpland permission to conduct a scientific expedition throughout the Spanish possessions in the Americas.

Humboldt and Bonpland sailed from the northern Spanish port of La Coruña in early June 1799. At a stop in Tenerife in the CANARY ISLANDS, they went ashore and climbed the 12,200-foot-high volcanic mountain Pico de Teide. In mid-July 1799, they landed at Cumana on the Caribbean coast of what is now Venezuela. That November, following preliminary scientific work along the coast, Humboldt and Bonpland set out to explore the ORINOCO RIVER from Caracas.

Over the next year, Humboldt made astronomical observations to clarify the geographic discrepancies found on many maps of South America. He also toured the savannahs of the Calabozo region and visited the natural hot springs of the Mariara region. Among the animals Humboldt studied in his Orinoco explorations was the large, swimming, rat-like animal called the capybara, the largest known rodent in the world. He also made observations of the electric eels of the lower Amazon Basin and noted the mass egg-laying carried on by up to a million turtles on the banks of one of the Orinoco's tributaries. Throughout 1800, Humboldt explored and charted the upper Orinoco and Río Negro. His canoe journey along the Casiquiare River from the Orinoco to the Río Negro, a tributary of the AMAZON RIVER, conclusively demonstrated that the Casiquiare linked the Amazon River system with the Orinoco, the only known connection between two major river systems in the world.

At the end of 1800, Humboldt and Bonpland went to Cuba, where they continued their botanical work. They assembled as many as 60,000 plant specimens, 6,300 of which were new to science, sending them back to Europe.

In spring 1801, Humboldt and Bonpland returned to the South American mainland, landing at Cartagena in present-day Colombia. From there, they ascended the Magdalena River into the interior and reached the eastern slopes of the ANDES MOUNTAINS. In his subsequent explorations of the Andes, Humboldt studied the effects of high altitude on the boiling point of water. In present-day Ecuador, Humboldt and Bonpland made an attempt to climb Mount Chimborazo, which, at 20,577 feet, was one of the world's highest peaks. They reached a point about 1,500 feet from the summit, where the thin atmosphere made them weak and forced them to turn back. Nevertheless, they had

reached a height of over 19,000 feet, a record not broken for another 30 years. English mountaineer EDWARD WHYMPER made the first successful ascent to the summit of Mount Chimborazo in 1880.

In his explorations of the Andes into Peru, Humboldt crossed the mountain range five times. He made geomagnetic observations and plotted the line of the magnetic equator, proving that the Earth's magnetic field decreases as one approaches the EQUATOR.

Humboldt and Bonpland followed the ancient Inca road southward to Cajamarca and Trujillo. They then sailed from the port of Guayaquil, Ecuador, and from there to Acapulco, Mexico. In his climatological study of the desert along the Pacific coast of Peru, Humboldt detected the strong, low-temperature ocean current that was later named the Humboldt Current in his honor.

In 1803, Humboldt carried out more scientific studies in Mexico, then sailed to the United States. He visited President Thomas Jefferson in Philadelphia, with whom he conferred on the planned expedition of MERIWETHER LEWIS and WILLIAM CLARK. In 1804, he returned to Europe. His explorations in South America, Cuba, and Mexico had covered more than 6,000 miles.

Humboldt resided in Paris from 1808 to 1827. He worked on his 23-volume *Personal Narrative of Travels to the Equinoctial Regions of America,* published from 1805 to 1834. In addition, he undertook diplomatic work in various European capitals on behalf of the Prussian government and served as the tutor of the Prussian crown prince.

It was not until 1829 that Humboldt made his next scientific expedition. Commissioned by Czar Nicholas I of Russia, he traveled across Russia and SIBERIA to survey Russia's mineral resources in central Asia. His journey took him across 10,000 miles in six months, as far as the Yenisey River and the Chinese frontier at Naryn. One result of the survey was Humboldt's correct prediction that diamonds would be discovered in the Ural Mountains.

In his later years, Humboldt wrote his five-volume *Kosmos* (1845–62), in which he attempted to formulate a uniform concept of nature based on the known scientific facts about the universe.

Alexander von Humboldt was called by CHARLES ROBERT DARWIN "the greatest scientific traveler who ever lived." His explorations were carried out not for commercial or political gain, but for the advancement of scientific knowledge about the world. His studies in South America were among the first to employ advanced meteorological techniques, including the use of isotherms. His geomagnetic observations expanded scientific knowledge about the Earth's magnetic field and contributed to an understanding of the actual shape of the planet. His contributions as the "father of modern geography" were recognized by explorers such as JOHN CHARLES FRÉMONT, who named the

Alexander von Humboldt *(New York State Library, Albany)*

Humboldt River and the Humboldt Sink in the American West in his honor.

Hume, Hamilton (1797–1873) *Australian explorer in New South Wales and Victoria*

Hamilton Hume was born in Parramatta, now a suburb of present-day Sydney, Australia. His father was among the original settlers of New South Wales, an administrator of convicts deported to the colony. In 1812, the family moved farther outside Sydney to Appin.

In 1814, at the age of 17, Hume undertook his first exploration into the Australian bush, examining the nearby Wingecarribee region. In 1817, he extended his surveys to Sutton Forest and the lands south and west of Sydney. The next year, in an exploration west of the colony, he charted Lake Bathurst.

Hume joined JOHN JOSEPH WILLIAM MOLESWORTH OXLEY in an 1819 exploration of the coast south of Sydney, in the course of which they surveyed the region around Jervis Bay. Two years later, Hume explored on his own into the lands southwest of Sydney, now known as the Yass Plains, north of the Australian capital city of Canberra.

Hume's exploration of the Clyde River in 1822 was followed two years later with an expedition across the southeastern corner of Australia with WILLIAM HILTON HOVELL, during which the two sighted the Australian Alps and reached the coast near the site of present-day Melbourne. Soon afterward, the New South Wales colonial government granted Hume a 1,200-acre tract of land near Yass, where he settled. In 1828, Hume helped blaze a road through the BLUE MOUNTAINS, and, in 1828–29, he accompanied CHARLES STURT in his exploration of the Macquarie and Castlereagh Rivers.

Hamilton Hume was one of the first native-born explorers of Australia. His investigations of the region southwest of the original New South Wales settlements ultimately led to the expansion of the colony into what is now Victoria. With Hovell in 1824, he made the first crossing of the continent's southeastern corner. His initial reports on the flow of the rivers of southeastern Australia later prompted Charles Sturt and others to seek their source in a large inland lake or sea.

Hunt, Wilson Price (ca. 1782–1842) *American fur trader, leader of the Overland Astorians, traveling to Pacific Northwest*

Wilson Price Hunt was a native of the Trenton, New Jersey, area. By 1804, he was a fur trader in St. Louis.

In 1810, Hunt was hired by JOHN JACOB ASTOR to undertake an expedition from St. Louis, up the MISSOURI RIVER, to the Oregon coast. Astor had initiated an earlier expedition by ship to the Pacific Northwest, during which Astoria had been founded at the mouth of the COLUMBIA RIVER in March 1811.

Hunt engaged a party of Canadian VOYAGEURS in Montreal. He took the group to St. Louis via Mackinac, Green Bay, and the Fox and Wisconsin Rivers to the MISSISSIPPI RIVER.

In St. Louis, Hunt hired PIERRE DORION, JR., as an interpreter and his Ioway Indian wife MARIE DORION as a guide. DONALD MACKENZIE, formerly of the NORTH WEST COMPANY, joined the expedition. EDWARD ROSE also joined as an interpreter and guide.

The Overland Astorians departed St. Louis in March or April 1811 and took their boats up the Missouri, stopping first at Fort Osage, then at the Arikara Indian villages of north-central South Dakota. English scientist JOHN BRADBURY and American botanist THOMAS NUTTALL traveled with Hunt's voyageurs for the earlier part of the journey.

During this leg of the journey, Hunt had been in direct competition with a group led by MANUEL LISA. At the Arikara villages, Hunt decided to leave the Missouri. He traded his boats to Lisa for horses, obtained additional mounts from the Arikara, and headed overland southwestward along the Cheyenne River, around the Black Hills.

By September 1811, Hunt and his party had reached the southern end of the Bighorn Mountains. They continued westward into the Wind River Mountains, then traveled through Teton Pass into the Snake River Valley.

Hunt explored the Snake as he made his way through what is now western Idaho, partly following the route of ANDREW HENRY to Henrys Fork. The expedition proceeded by CANOE until the rapids proved too dangerous, claiming boats and lives. On foot, the surviving Astorians followed the Snake to the Salmon River, then crossed the Blue Mountains to the Columbia River. Following the Columbia to the Pacific Ocean, they reached Astoria in February 1812.

Hunt explored the Pacific Northwest coast as far as southern Alaska. When the Astoria post was sold to the British-held NORTH WEST COMPANY in 1813, he returned to the East by ship around CAPE HORN, and he soon resumed his business career in St. Louis. The Astorians' 1811–12 overland expedition from St. Louis to the Oregon coast led by Wilson Price Hunt was the first since that of MERIWETHER LEWIS and WILLIAM CLARK. The Astorians made the first known crossing of the Continental Divide by way of the Snake River route. The final leg of Hunt's expedition pioneered the frontier thoroughfare that, 30 years later, developed into part of the Oregon Trail.

Huon de Kermadec, Jean-Michel (1748–1793) *French naval officer in the South Pacific*

Jean-Michel Huon de Kermadec was born in Brest, at that time the site of France's main naval station. He was descended from a long line of Breton seafarers and carried on the family tradition by going to sea and serving in the French navy.

By 1786, Huon de Kermadec was a senior naval officer. That year, he sailed to China aboard the *Resolution,* under the command of ANTOINE-RAYMOND-JOSEPH DE BRUNI, chevalier d'Entrecasteaux. Huon de Kermadec served again under d'Entrecasteaux in a voyage to the South Pacific Ocean in search of JEAN-FRANÇOIS DE GALAUP, comte de La Pérouse, and his expedition, missing since 1788. In command of the *Espérance,* Huon de Kermadec accompanied d'Entrecasteaux and the *Recherche,* embarking from Brest in September 1791. In December 1792, they reached the west coast of Australia at Cape Leeuwin, where a gale soon drove the ships eastward. While d'Entrecasteaux was driven into an island group he later named the Recherche Archipelago after his vessel, Huon de Kermadec found shelter in a bay, which he also named after his ship, calling it Esperance Bay.

The next spring, Huon de Kermadec and the d'Entrecasteaux expedition sailed into Adventure Bay in TASMANIA. By that time, SCURVY and dysentery had begun to take their toll on the crews, and, in early May 1793, while his ship was anchored at Balade Bay in New Caledonia, Huon de Kermadec died of these ailments.

Two months after Huon de Kermadec's death in New Caledonia, the expedition's commander, d'Entrecasteaux, also succumbed to scurvy and dysentery while en route to Batavia, the Dutch colony on Java. Neither ship returned to France, both having been seized by the Dutch in October 1793 soon after news of the outbreak of war between France and Holland had reached Java.

Jean-Michel Huon de Kermadec, one of the many French naval officers to participate in the exploration of the South Pacific, is considered the European discoverer of Esperance Bay.

Hutten, Philip von (1511–1546) *German soldier in northern South America*

German-born Philip von Hutten was a cousin of the noted scholar and humanist Ulrich von Hutten. In 1534, he arrived at the Spanish colony of Coro, which had been granted to the Welser family by Charles V, king of Spain and Holy Roman Emperor, in present-day Venezuela; he was accompanying the newly appointed governor GEORG HOHERMUTH VON SPEYER. In 1535–38, Hutten participated in Hohermuth's expedition to the south.

Hohermuth's and other German-led expeditions on behalf of the Welsers in the 1530s, those of AMBROSIUS ALFINGER and NIKOLAUS FEDERMANN, searched for the Indian riches rumored to exist in the fabled land of EL DORADO in Los Llanos (the plains) east of the ANDES MOUNTAINS as well as in the mountains themselves. In August 1541, Hutten led another such expedition of 100 horsemen from Coro, including a son of the director of the Welser banking firm sponsoring the expedition. Hutten retraced the earlier path he had taken with Hohermuth, as well as the 1537–39 path of Federmann, southward across the plains, further exploring the Río Meta and its tributaries and the Río Ariari in present-day eastern Colombia. Hutten's exact route beyond the Río Ariari is not known. The expedition returned to Coro in February 1546. Although it had had contact with numerous Indian peoples, it had discovered no wealthy civilization that could be exploited. Hutten was killed the following April in a dispute over the colony's governorship.

Philip von Hutten's expedition was the last German-led expedition in South America. The myth of El Dorado would continue to spur explorations in lands to the east into the next century.

I

Ibarra, Francisco de (ca. 1530–1575)
Spanish conquistador, colonial governor in Mexico

A native of Spain, Francisco de Ibarra was among the first generation of settlers to arrive in Mexico after the conquest. As a young man, he entered the military and took part in the subjugation of the Indian people north of Mexico City who had not yet come under Spanish domination.

In 1554, Ibarra set out with a small party of Spaniards to explore the lands above Zacatecas, spurred on by Indian reports of silver mines. During the next several years, he managed to establish Spanish control over the region, and, by 1562, he had established a series of settlements to exploit the territory's rich resources of silver and other minerals. These included the towns of Sombrerete, Durango, and Nombre de Dios. He also expanded Spanish influence westward, founding the town of Sinaloa, north of Culiacán and inland from the Gulf of California.

The territory that Ibarra had explored and colonized was organized in 1562 as the province of Nueva Viscaya, with Ibarra as its first governor. From his settlements in Nueva Viscaya, Ibarra led and sponsored additional exploring parties into the north in search of new sources of mineral wealth, reaching the Sonora River Valley.

Francisco de Ibarra's expeditions extended the northern frontier of Spanish-held territory in Mexico as far as southern Chihuahua.

Iberville, sieur de   See LE MOYNE, PIERRE.

Ibn Battutah, Abu Abd Allah Muhammad (Ibn Batuta, Ibn Battuta, Abu Abdullah Muhammed ibn Battuta, Muhammed ibn Abdallah ibn Battuta, Mohammed ibn Abdullah ibn Battuta, Abu Abdulla ben Batuta Lahuati, Sheik Muhammad ibn-Abdullah, Abu Allah Muhammed ibn Abd Allah al-Lawati at-Tanji ibn Battutah) (1304–1378)
Arab scholar in the Middle East, East Africa, central Asia, India, China, North Africa, and Spain

Abu Abd Allah Muhammad ibn Battutah was born in Tangier, Morocco, the son of a *qadi,* or Muslim judge. Educated in Islamic theology, he supplemented his studies with readings of texts about far-off places, which inspired him to take up a life of travel.

In 1325, at the age of 21, Ibn Battutah left Tangier on a pilgrimage to the holy city of Mecca. He made his way eastward by way of Tripoli and Misurata on the coast of Libya. From Alexandria, he continued to Cairo, then sailed down the NILE RIVER as far as Syene at present-day Aswan.

Ibn Battutah next journeyed to the RED SEA coast, where he planned to board a ship for Jidda, Arabia, the port of entry for Muslim pilgrims to Mecca. At the Egyptian port of Aidhab, he learned that no ships were sailing across the Red Sea to Jidda because of political turmoil in Arabia. He returned northward through Egypt and toured the lands of Syria and Mesopotamia, visiting Damascus and Hebron, where he saw the cave of Machpelah, the burial place of Abraham and Sarah and a site sacred to both Islam and Judaism.

After traveling southward from Damascus and across northern Arabia, Ibn Battutah finally reached Mecca. He then sailed to the Persian Gulf and ascended the Tigris and Euphrates Rivers to Baghdad. From there, he returned to Mecca, where he remained for three years, studying Islamic law. From the Gulf of Aden, he voyaged southward along the coast of East Africa to the ports of Kilwa and Mombasa, then once again returned to Mecca.

Ibn Battutah soon undertook a journey across Persia (present-day Iran) to Esfahan and Shiraz. He again visited Baghdad, from where he traveled to Constantinople (present-day Istanbul, Turkey), then went northward to the Black Sea, stopping at the port of Kaffa, a Genoese trading settlement in the Crimea and one of the few Christian places he visited. He attempted to travel northward into Russia from Bulgaria, but was turned back by cold weather.

Heading eastward, Ibn Battutah crossed the central Asian steppes, into the lands of the Mongolian Tartars, to Samarkand and the country of the Uzbeks. He reached Afghanistan by way of the Hindu Kush range, stopping at Kabul and Herat before making his way by the upper INDUS RIVER into India. At Delhi, he entered the service of Sultan Mohammed Tuglaq, for whom he worked as judge and legal scholar for seven years. He then was commissioned as the sultan's ambassador to the court of the Mongol emperor of China. He left Delhi with gifts for the emperor, but before he could embark from the Malabar Coast port of Goa, he was robbed. Afraid to return to Delhi without the gifts, he sailed for the Maldive Islands in the Indian Ocean, where he obtained another official post and several wives.

After less than two years in the Maldives, Ibn Battutah visited CEYLON (present-day Sri Lanka), then returned to the mainland of southeastern India at Madras. From there, he sailed to the Far East, stopping in Malaya and Sumatra, before finally reaching China.

Ibn Battutah began his homeward voyage in about 1346. Returning by ship from Canton (Guangzhou) to the Malabar Coast of southwestern India, he crossed the Arabian Sea and traveled up the Persian Gulf to Damascus, where he arrived in 1348 in the midst of an outbreak of bubonic plague, known as the Black Death. He arrived back in Tangier in 1350, where he was welcomed by the local ruler, or wazir, who provided him with a secretary, Ibn Juzayy, to whom he dictated an account of his epic journey.

In 1352, Ibn Battutah was commissioned by the sultan of Morocco to undertake a diplomatic mission southward across the SAHARA DESERT to TIMBUKTU in the kingdom of Mali. He crossed the Atlas Mountains and eventually reached the NIGER RIVER, on which he sailed to Timbuktu, later reporting on the river's east-flowing course. His return to Tangier took him across the Ahaggar Mountains.

In a subsequent journey, Ibn Battutah crossed the Strait of Gibraltar from Tangier and visited the Muslim cities of Spain. He also traveled throughout the lands of the western MEDITERRANEAN SEA, including a visit to the island of Sardinia.

Ibn Battutah's travels took him across 75,000 miles in Africa, Asia, and Europe, in the course of which he visited nearly every country in the Islamic world. In the east he reached as far as China, and to the south as far as Mali and the coast of East Africa. In the north, he traveled as far as the edge of the steppes of SIBERIA, and in the west he visited Spain. He was one of the first known explorers of the Sahara. His travel account, *Rihla* (Journey), completed in 1357, became known outside of the Arabic world after the French occupation of North Africa in the 19th century. The record of his travels provides a vivid description of the Middle East, East and West Africa, India, and China in the century before the onset of the age of European exploration. In it, he makes the first written reference to the mountains known as Hindu Kush.

Ibn Fadlan, Ahmad (Ahmad ibn Fodhlan)

(fl. 920s) Islamic scholar, traveler in early medieval Russia and eastern Europe

Ahmad ibn Fadlan lived in the region around Baghdad in what is now Iraq during the early 900s. All that is known of his early life is that he was a non-Arab and established a reputation as an Islamic scholar.

In 921–22, Ibn Fadlan served as a religious adviser on a diplomatic mission sent by the Abbasid caliph of Baghdad, al-Muqtadir, to the lands of the Eastern Bulgars, located near the confluence of the Volga and Kama Rivers.

Starting out from Baghdad, the delegation traveled into western Persia (present-day Iran), then headed northward into the Caucasus, west of the Caspian Sea. They continued westward into eastern Europe, territory that is now part of eastern Poland and Russia. Contact was made not only with the Eastern Bulgars, but also with other Turkic peoples, including the Khazars, who by that time had embraced Judaism. Ibn Fadlan also had the opportunity to observe the culture of the region's Scandinavian settlers, descended from the Vikings. Known as the Rus or Ruser, they had brought their Norse culture with them from the north and were ancestral to some modern Russians.

On his return to Baghdad some time after 922, Ibn Fadlan prepared an account of his travels. Entitled *Kitab* (Book), it details the life and culture of the early pagan Russians and the Turkic people of eastern Europe and western central Asia and provides the earliest record of the region in pre-Christian times.

Ibn Hawqal, Abu al-Qasim ibn Ali al-Nasibi (Abul Qasim ibn Hauqal, Abul Qasim ibn Haukal)

(fl. 940s–970s) *Arab traveler, merchant, and geographer in Europe, Middle East, and Africa*

Abu al-Qasim ibn Ali al-Nasibi ibn Hawqal, of Arab descent, was originally from the Mesopotamian city of Nasibin in what is now Iraq. He was known as a merchant as well as a religious scholar.

In 943, Ibn Hawqal embarked on what turned out to be a 30-year journey taking him through many of the Islamic lands of the Middle East, Europe, and North Africa. He visited Muslim cities from Armenia to Spain, as well as on the island of Sicily in the western MEDITERRANEAN SEA.

In North Africa, known to medieval Muslims as the Maghreb region, Ibn Hawqal journeyed across the SAHARA DESERT, reaching its southern edge, and entered the city of Kumbi in what is now the West African nation of Ghana. He later wrote about the trade in gold there. While in West Africa, he saw the NIGER RIVER; noting its apparent eastward flow, he thought it to be a western tributary of the NILE RIVER.

On his return to Mesopotamia in about 973, Ibn Hawqal wrote a geography, *Image of the Earth,* which revised an earlier geographic study made by the Muslim scholar al-Istakhri. Also known as *Of Ways and Provinces,* the work includes a map of the known world, as well as an account of the culture and economy of the lands he visited. Although mainly describing the Islamic people around the Mediterranean Sea and in eastern Europe, it also provides details on the non-Muslim nations adjacent, including the first account of the lands of West Africa, south of the Sahara.

Ibn Jubayr, Abu al-Hasan Muhammad (Mohammed ibn Jubair)

(1145–1217) *Islamic official and scholar in the eastern Mediterranean and Middle East*

Born in Valencia, on the Mediterranean coast of Spain, Abu al-Hasan Muhammad ibn Jubayr belonged to a well-established Muslim family; his father was a government official. Following an education in Arabic grammar and literature, in addition to Islamic theological studies, he went on to become the secretary to the Moorish governor of Granada.

In accordance with Islamic practice, Ibn Jubayr undertook a pilgrimage to Mecca and Medina in 1182. On his eastward journey across the MEDITERRANEAN SEA, he visited Sardinia and Crete before landing at Alexandria. He then continued to Cairo, from where he followed the usual pilgrim route to the holy cities on the RED SEA coast of the Arabian Peninsula.

Ibn Jubayr remained in Arabia for almost a year. He then traveled into what is now Iraq and returned to Spain by way of Sicily after an absence of three years. He made additional journeys to the Middle East in 1189 and 1191.

In 1217, while in Alexandria on his fourth trip to the eastern Mediterranean, Ibn Jubayr died. He left behind a written account of his 1182–85 journey to Arabia and Iraq, detailing his experiences as a pilgrim to Mecca. Known as the *Rihla* (Journey), the traditional Arabic title for travel writings, it includes a description of life and culture in the Middle East at a time when European influence was beginning to be felt as a result of the CRUSADES against Muslims. It also provides an account of the techniques of seamanship and navigation as practiced by medieval Arab seafarers on the Mediterranean. Ibn Jubayr's career in the government of Granada coincided with the last decades of Moorish domination of Spain.

Ibn Rusta, Abu Ali Ahmad (Ibn Rosteh)

(fl. early 900s) *Arab merchant in eastern and central Europe and Southeast Asia*

As an Arab merchant in the early 900s, Abu Ali Ahmad ibn Rusta traveled throughout much of the Islamic world. His business took him across southern Asia, as far as Malaya and the islands of present-day Indonesia. He also visited the lower Volga region of eastern Europe, where he observed the trade carried on between the Rus, a Viking people of Scandinavia, and the Volga Bulgars, with the Khazars acting as middlemen.

Ibn Rusta left an account of his travels, entitled *Kitab al-A'laq al-Nafisa,* in which he details the geography and culture of both the Islamic and non-Islamic lands he visited. His writings provide one of the earliest glimpses of life and commerce in eastern and central Europe during the early medieval period. They include a description of a Viking burial.

I-ching (Yijing, I-tsing) (634–ca. 700)

Chinese religious scholar in Indonesia and India

I-ching, a Buddhist scholar in China, inspired by the travels of HSÜAN-TSANG, set out in 671 on a journey to India to acquire authentic Sanskrit texts of Buddhist religious writings.

Unlike his contemporary Hsüan-tsang and his predecessor FA-HSIEN, I-ching was compelled to embark for India by ship from Canton (Guangzhou). The usual overland route across the HIMALAYAS and central Asia had become unsafe for Chinese travelers because of turmoil in Tibet and the Muslim conquests of the Pamir region and Afghanistan.

Sailing on a Persian vessel, I-ching first went to Palembang, the capital of the Srivijaya kingdom on the island of Sumatra and a center for Buddhist studies in Southeast Asia. He spent the next six months in Palembang learning Sanskrit, then traveled to the western end of Sumatra, beyond the Strait of Malacca, where he found passage on a Sumatran ship bound for the Bay of Bengal and India. Following a visit to the Nicobar Islands northwest of Sumatra, he sailed to the port of Tamralipiti at the mouth of the Hooghly River, near present-day Calcutta.

After an additional year of Sanskrit studies at Tamralipiti, I-ching set out to tour the sites sacred to Buddhism in the lower Ganges Valley. He reached Magadha, the place where Buddhism had first developed, where he remained for 10 years, studying and collecting Buddhist texts, including as many as half a million Sanskrit stanzas.

In about 682, I-ching returned to Palembang on Sumatra and began to translate the wealth of religious writings he had acquired. In 689, he sailed to Canton to recruit assistants to help him with the task. He returned with a staff of Buddhist scholars to Palembang, where he remained until 695, completing his work and preparing a detailed geographic study based upon his travels in India and what is now Indonesia.

I-ching had spent a considerable amount of time at the eastern terminus of the SPICE ROUTE. In his written account, which survives, he provides a description of the life and culture of the EAST INDIES and the coast of the Malay Peninsula as it was prior to the influx of Portuguese and Dutch explorers and traders in the 1500s. His travels carried on the tradition of Chinese explorations undertaken in the pursuit of religious knowledge established by Fa-hsien and Hsüan-tsang.

Idrisi, Abu Abd Allah Muhammad ash-Sharif al- (Abu Abdullah al-Shari al-Idrisi, al-Sharif al-Idrisi al-Qurtubi, Abu Abdullah Muhammed ibn Muhammed ibn Abdullah ibn Idris ash-Sharif, Abu Abd Allah Muhammed ibn Muhammed ibn Abd Allah ibn Idris al-Hammudi al-Hasani al-Edrisi, Dreses) (1099–ca. 1165) *Arab cartographer in Europe, North Africa, and the Middle East*

Abu Abd Allah Muhammad ash-Sharif al-Idrisi was probably born in Ceuta, in North Africa, although some sources cite Spain as his place of birth. He was a member of a noble Arab family, the Idrisids, who claimed descent from the prophet Mohammed and ruled the region around Fez, Morocco, and Malaga, Spain.

As a young man, Idrisi traveled widely in Europe, North Africa, and the Middle East, ranging over a wide area from England to Asia Minor. In 1145, he became court cartographer and geographer to Roger II, the Norman king of Sicily.

At Palermo, Idrisi set to work on a series of geographic projects for King Roger, including a PLANISPHERE, which projected an image of the celestial sphere onto a flat surface. He supplemented this work with his book *The Stroll of One Wishing to Traverse the Horizons of the Globe,* completed in 1154. Known also as *The Book of Roger,* in honor of his royal patron, it contains a series of 70 maps depicting the known world, as well as a narrative of Idrisi's travels and accounts of other world travelers. In addition to geographic data, it provides extensive details on the social and economic conditions of Europe and the Middle East in the 12th century.

The maps of the world drafted by Idrisi were considered to be the finest made in the Middle Ages. They showed the Earth as divided into seven climatic zones, in accordance with Islamic belief. With these maps, he introduced the use of the grid system into European mapmaking, enabling him to show geographic locations as they corresponded to celestial coordinates. This innovation originated in China and was taken to Europe and the Middle East by Arab navigators returning from Canton (Guangzhou).

Al-Idrisi's cartographic works presented a practical image of the world. Unlike existing maps of the time, which were based more on scriptural teachings than on geographic facts, his works could be used by mariners to determine the relative position of geographic points, laying the basis for the development of modern navigational charts.

Indicopleustes, Cosmas (Cosmas of Alexandria) (fl. 540s) *Egyptian merchant, monk, geographer in Ethiopia and India*

Originally a merchant of Alexandria, Egypt, Indicopleustes, whose name means "Indian Navigator," was a coastal trader along the shores of the Indian Ocean. In the course of his commercial travels, he visited ports south of the RED SEA in Ethiopia and east of the Persian Gulf as far as western India and Ceylon (present-day Sri Lanka).

In about 548, Indicopleustes converted to Christianity and became a monk, retiring to a monastery on Mount Sinai. He then undertook a 12-volume illustrated work entitled *Topographia Christiana* (Christian topography), in which he attempted to reconcile Christian religious teachings with concepts about world geography.

Although non-Christian writers had previously described the Earth as a sphere, Indicopleustes refuted these ideas, putting forth the belief that the world is a rectangular plane upon which rests the sky and the heavens. Basing his views on St. Paul the Apostle, who had written in the Bible that the Tabernacle of Moses is a true model of the world, Indicopleustes concluded that the world must be flat, like a table. He went on to describe the four great rivers of the Earth—the INDUS RIVER, NILE RIVER, Tigris River, and the Euphrates River—as all flowing from Paradise, and dividing the world into symmetrical quadrants. He supported his theological view of a flat Earth with a map of the world, one of the first Christian maps produced in the early Middle Ages.

Indicopleustes described the trade between India, Ceylon, and China. He was one of the first Westerners to present China as reachable by sea, identifying that country as the ultimate source of silk. He also mentioned Christian churches in India, a report that may have inspired later European missionaries and explorers to seek new routes to the East.

Irateba (ca. 1814–1878) *Mojave Indian chief, guide to U.S. government expeditions in Arizona and California*

Irateba was a leader of the Huttoh-pah band of the Mojave Indian tribe. He was born near present-day Needles, California.

During the early 1850s, Irateba guided a series of U.S. Army expeditions through western Arizona and southeastern California. This area, comprising the lower Colorado Basin and the Mojave Desert region, was newly acquired from Mexico and remained unexplored by non-Indians.

In 1851, Irateba guided Captain LORENZO SITGREAVES in his expedition across then uncharted parts of Arizona to San Diego, California.

Three years later, in 1854, Irateba guided Lieutenant AMIEL WEEKS WHIPPLE and a group of the U.S. Army Corps of Topographical Engineers across the Mojave Desert during the last leg of their expedition from Fort Smith, Arkansas, to Los Angeles, California. Irateba also accompanied Lieutenant JOSEPH CHRISTMAS IVES on his 1858 exploration of the COLORADO RIVER.

In 1859, Irateba became chief of his tribe following the end of the Mojave Uprising. In 1862–63, he made an official visit to Washington, D.C., where he met with President Abraham Lincoln.

Irateba's efforts as a guide for the U.S. Army Corps of Topographical Engineers in the Mojave Desert and lower Colorado Basin resulted in the first accurate maps of the region. The route he helped blaze across the southwestern desert soon led to the establishment of stagecoach and wagon routes providing more direct access to California for settlers and prospectors.

Irving, John Treat (1812–1906) *American traveler, writer in Kansas and Nebraska*

John Treat Irving was born in New York City, the son of an attorney and judge and nephew of the author Washington Irving. He was educated in preparatory schools in New York, and, in 1828, he graduated from Columbia College.

Irving, like his uncle, was interested in Indian life on the frontier, and it was with Washington Irving's influence that he was appointed a member of Henry Leavitt Ellsworth's expedition west of Fort Leavenworth in 1833.

In September 1833, Irving left Fort Leavenworth with Ellsworth who, as U.S. Indian Treaty Commissioner, had been assigned to establish diplomatic ties with the Otoe and Pawnee Indians of the Republican River and Platte River regions. On the return journey across the plains, Irving became separated from the rest of the expedition while hunting and traveled alone to Fort Leavenworth. He returned to New York City toward the end of November 1833.

In New York, Irving went on to study law and was admitted to the New York State Bar. He became a practicing attorney and leading real estate entrepreneur in the city, and also carried on a literary career, recounting his frontier experiences in his 1835 book *Indian Sketches,* followed by *The Hunters of the Prairie,* published in 1837.

In his written descriptions of the Indians who inhabited the prairies of what is now Kansas and Nebraska, John Treat Irving provides a glimpse of life on the frontier as it appeared to the first trappers and explorers.

Ives, Joseph Christmas (1828–1868) *U.S. Army officer, American topographical engineer in the American Southwest*

Born in New York City, Joseph C. Ives later lived in New Haven, Connecticut, where he attended Yale College. He went on to West Point, graduating as a second lieutenant in the ordnance department in 1852.

Ives transferred to the U.S. Army Corps of Topographical Engineers in 1853. That year, under the command of Lieutenant AMIEL WEEKS WHIPPLE, he took part in the government's survey for a proposed Pacific railroad route along the 35th parallel. Ives, in command of an auxiliary force, joined up with Whipple and the main column at Albuquerque in present-day New Mexico. The expedition then explored from the Zuni Indian villages of western New Mexico, to the COLORADO RIVER at Needles, and continued across the Mojave Desert along a wagon road to San Bernardino, California.

In 1857, Ives was placed in command of an expedition to determine the navigable limits of the Colorado River. Faced with an impending conflict with the Mormons in Utah's Great Basin, the army needed to know the feasibility of sending troops up the Colorado and Virgin Rivers to the Great Salt Lake.

Ives and his expedition assembled at San Francisco in October 1857. His group included geologist JOHN STRONG NEWBERRY, cartographer Baron F. W. Egloffstein, and artist Heinrich Baldwin Möllhausen. While most of the party traveled overland to the Colorado at Fort Yuma, Ives and a small detachment sailed from San Francisco to the head of the Gulf of California. Aboard the ship were parts for a small prefabricated shallow-draft steamboat, the USS *Explorer,* which Ives and his party assembled near Montague's Island at the mouth of the Colorado River.

Ives and his party traveled up the Colorado on the *Explorer*, joining the rest of his expedition at Fort Yuma in early January 1858. From there, he and his men steamed northward through Purple Hill Pass, Canebrake Canyon, the Red Gates of the Chocolate Mountains, and into the Great Colorado Valley, where they come upon Monument Mountain.

Proceeding farther upriver, Ives and his men reached the Mojave villages at Needles, where they were joined by the Indian IRATEBA, who agreed to act as their guide. At Black Canyon, about 500 miles up the Colorado, Ives determined that the river was no longer navigable and sent half his party back to Fort Yuma on the steamboat. After exploring Black Canyon in a small boat, he led a party overland to find a connection with the Mormon Road.

In April 1858, Ives and his party reached the floor of the Grand Canyon at Diamond Creek, where barometric readings indicated the canyon was more than a mile deep. They ascended the towering walls of the Grand Canyon by following dangerous Indian trails to the Colorado Plateau. Crossing the Painted Desert, they reached the Hopi Indian pueblos on May 11, 1858.

Ives and the expedition then attempted to head northward into Colorado, but they were unable to cross the desert. Instead, they went eastward across Arizona, through hostile Navajo (Dineh) Indian territory, and arrived at Fort Defiance on May 23. Ives returned to Fort Yuma by stagecoach, then went to San Francisco, where he boarded a steamer for Washington, D.C.

In the years just prior to the Civil War, Ives was an architect on the Washington Monument and took part in surveys in California, Nevada, and Oregon. In 1861, he resigned from the U.S. Army and became captain of engineers for the Confederacy, serving as chief aide to Confederate president Jefferson Davis. After the war, he settled in New York City, where he spent his remaining years.

In his 1858 exploration of the Colorado River, Joseph C. Ives and his party became the first non-Indians known to have set foot on the floor of the Grand Canyon. His route from Black Canyon to the Hopi pueblos traced that taken by Father FRANCISCO TOMÁS HERMENEGILDO GARCÉS in 1776. John Strong Newberry, the expedition's geologist, made stratigraphic studies of the Grand Canyon, which greatly increased the geologic understanding of the entire American West. Cartographer Baron F. W. Egloffstein subsequently created the first relief map of the Grand Canyon and the Colorado Plateau. The expedition's artist, Heinrich Möllhausen, produced the earliest pictorial representations of the canyon. In addition to determining the navigable limits of the Colorado River, Ives found a connection to the Mormon Road, which opened the lower Colorado to direct contact with the Great Basin. His official account, *Report Upon the Colorado River of the West* (1862), included one of the earliest detailed navigational studies of the Colorado River.

Izmailov, Gerasim Alekseyevich

(fl. 1770s–1790s) *Russian mariner in Siberia and Alaska*
Gerasim A. Izmailov was a Russian seafarer who sailed the Pacific coast of SIBERIA in the last half of the 18th century. In 1771, he was caught up in a mutiny at Bolsheretsk on the Kamchatka Peninsula along with DMITRY IVANOVICH BOCHAROV.

Izmailov returned to Kamchatka in 1775 on a voyage in which he explored the west and northeast coasts of the peninsula.

From 1783 to 1786, Izmailov served under GRIGORY IVANOVICH SHELIKOV in an expedition to Alaska during which he took part in the establishment of the first Russian fur-trading post on Kodiak Island.

In 1788, Izmailov again sailed with Bocharov, joining him in a voyage to Alaska on the *Three Saints*. They explored the north shore of the Gulf of Alaska and, in a series of landings, left marker plates laying Russian claim to the territory.

Izmailov returned to the northern Gulf of Alaska region in 1789 in an exploration of the Kenai Peninsula, the region around present-day Anchorage and Seward. He continued to explore the coastal regions of southern Alaska until 1797.

Gerasim A. Izmailov's explorations revealed many geographic details and provided navigational data important to subsequent Russian settlement.

J

Jackson, David E. (unknown–1837) *American fur trader, mountain man in northern Rocky Mountains*
David E. Jackson began his career as a fur trader with WILLIAM HENRY ASHLEY's first expeditions up the MISSOURI RIVER from St. Louis in the early 1820s.

By 1826, Jackson was a brigade leader in the northern ROCKY MOUNTAINS, and, at the rendezvous held that summer south of Bear Lake, near what is now the Utah-Idaho stateline, he entered into a partnership with JEDEDIAH STRONG SMITH and WILLIAM LEWIS SUBLETTE. They purchased Ashley's trade goods and took over management of the ROCKY MOUNTAIN FUR COMPANY's fur-trading brigades. The next fall, while Smith undertook his epic trek across the Southwest into the Sierra Nevada, Jackson and Sublette led a brigade into the Yellowstone country, where they witnessed the spectacular geysers in what is now Yellowstone National Park, among the first non-Indians to do so.

In 1831, Jackson again teamed up with Smith and Sublette as an investor in a wagon caravan transporting trade goods across the southern plains by way of the Santa Fe Trail. In the course of this expedition, Smith lost his life in an Indian attack in the Cimarron River region of what is now southwestern Kansas.

Jackson turned his attention to the Far West, journeying to California with EWING YOUNG in 1832, where he bought mules for resale to westward-bound settlers.

David E. Jackson was an associate of some of the most well-known MOUNTAIN MEN in the peak years of the FUR TRADE in the northern Rockies. His career, first as a fur trader, then as an entrepreneur in goods and livestock, reflected the rapid changes in the economic and social character of the American frontier of the 1820s and 1830s. Jackson Lake and Jackson Hole in Wyoming were named after him.

Jackson, Frederick George (1860–1938)
British explorer in Russian Arctic
British-born Frederick Jackson's earliest venture into the polar regions was a whaling expedition in 1886–87. Six years later, in 1893, Jackson undertook a scientific expedition into the Russian Arctic. He explored the tundra region that lies between the Pechora River and the Ob River, south of the Barents and Kara Seas. Traveling by sledge, he explored more than 3,000 miles of territory, across the Ural Mountains to the western edge of SIBERIA. He carried out additional explorations westward into Lapland.

Starting in 1894, and under the sponsorship of London newspaper publisher Alfred Harmsworth (Viscount Northcliffe), Jackson led a British scientific team on a three-year expedition to Franz Josef Land. Explored 20 years before by the Austrians KARL WEYPRECHT and JULIUS VON PAYER, the island chain lies at the northeastern rim of the Barents Sea and consists of the northernmost points of land in the Eastern Hemisphere.

On June 17, 1896, while exploring Cape Flora in Franz Josef Land, Jackson met up with Norwegian explorers FRIDTJOF NANSEN and Hjalmar Johannsen, who had wintered there after an unsuccessful attempt at reaching the NORTH POLE. Jackson took the two explorers back to his main camp and arranged for their return to Hammerfest, Norway, aboard his ship, the *Windward.*

After 1897, Jackson continued to explore the regions of the world still relatively unknown to Europeans, including parts of Africa and the deserts of Australia.

Jackson wrote of his experiences in the Russian tundra in his 1895 book *The Great Frozen Land.* His *A Thousand Days in the Arctic,* published in 1899, provides a detailed account of the Jackson-Harmsworth Arctic Expedition. His 1935 book, *Lure of the Unknown Lands,* recounts all his wide-ranging explorations.

The Jackson-Harmsworth Arctic Expedition of 1894–97 undertook the first major scientific study of Franz Josef Land. Moreover, Frederick Jackson's team was the first to use ponies in Arctic exploration.

Jacquinot, Charles-Hector (1796–1879)
French naval officer in the South Pacific and Antarctica

Born in the Loire Valley town of Nevers in central France, Charles-Hector Jacquinot entered the French navy when young. At the age of 19, he sailed, along with LOUIS-ISADORE DUPERREY, as an ensign on the *Uranie,* under the command of LOUIS-CLAUDE DE SAULCES DE FREYCINET in an 1817–20 expedition to Australia, New Guinea, and the South Pacific Ocean.

In 1822–25, Jacquinot served as an ensign under Duperrey on the *Coquille.* On this official French scientific voyage to the South Pacific, he was also the expedition's astronomer.

Starting in 1826, Jacquinot began his long association with JULES-SÉBASTIEN-CÉSAR DUMONT D'URVILLE. That year, he was promoted to the rank of lieutenant commander and was appointed second in command aboard the *Astrolabe* on Dumont d'Urville's expedition to the South Pacific in search of traces of the expedition of JEAN-FRANÇOIS DE GALAUP, comte de La Pérouse, which had disappeared nearly 40 years earlier. By March 1828, the wreckage of La Pérouse's ship was located at Vanikoro Island. Jacquinot, standing in for Dumont d'Urville, who was ailing from fever, officiated at a ceremony to dedicate a monument to the lost French navigator.

In 1837, after an eight-year period of routine naval assignments, Jacquinot joined Dumont d'Urville on his final voyage of exploration. With the rank of corvette captain, he commanded the *Zélée,* accompanying Dumont d'Urville on the *Astrolabe,* in an effort to locate the SOUTH MAGNETIC POLE.

Jacquinot returned from the voyage in 1840. Soon afterward, he was given command of the ship *Genereux.* He gave up this post later that year after Dumont d'Urville's death in a railroad mishap near Versailles, and assumed the responsibility of producing an account of Dumont d'Urville's 1837–40 expedition, a task that occupied him until 1854. Entitled *Voyage to the South Pole and Oceania,* it was published in 23 volumes with seven atlases.

Made a rear admiral in 1852, Jacquinot later commanded a French naval expedition against Piraeus, Greece, during the Crimean War of 1853–56. For this service, he was made a vice admiral. On retiring, he made his home near the French naval base at Toulon.

In the course of his naval career, Charles-Hector Jacquinot took part in some of the most important French scientific expeditions to the South Pacific and played a key supporting role in Dumont d'Urville's voyage of 1837–40, one of the earliest official explorations along the Antarctic mainland.

James, Thomas (ca. 1593–ca. 1635) *English mariner in Hudson Bay*

Born in Bristol, England, Thomas James was the son of a prominent citizen of that seaport, who served two terms as the city's mayor in the early 1600s. Trained for the law, he went on to become a wealthy Bristol attorney while still a young man. He was also drawn to a career to sea, acquiring to that end knowledge of mathematical navigation.

There is some evidence to suggest that James may have taken part in SIR THOMAS BUTTON's 1612 voyage to HUDSON BAY. Little is known of his exploits before 1631, the year in which he was commissioned by the Merchant Venturers' Society of Bristol to command an expedition to explore Hudson Bay. At that time, hope was still high for the discovery of the much-sought-after NORTHWEST PASSAGE, a water route that reportedly opened up on the fabled STRAIT OF ANIAN and led into a Western Ocean, across which lay the riches of China and Japan. By 1631, a rivalry had developed between Bristol and London commercial interests, both groups sponsoring voyages of exploration to ensure their respective trading rights for any routes or lands that might be found.

James, in command of the *Henrietta Maria,* sailed from Bristol on May 3, 1631, two days before LUKE FOXE, who had been commissioned to undertake a similar expedition to Hudson Bay, embarked from Deptford. More than two months later, the expedition, after negotiating the DRIFT ICE of Davis Strait, made its way through Hudson Strait, and, by mid-July, had sailed southwestward as far as Hubbert's Hope at present-day Churchill, Manitoba.

James continued to explore the coastline south of Cape Churchill. He named the southwestern mainland the New Principality of South Wales, and, on July 26, he located the estuary of a river that he dubbed the New Severn, now known as the Severn River in Ontario. Three days later,

James met up with Foxe off a point of land James had named Cape Henrietta Maria, in honor of both his ship and the wife of England's King Charles I. The commanders of the two rival expeditions met cordially for the next two days, exchanging information on their respective explorations of the west shore of Hudson Bay. Both had concluded that that part of Hudson Bay had no navigable western outlet.

James and his expedition then explored southward along the coast below Cape Henrietta Maria, into an arm of Hudson Bay that he named James Bay (although it had been first explored by HENRY HUDSON in 1610–11). Meanwhile, Foxe sailed back to England in fall 1631, fearing the onset of SCURVY and the prospect of being icebound for the winter. Failing to find a passage along the west shore of Hudson Bay, James probed southward to the foot of James Bay, hoping to find at least a route into the St. Lawrence River if not the Northwest Passage itself.

In early October 1631, James deliberately beached his ship on Charlton Island at the southern end of James Bay, in an effort to secure it against storms. He had his men then built shelters on Charlton Island, where they spent the winter. Four of them died of scurvy; all the survivors greatly suffered from that disease as well as from the severe cold. Despite the ordeal, James was able to record the effects of the extreme winter conditions, making the first scientific observations of the phenomenon of continuous low temperatures.

On June 24, 1632, James took formal possession of Charlton Island in the name of King Charles I. A week later, he sailed northward into Hudson Bay, stopping first at Danby Island, where he found what he believed to be traces of Hudson and his companions, who had been marooned in James Bay more than 20 years earlier.

James did not sail directly to England, but continued to explore northward into Hudson Bay for the Northwest Passage. He investigated Foxe Channel, explored by Luke Foxe the previous year, reaching as far as 65°30' north latitude before ice conditions forced him to return southward to Hudson Strait, and from there to England.

James and the *Henrietta Maria* arrived back in Bristol on October 22, 1632. Soon afterward, he was appointed commander of the British Navy's Bristol Channel Squadron.

With the support of King Charles, James wrote an account of his voyage to Hudson Bay. Published in 1635 as *The Strange and Dangerous Voyage of Captain Thomas James,* the work graphically describes the first planned wintering undertaken by Europeans in the Hudson Bay region. It was an immediate literary success. James's vivid account reportedly influenced Samuel Taylor Coleridge in his descriptions of the icebound ship in *The Rime of the Ancient Mariner,* written in 1798. Moreover, James's scientific data on the effects of extreme cold were later used by 17th-century English chemist Robert Boyle in formulating his conclusions on the relationship between temperature and pressure, later known as Boyle's Law.

Thomas James correctly surmised that no navigable outlet from Hudson Bay existed below 66° north latitude. This report, coupled with his harrowing account of the winter he spent at James Bay in 1631–32, served to discourage further exploration of Hudson Bay for decades afterward. Not until 1668 was the next major expedition into Hudson Bay made, that of MÉDARD CHOUART DES GROSEILLIERS, a fur-trading enterprise. The next explorer after James who actively sought the Northwest Passage in Hudson Bay was JAMES KNIGHT in 1719.

Jansz, Willem (Willem Janz, Willem Janszoon, Willem Janstzoon) (fl. early 1600s) *Dutch mariner in Australia*

An inhabitant of Amsterdam, Willem Jansz became a navigator for the DUTCH EAST INDIA COMPANY. About 1605, he sailed from the Netherlands to the East Indies, following the southern route across the Indian Ocean to the port of Bantam on Java. From there, he sailed his ship, the *Duyfken,* to New Guinea, hoping to locate the mainland of the GREAT SOUTHERN CONTINENT, or Terra Australis, then believed to exist in the high southern latitudes south of the EAST INDIES.

Sailing eastward, Jansz explored the south coast of New Guinea, as far as 140° east latitude. At that point, he turned southward and came upon the mainland of Australia's Cape York Peninsula. Cruising along the north Australian coast into the Gulf of Carpentaria as far as 13° south latitude, he wrongly concluded that the land, which he called New Holland, was a southern extension of New Guinea. He made at least one landing on the Australian mainland, where some of his men were killed in an encounter with Aborigines.

Just a few months after Jansz's voyage of 1605, Spanish navigator LUIS VÁEZ DE TORRES, sailing westward from Peru, charted the strait, now known as Torres Strait, separating New Guinea from Australia.

William Jansz made the European discovery of Australia. His name for the continent, New Holland, identified it on maps until MATTHEW FLINDERS explored it in the early 1800s and gave it its current name. Jansz's meeting with the Aborigines was the first recorded contact between the natives of Australia and Europeans.

Jenkinson, Anthony (unknown–1611) *English trade representative in Russia and central Asia*

In his early business career, Anthony Jenkinson was involved in trade between England and lands of the eastern MEDITERRANEAN SEA.

In 1556, Jenkinson succeeded RICHARD CHANCELLOR as chief trade agent of the London-based MUSCOVY COMPANY, organized to seek a NORTHEAST PASSAGE across the top of Europe and Asia to China. By that time, the company had succeeded in establishing trade relations with Russia under Ivan IV (also known as Ivan the Terrible).

In 1557, Jenkinson sailed from England to Archangel on the White Sea, then made his way overland to Ivan's court at Moscow, hoping to continue from Moscow to China on the first such journey ever attempted by an Englishman. After obtaining from Ivan letters of safe conduct and permission to explore the Russian-dominated region to the east, Jenkinson left Moscow accompanied by two English assistants—a pair of brothers named Johnson—and headed for the Kazan region and the Volga River. He descended the Volga to its mouth on the Caspian Sea at Astrakhan, then sailed along the northeast coast of the Caspian, beyond the mouth of the Ural River, landing finally at Mangyshlak.

At Mangyshlak, Jenkinson and his companions traveled eastward with a large camel caravan across the northern Kara-Kum Desert to the south shore of the Aral Sea and the Oxus River (the present-day Amu Darya). Ascending the Oxus, they reached the kingdom of Bukhara in present-day Uzbekistan. It became apparent to the Englishmen that the Mongols would block their progress eastward toward China; they decided to return to Moscow over the same route they had followed on the outward journey.

Jenkinson returned to England in 1559. He produced a map based on his first journey to Russia and central Asia; it was published in England in 1562. Although a direct overland trade route to China had proved unfeasible, Jenkinson saw the possibilities of crossing Russia southward and establishing trade contacts with Persia (present-day Iran), a region that was then emerging from Mongol domination. He soon organized follow-up trade expeditions to Persia, none of which met with much success due to the hazards of travel in the regions east of the Volga. In 1561, again with the backing of the Muscovy Company, he sailed to the White Sea coast, and from there traveled overland to Moscow and the Volga River.

Upon reaching the Caspian Sea, Jenkinson this time sailed southward along its west shore to Baku, where he traveled overland into northern Persia, arriving at the city of Qazvin, which at that time was the capital of Persian ruler Shah Tahmasp I. Jenkinson obtained commercial privileges for English traders from the shah, then returned to England by way of Russia and the White Sea, arriving in 1564.

While in Russia, Jenkinson heard reports on the disposition of the northern coastlines of Europe and Asia and surmised that an ice-free Northeast Passage to the Far East might be located. His conclusions were challenged by his contemporaries, among them SIR HUMPHREY GILBERT, who

still adhered to the idea of a NORTHWEST PASSAGE to the Orient across the top of the newly explored North American continent. During winter 1565–66, Jenkinson and Gilbert openly debated the issue before Queen Elizabeth I.

Anthony Jenkinson's travels into central Asia were an extension of English efforts to locate the Northeast Passage. His overland journeys resulted in the first direct contacts between England and Persia. On his 1557–59 journey, he and his companions became the first Englishmen to visit Bukhara.

Jiménez de Quesada, Gonzalo
(Gonzalo Ximenes de Quesada) (ca. 1509–1579)
Spanish conquistador in South America

Gonzalo Jiménez de Quesada was a native of either Granada or Córdoba, Spain. In about 1533, following his education at the University of Salamanca, he settled in Granada and practiced law.

In about 1535, Jiménez de Quesada embarked for the Americas as a member of a large expedition commanded by Pedro Fernández de Lugo, the newly appointed governor of the colonial province of Santa Marta on the Caribbean coast of present-day Colombia. Reports of the fabulously rich Indian city, known as EL DORADO, soon reached Lugo. Jiménez de Quesada was placed in command of an expedition along the Magdalena River into the interior. In addition to finding El Dorado, he was to locate a route connecting Santa Marta with Peru.

Jiménez de Quesada left Santa Marta on April 5, 1536, with 600 men. Rather than ascend the Magdalena River from its mouth west of Santa Marta and risk meeting Indian resistance along the river's lower course, the Spaniards chose to head eastward across the Sierra Nevada de Santa Marta mountains into what is now Venezuela. They would then head overland to the Magdalena and meet up with supply ships at its junction with the Cesar River. Following the Cesar River, Jiménez de Quesada stopped at Chiriguana before continuing to the rendezvous point at Tamalameque.

After a period of waiting, Jiménez de Quesada received word that the ships had been unable to ascend the river. The expedition continued along the Magdalena, hindered by the dense jungle as well as dwindling supplies. A second group of supply vessels managed to reach the Spaniards before they arrived at present-day Barrancabermeja, Colombia. At that point, attracted by reports of an advanced Indian civilization believed to exist on the eastern slopes of the ANDES MOUNTAINS, Jiménez de Quesada led his men away from the Magdalena and into the lands of the Chibcha Indians.

Starting in March 1537, Jiménez de Quesada began his two-year conquest of the Chibcha. He claimed the territory as the New Kingdom of Granada (New Granada); on August 6, 1538, he founded his capital, Santa Fe de Bogotá, derived from the name of the Chibcha tribal leader, Bacata, and known today as Bogotá.

By early 1539, Jiménez de Quesada had subjugated the natives and had acquired from them a fortune in gold and precious stones. At about that time, two other European exploring expeditions appeared in the Bogotá region. One, led by the Spaniard SEBASTIÁN MOYANO DE BENALCÁZAR, had arrived from Ecuador. The other, commanded by the German NIKOLAUS FEDERMANN, had traveled from the Welser family's colony in Venezuela. Although all three claimed the territory as their own, they agreed to allow the Council of the Indies in Spain to mediate the issue and decide who should govern New Granada.

Later in 1539 or early in 1540, Benalcázar, Federmann and Jiménez de Quesada sailed to Spain from Santa Marta. While awaiting the Spanish government's decision, Jiménez de Quesada traveled in France and Portugal, returning to Spain in 1545. The governorship of New Granada was awarded to Alonso Luis de Lugo, the son of his former commander in Santa Marta; Jiménez de Quesada was named marshal of the new province and councillor of Bogotá, to which he returned in 1551.

Jiménez de Quesada served as a colonial administrator in Bogotá over the next two decades. In 1569, although nearly 70 years of age, he set out on another attempt to find El Dorado. At his own expense, he outfitted a large expedition and led it across the Andes into the llanos, or plains region of eastern Colombia, as far as the junction of the ORINOCO RIVER and the Guaviare River. After three years, he returned to Bogotá without having found the fabled Indian city of great wealth.

In his final years, Jiménez de Quesada was afflicted with a skin malady, possibly leprosy. Nonetheless, although nearing the age of 80, he mounted a military campaign to put down an Indian revolt, during the course of which he was carried to the scene of the action on a stretcher.

Gonzalo Jiménez de Quesada was one of the few well-educated CONQUISTADORES. His eyewitness written account of the conquest of Colombia, although long since lost, was reportedly of literary value as well as accurate and objective. Some scholars suspect that a contemporary, Miguel de Cervantes, modeled his fictional hero, Don Quixote, after the life of Jiménez de Quesada, whose character was thought to embody the archetype of the gallant Spanish nobleman of the 16th century.

Jogues, Isaac (Saint Isaac Joques) (1607–1646)
French missionary, explorer of the Great Lakes and Lake George
Isaac Jogues was born in Orléans, France, into one of that city's leading families. In 1624, he was ordained a Jesuit priest and became a teacher of literature at the university in Rouen. In 1636, the Jesuit order sent him to Canada as a missionary to Native Americans. Soon after his arrival in Quebec, he traveled westward to Lake Huron and the Jesuit mission on Georgian Bay.

In 1641, Jogues explored north and west from Georgian Bay. From Lake Huron, he reached St. Marys River and followed it to the falls and rapids that empty into Lake Superior. Jogues named the falls Sault Sainte Marie (Saint Mary's falls). He also explored the north shore of Lake Michigan, becoming the first European missionary to visit that region.

In 1642, on the St. Lawrence River en route to Quebec, Jogues was captured by Mohawk Indians, who took him south into their lands in present-day New York State. The following year, Jogues was ransomed by Dutch officials and released to Fort Orange (present-day Albany, New York). He made his way to the Dutch colony of New Amsterdam (now New York City), from where he returned to France.

In Europe, Jogues was honored by both the French royal court and Vatican officials. He returned to Canada in 1644.

During the next two years, as a peace emissary to the Mohawk, Jogues made several trips to their territory south of Quebec. In 1646, tribal members took him to the southern end of Lake Champlain and through a narrows that

Isaac Jogues *(Library of Congress)*

led to a lake unknown to Europeans. Jogues named the body of water Lac du Sacrement. (Sir William Johnson renamed it Lake George in 1755, in honor of the English king.)

In October 1646, Mohawk again took Jogues captive. He was tortured and killed at the Caughnawaga Indian village near present-day Amsterdam, New York. He was subsequently named a Jesuit Martyr of North America, and he was canonized as Saint Isaac Jogues in 1930.

Isaac Jogues's explorations north and west of Georgian Bay established the locations of Lake Superior and Lake Michigan in relation to the known region of Lake Huron. His report of the location of Lake George and its connection to Lake Champlain provided geographic knowledge helpful to the French in their campaigns during the French and Indian Wars from 1689 to 1763.

John of Carpini   See CARPINI, GIOVANNI DA PIAN DEL.

John of Marignolli   See MARIGNOLLI, GIOVANNI DE.

John of Montecorvino (Friar John of Monte Corvino, Giovanni da Montecorvino) (1247–1328)
Italian missionary in India and China
An Italian Franciscan friar, John of Montecorvino undertook his earliest diplomatic assignment in the 1270s, as the emissary of the newly restored Byzantine emperor Michael VIII Palaeologus to Pope Gregory X.

In 1289, Pope Nicholas IV appointed John as his representative to the Persian capital at Tabriz. Two years later, the Italian priest set out on a journey through Persia (present-day Iran) to the mouth of the Persian Gulf. He sailed across the Arabian Sea and rounded the southern tip of India, landing near present-day Madras, where he established the first Catholic missions on the Indian subcontinent.

From India, John sailed southeastward, through the Strait of Malacca and into the South China Sea, then followed the coast of the Yellow Sea northward, landing on the mainland of China just east of Cambaluc, later known as Peking (Beijing). He made his way inland to the court of Kublai Khan in Cambaluc, where, in 1294, the Chinese emperor welcomed him and gave him permission to continue his missionary work in China.

Across from the emperor's palace in Cambaluc, John established a cathedral and church school, the first permanent Christian settlements in China. Over the next 30 years, he reportedly converted more than 6,000 Chinese to Christianity, although Kublai Khan himself resisted John's proselytizing efforts.

In 1307, John of Montecorvino was named the first Catholic archbishop of Peking, as well as patriarch of the Orient. The letters he sent back to Vatican officials in Rome provided a contemporary account of life in the Chinese capital in the early 14th century. Along with the writings of MARCO POLO, his reports made Europeans aware of China and inspired additional European travelers and traders to the Far East.

Johnston, Sir Harry Hamilton (1858–1927)
British diplomat, colonial official in Africa
Harry H. Johnston, from Kensington, England, attended London's King's College as well as the Royal Academy. In 1878, he toured Europe.

At the age of 21, Johnston visited the North African nation of Tunis, where he spent eight months sketching scenes of native life and writing articles on North African affairs for British newspapers.

In 1882, Johnston undertook his first trip to sub-Saharan Africa, accompanying the seventh earl of Mayo on a hunting expedition to Angola. After a year in the Portuguese colony, he was given permission to explore the CONGO RIVER (Zaire River) on his own. In the course of this journey, he visited with the Anglo-American explorer and journalist SIR HENRY MORTON STANLEY.

Johnston's experience in Africa, together with his proven ability as a scientific reporter, led to his appointment as leader of the British Kilimanjaro Expedition of 1884. Sponsored jointly by the ROYAL SOCIETY and the British Association, Johnston and his team explored the region around Africa's highest peak. He also conducted diplomatic meetings with indigenous leaders, resulting in the first treaties between the British government and the tribes of what is now Tanzania.

Johnston formally entered the British Consular Service in 1885, and, over the following years, served in a variety of diplomatic and colonial posts throughout Africa. In 1889, he explored the country east of Lake Nyasa in what is now Malawi; two years later, he was instrumental in bringing the region under colonial rule as the Central Africa Protectorate. In 1899, after two years as British consul general at Tunis, Johnston helped organize the Uganda Protectorate, where he was appointed special commissioner.

Johnston's disagreements with British Foreign Office policy in regard to Africa, together with health problems, led to his retirement in 1901. He returned to England and continued to write, concentrating on linguistic studies of the Bantu languages and other subjects relating to African culture.

Johnston went on to help found the African Society and establish a school of Oriental and African studies. His works on Africa include *British Central Africa* (1897), *Uganda Pro-*

tectorate (1902), and an account of the Kilimanjaro Expedition. He was also the author of several novels.

In addition to exploring central Africa and serving as a diplomat with tribal leaders, Sir Harry H. Johnston furthered African studies in England.

Jolliet, Louis (Louis Joliet) (1645–1700)
French explorer on the Mississippi River

Born at Beaupré, Quebec, Louis Jolliet entered the Jesuit college in Quebec in 1656, where he studied navigation and hydrography, as well as music. He took minor orders in 1662, but he left the priesthood in 1667 and traveled to France. Upon his return to Canada the following year, he entered the FUR TRADE.

In 1669, Jolliet traveled westward from Quebec by way of the CANOE and portage route to the Great Lakes, taking supplies to an expedition in search of copper deposits on Lake Superior. On the return trip, he pioneered a new portage route from Lake Huron to Lake Erie by way of the

St. Clair River, Lake St. Clair, and the Detroit River. Jolliet then crossed overland to western Lake Ontario. At the Jesuit mission near Niagara Falls, he first met Father JACQUES MARQUETTE.

Jolliet established a trading settlement at Sault Sainte Marie in 1670. Two years later, he was commissioned by Jean Talon, the governor of New France, to investigate Indian reports of a great river to the west. The French were interested in learning if this great south-flowing river drained into the Atlantic Ocean, the Gulf of California, or the Gulf of Mexico. Jolliet was also instructed to entice Indian tribes living beyond the Wisconsin River into the French fur trade.

Jolliet reached the Jesuit mission at St. Ignace on northern Lake Michigan's Mackinac Straits, where he was joined by Father Marquette. Well-versed in several Native American languages, Marquette was to serve as interpreter on the expedition.

Jolliet, Marquette, and a small party of VOYAGEURS and Miami Indian guides left St. Ignace on May 17, 1673, and

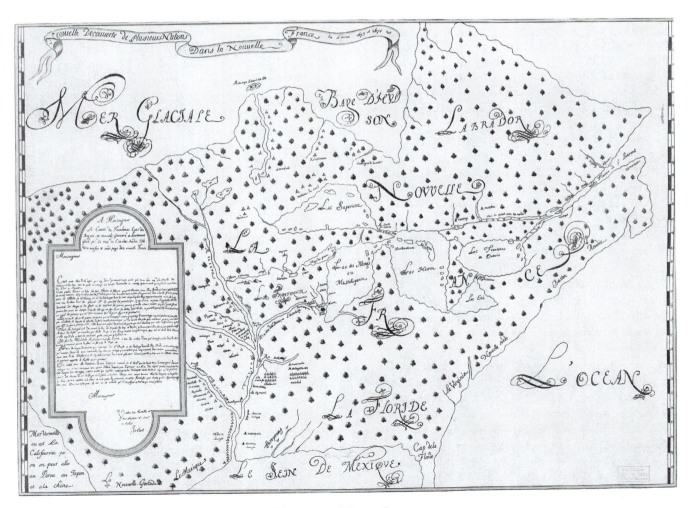

Map of eastern North America by Louis Jolliet (1674) *(Library of Congress)*

took their boats south to Green Bay on the west shore of Lake Michigan. From Green Bay, they followed the Fox River into Lake Winnebago, then crossed to the Wisconsin River, and descended it to its mouth on the MISSISSIPPI RIVER on June 17, 1673, near present-day Prairie du Chien.

The Jolliet-Marquette expedition descended the Mississippi to the mouth of the Arkansas River, midway between present-day Memphis, Tennessee, and Vicksburg, Mississippi. Quapaw Indians warned them that they faced monsters and hostile tribes if they ventured farther southward. Using his navigational skills, Jolliet determined that the river had taken them to a point far enough south that it must drain into the Gulf of Mexico. Heeding the Indians' advice, the expedition headed back upriver.

On the northward journey back to the Great Lakes, Jolliet led the group back up the Mississippi as far as its confluence with the Illinois River, about 25 miles north of present-day St. Louis, Missouri. At that point they left the Mississippi and ascended the entire length of the Illinois River to its junction with the Des Plaines River, near the present-day city of Joliet, Illinois, which was named for the explorer.

Jolliet then blazed a 50-mile portage through the site of present-day Chicago to the south shore of Lake Michigan. (A portion of Jolliet's route on this part of the journey was designated as the Chicago Portage National Historic Site in 1952.) In September 1673, after a five-month journey, Jolliet and his companions arrived at Green Bay, from where Marquette returned to St. Ignace.

Jolliet hurried back to Quebec with the results of his expedition. In January 1674, while he was negotiating the Lachine Rapids above Montreal, his CANOE capsized and most of his written records of the Mississippi journey were lost. However, he was able to reproduce his journals from memory and soon presented them to the French governor.

Jolliet returned to the fur trade after 1674, concentrating in the eastern St. Lawrence River region. Soon granted a trade monopoly on Anticosti Island, he explored the Gulf of St. Lawrence, producing navigational charts for the French government. Starting in 1679, he explored overland from Montreal to HUDSON BAY, where he established several trading posts. British raids, however, drove him from Hudson Bay after 1692.

In 1694, Jolliet explored the coast of Labrador for the French navy and produced one of the earliest scientifically accurate charts of that part of Canada. In recognition of his findings, he was appointed Royal Hydrographer in 1697.

Louis Jolliet and Jacques Marquette's four-month, 2,500-mile exploration of the Mississippi inspired the later expedition of RENÉ-ROBERT CAVELIER DE LA SALLE, who succeeded in reaching the river's delta in 1682. Jolliet also established important portage routes between the Great Lakes and the Illinois and Mississippi Rivers, which helped to ex-

pand French trade and settlement from the Great Lakes, along the Mississippi Valley to the Gulf of Mexico. His findings resulted in Green Bay and Prairie du Chien becoming key centers for the trade between Montreal, the Great Lakes, and the Mississippi.

Jörgenson, Jörgen (1780–1841) *Danish mariner in Tasmania and Iceland*

Born in Copenhagen, Denmark, Jörgen Jörgenson pursued a career as a mariner and found employ on British ships, working as a sealer and whaler in the waters around NEW ZEALAND, Australia, and Van Diemen's Land (TASMANIA) in the early 1800s. He may have participated in MATTHEW FLINDERS's expedition of 1801–03.

Jörgenson returned to Denmark in about 1805. He visited ICELAND in the next years, perhaps exiled there for debt or other crimes, but also claiming to liberate it, which led to his being known as the "king of Iceland." He also reportedly sailed with British PRIVATEERS and served as a spy for England in the Napoleonic Wars.

In 1825, because of debt, Jörgenson was transported to the penal colony at Hobart on Van Diemen's Land. He eventually earned a "ticket of leave," which allowed him to move about the island freely, and was hired by the Van Diemen's Land Company to explore the central and northern parts of the island and make contact with Aborigines, which he did in the Oyster Bay and Big River regions through 1832, it is thought. Jörgenson is known to have returned again to England, where he died in 1841.

Although some of Jörgen Jörgenson's activities may have been exaggerated in his own writings, his expeditions—as those of the Englishmen Thomas Laycock in 1807, John Helder Wedge in the 1820s, and George Augustus Robinson in the 1830s—contributed to the opening of Tasmania to non-Aboriginal settlement and development.

Jourdain, John (unknown–1619) *English mariner in the Indian Ocean, India, and the East Indies, cousin of Silvester Jourdain*

An English sea captain, John Jourdain was among the first members of the Council of India, the governing board of the BRITISH EAST INDIA COMPANY. He was the older cousin of seafarer SILVESTER JOURDAIN.

On March 25, 1608, Jourdain commanded the ship *Ascension* on the company's fourth expedition to India and the EAST INDIES. Sailing by way of the CAPE OF GOOD HOPE, he entered the Indian Ocean and stopped at the Seychelles, the first Englishman ever to do so.

Proceeding northward along the coast of East Africa, Jourdain next went to Socotra off the Horn of Africa and stopped at the port of Aden on the southwestern tip of the

Arabian Peninsula. He also made a trip inland, becoming the first Englishman to visit in Yemen.

By summer 1609, Jourdain had established trade contacts for the British East India Company at these strategic ports at the mouth of the RED SEA. He then sailed to India. At the Gulf of Cambay on the northwest coast of India, the *Ascension* was wrecked on some shoals; the crew survived, however, reaching the mainland in the ship's boats. From there, Jourdain made his way to the port of Surat, where he assumed command of the British East India Company's operations.

Following a visit to Agra in 1610–11, Jourdain sailed from Surat in the British East India company vessel *Trade's Increase.* On this voyage, he returned to the Red Sea ports, stopping at Mocha in Aden. He then undertook a voyage to the East Indies, establishing trade centers for his firm on Sumatra and at Bantam on Java. He also expanded the British East India Company's operations to include the islands of Ceram and Amboina off New Guinea. In 1612, while on a stopover in the SPICE ISLANDS (the Moluccas), Jourdain received a smuggled letter from British navigator WILLIAM ADAMS, who was being detained in Japan. Included with Adam's letter was a map of Japan, a land then little-known to the English.

Jourdain returned to England in summer 1617. The following November, he entered into a five-year contract with the British East India Company, receiving an appointment as president of the Council of India. He returned to Java the next year. Soon afterward, open hostilities broke out with the DUTCH EAST INDIA COMPANY. Despite these difficulties, Jourdain established a lucrative trade for the British East India Company, obtaining cloves from the Moluccas and pepper in Sumatra.

In July 1619, Jourdain embarked on a voyage to Pattani on the Malay Peninsula in what is now Thailand. En route, his vessel was attacked by Dutch ships and he was killed.

John Jourdain's trading expeditions resulted in the earliest British commercial presence in India and the East Indies as well as the first direct contacts for British merchants in the SPICE TRADE. His efforts helped break the trade monopolies held by the Dutch and the Portuguese over that part of the world and provided the basis for the eventual British domination of India.

Jourdain, Silvester (Silvester Jourdan)

(unknown–1650) *English seafarer in Bermuda, cousin of John Jourdain*

Silvester Jourdain was a native of Lyme Regis, a small English port town on the English Channel coast of Dorset. He came from a family of seafarers and merchants, among them his older cousin JOHN JOURDAIN, one of the original directors of the BRITISH EAST INDIA COMPANY.

Although few details exist of Jourdain's early life, business records indicate he was involved in the export business, shipping goods from the Dorset port of Poole as early as 1603.

In 1609, Jourdain sailed from England for Virginia, accompanying CHRISTOPHER NEWPORT and three of the Jamestown colony's newly appointed deputy governors. En route to America, the ship was wrecked on the island of Bermuda.

Although it had been explored by Spanish navigator Juan de Bermudez in 1515, the island was uninhabited when visited by Jourdain and his companions. Since no European nation had yet claimed it or the neighboring islands, the castaways took possession of the island group in the name of England.

Silvester Jourdain made his way back to England later in 1609. Soon afterward, he wrote an account of his voyage entitled *Discovery of the Buarmudas, otherwise Called the Isle of Devils.* Published in London in 1610, his descriptions soon appeared in the works of the period's leading playwrights. William Shakespeare included a direct reference to Bermuda as "Bermoothes" in *The Tempest,* produced only a few years after Jourdain's voyage. John Fletcher's *Women Pleased* and John Webster's *The Duchess of Malfi* also drew on Jourdain's image of Bermuda as the haunt of witches and other supernatural phenomena.

Joutel, Henri (ca. 1645–ca. 1730) *French soldier, colonizer in Texas and the lower Mississippi Valley*

Henri Joutel was born in Rouen, France. Although from a family of modest means, he was well educated and became a skilled journalist. His father was a gardener for an uncle of RENÉ-ROBERT CAVELIER DE LA SALLE.

By 1684, Joutel had served as a soldier in the French army for nearly 17 years. That year, while Joutel was at his family's home in Rouen, La Salle recruited him as his personal aide in a colonizing venture to the mouth of the MISSISSIPPI RIVER, which he had reached two years earlier.

In July 1684, Joutel sailed from La Rochelle with La Salle's fleet of four ships, carrying settlers and supplies for a colony on the lower Mississippi River. After a four-month voyage from France, during which one ship was captured by the Spanish, they reached the north coast of the Gulf of Mexico. Due to navigational errors, the three remaining vessels missed the mouth of the Mississippi and sailed westward, finally making a landing at Matagorda Bay, Texas, where La Salle and his expedition established a temporary base, Fort St. Louis.

Joutel was given command of the Matagorda Bay colony while La Salle and a small party searched in vain for the Mississippi River. In charge for three years, Joutel had to suppress several attempted uprisings.

In January 1687, Joutel joined La Salle on what turned out to be his final effort to reach the Mississippi from the Gulf Coast. From Matagorda, the party headed northeastward, reaching the Brazos River. In mid-March 1687, at an encampment near what is now Navasota, Texas, La Salle was shot to death by several of his own men. Joutel, who had been away from the camp, returned to find his commander murdered. As one of La Salle's most trusted assistants, he expected that he would also be killed, but he was instead allowed to escape, along with La Salle's brother and nephew.

Guided by sympathetic Indians, Joutel and his companions made their way eastward across what is now Arkansas to the lower Arkansas River. At the site of present-day Arkansas Post National Memorial on the Arkansas River, Joutel and his party met up with HENRI DE TONTI, who was heading a relief expedition from his post at Starved Rock on the Illinois River in search of La Salle along the lower Mississippi.

In May 1688, Joutel, escorted by Tonti, traveled up the Illinois, then followed the Great Lakes and Ottawa River route to Quebec, from where he sailed to France later that same year.

Joutel, who lived in Rouen the rest of his life, converted the extensive notes he had made of his experiences in Texas and the Mississippi Valley into an eyewitness account of La Salle's final expedition. The first English edition was published in London in 1714 as *A Journal of the Last Voyage Perform'd by Monsr. de la Sale to the Gulph of Mexico to Find out the Mouth of the Mississippi River.*

Henri Joutel's 1687–88 journey took him across little-known regions of present-day eastern Texas and western Arkansas. His subsequent voyage from Texas northward to Quebec was itself one of the earliest such journeys undertaken by a non-Indian. In his published account, Joutel was the second European, after JACQUES MARQUETTE, to report sighting the giant Indian paintings of legendary beings that adorn the steep cliffs of the east bank of the Mississippi River near present-day Alton, Illinois.

Jubayr, Abu al-Hasan Muhammad ibn

See IBN JUBAYR, ABU AL-HASAN MUHAMMAD.

Junker, Wilhelm Johann (William Junker)

(1840–1892) *German explorer on the upper Nile River and in East Africa*

Johann Wilhelm Junker was born in Moscow to a German family. In 1869, at the age of 29, he embarked on a career of travel and exploration, sailing to ICELAND. In 1873, he made his first trip to Africa, traveling in Tunisia for almost a year before journeying to Egypt and the Sudan region to the south.

Starting in 1876, Junker undertook a two-year exploration of the White Nile River, ascending the river as far as Malakal. He then headed overland into the region to the southwest, eventually reaching the Ubangi and Uele Rivers, both important as navigable northern tributaries of the CONGO RIVER (Zaire River).

In 1883, Junker headed eastward into the region around Lake Albert and Lake Victoria in present-day Uganda and Tanzania. He had intended to head northward and return to Khartoum by way of the White Nile, but the outbreak of the Mahdi Revolt two years earlier made that route too hazardous. Instead, he led a relief expedition to MEHMED EMIN PASHA, who was besieged at his headquarters at Lado in what is now southern Sudan.

Junker himself was forced to remain at Lado for several years, prevented by the Mahdi threat from venturing northward. Finally, in 1886, he undertook a journey to the coast of East Africa, arriving later that year at Zanzibar.

Back in Europe, Junker published an account in 1889–91 of his 11 years in North and East Africa, entitled *Reisen in Afrika* (Travels in Africa).

Johann Wilhelm Junker's explorations of the then little-known watershed region between the upper tributaries of the Congo River and NILE RIVER were made during a period of great political upheaval in northeastern Africa. He was among the first Europeans, after GEORG AUGUST SCHWEINFURTH, to visit the Uele River region in what is now northeastern Democratic Republic of the Congo.

Jusseaume, René (ca. 1789–ca. 1830)

French-Canadian interpreter, guide on the upper Missouri River

Little is known of French Canadian René Jusseaume before 1789, when he first came to live among the Mandan Indians of the upper MISSOURI RIVER in present-day North Dakota.

In November 1797, Jusseaume was hired as interpreter and guide by DAVID THOMPSON of the Canadian-based NORTH WEST COMPANY. With Thompson's party of voyageurs, he traveled southward on the Souris River in southern Saskatchewan into present-day North Dakota. They proceeded overland to the Mandan villages near the site of present-day Verendrye, North Dakota. While Thompson made a study of the Mandan, Jusseaume concentrated on convincing the tribe to break off with the Spanish traders from St. Louis and Santa Fe and to trade exclusively with the North West Company.

In winter 1804–05, Jusseaume was hired by MERIWETHER LEWIS and WILLIAM CLARK as an interpreter to the upper Missouri tribes. Jusseaume's ability as an Indian interpreter was often called into question, but he did provide the Corps of Discovery with valuable information on Indian customs.

When the expedition left for the ROCKY MOUNTAINS the following spring, Jusseaume remained among the Mandans and arranged for a delegation of the tribe's leaders to visit U.S. government officials in Washington, D.C. In his role as a liaison to Native American leaders, he traveled on occasion with PIERRE DORION, SR. In 1806–07, Jusseaume escorted Mandan chief Big White to Washington, D.C., where the tribal leader met with President Thomas Jefferson. On the journey back to the upper Missouri, Jusseaume was wounded in an attack by Sioux (Dakota, Lakota, Nakota) warriors, near the Arikara villages south of present-day Bismarck, North Dakota.

In 1809, Jusseaume apprenticed one of his sons to Meriwether Lewis. Jusseaume himself took part in MANUEL LISA's fur-trading expeditions into the northern plains and northern Rockies from 1809 to 1820.

In 1833–34, Jusseaume worked briefly for Missouri River explorer, ALEXANDER PHILIPP MAXIMILIAN, who later wrote disparagingly about Jusseaume's frontier abilities.

René Jusseaume's career as a guide and interpreter along the upper Missouri River, like those of other explorers and traders, helped open the region to non-Indian development.

K

Kaempfer, Engelbrecht (Engelbert Kampfer)
(1651–1716) *German, physician, diplomat in Asia*

Born in the northern German town of Lemgo, Engelbrecht Kaempfer was trained as a medical doctor, with a background in the natural sciences. In 1683, Kaempfer began a 10-year period of travel in Asia as a member of a Swedish diplomatic and trade mission. Starting from Moscow, he went first to the capital of Persia (present-day Iran) at Esfahan, at that time regarded as an international hub of commercial and diplomatic dealings between Europe and Asia. There he met diplomats representing the significant European powers of the time, including Russia, Poland, France, and the papacy. Also present were emissaries from all parts of Asia, including Arabia, central Asia, and the Far Eastern kingdom of Siam (present-day Thailand).

From Persia, Kaempfer continued his travels in southern Asia, visiting the island of CEYLON (present-day Sri Lanka), then sailing to Java in the EAST INDIES. In 1690, after a visit to Siam, he embarked for Japan, where he stayed two years. Although Japan had been closed to Europeans for decades, the Japanese government allowed Kaempfer freedom to travel throughout the country because of the services he could provide as a skilled physician.

Engelbrecht Kaempfer returned to Germany in 1694. He wrote of his experiences in the Far East in *History of Japan and Siam.* Published posthumously in 1728, it provided Europeans with one of the earliest accounts of the culture and geography of Japan.

Kane, Elisha Kent (1820–1857) *American physician, naval officer in the Arctic regions of Greenland*

Elisha Kent Kane was born in Philadelphia. His father was one of that city's leading attorneys; his mother was active in Philadelphia high society.

Following his early education, Kane entered the University of Virginia in 1838, planning a career in engineering. Later that year, he was stricken with rheumatic fever, which left his health in a weakened state. As a result, he changed his field of study to medicine (then considered a less physically demanding profession), graduating as a medical doctor from the University of Pennsylvania in 1842.

Following a short period as a medical researcher, Kane entered the U.S. Navy as an assistant surgeon in 1843. Despite his chronic health problems, he maintained an interest in traveling to distant places, and he accompanied the U.S. diplomatic mission to China and toured much of Asia.

After serving with a U.S. naval squadron off the coast of Africa, Kane was sent home because of a bout of tropical fever. In 1846, he saw action in Mexico in the U.S.-Mexican War; he was wounded and suffered from typhus.

After more than a year, Kane returned to active duty as a medical officer with a U.S. government survey in the Gulf of Mexico. He then sought and received an appointment as chief medical officer with the First U.S. Grinnell Expedition to the Arctic in search of SIR JOHN FRANKLIN and his expedition, who had been missing since 1845.

In 1850, under the command of Lieutenant EDWIN JESSE DE HAVEN, Kane sailed to Smith Sound, the southern end of the strait separating northern GREENLAND from the east shore of Ellesmere Island. After a year in the Arctic, Kane returned with the De Haven team to New York. He recounted his experiences in his book, *The U.S. Grinnell Expedition in Search of Sir John Franklin*. Published in early 1853, it was an immediate literary sensation, bringing Kane much renown as America's leading Arctic explorer, despite his limited experience.

Along with his book, Kane's series of lectures brought him public support for his next project. He was among the adherents of the existence of an ice-free polar sea north of the northernmost landmasses that would provide access to the NORTH POLE. Kane further speculated that Franklin had found a way northward through Smith Sound and that remnants of his expedition might still be located on the shores of the hypothetical polar sea.

With money raised by public subscription, and with the ship *Advance* donated by Henry Grinnell, the sponsor of the earlier De Haven voyage, Kane organized what came to be known as the Second U.S. Grinnell Expedition. Sailing from New York on May 31, 1853, the expedition was composed of a scientific team and a contingent of U.S. Navy men. On arriving in Smith Sound in summer 1853, Kane found its northern reaches frozen and unnavigable. He then sailed to the northeast, hoping to find an ice-free channel along the coast of northwestern Greenland. Another goal of the expedition was to explore northernmost Greenland to learn how far it extended northward and determine whether it could provide an overland route to the North Pole.

Kane and the *Advance* reached as far north as Rennsselaer Bay on the Greenland coast, where the ship soon became icebound. Kane sent out several exploring parties, one of which discovered Greenland's Humboldt Glacier, the largest known glacier in the world. In May 1854, ISAAC ISRAEL HAYES, the expedition's chief medical officer, crossed the frozen expanse that came to be known as Kane Basin to Ellesmere Island. Another member of the expedition, William Morton, undertook a trek northward along the east coast of Greenland, reaching as far as Cape Constitution. At 80°10' north latitude, it was at that time a northern record in the Western Hemisphere. In addition, the scientific team made studies of tides and glacial formation in the Arctic and made observations relating to astronomy and terrestrial magnetism. Inuit (Eskimo) culture was also examined, as was Arctic animal life. Although Kane had planned to spend only one winter in Smith Sound, it became apparent by August 1854 that the ship would remain icebound for at least another year. A shortage of food and an outbreak of SCURVY led Hayes and eight other members of the expedition to attempt an overland trek to the Danish Greenland settlements to the south. Storms and lack of experience in Arctic travel forced

Elisha Kent Kane *(Library of Congress)*

Hayes and the others to abandon the journey. They returned to the ship in December 1854, where Kane employed his medical skill to nurse his men back to health.

In May 1855, Kane took the decisive step of abandoning the *Advance* and led his men southward along 1,300 miles of the coast of northern Greenland, arriving after 83 days at the Danish settlement of Upernavik. They were soon met by a U.S. government relief expedition under Lieutenant H. J. Hartstene.

Upon his return to New York in October 1855, Kane began work on another book, *Arctic Explorations: The Second Grinnell Expedition in Search of Sir John Franklin in the Years 1853, '54, '55*. Published in 1856, it soon became a bestseller.

Following a voyage to England, where he met with JANE FRANKLIN, Kane sought to recover his health with a trip to Cuba. He died in Havana in 1857. At his funeral in Philadelphia, he was buried with honors befitting a national hero. Soon after his death, his career was marked with scandal when the American medium and spiritualist Margaret Fox claimed that she had had a romantic liaison with Kane between his two Arctic expeditions, claiming his estate as common-law wife. She also adopted his name and published his love letters to her as *The Love Life of Dr. Kane* (1866).

Elisha Kent Kane's Arctic explorations revealed little about the fate of the lost Franklin expedition, and, a half century later, the idea of the open polar sea was proven erroneous. Nonetheless, Kane's investigations into the unknown waters north of Smith Sound into Kane Basin, named in his honor, revealed an ice-free route through Kennedy Channel, which was later utilized in explorations undertaken by Hayes, CHARLES FRANCIS HALL, and ADOLPHUS WASHINGTON GREELY. ROBERT EDWIN PEARY finally succeeded in reaching the North Pole in 1909 by making a preliminary voyage to northern Ellesmere Island via Kane Basin.

Kane, Paul (1810–1871) *Irish artist in western Canada*

Paul Kane, a native of County Cork, Ireland, moved with his family to Canada in 1828. They settled in York (present-day Toronto), where Kane attended Upper Canada College.

In 1836, Kane went to the United States and traveled over a wide area, from Detroit to New Orleans, working at odd jobs and saving money for art studies in Europe. Kane sailed for Europe in June 1841. He studied art on his own for the next four years, visiting museums in Paris, Rome, Venice, Milan, and London, where he viewed a display of GEORGE CATLIN's paintings of American Indians.

In 1845, Kane was back in Toronto. In June of that year, he embarked on a sketching trip to the Huron (Wyandot) and Chippewa (Ojibway) lands around Lake Huron.

The Indian drawings he brought back greatly impressed HUDSON'S BAY COMPANY governor, SIR GEORGE SIMPSON. Kane was commissioned by Simpson to produce a series of paintings of western Indians.

In spring 1846, Kane left Sault Sainte Marie, soon joining the Hudson's Bay Company riverboats headed for western Canada. He traveled along the Rainy River to Lake of the Woods, and along the Winnipeg River to Fort Alexander on Lake Winnipeg's southern end.

From Fort Alexander, Kane traveled into the Red River region, where he lived with the Métis, a group of mixed-bloods. He accompanied the Métis westward onto the plains and took part in a buffalo hunt. During this trip, his party was attacked by Sioux (Dakota, Lakota, Nakota).

In late summer 1846, Kane returned to Lake Winnipeg and sailed to the northern end of the lake to Norway House. He traveled on Hudson's Bay Company riverboats westward along the Saskatchewan River to Carlton House, where his party of VOYAGEURS obtained horses and continued across the plains to Edmonton, Alberta.

Kane and the voyageurs crossed the ROCKY MOUNTAINS, traveling part of the way on snowshoes, then followed the COLUMBIA RIVER to Fort Vancouver, British Columbia, arriving on December 8, 1846.

Kane wintered on Vancouver Island, sketching scenes of Indian life. He set out for the East in July 1847. By December he was back in Edmonton. He spent the next several months sketching the natives and touring the region on a dogsled. Kane departed Edmonton in spring 1848, reaching Toronto by early October. He had produced hundreds of sketches as well as a journal of his western travels, and he subsequently produced more than 100 oil paintings based on these sketches. They were well received and launched him on a successful art career.

Paul Kane's account of this trip, *Wanderings of an Artist Among the Indians of North America,* was first published in 1849. His paintings were among the earliest to depict Native American life in the Canadian West.

Kan Ying (Gan Ying, Kan-ying) (fl. A.D. 90s)
Chinese diplomat in central Asia and the Middle East

Kan Ying was a diplomat in service to China in the last decades of the first century A.D. He may have been a native of the Turan Basin region in the Turkestan region of central Asia.

In A.D. 97, Chinese general Pan Ch'ao (Ban Chao) commissioned Kan Ying to undertake a diplomatic mission westward to the Roman Empire, known to the Chinese as Ta Ch'in (Daqin). At that time, China shared control of the 5,000-mile SILK ROAD, the vital trade route linking China with the Parthian and Kushana peoples of central Asia as well as with the Romans farther west. It was Pan Ch'ao's hope that Kan Ying could arrange a special agreement with the Romans to position China against its central Asian rivals.

Kan Ying's exact route westward is not known. He reached a seaport he called T'iao-chih, which may have been on the Mediterranean coast of present-day Syria. Other Chinese historical sources suggest he reached as far as the Parthian port of An-hsi (Anxi) on the Black Sea. Kan Ying reported that local seafarers warned him against making a crossing of the sea, because the return journey, if made under unfavorable winds, could take as long as two years, leading to death by homesickness. Heeding their advice, he returned to China, without having made any direct contact with the Roman Empire.

Kan Ying's diplomatic mission to Europe, although it fell short of its intended goal, marked the resurgence of Chinese control over its westernmost provinces and was among the first recorded journeys of a Chinese official to the Middle East.

Karlsefni, Thorfinn (Thorfinn Karlsevni)
(fl. 1010s) *Norse mariner, colonizer in North America*

Originally from ICELAND, Thorfinn Karlsefni was a Norse seafarer who engaged in the maritime trade between Norway and GREENLAND.

According to accounts in *Groenlendinga* (*Saga of the Greenlanders*) and in *Eiríks saga* (*Saga of Eric the Red*), Karlsefni visited the Norse settlement on the southwest coast of Greenland in about 1009, where he was hosted by the family of LEIF ERICSSON. While there, he met and married Gudrid, the widow of Leif's brother Thorstein, who had died in about 1003 on a reported voyage to what the Vikings referred to as VINLAND, somewhere in North America.

In about spring 1010, Karlsefni reportedly organized a large colonizing expedition planning to sail from Greenland and establish a permanent settlement in Vinland. Accounts in the sagas vary as to the number of colonists involved. One source relates that there were 60 men and five women, while another mentions that the colonizing expedition included as many as 160, with "all kinds of livestock." FREYDIS EIRÍKSDOTTIR was one of the women.

Karlsefni and his expedition sailed from Greenland's Western Settlement, eventually reaching sites on the coast of North America they identified as Helluland and Markland. At one of these, they located the keel of a ship left by THORVALD ERICSSON, who had been killed in an Indian attack on an earlier voyage.

At a site on the coat Karlsefni named Furdustrands (wonder strands), two Scottish slaves, a man and a woman, were sent ashore to reconnoiter. They returned after three days with wild grapes and wheat, evidence that the region had potential as an agricultural settlement.

Karlsefni and his colonists spent their first summer at the site of Leif Ericsson's former settlement on Vinland, where they collected grapes, fished, and hunted. A beached whale was discovered and slaughtered for food, although its blubber made many of the colonists ill.

In about 1011, Karlsefni's colony was visited by Native Americans, called Skraeling by the Norse (a derisive term meaning "wretches" or "uglies"). The Vikings traded with the Native Americans, bartering "milk" (which may have actually been mead, the intoxicating Norse beverage) and red cloth for furs. That spring, Karlsefni's wife, Gudrid, reportedly gave birth to a son, Snorri. If the account in the sagas is accurate, he is the first non-Indian child known to have been born in North America.

Although trade contacts with the natives had been initiated, relations soon deteriorated into open conflict, and Karlsefni decided to abandon his colony in spring, probably 1013. On the homeward voyage to Greenland, he stopped at Markland, believed by many to be present-day Labrador, where his men captured two native boys, who were taken to Greenland and taught the Norse language. They reportedly related to the Norse that an Irish monastic settlement had been established west of the Vinland settlement years earlier. From Greenland, Karlsefni, Gudrid, and their American-born son, Snorri, sailed to Norway and later settled in Iceland.

The only record of Thorfinn Karlsefni's expedition to North America is found in the Norse sagas, written several hundred years after the events described. Recent archaeological evidence suggests that the colony he established was located at present-day L'Anse aux Meadows, Newfoundland; some historians theorize, however, that geographic descriptions indicate territory along Cape Cod in present-day Massachusetts.

Thorfinn Karlsefni's expedition was the last major attempt by the Vikings to establish a permanent settlement in North America. He and his followers established what is possibly the earliest significant trading relationship between Europeans and Native Americans. A North American arrowhead found near the site of a farm owned by Karlsefni on Greenland provides credence to the story of the captured boys, who may have been the first Native Americans to be removed forcibly from their homeland by Europeans.

Kashevarov, Aleksandr Filippovich

(1808–1866) *Russian–Native American mariner in Alaska*
Aleksandr F. Kashevarov was born at the Russian fur-trading settlement on Kodiak Island in the Gulf of Alaska. His father, a Russian, was an employee of the RUSSIAN-AMERICAN COMPANY; his mother was a native Aleut woman.

While in his teens, the young Kashevarov was sent, at the Russian-American Company's expense, to St. Petersburg, where he underwent training as a navigator. In 1828–30, he sailed around the world on the Russian-American Company's ship *Elena,* stopping at the company's fur-trading bases in Alaska.

In 1832, Kashevarov returned to Alaska from Russia on the military transport *Amerika.* During the next 10 years, he took part in coastal surveys north of the Alaskan Peninsula. In 1838, aboard the *Polifem,* he explored Norton Sound on the west coast of Alaska, then sailed through BERING STRAIT, continuing along the coast to Cape Lisburne. At that point, he carried on his survey in an Aleut *baidarka,* a small open boat made of skins, reaching as far north as 30 miles beyond Point Barrow.

In 1845, after returning to St. Petersburg overland across SIBERIA, Kashevarov was appointed to a post in the Russian Naval Ministry's Hydrographic Department. His navigational findings contributed to the Russian navy's *Atlas of the Eastern Ocean Including the Okhotsk and Bering Seas,* published in St. Petersburg in 1850.

Starting in 1850, Kashevarov began six years of active duty in the Russian navy as a captain-lieutenant in command of Ayan, a seaport on the coast of SIBERIA in the Sea of Okhotsk. He returned to the Hydrographic Department in St. Petersburg in 1857, where he remained until 1862.

Aleksandr F. Kashevarov was one of the few native-born Alaskans to take an active part in the Russian exploration of

Alaska. His explorations above Norton Sound were among the first Russian attempts to investigate the territory north of their original settlements on the Gulf of Alaska.

Kearny, Stephen Watts (1794–1848)

U.S. Army officer, American explorer on the southern plains

Stephen Watts Kearny was a native of Newark, New Jersey. He attended Columbia College for one year, leaving to join the army at the outbreak of the War of 1812. He was commissioned a lieutenant and, after his capture and release at Niagara Falls, he was promoted to captain.

After the war, Kearny remained in the army. In 1819–25, he served under Colonel HENRY ATKINSON, during which time he helped establish Fort Atkinson on the MISSOURI RIVER near present-day Omaha, Nebraska. From Fort Atkinson, Kearny undertook official U.S. government explorations of the Great Plains west of the Missouri River.

In 1837, Kearny was promoted to colonel and placed in command of the First Dragoon Regiment. He led his mounted troops on patrols of the Indian Territory (present-day Oklahoma) and the known regions of the northern plains. During the early 1840s, he commanded the U.S. Third Military Department and oversaw posts throughout the Great Plains.

In spring 1845, Kearny left Fort Leavenworth, Kansas, in command of a small American force and explored the upper Platte and Arkansas Rivers. Mountain man THOMAS FITZPATRICK served as guide for part of the expedition. Kearny reached Fort Laramie and from there the SOUTH PASS. His expedition then headed southward to the Arkansas River in Colorado, as far as Bent's Fort in the eastern Rocky Mountains. Heading back eastward, he reached Fort Leavenworth in August 1845. The 2,200-mile journey had taken Kearny and his men 99 days. JOHN CHARLES FRÉMONT and JAMES WILLIAM ABERT led parties under Kearny's command during this expedition.

Kearny was promoted to brigadier general at the outbreak of the U.S.-Mexican War in 1846. He led 2,000 troops westward from Fort Leavenworth, along the Santa Fe Trail to New Mexico. WILLIAM HEMSLEY EMORY served under him and drafted maps of the Southwest. Arriving at Santa Fe in mid-August 1846, Kearny took the city. With about 300 men, he headed southward from Santa Fe along the Rio Grande River to Albuquerque. Along the way, he met up with CHRISTOPHER HOUSTON CARSON (Kit Carson), who was carrying military dispatches to the East. Kearny drafted Carson as a guide, then proceeded westward along the Gila River, across the southern Arizona desert, to San Diego, California.

Kearny played a decisive role in the conquest of California. Afterward, he became embroiled in a controversy with Frémont, which resulted in Frémont's court-martial. Toward the close of the U.S.-Mexican War, Kearny became military governor of Veracruz. After contracting yellow fever, he returned to St. Louis, where he soon died.

Stephen Watts Kearny's explorations of the Platte and Arkansas Rivers in 1845 provided valuable topographical information. His trek from Santa Fe to San Diego the following year helped establish the Gila River route across southern Arizona, which developed into a major trail for migrants heading for California during and after the gold rush of 1849.

Kelsey, Henry (Boy Explorer) (ca. 1670–1729)

British trader on Canadian Prairies

Born in England, probably near Greenwich, Henry Kelsey joined the HUDSON'S BAY COMPANY while in his teens. In about 1690, he was sent to York Factory, the company's main trading post on the southwest shore of HUDSON BAY.

In 1690–92, Kelsey explored the interior of Canada, hoping to expand the company's business to the Indians west of Hudson Bay. He traveled with Indian guides southwest from York Factory into present-day Manitoba and Saskatchewan. Crossing Lake Winnipeg, he spent the winter of 1690–91 near The Pas, Manitoba. In spring 1691, he traveled along the Assiniboine and Saskatchewan Rivers and became the first European known to have visited the Canadian Prairies.

Kelsey covered a vast area of central Canada, exploring west of the Touchwood Hills around present-day Saskatoon, Saskatchewan. He joined the Indians in a buffalo hunt, the first non-Indian to do so in this region. He reached as far as Red Deer in present-day Alberta, then returned to Hudson Bay in 1692.

Kelsey remained with the Hudson's Bay Company for the next 30 years. He became a governor of trading posts on Hudson Bay and for a time at Albany, New York. In 1719, aboard the ship *Prosperous,* he explored northward from York Factory along the west coast of Hudson Bay, as far as Marble Island. His mission was to search for the NORTHWEST PASSAGE, investigate reports of mineral deposits, and follow up the earlier expedition of JAMES KNIGHT. Kelsey made two later expeditions to the Marble Island region, in 1720 and 1721.

Henry Kelsey was the first European to see the Canadian prairies. His 1690–92 explorations of the Canadian West were the last undertaken by Hudson's Bay Company traders until the 1750s. His account of this expedition, written partly in verse, was not discovered until 1926. Kelsey's explorations of western Canada, undertaken when he was relatively young, earned him a reputation as the "Boy Explorer."

Kennedy, Edmund (1818–1848) *Australian explorer in Queensland*

Edmund Kennedy was born on Guernsey, one of the Channel Islands in the English Channel. He began his career as an explorer of eastern Australia as an assistant to THOMAS LIVINGSTONE MITCHELL, the surveyor-general of New South Wales, with whom he explored the Barcoo River region of what is now Queensland in 1845–46.

In 1847, Kennedy was sent by the Australian government back into the interior of Queensland to determine the course of a river previously located and named the Victoria by Mitchell. Kennedy's investigations revealed that the Victoria and the Barcoo rivers were one and the same. He further determined that the Barcoo followed a southwestward course into the interior of Australia; it was later proven that it flowed into Lake Eyre.

The next year, Kennedy led a team of 12 others on an expedition northward from Rockingham Bay, on the coast of Queensland, in an attempt to reach Cape York on the Torres Strait. They soon ran short of food, and Kennedy went on ahead of the main party northward in search of help. Along the way, he was killed in an attack by Aborigines. Of the 13 members of the expedition only three survived. They were picked up south of Cape York at Port Albany by a ship that had been sent to meet them.

Edmund Kennedy's explorations into the interior of Queensland helped shed light on the mystery of Australia's westward-flowing river. His final expedition into Queensland was the last attempt to explore northward to the Cape York region until the mid-1860s.

Kenton, Simon (1755–1836) *American explorer in Kentucky and the Ohio Valley*

Simon Kenton was born in Fauquier County, northeastern Virginia. In 1771, under the mistaken impression that he had killed a man in a fist fight over a woman, he fled to the upper Ohio River frontier. (For the next 10 years, he went under the assumed name of Samuel Butler.) Later that same year, Kenton traveled down the Ohio River on a hunting expedition with frontiersmen George Yeager and John Strader. For the next two years, Kenton and his two companions hunted and explored along the upper Ohio River, in search of a region known to the Indians as Kaintuckee, "the land of canes" or "meadow lands"—the modern Kentucky.

Indian attacks forced Kenton and his party out of the upper Ohio region in 1773. The next year, he served as a colonial scout in Lord Dunmore's War, during which he became friends with Kentucky pioneer DANIEL BOONE.

In 1775, after Lord Dunmore's War, Kenton established a temporary settlement at the confluence of the Ohio River and Limestone Creek (present-day Maysville, Kentucky). He then traveled to Boonesborough, where he joined Boone in defending the settlement against attacks by Shawnee Indians during the American Revolution. In 1778, Kenton joined Colonel George Rogers Clark's expedition from the Falls of the Ohio to the Illinois country and took part in attacks against the British and their Indian allies. In 1782, he participated in a military expedition against the Indians on the Great Miami River in what is now western Ohio.

Kenton then returned to his Virginia home and learned he had not killed the man he had fought with 10 years before. With his name cleared, he moved with his family to his original encampment in Kentucky at the mouth of Limestone Creek.

During the early 1790s, Kenton returned to fighting Indians in the Old Northwest under General "Mad" Anthony Wayne. In 1798, he moved with his family to Urbana, Ohio. He later took part in the War of 1812, fighting in the Battle of the Thames.

After 1820, Kenton lost most of his Kentucky and Ohio lands due to legal and financial problems.

Simon Kenton was one of the original settlers of Kentucky and western Ohio. His settlement at Limestone Creek on the Ohio River, like the CUMBERLAND GAP, became an important entry point for the influx of settlers into the Ohio Valley after the American Revolution. As an Indian fighter, hunter, and settler, he explored much of the Old Northwest, from present-day Louisville, Kentucky, to the MISSISSIPPI RIVER in southern Illinois.

Simon Kenton *(Library of Congress)*

Kerguélen-Trémarec, Yves-Joseph de (Yves-Joseph de Kerguélen de Trémarec, Yves-Joseph de Kerguélen-Trémec) (1734–1797)
French mariner in the southern Indian Ocean

Yves-Joseph de Kerguélen was a native of the seaport of Quimper in the Brittany region of northwestern France. In 1772, Kerguélen embarked from Île de France, present-day Mauritius, on a government-sponsored voyage in search of the hypothetical GREAT SOUTHERN CONTINENT, believed to exist in the high southern latitudes. With two ships, the *Fortune* and the *Gros-Ventre,* he sailed into the southern reaches of the Indian Ocean. On February 13, 1772, he sighted land (actually the largest of a group of about 300 islands), which he believed was the coast of the long-sought-after continent, also known as Terra Australis.

Claiming the region for France, Kerguélen sailed home, where he announced the discovery of what he called "la France Australe." His findings generated hopeful speculation that in the new lands would be found a race of men living in a "state of nature," a belief consistent with the myth of the noble savage prevalent at that time among French intellectuals. Kerguélen also fostered the hope that the newfound territory in the Indian Ocean would provide France with a source of mineral wealth and serve as an exclusive base for a French-dominated sea route to Asia and the Americas.

In 1773, on a second voyage to the Indian Ocean with the ships *Rolland* and *Oiseau,* Kerguélen had an opportunity to explore his earlier findings in greater detail. He soon determined that the island was barren and uninhabitable and devoid of any colonial value because of the severity of the climate. In response, he renamed the region the "Land of Desolation."

Kerguélen's voyages of 1772 and 1773 were undertaken at about the same time that British navigator JAMES COOK was engaged in his own explorations of the high southern latitudes in search of the Great Southern Continent. While on a stopover at Cape Town in November 1772, Cook learned the results of Kerguélen's first expedition, prompting him to carry on explorations for the fabled landmass in that part of the southern Indian Ocean. In February 1773, Cook searched the area but missed finding the lands Kerguélen had reported by five degrees of longitude. Three years later, in December 1776, while on his third voyage, Cook did manage to find Kerguélen's Land of Desolation, at which time he determined it was not a landmass but part of an island group.

In 1774, following his second reconnaissance of the land he had found in the southern Indian Ocean, Kerguélen returned to France. The French government, which had sponsored his expeditions, now charged him with fraud for his early favorable description of the lands he explored. Although convicted and sentenced to 20 years imprisonment, he was released in 1778 after serving four years.

The archipelago explored by Yves-Joseph de Kerguélen in 1772 is known today as the Kerguelen Islands, in honor of the French navigator, with the largest island of the group named Kerguelen Island. A unique variety of wild cabbage native to the islands was identified as the Kerguelen cabbage by British scientist SIR JOSEPH DALTON HOOKER while on a visit there with SIR JAMES CLARK ROSS's expedition in 1840.

Kermadec, Jean-Michel Huon de   See HUON DE KERMADEC, JEAN-MICHEL.

Kern, Benjamin Jordan (1818–1849) *American artist, physician, naturalist in the southern Rocky Mountains, brother of Richard Hovendon Kern and Edward Meyer Kern*

Benjamin Kern was born in Philadelphia, where he studied medicine, art, and natural science. He was a practicing doctor in Philadelphia in 1848, when he joined his younger brothers EDWARD MEYER KERN and RICHARD HOVENDON KERN in JOHN CHARLES FRÉMONT's ill-fated fourth expedition into the upper Rio Grande and southern ROCKY MOUNTAINS.

Kern and his brothers survived a blizzard in the San Juan Mountains northwest of Taos, New Mexico, despite being abandoned by Frémont at the height of the storm. They eventually made their way to Taos.

Soon afterward, Kern returned to the mountains, accompanied by Frémont's guide WILLIAM SHERLEY WILLIAMS. The two were killed by a band of Ute Indians.

Benjamin Kern was one of the many naturalists who helped record the non-Indian exploration of the West.

Kern, Edward Meyer (1823–1863) *American artist, topographer in the southern Rocky Mountains and the North Pacific, brother of Richard Hovendon Kern and Benjamin Jordan Kern*

Edward Kern was born in Philadelphia to a prominent family. He studied art and draftsmanship and became an accomplished painter and topographer.

In 1845–47, Kern served as topographer with JOHN CHARLES FRÉMONT's third expedition from eastern Colorado to the California coast. At the Great Salt Lake, Kern and guide JOSEPH REDDEFORD WALKER led part of the group along a section of the Hastings Cutoff into northern Nevada's Humboldt River region, then to Walker Lake. They crossed the Sierra Nevada into California through Walker Pass, rejoining Frémont and the rest of the group north of Monterey. The U.S.-Mexican War soon erupted, during which Kern took part in the California campaign under Frémont.

Kern was with Frémont on his fourth expedition to the upper Rio Grande and southern ROCKY MOUNTAINS during 1848–49, along with his older brothers, RICHARD HOVENDON KERN and BENJAMIN JORDAN KERN. In the aftermath of this trip, Benjamin Kern was killed by Indians in the San Juan Mountains northwest of Taos, New Mexico, while attempting to retrieve equipment left behind in a blizzard.

Based in Taos during 1849–51, Edward and his brother Richard worked as topographers with the U.S. Army's Corps of Topographical Engineers. In 1849, under Lieutenant JAMES HERVEY SIMPSON, they explored the Navajo (Dineh) Indian country around the Four Corners region of Colorado, Arizona, Utah, and New Mexico, accomplishing the first U.S. government survey of Canyon de Chelly.

In summer 1851, Edward Kern accompanied Lieutenant JOHN B. POPE on an expedition in search of an alternate route between Fort Leavenworth, Kansas, and Santa Fe, New Mexico.

From June 1853 to October 1855, Kern sailed the North Pacific with the Ringgold-Rodgers naval expedition to Japan, during which he produced maps of the Japanese coast.

For three years, starting in September 1857, Kern again explored the Pacific, this time with Lieutenant John M. Brook's expedition to China.

In March 1860, Kern returned to the United States, and he served with Frémont in the first year of the Civil War. Leaving the army in 1861, he returned to teach art in Philadelphia, where he died two years later from an attack of epilepsy.

The Kern brothers made valuable contributions to the scientific surveys of the American Southwest undertaken in the years immediately following the U.S.-Mexican War of 1846–48. Edward Kern's subsequent Pacific explorations provided the U.S. Navy with important data on sea routes between California and the Far East. The Kern River, north of present-day Bakersfield, California, was named by Frémont in honor of Edward Kern.

Kern, Richard Hovendon (1821–1853)

American artist, topographer, and naturalist in the southern Rocky Mountains, brother of Edward Meyer Kern and Benjamin Jordan Kern

Richard Kern, an artist and topographer from Philadelphia, joined his brothers EDWARD MEYER KERN and BENJAMIN JORDAN KERN on JOHN CHARLES FRÉMONT's disastrous 1848–49 expedition into the Sangre de Cristo Mountains of northern New Mexico.

Kern served as a topographer and naturalist on this expedition, which sought a year-round pass for a railroad route through the southern ROCKY MOUNTAINS. After Kern and his brothers were abandoned by Frémont in the midst of a severe snowstorm, they managed to make their way to safety in Taos. Soon afterward, Benjamin Kern and WILLIAM SHERLEY WILLIAMS were killed by Ute Indians when they returned to the mountains to pick up some equipment that had been left behind.

Richard Kern, with his surviving brother Edward, subsequently took part in several surveys of the Southwest with the U.S. Army Corps of Topographical Engineers. In 1849, the brothers explored the Navajo (Dineh) country around Canyon de Chelly, Arizona, with Lieutenant JAMES HERVEY SIMPSON. In 1851, Richard Kern explored the Little Colorado River with Lieutenant LORENZO SITGREAVES, while his brother explored the southern plains with Lieutenant JOHN B. POPE.

Richard Kern took part in JOHN WILLIAMS GUNNISON's 1853 survey for a proposed transcontinental railroad along the 38th parallel. Both Gunnison and Kern were among those killed in an attack by Ute Indians near Lake Sevier, Utah, on December 23, 1853.

Richard Kern produced sketches of the Southwest, many of which appeared in Simpson's 1850 report *Journal of a Military Reconnaissance from Santa Fe*. Kern also made archaeological and ethnological studies of the Navajo and Zuni Indians.

Khabarov, Yerofey Pavlovich (fl. 1650s)

Russian fur trader, explorer in southeastern Siberia

Originally from Ustyug in European Russia, Yerofey P. Khabarov settled in SIBERIA in 1636. After establishing himself in fur-trading and farming enterprises, he set out from Yakutsk in 1649 to explore south and east to the valley of the Amur River, a region unknown to European Russians. In command of an expedition of 150 men, he followed the Olekma and Tungir Rivers southward, then traversed southeastern Siberia's Yablonovy Range to the Amazar River, which eventually led him to the Amur. He returned to Yakutsk in early 1650.

At that time, the region north and south of the Amur was claimed by China; to avoid an international conflict, Khabarov decided to withdraw to Yakutsk. He later reported to government leaders in Moscow on the feasibility of a military campaign to take the Amur Valley region; the proposed military action, although planned, was never carried out.

Khabarov embarked on a second Amur River expedition later in 1650. He and his men settled at Albazin, a village on the Amur, and, in spring 1651, they continued downriver. They established a base called Achansk, where they spent the winter of 1651–52. Manchus from northern China launched an attack against the Russians in spring 1652, compelling Khabarov to withdraw with his men up the Amur, along which they founded a series of forts. Soon afterward, he was recalled to Moscow to face charges of cruelty to his men. Cleared of any wrongdoing, he was given command of another Siberian frontier post at Ilimsk.

Yerofey P. Khabarov was a pioneer in the expansion of Russia into what later became its Far Eastern Territory. Russia's Khabarovsk Territory, acquired from China in 1858, was named in his honor, as was the Amur River city of Khabarovsk, founded that same year.

Khan, Genghis See GENGHIS KHAN.

King, Clarence (1842–1901) *American geologist, surveyor in the American West*

Clarence King was born in Newport, Rhode Island. He studied geology at Yale College's (now Yale University) Sheffield Scientific School, graduating in 1862.

King soon spent time in California, participating in the state's geological survey of 1863–66. He explored much of the Sierra Nevada. In 1864, he determined its highest peak to be Mount Whitney, at 14,494 feet above sea level.

Clarence King *(Library of Congress)*

King was largely responsible for persuading Congress to fund the Fortieth Parallel Survey of 1867–72, which King himself directed. King's geological investigations in northwestern Colorado exposed a supposed diamond strike as a fraud (the Great Diamond Hoax of 1872).

In 1879, King organized the government-sponsored U.S. Geological Survey, and he served as its first director until 1881. Under his leadership, explorations were made of the silver deposits at Virginia City, Nevada, and Leadville, Colorado.

King left the U.S. Geological Survey in 1881, succeeded by JOHN WESLEY POWELL. King later became a mining engineer.

Clarence King's scientific explorations of the 1860s and 1870s yielded the first comprehensive portrait of the geology of the American West. His 1872 book, *Mountaineering in the Sierra Nevada,* made him one of the fathers of American mountaineering.

King, James (1750–1784) *British naval officer, astronomer in the South Pacific*

James King was born at Clitheroe in Lancashire, England, a town on the Ribble River, northwest of Liverpool. His father was an Anglican churchman.

At the age of 12, King entered the British navy. In his early years as a midshipman, he served with the Newfoundland fleet; during this time, he made the acquaintance of JAMES COOK, who was undertaking a survey of the Newfoundland coast.

In 1771, after serving in the Mediterranean Sea, King was promoted to the rank of lieutenant. Three years later, he moved to Paris to study scientific subjects, including astronomy. In about 1775, he joined his brother Walker King, who was then teaching at Corpus Christi College in Oxford. King's ability as an astronomer came to the attention of British scientist Thomas Hornsby, who recommended him to Cook for his planned third voyage.

In July 1776, King, as second lieutenant on the *Resolution,* sailed the South Pacific Ocean with Cook. Throughout the voyage, he conducted astronomical observations, including that of a solar eclipse on Eua in the Friendly Islands in July 1777, and another on Christmas Island in December of that year.

In February 1779, at the time Cook was killed in a skirmish with natives in the HAWAIIAN ISLANDS, King was ashore with some of the crew undertaking astronomical sightings. Isolated from the rest of the expedition, the party fought off the Hawaiian islanders for two hours until they were rescued by additional crew members.

In August 1779, King was given command of the *Discovery,* under the new expedition commander JOHN GORE, following the death of Cook's successor, CHARLES CLERKE.

On his return to England in August 1780, King was promoted to captain. Soon afterward, he commanded a convoy of 500 merchant vessels to the WEST INDIES.

Stricken with tuberculosis, King traveled to Nice, France, in 1783 to try to regain his failing health. He died there the following year.

James King's astronomical studies made on Cook's third voyage were published by the British navy's Board of Longitude in 1782; for that work he was made a fellow of the prestigious British scientific association, the ROYAL SOCIETY. King also completed Cook's journal of his last expedition, published in 1783.

King, Philip Parker (1793–1856) *British naval officer in Australia and South America*

Philip Parker King was born in the British colony on Norfolk Island in the South Pacific, about 1,000 miles northeast of Sydney, Australia. He was the son of Captain Philip Gidley King, the settlement's first governor.

At the age of 14, the younger King entered the British navy. Throughout the Napoleonic Wars of 1803–15, he served in Europe, seeing action in the Bay of Biscay, the North Sea, and the MEDITERRANEAN SEA. In 1814, he was promoted to the rank of lieutenant.

In 1817, King was sent to Australia to conduct a survey of the continent's northern and western coastlines. From 1817 to 1822, along with ALLAN CUNNINGHAM, he explored and charted the region between Arnhem Land, in what is now Australia's Northern Territory, westward to North West Cape on the central coast of present-day Western Australia. His main objective was to locate a gulf or river that led into the interior of Australia, and possibly a passage that cut through the continent all the way to the Pacific Ocean. The idea that such a passage existed had first been suggested by WILLIAM DAMPIER in the early 1700s; he had speculated that a water route into the interior of Australia might be found behind the island group on Australia's west coast that now bears his name. SIR JOSEPH BANKS had also theorized that there was a river system leading deep into the continent.

In four voyages, the first three on the *Mermaid* and the last on the *Bathurst,* King undertook a detailed hydrographic survey of the north shores of Australia. Yet he found no gulf or river providing passage inland, although he did establish a safe route from Sydney to the Torres Strait within the hazardous Great Barrier Reef. He also undertook a detailed survey of the coast of TASMANIA. Storms prevented him from studying the shoreline along the Eighty Mile Beach and the Buccaneer Archipelago on Australia's northwest coast, and King later speculated that the inland passage might exist in that uncharted region.

King returned to England in 1823, where he prepared the charts and written account of his explorations, first published in 1827 as *Narrative of the Survey of the Intertropical and Western Coasts of Australia.* For his efforts in exploring Australia, he was made a fellow of the ROYAL SOCIETY in 1824.

Given command of the *Adventure* in 1825, he joined Captain Pringle Stokes and ROBERT FITZROY on the *Beagle* (the ship on which CHARLES ROBERT DARWIN later undertook his scientific voyage of 1831–36) in a survey of the southern part of South America. In 1826–30, the expedition made an exhaustive survey from the mouth of the Río de la Plata on the east coast of South America, around the continent's southern tip, to Chiloé Island on the Pacific coast of Chile.

Returning to England in 1831, King presented his findings to the ROYAL GEOGRAPHICAL SOCIETY; then, in 1832, he published them as *Sailing Directions to the Coasts of Eastern and Western Patagonia, including the Straits of Magalhaen and Seacoast of Tierra del Fuego.* A less technical account of his South American voyage was published in 1839 as part of Fitzroy's *Voyages of the Adventure and Beagle.*

Leaving active service in the British navy after 1832, King settled in Australia, where he became a member of the legislative council of New South Wales as well as manager of the Australian Agricultural Society. In these capacities, he promoted additional explorations northward from Sydney into what is now Queensland. In 1855, a year before his death, he was promoted to rear admiral on the retired list.

In his earlier explorations of Australia's north coast, Philip Parker King had noted the possibilities of developing Port Essington, the northernmost point of Arnhem Land, as a base for maritime trade with Asia. To this end he dispatched several expeditions in search of an overland route there from Sydney and from the coast of Queensland, including those undertaken by THOMAS LIVINGSTONE MITCHELL and EDMUND KENNEDY in the late 1840s. His friend the geologist SIR PAUL EDMUND STRZELECKI named Lake King in southeastern Australia after him.

Kingsley, Mary Henrietta (1862–1900) *British traveler, writer in West and central Africa*

Born in London, Mary H. Kingsley was the daughter of British doctor and travel writer George H. Kingsley and a niece of novelist Charles Kingsley. She was educated at Cambridge University in sociology.

Soon after her father's death in 1892, Kingsley resolved to travel to Africa to study native fetish religions and collect specimens of fish. In 1893, she reached the Gulf of Guinea, and, after a visit to the island of Fernando Po, she landed on the mainland at Calabar in present-day Nigeria, from where she explored inland, visiting the region between the

Mary Kingsley *(Library of Congress)*

Cross River and NIGER RIVER. She then headed southward to the lower CONGO RIVER (Zaire) region of northern Angola, before returning to England in 1894.

Kingsley made her second visit to Africa late in 1894. She traveled to what was then French Equatorial Africa, now Cameroon and Gabon. Ascending the Ogowe River by steamer, she reached Lambarene, where Dr. Albert Schweitzer would establish his medical mission 20 years later. She continued up the river in a CANOE, accompanied by native guides and porters. She reached a region known as the Great Forest, where she observed the life and culture of the region's Fan people. Most of the territory she traversed in Gabon and Cameroon was then largely unknown to Europeans. She stayed with an agent of the French colonial government, then returned to the coast of Cameroon by way of the Rembwe River. Before leaving French Equatorial Africa, Kingsley climbed 13,350-foot Mount Cameroon, the region's highest peak.

Back in England in 1895, Kingsley wrote and lectured extensively on her travels. She became an outspoken critic of the practices of missionaries in West and central Africa, maintaining that European traders were a far more positive influence on the natives. Her first book on Africa, *Travels in West Africa,* was published in 1897 and was followed by two other works, *West African Studies* and *The Story of West Africa,* both published in 1899.

Although Kingsley had planned a third expedition to West Africa, the outbreak of the Boer War in 1899 led her to change her plans. She sailed to South Africa and worked as a nurse. At the age of 38, she died of typhoid fever, which she contracted while caring for Boer prisoners of war at Simonstown, just south of Cape Town.

In honor of Mary H. Kingsley's achievements as both an explorer of West and central Africa and a champion of native rights, her admirers in England established the Mary Kingsley Society, which later became known as the Royal African Society.

Kino, Eusebio Francisco (Eusebius Francisco Kino) (ca. 1645–1711) *Italian missionary in northern Mexico, southern Arizona, and Baja California*

Eusebio Francisco Kino was born near the northern Italian city of Trento. After studies in astronomy and mathematics, he was ordained a Jesuit priest in Germany in 1669.

Kino traveled to Mexico as a missionary in 1681. Two years later, he became the Spanish royal cosmographer for a colonizing expedition to Baja California, led by Admiral Isidro Atondo y Antillón.

In about 1687, the Baja California colony was abandoned, and Kino traveled to the Pimeria Alta region of what is now northern Mexico and southern Arizona. From 1691 to 1706, he established a series of missions and explored northward to the Gila River.

Kino searched unsuccessfully for a land route between Arizona and the Pacific coast. On one expedition, he explored the Gila River to its confluence with the COLORADO RIVER. The route was later known as El Camino del Diablo (the devil's highway). Kino also explored southern Arizona's San Pedro and Santa Cruz Rivers. In 1694, he located the Casa Grande Indian ruins near present-day Florence, Arizona.

In 1698, Kino explored the Colorado River to its mouth in the Gulf of California. Based on his observations at the northern end of the Gulf, he proved Baja California was not an island, as earlier explorers had believed.

After 1706, Kino worked out of his missionary headquarters, Nuestra Señora de los Dolores, in present-day Sonora, Mexico. He undertook more than 50 expeditions throughout the region south of the Gila River. He traveled more than 20,000 miles in his 25 years of exploring, establishing missions and producing the first accurate maps of southern Arizona and northern Mexico.

Eusebio Francisco Kino coordinated his geographic findings with other explorations and helped create the first comprehensive maps of the region between the Colorado River and the Gulf of Mexico. He is credited with naming

Statue of Eusebio Francisco Kino *(Library of Congress)*

During the 1870s, Kintup was recruited by British colonial authorities to take part in the Great Trigonometrical Survey of India, begun in the early part of the 19th century under SIR GEORGE EVEREST and others. The purpose of this project was to map and chart much of India and establish the heights and locations of the peaks of the Himalayas of northern India and Tibet. With European travel into Tibet restricted, the British relied on native explorers to venture into the region to obtain geographic information for the survey.

Kintup, although limited in his educational background and reportedly illiterate, was trained as one of the PUNDIT (Hindi for "learned expert") explorers by the British. In 1879, he was sent into Tibet, disguised as a Buddhist pilgrim and accompanied by a Mongolian lama. Kintup's main objective was to determine the connection, if any, between Tibet's major navigable river, the Tsangpo, and the Brahmaputra River of northeastern India. To accomplish this mission, he attached messages in metallic tubes to specially marked logs, which he then floated downstream.

Kintup was betrayed by his Mongolian lama companion, who sold him into slavery. He was held against his will for two years before managing to escape and return to India's northeastern Ganges Delta region in 1884. While there, he discovered that some of the logs he had sent down the Tsangpo River in Tibet several years earlier had reached the GANGES RIVER and Brahmaputra River outlets into the Bay of Bengal, thus establishing that the stream known as the Tsangpo in Tibet is in fact identical to the Brahmaputra River of the Bengal region, ultimately emptying into the Bengal bay.

Kintup, like NAIN SINGH and KISHEN SINGH, was among those few native explorers who worked independently of the Europeans who had hired them. His efforts contributed to the geographic knowledge of isolated regions forbidden to Europeans.

Kishen Singh   See SINGH, KISHEN.

Kittson, Norman Wolfred (1814–1888)
Canadian-born fur trader in the Red River of the North region
Norman Kittson was born in Chambly, Quebec, a small town near Montreal. His family background was English; his grandfather reportedly had served under General James Wolfe in the British victory over the French at Quebec in 1759.

Kittson received his only formal education at a grammar school in Sorel, Quebec. At the age of 16, he embarked on a career in the FUR TRADE, inspired by the tales of ad-

the Colorado River. Kino's charts were the basis for maps of the American Southwest that were used until well into the 19th century. He also made the first astronomical observations in the American West.

Kintup (Kinthup) (fl. 1880s) *Indian surveyor in Tibet, in service to Great Britain*
Kintup was a native of Sikkim, a northeastern state of India nestled in the HIMALAYAS between Nepal and Bhutan.

venture related to him by retired fur trader William Morrison. He became an apprentice with JOHN JACOB ASTOR's AMERICAN FUR COMPANY and served at the company's posts in present-day Wisconsin, Minnesota, and Iowa.

Kittson's abilities came to the attention of Henry Hastings Sibley, Astor's chief agent at the company's main upper Mississippi River post near Fort Snelling on the site of present-day St. Paul, Minnesota. In 1843, appointed as a special partner in Sibley's operations, Kittson was sent to trade with the Indians of the upper Minnesota and Red Rivers. Although the boundary north of Minnesota and the Dakotas between Canada and the United States had been established 25 years earlier, British-backed HUDSON'S BAY COMPANY traders were regularly making unlawful incursions into the region. To counter this competition, Kittson established an American Fur Company post at Pembina on the Red River, near the common border of present-day North Dakota, Minnesota, and Manitoba, Canada. He then set up outlying posts 300 miles east and west of Pembina in an effort to bring the first organized American presence into the region.

Over the next several years, Kittson took part in a ferocious trade war with the Hudson's Bay Company, sharing his profits as well as his losses with Sibley and the American Fur Company. During this period, Kittson began to organize his first transportation enterprises—ox-cart caravans carrying furs, hides, and other Indian products overland from Pembina to Sibley at the Fort Snelling post. Competition with the Hudson's Bay Company became so intense that Kittson resorted to purchasing from the Indians furs smuggled into the United States from Canada.

In 1851, a flood forced Kittson to move his headquarters in the Red River Valley from Pembina to nearby Walhalla. Three years later, when it became apparent that the Hudson's Bay Company was unwilling to buy him out and could continue the trade war indefinitely, he closed the business and settled in St. Paul, the territorial capital of Minnesota.

Kittson served as a delegate to the Minnesota territorial legislature in 1852–55, at times traveling to legislative sessions from his wilderness trading post by dogsled. In 1858, he was elected as a Democrat to the office of mayor of St. Paul. A few years later he began one of the earliest steamboat lines on the Red River of the North. He also served as the Hudson's Bay Company's forwarding agent at St. Paul. In 1872, Kittson entered into a partnership with James J. Hill that resulted in the formation of the Kittson Red River Transportation Company, a major steamboat line on the Red River. Six years later, along with Hill and several Canadian investors, he became one of the founders of the St. Paul, Minneapolis, and Manitoba Railroad, an enterprise that made him enormously wealthy. He retired in the early 1880s to raise horses.

Norman Kittson's fur-trading enterprise in what is now northwestern Minnesota and northeastern North Dakota helped assert U.S. control over the region at a time when the territory had only a handful of non-Indian settlers. Minnesota's northeastern Kittson County was named in honor of his pioneering efforts.

Knight, James (ca. 1640–ca. 1721) *British fur-trader in Hudson Bay*

Originally from London, James Knight worked as a shipwright's apprentice at the dockyards near Deptford. In 1676, he entered the service of the HUDSON'S BAY COMPANY as a staff carpenter, sailing to HUDSON BAY later that year.

By 1682, Knight had been promoted to chief factor at Fort Albany, the Hudson's Bay Company post on the west shore of James Bay. Following his return to England, he was dismissed from the company amid charges that he had engaged in unauthorized trading with the Indians for his personal gain.

Knight's separation from the Hudson's Bay Company proved temporary. In 1692, he was rehired to lead an expedition to retake the Fort Albany post, which had fallen into the hands of the French. Sailing from England with a fleet of four ships and 213 men in June 1692, he quickly reoccupied Fort Albany and served there as governor. In 1697, he returned to England as a principal shareholder of the Hudson's Bay Company, and in 1711, he was named as one of the directors of the firm's ruling council, the London Committee.

Knight returned to Hudson Bay in 1713 to accept from the French the surrender of York Factory at the mouth of the Hayes River in what is now northern Manitoba. Assuming the management of the post, he sent out fur-trading expeditions to the north and west in response to increased competition from French traders on the Albany River to the south. These expeditions, led by William Stuart, eventually made contacts with the Chipewyan Indian bands around Great Slave Lake. One woman, Thanadelthur, known as "the Slave Woman" because she had been held captive by Cree Indians, became a trusted guide and interpreter for Knight in his dealings with the Indians. In addition, she told the English fur trader tales of her homeland to the northwest of York Factory, where she said there were abundant mines of what sounded like gold, as well as a strait that opened up to a "Great Western Sea." Knight became convinced that these were references to the valuable mineral deposits reported by Indians and that the strait she spoke of might prove to be the NORTHWEST PASSAGE, or STRAIT OF ANIAN, which led to the coast of Asia.

Encouraged by this news, Knight sailed to England in 1718, where he succeeded in obtaining the Hudson's Bay Company's support for a seaward expedition to the northwest coast of Hudson Bay.

In June 1719, Knight sailed from London with two small vessels, the *Albany* and the *Discovery*, with a combined crew of 27 men and 10 passengers. Later that summer, he met up with supply vessels near York Factory, then sailed northward along the west coast of Hudson Bay. His expedition was never seen again.

Nearly 50 years later, in 1767, SAMUEL HEARNE, exploring Marble Island off the northwest coast of Hudson Bay, came upon the wreckage of Knight's ships and heard reports from local Inuit (Eskimo) that Knight's expedition had been wrecked in a storm on the island. The survivors had built shelters on the island, but in winter 1720–21, the last two men had perished. Three expeditions headed by Hudson's Bay Company factor HENRY KELSEY had explored the Marble Island region but found no evidence of Knight.

James Knight's 1719 voyage was one of the first seaward expeditions in search of the Northwest Passage undertaken by the Hudson's Bay Company, an endeavor called for under the terms of its original charter of 1670. Although his final effort was ill-fated, his earlier work led to the establishment in 1717 of Fort Prince of Wales at the mouth of the Churchill River on the southwest coast of Hudson Bay, which became a gateway for explorers of western Canada, including PETER POND and SIR ALEXANDER MACKENZIE.

Knight, John (unknown–1606) *English seafarer* *in Labrador*

Little is known of John Knight's origins or early life. By 1606, he was known as an accomplished mariner, and that year he was commissioned by Sir Thomas Smith, governor of the BRITISH EAST INDIA COMPANY, to command a voyage of exploration westward in search of the NORTHWEST PASSAGE. Smith had been involved in the earlier voyages of London's MUSCOVY COMPANY. Knight's 1606 voyage was to follow up the earlier explorations of MARTIN FROBISHER and JOHN DAVIS and the more recent explorations of GEORGE WEYMOUTH in 1602.

In command of the ship *Hopewell*, Knight sailed from England in spring 1606. By June 26, he had arrived off the coast of northern Labrador. While his ship underwent repairs for rudder damage from an iceberg, Knight went ashore with a surveying party that included his brother. They ventured inland and climbed over a hill, after which they were never seen again. With the loss of its commander and the other crew members, the *Hopewell* returned to England.

John Knight's ill-fated voyage in 1606 was one of the many prompted by the search for the elusive Northwest Passage. Four years later, in 1610, HENRY HUDSON found what came to be known as HUDSON BAY, fueling additional hopes that a direct sea route to the Orient through North America might soon be located.

Koldewey, Karl Christian (1837–1908) *German explorer in Spitsbergen and Greenland*

Karl Christian Koldewey was born in Bücken, near the German city of Hanover. Going to sea at the age of 16, he visited many parts of the world over the next 20 years.

In 1868, Koldewey led the first German expedition into the Arctic region north of Spitsbergen (in Svalbard), in an unsuccessful attempt to find a passage across the Arctic Ocean to the BERING STRAIT. At that time, the still-popular "open polar sea" theory of German geographer AUGUST HEINRICH PETERMANN posited the existence of an ice-free passage to the NORTH POLE in the region north of Scandinavia and eastern Russia, between Spitsbergen and Novaya Zemlya.

Koldewey followed up his Spitsbergen explorations with a second German expedition to GREENLAND in 1869–70. On the ship *Germania*, he advanced along the east coast of Greenland as far north as 77° north latitude before being forced back by the PACK ICE. He was accompanied by JULIUS VON PAYER.

Following his Arctic exploits, Koldewey was appointed to a high German government post in Hamburg dealing with navigation.

One significant result of Karl Christian Koldewey's Greenland expedition of 1869–70 was his discovery of a type of Siberian wood known as larchwood, which had washed ashore on the east coast of Greenland. This finding later provided Norwegian polar explorer FRIDTJOF NANSEN with evidence of the drifting patterns of ice in the frozen Arctic Ocean between SIBERIA, Alaska, and Greenland.

Kotzebue, Otto von (1787–1846) *Russian naval officer in Alaska and the South Pacific*

Otto von Kotzebue was born in the Baltic seaport city of Revel, present-day Tallinn in Estonia. His father, August von Kotzebue, was a German in service to the Russian government who went on to become an internationally acclaimed playwright.

The younger Kotzebue attended a military school in St. Petersburg until 1803, when, at the age of 15, he was recruited as a naval cadet for ADAM IVAN RITTER VON KRUSENSTERN's CIRCUMNAVIGATION OF THE WORLD. Aboard the expedition's lead vessel, the *Nadezhda*, he and his 14-year-old brother Moritz Kotzebue served as naval cadets in a three-year voyage that took them across the North Pacific to Kamchatka and along the western rim of the Pacific to Japan and China.

Kotzebue's next great maritime endeavor occurred in 1815 after the Napoleonic Wars. That year, Count Nicholas Romanzof, who at that time held the office of chancellor of the Russian Empire, personally financed and organized an expedition to explore the South Pacific Ocean and search the coasts of SIBERIA and Alaska for the NORTHEAST PASSAGE or NORTHWEST PASSAGE—an outlet connecting the North Pacific with Baffin Bay and the Atlantic. Kotzebue, by then a lieutenant commander in the Russian navy, was placed in charge and given command of the ship *Rurik* and its crew of 32. Among them were the naturalists LOUIS-CHARLES-ADÉLAÏDE CHAMISSO DE BONCOURT and JOHANN FRIEDRICH ESCHSCHOLTZ, and the draftsman LOUIS CHORIS.

Sailing from the Baltic port of Kronstadt, near St. Petersburg, at the end of July 1815, Kotzebue first stopped at the Canary Islands before continuing to the south coast of Brazil. He entered the Pacific by way of CAPE HORN and reached Concepción on the coast of Chile in February 1816. After a short stay in the Chilean port, he headed for Easter Island and located several previously uncharted islands nearby.

After a cruise that took him through the Gilbert and Marshall Islands of the Central Pacific, Kotzebue headed northward for the Kamchatka Peninsula on the Pacific coast of Siberia. In June 1816, he made a brief stopover at the port of Petropavlovsk Bay on Kamchatka, then sailed eastward across the Bering Sea. He visited Bering Island and St. Lawrence Island and finally reached the coast of Alaska. Arriving too late in the season to commence any extensive explorations, he remained only long enough to survey the coastline south of BERING STRAIT for suitable anchorages. He then sailed southward to spend the winter of 1816–17 in the HAWAIIAN ISLANDS and the Marshall Islands.

Kotzebue embarked on his second attempt to locate a northern sea route from the Pacific to the Atlantic in spring 1817. He returned to Alaskan waters, stopping at Unalaska Island, where he received equipment from employees of the RUSSIAN-AMERICAN COMPANY. He also took aboard several Aleut natives and their small skin boats, known as *baidarkas*, for the exploration of the coastline to the north. In July 1817, he came upon a promising inland arm of the sea, which he hoped would lead into an open-water passage to the Atlantic. It turned out to be Goodhope Bay on the south shore of an adjoining large inland gulf that Kotzebue named after himself: Kotzebue Sound.

Kotzebue had planned to sail northward through Bering Strait, but he decided to turn back in mid-July 1817. He later reported that concerns about his own health (possibly angina), as well as uncertainties about the ice conditions ahead, led to his decision to withdraw. On the return southward through the Bering Strait, he coasted along the Asian mainland, visiting with the Inuit of the Chukchi Peninsula. He again entered the Pacific. In his subsequent explorations, he located more uncharted atolls and islands in the Marshall, Mariana, and Gilbert groups.

Kotzebue arrived back in St. Petersburg in August 1818, having sailed around the CAPE OF GOOD HOPE in his second circumnavigation of the world. He was immediately promoted to the rank of captain lieutenant in the Russian Marine Guards.

Five years later, Kotzebue was directly commissioned by Czar Alexander I to command another Russian voyage to the Pacific. This expedition was intended as a political and scientific exercise, aimed partly at keeping an eye on Spanish, British, and American encroachment on Russian possessions in Alaska and the Pacific Northwest. He was also to patrol the Gulf of Alaska in an effort to protect the Russian-American Company's fur monopoly from the activities of smugglers. On the sloop *Predpriyatiye* (enterprise), he returned to the Pacific. After duty off the coast of North America, he once again cruised the islands of Oceania, making the European discovery of islands in the Tuamotu, Society, and Marshall groups.

Kotzebue and the *Predpriyatiye* returned to St. Petersburg in 1826, having completed his third round-the-world voyage. His account of his 1815–18 voyage was first published in 1821 as *A Voyage of Discovery into the South Sea and Bering Strait*. His third circumnavigation was recounted in his 1830 work *A New Voyage Round the World in the Years 1823–26*. He retired from active naval service in 1829, settling with his family in Estonia.

In the course of his South Pacific explorations in 1815–18 and 1823–26, Kotzebue charted more than 300 islands and atolls. Among them were a group of 36 islets in the Marshall chain, which he located in 1817 and called the Eschscholtz Islands, after the naturalist JOHANN FRIEDRICH ESCHSCHOLTZ. One of them later became known as Bikini Atoll and was made famous as the site of U.S. atomic bomb tests in 1946.

Krapf, Johann Ludwig (1810–1881)
German missionary in East Africa

J. Ludwig Krapf is thought to have been born in the Württemberg region of southwestern Germany. He attended the Basel Missionary Institute in Switzerland and eventually joined the Church Missionary Society, an Anglican organization.

Krapf's first missionary assignment was in Abyssinia (present-day Ethiopia), where he arrived in about 1837. He tried without success to establish a missionary presence in the country and he was expelled by government officials in 1842. He then headed southward to the port of Mombasa on the Indian Ocean coast of present-day Kenya. After establishing a mission, Neu-Rabai, he began preparations for a string of missions across the interior of central Africa in the hope of countering the SLAVE TRADE carried on by the Arabs.

Krapf decided that before founding any more missions, he had to explore the interior of the region inland from

Mombasa, still uncharted by Europeans. He learned the Swahili language and gathered geographic information from Arab traders passing through Mombasa on their slaving expeditions inland. Krapf learned of great mountains capped with a substance that he correctly deduced to be snow and ice. He also heard reports of great inland lakes, possibly Lake Victoria and Lake Tanganyika, filled with freshwater from these mountains. From these tales, Krapf speculated that he was hearing about the legendary MOUNTAINS OF THE MOON, the peaks mentioned by the ancient geographer PTOLEMY as the ultimate source of the NILE RIVER.

Before he could set out, Krapf was stricken with malaria. In about 1847, JOHANN REBMANN arrived at his mission as an assistant. The next year, while Krapf was still recovering, Rebmann undertook a journey into the interior, becoming the first European to see MOUNT KILIMANJARO, Africa's highest mountain.

Krapf regained his health, and, in 1849, he set out with a small band of Nyika and Swahili tribesmen. He had also been given a letter of safe conduct by the sympathetic Seyyid Said, the sultan of Oman and Zanzibar. In December 1849, after following a route northwestward from Mombasa, and also sighting Mount Kilimanjaro, he reached Nairobi and there made the first sighting by a European of Mount Kenya, Africa's second highest mountain. Like Kilimanjaro, it too was covered with ice and snow, confirming Krapf's earlier speculations about the interior lakes and the source of the Nile. From local natives he heard reports of the upper Congo River (Zaire River) and its course to the coast of West Africa.

In 1855, Krapf's map of the interior of eastern and central Africa appeared in the journal of the London Missionary Society. It sparked immediate controversy among professional geographers, with its clear delineation of interior high mountain ranges covered with snow lying nearly on the EQUATOR, and its suggestion that vast inland freshwater lakes were the source of the Nile. In 1856, the ROYAL GEOGRAPHICAL SOCIETY dispatched SIR RICHARD FRANCIS BURTON and JOHN HANNING SPEKE on an expedition to investigate these reports.

About that time, Krapf returned to Europe and published his account of his years in East Africa entitled *Travel, Researches, and Missionary Labours During Eighteen Years Residence in Eastern Africa*. In 1867, he returned to Africa as an interpreter for a British expedition to Abyssinia, and he subsequently introduced original Abyssinian manuscripts into Great Britain and Germany.

J. Ludwig Krapf was one of the first Europeans to venture into the interior of East Africa from the Indian Ocean coast. In his explorations, which included the European discovery of Mount Kenya, he relied on his ability to deal with natives in their own language and less on elaborate equipment or extensive supplies and an army of porters. His re-

ports on the interior of East Africa led to the European discovery of Lake Tanganyika and Lake Victoria and ultimately helped solve the mystery of the source of the Nile. In his 1849 expedition to Mount Kenya, he blazed a trail that was developed into a railroad route between Mombasa and Nairobi in 1902.

Krasheninnikov, Stepan Petrovich (1711–1755)
Russian naturalist in eastern Siberia

Stepan Krasheninnikov was born in Moscow. At the age of 13, he entered the Moscow Slavonic-Greek-Latin Academy, which he attended until 1732, before going on to the Academic University in St. Petersburg.

In 1733, Krasheninnikov left his studies to take part in the Great Northern Expedition. Organized that year by the Russian monarch, Empress Anna, and commanded by VITUS JONASSEN BERING, the expedition planned to make the first extensive exploration of central and eastern SIBERIA, which had only recently come under Russian control. From 1733 to 1737, as part of this undertaking, Krasheninnikov accompanied German naturalist JOHANN GEORG GMELIN and his scientific team in a survey of the natural history of Siberia.

By 1737, Krasheninnikov was on the Kamchatka Peninsula, along Siberia's Pacific coast, where, over the next three years, he took part in an extensive survey of the region's natural history, conducting comprehensive studies of Kamchatka's wildlife and geology. Krasheninnikov traveled throughout Kamchatka, observing the culture of the peninsula's native inhabitants. In 1741, Krasheninnikov returned to St. Petersburg. Under the sponsorship of the Academy of Sciences, he prepared a complete account of his findings and travels in the easternmost parts of the Russian Empire. Originally published in Russian in 1751, it was translated into English in 1972 as *Explorations of Kamchatka, North Pacific Scimitar*.

Stepan Krasheninnikov undertook one of the earliest anthropological studies of the native people of Kamchatka in the years just before their culture underwent dramatic changes as a result of increased contact with European Russia.

Krenitsyn, Pyotr Kuzmich (unknown–1770)
Russian navigator in the Aleutian Islands

Pyotr Krenitsyn was an officer in the Russian navy in the 1760s, during the first years of the reign of Catherine the Great, empress of Russia.

In 1768, Krenitsyn sailed from the mouth of the Kamchatka River on the Pacific coast of SIBERIA, in command of an expedition sent to explore the Aleutian Islands. Assisted by Mikhail D. Levashev, he cruised and charted the islands nearest the North American mainland, including Umnak,

Unalaska, and Unimak, as well as the western end of the Alaska Peninsula.

Soon after his return to Kamchatka in 1770, Pyotr Krenitsyn drowned in the Kamchatka River, near the port of Kamchatsk. Levashev, his assistant, returned to European Russia in 1771 with the expedition's geographic findings. Based on this information, cartographers in St. Petersburg were able to produce one of the earliest maps of the Aleutian chain. The Krenitzin Islands, which lie between Unalaska and Unimak Islands, were named in his honor.

Kropotkin, Peter (Prince Pyotr Alekseyevich Kropotkin) (1842–1921) *Russian geographer in Siberia, Finland, and Manchuria*

Peter Kropotkin was born in Moscow into a wealthy family of the Russian nobility. As a young prince, he served as a page at the court of the Russian czar; at about age 20, he became an army officer.

In 1862–65, as an officer, Kropotkin first traveled into SIBERIA, where he applied his background in geology and geography to develop theories on the development of Asia's mountain ranges.

Leaving the army in 1865, Kropotkin went on to high posts in the Russian government. He also actively pursued his interest in geography; by 1870, he had become secretary of the physical geography section of the Russian Geographical Society. In 1871–73, Kropotkin undertook a series of scientific expeditions into northern Finland, Siberia, and Manchuria in northeastern China, during which he made additional studies in the geography, natural history, and native culture of these regions.

Starting in 1872, Kropotkin began to concentrate his efforts in promoting the cause of revolutionary anarchism. He dropped his royal title, and for this action he was imprisoned by the czarist government. Soon afterward, he escaped to France, where his radical views again landed him in prison, from 1883 to 1886. His release came about as the result of a pardon secured through French statesman Georges Clemenceau.

During the 1890s, Kropotkin settled in England and continued to write and theorize about the anarchist cause. He made several lecture tours to the United States, appearing at Harvard University and Wellesley College. After the Russian Revolution of 1917, he returned to his native land, where the new Soviet government honored him as a hero.

Although chiefly known as the father of "anarchist communism," Peter Kropotkin was also an astute geographer. In 1870, he speculated that shifts in the ice of the frozen Arctic Ocean north of Siberia would eventually lead to the European discovery of uncharted lands. Soon afterward, in 1873, Austrian polar explorer JULIUS VON PAYER located Franz Josef Land north of the Siberian mainland, and, 40

Peter Kropotkin *(Library of Congress)*

years later, in 1913, Boris Andreyevich Vilkitsky discovered the Severnaya Zemlya archipelago, northeast of Novaya Zemlya.

Krusenstern, Adam Ivan Ritter von (Adam Johann von Krusenstern, Ivan Federovich de Krusenstern, Ivan Fyodorovich Krusenshtern) (1770–1846) *Russian naval officer in the South Pacific, Japan, and Alaska*

Adam Ivan von Krusenstern was born in Haggud, Estonia, then part of the Russian Empire, into a family of the Baltic German aristocracy. In 1785, he entered the Russian navy as a cadet, soon taking part in actions in the Russo-Swedish War of 1787–90.

At the outbreak of the French Revolution in 1793, Krusenstern served for a year aboard a British warship in the waters off Africa, Asia, and North America. In 1797, he sailed to the Orient on a British merchant ship, witnessing in Canton (Guangzhou) the trade in sea otter skins brought from northwestern North America by British and American ships.

Upon his return to St. Petersburg in Russia in 1799, Krusenstern presented to the Ministry of Trade his plan for a Russian CIRCUMNAVIGATION OF THE WORLD. His main reason for the expedition had grown out of his observations of the FUR TRADE, from which he had concluded that the Russian settlements on the Kamchatka Peninsula, in the Aleutian Islands, and in Alaska could only prosper by being supplied by sea from the Baltic ports, rather than by the expensive and time-consuming overland trek across SIBERIA from European Russia. He also wanted to carry American furs directly to Chinese markets from Alaska instead of trans-shipping them from the Kamchatka Peninsula.

With the help of Count Nicholas Romanzof, the Russian minister of trade, Krusenstern received a commission from Czar Alexander I to command a voyage to the northwest coast of North America and to the Far East. In London, he obtained two ships; in Germany, he recruited a small scientific team for the voyage, which included German naturalist GEORG HEINRICH VON LANGSDORFF.

Promoted to the rank of captain lieutenant, Krusenstern sailed on the *Nadezhda* from the Baltic port of Kronstadt, near St. Petersburg, in August 1803, accompanied by the *Neva,* under YURY FYODOROVICH LISIANSKY. Sailing as cadets aboard the *Nadezhda* were 15-year-old OTTO VON KOTZEBUE and his 14-year-old brother Moritz. After

Adam Ivan von Krusenstern *(Library of Congress)*

stopovers in the CANARY ISLANDS and on Santa Catarina Island off the south coast of Brazil, the expedition rounded CAPE HORN into the Pacific Ocean in March 1804. Although storms soon separated the two vessels, Krusenstern made for the Marquesas Islands, a prearranged rendezvous in case of such an event, and, in May 1804, he was reunited with Lisiansky. He befriended the native king of Nuku Hiva, Tapeya Kettenovie, and in his subsequent written account of the voyage he commented on the extensive tattoos that distinguished the nobility of the Marquesas. The next stopover was in the HAWAIIAN ISLANDS, where Krusenstern tried without success to buy supplies from native peoples. Lacking sufficient trade goods, he was compelled to head for Kamchatka to reprovision the *Nadezhda,* while Lisiansky and the *Neva* sailed to the Gulf of Alaska and the RUSSIAN-AMERICAN COMPANY's trading posts on Kodiak Island.

After obtaining supplies at Petropavlovsk on the Kamchatka Peninsula, Krusenstern headed southward for Japan. Traveling with Krusenstern was the czar's chamberlain, N. P. Rezanov, who planned to establish Russian trade relations with the Japanese at Nagasaki. Also aboard were some Japanese sailors who had been shipwrecked in the Aleutians and were now being returned to their homeland as a goodwill gesture.

On the voyage from Kamchatka to Japan, Krusenstern surveyed and charted the east coast of Kamchatka, the Kuril Islands, and Sakhalin Island. In October 1804, the *Nadezhda* arrived in Nagasaki, at that time the only Japanese port open to Europeans. Krusenstern remained there for the next five months, while Rezanov waited to see Japanese officials from whom he hoped to obtain trading privileges for Russian ships. Finally, in early April 1805, Krusenstern was told by the Japanese that the czar's representative would not be received by government officials and was advised to leave Nagasaki as soon as possible. Despite this setback, Krusenstern used the return voyage to Kamchatka as an opportunity to further explore the islands of northern Japan, where his men had contact with the non-Japanese aboriginal inhabitants of Hokkaido, known as the Ainu. He also stopped at the northern part of Sakhalin Island and visited with the native Tartar people. During this part of the voyage, he examined the Asian mainland opposite Sakhalin Island and there located the mouth of the Amur River.

Returning to Kamchatka in summer 1805, Krusenstern sent a courier overland across Siberia to St. Petersburg with a report of his expedition. He then sailed to Macao, where he rejoined Lisiansky and the *Neva* in December 1805. The two ships went on to Canton and sold the Russian furs to Chinese merchants. In February 1806, both ships set out on the homeward voyage. Sailing by way of Indonesia's Sunda Strait and the CAPE OF GOOD HOPE, they arrived in Kronstadt in August 1806, having circumnavigated the world in just over three years.

From 1810 to 1814, Krusenstern completed his multi-volume account of the expedition, first published in English in 1813 as *Voyage Around the World in the Years 1803, 1804, 1805, and 1806.* In 1815, Krusenstern sailed again to the North Pacific in an expedition exploring BERING STRAIT for the NORTHWEST PASSAGE. His comprehensive charting of the Pacific led to his *Atlas of the Pacific Ocean,* published in 1824–27. Named a rear admiral in 1826, he became director of Russia's naval cadet academy the next year. He carried on his navigational studies with the St. Petersburg Academy of Sciences and as a member of the scientific committee of Russia's naval ministry, and was promoted to vice admiral in 1829 and admiral in 1841. Krusenstern eventually settled on his estate near what is now the Baltic port of Tallinn.

In his 1803–06 voyage, Adam Ivan von Krusenstern commanded the first official Russian circumnavigation of the world and succeeded in establishing direct maritime links among European Russia, the Russian colonies in Alaska, and the fur markets in Canton, China. His successful expedition inspired Otto von Kotzebue's voyage of 1815–18. In recognition of his achievements as one of the foremost Russian navigators of his day, Cape Krusenstern, at the entrance to Alaska's Kotzebue Sound, was named in his honor.

Kupe (fl. ca. 950) *Polynesian seafarer in the South Pacific and New Zealand*

According to the Maori people, Kupe, a chieftain of the Polynesians, set out on a westward voyage from a central Pacific island by OUTRIGGER across some 2,000 miles of the Pacific Ocean in the mid-10th century. He and his followers reportedly reached two large mountainous islands, which later came to be known as North Island and South Island of NEW ZEALAND. According to the tale, Kupe and his followers eventually returned to their home island in OCEANIA known as Hawaiki—thought to be Rarotonga in the Cook Islands—where Kupe described his discovery of what the Polynesians called *Tiritiri o te moan* (the land shrouded in high mist). The account was passed down over subsequent generations. This oral tradition includes a recitation of the route taken and comprises the Polynesian settlement of New Zealand.

The tale has fantastic elements. Kupe supposedly set out on the journey to capture the Squid King who had stolen fish from his nets, when he eventually caught and killed in the waters between North Island and South Island (now called Cook Strait). It is taken as fact that the Polynesians settled New Zealand and were ancestral to the Maori people, who lived there long before its European discovery by the Dutchman ABEL JANSZOON TASMAN in 1642.

The legendary account of Kupe's voyage is one of many tales of POLYNESIAN EXPLORATION of the Pacific. If true, it stands out as a remarkable feat of seamanship, requiring the crossing of an expanse of ocean with only basic techniques of navigation.

Kurz, Rudolph Friederich (Rudolf Friedrich Kurz) (1818–1871) *Swiss artist on the upper Missouri River*

Rudolph Kurz was born in Berne, Switzerland. He studied art in Paris, then came to America in 1847, settling first in St Louis, Missouri.

That same year, Kurz traveled up the MISSISSIPPI RIVER from St. Louis and visited Indian lands to the west. During his travels he made sketches of western scenes and Ioway Indians. In 1848, Kurz went up the MISSOURI RIVER to Council Bluffs, then established an art studio at St. Joseph, Missouri.

In 1851, Kurz reached the Dakotas aboard a fur company steamboat, settling for a time at Fort Berthold, near present-day Garrison, North Dakota. While working as a clerk for a fur company, he made hundreds of sketches of the upper Missouri River Indians, including Mandan, Arikara, and Hidatsa.

Kurz left Fort Berthold when a cholera epidemic broke out, since the Indians believed his drawing had caused the sickness. He fled across the northern plains on horseback and reached Fort Union at the mouth of the Yellowstone River, where he stayed through the winter of 1851–52.

The following spring, Kurz left Fort Union and traveled down the Missouri to St. Louis and soon arranged passage to Europe. When back in Switzerland, Kurz taught art and produced paintings based on his sketches of the American frontier.

Rudolph Kurz's paintings are one of the earliest pictorial records of life on the upper Missouri frontier.

L

La Billardière, Jacques-Julien Houtou de

(1755–1834) *French naturalist in Australia, Tasmania, and the South Pacific*

Jacques de La Billardière was born in the northern French city of Alençon. He attended the university at Montpellier in the south of France, where he was trained as a doctor and also studied botany. In 1780, he became a botanist at the French Royal Botanical Gardens; soon afterward, he spent time with SIR JOSEPH BANKS in London and undertook botanical studies at Kew Gardens. In 1786–88, he took part in a botanical expedition to the Middle East.

In 1791, La Billardière was recruited as a naturalist by ANTOINE-RAYMOND-JOSEPH DE BRUNI, chevalier d'Entrecasteaux, for his voyage to the South Pacific in search of JEAN-FRANÇOIS DE GALAUP, comte de La Pérouse, whose expedition had been missing since early 1788. La Billardière sailed on the *Recherche* from Brest in September 1791. In spring 1792, he conducted a scientific exploration of TASMANIA. Among his scientific discoveries there were several varieties of eucalyptus trees, including the giant *Eucalyptus amygdalina*, capable of growing to a height of more than 300 feet.

In November 1792, La Billardière undertook a botanical survey of the southwest coast of Australia around Cape Leeuwin. Early in 1793, in an exploration of the coast of what was then known as Nuyts Land on the south coast of Australia, he discovered several varieties of flowering bushes, as well as several types of fruit-bearing bushes.

When La Billardière and the d'Entrecasteaux expedition reached the Dutch colony at Batavia (present-day Jakarta, Indonesia) in early 1794, news had arrived of the French Revolution. La Billardière, who strongly supported the Republican cause, was imprisoned by the Dutch at the nearby port of Semarang, although he was permitted to send his natural history collections to England. He also managed to send several living breadfruit trees to Île de France (present-day Mauritius) in the Indian Ocean; they were transplanted and eventually were shipped back alive to Europe.

La Billardière was not released from Dutch custody until March 1795. He made his way back to France by way of Île de France, arriving in Paris in spring 1796. He soon recovered his botanical specimens from England, with the help of Sir Joseph Banks. In 1799, he published his *Account of the Voyage in Search of La Pérouse* and was made a member of the French Academy of Sciences.

La Billardière remained a strong supporter of the Republican cause and an opponent of the regime of Napoléon Bonaparte. He lived in semiretirement in Paris, engaged in botanical research until his death in 1834.

Jacques de La Billardière helped publicize the scientific results of the d'Entrecasteaux expedition. A midget kangaroo, which the expedition's zoologists had discovered in southern Australia in 1792, was named *La Billardiere thylogale* in his honor; the Australian bushes he discovered were named *Billardiera* by British scientist ROBERT BROWN.

Lac, François-Marie Perrin du   See PERRIN DU LAC, FRANÇOIS-MARIE.

Lacerda, Francisco de (Francisco José de Lacerda e Almeida, F. J. M. De Lacerda)

(1753–1798) *Portuguese colonial official in central Africa*

Francisco de Lacerda was a Portuguese (or possibly Brazilian) colonial official in central Africa in the latter part of the 18th century. The Portuguese had been pioneers in exploration and settlement along the east and west coasts of Africa since the days of HENRY THE NAVIGATOR, prince of Portugal, in the 1400s. Yet they had not penetrated very far into the interior, even after a presence of more than 300 years on the coastline of the African continent, south of the SAHARA DESERT.

In 1787, Lacerda undertook one of the first European explorations inland into Angola. Ascending the Cunene River from the Atlantic coast, he reached the western edge of the Bihe Plateau in central Angola.

Soon after this expedition, Lacerda was appointed as colonial governor of what is now Mozambique on the Indian Ocean coast of central Africa. While in Mozambique, he recognized the need for direct overland contact between Portugal's possessions on the west coast of Africa and its colonies on the Indian Ocean. In 1798, he set out with an expedition of 70 men from the settlement of Tete on the ZAMBEZI RIVER in western Mozambique and headed northwestward, hoping to accomplish the first east-to-west crossing of central Africa by Europeans and locate a river route between Angola and Mozambique.

Lacerda and his party ascended the Zambezi River to a point above the Quebrabasa Rapids, then entered the Luangwe River into what is now Zambia. Although he traveled close to both Lake Nyasa (Lake Malawi) and the smaller Lake Bangweulu, he missed sighting them. He died of exhaustion and fever after reaching as far north and west as Lake Mweru in the land of a tribal ruler named Cazembe, present-day northeastern Zambia. With their leader dead, Lacerda's men returned southeastward to Tete on the Zambezi.

Although Francisco de Lacerda failed in his attempt to traverse the African continent, his 1798 expedition was the most extensive European penetration of sub-Saharan Africa up to that time. He produced a map of the area between Tete and Lake Mweru. It can be said that his expedition marked the beginning of colonial expansion into central Africa. In the decade after his death, PEDRO JOÃO BAPTISTA and Amaro José succeeded in making the first recorded east-to-west crossing from Luanda, Angola, to the lower Zambezi River.

Laclede, Pierre Ligueste (Pierre Laclede Liguest) (1724–1778) *French fur trader, founder of St. Louis, Missouri*

Born in Bedous, France, Pierre Laclede was educated at the French military academy at Toulouse. He arrived in New Orleans in 1755 and soon established himself in the Indian trade on the MISSISSIPPI RIVER, operating upriver as far north as Kaskaskia in present-day Illinois.

Laclede became associated with the Chouteau family through Marie Thérèse Bourgeois Chouteau. Her son RENÉ AUGUSTE CHOUTEAU became his protégé. In 1763–64, Laclede established a settlement and trading post on the west bank of the Mississippi River above Kaskaskia and Fort de Chartres. With France's loss of much of its eastern North America territory at the conclusion of the French and Indian War, many French settlers on the east bank of the Mississippi relocated to the new settlement.

Laclede carried on a lucrative trade with the Indians for the next two years, until his official monopoly was revoked by French authorities in New Orleans. Nonetheless, after 1765, Laclede continued to operate independently of French New Orleans interests while the Louisiana Country was under Spanish rule, becoming a significant commercial force in the lower MISSOURI RIVER and the Mississippi River FUR TRADE throughout the 1770s.

Pierre Laclede called his fur-trading post on the Mississippi River St. Louis, in honor of the medieval French king, Louis IX, who had been canonized as a saint. By 1810, the original settlement, constructed on the rocky bluff overlooking the river on the site of present-day downtown St. Louis, Missouri, had grown to become the focal point for trading and trapping along the upper Missouri River and in the ROCKY MOUNTAINS. Strategically located just below the mouth of the Missouri River, St. Louis became the starting point for the first official U.S. explorers of the American West, including MERIWETHER LEWIS and WILLIAM CLARK in 1804, ZEBULON MONTGOMERY PIKE in 1806, and STEPHEN HARRIMAN LONG in 1819.

La Condamine, Charles-Marie de (1701–1774)

French scientist, cartographer in Peru, Ecuador, and the Amazon Basin

Charles-Marie de la Condamine was born in Paris to a fairly affluent family. He entered the French army when he was 18 but left after a year to pursue his interest in mathematics, cartography, astronomy, and natural history. After he took part in a scientific expedition to the Middle East, La Condamine's reputation as a scientist grew in France. In 1730, he was elected to the French Academy of Sciences.

In late 1734, with the support and influence of his friend the French author and philosopher François Voltaire, La Condamine was appointed to lead an official French scientific expedition to South America, the express purpose of which was to measure the arc of a section of a meridian of longitude at the EQUATOR and thereby determine the true shape of the Earth. At that time, a scientific controversy was raging between the adherents of Sir Isaac Newton, who believed the planet to be flattened at the NORTH POLE and SOUTH POLE, and those who supported the contention of French-Italian mathematician Giovanni Cassini, who held that it flattened at the equator.

La Condamine was to head one of two expeditions involved in the Earth-measuring project. While one contingent went to Lapland to determine the variations in the curvature of the Earth near the Arctic Circle, La Condamine's group traveled to Quito in present-day Ecuador, then the most accessible point nearest to the equator, where they planned to make similar observations. Among his scientific team were French astronomer Louis Godin and his cousin Jean Godin des Odonais, who served as La Condamine's field assistant. A naval engineer by the name of Morainville, a doctor named Jean Seniergues, and the French botanist Joseph de Jussieu also participated. The expedition included a watchmaker, a man named Hugot, to maintain the project's scientific instruments, and two Spanish naval officers who were also mathematicians, Antonio de Ulloa and Jorge Juan y Santacilia.

Sailing from the French port of La Rochelle on May 16, 1735, La Condamine and his group first journeyed to the French Caribbean island of Martinique, then to Cartagena on the Caribbean coast of what is now Colombia. From there, they crossed the Isthmus of Panama, then headed southward along the Pacific coast of South America to the port of Manta in modern Ecuador, at that time part of northern Peru's Esmeraldas Province.

While traveling inland to Quito along the Rio Esmeraldas, La Condamine became one of the first Europeans to encounter the material we know today as rubber. Noting its resilient and elastic properties, he used it to fashion a protective casing for some of his most sensitive scientific instruments. Outside of Quito, on the Plain of Yarqui, the French scientists spent the next two years constructing observation posts and making calculations along a section of a meridian that measured an arc 3° north and south of the equator.

Difficulties with Spanish colonial authorities, who were suspicious of any foreigners in the region, caused extensive delays in La Condamine's scientific work. In 1736, he traveled to Lima with Juan y Santacilia for a meeting with the provincial governor to resolve these problems, a journey that took more than eight months. Soon after his return to Quito in 1737, word arrived from Europe that the French team in Lapland had finished its work, conclusively determining that Newton had been correct in his conclusions about the Earth flattening at the Poles.

Undaunted by this news, La Condamine and his associates continued their work, completing studies that later added to the understanding of the true shape of the Earth. Their research provided data on the variations in the readings of navigational instruments near the equator.

In 1738, La Condamine scaled Corazon in the ANDES MOUNTAINS. Two years later, he attempted unsuccessfully to reach the top of Chimborazo.

La Condamine also carried out scientific work in the area of natural history until 1743. By that time, most of the members of the French expedition had died or gone their separate ways. Jean Godin des Odanais had married a Peruvian, ISABELA GODIN DES ODONAIS. The doctor, Seniergues, had been killed in 1739 in a dispute arising out of his role as an intermediary in a jilted engagement between one of the members of the expedition and a local woman. The botanist, Jussieu, had a nervous breakdown when his collection of specimens was accidentally destroyed. The naval engineer, Morainville, was killed in a fall from a scaffold while helping to construct a church. The astronomer Louis Godin remained in Peru, having accepted a position at the University of San Marcos in Lima.

With his geodesic work completed in Quito, La Condamine decided to undertake a voyage down the Amazon Basin to the Atlantic coast of Brazil, rather than sail directly back to France. From Jesuit missionaries in Cuenca and Quito, he obtained maps of the AMAZON RIVER that had been prepared years earlier by Father SAMUEL FRITZ. In June 1743, he headed into the Andes, traveling across deep canyons and passes by way of rope bridges, of the type in use since the days of the Inca Indians. He reached the Marañón River, which he descended to its confluence with the Huallaga River, where he was joined by Pedro Maldonado, the governor of Esmeraldas Province. His downriver journey took him through the Pongo Pass, a narrow chasm through which the river surged in perilous rapids. Along the way, he made navigational calculations and studied the life of the Indians, noting for instance their hunting with arrows tipped with the poison curare.

On this journey, La Condamine was one of the first Europeans to hear reports of the link between the Amazon and the ORINOCO RIVER to the north—the Casiquiare Canal. He also investigated stories about the fabled women warriors and their matriarchal society (reported by FRANCISCO DE ORELLANA two centuries earlier), for whom the Amazon River was named. Among his findings was that the Rio Negro actually flowed into the Amazon from the northwest and not from the north as had previously been reported by Jesuit explorers. Near Pará (present-day Belem, Brazil), he explored Marajo Island. Before reaching the Atlantic coast, La Condamine used his geographic and mathematical skills to ascertain the coordinates of the demarcation line of the 1494 Treaty of Tordesillas separating Portuguese and Spanish possessions in South America, still in dispute as late as 1743.

After delays at Cayenne in French Guiana, La Condamine decided to sail to Europe from Paramaribo, a port in Dutch Guiana. Stopping over in Holland, he arrived back in Paris in February 1745. He immediately set to work on a map of his Amazon journey and a full account of his scientific work in Peru and Ecuador; it was published in

1751 as *Journal of a Voyage by Order of the King to the Equator.* La Condamine's later scientific efforts concentrated on trying, without success, to win acceptance of a universal unit of length based on his measurements with pendulum clocks near the equator.

Charles-Marie de la Condamine undertook the first scientific exploration of the Amazon. His work served as an inspiration for the expedition of ALEXANDER VON HUMBOLDT half a century later. He also introduced rubber to Europe, an event that would have a profound economic and social impact on the Amazon region 150 years after his visit.

La Cosa, Juan de   See COSA, JUAN DE LA.

Lagrée, Ernest-Marc-Louis de Gonzague Doudart de   See DOUDART DE LAGRÉE, ERNEST-MARC-LOUIS DE GONZAGUE.

La Harpe, Jean-Baptiste Bénard de (Bernard de la Harpe)   (fl. early 1700s) *French trader in the American Southwest*

Bénard de La Harpe, a Frenchman from the Louisiana country, was involved in the Indian trade in the region west of the lower MISSISSIPPI RIVER. The onset of the War of the Quadruple Alliance, in which Spain was pitted against France, prompted several French expeditions westward from Louisiana into the Spanish territory of Texas. One of these, a trading venture, was led by La Harpe in 1719. On reaching the Red River, he traveled with a small party of traders overland to the Arkansas and Canadian Rivers and attempted, without success to open up trade contacts with tribes of the southern plains. When he reached Santa Fe, Spanish officials became alarmed and took steps to curb further foreign encroachment into the region.

Bénard de La Harpe's 1719 trip to Santa Fe prompted Spanish colonial authorities in Mexico and New Mexico to counter the French threat. The Spanish realized that the only permanent bulwark against French expansion from Louisiana, as well as English expansion from Georgia, was to undertake a program of widespread colonization in Texas, which was begun in 1748 under JOSÉ DE ESCANDÓN.

Lahontan, Louis-Armand de Lom d'Arce de (Baron de Lahontan, Baron de la Hontan et Hesleche)   (ca. 1666–1716) *French army officer in the western Great Lakes region*

Baron de Lahontan was a captain in the French marines when he arrived in Montreal from France in 1683. During the next several years, he took part in the French campaign against the Iroquois (Haudenosaunee) Indians.

In 1687, Lahontan traveled westward into the eastern Great Lakes with DANIEL GREYSOLON DULUTH. Lahontan spent one year at Fort St. Joseph on the St. Clair River. In 1688, when this post was abandoned, he explored farther westward and reportedly reached Mackinac on Lake Michigan. He later claimed to have continued from there along the Fox and Wisconsin Rivers to the MISSISSIPPI RIVER.

Lahontan was back in Montreal in July 1689. He soon deserted from the military, returning to France in 1693.

In 1703, Baron de Lahontan's account of his travels, *New Voyages in North America,* was published in Holland. It relates his trip to the Mississippi and provides details about a great river flowing westward into a great inland salt sea with a highly advanced Indian civilization living on its shores. His accounts of North American geography were largely fictitious, but, until about 1750, his erroneous descriptions of the Mississippi country influenced mapmakers. His tales of a salt sea to the west fueled hopes of later explorers in search of an inland route to the Orient. Lahontan's description of the western prairies as suitable for agricultural development were accurate, however. Ironically, 130 years later, STEPHEN HARRIMAN LONG characterized the same region as the Great American Desert.

Laing, Alexander Gordon   (1793–1826) *British army officer in West Africa*

Gordon Laing was born in Edinburgh, Scotland, where he attended Edinburgh University before obtaining a commission as an officer in the British army's West India Regiment.

In 1822, Laing was stationed in the British West African colony of Sierra Leone. He commanded military expeditions into the Mandingo country northeast of Freetown in an effort to establish trade contacts with the native tribes as well as curtail the region's SLAVE TRADE. The next year, he took part in a military campaign to suppress an uprising of the Ashanti people in what is now the West African nation of Ghana. It was at this time, while commanding a patrol near the source of the NIGER RIVER north of the Ashanti region, that he first speculated on the true course of the NILE RIVER. From classical times to the beginning of the 19th century, most geographers had believed the Niger was a western tributary of the Nile, flowing eastward across Africa. From his observations of the low-lying terrain in what is now southern Mali, Laing concluded that this could not be the case, and he was one of the first to express the idea that the Niger was not connected to the Nile.

By 1824, Laing had been promoted to the rank of major, assigned as special assistant to Lord Bathurst, Great Britain's secretary of state for war and colonial affairs. With Bathurst's support, Laing was appointed to command an expedition to explore the interior of West Africa and determine the actual course of the Niger. Based on his earlier experience, Laing believed the best way to reach the Niger and descend it to its mouth was from the coast of West Africa. Bathurst was of the prevalent view that the most practical way to reach the region's interior was to head southward from the coast of North Africa, which Laing was compelled to do.

Laing arrived in Tripoli, Libya, in May 1825. He soon met and became enamored of Emma Warrington, daughter of the British consul in Tripoli, whom he married.

On July 18, 1825, Laing set out on his mission to explore the Niger. Accompanied by his West Indian servant, "Honest" Jack Le Bore, and two native West African carpenters who were to build a boat for the planned downriver journey once the SAHARA DESERT had been crossed, Laing headed southward from Tripoli. They soon reached the North African city of Ghadames, near the common border of present-day southern Tunisia, eastern Algeria, and northwestern Libya. Reportedly, Laing was the first European to visit this North African city.

While Laing's expedition was underway, another British group, led by HUGH CLAPPERTON, was also seeking to explore the Niger River, entering the region from the Bight of Benin on the coast of West Africa. From Ghadames, Laing and his three companions went southwestward across Algeria into the Fezzan region. Following a caravan route through the Grand Erg Oriental, they reached In Salah in the center of Algeria.

Laing and his party then skirted the western slopes of the Ahaggar Mountains and entered what is now Mali in early January 1826. An attack by Tuareg tribesmen in February left Laing severely wounded. By June 1826, his faithful servant, Le Bore, had succumbed to illness, and the two native boatbuilders had left him. Despite the hardships of traveling alone across the desert, he managed to reach the Niger River and the city of TIMBUKTU in Mali in August 1826.

Laing remained in Timbuktu for more than a month, until the local sheik, concerned about his safety amid a population outwardly hostile to non-Muslim visitors, convinced the Britisher to leave. Without a boat, Laing was forced to abandon his plan to sail down the river. He set out overland for the coast of West Africa on September 22, 1826, and was never seen alive again.

Two years later, French explorer RENÉ-AUGUSTE CAILLIÉ reached Timbuktu, where he learned that just two days after departing Timbuktu, Laing had been beaten to death by his Muslim guides, who believed him to be a Christian spy. A passerby had buried Laing in the desert. In 1910, French colonial authorities reburied his remains in Timbuktu.

Gordon Laing was the first European known to have visited the African cities of Ghadames and Timbuktu.

Lalemant, Gabriel (Saint Gabriel Lalement)
(1610–1649) *French missionary in the eastern Great Lakes region*

Born in Paris into a noble French family, Gabriel Lalemant was the son of a lawyer. At the age of 20, he embarked on a religious career as a novitiate, following his uncles Charles Lalemant and Jérome Lalemant, both prominent Jesuit missionaries in French Canada.

In 1632, the younger Lalemant entered the Jesuit order, committed to the idea of some day serving as a missionary in a foreign land. Nevertheless, he remained in France and nearby Belgium for the next 14 years, serving in a variety of academic positions at Jesuit schools in Moulins, Bruges, La Flèche, and Bourges.

Lalemant finally realized his goal of becoming an overseas missionary in 1646. In late September of that year, he arrived in French Canada, remaining in Quebec for two years. He then traveled to the southern Georgian Bay region of eastern Lake Huron, where he studied Indian languages at the Jesuit mission of Sainte-Marie-des-Hurons among the Huron (Wyandot). In February 1649, he joined Father JEAN DE BRÉBEUF at the St. Louis mission near the mouth of the Severn River at the southern end of Georgian Bay.

On March 16, 1649, Lalemant and Brébeuf were taken captive by the Iroquois (Haudenosaunee) who had overrun the mission with a force of 1,000 warriors. The two priests were led away and later killed by the Indians.

On June 29, 1930, both Gabriel Lalemant and Brébeuf were canonized by Pope Pius XI in a ceremony commemorating them and other missionary priests, including ISAAC JOGUES, as the Martyrs of North America. Along with fur traders, Lalemant was among the first Europeans to have extensive contact with the Indian population and explore the uncharted region of the eastern Great Lakes, west of the St. Lawrence and Ottawa Rivers.

La Mothe, Antoine Laumet de (sieur de Cadillac) (1658–1730) *French official in North America, founder of Detroit*

Antoine de La Mothe was born in Laumont, a village in Gascony, to middle-class parents. He would later claim to be of nobility, his father being the "seigneur de Cadillac," although in reality his father was a minor official. He traveled to New France in 1683, staying first at Port Royal (present-day Annapolis Royal, Nova Scotia) and then along the Union River in present-day Maine. Soon after his marriage in 1687, he came to the attention of the minister of the French colonies, Louis Phélypeaux de Pontchartrain, who recommended him to governor Louis de Buade, comte de Frontenac.

In 1692, Cadillac and cartographer Jean-Baptiste Franquelin sailed along the Atlantic coastline. The following year, he assumed command of a company and also received a ship's command. By the end of that year, he was given command of the frontier post Mackinac in the Great Lakes. His policies, including the distribution of alcohol, led to conflict with and among the area's Native American tribes and ended alliances that fur trader DANIEL GREYSOLON DU-LUTH had developed in the preceding years.

In 1698, in France, Cadillac won support for his plan of founding a colony on the Detroit River. In 1701, with 100 soldiers, missionaries, and colonists from Montreal, he founded Fort Pontchartrain on the site of present-day Detroit, Michigan. He did not assume full command of the post for another three years, but mismanagement of the post, including alleged trading with British interests, led to his being removed by Pontchartrain, who appointed him governor of French Louisiana in 1710, replacing JEAN-BAPTISTE LE MOYNE, sieur de Bienville. Cadillac did not travel to the southern territory until 1713. While governor, Cadillac sent French trader LOUIS JUCHEREAU DE ST. DENIS to Texas to open trade contacts with Indians, but his emissary was arrested by the Spanish.

Because of accusations of driving away colonists, Cadillac was recalled to France in 1716 and imprisoned for a time. Yet he again won royal favor and received the governorship of Castelsarrasin, a city near his native village. He lived the rest of his life in Gascony.

Antoine de La Mothe, despite the questions of character surrounding his career, is celebrated historically as the founder of Detroit.

Lancaster, Sir James (ca. 1554–1618)
English mariner, merchant in the Far East and South America, sponsor of expeditions in search of the Northwest Passage

Born in England, James Lancaster was a seafarer and merchant. In the early 1580s, he undertook commercial voyages to Portugal, where he first became acquainted with the great potential of direct trade with India and the EAST INDIES.

Lancaster was an associate of SIR FRANCIS DRAKE, with whom he served in England's great naval victory over the Spanish Armada in summer 1588. In 1591, he commanded Drake's ship, the *Edward Bonaventure,* in the first English trade expedition to the Far East. Sailing from Plymouth, he rounded the CAPE OF GOOD HOPE and entered the Indian Ocean. After a stopover at Zanzibar on the coast of East Africa, he visited ports on the west coast of India, as well as the island of CEYLON (present-day Sri Lanka). From there, he continued eastward to the Strait of Malacca and traded at Penang Island off the west coast of the Malay Peninsula. While in these waters, he operated as a privateer, preying on Spanish ships laden with valuable cargoes returning from the SPICE ISLANDS (the Moluccas of present-day Indonesia).

The voyage was cut short when his crew threatened to mutiny, and Lancaster and the *Edward Bonaventure* sailed back to England, arriving there in 1594. Later that year, he led an expedition of PRIVATEERS to South America, during which he succeeded in capturing the northeastern Brazilian port of Recife, as well as several Spanish and Portuguese ships. In 1595, he returned to England, his ship laden with a fortune in looted treasure.

In 1600, Lancaster's exploits as an overseas trader and mariner led to his appointment as one of the chief directors of the BRITISH EAST INDIA COMPANY, chartered that year by Parliament. On February 15, 1601, he sailed from Torquay on the southwest coast of England, in command of the British East India Company's first trading venture to the East Indies. The fleet of five ships included Lancaster's flagship, the *Sea Dragon,* piloted by English mariner JOHN DAVIS. On this voyage, Lancaster established trade with the kingdom of Atjeh on Sumatra, as well as with Bantam on Java.

Lancaster returned to England in 1603 with a valuable cargo of pepper. His subsequent reports suggested the existence of a NORTHWEST PASSAGE. This information sparked the interest of a group of leading English businessmen, who, in 1611, organized the COMPANY OF MERCHANTS OF LONDON DISCOVERERS OF THE NORTHWEST PASSAGE, with Lancaster as one of its directors.

Knighted by Queen Elizabeth I for his efforts in expanding both English seapower and overseas trade, Sir James Lancaster went on to sponsor and organize voyages in search of the Northwest Passage undertaken by WILLIAM BAFFIN, ROBERT BYLOT, and SIR THOMAS BUTTON. During their 1616 voyage, Baffin and Bylot briefly explored the strait between Baffin Island and Devon Island. They named the strait Lancaster Sound in honor of their chief patron, but they did not then realize that it led westward into the Barrow Strait and the Beaufort Sea, and ultimately to the Arctic coast of Alaska and the North Pacific Ocean. By the mid-19th century, however, British naval expeditions into the Canadian Arctic had established that Lancaster Sound was indeed the eastern entrance to the Northwest Passage.

Lander, Richard Lemon (1804–1834) *British explorer in West Africa*

Richard Lander was born at Truro in Cornwall, England, where his father was an innkeeper. At the age of 11, he traveled to the WEST INDIES as a merchant's apprentice, remaining there for three years. While in his teens, he worked as a servant to travelers, visiting many parts of Europe; he also served under a Major Colebrook on an expedition in South Africa.

In 1825, Lander won an appointment as an assistant with Captain HUGH CLAPPERTON's second expedition to

West Africa in search of the true course of the NIGER RIVER. That year, he sailed to the coast of what is now Nigeria with Clapperton, then traveled inland to Kano and Sokoto. When Clapperton died at Sokoto in April 1827, Lander was the only surviving European member of the expedition. Accompanied by Clapperton's Hausa guide, WILLIAM PASCOE, he made his way back to the coast despite great hardships. He finally reached England in 1828, where he edited Clapperton's journal, published in 1830 as *Records of Captain Clapperton's Last Expedition to Africa.*

Lander's African exploits came to the attention of the British Foreign Office. In 1830, under the sponsorship of Lord Bathurst, secretary of war and colonial affairs, Lander was sent again to West Africa to continue the search for the actual terminus of the Niger River. Sailing from Portsmouth on January 9, 1830, he was joined by his younger brother, John Lander. Lander's first stop on the Gulf of Guinea was Cape Coast in what is now Ghana, where he was reunited with the Hausa guide Pascoe, whom he recruited for the expedition. The group then continued to Badagri, near Lagos, in present-day Nigeria, where he disembarked for the trip into the interior. Traveling northward, he reached the Niger River at Bussa, where MUNGO PARK had drowned 24 years earlier.

Lander, his brother John, and Pascoe ascended the Niger from Bussa, exploring upriver without a compass for about 100 miles. They then headed downstream and soon reached the Niger's main tributary, the Benue. While investigating the myriad streams that make up the Niger's delta, Richard and John Lander were taken captive by Ibo tribesmen under King Obie. They were placed in the custody of another native trader, King Boy, with whom the Landers set out downriver, hoping to contact a European ship on the coast and obtain ransom for their freedom. With King Boy, the Landers eventually reached the Brass River, a southward-flowing branch of the Niger, and followed that stream to its outlet into the Bight of Benin, reaching the coast in mid-November 1830, thus determining the ultimate end of the Niger River.

While John Lander remained behind as a hostage at Brasstown on the coast, Richard attempted to obtain the ransom from a Captain Lake of the British ship *Thomas.* When Lander promised King Boy that Captain Lake would pay the ransom, the brothers were permitted to board the vessel. Although Captain Lake had actually refused to pay, Lander and his brother nonetheless sailed on the *Thomas,* leaving King Boy behind.

The Landers left the *Thomas* at the offshore island of Fernando Po in the Bight of Biafra, and found passage to Rio de Janeiro, Brazil, aboard the *Caernarvon.* From there, they sailed back to England, arriving in 1831, where they were hailed for having finally resolved the question of the course of the Niger River. Moreover, to redeem Richard Lander's good name on the Niger Delta, the British Colonial Office later arranged for King Boy to receive the ransom he had been promised in the form of 135 slaves.

In 1832, Lander published a report on his African explorations, entitled *Journal of an Expedition to Explore the Course and Termination of the Niger.*

Lander's reputation as an African explorer aroused the interest of a group of Liverpool merchants, led by Macgregor Laird, who commissioned him to lead a trading venture to the Niger to exploit the region commercially. Returning to the lower Niger in 1832, he undertook trading expeditions upriver over the next year. Pascoe, who again accompanied him, died on one of these journeys, probably poisoned by a jealous tribal leader. In early 1834, Lander was wounded in an attack by natives at Angiama, about 100 miles upstream from the coast. He sought aid on Fernando Po, where he died on February 2, 1834. Of the 48 men who had started out on Lander's last expedition, only eight survived.

Richard Lander, although without formal education and of a modest social background, nonetheless solved one of the great geographic mysteries of West Africa. Soon after he returned to England in 1832, the newly formed ROYAL GEOGRAPHICAL SOCIETY awarded him its first cash prize for his finding that the Niger River, long thought to be a western tributary of the NILE RIVER, actually flowed southward, emptying into the Gulf of Guinea at the western edge of the Bight of Benin.

Landsborough, William (1825–1886)
Scottish colonist in Australia

Born in Saltcoats, Ayrshire, Scotland, William Landsborough migrated to New South Wales in 1841. In 1856–59, he explored central Queensland, especially the areas around the Comet and Nogoa Rivers, from Mount Nebo to Bowen Downs Station.

In 1861, departing from the Gulf of Carpentaria with a camel, at first traveling along the Albert River, Landsborough searched for the missing Englishmen ROBERT O'HARA BURKE and WILLIAM JOHN WILLS, who had perished in their attempt to cross the continent from south to north. Landsborough reached Melbourne in New South Wales in 1862, completing a north-to-south crossing within a week of the Scotsman JOHN MCDOUALL STUART's successful south-to-north crossing of the continent.

Landsborough later received extensive land grants from the Queensland government for his explorations and served in various official posts. He died in Caloundra, Queensland.

William Landsborough's explorations opened up many parts of Queensland to settlement. The town of Landsborough, Landsborough Creek, and Landsborough Highway in Queensland are named after him.

Langford, Nathaniel Pitt (1832–1911)
American politician in Montana, first superintendent of Yellowstone National Park

Nathaniel P. Langford was born in Westmoreland, New York. In 1854, along with some other family members, he migrated westward to St. Paul, Minnesota, where he worked as a bank cashier for the next eight years.

In 1862, suffering from ill health and hoping a western trip would restore him, Langford joined Captain James L. Fisk and his Northern Overland Expedition to the goldfields of eastern Idaho's Salmon River region. When the group was forced to winter in the Prickly Pear Valley of central Montana, Langford and several others pushed westward on their own, reaching Bannack.

Langford's arrival in Bannack coincided with a major gold strike in that part of southwestern Montana. Over the next few years, he became prominent as the leader of a vigilante group that maintained law and order amid the rapid influx of thousands of prospectors.

In 1864, with the organization of the Montana Territory, Langford became a federal tax collector. In 1868, President Andrew Johnson nominated him as Montana territorial governor, but his appointment was not confirmed by the U.S. Senate.

In 1869, Langford heard of the geological marvels of the Yellowstone Park region from his friend D. E. Folsom. Folsom had attempted to explore the region but had been turned back by Indian war parties. Langford soon succeeded in organizing an official expedition under the protection of U.S. Army troops. With the help of General Henry D. Washburn, Langford obtained the services of a military escort, and, in August 1870, with 19 other civilians, he left Helena, Montana, and explored the parts of Idaho, Wyoming, and Montana that now comprise Yellowstone National Park.

Immediately after the 1870 expedition, Langford embarked on a campaign for the preservation of the Yellowstone region as a national wilderness treasure. He lectured widely and wrote articles for leading magazines. When the park was created by an act of Congress in 1872, Langford became its first superintendent, serving until 1876 without compensation. He then returned to St. Paul, where he lived the rest of his life.

In 1905, Nathaniel P. Langford published his account of the Yellowstone region, entitled *Diary of the Washburn Expedition to the Yellowstone and Fire Hole Rivers in the Year 1870.* In his years as superintendent of America's first national park, he consistently protected the integrity of the park from commercial exploitation. His work greatly contributed to maintaining Yellowstone National Park as it was intended.

Langlé, Paul-Antoine-Marie Fleuriot de
See FLEURIOT DE LANGLÉ, PAUL-ANTOINE-MARIE.

Langsdorff, Georg Heinrich Ritter von (George Henry Langsdorff, Grigory Ivanovich Langsdorff) (1774–1852) *German naturalist, diplomat in the Pacific, Alaska, California, Siberia, and South America, in service to Russia*

Georg Heinrich von Langsdorff was born in the southern German town of Wollstein. In 1797, after studying medicine at the University of Göttingen, he became a physician in service to the Prince of Waldeck.

In August 1803, Langsdorff won an appointment as the naturalist for a Russian expedition to the Pacific Ocean, under the command of ADAM IVAN RITTER VON KRUSENSTERN. He met up with Krusenstern's ship, the *Nadezhda,* in Copenhagen; they sailed to Santa Catarina Island off the south coast of Brazil. On the voyage across the South Atlantic Ocean, he observed that the sea at times became phosphorescent as a result of tiny marine organisms, which he studied with a microscope.

Langsdorff traveled around CAPE HORN with the Russian expedition, which, after stopovers in the HAWAIIAN ISLANDS and other Pacific island groups, arrived in Petropavlovsk on the Kamchatka Peninsula of eastern SIBERIA. From there, the expedition sailed to Japan.

In late 1805, Langsdorff returned to Petropavlovsk. Leaving the Krusenstern expedition, he accompanied Russian naval officer GAVRILL IVANOVICH DAVYDOV and N. P. Rezanov, a founder of the RUSSIAN-AMERICAN COMPANY, on a tour of the Russian settlements in Alaska. In spring 1806, he traveled to Spanish California. Returning to the Pacific coast of Siberia in 1807, he traveled overland across Asiatic and European Russia, arriving in St. Petersburg in March 1808.

Langsdorff spent the next few years preparing an account of his sea and land journey around the world, published in English in 1813 as *Voyages and Travels in Various Parts of the World, during the years 1803, 1804, 1805, 1806, and 1807.*

In 1812, Langsdorff entered the Russian diplomatic service, returning to Brazil, where he served as Russia's consul general at Rio de Janeiro. During the next 10 years, he undertook studies of the region's plant and animal life, sending specimens back to the Russian Academy of Sciences in St. Petersburg. He also reported on the region's potential for colonization, publishing his findings in 1820 as *Memoirs on Brazil, A Guide for Those Who Wish to Settle There.* He returned to Russia in 1823, where he made a scientific tour of the Ural Mountains.

In 1825, Langsdorff returned to South America as head of a Russian scientific expedition that undertook explorations into the largely uncharted interior regions of the Amazon Basin and the Mato Grosso country of south-central Brazil.

Stricken with an illness that left him mentally incapacitated in 1829, Langsdorff was forced to return to Europe.

He spent his remaining years in the German city of Freiburg.

Georg Heinrich von Langsdorff's CIRCUMNAVIGATION OF THE WORLD was one of the first combining both sea and land. His reports on his travels greatly added to modern scientific knowledge on many diverse parts of the globe, including the islands of the South Pacific, the interior of Siberia, the northwestern parts of North America, and the jungles and plains of South America.

La Noué, Charles Edouard de   See NOUÉ, CHARLES EDOUARD DE LA.

La Pérouse, comte de   See GALAUP, JEAN-FRANÇOIS DE.

Larpenteur, Charles   (1807–1872)   *French-American fur trader on upper Missouri River, northern plains, and northern Rocky Mountains*

Charles Larpenteur, a native of Fontainebleau, France, moved to the United States with his family in 1818, settling on a farm in Maryland. When in his teens, he headed westward for Missouri, attracted by the burgeoning FUR TRADE centered in St. Louis.

Larpenteur gained frontier experience as an employee of Indian agent and fur trader Benjamin O'Fallon. In 1833, he joined an expedition to the upper MISSOURI RIVER, led by WILLIAM LEWIS SUBLETTE and ROBERT CAMPBELL, and served as the bartender at that year's fur trappers' rendezvous on the Green River in present-day southern Wyoming. He then joined Campbell on an expedition to the Yellowstone region, where he took part in the construction of Fort William, close to the AMERICAN FUR COMPANY's post, Fort Union, in the northwestern corner of present-day North Dakota.

After Campbell sold his operation to the American Fur Company in 1834, it was merged with Fort Union, where Larpenteur remained for the next 15 years, working for fur trader KENNETH MCKENZIE. In that time, he had extensive contacts with the tribes of the northern Dakota country and also undertook trade expeditions to the Indians of present-day Saskatchewan.

In 1848–49, Larpenteur set off on his own fur-trading enterprise among the Flathead Indians of western Montana's Bitterroot River Valley. Supply problems and severe winter weather soon led him to abandon the fur trade. In the early 1850s, he again entered the fur trade, operating for the rest of the decade among the upper Missouri tribes, including the Assiniboine.

In 1860–61, Larpenteur, in partnership with HENRY A. BOLLER, worked the Yellowstone River region. In 1864, the American Fur Company commissioned Larpenteur to take charge of its operation at Fort Union, providing supplies for General Alfred Sully's military campaign against the Sioux (Dakota, Lakota, Nakota) Indians. He continued on as a merchant at Fort Buford in the Dakotas, until 1871, when he retired to a farm in Iowa.

Charles Larpenteur kept a journal of his life in the fur trade. This was later edited by Elliot Cous and was published in 1898 as *Forty Years a Fur Trader on the Upper Missouri: The Personal Narrative of Charles Larpenteur, 1833–1872*. Considered one of the most comprehensive accounts of the fur trade on the upper Missouri River, it provides everyday details of a frontier industry that contributed much to the exploration and settlement of the northern plains and northern ROCKY MOUNTAINS.

La Salle, René-Robert Cavelier de   (sieur de La Salle)   (1643–1687)   *French fur trader on the Great Lakes, explorer on the Mississippi River*

René-Robert Cavelier de La Salle was born in Rouen, France to a prominent and influential family. As a youth, he studied for the priesthood, entering the Jesuit order in 1658. After several years, however, he left the Jesuits to enter the FUR TRADE in French Canada.

La Salle arrived in Quebec in 1666, where he soon secured a land grant near Montreal through family connections. From Indians who came to Montreal to trade, La Salle heard reports of a great river to the west that emptied into the sea. He speculated that this river flowed into the Gulf of California and, if found, would provide France with a water route from Canada to the Orient.

In summer 1669, La Salle made his first foray into the Great Lakes region. He departed Montreal with a group of missionaries and fur traders, including FRANÇOIS DOLLIER DE CASSON and RENÉ DE BRÉHANT DE GALINÉE, heading westward along the St. Lawrence River to Lake Ontario. He explored the south shore and inland regions of this body of water. At a Seneca Indian village near present-day Rochester, New York, a captive from an Ohio Valley tribe told him of great open prairie lands to the west.

Near Niagara Falls, La Salle encountered LOUIS JOLLIET, returning from Lake Superior. La Salle left his companions and ventured southward into the Ohio Valley. According to his own account, he explored Lake Erie and located the Ohio River, which he explored as far as present-day Louisville, Kentucky. He may have reached as far west as the Illinois River.

In 1670, La Salle returned to Montreal and sought the French colonial government's support for his plan to establish a series of fur-trading posts between the Great Lakes and the upper MISSISSIPPI RIVER.

In 1673, Comte de Frontenac, the governor of New France, appointed La Salle commander of Fort Frontenac, a

René-Robert Cavelier de La Salle on the lower Mississippi River *(Library of Congress)*

post La Salle had established that year on the northeastern end of Lake Ontario, near the head of the St. Lawrence River (now the site of Kingston, Ontario). La Salle returned to France in 1674, where he received a grant of nobility from French king Louis XIV. Back in Canada, he developed the fur trade around Fort Frontenac. In 1677, La Salle made another trip to France and obtained royal authorization to explore the lands west of Lake Ontario and to develop the region's fur trade.

La Salle returned to Canada in 1678, accompanied by HENRI DE TONTI, who would become his chief lieutenant in subsequent explorations. In 1679, La Salle traveled to the eastern end of Lake Erie and established Fort Niagara (near present-day Buffalo, New York). He and Tonti directed the construction of the sailing ship the *Griffon.* Launched in August 1679, it was the first European-built sailing vessel to ply the Great Lakes west of Lake Ontario.

La Salle and his party sailed across Lake Erie to the Detroit River; northward to Lake St. Clair and the St. Clair River and into Lake Huron; then northward through the Straits of Mackinac into Lake Michigan. La Salle established a trading post at Green Bay on the west shore of the lake, then traveled by CANOE down Lake Michigan to its southern end and to the mouth of the St. Joseph River, where he established Fort Miami (present-day St. Joseph, Michigan).

Meanwhile, the *Griffon,* which had been sent back from Green Bay with a rich cargo of furs, failed to reach Fort Niagara. No trace of the ship has ever been found.

From Fort Miami, La Salle led the expedition across the Kankakee Portage to the Illinois River, where he established Fort Crévecoeur (near present-day Peoria, Illinois). From Fort Crévecoeur, La Salle dispatched the expedition's chaplain, Father LOUIS HENNEPIN, along with MICHEL ACO to explore the Wisconsin, Mississippi, and Minnesota Rivers to the north.

La Salle then undertook an early spring trek back to Fort Frontenac to obtain additional supplies, reaching the post after two months. In August 1680, he organized another expedition to Green Bay and Fort Crévecoeur, this time traveling by canoe via Lake Simcoe to Lake Huron and Lake Michigan.

When La Salle finally reached Fort Crévecoeur, he found it deserted. Tonti, who had been left in charge the year before, had fled with his men in the face of a new Indian uprising. La Salle met up with Tonti and the rest of his party at Mackinac in May 1681.

Early in 1682, La Salle was back at the Illinois River post, from where he launched an expedition to the Mississippi River. His party was delayed by ice and did not reach the Mississippi until February 1682. They descended the river, reaching the Gulf of Mexico on April 9, 1682. La Salle claimed the entire Mississippi Valley for France, naming the region Louisiana in honor of Louis XIV.

On the return trip up the Mississippi, La Salle initiated the construction of Fort St. Louis at Starved Rock on the Illinois River near what is now Ottawa, Illinois. He left Tonti in charge, then headed back up the Illinois River and returned to Montreal.

In 1683, La Salle traveled to France and reported his discoveries to King Louis. The king appointed La Salle viceroy of North America and authorized the founding of a fortress and colony at the mouth of the Mississippi River.

La Salle led a major colonizing expedition from France in late July 1684. He commanded four ships with more than 300 colonists, sailing from La Rochelle. One of the ships was soon captured by Spanish pirates. La Salle and his remaining three ships reached the Gulf Coast but missed the Mississippi Delta, landing instead at Matagorda Bay about 400 miles to the west, in present-day Texas, on February 20, 1685. Problems continued to plague the expedition. By the end of 1686, a second ship had been lost, and a third had departed for France with disenchanted colonists. In late winter 1686, the fourth ship, the *Belle,* was wrecked by a squall.

La Salle and his colonists established a settlement, Fort St. Louis. In 1685–86, he led several overland expeditions into central Texas, vainly looking for the Mississippi River. In March 1687, on still another third attempt to find the Mississippi from the Gulf Coast, his men mutinied. One of them killed him at an unknown site along the Brazos River. The Texas colony was abandoned, and the surviving settlers under HENRI JOUTEL returned on foot to Canada.

René-Robert Cavelier de la Salle's journeys to the western Great Lakes established an inland water route from the St. Lawrence River, leading to intensified exploration of the region and a new southern outlet for the French fur trade. Moreover, his exploration of the last 700 miles of the Mississippi River and his finding that it flowed into the Gulf of Mexico provided France with a southern base for its North American empire.

Laudonnière, René Goulaine de (fl. 1560s)

French colonizer in South Carolina and Florida

René de Laudonnière was a French Huguenot who took part in JEAN RIBAULT's unsuccessful colonizing attempt on the South Carolina coast in 1562, along with artist JACQUES LE MOYNE DE MORGUES.

In 1564, Laudonnière abandoned the first site and commanded a second North American colonizing attempt on the St. Johns River, near present-day Jacksonville, Florida. They found Timucua Indians worshiping a stone monument that had been erected by Ribault when he had explored the region two years earlier. Laudonnière made an alliance with tribal leaders and enlisted their help in building his new settlement, Fort Caroline.

Hardship soon befell the French colonists. They declined to work or grow food, choosing instead to search for gold and precious stones. Laudonnière was forced to introduce rationing. The colonists mutinied and made two unsuccessful attempts on Laudonnière's life, first trying to poison him, then to blow him up with gunpowder.

Laudonnière's colony incurred the enmity of Spain when a group of colonists stole one of the ships, took it to Cuba, and attacked a Spanish GALLEON. The Spanish made plans for retaliation.

English privateer SIR JOHN HAWKINS visited Fort Caroline in August 1565; Laudonnière bought food supplies and a ship from him. That same month, Ribault arrived, with plans to take Laudonnière back to France to face charges of misconduct. In September, a large Spanish force under PEDRO MENÉNDEZ DE AVILÉS launched an attack against Laudonnière and his colony. Two-thirds of the colonists were killed. Laudonnière escaped by fleeing into the woods and was later rescued by an English ship. He returned to France in 1566, where he wrote an account of the French colonizing effort, *L'Histoire notable de la Floride* (Notable history of Florida), published in 1856.

Laudonnière's failed attempt at colonizing northern Florida put an end to French settlement on the east coast of the present United States. Spain continued to dominate the region for the next two centuries.

La Vérendrye, Louis-Joseph Gaultier de

(1717–1761) *French-Canadian fur trader on the upper Missouri River and northern plains, son of Pierre Gaultier de Varennes de la Vérendrye*

Son of French-Canadian explorer and soldier PIERRE GAULTIER DE VARENNES DE LA VÉRENDRYE, Louis-Joseph de La Vérendrye was born at Île aux Vaches on the St. Lawrence River in present-day Quebec.

In 1735, La Vérendrye joined his father in expanding the FUR TRADE westward into the Assiniboine River region of southern Manitoba, taking part in the establishment of Fort La Reine and Fort Maurepas. In 1738, he and his father traveled southward into present-day North Dakota, where they made the earliest fur-trading contacts with the Mandan Indians, visiting their villages on the MISSOURI RIVER (near modern Bismarck, North Dakota).

In 1739–40, La Vérendrye returned northward and circled Lake Winnipeg and reached the forks of the Saskatchewan River. In 1742, accompanied by his brother François and two other French fur traders, he set out south and west of the Mandan, hoping to locate a river leading to the Pacific coast. They possibly traveled as far west as the Black Hills in what is now western South Dakota or eastern Wyoming, before turning back along the Cheyenne and Bad Rivers. By late 1743, they were at an encampment near present-day Pierre, South Dakota.

La Vérendrye took part in French military actions against the Mohawk Indians in eastern Canada and northern New York in the last year of King George's War of 1744–48. He went on to fight in the French and Indian War of 1754–63, seeing action against the British and their Iroquois (Haudenosaunee) Indian allies in the Lake Champlain region. He died in a shipwreck off the north coast of Cape Breton Island in 1761.

Louis-Joseph de La Vérendrye led the first party of Europeans across the Missouri River and into the Great Plains, exploring what is now western Manitoba and western Minnesota, the Dakotas, Montana, Wyoming, and parts of the western Canadian provinces of Saskatchewan and Alberta. His western travels indicated to non-Indians the vast westward extent of the North American continent beyond the Great Lakes. On their return from the northern plains, the La Vérendrye brothers commemorated their western explorations by placing an engraved lead plaque on the prairie near the site of present-day Pierre, South Dakota. The plaque was found 270 years later, in 1913, by a group of schoolchildren on a field trip.

La Vérendrye, Pierre Gaultier de Varennes de (sieur de La Vérendrye) (1685–1749)

French-Canadian soldier and fur trader in central Canada and on the upper Missouri River, father of Louis-Joseph Gaultier de La Vérendrye

Pierre Gaultier de La Vérendrye was born at Trois Rivières in present-day Quebec, Canada, where his father, a French nobleman, served for a time as governor. At the age of 12, he entered the French army. He took part in that phase of the French and Indian Wars in North America known as Queen Anne's War of 1702–13, including the French raid on the English settlement at Deerfield, Massachusetts, in 1704.

La Vérendrye's military career then took him to Europe, where the conflict was known as the War of the Spanish Succession. At Flanders, in the Battle of Malplaquet in 1709, La Vérendrye was wounded and taken prisoner by the British. Released in 1710, he returned to Canada by 1712, where he married into a prominent French-Canadian family and settled on his wife's lands near Trois Rivières.

Starting about 1717, La Vérendrye operated out of Trois Rivières as a fur trader along the St. Maurice River to the north. In 1726, he went westward to join his brother, Jacques René, then in command of the fur-trading posts on the north shore of Lake Superior. La Vérendrye helped develop French influence over the FUR TRADE in the region around Lake Nipigon, and, by 1728, he had succeeded his brother as commander.

From Indians at Lake Nipigon, La Vérendrye heard reports of a west-flowing river that led into a "Western Sea," and he theorized that an inland gulf of the Pacific

Ocean could be reached by following this river westward. In 1729, he returned to Quebec and succeeded in gaining French governmental support to explore west of the Great Lakes in search of a NORTHWEST PASSAGE to the Pacific.

Starting in 1731, La Vérendrye, along with three of his sons (Jean-Baptiste, Pierre, and François) and a nephew (François-Christophe Dufrost de la Jémerais), undertook a series of expeditions from Lake Nipigon west to Rainy Lake, the Lake of the Woods, and the upper Red River. They established the first trading posts in this region and pioneered an improved CANOE route along the Pigeon River that became part of the Grand Portage, the gateway to the Canadian West.

La Vérendrye's eldest son, Jean-Baptiste, and a party of trappers were killed by Sioux (Dakota, Lakota, Nakota) Indians at Massacre Island on the Lake of the Woods in summer 1736. In 1738, La Vérendrye and his eldest surviving son, LOUIS-JOSEPH GAULTIER DE LA VÉRENDRYE, set out from Fort St. Charles, his post at the Lake of the Woods, and headed up the Red River to its junction with the Assiniboine River. There they established a post, Fort Rouge, near the site of what would become the city of Winnipeg, Manitoba. They explored Lake Winnipeg, then went south along the Red River into what is now North Dakota, reaching the Mandan Indian villages on the MISSOURI RIVER. On this expedition, they became the first non-Indians to cross overland west of the 100th meridian of longitude in what is now Canada. In 1739, while returning to Fort La Reine (Portage la Prairie), the La Vérendryes reportedly also became the first non-Indians to see Lake Manitoba.

After 1742, La Vérendrye organized and financed the expeditions of his sons across the Great Plains. In 1744, he gave up the fur trade and returned to Quebec. In 1749, the French government awarded him the Cross of St. Louis for his accomplishments as an explorer. His plans to set out again in search of the Western Sea were cut short by his death in Quebec.

Sieur de La Vérendrye's efforts to find the Northwest Passage and the Western Sea, while not successful in themselves, led to the development of fur-trading posts throughout southern Manitoba. He was among the first non-Indians to visit the Dakotas, and his explorations in that region led to the first maps of the upper Missouri River. La Vérendrye's sons, whose expeditions in the 1740s he supported, may have been the first non-Indians to explore what is now Wyoming and Montana.

Lawrence, Thomas Edward (T. E. Lawrence, Lawrence of Arabia, John Hume Ross, T. E. Shaw)

(1888–1935) *British scholar, army officer in the Middle East*
T. E. Lawrence was originally from Wales. At Oxford University, he studied Arabic literature and became interested in Middle Eastern antiquities. In 1910, he first traveled to the Middle East and undertook a walking tour of Syria.

In 1911, Lawrence joined a British Museum archaeological expedition to the site of the ancient city of Carchemish, on the Euphrates River in what is now Syria, which he reached by ascending the Euphrates from the Persian Gulf. Two years later, in 1913, he began a year-long archaeological study of the northern part of the Sinai Peninsula, during which he learned much about the native bedouin way of life and learned to speak colloquial Arabic.

At the outbreak of World War I in 1914, Lawrence was attached to the British army's intelligence department in Cairo. In 1915, he undertook a mission up the NILE RIVER going as far as Asyut, where he evaluated the potential for an Arab uprising against Turkey, which was then allied with Germany and the Central Powers against Great Britain. The next year, he sailed across the RED SEA to the Arabian port of Jidda; soon afterward, he made contact with Hussein ibn Ali and his son Faisal ibn Hussein. Without direct British military support, he helped these Arab leaders raise an army, which waged a successful campaign against the Turks in the Hejaz region, the northwestern part of what is now Saudi Arabia. Arab forces under Lawrence destroyed vital links of the Turkish-run Hejaz Railroad and captured and occupied the strategically important port of Aqaba at the northern end of the Red Sea. While engaged in this campaign, Lawrence undertook explorations of the little-known Hejaz region, determining the longitude of important points along the railroad line and noting the territory's geological features.

For his efforts, Lawrence was promoted to major; by the war's end in 1918, he had been made a lieutenant colonel. That year, he rode into the Syrian capital of Damascus with the victorious Arab armies, and, in 1919, he attended the peace conference in Paris as a delegate representing Arab interests.

Lawrence served as an adviser on Arab affairs with the British Colonial Office in 1921–22. Although he had promised his Arab allies his support for their independence movement, when World War I ended, Turkish colonial rule was replaced with colonial rule by Great Britain and France.

Believing he had unwittingly betrayed his Arab comrades, Lawrence left public life and sought obscurity, enlisting in the Royal Air Force under the alias of John Hume Ross in 1922. He left that branch of the service after a year and entered the Royal Tank Corps, having legally changed his name to T. E. Shaw. In 1925, he transferred back to the Royal Air Force and was stationed at times on the northwestern frontier of India. In 1929, he proposed to the Royal Air Force a plan to use an AIRSHIP to explore the largely unknown Rub' al-Khali—the EMPTY QUARTER—of the southeastern Arabian Peninsula. Two years later, the desert was explored by BERTRAM SYDNEY THOMAS, who crossed the region by camel.

Lawrence had written an account of his experiences in Arabia, *Revolt in the Desert.* Although the manuscript was first completed in 1919, Lawrence lost it in Paris that year and had to rewrite the entire work from memory. It appeared in 1927; an expanded version, *The Seven Pillars of Wisdom,* was published in 1935. That same year, Lawrence was killed in a motorcycle accident on an English country road.

Known as Lawrence of Arabia, T. E. Lawrence was one of the most enigmatic public figures of the first part of the 20th century. As an archaeological explorer turned military leader, he waged a victorious campaign on an all but forgotten front of World War I. His political dealings with the Arab leaders of what is now Iraq and Saudi Arabia had a long-range impact on relations between the people of the Middle East and the Western powers.

Lawson, John (unknown–1711) *British surveyor in the Carolinas*

The Englishman John Lawson arrived at Charleston in the Carolina colony in 1700. During the next several years, he explored the Santee River as far as present-day Columbia, South Carolina. From there, he traveled along Native American paths into North Carolina, as far as present-day Durham. In prior years, HENRY WOODWARD had opened up other trade routes to the west.

In 1708, Lawson was appointed surveyor general of North Carolina. Two years later, Lawson and Baron Christoph De Graffenried founded a settlement for Swiss colonists on the Neuse River called New Bern, in Tuscarora Indian country. In 1711, Lawson was captured and killed by Indians in the Tuscarora War.

John Lawson described his explorations in his 1709 book *A New Voyage to Carolina.* His penetration inland from the coast helped spark future settlement westward to the APPALACHIAN MOUNTAINS.

Lazarev, Mikhail Petrovich (1788–1851) *Russian naval officer in the South Pacific and Antarctica*

In 1803, at the age of 15, Mikhail Petrovich Lazarev traveled to England, where, along with 30 other Russian naval cadets, he underwent five years of training with the British navy, serving on British warships in the Atlantic Ocean and in the Caribbean Sea.

Lazarev embarked on his first round-the-world voyage in 1813, sailing for the Russian fur-trading monopoly in Alaska, the RUSSIAN-AMERICAN COMPANY. Aboard the *Suvorov,* he sailed from the Russian Baltic Sea port of Kronstadt to the company's settlement of Sitka, off the coast of Alaska's southeastern panhandle, and returned to Russia in 1816, completing a CIRCUMNAVIGATION OF THE WORLD.

Starting in 1819, Lazarev joined Russian navigator BARON FABIAN GOTTLIEB BENJAMIN VON BELLINGSHAUSEN on a voyage of exploration to the South Pacific Ocean and Antarctica in which he completed his second voyage around the world. In command of the *Mirny* (Peaceful), Lazarev accompanied Bellingshausen and the *Vostok* on a two-year expedition that reached as far south as 69° south latitude. With Bellingshausen, he made one of the earliest sightings of the Antarctic mainland and made the European discovery of two Antarctic islands, which they named after Russian monarchs Peter I and Alexander I. The Russian navigators later undertook an exploration of Antarctica's coastline during which they followed a course opposite to that taken by JAMES COOK in the 1770s, completing one of the earliest surveys of the Antarctic mainland.

In 1822, a year after he had returned from his voyage to Antarctica with Bellingshausen, Lazarev commanded the Russian frigate *Kreiser* on a third voyage around the world.

Lazarev went on to a distinguished career as a commander of Russian naval forces, taking part in naval operations against the Ottoman Empire in the Greek War of Independence, including the Battle of Navarino in 1827. He later commanded Russia's fleet in the Black Sea; in 1843, he was promoted to the rank of admiral.

Mickhail Petrovich Lazarev's career in exploration began with the FUR TRADE in Alaska and evolved into voyages of exploration in the South Pacific and Antarctica.

Leavenworth, Henry (1783–1834) *U.S. Army officer on the upper Mississippi frontier and southern plains*

Henry Leavenworth was born in New Haven, Connecticut. He spent his early years in Vermont, then moved to Delhi, New York, where he studied law. He was admitted to the New York State Bar in 1804, but he left his law practice for the army at the outbreak of the War of 1812. At the war's end, he resigned from the military at the rank of colonel.

After a brief period as a legislator in New York, Leavenworth rejoined the army in 1818. In 1819, he was sent to the upper MISSISSIPPI RIVER frontier, where he helped establish Fort Snelling at the confluence of the Mississippi and Minnesota Rivers, near present-day Minneapolis, Minnesota. For a time, it was the northwesternmost outpost of the United States.

In 1821, Leavenworth took command of Fort Atkinson on the MISSOURI RIVER near present-day Omaha, Nebraska. Two years later, he mounted a military expedition against the Arikara Indians on the Missouri, near the present-day border between North and South Dakota. In addition to regular army troops under Leavenworth, the operation included WILLIAM HENRY ASHLEY, JOSHUA PILCHER, and a host of MOUNTAIN MEN known as the "Missouri Legion," as well as about 400 Sioux (Dakota, Lakota, Nakota) warriors. In 1824, Leavenworth commanded U.S. troops on Lake Michigan at Green Bay. Three years later, he undertook a military expedition from St. Louis into what is now eastern Kansas, where he founded Fort Leavenworth on the Missouri River.

In 1834, Leavenworth was made a general and placed in command of the southwestern frontier. That year, in conjunction with Colonel HENRY DODGE, Leavenworth led an expedition of dragoons into the southern plains to establish peaceful relations with the Comanche and Kiowa Indians. He left Fort Gibson in the Indian Territory (present-day Oklahoma) and explored the upper Arkansas River and Red River region of what is now western Oklahoma and northern Texas. Traveling with this expedition was frontier artist GEORGE CATLIN.

During Leavenworth's 1834 expedition to the southern plains, his men were stricken with "bilious fever." Leavenworth himself became ill and died at an encampment on the Washita River in Oklahoma.

Henry Leavenworth's military expeditions during the early 1820s were among the first organized explorations of the U.S. frontier following the War of 1812. He was instrumental in establishing the chain of frontier forts that ran from Fort Snelling on the upper Mississippi River in the north, to Fort Smith on the Arkansas River in the south. In addition, he established Fort Leavenworth in present-day Kansas, which became an important staging area for subsequent military explorations into the Southwest.

Lederer, John (fl. 1660s–1670s) *German physician, explorer of the Piedmont and Blue Ridge regions of the American Southeast, in service to colonial Virginia*

German physician John Lederer arrived in the Virginia colony in the 1660s. His interest in exploring the uncharted regions west of Virginia's coastal plain soon came to the attention of the colonial governor, Sir William Berkeley.

With Berkeley's support, Lederer embarked on three expeditions across the Virginia and Carolina Piedmont regions between 1669 and 1670. Berkeley, unsure of the extent of the North American continent, believed the Pacific coast and the gold and silver mines of Mexico were just beyond the western mountains, and he commissioned Lederer to find a route through the APPALACHIAN MOUNTAINS.

In March 1669, Lederer, with a small party, left Chickahominy, the English post near the headwaters of the York River, and traveled northwestward as far as the top of Eminent Hill, becoming the first non-Indians to see the mountains of the Blue Ridge.

In May 1670, Lederer's second expedition left Fort Charles, the English settlement at present-day Richmond, and followed the eastern slopes of the Blue Ridge southward into present-day North Carolina. The 21 non-Indians accompanying him turned back soon after leaving Fort Charles, but Lederer continued on with an Indian guide. He reportedly explored North Carolina as far as the Catawba River, near present-day Charlotte. According to his later account, Lederer crossed broad savannahs and a wide desert and came upon a large lake of brackish water.

In the course of his second expedition, Lederer had contact with displaced Erie Indians. From descriptions of their homeland, he wrongly deduced that they came from the Pacific coast of California, rather than from the eastern Great Lakes. In mid-July, he reached the Virginia frontier post, Fort Henry, on the Appomattox River.

Lederer's third expedition started out from Talifer's House, a settlement south of the Rappahannock River. With a party of 10 colonists and five Indians, he followed the Rappahannock River Valley northwestward, climbed the Blue Ridge, and sighted the Appalachians beyond the Shenandoah Valley.

In 1671, Lederer settled in Maryland. The next year, an account of his explorations was published in London, entitled *The Discoveries of John Lederer, in Three Several Marches from Virginia, to the West of Carolina, and Other Parts of the Continent.* . . . In addition to detailed descriptions of Southeast Indians, he included reports of an inland arm of the Pacific Ocean, or "South Sea," which he believed could be reached by a pass through the Appalachians.

Although John Lederer failed to find a route through the Appalachians, he did ascertain the southern extent of the Blue Ridge into the Piedmont region of the Carolinas. His book, with its erroneous information on the geography of inland Virginia and the Carolinas, influenced mapmakers for the next century.

Ledyard, John (1751–1789) *American sailor in the South Pacific and South Atlantic, traveler in Siberia*

John Ledyard was born in Groton, Connecticut. He attended Dartmouth College in New Hampshire in 1772–73, but he left and lived with the Iroquois (Haudenosaunee) Indians for four months.

In 1774, Ledyard worked his way to England on a merchant ship. Two years later, as a British Royal Marine, he joined JAMES COOK's third voyage of 1776–80. When the Cook expedition reached Unalaska Island in the Gulf of Alaska, Ledyard was sent ashore alone to meet with the Russian fur traders.

Ledyard returned to England in 1780, during the American Revolution. Two years later, he volunteered for service in America. Once there, he deserted from the British and hid out until the end of the war.

In 1783, Ledyard published one of the earliest accounts of Cook's third expedition, entitled *A Journal of Captain Cook's Last Voyage to the Pacific Ocean.*

Ledyard was among the first Americans to recognize the tremendous potential of the FUR TRADE with the Indians of the Pacific Northwest. Over the next several years, he tried unsuccessfully to get backing from New England merchants for a seaward expedition to the northwest coast of North America. He next traveled to England, then to France, where his plan was received with great enthusiasm by then U.S. foreign minister Thomas Jefferson and naval hero John Paul Jones. At Jefferson's suggestion, Ledyard revised his plan to include an overland journey from the Pacific coast of North America to the MISSISSIPPI RIVER, providing a transcontinental route for U.S. trade. Ledyard received some funding for his proposed journey through English naturalist SIR JOSEPH BANKS.

In December 1786, Ledyard left England for Hamburg, then walked across Scandinavia to St. Petersburg. Through the influence of Thomas Jefferson, he received official permission to cross Russia and traveled into SIBERIA with a Scottish doctor in the service of Russian empress Catherine the Great.

Ledyard reached Irkutsk, from where he traveled northward on the Lena River in a native boat. At Yakutsk, Russian officials arrested Ledyard, then deported him to Poland. His arrest and expulsion from Russia may have been at the prompting of Russian fur entrepreneur GRIGORY IVANOVICH SHELIKOV, who feared foreign encroachment in the Pacific coast fur trade. From Poland, Ledyard returned to London in 1788.

That year, the newly founded AFRICAN ASSOCIATION commissioned Ledyard to explore the SAHARA DESERT between Egypt and the NIGER RIVER. Ledyard reached Cairo, where he died of fever.

Ledyard was one of the earliest proponents of U.S. involvement in the lucrative Pacific Northwest fur trade. Fifteen years after his death, his writings and his unrealized plans gave impetus to the expedition of MERIWETHER LEWIS and WILLIAM CLARK organized by President Thomas Jefferson, as well as to JOHN JACOB ASTOR's enterprise to Astoria.

Legazpi, Miguel López de (Miguel López de Legaspi) (1510–1572) *Spanish mariner, conquistador in the Philippines*

Miguel López de Legazpi was born in Zubarraja, a town in the Basque province of Guipúzcoa on Spain's Atlantic coast. In 1545, after pursuing a career as a seafarer and navigator, he settled in Mexico, where he received an appointment as a minor official in the colonial government under Spanish viceroy Luis de Velasco.

In 1563, Legazpi was commissioned by King Philip II of Spain to command a small fleet on a voyage to the western Pacific Ocean, on the recommendation of a prominent Basque geographer and Augustinian friar, ANDRÉS DE URDANETA, who also accompanied him on the expedition. One of the principal objectives of the voyage was to locate new sources of spices in the EAST INDIES not yet under the control of Portugal. Another major aim was to assert Spain's dominion over islands explored on the earlier voyages of Spanish navigators FERDINAND MAGELLAN and JUAN SEBASTIÁN DEL CANO. Legazpi was also directed to find out at what latitude ships could regularly sail eastward across the Pacific. Until that time, the unfavorable winds in the known southern latitudes had made a passage eastward from Asian ports to the Pacific coasts of Spain's possessions in Mexico, CENTRAL AMERICA, and Peru nearly impossible for 16th-century sailing ships.

Legazpi and his fleet of five ships sailed westward into the Pacific from Navidad, Mexico, on November 21, 1564. He made landings in the Marianas (originally named the Ladrones, or "Thieves'" Islands, by Magellan), where he declared formal Spanish possession of Saipan, Tinian, and Guam. He came upon some uncharted islands as well, including Los Barbudos (island of bearded men), known today as Mejit, in the Marshalls.

On February 13, 1565, Legazpi and his fleet arrived off the coast of Samar in the Philippines. Although it had been visited 44 years earlier by Magellan, who had been killed there in 1521, no permanent Spanish presence had yet been established. Without resorting to much armed force, Legazpi was soon able to bring the Filipino natives under Spanish colonial rule. The Spanish conquest of the Philippines was largely nonmilitary due to Legazpi's skill as a diplomat and because the Filipino natives did not have a strong central government with which to mount any organized resistance. San Miguel, the first permanent Spanish settlement and colonial capital, was established on the Philippine island of Cebu later in 1565.

On June 1, 1565, Legazpi sent one of his ships, the *San Pedro,* under the command of Felipe de Salcedo (with Urdaneta as navigator), back toward Mexico in an attempt to find out at what latitude a successful eastward crossing of the Pacific could be made. Unknown to Legazpi at that time, another one of his ships, the *San Lucas,* under the command of Alonso de Arellano, which had become separated from the fleet on the outward bound voyage, was already returning eastward across the Pacific. It arrived back in Navidad on August 8, 1565, having been greatly aided by the northeastward-flowing Japan Current. Salcedo and Urdaneta, who had also ridden the Japan Current, arrived one month later at San Miguel Island off the California coast, from where they soon reached Acapulco, Mexico.

Meanwhile, back in the Philippines, Legazpi continued to expand Spanish hegemony over the region and succeeded in bringing most of the islands under the control of his centralized colonial administration by 1571. That year, he occupied the large northern Philippine island of Luzon, where he established Manila as the new capital. He died there of a stroke the following year.

Miguel López de Legazpi completed the Spanish conquest of the Philippines in less than six years. His important role in the history of the Philippines is commemorated in the city on the southern end of Luzon that bears his name. Spain remained in control of the islands for the next 227 years, until forced to cede them to the United States at the conclusion of the Spanish-American War in 1898. Until that time, the Philippines served as Spain's most important link in its trade with Asia. The charting of an eastward sea route across the Pacific to California and Mexico enabled Spain to establish direct trade links with the Far East through its American colonies. By the 1580s, an annual commercial fleet known as the Manila Galleon was sailing eastward through the latitudes of the Japan Current, carrying valuable cargoes from the Orient to Mexico and Panama for trans-shipment to Spain.

Leichhardt, Friedrich Wilhelm Ludwig

(1813–ca. 1848) *German naturalist in northern Australia*
Ludwig Leichhardt was born in the northern German city of Trebatch, in what was then the Prussian province of Brandenburg. In 1831, he began two years of study at the University of Berlin, studying natural science, and in 1833, he attended the University of Göttingen. He returned to the University of Berlin in 1834 for two more years. Leichhardt soon entered the Prussian army, but he deserted sometime before 1842. That year, he arrived in Sydney, Australia, around which he studied rocks, animals, and plants. He also tried without success to obtain the support of SIR THOMAS LIVINGSTONE MITCHELL, surveyor general of New South Wales, for a proposed exploration into the northeastern part of Australia.

Leichhardt next sought backing from private sources. At that time, commercial interests in Sydney hoped to develop the natural harbor at Port Essington, on Australia's north coast, near present-day Darwin, in order to create a trade link with India. For Sydney businessmen to reap any benefit, an overland route northwest to the Gulf of Carpentaria first had to be established, and this was precisely what Leichhardt proposed to do. After receiving the financial support he needed for the project, he undertook a preliminary journey in 1843, traveling overland by foot from Newcastle, north of Sydney, 480 miles northward along Australia's east coast to Moreton Bay, near present-day Brisbane. In the course of this expedition, he undertook botanical and geological studies.

In August 1844, Leichhardt set out on his exploration of northern Australia. He first sailed from Sydney to Moreton Bay, where he met up with ornithologist John Gilbert, who was to be the expedition's naturalist. On October 1, he left Jimbour, in the Darling Downs region west of Brisbane, accompanied by Gilbert, two Aborigine guides named Charley Fisher and Harry Brown, plus four other men.

Since his small party could not carry a large supply of water, Leichhardt planned to travel along a route that took them no more than 10 miles from a river. Accordingly, they followed the Condamine River to its headwaters, then proceeded northwestward, along the eastern slopes of the GREAT DIVIDING RANGE, to the Burdekin and Warrego Rivers. They eventually reached the Cape York Peninsula, and, in June 1845, after descending the Mitchell River, they arrived on the shores of the Gulf of Carpentaria. It was during this part of the journey that John Gilbert was killed in an attack by Aborigines, and two other members of the party were wounded.

Although critically short on supplies and two of his expedition having been injured, Leichhardt pushed onward along the south coast of the Gulf of Carpentaria. After traversing the heart of Arnhem Land, he reached Van Diemen Gulf and Port Essington on December 17, 1845, where the expedition was met by a ship that took them back to Moreton Bay.

Leichhardt returned to Sydney in March 1846. The news of his successful 3,000-mile trek across northeastern Australia quickly brought him fame, and he soon received word that the king of Prussia, in recognition of his accomplishment as an explorer, had granted him a royal pardon for his earlier desertion. In addition, for making the first overland crossing from Queensland to the north coast, Leichhardt was awarded a sizable cash prize. Although he had followed a circuitous route, not feasible for commercial purposes, he had accomplished the European discovery of uncharted rivers and, more importantly, large tracts of fertile grazing lands in the interior of northern Queensland. His account of this exploit, *Journal of an Overland Expedition in Australia from Moreton Bay to Port Essington,* was published in 1847.

In December 1846, Leichhardt again left Moreton Bay on an expedition in which he hoped to explore the east, north, and west coasts of Australia. Within six months, after traveling northward about 500 miles as far as the TROPIC OF CAPRICORN, he was forced to turn back because of food shortages.

Undaunted by this setback, Leichhardt soon made another attempt at the first east-to-west crossing of the Australian continent. His eight-man expedition, including a relative named Adolf Classen, was equipped with 77 pack animals. They left McPherson Station west of Brisbane in April 1848, planning to follow a route that

Surveyor General Mitchell had previously taken into the Barcoo River region, then head southwestward and eventually reach the Swan River and Perth on the southwest coast. Leichhardt and his expedition were never heard from again.

The disappearance of Ludwig Leichhardt and his companions remains one of the great unsolved mysteries of Australian exploration. It inspired numerous expeditions, including one undertaken by SIR AUGUSTUS CHARLES GREGORY in 1855 and another by JOHN FORREST in 1869. Although his critics often cited his incompetence as a planner and leader as the reason behind the failure of his 1846 expedition, as well as the probable cause of his final failure, Leichhardt is nevertheless credited with making the first European crossing of northeastern Australia and revealing the region's great potential for agricultural development. The Leichhardt River in northern Queensland was named in his honor.

Leif Ericsson   See ERICSSON, LEIF.

Le Maire, Jakob (Jacob le Maire, Jacques le Maire, James le Maire, Jacob la Maire)

(ca. 1565–1616) *Dutch mariner in the South Atlantic and South Pacific*

Born in Holland, Jakob Le Maire was the son of Amsterdam merchant Isaac Le Maire. The elder Le Maire was born in the city of Tournai in what is now western Belgium but, as a Jew, had been forced to flee to Amsterdam after the onset of the religious persecutions of non-Catholics instituted by Fernando Álvarez de Toledo, the duke of Alba, during the early 1570s.

In Amsterdam, Isaac Le Maire prospered as a merchant engaged in overseas trade, becoming the largest shareholder of the DUTCH EAST INDIA COMPANY by 1602. He soon became disenchanted with the Dutch East India Company's stranglehold on foreign commerce, which it exercised through its domination of the trade routes to the Far East by way of both the CAPE OF GOOD HOPE and the STRAIT OF MAGELLAN. In 1610, with the support of the Dutch legislature, the States-General, he formed a new firm, the Australian Company, chartered to engage in trade with China, Tartary (northeastern Asia), Japan, New Holland (Australia), and the islands of the South Pacific. In 1615, Isaac Le Maire organized an expedition to find an alternate route from Europe to the Pacific and Indian oceans, hoping to circumvent the Dutch East India Company's monopoly over both the Cape of Good Hope and Strait of Magellan sea routes to India and the Far East. Much of the financing for the enterprise came from leading businessmen of the city of Hoorn in northern Holland.

Jakob Le Maire, named director general of the enterprise, was joined in the voyage by his brother Daniel Le Maire and by WILLEM CORNELIS SCHOUTEN, a native of Hoorn and an experienced navigator. Based on reports of an earlier voyage to the South Atlantic undertaken by SIR FRANCIS DRAKE, Schouten believed that a passage into the Pacific could be found south of the Strait of Magellan.

Equipped with two ships, the *Eendracht* and the smaller *Hoorn,* Le Maire and Schouten set sail from Hoorn on June 15, 1615. They made a stop at Sierra Leone on the coast of West Africa, where they took on a cargo of lemons, used on the voyage to prevent SCURVY among the crew. They then sailed to Puerto Deseado on the Patagonian coast of southeastern South America to make repairs. While there, the *Hoorn* accidentally caught fire and burned to the waterline, whereupon the crew and salvageable supplies were transferred to the *Eendracht.*

Le Maire and Schouten continued southward along the east coast of South America, beyond the entrance to the Strait of Magellan. On January 25, 1616, they sighted what they believed was the coast of a large southern landmass, which they called Staten Landt, later known as Staten Island (Esla de los Estados) after its insularity was revealed by subsequent navigators. They soon located an eight-mile-wide strait separating Staten Island from the mainland of Tierra del Fuego, and passed through it. (It later became known as Le Maire Strait.) Proceeding westward, they rounded a point of land extending from an island. This they named Cape Hoorn (later modified to CAPE HORN) after Schouten's hometown, whose leading citizens had provided much of the financing for the expedition. The island became known as Horn Island.

Le Maire and Schouten, on finding that the mainland extended to the north, realized that they had indeed located an uncharted sea route into the Pacific. Off the coast of Chile, they made the European discovery of the Juan Fernandez Islands, and, unable to continue farther northward because of unfavorable winds, headed westward toward the Orient. On the transpacific voyage, they came upon some uncharted islands of the Tuamotu group, as well as the Horn Islands and the Coco Islands of what later came to be known as Samoa. After stops at Fiji, where they came into contact with natives, they continued westward into the islands of Melanesia. Le Maire and Schouten incorrectly surmised that the long, narrow island of New Ireland was an extension of Terra Australis, the much-sought-after GREAT SOUTHERN CONTINENT, thought by 17th-century geographers to exist in the extreme southern latitudes.

On September 17, 1616, the expedition reached the island of Ternate in the SPICE ISLANDS (the Moluccas) of present-day Indonesia; at the end of the following month it arrived at the Dutch East India Company port of Batavia (present-day Jakarta) on Java. Jan Pieterzoon Coen, the

Dutch East India Company governor at Batavia, discounted as untrue Le Maire and Schouten's account that they had located a passage into the Pacific south of the Strait of Magellan. Believing that they had actually used the Strait of Magellan without the company's permission, Coen confiscated the *Eendracht* and had Le Maire and Schouten sent back to the Netherlands under arrest.

Although Le Maire died on the homeward voyage, his brother Daniel and Schouten pleaded the case before the Dutch legislature, and, with the help of Isaac Le Maire, recovered their ship and its cargo from the Dutch East India Company. Subsequent expeditions proved that the channel located on their 1615–16 voyage indeed provided a new passage into the Pacific. It was named Le Maire Strait in his honor.

Jakob Le Maire commanded the second European expedition to round Cape Horn after Drake and successfully navigate through the maelstrom caused by the collision of waters flowing from the Pacific and Atlantic oceans and the Antarctic seas. His subsequent explorations in the western Pacific revealed the eastern extent of the large island of New Guinea. Most significantly, in rounding Cape Horn, he showed that South America was not contiguous with any landmass to the south and provided European mariners with a sea passage into the Pacific as an alternative to the winding and treacherous 370-mile-long Strait of Magellan. A Dutch mission in 1675 under the German SIGISMUND NIEBUHR thoroughly charted Le Maire Strait and made depth soundings.

Le Moyne, Jean-Baptiste (sieur de Bienville)

(1680–1768) *French colonizer of the lower Mississippi River, brother of Pierre Le Moyne, sieur d'Iberville*

Jean Baptiste Le Moyne, sieur de Bienville, was born in Ville-Marie near Montreal, Quebec. He was the son of French colonial leader Charles Le Moyne and brother of French naval commander PIERRE LE MOYNE, sieur d'Iberville.

Bienville served as a midshipman under his brother Iberville during King William's War of 1689–97, taking part in raids against British fur-trading posts on HUDSON BAY. In 1698, with his brother, he received a patent to colonize the lower MISSISSIPPI RIVER region and locate that river's mouth in the Gulf of Mexico.

The brothers set sail for the Gulf of Mexico in late 1698, leading an expedition of four ships with 200 colonists and soldiers. They landed at Dauphin Island in Mobile Bay in March 1699. From there, Bienville and Iberville left the main contingent of colonists and, with a company of 50 men traveling by CANOE and longboat, explored the Gulf Coast westward until they reached the actual mouth of the Mississippi. A group of Indians they encountered in the region showed them a letter written by explorer HENRI DE TONTI and left for RENÉ-ROBERT CAVELIER DE LA SALLE, some 13 years earlier. (Tonti would later help in establishing settlements in the region.) Bienville and Iberville continued to explore the lower Mississippi for a distance of about 100 miles upriver before returning to the Gulf.

In 1700, the brothers established a permanent settlement on Dauphin Island in Biloxi Bay, then known as Massacre Island because of the large number of bleached human bones found there. Iberville returned to France for supplies and more colonists, leaving Bienville in charge.

In 1700–02, Bienville continued to explore the interior of the lower Mississippi Valley and also penetrated to the west into the Red River region of present-day northeastern Texas. During that time, Bienville moved the settlement from Dauphin Island to the mainland, where he founded Fort Maurepas on the site of present-day Ocean Springs, Mississippi. Other settlements were also established, including Fort de la Boulaye in 1707, the first permanent French settlement in what is now the state of Louisiana, south of what is now New Orleans; and Fort Louis, on the site of what is now Mobile, Alabama, at the head of Mobile Bay, in 1710 (renamed Fort Conde in 1720).

Iberville returned to the Mobile Bay colony briefly in 1702, but he soon left again for France to obtain support for

Jean-Baptiste Le Moyne, sieur de Bienville *(Library of Congress)*

a military campaign against the Spanish in Florida and the British along the southeast Atlantic coast. He never returned to the French Gulf Coast settlements, dying in Havana, Cuba, from yellow fever in 1706. Bienville assumed leadership of French Louisiana, as the area became known.

ANTOINE LAUMET DE LA MOTHE, sieur de Cadillac, was appointed to the governorship in 1712, but Bienville continued to serve in a leadership capacity. In 1714, he explored the Alabama River and established Fort Toulouse at the junctions of the Coosa and Tallapoosa Rivers, which developed into an important fur-trading center in the early 18th century.

As a military leader, Bienville conducted several campaigns against the Natchez and Chickasaw Indians. During one such campaign in 1716, he established Fort Rosalie on the site of what was to become the modern city of Natchez, Mississippi. He was appointed governor of Louisiana in 1717.

In 1718, Bienville realized his long-sought-after goal of establishing a permanent settlement at the Indian portage between Lake Pontchartrain and the Mississippi River. This settlement of New Orleans became the capital of French Louisiana three years later.

Administrative differences and internal conflicts with the colonists led to Bienville's recall as governor of Louisiana in 1725. He lived in France until he was eventually reinstated in 1732.

In 1736, back in North America, Bienville led a military expedition of 600 French soldiers, along with 1,000 Choctaw auxiliaries, northward along the Tombigbee River. His objective was to join up with another French force heading southward down the Mississippi to the Chickasaw stronghold in western Tennessee. But both French columns were defeated in separate engagements with the Indians. During this campaign, a settlement in the interior of Alabama, Fort Tombigbee, was established. In 1739, Bienville attempted yet another, larger invasion of Chickasaw lands, which was abandoned because of heavy rains.

In 1742, Bienville departed Louisiana for France, where he remained for the rest of his life. In 1763, he unsuccessfully lobbied against the cession of French Louisiana to Spain.

By establishing numerous forts and settlements along the Mississippi Gulf Coast, including the city of New Orleans, Jean-Baptiste Le Moyne, sieur de Bienville, helped open the way for French settlement into Alabama, Tennessee, and Arkansas. His influence also extended to the legal and governmental system of Louisiana, even after that region became part of the United States in 1803.

Le Moyne, Pierre (sieur d'Iberville) (1661–1706)

French naval officer on the lower Mississippi River, brother of Jean-Baptiste Le Moyne, sieur de Bienville

Pierre Le Moyne, sieur d'Iberville, was born in the Ville Marie section of Montreal to a prominent French colonial family. In 1675, he was commissioned an officer in the French navy.

In September 1697, during King William's War of 1689–97, Iberville led French naval campaigns against the British throughout northeastern North America. He also undertook several overland military expeditions from Montreal through the wilderness to HUDSON BAY and James Bay.

In 1698, Iberville was granted a patent by French king Louis XIV to establish a French colony at the mouth of the MISSISSIPPI RIVER. RENÉ-ROBERT CAVELIER DE LA SALLE had failed to do so in his attempt 13 years earlier.

In October 1698, Iberville sailed from Brest, France, in command of the *Badine* and the *Marin,* plus two smaller vessels. His small fleet carried about 200 French colonists. Iberville's brother, JEAN-BAPTISTE LE MOYNE, sieur de Bienville, was second in command of the expedition.

Iberville and his fleet stopped first at Santo Domingo and, in January 1699, they landed at Pensacola Bay. He continued westward along the Gulf Coast and located and named Mobile Bay, where he established Fort Louis de Mobile. At the mouth of the bay, Iberville explored an island with piles of bleached human bones, and named it Massacre Island (later Dauphin Island). Off the coast of present-day Mississippi, he located and named Cat Island and Ship Island. He left the two larger ships and the colonists at Ship Island and continued his explorations with the two smaller vessels.

Iberville located the Mississippi's outlet to the Gulf of Mexico on March 3, 1699. He encamped at a place he named Mardi Gras Island, then explored upriver as far as the mouth of the Ohio River.

On Iberville's return to the Mississippi Delta, he established a settlement called Fort de la Boulaye, 40 miles below the future site of New Orleans. On the way to the Gulf, he made the European discovery of Lake Pontchartrain, which he named in honor of Louis Phelypeaux, comte de Pontchârtrain, head of the French navy.

Iberville returned to the main body of his expedition at Ship Island and took the colonists to the mainland, where they established the first permanent French settlement in French Louisiana. Called Fort Maurepas or Old Biloxi, it was located at the present-day site of Ocean Springs, Mississippi.

Iberville sailed to France later in 1699, but he returned to the Gulf of Mexico in 1700 and 1701. He established additional settlements at Biloxi Bay, at present-day Mobile, Alabama, and on Dauphin Island.

At the outbreak of the War of the Spanish Succession in 1702, Iberville returned to active service in the French navy, whereupon Bienville assumed charge of the Louisiana colony. Iberville never returned to Louisiana. He contracted yellow fever while serving in the Caribbean and died aboard his ship in Havana harbor in 1706.

Pierre Le Moyne, sieur d'Iberville, along with his brother Bienville, made the first European approach to the mouth of the Mississippi River from the Gulf of Mexico, henceforth providing New France with another trade route to the sea. Iberville reestablished French sovereignty over Louisiana and the lower Mississippi Valley and founded the first permanent settlements along the Gulf Coast of what is now Alabama, Mississippi, and Louisiana.

Le Moyne, Simon (Ouane) (1604–1665)
French missionary in Quebec and upstate New York
Simon Le Moyne was born in the French cathedral town of Beauvais, north of Paris. After entering the Jesuit order at the age of 18, he undertook a course of study in philosophy at the College de Clermont in Paris. Starting in 1627, he taught for 10 years at the Jesuit college in Rouen, and, in 1637, he took holy orders, committing himself to a career as a Jesuit missionary priest.

In June 1638, Le Moyne arrived in Quebec; less than two months later, he headed westward into Huron (Wyandot) country with Indian guides. His guides soon deserted him, and he was left in the wilderness with another Frenchman. They wandered in the forest, surviving on whatever they could hunt, until, after about two weeks, a Jesuit associate, Father François du Peron, came upon them. With his party, they continued to the Huron villages on the east shore of Lake Huron's Georgian Bay.

Known as "Ouane" by the Huron, Le Moyne lived among them until 1649, when he was compelled to return to Quebec at the outbreak of war between the Huron and tribes of the Iroquois Confederacy. He served at the Jesuit center at Trois-Rivières, where he studied the Iroquoian and Algonquian languages.

Le Moyne's ability to deal with Indians was again called upon in 1654, when he led a diplomatic mission to the Iroquois (Haudenosaunee) Indians. Departing Quebec in early July of that year, he reached the headquarters of the Iroquois Confederacy in the lands of the Onondaga in present-day upstate New York, where he remained most of the summer. On his return to Quebec in September 1654, he reported having visited a saltwater lake fed by a salt spring near the Onondaga village, which the Onondaga believed to be inhabited by an evil spirit because of the strange taste of the water.

During the next seven years, Le Moyne made five more trips into the lands of the Iroquois, successfully establishing ties with some prominent tribal leaders and obtaining permission to send Jesuit missionaries into the region. He was also instrumental in winning the release of several dozen French captives, who otherwise would have been tortured and burned at the stake.

The saltwater lake that Simon Le Moyne visited on his 1654 journey is known today as Lake Onondaga; it spurred the development of the region's salt-making industry in the early 19th century and led to the growth of the adjacent central New York State city of Syracuse. Le Moyne College, a Jesuit-run institution in Syracuse, was named in his honor.

Le Moyne de Morgues, Jacques (Jacques le Moine) (d. 1588) *French artist, colonist in Florida*
French artist Jacques Le Moyne was a member of the French colonizing expedition under RENÉ GOULAINE DE LAUDONNIÈRE to North America. With Laudonnière, he helped establish Fort Caroline near present-day Jacksonville, Florida, in 1564. Over the next 15 months, he made drawings of the Indians, plants, and animals of northern Florida.

Le Moyne survived a Spanish attack under PEDRO MENÉNDEZ DE AVILÉS on the Fort Caroline settlement in September 1565, in which most of the inhabitants were massacred. He fled with the other survivors into the woods and was later rescued by an English ship. He sailed to England with his rescuers and subsequently settled there. He produced paintings of the unique animals and plants he had seen and sketched in Florida, as well as depictions of the Indians. Flemish artist Theodore de Bry made engravings from Le Moyne's watercolors, which appeared as illustrations for an account of the Fort Caroline colony, written by the expedition's carpenter, Nicolas le Challeux. In England, Le Moyne's paintings came to the attention of SIR HUMPHREY GILBERT and his half brother SIR WALTER RALEIGH, probably giving impetus to their later colonizing efforts in Virginia.

Jacques Le Moyne was the first European artist to paint scenes in what is now the continental United States. His work led to continuing European interest in the exploration of North America.

Lenz, Oskar (Oscar Lenz) (1848–1925)
German explorer in Africa
Oskar Lenz was born in the German city of Leipzig. Soon after completing his education, which included training as a geologist, he traveled to Africa, where, over the next 13 years, he undertook a series of expeditions that penetrated deep into the continent's little-known interior regions.

Lenz's first African expedition began in 1874 at the mouth of Gabon's Ogowe River on the Atlantic coast of central Africa. For three years, he traveled up the Ogowe, along a route that took him eastward, just south of the equator, toward the lower CONGO RIVER (Zaire River).

Lenz next turned his attention northward to the SAHARA DESERT. In 1879, he set out from the North African port of Casablanca in Morocco and traveled southward into high country. He then made a southward crossing of the Sahara, reaching TIMBUKTU in what is now the West African nation of Mali in 1880, having traversed more than 1,500 miles of rugged mountain and desert terrain.

After a three-week stay in Timbuktu, Lenz began his return journey. He followed the NIGER RIVER westward, then made an overland crossing to the Senegal River, which he followed to the coast of West Africa.

Lenz's most extensive exploration of Africa began in 1885, when he set out from the mouth of the Congo River in command of a relief expedition sent to aid German explorer WILHELM JOHANN JUNKER and his companions, who were trapped in the southern Sudan region by the outbreak of the Mahdi revolt in Egypt. After ascending the Congo into the African interior, Lenz located its confluence with the Lualaba, which he followed to its headwaters. He then traveled overland to the northern end of Lake Tanganyika. Unable to reach Junker and his party, Lenz led his expedition to Lake Nyasa (Lake Malawi), and from there reached the coast of East Africa and the Indian Ocean in 1887.

Oskar Lenz spent his last years in the Austrian town of Sooz. In his 1879–80 Sahara expedition from Casablanca to Timbuktu, he duplicated in reverse the journey of RENÉ-AUGUSTE CAILLIÉ, who had reached the fabled city from the coast of West Africa a half-century earlier. Lenz's 1885–87 cross-continental expedition up the Congo River and across the width of Africa also partly retraced, in the opposite direction, the route taken by SIR HENRY MORTON STANLEY, who had descended the Congo in 1876–77. Lenz was among the few 19th-century African explorers to venture into both the Saharan and sub-Saharan regions of the continent.

Leo Africanus (Leo the African, John Leo de Medicis, Giovanni Leone, Johannes Leo, al-Hassan ibn Muhammed al-Wazzan al-Zaiyati, el-Hasen ben Muhammed el-Wazzan-ez-Zayyati)

(ca. 1485–ca. 1554) *Arab diplomat, traveler in Africa and Asia*

Leo Africanus was born al-Hassan ibn Muhammed in the Moorish city of Granada, Spain. After the reconquest of Spain by Christian forces in 1492, he fled with his Muslim family to Fez, Morocco, where he was educated.

Trained in law and science, Leo Africanus entered the diplomatic service of the sultan of Morocco in about 1507, and, in that capacity, he traveled widely throughout northern and central Africa. He also undertook diplomatic expeditions to the Middle East and central Asia, journeying as far as Armenia, according to his later account.

In 1512–14, Leo Africanus made several journeys across the SAHARA DESERT to TIMBUKTU on the NIGER RIVER in what is now Mali. On one trip to Timbuktu, he returned to Egypt by way of Lake Chad, thus practically traversing the width of the African continent.

In 1518, while returning to Morocco from an official visit to the sultan of the Ottoman Empire in Constantinople (present-day Istanbul, Turkey), Leo Africanus was captured by the Sicilian pirate Pietro Bovadiglia and taken to Italy. In Rome, he was presented as a slave to Pope Leo X, who freed him on learning of his background. Leo Africanus remained near the Vatican, where for two years he was tutored by three bishops in Latin, Italian, and the basic principles of Catholicism.

In 1520, Leo Africanus was converted to Christianity in a ceremony at St. Peter's Church at the Vatican, during which he was personally baptized by Pope Leo, who bestowed his own Christian name upon him, Giovanni Leone (John Leo) de Medicis. Afterward, he was also known as Johannes Leo, but he was commonly referred to as Leo Africanus, Latin for "Leo the African."

Over the next nine years, Leo Africanus taught Arabic in Rome and wrote of his travels throughout Africa and Asia. In 1526, he published an account of his African travels, entitled *Descrittione dell' Africa et delle cose notabili che quivi sono* (published in English as *A Geographical Historie of Africa* in 1600, now commonly known as *Description of Africa*). In 1529, he was allowed to leave Italy and returned to Africa, eventually settling in Tunis, where he re-embraced the Islamic faith.

In 1559, an account by Leo Africanus was published of the wealth to be found in the West African caravan trading center of Timbuktu. Through his writings, Timbuktu soon earned a reputation in Europe as a city of fabulous riches.

An English edition of Leo Africanus's writings on Africa first appeared in 1600. For many years afterward, this work was the primary source of geographic knowledge of Africa south of the Sahara, a region known as the Sudan.

León, Alonso de (ca. 1640–1691) *Mexican army officer, colonial administrator in Texas, in service to Spain*

Alonso de León was a native of Mexico. He became a career officer with Spanish colonial forces in northern Mexico, rising to the rank of captain. In about 1680, he was named colonial governor of the northeastern province of Coahuila, just south of the Rio Grande. Over the next several years, he commanded a series of exploring expeditions into the neighboring Nuevo León region to the east.

In 1689, León was directed to investigate reports received by Mexico's chief colonial administrator, the Count of Galve, that the French were establishing settlements on the Gulf Coast, north of the Rio Grande, on lands claimed by Spain. He set out from Monclova, the provincial capital of Coahuila, in command of a small military force, and, after a northeastward trek across the desert region of what is now southeasternmost Texas, he arrived on the Gulf Coast, about midway between Corpus Christi and Matagorda Bay.

At a site identified as San Bernardo Bay (known later as Lavaca Bay), León came upon a fort and, based on information provided by local Indians, soon located a party of Frenchmen nearby. His men managed to capture two of the French settlers, Jacques Grollet and Jean l'Archevêque, who were survivors of RENÉ-ROBERT CAVELIER DE LA SALLE's last expedition to North America. Placed under arrest, they were taken to Mexico City and later sent to Spain. Meanwhile, León burned the French base, Fort St. Louis, which had been established five years earlier by La Salle.

In 1690, under orders from the king of Spain, León commanded a second and larger expedition into eastern Texas, planning to set up additional presidios and missions to discourage further French encroachment from the lower Mississippi Valley. Later that year, León and Father Damian Massanet founded the San Francisco de los Tejas Mission in the Neches River region near Houston, and, in 1691, they established Santísimo Nombre de María nearby.

León's harsh treatment of the Tejas Indians soon provoked a native uprising against the Mexican colonists, and by 1693, nearly all the missions he had established were destroyed. That year, he was recalled from office. He went on to found the city of Cadereita in the newly organized Mexican province of Nuevo León.

In his earlier contact with the French in Texas in 1688, Alonso de León stemmed the short-lived attempt by French settlers to colonize the region, which had been inadvertently begun by La Salle in the course of his last expedition of 1684–87. Although León's own missions and presidios also were short-lived, they were among the earliest European attempts at settlement in the interior of eastern Texas.

León, Francisco de Montejo y   See MONTEJO Y LEÓN, FRANCISCO DE.

León, Juan Ponce de   See PONCE DE LEÓN, JUAN.

Leonard, Zenas (1809–1857) *American fur trader in the American West*

Zenas Leonard was originally from the central Pennsylvania town of Clearfield. In 1820, he left home to work at his uncle's store in Pittsburgh.

In 1830, Leonard headed westward for St. Louis; the next year, he joined a fur-trading expedition up the MISSOURI RIVER and into the northern ROCKY MOUNTAINS. He took part in the annual fur trappers' rendezvous at Pierre's Hole in the Teton Mountains in summer 1832, where he helped fight off an Indian attack on July 18.

At the summer 1833 rendezvous on the Green River, near the present Wyoming-Utah border, Leonard joined Captain BENJAMIN LOUIS EULALIE DE BONNEVILLE's expedition into the central Rockies. As part of a contingent of MOUNTAIN MEN led by JOSEPH REDDEFORD WALKER, Leonard explored the unknown regions of northern Utah and Nevada. The group traveled along the Humboldt River into northern California's Yosemite Valley. Along the way, they successfully repelled an Indian raid.

After reaching the Pacific coast, Leonard and the Walker party made an eastward crossing of the Sierra Nevada and the southern Rockies, rejoining Bonneville in July 1834 at the fur trapper's rendezvous on the Bear River in what is now northeastern Utah.

Leonard remained in the western FUR TRADE for another year, then returned to his home in Pennsylvania, where he wrote an account of his adventures with Bonneville and others in the Rockies, entitled *Narrative of the Adventures of Zenas Leonard*. It was published in 1839.

Soon afterward, Leonard settled at Sibley, Missouri, near Kansas City, where he was involved in trading with the Indians and the commerce of the Santa Fe Trail. He also operated a steamboat on the Missouri River.

As a member of Joseph Walker's expedition of 1833–34, Zenas Leonard was among the first non-Indians to cross the deserts of what is now Utah and Nevada, explore the Yosemite Valley of California, and see the giant sequoia trees of the Merced region.

Leonov, Alexei Arkhipovich (Alexey Leonov, Aleksei Leonov, Aleksey Leonov) (1934–   )
Soviet cosmonaut, first human to walk in space

Born in Listvyanka, SIBERIA, Alexei Leonov attended the Kremenchug preparatory school for pilots and the Chuguyev Higher Air Force School in Ukraine, graduating in 1957. He served in East Germany as a pilot in the air force of the Union of Soviet Socialist Republics (USSR, or Soviet Union). In addition to aviation, he developed an interest in painting. In 1959, Leonov was a student at the Zhukovsky Air Force Engineering Academy when the USSR was recruiting cosmonauts (*see* ASTRONAUTS) for its space programs; Leonov was one of the first 20 selected. In 1962, he was selected to train for the first "walk" in space (or EVA, for "extravehicular activity") as part of the VOSKHOD PROGRAM.

On the *Voskhod 2* mission, Leonov flew with Pavel Belyayev as pilot on March 18, 1965. During the mission of 17 orbits, Leonov became the first human to walk in space, exiting his capsule through an inflatable airlock and floating outside for 10 minutes before attempting to reenter. His spacesuit had become rigid, however, because of the pressure difference between the air inside it and the vacuum in space, and he was forced to bleed air from it, exposing him to the vacuum for an additional 10 minutes before he was safely inside. The mission later suffered a guidance control malfunction, forcing Belyayev to pilot the capsule manually. The parachuted landing was 600 miles off course in the deep snow at the foot of the Ural Mountains. Leonov and Belyayev spent two days and a night there, their capsule surrounded by wolves part of the time, before being rescued.

Because of his accomplishment—the first walk in space, beating American EDWARD HIGGINS WHITE II's spacewalk by three months—Leonov was named deputy commander of the cosmonaut program and helped train other cosmonauts in preparation for spacewalks. He and a copilot, Valerei Kubasov, trained for a 1969 lunar mission that never happened. They also trained for the Salyut SPACE STATION project and were assigned to the *Salyut 1* mission, but, when Kubasov became sick, a backup crew was assigned. The three cosmonauts on this mission died when an air valve failed during reentry.

It was not until 1975 that Leonov flew into space again, this time as commander of the *Soyuz 19* mission, part of the SOYUZ PROGRAM and the first Soviet-U.S. space endeavor, known as the Apollo-Soyuz Test Project in the United States. (It used existing Apollo spacecraft but was not part of the APOLLO PROGRAM.) Liftoff of both Soyuz and Apollo spacecraft occurred on July 15; the first international rendezvous and docking in space occurred two days later. While linked for 47 hours, Leonov and Kubasov conducted joint experiments with the *Apollo 18* crew—Thomas P. Stafford, Deke Slayton, and Vance DeVoe Brand.

After his second and final mission, Leonov served as commander of the cosmonaut team until 1982. He also served as deputy director of the Gagarin Cosmonaut Training Center until his retirement at the rank of major general in 1991. During this time, he became known as a painter; some of his works involving space themes are on display at the National Air and Space Museum in Washington, D.C. He has also worked as editor, designer, and cartoonist for *Apogee,* a newsletter for astronauts.

Alexei Leonov achieved two firsts in SPACE EXPLORATION: his spacewalk and his participation in the first U.S.-Soviet space mission. When he and Stafford met at the edge of the docking tunnel, the first international handshake in space occurred. For each of his missions, Alexei Leonov received the Hero of the Soviet Union award. When visiting the Johnson Space Center in Houston, Texas, in preparation for the Apollo-Soyuz mission, as well as during the mission itself and a subsequent international tour by both teams, he reportedly helped further goodwill by his warm personality and sense of humor.

Lesseps, Jean-Baptiste-Barthélemy de (baron de Lesseps) (1766–1834) *French interpreter, diplomat in the Pacific and Siberia*

Jean-Baptiste-Barthélemy de Lesseps was born in the French Mediterranean seaport city of Sète. His mastery of the Russian language came through his father, who was France's consul general to the Russian government in St. Petersburg. At the age of 18, the younger Lesseps entered the French diplomatic service with an appointment as vice consul at the Russian Baltic port of Kronstadt, near St. Petersburg.

In August 1785, Lesseps sailed from France on the *Astrolabe* as the Russian interpreter for an official French scientific voyage to the Pacific Ocean, commanded by JEAN-FRANÇOIS DE GALAUP, comte de La Pérouse. In September 1787, he arrived with the La Pérouse expedition in Petropavlovsk, the Russian settlement on the Pacific coast of eastern SIBERIA's Kamchatka Peninsula.

After a month, when the *Astrolabe* and the expedition's other vessel, the *Boussole,* sailed for Botany Bay, Australia, Lesseps stayed behind in Petropavlovsk, directed to report back to France on the expedition's progress until its arrival on the Kamchatka coast. For the next year, he made his way westward, across the width of Siberia and European Russia. When he arrived in Paris on October 17, 1788, he had completed a combined sea and overland CIRCUMNAVIGATION OF THE WORLD. At Versailles, he conferred with the La Pérouse expedition's chief sponsor, King Louis XVI.

Lesseps resumed his diplomatic career with an appointment as French consul in Kronstadt in 1789. The next year, he published an account of his 1787–88 journey from Kamchatka to Paris.

In 1793, Lesseps was appointed French consul general at St. Petersburg, his father's former post, and five years later he became French chargé d'affaires in Constantinople (present-day Istanbul). Soon after taking this post in 1798, he was briefly imprisoned by the Ottoman government when French forces, under Napoléon, invaded Turkish-controlled Egypt. From 1802 to 1812, Lesseps served as France's chief official in charge of trade relations with Russia. His last diplomatic post was in 1814, as French chargé d'affaires in Lisbon.

Jean de Lesseps was one of the few survivors of the La Pérouse expedition still living when wreckage of the *Astrolabe* was finally discovered in the South Pacific and recovered by JULES-SÉBASTIEN-CÉSAR DUMONT D'URVILLE in 1828, 40 years after the expedition had vanished. He identified the objects brought back by Dumont d'Urville as belonging to the *Astrolabe,* and, in 1831, he published an updated account of the 1785–88 voyage with new information on what probably had happened to La Pérouse.

Lesson, René-Primevère (1794–1849)
French naturalist in the South Pacific

Born in the French port city of Rochefort on the Bay of Biscay, René Lesson was trained as a pharmacist, with a background in medicine and botany. At the age of 20, he was placed in charge of medical and pharmacological research at the botanical garden in his hometown.

In 1822, Lesson sailed on the *Coquille* under the command of LOUIS-ISADORE DUPERREY, part of an official French scientific expedition to the EAST INDIES. Along with his duties as assistant surgeon, he served with Prosper Garnot as one of the expedition's zoologists. In the course of the voyage, which lasted nearly three years, he made an extensive study of the varieties of seals he observed in different parts of the globe.

While exploring Waigeo Island in the Moluccas in September 1823, Lesson first encountered live specimens of the fabled "birds of paradise." He continued his research on these rare birds at Port Dorey in New Guinea the following summer, where he also cataloged several previously unknown species of mound birds, as well as a type of wild boar, a kangaroo, and a scrub wallaby. A species of algae, discovered in the Falkland Islands by the expedition's second in command, JULES-SÉBASTIEN-CÉSAR DUMONT D'URVILLE, was named *lessonia* in Lesson's honor.

In 1829, four years after he had returned to France with the Duperrey expedition, Lesson published a scientific account of his CIRCUMNAVIGATION OF THE WORLD, and, the following year, he published an illustrated journal of the expedition. He became a professor of botany at the naval academy in Rochefort, a position he held for the remainder of his life. He also served as chief pharmacist for the French navy.

As a zoologist, René Lesson won international fame as the first scientist to report accurately on the "birds of paradise" of the East Indies. In bringing to France live specimens of these creatures, he dispelled as erroneous a legend begun by Dutch navigator JAN HUYGHEN VAN LINSCHOTEN, who had reported in 1596 that these birds were born without feet and consequently were hatched in flight and spent their entire lives airborne.

Lesueur, Charles-Alexandre (1778–1846)
French naturalist, artist in Australia, Tasmania, the East Indies, and North America

Charles-Alexandre Lesueur was born in the port city of Le Havre, on the northeast coast of France. Joining the French navy, Lesueur was assigned in 1800 as an assistant gunner on the *Géographe*. Under the command of THOMAS-NICOLAS BAUDIN, he sailed from Le Havre on a three-and-a-half-year voyage to Australia, TASMANIA, and the EAST INDIES.

Lesueur's ability as an artist was soon recognized by the expedition's zoologist, FRANÇOIS PÉRON, to whom he became an assistant. In the course of the voyage, Lesueur produced more than 1,500 drawings and paintings of animal specimens. In addition, he painted landscapes and views of the newly established British settlement of Port Jackson, at present-day Sydney, Australia. Lesueur accompanied Péron on specimen-collecting expeditions throughout the voyage, including one undertaken in Timor, in what is now Indonesia, where they hunted crocodiles in order to take a preserved skin back to France.

After his return from the Baudin expedition in 1804, Lesueur worked with Péron, and, after Péron's death in 1810, with LOUIS-CLAUDE DE SAULCES DE FREYCINET in preparing an account of the expedition, the first volume of which appeared in 1807 as *Voyage aux terres australes sur le* Géographe *et* Naturaliste (Voyage to the southern lands on the *Géographe* and the *Naturaliste*).

In 1815, Lesueur traveled to the United States. He settled in Philadelphia and continued his work as a naturalist and painter, sending back numerous items of scientific interest to the Museum of Natural History in Paris. In 1816–17, he undertook a voyage on the MISSISSIPPI RIVER for an extensive study of North American fish, and he became acquainted with the American naturalist and artist JOHN JAMES AUDUBON.

Lesueur joined Robert Owen's utopian community at New Harmony, Indiana, in 1826, where he taught art and continued his studies of American fish and other wildlife for the next 10 years. Soon after his return to France in 1836, he became director of the Museum of Natural History in his native city of Le Havre.

With Péron, Charles Lesueur is credited with bringing back from the 1800–1804 Baudin expedition more than 10,000 zoological specimens, including 2,500 that were new to science.

Le Sueur, Pierre-Charles (ca. 1657–ca. 1705)
French trader in present-day northern Wisconsin and southern Minnesota

Sources vary on the details of Pierre-Charles Le Sueur's origins and early life. Some indicate he was a native of France, while others suggest he was born in French Canada.

In the 1670s, Le Sueur served as a lay assistant to the Jesuit missionaries operating out of Quebec and Montreal. In 1679, he set out as an Indian trader along the CANOE-and-portage route westward into the Great Lakes. Traveling westward across the length of Lake Superior, he reached Chequamegon Bay, on the shore of what is now northern Wisconsin. He soon established friendly relations with both Chippewa (Ojibway) and Sioux (Dakota, Lakota, Nakota) bands, helping to maintain peace between these traditional enemies.

In 1693, Le Sueur founded a trading post on the site of present-day La Pointe on Madeline Island, the largest of

Chequamegon Bay's Apostle Islands. After hearing reports of what he believed were valuable deposits of copper ore south of Lake Superior, he traveled to France in 1697, where the French government granted him permission to mine these resources.

On his return voyage to North America, Le Sueur was taken prisoner by the British. Released soon afterward, he traveled to the French colony at Biloxi, on the Gulf Coast of what is now the state of Mississippi, where he entered the service of PIERRE LE MOYNE, sieur d'Iberville, taking part in a 1699 exploration of the lower MISSISSIPPI RIVER.

In spring 1700, Le Sueur was commissioned by Iberville to lead a 20-man expedition up the Mississippi River on a small vessel to establish a French foothold in Sioux country as well as to explore for the copper deposits he had learned of previously. By September 19, 1700, he had reached St. Anthony's Falls, near present-day St. Paul, and before long he came to the St. Peter's River. He next came upon a stream flowing into the St. Peter's River; he named it Green River (now the Blue Earth River) after the color of its water, which he believed was caused by copper ore deposits farther upstream.

Near what is now Mankato, Minnesota, Le Sueur founded Fort L'Huiller to serve as a headquarters for trade with the Sioux and for his planned mining operations. Over the next year, he supervised the extraction of mineral ore, collecting as much as 15 tons by spring 1701. At great expense, he transported two tons of the material back to France, where assayers soon determined that it was not copper ore, as Le Sueur had hoped, but only worthless blue clay. Soon afterward, Le Sueur died at sea while on the return voyage from France to North America.

Pierre-Charles Le Sueur's fort at La Pointe was one of the earliest permanent non-Indian settlements in the western Lake Superior region of present-day northern Wisconsin. With the establishment of Fort L'Huiller, he was also one of the original non-Indian settlers of what is now southern Minnesota. Although he was unsuccessful in locating mineral wealth, Le Sueur's 1700 expedition up the Mississippi from the Gulf of Mexico revealed much about the little-known geography of the lower and upper Mississippi Valley. In his earlier travels in the Great Lakes region, along with his ascent of the Mississippi in 1700, he explored thousands of miles of the interior of North America. Southern Minnesota's Le Sueur County, the Le Sueur River near Mankato, as well as the town of Le Sueur, Minnesota, are all named after him.

Lewis, Meriwether (1774–1809) *U.S. Army officer, coleader with William Clark of the Corps of Discovery in the Lewis and Clark Expedition to the American West*

Meriwether Lewis was born on his family's plantation near Charlottesville, Virginia. In the early 1790s, he entered the Virginia militia and took part in the Indian wars in the Ohio Valley as well as the suppression of the Whiskey Rebellion of 1794. By 1801, he was a captain in the regular army. That year, he became private secretary to his long-time friend and Virginia neighbor, newly elected president Thomas Jefferson.

In January 1803, Lewis won an appointment for a proposed government-funded expedition to explore westward from the MISSOURI RIVER and establish an overland route to the Pacific Ocean.

Lewis studied natural sciences at the University of Pennsylvania in preparation for the expedition. In the meantime, the Louisiana Purchase was finalized with France, giving the expedition the added purpose of exploring new holdings and establishing diplomatic contacts with Indian tribes. Lewis requested his former army comrade WILLIAM CLARK as coleader.

In Pittsburgh, Lewis obtained a KEELBOAT and, with some crew members, headed down the Ohio River to

Meriwether Lewis *(Library of Congress)*

Meriwether Lewis and William Clark holding a council with Native Americans *(Library of Congress)*

Louisville, Kentucky, where he was joined by Clark. Lewis took his party to the mouth of the Ohio and entered the MISSISSIPPI RIVER, following it to Camp Wood River, Illinois, opposite St. Louis. He and Clark assembled a group of MOUNTAIN MEN, soldiers, and VOYAGEURS, including JOHN COLTER, GEORGE DROUILLARD, PIERRE DORION, SR., and PIERRE DORION, JR.

On May 14, 1804, the Corps of Discovery, as it was known, started up the Missouri from St. Louis. At Council Bluffs they met with Sioux (Dakota, Lakota, Nakota) tribal leaders. They continued into the Dakotas and camped for the winter at the Mandan Indian villages near present-day Bismarck, North Dakota. The encampment they constructed was called Fort Mandan. The French-Canadian interpreter TOUSSAINT CHARBONNEAU and his Shoshone wife SACAJAWEA (Sacagawea) joined the expedition at this location. Before departure, Sacajawea gave birth to JEAN-BAPTISTE CHARBONNEAU, who was known as Pomp to the explorers.

In April 1805, the Lewis and Clark Expedition left the Mandan and continued up the Missouri with their men in boats. About 1,200 miles upriver, the Missouri forked north and south, and Lewis left the main group and explored the northern branch, which he called the Marias River, after his cousin Maria. Clark continued with the rest of the expedition along the southern branch. Lewis discovered that the Marias River was unnavigable after 70 miles and rejoined

Clark at the Great Falls of the Missouri. The expedition soon reached the Three Forks of the Missouri, which Lewis named the Gallatin, Jefferson, and Madison Rivers. They followed the westernmost stream, the Jefferson, to its headwaters, then headed into the ROCKY MOUNTAINS on foot.

Lewis led his men across the Continental Divide and reached the Lemhi River. They soon encountered the Lemhi Shoshone band of Sacajawea's brother Cameahwait, who provided them with horses, which they used to continue their journey across the Bitterroot Range of the Rockies into the Clearwater River Valley. By CANOE, they followed the Clearwater westward into the Snake, which took them into the COLUMBIA RIVER.

The Lewis and Clark Expedition reached the Columbia's mouth on the Pacific coast on November 15, 1805. They had planned to return from Oregon by sea, but the season's last trading vessels had already departed. They wintered at Fort Clatsop, the post they constructed near present-day Astoria, Oregon.

In late March 1806, Lewis and Clark began their journey back to St. Louis. They first retraced their outward-bound route, but separated for a time in early June. Lewis went with a small party to explore the Marias River and see whether it led northward to the Saskatchewan River. During this side trip, Lewis and his party were involved in a clash with a band of Indians, probably Blackfeet. This was the only hostile encounter with Native Americans in the course of the entire expedition, largely due to Sacajawea's presence and linguistic and diplomatic skills.

After a month of exploring, Lewis rejoined Clark at the mouth of the Yellowstone River. They traveled down the Missouri, stopping briefly at the Mandan villages, and proceeded to St. Louis, arriving on September 23, 1806.

Lewis soon headed for Washington, D.C., where he presented the results of his explorations to President Jefferson. In 1807, he was named territorial governor of upper Louisiana Territory, assuming the post the following year. In 1809, at a stopover in Tennessee while en route to Washington, D.C., to answer official criticism relating to his governmental and Indian policies and to arrange for the publication of his journal of the expedition, he was shot to death. The exact circumstances of his death are unknown.

Meriwether Lewis, with William Clark, undertook the earliest exploration of the country between the Missouri River and the northwest coast by Americans. They covered almost 8,000 miles in over three years of exploring. The expedition made contact with more than 50 Indian tribes and brought back a large number of botanical species. They also reaffirmed U.S. claims to the Pacific Northwest and led the way for the fur traders and mountain men, who would follow their route into the northern Rocky Mountains. The map of their expedition, published in 1814, was the first to show clearly a route westward from the northern Rockies to the Pacific. Lewis was the first to refer to the open territory west of St. Louis as the "Great Plains."

Linschoten, Jan Huyghen van (1563–1611)

Dutch geographer in India, explorer in the Arctic Ocean

Jan Huyghen van Linschoten was a native of Enkhuizen, a fishing port in northern Holland. His family were farmers.

In 1583, Linschoten sailed around the CAPE OF GOOD HOPE to Goa, the Portuguese colony on India's west coast. For the next five years, while serving as bookkeeper to the Portuguese archbishop, he learned much about Portuguese trading practices in the Far East and gained knowledge of sea routes to the EAST INDIES, especially the Moluccas, then known as the SPICE ISLANDS. Linschoten returned to Holland in 1588.

In his book *Itineraio,* published the following year, Linschoten presented a firsthand account of the trade carried on between the Far East, India, and Portugal, illustrated with maps detailing sea routes from India to the East Indies, the eastern terminus for the lucrative trade in spices. Much of the information he revealed had been kept secret by the Portuguese for most of the 16th century.

In Holland, Linschoten became known as one of the foremost authorities on trade with the Far East. He soon became involved with Dutch efforts to discover a NORTH-EAST PASSAGE around the top of Russia and Asia, to China, Japan, and the East Indies.

In 1594, Linschoten commanded a ship in an expedition in search of the Northeast Passage, financed in part by the merchants of Enkhuizen. Another vessel in the small fleet was captained by Dutch navigator WILLEM BARENTS, who served as the expedition's chief pilot and commander. On this voyage, which embarked from Enkhuizen, Barents found the route around the northern end of Novaya Zemlya blocked by ice, while Linschoten managed to navigate his ship eastward for a short distance beyond the southern end of Novaya Zemlya and into the Kara Sea, where he too was turned back by ice.

The following year, Linschoten took part in a second attempt to navigate the Northeast Passage, again with Barents. On this voyage, the two attempted a southern passage around Novaya Zemlya, but were halted by ice near Vaigach Island, between Novaya Zemlya and the Russian mainland.

Jan Huyghen van Linschoten produced an atlas in 1596 with maps depicting all that had been learned by Dutch and English navigators in their explorations for a navigable sea route across the top of Asia. His account of the lucrative SPICE TRADE with the East Indies and his descriptions of key trade routes greatly influenced the voyages of CORNELIUS HOUTMAN and FREDERIK HOUTMAN in 1596 and OLIVER VAN NOORT in 1598 and ultimately gave impetus to the formation of the DUTCH EAST INDIA COMPANY in 1602.

Lisa, Manuel (1772–1820) *American fur trader*

on the upper Missouri River

Manuel Lisa was born in New Orleans, where his father was an official with the Spanish colonial government. In about 1790, he settled in St. Louis and soon obtained a trade monopoly with the Osage Indians of the lower MISSOURI RIVER.

In 1803–04, Lisa provided supplies and equipment for the Corps of Discovery under MERIWETHER LEWIS and WILLIAM CLARK. In spring 1807, encouraged by the expedition's success, Lisa launched the first American fur-trading venture to the upper Missouri River and northern plains.

On April 19, 1807, Lisa and 42 trappers left St. Louis and traveled up the Missouri by KEELBOAT. His partner, who remained in St. Louis during this first expedition, was ANTOINE PIERRE MENARD. Among the crew were a number of veterans of the Lewis and Clark Expedition, including John Potts, RENÉ JUSSEAUME, and the interpreter GEORGE DROUILLARD. At the mouth of the Platte River, Lisa recruited JOHN COLTER, who had also traveled west with Lewis and Clark.

Lisa and his party continued up the Missouri into the Dakotas, then entered the Yellowstone River. They traveled along the Yellowstone to its junction with the Bighorn

River, where he established Fort Manuel (also known as Fort Raymond), the first non-Indian settlement in what is now Montana.

During the next several months, Lisa sent out trappers from Fort Raymond, including John Colter, who explored the region of present-day Yellowstone National Park.

Lisa and his party returned to St. Louis in August 1808 after a highly profitable season of trading furs with Plains Indians. In February 1809, he organized the ST. LOUIS MIS-SOURI FUR COMPANY. His partners included Missouri terri-torial governor William Clark, Reuben Lewis (brother of Meriwether Lewis), JEAN PIERRE CHOUTEAU, AUGUSTE PIERRE CHOUTEAU, and ANDREW HENRY, among others.

In spring 1809, Lisa, his partners, and 172 fur trappers traveled up the Missouri into the Mandan Indian lands of present-day North Dakota. At the mouth of the Knife River, near what is now Bismarck, they established Fort Mandan. From this post, Lisa mounted several expeditions into the lands of the Blackfeet and Crow Indians.

Lisa soon faced stiff competition from WILSON PRICE HUNT of JOHN JACOB ASTOR's AMERICAN FUR COMPANY. In spring 1811, in an effort to corner trade with the Arikara Indian villages in the Dakotas, Lisa and his keelboat crew raced Hunt and his party along 1,200 miles of the Missouri River. Naturalist HENRY MARIE BRACKENRIDGE was a pay-ing guest on Lisa's boat. Hunt and the Overland Astorians then continued westward to Oregon, while Lisa continued to develop the FUR TRADE on the northern plains.

In 1812, Lisa established Fort Lisa, near present-day Omaha, Nebraska. During the War of 1812, as a U.S. In-dian agent, Lisa succeeded in keeping the central Missouri River tribes from siding with Great Britain. After the war, he expanded his trade into the Arkansas River and Canadian River region of what is now northern Texas and southern Oklahoma. The St. Louis Missouri Fur Company stayed in business into the 1820s.

Manuel Lisa undertook the first American-based fur-trading expedition to the northern plains and eastern Rock-ies. His 1807 endeavor marked the first commercial application of the explorations of Lewis and Clark and led to St. Louis becoming the focus of the western fur trade for the next 30 years.

Lisiansky, Yury Fyodorovich (Yuri Lisianski, Yuri Lisyanskii) (1773–1839) *Russian naval officer in Alaska and the Pacific*

Yury Lisianksy entered the Russian navy following his train-ing with the Royal Naval Cadet Corps. While still in his teens, he took part in naval operations against Swedish forces in 1788; by 1793, he had been promoted to the rank of lieutenant. That year, he was selected by Empress Cather-ine II to serve with the British navy, along with 15 other Russian naval officers, including ADAM IVAN RITTER VON KRUSENSTERN.

During the next five years, Lisiansky sailed on British naval vessels over a wide area of the globe, taking part in campaigns in the French Revolutionary Wars of 1793–98, in the Caribbean, North America, and India. Upon his re-turn to Russia in 1798, he was made a captain lieutenant in the Russian navy; three years later, he was given his first command, a frigate.

In 1802, Lisiansky was chosen by Krusenstern to ac-company him as second in command on the first Russian CIRCUMNAVIGATION OF THE WORLD. In preparation for the project, Lisiansky traveled to England, where he pro-cured two ships for the expedition, the *Nadezhda* and the *Neva*. In early August 1803, the ships sailed from the Rus-sian Baltic port of Kronstadt, with Krusenstern on the *Nadezhda* and Lisiansky commanding the *Neva*.

By the following summer, Lisiansky and Krusenstern had rounded CAPE HORN and arrived in the HAWAIIAN IS-LANDS. The two ships separated, with Krusenstern sailing to the Pacific coast of SIBERIA and Japan, and Lisiansky and the *Neva* heading to the RUSSIAN-AMERICAN COMPANY's fur-trading settlements on the Gulf of Alaska.

Lisiansky first visited Kodiak, then went on to the Rus-sian settlement of New Archangel on Sitka, where he helped the Russian-American Company's director, ALEKSANDR AN-DREYEVICH BARANOV, retake the trading post from the Tlingit Indians, who had captured and destroyed it in 1802. After spending the winter of 1804–05 at Kodiak, Lisiansky and the *Neva* sailed back to the South Pacific Ocean, headed for China with a cargo of furs. On this leg of the voyage, he came upon a previously uncharted outlying island in the Hawaiian chain, known afterward as Lisianski Island in his honor, as well as two reefs that he called Neva Reef and Krusenstern Reef.

After selling the furs in Canton, Lisiansky rejoined Krusenstern and the *Nadezhda* at the Portuguese colony of Macao near Hong Kong. The ships then sailed to Indonesia and into the Indian Ocean, completing their round-the-world voyage by way of the CAPE OF GOOD HOPE and re-turning to Kronstadt in August 1806, after a voyage of almost exactly three years.

Yury Lisiansky retired from active naval service in 1809 at the rank of full captain. His account of the expedition to the Pacific, *A Voyage Round the World in the Years 1803, 4, 5, & 6*, was first published in English in 1814. In addition to playing a significant role in the first Russian circumnavi-gation of the world, Lisiansky opened up direct links be-tween Russian fur traders in Alaska and markets in China. Moreover, he pioneered the practice of supplying Russian settlements in Alaska with ships sailing from Russia and around Cape Horn, a more practical alternative to the route then in use, which necessitated a difficult and costly overland trek through Siberia, followed by transshipment by boat across the Bering Sea.

Litke, Fyodor Petrovich (Count Fedor Petrovich Lütke) (1797–1882) *Russian naval commander in the Arctic and Pacific*

Fyodor Litke was born in St. Petersburg to a Russian aristocratic family. After undergoing training at the Naval Cadet Academy, he entered the Russian navy as a midshipman in 1812.

In 1817–19, Litke made his first trip around the world, serving on the *Kamchatka* under the command of VASILY MIKHAILOVICH GOLOVNIN, visiting ports in Alaska and on the Kamchatka Peninsula of eastern SIBERIA.

Promoted to lieutenant while on the Golovnin voyage, Litke went on to command the *Novaya Zemlya* (or possibly the *Apollo*) on an expedition into the Arctic regions of Murmansk in 1821. During the next three years, he charted the Arctic seas north of Russia, along the shore of the Barents Sea eastward to Novaya Zemlya.

Litke's published account of his exploits in the Russian Arctic, entitled *Four Voyages in the Polar Seas from 1821 to 1824,* appeared soon after his return to St. Petersburg in 1825. That same year, he was appointed aide-de-camp to Czar Nicholas I. On a direct order from the czar, he was promoted to captain lieutenant, and, in 1826, he was placed in command of the *Senyavin,* with a commission for a scientific voyage to the Pacific Ocean and around the world. KARL HEINRICH MERTENS was one of the naturalists.

Sailing from the Russian Baltic port of Kronstadt in September 1826, Litke entered the Pacific by way of CAPE HORN. After a stopover in Valparaiso, Chile, he sailed northward along the Pacific coasts of the Americas to New Archangel, the RUSSIAN-AMERICAN COMPANY's trading settlement at Sitka Bay, off the coast of Alaska's panhandle.

In summer 1827, Litke explored westward into the Bering Sea, visiting Unalaska Island in the Aleutians and reconnoitering St. George and St. Paul Islands in the Pribilof group, as well as St. Matthew Island to the north.

With the onset of winter, Litke sailed the *Senyavin* southward into the tropics. He first cruised the Caroline Islands of Micronesia and made the European discovery of an island group he named the Senyavin Islands after his ship. Reprovisioning in Guam, he sailed northwestward toward Japan and reached the little-known Bonin Islands, off the coast of the Japanese island of Kyushu. On Peel Island in the Bonins, he learned from two shipwrecked sailors from a whaling ship that British navigator FREDERICK WILLIAM BEECHEY had charted the islands the previous year. Although the sailors, for some reason, had previously declined to leave with Beechey, they now accepted passage aboard the *Senyavin* with Litke.

In summer 1828, Litke went northward to Kamchatka. From Petropavlovsk, he continued northward along the Pacific coast, rounded Cape Kronotksi, and sighted the giant volcano Klyuchevskaya Sopka. He then explored around Karaginsky Island, charting the channel separating it from the mainland, known afterward as Litke Strait. Retracing the route of VITUS JONASSEN BERING's final voyage of 1740–41, Litke explored the coast of the Chukchi Peninsula, the northeasternmost region of Siberia, where he located the strait separating Arakamchechen and Itygran islands from the Siberian mainland, naming it the Senyavin Strait. He also undertook a study of the native Chukchi people.

In winter 1828–29, Litke returned to the South Pacific and resumed his explorations in the Carolines, coming upon an additional number of uncharted atolls. Sailing eastward by way of the Philippines and Sumatra, he crossed the Indian Ocean, rounded the CAPE OF GOOD HOPE, and returned to Kronstadt in September 1829, thus completing his second CIRCUMNAVIGATION OF THE WORLD.

The next year, after his arrival back in Russia, Litke again set out on the *Senyavin* for an expedition to Iceland, exploring its coastline.

Litke went on to become one of the founding members of the Russian Geographical Society in 1845. In 1850, he was named maritime governor of the Baltic port of Revel (Tallinn, Estonia), and he later assumed command of the port of Kronstadt, reaching the rank of full admiral in 1855. The Paris Academy of Science appointed him as a corresponding member in 1861.

Fyodor Litke's voyage to the Pacific in 1826–29 was hailed as a great success for the wealth of scientific data brought back by the expedition's naturalists. His account of the expedition, *Voyage Around the World,* was published in 1835. In 1934, the Canadian-built icebreaker, the *Litke,* named in honor of his contributions to the exploration of the Russian Arctic, sailed from Vladivostok to Murmanskin the first east-to-west voyage through the NORTHEAST PASSAGE.

Livingstone, David (1813–1873) *Scottish missionary in Africa, husband of Mary Moffat Livingstone*

David Livingstone was born in Blantyre, Scotland, near Glasgow, the son of an itinerant tea salesman. At the age of 10, he went to work in a textile factory, studying Latin and other basic subjects in his spare time and eventually working his way through Glasgow University.

In 1836, Livingstone resolved to become a medical missionary, largely due to the influence of his father, a highly religious man, who distributed religious tracts along with each order of tea he delivered. He studied medicine at Edinburgh University, and, after additional training at hospitals in London, received a medical degree from the Faculty of

Physicians and Surgeons in Glasgow in 1840. Soon afterward, he was accepted by the London Missionary Society.

Although Livingstone had originally planned on a career as a medical missionary in China, the outbreak of the Opium War of 1839–42 caused him to change his plans. While training in England, he had met the missionary ROBERT MOFFAT; at Moffat's suggestion, he decided to pursue a career in Africa instead. He arrived at Algoa Bay, on the south coast of Africa near Port Elizabeth, in March 1841, from where he traveled northward to Kuruman, Moffat's mission on the southern edge of the Kalahari Desert in present-day South Africa.

Livingstone remained at the Kuruman outpost for most of the 1840s, marrying Robert and MARY MOFFAT's eldest daughter, Mary (MARY MOFFAT LIVINGSTONE), in 1844. He established a new mission at Mabotsa, deeper into what is now northeastern South Africa. By 1849, however, Boers had started settling in the region, enslaving and abusing the native people to whom Livingstone was ministering. In order to establish a new mission in the unexplored region to the north, he made a crossing of the Kalahari Desert in 1849, accompanied by British sportsman William Oswell. After three months, they reached the Zouga River, and, soon afterward, they came upon Lake Ngami, becoming the first Europeans to see it. Two years later, he made another crossing of the Kalahari, this time with his pregnant wife and three small children, reaching a tributary of the upper ZAMBEZI RIVER, where he was welcomed by a local tribal leader.

While exploring the upper Zambezi, Livingstone had a chance to observe the horrors of the central African SLAVE TRADE, carried on by both black African and Arab traders. He determined that the only way to eradicate the practice was to bring alternative commerce into the African interior.

In 1853, after escorting his wife and children to Cape Town, from where they sailed to England, Livingstone embarked on the first of his great expeditions into the heart of the African continent. He made his way back northward to the Linyote and upper Zambezi region, then set out westward for the Atlantic coast of central Africa, reaching the Portuguese trading port of Luanda in what is now Angola at the end of May 1854. Although he had succeeded in reaching the coast, the route he had followed did not seem suitable for commercial development, and, after a three-month rest at Luanda, he set out eastward to seek a more feasible route to the Indian Ocean. By 1855, he had returned to the upper Zambezi, hoping that river would prove to be a navigable route to the Indian Ocean. Later that year, he became the first known European to see the 420-foot-high waterfalls of the Zambezi, which he named Victoria Falls in honor of the queen of England. On May 20, 1856, he arrived at Quelimane on the Indian Ocean coast of Mozambique, from where he returned to England.

Back in England, Livingstone was hailed as a national hero, the first European known to have made a coast-to-coast crossing of south-central Africa. His account of his experiences, *Missionary Travels,* became an immediate bestseller, and, in honor of his accomplishment, the ROYAL GEOGRAPHICAL SOCIETY awarded him a gold medal.

In 1858, Livingstone left the London Missionary Society to devote himself full time to African exploration. Later that year, having been appointed Great Britain's General Consul to Inner Africa at Quelimane, he returned to central East Africa. During the next five years, he led a series of expeditions exploring up the Zambezi and Ruvuma Rivers, at times using a paddlewheel steamship. He also explored the Shire River, and, in 1859, he located Lake Nyasa (Lake Malawi), which had been reached by Portuguese explorers in 1616 but had been forgotten thereafter. The artist THOMAS BAINES traveled with him in 1858–59.

Mary Livingstone died in 1862, while traveling the Zambezi with her husband. Recalled by the British government in 1863, Livingstone sailed his small steamer, the *Lady Nyasa,* from East Africa across the Indian Ocean to Bombay, India, where he sold the vessel, then returned to England.

In 1865, Livingstone published an account of his explorations into the waterways of East Africa, *The Zambezi and Its Tributaries.* The next year, he returned to Africa to investigate the continent's central watershed, hoping to determine the source of the NILE RIVER. From Mikindani on the coast of what is now Tanzania, he set out up the Ruvuma River, and, over the next years, he explored the southern end of Lake Nyasa and the upper CONGO RIVER (Zaire River). He located Lake Mweru and Lake Bangweulu, in present-day Zambia, which had been reached by Portuguese explorer FRANCISCO DE LACERDA in 1798.

Livingstone heard reports of the Lualaba River, which he suspected was a source of the Nile, although it is actually a tributary of the Congo. He set out to investigate it in 1869, reaching the Nyangwe region on the Lualaba two years later.

By that time, the outside world had not heard from Livingstone for over three years. Publisher James Gordon Bennett, Jr., of the *New York Herald* newspaper had instructed the journalist SIR HENRY MORTON STANLEY to find Livingstone. Stanley departed the coast on March 21, 1871, and, on November 10, 1871, Stanley met up with the Scottish explorer, impoverished and in poor health, at Ujiji on the east shore of Lake Tanganyika.

Livingstone recovered his strength sufficiently to explore the northern end of Lake Tanganyika with Stanley, determining that it was not a source of the Nile, but that the Ruzizi River flowed into it.

Although Stanley wanted him to return to England, Livingstone decided to remain in Africa and continue exploring for the Nile's source. He reached Tabora in central

Tanzania, and, after surveying Lake Bangweulu, succumbed to dysentery at a nearby native village on May 1, 1873. The natives who had assisted him in his explorations removed and preserved his heart and other vital organs, embalmed his body in salt, and carried it overland to the Indian Ocean coast, an arduous nine-month journey. Livingstone's remains were then transported by ship to England and interred at London's Westminster Abbey with all the honors of a state funeral on April 18, 1874.

David Livingstone's explorations of central Africa revealed that the interior of the continent was not an arid wasteland as 19th-century geographers had speculated, but a fertile country, inhabited by a large population of highly diverse peoples, skilled in commerce, crafts, and farming. His earlier travels in southern Africa across the Kalahari Desert helped develop what became known as the Missionary Road, a route that later contributed to the settlement of South Africa's Transvaal region and Rhodesia, present-day Zimbabwe. In addition to being recognized as the first European known to have crossed the southern part of the African continent, Livingstone will always be associated with Stanley's heroic efforts to find him.

Livingstone, Mary Moffat (Ma-Robert)

(1821–1862) *Scottish traveler in Africa, daughter of Robert Moffat and Mary Moffat, wife of David Livingstone*

Mary Livingstone, née Moffat, was the eldest daughter of British missionaries ROBERT MOFFAT and MARY MOFFAT. She was born at her parents' missionary settlement in Bechuanaland, the frontier region between Cape Province and the Kalahari Desert.

In 1830, Moffat was sent to school at Grahamstown, on the south coast of Africa, near Port Elizabeth. Nine years later, at the age of 18, she made her first trip outside Africa, sailing to England with her family. In England, she met DAVID LIVINGSTONE.

The Moffat family returned to Bechuanaland in 1843. David Livingstone arrived at the Kuruman mission soon afterward and in 1845, he married Mary. During the next six years, she resided with her husband at a series of missions he established in the country north of Kuruman, and, by 1851, she had had three children and was pregnant with a fourth. That year, she and her children accompanied David Livingstone on his expedition northward across the Kalahari Desert, all nearly dying of thirst before reaching the Linyote River (then known as the Chobe), a tributary of the upper ZAMBEZI RIVER.

Soon afterward, the Livingstones headed southward on a six-month journey to Cape Town, Mary giving birth to her fourth child along the way. From there she sailed to England, where she remained for the next six years while her husband carried on his explorations of south-central Africa.

In 1858, Mary Livingstone and her children rejoined her husband at Quelimane on the coast of what is now Mozambique. She then accompanied her husband on his trips up the Zambezi and Ruvuma Rivers. In 1862, she contracted a tropical fever and died while traveling on the Zambezi. The children soon returned to Cape Town and then to England.

Mary Livingstone was one of the first European women to travel deep into the interior of south-central Africa, taking part in her husband's early explorations north of Bechuanaland and joining him in his later journeys along the waterways inland from the Indian Ocean. As the mother of the Livingstones' eldest son, Robert, she was known among the native people as "Ma-Robert," a name they also applied to the steamboat with which her husband explored the lower Zambezi River.

Llewellyn, Martin (unknown–1634)

English cartographer

There are few details of Martin Llewellyn's origins or early life, although his name suggests he was of Welsh background. In 1598, Llewellyn produced an atlas of 16 maps depicting sea routes to the Far East. His charts, which detailed the CAPE OF GOOD HOPE, the EAST INDIES, the Philippines, Japan, and the Marianas, contained the same place names used by CORNELIUS HOUTMAN and FREDERIK HOUTMAN in their voyages of 1595 and 1598, suggesting that Llewellyn either sailed with the Houtmans or had direct knowledge of their exploits.

From 1599 to 1634, Martin Llewellyn served as the Steward of St. Bartholomew's Hospital. Although forgotten after his death, his cartographic works were rediscovered in Oxford, England, in the 1940s. His atlas is considered one of the earliest major cartographic works to have been produced in England.

Lobo, Jerónimo (1593–1678) *Portuguese missionary in Ethiopia*

A native of Portugal, Jerónimo Lobo entered the Jesuit order at the age of 16. He was ordained a priest in 1621 and, soon afterward, embarked on a career as a missionary.

In 1624, Lobo traveled to the Ethiopian city of Assab at the southern end of the RED SEA. From there, he traveled to Gondar and the region around Lake Tana in the northwestern part of the country. He visited the Tisisat Falls and came upon the source of the Blue Nile, which he observed flowing out of two springs in the ground.

Jerónimo Lobo also carried on his missionary work in India. His account of his explorations around Lake Tana was translated into French as *Voyage historique d'Abissinie*, first published in 1728. His journey to the source of the Blue

Nile followed the 1613 visit of the Spanish Jesuit missionary PEDRO PÁEZ. The next European to explore the region was the Scotsman JAMES BRUCE in 1770.

Long, George Washington de   See DE LONG, GEORGE WASHINGTON.

Long, Stephen Harriman (1784–1864)
U.S. Army officer in the American West
Stephen H. Long, a native of Hopkinton, New Hampshire, graduated from Dartmouth College in 1809. Entering the army in 1814, he was commissioned a lieutenant in the U.S. Army Corps of Engineers the next year. He taught mathematics at West Point until 1816, when he was breveted a major in the U.S. Army Corps of Topographical Engineers.

In 1817, the Department of War sent Long on a military and scientific expedition into the upper MISSISSIPPI RIVER region. His mission was to collect topographic and scientific information, and to report on the presence of British traders on the upper Mississippi frontier.

Long explored the portages between the Fox and Wisconsin Rivers and the Mississippi River as far as the Falls of St. Anthony, near present-day Minneapolis, Minnesota. While there he also surveyed the site of Fort St. Anthony (later known as Fort Snelling), established in 1823.

In 1819, HENRY ATKINSON organized the first Yellowstone Expedition, which was intended to establish a military post at the junction of the MISSOURI RIVER and Yellowstone River. He assembled a group of naturalists and artists at Pittsburgh, including zoologist A. E. Jessup, naturalist Titian Ramsey Peale, and artist Samuel Seymour. Long commanded a contingent. Intending to travel up the Missouri to the Yellowstone by steamboat, he supervised the construction of five steam-powered vessels, including the *Western Engineer,* which became the first steamboat on the Missouri River.

Long and the expedition left St. Louis on June 21, 1819. At a site called Engineer Cantonment near present-day Omaha, Nebraska, the expedition wintered. Problems with the steamboats, as well as an outbreak of SCURVY, soon led Long to seek a change in plans. He went to Washington, D.C., over the winter, where he worked out new goals for the expedition with government officials. Instead of heading for the Yellowstone, he was to explore the ROCKY MOUNTAINS and locate the source of the Red River of the South.

On June 6, 1820, Long and a party of 19 men departed Engineer Cantonment (now Fort Atkinson), and headed westward along the Platte River to the South Platte. In central Nebraska, he engaged several French guides. His Indian interpreter was TOUSSAINT CHARBONNEAU, who had served with MERIWETHER LEWIS and WILLIAM CLARK. On June 30, 1820, they sighted the Rocky Mountains and what later became known as Longs Peak.

Long left the South Platte and headed southward through what is now the Denver, Colorado, area and across the Continental Divide. En route, Dr. Edwin James, a naturalist and geologist with the expedition, made the first successful climb of Pikes Peak, named after ZEBULON MONTGOMERY PIKE.

Long and his expedition reached the Arkansas River near Pueblo, Colorado, where the group divided. Long and some of the men explored southward in search of the Red River, while the rest headed eastward on the Arkansas River.

At Raton Pass, New Mexico, Long found a waterway he thought was the Red River. He followed it through what is now eastern New Mexico, the Texas Panhandle, and Oklahoma, and soon found himself back on the Arkansas River. He realized he had not found the Red River but instead had traveled along the Canadian. He rejoined the rest of the expedition at Fort Smith, Arkansas, on September 13, 1820. Although he failed to find the source of the Red River of the South, the expedition's scientists brought back 200 species of newly discovered plants, animals, and insects.

In 1823, Long made an exploration of the region between the upper Mississippi and Missouri Rivers. With a detachment of army topographers and scientists, he traveled from Philadelphia to Fort St. Anthony. They explored the Minnesota River and the Red River of the North. Long also surveyed the U.S.-Canada boundary north of present-day Pembina, North Dakota. He followed the Red River into Lake Winnipeg, portaged to Lake Superior, then continued by way of the Great Lakes to New York State. His expedition returned to Philadelphia on October 26, 1823.

Long remained in the army until 1863, involved in railroad surveys and civil engineering projects.

Stephen H. Long's report of his 1820 exploration of the Platte and Arkansas River region, assembled by Dr. Edwin James, described the Great Plains as the "Great American Desert," unsuitable for agricultural development. This characterization of the present-day wheat-belt states of Kansas, Oklahoma, and Nebraska appeared on maps of the West for the next 50 years and dissuaded settlement of the region until after the Civil War. Twenty-five years after Long explored the southern plains, JOHN CHARLES FRÉMONT would begin to dispel the myth of the Great American Desert.

López de Cárdenas, García (fl. 1540s)
Spanish conquistador in the American Southwest
García López de Cárdenas was a Spanish conquistador in North America who, in 1540, took part in FRANCISCO

VÁSQUEZ DE CORONADO's exploration into what is now the southwestern United States.

On August 25, 1540, soon after the Spanish had subdued the Zuni Indians in what is now western Mexico, López de Cárdenas and a small party of soldiers were sent westward to investigate Indian reports of a large river. By mid-September 1540, they had reached the rim of the Grand Canyon in present-day Arizona. Almost a mile below they could see the COLORADO RIVER. They tried to descend the canyon but abandoned the attempt after three days and returned eastward to rejoin Coronado's main force at the Zuni pueblos. At about this time, the seaward portion of Coronado's expedition, under HERNANDO DE ALARCÓN, was exploring the Colorado River from its mouth in the Gulf of California. Following his participation in Coronado's expedition, López de Cárdenas is believed to have returned to Spain.

García López de Cárdenas and his small party of Spanish soldiers were the first non-Indians to see the Grand Canyon. The next European visit to the Grand Canyon occurred more than two centuries later when missionary FRANCISCO TOMÁS HERMENEGILDO GARCÉS journeyed there in 1776.

Lozier, Jean-Baptiste-Charles Bouvet de

See BOUVET DE LOZIER, JEAN-BAPTISTE-CHARLES.

Lyon, George Francis (1795–1832) *British naval office in North Africa*

George Lyon, a British naval officer, was commissioned by second secretary of the Admiralty SIR JOHN BARROW to travel southward across the SAHARA DESERT from Tripoli in order to ascertain the true course of the NIGER RIVER with British surgeon JOSEPH RITCHIE.

In 1818, Lyon and Ritchie set out from the North African port of Tripoli on the coast of Libya, heading southward into the Fezzan region. At the southern Libyan city of Murzuk, in November 1819, Ritchie died.

Left with only a native guide, a Tuareg from Ghat named Hatita ag-Khuden, Lyon attempted to continue southward across the Sahara, hoping to reach the Niger River. He was able to reach only as far as Tejerri, 200 miles farther to the south.

Before he returned to England, George Lyon obtained information from local natives about Lake Chad to the south. Based on these reports, he wrongly concluded that the Niger River flowed into Lake Chad, and from there into the NILE RIVER. The true course of the Niger remained a mystery for another 12 years until the explorations of RICHARD LEMON LANDER and his brother John, who, in 1830–31, sailed down the river into the Gulf of Guinea.

Mackenzie, Sir Alexander (1764–1820)
Scottish-Canadian fur trader in the Canadian Northwest,
cousin of Donald Mackenzie

Alexander Mackenzie was born at Stornoway, Scotland, in the Outer Hebrides. At the age of 10, he was taken to New York by his widowed father. With the onset of the American Revolution, his father, a Loyalist, sent the young Mackenzie to school in Montreal.

In about 1780, Mackenzie joined the Montreal fur-trading firm of Finlay, Gregory & Co. Five years later, he was a partner in the NORTH WEST COMPANY and served at the company's posts at Detroit and at Grand Portage on western Lake Superior. In 1788, he joined PETER POND at Fort Chipewyan, the North West Company's post on Lake Athabasca.

On June 3, 1789, Mackenzie embarked on an expedition north from Fort Chipewyan in search of a water route to the Pacific Ocean. If found, it would enable the North West Company to supply its far western posts from the sea and avoid the long overland trek from Montreal. In addition, an outlet to the Pacific coast would provide access to the lucrative sea otter trade.

With a crew of VOYAGEURS and Indian guides, Mackenzie traveled by CANOE along the Great Slave River north to Great Slave Lake. Pond had previously located a river flowing out of the western end of Great Slave Lake and hypothesized that it led to Cook Inlet on the Alaskan coast. By following this river, Mackenzie planned to reach the Russian trading fort on Unalaska Island, then travel to

Kamchatka on the Siberian coast, and across Russia to England. From Great Slave Lake, Mackenzie and his party followed the river northward along the eastern slopes of the ROCKY MOUNTAINS. By mid-July, he had reached the river's outlet into the Beaufort Sea, an arm of the Arctic Ocean. The river had not taken him to the Pacific coast as hoped, and Mackenzie called it the River of Disappointment. It was later named the Mackenzie River in his honor.

In 1791–92, Mackenzie went to England, where he prepared for his next expedition. He studied astronomy and navigation and became familiar with the charts of the northwest coast of North America brought back from JAMES COOK's final voyage.

By fall 1792, Mackenzie had returned to Lake Athabasca and Fort Chipewyan. From there, he explored the Peace River and made the European discovery of the Smoky River, at the mouth of which he established a new trading post.

On May 9, 1793, Mackenzie set out from the Peace River post, once again in search of a water route to the Pacific. His party of voyageurs and Indian guides traveled in a lightweight canoe carrying over a ton of trade goods and supplies. They reached the Parsnip River. Near its headwaters in the Rocky Mountains, Mackenzie made a short portage and crossed the Continental Divide.

Mackenzie soon found the West Road (Blackwater) River. When he reached the turbulent and impassable upper Fraser River, Mackenzie led his party on foot back to the Blackwater, then across the Coast Range, and on to the Bella Coola River. After obtaining canoes from local Indians, the party rapidly descended the Bella Coola to the Pacific coast at Dean Channel.

On this site, Mackenzie used vermillion and melted animal fat to write on a large rock the words: "ALEXANDER MACKENZIE, FROM CANADA, BY LAND, THE 22ND OF JULY, 1793." Coincidentally, British naval explorer GEORGE VANCOUVER had explored this part of Queen Charlotte Sound only six weeks earlier. Mackenzie and his party retraced their route. A month later, they reached the Peace River post.

Not long after his successful expedition to the Pacific, Mackenzie returned to eastern Canada. In 1801, he published an account of his exploits in the Canadian Far West, *Voyages from Montreal through the Continent of North America to the Frozen and Pacific Oceans.* His accomplishments won him a knighthood the following year. He remained in the FUR TRADE and served as a legislator in Canada before returning to Scotland in 1808.

Sir Alexander Mackenzie's 1789 expedition to the Arctic coast of Canada showed that the Rocky Mountains extended farther north than was thought, and cast severe doubt on the idea of a NORTHWEST PASSAGE west of HUDSON BAY. Mackenzie also brought back the first reports of the coal deposits north of Great Slave Lake. Mackenzie's expedition of 1792–93, taking into account the preliminary trip from Montreal to Lake Athabasca, constituted the first overland journey across North America north of the Rio Grande. His accomplishment was the first recorded transcontinental journey since ALVAR NÚÑEZ CABEZA DE VACA in 1536. Mackenzie's writings on the voyages came to the attention of Thomas Jefferson and gave impetus to the subsequent overland expedition of MERIWETHER LEWIS and WILLIAM CLARK.

Mackenzie, Donald (Donald McKenzie)

(1783–1851) *Scottish fur trader in the Pacific Northwest, cousin of Sir Alexander Mackenzie*

Donald Mackenzie, a native of the Scottish Highlands, was a cousin of SIR ALEXANDER MACKENZIE, the explorer of northwestern Canada. Although he had planned to enter the ministry, he decided at the age of 17 to follow his brother Roderick to North America and join him in the FUR TRADE.

In 1800, Mackenzie arrived in Montreal and went to work for the NORTH WEST COMPANY as a clerk. Then, in June 1810, he was hired by JOHN JACOB ASTOR to take part in a venture to the Pacific Northwest, organized as the Pacific Fur Company, a subsidiary of the AMERICAN FUR COMPANY.

In 1811, Mackenzie accompanied WILSON PRICE HUNT and his Astorians on a trek from St. Louis up the Missouri River, then across the northern Rocky Mountains. He arrived at Astoria on the Oregon coast in early 1812, hav-

ing explored much of the Snake River region en route. That spring, he embarked on a series of fur-trapping expeditions along the Willamette River, COLUMBIA RIVER, and Snake River.

In March 1813, Mackenzie led a large party of fur trappers into the region between the Okanogan and Spokane Rivers, now part of north-central Washington. Through a trader with the North West Company, he learned of the outbreak of hostilities between the United States and Great Britain, later known as the War of 1812. With Astoria facing imminent capture by a British naval force then on its way to the Pacific coast, Mackenzie and the other managers of the Pacific Fur Company opted to sell the post to the North West Company. The sale was completed in April 1814, after which they headed back to New York to report to Astor.

Mackenzie tried without success to obtain another appointment with Astor, who declined to reengage him, believing Mackenzie and his associates had accepted too low a price for the Astoria post. In 1816, Mackenzie rejoined the North West Company and again traveled to the Oregon Country, operating out of Fort George and Fort William on the Columbia River. Rather than rely on Indians bringing furs to central locations, he began sending out brigades of traders and trappers over extensive territory in the Pacific Northwest. By 1819, he had established Fort Nez Perce at the junction of the Columbia and Walla Walla Rivers, near present-day Walla Walla, Washington, from where he directed extensive fur-trading operations into the interior of what is now Oregon, Washington, and southern Idaho, as well as into the south to western Wyoming and northern Utah.

Mackenzie went on to work for the HUDSON'S BAY COMPANY after it merged with the North West Company in 1821. In 1824, he became director of the company's operations near what is now Winnipeg, Canada, and, soon afterward, he was named governor of the Red River Colony, extending over a vast region of what is now Minnesota, North Dakota, and Canada's Manitoba province. He retired in 1833 and settled on an estate near Mayville in western New York State.

Donald Mackenzie had a leading role in the first great commercial expedition to cross North America in 1811–12 and was later instrumental in reviving the British fur trade in the Oregon Country following the War of 1812. Reportedly a large and imposing figure, weighing over 300 pounds, he was nonetheless a man of great action, nicknamed "Perpetual Motion" by his colleagues. Fur traders under his command explored a wide area of the Pacific Northwest.

Macomb, John N. (1811–1889) *U.S. Army officer in the American Southwest*

In 1855, Captain John N. Macomb of the U.S. Army Corps of Topographical Engineers was placed in command of U.S.

government wagon roadbuilding projects in northern New Mexico. Under his supervision, the route between Taos and Santa Fe, known as the Camino Militar, was developed, as well as the road between Albuquerque and Tecolote.

In summer 1859, Macomb commanded an official U.S. exploring expedition into the San Juan Mountains in search of a route into Utah from the south. He led his men along the Old Spanish Trail from Santa Fe to the Rio Chama, then traced the course of the San Juan River to its headwaters. In the Sierra de La Plata, Macomb and his party located ruins of the ancient Anasazi Indian civilization, near what is now Mesa Verde National Park in southwestern Colorado. At Cañon Pintado, Macomb came upon a complete petrified dinosaur skeleton, which he sent back East for study.

Macomb and a small staff of assistants left the main body of the expedition and explored the Colorado Plateau. They soon reached the junction of the Grand and Green Rivers in eastern Utah, which they determined was the source of the COLORADO RIVER. The Grand River is now considered part of the Colorado itself, and the name has been abandoned. The source of the Colorado is now considered the Grand Lake to the northeast in northern Colorado.

Macomb went on to serve in the Civil War as a commander in a Union army balloon reconnaissance unit.

John N. Macomb surveyed and constructed some of the first major wagon roads in northern New Mexico, which greatly improved communications and accelerated settlement. His 1859 explorations of the Colorado Plateau and Great Basin region of southern Utah and Colorado advanced the knowledge of the river system of the Southwest and determined the source of the Colorado River. The ruins Macomb located at Mesa Verde proved to be one of the foremost sites of Anasazi civilization. His work, *Exploring Expedition from Santa Fe, New Mexico to the Grand and Green Rivers of the Great Colorado of the West in 1859*, was published in 1876.

Magellan, Ferdinand (Fernando Magellanes, Fernão de Magalhães, Fernando de Magallanes)

(ca. 1480–1521) *Portuguese mariner, commander of first expedition to circumnavigate the world, in service to Spain* Ferdinand Magellan was born in northern Portugal in the vicinity of Oporto and Saborosa. Known in Portugal as Fernão de Magalhães, he was a member of a family of the minor nobility. In 1492, at the age of 12, he became a page at the court of Queen Leonora, consort of Portuguese monarch John II.

Magellan embarked on his first overseas adventure as a member of FRANCISCO DE ALMEIDA's 1505 expedition to India, along with his friend FRANCISCO SERRANO. He took part in Portuguese campaigns that secured the port of Diu on the northwest coast of India, and later served under Almeida's successor, AFONSO DE ALBUQUERQUE, in naval actions against Muslim forces at Goa and Calicut on southwestern India's Malabar Coast.

In 1508–09, Magellan and Serrano sailed under DIEGO LÓPEZ DE SEQUIRA in an unsuccessful attempt to take the Malayan port city of Malacca on the southern end of the Malay Peninsula. Two years later, Magellan may have accompanied Serrano on an expedition to the Moluccas, then known as the SPICE ISLANDS, where Serrano established contacts with the Muslim ruler of Ternate.

After returning to Portugal in 1512, Magellan was made a captain in the army and given a noble rank. Later that year, he fought against the Moors in Morocco, where he suffered a wound in the knee that left him lame for the rest of his life. Despite his gallantry in battle, Magellan soon fell out of favor with Portuguese king Manuel I, reportedly over his role in an unauthorized sale of some cattle to the Moroccans. He returned to Lisbon, where he sought royal backing for a proposed expedition to the East Indies, hoping to join his friend Serrano and reap the tremendous profits in the trade in cloves and other spices. When refused a raise in salary by his king, Magellan decided to seek support for his project in Spain; he renounced his Portuguese citizenship and crossed the border into Spain in 1517.

From reports brought back from survivors of JUAN DÍAZ DE SOLÍS's expedition to the southeast coast of South America, Magellan learned that the continent appeared to curve southwestward. With this information, together with secret Portuguese navigational charts to which he probably had access, he speculated that South America was separated from the conjectured GREAT SOUTHERN CONTINENT by a strait providing a westward passage to the Far East.

Magellan proposed to Charles I of Spain (later Holy Roman Emperor Charles V) that he could reach the Moluccas by sailing westward around South America and continue on a westward course back to Spain, thus avoiding Portuguese territory on the homeward voyage. At that time, it was not known on which side of the demarcation line, established in the 1494 Treaty of Tordesillas between Spain and Portugal, the Moluccas were located. Based on MARTIN BEHAIM's GLOBE of 1492 and data provided by an associate, astronomer and cosmographer Ruy Faleiro, Magellan suggested that the distance from the west coast of South America to the Moluccas was not great and that the Moluccas actually fell within the part of the world allocated to Spain in the treaty.

Hoping to gain control of the lucrative SPICE TRADE in the Moluccas, the Spanish Crown offered Magellan the support he needed. Additional financing for the expedition came from the German banking firm the House of Fuggers. Five ships were provided for the expedition: the *Trinidad*,

Ferdinand Magellan *(Library of Congress)*

Magellan's flagship, the *San Antonia,* the *Concepcíon,* the *Victoria,* and the *Santiago.*

Magellan's fleet, with a combined crew of 237 men, sailed from Sanlúcar de Barrameda, south of Seville, on September 20, 1519. After stopovers at Madeira and the CANARY ISLANDS, the expedition followed the coast of West Africa to Sierra Leone, then crossed the Atlantic Ocean to South America. Seeking a passage through the continent, Magellan explored along the coast of Brazil, examining the Bay of Guanabara at present-day Rio de Janeiro. He also explored the estuary of the Rio de la Plata, where he sighted a high mountain and exclaimed "monte video!" ("I see a mountain!"), which became the name of a settlement in the region two centuries later—Montevideo, Uruguay.

With the onset of the Southern Hemisphere's winter season, Magellan and his ships put in at the bay of San Julian along the southeast coast of present-day Argentina. The region came to be known as Patagonia, or "Land of Big Feet," after the Telhuelche Indians, who not only appeared to be of greater than normal stature, but whose footgear made their feet seem enormous. Over the next five months, Magellan attempted to keep his men occupied, but dissension soon developed, with many of the Spanish members resenting their Portuguese commander. A mutiny erupted, which Magellan quelled with the execution of one of the ringleaders. Soon afterward, the *Santiago* was wrecked while surveying the coast of Patagonia.

With his four remaining vessels, Magellan set out before the end of the winter to seek the passage that he believed would lead him to the South Sea. On October 21, 1520, the feast day of St. Ursula of the 11,000 Virgins, a strait was sighted beyond a cape, which he named Cape Vírgenes in honor of the occasion. Over the next 38 days, Magellan's ships made their way through the passage, since named the STRAIT OF MAGELLAN, negotiating channels that varied from two to 15 miles in width. While in the strait, a rebellion erupted aboard the *San Antonia,* and the ship deserted the fleet and returned to Spain. Along the shore to the south, many fires were seen, and for this reason, it was called Tierra del Fuego ("Land of Fire").

On November 28, 1520, Magellan and his ships reached the western end of the strait at a point he named Cape Deseado ("Desired Cape") and entered an ocean, which he called the "Pacific" after its apparent calmness. After exploring northward along the west coast of South America, he set out westward across the Pacific, expecting to encounter before long the Moluccas and the rest of the EAST INDIES. Although his exact route is not known, his course took him north of the numerous islands of the South Pacific. During this period, he sighted land only once, and these were several barren and uninhabited atolls of the Tuamotu Islands, which he dubbed the Islands of Disappointment. With the westward passage across the Pacific taking

much longer than anticipated, supplies of fresh food and water dwindled, and the men began to die of SCURVY. At one point, Magellan's sailors resorted to boiling and eating leather sailing gear, as well as sawdust and rats.

Finally, on March 6, 1521, after nearly 100 days out of sight of land, Magellan came upon an island group and obtained fresh provisions. The natives, although friendly, proved to be larcenous, stealing anything on the ships that they could carry away, and for this reason Magellan called the islands the Ladrones, or "Islands of Thieves," later known as the Marianas.

After a short respite on Guam in the Marianas, Magellan continued his westward search for the Moluccas, not realizing he was well north of those islands. After 10 days of sailing, he reached Samar in the Philippines, making the European discovery of these islands. After a brief exploration of Samar, he continued on to Cebu, where he succeeded in winning the allegiance of the natives and Christianizing their ruler. Soon afterward, he accompanied the native king of Cebu on a military campaign against the nearby island of Mactan. On April 27, 1521, Magellan was fatally wounded by poison-tipped arrows.

Command of Magellan's three remaining ships went first to Duarte Barbosa, Magellan's brother-in-law, and Juan Rodríguez Serrano, probably a brother of Magellan's friend Francisco Serrano. By that time, more than half of the expedition's 250 men had either died of scurvy or been killed in native attacks. Shorthanded, they decided to burn one of the ships, the *Concepcíon,* and continue with the *Victoria* and the *Trinidad.* Barbosa and Serrano were soon killed in another attack by the natives, and the expedition's pilot, João Lopes de Carvalho, took command. He cruised the East Indies but was unable to locate the Moluccas. Eventually, JUAN SEBASTIÁN DEL CANO assumed leadership and managed to lead the two remaining ships to Tidore in the Moluccas.

At Tidore, it was soon learned that Francisco Serrano had been murdered, and that a Portuguese fleet was on its way. Fearing arrest by the Portuguese, Cano promptly took on a load of spices aboard the *Victoria* and sailed for Spain by way of the CAPE OF GOOD HOPE. Meanwhile, the *Trinidad,* having tried unsuccessfully to sail eastward back across the Pacific, was captured by the Portuguese, and its Spanish crew members were held as prisoners for several years afterward.

The *Victoria* sailed into the harbor at Sanlucar de Barrameda, Spain, on September 6, 1522, the only one of Magellan's ships to complete the first round-the-world voyage. Aboard were only 18 men, the rest having died on the voyage or been taken into custody by the Portuguese during a stopover in the Cape Verde Islands. Among the survivors was the Italian gentleman adventurer FRANCESCO ANTONIO PIGAFETTA, who later published his journal of the voyage. Although most of the ships had been lost, the spices taken on in the Moluccas more than paid for the initial investment for the expedition. Moreover, with knowledge of the Strait of Magellan, Portugal's monopoly over trade with the East Indies by way of the Cape of Good Hope had been broken.

Ferdinand Magellan did not live to complete the historic voyage he initiated. Nevertheless, if his westward passage across the Pacific to the Philippines is considered together with his earlier voyages to India and the East Indies, he was among the first explorers known to have circled the world. The Magellan voyage of 1519–22 linked the earlier explorations of VASCO DA GAMA and CHRISTOPHER COLUMBUS, proving beyond any doubt that the Earth was a sphere, and that the world's oceans were connected, including the Indian Ocean, which had been thought to be a landlocked sea since the days of PTOLEMY in the first century A.D. Moreover, Magellan's explorations along both the east and west coasts of South America enabled European geographers to determine more accurately the true dimensions of that continent. Magellan's voyage also revealed the true vastness of the Pacific Ocean and the extent of the distance between Asia and the Americas.

Maire, Jakob le   See LE MAIRE, JAKOB.

Malaspina, Alessandro (Alejandro Malaspina)
(ca. 1755–1810) *Italian-born Spanish naval officer in the Americas and the South Pacific*

Alessandro Malaspina was born in Italy's Lombardy region. In about 1770, he traveled to Spain and entered the Royal Naval Academy at Cádiz, eventually becoming a captain in the Spanish navy.

In 1789, Malaspina and fellow naval officer José Bustamante y Guerra won approval from the Spanish government for their proposed scientific CIRCUMNAVIGATION OF THE WORLD. Two ships were built for the enterprise, the *Discubierto* (discovery) and the *Atrevida* (daring). For planning and advice, Malaspina consulted Spanish naval officers who had conducted earlier explorations of South America.

The ships left Cádiz, Spain, on July 30, 1789. Along with a full complement of officers and sailors, the 200-man expedition included scientists, ethnologists, and artists. Its purpose, in addition to scientific research, was to evaluate the status of Spanish possessions in South and North America and reassert Spanish claims to the Pacific islands.

Malaspina's first destination was South America. He reached the coast of Brazil and proceeded to the estuary of the Río de la Plata. While some of the expedition's scientists explored that region, others went overland into Argentina and made a study of the Pampas. A scientific station was established near Montevideo in present-day Uruguay, where astronomical and gravitational observations were undertaken.

The Malaspina expedition sailed southward along the South American coast and visited the Falkland Islands (Malvinas), Patagonia, and Tierra del Fuego. The ships rounded CAPE HORN and followed the coast of Chile and Peru. Malaspina made stops at San Carlo de Chiloé, Puerto Concepción, and Valparaíso, where the team of scientists undertook expeditions into the ANDES MOUNTAINS and the upper Amazon Basin. Similar inland expeditions were made from Guayaquil, Ecuador.

In spring 1791, Malaspina and his ships arrived in Acapulco, Mexico. There, Malaspina received dispatches from Spain that altered the course of the expedition. The papers of 16th-century Spanish navigator Lorenzo Ferrer Maldonado had recently been uncovered in Catalan, indicating the existence of a passage through North America, with an outlet supposedly in the Gulf of Alaska. Rather than head westward across the Pacific Ocean to the HAWAIIAN ISLANDS as planned, Malaspina was instructed to head northward along the coast of North America and seek the long-sought NORTHWEST PASSAGE, known since the early 1500s also as the STRAIT OF ANIAN.

Malaspina's expedition headed northward from Acapulco on May 2, 1791. By June 1791, his ships had reached Alaskan waters. The Spanish explored westward along the Gulf of Alaska almost as far as the Kenai Peninsula. They then headed eastward to Mulgrave Sound (now Yakutat Bay). A scientific station was established there, in order to study the region's plant and animal life, as well as the culture of the Tlingit Indians.

In small boats, Malaspina explored Yakutat Bay with cartographer Felipé Bauza and crew member Antonio de Tova. They soon found there was no eastern outlet for the Strait of Anian, and Malaspina dubbed the region the "Port of Disappointment." The glacier he discovered on the bay is now called Malaspina Glacier.

In mid-summer 1791, Malaspina's expedition headed southward for Vancouver Island. In 1789, the Nootka Sound controversy had erupted between Spain and England, and the Spanish government wanted Malaspina to assert Spanish sovereignty at its base at Santa Cruz de Nutka (present-day Friendly Cove, British Columbia).

Upon reaching Nootka Sound, off the west coast of Vancouver Island, Malaspina and his party established another scientific station. They studied the region's Nootka Indians and again made a search for an inland passage. But the coastline of Vancouver Island had too many shallow inlets and bays for his large ships to explore adequately, and plans were made for a follow-up expedition.

From Nootka Sound, Malaspina sailed southward along the Pacific coast of North America, exploring Puget Sound. His cartographers made the first charts of the Washington,

Oregon, and California coasts based on triangulation. The expedition's artists, including Manuel José Cardero and Tomás de Suria, produced coastal profiles that detailed how various sections of the Pacific coast looked to approaching ships.

Malaspina's ships arrived at Monterey, California, on September 11, 1791. Another scientific station was established, and his naturalists and scientists explored the interior of central California. Among them was Bohemian botanist Tadeo Haenke, who made the first scientific description of California's giant redwood trees.

In late September 1791, the expedition left Monterey and followed the coastline back to Acapulco. In summer 1792, Malaspina sent two sloops from Acapulco, the *Mexicana* and the *Sutil*, which succeeded in making the first circumnavigation of Vancouver Island.

Malaspina himself set sail westward across the Pacific. The expedition reached Guam and visited the Philippines, Macao, NEW ZEALAND, and Australia. Malaspina then headed eastward across the Pacific, stopping at the Fiji Islands, then retraced the expedition's outward-bound route around the west and east coasts of South America.

Malaspina arrived back in Cádiz, Spain, on September 21, 1794, after a voyage of over five years. Not long after his return, he became embroiled in a political intrigue and was found guilty of plotting a coup against the Spanish government. He served eight years in prison, then was exiled to his native Italy, where he spent the remainder of his life. Most of the seven-volume report of his expedition was suppressed by the Spanish government for nearly a century.

Alessandro Malaspina did not circumnavigate the world as planned. Nevertheless, his five-year voyage, undertaken in the spirit of scientific inquiry, complemented the late-18th-century Pacific explorations of British captain JAMES COOK and French navigator JEAN-FRANÇOIS DE GALAUP, comte de La Pérouse. In addition to scientific studies of the flora, fauna, and native culture of the Americas, Malaspina brought back the first scientifically based navigational charts of the west coast of North and South America. Previous charts of much of these shores had not been revised since the voyages of 17th-century Spanish explorers.

Malinche (Malintzin, "the tongue," Doña Marina, Marina) (ca. 1508–ca. 1528) *Aztec interpreter in the Spanish conquest of Mexico*

Malinche was a young Aztec woman living in Mexico at the time of the Spanish conquest. She was born in Painalla, a village in the province of Coatzacualco, a region adjacent to Aztec territory.

Malinche's father, a rich and powerful native chief, died when she was still an infant; her mother remarried and bore a son by her second husband. In an attempt to take away Malinche's rightful inheritance on behalf of her newborn son, Malinche's mother falsely reported that Malinche had died. The corpse of a dead slave child was used to verify the death, while Malinche herself was secretly sold into slavery to an itinerant trader from Xicallanco. Eventually, Malinche was sold to Maya Indians living near the mouth of the Tabasco River on Mexico's Gulf Coast, west of the Yucatán Peninsula.

By 1519, Malinche had grown into a beautiful young woman. That year, HERNÁN CORTÉS and his army of conquistadores arrived on the Mexican mainland. When the Spaniards reached the island of San Juan de Ulúa, off the coast of the Tabasco region, the local chiefs presented Cortés with a group of young Indian women, among whom was Malinche. Possessing intelligence as well as great beauty, she soon came to the attention of Cortés.

Malinche knew both Nahuatl, the language of the Aztec, as well as Mayan dialects. Prior to his landing on the Yucatán mainland, Cortés had stopped at offshore Cozumel Island, where he had picked up the missionary priest Jerónimo de Aguilar, who, in the course of his eight years among the Indians, had learned Mayan. With Aguilar's knowledge of Spanish and Mayan, together with Malinche's ability in Nahuatl and Mayan, Cortés could learn about the Aztec Empire. Malinche informed Cortés of the Aztec belief in the return of the white god Quetzalcoatl and told him that many of the Aztec already believed Cortés and his Spanish forces to be the living embodiment of this divinity and his entourage.

Malinche, who was baptized a Christian as Doña Marina, rapidly learned Spanish and eventually acted as Cortés's interpreter in his dealings with the Aztec ruler Montezuma (Moctezuma). During the conquest of 1519–21, she exposed spies of hostile Aztec forces within his camp and revealed a plot by the Aztec rulers to exterminate Cortés and his men in a secret attack.

By 1525, Malinche and Cortés had had a son, Don Martín Cortés, who grew to be a military leader among the Spanish forces in Mexico. That year, Malinche was reunited with her mother, whom she forgave for abandoning her to slave traders, bestowing upon her gifts of jewels. Also in 1525, Cortés took Malinche with him on his conquest of present-day Honduras, and, in the course of that campaign, he presented her as a gift to one of his military colleagues, Don Juan Xamarillo, a knight from Castile.

Malinche settled on lands she was granted in her native Coatzacoalcos province, where she spent the rest of her short life (although some sources suggest she went to live in Spain with Xamarillo), dying at the age of 20. The details of her life and the role she played for the Spanish were recorded by BERNAL DÍAZ DEL CASTILLO in his account of the conquest.

Malinche greatly aided the Spanish in their swift victory over the Aztec by providing her skills as an interpreter and by informing Cortés that the Aztec perceived the Spaniards as divine beings.

Mallet, Pierre-Antoine (Pierre-Antoine Maillet, Pierre-Antoine Mailhet, Pierre-Antoine Malet) (1700–ca. 1751) *French Canadian fur trader on the northern and southern plains*

French-Canadian Pierre-Antoine Mallet moved to Detroit with his parents, Pierre Mallet and Madeleine Thuney, as a young child. His brother, Paul, was baptized there in 1711.

In the early 1730s, the two brothers relocated to the Illinois country, becoming fur traders on the central MISSISSIPPI RIVER. In 1734, they left a French trading post in the Illinois country and ascended the MISSOURI RIVER into the Dakotas, where they established trade contacts with the Mandan Indians. They also established a trade route between the French merchants of St. Louis and New Orleans and Native Americans of south-central Canada.

In 1739, the Mallet brothers and a small trade caravan set out from the Illinois country, intending to reach the Spanish settlements in New Mexico by way of the Missouri River. They erroneously believed the Missouri would lead them directly to Santa Fe.

The Mallets followed the Missouri to its junction with the Niobrara River in northern Nebraska. They explored the Niobrara and, guided by Pawnee Indians, crossed present-day Nebraska southwestward to a river they named "La Rivière Plate"—the "Flat River"—and known afterward as the Platte River. They continued southward beyond the Platte, exploring into present-day Kansas. From the Republican and Smoky Hill Rivers, they crossed into the valley of the Arkansas River. The Mallets followed the Arkansas River and reached the Apache Indian settlement at El Cuartelejo in western Kansas. From there, they were guided by an Indian into the southeastern Colorado ROCKY MOUNTAINS and the Raton Mountains of northern New Mexico. They crossed the Raton Mountains, possibly through Raton Pass, stopped at Taos, then entered Santa Fe on July 22, 1739.

Even though visits by foreign traders were forbidden by the Spanish government, the Mallets were welcomed in Santa Fe, having brought with them a shipment of sought-after French manufactured goods, available at considerably lower prices than similar items imported from Mexico.

The Mallet brothers and their six companions were guests of prominent Santa Fe merchants for the next nine months. The colonial governor of New Mexico petitioned Spanish authorities in Mexico City for the Mallets to trade openly out of New Orleans with the Spanish. Permission was denied, however, and the Mallets and the rest of their party were ordered out of New Mexico.

In May 1740, the Mallets headed eastward into the upper Pecos Valley. They explored the Texas Panhandle and, on June 14, came upon a river that was later named the Canadian in their honor. The Canadian River took them back to the Arkansas, which they followed to the Mississippi and New Orleans.

In New Orleans, French colonial governor JEAN-BAPTISTE LE MOYNE, sieur de Bienville, engaged the Mallets to lead André Fabry de la Bruyère's trade expedition to New Mexico.

Starting out in August 1741, the Mallets led the expedition up the Mississippi to the Arkansas, then attempted to cross the southern plains. But the water level on the southwestern rivers was too low for their boats. The brothers separated from the main party and sought an overland route, but failed to reach Santa Fe.

The Mallets settled near a trading post on the Arkansas River, using it as their base of trading operations at least until 1750. Pierre Mallet headed another expedition out of New Orleans that year, organized by Louis-Xavier Martin de Lino de Chalmette, head of the Arkansas post, and Pierre de Rigaud de Vaudreuil, the new governor of New Orleans. Pierre Mallet and three companions were arrested by Spanish officials at Pecos in November 1750, then taken to Santa Fe, then El Paso, and, in February 1751, to Mexico City. It is thought that he died a prisoner in Spain. His brother Paul died at the Arkansas post in 1753.

Pierre and Paul Mallet's expeditions into the Dakotas opened the Indian trade of the northern plains to the French on the lower Mississippi. Their 1739–40 exploration of what is now Kansas, Nebraska, Colorado, and New Mexico laid the basis for the development of the Santa Fe Trail, which remained a major trade and transportation conduit into the Southwest for more than a century.

Mallory, George Herbert Leigh (George Leigh-Mallory) (1886–1924) *British mountain climber on Mount Everest in the Himalayas*

British-born George Mallory, the son of a clergyman, became a teacher as a young man. In World War I, he served as a gunner for British forces. He became an accomplished rock climber and ice climber in his spare time and established his reputation in MOUNTAIN CLIMBING with ascents in the Alps.

In 1921–22, Mallory participated in two British pioneering expeditions on the north side of MOUNT EVEREST, the tallest mountain in the world at 29,035 feet above sea level in the HIMALAYAS. Plagued by strong winds and avalanches and without oxygen bottles to assist in breathing the thin air, the teams were unable to reach the summit, falling only 2,000 feet short on the second climb.

In 1924, Mallory participated in a third expedition. His climbing partner was 22-year-old Andrew "Sandy" Irvine, who, although he had little high-altitude climbing experience, was an expert in the supplemental oxygen rigs that Mallory now considered essential for the expedition. The first part of their ascent up the north side was successful, but they ran into problems near the top. The last person to see them alive was Noel Odell, who reported that they were possibly within a few hours of the summit—maybe as close as 80 feet—at about 1:00 P.M. on June 8.

In 1999, Mallory's body was found by an expedition filming a television special for *NOVA,* a program of the Public Broadcasting Service (PBS). The location of the body, at the point where he was last seen, began a debate as to whether he and Irvine had died after rather than before reaching the summit. Mallory's body was left on the mountain, as were those of many others who died in ensuing years, because of the difficulty of recovering bodies from that particular location.

George Mallory, legendary because of his pioneering attempts on Mount Everest as well as the mystery surrounding his disappearance, was once asked why he wanted to climb Mount Everest. He replied with the now-famous quote, "Because it is there." SIR EDMUND PERCIVAL HILLARY and TENZING NORGAY finally reached Mount Everest's summit in 1953, via the south side.

Manning, Thomas (1772–1840) *British traveler in Tibet*

In 1811, Thomas Manning, an employee of the BRITISH EAST INDIA COMPANY in Calcutta, endeavored to undertake a journey northward across the western HIMALAYAS into Tibet, which had been closed to British travelers since 1791.

At first Manning sought support for his expedition from his employers, proposing to travel to Tibet as the official representative of the British East India Company. When this plan was rejected, he set out on his own in late summer 1811, accompanied only by a Chinese servant. He made his way northward across the Himalayas in Bhutan, disguised in Oriental clothing, and he reached the Tibetan capital of LHASA in December 1811.

Manning remained in Lhasa for more than three months, during which he conferred with the seven-year-old Ninth Dalai Lama, the spiritual leader of Tibetan Buddhism, and toured the Buddhist palace, the Potala. In April 1812, compelled by occupying Chinese forces to leave Lhasa, he returned southward to India.

Thomas Manning later prepared a detailed account of his impressions of Lhasa and the Tibetans, especially of the young Dalai Lama. He was the first Englishman to enter Lhasa, as well as the first European to visit the Tibetan capital, since the visit of Italian Jesuit missionary IPPOLITO DESIDERI in 1716. Nearly a century elapsed before the next Englishman, SIR FRANCIS EDWARD YOUNGHUSBAND, ventured into the forbidden city of Lhasa in 1904.

Marchand, Jean-Baptiste (1863–1934) *French army officer in Africa*

Jean-Baptiste Marchand was born in Thoisey, near Lyon in eastern France. At the age of 20, he enlisted in the French army, and, four years later, he was commissioned a sub-lieutenant.

In 1889, Marchand undertook his first tour of duty in France's colonial possessions of West Africa. In addition to military actions in what is now Senegal, he undertook exploring expeditions to the source of the NIGER RIVER and into the region inland from the Ivory Coast.

Marchand returned to France in 1895, where he was promoted to the rank of major. He returned to Africa in command of a military expedition aimed at reinforcing French forces in the territory between the Ubangi and Bahr El Ghazal Rivers, now parts of the Central African Republic and southern Sudan.

From the mouth of the CONGO RIVER (Zaire River) on the west coast of central Africa, Marchand led his command northeastward across the continent. Via the Ubangi and Uele Rivers, he traveled eastward across what is now northern Democratic Republic of the Congo. By late summer 1898, he had crossed the watershed region between the upper Congo and upper Nile Rivers and reached Fashoda (now Kodok) on the White Nile, in southern Sudan. Britain's general Horatio Herbert Kitchener, commander of Anglo-Egyptian forces in Sudan, protested the presence of the French troops at Fashoda and ordered Marchand to withdraw. Marchand's refusal to leave the upper White Nile region resulted in a major international crisis, known afterward as the Fashoda Incident, which brought England and France to the brink of war.

After intense diplomatic negotiations, the French government ordered Marchand's withdrawal. In November 1898, he led his expedition southeastward along the Sobat River, reaching Djibouti on the Gulf of Aden by May 1899.

Soon afterward, Marchand returned to France, where he was hailed as a hero for his great journey across Africa. In 1900, he took part in the suppression of the Boxer Rebellion in China. Promoted to the rank of general by the outbreak of World War I in 1914, he went on to command French forces in the Battle of the Somme and in the Battle of Verdun. He retired from military service in 1919.

Jean-Baptiste Marchand's explorations in the last decades of the 19th century took him across both West and East Africa. In the course of his transcontinental march, he led the first major expedition to the upper NILE RIVER region from the coast of West Africa.

Marco Polo   See POLO, MARCO.

Marcos de Niza   See NIZA, MARCOS DE.

Marcy, Randolph Barnes (1812–1887) *U.S. Army officer in the American Southwest*

Randolph B. Marcy was born in Greenwich, Massachusetts. He graduated from West Point in 1832 as a second lieutenant in the infantry and was assigned to Fort Howard, a frontier post on the west shore of Lake Michigan, near present-day Green Bay, Wisconsin. He served in the last phase of the Black Hawk War of 1832, then went on to a long military career on the frontier.

In 1849, Marcy, as a captain in the U.S. Fifth Infantry, commanded a military escort for an emigrant wagon train bound for the California goldfields from Fort Smith, Arkansas. He was to accompany the wagon train as far as Santa Fe, New Mexico, and en route blaze a trail across the Indian Territory (present-day Oklahoma) and northern Texas, along the south bank of the Canadian River. Attached to his expedition was army topographer Lieutenant JAMES HERVEY SIMPSON. Marcy left Fort Smith on April 4, 1849. Leading his command in advance of the wagon train, he traversed the Cross Timbers region of northern Texas. He then explored the Llano Estacado (staked plains) region of western Texas and eastern New Mexico, which he later characterized as the "Great Sahara of North America." Marcy and his party reached Santa Fe on June 28, 1849, after crossing 800 miles of the southern plains.

On his return to the Indian Territory, Marcy followed a more southern route through Texas. He crossed the Organ, Sacramento, and Guadalupe Mountains of central Texas, followed the Pecos River to the Brazos, then headed northward to the Red River and Fort Washita. In his official report of the expedition, Marcy declared that the southern route from western Arkansas to New Mexico was highly suitable for emigrant wagon traffic, and before long, Fort Smith became a major gateway for overland travel into the southern plains.

On an 1852 military reconnaissance, Marcy located the source of the Red River near present-day Amarillo, Texas. He then explored what is now Arizona and New Mexico, making contact with previously isolated Indian bands. Based on his explorations, Marcy made recommendations to the army that led to the establishment of a chain of forts stretching from Oklahoma to western Texas.

Captain Marcy served in western Wyoming and northeastern Utah during the Mormon War of 1857–58.

In November 1857, with Fort Bridger in southwestern Wyoming cut off by Mormon insurgents, Colonel Albert Sidney Johnston ordered Marcy to lead a detachment of 60 mounted soldiers and a contingent of MOUNTAIN MEN southward to obtain supplies and fresh horses at Fort Massachusetts in southwestern Colorado's San Luis Valley.

Marcy and his command made their way southward through the winter snows of the southern Rocky Mountains, at times forcing their way through snowdrifts as high as 10 feet. Through some stretches the route was passable only after some of the soldiers broke a path through the high snows by crawling on their hands and knees. They became lost in the Sangre de Cristo Mountains while searching for Cochetopa Pass, but were saved by a Mexican mule driver named Manuel Aleno, who managed to guide them to it.

By the time Marcy and his men had entered the San Luis Valley, they were short of food and in an exhausted state. Facing death from starvation and exposure, they nevertheless pushed on, and after another 10 days, reached Fort Massachusetts. Their harrowing north-south trek had traversed most of the present state of Colorado in severe winter weather, a distance of more than 600 miles across snow-covered mountains. On the last part of the journey, they had succeeded in making a winter crossing of the San Juan Mountains, the same range in which JOHN CHARLES FRÉMONT and his expedition had met disaster in the winter of 1848–49.

Although Marcy's heroic march through the southern Rockies ultimately succeeded in securing aid for beleaguered Fort Bridger to the north, the extreme difficulty of the journey also underscored the need for better north-south travel routes across the Colorado Plateau and Great Basin. As a result, Marcy's relief expedition prompted the first formal reconnaissance of the San Juan Mountains, which was undertaken by Captain JOHN N. MACOMB of the U.S. Army Corps of Topographical Engineers in 1859.

In the Civil War, Marcy was breveted a brigadier general of volunteers and served as chief of staff for his son-in-law, General George B. McClellan. After the war, Marcy became inspector general of the army, retiring from active duty in 1881.

Randolph B. Marcy's 1849 wagon route across Texas to Santa Fe provided an eastern connection for the established route from the Rio Grande to the Pacific coast. He traced the Red River to its source in 1852, which the earlier explorations of both ZEBULON MONTGOMERY PIKE and STEPHEN HARRIMAN LONG had been unable to do. Marcy's military career on the American frontier spanned the period from the Mexican Cession of 1848 to the settlement of the southern plains after the Civil War. He wrote a number of official reports and personal accounts of his explorations, including *Exploration of the Red River in 1852* (1853), *The Prairie Traveller, a Handbook for Overland Emigrants* (1859), *Thirty*

Years of Army Life on the Border (1866), and *Border Reminiscences* (1871).

Marignolli, Giovanni de (John of Marignolli)

(ca. 1290–unknown) *Italian envoy, missionary in China*
Giovanni de Marignolli became a Franciscan friar in Florence, Italy, at a young age. He later taught theology at the University of Bologna.

In December 1338, Marignolli set out from Avignon in southeast France as part of a papal mission to the emperor of China, arriving in Constantinople (present-day Istanbul) in early 1339, then continuing on to the Crimea on the north shore of the Black Sea and to Sarai near present-day Volgograd. At Sarai, he met with Usbek, khan of Kiptchak, who provided an escort as far as Armalec, which he reached in the winter of 1340–41. He remained there about a year and crossed the GOBI DESERT to Peking (Beijing), arriving in 1342. He stayed there three years, continuing the missionary work begun by JOHN OF MONTECORVINO.

Marignolli next traveled in southern China, India, CEYLON (Sri Lanka), as well as Java and Sumatra in present-day Indonesia. He departed India from the Malabar Coast and sailed to the Persian Gulf. After travels in the Middle East and Egypt, he returned to Italy in 1353.

Marignolli became the bishop of Bisignano in 1354 and papal legate in Avignon two years later. The next year, he became a chaplain to Charles IV, Holy Roman Emperor and king of Bohemia. He also served as court historian. The date of his death is unknown.

Giovanni de Marignolli's *Bohemian Chronicle,* in which he relates his travels, educated Europeans on lands to the east.

Marquette, Jacques

(1637–1675) *French missionary, interpreter in the Great Lakes and Mississippi Valley regions*
Jacques Marquette was born in Laon, France. In 1654, he entered the Jesuit order. In 1666, he was ordained a missionary priest and went to French Canada to work among

Jacques Marquette and Louis Jolliet entering the upper Mississippi River *(Library of Congress)*

Native Americans. He studied Indian languages for two years at the Jesuit center in Trois Rivières on the St. Lawrence.

In 1668, Marquette went west to Sault Sainte Marie, where he established a mission to the Ottawa Indians. The next year, he traveled to the western end of Lake Superior and established La Pointe mission on Chequamegon Bay. It was here he first met fur trader LOUIS JOLLIET. From the Indians of the western Great Lakes, Marquette and Jolliet heard reports of a great south-flowing river.

Sioux (Dakota, Lakota, Nakota) Indian attacks caused Marquette to relocate to Mackinac Island in 1670, where he established the St. Ignace mission. In late 1672, Jolliet joined Marquette at Mackinac. The French colonial government had commissioned Jolliet to search for the great south-flowing river and determine its outlet. Marquette, with his expertise in Indian languages, was chosen as the expedition's interpreter.

In May 1673, Marquette and Jolliet left Mackinac with a part of VOYAGEURS and Miami Indian guides and traveled by CANOE south to Green Bay. They then traveled by way of the Fox and Wisconsin Rivers to the MISSISSIPPI RIVER, which they descended as far as the mouth of the Arkansas River. At that point, warnings from local Indians—probably the Quapaw—of hostile natives farther downstream led Marquette and Jolliet to turn back; they eventually reached Lake Michigan by way of the Illinois River.

In fall 1673, Marquette returned to Mackinac and resumed his missionary work. In 1674, he embarked on an expedition to the Illinois Indian bands he had contacted on the Mississippi expedition. He explored the region of what is now northeastern Illinois, visiting the site of present-day Chicago. His health began to fail, however, and during his return journey to Mackinac and St. Ignace, he died on the east shore of Lake Michigan, near present-day Ludington, Michigan.

Jacques Marquette played a key role in the first European descent of the Mississippi River from the Great Lakes. He obtained important geographic information from the Indians, which helped the expedition locate the portage route between the Fox and Wisconsin Rivers. With Louis Jolliet, he helped determine that the Mississippi most likely flowed into the Gulf of Mexico, which was proven conclusively by RENÉ-ROBERT CAVELIER DE LA SALLE in the years to come.

Marsden, Samuel (1764–1838) *British clergyman in Australia and New Zealand*

Born in Horsforth, near Leeds, England, Samuel Marsden was the son of a retail merchant. Following his early education at Hull Grammar School, he worked briefly for his father, then was granted a scholarship to study at Cambridge University's Magdalene College, which he entered in 1790.

While at Cambridge, Marsden was ordained a minister in the Anglican Church, and, in January 1793, he received a royal commission as assistant chaplain to the newly established penal colony at New South Wales, Australia.

In March 1794, Marsden arrived at New South Wales, settling at Parramatta near present-day Sydney. In addition to overseeing the religious life of the convict population, he was instrumental in creating the first separate penitentiaries for women prisoners and in establishing schools for the colony's orphans.

Marsden returned to England in 1807, where he met with King George III and informed the British monarch on the progress of the New South Wales settlement. The king presented him with five Spanish or Merino sheep from the royal flock. Upon his return to Australia in 1809, Marsden used these animals to breed his own flock of wool-bearing sheep, which formed the basis for the Australian sheep-raising and wool industry.

In 1814, Marsden outfitted the ship the *Active,* which sailed from New South Wales to NEW ZEALAND's North Island. The two missionaries aboard were the first ever to visit New Zealand. Marsden himself arrived soon afterward, accompanied by six Maori chiefs, who had been residing in Parramatta. Later that year, he gained permission from the Maori to establish the first Christian mission at the Bay of Islands on the North Island.

Over the next 23 years, Marsden made seven voyages from Australia to the North Island of New Zealand. Although his main purpose was to win converts among the Maori, he also undertook extensive explorations along the northern part of the North Island. He investigated the region between the Bay of Plenty and the Firth of Thames and located the narrow strip of land joining the northern peninsula with the rest of the island. The city of Auckland, New Zealand's first capital, was founded on this strip in 1840.

Called the "Apostle of New Zealand," the Reverend Samuel Marsden was also known as the "Flogging Parson" for his propensity for meting out severe punishments to rebellious convicts in New South Wales, especially Irish Catholics. He became one of the largest landowners in New South Wales during its initial period of colonization and, with his wife Ellen, founded one of the colony's leading families. On his final visit to New Zealand in 1837, he entered into a peace treaty with the Maori, which soon led to the founding of the first European settlements on the North Island.

Marsili, Luigi Ferdinando (Count Marsili, Luigi Ferdinando Marsigli) (1658–1730) *Italian naturalist, oceanographer*

Luigi Ferdinando Marsili, born into an Italian noble family, served as a surveyor in Emperor Leopold's Austrian army in campaigns against Turkey. During his military career, he wrote a history and geography of lands along the Danube River.

After leaving the military, Count Marsili devoted himself to scientific pursuits. In 1706–08, living in Montpellier in southern France, he began a survey and study of the MEDITERRANEAN SEA's coastline, floor, and features, including waves, tides, and currents. Accompanying fishing boats that harvested corals with scoops and nets, he collected specimens and later examined them under a microscope. He defined them as marine plants, which was later disproved (corals are a coelenterate, or invertebrate animal, of the class Anthozoa). In 1712, Count Marsili founded the Academy of Science in Bologna, Italy, and in 1722, was elected a member of the ROYAL SOCIETY.

Luigi Ferdinando Marsili carried out the first scientific underwater exploration. His book *Histoire physique de la mer* (Physical history of the sea), published in 1725, was the first scientific text devoted entirely to oceanography.

Martínez de Irala, Domingo (Domingo Martínez de Iraola, Captain Vergara)

(ca. 1509–1557) *Spanish conquistador, colonial governor in Paraguay*

Domingo Martínez de Irala was born in the town of Vergara, in the Basque region of northeastern Spain. In 1535, Martínez de Irala sailed to South America in an expedition commanded by PEDRO DE MENDOZA, and, in February 1536, he took part in the founding of the original settlement of Buenos Aires in present-day Argentina, at the mouth of the Río de la Plata.

In 1536, Martínez de Irala served as second in command under JUAN DE AYOLAS in an exploration farther up the Río de la Plata, to the Paraná and Paraguay Rivers. He took over command of the newly established colony of Asunción, and, in 1538, he was elected by the colonists as the settlement's governor.

In 1540, Martínez de Irala was replaced as governor by ÁLVAR NÚÑEZ CABEZA DE VACA. Appointed as Cabeza de Vaca's deputy, he was sent on a voyage of exploration in 1542 to the upper Paraguay River, reaching a point 250 miles above Asunción, at a place he called Puerto de los Reyes. Soon after his return in 1543, the colonists at Asunción rose up against Cabeza de Vaca and imprisoned him; the next year, they reinstalled Martínez de Irala as governor.

Martínez de Irala set out on another exploration of the Paraguay River in 1546, hoping to find an overland route to Peru. Reaching his previous outpost at Puerto de los Reyes, he left his boats and, with a company of 300 Spaniards and 3,500 Indians, pushed into the interior as far as the eastern slopes of the ANDES MOUNTAINS. There,

he made contact with Indians allied with Spanish forces engaged in the war against rebel leader GONZALO PIZARRO. His soldiers refused to continue northwestward, and he was compelled to return to the Paraguay River and Asunción in a trek made even more arduous because the boats left behind at Puerto de los Reyes had been stolen.

An expedition Martínez de Irala sent out from Asunción in 1548 managed to reach the high plains of what is now Bolivia, and several of its members arrived in Lima, completing one of the earliest east-to-west crossings of the South American continent.

Martínez de Irala led his last foray into the upper Paraguay region in 1550. This journey was so fraught with hardships that it was later dubbed the "Mala Entrada," or "unfortunate invasion." Throughout his governorship in the 1550s, Martínez de Irala continued to consolidate Spanish rule over peoples of the upper Paraguay and Paraná Rivers, and in 1557, he sent out an expedition that founded the town of Ontiveros.

Domingo Martínez de Irala, also known as Captain Vergara after his birthplace, has the distinction of being the first freely elected colonial governor in the Americas. His colonizing efforts in what is now Paraguay made Asunción a center for trade and one of the most important cities of the Río de la Plata region prior to the development of Buenos Aires.

Martius, Carl Friedrich Phillipp von (Charles Frederic Philip de Martius; Karl Martius)

(1794–1869) *German botanist in South America*

Carl Friedrich von Martius was born in Erlangen, a German city in northern Bavaria. He attended the University of Munich, graduating in 1816 as a surgeon, with a background in botanical studies.

In 1817, Martius was appointed as physician and botanist for a scientific expedition to eastern Brazil, jointly sponsored by the governments of Austria and Bavaria. Sailing later that year from Trieste, which was then an Austrian port, Martius and the expedition accompanied Archduchess Leopoldina of Austria, who was then en route to South America to join her fiance, the crown prince of Brazil.

Martius, along with another German, Johann Baptist von Spix, the expedition's zoologist, traveled first to the southeastern Brazilian city of São Paulo, and from there headed northward across eastern Brazil. While Spix studied fauna, Martius undertook a thorough examination of the region's natural history, concentrating on flora as well as the life and customs of the native people.

Martius and Spix eventually reached the AMAZON RIVER, which they ascended to its junction with the Japura

River, west of Manaus, near the border with Peru and Colombia. At that point, they separated, with Spix continuing up the Amazon, and Martius up the Japura River into the eastern slopes of the ANDES MOUNTAINS.

After nearly three years in the Amazon Basin, Martius and Spix returned to Europe, where Martius set to work on a three-volume account of his explorations, *Journey to Brazil,* published in Munich from 1824 to 1832. In 1826, he was appointed professor of botany at the University of Munich, a position he held until 1860. He also served for many years as the director of Munich's botanical gardens. Over the next 30 years, Martius wrote many scientific and general studies of Brazil, including a 10-volume work published by the Bavarian government from 1840 to 1857, entitled *Flora Brasilliensis* (Brazilian flora).

Carl Friedrich von Martius, along with Johann Baptist von Spix, conducted one of the most extensive scientific surveys of South America since the 1799–1803 explorations of ALEXANDER VON HUMBOLDT. Their 1817–20 expedition into eastern Brazil and the upper Amazon River yielded 6,500 different plants, as well as 3,300 animal specimens. They brought back the earliest reports of the Amazon rain forest's giant trees, one of which they measured as having a circumference of 82 feet.

Masudi, Abu al-Hasan Ali al- (Abul Hasan Ali ibn Husain Ibn Ali al-Masudi, Abul Hasan Ali Ibn al-Husain al-Masudi, Abul Hasan Ali al-Masudi, Abu al-Hasan Ali al-Husayn al-Masudi, Masoudi, al-Masuid, Masudi) (d. 956 or 957) *Arab traveler, writer in central Asia, the Far East, Africa, and Europe*

The Arab historian, geographer, and world traveler Abu al-Hasan Ali al-Masudi was born at Baghdad in present-day Iraq. According to his own account, one of his ancestors was Masud, an associate of the prophet Mohammed, the founder of Islam.

In about 914, al-Masudi embarked on a career of travel, and, over the next 20 years, he visited every country in the Islamic world. From Baghdad, he traveled across Persia (present-day Iran) to the south shore of the Caspian Sea. He then sailed across the Caspian to Armenia, and also visited the Turkistan region of central Asia. On another journey, he sailed westward across the MEDITERRANEAN SEA to Muslim cities in Spain and North Africa.

One of Masudi's longest trips was a sea voyage he made from the South China Sea westward across the Indian Ocean. After stopping at CEYLON (present-day Sri Lanka), India, and the islands of Madagascar and Zanzibar off central Africa, he returned to the Middle East. He also visited Syria and what is now Israel.

After settling in Egypt in about 943, al-Masudi wrote his 30-volume *Akkbar al-Zaman* (History of time) and a shorter work, *Kitab al-Tanbih wa al-Isharf* (Book of warning and supervision). In his history of the universe from the creation until the period in which he lived, he included a description of the world as revealed to him in his travels, as well as from the accounts of scholars he had met in distant lands.

Maternus, Julius (fl. A.D. 50s) *Roman army officer in North Africa*

Julius Maternus was a Roman military leader in North Africa during the first century A.D. From the Roman city of Jerma, in what is now either northern Libya or Tunisia, Maternus led a military expedition southward across the SAHARA DESERT in about A.D. 50.

Maternus and his command advanced deep into the Sahara and, after four months, arrived in a country known as Agisymba, a region he later characterized as a central breeding ground for the rhinoceros.

The exact route that Julius Maternus followed into the Sahara is not known. Nevertheless, based on the amount of time he spent traveling southward and his description of the animals he saw, historians have speculated that he may have made the first known north-to-south crossing of the Sahara, reaching as far south as what is now Lake Chad. If he did indeed see Lake Chad, he would have predated by almost 1,800 years its discovery in 1823 by British naval officer HUGH CLAPPERTON.

Matonabbee (ca. 1736–1782) *Chipewyan guide to British explorations of northern Canada*

Matonabbee was born near the HUDSON'S BAY COMPANY post, Fort Prince of Wales, on the southwest shore of HUDSON BAY near the mouth of the Churchill River. His father was a Chipewyan Indian; his mother a captured Indian from a southern tribe.

Left fatherless soon after his birth, Matonabbee was adopted by the governor of Fort Prince of Wales, Richard Norton. Although he was raised by non-Indians during his early years, he returned to live with the Chipewyan of Canada's Barren Grounds when Norton returned to England.

Matonabbee returned to Fort Prince of Wales by about 1752, working as a hunter for the Hudson's Bay Company. With his Chipewyan band, he roamed the Barren Grounds in search of game, possibly as far west as the Continental Divide, and as far north as the Arctic coast. He also traveled aboard Hudson's Bay Company ships on expeditions along the west coast of Hudson Bay.

In the late 1760s, Matonabbee became acquainted with Hudson's Bay Company trader SAMUEL HEARNE at Fort Prince of Wales. In late September 1770, Matonabbee met up with Hearne at the Englishman's encampment south of Aberdeen Lake. Hearne was on his way back to Fort Prince of Wales after a second attempt at locat-ing the fabled Northwest Passage, or the STRAIT OF ANIAN. When Maton-abbee arrived, Hearne's party was dangerously short of food and proper clothing for the trip back to the Churchill River post. With Matonabbee's influence, Hearne obtained the necessary supplies from the Chipewyan. Matonabbee then guided Hearne safely back to Fort Prince of Wales. He also agreed to help Hearne undertake another expedition to find the Coppermine River.

Hearne and Matonabbee left Fort Prince of Wales on the Third Coppermine Expedition in December 1770. Ma-tonabbee led a number of Chipewyan families, with women as bearers and workers for the trip. While Hearne kept track of the route they followed, Matonabbee was responsible for the daily progress across the Barren Grounds, as well as the party's survival.

After traveling northward from Fort Prince of Wales, Matonabbee, Hearne, and the Indians headed northwest-ward from the Egg and Seal Rivers across the Barren Grounds, exploring Nueltin Lake, then Kasba Lake and Snowbird Lake. Chipewyan men hunted in separate parties in order to locate enough food for the expedition. In June 1771, Matonabbee brought Hearne to Contwoyto Lake, near the Arctic Circle, where they were joined by a band of Copper Indians.

In early July 1771, Matonabbee and Hearne reached the Coppermine River at Sandstone Rapids. On July 15, at a place later called Bloody Falls by Hearne, Matonabbee and band members launched a surprise attack on a band of Inuit (Eskimo), their traditional enemies, killing all of them. The expedition continued the remaining length of the Cop-permine River to the Arctic coast at Coronation Gulf.

Hearne found that the shallow Coppermine River was unsuitable for shipping. He also concluded that he had jour-neyed far enough north to prove that an east-west passage did not traverse the North American continent. After Ma-tonabbee showed Hearne the copper deposits east of the Coppermine River, the expedition set off on the return jour-ney to Fort Prince of Wales.

Matonabbee led Hearne on a circuitous trip back, head-ing southwestward onto the northern Canadian prairies be-fore going eastward to Hudson Bay. Along the way, they stopped at Great Slave Lake, where Hearne named Maton-abbee Point after the Chipewyan.

Matonabbee and Hearne eventually reached the Egg and Seal Rivers, then followed the west coast of Hudson Bay south to Fort Prince of Wales, arriving there on June 30, 1772. The last part of the journey was fraught with hard-ship, and a number of Indians died of starvation.

In the years that followed, Matonabbee continued to hunt and trade at Fort Prince of Wales, and Hearne became

the post's governor. In 1782, he surrendered the fort to an overwhelming French naval force under JEAN-FRANÇOIS DE GALAUP, comte de La Pérouse, and was taken back to France as a prisoner. Soon afterward, a smallpox epidemic took a heavy toll among the Churchill River Chipewyan. Faced with these disasters, Matonabbee took his own life by hanging himself.

Matonabbee's participation in the Third Coppermine Expedition contributed to its success and enabled Samuel Hearne to reach the Arctic coast, as well as make the Euro-pean discovery of Great Slave Lake, the 10th largest lake in the world.

Maury, Matthew Fontaine (1806–1873)
American naval officer, meteorologist, oceanographer
Matthew Fontaine Maury was born near Fredericksburg, Virginia, and grew up in Tennessee. Following in the footsteps of an older brother, a naval officer, he joined the navy and reached the rank of lieutenant. From 1825 to 1834, he traveled extensively on active duty, circumnavi-gating the world on one of his trips. He kept notes on his travels and later wrote about the history and science of navigation.

In 1839, Maury was injured in a stagecoach accident, which forced him from active service. In 1842, he was ap-pointed superintendent of the Depot of Charts and Instru-ments (the predecessor of the U.S. Naval Observatory and the U.S. Naval Oceanographic Office), based in Washing-ton, D.C. Requesting data from current captains of both naval and merchant marine ships, and using old ship logs as well, Maury compiled charts on wind and currents. He also sought information on deep soundings. In 1855, Maury's work was published under the title *The Physical Geography of the Sea*.

During the Civil War, which interrupted his scientific work, Maury served as a captain in the Confederate States navy. He traveled to England as a spokesperson for the Con-federate cause and was successful in acquiring warships. He also engaged in research in torpedoes and electrical mines. After the war, he became a professor of meteorology at the Virginia Military Institute in Lexington.

Matthew Fontaine Maury's *Physical Geography*, al-though containing many inaccuracies, is considered the first textbook of modern oceanography. His work also helped bring about the first international conference on oceanog-raphy, held in Brussels in 1853.

Mawson, Sir Douglas (1882–1958) *Australian scientist in the Antarctic*
Douglas Mawson was born in Bradford, England. When still young, he immigrated to Australia with his family.

Trained in science, Mawson had a background in both physics and geology. In 1903, he took part in his first scientific expedition, serving as a geologist with an Australian team in the New Hebrides, the island group east of Australia.

In 1907, while serving as a professor of physics at the University of Adelaide, Mawson was recruited by SIR ERNEST HENRY SHACKLETON for a voyage to Antarctica. The expedition sailed from NEW ZEALAND later that year, arriving on the Ross Sea coast of Antarctica in summer 1908. With two other members of Shackleton's expedition, T. W. Edgeworth David and Dr. A. F. Mackay, Mawson made the first ascent of 12,280-foot Mount Erebus, the volcanic peak on the Ross Sea that had been sighted by SIR JAMES CLARK ROSS in 1841.

In October 1908, Mawson set out again with David and Mackay to explore Victoria Land in search of the SOUTH MAGNETIC POLE. They originally planned to use an automobile equipped with skis. The vehicle broke down, however, and the men resorted to pulling their 2,200 pounds of equipment across the ice. Their trek took them from Terra Nova Bay and across the Larsen Glacier. On Jan-

uary 16, 1909, they reached a point 190 miles inland from the west shore of the Ross Sea, where they determined by their compass readings that they were at the South Magnetic Pole. They then headed back to the coast, where the expedition's ship, the *Nimrod,* picked them up in early March 1909, then took them to England.

In 1911, Mawson was placed in command of an official Australian government-sponsored exploration of Antarctica, known as the Australasian Antarctic Expedition. Aboard the *Aurora,* Mawson and his team sailed to Antarctica's Adelie Coast in late 1911. By January 1912, they had established a base camp at Cape Denison. On this expedition, Mawson had brought the first aircraft to be used in Antarctica. Although the airplane was wingless, having been damaged in an accident at Adelaide, the explorers planned to use it as a propeller-driven tractor to haul equipment. Mechanical problems led Mawson to abandon the attempt and resort to the old standby of sledges pulled by dog teams.

In January 1913, accompanied by Swiss mountaineer and champion skier Dr. Xavier Mertz and Lieutenant B. E. S. Ninnis of the British army, Mawson set out to explore the inland region east of Commonwealth Bay. They soon came upon a previously uncharted part of the Antarctic coast, which they called George V Land (afterward George V Coast). On their way back to Commonwealth Bay, Ninnis fell into a deep crevasse with his sledge and dog-team and was lost; soon afterward, Mertz died of exhaustion. Left alone, Mawson overcame great hardships caused by frostbite and shortages of food and managed to return to the Cape Denison camp. He spent another winter there, then returned to Australia on the *Aurora.* According to Mawson, the Cape Denison site was the windiest place on Earth, with frequent storms. He referred to it as "Home of the Blizzard," which became the title of his account of the expedition, published in 1915.

In 1915, soon after his return from Antarctica, Mawson was awarded a gold medal by the ROYAL GEOGRAPHICAL SOCIETY. He was appointed professor of geology at the University of Adelaide in 1920, a position he held for 32 years.

In 1929, Mawson returned to Antarctica in command of a joint British, Australian, and New Zealand expedition. During the next two years, he undertook a series of aerial reconnaissance flights over Antarctica, in the course of which he made the European discovery of the MacRobertson Coast. At one point, he met up with a Norwegian expedition at Enderby Land, a region that had not been explored since it was sighted in the first half of the 19th century. Mawson reached an agreement with the Norwegians that set the 45th meridian of longitude as the boundary between Australian and Norwegian exploration and territorial claims.

Matthew Fontaine Maury *(Library of Congress)*

Sir Douglas Mawson's aerial explorations of Antarctica, along with the aerial surveys of LINCOLN ELLSWORTH and Admiral RICHARD EVELYN BYRD, provided a complete picture of the continent's coastline. On his 1911–14 expedition, Mawson was the first to use a radio in Antarctic exploration. Ninnis Glacier Tongue and Mertz Glacier Tongue on the George V Coast were named in honor of the two companions he lost while exploring that part of Antarctica. Mawson Coast on the Indian Ocean is named after him. One of Mawson's most significant findings was made early in his Antarctic career in 1909, when he reached the South Magnetic Pole and determined that it was not a fixed point but periodically shifted its location.

Maximilian, Alexander Philipp (Prince Maximilian, Maximilian, prinz zu Wied-Neuwied) (1782–1887) *German naturalist, ethnologist in the Americas*

Prince Alexander Philipp Maximilian was a German nobleman from the Prussian principality of Wied, near Coblenz. He served in the Napoleonic Wars with the Prussian army and was captured after the Battle of Jena in 1806.

Maximilian became an avid student of the natural sciences—geology, zoology, and botany. He was also interested in studying the cultures of aboriginal peoples. Among his friends in German scientific circles was naturalist and explorer ALEXANDER VON HUMBOLDT.

In 1815, Maximilian took part in an expedition to South America with two other German scientists. During the next two years, he explored the coastal forest of Brazil and studied the culture of the inhabitants. He also made sketches of Native Americans that served as the basis for illustrations in his later published account of the expedition.

In 1832, Maximilian engaged Swiss artist KARL BODMER to accompany him on a trip to North America and produce drawings and watercolors of wilderness themes. Later that year, they traveled to Boston, then to New York, where they were the guests of German-American financier JOHN JACOB ASTOR, who arranged a tour for them of his upper MISSOURI RIVER fur-trading posts.

Maximilian, Bodmer, and Maximilian's retainer, David Dreidoppel, left St. Louis in April 1833 aboard the AMERICAN FUR COMPANY steamboat *Yellowstone*. They traveled up the Missouri into the Dakotas. Over the next 13 months, they visited trading posts on the upper Missouri, including Fort Clark near present-day Pierre, South Dakota, Fort Union at the mouth of the Yellowstone River, and Fort McKenzie at the mouth of present-day Montana's Marias River.

Maximilian's trip up the Missouri was undertaken with the help and cooperation of Indian Superintendent WILLIAM CLARK, as well as American Fur Company officers PIERRE CHOUTEAU, JR., and KENNETH MCKENZIE. TOUSSAINT CHARBONNEAU, who had traveled with Clark and MERIWETHER LEWIS in the Lewis and Clark Expedition 30 years earlier, served as interpreter to the Indians.

Throughout his tour of the upper Missouri region, Maximilian made ethnological studies of Indian peoples, especially the Mandan. Bodmer recorded their culture in drawings and paintings.

In spring 1834, Maximilian and Bodmer returned eastward from St. Louis by way of the MISSISSIPPI RIVER, the Ohio River, and the Erie Canal. They sailed from New York for Europe, returning to Germany with hundreds of sketches of Indians, as well as botanical specimens, including several bears captured during the expedition. Their 13-month odyssey had covered more than 5,000 miles of the Missouri frontier.

During the next several years, Maximilian worked with Bodmer on producing an illustrated account of the upper Missouri expedition. It was first published in 1839 as *Travels in the Interior of North America*.

Maximilian's North American expedition was his last. He settled at his family's estate in Wied along the Rhine River, where he spent the rest of his life in ethnological and naturalist studies.

Among his scientific observations, Prince Alexander Philipp Maximilian remarked on the fertility of the northern plains, noting that only a rich soil could provide the extensive grasslands that supported the region's huge buffalo herds and other abundant wildlife. He was among the first to predict the region's great agricultural potential at a time when the area was widely considered a wasteland. Maximilian and Bodmer traveled as scientists and artists in the upper Missouri frontier only a generation after the area was first explored by non-Indians. Maximilian's written account, coupled with Bodmer's illustrations, provides an image of the trans-Mississippi region as it was in the last decades before the influx of settlers and the advent of railroads changed it forever.

Mazuchelli, Elizabeth Sarah (Nina Mazuchelli) (1832–1914) *British traveler, writer in Nepal and northern India*

Elizabeth Sarah "Nina" Mazuchelli was the wife of Anglican clergyman Francis Mazuchelli. In 1858, she went to India with her husband, who had been sent there to serve as a chaplain to the British army.

Mazuchelli spent the next 10 years with her husband at garrisons on the plains of central India. In 1869, she and Francis moved to Darjeeling in the foothills of the HIMALAYAS, where he had been transferred.

In 1872, the Mazuchellis undertook a 600-mile, two-month expedition from Darjeeling into the Himalayas of northern Sikkim and eastern Nepal. Along the way, Mazuchelli made sketches of MOUNT EVEREST and Mount Kanchenjunga. They traveled through the unmapped regions of the Singalila Mountains, which Mazuchelli dubbed the "Indian Alps." At some locations, they suffered from the ill effects of the high altitude's rarefied atmosphere, as well as snow blindness.

The Mazuchelli party traveled into northern Sikkim as far as the base of 25,311-foot Mount Junnoo. They returned to Darjeeling on ponies, following the Great Rangit River southward.

In 1875, the Mazuchellis returned to England and eventually settled in Wales. The next year, Mazuchelli's account of the Himalayan journey was published, entitled *The Indian Alps and How We Crossed Them.* She subsequently toured the Carpathian Mountains of central Europe and wrote about the experience in her 1881 book *Magyar Land.*

Nina Mazuchelli's journey through the eastern Himalayas took her across some uncharted regions without roads or paths. She was the first known European woman to travel the entire length of the Singalila Mountains of eastern Nepal and northern Sikkim.

McClintock, Sir Francis Leopold (1819–1907)
Irish-born British naval officer in the Canadian Arctic

Francis Leopold McClintock was born in Dundalk on the northeast coast of Ireland. In 1831, in his 13th year, he enlisted in the British navy as a midshipman. Over the course of his early naval career, McClintock served on British naval vessels in the coastal waters of both North and South America.

In 1845, soon after his completing of a two-year cruise in the Pacific Ocean, McClintock was promoted to the rank of lieutenant. His first Arctic assignment came in 1848, when he was attached to SIR JAMES CLARK ROSS's voyage in search of SIR JOHN FRANKLIN, missing since 1845. With Ross, McClintock conducted several reconnaissance expeditions from Somerset Island, at the western outlet of Lancaster Sound, traveling by sled southward into Peel Sound and westward to Prince of Wales and Melville Islands. The expedition returned to England in fall 1849.

Although no trace of Franklin was found, the experience taught McClintock much about Inuit (Eskimo) sledging techniques, as well as the deployment of food depots and relays, essential for exploration on the Arctic ice.

McClintock made his second voyage to the Canadian Arctic in 1850, serving under Captain Horatio Austin. From the expedition's winter quarters at Barrow Strait, at the western end of Lancaster Sound, he undertook a sledge journey westward and southward to Prince of Wales Island, Bathurst Island, Byam Martin Island, and Melville Island, covering more than 770 miles in 80 days.

In 1852, McClintock took part in SIR EDWARD BELCHER's effort to find Franklin. They also searched for SIR ROBERT McCLURE and RICHARD COLLINSON, who had been missing since their own search for Franklin. In spring and summer 1853, McClintock undertook several explorations by sledge from the expedition's base on Melville Island and covered more than 1,400 miles. West of the base, he made the European discovery of Eglington Island and Prince Patrick Island on the eastern edge of the Beaufort Sea.

McClintock returned to England in 1854, where he was promoted to the rank of captain. That year, the British Admiralty ended its official search efforts for Franklin. Nevertheless, JANE FRANKLIN was not satisfied with reports brought back by JOHN RAE of the HUDSON'S BAY COMPANY, which indicated her husband's expedition had perished near King William Island, and she commissioned McClintock to lead another effort.

In command of Lady Franklin's steam yacht the *Fox,* in 1857, McClintock sailed to the west coast of GREENLAND, where he put in at Upernavik and acquired sled-dogs and Inuit guides. He attempted to negotiate into Lancaster Sound, hoping to retrace Franklin's conjectured route, but advancing PACK ICE drove the *Fox* back into Baffin Bay. Finally, after eight months, he managed a passage through Lancaster Sound. He stopped at Beechey Island and erected a monument commemorating Franklin's Arctic exploits, then headed southward into Peel Sound. He located a passage through Bellot Strait, which took him into an open stretch of water north of King William Island, named McClintock Channel in his honor.

By 1859, McClintock and his men had reached the north coast of King William Island, which he circumnavigated, proving that it was truly an island, separated from the Canadian mainland by Simpson Strait. While on King William Island, McClintock found a sledge and several skeletons of crew members of Franklin's expedition, some still clad in the tattered remains of British navy uniforms. Another party under his command, led by Lieutenant W. R. Hobson, crossed Simpson Strait and, at the mouth of the Back River, found letters written by Franklin's men. The letters indicated that Franklin himself had died in spring 1847 and that the remaining men had attempted to reach a Hudson's Bay Company outpost on the lower Back River in 1848. Accounts by Inuit and the discovery of more skeletal remains revealed that all had perished in the attempt.

McClintock returned to England later in 1859. That same year, he published his account of the expedition, *The Voyage of the Fox,* in which he described his own explorations in the Canadian Arctic, reconstructed what had happened to Franklin and his expedition, and suggested that Franklin had located the eastern entrance to the NORTHWEST PASSAGE, dying before he could explore it.

Both Lady Franklin and McClintock were awarded gold medals by the ROYAL GEOGRAPHICAL SOCIETY in 1859; the following year, McClintock was knighted by Queen Victoria.

McClintock went on to a long and distinguished naval career, remaining on active duty until age 75. He was made an admiral in 1884, retiring from the navy soon afterward.

Sir Francis Leopold McClintock served as an adviser to subsequent Arctic explorers, including SIR GEORGE STRONG NARES and FRIDTJOF NANSEN. ROALD ENGEL-BREGT GRAVNING AMUNDSEN used *The Voyage of the Fox* as a guide in his successful voyage through the Northwest Passage in 1903–06. In his 1915 Arctic expedition, VILHJAL-MUR STEFANSSON recovered a canister with letters left by McClintock in 1853 on Prince Patrick Island, at a site since known as Cape McClintock. In addition to shedding light on the true fate of Sir John Franklin and his expedition, McClintock is credited with introducing sledging techniques adapted from the Inuit, which proved invaluable in later Arctic and Antarctic explorations.

McClure, Sir Robert John Le Mesurier

(1807–1873) *Irish-born British naval officer in the Canadian Arctic*

Born in Wexford, on the southeast coast of Ireland, Robert McClure was educated in England at Eton before going on to the Royal Military Academy at Sandhurst. He entered the British navy at the age of 17 and served in many regions of the world.

McClure had his introduction to Arctic exploration in 1836–37, while serving as mate under Captain GEORGE BACK on the *Terror* in a voyage to HUDSON BAY. On his return to England, he was promoted to lieutenant. Attached to the Coast Guard, he then took part in patrols in the Great Lakes region of Canada, as well as in the Caribbean Sea.

In 1848, McClure was assigned to the British navy's first search efforts for SIR JOHN FRANKLIN and his expedition, which had been missing in the Canadian Arctic since 1845. Under the command of SIR JAMES CLARK ROSS, he sailed with SIR FRANCIS LEOPOLD McCLINTOCK in an attempt to locate Franklin and his ships by retracing the route they were thought to have taken westward through Lancaster Sound. The British ships were beset by ice at Somerset Island at the western end of Lancaster Sound and blocked for the winter; they returned to England after the spring thaw.

Late in 1849, McClure was placed in command of the *Investigator* in a second attempt to find Franklin. Sailing from England on January 31, 1850, he was accompanied by the *Enterprise* under SIR RICHARD COLLINSON, the commanding officer for that part of the search. Acting on the assumption that Franklin may have actually navigated westward through the NORTHWEST PASSAGE, Mc-Clure and Collinson planned to approach the Canadian Arctic from the north coast of Alaska and locate its western entrance.

McClure and Collinson sailed around South America by way of CAPE HORN, then headed northward along the coasts of South and North America. En route to the Arctic, the ships became separated. Instead of waiting for Collinson at BERING STRAIT as planned, McClure made his way through the Strait and around Point Barrow before winter ice conditions blocked the way. Collinson, who arrived at Bering Strait just 10 days later, could not continue because of the ice and wintered there.

Meanwhile, McClure had managed to proceed well east of the north coast of Alaska, reaching the south shore of Banks Island, east of the Yukon mainland. He made the European discovery of a channel, Prince of Wales Strait, between Banks Island and Victoria Island to the east, although by early September 1850, as he approached Melville Island to the north, his ship became trapped in the ice.

Taking to sledges, McClure and his men explored northward around Banks Island and reached the shore of Viscount Melville Sound on October 26, 1850. On sighting Melville Island and the westernmost point reached by SIR WILLIAM EDWARD PARRY in his 1819 expedition, McClure declared that he had found the long-sought Northwest Passage. At the site on the north coast of Banks Island, in a cannister beneath a small monument, he left a letter announcing his accomplishment, which was found by VIL-HJALMUR STEFANSSON in his Arctic expedition of 1917.

With the route to the north and east blocked by ice, McClure made a counterclockwise circumnavigation of Banks Island, making the European discovery of a wide ice-free stretch of water on its north coast, known afterward as McClure Strait. Seeking shelter at an inlet he called Mercy Bay, the *Investigator* was again trapped by advancing ice, this time inextricably.

In spring 1853, McClure decided to abandon the ship and lead his expedition over frozen Viscount Melville Sound to Melville Island, in the hope of joining other British vessels penetrating the Canadian Arctic from the east at Lancaster Sound. Soon after McClure and his men had set out on their sledges, they encountered another sledge-borne party sent westward by McClintock. They then all returned to SIR EDWARD BELCHER's fleet at Beechey Island, at the western end of Lancaster Sound, from where they sailed back to Baffin Bay and eventually to England.

McClure and his men were hailed for their crossing of the Canadian Arctic and their finding the Northwest Passage. He had not made a continuous sea passage. But Mc-Clure's eastward journey, taken together with the earlier voyages of Parry and the explorations undertaken by Collinson in 1851–52, demonstrated that a navigable northwest passage existed between the Atlantic and Pacific Oceans.

Soon after his triumphant return to England in 1854, McClure was knighted and promoted to the rank of captain. He then served in the Pacific, reaching the rank of rear admiral in 1857. In 1873, the year of his death, he was elevated to vice admiral.

Sir Robert McClure's journal of his historic Arctic expedition was edited by Sherard Osborn and published in 1856 as *The Discovery of the Northwest Passage by H.M.S. "Investigator," Capt. R. M'Clure, 1850, 1851, 1852, 1853, 1854*. Whether he actually was the first to find the Northwest Passage has become a matter of dispute. McClintock, based on the findings of his 1857–59 expedition, later maintained that Franklin had found open channels that he could have followed from Prince William Island westward to the Beaufort Sea and Bering Strait, had he and his men not perished. Nonetheless, McClure commanded the first known circumnavigation of both South and North America, and, in his 1853 sledge journey, he and his men made the first known crossing of North America north of the ARCTIC CIRCLE.

McKenzie, Kenneth (Kenneth Mackenzie)

(ca. 1800–1861) *Scottish-Canadian fur trader in the American West*

Kenneth McKenzie was born at Rosshire in Inverness, Scotland. He moved to Canada while still in his teens and went to work for the NORTH WEST COMPANY, the trading firm based in Montreal.

In 1821, McKenzie left the North West Company on its merger with the HUDSON'S BAY COMPANY and joined the American-owned Columbia Fur Company. By 1825, he was president of the Columbia Fur Company, and he made it a leading competitor in the FUR TRADE of the Great Lakes and the upper Mississippi and upper Missouri rivers.

McKenzie's success led to a merger, in 1827, between the Columbia Fur Company and JOHN JACOB ASTOR's AMERICAN FUR COMPANY. McKenzie then took charge of the American Fur Company's Upper Missouri branch.

In fall 1829, McKenzie established Fort Union near the junction of the Yellowstone River and MISSOURI RIVER, 1,800 miles upstream from St. Louis. This post soon dominated the upper Missouri fur trade, and McKenzie sent out traders and trappers southwestward into the ROCKY MOUNTAINS. JAMES PIERSON BECKWOURTH and CALEB GREENWOOD worked for McKenzie.

During the next several years, McKenzie established more trading centers in present-day Montana, including Fort Cass on the Bighorn River and Fort McKenzie at the mouth of the Marias River. The latter, established in 1832, became the principal post for the American Fur Company's penetration of the Rocky Mountains. Traders, among them

ÉTIENNE PROVOST and WILLIAM HENRY VANDERBURGH, ranged into present-day Wyoming and Utah.

Meanwhile, Fort Pierre and Fort Clark, McKenzie's posts on the Missouri in the Dakotas, dominated much of the trade above Old Council Bluffs.

In 1832–33, McKenzie had a whiskey still constructed at Fort Union, in response to a law enacted by the U.S. government forbidding the importation of liquor into Indian territory. Rival traders reported the still to American authorities in St. Louis, and McKenzie was forced to resign his post with the American Fur Company.

Sometime after 1834, McKenzie traveled to Germany, where he visited ALEXANDER PHILIPP MAXIMILIAN. The prince and Swiss artist KARL BODMER had been McKenzie's guests at Fort Union and Fort McKenzie during their 1833–34 tour of the upper Missouri. Upon his return to the United States, McKenzie settled in St. Louis, where he became a wholesale liquor importer.

Kenneth McKenzie expanded the influence of the American Fur Company to the headwaters of the Missouri River, as well as into the northern plains and northern Rockies. His traders brought back reports of the geography of the Rockies and the Great Basin. He also initiated the trade in buffalo hides, which provided further impetus for exploration of the northern plains. At the height of his career in the fur trade, he was known as the "King of the Missouri."

McLeod, William C. (unknown–1880) *British army officer in Southeast Asia*

In December 1836, William C. McLeod, a British army captain who had served in India, set out from Moulmein, the principal city of British-controlled Burma (present-day Myanmar), in search of a feasible travel route northward into China's southeastern Yunnan province. Ten years before, Burma had ceded much of its southern region to Great Britain as a consequence of the First Anglo-Burma War of 1824–26, leaving only the still semi-autonomous Shan States of northern Burma between British territory and a direct trade link with southern China.

McLeod first followed the Salween River northward from its mouth near Moulmein to a point upstream where it becomes unnavigable. Traveling overland, he then headed eastward into what is now northwestern Thailand, arriving at the city of Chiang Mai in January 1837. From there, he embarked northward across the Shan States, making his way on the back of an elephant into the mountainous, little-known region of northern Burma.

By March 1837, McLeod had reached the northern Burmese city of Keng Tung, not far from the Chinese border. Although he was close to reaching his goal, Chinese officials denied him permission to enter the country.

Although political problems prevented Captain William C. McLeod from making one of the earliest crossings into Yunnan, China, from the south, he was nonetheless the first European to explore the territory between northern Burma and southeastern China since the 13th-century travels of MARCO POLO. For another 100 years after McLeod's expedition, there was still no regular travel route through this country. Then, in 1937–38, with the outbreak of the Sino-Japanese War, in which China's Pacific ports fell into Japanese hands, the Chinese constructed the Burma Road, finally establishing a link between Yunnan and lower Burma.

McLoughlin, John (1784–1857) *Canadian-born fur trader, physician in the Pacific Northwest*

Born in Rivière-du-Loup, Quebec, John McLoughlin came from a family with extensive ties to Canada's FUR TRADE. He studied medicine under his uncle, Alexander Fraser, a celebrated Canadian doctor, and was licensed as a physician in 1803.

In 1814, McLoughlin's family connections led to his appointment as a physician at the NORTH WEST COMPANY's trading post, Fort William, on the northwest shore of Lake Superior in present-day Ontario, Canada. While there, he engaged in fur trading with the Indians of the Kaministik-wia River region, gaining valuable experience that soon led to his partnership in the company.

After the North West Company merged with the HUDSON'S BAY COMPANY in 1821, McLoughlin was named director of operations at Lac la Pluie, and, in 1824, he was put in charge of the Hudson's Bay Company fur-trading enterprise in the Pacific Northwest. The following year, he established Fort Vancouver on the COLUMBIA RIVER, opposite present-day Portland, Oregon, where his associate was PETER SKENE OGDEN.

From his base on the Columbia River, McLoughlin directed trading expeditions into the Snake River country of what is now eastern Washington and southern Idaho, and, until the late 1830s, into the Sacramento Valley region of northern California. He also played host and rendered help to the earliest American trappers to explore the Oregon Country, including JEDEDIAH STRONG SMITH and his party of mountain men, who arrived at Fort Vancouver in 1828.

McLoughlin provided help and lent his support to settlers from the East who began arriving in the mid-1830s, attracted by the great farming potential of the Cascade region. Among those he assisted at Fort Vancouver were Methodist missionaries MARCUS WHITMAN and HENRY HARMON SPALDING. Concerned that increased non-Indian settlement of the Oregon Country would lead to a decline in fur trade with the Indians, McLoughlin di-

John McLoughlin *(Library of Congress)*

rected many of the settlers south of the Columbia, to the Willamette River region around present-day Salem, Oregon.

In 1841, McLoughlin became director of the Hudson's Bay Company's new trading center on Vancouver Island in present-day British Columbia, where the headquarters of its Pacific Northwest operations had been moved when it seemed likely that the lower Columbia River region would become U.S. territory. McLoughlin served there until 1845, when he retired from the fur trade and settled in the Willamette Valley. He became an American citizen and helped establish the community that became Oregon City, Oregon.

John McLoughlin was an important figure in the early settlement of the Pacific Northwest. As director of fur-trading operations on the Columbia, he provided organization and support for the explorations of Peter Skene Ogden into the Great Basin Region, as well as invaluable assistance to the first mountain men and settlers to venture into the interior of the Oregon Country. The site of his original Columbia River post, at Fort Vancouver in southwestern Washington, was declared a National Historic Site in 1948 by the U.S. National Park Service.

Mee, Margaret Ursula (Margaret Ursula Brown) (1909–1988) *British botanical painter in Brazil*

Margaret Mee, née Brown, was born near Chesham, in Buckinghamshire, England. As a young girl, she was inspired to draw by an aunt who had illustrated children's books, and she later studied art at St. Martin's School of Art in London, where she met her second husband, Greville Mee, then at the Camberwell School of Art, also in London. In the 1940s, while on a visit to Brazil to see her sister, she was hired to teach art at St. Paul's, a British school in São Paulo. Her husband eventually joined her there and built a successful career as a commercial artist.

In 1956, when she was in her late 40s, Mee first traveled into the Amazon rain forest to paint plants, especially flowers. She undertook a total of 15 such expeditions by dugout CANOE, each trip lasting months. Her travels took her along the AMAZON RIVER and its tributaries, among them the Arinos, Içana (Isana), Maués, and Tefé. She worked in the medium of gouache, a method of painting using opaque watercolors, in the field or from sketches in the studio. She also collected live specimens to take home and would wait for them to blossom before painting them and kept a diary with notes about plant she painted.

Mee corresponded with botanists from around the world. Her paintings appeared in *Flowers of the Brazilian Forest, Collected and Painted by Margaret Mee* (1968) and in *Flores do Amazonas/Flowers of the Amazon* (1980). *Margaret Mee: In Search of Flowers of the Amazon Forests* (1988) includes excerpts from her diaries. She died in an automobile accident during a visit to England in 1988.

In addition to her contributions to the field of botany, Margaret Mee became an early advocate of preservation of the rain forest, having witnessed over the course of three decades the impact of growing settlement and development. Many of her paintings are kept at Kew Gardens in London.

Meek, Joseph L. (Joe Meek) (1810–1875)
American fur trader, trapper in the American West, Oregon pioneer

Joseph Meek spent his early years in the mountains of southwestern Virginia's Washington County. At the age of 18, he moved to St. Louis, Missouri, where he joined his brothers, Hiram and Stephen.

In 1829, Meek traveled into the northern and central ROCKY MOUNTAINS as a trapper with WILLIAM LEWIS SUBLETTE. That year, he took part in the annual fur trappers' rendezvous at Pierre's Hole, on the western slopes of the Teton Mountains. He also attended the 1832 Pierre's Hole rendezvous with such famous MOUNTAIN MEN as THOMAS FITZPATRICK and JAMES BRIDGER, as well as two nephews of legendary frontiersman DANIEL BOONE. In 1833–34,

Meek was a member of JOSEPH REDDEFORD WALKER's expedition that crossed the Sierra Nevada into California's Yosemite region.

During most of the 1830s, Meek was active as a fur trader and mountain man throughout a wide area of the west. With his brother, Stephen, he ranged from the Snake River of Idaho south into the Great Basin region of central Utah. During this period, he joined CHRISTOPHER HOUSTON CARSON (Kit Carson) in hunting expeditions on the northern plains and hunted and trapped around Yellowstone Lake.

With the decline in the FUR TRADE after 1838, Meek settled at Fort Hall in what is now southeastern Idaho, where he lived for a short time with his Indian wife. In 1840, Meek, with his wife and children, left Fort Hall for the Oregon Country, accompanying one of the earliest wagon trains to cross the mountains on the Oregon Trail.

Meek and his family settled in Oregon's Willamette Valley. In 1847, in the wake of the killing of MARCUS WHITMAN and others by Cayuse Indians under Chief Tiloukaikt, Meek was dispatched to Washington, D.C., by a group of concerned Oregon settlers seeking federal military support from President James Polk (whose wife was Meek's cousin). Meek made the transcontinental journey in the middle of an exceptionally severe winter, arriving in Washington in spring 1848. Partly through his efforts, Oregon was given territorial status. Meek, appointed a U.S. marshal, escorted Oregon's newly appointed territorial governor, Joseph Lane of Indiana, back to Oregon. They reached St. Louis, from where they headed westward by way of the Santa Fe Trail and the Gila River across the Mojave Desert to Los Angeles. From there, they reached Oregon by ship. Meek went on to become prominent in Oregon territorial and state politics.

As a mountain man in the 1830s, Joseph Meek played an active role in the exploration of the trans-Mississippi West. His later exploits as a pioneer in the Pacific Northwest contributed directly to the settlement of Oregon.

Megasthenes (fl. 290s B.C.) *Greek diplomat in India*

Megasthenes was a Greek from Ionia, now the Mediterranean coast of present-day Turkey. He became a diplomat in the service of Seleucus I, the king of ancient Syria and one of the inheritors of the empire of ALEXANDER THE GREAT. In about 302 B.C., he was sent as an ambassador to the court of King Chandragupta, the ruler of the Mauryan Empire of northeastern India.

Megasthenes spent several years at Chandragupta's capital city of Palibothra (on the site of present-day Patna, India) and traveled widely in northern India, recording his observations on the region's geography, politics, and social institutions, including the Hindu caste system. He also wrote about the natural history of the region between the INDUS RIVER and GANGES RIVER.

On his journey from the eastern edge of Seleucus's domain, Megasthenes traveled eastward to Patna along India's Grand Road, a well-maintained trade route stretching from Patna in the east, northwestward across India into the Punjab, as far as the Kabul region in present-day Afghanistan.

Only fragments of Megasthenes's account, called *Indica*, survived. The work provided the ancient Mediterranean world with the earliest account of India, including such details as the correct shape of the Indian subcontinent. It also contained the earliest reports on the existence of Tibet and the island of CEYLON (present-day Sri Lanka), the latter referred to by Megasthenes as Taprobrane.

Megasthenes was probably the first Greek, as well as the first Westerner, to see the Ganges River, fulfilling the aspirations of Alexander the Great from a generation earlier. In his speculations on the source of the Ganges, Megasthenes correctly surmised that the river originated in the HIMALAYAS, a mountain range he called the "Indian Caucasus." With the decline of the Hellenistic empires of the eastern Mediterranean and the Middle East two centuries after Megasthenes's journey to Patna, connections between India and the West withered, and they were not revived until the emergence of the Roman Empire in the first century A.D.

Menard, Antoine Pierre (1766–1844)
Canadian fur trader on the upper Missouri

Pierre Menard was born in St. Antoine, Quebec. After spending his early years in Montreal, he moved west to Vincennes on the Indiana frontier, where he found work under Indian trader Francis Vigo.

In 1789, Menard moved to the Illinois country and settled at Kaskaskia, a settlement on the MISSISSIPPI RIVER just below St. Louis. Along with Toussaint DuBois, he established a mercantile business, dealing with both Indians and non-Indian settlers. During the 1790s, Menard became prominent in the territorial militia and served as a magistrate in the territorial government.

In 1806, Menard married a sister-in-law of JEAN PIERRE CHOUTEAU, head of a leading St. Louis merchant family. That same year, he joined fellow Kaskaskia businessman William Morrison in a partnership with St. Louis entrepreneur MANUEL LISA. Menard was one of the backers and key suppliers of Lisa's spring 1807 expedition up the MISSOURI RIVER to the Dakotas and the Bighorn River region of present-day Montana. Menard did not personally take part in the expedition; GEORGE DROUILLARD, a veteran of the Corps of Discovery under MERIWETHER LEWIS and WILLIAM CLARK, went along as Menard and Morrison's agent.

In 1809, Menard was one of the founding partners of the ST. LOUIS MISSOURI FUR COMPANY. Manuel Lisa and William Clark also participated.

On June 15, 1809, Menard left St. Louis with the company's 200-man expedition to the Dakotas and northern ROCKY MOUNTAINS. By early September, the expedition had reached the mouth of the Knife River in present-day central North Dakota, where the fur traders constructed Fort Mandan.

In late November 1809, Menard departed Fort Mandan and traveled overland into Montana, accompanied by Andrew Henry, George Drouillard, and a party of trappers. Menard and his party wintered at Fort Raymond, the post Lisa had established at the confluence of the Bighorn and Yellowstone Rivers during his first expedition in 1807.

In March 1810, guided by JOHN COLTER and EDWARD ROSE, Menard's party headed westward through the Bozeman Pass to the Three Forks of the Missouri. They constructed a stockade, the first such post at that location, and began trapping beaver and trading with the Indians. Attacks by Blackfeet Indians plagued the enterprise from the start. Shortly after Drouillard and some other trappers were killed near the fort in May, Menard headed back to St. Louis, arriving in July 1810.

Menard returned to Kaskaskia, Illinois, and subsequently became a leading political figure. He was president of the Illinois territorial legislative council from 1812 to 1818. When Illinois was admitted to the Union in 1818, Menard became the state's first lieutenant governor.

Pierre Menard provided the financial support for the first commercial expedition into the upper Missouri and northern Rockies. With the 1809–10 expedition into central Montana, he took part in one of the earliest organized ventures into the Three Forks of the Missouri area.

Ménard, René (1604–1661) *French missionary in the Great Lakes region*

Born in Paris, René Ménard studied to be a Jesuit priest. After serving in France, he traveled to Quebec in 1640. His first assignments were among the Nipissing and Huron (Wyandot) Indians of present-day Ontario and among the Cayuga of present-day New York. He also ministered to Indians at Trois-Rivières, Quebec.

In 1659, at the age of 55, Ménard joined up with a party of Ottawa Indians who had visited the St. Lawrence settlements for the purpose of trade, and along with five French traders, set out westward on the traders' return CANOE journey to their homeland by the Ottawa River, Lake Huron, and Lake Superior. On the south shore of Lake Superior in present-day Michigan, Ménard founded a mission at a place he called Chassahamigan, thought to be Keweenaw Bay, located about 190 miles west of Sault Sainte

Marie. In July 1661, Ménard embarked on a journey farther to the west in the hope of preaching to Sioux (Dakota, Lakota, Nakota) Indians. He traveled with one other Frenchman, thought to be a blacksmith. That August, however, the two became separated in the woods. Ménard, never heard from again, was most likely killed by Indians in present-day Wisconsin.

René Ménard, along with MÉDARD CHOUART DES GROSEILLIERS and PIERRE-ESPRIT RADISSON, was one of the first known Europeans to visit the lands and Indians of the western Great Lakes. The work he started was continued by fellow Jesuit CLAUDE-JEAN ALLOUEZ, who founded a mission farther to the west at Chequamegon Bay.

Mendaña, Álvaro de (Álvaro Mendaña de Neira, Álvaro Mendaña de Neyra, Álvaro Mendeña de Nehra) (ca. 1541–1595) *Spanish mariner in the South Pacific*

The navigator Álvaro de Mendaña, born in Saragossa, Spain, was an associate of PEDRO SARMIENTO DE GAMBOA, a cosmographer who had commanded an expedition to Peru in 1557 and had become a recognized authority on Inca Indian history.

Both Mendaña and Sarmiento held the view that Terra Australis, the GREAT SOUTHERN CONTINENT, existed in the high southern latitudes as a counterbalance to the landmasses of the Northern Hemisphere. Moreover, in his study of Inca legends, Sarmiento had come upon an account of an Inca king who had undertaken a westward voyage across the Pacific Ocean, reached the "Western Lands," and returned from there with a treasure in silver and gold. Sarmiento concluded that the "Western Lands" of Inca tradition were actually the biblical lands of OPHIR and Tarshish, the site of King Solomon's mines. He further speculated that these islands lay off the coast of Terra Australis, somewhere west of Tierra del Fuego.

Mendaña and Sarmiento organized an expedition to reach these fabled islands, discover Terra Australis, and Christianize its inhabitants. Outfitted with two ships under Mendaña's general command, they sailed from the port of Callao, near Lima, Peru, in November 1567.

After sailing almost due westward across the Pacific for 80 days, Mendaña and his ships made their first sighting of land, Nui Island in the Ellice group. About a month later, in February 1568, after coming upon Ontong Java and Roncador Reef, he made a landing on a larger island nearby, which he named Santa Isabel in honor of his wife's patron saint. At first, Mendaña believed he had reached the mainland of Terra Australis, but upon further exploration in a small boat, he learned that the landmass was an island. Yet Mendaña was certain that he was at least near the mainland of a southern continent and named the island group the Solomons, believing they were the fabled lands mentioned in the Bible's Book of Solomon.

Mendaña conducted further explorations in the Solomons, making the European discovery of islands he named Guadalcanal and San Cristobal. In August 1568, he headed northward and reached the Marshall Islands, as well as an island he called San Francisco, between Guam and the HAWAIIAN ISLANDS. He continued eastward, across 4,000 miles of the Pacific, and reached the Santa Barbara Islands, off the coast of present-day Los Angeles, California. He then followed the coastline to Acapulco and beyond, returning to Peru in early 1569.

It was not until 1595, three years after Sarmiento's death, that Mendaña was able to mount a follow-up voyage to the Solomons. The Spanish government had lost interest in the findings of his first expedition when he failed to return with gold in 1569. By 1595, however, SIR FRANCIS DRAKE and other English PRIVATEERS were causing serious problems for Spanish shipping off the Pacific coast of South America, leading the Spanish to seek additional lands in the western Pacific as colonies and naval bases.

Mendaña was given command of a four-ship fleet, with the Portuguese-born navigator PEDRO FERNÁNDEZ DE QUIRÓS as chief pilot. In June 1595, the expedition sailed from Callao, Peru, as on his earlier voyage. The 378 people aboard included soldiers and colonists. Among them was his wife, Doña Isabela Bareto de Mendaña, nicknamed "the Governess," who was accompanied by her three brothers.

On July 26, 1595, after about a month at sea, Mendaña came upon an island group he dubbed Las Marquesas de Mendoza, in honor of the viceroy of Peru, who had sponsored the expedition. The islands were afterward known as the Marquesas. At one of these islands, which he had called Magdalena Island, the Spanish massacred about 200 native islanders.

On his earlier voyage, Mendaña had incorrectly plotted the Solomon Islands, largely because an accurate technique for establishing longitude had not yet been perfected. Over the next several weeks, he tried in vain to locate them, until finally, short on supplies, he was compelled to stop in another South Pacific island group, the Santa Cruz chain. One of his ships, the *Almirante,* was lost while exploring these islands. The chain was claimed for Spain and an attempt was made to establish a colony on Ndeni. The Spanish discovered breadfruit growing there, becoming the first Europeans known to eat it.

After a few months, dissension among the members of Mendaña's colony erupted into a mutiny, resulting in some deaths. Soon afterward, Mendaña was taken ill and died. Command of the ships then went to Quirós. With food running short, the colonists opted to leave the Santa Cruz Islands and head for the Philippines. Under the command of

Quirós, they sailed for Manila on November 15, 1595. Many succumbed to SCURVY on this part of the voyage, although the Governess and her brothers survived on hoarded stores of food.

Alvaro de Mendaña was one of the earliest European navigators to search for Terra Australis and attempt to colonize the South Pacific. Nevertheless, many of the lands he explored were lost to subsequent European seafarers until the late 1760s. British naval officer PHILIP CARTERET, as well as French navigator LOUIS-ANTOINE DE BOUGAINVILLE, came upon the Solomon Islands during their separate Pacific explorations, and each thought he had located an unknown archipelago. In 1792, French explorer ANTOINE-RAYMOND-JOSEPH DE BRUNI, chevalier d'Entrecasteaux, finally determined that these islands were actually the Solomon Islands group, mistakenly charted by Mendaña two centuries earlier. The Marquesas were located again by JAMES COOK in 1774. San Francisco Island was not precisely charted until 1841, when it was found by Lieutenant CHARLES WILKES of the U.S. Navy, who named it Wake Island.

Mendoza, Antonio de (ca. 1490–1552)
Spanish colonial official in Mexico, organizer of expeditions to the American Southwest

Born in Spain, Antonio de Mendoza was a member of a noble family. In 1535, after holding high posts in the Spanish government, he was sent to Mexico as the first viceroy of New Spain, superceding the administration of HERNÁN CORTÉS, who had been ruling Mexico as governor since the conquest of 1519–21.

Soon after his arrival, Mendoza directed the construction of what became Mexico City on the site of the old Aztec capital. In 1539, he sent out the friar MARCOS DE NIZA and the slave ESTEVANICO to investigate the accounts of a wealthy Indian civilization north of Mexico reported by ÁLVAR NÚÑEZ CABEZA DE VACA. Soon afterward, Mendoza organized the first large-scale expedition to explore what is now the southwestern United States, commanded by FRANCISCO VÁSQUEZ DE CORONADO. He also dispatched HERNANDO DE ALARCÓN to explore the northern end of the Gulf of California, and he sponsored a seaward expedition along the coast of California under the command of JUAN RODRÍGUEZ CABRILLO.

After 15 years in Mexico, Mendoza was named as viceroy of Peru. He died after having served there for only one year.

Known as the "Good Viceroy," for his attempts to limit the exploitation of the conquered Indians, Antonio de Mendoza also supervised Spanish forces in putting down a revolt of the Indians in the Mixtón War of 1541 in the Nueva Galicia region of western Mexico. His administration provided a foundation for Spanish colonial rule in Mexico that endured for almost 300 years and fostered Spanish explorations northward into present-day California, Arizona, New Mexico, Texas, Oklahoma, and Kansas.

Mendoza, Pedro de (ca. 1487–1537)
Spanish conquistador in South America

Pedro de Mendoza was born at Gaudix in southern Spain. Born into a noble and wealthy family, he embarked on a military career as an officer in the army of Charles I of Spain (later Holy Roman Emperor Charles V) in campaigns on the Italian Peninsula.

In 1534, Mendoza was appointed as the first military and civil governor of the country between the Río de la Plata and the STRAIT OF MAGELLAN, a territory comprising most of what is now Argentina. Commissioned by Charles to colonize and explore the region, he outfitted at his own expense a large expedition of 14 ships and recruited more than 2,000 colonists, among them many Germans and Flemings.

On August 24, 1535, Mendoza and his expedition sailed from the port of Sanlúcar de Barrameda, near Seville, and by early January 1536 they had reached the estuary of the Río de la Plata. On February 22, 1536, he founded a city at the mouth of the Riachuelo River he called Santa María del Buen Aire (Our Lady of the Fair Wind), known afterward as Buenos Aires.

In addition to colonizing this vast region of South America, Mendoza had been instructed to explore inland to seek an overland route through the continent to Peru and to investigate stories of a source of gold and silver in the interior reported by English explorer SEBASTIAN CABOT. To this end, he sent out his lieutenants JUAN DE AYOLAS and DOMINGO MARTÍNEZ DE IRALA to travel up the Paraná River.

Pedro de Mendoza died at sea on a return voyage to Spain in 1537. Although his original settlement at Buenos Aires was abandoned two years later because of repeated attacks by Querandí Indians, it was reestablished in 1580 and endured to become one of the largest and most important cities of South America.

Menéndez de Avilés, Pedro (1519–1574)
Spanish naval officer, colonizer in Florida

Pedro Menéndez de Avilés was a native of Avilés, a port on the Bay of Biscay in Asturias, Spain. At the age of 13, he left his affluent family and embarked on a maritime career.

Menéndez rose to prominence in the Spanish navy. In 1549, Spanish king Charles I (Holy Roman Emperor Charles V) commissioned him to drive out the French pirates and PRIVATEERS then preying on ships in Spanish waters.

Pedro Menéndez de Avilés *(Library of Congress)*

In 1554, Menéndez was appointed captain general of the Indies Fleet. From 1555 to 1563, he made three trips to the Americas and commanded the convoys of treasure-laden galleons returning to Spain.

Menéndez was imprisoned for political reasons in 1563 but was released in 1565. On March 20, 1565, Spanish monarch Philip II named him *adelantado* (governor) and captain general of Florida.

Specifically, Menéndez's mission was to drive out the recently established French colony on the east coast of Florida. The Spanish considered the French presence there a direct threat to their ships returning with gold and silver from South America and Mexico. By spring 1565, pirates based at the French settlement of Fort Caroline, Florida, had already raided Spanish shipping in the Caribbean Sea.

On June 29, 1565, Menéndez, in command of 2,000 men on 11 ships, including soldiers, priests, slaves, and colonists, set out from Spain. Part of his fleet reached Puerto Rico in late July. After a daring crossing of the Caribbean Sea by way of a shortcut through the Bahamas, his five ships sighted the Florida coast on August 28, 1565, the feast day of St. Augustine. Menéndez soon located a suitable harbor, which he

called St. Augustine. He quickly set some of his party ashore and sailed northward along the coast. With him was a force of 700 soldiers.

On September 4, 1565, Menéndez made an unsuccessful assault on Fort Caroline, at the mouth of the St. Johns River, 40 miles up the coast from St. Augustine. The French ships, under JEAN RIBAULT, escaped.

Menéndez and his men returned to St. Augustine and completed construction of the settlement. Meanwhile, Ribault and his fleet attempted a seaward counterattack against St. Augustine. The French ships were wrecked in a hurricane, leaving Fort Caroline undefended. Taking advantage of this turn of events, Menéndez led his forces overland in an assault on the French colony. The unprotected settlement quickly fell to the Spanish, who massacred most of the Huguenot inhabitants. Colonial leader RENÉ GOULAINE DE LAUDONNIÈRE and artist JACQUES LE MOYNE DE MORGUES escaped, however.

Menéndez turned his attention to the survivors of Ribault's fleet. They had come ashore near present-day Cape Canaveral and were marching against St. Augustine to the north. Although his forces were outnumbered, Menéndez tricked the French into surrendering. He put most of his 500 prisoners to death, sparing only the Catholics among them. Ribault himself was executed. The site of this massacre became known as Matanzas, which means "slaughters" in Spanish.

Soon after destroying the French colony, Menéndez occupied Fort Caroline and renamed it San Mateo. During the next two years, he explored the Atlantic and Gulf coasts of Florida and established Spanish garrisons at Tampa Bay and Charlotte Harbor and on the Miami River and St. Lucie River. He also founded settlements on the coastal islands of present-day Georgia and the Carolinas, as well as on Chesapeake Bay to the north.

In 1566, Menéndez sent Captain Juan Pardo from Santa Elena Island (St. Helena Island) on the Carolina coast up the Broad River to explore for gold in the APPALACHIAN MOUNTAINS. Pardo and his party also explored the upper reaches of the Chattahoochee River in present-day Georgia.

In 1567, Menéndez was recalled to serve in the naval war against England. He made two brief visits to Florida in 1568 and 1571. He died in 1574, still serving in the Spanish navy.

The brutal campaign of Pedro Menéndez de Avilés against the French resulted in Spanish sovereignty in Florida. Unlike his predecessors, JUAN PONCE DE LEÓN and PÁNFILO DE NARVÁEZ, Menéndez succeeded in establishing a Spanish presence in Florida that provided a base from which the treasure route back to Spain could be protected. Although most of Menéndez's Florida posts were soon abandoned, St. Augustine endured, the first permanent non-Indian settlement in what is now the United States.

Mercator, Gerardus (Gerhardus Mercator, Gerard Mercator, Gerhard Kremer) (1512–1594)

Flemish cartographer

Born as Gerhard Kremer in the Flemish town of Rupelmonde, Gerardus Mercator adopted the Latin form of his name (after the fashion of 16th-century humanists) in 1530, during his university studies at Louvain, in what is now central Belgium. Among his studies at Louvain were mathematics and philosophy. Mercator also worked with engraver Gaspar a Myrica, under whom he learned basic graphic arts skills. In 1534, he embarked on a career as a cartographer, establishing his first workshop in the university town.

After producing a map of the Holy Land in 1537, Mercator was commissioned by King Charles I of Spain (Holy Roman Emperor Charles V) to create a map of the Earth and the heavens. In 1538, he published his first world map, in the style of the second century A.D. cartographer PTOLEMY.

Mercator constructed a world GLOBE in 1541, the details of which may have run contrary to Catholic Church doctrine, for in 1544, he was accused of heresy and imprisoned for seven months. In 1551, he produced a celestial globe. The following year, he moved to the German city of Duisberg, accepting a professorship in cosmography at that town's university.

Establishing a new cartography workshop at Duisberg, Mercator produced a six-part map of Europe in 1554, further establishing his reputation. In 1564, he was appointed as the official cartographer to the court of Wilhelm, the duke of Cleve.

Mercator's most famous work, a projection map of the world, was published in 1569. At that time, European cartographers were faced with the difficult task of depicting the explorations then being made by Spanish, French, English, and Portuguese mariners on two-dimensional maps. Mercator (and perhaps others of his age) approached the problem by projecting a globe of the world onto a cylinder wrapped around it. Although the extreme northern and southern regions of the world were distorted, the temperate, subtropical, and equatorial regions, where most travel and commerce took place, were accurately depicted. Moreover, the lines of LATITUDE AND LONGITUDE from the globe were projected onto Mercator's two-dimensional map as lines that intersected at right angles, enabling navigators to plot courses between two geographic points. Although the course set was not exactly a straight line between the points, a COMPASS would give a steady reading when sailing from one point to the other. As a result, Mercator's projection map of the world became extremely popular among both navigators and geographers.

Mercator was a proponent of the idea that the great landmasses of the Northern Hemisphere had to be counterbalanced by equally large continents in the Southern Hemisphere. He included on his map a region known as Terra Australis, the GREAT SOUTHERN CONTINENT, which he showed as taking up much of the as yet unexplored South Pacific Ocean. One curious feature of Mercator's 1569 projection map was that it showed the known coast of northern Australia as separate from the large island of New Guinea, although the Torres Strait that divides these two bodies of land had not yet been charted by Europeans.

Mercator became known as one of the foremost cartographers of his day. In 1580, a group of London merchants and navigators, including STEPHEN BOROUGH, consulted him on the feasibility of seeking a NORTHEAST PASSAGE from Europe to the Far East, around the top of Russia, an idea that he strongly supported.

Mercator's final project, a comprehensive world atlas, was begun in 1585 and completed in 1595, a year after his death, by his son Rumold.

The cartographic technique developed (if not entirely invented) by Gerardus Mercator, the MERCATOR PROJECTION, revolutionized mapmaking. His innovations in cartography resulted from the need to portray accurately the

Gerardus Mercator *(Library of Congress)*

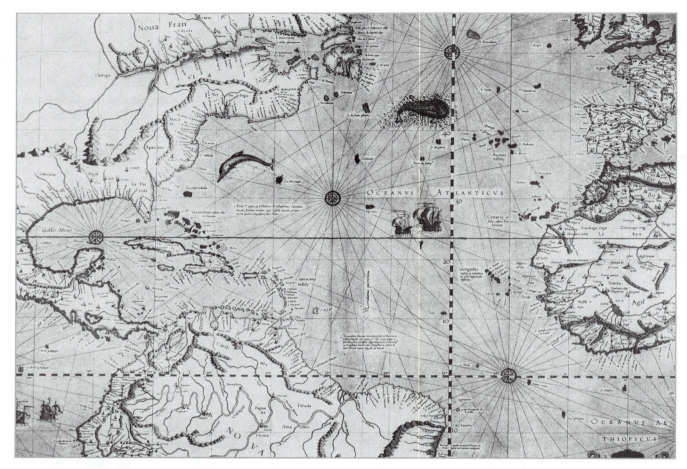

Detail of map of the world by Gerardus Mercator (1569) *(Library of Congress)*

new image of the world stemming from the great discoveries then being made. His maps, as practical aids to navigation, enabled explorers to expand geographic knowledge. Decades after MARTIN WALDSEEMÜLLER had applied the name "America" to the newly explored continent in the Southern Hemisphere, Mercator was the first to apply this name to the adjoining continent to the north, known afterward as North America. He was also the first to use the word *atlas* in reference to a group of maps.

Mertens, Karl Heinrich (1796–1830)
German physician, naturalist in South America, Alaska, and the South Pacific, in service to Russia

Karl Heinrich Mertens was born in the German city of Bremen, the son of noted botanist Francis Karl Mertens. The younger Mertens's own keen interest in natural history took him to Paris, where he studied at the Museum of Natural History. He soon established contacts with the leading naturalists of the day, including ALEXANDER VON HUMBOLDT, SIR JOSEPH BANKS, ROBERT BROWN, and JOHANN REIN-

HOLD FORSTER, each of whom had made great contributions in his respective field after conducting research in distant lands.

Mertens also studied medicine, graduating with a medical degree in 1820. Soon afterward, he moved to St. Petersburg, where he worked as a doctor. There he came to the attention of Russian navigator ADAM IVAN RITTER VON KRUSENSTERN of the St. Petersburg Academy of Sciences. With Krusenstern's assistance, Mertens won an appointment as surgeon and naturalist with FYODOR PETROVICH LITKE's scientific expedition to the Pacific Ocean.

Sailing from the Russian Baltic port of Kronstadt on the *Senyavin* in September 1826, Mertens spent the next three years on a voyage that took him to the coasts of Chile, Alaska, and the Kamchatka Peninsula of eastern SIBERIA. In the summer seasons, he conducted extensive botanical and other naturalist studies throughout the Caroline Islands of the western South Pacific.

Mertens returned to St. Petersburg in September 1829, having circumnavigated the world, as well as having collected more than 4,000 plant specimens. He also had conducted a study of crustaceans, discovering 150 new species, and identified 700 different types of insects. Moreover, he had produced more than 300 drawings relating to the natural history of the places he visited.

Soon after his return from the Pacific expedition, Mertens again joined Litke as surgeon and naturalist in a second voyage on the *Senyavin*, this time to the coast of Iceland. On this expedition, Mertens's medical skills were called upon to tend sick crew members when an epidemic of fever erupted on board. He himself became ill and died in September 1830, less than two weeks after returning to St. Petersburg.

One of Dr. Karl Heinrich Mertens's most significant contributions to science was his study of algae throughout the Pacific, from Chile to the Caroline Islands. By the time he had returned to St. Petersburg in 1829, he had accumulated the largest collection of algae specimens until that time.

Messerschmidt, Daniel Gottlieb (1685–1735)

German physician, naturalist in central Siberia, in service to Russia

Originally from the Prussian city of Danzig (present-day Gdańsk, Poland), Daniel Messerschmidt attended the University of Halle, where he studied medicine as well as geography, archaeology, and natural history.

Messerschmidt's diversified scientific background came to the attention of Czar Peter I (the Great) of Russia, who invited him to St. Petersburg in 1716. The Prussian doctor was then commissioned by the czar to undertake an extensive exploration into central SIBERIA. He was to study the geography of this vast unknown region, its plant and animal life, as well as the ethnography of the Siberian people. As a medical man, he was to note the diseases prevalent among the Siberians as well as the medicinal plants they used.

In 1719, Messerschmidt set out from St. Petersburg. After first traveling to Moscow, he made his way across the Ural Mountains to the western Siberian city of Tobolsk, from where he entered the lower Ob River region. He was soon assigned an assistant, a Swedish war prisoner named Tabbert (also known as Strahlenberg). During the next eight years, Messerschmidt covered a wide area of Siberia, from the Arctic regions of the lower Lena and Yenisey Rivers in the north to Lake Baikal and the upper Amur River in the south. While exploring the Tom River region, he located a complete mammoth skeleton, which he had transported back to St. Petersburg. His scientific work took him into the Lake Dalai Nor region of inner Mongolia. In the course of his explorations around Lake Baikal, he discovered significant deposits of mineral resources. Throughout his travels in Siberia, he made astronomical observations on the height of the NORTH STAR, and his findings were later applied by geographers to fix definite points in the great landmass.

In 1727, Messerschmidt returned to St. Petersburg with a collection of animal and plant specimens, plus drawings depicting the natural history and ethnography of central Siberia. He also obtained several ancient Tatar and Kalmyk manuscripts, which enabled him to deduce the connections between the various languages of the nomadic people of the Siberian steppes.

Messerschmidt wrote a 10-volume account of his Siberian explorations. He wrote in Latin, however, and the work was never translated or published; he thus found little support for further scientific work in Russia. He spent his remaining years in St. Petersburg in relative poverty and obscurity.

Although much of Daniel Messerschmidt's scientific work was overlooked in his lifetime, he is recognized as having initiated the Russian government's program of planned Siberian exploration. In addition, he provided the earliest accurate description of permafrost, an Arctic phenomenon in which the soil and subsoil remain permanently frozen to depths of several hundred feet.

Meyer, Hans (1858–1929) *German mountain climber, geographer in East Africa and South America*

Born in the central German city of Hildburghausen, Hans Meyer was the grandson of 19th-century publishing magnate and industrialist Joseph Meyer. In 1884, the younger Meyer entered his family's reference book publishing firm, Bibliographisches Institut, becoming its director the following year.

Meyer was a world traveler and mountaineer, who spent time in the late 1880s exploring German East Africa, the region comprising what is now Tanzania. In 1887 and 1888, he made two unsuccessful attempts at climbing MOUNT KILIMANJARO, Africa's highest mountain at 19,341 feet above sea level. On a third try in 1889, he made it to the top with the Austrian Ludwig Purtscheller.

Nine years later, Meyer returned to East Africa, where he undertook an extensive exploration of the region around Mount Kilimanjaro. In 1901, he was named as a member of the German Colonial Council, which then oversaw the administration of this part of Africa. In 1903, Meyer turned his attention to the ANDES MOUNTAINS of Ecuador, where he undertook geological studies of volcanoes and glaciation.

Meyer revisited German East Africa in 1911. In 1915, he accepted an appointment as professor of colonial geography at the University of Leipzig.

In his 1889 climb of Mount Kilimanjaro's highest point, the peak known as Kibo, Hans Meyer discovered a crater at the top, from which he determined that the highest mountain in Africa was an extinct volcano.

Middleton, Christopher (ca. 1700–1770)
British mariner in Hudson Bay

In his early maritime career, Christopher Middleton sailed with PRIVATEERS. Then, in the 1730s, he entered the service of the HUDSON'S BAY COMPANY, as second mate on the supply ship *Hannah;* soon afterward, he was given command of the vessel.

Middleton believed that HUDSON BAY was actually a strait whose western outlet provided access to a NORTHWEST PASSAGE to the Pacific Ocean. His ability as a mariner and his sailing experience in Hudson Bay brought him to the attention of the former surveyor general of Ireland, Arthur Dobbs, an outspoken critic of the Hudson's Bay Company's monopoly. Dobbs shared the view that a Northwest Passage could be found on the western side of Hudson Bay. Throughout the 1730s, Dobbs had challenged the Hudson's Bay Company to live up to the terms of its original charter and search for the Northwest Passage. By 1741, through contacts in the British Board of Trade and Plantations and in the Admiralty, Dobbs had succeeded in promoting an official naval expedition for that purpose.

Middleton offered to command the expedition, and, through Dobbs's influence, and with the approval of King George II, received the appointment. Outfitted with two naval vessels, the *Furnace* and the *Discovery,* Middleton sailed from England in June 1741. He and his men spent the following winter on the southwest shore of Hudson Bay near Prince of Wales Fort at the mouth of the Churchill River.

In June 1742, Middleton set out to explore northward. He soon came upon a large opening to the west, which, upon further exploration, proved to be a closed inlet, which he named Wager Bay after then first lord of the Admiralty, Sir Charles Wager. He continued northward into Roes Welcome Sound, which separates Southampton Island from the northwest coast of Hudson Bay. At the closed northern end of Roes Welcome Sound, Middleton came upon another opening, which also proved to be closed at its western end, and named it Repulse Bay.

Middleton reached Frozen Strait at the northern tip of Southampton Island before turning southward to reexamine the bay's west coast. Finding no evidence of a Northwest Passage in either the southern or northern sections of western Hudson Bay, he sailed back to England.

Later in 1742, in recognition of his explorations in Hudson Bay, Middleton was awarded the Copely Medal by the ROYAL SOCIETY, which had elected him as a member. In addition, his study of the magnetic variations of the compass he had observed in Hudson Bay appeared in the Royal Society's publication, *Philosophical Transactions.* Nevertheless, he received only scorn from his former sponsor, Dobbs, who accused him of having taken a bribe from the Hudson's Bay Company to fail in the search for the Northwest Passage.

Middleton retired from the Hudson's Bay Company in 1750. An expedition sent out by Dobbs under WILLIAM MOOR in 1746, along with other expeditions, revealed that Middleton had correctly surmised that Hudson Bay's west coast offered no outlet.

Captain Christopher Middleton commanded the first expedition in search of the Northwest Passage to be mounted by the British navy. He proceeded farther north along the west coast of Hudson Bay than had any European before him.

Miletus, Hecataeus of   See HECATAEUS OF MILETUS.

Miller, Alfred Jacob (1810–1874) *American artist on the Great Plains and in the northern Rocky Mountains*

Alfred Jacob Miller was born in Baltimore, Maryland, where his father was a grocer. He exhibited a talent for art and studied under Thomas Sully in Philadelphia. In 1833, Miller went to Europe to complete his formal art training, studying at the École des Beaux Arts in Paris, and also in Florence and Rome.

Back in Baltimore in 1834, Miller attempted to establish himself as a professional artist, specializing in portraits. He moved to New Orleans in 1837. Soon afterward, he met adventurer and hunter Sir William Drummond Stewart, a Scottish nobleman and former captain in the British army. Stewart engaged Miller to accompany him on an expedition to the Great Plains and ROCKY MOUNTAINS, during which he was to make sketches for later paintings of western scenes.

From New Orleans, Miller traveled with Stewart to St. Louis, where they joined up with an AMERICAN FUR COMPANY trade caravan and headed westward across the Great Plains, along the Oregon Trail, to Fort Laramie. Miller made a sketch of Fort Laramie as it appeared that summer. Miller and Stewart then crossed the Continental Divide via the SOUTH PASS and spent a month at the fur trappers' rendezvous in the Green River Valley in what is now western Wyoming. Miller made sketches of Native Americans and Rocky Mountain landscapes. More than 3,000 Snake Indians attended the Green River rendezvous that year, as well as mountain men such as CHRISTOPHER HOUSTON CARSON (Kit Carson) and JAMES BRIDGER, both of whom Miller had the opportunity to meet.

In fall 1837, Miller returned to New Orleans by way of St. Louis, and soon set to work producing oil paintings based on his western travels. The next year, he showed his paintings in Baltimore and New York. In 1840, he sailed to Scotland, where he stayed at Stewart's family home, Murthly Castle, and completed additional western pictures. In 1842, Miller moved back to Baltimore permanently and continued his artwork.

Alfred Jacob Miller's painting reflected a crucial turning point in the development of the American West. The Plains Indians, whose images he preserved in his art, were in the final decades of relatively peaceful coexistence and profitable trade with non-Indians. Over the next 30 years, the influx of settlers, along with the development of cattle ranching and railroads, greatly altered the Plains Indian way of life.

Milton, William-Wentworth Fitzwilliam
(Viscount Milton, Lord Milton) (1839–1877)
British traveler in the Canadian West
William-Wentworth Fitzwilliam, an English nobleman and descendant of the old and prominent Fitzwilliam family, was born in London and studied at Eton College and Cambridge University. He first visited the Canadian West in 1860, when he took part in a buffalo hunt in the region of the Red River in southern Manitoba.

In summer 1862, Viscount Milton accompanied the physician WALTER BUTLER CHEADLE on a journey across Canada in an attempt to find a direct east-west route to the Cariboo goldfields in eastern British Columbia. They crossed the ROCKY MOUNTAINS by way of Yellowhead Pass.

Back in England, Viscount Milton wrote and lectured about his experiences in the Canadian West and, with Cheadle, coauthored an account of their trans-Canada journey. It was first published in 1865. Starting that year, until 1872, he sat in the British House of Commons.

Viscount Milton, along with Walter Cheadle, helped establish a more direct route through the Canadian Rockies.

Mitchell, Sir Thomas Livingstone (1792–1855)
British army officer, government official in Australia
Thomas Mitchell was born in Craigend, a town in the former Stirlingshire county of central Scotland. As a teenager, he went to work for his uncle's coal-mining business, and when about 18, he enlisted in the British army. In 1810–13, Mitchell served in Portugal and Spain as a surveyor and draftsman in the Peninsular War under the command of Arthur Wellesley, duke of Wellington.

Mitchell left the army at the rank of major and, in 1827, he was appointed deputy surveyor general for New South Wales, Australia. In May 1828, the surveyor general of New South Wales, JOHN JOSEPH WILLIAM MOLESWORTH OXLEY, died, and Mitchell was appointed his successor.

In his first years as surveyor general, Mitchell supervised bridge- and road-building projects throughout New South Wales. Then, in 1831, spurred on by the explorations of CHARLES STURT into the interior, Mitchell organized a series of expeditions of his own, hoping to locate a great navigable northwestward-flowing river, which could be used as a trade link between New South Wales, the north coast of Australia, and the riches of India and Southeast Asia.

Mitchell heard from the Aborigines reports of just such a river, which they called Kindur. On his first two expeditions into the region of the upper Darling River in 1831–35, he made the European discovery of the Peel, Namoi, and Gwydir Rivers. In 1835, he made a concerted effort to determine the true course of the Darling River, believing that it flowed northwestward into the Gulf of Carpentaria more than 1,000 miles distant. Mitchell established a post on the Darling, Fort Bourke, from where he descended the river for about 300 miles, eventually becoming resigned to the fact that it did not turn northward. Losing two of his men in a native attack, he returned to Sydney.

On a third expedition in 1836, Mitchell searched for a connection between the Murray and Darling Rivers. After finding a junction between them, he pushed far to the south and came upon a large fertile region in the interior of what is now western Victoria, which he named "Australia Felix." On this expedition, he reached the south coast of Australia at Portland Bay and also climbed Mount Macedon.

In 1845, Mitchell mounted his largest expedition in an attempt to make the first crossing of the Australian continent, from Sydney to Port Essington, on the north coast near present-day Darwin. Soon after his departure, he received word that German explorer FRIEDRICH WILHELM LUDWIG LEICHHARDT had already succeeded in making the northwestern traverse from Darling Downs to the north coast. Instead of turning back, Mitchell went on to explore the central region of what is now Queensland and came upon large areas of previously uncharted lands suitable for agriculture and sheep raising.

On the return journey, Mitchell made the European discovery of a river, which he named Victoria in honor of the queen. The stream seemed to flow northwestward, leading Mitchell to speculate that he had at last found the northern river that would connect Joseph Bonaparte Gulf on the north coast with settled regions of southeast Australia. A follow-up expedition carried out in 1847 under his assistant EDMUND KENNEDY revealed that Mitchell's Victoria River was actually the Barcoo, which eventually flowed into the desert region around Lake Eyre to the southwest.

Mitchell returned to England in 1848, where he published his journals, received a knighthood, and was rewarded by the British government for locating new areas for agricultural settlement. He was back in Sydney in 1855, when his survey department came under investigation by a royal commission. He died of pneumonia later that year.

Sir Thomas Mitchell managed the official exploration of New South Wales, Victoria, and Queensland for 27 years. In that time, he personally undertook extensive explorations into the interior, which revealed much about the river system of eastern Australia. While he did not fulfill his goal of finding the great water route through the continent that would link Sydney with Asia, his investigations into the continent resulted in the European discovery of vast areas of fertile lands for future settlement.

Moffat, Mary (1795–1871) *British missionary in South Africa, wife of Robert Moffat, mother of Mary Moffat Livingstone*

Mary Moffat was born Mary Smith in Salford, near Manchester, England. Her family was deeply involved with Methodism, and two of her brothers became missionaries. Mary herself developed strong religious convictions in her education at the Moravian school in Fairfield.

In 1815, Mary first met ROBERT MOFFAT, who had come to work for her father's garden nursery in Dukinfield, near Manchester, where her family had settled. Although the two became engaged, Mary's parents objected to the match. The following, Robert Moffat sailed to South Africa to begin his work as a missionary.

By 1819, Mary had won her parents' consent to marry Robert Moffat, and she sailed to Cape Town. Soon after her arrival, she and Moffat were wed, and almost immediately the couple set out northward into the interior regions of Bechuanaland (present-day Botswana) as missionaries to the tribes of southern Africa. In 1825, the Moffats established the first Christian mission at Kuruman, on the edge of the Kalahari Desert.

In 1870, after a half century in Africa, Mrs. Moffat returned to England with her husband. They settled at Brixton, then a suburb of London, where she died the following year.

Mary Moffat accompanied her husband on his travels and explorations in Africa and, according to contemporary accounts, was a motivating force both for the missionaries who worked with her husband and for the natives to whom they ministered. While in Africa, she and her husband raised a family of two girls and one boy. In 1844, her eldest daughter, also named Mary (MARY MOFFAT LIVINGSTONE), married the Scottish missionary-doctor and African explorer DAVID LIVINGSTONE.

Moffat, Robert (1795–1883) *Scottish missionary in South Africa, husband of Mary Moffat, father of Mary Moffat Livingstone*

Robert Moffat was born at Ormiston in southern Scotland. As a child, he moved with his family to Falkirk, north of Glasgow, where his father, a customs officer, had been assigned. At the age of 14, after schooling in Falkirk, Moffat began an apprenticeship as a gardener, and, in 1812, he went to work on the estate of Scottish nobleman Lord Moray in Fifeshire.

Moffat moved south to England in 1813, and two years later, he obtained a position as gardener for James Smith at his nursery near Manchester. While there, he became engaged to Smith's daughter, Mary.

Moffat, who had come from a religious family, found himself drawn to Methodism in his first years in the Manchester area. He resolved to become a missionary, and in September 1816, he was accepted by the London Missionary Society. After his admission to the Methodist ministry, he was commissioned to undertake a mission to the tribes of South Africa; he sailed for Cape Town on the *Alacrity* in October 1816, arriving three months later.

Although he had intended to head northward beyond the settled district around the CAPE OF GOOD HOPE, Moffat was at first denied permission by Cape Town authorities to cross the frontier. During the next nine months, while waiting for authorization to proceed into Namaqualand, he studied the Afrikaans language.

In September 1817, Moffat was allowed to travel northward. He traveled first to Namaqualand on the Atlantic coast, from where he set out eastward into the Kalahari Desert, reaching as far as Griquatown and Lattakoo, near present-day Kimberly, South Africa. Moffat undertook several explorations north of Lattakoo before returning to Cape Town in 1819. He was joined there by Mary Smith, who had arrived from England, having won her parents' permission to marry him. The two were soon wed, and Moffat was appointed as superintendent of missions for Lattakoo, where the Moffats returned in March 1820.

By 1821, Moffat had established a mission settlement at Lattakoo. During this period, he studied native languages and undertook explorations into the Kuruman River region. An outbreak of tribal strife drove Moffat and his wife from Lattakoo in 1825, and they relocated their mission to the largely unsettled country along the Kuruman River.

Moffat pursued his missionary work at Kuruman for the next several years, undertaking a translation of the Old Testament into the Sechwana language. In 1830–31, he traveled to Cape Town, where he arranged to have the work printed, and returned to Kuruman with one of the first printing presses to be taken into the interior of Africa.

In 1835, Moffat accompanied a British scientific team in an expedition into the land of the Matabele people. Two years later, an influx of Boer settlers caused problems for Moffat and his native following, and he was compelled to leave the area. He traveled with his family to Cape Town, from where they sailed for England, arriving in June 1839.

Moffat published another edition of the New Testament, which he had translated into native African languages, as well as an account of his experiences as a missionary in Africa, *Labours and Scenes in South Africa* (1842). He also went on a lecture tour, in the course of which he met DAVID LIVINGSTONE, whom he inspired to embark on a career as a missionary in Africa.

Moffat and his wife returned to Africa in 1843, and, with Livingstone, reestablished the Kuruman mission. The following year, Moffat's eldest daughter, Mary, and Livingstone were married.

During the next decade, Moffat continued his missionary work and produced more translations into Sechwana of religious writings, including *The Pilgrim's Progress.* He also continued to explore the outlying regions around Kuruman, visiting the Highveld, the Drakensberg Escarpment, and the Transvaal, and traveling northeastward to the Zimbabwe River. In 1854, he joined British sportsmen James Chapman and Samuel Edwards in an expedition along the edge of the Kalahari Desert.

In 1870, Moffat and his wife returned to England, after nearly 50 years engaged in missionary work in Africa. In England, Moffat continued to lecture and promote missionary work. When David Livingstone's remains arrived at Southampton in 1874, it was Moffat who identified them. He later attended Livingstone's state funeral at Westminster Abbey, and, in 1876, he officiated at the unveiling of a statue of Livingstone in Edinburgh. In 1882, Moffat met with Zulu leader Ketchwayo during his visit to England.

In his missionary work, Robert Moffat was one of the first Europeans to venture into what is now Botswana. He made several long overland trips northward from Cape Town and was one of the earliest European explorers of the region around the Kalahari Desert. He is also known for the influence he had on David Livingstone.

Montecorvino, John of   See JOHN OF MONTECORVINO.

Montejo, Francisco de   (1508–1565)
Spanish conquistador in Mexico's Yucatán Peninsula, son of Francisco de Montejo y León
Francisco de Montejo the Younger was born in Salamanca, Spain, son of FRANCISCO DE MONTEJO Y LEÓN, veteran of the Spanish conquests of Panama and the Aztec Empire in Mexico.

In 1537, Montejo's father directed him to carry on the conquest of the Yucatán. The campaign, begun by the elder Montejo in 1528, had come to a halt two years earlier in the face of fierce resistance by the Maya Indians, who by 1535, had succeeded in driving all the Spaniards out of the region.

Montejo established a stronghold at the former Maya settlement of Champotan on the west coast of the Yucatán Peninsula. He then advanced northeastward, and by 1540, he had captured the ancient Maya stronghold of Kimpech, where he then founded a city known today as Campeche. From there, he penetrated into the interior of the peninsula and, in 1542, after taking control of most of western Yucatán, founded the city of Mérida on the ruins of another Maya city. By 1546, after suppressing a final uprising by a coalition of Maya tribes, he had the rest of the Yucatán Peninsula's eastern region firmly under Spanish control.

Montejo was appointed assistant governor of Yucatán and nearby Cozumel Island by his father in 1545. He settled in Mérida, which later became the principal city of the region and, after 1821, was capital of Mexico's Yucatán State.

Francisco de Montejo, part of the first wave of CONQUISTADORES in Mexico, participated in the subjugation of Indian peoples of the Yucatán, which opened the region to Spanish settlement.

Montejo y León, Francisco de
(ca. 1479–ca. 1549) *Spanish conquistador in Mexico and Central America, father of Francisco de Montejo*
Born in Salamanca, Spain, Francisco de Montejo was a member of a noble family. There are few details of his early years until 1514, when he sailed to the coast of Panama as a member of PEDRO ARIAS DE ÁVILA's expedition.

After a brief stay at Ávila's settlement at Nombre de Dios in Panama, Montejo went on to Cuba, where he entered the service of the island's colonial governor, DIEGO DE VELÁSQUEZ. In May 1518, he was given command of the soldiers who were sent under JUAN DE GRIJALVA to explore reports of a rich Indian civilization to the west. With Grijalva, Montejo explored the coast of Yucatán; he was among the first Europeans to learn of the Aztec Indian civilization of Mexico.

In 1519, Montejo served as an officer under HERNÁN CORTÉS in his expedition to the mainland of Mexico. Among the original landing party on the Yucatán Peninsula, he was later sent northward along the coast to discover a suitable landing site. He soon located a natural harbor where Cortés's ships were able to anchor. Cortés organized a permanent settlement, which he named Veracruz (true cross), and appointed Montejo as one of its administrators.

In July 1519, Montejo was sent back to Spain by Cortés to report personally to the Spanish monarch, Charles I (Holy Roman Emperor Charles V) on his contacts with the Aztec and to present him with gifts of gold, silver, and jewels acquired from the Indians. Charles appointed Montejo as governor of Veracruz.

Returning to Mexico in 1522, Montejo went on to assist Cortés in his conquest of the Aztec, leading the Spanish advance into Coatzacoalcos province, as far as the Gulf of Honduras and present-day Belize.

Montejo again returned to Spain in 1526, where he was commissioned to undertake the conquest of the Yucatán, which was then thought to be an island. In May 1528, he sailed from the port of Sanlúcar de Barrameda, near Seville, in command of a fleet of three ships and a force of 500 soldiers. His first attempt to subdue the Maya Indians from the east failed, and, in 1530, the CONQUISTADORES were forced to withdraw to Mexico.

In the meantime, Montejo succeeded in conquering the Tabasco region of southern Mexico, and, in 1531, he launched a second offensive against the Maya. This too met with little success in the face of stiff resistance. His men, disappointed at not finding wealth among the Maya comparable to the riches of the Aztec, deserted him in 1535, and he again returned to Mexico.

In 1540, Montejo's son, also named FRANCISCO DE MONTEJO, mounted a successful campaign that resulted in the total subjugation of the Maya and other native peoples of Yucatán.

The elder Montejo received the surrender of the Yucatán's most powerful native chief, Tutulxin, on January 23, 1541. The following year, he was appointed governor of Honduras, where he established the cities of Caballos and Comayagua. In 1547, he took charge of the Chiapas region of southern Mexico and became governor of Guatemala, where he founded the cities of New Sevilla and Olancho.

Montejo's colonial administration was investigated by a royal commission in 1546. To clear his name, he sailed to Spain in 1548, where he died the following year.

Francisco de Montejo served as one of Cortés's leading officers in the conquest of Mexico. He is credited with helping found Veracruz, one of the earliest permanent Spanish settlements on the North American mainland, and with initiating the conquest of the Yucatán, the last part of Mexico to fall under Spanish domination.

Moor, William (unknown–1765) *British mariner in Hudson Bay*

William Moor, who had served as a mate on HUDSON'S BAY COMPANY supply ships, was selected in 1746 to lead an expedition in search of an entrance to the NORTHWEST PASSAGE on the west coast of HUDSON BAY.

Moor was given command of the *Dobbs*, named after the enterprise's chief promoter, Arthur Dobbs, a politically well connected former Irish parliamentarian and surveyor general, who had won the support of the British Admiralty for this and a previous venture commanded by CHRISTOPHER MIDDLETON in 1741–42. A year before Moor sailed in 1746, the British Parliament had offered a prize of £20,000 to anyone who found the Northwest Passage. The expedition included another vessel, the *California*, commanded by Francis Smith, also a seafarer from the Hudson's Bay Company's supply fleet.

After wintering on the southwest shore of Hudson Bay at York Factory, Moor cruised northward along the bay's west coast and explored what first seemed to be a passage westward. Upon further exploration, the passage proved to be a closed-end bay, later known as Chesterfield Inlet. To the north, he made a thorough investigation of Wager Bay, located by Middleton in 1742. Using longboats, Moor and his men went more than 150 miles up Wager Bay, reaching Brown Lake at its western end, where they found the mouth of an unnavigable stream. Finding no other major openings to the west, Moor and his ships returned to England.

William Moor's expedition of 1746–47 served to convince many English navigators and geographers that Hudson Bay was not the gateway to the Northwest Passage. In the decades that followed, maritime explorers seeking the elusive waterway through North America concentrated their efforts on the coast of the Pacific Northwest.

Moorcroft, William (1765–1825) *British veterinarian in central Asia*

William Moorcroft, of Lancashire, England, studied medicine at the Liverpool Infirmary and, while still a student, was called upon to help determine the cause of a livestock epidemic known as the Derbyshire Cattle Plague of 1783. The experience led him to pursue a career in veterinary medicine, for which he went to France for additional training.

Moorcroft settled in London and developed a highly successful practice as an animal doctor. Then, in the late 1790s, he began to suffer financial losses as a result of problems arising from a patent he had obtained for a mechanical horse-shoeing process. In 1808, he accepted a position as a veterinary surgeon with the British-controlled Bengal government in northeastern India, caring for Bengal army horses; he also was engaged as the superintendent of the BRITISH EAST INDIA COMPANY's horse-breeding operations near the city of Kanpur.

It was in connection with his duties as an army veterinarian and horse breeder for the British East India Company that Moorcroft first became involved in the exploration of central Asia. In an effort to improve the quality of the native cavalry horses, he sought to travel overland into Turkistan to acquire breeding stock from the central Asian steppes. In 1812, he accompanied British army officer HYDER JUNG HEARSEY on an expedition, undertaken as part of the British government's Great Trigonometrical Survey of India, in which they searched for the source of the GANGES RIVER and crossed the HIMALAYAS into Tibet.

In 1819, Moorcroft embarked on a trade mission northwestward from Calcutta, seeking to open the independent states of northern India to trade with the British East India Company. Accompanied by a young English geologist, George Trebeck, he traveled to the city of Leh in the Ladakh region (now part of Kashmir), where he remained for more than two years, establishing diplomatic and commercial ties. In 1822, the company showed its displeasure at his overly long stay in Leh by suspending him from its payroll.

Undaunted, Moorcroft set out to implement his plan to obtain larger and stronger horses in Turkistan for the Bengal Army. He had first intended to travel by way of western China but he was denied permission to cross the border. Instead, he set out from Leh for Kashmir, where he arrived in early November 1822. While there, he arranged to send back several live "shawlwool goats," whose offspring eventually reached England.

From Kashmir, Moorcroft and Trebeck traversed the Punjab region of what is now northern Pakistan on a route not traveled by Europeans in modern times, and reached Peshawar. After crossing the Hindu Kush range and the KHYBER PASS, then following the Kabul River, they reached Kabul, Afghanistan. Moorcroft then traveled to the Turkistani kingdom of Bukhara, again through country not visited by Europeans since the days of ALEXANDER THE GREAT. In Bukhara, he met with the region's king and sold a shipment of trade goods.

In August 1825, Moorcroft set out from Bukhara for the city of Meymaneh on the northern Afghani border, hoping to find the finest horses in the world. While en route, he was captured by bandits. He died soon afterward, either from the effects of poison or from fever. His body was transported to the city of Balkh, where he was buried. Trebeck died of fever not long afterward at the Afghani city of Mazar.

In his 1812 expedition with Hearsey, William Moorcroft became one of the first Englishmen to cross the Himalayas. His account of this journey was published in England in the journal *Asiatic Researches* in 1816. At the time of his death in Afghanistan in 1825, he was still under suspension by the British East India Company, a fact that later led to a dispute over who actually had a claim to the journals of his last expedition. They remained unpublished for more than 20 years, and later British travelers from India, covering much of the same territory through which Moorcroft had already explored, mistakenly believed they were the first Europeans to visit northern Afghanistan and the Turkistan region. Finally, in 1841, the ROYAL GEOGRAPHICAL SOCIETY published Moorcroft's account of the six years he spent in northern Pakistan and Turkistan, entitled *Travels in the Himalayan Provinces of Hindustan and the Punjab, from 1819 to 1825*. Even though he did not obtain the Asian horses for the Bengal army as planned, the "shawlwool" goats he sent back had a great impact on the British woolen industry and led to the introduction into western markets of what is known today as cashmere (Kashmir) wool.

Moreno, Francisco (1827–ca. 1905)

Argentine naturalist in the Andes Mountains and Patagonia

Born in Buenos Aires, Francisco Moreno attended Argentina's University of Córdoba, then went on to the University of Buenos Aires, graduating in 1854 as a doctor of natural science.

Moreno became a professor in the department of natural history at the University of Buenos Aires, where he concentrated in anthropology. In 1872, he undertook the first of a series of explorations, which would take him through much of the little-known regions south and west of Buenos Aires.

In 1876–77, Moreno traveled into the southern Andes Mountains and Patagonia to study the life and culture of the region's native peoples. After exploring Lake Nahuel Haupí, he continued southward, and on February 14, 1877, he became the first non-Indian to see Lake San Martín; two weeks later, he explored Cerro Chaltel (Mount Fitzroy).

On his second Patagonian expedition in 1880, Moreno was taken captive by the Tehuelche Indians (the "fabled Patagonian giants" reported by FERDINAND MAGELLAN and other earlier explorers of South America). He managed to escape just before his captors planned to kill him.

In 1882–83, Moreno undertook his most extensive exploration of the ANDES MOUNTAINS, traveling southward along the length of the mountain range, from Bolivia into the frontier region between Chile and Argentina. In 1884–85, he explored southwestward into the region south of Argentina's Río Negro, and into the Andean country around Lake Buenos Aires.

Francisco Moreno wrote many books based on his explorations into southern Argentina and the Andes Mountains. He was named chief of the Argentine government commission on the exploration of the country's southern territories and became director of Buenos Aires's anthropological museum. His work carried on the tradition of scientific study of the natural history of Patagonia begun by CHARLES ROBERT DARWIN and GEORGE CHAWORTH MUSTERS.

Morgues, Jacques Le Moyne de See LE MOYNE DE MORGUES, JACQUES.

Morozko, Luka (Luka Moroskoi)

(unknown–ca. 1699) *Russian Cossack in eastern Siberia*

In the late 1690s, the Russian Cossack Luka Morozko participated in the exploration and conquest of northeastern SIBERIA. Morozko served under VLADIMIR VASILYEVICH ATLASOV at Anadyr, which at that time was Russia's main settlement on the Pacific coast of Siberia, located at the mouth of the Chukchi Peninsula's Anadyr River. In 1696, under the direction of Atlasov, Morozko led a detachment of 16 Cossacks to investigate reports of a land to the south rich in fur and minerals. Morozko and his men penetrated the Kamchatka Peninsula, the only part of Siberia still unknown to Europeans, exploring along its west coast as far as the Tigil River.

Back at Anadyr later that year, Morozko reported to Atlasov on his findings, including accounts he had heard of the Kuril Islands, a chain of islands that stretch off the southern tip of Kamchatka, all the way to northern Japan. Starting in 1697, Morozko took part in Atlasov's campaign to bring the newly explored Kamchata Peninsula under Russian control. He was killed in about 1699 in a battle with the Kamchadal natives of eastern Kamchatka.

With Luka Morozko's penetration of the Kamchatka Peninsula in 1696, the full extent of Russia's vast Siberian domain was revealed.

Moscoso, Luis de (Luis de Moscoso de Álvara, Luis de Moscoso de Alvarado, Luys Moscoso)

(fl. 1530s–1540s) *Spanish conquistador in the American Southeast and Southwest*

Luis de Moscoso was born at Zafra in southwestern Spain, the son of a local government official. From 1530 to 1535, Moscoso, having become a professional soldier, served as an officer under PEDRO DE ALVARADO in campaigns of conquest in present-day Guatemala and in the northern Inca province of Quito, part of present-day Ecuador.

In April 1538, Moscoso left Spain with HERNANDO DE SOTO's expedition to explore Florida and adjacent lands for new sources of wealth. He sailed with de Soto's fleet, in command of the GALLEON *Concepcíon,* and after a long stopover in Cuba, landed with the expedition in the Tampa Bay area in May 1539. As de Soto's *maestro de campo,* or second in command, Moscoso undertook reconnaissance missions ahead of the main body of Spanish forces as they traveled through what is now northwestern Florida and into the southern APPALACHIAN MOUNTAINS of present-day Georgia, the Carolinas, and Tennessee. He was frequently sent ahead to confer with local native leaders and to announce de Soto's arrival.

In fall 1540, Moscoso warned de Soto that the Creek Indians were planning to attack the Spaniards while they were encamped near present-day Mobile, Alabama. His warning went unheeded, and although de Soto and his forces were able to repel the Indians, they suffered losses in both men and equipment. De Soto replaced Moscoso as chief lieutenant with Baltasar Gallegos following a defeat at the hands of the Chickasaw Indians near present-day Pontotoc, Mississippi, in March 1541. Nevertheless, as de Soto was dying of fever in May 1542, he appointed Moscoso as his successor.

Moscoso tried, without much success, to convince local Indian leaders that de Soto had not really died but had ascended into heaven and would soon return. For this reason, he had his men weight de Soto's body with rocks and dispose of it secretly in the MISSISSIPPI RIVER.

After conferring with his officers, Moscoso determined that the expedition, with severe losses in men, livestock, food, and equipment, was in no condition to continue the quest for riches among the Indians, and he decided to lead survivors to safety in New Spain (Mexico). In late spring 1542, from a site near what is now Texarkana, Arkansas, he led them westward into eastern Texas. From Indians in Texas, Moscoso heard legend-like accounts of ÁLVAR NÚÑEZ CABEZA DE VACA and his companions, who had wandered through much of Texas and the American Southwest in the early 1530s.

By fall 1542, after reaching as far westward as the Trinity and Brazos Rivers, near the present-day Dallas–Fort Worth area, Moscoso abandoned his attempt to reach Mexico overland across the seemingly endless southern plains. He led his men back eastward along the Arkansas River and returned to the Mississippi River, where the expedition wintered in 1542–43, near present-day Natchez, Mississippi. While there, seven crude barges were built under the direction of a Genoese shipwright and, on July 2, 1543, Moscoso and his men sailed down the Mississippi River into the Gulf of Mexico, then followed the Gulf Coast southward. After a voyage of 52 days, they reached the mouth of the Pánuco River, near the newly established Spanish settlement of Tampico, Mexico, on September 10, 1543. Reequipped with food and clothing, they walked from there to Mexico City, where Moscoso was received by the Spanish viceroy, ANTONIO DE MENDOZA, to whom he presented an official narrative of the expedition, written by Luis Hernández de Biedma and sent back to King Charles I in Spain. Of the more than 600 men who had started out with de Soto, only 311 returned to Mexico with Moscoso.

As de Soto's second in command and as his successor, Moscoso had covered more than 4,000 miles of territory through what is now the southeastern United States and eastern Texas and had commanded the first vessels to be sailed by Europeans down the Mississippi River into the Gulf of Mexico.

Luis de Moscoso's explorations, taken together with those of de Soto and Coronado, provided Spain with much information on the interior of the vast country north and east of Mexico. Yet Moscoso's return to Mexico marked the end of European exploration into the lower Mississippi River Valley and the southeastern United States for 140 years. The next major European penetration into the region did not occur until the 1682 expedition of RENÉ-ROBERT CAVELIER DE LA SALLE.

Mothe, Antoine Laumet de la   See LA MOTHE, ANTOINE LUMET DE.

Mouhot, Henri (Alexandre-Henri Mouhot)

(1826–1861) *French naturalist in Southeast Asia*

Henri Mouhot was born at Montbeliard in eastern France, the son of an official in the French government. With his father's support, Mouhot embarked on a career of full-time scholarship. In the early 1850s, after studies in natural history at various European universities, as well as philology studies in Russia, he became involved in an early form of photography. He traveled throughout Europe with his brother, producing daguerreotype pictures of well-known natural scenes and works of art.

In 1856, Mouhot settled on Jersey in the Channel Isles, with his English wife, a descendant of the Scottish explorer of Africa, MUNGO PARK. Mouhot continued his work as a naturalist, concentrating on ornithology and on conchology, the study of shells. Not long afterward, inspired by reading about the kingdom of Siam (present-day Thailand), Mouhot resolved to attempt a scientific expedition into the upper Mekong River region of Southeast Asia, an area little known to Europeans.

With the support of Great Britain's ROYAL GEOGRAPHICAL SOCIETY and Royal Zoological Society, Mouhot sailed to Singapore in April 1858, from where he traveled to Bangkok and met with the king of Siam. Mouhot was one of the first Europeans to report that the native people of Siam called themselves and their land "Thai," meaning "free" in the Thai language.

Mouhot made his first scientific foray into the jungles of Southeast Asia in October 1858 on a voyage up the Mae Nam River, during which he collected specimens of fish, reptiles, and mammals. After several weeks, he returned to Bangkok. That December, he set out for Phnom Penh, capital of the neighboring kingdom of Cambodia. He was also received by this country's ruler.

Soon afterward, Mouhot embarked on his first expedition up the Mekong River. West of the river, in early 1860, he came upon the ruins of the ancient temples at Angkor. Extending over 100 square miles, they comprise the largest complex of religious buildings ever constructed. Erected from about A.D. 880 to 1434 by the Khmers, they had since been abandoned and overgrown with dense jungle. Mouhot sent back to England and France a written description and sketches of the site.

In October 1861, Mouhot traveled into northern Laos and made a study of the region's animal life. He visited additional sites of ancient ruins, accompanied at times by French missionary priests. He also explored the upper Mekong River and some of its tributaries. While traveling through the Plain of Jars region of northern Laos, he was stricken with tropical fever, dying near Louangphrabang on November 10, 1861.

Henri Mouhot's account of his explorations in Southeast Asia, *Journey to the Kingdoms of Siam, Cambodia, Laos and Parts of Indochina,* was first published in France in 1863. The Angkor ruins were hailed in Europe as one of the greatest archaeological finds of all time. Moreover, Mouhot's explorations in Laos immediately prompted the French government to sponsor efforts to find the source of the Mekong River. The most important of these efforts was the Mekong River Expedition of 1866, undertaken by ERNEST-MARC-LOUIS DE GONZAGUE DOUDART DE LAGRÉE and FRANÇOIS GARNIER.

Muir, John (1838–1914) *American naturalist, preservationist, writer*

John Muir was born in Dunbar, Scotland. When he was 11 years old, his family immigrated to the United States and settled on a farm in Portage, Wisconsin. He attended the University of Wisconsin in 1860–63, leaving before obtaining a degree. He pursued an interest in natural science on walking trips through the countryside, studying geography, geology, and wildlife. In 1867, he hiked from Indianapolis, Indiana, to the Gulf of Mexico.

In 1868–74, Muir spent time in the West, exploring and studying Yosemite Valley and the peaks of the Sierra Nevada in California and Glacier Bay in Alaska. In 1880, he settled on a fruit ranch in Martinez, California, and became successful in horticulture. In the 1890s, he traveled to and studied the forests of Australia, Africa, Europe, and South America.

Muir became active politically as a preservationist of wilderness areas and wildlife. His efforts led to the founding of Yosemite and Sequoia National Parks in 1890. He also was one of the founders of the Sierra Club in 1892, an environmental organization still active at present. His books include *The Mountains of California* (1894), *Our National*

John Muir *(Library of Congress)*

Parks (1901), *My First Summer in the Sierra* (1911), and *The Yosemite* (1912). His journals, *Travels in Alaska* (1915) and *A Thousand Mile Walk to the Gulf* (1916), were published posthumously.

John Muir's work was central to the shaping of the environmental movement in the United States and around the world and influenced President Theodore Roosevelt to set aside national forest reserves, national parks, and national monuments. Muir Glacier, which Muir located in Glacier Bay, Alaska, was named after him. In 1964, Muir's California home, some of his fruit orchards, and his gravesite were designated the John Muir National Historic Site.

Munk, Jens Eriksen (Eriksen Munk, Eriksen Munke, Jens Muncke) (1579–1628) *Danish mariner in Hudson Bay*

Jens Munk was born in Barbo on the south coast of Norway, at that time under the sovereignty of Denmark. He went to sea when very young, serving as a merchant sailor in Portugal and Brazil, as well as with the Dutch merchant fleet. By the age of 25, he had become an experienced mariner and shipowner.

In 1609, Munk attempted a voyage to Novaya Zemlya, but, in the Barents Sea, he lost his ship to the ice. On Kolguyev Island, he and his men constructed a boat from the wreckage and used it to reach Archangel 580 miles away. From there, they returned to Copenhagen.

Munk was commissioned as a captain in the Danish navy in the Kalmar War of 1611–13 with Sweden. Afterward, he remained in service to Danish king Christian IV, carrying out a campaign against PIRATES along the North Sea coast of Norway. Munk was one of the first Danes to recognize the profits to be gained from Arctic whaling, and, in about 1618, he established the first Danish whaling facility on Spitsbergen (present-day Svalbard).

In 1619, Munk was directed by Christian IV to explore HUDSON BAY's west shore for a NORTHWEST PASSAGE to India. King Christian, known as the Danish Sailor King for his efforts to make Denmark a maritime power, decided upon this expedition after learning of the explorations of the Greek seafarer known as JUAN DE FUCA, who reportedly had located the STRAIT OF ANIAN, a fabled opening on the west coast of North America providing a passage between the Pacific and Atlantic Oceans.

Outfitted with two naval vessels, the frigate *Unicorn* and a sloop the *Lamprey,* Munk and a combined crew of 63 men sailed from Denmark in May 1619. Following a course north of the Shetlands, they passed the Faeroe Islands and sighted Cape Farewell, GREENLAND's southern tip, in late June 1619. Sailing northwestward across Davis Strait, Munk and his ships entered closed-end Frobisher Bay, which they mistook for Hudson Strait.

Although Munk soon realized his error and managed to locate the entrance to Hudson Strait, he then sailed too far to the south, into Ungava Bay on the north coast of present-day Quebec, mistaking it for HUDSON BAY. He went ashore on land he called "Rinsund," where he met with a band of Inuit (Eskimo) and hunted reindeer. He took possession of the region in the name of King Christian.

By August 1619, Munk had managed to correct his navigational errors and negotiate the length of Hudson Strait, rounding Cape Wolstenholme and Digges Island. He then made a southwestward crossing of the bay, reaching the estuary of the Churchill River, near present-day Churchill, Manitoba, in early September 1619. The ships were beached to protect them from storms, and Munk and his men settled in for the winter.

During his stay, Munk undertook the first scientific studies to be made in Hudson Bay, noting bird migrations, making astronomical observations, and recording his own speculations on the origins of the icebergs he had encountered while negotiating Davis and Hudson Straits. By noting the exact time of an eclipse on December 20, 1619, and later correlating it with the time the same eclipse was observed in Paris, he was able to determine accurately the exact meridian of longitude of his winter base at Churchill.

By mid-January 1620, SCURVY had begun to take its toll among the crew; by the end of June 1620, only Munk and two others remained alive. Some sources suggest that the crew may have actually succumbed to an outbreak of trichinosis resulting from eating undercooked polar bear meat. Munk had commented in his journal that he preferred his meat cooked well-done, a factor that may have saved his life.

Munk and the other two survivors recovered by eating grass and other plants on shore. They refloated the *Lamprey* and sailed back to Norway, which they reached in September 1620. From there, Munk returned to Denmark.

Despite the disastrous outcome of his Hudson Bay voyage, Munk planned a second expedition to the Churchill River region, where he intended to establish a fur-trading colony. Called back to naval service in 1623, he never did return to Hudson Bay. He served on the Weser River in the Thirty Years' War of 1618–48, reaching the rank of admiral in 1625. He died three years later at the age of 49.

Jens Munk's 1619–20 expedition to Hudson Bay was the only known Danish attempt to find the Northwest Passage. He and his men were the first to winter in the Churchill River estuary in 1625, a region that had been visited but not thoroughly explored by SIR THOMAS BUTTON in 1612–13. Munk's account of his voyage and the harrowing winter he spent on Hudson Bay was published in 1624. His map was the first to depict Hudson Bay in its entirety and identify it as a single inland sea, which he had named the Novum Mare Christian (new Christian sea). European exploration of Hudson Bay resumed 10 years after Munk's expedition, with the 1631 voyages of THOMAS JAMES and LUKE FOXE.

Musters, George Chaworth (1841–1879)

British naval officer in South America

Born in Naples, Italy, George Musters was the son of a former British army officer, whose family was among the landed gentry of Nottinghamshire, England. Orphaned by the time he was four, he was raised by his uncles, one of whom, Robert Hammond, had sailed the Pacific Ocean and the coasts of South America on the *Beagle* with Admiral ROBERT FITZROY.

Musters underwent schooling on the Isle of Wight, then at a naval academy near Portsmouth; he entered the British navy as a cadet in 1854. His first assignment took him to the Black Sea, where he participated in naval actions in the Crimean War of 1853–56. By the war's end, at the age of 15, he had been awarded medals for valor by both the British and Turkish governments.

In 1861, Musters was promoted to lieutenant while serving on Queen Victoria's yacht; soon afterward, he was assigned to the *Stromboli,* on which he took part in a five-year cruise in South American waters. While ashore at Rio de Janeiro in 1862, he and a midshipman from the *Stromboli* scaled Sugarloaf Mountain and, as a prank, planted a British flag at the mountain's peak. The flag remained there for several years, despite efforts by Brazilian authorities to remove it.

Musters purchased lands around Montevideo, Uruguay, where he established a sheep ranch while still with the British navy. Leaving active naval service at the rank of commander by 1869, he settled briefly in the Falkland Islands in the Atlantic Ocean. He became interested in the natives of Patagonia, the Tehuelche, whom FERDINAND MAGELLAN and other explorers had described as giants.

In 1869, Musters embarked on an expedition to explore the little-known interior regions of Patagonia and to study the life and culture of the Patagonian natives. From the Falklands, he first sailed to Punta Arenas on the STRAIT OF MAGELLAN. He then traveled northward to Santa Cruz on the southeast coast of Argentina. Accompanied by a band of

Tehuelche (who came to regard him as their king), he traced the course of the Río Chico westward almost to its source, then followed the eastern slopes of the southern ANDES MOUNTAINS northward. After crossing Argentina's Pampas, he followed the Río Negro to its mouth on the South Atlantic, which he reached in 1870, having covered more than 1,400 miles through the interior of southernmost South America.

Musters returned to England, where he wrote an account of his journey, entitled *At Home With the Patagonians, a Year's Wanderings on Untrodden Ground from the Straits of Magellan to the Rio Negro.* It was published in London in 1871. The work provided his contemporaries with a full description of the customs of the Tehuelche, distinguishing them from the Araucanian tribes to the north and the Tierra del Fuego people to the south. In addition, it added much to the geographic knowledge of the interior of southern Argentina, which until that time had remained largely unknown to Europeans. Musters's achievements in exploring South America were officially recognized by the ROYAL GEOGRAPHICAL SOCIETY, which awarded him a gold watch in 1872.

Musters made a visit to Vancouver Island, British Columbia, where he lived among the Indians and studied their life and culture. Afterward, he returned to South America, planning to make a west-to-east crossing of the continent from Chile to Patagonia. Circumstances led him to abandon this venture, however. He soon married the daughter of a British family living in Bolivia and settled there, traveling throughout that country and adjoining regions.

In 1876, Musters returned to his family's home, Wiverton Hall, in Nottinghamshire. Two years later, he was appointed Great Britain's diplomatic representative in Mozambique, but he died in early 1879 before he could travel there.

Nicknamed the "King of Patagonia" for his exploits among the Tehuelche, George Musters provided one of the first modern descriptions of the aboriginal people of southern Argentina. Lake Musters, near the headwaters of the Chico River, was named in honor of his explorations along the southeastern slopes of the Andes and the upper Chico River region.

Mylius-Erichsen, Ludwig (Ludvig Erichsen)
(1872–1907) *Danish explorer in Greenland*

Born in Denmark, Ludwig Mylius-Erichsen commanded the Danish Greenland Expedition of 1902–04. His team of anthropologists, scholars, and scientists traveled to GREENLAND's northwest coast, at the upper end of Melville Bay, where they made a study of the language and customs of the Inuit. They also explored the uncharted shores of the Hayes Peninsula, near what is now Thule Air Force Base, Greenland, reaching as far north as Cape York.

In an expedition aboard the Arctic exploring vessel *Danmark,* Mylius-Erichsen led another Danish scientific expedition to Greenland's northeast coast in 1906. He reached a point farther north than the one achieved by KARL CHRISTIAN KOLDEWEY in a 1869–70 expedition to eastern Greenland. In 1907, Mylius-Erichsen reached the Northeast Foreland, a peninsula jutting out of Greenland's northeastern corner. While exploring Northeast Foreland, he and two members of his expedition perished of cold, hunger, and exhaustion.

The peninsula Ludwig Mylius-Erichsen located at 82° north latitude, Greenland's northeasternmost point, was renamed Mylius-Erichsen Land in his honor. One of the survivors of the expedition was the German meteorologist and geophysicist ALFRED LOTHAR WEGENER, who undertook subsequent explorations in Greenland.

N

Nachtigal, Gustav (1834–1885) *German physician, diplomat in North and West Africa*

Gustav Nachtigal was born in the Bavarian town of Eichstatt, the son of a Lutheran pastor. He studied medicine at several German universities and eventually became an army surgeon.

With the onset of tuberculosis, Nachtigal traveled to Algeria in 1862 to recover his health in the dry desert climate. While there, he made his first explorations into the SAHARA DESERT. Two years later, he was appointed court physician to the bey of Tunis. Learning enough Arabic to travel among the Arabs as one of them, he took part in a yearlong military expedition with the Tunisian army against marauding desert nomads.

In 1868, the German explorer GERHARD ROHLFS of North Africa contacted Nachtigal in Tunis, arranging a commission from Wilhelm I of Prussia for a diplomatic mission to the Sultanate of Bornu in what is now northeastern Nigeria. Nachtigal set out from Tripoli and, traveling southward into the Fezzan, reached the desert city of Murzuk in southwestern Libya, where he was joined for a short time by the Dutch woman explorer of North Africa, ALEXANDRINE PETRONELLA FRANCINA TINNÉ. From Murzuk, Nachtigal headed southeastward across nearly 500 miles of desert into the 11,000-foot-high Tibesti range of what is now northwestern Chad, becoming the first European to visit the region.

Nachtigal eventually reached Kukawa, the capital of Bornu, where he presented the sultan with gifts from the Prussian monarch, among which was a type of portable organ known as a harmonium. He then proceeded to Lake Chad, disguised as a Muslim pilgrim, and after exploring the Chari River, he journeyed to TIMBUKTU and into central Africa before traveling into the eastern Saharan states of Wadai, Darfur, and Kordofan. He then made a southeastward crossing of the Sahara Desert. By summer 1874, he had reached Khartoum on the White Nile River, from where he traveled to Cairo, then back to Europe. In Germany, Nachtigal wrote a three-volume account of his explorations in North Africa, *Sahara and Sudan,* published from 1879 to 1889.

Nachtigal became German general consul of Tunisia in 1884, soon after it had become a French protectorate. After a subsequent appointment as German imperial commissioner to West Africa, he headed a diplomatic expedition to Togoland and Cameroon, which by then were among the last regions of West Africa not yet under European colonial rule. In July 1884, Nachtigal successfully negotiated a treaty with the native ruler of Togoland, making the region a German colony. In the same month, he entered into an agreement with the tribal leaders of Cameroon under which that land became a German protectorate. While returning to Germany, he died at sea off the Ivory Coast and was buried ashore at Grand-Bassam.

Gustav Nachtigal was the first European to make a southeastward crossing of the Sahara and travel through the region between Lake Chad and the White Nile. He revealed much about the relationship between the dominant geographic features of the eastern and western regions of North Africa.

Naddod (Naddod the Viking, Naddoc)

(fl. 860s–870s) *Norse mariner in Iceland*

Naddod the Viking appears in several traditional Norse historical accounts as a seafarer. In about A.D. 860 (according to events reconstructed from one version of the Norse *Book of the Settlements*), Naddod sailed from Norway on a voyage to the Faeroe Islands. After being driven by a storm about 250 miles northwest of the northernmost of the Faeroes, he came upon the east coast of ICELAND.

Naddod and his crew landed at a point that may have been near Reydharfjordhur and briefly explored the surrounding countryside. They scaled a mountain, hoping to find some sign of human habitation. Failing to do so, they set sail for the Faeroes. As they left, snow began to fall, whereupon Naddod and his men named the land Snaeland, meaning "snow land" in Old Norse.

In another version of the *Book of the Settlements,* the Swedish Viking GARDAR SVARSSON is credited with landing in Iceland at about the same time as Naddod. Although one of them may have been the first Norseman to reach Iceland, traditional Irish sources suggest that Irish monks may have made voyages there earlier.

Nain Singh   See SINGH, NAIN.

Nansen, Fridtjof (1861–1930) *Norwegian zoologist, oceanographer, statesman in Greenland and the Arctic Ocean*

Fridtjof Nansen was born in Store Froen, Norway, near Christiania (present-day Oslo). In 1880, he entered the University of Oslo, where he concentrated in zoological studies.

In 1882, while still a student, Nansen undertook his first venture to the Arctic, sailing on the Norwegian sealing vessel the *Viking* to Spitsbergen (present-day Svalbard), where he collected zoological specimens. On the return voyage, he sailed by way of the east coast of GREENLAND, where the vessel was trapped in the PACK ICE for three weeks. Soon after his return to Norway, Nansen was appointed as curator of the Museum of Natural History in Bergen.

In 1888, a year after he had received his doctorate in zoology, Nansen, inspired by the accounts of NILS ADOLF ERIK NORDENSKJÖLD, organized an expedition to explore the southern part of Greenland. He designed special equipment for the venture, including an ultralight sledge and a portable stove that used a minimum of fuel, which came to be known as the "Nansen Cooker."

Among the five men Nansen had recruited to accompany him were two Laplanders (Sami) and three Norwegians, including OTTO NEUMANN SVERDRUP. Aboard the sealing ship the *Jason,* they sailed from Oslo in May 1888. Upon reaching the uninhabited southeast coast of Greenland, they approached the shore in two small boats, making a landing at Kjoge. Using snowshoes and what are known today as cross-country skis, Nansen and his companions then traveled westward, and, by mid-August 1888, they had ascended Greenland's ice cap to an altitude of 9,000 feet. On September 27, they reached Greenland's west coast at Ameralikfjord, then made their way to the Danish settlement at Godthaab (present-day Nuuk). While wintering there in 1888–89, Nansen made a study of the Inuit (Eskimo) and their Arctic survival techniques.

Nansen returned to Norway in 1889, having proven that Greenland's ice cap extended all the way into the interior. Soon afterward, he married Eva Sars, the daughter of a university professor. His account of the expedition, *The First Crossing of Greenland,* was published in 1890.

In 1884, Nansen had learned that wreckage from the *Jeannette,* American Arctic explorer GEORGE WASHINGTON DE LONG's ship, which had been crushed and sunk by the ice in the polar seas off the New Siberian Islands in 1881, had been found on the southwest coast of Greenland. Based on this information, he speculated that a specially designed vessel could be deliberately set in the ice near where the *Jeannette* had been stranded and drift enough northward through the frozen Arctic Ocean to serve as a base for a successful expedition by sledge across the ice to the NORTH POLE.

Although Nansen's plan was at first met with some skepticism, by 1893 he had gained enough financial support from the Norwegian government, King Oscar of Norway, and Great Britain's ROYAL GEOGRAPHICAL SOCIETY to mount an attempt. A ship, the *Fram,* built under the direction of Scottish naval architect Colin Archer, was equipped with a saucer-shaped hull designed to withstand the pressure of advancing ice and force the vessel on top of the surface of the frozen Arctic Ocean.

In June 1893, Nansen and the *Fram* sailed from Oslo with a crew of 12, including a member of the earlier Greenland expedition, Otto Sverdrup, as second in command. On rounding North Cape, they made their way into the NORTHEAST PASSAGE along the Arctic coast of Russia and SIBERIA. Before entering the Kara Sea, they stopped at Khabarova, near Vaigach Island, where Russian Arctic explorer EDUARD VON TOLL provided them with dogs for the planned sledge journey to the North Pole.

Sailing eastward beyond Cape Chelyuskin, Asia's northernmost point, they entered the Sea of Laptev, and, on September 26, 1893, they achieved their goal of being icebound near the New Siberian Islands, at 77° north latitude. After a year, the ship had drifted only 5° northward and had begun to trend more to the west. In March 1895, with the *Fram* still heading too much to the west, Nansen de-

Fridtjof Nansen *(Library of Congress)*

cided to leave the ship and make an attempt on the North Pole, then 400 miles to the north. Leaving Sverdrup in charge, on March 14, 1895, he and Frederik Hjalmar Johansen embarked across the ice equipped with two kayaks, three sledges, and 24 dogs.

On April 8, 1895, at a point 240 miles from the North Pole, Nansen decided to turn back when ice conditions made progress northward by either sledge or kayak impossible. He had reached 86°14' north latitude, a record at that time.

Realizing that they would be unable to locate the still drifting *Fram,* Nansen and Johansen traveled southward toward the Siberian mainland. On July 24, 1895, they reached the northernmost islands of Franz Josef Land, where they built a hut of stone and moss, with a roof of walrus skins. They wintered there, hunting polar bear and walruses. On June 17, 1896, Nansen met up with British Arctic explorer FREDERICK GEORGE JACKSON, then in Franz Josef Land with the Jackson-Harmsworth Expedition. Anticipating such a meeting, Jackson had brought along letters from both the Norwegian government and Nansen's wife, Eva, which he presented to Nansen at his base at Cape Flora. Soon afterward, Nansen and Johansen were picked up by Jackson's relief ship, the *Windward,* on which they sailed to the northern Norwegian port of Vardo. There, they learned of the arrival of the *Fram* at Tromso a few days later. The *Fram* had drifted to Spitsbergen, where Sverdrup had managed to free it from the ice.

Hailed as a national hero in Norway, Nansen returned to academic life as a professor of zoology. He was honored with degrees from both Oxford and Cambridge Universities in England, where an English edition of his account of his attempt on the North Pole, *Farthest North,* was published in 1897. Having achieved national prominence, he went on to play an important political role in the dissolution of Norway's union with Sweden in 1905, and, that year, he was appointed modern Norway's first ambassador to Great Britain.

In 1908, Nansen became professor of oceanography at the University of Oslo. Ten years later, he became involved in relief efforts to aid displaced persons and war prisoners in the aftermath of World War I, for which he was awarded the Nobel Peace Prize in 1922. He had planned another Arctic exploit, a flight over the North Pole in an AIRSHIP, the *Graf Zeppelin,* before he died in May 1930, at his home outside of Oslo.

Fridtjof Nansen made the first known crossing of Greenland in 1888. Although he did not reach the North Pole in his Arctic expedition of 1893–96, the oceanographic studies he conducted revealed the Arctic Ocean to be much deeper than was thought, containing neither large landmasses nor a large number of islands, as some geographers and scientists had speculated. Among his numerous published works on oceanography and Arctic exploration, he wrote *Northern Mists* (1911), which recounts the history of Arctic exploration, dating from the ancient voyages of PYTHEAS and the medieval voyages of the VIKINGS. Nansen's ship, the *Fram,* was used by ROALD ENGELBREGT GRAVNING AMUNDSEN on his successful 1910–12 expedition to Antarctica and the SOUTH POLE.

Nares, Sir George Strong (1831–1915)
British naval officer in the Canadian Arctic

George Nares was born in Aberdeen, Scotland, the son of a British naval officer. At the age of 15, he entered the British navy as a midshipman.

In 1852, Nares was appointed as second in command aboard the *Resolute,* one of the fleet of ships under SIR EDWARD BELCHER searching for SIR JOHN FRANKLIN, who had been missing in the Canadian Arctic since 1845. He undertook several long sledge journeys over the next two years, surveying more than 1,100 miles to the north and west of Devon Island.

Nares next took part in naval actions in the Black Sea in the Crimean War of 1853–56. During the late 1860s, he undertook coastal surveys for the British Admiralty in Australia as well as in the Gulf of Suez.

In 1872, at the rank of captain, Nares was given command of the steamer *Challenger* and sailed around the world on one of the first oceanographic research voyages in history. In charge of the expedition's scientific team was SIR CHARLES WYVILLE THOMSON. After three crossings of the Atlantic Ocean, Nares directed the expedition to the Pacific Ocean by way of the CAPE OF GOOD HOPE. The team made oceanographic observations in the waters off Australia, NEW ZEALAND, and Japan, as well as in Polynesia. The expedition then headed southward, and, in February 1874, the *Challenger* became the first steamship to cross the ANTARCTIC CIRCLE. From the findings of his subsequent coastal survey, geographers were able to determine that Antarctica was a continent.

Later in 1874, Nares was called back to England and placed in command of the British Arctic Expedition, the major aim of which was to plant the British flag at the NORTH POLE. With two ships, the *Alert* and the *Discovery*, he was to explore the region north of Smith Sound and the channel between northern Ellesmere Island and northwestern GREENLAND, from where he could make an attempt on the North Pole. On May 29, 1875, he sailed with his ships from Portsmouth, England. After a stopover for sledge dogs at Proven, Greenland, he headed into Baffin Bay and then to Smith Sound, which he reached in July 1875. He then crossed westward to Ellesmere Island and northward to Cape Frazier.

Leaving the *Discovery* at the southern end of Kennedy Channel to serve as a relief ship, Nares, on the *Alert*, continued northward into Robeson Channel. He reached a point on the north coast of Ellesmere Island, adjacent to the edge of the frozen Arctic Ocean, where he and his men wintered.

Under Nares's command, sledging parties explored westward along the north coast of Ellesmere Island. The sledging expedition on the polar attempt was led by Commander Albert Markham, who managed to reach 83°20'26" north latitude, the northernmost record until that time. At that point, on encountering impassable stretches of ice, the team was forced to return.

Nares and his ships returned to England on October 27, 1876. He again commanded the *Alert* in an 1878 survey of the STRAIT OF MAGELLAN. Knighted for his achievements in Arctic exploration, he was made a vice admiral in 1892.

Based on his 1875–76 expedition, Sir George Nares reported that he had proved the nonexistence of an ice-free polar sea, and he concluded erroneously that the impassable permanent ice fields north of Ellesmere Island and Greenland made any attempt on the North Pole futile. He confirmed and corrected the locations of earlier geographic discoveries made by the Americans ISAAC ISRAEL HAYES and CHARLES FRANCIS HALL, and established that Greenland was an island. In addition, his study of the ice north of Ellesmere Island revealed it to be nearly identical to the type of ice encountered around Banks Island, farther to the west, demonstrating that the Arctic Ocean was a single, unified, frozen expanse. On the site of the north coast of Ellesmere Island where Nares and his expedition spent the winter of 1875–76, a radio and meteorological base was later established by the U.S. and Canadian governments. Named Alert in honor of Nares's ship, the base is the most northerly permanent settlement in the world. The body of water that separates northwestern Greenland from Ellesmere Island is named Nares Strait.

Narváez, Pánfilo de (ca. 1478–ca. 1528)
Spanish soldier, colonial official in the Caribbean, Mexico, and Florida

Pánfilo de Narváez was born in Valladolid, Spain. A soldier by profession, he traveled to the Americas in about 1500, where he took part in the Spanish conquests of Jamaica and Hispaniola (present-day Haiti and the Dominican Republic). In 1511–14, he was DIEGO VELÁSQUEZ's chief lieutenant in the conquest of Cuba.

In 1520, Narváez was sent from Cuba by Velásquez to arrest conquistador HERNÁN CORTÉS, who had disobeyed official orders in his advance on the Aztec. That May, Narváez landed near Veracruz, Mexico, with a 900-man military force. Cortés launched a surprise counterattack against Narváez at Veracruz. Narváez lost an eye in battle and was taken prisoner, whereupon most of his men deserted to join Cortés in the conquest of Mexico. In 1521, after his release, Narváez returned to Spain.

In 1526, Narváez was appointed *adelantado* (governor) of Florida by Spanish king Charles I (Holy Roman Emperor Charles V) and was empowered to explore and conquer the lands between the Río de las Palmas in northeastern Mexico and the Cape of Florida. With a fleet of five ships, carrying 600 soldiers and colonists, Narváez left the Spanish port of Sanlúcar de Barrameda in June 1527. He stopped first at the Spanish settlements in Cuba and Santo Domingo, where one-third of the colonists deserted. In April 1528, his expedition, now reduced to 400 men, attempted to reach the Mexican coast at Tampico, but the ships were blown off course by storms. He instead made a landing at Tampa Bay on Florida's Gulf Coast.

Narváez stayed ashore with 300 men, sending his ships with the rest of his forces northward. He planned to rejoin the ships after a short exploratory march and sail to a Spanish settlement at the mouth of the Pánuco River on the east coast of Mexico.

Narváez led his reduced expedition inland into the Florida Panhandle. From the Indians, he heard tales of gold and other riches at the town of Apalachen to the north. This site, near present-day Tallahassee, Florida, proved to have only an abundance of food. The Spanish pillaged Apalachen, thus earning the hostility of the Indians. After engaging the Indians in several battles and losing some of his men to Indian arrows as well as to tropical fever, Narváez headed for the Gulf Coast, where he believed his ships were waiting.

Narváez reached Apalachicola Bay, but the ships had since departed for Mexico. When food ran out, his men were forced to eat the last remaining horses at Apalachicola Bay, referred to as the "Bay of Horses." With no gold to be found and supplies critically low, Narváez decided to abandon the enterprise and try to reach Mexico by sea, still believing it to be only a few days' journey away. His men undertook the construction of five crude barges.

On September 22, 1528, Narváez and his 242 remaining men set sail into the Gulf of Mexico, intending to follow the shoreline to the Pánuco River. At a point below the outlet of the MISSISSIPPI RIVER, the barges were driven farther offshore by the river's currents. Narváez, in command of one barge, was caught in a storm and never seen again. Only a handful of the expedition later reached the Texas mainland and Mexico, including the expedition's treasurer, ÁLVAR NÚÑEZ CABEZA DE VACA, and a former slave, ESTEVANICO.

Pánfilo de Narváez' 1528 attempt to conquer and colonize Florida ended in disaster. Nevertheless, his explorations resulted in the first significant land penetration by Europeans into the present-day United States. The expedition's few survivors brought back the first reports by Europeans of a great river—the Mississippi—flowing into the Gulf of Mexico.

Nearchus (Nearchos) (ca. 360–312 B.C.)
Greek mariner under Alexander the Great in the Arabian Sea, Gulf of Oman, and Persian Gulf

Nearchus was a native of the island of Crete in the Mediterranean Sea. He settled at Amphipolis in the northern Greek kingdom of Macedon, where he was befriended by ALEXANDER THE GREAT. Starting in 334 B.C., he joined Alexander in his campaign against the Persian Empire, and, following the victory over Darius III at Granicus that same year, he was appointed governor of Lycia, a town on the Mediterranean coast of present-day Turkey.

In 329, Nearchus traveled east into Bactria (present-day Afghanistan), bringing reinforcements for Alexander's campaign to India. By 325, Alexander had reached western India's Hydaspes (the Jhelum River), where his army refused to continue. A fleet of 150 ships was constructed for a voyage of exploration, and a force of 5,000 men, including Macedonian officers, plus Greek, Cypriot, and Egyptian soldiers, was placed under Nearchus's command.

By September 325, Nearchus had reached the mouth of the INDUS RIVER near modern-day Karachi, Pakistan. The expedition was delayed in the Indus Delta by unfavorable monsoon winds for about three weeks. Nearchus then headed westward along the coast of what is now Pakistan. The fleet made daily stops for food and water, putting in at Gwadar Bay near the present-day Pakistan-Iran border.

Nearchus sailed into the Gulf of Oman, then passed through the Strait of Hormuz and entered the Persian Gulf. During one of his frequent stops along the west shore of the Persian Gulf, he met up with Alexander's lieutenant Leonnatus, with whom he made a five-day march inland to present-day Kerman, Iran. With fresh supplies from Alexander's army, Nearchus returned to his fleet on the Persian Gulf.

Sailing along the Makran Coast—the Persian Gulf coast of what is now Iran—Nearchus came into contact with several different primitive peoples, whom he described in his subsequent report to Alexander. He reported seeing "hairy men," who used their long fingernails as tools, as well as a people he called the Ichtyophagi (literally, "fish eaters"), who subsisted entirely on fish and built houses from whale bones. At one point, the fleet had an encounter with a group of large whales, creatures unknown to his Mediterranean sailors. Nearchus made a visit to the island of Astola, which, according to legend, was inhabited by mermaids.

Nearchus journeyed inland to meet with Alexander at Gulashkird, then returned to the Persian Gulf and his ships. He sailed to the head of the Persian Gulf and the mouth of the Euphrates River, which he ascended to the Tigris, rejoining Alexander at Susa.

Nearchus had intended to undertake additional voyages of exploration, including a proposed voyage around the Arabian Peninsula and a circumnavigation of Africa, but Alexander's death in 323 put an end to these plans. Nearchus resumed his governorship of Lycia.

Alexander had hoped Nearchus's coastal voyage from western India to the head of the Persian Gulf would establish a sea route connecting the Asian and Mediterranean portions of his empire. Following the breakup of Alexander's empire after 323, a better route to India was established that made use of the monsoon winds of the Indian Ocean. Nonetheless, an account of Nearchus's expedition, written in the second century A.D. by the Greek historian Arrian in his work *Indica*, survives as one of the earliest records of nonmilitary exploration.

Necho II (Neco, Nechoh) (unknown–593 B.C.)
king of ancient Egypt, organizer of expedition along coastal Africa

Pharaoh Necho II, who ruled Egypt from 609 to 593 B.C., was the son of Psamtik, founder of the XXVI dynasty.

Soon after his ascent to the throne, Necho launched a campaign of expansion eastward into what is now Israel and

Syria, decisively defeating King Josiah of Judah and his army at Megiddo in 608. Three years later, Necho himself was defeated at Carchemish on the Euphrates River by the Babylonians under Nebuchadnezzar, and withdrew to Egypt.

From his capital in the ancient Nile Delta city of Saïs, Necho turned his attention to establishing a trade link between the MEDITERRANEAN SEA and the RED SEA. He first attempted to re-excavate an old canal that had run from the city of Bubastis, on the NILE RIVER north of Cairo, eastward to the Red Sea. He abandoned the project after an oracle warned him of its dire consequences.

In about 600, Necho commissioned a group of Phoenician seafarers to undertake a voyage from the Gulf of Aqaba southward into the Red Sea and Indian Ocean, in an attempt to find an alternate sea route from Egypt to the Mediterranean. The Phoenicians reportedly followed the coastline of Africa, and, on rounding the continent's southern end from east-to-west, sailed northward to the STRAIT OF GIBRALTAR, from where they crossed the Mediterranean eastward to Egypt's Nile Delta.

According to an account of the expedition by HERODOTUS, written more than 100 years later, the voyage Necho had commissioned took almost three years to complete, during which the Phoenicians stopped each fall to plant a crop of grain, remaining until the following spring to harvest it. The sailors' descriptions of the relative position of the sun as they rounded southern Africa from east to west strongly suggests that they were the first people from the Mediterranean world to travel south of the EQUATOR and circumnavigate Africa.

Although the expedition Necho II had sent out located no practical alternate sea route between Egypt and the Mediterranean, the geographic information it brought back led Herodotus to conclude correctly that Africa, except where it is connected to Asia, is surrounded by a continuous sea. Almost 2,000 years afterward, surviving fragments of Herodotus's account inspired Portugal's HENRY THE NAVIGATOR, prince of Portugal, to launch a program of exploration, which culminated in the voyage around Africa under VASCO DA GAMA in 1497–99.

Needham, James (unknown–1673) *English colonist in North Carolina and Tennessee*

In April 1673, Carolina colonist James Needham accompanied GABRIEL ARTHUR on a voyage of exploration of the Occaneechi Path, an Indian trail that followed the Blue Ridge southwest from Fort Henry, present-day Petersburg, Virginia. Their expedition was organized by prominent Virginia colonist Major General ABRAHAM WOOD.

At the headwaters of the Roanoke River, Needham and Arthur were turned back by Occaneechi Indians, who resented the intrusion of Englishmen into their lucrative trade with the inland Cherokee. Needham and Arthur again set

out from Fort Henry in May 1673 and traveled southwestward across present-day North Carolina into Cherokee territory at the headwaters of the Tennessee River. Needham left Arthur with the "Tomahitan" Indians (probably Cherokee) to learn their language, and headed back to Fort Henry.

In September 1673, Needham departed Fort Henry to rejoin Arthur. His Ocaneechi guide, John Hasecoll, fearing that his tribe's trade with the Cherokee would be jeopardized by English interlopers, murdered Needham at a point southwest of present-day Winston-Salem, North Carolina. Arthur, after being held captive, wandered for several months through a wide area of the western APPALACHIAN MOUNTAINS.

James Needham participated in one of the earliest explorations of the Blue Ridge southwest of the early English Virginia settlements. He was among the first Englishmen to enter what is now Tennessee and make contact with trans-Appalachian tribes.

Nevelskoy, Gennady Ivanovich (Genadii Nevelskoi) (1814–1876) *Russian naval officer in southeastern Siberia and the Russian Far East*

Gennady Nevelskoy was a captain-lieutenant in the Russian navy in 1848, when he commanded the *Baykal* on a voyage from the Baltic port of Kronstadt, by way of CAPE HORN, to Kamchatka on the Pacific coast of SIBERIA.

In 1849, Nevelskoy undertook explorations southward from Kamchatka to the region around the mouth of the Amur River and the northern end of Tatar Strait. He then cruised around the northern end of Sakhalin, proving it to be an island.

Nevelskoy traveled westward across Siberia and European Russia and returned to St. Petersburg in 1850, thus completing a journey around the world. He reported that the lower Amur River was navigable, and that a strait separated Sakhalin from the mainland, indicating the existence of a short sea route from the mouth of the Amur River into the Sea of Okhotsk and the North Pacific Ocean.

In 1851, Nevelskoy, as commander of the Amur Expedition, again traveled to the region southwest of the Sea of Okhotsk and claimed for Russia the territory around the lower Amur River, as well as all of Sakhalin. He established Nikolayevsk, an outpost near the mouth of the Amur, and, during the next four years, directed further explorations of Sakhalin and the regions inland from Tatar Strait. These expeditions located new harbors, including one that came to be known as Nevelskoy Bay. The results of the land explorations were later used to establish a portion of the Russian-Chinese border in the early 1860s.

Nevelskoy returned to European Russia in 1856. Soon afterward, he left active naval service, taking up residence in Paris.

Gennady Nevelskoy's explorations revealed Sakhalin to be an island, not a peninsula, as had been previously reported by JEAN-FRANÇOIS DE GALAUP, comte de La Pérouse, and ADAM IVAN RITTER VON KRUSENSTERN. His finding that the lower Amur River was navigable soon led to the development of Nikolayevsk as an important Pacific port for Russia.

Newberry, John (unknown–ca. 1585)
English merchant, traveler in Persia and India

In 1580, John Newberry, an English merchant, was sent by the London-based LEVANT COMPANY to revive direct overland trade links between India, the Persian Gulf ports, and the MEDITERRANEAN SEA. His sponsors hoped to establish an alternative to the sea route around Africa, which was then dominated by Portugal and Spain.

Newberry descended the Euphrates River to Baghdad, and then Basra, reaching the Persian Gulf. He sailed down the gulf to Portuguese-controlled Hormuz, from where he traveled northward into western Persia (present-day Iran), visiting the cities of Shiraz, Esfahan, Qazvin, and Tabriz. On his return trip to England, he made a westward crossing of what is now Turkey to Constantinople (present-day Istanbul), and sailed for England, reaching it in 1581.

In 1583, Newberry acted as guide for an English diplomatic and trade expedition to the court of Akbar, the Mogul emperor of India. The group, which included merchant and diplomat RALPH FITCH, sailed to Syria, then reached the Persian Gulf by way of the Euphrates River.

At Hormuz, Newberry and his party were arrested by the Portuguese and taken across the Arabian Sea to Goa, the Portuguese colony on India's southwest coast. Yet they soon managed to gain their release.

Newberry then accompanied Fitch and another Englishman to the court of Akbar at Fatehpur Sikri, near Agra, India, and presented the Mogul ruler with letters from Queen Elizabeth I.

In 1585, Newberry began the return trip to England on his own, having left his companions at the Mogul capital. Soon after his departure for Lahore to the northwest, he disappeared without a trace.

John Newberry was the first Englishman to descend the Euphrates and to travel across Persia. Along with Ralph Fitch, he initiated trade contacts leading to the organization of the BRITISH EAST INDIA COMPANY in 1600.

Newberry, John Strong (1822–1892)
American physician, geologist in the American West

John Strong Newberry was born in Windsor, Connecticut. He attended Western Reserve College (now Case Western Reserve University) in Cleveland, graduating in 1846. He continued his studies at Cleveland Medical College, receiving a degree as a doctor in 1848. After two years of travel and additional studies in Europe, he returned to Cleveland, where he set up a medical practice.

In May 1855, Newberry served as assistant surgeon and geologist for an official U.S. government expedition exploring the country between San Francisco and the mouth of the COLUMBIA RIVER, as part of a survey for a proposed transcontinental railroad route. Under the command of Lieutenant Robert S. Williamson of the U.S. Army Corps of Topographical Engineers, he made a detailed study of the geology, plant life, and animal life of northern California and the Pacific Northwest, which was incorporated into the official account of the expedition, published in 1857, *Reports of Explorations and Surveys to ascertain the most Practical and Economical Route for a Railroad from the Mississippi River to the Pacific ocean, made in 1853–6.*

Newberry took part in a subsequent topographical expedition in 1857–58, accompanying Lieutenant JOSEPH CHRISTMAS IVES in a journey by steamboat 500 miles up the COLORADO RIVER. He then spent nearly a year studying the natural history of the Grand Canyon and the surrounding territory; he contributed much to the expedition's official report, *Report Upon the Colorado River of the West, explored in 1857–58,* which was published in 1861.

In summer 1859, Newberry served under Captain JOHN N. MACOMB in a Topographical Corps expedition to the San Juan and upper Colorado River regions of what is now southwestern Colorado, southern Utah, and northern New Mexico and Arizona. While traveling across hundreds of square miles of unknown territory, he collected thousands of fossil specimens and made several discoveries of mineral deposits. His findings were included in *Report of the Exploring Expedition from Santa Fe to the junction of the Grand and Green Rivers,* published in 1876.

During the Civil War, Newberry directed the supply and administration of the Union army's hospitals. At the war's end, he became a professor of geology and paleontology at New York's Columbia College (now Columbia University). In 1869, he was appointed state geologist of Ohio, and he later worked as a consultant to mining operations throughout the United States. In 1884, he joined the U.S. Geological Survey as a paleontologist.

In the course of his scientific work in the American West, John Strong Newberry amassed more than 100,000 fossil and geological specimens, which later became part of the natural history collection at Columbia University.

Newell, Robert (1807–1869) *American fur trader, trapper, pioneer in Oregon*

Robert Newell was originally from Ohio. While in his early 20s, he became a trapper, and, in 1829, he traveled from St. Louis up the MISSOURI RIVER with one of JEDEDIAH STRONG SMITH's fur-trading expeditions to the northern ROCKY MOUNTAINS.

After about 10 years in the fur trade, Newell decided to head into the Oregon Country. In 1839, he set out with his family from Fort Boise and took his wagons along the difficult last leg of the Oregon Trail northwestward to Walla Walla. The following year, he continued his trek westward, arriving in the Willamette Valley, south of present-day Portland, Oregon, in early 1841.

Newell was one of the founders of Oregon's first provisional government in 1843, several years before the region was organized as a U.S. territory. His memoirs of his career as a mountain man in the Rockies, and of his later life as a pioneer in Oregon, were edited by D. O. Johansen and published in 1959 as *Memoranda*.

In his journey from Fort Boise into what is now southeastern Washington in 1839–41, Robert Newell became the first settler to lead wagons along the entire length of the Oregon Trail, having blazed a wagon road through northeastern Oregon's Blue Mountains, a barrier over which previous Oregon Trail travelers had passed only on horses and mules, or by foot.

Newport, Christopher (ca. 1565–1617)
English mariner in Virginia and the East Indies

Christopher Newport, an English sea captain and privateer, took part in SIR FRANCIS DRAKE's raid of PRIVATEERS on the Spanish port of Cádiz in 1587.

In 1590–91, Newport commanded one of the ships in the fleet sent by JOHN WHITE to bring relief to the Roanoke Colony off the coast of what is now North Carolina. The ships sailed first to the WEST INDIES, where Newport and his ship, the *Little John,* remained behind to attack Spanish settlements on Hispaniola (present-day Haiti and the Dominican Republic) and along the coast of Honduras. The next year, while in the AZORES, Newport aided in the capture of the Spanish galleon the *Madre de Dios,* which proved to be the richest prize ever taken by Queen Elizabeth I's privateers.

During the next 10 years, Newport commanded several more voyages to the Caribbean in which he continued to prey on Spanish shipping. In September 1605, he was back in England, where he presented King James I with two live young crocodiles and a wild boar captured in the West Indies.

A year later, Newport was engaged by the London Company as commander of its colonizing expedition to Virginia. BARTHOLOMEW GOSNOLD was his vice admiral. In December 1606, he sailed from England with a fleet of three vessels, the *Discovery,* the *Godspeed,* and the *Susan Constant,* carrying 120 colonists. After the Atlantic crossing to the West Indies, Newport sailed north to Chesapeake Bay, which he entered in April 1607. The colonists disembarked near the mouth of the James River, where,

on May 14, 1607, they founded the settlement of Jamestown.

Newport had been instructed by the VIRGINIA COMPANY to explore inland from the settlement for a waterway to the Far East, the much-sought-after NORTHWEST PASSAGE. In May 1607, he sailed about 100 miles up the James River to its head of navigation, near what later became Richmond, Virginia. At the same time, the settlement's military leader, Captain JOHN SMITH, explored along the shores of Chesapeake Bay.

In late July 1607, Newport returned to England with mineral samples from Virginia that he believed to be gold. Upon analysis, they proved to be worthless.

In January 1608, Newport arrived back in Jamestown in command of the "First Supply," the Virginia Company's first follow-up expedition, carrying an additional 100 colonists. More than half of the original Jamestown settlers had since died; the colony's director, E. M. Wingfield, had been jailed, and John Smith was about to be hanged. Newport soon freed Wingfield and Smith and restored order to the colony. Less than a week later, another crisis developed when a fire swept through the settlement. With their food supplies destroyed, Newport and Smith were compelled to seek aid from the Indian leader Powhatan. They journeyed to his village, Werowocomoco, on the York River in late February 1608, where they were able to obtain a supply of corn. Having seen the Jamestown colony survive through its first difficult year, Newport sailed back to England.

On his third trip to Virginia, in 1608–09, Newport presented Powhatan with gifts, including a crown, which he used in a coronation ceremony for the Indian leader. Newport later undertook an overland exploration along the upper James River, probing beyond the point he had sailed to in 1607, possibly reaching as far inland as the mouth of the Rivanna River near present-day Columbia, Virginia.

In 1609, at the rank of vice admiral, Newport sailed from England for Virginia in command of a nine-ship fleet. Along with him were Sir Thomas Gates, the deputy governor of the Virginia colony; Sir George Somers, a founder of the Virginia Company; and SILVESTER JOURDAIN, British mariner. On September 28, 1609, Newport's ship was wrecked off Bermuda, and he, Gates, Somers, and some of the colonists were stranded on the island for 10 months. Somers took the opportunity to claim Bermuda and the neighboring islands for Great Britain. By the following spring, they had constructed several small sailboats, with which they managed to reach Virginia in May 1610.

Newport commanded a fourth colonizing expedition to Virginia in 1611, then left the Virginia Company for the BRITISH EAST INDIA COMPANY. He made his first voyage to the EAST INDIES in 1613–14, in which he took the shah's ambassador, the Englishman Sir Robert Sherley, brother of SIR ANTHONY SHERLEY, back to Persia (present-day Iran) from a diplomatic mission in Europe. Traveling with Newport on his second voyage for the British East India Company in 1615–16 was SIR THOMAS ROE, on his way to India as England's ambassador to the court of the Mogul emperor. In August 1617, while on his third voyage to the Far East, Newport died at Bantam, in the East Indies.

Christopher Newport played a part in establishing what was to become the first permanent English settlement in North America. He also carried out the earliest European explorations deep into the interior of Virginia, and he was among the first to realize that the rivers that emptied into Chesapeake Bay led inland only as far as the barrier of the Blue Ridge. Accounts of the shipwreck and time in Bermuda in 1609–10 by Silvester Jourdain and fellow crew member William Strachey reportedly served as inspiration for William Shakespeare's 1611 play *The Tempest*.

Nicolet, Jean (Jean Nicollet de Bellesborne)

(ca. 1598–1642) *French fur trader, interpreter in Lake Michigan and Green Bay areas*

Jean Nicolet was born in Cherbourg, France. In 1618, he arrived in French Canada, as a protégé of SAMUEL DE CHAMPLAIN and as an agent in the FUR TRADE for merchants in Rouen and St.-Malo, France.

From 1618 to 1620, Nicolet lived among the Algonkin Indians on Allumette Island in the Ottawa River. He then spent nine years with the Nipissing Indians, a subgroup of the Chippewa (Ojibway), in the Georgian Bay region of Lake Huron.

By 1634, Nicolet had learned a variety of Indian languages and had become an important intermediary between French traders and the region's tribes. That year, Champlain sent him to investigate reports of a great "bad-smelling" sea that lay to the west of Lake Huron. After escorting a group of Jesuit missionaries to the Huron (Wyandot) Indian settlements on Georgian Bay, Nicolet set out by CANOE with seven Huron and retraced ÉTIENNE BRULÉ's route to Sault Sainte Marie. He explored the entrance to Lake Superior, located the Straits of Mackinac, and entered Lake Michigan.

Nicolet had been instructed to make contact with the Winnebago (Ho-Chunk) Indians. He followed the north shore of Lake Michigan, entered Green Bay, and came upon a Winnebago band living at the mouth of the Fox River. Under the impression that he was not far from the East China Sea and China, Nicolet believed the Indians were subjects of the Great Khan. He reportedly dressed in a Chinese damask robe in preparation for a meeting with Chinese officials.

From Green Bay, Nicolet explored the Fox River and the watershed above the Wisconsin River. From the Indians, he heard of a great river to the south, which he speculated flowed into the Pacific Ocean.

Nicolet returned to Trois Rivières on the St. Lawrence River, where he became prominent in the fur trade. In 1642, while he was traveling on the St. Lawrence, his small boat capsized and he was drowned.

Jean Nicolet was the first non-Indian to report the existence of Lake Michigan. He also brought back Indian accounts of what turned out to be the MISSISSIPPI RIVER. Twenty years after Nicolet's visit to Green Bay, French fur traders MÉDARD CHOUART DES GROSEILLIERS and PIERRE ESPRIT RADISSON followed his route and developed a lucrative fur-trading business with the Indians. Green Bay, in the 1670s, would become a key staging area for French explorations of the Mississippi Valley undertaken by LOUIS JOLLIET, JACQUES MARQUETTE, and RENÉ-ROBERT CAVELIER, DE LA SALLE.

Nicollet, Joseph Nicolas (Jean N. Nicollet)

(1786–1843) *French mathematician, astronomer in North America*

Joseph Nicollet was born at Cluses in southeastern France. As a child, he exhibited talent for mathematics and astronomy, and he went on to become a professor at the Collège Louis-le-Grand. His academic career in France came to an end in 1832 with his immigration to the United States, resulting from a series of financial setbacks. He settled in New Orleans, where he was received by the French community as an internationally known scientist.

Seeking to carry on the tradition of French exploration in North America, Nicollet, in 1836–37, organized and led an expedition in search of the source of the MISSISSIPPI RIVER (although HENRY ROWE SCHOOLCRAFT had correctly determined the river's source four years earlier).

In 1838, Nicollet traveled to Washington, D.C., where he accepted an appointment with the U.S. Army Corps of Topographical Engineers, and, in 1838–39, he headed two government surveying expeditions into the prairies between the upper Mississippi River and MISSOURI RIVER, assisted by the young lieutenant JOHN CHARLES FRÉMONT. Nicollet and Frémont explored up the Minnesota River from Fort Snelling to the Red Pipestone Quarry in what is now southwestern Minnesota, a site sacred to a number of tribes.

Nicollet's later work was devoted to astronomy and mathematics, including the calculation of actuarial charts for life insurance companies. During a visit to St. Louis, Nicollet became interested in exploration of the American West, and in 1842, he was chosen to command a Topographical Corps expedition into the ROCKY MOUNTAINS. Because of serious illness, however, he was replaced by Frémont. Nicollet died the following year.

Joseph Nicollet's report of his explorations in the upper Mississippi River region was published in 1843. The maps he produced of the territory between the upper Mississippi and the Missouri Rivers were the first to be based on mathematical calculations and astronomical observations. While serving with Nicollet in 1838–39, John C. Frémont learned the skills necessary for his subsequent explorations into the Rocky Mountains and California.

Nicuesa, Diego de (unknown–1511)
Spanish conquistador in Central America

Diego de Nicuesa was born at Baeza in the Andalusia region of southern Spain into a noble family. He was well connected to the Spanish ruling family, serving in the household of an uncle of King Ferdinand II, and was known in Spain as an accomplished lute player. His involvement in the early Spanish settlement of Hispaniola (present-day Haiti and the Dominican Republic) brought him considerable wealth.

In 1508, King Ferdinand granted Nicuesa a license to establish a colony on the mainland of CENTRAL AMERICA in what is now Panama, west of the Gulf of Urabá. At the same time, the coastal region to the east in the vicinity of present-day Cartagena, on the Caribbean coast of present-day Colombia, had been granted to ALONSO DE OJEDA.

Both Nicuesa and Ojeda launched their colonizing expeditions from Hispaniola in 1509. The first to sail was Ojeda, whose men were attacked by Indians soon after landing at Cartagena. Nicuesa arrived there not long afterward and aided Ojeda in a counterstrike against the native peoples. He then sailed westward across the Gulf of Darien for the coast of Panama.

Nicuesa's fleet of four ships, carrying more than 700 men, became separated in a storm, leaving him with only one ship and fewer than 100 men. He tried to reach the site of his proposed colony at the mouth of the Darién River, but his ship ran aground and was wrecked. Nicuesa and his men then set out westward along the coast, although the site of the proposed colony lay in the opposite direction. With supplies of food running short, and having suffered repeated attacks by Indians, the Spaniards were relieved to come upon a natural harbor. Nicuesa decided to found his settlement on the site and reportedly exclaimed, "Here let us stop, in the name of God." His men called the site Nombre de Dios (name of God) after Nicuesa's remark. Soon afterward, contact was made with the other members of the expedition, who had reached the mouth of the Darién River to the west.

Nicuesa promptly sailed there to claim governorship over the newly established colony, Santa María la Antigua del Darién, but he found members of Ojeda's expedition in control. The colonists, under the leadership of VASCO NÚÑEZ DE BALBOA, refused to accept Nicuesa as their ruler. They sent him and 17 of his followers out to sea in an unseaworthy vessel. They were never seen or heard from again.

Diego de Nicuesa's settlement at Nombre de Dios later became the eastern terminus of the main route across the Isthmus of Panama from the Pacific coast, serving as the transshipment point for Spanish gold and other treasure from Peru and the Philippines.

Niebuhr, Carsten (Karsten Niebuhr)
(1733–1815) *German traveler in Arabia, Yemen, and the Persian Gulf, in service to Denmark*

Carsten Niebuhr was born into a German family at Holstein, which then was under the dominion of Denmark, and later became part of northern Germany. Following his early education, he went on to advanced studies in astronomy and mathematics, and, by the age of 27, he had applied his skills to become an accomplished surveyor, topographer, and cartographer.

At the invitation of Frederick V, King of Denmark, Niebuhr joined a Danish government-sponsored scientific expedition to explore the once-fertile southwestern corner of the Arabian Peninsula, a region known to Europeans since classical times as Arabia Felix, and comprising the Arab kingdom of Yemen. Although the expedition was loosely organized, without an appointed leader, Niebuhr held the position of "Engineer-Lieutenant." Along with the scientific aim of the project, a thorough study of the topography and animal and plant life of the region, the expedition was also charged with determining if Denmark could enter into trade contacts with Yemen, a region where foreign commerce was then dominated by the English and the Dutch.

In fall 1761, Niebuhr left Copenhagen with the five other members of the expedition: Peter Forrskal, a Swedish naturalist; Christian Kramer, a Danish physician and zoologist; George Baurenfeind, a German artist; Friedrich von Haven, a Danish linguist; and a former Swedish military man named Berggren. They first traveled to Egypt, where they remained until October 1762. Then, disguised as Muslims, they sailed on a ship carrying pilgrims to the Arabian port of Jidda on the RED SEA.

From Jidda, Niebuhr and his companions continued their journey to southern Arabia in a type of open boat known as a *tarrad*. During nightly stops, Niebuhr went ashore and made astronomical observations and calculations, upon which he based his later map of Yemen. The naturalists Forrskal and Kramer collected specimens of the region's fauna and flora, sending them back to Europe.

On December 29, 1762, Niebuhr and the Danish expedition arrived at Luhaiya, a port on the Red Sea coast of northern Yemen in what is now the Yemen Arab Republic. They proceeded inland, heading southward on donkeys along the coastal plain of the Tihama region. Niebuhr continued to make stellar and solar observations en route. In February 1763, the expedition reached the coastal city of Bait al-Faqih, where Niebuhr and von Haven both contracted malaria. At the port city of Mocha on the southwestern corner of the Arabian Peninsula, von Haven died.

In late June 1763, Niebuhr and the four remaining expedition members headed inland from Mocha across the desert toward the Yemeni capital Sanaa, where they hoped to meet with the ruler of Yemen, known as the imam. During this leg of the journey, the naturalist Forrskal died of malaria, and Niebuhr, himself weakened by the disease, was unable to record their route on his map. Despite his illness, he managed to reach Sanaa and also explored the region to the east, on the edge of the Rub' al-Khali Desert, the great waterless region of southern Arabia known as the EMPTY QUARTER.

After meeting with the imam in late July 1763, Niebuhr, Baurenfeind, Kramer, and Berggren made their way back to Mocha on camels just in time to catch the yearly ship to Bombay, India, as planned. Both Baurenfeind and Berggren died on the voyage to India. In Bombay, in February 1764, Kramer also died, leaving Niebuhr as the expedition's sole survivor.

Niebuhr remained in India until late 1764, sailing to the Persian Gulf aboard a British naval vessel in December of that year. He made his way overland through southwestern Persia (present-day Iran), then traveled up the Tigris River through present-day Iraq into Syria and what is now Israel, returning to Copenhagen by way of Constantinople (present-day Istanbul, Turkey) in 1767.

Carsten Niebuhr's account of his journey in Arabia and the Persian Gulf was first published in German in 1772–74, with an English edition, *Travels through Arabia,* published in Edinburgh in 1792. His work provided Europeans with the first comprehensive descriptions of the region from an 18th-century rationalist viewpoint. Niebuhr was also the first European to report on the spread of the Wahhabi revolution, an Islamic fundamentalist movement that had begun to sweep through Yemen and subsequently had a tremendous impact on the history of Arabia and adjoining lands. His map of Yemen was the first to detail scientifically that portion of the Arabian Peninsula.

Niebuhr, Sigismund (1631–1699)
German navigator along the south coast of South America, in service to Holland

Sigismund Niebuhr was born near the southwestern German town of Breisach on the Rhine. He became a skilled mariner and navigator, and, in about 1670, he entered the service of the Dutch government, the States-General.

In 1675, commissioned by the States-General, Niebuhr left Holland to explore the southernmost coast of South America. He first sailed to Rio de Janeiro, then made his way southward to Le Maire Strait off the south coast of Tierra del Fuego (explored in 1616 by JAKOB LE MAIRE and WILLEM CORNELIS SCHOUTEN). He undertook depth soundings and plotted the exact locations of dangerous rocks and other hazards to navigation. Niebuhr made a landing on Tierra del Fuego, where he befriended the natives and convinced two of them to accompany him back to Holland. Although Niebuhr's ship was wrecked in a storm off Los Reyes Island, he and his crew managed to construct another vessel, on which they returned to Holland in October 1677.

The next year, Sigismund Niebuhr published an account of his explorations around CAPE HORN and Tierra del Fuego. He also produced a navigational chart of Le Maire Strait, which greatly aided subsequent mariners in using that passage as a more practical alternate route around the tip of South America than the maze of channels that make up the STRAIT OF MAGELLAN.

Niño, Andrés (1475–ca. 1530) *Spanish mariner in Central America*

Born at Moguer in southwestern Spain, Andrés Niño went to sea when young. His first maritime exploits were on Portuguese ships along the coast of Africa and in the EAST INDIES. In 1515, he went to the newly established Spanish colony in Panama, where he became known as a skilled pilot.

When Spanish conquistador Gil González de Ávila set out to explore and conquer the Pacific coast of CENTRAL AMERICA in 1521–22, Niño was named as chief pilot for the seaward part of the expedition. In January 1522, at Tararegui, the expedition embarked on four ships that had been constructed on the Bay of San Miguel along the eastern end of Panama's Pacific coast.

After González de Ávila and his forces had gone ashore at the Bay of San Vicente to explore the interior, Niño and the small fleet continued northward along the coast, hoping to locate a strait that, according to reports by Indians, linked the Pacific Ocean and the Atlantic Ocean. He reached as far as 17°50' north latitude, off the Pacific coast of southern Mexico, and, finding no inland passage to the Atlantic, returned southward.

Niño found González de Ávila and his men under attack by a large force of Indians, reportedly numbering 4,000. He helped fight them off, then joined González de Ávila in exploring the coastal region around Cape Blanco and the Gulf of Papagayo, on the Pacific coast of what is now northwestern Costa Rica. They became the first known Europeans to reach the Possession River, and on the coast of what is now Honduras, they came upon a large bay, which they named the Gulf of Fonseca in honor of Bishop Juan Rodríguez de Fonseca, the head of the Council of the

Indies (which then supervised all Spanish explorations in the Americas).

Niño and González de Ávila's expedition next explored southward into the lands of an Indian chieftain known as Nicarao. They came upon a large body of freshwater, which they named Mar Dulce (sweet sea), later known as Lake Nicaragua after Nicarao. North of the lake, the Spaniards sighted the volcano called Masaya, near the present-day Nicaraguan city of the same name.

After exploring the interior of what is now western Nicaragua, Niño and González de Ávila returned to the Panama colony by sea, arriving on December 29, 1522. The gold, precious stones, and other valuables they obtained from the natives led them to compare the lands they had explored to the "paradise of Mohammed."

In 1523, Andrés Niño and González de Ávila returned to Spain with their treasure. Soon afterward, the region of Central America that they had explored was colonized by FRANCISCO FERNÁNDEZ DE CÓRDOBA. Lake Nicaragua, which Niño reached with González de Ávila in 1522, is the largest lake in Central America.

Niza, Marcos de (Fray Marcos, Fray Marcos of Nizza, Marco de Nica, Sayota) (ca. 1495–1558)
Italian missionary in Peru and the American Southwest
Marcos de Niza, born in Nice, then part of the Italian principality of Savoy, grew up to become a Franciscan missionary priest. In 1531–35, he served with FRANCISCO PIZARRO in the conquest of the Inca Indians of Peru in South America.

After time in Guatemala, Niza was assigned to Culiacán, Mexico, in 1537. Two years later, he was commissioned by ANTONIO DE MENDOZA, viceroy of New Spain, to undertake a reconnaissance of Sonora and investigate the reports, brought back by ÁLVAR NÚÑEZ CABEZA DE VACA and ESTEVANICO, of fabulously rich Indian cities to the north.

Niza was chosen by Mendoza because of the priest's earlier experience among the Inca of Peru. It was thought that a priest would be better received by the Indians. Additionally, sending Niza was much less expensive than mounting a military expedition led by a knight.

In March 1539, Niza, accompanied by Estevanico and another priest named Honorato, journeyed north from Culiacán on the west coast of Mexico, along the Sonora and San Pedro Rivers, into present-day Arizona. Among Indians he encountered, Niza became known as Sayota, or "Man from Heaven."

Niza sent Estevanico ahead, with instructions to send back crosses of varying sizes indicating the relative importance and wealth of any cities he came upon. Estevanico, at times two weeks ahead of Niza, sent back a cross the size

of a man, signifying that he had found cities that contained greater riches than those of the Aztec Indians. Soon afterward, Niza received news of Estevanico's death at the hands of Zuni Indians at Hawikuh Pueblo near present-day Zuni, New Mexico. The priest proceeded northward and espied from a distance what he thought must be cities of gold—the legendary Seven Cities of CIBOLA. They were actually adobe pueblos whose turquoise decorations glistened in the sun. Niza then went to Mexico City, where he presented his exaggerated report to Mendoza.

In spring 1540, Niza guided FRANCISCO VÁSQUEZ DE CORONADO and an advance party of about 100 soldiers and Indians from Culiacán, back across the Colorado Plateau, into present-day western New Mexico. After a battle, the Spaniards subjugated Hawikuh and learned it was not the hoped-for Cibola. Coronado, concerned that his disappointed soldiers would vent their anger against Niza, whose misinformation had led them there, sent the priest back to Sonora, Mexico, with one of his lieutenants.

Niza remained in Mexico for the rest of his life, serving as father provincial of Franciscan missionaries in New Spain. He later wrote of his explorations in what is now northern Mexico, the Gila River region of Arizona, and western New Mexico, in his published account, *Descubrimiento* (Discovery). In addition to erroneous descriptions of the Indians, he also reported seeing elephants, camels, unicorns, and other fabulous creatures.

Marcos de Niza was one of the earliest Europeans to explore north of Mexico. His report that the region's Indian pueblos were the fabled Seven Cities of Cibola, inspired Coronado's subsequent extensive explorations of the American Southwest and Great Plains.

Nobile, Umberto (1885–1980) *Italian air force officer, aviator, aeronautical engineer in the Arctic*
Umberto Nobile was born in the southern Italian city of Avellino near Naples. Trained as an aeronautical engineer, he became a high-ranking officer in the Italian Military Aeronautic Corps during World War I, supervising Italian aircraft production.

After the war, Nobile became an accomplished pilot and designer of AIRSHIPs, in particular the semi-rigid variety with a longitudinal keel providing support for the bags holding hydrogen gas. In 1925, Norwegian polar explorer ROALD ENGELBREGT GRAVNING AMUNDSEN and his partner, American millionaire LINCOLN ELLSWORTH, purchased from the Italian government the airship *N-1,* which Nobile had designed. Planning to use the airship for a flight over the NORTH POLE, they engaged Nobile as pilot for the expedition.

Nobile flew the airship, which had been rechristened the *Norge* by Amundsen, from Italy northward across

Europe. At the port of Vadso, on Norway's Arctic coast, he left the mainland and crossed over the Arctic Ocean to King's Bay, Spitsbergen (in Svalbard), arriving in early May 1926. He was met by Amundsen and Ellsworth, who had been on the Arctic island since the previous October, supervising the construction of a huge hangar for the airship.

While Nobile, Amundsen, and Ellsworth were making final preparations before take-off, RICHARD EVELYN BYRD and Floyd Bennett arrived at King's Bay, and they soon reportedly made a successful flight to the North Pole and back in an airplane on May 9, 1926. On May 11, 1926, the *Norge* lifted off from King's Bay, and, the next day, flew over the North Pole and continued over the ice cap to Teller, Alaska, completing the first Europe-to-America flight by way of the North Pole (and perhaps the first flight over the Pole since there is some question as to whether Byrd and Bennett passed directly over it). While over the Pole, the explorers dropped the flags of the United States, Norway, and Italy onto the ice. The flight had taken them across more than 3,400 miles in two and a half days. Inuit who had viewed the *Norge* from the ground later described it as a great "flying whale."

In the following weeks, Nobile grew to resent that the international press had overlooked his important contributions to the mission as both the pilot and designer of

Umberto Nobile *(Library of Congress)*

the *Norge.* Instead, public attention concentrated on Amundsen, now acclaimed as the first man to have reached both South and North Poles. Nobile's cause was taken up by the Italian press, who supported his contention that he had not been sufficiently credited for his role. A falling-out developed between Nobile and Amundsen after the latter openly criticized Nobile's ability as an aviator, claiming he had made several serious navigational errors during the flight. He characterized Nobile as a "boasting dreamer" and an "epauletted Italian." Nobile was affronted even more when Amundsen expressed the view that dirigibles were unreliable and impractical, and that future polar exploration from the air should be with airplanes with at least four engines.

Nobile reacted by organizing an Italian-sponsored dirigible flight over the North Pole under his command. Money for the venture was raised by public subscription in Milan; additional support came from Great Britain's ROYAL GEOGRAPHICAL SOCIETY. Nobile designed the airship *Italia,* specially equipped for the polar regions. He also received the backing of the Italian government under Mussolini, who provided the expedition with the naval vessel *Citta' di Milano* as an escort ship. Nobile recruited a mostly Italian crew of expert mountaineers from the Alps, and, intending to make scientific studies while at the North Pole, took along three internationally known scientists: Czechoslovakian radium specialist Franz Behounek, Italian physicist Aldo Pontremolli, and Swedish meteorologist Finn Malmgren. Spiritual support for the enterprise came from Pope Pius XI, who blessed the *Italia* and gave Nobile a large cross to drop at the North Pole.

In May 1928, almost exactly two years after his flight with Amundsen, Nobile arrived in Spitsbergen with the *Italia.* A planned preliminary flight over the Siberian archipelago of Nicholas II Land was called off because of bad weather. On May 23, Nobile and the *Italia* took off from Spitsbergen and headed for the North Pole, which he reached at one o'clock the next morning. As he flew over the Pole, the flag of Italy and the pope's cross were thrown out of the airship, and a message was radioed to Mussolini announcing that "the standard of Fascist Italy is floating in the breeze over the ice of the Pole." The *Italia* circled the North Pole for two hours, but it did not land to make oceanographic observations as planned. Because the airship's aerial had become ice-encrusted, and radio contact had been lost, Nobile decided instead to return to Spitsbergen.

With intense cold and winds, the airship was iced over on the return flight. The added weight of the ice and conditions of dense fog forced a crash landing onto the frozen sea, 180 miles northwest of Spitsbergen. On hitting the ice, the *Italia*'s control gondola, carrying Nobile and eight others, broke free, while the lighter-than-air portion of the airship, carrying seven other crewmen, became airborne once again and drifted out of control. No trace of it or the men aboard was ever found.

Nobile suffered a broken leg and broken arm in the crash, and one of the crewmen in the gondola was killed on impact. The others suffered a variety of injuries. Although the *Italia* had landed only 180 miles northwest of Spitsbergen, the PACK ICE was too rugged for most of the survivors to cross on foot, and Nobile decided to remain in that location and radio for help. After two weeks, three of the survivors, two Italians, Zappi and Mariano, and the Swedish meteorologist Malmgren, set out over the ice to obtain help, while Nobile and the others continued to transmit a distress call on the gondola's emergency radio set.

On June 6, 1928, an amateur radio operator near Arkhangelsk, Russia, picked up the signal from Nobile's party. The Soviet icebreaker *Krassin* was dispatched, and its reconnaissance plane sighted Zappi, Mariano, and, reportedly, Malmgren. Yet, when the ship reached them several weeks later, only Zappi and Mariano were found. Zappi reported that there were only two of them left, contrary to what the Soviet pilot had seen, and claimed that Malmgren had died a month earlier. The contradictory accounts led to charges that Malmgren may have met with foul play, and that Zappi may have committed cannibalism.

Sixteen ships, 21 airplanes, and more than 1,500 men from Italy, Norway, Sweden, and the Union of Soviet Socialist Republics (USSR or Soviet Union) took part in the search and rescue efforts for Nobile and his crew. Amundsen, despite his previous differences with Nobile, agreed to the Norwegian government's request that he join the search; he perished when his plane disappeared en route to Spitsbergen.

On June 24, 1928, Nobile's red tent was sighted from the air by Swedish aviator Einar Lundborg, who then made a landing on the ice. With room in his plane for only one passenger, Lundborg took Nobile back first, reportedly so that the commander of the expedition could more effectively supervise the rest of the rescue effort. The others were later rescued by ship. Nonetheless, with charges of cannibalism already leveled against one member of the expedition, Mussolini took a dim view of the fact that Nobile had been the first to be saved, and he ordered the aviator to be put under arrest for allegedly deserting his men.

Back in Italy in 1929, Nobile faced a board of inquiry that ultimately found him at fault for the disastrous outcome of the expedition. His reputation became further clouded amid reports that the real reason why he was the first to be rescued was because his life had been heavily insured and that underwriters at Lloyds of London had offered Lundborg a substantial cash reward for his rescue.

With his conduct officially condemned, Nobile was compelled to resign his commission as general in the Italian air force. He also lost his post as professor at Italy's Aero-

nautical Institute, and, in 1931, he went into voluntary exile in the Soviet Union. He lived there for the next five years, teaching aeronautics and advising the Soviet government on airship construction. In 1936, Nobile moved to the United States, where he became head of the aeronautical engineering department at Lewis College of Science and Technology (now Lewis University) near Chicago, Illinois.

At the end of World War II, Nobile returned to Italy, where the newly installed democratic government, having reconsidered his role in the 1928 Arctic disaster, cleared him of any wrongdoing and reinstated him in the air force. In 1946, he was elected as a deputy in the Italian parliament.

Several firsthand accounts were written about the *Italia* expedition, including Nobile's own *With the Italia to the North Pole* (1930), Einar Lundborg's *The Arctic Rescue* (1929), and *The Truth About the Red Tent* (1929), written by one of the survivors, Czech scientist Franz Behounek.

Umberto Nobile's Arctic exploit marked the last time aircraft were used to explore large stretches of uncharted territory in the Arctic. In the years that followed, such flights were made mainly to establish new air travel routes between specific points.

Noort, Oliver van (Olivier van Noort)

(1568–ca. 1622) *Dutch mariner on the coasts of South America and in the South Pacific*

A native of Utrecht in the Netherlands, Oliver van Noort became well known in Holland as an accomplished seafarer and navigator. In 1598, a group of Dutch merchants commissioned van Noort to command two commercial fleets on a voyage to the Far East by way of the STRAIT OF MAGELLAN. He sailed from Rotterdam on September 13, 1598, and reached the South American coast at Rio de Janeiro. When his ships were driven back by storms, he sought shelter along the coast of Brazil, where he lost some of his men in Indian attacks.

Van Noort came upon uninhabited Santa Clara Island, on which he and his men spent the winter of 1598–99. Resuming the voyage on June 2, 1599, he continued southward to the coast of Patagonia, and, three weeks later, he came upon an uncharted island, where his ships put in for repairs.

Van Noort's expedition entered the eastern approach to the Strait of Magellan on November 23, 1599. During the next two months, he made landings along the strait's north shores, during which he suffered additional losses in repeated Indian attacks. In the Penguin Islands, he located three uncharted bays, which he named Mauritius, Henry, and Oliver.

Van Noort and his ships left the Strait of Magellan and entered the Pacific Ocean on February 6, 1600. He then followed the coast of Chile northward, attacking Spanish ports and ships as far as the coast of Peru. Although the Spanish viceroy of Peru, Luis de Velasco, sent a naval force after the Dutch, they eluded capture and made their way westward across the Pacific to Guam in the Mariana Islands. From there, they resumed their attacks on the Spanish in the Philippines, then visited the Indonesian islands of Java and Borneo. The expeditor continued westward across the Indian Ocean, and, after rounding the CAPE OF GOOD HOPE, arrived back in Rotterdam on August 26, 1601.

Oliver van Noort commanded the first Dutch ships in a CIRCUMNAVIGATION OF THE WORLD and was among the first northern European navigators to probe the Pacific Ocean, a part of the world that had been explored mainly by the Spanish and Portuguese. A Dutch narrative of his voyage was published in Amsterdam in 1612, with translations in French and German appearing in 1613.

Nordenskjöld, Nils Adolf Erik
(Baron Nordenskjöld, Adolf Nordenskiöld)

(1832–1901) *Swedish-Finnish geologist in the Arctic regions of Spitsbergen, Greenland, and Siberia, explorer of Northeast Passage, uncle of Nils Otto Gustaf Nordenskjöld*

Adolf Nordenskjöld was born in Helsinki, Finland, the son of prominent Swedish parents. He attended Helsinki University, specializing in chemistry, mineralogy, and geology.

In 1858, Nordenskjöld left Finland, which was then under Russian rule, and moved to Stockholm, Sweden, where he accepted both an appointment as head of the mineralogy department of the National Museum of Natural History and a professorship at the University of Stockholm. That year, he began his career in Arctic exploration with a Swedish scientific expedition, led by Otto Martin Torell, to Spitsbergen (in Svalbard), midway between the north coast of Norway and the NORTH POLE. In 1861, he accompanied Torell on a second expedition to Spitsbergen, exploring the northern islands of the group by dogsled and producing one of the first scientifically based maps of the region.

Nordenskjöld led his own expedition to Spitsbergen in 1864, then again in 1868, in command of the First Swedish North Polar Expedition. On the steamer *Sofia*, accompanied by naval officer F. W. von Otter (who went on to become a prime minister of Sweden), Nordenskjöld reached 81°42' north latitude, the northernmost point a ship had reached in the Eastern Hemisphere until that time. For his achievement, Great Britain's ROYAL GEOGRAPHICAL SOCIETY awarded him a gold medal the following year.

In 1870, Nordenskjöld turned his attention to western GREENLAND, where he made an attempt at an inland penetration by dogsled. Although he traveled only 30 miles inland from Disko Island, he reached an elevation of 2,200 feet and undertook the first scientific investigation of the Greenland ice cap.

Nordenskjöld returned to Spitsbergen in command of the Second Swedish North Polar Expedition in 1872. He had planned to use reindeer to pull his sledges over the frozen expanse of the Arctic Ocean to the North Pole, but the PACK ICE proved to be too rugged, and his ship was later frozen in for the winter. Unable to make an attempt on the Pole, he instead explored Nordaustlandet, the northernmost of Spitsbergen's islands.

Back in Sweden in 1873, Nordenskjöld became interested in finding a navigable sea route from Europe, along the Arctic coast of Russia and SIBERIA, to the Bering Sea and the Pacific Ocean—the long-sought NORTHEAST PASSAGE. After familiarizing himself with the history of earlier unsuccessful attempts, he sailed on the walrus-hunting ship *Proeven* in 1875, across the Barents Sea to the islands of Novaya Zemlya. The next year, with the financial support of Swedish merchant Baron Oscar Dickson, he sailed on the steamer *Ymer*, halfway across the Kara Sea, to the mouth of the Yenisey River. Nordenskjöld came upon a natural harbor, which he named Port Dickson after his sponsor, reporting that it could become an important seaport if an ice-free Northeast Passage route were established.

With his reports that the Kara Sea's coastal waters were generally ice-free, Nordenskjöld gained additional support for a Northeast Passage expedition from King Oscar II of Norway and Sweden, as well as from Aleksandr Sibiryakov, a Russian mining and shipping tycoon. The expedition was outfitted with a 300-ton converted whaler, the *Vega*, which was driven by sails as well as a steam engine. Nordenskjöld sailed aboard the *Vega*, equipped with coal and provisions for two years, from Tromsö on Norway's Arctic coast on July 21, 1878, accompanied by three Russian merchant vessels. The expedition headed eastward around North Cape, then proceeded across the Barents Sea to the Kara Sea. At Port Dickson, two of the Russian ships left the group to ascend the Yenisey River, planning to return to Sweden with a cargo of Siberian wheat. Nordenskjöld and the *Vega*, along with the remaining merchant vessel, the *Lena*, continued to follow the coast eastward, and, on August 19, 1878, they rounded Cape Chelyuskin, making Nordenskjöld and his expedition the first men known to have sailed past the Asian mainland's northernmost point.

By August 28, 1878, Nordenskjöld had reached the Arctic delta of eastern Siberia's Lena River, where the *Vega* and the remaining merchant ship parted. While the *Lena* proceeded to ports on the upper Lena River, Nordenskjöld, aboard the *Vega*, made an attempt to reconnoiter the New Siberian Islands to the north. Pushed back to the Siberian mainland by the advancing pack ice, he resumed the voyage eastward.

On September 27, 1878, Nordenskjöld was off North Cape (now Cape Shmidta), the westernmost point JAMES COOK had reached from the Pacific Ocean in his search for the Northeast Passage in 1778. The next day, the last remaining ice-free channel also became choked, and, at a point only 120 miles from BERING STRAIT, the *Vega* became icebound. During the next 10 months, friendly contacts were made with the region's natives, the Chukchi people of northeastern Siberia, whose customs were studied by the expedition's scientific team. Extensive scientific work was also undertaken in the areas of zoology, botany, oceanography, and geophysics.

The *Vega* was able to break free of the ice on July 18, 1879, and, on July 20, Nordenskjöld sailed southward into Bering Strait, thus completing the first voyage from the Atlantic Ocean to the Pacific by way of the Northeast Passage. After stops in Japan and CEYLON (present-day Sri Lanka), the *Vega* returned to Europe by way of the recently opened Suez Canal, arriving in Stockholm on August 24, 1880.

Nordenskjöld was made a baron for his achievement and soon published an account of the voyage, *The Voyage of the Vega Round Asia and Europe, With a Historical Review of Previous Journeys Along the North Coast of the Old World* (1881). The book became a best-seller and was followed by a five-volume report on the expedition's scientific work, *Scientific Observations of the Vega Expedition*. Published from 1882 to 1887, it served as a model for subsequent polar studies.

Nordenskjöld resumed his explorations of the Greenland ice cap in 1882–83, hoping to locate an ice-free region, which he theorized lay within the interior. He again scaled the glacier on the mainland at Disko Bay, reaching about 75 miles inland.

In addition to his Arctic exploits, Nordenskjöld also undertook studies on the history of geographic exploration. His *Facsimile-Atlas to the Early History of Cartography* (1889) and his *Periplus: An Essay on the Early History of Charts and Sailing Directions* (1897), published simultaneously in English and Swedish editions, were important early works on the history of mapmaking and exploration.

Baron Adolf Nordenskjöld led the first successful navigation through the Northeast Passage, a feat that had challenged mariners since the voyages of SIR HUGH WILLOUGHBY, WILLIAM BOROUGH, and STEPHEN BOROUGH in the 1550s, and WILLEM BARENTS in the 1590s. On his return voyage to Sweden, Nordenskjöld completed the first circumnavigation of Europe and Asia. In the years following the Russian Revolution of 1917, the Soviet government developed the Northeast Passage into a viable commercial waterway, which became known as the Northern Sea Route. As Nordenskjöld had predicted, the once uninhabited Port Dickson (known today as Dikson), strategically located

midway between the Atlantic and Pacific entrances of the Northeast Passage, became a vital stopover point and Arctic gateway to central Siberia. The Laptev Sea, the arm of the Arctic Ocean east of the Kara Sea, was known for a time as the Nordenskjöld Sea in his honor, and April 24 is still celebrated in Sweden as Vega Day, in recognition of his triumphant return from his 1878–79 Northeast Passage voyage. His nephew NILS OTTO GUSTAF NORDENSKJÖLD became a renowned geologist.

Nordenskjöld, Nils Otto Gustaf (Otto Nordenskiöld) (1869–1928) *Swedish geologist in Antarctica, South America, Greenland, and Alaska, nephew of Nils Adolf Erik Nordenskjöld*

Otto Nordenskjöld, born in Sweden, like his famous uncle, the NORTHEAST PASSAGE pioneer NILS ADOLF ERIK NORDENSKJÖLD, was a distinguished geologist who embarked on a career of scientific exploration.

In 1895–97, Nordenskjöld led a scientific team to southernmost South America, where he undertook geological studies in Patagonia and Tierra del Fuego.

In 1898, Nordenskjöld conducted geological research in Alaska and the adjoining Klondike region of the Yukon Territory, and, in 1900, he visited GREENLAND. That same year, the International Geographical Congress was held in Berlin, where the world's leading scientists declared 1901–03 to be the Antarctic Year, with scientific expeditions to Antarctica planned by Germany, France, Scotland, and Sweden.

Appointed to lead the Swedish expedition, Nordenskjöld sailed from Gothenburg, Sweden, in October 1901 on the *Antarctic,* captained by C. A. Larsen. After stopovers in the New Hebrides and in Argentina, the *Antarctic* went to the South Shetland Islands off the Antarctic Peninsula. In exploring the southwestern South Shetlands, the expedition corrected some errors made by SIR JAMES CLARK ROSS and JULES-SÉBASTIEN-CÉSAR DUMONT D'URVILLE when they charted the Antarctic archipelago more than 60 years earlier.

After surveying the Antarctic coast of Louis Philippe Land, Nordenskjöld and his expedition landed on the Weddell Sea coast of Grahamland, where he planned to undertake geological studies to determine if northeastern Antarctica had ever been joined to the southern end of South America. While a base was established at Snow Hill Island, Larsen sailed the *Antarctic* back toward South America, planning to return the following Antarctic summer. Although the ship failed to arrive after a year, Nordenskjöld and his men, equipped for only one winter in the Antarctic, nevertheless managed to comfortably survive through a second winter, living on birds and animals they hunted and whatever edible vegetation they could forage.

In October 1903, Nordenskjöld explored nearby Mount Haddington, which he found to be an island surrounded by ice. He encountered three members of the expedition who had sailed with the *Antarctic* and learned from them that the ship had been unable to breech the PACK ICE the previous year. A month later, Captain Irizar of the Argentine navy arrived on the ship *Uruguay,* having been dispatched to rescue the Swedish expedition when the *Antarctic* failed to arrive in Argentina. As it turned out, the *Antarctic* had sunk in February 1903, crushed in the ice on its second attempt to reach Snow Hill Island. Larsen and the rest of the *Antarctic* crew arrived at Nordenskjöld's encampment soon afterward, and all expedition members were safely taken back to South America by the *Uruguay.*

Nordenskjöld continued his geological studies of South America with scientific expeditions to the Andes in 1904–05 and again in 1920–21. He made another visit to Greenland in 1909.

In 1905, Otto Nordenskjöld was appointed as professor of geography at the University of Gothenburg. His geological investigation in Antarctica in 1901–03 revealed an abundance of fossil evidence suggesting that Graham Land had been covered with lush forests during the Jurassic period and was probably once connected to Tierra del Fuego or TASMANIA.

Norgay, Tenzing   See TENZING NORGAY.

Noué, Charles-Edouard de la   (1624–1691)
French priest in South America
Charles-Edouard de la Noué was born in the Anjou region of western France. Although he had entered the priesthood, he involved himself more in the study of scientific matters than in the practice of religion.

In 1665, the French government sent Noué to explore Tierra del Fuego and the Pacific coast of southern Patagonia in what is now southern Chile. The region, nominally part of Spanish territory, had not yet been settled by Europeans, and France hoped to claim it.

Noué traveled in Patagonia and Tierra del Fuego for a number of years. Taken captive by the Indians, he learned their language and customs and adopted their mode of dress. The natives came to accept him as an equal and eventually allowed him to depart on a passing European ship.

Back in France, Charles-Edouard de la Noué recorded his experiences in South America in his two-volume *Mémoire,* published in 1675. Its stark portrayal of the region's rugged terrain, inhospitable climate, and primitive native population served to discourage any further attempts by the French to settle that part of South America.

Núñez de Balboa, Vasco   (1475–1519)
Spanish conquistador, colonizer in Panama, brother-in-law of Hernando de Soto
Vasco Núñez de Balboa was born in the Estremadura region of west-central Spain. Although of a humble family, he became well-connected among the Spanish nobility, serving in his early years as a page in the court of Don Puertocarrero, the lord of Moguer.

In 1501, Núñez de Balboa embarked on a career as a conquistador in the Americas. He left Spain as part of RODRIGO DE BASTIDAS's expedition to the north coast of South America in search of pearls. With Bastidas, he explored the harbor around what is now Cartagena, Colombia, and also visited the Gulf of Urabá, at the lower end of the Isthmus of Panama. Problems with the ships forced the expedition to head for the Spanish settlements on the island of Hispaniola (present-day Haiti and the Dominican Republic). Núñez de Balboa settled there and attempted to establish a plantation.

By 1510, Núñez de Balboa found himself seriously in debt. To escape his creditors, he stowed away on a ship headed for San Sebastián, on the eastern end of the Gulf of

Vasco Núñez de Balboa *(Library of Congress)*

Vasco Núñez de Balboa at the Pacific Ocean *(Library of Congress)*

Urabá, to commence an expedition. With him, he had few possessions other than his sword and his dog, Leoncico. The leader of the expedition, Martín Fernández de Encisco, agreed reluctantly to allow Núñez de Balboa to remain with it. Upon reaching San Sebastián, they discovered the colony had been abandoned. Drawing upon his earlier experience on the Panama coast with Bastidas, Núñez de Balboa directed the expedition and the remaining colonists to the western side of the Gulf of Urabá and established the settlement of Santa María de la Antigua del Darién.

By 1511, Núñez de Balboa had consolidated his control over the new colony, deposing the former Spanish rulers, DIEGO DE NICUESA and ALONSO DE OJEDA. The Spanish king commissioned him as interim governor and captain general of Darién, as Panama was then known. Núñez de

Balboa penetrated the interior of the isthmus, battling Indians and expanding the colony. His chief lieutenant at this time was FRANCISCO PIZARRO.

Núñez de Balboa was skillful in his diplomatic relations with native peoples. He made alliances with Indian leaders Careta and Comogre, from whom he first heard reports of tribes to the south and west who possessed gold and pearls. He was told that if he could defeat the powerful chief Tubanamá, these riches could be his. He also learned from the Indians of a great sea on the other side of the Sierra de Quareca Mountains.

In early September 1513, Núñez de Balboa set out from Darién with a force of almost 200 Spaniards and 1,000 Indians and slaves. Crossing the lower part of the isthmus, his men struggled through some of the densest jungles and most rugged mountains in CENTRAL AMERICA. On September

25, 1513, they came to a hill that appeared to afford an un-obstructed view to the south and west. Núñez de Balboa ascended it, accompanied only by his dog, and viewed the PACIFIC OCEAN.

Núñez de Balboa and his men pushed onward through the jungle and reached the shores of the Pacific on September 29. He called it the Great South Sea and, in a solemn ceremony, claimed it and all the lands it touched for the king of Spain. He named the bay there the Gulf of San Miguel. On this expedition, he and Pizarro heard the earliest reports of the Inca civilization to the south in present-day Peru. Núñez de Balboa obtained gold and pearls on the Pacific coast of Panama, then returned to the Atlantic side of the isthmus and, following a different route, conquered more Indian towns and obtained more riches.

Núñez de Balboa arrived back at the Darién settlement in January 1514. Meanwhile, court intrigues in Spain led to his being superceded in command in Panama by PEDRO ARIAS DE ÁVILA, who arrived at the colony later that year.

In 1516, Núñez de Balboa directed another expedition across Panama to the Pacific. On this occasion, the parts of disassembled ships were carried across the isthmus from Acla, a town Núñez de Balboa had established as his base on the Atlantic coast of Panama, near Puerto Careta. Transporting the ships through the mountains and jungles was accomplished with great difficulty and succeeded only because of Núñez de Balboa's great organizational skills. Núñez de Balboa himself had to make 20 crossings of the isthmus in the course of this project. Nearly 500 Indian laborers lost their lives. Two brigantines were eventually launched into the Gulf of San Miguel, and Núñez de Balboa sailed to the Perlas Islands, where he obtained pearls and undertook a few short explorations southward along Panama's Pacific coast.

Meanwhile, back on the Atlantic coast, intrigues against Núñez de Balboa continued. He was lured to Acla by Arias de Ávila and was arrested by his former lieutenant, Pizarro. In late January 1519, Núñez de Balboa was tried and found guilty of treason, stemming from trumped-up charges that he planned to establish his own colony on the Pacific side of the isthmus. Along with four of his chief supporters, he was publicly beheaded.

Vasco Núñez de Balboa was the first European to see the Pacific Ocean from the west coast of the Americas. His exploit had a profound influence on subsequent explorers, encouraging hopes that the newfound continent was narrow enough to provide an all-water route to the Pacific. His explorations also revealed that the riches of the Far East lay much farther west of the American landmass than previously believed. Núñez de Balboa established the first overland trail across the Americas, which subsequently provided the Spanish with a direct route to the west coast of South America and the gold and silver of Peru.

Nuttall, Thomas (1786–1859) *British naturalist in North America*

Born in the town of Settle in Yorkshire, England, Thomas Nuttall grew up in a family of modest means. After serving as an apprentice in the printing trade, he went to work at his uncle's printing shop in Liverpool.

In 1808, at the age of 22, Nuttall traveled to the United States, settling in Philadelphia. He became acquainted with the physician and naturalist Benjamin S. Barton, who encouraged him to pursue his interest in natural history. Nuttall soon began making field trips southward into the Delaware River Valley, as well as northward to the New Jersey Pine Barrens. His specimen-collecting expeditions eventually took him into the Delaware-Maryland Peninsula, coastal Virginia, the lowlands of North Carolina, and as far south as Mississippi and Florida.

In 1811, Nuttall, along with Scottish naturalist JOHN BRADBURY, accompanied WILSON PRICE HUNT and his fur-trading expedition from St. Louis up the MISSOURI RIVER by keelboat, reaching a point on the river above the Mandan Indian villages in what is now North Dakota.

Nuttall was back in Philadelphia in 1811, where he prepared a detailed study of his botanical specimens from the West. In 1813, he was elected a fellow of London's prestigious Linnaean Society, and, in 1817, he was made a member of the Philadelphia-based American Philosophical Society and correspondent of Philadelphia's Academy of Natural Sciences.

In 1818–20, Nuttall returned to scientific exploration in the American West, traveling along the Arkansas and Red Rivers into the remote parts of what is now Arkansas, Louisiana, and eastern Oklahoma. His *Journal of Travels into the Arkansas Territory, during the Year 1819,* published in 1821, includes information on the history of the region's Indian tribes as well as meteorological observations.

Nuttall's major botanical work, *The Genera of North American Plants, and a Catalogue of the Species, in the Year 1817,* first published in 1818, brought him fame in American scientific circles. In 1822, he was appointed a professor of natural history at Harvard, where he also served as curator of the botanical gardens.

Nuttall left his post at Harvard in 1834 to travel with NATHANIEL JARVIS WYETH's fur-trading expedition to the mouth of the COLUMBIA RIVER. He was accompanied by another naturalist, ornithologist John Townsend, as well as by Jason Lee and his small band of missionaries on their way to the Oregon Country. After the overland crossing to the Pacific coast, Nuttall returned to the East the following year by ship, sailing via the HAWAIIAN ISLANDS and CAPE HORN.

Nuttall returned to England in 1842 to live on an estate near Liverpool called Nutgrove, left to him by his uncle, where he cultivated exotic plants. He returned to Philadelphia for a visit in 1847–48, during which he studied a natural history collection that had recently arrived at the Academy of Sciences from the Far West. He spent his remaining years in England.

With the publication in 1832 of his *Manual of the Ornithology of the United States and Canada,* Thomas Nuttall, like his contemporary JOHN JAMES AUDUBON, was acclaimed as one of the foremost authorities on the birds of North America. The first ornithological association in the United States was subsequently named in Nuttall's honor. In addition to his work in botany and bird studies, Nuttall was a pioneer paleontologist, and he was among the first to cite the similarities in the geological makeup of such widely separated regions as Iowa and Derbyshire, England. He was one of the best-traveled naturalists to study the flora and fauna of North America in the first half of the 19th century. His explorations in search of plant and bird specimens took him into almost every state in the Union as well as into uncharted territory of the American West.

Odanais, Isabela Godin des See GODIN DES
ODANAIS, ISABELA.

**Odoric of Pordenone (Friar Odoric, Friar
Oderic)** (ca. 1265–1331) *Italian missionary in India,
China, and Tibet*

Odoric of Pordenone was probably born in the northeastern
Italian city of that name, north of Padua. He took holy orders as a Franciscan friar, becoming a missionary priest
committed to winning converts to Christianity in Asia.

In about 1318, Odoric left Italy on a missionary expedition to the Far East. From Constantinople (present-day Istanbul, Turkey), he traveled overland across Asia Minor and
Persia (present-day Iran) to the mouth of the Persian Gulf
and the port of Hormuz, from where he continued his eastward journey by ship. He sailed first to Thana on India's
northwest coast, north of Bombay, where he collected the
bones of some recently martyred Christian missionaries. On
southwestern India's Malabar Coast, he visited the port of
Quilon and witnessed the trade carried on in the city's pepper and ginger markets.

Odoric then sailed to the island of CEYLON (present-
day Sri Lanka); he later reported seeing a two-headed bird,
probably a variety of hornbill whose long, curved bill
confused him. After stopping at the Nicobar Islands of
the eastern Indian Ocean, he reached Sumatra and the Strait
of Malacca, from where he sailed to Borneo and Java, then
landed on the East Asian mainland of Cochin China (present-
day Vietnam).

In about 1322, Odoric arrived at the Chinese port of
Hangchow, then proceeded inland along the Grand Canal
to Peking (Beijing). He stayed with JOHN OF MON-
TECORVINO, who had founded a Franciscan mission and
church in the Chinese capital.

The bones of the martyred missionaries Odoric had carried from India were interred in Peking. Odoric remained in
northern China until about 1328, then set out overland for
his return journey to Europe. From Peking, he traveled
northward, beyond the Great Wall of China into Inner
Mongolia, then made his way southwestward across central
China and entered Tibet. He reportedly reached the Tibetan
capital of LHASA, the first Christian to do so. He later described the Tibetan people in critical terms, stating that they
practiced cannibalism and that they drank out of the skulls
of their ancestors.

Odoric's homeward journey took him along the northern slopes of the HIMALAYAS and through the Hindu Kush.
He passed through Persia again, traveling along the south
shore of the Caspian Sea, and, in about 1330, he arrived
back in Padua. His route to the Far East and back followed
in reverse that taken by MARCO POLO some 40 years earlier.

Soon after returning to Italy, Odoric wrote, with the help
of another Franciscan friar, an account of his 12-year odyssey
to the Far East. In the course of his travels, he reportedly
had made as many as 10,000 converts to Christianity.

Odoric of Pordenone died in 1331, one year after his return from China. At the time of his death, he was planning a second proselytizing mission to Asia. The narrative of his travels, along with that of Marco Polo, fueled European interest in Asia, with its descriptions of the great size and marvels of such Chinese cities as Hangchow (Hangzhou) and Zaiton (Quanzhou), and the SPICE TRADE in India and Sumatra. It also provided Europeans with new geographic information about the Orient, much of which was incorporated by cartographer ABRAHAM CRESQUES in his *Catalan Atlas* of 1375. Odoric's account seems to have been a source for the 14th-century travel book *The Travels of Sir John Mandeville* by Sir John Mandeville, thought to be a pseudonym. After Odoric, 300 years elapsed before the next European visited Tibet; Jesuit missionary ANTONIO DE ANDRADE entered the region from India in 1624.

Ogden, Peter Skene (M'sieu Pete) (1794–1854)

Canadian fur trader in the American West

Peter Skene Ogden was born in Quebec City, Canada, to a Loyalist family who had settled there during the American Revolution. He was raised and educated in Montreal, where his father was a magistrate.

Although trained as a lawyer, Ogden decided against a legal career in favor of a life of travel and adventure in the FUR TRADE. In 1811, he joined the Canadian-owned NORTH WEST COMPANY and took part in fur-trading and trapping operations in the Great Lakes region.

Ogden journeyed to the Pacific Northwest in 1818. In 1824, three years after the North West Company's merger with the HUDSON'S BAY COMPANY, he became chief lieutenant to the Hudson's Bay Company's factor, JOHN McLOUGHLIN, in the COLUMBIA RIVER region.

In late 1824, Ogden, with a party of 75 trappers and about 400 pack animals, embarked on an expedition to the south and east of the Hudson's Bay Company's Flathead Post in present-day northern Idaho. He was directed to deplete the area's beaver resources in an effort to discourage American trappers who were then penetrating the region from the upper MISSOURI RIVER. Driven out of the Three Forks of the Missouri area by Indian attacks, Ogden and his men explored the upper Jefferson River, then headed southward to the Salmon River, crossing the Continental Divide en route.

By May 1825, Ogden reached the northern Wasatch Mountains, near the site of present-day Ogden, Utah. From there, he explored the Weber River and the Bear River to its outlet into the Great Salt Lake. He returned to the Three Forks of the Missouri, and, after exploring and trapping along the Marias River, he reached Fort Vancouver, the Hudson's Bay Company's main post on the Columbia, in late 1825.

Ogden soon embarked on a second wide-ranging fur expedition. Starting from Fort Vancouver in winter 1825–26, he led a group of traders and trappers southward from the Columbia along Oregon's Deschutes River, then explored the region of the Blue Mountains to the east, as far as the Snake River.

In 1826–27, Ogden again headed southward from Fort Vancouver to Klamath Lake and northern California. While trapping and exploring there in 1827, Ogden and his party became the first non-Indians to sight Mount Shasta, which he named.

Ogden undertook an expedition into Utah's Great Basin in 1828–29. He and his men explored the north and west shores of the Great Salt Lake, then traced a previously unknown stream to its sink in what is now western Nevada, which Ogden named the Marys River. Fifteen years later, it was located by JOHN CHARLES FRÉMONT, who renamed its lower course the Humboldt River.

The next season, 1829–30, Ogden led his men from the Columbia southward across the Great Basin to the COLORADO RIVER, which he followed to its outlet into the Gulf of California. He and his party crossed the Sierra Nevada into California via Walker Pass, then returned northward to the Columbia through the San Joaquin and Sacramento Valleys. Along the way, Ogden was joined at times by EWING YOUNG and his men.

Throughout the 1830s, Ogden continued to expand the Hudson's Bay Company's operations in the Pacific Northwest. For a time, he supervised the fur trade in the Stikene River region of southeastern Alaska, and he was subsequently appointed as chief factor at Fort Vancouver. In 1847, he helped negotiate the release of non-Indian captives held by Cayuse Indians following the attack on missionary MARCUS WHITMAN and his followers.

After retiring from the fur trade, Ogden settled in Oregon City, Oregon, with his Indian wife. His explorations of the American West had brought him into contact with a wide variety of Native Americans, and he wrote about these experiences in his book *Traits of American Indian Life and Character. By a Fur Trader,* published posthumously in 1855.

Peter Skene Ogden's trading expeditions took him over a vast area of the American West. He was among the first non-Indians to report the existence of the Great Salt Lake. His 1828–29 exploration along the Humboldt River to the Humboldt sink in Nevada confirmed that it was not the fabled Bonaventura River and ended speculation that the Great Salt Lake was an arm of the Pacific Ocean. His 1829–30 expedition took him from the Columbia River as far south as the Gulf of California and constituted the first north-south crossing by non-Indians of the North American continent west of the Continental Divide. Utah's Ogden City, Ogden River, Ogden Valley, and Ogden Canyon were named in honor of his extensive explorations of the Great Basin.

Ojeda, Alonso de (Alonso de Hojeda)

(ca. 1465–ca. 1515) Spanish conquistador in the West Indies, South America, and Panama

Alonso de Ojeda was born in Cuenca, Spain, the son of aristocratic parents. In his early years, he was a member of the household of the Duke of Medina Celi and took part in Spain's final campaigns of reconquest against the Moors.

In 1493, Ojeda commanded one of the ships in CHRISTOPHER COLUMBUS's second voyage of exploration, sailing to the island of Hispaniola (present-day Haiti and the Dominican Republic), where he helped establish the settlement of Isabela. He then explored the interior of the island, discovering gold mines near Cibao. In April 1494, Ojeda led a military expedition against Indians in the La Vega Real region of Hispaniola, defeating the leader Caonabo at the Battle of La Vega the following March.

In 1497, Ojeda returned to Spain and sought royal authority for an expedition of his own to the Americas. In 1499, he received permission to explore along the coast of South America, reached by Columbus on his third voyage in 1498. On May 16, 1499, Ojeda sailed with several ships from the Spanish port of Santa María, near Cádiz. Accompanying him were Columbus's former pilot, JUAN DE LA COSA, and AMERIGO VESPUCCI, a representative of the Italian banking interests that had partly financed the voyage.

Ojeda's small fleet reached South America at about 5° north latitude, off the coast of what later became French Guiana. While Vespucci explored to the south and east, Ojeda coasted to the north and west, making stops at Margarita Island and Trinidad. On the mainland, along a coastal inlet, he came upon an Indian settlement of houses supported by piers in the water. The scene reminded Ojeda of Venice with its canals and he named the place Venezuela, "Little Venice" in Spanish. He also came upon a similar village at what is now Maracaibo, which he called San Bartolomé.

After exploring the northeast coast of South America as far as Cape Vela, Ojeda sailed to Hispaniola for ship repairs. He soon ran afoul of Columbus's lieutenants, who ordered him to leave Hispaniola, accusing him of trespassing on territory already claimed by Columbus. In response, Ojeda attempted, without success, to mount an uprising against Columbus's rule on Hispaniola. He then sailed to Jamaica, and, on a stopover in the Bahamas, he captured a number of Indians whom he sold as slaves upon his return to Cádiz in June 1500. He also took back a cargo of brazilwood, used for dying cloth, as well as a quantity of pearls from the Gulf of Paria.

In January 1502, Ojeda led another expedition to the northeast coast of South America, intending to establish a colony on the coast of Venezuela. The settlement, which he called Santa Cruz, was constantly besieged by the Indians. After about nine months, when supplies became low, his men mutinied. They arrested Ojeda and sent him in chains to Spanish authorities in Hispaniola, charging him with being despotic and brutal in his treatment of both his own men and the region's Indians. Bishop Fonseca, president of the Council of the Indies, which directed all Spanish exploration and settlement in the Americas, interceded on Ojeda's behalf and won his release. In 1505, Ojeda again unsuccessfully attempted to establish a colony on the Venezuelan mainland.

In 1508, Ojeda sent Cosa to Spain to seek another royal commission for a colony in South America. As a result, Ojeda was named governor of New Andalusia, a colonial province extending from Cape Vela to the Gulf of Darien, comprising most of the Atlantic coast of what is now Colombia and eastern Panama.

Among the men Ojeda recruited on Hispaniola for this enterprise was FRANCISCO PIZARRO, the future conqueror of Peru. HERNÁN CORTÉS, who later commanded the conquest of Mexico, also planned to accompany Ojeda, but he was forced to stay behind due to an injury. In November 1509, Ojeda sailed from Hispaniola's port of Santo Domingo with four ships, carrying 300 men and supplies. He landed at what is now Cartagena, Colombia, where his men suffered a devastating defeat in an Indian attack; Cosa, who had partly financed the expedition, was killed. Soon afterward, DIEGO DE NICUESA, in command of a rival expedition, arrived at Cartagena, rescued Ojeda, then helped him launch a counterattack against the Indians.

Unable to subdue the native peoples around Cartagena, Ojeda moved his colony westward along the coast, establishing San Sebastian on the east shore of Colombia's Gulf of Urabá. The relief ship supposedly sent by the principal backer, Spanish lawyer Martín Enciso, failed to arrive, and Ojeda decided to return to Hispaniola. Leaving Pizarro in command, he sailed with Bernardino de Talavera (or Calavera), one of the Spanish PRIVATEERS active in the region. The ship was wrecked off the coast of Cuba. A message sent by CANOE to Jamaica was received there by PÁNFILO DE NARVÁEZ, who sent a ship to pick up Ojeda and take him back to Hispaniola. Meanwhile, Enciso had already sailed for the mainland, and VASCO NÚÑEZ DE BALBOA, in Ojeda's absence, usurped his authority and reorganized the Panama colony under his own leadership.

Left without financial backing to reestablish his claim on New Andalusia, Ojeda spent his last years on Hispaniola in poverty. His death was reportedly due to the effects of a poison-tipped arrow with which he had been wounded on his final expedition to the mainland of South America and the Isthmus of Panama.

Alonso de Ojeda was among the first generation of Spanish adventurers to colonize the lands explored by Columbus between the mouths of the ORINOCO RIVER and Panama's Gulf of Urabá. Based on his 1499 voyage with

Ojeda, Cosa produced the first map to depict the mainland of northern South America. Although Ojeda's own colonizing efforts were unsuccessful, they soon led to permanent European settlements on the coast of what is now Venezuela, Colombia, and Panama. His son, also named Alonso, played a leading role in the Spanish conquest of Mexico under Cortés in 1519–21.

Oñate, Juan de (ca. 1550–ca. 1630)
Spanish colonizer of New Mexico

Juan de Oñate was probably born in western Mexico, in the old colonial province of Nueva Galicia. His father, Cristóbal de Oñate, was one of the original European discovers of the silver mines of Zacatecas. The younger Oñate married a direct descendant of HERNÁN CORTÉS, the leader of the Spanish conquest of Mexico.

In 1595, Juan de Oñate was commissioned by the Spanish government to undertake a colonizing expedition north of the Rio Grande into what is now New Mexico. Three years later, in late 1598, he led several soldiers, settlers, and Franciscan missionaries north from Nueva Gali-

cia into what is now western Texas. Oñate and his expedition reached the Rio Grande near present-day El Paso, Texas, and followed it to its confluence with the Chama, where they established the settlement of San Juan de los Caballeros, near present-day Santa Fe. He claimed New Mexico for Spain and became the province's first Spanish governor. Soon afterward, he established a permanent settlement nearby at San Gabriel de Yungue-Ouinge, at what became known as the San Gabriel Pueblo, the first colonial capital of the province of New Mexico.

Beginning in 1601, Oñate undertook a series of explorations in the lands surrounding his New Mexico settlements, in search of mineral wealth and the fabled Seven Cities of CIBOLA and QUIVIRA. He explored the Texas Panhandle and the Canadian and Arkansas Rivers, crossing what is now Oklahoma, and penetrated the southern plains as far as present-day Wichita, Kansas.

In 1604–05, Oñate explored westward from the San Gabriel settlement into the Gila River region of present-day Arizona, in search of a direct route to the "South Sea." He reached the COLORADO RIVER and followed it to the northern end of the Gulf of California.

Juan de Oñate's inscription at El Morro in New Mexico *(Library of Congress)*

Oñate served as Spain's first colonial governor of New Mexico until 1609. After he resigned, he was charged with mismanagement and excessive cruelty in suppressing Indian uprisings, especially at Acoma Pueblo in 1598–99. In 1609, he founded a settlement at Santa Fe. In 1614, he was exiled from New Mexico. He later traveled to Spain, where he won a reversal of his sentence.

Juan de Oñate explored much of the same territory covered by FRANCISCO VÁSQUEZ DE CORONADO in 1541. He founded the first permanent European settlements west of the MISSISSIPPI RIVER in what is now the United States. Oñate's 1604–05 expedition across what is now western New Mexico took him to the famous inscription rock, El Morro, where he was the first European to record his name at the base of the 200-foot-high natural sandstone monument.

Orbigny, Alcide-Charles-Victor Dessalines d'

(1802–1857) *French naturalist in South America*
Alcide d'Orbigny was born in Coueron, France. In 1825, when he was just 23 years old, his studies of foraminifera (a class of shelled, near-microscopic, protozoa-type creatures) so impressed the directors of the Paris Museum of Natural History that they commissioned him to lead a scientific expedition to South America.

In 1826–27, Orbigny traveled across Brazil and Uruguay, collecting zoological and botanical specimens. In 1827–28, he undertook an exploration of the Paraná River and its tributaries in southeastern Brazil, Paraguay, and Argentina.

In 1828, Orbigny was commissioned by the government of Argentina to explore the Pampas and prepare a report on its potential for agricultural development. That year, he went south to Patagonia to conduct natural history studies. While there, he was adopted by a native band and fought on their side in an intertribal war. He then spent several years exploring Bolivia and traveling in Peru, during which he carried out additional scientific studies and collected plant and animal specimens.

Orbigny returned to France in 1834. The extensive natural history collection he had amassed in his travels in South America brought him the Grand Prize from the Geographical Society of Paris, and the French government published his nine-volume report of the expedition, *Voyage dans l'Amérique Meridionale* (1834–47). In the course of his explorations in South America, Orbigny had also collected and studied microscopic fossils, work that became the foundation for the science of stratigraphical paleontology.

Alcide d'Orbigny's explorations through nearly every part of South America yielded much new geographic information, and, in 1842, he produced the first comprehensive map of the continent.

Ordaz, Diego de (Diego de Ordás) (1480–1535)

Spanish conquistador in the Americas
Diego de Ordaz was born at Zamora in northwestern Spain. While in his early 20s, he sailed to the WEST INDIES. In 1509, he embarked from Hispaniola (present-day Haiti and the Dominican Republic) with ALONSO DE OJEDA's abortive colonizing expedition to the coast of what is now Colombia and Panama.

Ordaz took part in the conquest of Cuba under DIEGO DE VELÁSQUEZ in 1511 and he later served in Velásquez's household after the latter was appointed as the island's first colonial governor.

Ordaz served as an officer under HERNÁN CORTÉS in his conquest of Mexico in 1519–21. In the early stages of that campaign, he commanded a reconnaissance of the Yucatán coast. Later, as Cortés and his army approached the Aztec capital, Ordaz led a number of men part way up 17,930-foot Popocatépetl, an active volcano on the outskirts of what is now Mexico City. He thus became one of the first Europeans to catch a glimpse of Tenochtitlán, the Aztec capital. Soon afterward, Ordaz accompanied Cortés in his first meeting with the Aztec emperor Montezuma (Moctezuma).

In 1521, Ordaz returned to Spain and reported on the conquest of Mexico to King Charles I (Holy Roman Emperor Charles V). In honor of Ordaz's having made the climb of Popocatépetl, the Spanish monarch permitted his family to display a burning mountain in its coat of arms.

Ordaz became the commander of his own expedition in 1530. He was commissioned by the king to explore, conquer, and colonize a large portion of the northeast coast of South America, stretching from the mouth of the AMAZON RIVER to Cape de la Vela, a region comprising part of what is now eastern Colombia, Venezuela, the Guianas, and northeastern Brazil.

Ordaz sailed from Spain with three ships carrying 500 men. Although he located the mouth of the Amazon, he was unable to make a landing, and instead he sailed westward along South America's northeast coast to the Gulf of Paria. He learned from the natives of another great river, which the natives called the Huyapari. By June 1531, Ordaz had succeeded in finding the delta of this river, now known as the ORINOCO RIVER. He explored upriver for about 800 miles, reaching its junction with the Meta River, which he briefly investigated.

From the region's Indians, Ordaz learned of a mysterious people called the "Guiana," who supposedly possessed vast amounts of gold and other riches and were said to be white, like Europeans. Ordaz searched in vain for this fabled land of wealth before returning to the coast. On nearby Cubagua Island he ran afoul of Spanish settlers, who charged him with trespassing in lands that had already been claimed in that part of what is Venezuela.

Placed under arrest, Ordaz was transported to Santo Domingo on Hispaniola, where he was soon released. In 1532, he sailed for Spain to assert his claim on the lands he had explored, but he died on the homeward voyage.

Diego de Ordaz, who played a significant role in the early stages of the Spanish conquest of Mexico, became the first European to explore the Orinoco River, one of the longest in South America, ascending it to a point about 600 miles inland from the Caribbean coast of present-day Venezuela. The reports he related of a rich Native American civilization rumored to exist in the region encouraged subsequent explorations of the Orinoco, in search of the fabled land of EL DORADO.

Orellana, Francisco de (ca. 1490–ca. 1546)
Spanish conquistador in Peru, Ecuador, and the Amazon Basin

Born at Trujillo in the Estremadura region of western Spain, Francisco de Orellana was a relative and boyhood friend of FRANCISCO PIZARRO. In 1527, he left Spain to seek his fortune in the WEST INDIES. In the years that followed, he took part in campaigns of conquest on the mainland.

Orellana joined his kinsman Pizarro in the conquest of Peru in 1533–35, during which he fought in battles against the Inca at Lima, Trujillo, and Cuzco, suffering the loss of an eye in one engagement. In 1538, he led Spanish forces in the conquest of the Inca province of La Culata, and soon afterward he helped reestablish the city of Guayaquil near the Pacific coast of what is now Ecuador. Orellana also aided Pizarro and his forces in defeating DIEGO DE ALMAGRO in the civil war that same year.

Orellana settled for a time at Puerto Viejo (present-day Portoviejo, Ecuador) near Guayaquil, where he had been appointed governor by Pizarro. In early 1541, he organized at his own expense a small force of about 20 Spaniards and a number of Indians and set out eastward from Quito, across the northern ANDES MOUNTAINS, hoping to join up with a larger expedition under the command of GONZALO PIZARRO, Francisco Pizarro's younger brother. The younger Pizarro was at that time in search of La Canela (the land of cinnamon), reportedly an abundant source of that highly prized spice, and of the fabled kingdom of EL DORADO, a land that, according to Indian stories, was rich with gold.

In March 1541, Orellana met up with Gonzalo Pizarro and his men on the upper Coca River in what is now northern Ecuador; he was immediately named second in command. Pizarro had located some cinnamon trees in the region, but not enough to be of any commercial value. The search for El Dorado persisted, and, by late 1541, the combined expedition was facing a critical shortage of food and supplies. A brigantine-type boat, the *San Pedro*, was constructed with improvised materials, and on Christmas Day 1541, Orellana, accompanied by 56 men and a number of natives traveling by CANOE, headed down the Coca, hoping to find an Indian village with food.

Although he had been instructed by Pizarro to return within 12 days, Orellana and his men were soon swept into the upper Napo River. At the confluence of the Napo and the Aguarico Rivers, they came upon an Indian village called Aparia, where they found ample food, and it was there that Orellana decided not to attempt a return journey upstream to rejoin Gonzalo Pizarro. Instead, he resolved to construct a larger vessel and continue downstream into the AMAZON RIVER, then known as the Marañon (maze), intending to explore it to its mouth on the Atlantic Ocean. After two months, the second boat, the *Victoria*, was completed, and, on April 24, 1542, Orellana resumed his downriver journey.

In mid-May 1542, Orellana and his men successfully fought off a series of Indian attacks as they made their way downstream. In early June, after locating the mouth of the Río Negro (so named after the darker appearance of its water as it combined with the main stream of the Amazon), the Spaniards were reportedly besieged by a group of women warriors, likened by the expedition's chronicler, Dominican friar Gaspar de Carvajal, to the Amazon women of Greek legend.

On July 28, 1542, Orellana and his men reached the tidal basin of the Amazon. After rigging sails made from blankets, they continued into the mouth of the Amazon, entering the Atlantic on August 26, 1542. While following the northeast coast of South America, along the shores of what is now the Guianas and Venezuela, the ships were separated. They were not reunited until September 11, when they met up at Nueva Cádiz on Cubagua Island off the central Caribbean coast of what is now Venezuela.

Meanwhile, Gonzalo Pizzaro, having managed to return to Quito with the remnants of his expedition, charged Orellana with deserting him. Amidst the political turmoil that soon erupted in Peru, and which resulted in the end of the Pizarro family's domination of the region, the accusations were overlooked.

In 1543, Orellana returned to Spain to seek royal sponsorship for another voyage of exploration. King Charles I (Holy Roman Emperor Charles V) appointed him governor of the region around the river he had descended and commissioned him to lead a colonizing expedition to New Andalusia, as it was named. In May 1545, Orellana sailed from the Spanish port of Sanlúcar de Barrameda with four ships and about 350 men. By the time he had returned to the mouth of the Amazon in December 1545, he had only two ships remaining. He explored the great river's estuary, searching for the river's main channel, until December 1546, when he reportedly died of tropical disease.

Although it was not his intention, Francisco de Orellana led the first known journey down the Amazon River, traveling along it for 2,000 miles, from a point near its source in the Andes to its outlet on the Atlantic. Taken together with his preliminary trek over the Andes from Guayaquil in 1541–42, he and his men had also made the first complete crossing of the South American continent. Friar Carvajal's eyewitness account of the expedition, entitled *Account by Friar Gaspar de Carvajal of the Voyage down the River that Captain Francisco de Orellana Discovered,* appeared in Spain soon afterward. Carvajal referred to the river as the "Orellana," although VICENTE YÁÑEZ PINZÓN had actually reached the mouth of the river in 1500 and had named it La Mar Dulce (the freshwater sea). By the early 1600s, because of Carvajal's report on the women warriors, whom he had likened to the Amazons of Greek legend, the river had come to be known as the Amazon. Carvajal also described the so-called Amazons as being fair-skinned and reported other white inhabitants in the rain forest. Similar sightings of white-skinned native people in the Amazon Basin persisted well into the 20th century. Orellana's voyage of 1542 initiated exploration of the Amazon and revealed for the first time the full extent of the river. The geographic knowledge resulting from his expedition was incorporated into the first comprehensive map of the South American continent, produced by DIEGO GUTIÉRREZ in 1562.

Ortelius, Abraham (Abraham Oertel, Abraham Ortell, Abraham Ortel) (1527–1598)
Flemish cartographer, geographer

Abraham Ortelius was born at Antwerp in present-day Belgium, which was then under Spanish rule. His original family name, Oertel or Oertell, was later Latinized in the humanist tradition. He became involved with cartography early in his life, becoming a skilled illuminator of maps by the time he was 20 years old.

The death of Ortelius's father left him as the sole support for his widowed mother and two sisters, and, to augment their income, he became an itinerant dealer in maps. The maps he acquired were mounted on linen by his mother and sisters and sold on his commercial trips to Germany, France, Italy, and England. Ortelius also collected locally produced maps in the course of his travels, which he brought back to Antwerp, illuminated, and resold.

In about 1549, Ortelius was commissioned by Dutch merchant Aegidus Hooftman to put together a comprehensive collection of European maps in book form. Hooftman and other businessmen of that time needed such a portable reference work to aid in determining the best routes with which to carry on trade during the nearly constant political and religious warfare then raging between the nations of Europe. Demand for more such works soon followed, and over the next 10 years, Ortelius published maps he had collected in bound, uniform-sized sheets. He became a friend and associate of Flemish cartographer GERARDUS MERCATOR, who assisted him in acquiring maps and with whom he corresponded about the latest geographic information.

On May 20, 1570, Ortelius published what amounted to the first modern geographic world atlas. Entitled *Theatrum Orbis Terrarum* (Picture of the world), it contained 53 maps printed from newly etched copperplates. It was an immediate commercial success. During the next 28 years, Ortelius regularly produced annual editions; by 1598, the year of his death, the work included more than 100 maps with an accompanying text.

Ortelius's reputation as one of the leading cartographers of his day spread across Europe. Editions of his books of maps were soon published in Dutch, German, French, Italian, and English translations from the original Latin, and in 1575, he was appointed as royal geographer to King Philip II of Spain. In addition to his cartographic work, Ortelius produced a geography, *Thesaurus Geographicus,* first published in 1587.

Abraham Ortelius *(Library of Congress)*

Map of the world by Abraham Ortelius (1570) *(Library of Congress)*

The maps included in Abraham Ortelius's published works were based more on actual explorations and reports of mariners and less on the traditional geographic dogma handed down since the days of PTOLEMY. Although his charts did continue to depict such traditional inaccuracies as Tierra del Fuego being an extension of Terra Australis (the hypothetical GREAT SOUTHERN CONTINENT), some features were inexplicably accurate. His map of North America, published in 1570, details what appears to be HUDSON BAY, yet that feature was not reported until after HENRY HUDSON's last voyage 41 years later in 1611. In addition, Ortelius's atlases were among the first to list the Americas among the continents of the world and to reflect the rapid gains in geographic knowledge that were made in his lifetime. With his annually updated atlases, Ortelius made the latest findings of such explorers as CHRISTOPHER COLUMBUS, VASCO NÚÑEZ DE BALBOA, FERDINAND MAGELLAN, and SIR FRANCIS DRAKE available to the European public. Prior to his work, such information had been included only on charts used by mariners or in lavishly produced works privately commissioned by wealthy, usually royal, patrons.

Orville, Albert d' (1621–1662) *Flemish missionary in China, Tibet, and India*

Albert d'Orville was a native of Flanders, territory now part of Belgium. After entering the Jesuit order, he dedicated himself to a career as a missionary priest in the Far East.

Orville was in Peking (Beijing) in 1658, when fellow Jesuit missionary JOHANN GRUEBER arrived there from Europe. In 1661, the two set out on a journey westward across China, which took them across the Ordos desert country to Lake Koko Nor, then southward into Tibet.

After a brief visit to LHASA, the Tibetan capital, Orville and Grueber crossed the HIMALAYAS into Nepal and India. While on a stopover at Agra in north-central India, Orville died, and soon afterward, Grueber resumed his journey, traveling back to Europe by way of the Middle East and the MEDITERRANEAN SEA.

Albert d'Orville, together with Johann Grueber, made one of the first extensive journeys across China and into Tibet since the travels of MARCO POLO in the late 1200s and ODORIC OF PORDENONE in the early 1300s. Grueber survived to take back to Europe much updated information about the geography and people of central Asia.

Oudney, Walter (1790–1824) *Scottish physician, naturalist in North and West Africa*

Walter Oudney was born into a family of modest means in Edinburgh, Scotland. As a youth, he acquired some knowledge of medicine, and in 1810, he entered the British navy as a surgeon's mate. In 1814, after serving in the EAST INDIES, he was made a naval surgeon. Soon after the conclusion of the Napoleonic Wars in 1815, Oudney left the navy and began a course of medical studies at Edinburgh University. He also undertook studies in chemistry and natural history and pursued an interest in botany. Soon after receiving his medical degree in 1817, he opened a private practice in Edinburgh and also carried on independent studies in chemistry and natural history, hoping to someday secure a university professorship in botany.

In 1820, Oudney accepted the British government's proposal to determine the course of West Africa's NIGER RIVER. Accompanying him on this venture was British naval officer HUGH CLAPPERTON, with whom he sailed to Tripoli in present-day Libya, arriving there in October 1821. They were soon joined by British army officer DIXON DENHAM, as well as by an English shipbuilder named William Hillman.

Oudney, having been instructed to trace the course of the Niger River through the kingdom of Bornu in what is now northern Nigeria, almost at the opposite end of Africa's great western bulge from Tripoli, led his expedition southward across the SAHARA DESERT. By April 1822, they had reached Murzuk in the Fezzan region of present-day southwestern Libya. They remained there for the next seven months, exploring the surrounding territory while waiting to arrange for an armed escort from the bey, the region's local ruler. In December 1822, Oudney and his companions managed to get the support they needed from a wealthy native merchant, Abu Bakr bu Khullum, and they soon crossed the border into the kingdom of Bornu.

On February 4, 1823, Oudney, Clapperton, Denham, and Hillman became the first confirmed Europeans to see Lake Chad. On a reconnaissance around the lake with Clapperton, Oudney went on to locate the Chari River, Lake Chad's principal tributary.

Oudney and the expedition next visited the Bornu capital at Kuka (now the Nigerian city of Kukawa), where they remained until the following fall. He began his quest for the Niger on December 14, 1823, when he left Kuka and headed into western Bornu, believing that the river flowed from somewhere in a region called Nupe to the southwest. Clapperton alone accompanied him, while Denham and Hillman remained at the Bornu capital.

Exposed to extreme cold, Oudney contracted pneumonia and died at Katagum on January 12, 1824, barely a month after setting out from Kuka. Clapperton continued on alone but returned to Kuka after native rulers warned him that to proceed to Nupe would be too hazardous. With Denham and Hillman, he then returned to Tripoli, from where they sailed to England, arriving in June 1825.

Some of the mineralogical studies made by Walter Oudney on his crossing of the Sahara in 1821–22 were later incorporated into Dixon Denham's published account of the expedition, as was Oudney's account of the journey from Murzuk to Bornu. Further exploration to determine the true course of the Niger River resumed with Clapperton's expedition of 1825 and ended in 1830 when RICHARD LEMON LANDER and his brother John followed the river to its outlet into the Gulf of Guinea.

Overweg, Adolf (1822–1852) *German geologist, astronomer in North and central Africa*

A native of Germany, Adolf Overweg had, by his late 20s, achieved a reputation as an accomplished geologist and astronomer. In 1849, he joined German geographer HEINRICH BARTH in an expedition into central and West Africa, sponsored by the British government and led by antislavery activist and explorer JAMES RICHARDSON.

Overweg and Barth arrived in Tripoli along the North African coast on January 18, 1850. They were soon joined by Richardson, and the three set out southward across the SAHARA DESERT to the oasis city of Murzuq in the Fezzan region of what is now southwestern Libya. In October 1850, they arrived at Agades in what is now central Niger, from where they continued into the sub-Saharan region, traveling with a salt caravan. They then separated, each taking a different route southward to Lake Chad, with Overweg approaching the lake from the northwest.

In April 1851, Overweg rejoined Barth in Kuka, the capital of the black Muslim kingdom of Bornu in what is now northern Nigeria. They learned there that Richardson, who had been sent to Bornu on a semidiplomatic mission, had died en route to Lake Chad.

Overweg returned to his explorations around Lake Chad, while Barth independently explored the Chari River, as well as the Benue River. In summer 1851, Overweg completed his survey of the west and north shores of Lake Chad. From his continuous exposure to the swampy regions around the lake, he developed a fever, dying on September 27, 1852. The inhabitants of the lakeside village, with whom he had become friends, buried him on the shore of the lake he had explored, according to his final wishes.

In the course of his explorations, Adolf Overweg mapped the entire perimeter of Lake Chad from a small boat and was the first known European to sail completely around the lake. Barth, who continued to explore in West and North Africa until 1855, sent Overweg's maps back to Europe.

Oxley, John Joseph William Molesworth

(ca. 1783–1828) *British explorer, government official in Australia*

Born at Westow in Yorkshire, England, John Oxley entered the British navy as a teenager. After 12 years of service, he left the navy at the rank of lieutenant. He sailed to Australia in 1812, where he had been appointed surveyor general of New South Wales.

Oxley undertook his first major exploration into the interior of southeastern Australia in 1817, when he was sent by New South Wales governor Lachlan Macquarie to explore the Lachlan River, southwest of Bathurst. Macquarie hoped to determine if the Lachlan led to an internal network of rivers, similar to the MISSISSIPPI RIVER and its tributaries in North America. If so, he speculated that such a river system could provide a water route through the continent from Sydney to either the Indian Ocean to the west or to Spencer Gulf on the south coast.

Oxley and his expedition left Bathurst on April 28, 1817. Second in command was George W. Evans, who had made the European discovery of the Lachlan River five years earlier. Along with Oxley and Evans were 11 other men, including botanist ALLAN CUNNINGHAM. Equipped with packhorses and boats, it was the largest expedition to penetrate the Australian interior until that time. Evans led Oxley to the point he had reached on the Lachlan in his earlier exploration. From there, the expedition attempted to trace the river's westward-flowing course. After several hundred miles, the river opened up into a vast and impassable morass of reedy marshlands they called Field's Plains. Oxley led the expedition overland to the southwest, hoping to find a navigable stretch of the Lachlan downstream, but he once again found it blocked by swamps. Without realizing it, Oxley had reached a point only 25 miles from the mouth of the Murrumbidgee River, a major tributary of the Murray and one of southeastern Australia's longest rivers.

Deciding that further exploration through the Lachlan's swampy lower reaches would be impossible, Oxley proceeded overland to the Macquarie River, which he followed back to Bathurst, arriving on August 29, 1817.

In April 1818, Oxley, again accompanied by Evans, led a larger expedition in an exploration of the upper Macquarie River, northwest of Bathurst. In June, 220 miles downriver,

they were again halted by a great expanse of marshes. In an attempt to skirt southward around the region, Oxley came upon a chain of mountains he called the Arbuthnot Range, as well as an expanse of fertile grazing land he called the Liverpool Plains. After crossing the GREAT DIVIDING RANGE, the expedition headed southward down the Hastings River and reached the Pacific coast, then returned to Sydney.

In 1819, Oxley, with HAMILTON HUME, undertook an exploration by boat along the shores of Jervis Bay and the Illawarra District, south of Sydney. Four years later, in 1823, New South Wales governor Thomas Brisbane sent Oxley northward from Sydney to explore Moreton Bay, hoping to find a suitable site for a new penal colony. Although Moreton Bay had been charted 50 years earlier by JAMES COOK, Oxley conducted the first thorough reconnaissance of the bay, locating the mouth of the Brisbane River. He came upon two shipwrecked sailors who, having been adopted by Aborigines, had survived on the abundant supply of fish and birds in the region. On his return to Sydney, Oxley reported that the region contained rich soil and adequate freshwater. Although he recommended that the Moreton Bay area be colonized by free settlers, a penal colony was nonetheless established the following year.

John Oxley was active in the early political life of the New South Wales colony, and was one of the pioneer settlers of the coastal Bowral District, south of Sydney. From his explorations of both the Lachlan and Macquarie Rivers in 1817–18, he speculated that the interior of the Australian continent was not crisscrossed by a network of interconnecting rivers but contained a large, landlocked inland sea. This view, which had been expressed previously by MATTHEW FLINDERS and others, was based on Oxley's having found great marshes in his explorations of both the Lachlan and Macquarie, which he concluded defined the inland sea's shoreline. His theories inspired the subsequent expeditions of CHARLES STURT and THOMAS LIVINGSTONE MITCHELL, who also searched for the hypothetical sea. The Oxley Highway, which crosses New South Wales along the route of his 1818 expedition, was named in honor of Oxley's contributions to the exploration of southeastern Australia, as was the town of Oxley on the Lachlan River, near its junction with the Murrumbidgee.

P

Pacheco, Duarte (Duarte Pacheo Pereira)

(unknown–ca. 1530) *Portuguese mariner, soldier in Africa and India*

Duarte Pacheco was born at Santarem, near Lisbon, into a family of nobles with close ties to the Portuguese ruling family. He was well educated and, in his early career, served as a personal assistant to King John II of Portugal.

Pacheco took part in Portuguese voyages of exploration along the southwest coast of Africa during the 1480s. In 1488, he was shipwrecked with his crew on the island of Principe in the gulf of Guinea. He and his men were rescued later that year by BARTOLOMEU DIAS, who was returning to Portugal from the CAPE OF GOOD HOPE.

According to some sources, Pacheco first sailed to India with PEDRO ÁLVAREZ CABRAL's fleet in 1500, which also landed along the coast of Brazil. In 1503, he accompanied AFONSO DE ALBUQUERQUE on his expedition to the ports of southwestern India's Malabar Coast, where he played a major role in naval victories against Calicut. In 1504–05, he successfully defended the port of Cochin against a year-long siege.

Proclaimed a hero, Pacheco returned to Lisbon in 1505, where he was personally greeted by King Manuel I. Four years later, he added to his naval triumphs with a decisive victory over the pirate Mondragon, who had long been preying on Portuguese treasure ships along the African coast.

In 1520, Pacheco was appointed military governor at the fortress of São Jorge da Mina, the Portuguese trading settlement on the Gulf of Guinea coast (present-day Elmina, Ghana). After two years, he was sent back to Lisbon in chains, accused of embezzlement. Although he managed to prove his innocence and regain his freedom, the scandal ruined his reputation. Poverty-stricken, he lived out the rest of his days in obscurity.

Pacheco wrote an account of Portuguese explorations, entitled *Principio do Esmeraldo de Situ Orbis*. The work, which contained valuable geographic information, as well as sailing and navigational directions for voyages to India, was long suppressed by the Portuguese government under its policy of keeping all such information secret.

In the 1570s, nearly 50 years after his death, Duarte Pacheco's fame as a hero was revived in the works of the Portuguese epic poet Luíz Vaz de Camões, who bestowed on Pacheco the sobriquet Aquiles Lusitano—the "Portuguese Achilles."

Padilla, Juan de (ca. 1500–1542) *Spanish missionary in Mexico and the American Southwest and Midwest*

Spanish Franciscan missionary Friar Juan de Padilla arrived in Mexico in 1528. He accompanied HERNÁN CORTÉS on an expedition into southern Mexico in 1533, and, in 1540, he was attached to FRANCISCO VÁSQUEZ DE CORONADO's expedition northward from western Mexico into what is now Arizona and New Mexico. He hoped to prove the truth of the legendary, fabulously rich Seven Cities of Antillia, which now were thought to be the Seven Cities of CIBOLA.

In July 1540, after finding no great wealth among the Zuni Indians, Padilla, along with one of Coronado's officers, PEDRO DE TOVAR, explored into what is now eastern Arizona. They came upon seven Hopi Indian villages and returned to Coronado with reports of a great river to the west. A follow-up expedition, led by GARCÍA LÓPEZ DE CÁRDENAS, further investigated the region and made the European discovery of the COLORADO RIVER, as well as the Grand Canyon.

Padilla was among the friars who traveled with Coronado and his army of CONQUISTADORES in search of QUIVIRA, an Indian land that, according to the account of the captured Indian TURK, contained an abundance of gold and silver and that Padilla believed might be Antillia. In April 1541, the expedition departed Tiguex in the upper Rio Grande Valley of what is now north-central New Mexico and marched across the Texas Panhandle into present-day western Oklahoma.

Padilla may have remained with Coronado until his expedition reached what was thought to be Quivira, near present-day Lindsborg in central Kansas. Finding no riches, Coronado led his men back to Tiguez on the Rio Grande, from where he planned to return to Mexico. With the prospect of winning new Christian converts, Padilla decided not to return to Mexico with Coronado but instead to proselytize among the Plains Indians. He may have been joined by two other missionaries, Juan de la Cruz and Luis de Escalona. Soon after traveling back onto the plains, he was murdered by the native people.

Friar Juan de Padilla's explorations with Pedro de Tovar led to the Spanish discovery of the upper Colorado River. Padilla was the last known European to visit the plains of central Kansas until JUAN DE OÑATE sent his reconnaissance expeditions into the region more than a half century later.

Páez, Pedro (Pedro Páez Xaramillo) (1564–1622)
Spanish missionary in Ethiopia, in service to Portugal
Pedro Páez was a native of Spain. In about 1586, after entering the Jesuit order, he sailed to Goa, the Portuguese colony on the west coast of India, where he worked as a missionary.

In 1589, Páez set out from Goa for Ethiopia, drawn there by reports of a Christian kingdom, possibly that of the fabled PRESTER JOHN. While sailing across the Arabian Sea, Páez's ship was attacked by Turkish pirates, and he was taken captive and sold into slavery. He then spent seven years as a slave in Yemen before his release, returning to Goa in 1596.

In 1603, Páez again left Goa for Ethiopia, and he soon reached the northern Ethiopian port of Massawa on the RED SEA. During the next 10 years, he made numerous journeys inland, including one in 1613 in which he traveled from Gondar to Lake Tana and the nearby Springs of Geesh, which he determined were the principal source of the Blue Nile, which feeds the NILE RIVER. By the time of his death in 1622, Páez had succeeded in converting the emperor of Ethiopia, Negus Susenyos, and his family to Catholicism.

Although Pedro Páez was the first European known to have reached Lake Tana and to have determined that the Blue Nile flowed from it, his finding was long suppressed by the Portuguese, who, with their traditional policy of keeping new geographic information secret, then dominated European contacts with East Africa. A century and a half later, Scottish explorer JAMES BRUCE, in his travels in Ethiopia during the early 1770s, finally confirmed Páez's earlier finding that Lake Tana was the true source of the Blue Nile.

Palgrave, William Gifford (1826–1888)
British missionary, diplomat, writer in Arabia, in service to France
William Palgrave was born in London, England, the son of prominent upper-class parents. His father was the historian Sir Francis Palgrave, and his grandfather, Meyer Cohen, was a member of the London Stock Exchange. Palgrave's early education at Charterhouse School was followed by several years at Oxford University, where he studied modern and classical languages, graduating in 1846. Having developed an interest in Eastern studies, he traveled to India and entered the Eighth Bombay Infantry Regiment as a lieutenant. After only a few years, he left the military and converted to Catholicism. In 1848, he began studies at a Jesuit college near Madras. He eventually undertook missionary work in southern India.

In 1853, Palgrave sailed back to Europe, where he continued his religious studies in Italy at the Colegio Romano in Rome. He was assigned to Beirut, Lebanon, where he served as a priest and teacher in the Maronite Christian community. He became proficient in Arabic, and, in 1857, he was ordained a priest.

Palgrave remained in Lebanon until 1860, when he was forced to flee to France amid a widespread outbreak of persecution and violence against the Christian minority. In 1861, he conceived a plan to undertake a missionary expedition into the heart of the Arabian Peninsula. His idea came to the notice of French emperor Napoléon III, who, anticipating the construction of the Suez Canal, sought to extend French hegemony over the region and was willing to provide financial backing. French businessmen were also interested in exploring the possibility of trade in Arabia, as well as in the prospect of increased imports of the region's cotton, for cotton was in short supply in Europe because shipments from the United States had been interrupted with the outbreak of the Civil War. European horse breeders also gave their support to Palgrave, hoping his expedition would facilitate the importation of pure-blood Arabian breeding stock.

Palgrave left Europe for the Middle East on June 24, 1861. After a stopover in Egypt, he continued to the city of Ma'an in what is now southern Jordan; in July 1862, he left there and headed into the Arabian Peninsula. Disguised as a Syrian doctor and accompanied by a Syrian-Greek Christian priest and teacher named Barakat Jurayjuray, Palgrave traveled southeastward across the Nafud Desert into the land of the Shammar people. After a visit to the Shammar capital at Hai'l, where he was welcomed by the emir, he continued to Riyadh, finally reaching the Persian Gulf coat at Qatif, north of Qatar.

Back in England, Palgrave lectured on his Arab exploits before the ROYAL GEOGRAPHICAL SOCIETY, and, in recognition of his accomplishment, Napoléon III and the French government awarded him a grant of 10,000 francs. In 1865, he published an account of his 13-month, 1,500-mile trek from Jordan to the Persian Gulf, entitled *Narratives of a Year's Journey Through Central and Eastern Arabia*. The book was immediately translated into French and became a bestseller throughout Europe.

In 1865, Palgrave left the priesthood and began a diplomatic career with the British Foreign Office. That year, he was dispatched to Ethiopia, where he obtained the release of the British consul and his staff, who had been taken hostage by the Abyssinian ruler, King Theodore. Soon afterward, he assumed consular duties at Trabzon, on the Black Sea coast of the Ottoman Empire, and while stationed there, he undertook explorations into various regions of Asia Minor. During the next 20 years, he served in diplomatic posts in the Philippines, Japan, Bulgaria, Thailand, and the WEST INDIES. His last assignment was in Montevideo, Uruguay, where he died of bronchitis in September 1888.

William Palgrave was the second European known to have crossed the Arabian Peninsula, the first being British officer GEORGE FOSTER SADLIER in 1819. While Sadlier had made the first east-to-west crossing of Arabia, Palgrave was the first to traverse the region from west to east.

Palliser, John (1807–1887) *Irish sportsman, traveler in the Canadian West*

Born into a family of wealthy landowners in Waterford County, Ireland, John Palliser attended schools in Europe before going on to Trinity College in Dublin. While serving as a captain with the Waterford Artillery Militia in the mid-1840s, he was probably exposed to modern topographic mapping techniques, knowledge of which was vital in his subsequent explorations into the Canadian West.

Palliser was a sportsman as well as a hunter, and in 1847–48, he undertook a hunting expedition up the MIS-SOURI RIVER into the Great Plains, where he hunted buffalo while living with Indians. Upon his return to Great Britain, he wrote an account of the experience, published in 1853 as *Adventures of a Hunter in the Prairies*. The book became a bestseller, and, in 1856, Palliser was elected as a fellow of the ROYAL GEOGRAPHICAL SOCIETY.

Later in 1856, Palliser received the support of the Royal Geographical Society for a planned expedition into the Canadian West. At that time, much of the vast prairie country extending across what was to become southern Saskatchewan and Alberta was largely unknown to non-Indians, and there was great interest in learning whether the region had potential for agricultural development.

The British government provided financial backing for the proposed expedition through the influence of Palliser's friend John Ball, then undersecretary of state for the colonies. The government wanted Palliser to undertake a topographic survey along the 49th parallel, westward from Lake Superior to the Pacific Ocean, and thereby determine the international border between western Canada and the United States. He was also instructed to explore and evaluate the lands of the Canadian West and investigate the old CANOE route of the NORTH WEST COMPANY between Lake Superior and the Red River Settlement (present-day Winnipeg, Manitoba), in order to determine whether it could be revived as a transportation and communications link. The British government also provided Palliser with a scientific team: John William Sullivan, an astronomer; James Hector, a geologist; Eugène Bourgeau, botanist; and Thomas Wright Blakiston, an ornithologist. A simultaneous expedition under HENRY YOULE HIND also was to explore the region.

In May 1857, the expedition arrived in New York and from there headed westward to Sault Sainte Marie and the Lake Superior shore of Michigan's Upper Peninsula. At Isle Royale, they met up with VOYAGEURS with canoes provided with the help of HUDSON'S BAY COMPANY governor SIR GEORGE SIMPSON. After examining eastern Lake Superior's White Fish Bay and the White Fish River, the party headed north and west along the Rainy River and Lake of the Woods canoe and portage route to what is now Winnipeg, Manitoba. From there, the expedition traveled southward to the 49th parallel at present-day Pembina, North Dakota, which they surveyed westward as far as the Turtle Mountains along the present-day border between western Manitoba and north-central North Dakota.

While the rest of the expedition spent the winter of 1857–58 at Fort Carlton in what is now north-central Saskatchewan, Palliser traveled to New York, where he conferred with British government officials in an attempt to get more funding for the project. In spring 1858, he rejoined the expedition, which proceeded westward into the ROCKY MOUNTAINS.

Accompanied by the expedition's astronomer, John W. Sullivan, Palliser crossed the Buffalo Prairie of southern Alberta and made his way through the Rockies by way of the North Kananaskis and North Kootenay Passes. He then returned to Edmonton, Alberta, where he was reunited with the other members of the expedition, who had explored South Kootenay and Kicking Horse Passes. After wintering at Edmonton, Palliser and his companions headed eastward to explore the region around the confluence of the Red Deer and South Saskatchewan Rivers on the present-day border of Saskatchewan and Alberta. He thus completed a wide circuit around an expanse of the Canadian prairies, which, except for fur traders, was largely unknown to non-Indians.

From the Red Deer River, Palliser and his expedition returned westward, crossed western Canada's Blackfeet country, and traversed the Rockies by way of North Kootenay Pass. West of the COLUMBIA RIVER, they traveled overland to New Westminster, where the 49th parallel meets the Pacific coast. Palliser had surveyed nearly 2,000 miles of the border, as well as having undertaken an exploration of the prairies and the key passes through the Rockies.

In 1859, Palliser was awarded a gold medal by the Royal Geographical Society for his wide-ranging explorations. He returned to England in 1860, then traveled to North America again in 1862–63, visiting the American South, which at the time was embroiled in the Civil War. In 1869, he sailed to the Russian and Siberian Arctic, where he hunted and explored along the Kara Sea and the islands of Novaya Zemlya.

John Palliser completed the first scientific survey of western Canada, topographically determining the present-day U.S.-Canada boundary from the western end of Lake Superior to the Pacific coast. Based on his recommendations, Canada's first transcontinental railroad used Kicking Horse Pass as its principal route through the Rocky Mountains. The semiarid prairies of southern Saskatchewan and Alberta that he surveyed came to be known as Palliser's Triangle. The maps resulting from Palliser's topographic survey were of great help to subsequent geological expeditions, as well as to the region's first civil authority, the North West Mounted Police.

Palmer, Nathaniel Brown (Captain Nat)

(1799–1877) *American mariner, sealer in Antarctica*
Nathaniel Palmer was born in Stonington, Connecticut, a small seaport at the eastern end of Long Island Sound. He was a descendant of one of the town's original 17th-century settlers and the son of a shipbuilder and lawyer.

At the age of 14, Palmer went to sea, and, during the next four years, he served on vessels plying the coastal waters between Maine and New York. In 1819, he sailed with Stonington's sealing fleet to the South Shetland Islands south of

CAPE HORN in the South Atlantic Ocean, serving as second mate aboard the *Hersilia* under Captain James P. Sheffield. The voyage proved highly profitable, and, the next year, Palmer again sailed to the South Shetlands with the Stonington fleet, this time as captain of the sloop *Hero*.

In November 1820, after a sighting of what appeared to be mountains, the fleet's commodore, Captain Benjamin Pendleton, sent Palmer and the *Hero* to explore southward from Deception Island in the South Shetlands. Palmer soon sighted an archipelago of barren, snow-covered islands, about 700 miles southwest of CAPE HORN, just north of the ANTARCTIC CIRCLE. Since there were no seals to be found there, he continued south and west. After a month, he encountered what appeared to be a contiguous mainland, which later proved to be a peninsula extending from the Antarctic continent.

In February 1821, on his way back to the fleet in the South Shetlands, Palmer met up with the Russian navigator FABIAN GOTTLIEB BENJAMIN VON BELLINGSHAUSEN and his vessels, which were then engaged in exploring the waters around Antarctica. When Palmer informed the baron of his recent findings, Bellingshausen insisted on naming the new islands the Palmer Archipelago and the new coastline Palmer Land in honor of the young American seafarer, and he indicated them as such on the charts he published in Europe. Before rejoining the Stonington vessels, Palmer came upon another group of uncharted islands near the Falklands, now known as the South Orkneys.

Palmer commanded the *James Monroe* on another sealing voyage to the Antarctic in 1821. After again reaching the coast of Palmer Land, he proceeded eastward and located a strait that he named Washington Strait. Upon further examination, he found that the strait led into a bay, which he named Monroe Bay. A good natural anchorage he found there became known as Palmer's Harbor. He made a landing on an offshore island teeming with leopard seals and king penguins. Although he found no vegetation, Palmer was certain he had come upon a continuation of the large landmass he had located the previous year, having sighted rocky peaks projecting from the ice and snow along the coast.

Palmer then undertook voyages to the Caribbean Sea and the northeast coast of South America, during which he reportedly carried troops and supplies for Simón Bolívar in his struggle for independence. Palmer returned to the Antarctic in 1829, on a voyage that included a scientific team, and attempted, without success, to locate uncharted lands west of Palmer Land.

In 1833, Palmer received his first appointment as captain of a packet, plying the sea route between New York and New Orleans. Over the next several years, he became one of the most accomplished sea captains in New England, commanding clipper ships between New York and Liverpool, England, and eventually to China. In 1845, Palmer became one of the founding members of the New York Yacht Club. After commanding the steamship *United States* on a voyage to Bremen, Palmer retired from the sea in 1850. Thereafter, he became director of a major New England-based steamship line. He remained active in yacht racing, becoming well known as a ship designer. "Captain Nat," as he was known through much of his career, died in San Francisco while returning from a voyage to China in 1877.

Nathaniel Palmer was only 21 years old when he was credited with sighting the Antarctic mainland. Although the land he reached in 1820 was called Palmer Land on American, Russian, and other charts in the years that followed, Great Britain claimed that the peninsula had actually been first sighted by British naval officer EDWARD BRANSFIELD in January 1820. Accordingly, Palmer Land was for years depicted on British charts as Graham Land, in honor of then lord of the Admiralty, James R. G. Graham. The dispute over just which seafarer the land should be named after was finally resolved in 1964 when Great Britain and the United States agreed to call that part of the continent the Antarctic Peninsula.

Park, Mungo (1771–1806) *Scottish physician, explorer in West Africa*

Mungo Park was born at Foulshiels, near Selkirk, in southern Scotland, the son of a tenant farmer and the seventh in a family of 13 children. He attended Edinburgh University, studying medicine and botany.

In 1792, Park's brother-in-law, botanist James Dickson, arranged for him to sail to the EAST INDIES as assistant ship's surgeon aboard the BRITISH EAST INDIA COMPANY vessel the *Worcester*. Park's study of Sumatra's plant and animal life, published upon his return to England the following year, came to the attention of the naturalist SIR JOSEPH BANKS, president of the ROYAL SOCIETY and principal founder of the AFRICAN ASSOCIATION.

Prompted by Banks's recommendations, the African Association commissioned Park to undertake an exploration into the interior of West Africa. His main objectives were to find the NIGER RIVER and determine its course, then follow it to the legendary city of TIMBUKTU and return to the African coast by way of the Gambia River or by some other route that he might locate. At that time, Europeans knew of the Niger only from the reports of the medieval Arab travelers ABU ABD ALLAH MUHAMMAD IBN BATTUTAH and LEO AFRICANUS and from descriptions attributed to ancient Greek historian and geographer HERODOTUS. As late as the last decade of the 18th century, European geographers were not certain if the Niger flowed east or west, or whether it was a western tributary of the NILE RIVER.

Park sailed from England aboard the MERCHANT SHIP *Endeavor*, arriving at the mouth of the Gambia River along the coast of West Africa in June 1795. He made contact with an English trader, Dr. John Laidley, at his Gambia River trading post at Pisania (present-day Karantaba, Gambia), and there was soon stricken with tropical fever. While recovering, Park studied the native Mandingo language and engaged an interpreter, a former slave named Johnson, who had lived for a time in Jamaica.

On December 2, 1795, Park set out from Pisania, accompanied by the interpreter Johnson, a slave boy named Demba, and several servants. His party first headed up the Gambia with a group of native slave traders. Park then crossed from the swampy Gambia River Valley into the semiarid Kaarta region of what is now eastern Senegal. At Nioro, he was shown the place where another explorer sent by the African Association, Major DANIEL HOUGHTON, had died four years previously. Park then entered the kingdom of Bondou, where he was treated well by the native ruler. Nevertheless, as he continued north and east toward the Niger and Timbuktu, the natives proved to be far less hospitable and increasingly larcenous, and, by the time he had entered the lands of hostile Muslim tribesmen, he had been robbed of most of his possessions. Deserted by most of his servants, including his interpreter Johnson, Park was left with only the slave boy Demba. In spring 1796, the two were taken captive at Benowm by the Moorish chief Ali, king of Ludamar.

Mungo Park *(Library of Congress)*

Park was held prisoner by Ali and his people for three months, traveling with the nomadic tribe through the arid regions of western Mali. On July 1, 1796, at Quiera, after suffering much ill treatment at the hands of his Moorish captors and learning that he was about to be put to death as a Christian spy, he managed to escape. Instead of fleeing for the safety of European settlements on the coast, he continued inland, traveling alone and totally impoverished, in search of the Niger River and Timbuktu. At a native village, Park received help in the way of food and cowrie shells with which to trade. Traveling by horseback, he finally sighted the Niger River at Segou on July 21, 1796.

Park determined that the Niger indeed flowed eastward, as had been reported by Ibn Battutah in the 14th century. He then headed downstream toward Timbuktu, hoping to determine if the river led to the Nile River, the Atlantic Ocean, or, as he himself had theorized, to the CONGO RIVER (Zaire River). After about 300 miles, at a village called Silla, he was informed by friendly natives that Muslims controlled the region downriver, including Timbuktu. Rather than face more hostile tribesmen, and with his resources running low, Park headed back upriver to Bamako, and from there crossed overland to the Gambia River. His westward journey was halted for seven months at Kamalia, where he was again stricken with fever. By the time he had reached Pisania, near the Gambia River's mouth, in spring 1797, no one had heard from him for 18 months and he had been given up for dead.

In June 1797, Park left the coast of West Africa aboard an American slave ship, the *Charleston,* and, by way of the WEST INDIES and the South Carolina coast, he arrived back in England in December. In 1799, his account of his African explorations, *Travels in the Interior Districts of Africa,* was published and became an immediate bestseller.

Park returned to Scotland, married, and settled down to a medical practice in the town of Peebles, near Selkirk. Although he wanted to return to Africa and further explore the Niger, the African Association was not forthcoming with additional support. In 1801, Park was offered a post with the British navy on a scientific voyage to Australia, under the command of MATTHEW FLINDERS, a position he declined and which was later filled by naturalist ROBERT BROWN.

In 1803, the British Colonial Office proposed to Park that he lead a second exploration of the Niger. By then, the British government, concerned about French expansion into Africa south of the Sudan, wanted to establish a colonial presence of its own in West Africa. After a series of delays, Park sailed from England in January 1805. As commander of the expedition, he had been commissioned a captain, and, at the British garrison on Goree Island, off the coast of Dakar and Cape Verde, he recruited 35 soldiers to accompany him into the African interior. Joining him as well were two ship's carpenters, who were to supervise the construction of a boat for the voyage down the Niger. Second in command was fellow surgeon Alexander Anderson, who was also Park's brother-in-law.

In April 1805, Park led his expedition eastward up the Gambia from the river port of Kaiaf, then crossed the mountains to the Senegal River. Continuing eastward across southwestern Mali, Park and his expedition reached the Niger at Bamako. By that time, tropical fever and dysentery had taken their toll on Park's men. More than 30 had died, including Anderson. The survivors continued downriver to Sansanding, at which point their interpreter, a Mandingo priest named Isaaco, was sent back to the coast with journals of the expedition's progress to date. A boat was constructed from two native canoes fitted together, which Park named the *Joliba* after the Mandingo name for the Niger River. On November 19, 1805, Park, three surviving soldiers, several slaves, and a native guide and interpreter named Amadi Fatouma set out on the Niger, planning to discover where it ultimately led.

No word was heard of Park or any of his expedition until nearly three years later, when, in 1808, British colonial authorities sent Park's former interpreter Isaaco to investigate what had happened. Isaaco located Fatouma, Park's last interpreter. According to his account, in April 1806, the boat had been attacked as it descended the rapids at Bussa in what is now northern Nigeria. When the *Joliba* ran aground on a rock, Park and the three remaining Europeans attempted to escape from the native people by jumping into the raging waters but were drowned. Since this was at a point about 500 miles upstream from the Niger's outlet into the Gulf of Guinea, if he indeed had reached this far, he had gone by Timbuktu, although there is no record of his having stopped there.

One of the objects of the Bornu Mission, the British expedition into West Africa undertaken in 1821 by HUGH CLAPPERTON, WALTER OUDNEY, and DIXON DENHAM, was to find out what had happened to Park. In 1827, Park's son Thomas, who had become a naval officer, attempted to find some trace of his father, but he died of fever en route to Bussa.

Mungo Park was the first European known to have reached the Niger River in modern times. On his return from his first expedition in 1797, he was acclaimed "the Great African Traveler." Park's explorations led to a series of journeys into West and central Africa sponsored by European governments. His published account of his travels into the interior of West Africa revealed to Europeans for the first time the varied cultures of the region. Park added to the geographic knowledge of Africa by identifying the southern limit of the SAHARA DESERT and demonstrated that there was a feasible route into the southern Sudan from the coast of West Africa, a finding that had great impact on the future of European trade and colonial expansion south of the Sahara.

Parke, John Grubb (1827–1900) *U.S. Army officer, American topographer in the American Southwest*

John G. Parke was born in Coatesville, Pennsylvania, and raised in Philadelphia. He attended the University of Pennsylvania, then went on to West Point, graduating in 1849 as a second lieutenant in the U.S. Army Corps of Topographical Engineers.

In 1851, after taking part in a survey of the Minnesota-Iowa boundary, Parke went to the Southwest, where he assisted Captain LORENZO SITGREAVES in an expedition that explored westward from Santa Fe to Fort Yuma on the COLORADO RIVER, and across the Mojave Desert and Sierra Nevada to San Diego. Just prior to this expedition, Parke, with RICHARD HOVENDON KERN, prepared an updated map of the Southwest based on the explorations by JOHN CHARLES FRÉMONT, as well as information provided by mountain men WILLIAM SHERLEY WILLIAMS and Antoine Leroux.

Parke undertook several important explorations for the Pacific Railroad Surveys of 1852–55. He explored along the coastal ranges of California and Oregon with Lieutenant HENRY LARCOM ABBOTT, seeking connections between Pacific ports north and south of any proposed western terminus for the planned transcontinental railroad.

In January 1854, Parke commanded an expedition that examined the possibility of a railroad route along the 32nd parallel, from San Diego, California, to El Paso, Texas. Parke and his party traveled along the Gila River from the Pima (Akimel O'odham) Indian villages of south-central Arizona, through Tucson, and into the Chiricahua Mountains. Along the way, he ascertained the correct location of an emigrant trail known as Nugents Wagon Road. He then followed part of Cooke's Wagon Road to the Rio Grande, undertaking a side expedition that revealed a more direct route to El Paso. In spring 1855, on a second exploration of the Gila River country, Parke found a pass through the Chiricahua Mountains near Mount Graham, which shortened the 32nd parallel route.

From 1857 to 1861, Parke was chief astronomer and surveyor in the Canada-U.S. boundary survey. He worked directly with the British Royal Engineers and helped establish the last segment of the international border, from the ROCKY MOUNTAINS to the Pacific coast of Washington.

In the Civil War, Parke commanded Union troops in campaigns throughout the South and was breveted a major general. He returned to the Topographical Corps after the war and went on to become superintendent of West Point. After his retirement from the army in 1889, he was involved in railroad development and banking.

Parke's official account of his explorations along the 32nd parallel in 1854–55 were included in the U.S. government's *Pacific Railroad Reports* (1855–59). He described the territory from southern Arizona to the Rio Grande as generally level and practical for a railroad, the only drawbacks being lack of a water supply and a scarcity of timber.

Parry, Sir William Edward (1790–1855)
British naval officer in the Canadian Arctic

Born in Bath, England, Edward Parry entered the British navy in 1803, at the age of 13. After serving for five years on the English Channel, he took part in naval operations in the Baltic Sea. In 1810, as a lieutenant, he made his first voyage to the Arctic aboard a naval escort for British whalers in the Spitsbergen (present-day Svalbard) region, north of Norway.

In 1818, Parry was named second in command to SIR JOHN ROSS in a British naval expedition in search of the NORTHWEST PASSAGE. In command of the *Alexander*, he accompanied Ross on the *Isabella* to GREENLAND's west coast, then headed northward into Baffin Bay, in an attempt to verify the early-17th-century findings of ROBERT BYLOT and WILLIAM BAFFIN. Sailing westward to the northern end of Baffin Island, the expedition examined the entrance to Lancaster Sound; soon afterward, Ross ordered the ships to turn back, having sighted what he believed was a mountain range blocking further progress westward. Parry and some other officers later reported to the British Admiralty that they had seen a clear channel ahead, which they would have explored had they not been ordered back by Ross.

By 1819, Parry had been elected to the ROYAL SOCIETY for his studies on nautical astronomy. That year, SIR JOHN BARROW, second secretary of the Admiralty, and Lord Melville, the first lord of the Admiralty, put Parry in command of a Northwest Passage expedition of his own, instructing him to navigate through Lancaster Sound, and thereby resolve the controversy that had arisen from Ross's voyage of the previous year.

In command of two ships, the *Hecla* and the *Griper,* he sailed from Yarmouth on May 11, 1819, heading westward back to Baffin Bay and Lancaster Sound.

By August 1, 1819, Parry had managed to sail through Lancaster Sound, establishing that it was actually a strait. He then made the European discovery of Barrow Strait, which he named after Sir John Barrow. Continuing westward, he reached the south coast of a large island he named Melville Island after Lord Melville. Parry and his men had sailed west of the 110th meridian of longitude, half the distance of the Northwest Passage, and thereby won a prize of £5,000, which Parliament had offered as an incentive for its discovery.

Frozen in at Melville Island, Parry and his expedition were well equipped for the first deliberate wintering by a naval expedition above the ARCTIC CIRCLE. At an anchorage they called Winter Harbor, the decks of the ship were covered with an insulated roof. Heat was supplied by coal-fueled stoves, and dietary precautions were taken against SCURVY. Recreation among the men was encouraged, and the officers published a newspaper. A theatrical troupe was organized, with Parry himself writing a musical play entitled *The Northwest Passage,* a light-operatic satire of the expedition that was staged by the crew and directed by one of Parry's officers, FREDERICK WILLIAM BEECHEY.

In spring 1820, Parry undertook a two-week land exploration of Melville Island. He observed such Arctic animals as musk oxen, reindeer, wolves, and foxes, and found patches of grass and moss, as well as traces of abandoned Inuit (Eskimo) encampments. Having trekked as far westward as Cape Dundas, at 113°48' west longitude, he was just 250 miles from the Beaufort Sea, which subsequently proved to be the western outlet of the Northwest Passage. With the southeastward drift of the PACK ICE making further progress westward impossible, Parry sailed back to England, arriving in fall 1820.

Sir William Edward Parry *(Library of Congress)*

Parry's encouraging reports of ice-free channels leading far to the west of Lancaster Sound soon led to his appointment as commander of yet another Northwest Passage expedition. On this voyage, which sailed from England in May 1821, he had under his command the *Hecla,* as well as an identical vessel, the *Fury.* Instead of returning to Lancaster Sound, he directed the expedition into HUDSON BAY by way of Hudson Strait and toward its north shore at Foxe Channel and Foxe Basin, hoping to find an ice-free passage into Prince Regent Inlet from the south.

The expedition explored around Southampton Island in the northwestern corner of Hudson Bay, then wintered at Winter Island off the south coast of the Melville Peninsula. Overland exploring parties probed inland along the coast, with one group discovering the complete skeleton of a whale, inexplicably perched atop a rocky cliff, 100 feet above sea level. In July 1822, Parry resumed his explorations for a western outlet from Hudson Bay, reaching a strait that he named Fury and Hecla Strait after his ships. Although unobstructed by land, it proved to be ice-choked the year round and unnavigable for sailing ships even in summer. After only a month of open-sailing conditions, the ships were again iced in for the winter in August 1822. They anchored near the Inuit settlement Igloolik at the northern end of the Melville Peninsula along the eastern end of Fury and Hecla Strait.

Over the winter, Parry and his men established good relations with the Inuit, who constructed an igloo village on the ice alongside the ship. Parry made a study of Inuit customs, observing how efficiently their survival skills enabled them to thrive even in wintertime. He also entertained the Inuit, delighting them with an organ recital aboard one of his ships. Over the winter of 1822–23, Parry purchased a dog team from the Inuit, which he used in the first British naval explorations of the Arctic by dogsled.

In July 1823, Parry sailed back to England. Although he had established Fury and Hecla Strait as the long-sought western outlet from Hudson Bay, its icebound condition made it unusable for the Northwest Passage.

Parry led another expedition with the *Fury* and *Hecla* to the Canadian Arctic in 1824, in search of an ice-free route west of Lancaster Sound that would ultimately lead to the Bering Sea and the Pacific Ocean. After sailing through Lancaster Sound in 1824, he headed southward into Prince Regent Inlet, hoping again to locate the Northwest Passage by skirting Canada's Arctic mainland. After exploring the Gulf of Boothia, south of Lancaster Sound and Somerset Island, the *Fury* became entrapped in the ice and was wrecked. Left with only one vessel for his combined crews, and short on supplies, Parry was compelled to cut short his search for the Northwest Passage in spring 1825 and return to England.

After 1825, Parry's exploits won him national renown as the British navy's foremost Arctic explorer and navigator. In

1827, he won the support of both the Admiralty and the Royal Society for an attempt on the NORTH POLE. In April 1827, he sailed from England with the *Hecla,* and at Spitsbergen he set out across the frozen Arctic Ocean with flat-bottomed, amphibious sledges and boats hauled by a party of 24 sailors and marines. Among the officers accompanying him were SIR JAMES CLARK ROSS, who had been with Parry on all of his previous Arctic expeditions, and FRANCIS RAWDON MOIRA CROZIER, a veteran of Parry's second and third voyages.

Although Parry and his men traversed more than 700 miles, the actual distance they advanced from Spitsbergen northward to the pole was less than 200 miles, due to the southward drift of the pack ice. At 82°45' north latitude, the latitude of Greenland's northernmost point, and less than eight degrees from the North Pole, Parry turned back, having concluded he was being pushed southward faster than he was progressing northward. Nonetheless, he had set a farthest-north record that stood for years, until CHARLES FRANCIS HALL's expedition of 1871.

Parry, who had married a daughter of Lord Stanley, was knighted in April 1829. Soon afterward, he left the navy to supervise a private agricultural enterprise in New South Wales, Australia. He returned to England in 1837, where he was appointed to a government post in Norfolk, and he subsequently returned to the navy and directed the development of steam machinery for ships. He went on to serve as governor of Greenwich Hospital. In 1852, he was made a rear admiral.

Parry's *Journal of a Voyage for the Discovery of a North-West Passage from the Atlantic to the Pacific; performed in the years 1819–20 in his Majesty's Ships Hecla and Griper, under the orders of William Edward Parry, R.N., F.R.S., and commander of the Expedition* was published in London in 1821. His *Narrative of an Attempt to Reach the North Pole in Boats Fitted for the Purpose, and Attached to his Majesty's Ship Hecla, in the year MCCCXXVII* was first published in 1828.

Sir William Edward Parry's feat of reaching as far west as Melville Island in one season was not equaled until 1969 by the steel-hulled tanker *Manhattan.* As a result of Parry's 1819–20 voyage, the islands and channels of the Canadian Arctic archipelago north of the North American mainland were revealed to Europeans for the first time. The westernmost islands of this group are known today as the Parry Islands in his honor. The techniques Parry developed for wintering in the Arctic were adopted by later British naval expeditions, including Franklin's in 1845, as well as those sent to search for Franklin in the 1850s. Parry's explorations in the Canadian Arctic firmly established that Lancaster Sound was the only practical eastern entrance to the Northwest Passage. As the leading Arctic explorer of his time, Parry had traveled farther westward through the Northwest Passage and reached a point closer to the North Pole than anyone before him. His 1827 North Pole attempt was the first Arctic expedition the main objective of which was not the discovery of a Polar Sea route between the Atlantic and Pacific Oceans, but the attainment of the pole itself.

Pascoe, William (Pasko, abu-Bakr)
(unknown–1833) *African guide and interpreter in West Africa*

William Pascoe was born in the Gobir region of what is now northern Nigeria. The Hausa, his tribe, are a Muslim people, and his name among them was abu-Bakr. As a young man, he was kidnapped and sold into slavery to the Portuguese but was liberated in a British naval attack on the slaver ship. He served with the Royal Navy for a time, but, in 1823, at Cape Coast, in present-day Ghana, he left to work as a guide and interpreter for an Italian by the name of Giovanni Belzoni on an expedition to locate the NIGER RIVER. Belzoni died soon afterward, however.

Pascoe was eventually hired by the Englishman HUGH CLAPPERTON for an expedition undertaken with RICHARD LEMON LANDER to locate the true source of the Niger. In 1825, with Pascoe serving as a cook as well as a guide and interpreter, they set out from the Gulf of Guinea, which Clapperton believed to be the outlet of the Niger—not the NILE RIVER, a prevalent theory. They reached the Niger in early 1826. Pascoe deserted more than once because of disputes with Clapperton and was dismissed by the Englishman once. But when Clapperton succumbed to dysentery in Sokoto in spring 1827 before an attempt to reach TIMBUKTU, Lander—the only surviving European member of the expedition—hired Pascoe to help him return to the coast, which they accomplished despite great hardship. Lander hired Pascoe for a subsequent expedition in 1830, during which it was determined that the Niger did indeed flow into the Gulf of Guinea, as Clapperton had theorized. Lander and Pascoe also located the Niger's main tributary, the Benue.

In 1832, on a third expedition, this one organized by a group of Liverpool merchants to develop commercial interests along the Niger, Pascoe again accompanied Lander into the interior. The next year, because of disputes over trading, he was reportedly poisoned by a local ruler because he recommended trading with another people farther upriver.

William Pascoe, like fellow African guide SIDI BOMBAY, proved indispensable to the efforts of the Europeans for whom he worked and helped solved the mystery of the source of the Niger River.

Pasha, Mehmed Emin   See EMIN PASHA, MEHMED.

Pattie, James Ohio (ca. 1804–ca. 1851)

American fur trapper, trader in the American West

James Ohio Pattie, son of frontiersman Sylvester Pattie, was born in Bracken County, Kentucky. He moved to the Missouri frontier with his father in 1812. In 1824, the Patties became traders on the MISSOURI RIVER. In July of that year, the two joined up with Silvestre Pratte's trade caravan near what is now Omaha, Nebraska, and traveled across the southern plains to Santa Fe, arriving there in November 1824.

While his father operated a copper mine at Santa Rita in southwestern New Mexico, James Ohio Pattie embarked on a career in the FUR TRADE in the southern ROCKY MOUNTAINS. In 1826, Pattie trapped the Gila River region with EWING YOUNG and his party. He explored the COLORADO RIVER into the Grand Canyon and established an overland route from New Mexico to the eastern edge of California, south of the Old Spanish Trail. Pattie also reportedly traveled northward along the Rockies as far as the Bighorn and Yellowstone Rivers of present-day Montana and Wyoming. He returned to Santa Fe via the Arkansas River and the Rio Grande in September 1827.

In winter 1827–28, Pattie, accompanied by his father, again trapped the Gila River into northern Mexico, then followed the Colorado River to its outlet on the Gulf of California. They crossed the northern end of the Baja California peninsula to the Pacific coast at Santa Catalina mission, arriving in March 1828. They were taken into custody by Mexican officials for unauthorized trapping in California. The elder Pattie died after a month of imprisonment in San Diego. The younger Pattie won his release from the Mexicans in 1829, after helping stem an epidemic of smallpox with vaccine he and his father had brought from New Mexico.

Pattie returned to U.S. territory in 1830, settling for a time near his Kentucky birthplace. He collaborated with Cincinnati journalist Timothy Flint in writing an account of his adventures and explorations in the American West, entitled *The personal narrative of James O. Pattie of Kentucky, During an Expedition from St. Louis, through the Vast Regions Between That Place and the Pacific Ocean.* First published in 1831, it was an immediate success.

Pattie returned to California during the gold rush of 1849. In winter 1850–51, he left a mining camp in the Sierra Nevada, and he was never seen or heard from again.

James Ohio Pattie was one of the first Americans to travel widely through the entire Rocky Mountain frontier. The route he blazed from New Mexico to California became a well-traveled path for traders and trappers in the 1830s, and for California-bound emigrants following the U.S.-Mexican War of 1846–48.

Paulinus, Suetonius (Caius Suetonius Paulinus)

(unknown–ca. A.D. 70) *Roman general in North Africa*

Suetonius Paulinus, a Roman general under Emperor Claudius I, served in Rome's Mauretanian provinces in North Africa, now comprising the coastal regions of northeastern Morocco and western Algeria. In A.D. 42, soon after the Romans had subdued a native rebellion and organized the region into provinces, Paulinus led a company of soldiers inland from the MEDITERRANEAN SEA to investigate the country to the south. He crossed the Atlas Mountains somewhere between Tangier and Algiers and came upon the northern edge of the SAHARA DESERT. Determining that the Roman provinces of North Africa were bounded by a vast arid expanse, he returned to the Mediterranean Sea and Rome, where he was hailed for having explored beyond the southern frontiers of the empire.

Paulinus's later career took him to Britain, where from 59 to 61, as military governor, he commanded Roman forces in suppressing a revolt by the Druids, as well as by Queen Boudicca of the Iceni. GNAEUS JULIUS AGRICOLA served under him. He later played a leading role in the military revolt against Emperor Nero in A.D. 69.

Suetonius Paulinus was one of the first Europeans known to have traveled beyond the barrier of the Atlas Mountains; his reports indicated the vast extent of the African continent, stretching southward from the Mediterranean. His expedition marked one of the few recorded instances of official Roman exploration.

Pavie, Auguste-Jean-Marie (1847–1925)

French diplomat in Southeast Asia

Originally from France, Auguste Pavie arrived in Southeast Asia as a member of a French marine regiment in the early 1860s, when the French government first began to bring the region around the lower Mekong River within its colonial sphere.

In 1868, Pavie went to work for the French colonial government of Cochin China (present-day Vietnam), serving at Kampot on the Cambodian coast of the Gulf of Thailand. While there, he made sojourns into the countryside, traveling through territory little known to Westerners, and undertook a study of the Cambodian language and culture.

Pavie's interest in further exploring the interior of Indochina (present-day Cambodia, Thailand, Laos, and Vietnam) came to the attention of the French colonial authorities in Cochin China. In 1880, they commissioned him to direct the construction of the first telegraph line between Phnom Penh and Bangkok.

Starting in 1881, Pavie directed a series of surveys into the interior of what is now Cambodia and Laos, as well as the upper Mekong River. Over the next 14 years, he and his associates traversed 18,000 miles of Southeast Asian territory, much of which was unknown to Europeans.

In 1886, Pavie was appointed as French vice consul at Louangphrabang, capital of the northern Laotian principality. During the next five years, he oversaw the demarcation of the Laotian kingdom's border with Siam (present-day Thailand) in the upper Mekong Valley, and was instrumental in the establishment of a French protectorate over the region in 1893, as part of French Indochina. He also served as French consul general at Bangkok from 1891 to 1893.

Auguste Pavie's extensive program of exploration from 1881 to 1895 became known as the Pavie Mission. As a result of his efforts, few areas of Southeast Asia, outside of some remote mountain and highland regions, remained unknown to Europeans by the beginning of the 20th century. Pavie was the editor of the expedition's official record, *Mission Pavie* (1898–1919), an 11-volume study of Southeast Asia that included scientific information as well as linguistic and cultural profiles of the region's native peoples.

Pavy, Octave (1844–1884) *American physician and naturalist in the Arctic*

Born in New Orleans, Octave Pavy was the son of Creole parents and a descendant of Louisiana's original French settlers. He was educated in France, attending the University of Paris, where he studied science, art, and medicine; he regularly took time out from his studies for travel in Europe.

In 1869, Pavy was named second in command of a French government-sponsored Arctic expedition that was to have been led by Gustave Lambert. The following year, before the expedition could leave France, it was called off due to the outbreak of the Franco-Prussian War. In that conflict, Pavy, along with a nephew of Confederate general Pierre G. T. Beauregard and a number of other Americans of French descent, served in the French army with the Zouave Corps, a volunteer unit that he had helped to organize.

At the war's end in 1871, Pavy returned to the United States, where he was soon named a member of a privately backed Arctic expedition that planned to reach the NORTH POLE by way of the BERING STRAIT. This endeavor was also abandoned before it could get under way when its chief financial sponsor suddenly died.

Nearly 10 years elapsed before Pavy was to reach the Arctic. In the meantime, he completed his medical studies at the Missouri Medical College, and, in 1878, he married Lilla May Stone, a woman from Lebanon, Illinois. They resided in St. Louis, where he served as a physician at an iron works and lectured about the Arctic.

Finally, in June 1880, Pavy sailed for GREENLAND on the *Gulnare,* as surgeon and naturalist in H. W. Howgate's Arctic expedition. It seemed like another false start for Pavy when, soon after the *Gulnare* had arrived off the west coast of Greenland, the vessel was found to be unsuitable for navigation northward into the ice-choked channels above Baffin Bay and was forced to return to the United States. Pavy, however, opted to stay behind in Greenland. Over the next year, he explored the west-central coast, learned Inuit survival and travel techniques and undertook a study of the region's animal and plant life. In July 1881, at Godhavn, Pavy joined ADOLPHUS WASHINGTON GREELY and his U.S. government expedition to northwestern Ellesmere Island's Lady Franklin Bay. In April 1882, after a winter at the expedition's base at Lady Franklin Bay, Pavy undertook a sledge exploration northward in which he reached the north coast of Ellesmere Island and rounded Cape Joseph Henry. Although he had neared the northernmost point reached by members of SIR GEORGE STRONG NARES's 1876 expedition, he was unable to proceed farther northward or westward when the PACK ICE on which he had been traveling began to break up and drift away from the coast.

When a relief ship failed for a second time to reach the expedition in 1883, Pavy and the rest of the expedition withdrew southward to Smith Sound. At Cape Sabine, they awaited a third rescue attempt. With their food supply all but exhausted, the men began to succumb to starvation and exposure. Pavy died on June 6, 1884, just 16 days before a relief ship finally reached Cape Sabine to pick up Greely and the other survivors.

In his sledge journey in spring 1882, Dr. Octave Pavy reached the north coast of the Ellesmere Island, one of the northernmost points of land on Earth. He later reported that the frozen sea ice stretching northward to the pole was subject to drift and broke up regularly, demonstrating that it was not a solid and immovable mass as had been previously thought. In Greely's official account of the expedition, he reported that Pavy had been insubordinate in questioning some of his commander's decisions, and, at one point, Greely had placed the doctor under arrest. Yet Pavy's medical skill helped maintain the health of the expedition's surviving members during their last two difficult years.

Payer, Julius von (1842–1915) *Austrian army officer in the Arctic*

Julius von Payer was born in Schoenau, Bohemia, in what is now the Czech Republic. After his education at the military academy in Vienna, he entered the Austrian army as a lieutenant in 1859. In 1866, after serving briefly as a history professor at the military academy, he conducted a survey for the army's general staff in which he determined the altitude of most of the peaks in the Austrian Alps.

Payer first visited the Arctic in 1869–70, when he took part in a German expedition to GREENLAND, led by KARL CHRISTIAN KOLDEWEY, during which he discovered a mountain range in the interior with summits as high as 11,000 feet above sea level.

Soon after his return from Greenland, Payer was commissioned by the Austrian government to explore the Arctic coast of Russia on the Austro-Hungarian Arctic Expedition. The goal was to locate an open "polar sea," extending eastward from Spitsbergen to North America–the long-sought NORTHEAST PASSAGE. In spring 1871, Payer, along with German Arctic explorer KARL WEYPRECHT, undertook a preliminary voyage on the ship *Isbjorn* to Novaya Zemlya, the islands extending northward from the Arctic coast of eastern Russia. They speculated that if the ice-free polar sea opened to the north of these islands, it might provide access not only to the Northeast Passage, but also to the NORTH POLE itself.

Payer and Weyprecht left for Novaya Zemlya once again in June 1872, sailing from Bremen aboard the *Tegethoff*, a ship equipped with both sails and steam power. There were 23 others in the expedition, which had been outfitted with provisions for three years. Off the northwest coast of Novaya Zemlya, the *Tegethoff* became entrapped in the ice of the eastern Barents Sea. Payer and the Austrian expedition drifted northward with the ice until August 1873, when they came upon an uncharted chain of islands, which they christened Franz Josef Land in honor of the Austrian emperor.

In spring 1874, after wintering off Franz Josef Land, Payer explored the archipelago, reaching as far north as 82°5' north latitude. Soon afterward, convinced that the *Tegethoff* was likely to remain trapped in the ice for another winter, Payer and Weyprecht decided to abandon the vessel and return across the frozen sea to the continental mainland. After leading the expedition on a 300-mile sledge journey southward, they reached the southern limit of the PACK ICE, then continued across the open water in small boats they had hauled over the ice. The Austrian explorers soon encountered the Russian whaling ship *Nicholas*, which took them safely to the coast of northern Lapland.

Payer was back in Vienna by July 1874. He retired from the military the following year. In 1876, he published an account of his attempt on the Northeast Passage and the North Pole from Novaya Zemlya. He later settled near Frankfurt, Germany, where he undertook scientific research and painted pictures depicting his experiences in the Arctic.

In their 1872–74 voyage, Julius von Payer and Karl Weyprecht demonstrated that the seas north of Novaya Zemlya were frozen year round, a finding that helped disprove the idea that an open polar sea surrounded the North Pole. Along with Weyprecht, Payer was one of the European discoverers of Franz Josef Land, the northern islands of which constitute the northernmost points of land in the Eastern Hemisphere.

Peary, Robert Edwin (1856–1920) *U.S. naval officer in the Arctic*

Born in Cresson, Pennsylvania, Robert E. Peary grew up in Maine, where he attended Bowdoin College, graduating in 1877 with a background in engineering. After working as a draftsman for the United States Coast and Geodetic Survey in Washington, D.C., he entered the U.S. Navy as a commissioned officer and civil engineer in 1881.

In 1884–85, Peary was in Nicaragua, where he took part in a survey for a proposed canal route across Central America. In 1886, inspired by the accounts of Norwegian polar explorer NILS ADOLF ERIK NORDENSKJÖLD, Peary made his first trip to the Arctic, in which he attempted a west-to-east crossing of GREENLAND from Disko Bay. Although he managed to ascend the ice cap to a height of 7,500 feet, he was able to reach only 125 miles inland before bad weather forced him back. Nevertheless, he had penetrated the interior of Greenland farther than any expedition before him.

Back in Washington, D.C., in 1887, Peary hired as his butler MATTHEW ALEXANDER HENSON, who, for the next 22 years, accompanied and assisted Peary in all his Arctic expeditions. After a surveying assignment in Nicaragua later in 1887, Peary returned to the United States and sought support for other Arctic explorations. He married Josephine Diebitsch in 1888. In 1891, the Philadelphia Academy of Natural Sciences appointed him to lead an expedition to the northwest coast of Greenland. That year, with his wife and Henson, Peary sailed aboard the *Kite* to Inglefield Gulf on Greenland's west coast north of Baffin Bay. En route, he suffered a broken leg in an accident aboard the ship and was treated by the expedition's medical officer, FREDERICK ALBERT COOK. At Inglefield Gulf, a portable house was set up, and, during the next 13 months, Peary and his expedition lived among the region's Inuit (Eskimo) and made a study of their Arctic survival techniques.

In spring 1892, Peary set out to explore eastward by sledge. After traveling 500 miles across the north of Greenland, he came upon an inlet along the east coast on July 4, 1892, which he named Independence Bay. Peary made another trek across Greenland to the same region in 1893. In the fall of that year, his wife gave birth to a daughter, Marie Ahnighito Peary, while at the Inglefield Gulf base.

By 1895, Peary had reached Greenland's northernmost extension, a peninsula that came to be known as Peary Land in his honor. On expeditions to Independence Bay and northern Greenland from 1895 to 1897, he found several large meteorites, which had previously been reported as an "iron mountain." Peary shipped them to the United States.

The Peary Arctic Club, organized in 1898 by a group of wealthy New Yorkers, provided funding for Peary's later Arctic expeditions. The AMERICAN GEOGRAPHICAL SOCIETY also offered support. In 1898–99, Peary explored Grant Land on Ellesmere Island. At Fort Conger (ADOLPHUS WASHINGTON GREELY's former base near Lady Franklin Bay), he lost eight of his toes to frostbite.

In 1900, Peary demonstrated conclusively that Greenland was an island on reaching its northernmost point, which he named Cape Morris Jesup in honor of the president of the American Museum of Natural History and one of his chief patrons. By that time, he had resolved to make an attempt on the NORTH POLE and had determined that the only feasible starting point was the north coast of Ellesmere Island.

Peary set out for the Pole from Cape Hecla on northern Ellesmere Island in 1902, and, although he was forced back by DRIFT ICE 340 miles short of his goal, he nonetheless set a farthest-north record for the Western Hemisphere by reaching 84°17'27" north latitude.

In 1905, Peary sailed from New York on the *Theodore Roosevelt,* a steam-powered vessel specially designed for Arctic navigation. Planning to penetrate Robeson Channel, the northern part of the passage between Ellesmere Island and Greenland, he hoped to reach the Lincoln Sea and the North Pole beyond. Peary set yet another farthest-north record on this voyage, reaching 87°6' north latitude, within 200 miles of the North Pole. Nevertheless, the ship had become badly damaged in its forced passage through the ice, and, with the onset of rough weather, the expedition was forced to turn back.

Two years passed while the *Theodore Roosevelt* underwent repairs, and Peary raised the additional support he needed for another polar attempt. He sailed on the *Theodore Roosevelt* from New York on July 6, 1908, and, by early September of that year, he had set up his base camp at Cape Sheridan on Ellesmere Island. En route, he had stopped at Etah, Greenland, where he had taken on a number of Inuit families and several hundred sled dogs. Over the next several months, supply depots were set up along a trail to the north coast of Ellesmere Island, terminating at Cape Columbia. From there, on March 1, 1909, Peary, Henson, and four Inuit set out northward with sledges and dogs. After a month-long trek across the frozen sea, they reached the North Pole on April 6, 1909.

Peary and his companions unfurled five flags at the Pole: the U.S. flag, the U.S. Navy flag, the official banner of his Delta Kappa Epsilon fraternity chapter at Bowdoin College, a Red Cross flag, and the "World Ensign of Liberty and Peace." Soundings were made of the ocean depths beneath the ice, revealing that they were atop 10,000 feet of water, thus proving that no continental shelf lay beneath the North Pole. Peary, Henson, and their Inuit companions then made a safe dash back to Cape Columbia, from where they returned with the rest of the expedition to the *Theodore Roosevelt* at Cape Sheridan.

The news that Peary had reached the North Pole could not be communicated to the outside world until July 17, 1909, when the *Theodore Roosevelt* put in at Indian Harbor, Labrador. There, Peary learned that Dr. Frederick Cook, the medical officer on his 1891–92 expedition, had announced five days earlier that he had reached the North Pole in April 1908, a full year ahead of Peary. Upon Peary's return to New York, a bitter controversy ensued over who had actually reached the Pole first, with many doubting that Cook had reached it at all. Scientists and Arctic explorers continued to take sides in the dispute, although, in 1911, Peary received official recognition from the U.S. Congress for his achievement (although Peary may have missed the Pole by a couple of miles). He retired from the navy that year with the rank of rear admiral and spent his latter years promoting the advancement of U.S. air power.

Peary published accounts of his Arctic explorations, including *Northward over the "Great Ice"* (1898), about his experiences in Greenland; *Nearest the Pole* (1907), an account of his 1905–06 North Pole attempt; *The North Pole* (1910), about his final success in 1909; and *Secrets of Polar Travel* (1917). Josephine Peary recounted her own experience in northern Greenland in *My Arctic Journal* (1894) and *The Snow Baby* (1901).

Admiral Robert E. Peary, along with Henson and their four Inuit companions, were the first men known to have stood at the North Pole. Peary is also credited with having clearly established that Greenland is an island and not part of a continental landmass extending northward to the Pole. Peary's consistent success in his Arctic expeditions was due largely to what he called the "Peary System," which freely adapted the Arctic survival techniques of the Inuit to his own method of establishing food depots and shelters in advance of the main exploring party.

Peck, Annie Smith (1850–1935) *American mountain climber in the Alps and Andes Mountains*

Annie Peck was born in Providence, Rhode Island. In 1870–72, she attended the Rhode Island State Normal School (now Rhode Island College) and, in 1874–78, the University of Michigan, graduating with honors. She earned a master's degree from Michigan in 1881. She went on to teach Latin at Purdue University, then continued her studies in Germany. In 1885, she became the first woman to attend the American School of Classical Studies in Athens, Greece. In 1886–87, she taught at Smith College in Massachusetts as a professor of classics.

During a visit to the Alps, Peck, who had participated in sports with her older brothers, decided to pursue MOUNTAIN CLIMBING as a hobby. Her first climb, in 1888, at the age of 38, was Mount Shasta in the Cascade Range in northern California. In 1895, she climbed the Matterhorn in the Swiss Alps, first summitted by EDWARD WHYMPER 30 years

Annie Peck *(Library of Congress)*

before, and by only two women before Peck. With her reputation as a woman mountaineer growing, she ascended two volcanoes in Mexico in 1897, Popocatépetl and Citlaltépetl (Pico de Orizaba), the latter the highest peak (18,700 feet) in the Western Hemisphere ascended by a woman to that time.

Peck lectured and wrote magazine articles to raise money for her climbs. She completed other climbs in Europe and founded the American Alpine Club in 1902. In the years to follow, she turned her attention to South American peaks. In 1904, she ascended Illampu, a peak on Mount Sorata in Bolivia's Cordillera Real. In 1906, after failing to reach the top of Huascarán in Peru's ANDES MOUNTAINS, she pursued the source of the AMAZON RIVER, traveling up the Marañón and Ucayali tributaries. In 1908, on her sixth attempt, she finally reached the summit of Huascarán. In 1911, she climbed the north peak of the Coropuna volcano, also in the Peruvian Andes. At the age of 82, Peck made her last climb, ascending Mount Madison in New Hampshire's White Mountains.

Peck also had an interest in the development of South America and researched the possibilities of commercial aviation there, flying 20,000 miles at the age of 80. Peck's books include *A Search for the Apex of South America* (1911), *The South American Tour* (1913), *Industrial and Commercial South America* (1922), and *Flying over South America—20,000 Miles by Air* (1932).

Annie Peck's fame as a mountain climber in Victorian times helped further the cause of women's rights. Already controversial for wearing pants when mountain climbing, Peck raised a "Votes for Women" banner at the summit of Mount Coropuna. In 1927, the Lima Geographical Society named the north peak of Huascarán in her honor—Cumbre Ana Peck.

Pedrarias Dávila   See ÁVILA, PEDRO ARIAS DE.

Penha, Joseph de la   (fl. 1680s–1690s)
Dutch explorer in eastern Canada

In about 1685, Joseph de la Penha, a Dutch Jew from Rotterdam, reportedly explored and settled parts of northeastern Canada, including Labrador, as well as regions he identified as Corte Real Land and Estotis Land.

In 1697, King William III of England, who also ruled the Netherlands, granted Penha and his descendants ownership of Labrador, in recognition for his having claimed the region in the name of the House of Orange.

Joseph de la Penha's heirs never attempted to gain title to the region, although their claim to it was officially recognized by Prince William of Orange, the Dutch monarch, in 1768.

Pérez Hernández, Juan Josef   (Juan Pérez)
(ca. 1725–1775) *Spanish naval officer in California and the Pacific Northwest*

Juan Pérez was born in Majorca, Spain. A trained pilot, he served aboard Spanish naval vessels in the Pacific Ocean, along the Manila Galleon route between the Philippines and the west coast of Mexico and South America.

In 1767, Pérez was assigned to San Blas, then the main Spanish naval base on Mexico's Pacific coast and the administrative center for all settlements to the north. At about that same time, Spanish colonial authorities in Mexico, alarmed by reports of Russian encroachment southward from the Aleutian Islands and Alaska into Spanish territory, initiated a full-scale program to colonize California. In 1769, Pérez took part in the earliest of these efforts, commanding the packet boat *Príncipe,* which carried some of the first colonists to the newly established settlements at San Diego and Monterey.

Although not a high-ranking naval officer in 1774, Pérez was nonetheless the most senior officer at San Blas and, as such, was commissioned to lead a voyage of exploration north of the known sections of the California coast. Spanish viceroy Antonio María Bucareli y Ursúa instructed him to sail as far northward as the 60th parallel and thereby determine the geography of the coastline north of California, as well as evaluate the extent of Russian settlement southward from the Gulf of Alaska. On his return southward, he was to land at various points along the coast and make formal acts of possession of the mainland in the name of Spain. In addition, he was to study the coastal Indians and try to establish friendly relations with them.

Pérez departed San Blas on January 25, 1774, in command of the frigate *Santiago*. After stops at San Diego and Monterey, he headed northwestward in June 1774. He sailed out of sight of land for several weeks, then changed his course to due north. On July 15, 1774, the North American mainland came in sight again at 55°30' north latitude, near Dixon Entrance and the southernmost point of the Alaskan Panhandle. Pérez and a landing party went ashore on one of the northernmost of the Queen Charlotte Islands, where he and his men encountered the Haida Indians. The Spaniards, the first Europeans to come in contact with the Haida, established friendly contacts with these coastal Indians and traded copper, cloth, and beads for furs.

Faced with unfavorable winds, Pérez decided not to sail any farther to the north. On his return along the coast, the mainland was shrouded in fog, and a thorough reconnaissance near the coastline was not possible due to currents and hazardous rocks. Pérez did manage to examine the west coast of Vancouver Island, although he was unaware that it was separated from the mainland. There, on August 8, 1774, he made the European discovery of an inlet he named Surgidero de San Lorenzo, later known as Nootka Sound. A landing was made; Pérez and his crew became the first Europeans to meet the Nootka Indians, with whom they also traded for furs. At that point in the voyage, the crew was weakened by SCURVY, so Pérez decided against additional landings and set sail for Mexico. Soon after leaving Nootka Sound, his second in command, Esteban José Martínez, reportedly sighted what he believed was the much-sought-after entrance to the Strait of Juan de Fuca, but Pérez declined to investigate, having determined that the offshore breakers and coastal fog posed too great a risk. Within a short time, they sighted a snow-capped peak rising eastward beyond the coastline of what is now Washington State. Named Sierra Nevada de Santa Rosalía by Pérez, it is known today as Mount Olympus. The expedition then continued back to San Blas.

In spring and summer 1775, Pérez took part in a second voyage of exploration north of California, serving with JUAN FRANCISCO DE LA BODEGA Y QUADRA under BRUNO DE HECETA. On the return trip to San Blas, in November 1775, Pérez died of scurvy off the California coast and was buried at sea with full naval honors.

Juan Pérez commanded the first known European expedition along the Pacific coast of what is now British Columbia. His exploration of Nootka Sound in 1774 provided the basis for Spain's claim in the Nootka Sound Crisis of 1789. In 1778, a landing party from JAMES COOK's expedition visited Nootka Sound, where they found the natives to be in possession of several silver spoons that had been stolen from one of Pérez's officers four years earlier. This was cited by Cook's own officers as proof that the Spanish had been there earlier, even though later accounts incorrectly credited Cook with having made the European discovery of Nootka Sound. In addition to geographic data, Pérez's written accounts of the Haida and Nootka tribes provide an image of the pre-contact life and culture of these coastal Indians.

Péron, François (1775–1810) *French naturalist in Australia and Tasmania*

François Péron was born and raised at Cerilly in central France near Vichy. With the onset of the French Revolutionary Wars in 1792, the 17-year-old Péron abruptly ended his theological studies to enlist in a local militia unit. In the ensuing conflict, he lost his right eye and was discharged from the army. Soon afterward, a woman he had planned to marry broke off their engagement. He then undertook medical studies in Paris, pursuing also an interest in natural history.

Péron's abilities as a naturalist came to the attention of French botanist Antoine-Laurent de Jussieu, who recommended him for the scientific team on a proposed French government-sponsored voyage of exploration to Australia and the South Pacific Ocean. Appointed as one of the expedition's zoologists, Péron sailed on the *Géographe* from Le Havre in October 1800, under the command of THOMAS-NICOLAS BAUDIN. The *Géographe,* accompanied by the *Naturaliste,* reached the west coast of Australia in July 1801, after a voyage around the CAPE OF GOOD HOPE and across the Indian Ocean.

Péron went ashore on Bernier Island at the mouth of Western Australia's Shark Bay, where he made a study of a species of red-headed marine snakes that lived on the rocky shoreline. At a stopover at Kupang on the island of Timor, Péron became friends with the headman of local natives.

In January 1802, Péron went ashore on Van Diemen's Land (TASMANIA), becoming one of the first Europeans to encounter the island's natives. Soon afterward, he took part in a specimen-gathering expedition on King Island, off southeastern Australia, in which he collected 180 different types of mollusks and zoophytes and undertook a study of elephant seals. He also made contact with King Island's natives.

Baudin's expedition next visited the British colony at Sydney, which Péron, in his later published account of the voyage, described in glowing terms, citing the penal settlement's great success in transforming its population of transported convicts and prostitutes into productive citizens. On a second visit to Timor in 1803, Péron joined the expedition's naturalist artist, CHARLES-ALEXANDRE LESUEUR, in a crocodile hunt.

By the time the *Géographe* arrived back in France in March 1804, Péron was the last remaining zoologist among the scientists, the others having died or left the expedition due to illness. Péron took on the task of classifying and cataloging the more than 100,000 zoological specimens, which had been collected in the four years of the Baudin voyage. His finished work, presented to the French Academy of Sciences in June 1806, included as many as 2,500 species new to science.

Acclaimed for his efforts, Péron was elected in 1806 to the Institute of France, the prestigious governmental body that, under the direction of Napoléon, had organized the Baudin expedition. He was then commissioned to write an official account of the expedition, the first volume of which appeared in 1807 as *Voyage aux terres australes sur le "Géographe" et le "Naturaliste"* (Voyage to southern lands on the *Géographe* and *Naturaliste*).

François Péron was unable to finish his account. He developed tuberculosis and died at his home at Cerilly in 1810. His work was later completed by his friend LOUIS-CLAUDE DE SAULCES DE FREYCINET, who had served as a naval officer on the Baudin expedition, and was published from 1811 to 1816. Although it was soon revealed that many of the geographic discoveries attributed to Baudin had actually been made a year earlier by British naval officer MATTHEW FLINDERS, Péron's zoological studies based on the 1800–1804 voyage remained a standard source on Australia's animal life for years afterward.

Perrin du Lac, François-Marie (1766–1824)

French government official, traveler on the Missouri River

François Perrin du Lac was born at La Chaux de Fonds, Neuchatel (now part of Switzerland), into a noble French family. In 1789, he was appointed to an administrative post with the French colonial administration in Haiti, attached to the colony's treasury department. Soon after his arrival, civil strife erupted between the slaves, the mixed-bloods, and the French colonists.

In 1791, Perrin du Lac was part of an official French delegation to Washington, D.C., requesting military help from the U.S. Congress in suppressing the slave rebellion. With the situation still unsettled in Haiti, and the outbreak of war between France and England in 1792 preventing his return to Europe, Perrin du Lac decided to remain in the United States. During the next years, he traveled widely throughout the valleys of the lower MISSISSIPPI RIVER and Ohio River, exploring Pennsylvania and Spanish-held Louisiana.

On May 18, 1802, Perrin du Lac, accompanied by a former fur trader, set out from St. Louis up the MISSOURI RIVER. He reached as far as the river's junction with the White River in what is now south-central South Dakota before returning to St. Louis.

Perrin du Lac returned to France in 1803, where he accepted a position with Napoléon's government in Hamburg, a post he held only briefly. He retired from government service until the restoration of the monarchy in 1814, when he was granted an appointment with the navy; in 1819, he accepted a government administrative post near Paris.

François Perrin du Lac included an account of his 1802 Missouri River trip in his book on his travels in North America: *Voyage dans les deux Louisianes, et chez les nations sauvages du Missouri . . .* (Journey in the two Louisianas and among the Indian nations of the Missouri River . . .). Published in Paris in 1805, it was the first written report describing the upper Missouri River. It was in print a full year before the first official American expedition into the region, under MERIWETHER LEWIS and WILLIAM CLARK, returned to St. Louis.

Perrot, Nicolas (ca. 1644–1717) *French fur trader, interpreter in the western Great Lakes and upper Mississippi Valley regions*

Nicolas Perrot was born in the Burgundy region of France, the son of a government law enforcement officer. Arriving in French Canada in 1660, he served for a few years as an assistant to the Jesuit missions, during which he learned several Indian languages.

In about 1667, Perrot embarked on a career in the FUR TRADE. He undertook an expedition west from Quebec to the Great Lakes, where he visited the Potawatomi and Fox (Mesquaki) Indians around Green Bay in present-day Wisconsin. He introduced the first European trade goods to the Indians of the western Great Lakes and may have been the first Frenchman to trade directly with the Sioux (Dakota, Lakota, Nakota). Perrot not only succeeded in convincing the Green Bay tribes to trade directly with the French, but also won their allegiance in the French wars against the Iroquois (Haudenosaunee) Indians.

From Green Bay, Perrot explored the Fox and Wisconsin Rivers, then became one of the earliest Europeans to see the upper MISSISSIPPI RIVER. In 1669–70, he served as an interpreter for the French colonial government in an expedition to the Indians of the Great Lakes. He traveled to northern Lake Huron by way of the Ottawa River and Lake Nipissing, and, after wintering on Manitoulin Island, went to Green Bay.

At Green Bay, Perrot induced the Potawatomi and other Wisconsin tribes to attend a ceremony at Sault Sainte Marie in which French colonial official Simon Francis Daumont, sieur de St. Lusson, formally took possession of the Great Lakes and upper Mississippi Valley in the name of King Louis XIV. This event, which occurred in June 1671, was attended by major tribal leaders of the Old Northwest, as well as Perrot, LOUIS JOLLIET, and missionary CLAUDE-JEAN ALLOUEZ.

Later in 1671, Perrot returned to Quebec, where he married and continued to develop his fur trading. In the 1680s, he used his influence among the western Great Lakes tribes to win their military support in the French conflicts with the Iroquois and English. In 1685, he was named commander of the French fur-trading and military settlement at Green Bay. He then made peace between warring Chippewa (Ojibway) and Fox bands by winning the release by the Fox of a Chippewa Indian girl, who otherwise would have been burned at the stake.

While in Green Bay in 1685, Perrot explored the Fox River to the lands of the Miami and Illinois Indians, then descended the Wisconsin River to the Mississippi.

In 1687, Perrot led a large force of Great Lakes Indians eastward in a raid against the Seneca Indians. While he was away, his stock of furs, stored at a Jesuit mission, was destroyed in a fire. Financially ruined, he returned to Montreal, where he served as an interpreter to delegations of Sac, Miami, and Potawatomi Indian leaders.

Two years later, in 1689, Perrot again ventured west of Lake Michigan. He explored the Fox, Wisconsin, and Mascouten Rivers and established trading forts at Lake Pepin and at the mouth of the Wisconsin River, near present-day Prairie du Chien, Wisconsin. The next year, he explored parts of present-day northern Iowa and discovered lead deposits.

With the revocation of independent trading licenses in 1696, Perrot was forced to leave the fur trade. He settled in

Montreal and continued to serve as an important intermediary with the Indians.

Nicolas Perrot's efforts helped open up the western Great Lakes and the upper Mississippi Valley to French trade interests. He made a significant impact on the life and culture of the Indians of the region by introducing tools and implements made of iron.

Petermann, August Heinrich (1822–1878)
German geographer

August Petermann was born in the central German town of Bleicherode near Weimar. After studying geography in Potsdam, he continued his studies in Edinburgh, Scotland, where he also was trained as a cartographer.

Petermann opened a small London map-publishing business in 1847. After seven years he returned to Germany, where he had been appointed director of the Perthes Geographical Institution in Gotha. The following year, 1855, he launched his journal, *Petermann's Geographische Mitteilungen,* which, in the latter part of the 19th century, became an important record for new geographic knowledge.

Petermann became an internationally recognized authority on the geography of central Africa and the Arctic. In 1852, he speculated that SIR JOHN FRANKLIN and his expedition, missing in the Canadian Arctic Archipelago since 1845, may have actually navigated the ice-choked channels northward into what he theorized was an "open polar sea." If this were the case, he theorized, Franklin and his men could be found somewhere between the NORTH POLE and the Bering Sea.

Petermann persisted in advancing his idea of an open polar sea for the next 20 years. In the late 1860s, he cited the unexplored Arctic region north of European Russia, between Spitsbergen (in Svalbard) and Novaya Zemlya, as a likely place where an ice-free entrance to such a body of water could be found. Prompted by Petermann's ideas, KARL CHRISTIAN KOLDEWEY led explorations into the region between Spitsbergen and GREENLAND from 1868 to 1870. Also influenced by Petermann were Austrian Arctic explorers JULIUS VON PAYER and KARL WEYPRECHT, who probed the frozen Arctic seas north of Novaya Zemlya. Although they found no ice-free passage to the Arctic Basin, they nonetheless made the European discovery of Franz Josef Land.

By the mid-1870s, Petermann had formulated a new concept of the geography of the Arctic, suggesting that Greenland, the northern limits of which were yet to be determined, extended northward across the North Pole, to the East Siberian Sea, where it was known as Wrangel Island.

August Petermann died in 1878, a suicide. A year later, American naval officer GEORGE WASHINGTON DE LONG, prompted by Petermann's last Arctic theory, undertook an attempt on the North Pole by way of BERING STRAIT and Wrangel Island. This expedition, which ended disastrously in 1881, nevertheless showed that Petermann's theory of a polar landmass extending from Arctic SIBERIA to Greenland was as erroneous as his earlier ideas about the open polar sea. Although he was ultimately wrong in his views on Arctic geography, Petermann nonetheless gave impetus to American and European expeditions to the Arctic and helped promote modern geographic investigations in central Africa. Significant among his works were his atlas of physical geography and his maps of Africa, which provided details on the continent's interior based on the most recent European explorations.

Pethahia of Regensburg (Petahiah of Regensburg) (fl. 1180s–1190s) *German traveler, writer in eastern Europe and Middle East*

Pethahia was a German Jew from the Bavarian city of Regensburg. In about 1180, he left Prague and journeyed eastward through Europe, the Crimea, and Armenia, into the Middle East, visiting Jewish communities in the lands of present-day Syria, Iraq, Jordan, Israel, Turkey, and Iran.

Soon after Jerusalem fell to MUSLIMs in 1187, Pethahia returned through Greece to Prague, where an account of his travels was recorded in Hebrew in a work entitled *Sibbuv* (Circuit).

Although mainly concerned with the Jewish legends and traditions that Pethahia had collected in the course of his journey, his report also included geographic and cultural information on the Middle Eastern lands he had visited, including contemporary descriptions of the Holy Land's sacred sites. His work became an important source of information for Western Europeans when contacts with the region accelerated with the initiation of the third of the CRUSADES in 1189.

Pfeiffer, Ida Reyer (1797–1858) *Austrian world traveler, writer*

Ida Pfeiffer, née Reyer, was born in Vienna, the daughter of a wealthy merchant. She had a liberal upbringing and was educated at home by tutors. At the age of 22, she married a Swiss-born lawyer named Pfeiffer who was many years her senior; they had two sons together.

Starting in 1842, at the age of 45, after her children had grown and her husband had gone to live with a son from a former marriage, Pfeiffer embarked on a career of world travel. She first went to the Middle East, where she visited Jerusalem and Egypt, crossing the desert region between Cairo and Suez. After nine months in the region, she returned to Vienna where her journal of the trip was published in 1843. (The first English edition of this work was published in London in 1852 as *Visit to the Holy Land, Egypt and Italy*.)

With the money from this work, Pfeiffer was able to finance a trip to ICELAND in 1844. During a stay of six months, she collected geological and plant specimens that she later sold to museums. With this money, along with what she earned from the publication of her account of the trip (published in an English edition in 1852 as *Visit to Iceland*), she was able to undertake a trip around the world.

Leaving in spring 1847, Pfeiffer sailed to Brazil; from Rio de Janeiro, she traveled inland to the town of Petropolis. In the surrounding forest area she visited with the Puri Indians, with whom she took part in a monkey hunt. She next sailed to Tahiti, where she remained for several weeks before continuing across the Pacific Ocean to Hong Kong, then sailed by a Chinese JUNK to Canton (Guangzhou), China, where she toured the city and the surrounding countryside.

Pfeiffer's next destination was India, where she visited nutmeg groves and a sugar cane processing plant. She also took part in a tiger hunt. In her travels in India, she collected plants and insect specimens for sale to European museums. She then went on to the Persian Gulf region, where she ascended the Tigris River to Baghdad. After traveling by camel caravan 300 miles to Mosul in what is now northern Iraq, she continued to the Persian city of Tabriz in present-day northern Iran. Pfeiffer proceeded northward into the Kurdistan region of eastern Turkey and crossed into Russia, where Cossack authorities detained her briefly due to some misunderstanding concerning her passport. She then returned home by way of Greece and Italy, reaching Vienna in November 1848. In all, she had traversed some 2,800 miles by land, and 35,000 miles by sea.

Pfeiffer's account of her trip was published soon afterward, the first English edition of which appeared in 1852 as *A Woman's Journey Round the World*. The book earned her wide acclaim, and shipping companies offered her free passage on trans-oceanic vessels in recognition of her accomplishments as a world traveler.

Pfeiffer began her second round-the-world journey in May 1851. From London, she sailed to Cape Town, and, following a month-long stay, she continued across the Indian Ocean to the Dutch East Indies (present-day Indonesia). At Sarawak on the island of Borneo, she was hosted by the territory's British-born rajah, Sir James Brooke.

During her six months on Borneo, Pfeiffer undertook several forays into the interior, making contact with the Dyak, a tribe of headhunters. She also went to Sumatra where she visited with another tribe, the Batak. On Ceram, she spent time among the Alfora.

Pfeiffer next sailed across the Pacific Ocean to San Francisco, California, from where she left for additional travels in South America. Before returning home, she undertook a tour of the United States. In June 1855, she arrived back in London, having circled the world for the second time. She chronicled her four-year odyssey in another travel book, published in an English edition in 1856 as *A Woman's Second Journey Round the World, from London to the Cape of Good Hope, Borneo, Java, Sumatra, Celebes, Ceram, the Moluccas etc., California, Panama, Peru, Ecuador, and the United States*.

Pfeiffer's last journey was to Madagascar, where she joined several other Europeans in an abortive plot to overthrow the island's tyrannical ruler, Queen Ranavalona. After the plot failed, she and the other Europeans were expelled. She had become ill with fever and was still ailing when she reached Vienna, where she died in October 1858.

Although without great financial resources, Ida Reyer Pfeiffer managed to travel on her own around the world two times, both west to east as well as east to west. The exotic places she visited and described in her highly popular travel accounts had rarely been seen by European women.

Philby, Harry St. John Bridger (1885–1960)

British diplomat, traveler in Arabia

Harry St. John Philby was born on the island of CEYLON (present-day Sri Lanka) into a British colonial family who operated a tea plantation. After attending Westminster School in London, he went on to Cambridge University's Trinity College, where he studied classical and modern languages, including Persian and Arabic, as well as Urdu and Hindi, two of the major languages of India.

In 1908, Philby entered the British diplomatic service in India. Soon after the outbreak of World War I in 1914, he was sent to the Middle East, attached to the British army as a political officer in Baghdad.

Philby made his first long journey into the Arabian Peninsula in 1917, when he was sent to Riyadh to meet with Ibn Saud, a local Arab leader, in an attempt to gain his support for the Arab rebellion against Turkish rule that had erupted the year before. From Baghdad, Philby traveled to the Persian Gulf coast of Arabia, then headed inland at Qatar, and, from Hofuf, proceeded to Riyadh. After conferring with Ibn Saud, Philby made his way westward across the interior of Arabia, visiting ancient ruins at Dariyan. He then went through the Sagta Pass and followed the Muslim pilgrim route toward Mecca, arriving on the coast of the RED SEA at Jidda. He thus completed an east-to-west crossing of the Arabian Peninsula, the first European to do so since GEORGE FOSTER SADLIER, who had made a similar journey a century earlier in 1819.

From Jidda, Philby sailed to Bombay, India, then returned to Basra (present-day Iraq), at the head of the Persian Gulf. In 1918, he again traveled southward into Arabia and explored the southern provinces of the Nejd region, as far as the northern edge of southeastern Arabia's vast Rub' al-Khali

—known as the EMPTY QUARTER—one of the largest sand deserts in the world.

In 1920, the ROYAL GEOGRAPHICAL SOCIETY awarded Philby a gold medal for his explorations into the little-known regions of Arabia. He remained in the diplomatic service in the Middle East for the next few years. In 1920–22, he explored the Syrian Desert, covering the territory between Amman, Jordan, and the upper Euphrates River.

In 1924, Philby left the British diplomatic corps to pursue private business ventures in Arabia. He returned to the Riyadh region, and, over the next five years, as an agent for Western oil and mining interests, he sought the cooperation and support of Ibn Saud, who was then emerging as the dominant leader on the Arabian Peninsula.

By 1930, Philby had become disenchanted with British foreign policy in regard to Arabia; after converting to Islam, he became a trusted political adviser to Ibn Saud. Soon afterward, Ibn Saud succeeded in consolidating his rule into the present-day Kingdom of Saudi Arabia.

In 1931, Philby received permission from the Saudi king to undertake an exploration into the Rub' al-Khali in search of the ruins of the legendary city of Wabar, which, according to Muslim tradition reminiscent of the biblical account of Sodom and Gomorrah, had been destroyed by God for its wickedness. On January 7, 1932, Philby set out from the wells at Dulaiqiya, west of Qatar near Hofuf, and traveled southward into the Empty Quarter. In the middle of this great desert, he located several large craters near a site known as Al Hadida. There, he discovered quantities of iron, which he later determined were fragments of a giant meteor, and which some Muslim authorities judged to be remnants of the fabled Wabar. From this site, Philby headed westward across the desert wastes, and, on March 11, 1932, he arrived at the mouth of the Wadi Dawasir, near the Arabian oasis settlement at Sulaiyil.

In 1936, Philby undertook additional explorations in southwestern Arabia, traveling from Mecca southward into the Hadhramaut region of what is now the People's Democratic Republic of Yemen.

Philby remained as an adviser to the Saudi royal family in the years after the discovery of great oil reserves in Arabia in 1936, guiding the kingdom through the massive changes that resulted from the sudden influx of western capital and technology.

Harry St. John Philby, whose epitaph hails him as the "Greatest of Arabian Explorers," was one of the last Europeans to explore vast areas of Arabia before oil companies began to probe the remote regions of the interior with motorized vehicles and aircraft. Although Englishman BERTRAM THOMAS had been the first European to cross the Empty Quarter in 1931, Philby's journey a year later, in which he traversed far more difficult terrain, is considered to have been a more thorough exploration. In his travels in Arabia, Philby amassed hundreds of plant, animal, and fossil specimens that later became part of the natural history collections of major museums in Great Britain and the United States. Among Philby's works on the region are *Heart of Arabia* (1923), *The Empty Quarter* (1933), *Sa'ud Arabia* (1955), and *Forty Years in the Wilderness* (1957). His son, Kim Philby, was exposed in 1963 as having been a long-time Soviet spy within the British intelligence establishment.

Phillip, Arthur (1738–1814) *British naval officer in Australia*

Arthur Phillip, a British naval officer, received command of the *Sirius,* the flagship of First Fleet, consisting of 11 ships on what was to be first colonizing expedition to Australia. The excursion was planned as a follow-up to JAMES COOK's landing in Botany Bay in 1770.

Commissioned by Thomas Townsend, Viscount Sydney, the First Fleet departed Portsmouth, England, on May 13, 1787, with 450 crew members; 564 male and 192 female convicts, plus 58 wives and children; and two years' worth of supplies. Sailing via Rio de Janeiro in Brazil around Africa's CAPE OF GOOD HOPE and past Van Diemen's Land (TASMANIA), the First Fleet arrived in Botany Bay on the east coast of Australia and then continued northward to Port Jackson (present-day Sydney) and founded a colony on January 26, 1788. Despite great hardship, the colony survived with Phillip serving as governor until 1792, when he returned to England because of failing health.

Arthur Phillip's expedition led to the first permanent European settlement in Australia and the New South Wales colony. January 26 is celebrated as Australia Day.

Phipps, Constantine John (1744–1792) *British naval officer in the Arctic*

Constantine Phipps, an experienced British naval officer, received command of an early expedition to the NORTH POLE, proposed by John Montagu, earl of Sandwich, and sponsored by the ROYAL SOCIETY, with the support of the Lords of the Admiralty and King George III. The hulls of two warships, the *Racehorse* and the *Carcass,* were reinforced for DRIFT ICE. It was believed at the time that the North Pole could be reached by a water route.

Captain Phipps and his expedition departed England in June 1773, sailing due north. Between GREENLAND and the Spitsbergen island group (part of present-day Svalbard), Phipps found passage blocked by ice. While skirting the ice barrier, Phipps attempted to carry out planned experiments, using a thermometer for measuring water temperature and an apparatus for distilling freshwater from the sea. The expedition reached 80'48" North latitude.

Phipps wrote about the expedition in *A Voyage Towards the North Pole Undertaken by His Majesty's Command 1773*, published in 1774. His observations on Arctic navigation as well as on natural science, including a discussion of polar bears, proved helpful to subsequent Arctic explorers sent out by the British Admiralty, including DAVID BUCHAN and SIR JOHN ROSS in 1818.

Piccard, Auguste (1884–1962) *Swiss physicist, aviator, oceanographer, father of Jacques Ernest-Jean Piccard*

Auguste Piccard was born in Basel, Switzerland. In 1922, he became a professor of physics at the Polytechnic Institute of the University of Brussels in Belgium.

Piccard, interested in lighter-than-air flight, pioneered the use of the pressurized cabin to enable a high-altitude ascent in a BALLOON. In 1931, he and Paul Kipler, in a sealed spherical gondola lifted by a hydrogen-filled balloon, set a new world altitude record of 51,793 feet, becoming the first humans to penetrate the stratosphere. In 1932, Piccard reached 55,577 feet. In these ascensions, he studied temperature and cosmic rays in the stratosphere. His twin brother, Jean-Félix Piccard, ascended with his wife to an altitude of 57,564 feet in 1934.

Auguste Piccard next turned his attention to undersea exploration and the SUBMERSIBLE. In 1947, applying the principles of an AIRSHIP, he built his first BATHYSCAPH (an improvement on the BATHYSPHERE), an envelope filled with heptane (an aviation petrol), bearing a steel watertight cabin. In 1954, after a series of dives, he accomplished a descent to a depth of 13,125 feet.

In 1957, the U.S. Navy financed a series of dives in Piccard's bathyscaph, refurbished and renamed the *Trieste II*, off the island of Capri, Italy. Piccard's son JACQUES ERNEST-JEAN PICCARD was hired to join the team. In 1959, the bathyscaph was brought to the island of Guam in the Pacific Ocean. After a series of engineering trials, on January 23, 1960, Jacques, as pilot, along with Donald Walsh, a navy lieutenant, dove in the *Trieste II* about 35,810 feet to the bottom of the Challenger Deep of the MARIANAS TRENCH, the deepest point on Earth, and set the world record in depth.

Auguste and Jacques Piccard also designed a mesoscaph for diving to 6,000 feet. The mesoscaph used helicopter-like propellers to maintain its depth.

Auguste Piccard was a pioneer in both aviation and oceanography. He also collaborated with Albert Einstein on the development of instruments for measuring radioactivity. His grandson Bertrand Piccard participated in the first nonstop balloon flight around the world in 1999.

Piccard, Jacques Ernest-Jean (1922–)
Swiss oceanographer, engineer, son of Auguste Piccard

Born in Brussels, Belgium, the son of the Swiss physicist AUGUSTE PICCARD, Jacques Piccard originally pursued a career in economics, graduating from the University of Geneva in Switzerland in 1946 and then becoming an assistant professor there.

Moving to Italy and working as an economist in Trieste, Piccard was invited to join the team building the BATHYSCAPH, a type of BATHYSPHERE, designed by his father. In 1957, the U.S. Navy purchased Auguste Piccard's second bathyscaph, the *Trieste,* completed five years earlier, and hired Jacques as a scientific consultant. Starting in 1959, off Guam in the Pacific Ocean, more engineering trials were carried out. On January 23, 1960, Jacques, as pilot, and Donald Walsh, a navy lieutenant, dove in the renamed *Trieste II* some 35,810 feet (seven miles), nearly to the bottom of the Challenger Deep of the MARIANAS TRENCH, the deepest point on Earth, setting the world record in depth.

Piccard, working in Lausanne, Switzerland, designed an exploratory SUBMARINE, the *Auguste Piccard.* In 1964, some 33,000 visitors of the Swiss National Exhibition, were taken on sight-seeing dives in Lake Geneva to a depth of 330 feet. Piccard designed another submarine, the *Ben Franklin* (PX-15), for the purpose of studying OCEAN CURRENTS. In 1969, he and a team of five observers drifted in the GULF STREAM along North America's Atlantic coast from Palm Beach, Florida, to Cape Hatteras, North Carolina.

For their record-setting dive in the *Trieste,* Piccard and Walsh were awarded the Distinguished Public Service award by the U.S. government. Piccard's writings include *Seven Miles Down* (1961, with American oceanographer Robert Dietz) and *The Sun Beneath the Sea* (1971).

Jacques Piccard's dive in the Pacific Ocean's Marianas Trench—more than 6,000 feet deeper than the highest point on Earth from sea level, MOUNT EVEREST—still stands as a world record. His son, Bertrand Piccard, participated in the first nonstop BALLOON flight around the world in 1999.

Pigafetta, Francesco Antonio
(ca. 1491–ca. 1535) *Italian author, traveler in South America and the South Pacific, in service to Spain*

Antonio Pigafetta was born at Vicenza in northern Italy's Lombardy region, the son of noble parents. He received a good education, and, with his talent for languages, planned a career as a diplomat.

In 1518, Pigafetta toured the major European capitals with a Vatican diplomatic mission. He had become interested in the explorations then being undertaken by Portuguese and Spanish navigators, and, while in Spain with the papal delegation, he learned of FERDINAND MAGELLAN's planned expedition to the EAST INDIES. He offered his services to Spain's king Charles I (Holy Roman Emperor Charles V), the expedition's chief sponsor, and received a royal commission as a "gentleman volunteer" to be Magellan's private secretary.

Pigafetta arrived in May 1519 in Seville, where he spent the next few months studying navigational techniques in preparation for the voyage. On September 20, 1519, he sailed from the nearby port of Sanlúcar de Barrameda on Magellan's flagship, the *Trinidad,* one of a fleet of five vessels.

During the next three years, Pigafetta kept a daily record of this historic voyage in which the STRAIT OF MAGELLAN was located and the world was first circumnavigated. He was one of the 18 survivors of the expedition to return to Spain on the *Victoria* in September 1522. As it turned out, Pigafetta's journal was the only surviving eyewitness written record of the historic voyage, the Portuguese having confiscated Magellan's own log when they seized the *Trinidad* in the East Indies in 1521.

Soon after his return to Spain, Pigafetta presented his journal to King Charles I. He then went to Rome, where he was received by Pope Clement VII. Through the pope's influence, in 1524, Pigafetta became a member of the Knights of Rhodes (later the Knights of Malta), a military-religious order. At the request of Pope Clement and King Charles, Antonio Pigafetta wrote an account of the Magellan voyage, *Primo viaggio intorno al mondo* (First journey around the terrestrial globe), which was first published in an abridged form in Paris in 1540.

The work describes the mutiny on the South American coast and Magellan's death in the Philippines. Although JUAN SEBASTIÁN DEL CANO was initially hailed as having completed the first CIRCUMNAVIGATION OF THE WORLD, since he commanded the *Victoria* on its return voyage to Spain after Magellan's death in 1521, the accomplishment, according to Pigafetta, was largely due to Magellan's skill as a navigator and leader. With his background in navigation, Antonio Pigafetta was able to provide details on the locations of the various islands he visited. The work relates that Magellan first learned of the passage at the southern end of South America (afterward known as the Strait of Magellan) from a secret GLOBE or chart he had seen in Lisbon, produced by MARTIN BEHAIM in 1492.

In addition to revealing to European geographers the vast extent of the Pacific Ocean, Antonio Pigafetta was among the first to comment on the phenomenon of having lost a day in the westward journey around the world. Although he had kept an accurate record of all the days that had transpired on the three-year voyage, Pigafetta nonetheless failed to take into account that the expedition had sailed westward across the 180th meridian of longitude in its passage across the Pacific Ocean and, in so doing, had traversed what has since been designated as the INTERNATIONAL DATE LINE. Pigafetta also provided European leaders with valuable information on trading practices in the East Indies and described the native peoples he had encountered.

Pike, Zebulon Montgomery (1779–1813)

U.S. Army officer, American explorer of the upper Mississippi, eastern Colorado Rockies, and Arkansas River

Zebulon Pike was born in Lamberton, near Trenton, New Jersey. His father, who had the same name, was an American army officer in the Revolutionary War. The younger Pike joined the army in about 1793, serving alongside his father under General "Mad" Anthony Wayne in campaigns against the Ohio Valley tribes in the Miami War, or Little Turtle's War, of 1790–94. Pike remained in the army and was subsequently stationed at garrisons throughout the Old Northwest. By 1799, he had been commissioned a second lieutenant.

In 1805, General James Wilkinson sent Pike on an expedition to explore the headwaters of the MISSISSIPPI RIVER. In addition to locating the Mississippi's source, Pike was ordered to assert U.S. sovereignty over the upper Mississippi and Great Lakes region and to enforce the terms of Jay's Treaty of 1794, under which British traders and military personnel were to leave U.S. territory. Pike was also instructed to establish peaceful contacts with Indians in the region and survey fur and mineral resources.

Pike's expedition of 20 soldiers departed St. Louis on August 9, 1805, and traveled up the Mississippi aboard a 70-foot KEELBOAT. After meeting with leaders of the Sac tribe at

Zebulon Pike *(Library of Congress)*

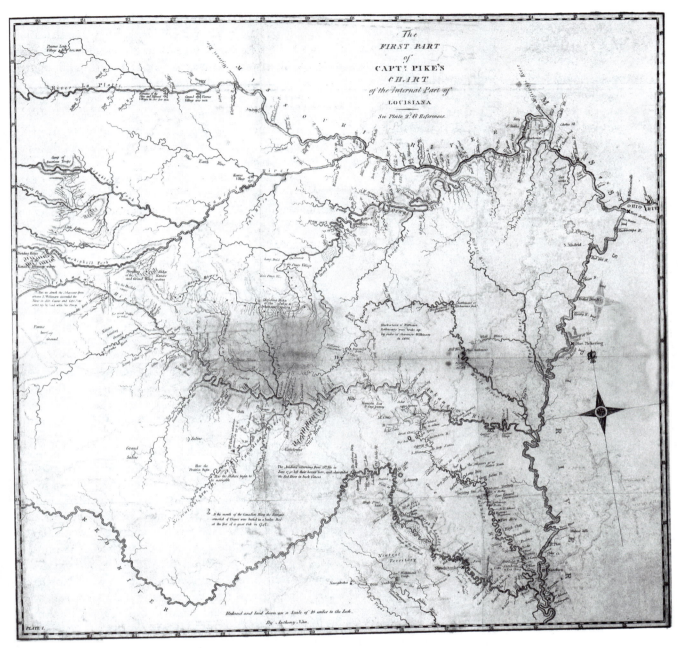

Map of the Louisiana Territory by Zebulon Pike (1807) *(Library of Congress)*

present-day Keokuk, Iowa, and surveying the lead deposits at Dubuque, Pike continued upriver to Prairie du Chien. At this point, he left his keelboat, proceeding with his expedition on two smaller and faster boats. He negotiated a purchase of 100,000 acres of land in Minnesota from the Sioux (Dakota, Lakota, Nakota) Indians, which later became the site of Minneapolis.

About 230 miles above the Falls of St. Anthony, Pike established winter quarters for most of his party. In December 1805, accompanied by some of his men, he pushed onward into northern Minnesota, seeking the source of the Mississippi. The river was frozen in some places, and his expedition traveled alternately by CANOE and sled. In February 1806, Pike and his men reached Red Cedar Lake (Cass Lake) and Leech Lake, which he wrongly concluded were the sources of the Mississippi River. The actual source of the Mississippi, Lake Itasca, was determined by HENRY ROWE SCHOOLCRAFT in 1832.

Pike returned to his expedition's winter encampment at present-day Little Falls, Minnesota, and from there descended the Mississippi, arriving back in St. Louis on April 30, 1806.

Two months later, Wilkinson again dispatched Pike. This time, he was to search for the sources of the Arkansas and Red Rivers and survey the southern boundary of the newly acquired Louisiana Territory. On July 15, 1806, with 23 soldiers and 51 recently freed Osage Indians, whom he was to escort back to their homeland, plus Wilkinson's son James Biddle, also a U.S. army lieutenant, and a naturalist, Dr. John Robinson, Pike left Fort Belle Fontaine, near St. Louis, and headed up the MISSOURI RIVER on two riverboats. By way of the Osage River, Pike and his men reached the Osage lands, then traveled on horseback overland to the Republican River in what is now western Nebraska. On learning that a Spanish military force had been sent to intercept him, Pike led his men southward to the Great Bend of the Arkansas River. While the younger Wilkinson and a small party explored the Arkansas to its junction with the Mississippi, Pike and the rest of his command ascended the Arkansas into Colorado.

In November 1806, Pike and his men first sighted the Front Range of the ROCKY MOUNTAINS, near what is now Pueblo, Colorado. From a distance, they espied the 14,110-foot mountain that would later be known as Pikes Peak. Pike and a small party attempted to climb the mountain, but early winter snows prevented an ascent. The expedition headed southward and returned to the Arkansas, tracing it to its source in the Royal Gorge.

Pike then attempted to reach the Red River. He crossed the Sangre de Cristo Mountains into the San Luis Valley. On the Conejos River, a tributary of the Rio Grande, he established a stockade, where he and his men spent the winter.

In spring 1807, Spanish military authorities arrested Pike's party for illegally crossing into Spanish territory. They suspected that the expedition had been sent to spy on Spanish defenses in the Southwest. The prisoners were taken to Santa Fe, then to Chihuahua, Mexico. Pike maintained that he had mistaken the Rio Grande for the Red River and had entered Spanish territory accidentally. Historians have speculated that Pike knew his true location and was indeed engaged in a spying operation against the Spanish. After being held in custody for several months, Pike and his men were taken across Texas and returned to the United States at Natchitoches, Louisiana, on June 30, 1807.

Pike was subsequently implicated along with Wilkinson in Aaron Burr's plot to establish a separate empire in the American Southwest, but he was soon acquitted of any wrongdoing. He went on to serve as a brigadier general in the War of 1812. In April 1813, while leading an attack against Toronto, he was killed in an explosion of a British powder magazine.

The charts and journals that Pike made on his Colorado expedition were confiscated by the Spanish. Nevertheless, he was able to reproduce most of his observations from memory and from private papers he had smuggled back to St. Louis.

Zebulon Pike's report of his expeditions up the Mississippi and into the Rockies was published in 1810 as *An Account of the Expeditions to the Sources of the Mississippi and through the Western Parts of Louisiana.* It was translated into French, German, and Dutch. In it, Pike described the southern plains as too arid for agricultural settlement. His findings were confirmed by STEPHEN HARRIMAN LONG in his 1819 expedition and helped lay the foundation for the myth of the "Great American Desert." Yet Pike's descriptions of the Spanish settlements in New Mexico encouraged St. Louis traders to develop commerce by way of the Santa Fe Trail. Pike's explorations of the southern plains began at the same time that the expedition of MERIWETHER LEWIS and WILLIAM CLARK was returning from the Pacific Northwest. His account, along with that of Lewis and Clark, provided the first complete picture of the American trans-Mississippi West.

Pilcher, Joshua (1790–1843) *American fur trader on the upper Missouri and in the Rocky Mountains*

Born in Culpeper County, Virginia, Joshua Pilcher moved with his family to western Tennessee while young. He studied medicine for a short time, but gave it up to become a frontier merchant.

In 1815, Pilcher arrived in St. Louis, Missouri, where he soon became prominent in business as a director of the Bank of St. Louis. He entered the FUR TRADE, and, by 1819, he had become a partner with MANUEL LISA in the ST. LOUIS MISSOURI FUR COMPANY.

Following Lisa's death in 1820, Pilcher became president of the company and directed its trading operation on the upper MISSOURI RIVER. In spring 1823, one of his fur brigades was attacked and annihilated by Arikara Indians in the Dakota country. That summer, Pilcher led a battalion of fur traders and allied Sioux (Dakota, Lakota, Nakota) Indians as part of Colonel HENRY LEAVENWORTH's punitive military expedition against the Arikara at their villages on the Missouri near the present border between North and South Dakota. During this operation, Pilcher's men, without authorization from Leavenworth, destroyed the Arikara villages. That same year, another of his trading parties was wiped out by marauding Blackfeet Indians in western Montana.

With the upper Missouri effectively closed by Indian resistance, the St. Louis Missouri Fur Company continued to suffer losses and went out of business by 1825. He subsequently organized a new trading outfit in 1827. That year, he led 45 traders and trappers into the ROCKY MOUNTAINS by way of the Platte River. Pilcher's explorations across the northern plains and into the northern Rockies continued for the next three years. He and his men eventually reached the Columbia River Basin and the HUDSON'S BAY COMPANY post, Fort Vancouver.

Pilcher returned to St. Louis in 1830, and, the following year, he took charge of the AMERICAN FUR COMPANY's trading fort on the Missouri at Council Bluffs.

In 1833, he accompanied ALEXANDER PHILIPP MAXI-MILIAN and artist KARL BODMER on their tour of the upper Missouri.

Through his fur-trading operations, Pilcher developed extensive contacts with the upper Missouri Indian tribes, and in 1837, he was appointed Indian subagent to the Sioux, Ponca, and Cheyenne. In 1839, he succeeded WILLIAM CLARK as superintendent of Indian affairs at St. Louis, serving until 1841. He remained prominent in St. Louis political and business affairs and was a friend and associate of Missouri senator Thomas Hart Benton.

Joshua Pilcher's report on his explorations was later published by the U.S. Congress. In it, he commented on the Oregon Country's potential for agricultural settlement, pointing out that emigrants could easily reach it by way of the Platte River route and the SOUTH PASS. His account gave impetus to the development of the Oregon Trail as a major migration route across the Great Plains and northern Rockies to the Pacific Northwest.

Pinto, Fernão Mendes (Fernando Pinto)

(1509–1583) *Portuguese traveler in India and the Far East*
Born at Montemor-o-Velho in southern Portugal, Fernão Pinto came from a family of modest means. As a teenager, he served as a page in the households of nobles.

In about 1537, Pinto traveled to India with Cristoval da Gama, a son of VASCO DA GAMA, and was taken captive by Turks, who sold him into slavery. He eventually regained his freedom in Malaya, from where he went to China with a European trading expedition.

In about 1541, Pinto arrived in Peking (Beijing), where he entered the diplomatic service of the Chinese government. He accompanied an official Chinese delegation to Cochin China (present-day Vietnam), visiting the lower Mekong River region and Hainan Island in the South China Sea. From there, he sailed to Japan, arriving in 1542. While in Japan, he became associated with FRANCIS XAVIER, with whom he traveled for a time.

After 20 years as a trader and adventurer in Southeast Asia, China, Indonesia, and India, Pinto returned to Europe, arriving in Portugal in 1558. He settled near Lisbon and wrote an account of his travels, entitled *Peregrinação* (Peregrinations, or Wanderings). It was published in 1614, 30 years after his death.

Although many of his described adventures were too fantastic to be believed and earned him the sobriquet "Prince of Lies," Fernão Pinto is nonetheless credited as being the first known European to visit Japan.

Pinzón, Arias Martín (1465–1510) *Spanish mariner in the West Indies and South America, nephew of Francisco*

Martín Pinzón, Martín Alonso Pinzón, and Vicente Yáñez Pinzón
Arias Pinzón was born at Palos de Moguer in the Andalusia region of southwestern Spain. A member of a family of well-established seafarers and shipowners, he was the son of an older brother of FRANCISCO MARTÍN PINZÓN, MARTÍN ALONSO PINZÓN, and VICENTE YÁÑEZ PINZÓN.

By 1492, Pinzón had become an accomplished mariner and pilot. He sailed on CHRISTOPHER COLUMBUS's first voyage to the WEST INDIES as a crewman on the *Niña*, commanded by his uncle Vicente. Also along on this expedition were his uncle Martín, who commanded the *Pinta*, as well as his uncle Francisco, who was the first mate on the *Pinta*.

The next year, 1493, Pinzón joined Columbus on a second exploration of the West Indies, taking him to Hispaniola (present-day Haiti and the Dominican Republic), Puerto Rico, the south coast of Cuba, and the north coast of Jamaica. Five years later, in 1498, he sailed again with Columbus to the northeast coast of South America and the island of Trinidad.

In 1499, together with his uncles Vicente and Francisco, Pinzón commanded several ships exploring the South American coast north and south of the mouth of the AMAZON RIVER. On the westward voyage across the Atlantic Ocean from the Cape Verde Islands, Pinzón's ships and those of Vicente became separated in rough weather. They met up again in late January 1500, off Cape São Augustinho, just south of South America's great eastern bulge, near what is now Recife, Brazil. They then headed northwestward along the coast to the mouth of the Amazon. While Vicente continued to probe northward along the coast of the Guianas, Pinzón returned southward and may have cruised along the Brazilian shore as far as what is now Rio de Janeiro. He later rejoined his uncle in the Gulf of Paria, on the coast of present-day Venezuela, from where they returned to Spain by way of Hispaniola.

Over the next several years, Pinzón became wealthy as one of the first traders to develop commercial ties between his home at Palos de Moguer in Spain, and Spanish colonies in the West Indies. In 1506–07, together with his uncle Vicente and JUAN DÍAZ DE SOLÍS, he explored along the coast of the Yucatán Peninsula, and, in 1509–10, he returned to the South American coast in search of an interoceanic strait through the continent.

Arias Pinzón, while not the best known of the Pinzóns, was nevertheless instrumental in the early exploration of the West Indies and the mainland of South America.

Pinzón, Francisco Martín (1462–1500)

Spanish mariner in the West Indies and South America, brother of Martín Alonso Pinzón and Vicente Yáñez Pinzón, uncle of Arias Martín Pinzón
Born at Palos de Moguer in southwestern Spain, Francisco Pinzón was the youngest of the three Pinzón brothers whose

shipbuilding firm provided the *Niña* and the *Pinta* for CHRISTOPHER COLUMBUS's first voyage to the Americas.

On that 1492 voyage, in which Columbus reached the Bahamas, Hispaniola (present-day Haiti and the Dominican Republic), and other islands in the WEST INDIES, Pinzón sailed as first mate and pilot on the *Pinta,* under the command of his brother MARTÍN ALONSO PINZÓN. He supported his brother's attempt to desert the expedition with the *Pinta* off the coast of Cuba, despite the fact that another brother, VICENTE YÁÑEZ PINZÓN, commander of the *Niña,* remained loyal to Columbus.

With Martín's death in 1493, Pinzón became managing partner of the family shipbuilding business. In 1499–1500, he joined his brother Vicente and their nephew ARIAS MARTÍN PINZÓN in an exploration of the northeast coast of South America, during which they made the European discovery of the AMAZON RIVER. On the homeward voyage, he was lost with all his crew when the ship he commanded went down in a hurricane off Hispaniola.

Francisco Pinzón, together with his brothers and nephew, provided the ships and navigational expertise essential for the success of Columbus's 1492 voyage. In his final voyage with Vicente and Arias, he took part in the first European exploration of the South American mainland south and east of Trinidad.

Pinzón, Martín Alonso (Martín Alonzo Pinzón)

(ca. 1441–1493) *Spanish mariner in the West Indies, brother of Francisco Martín Pinzón and Vicente Yáñez Pinzón, uncle of Arias Martín Pinzón*

Martín Pinzón was a native of Palos de Moguer, near the former seaport of Palos de Frontera, on the Andalusian coast of southwestern Spain. A descendant of a long line of seafarers, he became an accomplished mariner and ship's pilot, taking part in trading voyages throughout the MEDITERRANEAN SEA and along the coast of West Africa.

According to some accounts, Pinzón sailed with a French navigator named Cousin in a 1488 voyage to the coast of West Africa; after a storm had driven their vessel far to the southwest, they reportedly came within sight of uncharted land and reached the mouth of large river.

Another source relates that, by the late 1480s, Pinzón had retired from the sea and joined his brothers FRANCISCO MARTÍN PINZÓN and VICENTE YÁÑEZ PINZÓN in the family's shipbuilding business in Palos de Frontera, as the senior partner. The Pinzón brothers befriended CHRISTOPHER COLUMBUS and supported his idea that Japan and China could be reached by sailing westward across the Atlantic Ocean. On a visit to Rome about 1490, Pinzón reportedly came across records that papal taxes, or tithes, had been collected from a land called VINLAND until about 1400, and found references to this place on old Norman charts, indicating that it was located westward across the Atlantic.

Pinzón was well respected in the Spanish royal court as an authority on maritime matters, and on his return to Spain, he presented these findings to the advisers of King Ferdinand II and Queen Isabella I. His report may have influenced the Spanish monarchs' ultimate decision to sponsor Columbus in 1492.

Pinzón provided one-eighth the cost of mounting the expedition, helped recruit the crews from his native Palos de Moguer and Palos de Frontera, and was instrumental in obtaining two of the ships for the voyage, the *Niña* and the *Pinta.* He sailed with Columbus in early August 1492, as captain of the *Pinta,* assisted by his brother Francisco. His brother Vicente commanded the *Niña,* while Columbus commanded the expedition's flagship, the *Santa María.*

In early October 1492, Pinzón convinced Columbus to follow flocks of birds migrating southward, a sign that land was probably in that direction. He had determined that they had traveled westward beyond the point where Japan was thought to be; the decision to head toward a possible landfall calmed the fears of the men on all the ships, who had become alarmed at not having come upon land since leaving the CANARY ISLANDS three weeks earlier.

On the morning of October 12, 1492, one of Pinzón's crewmen on the *Pinta,* Roderigo de Triano, sighted land, one of the Bahama Islands. Columbus named it San Salvador (also known as Watling Island).

Pinzón and the *Pinta* abruptly left Columbus and the other two ships off the east coast of Cuba on November 21, 1492. The natives on Cuba had reported that gold could be found in abundance on a nearby island, and it was there that Pinzón had gone. He later reported that he had landed on Great Inagua Island, off Cuba's eastern tip, but found no gold there. He then explored the Cibao region along the north coast of the island of Hispaniola (present-day Haiti and the Dominican Republic), where he found some gold and learned from the natives that the *Santa María* had been wrecked. On January 6, 1492, off northern Hispaniola's Monte Cristi Peninsula, Pinzón rejoined Columbus and his one remaining ship, the *Niña.*

Pinzón sailed back toward Europe with Columbus as far as the AZORES, where their ships were again separated, this time by a storm. The *Pinta,* driven northward, reached the northwest coast of Spain near Vigo. King Ferdinand and Queen Isabella refused Pinzón's request for an audience to report on his findings. Instead, they ordered Pinzón not to leave his ship until he had returned to Palos de Frontera, where he was to wait for Columbus, who had stopped in Portugal. Pinzón and the *Pinta* reached Palos de Frontera on March 15, 1493, just hours after Columbus had arrived. Reportedly, the snub by the Spanish court, coupled with Columbus's accusations of disloyalty, further undermined his health, already weakened by the voyage, and Pinzón died in Palos de Moguer several weeks later. Some sources suggest that Pinzón may actually have succumbed to a particularly virulent strain of syphilis, contracted in his contacts with the natives in the WEST INDIES, which would make him one of the first Europeans to die of that disease.

The fact that Martín Pinzón apparently deserted Columbus on the Cuban coast has cast a shadow on his reputation as one of the European discoverers of the Americas. Nonetheless, Pinzón's support was essential for the success of Columbus's first voyage. He had helped Columbus gain the backing of the Spanish court and had contributed his own money to the venture. As second in command, he served as an intermediary between Columbus and his men, most of whom, like Pinzón, were from the Palos area and regarded the Italian-born Columbus as a foreigner. In his independent explorations in the West Indies, Pinzón may have actually preceded Columbus in reaching the island of Hispaniola.

Pinzón, Vicente Yáñez (Vicente Anes Pinzón)

(1463–ca. 1523) *Spanish mariner in the West Indies, South America, and Central America, brother of Francisco Martín Pinzón and Martín Alonso Pinzón, uncle of Arias Martín Pinzón*

Vicente Pinzón was born at Palos de Moguer on the Andalusian coast of southwestern Spain, a member of a prominent family of seafarers and shipbuilders that included his brothers FRANCISCO MARTÍN PINZÓN and MARTÍN ALONSO PINZÓN.

Along with his brothers, Pinzón was a friend of CHRISTOPHER COLUMBUS and a backer of his plan to reach Japan and China by sailing westward across the Atlantic Ocean. All three brothers took part in Columbus's first voyage, which sailed, in August 1492, from the seaport of Palos de Frontera, near their home. On the historic voyage, Pinzón commanded the *Niña*, on which he was assisted by his nephew ARIAS MARTÍN PINZÓN.

Pinzón remained loyal to Columbus after his brother Martín, captain of the *Pinta*, deserted the expedition off the coast of Cuba in November 1492. A month later, when the *Santa María* was wrecked off the north coast of Hispaniola (present-day Haiti and the Dominican Republic), Pinzón rescued Columbus and his crew, and it was his ship, the *Niña*, on which Columbus triumphantly returned to Spain in March 1493. Pinzón may have sailed again with Columbus on his second voyage of 1493 and on his third voyage of 1498, but there is no accurate record of his having done so.

Although the Spanish government had granted him permission to undertake an additional voyage of exploration on his own in 1495, Pinzón apparently did not sail until November 13, 1499. His fleet of four ships embarked from Palos de Frontera, on a voyage in which he was joined by his brother Francisco and his nephew Arias. After first sailing to the Cape Verde Islands, where the ships were resupplied, Pinzón headed southwestward. According to his astronomical observations, he lost sight of the NORTH STAR,

indicating that he had gone south of the EQUATOR. On January 20, 1500, he sighted a cape on the mainland of South America, which he named Santa María de la Consolación, later known by the Portuguese as São Augustinho, near present-day Recife, Brazil.

Proceeding northwestward, Pinzón made the European discovery of the mouth of the AMAZON RIVER, which he named La Mar Dulce (the freshwater sea), having noted that the river's water flowed well out to sea, where it was still fit to drink. He explored up the Amazon for about 50 miles, then continued along the Caribbean coast of the Guianas and what is now Venezuela. He explored the Gulf of Paria, where he made the European discovery of the island of Tobago, which he called Isla de Mayo.

Pinzón then examined the coast of CENTRAL AMERICA, sailing as far northward as what is now Honduras and Costa Rica. Some accounts suggest that on this voyage, Pinzón made one of the first known circumnavigations of Cuba, thus establishing that it was an island, contrary to Columbus's previous assertion that it was part of the mainland of Asia.

Pinzón's ships were struck by a hurricane off Hispaniola in July 1500. Two of his four vessels were lost with all hands, including the one commanded by his brother Francisco. He returned to Spain on September 30, 1500, with a cargo of tropical wood and 20 Indian slaves. He also brought back an opossum from South America, the first marsupial ever to be seen by Europeans.

Pinzón returned to the northeast coast of South America in 1502. Over the next two years, he traded with the Indians along the Gulf of Paria, from whom he obtained gold, woven cotton fabrics, and parrots, which had become popular pets in Europe soon after the European discovery of the Americas.

In 1504, Pinzón visited the Spanish settlement on Hispaniola, where he met with Columbus. The next year, he was named governor of Puerto Rico, an appointment that lapsed when he made no attempt to colonize that island.

In 1506, Pinzón joined JUAN DÍAZ DE SOLÍS in an exploration of the coast of Central America. Together they retraced the route of Columbus's last voyage of 1502, landing on Guanaja Island, off the coast of what is now Honduras. From there, they sailed into the Gulf of Mexico and were among the first Europeans to explore the coast of the Yucatán Peninsula and Bay of Campeche.

Pinzón returned to Spain in 1507, where he conferred with AMERIGO VESPUCCI on the findings of his recent voyage. In 1508, he sailed again with Díaz de Solís, leaving Spain with two ships, the *Isabeleta* and the *Magdalena*. Pinzón and Díaz de Solís had been commissioned by the Spanish government to follow the coast of South America southward in hopes of locating a strait leading to the Indian Ocean and the SPICE ISLANDS, the present-day Moluccas of Indonesia. (The fact that the Pacific Ocean lay on the other side of South

America was then unknown to Europeans.) From Cape São Augustinho on the Brazilian coast, Pinzón and Díaz de Solís explored southward as far as 40° south latitude, where they reached the mouth of the Río Negro, on the central coast of what is now Argentina.

Pinzón returned to Spain in 1509, having had a falling-out with Díaz de Solís during the voyage, and he undertook no further voyages of exploration. In 1518, King Charles I of Spain (Holy Roman Emperor Charles V) granted Pinzón and his heirs a hereditary title of nobility.

In addition to his vital role in the Columbus voyage of 1492, Vicente Pinzón became well known as an explorer in his own right. Although generally credited with the European discovery of the Amazon River, his reported sighting of the Brazil coast to the south in 1500 has been disputed by Portuguese and Brazilian historians. They maintain that Pinzón never went south of the equator, and that the European discoverer of Brazil was Portuguese navigator PEDRO ÁLVARS CABRAL, who reached the southern Brazilian coast in April 1500, several months after Pinzón's reported landing.

Pires, Tomé (ca. 1468–ca. 1540) *Portuguese apothecary, diplomat in the East Indies and China*

Portuguese-born Tomé Pires was the son of the apothecary to King João II. In 1490, he himself became an apothecary in the Portuguese royal household.

Pires traveled to India in 1511, with what is assumed to be a royal commission to study medicinal spices of the Orient. After a year amassing a fortune in the SPICE TRADE, he participated in expeditions under the Portuguese viceroy of the region, AFONSO DE ALBUQUERQUE, visiting Java in 1513, and Sumatra and Malacca on the Malay Peninsula in the South China Sea two years later.

In 1516, the new viceroy, Lopo Soares de Albergaria, chose Pires as an envoy to the Chinese. The fleet failed to reach China, after being driven off course south of present-day Vietnam in September of that year. A second attempt succeeded in August 1517, and it is thought that Pires stayed at the Chinese court in Peking (Beijing) for some 20 years.

In the *Suma Oriental*, written in India and Malacca in 1512–15, Tomé Pires gives an account of the Far East from his travels and those of others. Although his writings on China have not survived, his visit there is important in that it represents the first opening of diplomatic relations between Portugal and China.

Pizarro, Francisco (ca. 1475–1541)
Spanish conquistador in South America, half brother of Gonzalo Pizarro and Hernando Pizarro

Francisco Pizarro was born at Trujillo in the Estremadura region of west-central Spain. He was born out of wedlock; his father was a nobleman and officer in the Spanish army, and his mother was a local peasant girl. Raised outside his father's aristocratic household, he remained uneducated in his early years, during which he worked as a swineherd tending his father's pigs. Some sources suggest he gained his earliest military experience while serving with his father in campaigns in Italy.

In about 1500, Pizarro ran away to Seville, then a major staging area for colonizing expeditions to the newly explored WEST INDIES. He soon entered the service of Nicolas de Ovando, who had just been appointed governor of Hispaniola (present-day Haiti and the Dominican Republic), succeeding CHRISTOPHER COLUMBUS, and sailed with Ovando's fleet to the West Indies in 1502. In 1509, he made his first landing on the South American mainland as part of ALONSO DE OJEDA's expedition to the Caribbean coast of what is now Colombia. Left in charge at San Sebastián, he later moved the colony to Panama's Gulf of Urabá, where he helped to found the settlement of Santa María de la Antigua.

Pizarro accompanied VASCO NÚÑEZ DE BALBOA in his explorations of the Isthmus of Panama, including the 1513 expedition in which Europeans first sighted the Pacific Ocean. From Native Americans encountered on these expeditions, Pizarro heard of a fabulously rich native kingdom to the south, called by the natives Biru and known afterward as Peru.

It was Pizarro who later arrested Núñez de Balboa on behalf of Panama's colonial governor PEDRO ARIAS DE ÁVILA. In the years following Núñez de Balboa's execution in 1519, Pizarro rose to prominence in Panama, becoming mayor of Panama City and receiving grants of land. He also explored the Pearl Islands off Panama's Pacific Coast. In 1522, he learned more about an advanced Indian civilization south of Panama from the accounts of Spanish navigator PASCUAL DE ANDAGOYA. The next year, he entered into a partnership with DIEGO DE ALMAGRO to undertake the exploration and conquest of the fabled land of Biru. Another partner was a priest named Hernando de Luque, who provided financing for the venture.

In 1524, Pizarro sailed from Panama southward along the Pacific coast of what is now Colombia to Cabo Corrientes and the San Juan River. His explorations along Colombia's Buenaventura Bay were soon curtailed when he lost two-thirds of his 80-man expedition to disease and Indian attacks.

Pizarro's losses were so great that Spanish authorities forbade his undertaking any additional explorations. Undaunted, he and Almagro continued their probings southward, and in 1526, they reached as far as the Gulf of Guayaquil on the coast of what is now southern Ecuador. A landing was soon made at the Inca town of Tumbes, where Pizarro's men saw evidence of an advanced civilization rich with gold and jewels. A further seaward reconnaissance along the coast by Pizarro's chief mariner, Bartolomeo Ruiz, confirmed that there were greater Inca Indian cities southeast of Tumbes.

In 1528, Pizarro returned to Spain to seek royal backing for a large-scale expedition of exploration and conquest. In Toledo, he met with King Charles I (Holy Roman Emperor Charles V), to whom he presented gold and jewels from Peru; several captured Indians; several llamas, an animal that had been unknown in Europe; and samples of a silk-like cloth produced from the wool of the vicuña, a species of wild camel found in the ANDES MOUNTAINS. Coincidentally, HERNÁN CORTÉS, a distant relative of Pizarro, was visiting the Spanish royal court, reporting on his recent conquest of the Aztec Indians of Mexico. Encouraged by Cortés's success, the king agreed to sponsor Pizarro's planned expedition, naming him captain general and governor of New Castile, as the yet-to-be explored region of what is now Peru had been designated. Pizarro's partner, Almagro, who had remained behind in Panama, was given a subordinate position as commandant of Tumbes.

Along with his half brothers GONZALO PIZARRO, HERNANDO PIZARRO, Juan Pizarro, and Martín Pizarro, Pizarro returned to Panama in 1530. In January 1531, he set out by boat with a force of 180 men and 27 horses. They landed at San Mateo Bay on the coast of present-day Ecuador, and, soon afterward, they occupied the Inca Indian town of Tumbes without resistance. The Inca emperor, Atahualpa, had recently consolidated his rule by defeating his half brother Huascar in a civil war. On learning of the arrival of Pizarro and his forces, Atahualpa decided to allow the Spaniards to penetrate the interior of his realm, where they could then be easily contained. The Inca may also have mistaken the Spaniards for legendary white gods, who, according to traditional beliefs, were expected to arrive soon after the death of Atahualpa's father, which had occurred at about that time.

Pizarro was joined by additional forces at Tumbes, led by HERNANDO DE SOTO and SEBASTIÁN DE BENALCÁZAR. After establishing a base he called San Miguel, south of Tumbes, near the mouth of Peru's Piura River, he led his men along the Royal Inca Road, eastward into the Andes and the Piura Valley. Unopposed by the Inca, he crossed the Sechura Desert and proceeded through the high passes of the Western Cordillera to the central plateau region of the Andes.

On November 15, 1532, Pizarro entered the city of Cajamarca, which he found to be deserted. Nearby, the Inca ruler, Atahualpa, had encamped with 50,000 of his men. Pizarro's half brother Hernando, the only one of them of legitimate and noble birth, was sent as an emissary to Atahualpa. He presented the Inca leader with a Bible and asked him to embrace Christianity and pledge his allegiance to Charles V. On hearing that the Bible would teach him about Christ, the Inca leader reportedly held it to his ear, expecting it to speak to him; when it did not, he cast it to the ground. This gesture was taken by the Spaniards as an insult to their faith and provided them with an excuse to launch a surprise assault on the Inca, charging them with horses and firing upon them with cannon. Thousands of the Inca were killed in the attack, and Atahualpa was taken captive. The Spaniards, numbering fewer than 200 men, suffered minimal casualties.

Atahualpa, knowing how interested Pizarro and his men were in acquiring gold, offered to ransom himself for an amount of the metal that would fill the room of the building in which he was being held (a space measuring 22 by 17 feet) to a height equal to his own. Pizarro ostensibly agreed to these terms, and during the next several months, gold was brought from all parts of the Inca Empire. Many of the objects were artistic and religious works, which were nevertheless melted down into gold bars by the Spaniards. The total amount of gold brought to rescue Atahualpa in Cajamarca amounted to 1,325 pounds.

Pizarro betrayed his word and kept Atahualpa prisoner. Atahualpa had meanwhile ordered the murder of his half brother Huascar to prevent him from forming an alliance with the Spaniards. Pizarro used this act as a pretext to try Atahualpa and condemn him to death for conspiring against the Spanish. Both de Soto and Pizarro's half brother Hernando protested against the killing of the Inca ruler, but to no avail. Although Atahualpa had been sentenced to be burned, Pizarro had him garroted after the Inca ruler agreed to embrace some measure of the Christian faith. Just prior to his death in July 1533, he reportedly uttered a curse on Pizarro and all his descendants.

On November 15, 1533, Pizarro's forces captured the Inca capital at Cuzco, seizing all its gold and enslaving many of its inhabitants. Pizarro then founded a new capital for his domain nearer to the coast, which he called Ciudad de Los Reyes (city of kings), at the mouth of the Rimac River. Established on January 18, 1535, it later came to be known as Lima (after a corruption of the name of the nearby Rimac River) and is one of the oldest capital cities in South America.

Pizarro's partner, Almagro, suppressed an Inca revolt at Cuzco in 1538, and, soon afterward, he attempted to seize control of Peru for himself. He was captured and executed by forces loyal to Pizarro.

Pizarro was made a marquis in his last years. He sent his brother Gonzalo on an expedition across the Andes to the headwaters of the AMAZON RIVER, in an expedition under FRANCISCO DE ORELLANA. In June 1541, followers of the late Almagro's half-Indian son and heir, Don Diego Almagro, assassinated Pizarro at his residence at Lima.

The high level of culture that the Inca had reached at the time of European contact facilitated Pizarro in his conquest. Specifically, their highly centralized system of roads, spanning more than 2,000 miles and connecting every part of their empire, enabled the Spaniards to subjugate rapidly a large portion of western South America, equal in size to the eastern seaboard of the United States (with the spread of European diseases among the native population being a major factor in the conquest). The Spanish had by then realized that the Indians of the Americas were not subjects of the great powers of the Orient, as had previously been thought, and therefore could be conquered without instigating the wrath of the rulers of China and central Asia. In the subsequent years of colonial rule, the Spanish suppressed all active traces of the Inca civilization. Nevertheless, contact with the Inca had a long-ranging impact on Europe, where the sudden influx of vast quantities of gold led to severe inflation, with dire economic consequences, especially in Spain.

The tremendous wealth that Francisco Pizarro and his followers reaped in their conquest of Peru inspired the subsequent explorations of de Soto into the American Southeast and those of FRANCISCO VÁSQUEZ DE CORONADO into the American Southwest. Another of his officers, Benalcázar, went on to undertake an exploration into what is now central Colombia.

Pizarro, Gonzalo (ca. 1506–1548)

Spanish conquistador in South America, half brother of Francisco Pizarro and Hernando Pizarro

Born at Trujillo in Estremadura, Spain, Gonzalo Pizarro was the youngest of FRANCISCO PIZARRO's four half brothers. As a youth, he served with his father, a nobleman and army officer, in military campaigns in Italy during the 1520s. In 1530, he arrived in Panama with Francisco, along with HERNANDO PIZARRO, Juan Pizarro, and Martín Pizarro. Over the next four years, he served with them in the Spanish conquest of Peru.

After taking part in the suppression of the Inca uprising in 1536–37 and in the defeat of DIEGO DE ALMAGRO in 1538, Gonzalo was appointed by Francisco as governor of the northern Inca province of Quito, comprising most of present-day Ecuador.

From the Indians in the Quito region, Pizarro learned of La Canela (the land of cinnamon), located east of the ANDES MOUNTAINS, which was said to contain extensive forests of cinnamon, a spice highly prized in Europe. The Indians also reported the existence of the kingdom of EL DORADO, the fabled land of the Gilded One, where there was supposedly a lake with a bottom lined in gold and jewels. In 1540, Pizarro was authorized by Francisco to undertake an expedition eastward into the Andes to locate and conquer both these places.

Pizarro recruited about 300 Spanish adventurers, and, along with nearly 4,000 enslaved Indians, left Quito in February 1541, heading eastward into the Andes. The Spaniards took along a large herd of pigs as a mobile source of fresh food, plus a number of llamas as pack animals. They also had a pack of hunting dogs, used to terrorize the natives.

Many of the Indians died of the cold in the high altitudes of the Andes, and Pizarro's men soon ran short of supplies when most of the pigs and llamas died or ran away into the jungles beyond the eastern slopes of the mountains. At the Valley of Zumaco, Pizarro was joined by the lieutenant governor of Guayaquil, FRANCISCO DE ORELLANA, and a small contingent of Spaniards. After seven months, they reached the upper Coca River, where Pizarro located some cinnamon trees, but not in sufficient quantity to be of any commercial value. With his men facing starvation, he decided to send Orellana, whom he had named as his second in command, downriver to search for an Indian village where food could be obtained. The Spaniards constructed a brigantine-type riverboat with which to proceed farther downstream, the jungle having by that time become flooded and made impassable by the seasonal rains. On December 26, 1541, Orellana and his men left Pizarro and continued down the Coca, eventually reaching the Napo River and the AMAZON RIVER, which they followed all the way to its outlet on the Atlantic Ocean.

Meanwhile, Pizarro and his men suffered great privations in the jungle. Believing he had been deserted by Orellana, Pizarro decided to head back westward across the Andes to Quito, which they reached in June 1542. Only 80 of his 300 men had survived, and nearly all of the Indians with the expedition had perished.

On his arrival in Quito, Pizarro learned of his half brother Francisco's murder in Lima the year before. Although he had been designated by the elder Pizarro as his successor, the administration of Peru had been given to a royal viceroy, Blasco Núñez Vela, appointed by the king of Spain. During the next six years, Pizarro and his followers attempted to seize control of Peru, but they were ultimately defeated in 1548. Soon afterward, Pizarro was taken prisoner by the royal viceroy's forces and executed in Cuzco.

Gonzalo Pizarro was the first of many European explorers to seek the fabled land of El Dorado. His expedition took him across the Andes from Quito, to the western edge of the Amazon Basin, and ultimately led to the first known descent of the Amazon River and the first known crossing of the South American continent, accomplished by Orellana in 1542.

Pizarro, Hernando (ca. 1478–1578)

Spanish conquistador in South America, half brother of Francisco Pizarro and Gonzalo Pizarro

Hernando Pizarro was born at Trujillo in the Estremadura region of Spain. A half brother of FRANCISCO PIZARRO, GONZALO PIZARRO, Juan Pizarro, and Martín Pizarro, he was the only one of the five to be of legitimate birth and the only one to receive any sort of formal education. With his father, a nobleman and colonel in the Spanish army, he was part of military campaigns in Italy in 1502–03 and in the Navarre region of Spain in 1512.

In 1530, Pizarro accompanied Francisco and his other three half brothers to Panama, and soon afterward, he took part in the conquest of the Inca Empire in Peru. He returned to Spain in 1533 to present the king of Spain, Charles I (Holy Roman Emperor Charles V), with his share of the treasure obtained as ransom for the Inca ruler Atahualpa. After being received at court and knighted, Pizarro organized an expedition of his own and returned to Peru in 1535. Named governor of Cuzco, he defended that city when it was besieged by its former Inca inhabitants the following year.

In the civil war that erupted between the Pizarros and DIEGO DE ALMAGRO in 1537, Pizarro was taken prisoner. Released soon afterward, he promptly breeched the terms of his parole and led his troops against Almagro, whom he captured and executed in 1538.

In 1539, Pizarro returned to Spain to answer charges against himself and his half brothers in connection with the execution of Almagro and their administration of Peru. He appeared before Charles I, to whom he presented an additional large quantity of Inca gold as a gift. Although not actually sentenced for any wrongdoing, Pizarro was nonetheless held as a prisoner until 1568. During his incarceration at the fortress of Medina del Campo in León, he was allowed a fair amount of liberty and was able to marry a niece in 1551. Upon his release, he returned to his native Trujillo, where he reportedly lived until the age of 100.

Hernando Pizarro, as the sole legitimate half brother among the Pizarros, was the only one deemed suitable to act as the official emissary to the Inca emperor Atahualpa at Cajamarca in 1532. The next year, he was one of the few Spanish officers to protest the execution of the Inca ruler when Francisco betrayed his promise to release Atahualpa and had him put to death, despite the payment of an enormous ransom in gold.

Pliny the Elder (Pliny, Gaius Plinius Secundus)
(ca. A.D. 23–79) *official, geographer in ancient Rome*
Born near Lake Como in what is now northern Italy, Pliny went to Rome as a young man and embarked on a military career in which he served as a cavalry officer in Africa and Germany. He was a friend of the Roman emperor Vespasian and of Titus, who also went on to become emperor.

Known as Pliny the Elder to distinguish him from his adopted nephew, the Roman orator and statesman Pliny the Younger, he served as a Roman government official in what is now Spain, France, and northern Italy. He was an industrious scholar as well, producing many literary works detailing information about the known world. Pliny the Elder died of asphyxiation near Mount Vesuvius during a visit to observe the volcano's eruption in A.D. 79.

The only one of Pliny's works to survive was his *Historia Naturalis,* a comprehensive study of the physical world as

Pliny the Elder *(Library of Congress)*

it was known in his day. Completed in 77, it includes much geographic information about the Mediterranean world, western and northern Europe, Asia, and Africa. He is known as the first writer to have referred to what is now Norway and Sweden as Scandinavia, although he depicted that region as an island, not a peninsula. Relying on secondhand sources for his accounts of Asia, he makes references to the Tigris and Euphrates Rivers, northern India, and the island of CEYLON (present-day Sri Lanka), as well as the SILK ROAD between the Black Sea and central Asia. In his descriptions of West Africa, Pliny the Elder made the earliest known reference to a great river south of the SAHARA DESERT, which he called the "Nigris," which came to be referred to as the NIGER RIVER. Pliny the Elder's geographic works, along with MARCO POLO's account of his travels to the Far East, influenced CHRISTOPHER COLUMBUS. In addition, his accounts of the interior of North and West Africa, largely unknown to Europeans until the early 19th century, inspired German explorer HEINRICH BARTH in his archaeological investigations in the Sahara during the 1850s.

Polo, Maffeo (Matteo Polo) (fl. 1260s–1290s)
Italian merchant, traveler in central Asia and the Far East, brother of Niccolò Polo, uncle of Marco Polo
Maffeo Polo was a minor Venetian nobleman and merchant. With his brothers Marco and NICCOLÒ POLO, he operated

a lucrative trade in jewels and precious stones in Constantinople (present-day Istanbul, Turkey).

In 1260, Maffeo and Niccolò sailed across the Black Sea to Soldaia in the Crimea, where the family operated a trading establishment. Unable to obtain an adequate price for the jewels they had brought from Constantinople, they headed eastward across the Crimea to the north shore of the Caspian Sea and the court of Barka Khan at Serai, near the mouth of the Volga River.

Barka Khan welcomed the Polo brothers and bought their entire stock of jewels for a price that netted them a 100 percent profit. While they were at Serai, a war broke out between Barka Khan and the khan of Persia, to the south. The conflict made a trip back across the Crimea to the Black Sea too hazardous to consider. Cut off from any homeward route, the Polo brothers headed eastward again in 1263. After a 17-day trek across the Kara-Kum desert, they arrived at the city of Bukhara in what is now Uzbekistan.

The Polo brothers remained in Bukhara, at that time a major center of the caravan trade, from 1263 to 1266. Their planned return to Italy by way of Persia (present-day Iran) and the MEDITERRANEAN SEA was still impossible because of warfare and uncertainty to the west. They then met up with a group of Tartar envoys who were on their way to visit the court of Kublai Khan—the Great Khan, ruler of the vast Mongol Empire—at his capital at Cambaluc (present-day Beijing, China). The envoys invited the Polos to travel with them eastward across China to Cambaluc, and, encouraged by the prospect of great profits to be made there, Maffeo and Niccolò agreed.

In their eastward journey across central Asia and China, the Polo brothers followed the well-established SILK ROAD. They stopped at Samarkand, crossed Turkistan, and, after skirting the northern rim of the Tarim Basin and the desert regions north of Tibet, traversed the Mongolian steppes, arriving at Cambaluc in 1266.

In Cambaluc, the Polos met with Kublai Khan, who had never seen Europeans before and was very interested in the culture of the West, especially Christianity. Since the Mongols had no strong religious institution of their own, and were continually threatened by the Islamic armies to the South, he wanted to bring Christianity to his empire, hoping it would have a unifying and civilizing effect on the Mongols, as well as the other diverse peoples he now ruled. After a year in the Chinese capital, the Polo brothers were given leave by Kublai Khan to return home. He gave them a passport, made of a large slab of gold, which ensured safe passage and hospitality as they traveled westward through his vast empire stretching from the Pacific coast of China to the Black Sea. Moreover, he made them his envoys to Pope Clement IV. He entrusted them with a letter to the pontiff requesting that 100 missionary priests be sent to China to teach his people the ways of Christianity. He also wanted some holy oil from the Church of the Holy Sepulcher in Jerusalem.

It took the Polo brothers three years to reach Europe, traveling westward to Bukhara, then southwestward across Persia and Syria to the northeastern corner of the Mediterranean. From there, they headed southward to Palestine, reaching Acre, north of Jerusalem, in April 1269. From the papal legate Teobaldo Visconti, they learned that Pope Clement IV had died the year before, and that conflicts between factions in the Church would delay the election of his successor for some time. They returned to Venice, where they remained for the next two years.

In 1271, the Polo brothers left Venice for China, accompanied by Niccolò's 17-year-old son, MARCO POLO. Even though a new pope had not yet been elected, they were eager to reestablish their contacts with the Mongol emperor. This time, the Polos remained in China until 1292, acquiring great wealth, which they carried with them in the form of jewels and precious stones sewn into their Mongol-style garments.

In his famous account of his travels, Marco Polo relates little about his father and uncle's experiences in China, because he traveled apart from them much of the time. He did mention, however, that at one point they helped design siege engines for an assault on the city of Siang Yang Fou near present-day Yangzhou. He does not describe how the Polo brothers acquired the great riches they carried back to Europe by 1295.

Maffeo and Niccolo Polo were the first Europeans to visit what is now Beijing, China. Their 1260–69 journey to the Far East marked the beginning of a century of open contacts between East and West resulting from the stabilization of the Mongol Empire.

Polo, Marco (1254–1324) *Italian traveler in central Asia and the Far East, son of Niccolò Polo, nephew of Maffeo Polo*

A native of Venice, Marco Polo was the son of NICCOLÒ POLO, a minor nobleman and merchant in jewels. Just prior to Marco's birth, his father and his uncle MAFFEO POLO had left for Constantinople (present-day Istanbul, Turkey), from where they subsequently embarked on a journey across Asia to Cathay and the court of Kublai Khan, the Great Khan, ruler of the Mongols, at Cambaluc (present-day Beijing, China). Marco's mother had died in childbirth, and he was 15 before his father returned to Venice in 1269.

In 1271, 17-year-old Polo accompanied his father and uncle on their second journey to the East. From Venice, they sailed to the east shore of the MEDITERRANEAN SEA, and at Acre, north of Jerusalem, they met with papal legate Teobaldo Visconti. He gave them a letter for Kublai Khan explaining that the delay in the election of a new pope had precluded the sending of 100 missionary priests, which the Mongol emperor had requested on the elder Polos' earlier trip to China. Soon afterward, Visconti himself was elected

Marco Polo *(Library of Congress)*

to the papacy as Pope Gregory X, and the Polos, recalled to Acre upon hearing the news, were joined there by just two Dominican friars, William of Tripoli and Nicolas of Vicenza, who planned to carry Christian learning to Kublai Khan's domain. Not long after they had left Acre, the two priests decided not to risk the hazards of a long journey to the East, and they turned back to the Mediterranean coast. The Polos nevertheless continued eastward across

Mesopotamia to Baghdad and into Persia (present-day Iran), then went southward to Hormuz, at the mouth of the Persian Gulf, carrying with them a flask of holy oil from the Holy Sepulcher in Jerusalem for Kublai Khan.

Although the Polos had planned to continue their journey by sea, they were unable to find a boat at Hormuz on which they were willing to embark. Instead, they decided to undertake an overland journey, and, in 1272, they traversed the desert of Persia's southern Kerman region, traveling northeastward into the mountains of Khorasan. From there, they entered northern Afghanistan, visiting the cities of Herat and Balkh, the easternmost point reached by ALEXANDER THE GREAT in his conquests 1,500 years earlier. En route to the caravan trade center at Kashgar on the Chinese frontier, the young Polo fell ill, and his father and uncle took him to the mountains of Badakhsan in northeastern Afghanistan, where they remained a year while he recovered his health.

From the mountains of northern Afghanistan, the Polos continued their journey to Cathay by following the Oxus River (the Amu Darya) northward toward Samarkand and around the northern Hindu Kush mountain range to the 15,600-foot-high Pamir Plateau, where Marco noted the effects of the high altitude and also observed a peculiar type of large wild sheep. They then traveled along the edge of the Taklimakan desert to the remote western Chinese city of Lop Nor on the edge of the GOBI DESERT.

Polo and his father and uncle crossed the desert region of northwestern China with a camel caravan. In the middle of inner Mongolia, a 40-day journey from the court of Kublai Khan, they were met by representatives of the Mongol emperor, who escorted them to the royal palace, Shangdu, northwest of Cambaluc, which they reached in 1275, after a three-and-a-half-year journey from Europe.

The Mongol emperor, much impressed by Polo, who by then was a young man of 21, appointed him to a diplomatic post. Over the next 17 years, the emperor sent Polo on missions throughout his vast empire. Adept at languages, Polo quickly mastered several Mongol dialects. His official travels took him all over China and Southeast Asia. He visited Tibet and the provinces along the YANGTZE RIVER (Chang), YELLOW RIVER (Huang He), and upper Mekong River, and he was the first known European to visit the interior of Burma and what is now Thailand and Vietnam. At one point, he undertook a seaward expedition on behalf of Kublai Khan in which he sailed to the islands of Indonesia. In the north, he visited the former Mongol capital at Karakorum in what is now modern Mongolia, and he may have journeyed into eastern SIBERIA. For three years of his stay in China, 1282 to 1285, Polo served as governor of the city of Yangchow (Yangzhou).

While Marco had been in service to the emperor, his father and uncle had become wealthy from their trading activities. By 1292, however, all three were concerned about their future in China after the death of the emperor, who by that time was well advanced in years, and they were anxious to return to Italy. That year, they accepted an opportunity to return to the West as escorts for the Mongolian princess Cocachin, who had been betrothed to the khan of Persia, Arghun. Since warfare still raged along the overland route to Persia, it was decided to travel by sea. The Polos, provided with a 14-ship fleet, carrying combined crews of 600, sailed from the Chinese port of Zaiton (Quanzhou) and, after a long passage around Sumatra, entered the Indian Ocean by way of the Strait of Malacca. The voyage across the Indian Ocean included stops at the Nicobar and Andaman Islands, as well as a visit to CEYLON (present-day Sri Lanka).

In 1294, Polo, his father, his uncle, and the princess arrived safely in Hormuz after a two-year voyage. All but 18 of the 600 members of the expedition had perished, either in shipwrecks or from SCURVY. Since Arghun, the khan of Persia to whom Cocachin had been promised, had died a year before they arrived, she became the bride of his son and successor, Ghazan.

The Polos remained at the Persian court at Tabriz for some months, then continued their homeward trek to Trabzon on the Black Sea, from where they sailed to Constantinople (present-day Istanbul, Turkey). They then headed for Venice, arriving in late 1295, after an absence of 24 years.

In 1298, Marco took part in a naval war between Genoa and his native Venice, serving as a commander of a Venetian galley. On September 6, 1298, he was captured along with 7,000 other Venetians following a naval engagement at Curzola on the Dalmatian coast of what is now Croatia. In the Genoese prison where he was confined, Polo met a writer of romances, Rustichello (or Rusticano) of Pisa, also a prisoner of war. Polo related his experiences in the Far East to him, and Rustichello recorded them in a work that came to be known as *The Book of Ser Marco Polo, the Venetian, Concerning the Kingdoms and Marvels of the East* (also known in various editions and languages as *The Travels of Marco Polo, The Book of Marco Polo, The Book of Marvels, The Description of the World*, and *Il Milione*, the last referring to Marco Polo himself, "the man with a million stories").

Released after a year, Polo returned to Venice, where he married and lived the life of a wealthy merchant, dying in 1324 at the age of 70.

During the next two centuries, Marco Polo's book became the principal source of information about the Far East for medieval Europeans. Many of the places and customs he described were unknown in Europe, where contact with the Orient had been severed by the Muslim conquests five centuries earlier. His depictions of the great cities of China, with populations far exceeding any in Europe, as well as his account of the huge palaces of the Mongols and other wonders of the East, were met with skepticism. For his repeated use of the term *millions* in his expansive descriptions of the Orient, he later became known as "Marco Millions." He was the first European to mention the use of paper, the Chinese method of printing from blocks of carved type, how coal was used as a fuel, and the Chinese practice of using paper money, all of which were unknown in Europe until that time. Many of his observations were rejected by his contemporaries as outlandish exaggerations, although his geographic descriptions of Asia were more readily accepted and were incorporated by ABRAHAM CRESQUES in his *Catalan Atlas* of 1375. In the late 1400s, CHRISTOPHER COLUMBUS, influenced by Polo's writings, grossly underestimated the distance between the west coast of Europe and the easternmost point of Asia, and, based on this determination, undertook his historic voyage in 1492. When he arrived in the WEST INDIES that year, he believed he had reached CIPANGU, as described by Marco Polo (probably referring to Japan or some other outlying islands of Asia). Parts of Burma, Southeast Asia, and western China that Marco Polo visited during his long sojourn in the Far East were not seen again by Europeans until the 19th century. The type of long-horned sheep he described in the Pamir region was later named *Ovis polis*, in his honor, by British zoologist Edward Blyth in 1840.

Polo, Niccolò (Nicolò Polo) (fl. 1260s–1290s)
Italian merchant, traveler in central Asia and the Far East, brother of Maffeo Polo, father of Marco Polo

Niccolò Polo, a Venetian merchant and minor nobleman, made two journeys to China. In his first, he and his brother MAFFEO POLO were the first Europeans to reach what is now Beijing, China (then known as Cambaluc), in 1266, after an overland journey eastward across Asia from Constantinople (present-day Istanbul, Turkey).

On a second visit to China in 1275, in which he was again joined by his brother Maffeo, as well as by his son, MARCO POLO, he remained for 17 years, and returned to Venice in 1295, after a two-year sea voyage through the islands of Indonesia and across the Indian Ocean to Persia (present-day Iran).

Although his son became known as the greatest medieval traveler to the Orient, Niccolò Polo, along with his brother, may have actually traveled over a much wider territory of central Asia. They followed a northern route around the Caspian Sea on their first voyage in 1260–66 and took a more southern route through the Hindu Kush mountain range on their second journey to the East with Marco in 1271–75. In any event, with Maffeo, Niccolò Polo was the first European known to have made a complete west-to-east crossing of Asia and an east-to-west trek back to Europe.

Ponce de León, Juan (ca. 1460–1521) *Spanish colonial official in Puerto Rico, conquistador in Florida*

Juan Ponce de León was born in Tierra de Campos in the León province of Spain (although some sources say he was born at Santervas del Campo in the province of Valladolid). As the son of a noble family, he served as a page at the Spanish royal court at Aragon. He went on to a military career, taking part in the reconquest of Spain from the Moors. In 1490, he participated in the recapture of the city of Granada.

In 1493, Ponce de León sailed with CHRISTOPHER COLUMBUS on his second voyage to the WEST INDIES. He eventually settled in the Spanish colony on Hispaniola (present-day Haiti and the Dominican Republic). In 1502, he served as a deputy to Spanish colonial governor Nicolás de Ovando, and, during the next two years, he fought the Arawak (Taino) Indians in the conquest of the eastern part of the island.

In 1508, on orders from Ovando, Ponce de León undertook an expedition to Puerto Rico, which he had visited with Columbus in 1493. Columbus had named the island San Juan de Boriquen, but, after Ponce de León reportedly discovered gold there, it became known as Puerto Rico, Spanish for "rich port."

By 1509, the island of Puerto Rico had been subjugated by Ponce de León. That year, King Ferdinand of Spain appointed him governor of Puerto Rico, and Ponce de León established Caparra, the first Spanish settlement on Puerto Rico, near the site of what later became the city of San Juan on an offshore island.

Over the next several years, Ponce de León prospered on Puerto Rico, making his fortune in gold, slaves, and land. He heard tales from the Indians about an island to the north, called Bimini, which he was told possessed great riches. He supposedly also heard that on Bimini was a fabled FOUNTAIN OF YOUTH, the waters of which had great restorative powers, providing anyone who drank from it with the gift of perpetual youth.

In 1512, Ponce de León lost his position as governor of Puerto Rico when Diego Columbus, son of Christopher, asserted his exclusive right to make official appointments in the newly explored West Indies. To compensate for his loss, King Ferdinand commissioned Ponce de León to search for Bimini and conquer and colonize it.

Ponce de León's expedition left the port of San Germán, Puerto Rico, on March 3, 1513. His three ships, the *Santa María de la Consolación*, the *Santiago*, and the *San Cristóbal*, sailed northwestward through the Turks and Caicos Islands and into the Bahamas. On March 13, 1513, the expedition made a brief stop at the island then known as San Salvador, where Columbus possibly had made his first landing in the Americas in 1492. From there, they approached the coast of what is now Florida.

Ponce de León and some of his men landed on the Florida mainland on April 2, 1513, below the mouth of the St. Johns River, where the city of St. Augustine would be

Juan Ponce de León *(Library of Congress)*

founded 52 years later. (Some sources indicate Ponce de León's landing place was at what is now known as Ponce Inlet near Daytona Beach, Florida.) The next day, Easter Sunday, he officially claimed it for Spain, naming it Florida after the Spanish name for Easter—Pascua Florida.

According to some sources, Ponce de León and his ships explored the Atlantic coast as far north as the Okefenokee Swamp. In any event, soon after his initial landing on the Florida mainland, he sailed southward and made additional stops at Jupiter Inlet, where his men obtained fresh water from the Santa Cruz River. He also made a landing at what is now Cape Canaveral. After exploring Biscayne Bay, he headed into the Florida keys, then reached a group of islands he called the Dry Tortugas because of the quantity of sea turtles his men captured there. On this part of the expedition, Ponce de León made an early observation of the GULF STREAM, a current that seemed to drive his ships more forcefully than the wind.

At the time of his voyage, Ponce de León believed Florida to be an island. To confirm this, he sailed up the Gulf Coast of the Florida peninsula and made a landing at Pine Island, off the shores of Charlotte Harbor, between what is now Sarasota and Fort Myers, Florida. A Calusa Indian attack soon cut short his inland explorations.

Ponce de León continued along the west coast of Florida, possibly sailing as far north as Pensacola Bay. He turned to the southwest and reached what he thought was the unexplored coast of Cuba (although some historians believe it was the Yucatán). From there, he returned to the southern end of Florida, explored Miami Bay and, after stopping at Cuba, returned to Puerto Rico on September 21, 1513.

The next year, Ponce de León was involved in the suppression of a revolt on Puerto Rico. In September 1514, he was named captain general of Puerto Rico. Soon afterward, he returned to Spain, where he presented an account of his explorations in Florida to King Ferdinand. The king then appointed Ponce de León *adelantado* (governor) of Florida, commissioning him to return there and establish a colony.

Ponce de León returned to the West Indies in 1517. Before undertaking a second expedition to Florida, he was involved in a military expedition against the Carib Indians of Guadeloupe and also participated in the conquest of Trinidad. In the meantime, expeditions by Spanish explorers LUCAS VÁSQUEZ DE AYLLÓN and ALONSO ÁLVAREZ DE PINEDA had explored the Florida coast in 1519 and 1520, determining it was an extension of a much larger mainland.

Ponce de León's royal appointment as *adelantado* had granted him control over Florida and all lands contiguous to it. Fearing encroachment by other CONQUISTADORES, he set about organizing a new colonizing expedition. In spring 1521, with two ships carrying 200 soldiers and settlers, as well as a number of farm animals and agricultural tools and supplies, he sailed from Puerto Rico to the west coast of Florida. Ponce de León and his expedition landed on Sanibel Island in the mouth of the Caloosahatchee River, where they were soon attacked by Indians, possibly Calusa.

After Ponce de León was wounded by an Indian arrow, the attempt to colonize Florida was abandoned, and the expedition withdrew to Cuba. There, in July 1521, he died of his wounds. His remains were subsequently moved to San Juan, Puerto Rico. The city of Ponce, the second largest in Puerto Rico, was named in his honor.

Juan Ponce de León was one of the first generation of Spanish conquistadores to travel to the New World after Columbus's earlier voyages. In the course of his expedition to Florida, he unwittingly made the first recorded European exploration of what is now the mainland United States. Moreover, he founded the first settlement on Puerto Rico. His attempt to colonize Florida in 1521 was soon followed by the expeditions of PÁNFILO DE NARVÁEZ and HERNANDO DE SOTO. Almost as significant as his expedition to Florida was Ponce de León's report of the Gulf Stream, which soon was used by treasure-laden Spanish ships in their northeastward journey across the Atlantic to Europe. Two small islands of the Bahamas east of Florida were named the Bimini Islands after the mythical land.

Pond, Peter (1740–1807) *American fur trader in the Canadian Northwest*

Peter Pond was born in Milford, Connecticut, the son of a shoemaker. In 1756, he enlisted in the colonial militia and took part in the final years of the French and Indian War. In the campaign against Montreal of 1760, he was commissioned an officer.

Pond left the military after the war and entered the fur trade in the Great Lakes region. From 1765 to 1771, he operated out of Detroit in present-day Michigan. During this period, he killed a man in a duel, the first in a series of violent episodes that would mark his career.

In 1772, Pond went to Mackinac, from where he undertook fur-trading expeditions into the upper MISSISSIPPI RIVER region of what is now Wisconsin and Minnesota.

Pond first traveled to western Canada in 1775. Accompanied by fellow trader ALEXANDER HENRY (the elder), he traveled to the Saskatchewan River region by way of Lake Superior, Grand Portage, and Lake Winnipeg. From there, he went on by himself to Dauphin Lake, south of Lake Winnipegosis.

In 1777, Pond entered into a partnership with Simon McTavish, the Frobisher brothers, and the McGill brothers, which eventually developed into the NORTH WEST COMPANY. That year, Pond established a trading fort on the Saskatchewan River that brought the FUR TRADE to the Indians of western Canada and cut into the monopoly of the HUDSON'S BAY COMPANY outposts to the east.

In spring 1778, Pond led a trading expedition northwest of Cumberland House on the lower Saskatchewan River. His party of 16 VOYAGEURS, traveling by CANOE, carried several tons of supplies and trade goods. In summer 1778, they reached the Methye Portage, which they crossed, becoming the first non-Indians to traverse the watershed between the rivers draining into HUDSON BAY and those emptying into the Mackenzie River Basin and the Arctic Ocean. The Methye Portage took them to the Clearwater River, which they followed into the Athabasca River. Thirty miles below the entrance to Lake Athabasca, Pond and his men established winter quarters. He traded with the Chipewyan Indians and was able to obtain twice as many fur pelts as

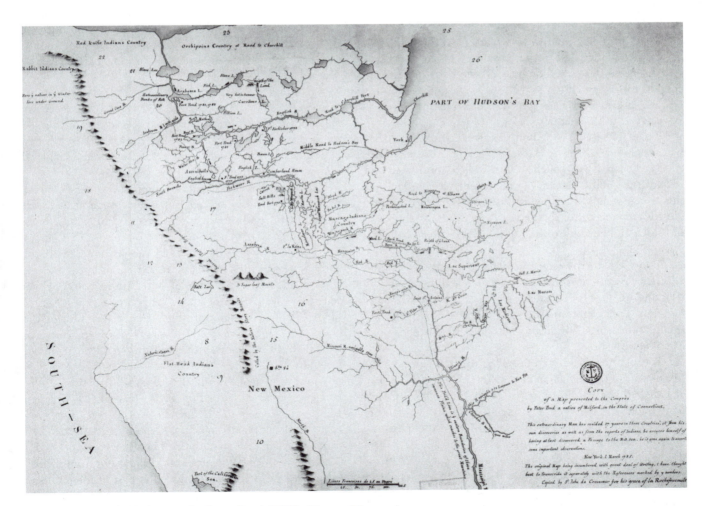

Map of western North America by Peter Pond (1775) *(Library of Congress)*

expected. He returned to the lower Saskatchewan post at Cumberland House in summer 1779.

Pond made his next trip to the Lake Athabasca region in 1780. The next year, he was caught in early winter weather and remained at Lac La Ronge. While there, he was involved in another killing, this time of a competing trader. He returned to Montreal in 1782, where he was tried and acquitted of murder. Soon afterward, he left Canada and returned to the United States.

While in the Lake Athabasca region, Pond had heard from the Indians of a river flowing eastward from the ROCKY MOUNTAINS, now known as the Peace River. He incorrectly surmised that from Lake Athabasca the distance to the Pacific Ocean was less than 400 miles. His error was based on his incorrect determination of the longitude of Lake Athabasca, which Pond placed 700 miles farther west than it really was. In 1784, the first published reports of JAMES COOK's 1778 exploration of the coast of the Pacific Northwest appeared. Based on the maps included in Cook's account, coupled with tales from the Chipewyan Indians, Pond speculated that there was a water route that linked the rivers north of Lake Athabasca with the Pacific coast of Alaska, near present-day Anchorage.

In 1785, Pond went to New York City, then the U.S. capital, where he tried to present a map of the Canadian Northwest to the U.S. Congress, in the hope of winning support for an expedition to the lucrative sea otter resources on the Alaskan coast. Failing to gain governmental support, he returned to Lake Athabasca.

From 1785 to 1788, Pond explored the Lake Athabasca region, reaching Great Slave Lake. He observed there the Mackenzie River, which seemed to flow southwestward toward the Pacific Ocean. He mistakenly concluded that this stream would link up with the Cook River, thus providing a canoe route to the sea otter trade in the Gulf of Alaska and beyond to the Kamchatka Peninsula of eastern SIBERIA.

Pond left northwestern Canada in about 1788, after another violent confrontation in which a rival trader was shot and killed. He reportedly returned to Milford, Connecticut, where he remained for the rest of his life, although other sources indicate that he returned to the upper Mississippi.

Peter Pond's 1785 map provided the first comprehensive picture of the Canadian Northwest. During his last year at Lake Athabasca, he conferred with North West Company trader and explorer ALEXANDER MACKENZIE, who, in 1789, explored Great Slave Lake and followed the river previously reached by Pond. This was the Mackenzie River, which led to the Arctic Ocean, not the Pacific. Nevertheless, several years later, Mackenzie, based on Pond's reports of the Peace River, was able to trace a canoe-and-portage route from Lake Athabasca to the Pacific coast.

Pope, John B. (1822–1892) *U.S. Army officer, American topographer in the American Southwest*

Born in Louisville, Kentucky, John B. Pope graduated from West Point in 1842. During the next four years, as a second lieutenant in the U.S. Army Corps of Topographical Engineers, he conducted government surveys of Florida as well as the northeastern part of the U.S.-Canada boundary.

During the U.S.-Mexican War of 1846–48, Pope served under General Zachary Taylor in the Texas and Mexico campaigns. After the war, Pope returned to the Topographical Corps. In 1849, he undertook a survey of the Red River of the North in the Minnesota Territory.

In 1851, Pope became chief topographical engineer for the Department of New Mexico. That year, he surveyed a route between Santa Fe, New Mexico, and Fort Leavenworth, Kansas, that was to serve as an alternative to the established Santa Fe Trail.

In February 1854, as part of the Pacific Railroad surveys, Pope led an expedition eastward from Dona Ana on the Rio Grande, across central Texas, to Fort Washita on the Red River. The expedition explored the eastern segment of the proposed 32nd parallel transcontinental railroad route, while another expedition, under the command of Lieutenant JOHN GRUBB PARKE, explored the western segment from the Rio Grande to the Pacific Ocean.

Heading eastward from the Rio Grande, Pope located a pass over western Texas's Guadalupe Mountain. He sent two small parties northward to explore the arid Llano Estacado (Staked Plain) region. The expedition reached Fort Washita by following a route that closely paralleled a well-established emigrant wagon road.

In 1855, Pope returned to western Texas, where he supervised the drilling of experimental artesian wells in the Staked Plain region to determine if the 32nd parallel route was viable for a railroad.

Pope rose to prominence as a Union commander in the early battles of the Civil War. Yet, after suffering a severe reversal at the second battle of Bull Run in 1862, he was sent to western Minnesota to help suppress the Santee Sioux (Dakota) Indian uprising. After the war, during the late 1860s, he commanded the army's vast Department of the Missouri. He retired from the army in 1886 as a major general.

John B. Pope's contribution to North American exploration is somewhat tainted by the fact that his 1849 map of Minnesota was revealed by Lieutenant HENRY LARCOM AB-BOTT to be a plagiarism of JOSEPH NICOLAS NICOLLET's map of the same region, published in 1843. Nonetheless, his subsequent official account of his explorations from the Rio Grande to the Red River, included as part of the results of the Pacific Railroad surveys, widened geographic knowledge of the southern plains.

Popham, George (ca. 1550–1608) *English mariner, colonizer in the Americas*

Born at Huntsworth in Somerset, England, near Bristol, George Popham was a nephew of Sir John Popham, England's lord chief justice. In 1594–95, Popham commanded a ship of British PRIVATEERS to the WEST INDIES and the mainland of northeastern South America, where he took part in raids on Spanish ships and ports. From a captured Spanish vessel, he recovered documents detailing the interior of the region known as Guiana, which he later gave to SIR WALTER RALEIGH.

In 1606, Popham was one of the original organizers of the VIRGINIA COMPANY of Plymouth, which, with the VIRGINIA COMPANY of London, had received from King James I grants of land in what is now New England and Virginia. That year, with the help of his uncle Sir John Popham and Sir Ferdinando Gorges, he organized a colonizing expedition to North America.

On May 31, 1607, Popham sailed from Plymouth in command of the *Gift of God,* accompanied by the *Mary and John* captained by Raleigh Gilbert, a son of SIR HUMPHREY GILBERT and a nephew of Sir Walter Raleigh. The ships, carrying about 100 colonists, reached Maine in late July. After exploring along the coast, they made an initial landing on Monhegan Island on August 9, 1607. One week later, they established a colony at the mouth of the Kennebec River (then known as the Sagadahoc), near what is now Phippsburg, Maine. The settlement consisted of 15 huts and a church. Popham was elected governor of the colony, which was called Fort St. George.

Popham, Gilbert, and about 45 colonists remained in the Maine colony when the ships sailed back to England on December 5, 1607. Before long, however, a fire destroyed most of their provisions, and, on February 8, 1608, Popham died. Gilbert soon sailed for England, and, the following summer, the remaining colonists abandoned the settlement and also returned to England.

Short-lived as it was, George Popham's settlement on the Maine coast was the first English colony in New England. At the same time, a more successful settlement had been established by the London Company at Jamestown on the Virginia coast. Popham Beach, Maine, near the site of the abandoned colony, was named in his honor.

Popov, Fyodot Alekseyev (Feodot Alekseyev Popov) (fl. 1640s) *Russian trader in Siberia*

Fyodot Alekseyev Popov was a merchant from the Northern Dvina River port of Veliki Ustyug, north of Moscow and then an important trade and transportation center on the road from European Russia to SIBERIA. Popov became a pioneer Russian trader along the Arctic coast of eastern Siberia. In 1647, he organized an expedition planning to travel by sea from Nizhnekolymsk, a settlement near the mouth of the Kolyma River, around the Chukchi Peninsula, to Anadyr Island off the Siberian coast of the Bering Sea, which had been reported as a rich source of walrus ivory.

Turned back by ice at the mouth of the Kolyma River in his first attempt, Popov set out again in 1648, accompanied by SEMYON IVANOVICH DEZHNEV, a Cossack in service to the czar. With six small boats, carrying about 90 men, he left Nizhnekolymsk and managed to travel eastward around what later came to be known as Cape Dezhnev, to the mouth of the Anadyr River and Anadyr Island. Afterward, he reportedly went south into the northern Kamchatka Peninsula.

In their 1648 voyage, Fyodot Alekseyev Popov and Dezhnev unwittingly located the northeasternmost extent of the Asian continent, a finding that eventually led Russian geographers to conclude that Asia and North America were separated by open sea.

Pordenone, Odoric of   See ODORIC OF PORDENONE.

Porte, François de la (comte de Castelnau, Francis de la Porte, count of Castelnau) (1812–1880) *French naturalist in the Americas*

François de la Porte, comte de Castelnau, was born in London, England, to French nobility. His interest in geography and the natural sciences led him to an appointment as head of an 1837 French scientific expedition to North America. During the next four years, Castelnau and his team of scientists undertook a study of the lakes of Mexico, the United States, and Canada.

In 1843, Castelnau led a French scientific team in an expedition to South America. From Rio de Janeiro, he traveled to the Río de la Plata, which he ascended in his exploration of the interior of Brazil. He then surveyed the watershed between the AMAZON RIVER and the Río de la Plata, and explored the Paraguay River, locating its source in the Mato Grosso region of western Brazil. Proceeding westward from Brazil, he became one of the few 19th-century European explorers to traverse the difficult and uninhabited Gran Chaco region. While in Brazil, he also explored the Araguaia and Tocantins Rivers. Entering Bolivia from the east, Castelnau continued on to Potosí, eventually reaching Lake Titicaca, near the Pacific coast.

Starting in 1846, Castelnau began his second great exploration of South America. From Urubamba, north of Cuzco, Peru, he traveled along the eastern slopes of the ANDES MOUNTAINS to the Urubamba and Ucayali Rivers into the Amazon. Eventually reaching the Pará River, he followed it to the Atlantic Ocean, arriving in 1847.

Comte de Castelnau's two explorations of the South American continent revealed much about the geography of the little-known area lying between the Amazon and Río de la Plata. In his second expedition of 1846–47, he made the first west-to-east crossing of South America by way of Peru and Brazil.

Porto, Antonio Silva   See SILVA PORTO, ANTONIO.

Portolá, Gaspar de (ca. 1722–ca. 1784)
Spanish army officer, colonial governor in California
Gaspar de Portolá was born at Balaguer in the Catalonia region of Spain, into a noble family. While in his early teens, he entered the Spanish army as a commissioned officer, and during the next 30 years, he served in assignments in Portugal and Italy, attaining the rank of captain in 1764.

In 1767, Portolá was named governor of the Spanish-held province of California, which then comprised Mexico's Baja California as well as what is now the state of California. Two years later, on May 15, 1769, he left Velicate, the Spanish settlement in Baja California, in command of a colonizing expedition northward into present-day southern California. Accompanied by Franciscan missionary Father JUNÍPERO SERRA, Portolá led a group of 126 soldiers, colonists, and Franciscan friars, along with pack animals and a large herd of cattle, northward across several hundred miles of unexplored desert.

On July 1, 1769, after an overland trek of six weeks, Portolá and his party arrived at San Diego. They met up with another contingent of colonists there, who had arrived by ship several weeks earlier. Two weeks later, Portolá set out with a party of 40 soldiers, heading northward along California's coastal valleys and mountains, seeking the great bay that SEBASTIÁN VISCAÍNO had reported finding in 1602. Serra stayed in San Diego for the time being.

On October 1, 1769, Portolá and his party arrived at the mouth of the Salinas River on the shores of Monterey Bay, although at the time the Spaniards did not recognize it as the one Viscaíno had described. Instead, they continued to search northward. After several more weeks, a reconnaissance team reached Drakes Bay, a site already known to Spanish navigators. Soon afterward, on November 1, 1769, Portolá's scouts came upon a huge natural harbor, which one member of the expedition later described as big enough to hold the ships of all the navies of Europe. Portolá took possession of the harbor and the surrounding territory for the Spanish Crown, naming it San Francisco Bay. He then led his men southward, back to San Diego, which they reached on January 24, 1770.

After a rest at San Diego, and the arrival of a ship carrying much-needed supplies, Portolá set out again in search of Monterey Bay. On May 24, 1770, he reached Monterey Bay a second time, and, from the height of a mountain overlooking the coast, he was able to discern that it was indeed the shape of the bay that Viscaíno had described. One week later, Portolá established the mission and presidio of San Carlos Borromeo on the shores of the bay. The next year, it was moved to the north near present-day Carmel, California.

With a permanent Spanish presence firmly established in California, Portolá returned to Mexico. In 1776, he was appointed governor of the city of Puebla, a post he held until 1784. He may have then returned to Spain, although some sources suggest he spent his last years in Mexico.

Gaspar de Portolá, along with Serra, played an important role in establishing the first European settlements in California. His overland explorations in 1769–70 resulted in the first European penetration into California's interior, and his northward route from San Diego to San Francisco later developed into the California Mission Trail. It was Portolá's landbased expedition that made the European discovery of San Francisco Bay in 1769, a find that had eluded European navigators through more than 200 years of exploration along that part of the California coast by sea, beginning with JUAN RODRÍGUEZ CABRILLO's voyage of 1542.

Pottinger, Sir Henry (1789–1856) *Irish-born*
British army officer in southwestern Asia
A native of Ireland, Henry Pottinger's military and diplomatic career began in the early 1800s with the British army in India. In 1810, Pottinger and a military surveyor, Captain CHARLES CHRISTIE, were sent from Bombay to the Baluchistan coast of what is now southern Pakistan to explore northward as far as the Afghan frontier, territory then little known to Europeans. The expedition had been spurred on by British concern that the French, under Napoléon, might get military support from Russia and Persia (present-day Iran) for an assault on India. Essential to meeting this possible challenge to British influence in southwestern Asia was updated and accurate geographic information about the territory between the Persian Gulf and western India.

Pottinger and Christie sailed from Bombay, and after landing at Karachi, they explored inland disguised as horse traders. They traversed the interior of Pakistan northward to Nushki on the Afghan border, where they separated. While Christie crossed Afghanistan to Herat, Pottinger made his way westward through the Kerman region of Persia, present-day southeastern Iran. He reached Bushehr, midway up the Persian Gulf, from where he went northward to Esfahan and rejoined Christie.

From there, Pottinger and Christie traveled northward to the city of Qazvin, where they again parted. Christie surveyed the region around Baku, west of the Caspian Sea, and

Pottinger went southward to Baghdad, then proceeded down the Euphrates River to Basra and the Persian Gulf.

In his later career, Pottinger took part in military campaigns in west-central India, and, following the consolidation of British rule there, held diplomatic positions in southern Pakistan's Sindh region. He went on to command British forces in the Far East in the Opium War of 1839–42, and, in 1843, he became the first British governor of Hong Kong. In 1846, he served as British colonial governor at the CAPE OF GOOD HOPE, returning to India the following year to become governor of Madras. Pottinger described his early travels in Persia and Pakistan in his book *Travels in Beloochistan and Sinde,* first published in 1816.

Sir Henry Pottinger and Charles Christie were among the first modern European explorers of southwestern Asia, a part of the world that had remained largely unknown to Europeans since medieval times.

Powell, John Wesley (1834–1902)

American geologist, ethnologist, explorer of the Grand Canyon
John Wesley Powell was born at Mount Morris in western New York State's Genesee Valley region. His father, who had come from England in 1830, was an exhorter for the Methodist Episcopal Church. While still young, Powell moved with his family to Jackson, Ohio, where he first studied the natural sciences as a student of naturalist George Crookham. The family subsequently moved west to Wisconsin, finally settling in Wheaton, Illinois.

Starting in 1852, Powell attended what later became Wheaton College, while supporting himself as a schoolteacher. He went on to Illinois College at Jacksonville and also studied at Oberlin College in Ohio. Powell planned to follow his father in a career as a Methodist minister, but instead embarked on a study of natural science, concentrating on geology.

From 1855 to 1858, while studying at Oberlin and Wheaton, Powell undertook solo expeditions in a small boat along the MISSISSIPPI RIVER and Ohio River.

With the onset of the Civil War in 1861, Powell enlisted in the army and received a commission as a lieutenant. He organized an artillery unit in 1862, and that year, at the battle of Shiloh, suffered a wound in which he lost the lower part of his right arm. In 1865, Powell left the army at the rank of major and became a professor of geology at Illinois Wesleyan College in Bloomington, Illinois.

In summer 1867, Powell took a group of his geology students and a party of scientists on a field trip to the Colorado ROCKY MOUNTAINS. On a second field trip the following summer, he visited the gorge of the Green River in present-day Wyoming and the Grand Canyon in present-day Arizona, which inspired him to obtain federal funding for an exploration of the COLORADO RIVER.

John Wesley Powell *(Library of Congress)*

On May 24, 1869, Powell's expedition of 11 men entered the Flaming Gorge of the Green River at the Union Pacific Railroad's crossing near the town of Green River, Wyoming. In four specially constructed boats, Powell and his men traveled southward through what is now eastern Utah to the Green River's confluence with the Colorado, which they descended into what is now northern Arizona. At the entrance to the Grand Canyon, three of his party decided not to continue. Powell and the remaining eight men then proceeded in boats down the rapids and through the mile-high walls.

In 1871, Powell led a government scientific expedition that explored and charted the Colorado Plateau in Utah and Arizona. Over the next four years, he undertook topographic and geological surveys of the Uinta Mountains. In 1875, he became a director of the U.S. Geological and Geographical Survey of the Territories, then went on to succeed CLARENCE KING as director of the U.S. Geological Survey in 1881.

Powell's interest in the American West also included the study of the culture of Pueblo Indians. In 1894, he became the director of the Smithsonian Institution's Bureau of American Ethnology and supervised anthropologists in studies of Indian tribes. Powell's account of his 1869 exploration of the Grand Canyon is included in his *Explorations of the Colorado River of the West and Its Tributaries,* first published in 1875.

John Wesley Powell led the first successful navigation down the Colorado River through the Grand Canyon. His subsequent efforts helped promote and consolidate U.S. government-sponsored scientific explorations in the American West. His studies of topography and geology in Arizona and Utah led to his theories on the origins of the Uinta Mountains and other ranges in the West, and laid the foundation for the science of geomorphology, the branch of geology that studies the origins of the Earth's land forms.

Poyarkov, Vasily Danilovich (Vasili Poyarkov)
(fl. 1640s) *Russian Cossack in eastern Siberia*
Vasily Poyarkov was a Russian Cossack leader in service to the czarist government in eastern SIBERIA. In 1643, he was commissioned to lead a military expedition from Yakutsk in search of the Shilka (black dragon), a river thought to lead southward into China. He was also to investigate the region's mineral resources and collect taxes from the area's fur traders.

From Yakutsk, Poyarkov and his command traveled along the Lena River to its junction with the Aldan, which they followed eastward and southward to the edge of the Aldan Plateau. At the Gonam River, he established a small garrison, leaving a contingent of men, then continued southward across the mountains. He came upon the Zeya River, an uncharted tributary of the Amur.

Poyarkov and his men wintered on the Zeya, and, in spring 1644, the rest of his command arrived from the Gonam River post with fresh supplies. Soon afterward, Poyarkov led his expedition down the Zeya and reached the Amur River, near what is now the Russian city of Blagoveshchensk on the Chinese border. The Cossack leader's brutal treatment of the region's native Daurian people aroused hostility, instigating attacks in which Poyarkov lost half his force.

Poyarkov and the survivors descended the Amur in small boats; after three months, they reached its mouth on the Sea of Okhotsk. In summer 1645, following delays because of ice at the mouth of the Amur, they sailed into Sakhalin Gulf and sighted the north coast of Sakhalin Island. They followed the shore of the Sea of Okhotsk northward, eventually reaching the mouth of the Ulya River, where they encamped for the winter.

Poyarkov and his men began the last leg of their journey homeward in spring 1646, with a trip up the frozen Ulya River on skis. They eventually reached the Aldan River, which led them back to the Lena and Yakutsk by June 1646.

Vasily Poyarkov is the first European known to have descended the length of the Amur River to the Sea of Okhotsk and the Pacific. The information he brought back about the Amur River and the surrounding territory was used by the Russian government in planning its conquest of the region in the 18th and early 19th centuries. His combined river and overland explorations took him across a vast area of southeastern Siberia.

Pribylov, Gavrilo Loginovich (Gavril Pribylov, Gerasim Pribilof) (fl. 1780s) *Russian mariner in the Bering Sea*
During the 1780s, sea captain Gavrilo Pribylov sailed the Bering Sea for a Russian fur-trading company in search of new sources of seal and sea otter fur. In 1786, two years after the establishment of the first Russian fur-trading colony in Alaska on Kodiak Island, Pribylov reached a group of four volcanic islands, approximately 230 miles north of Unalaska. Although previously sighted by earlier mariners, they had not been visited by Europeans. These islands proved to be the main breeding grounds of the Alaska fur seal, a type of eared seal, related to the California sea lion and highly prized as a source of fur.

Gavrilo Pribylov named the uninhabited islands after himself (later spelled Pribilof). Russian fur traders soon took some Aleut there to hunt the fur seals for their valuable pelts as well as for their sex glands, which were then in great demand in China, where they were believed to have rejuvenative powers. Seal hunting in the Pribilofs became so extensive in the next two decades that by 1810 the seal population there had been reduced by 90 percent. In 1868, the year after the United States took possession of the islands as part of its purchase of Alaska, the Pribilofs became a seal preserve. Nevertheless, open-sea hunting of seals migrating to the Pribilof Islands in the spring continued on a wide scale so that, by 1911, the herd was threatened with extinction. The situation changed that year, when the United States, Japan, and Russia entered into the North Pacific Sealing Convention under which the three nations agreed to prohibit open-sea seal hunting; as a result, the seal herd was gradually built up again.

Pring, Martin (fl. 1603–1606) *English mariner on the New England coast*
Martin Pring was originally from Devonshire, England. By the early 1600s, he had developed a reputation as an able navigator and sea captain. In 1603, a group of Bristol merchants commissioned a followup of BARTHOLOMEW GOSNOLD's 1602 voyage to the New England coast. The expedition was organized by English geographer RICHARD HAKLUYT and was to be headed by Pring.

In April 1603, Pring departed England in command of the ship the *Speedwell.* A smaller ship, the *Discoverer,* commanded by William Brown, was also part of the expedition. Pring followed Gosnold's route to North America, reaching the coast of Maine in June 1603. From there, he sailed southward around Cape Cod and made a landing at what is now Edgartown on Martha's Vineyard. He proceeded along the Massachusetts coast to New Bedford, then explored the New England coast of Long Island Sound.

Pring traded with the Indians, obtaining furs and sassafras, which he sent back to England aboard the *Discoverer*. On locating a good harbor, he sent a party ashore to investigate the fertility of the soil. His men planted wheat, barley, oats, peas, and other garden vegetables. After seven weeks, the crops started to sprout, confirming earlier reports that the New England coastal region was highly suitable for an agricultural colony.

In August 1603, Martin Pring and the rest of his party sailed for England, reaching Bristol about nine weeks later. He made another voyage to the Maine coast in 1606. The success of Pring's agricultural experiment, the first such undertaking in New England, inspired the establishment of an English colony under GEORGE POPHAM on Maine's Kennebec River in 1607.

Provost, Étienne (1782–1850) *French-Canadian fur trader in the American West*

Born in Montreal, Canada, Étienne Provost arrived in St. Louis in 1815, where he entered the FUR TRADE as a trapper with AUGUSTE PIERRE CHOUTEAU. He took part in Chouteau's 1815–17 expedition up the Arkansas River into present-day Colorado. When his party wandered into Spanish-held New Mexico, he was arrested along with them and briefly jailed in Santa Fe.

Provost remained in New Mexico after Mexican independence had been won in 1821, and he undertook fur-trapping expeditions into the ROCKY MOUNTAINS north of Taos, New Mexico. He may have been with an 1823 fur-trapping expedition under JEDEDIAH STRONG SMITH that rediscovered the SOUTH PASS in what is now southern Wyoming. In 1824, Provost and a party of trappers explored the Wasatch Mountains, into the area around present-day Provo, Utah, and may have continued northward as far as the Great Salt Lake.

Indians later attacked the trappers in the Wasatch Mountains, killing several. Provost and the other survivors fled to their encampment on the Green River in northeastern Utah. In 1825, Provost joined with WILLIAM HENRY ASHLEY on the way to the first trappers' rendezvous on the Green River at Henrys Fork.

In 1837, Provost traveled with THOMAS FITZPATRICK and frontier artist ALFRED JACOB MILLER along the Oregon Trail to Fort Laramie on the Laramie River in present-day Wyoming. Two years later, in 1839, he guided JOHN CHARLES FRÉMONT and JOSEPH NICOLAS NICOLLET in their exploration of the territory between the upper MISSISSIPPI RIVER and upper MISSOURI RIVER. Then, in 1843, he served as a guide for JOHN JAMES AUDUBON's expedition to the upper Missouri.

The city of Provo, Utah, although spelled differently, was named in honor of Étienne Provost, as were a Utah river and mountain peak. His career as a mountain man and fur trader took him across a wide area of the Rocky Mountains and brought him in contact with some of the best-known explorers of the American West.

Przhevalsky, Nikolay Mikhailovich (Nikolai Mikailovich Prejevalski, Nicholas Michailovitch Prjevalsky, Nicholas Przevalskii, Nikolai Przewalksi) (1839–1888) *Russian army officer, naturalist in central Asia*

Born in the Russian town of Otradnoe, near Smolensk, west of Moscow, Nikolay Przhevalsky was of Cossack descent, born into a family of landed gentry. He attended secondary school in Smolensk; in 1855, at the age of 16, he entered the Russian army as a career military officer. He served with a Moscow-based regiment, then became a teacher of geography at the army's military academy in Warsaw.

In 1867, on volunteering for an assignment in eastern SIBERIA, Przhevalsky was sent to the frontier region along the Ussuri River on the Russia-China border, 200 miles inland from the Pacific coast. He conducted a census of the native inhabitants and took part in military actions against the gangs of marauding Chinese bandits infiltrating Russian territory from Manchuria. Przhevalsky also studied the region's natural history, and, in his subsequent report, he detailed the plant and animal life around the Ussuri River region, as well as the life and culture of its native people.

Highly impressed with Przhevalsky's account, the Russian Imperial Geographical Society agreed to sponsor his plan to conduct a series of extensive explorations into the interior of Mongolia and China. A leave of absence from the army was arranged, and in 1870 he set out on his first expedition from the southeastern Siberian city of Irkutsk, accompanied by two Russian companions. The group traveled southward around Lake Baikal to Kyakhta along Mongolia's north-central frontier, continuing on to Ulan Bator, where they obtained camels for the journey across the GOBI DESERT to Peking (Beijing) in China. Przhevalsky and his party followed the traditional caravan route across northeastern China, crossing the Great Wall at Kalgan. They completed the last leg of the trip to Peking on horseback, arriving in early 1872. From there, he assembled another camel caravan for an expedition into northern and western China.

Following the east-west caravan route, Przhevalsky reached Koko Nor, a large salt lake, and the Tsaidam Swamp (depression) in western China. By that time, he had run out of funds to continue his explorations southwestward into the Tibetan Plateau and to LHASA. He made an arduous return journey across the Ordos desert to the Russia-Mongolia frontier at Kyakhta. On this expedition, he had traversed Mongolia from north to south, and had traveled along a wide arc through eastern, western, and southern China.

Przhevalsky's next expedition penetrated China from the west. In 1876, he set out from Kuldja (present-day Yining, China), then a Russian-held city on China's northwestern frontier with Russia. He crossed the Tian Shan range and the Taklimakan Desert; after exploring the Tarim River Basin, he came upon Lop Nor, the dried-up bed of an immense salt lake whose location had mysteriously shifted over the last six centuries. Afterward, in an attempt to reach Tibet, he entered the previously uncharted Astin Tagh mountains. With the onset of winter in the difficult mountain terrain, he was again forced to abandon his planned trip to Lhasa, and he returned to Kuldja.

In 1879, Przhevalsky undertook another exploration of the Chinese interior from the west, starting out from Zaysan in what is now Kazakhstan. On this exploration, he explored the upper Yellow River (Huang He) region and approached the Tsaidam Swamp and Koko Nor from the west. He then traveled southward across southwestern China's Dzungaria region into Tibet. He reached within 150 miles of Lhasa, when Tibetan authorities, suspicious of all Westerners, ordered him out of the country. The next year, he returned to Russian territory.

In 1883–85, in his fourth and final expedition, Przhevalsky again crossed the Gobi Desert from northern Mongolia and traversed China westward to Koko Nor. He proceeded westward through the Kunlun and Tian Shan Mountains to Karakul, on Issyk Kul, a lake in what is now Kyrgyzstan. He had planned a fifth expedition to Tibet in 1888, but he died that year, shortly after setting out from Karakul.

Nikolay Przhevalsky is credited with making the first scientific exploration of central Asia. His expeditions were undertaken amid Russian apprehensions over possible British encroachment into central Asia from India and Afghanistan, making his reports on the region's geography politically significant as well. In his nine years of explorations, he traveled more than 20,500 miles in Mongolia, China, and Tibet, covering a vast area ranging from the edge of the Pamirs in the west, eastward to Peking, and from Mongolia southward to Tibet. Among the species new to science that he encountered were a type of wild camel, a type of wild sheep, a long-eared pheasant, and a type of wild horse, known today as Przhevalsky's horse, which in its pure-bred state is believed to be a "living ancestor" of the domestic horse. A city in the Kirghiz region where Przhevalsky died has since been named Przhevalsk in his honor. Przhevalsky's visit to Lop Nor in 1876 marked the first time a European ventured to that region since the travels of

MARCO POLO, 600 years earlier. Although he did not achieve his goal of reaching the city of Lhasa, which was then forbidden to most foreigners, he is nonetheless considered the greatest Russian explorer of central Asia. His published accounts of his travels include *From Kulja, Across the Tian Shan to Lop-Nor* (1879) and the two-volume *Mongolia, the Tangut Country and the Solitudes of Northern Tibet* (1876).

Ptolemy (Ptolemy of Alexandria; Claudius Ptolemaeus) (ca. A.D. 90–ca. A.D. 150)

Hellenized Egyptian geographer, astronomer, mathematician in ancient Alexandria, Egypt

A hellenized Egyptian, Ptolemy was a native of Alexandria, Egypt, and a leading scholar and scientist among that city's Greek intellectual community in the second century A.D. His exact heritage is not known. He may have had Egyptian, Greek, or Roman ancestry, or a combination. He conducted studies in and wrote works on mathematics, astronomy, and geography.

From A.D. 127 to 147, Ptolemy produced an eight-volume work summarizing the geography of the known world. Known as *Geographia*, or *Introduction to the Description of the Earth*, it includes a compilation of 8,000 places, along with their coordinates of LATITUDE and LONGITUDE, with relative distances obtained from travel reports and some astronomical observations.

Like other learned Greeks of his day, Ptolemy conceived the world as spherical, although he rejected the notion that all the lands on Earth were surrounded by a great "Ocean Stream," and instead suggested that uncharted lands could be located across the unexplored seas.

Ptolemy's *Geographia* was fairly accurate about the Mediterranean region and correctly located Ireland as lying west of Britain. His northernmost point, known as ULTIMA THULE, has since been hypothesized as one of Scotland's Shetland Islands. He also mentions eastern Europe's Volga River and makes the first known reference to the Carpathian Mountains. He was also aware of the lands of western China, citing that region as the ultimate source of silk that was transported along the SILK ROAD. Much of his work was drawn from earlier Greek geographers, including Marinus of Tyre and STRABO.

Ptolemy's larger view of world geography, based more on traditional beliefs than on actual travel accounts, was far less precise. In later world maps based directly on his work, Africa is shown to be joined to eastern Asia, thus depicting the Indian Ocean as an entirely enclosed inland sea. He also believed that a great unknown landmass had to exist in the Southern Hemisphere to counterbalance the known continents of the Northern Hemisphere, an idea that later prompted European exploration of the Pacific Ocean in

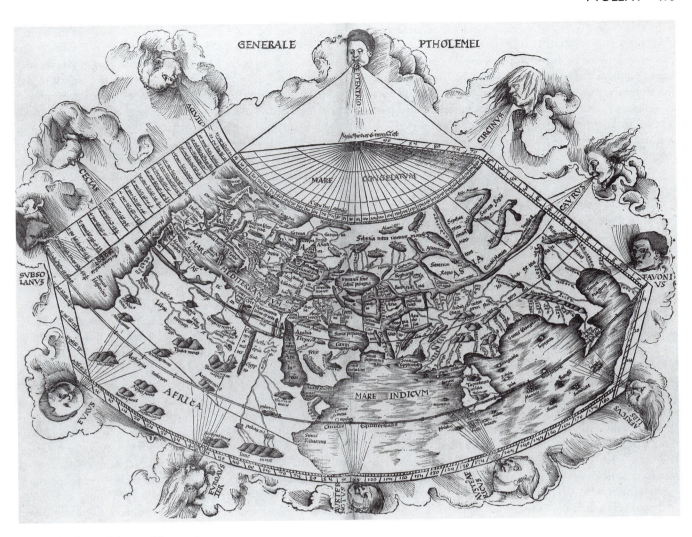

Map by Ptolemy *(Library of Congress)*

search of the GREAT SOUTHERN CONTINENT, or Terra Australis, including the first two voyages of JAMES COOK in the early 1770s. Yet Ptolemy accurately portrayed the NILE RIVER as flowing from two large lakes in the interior, fed by snow melting off the fabled MOUNTAINS OF THE MOON. This idea, rejected by later geographers, was later proven to be true with the African expeditions of SIR HENRY MORTON STANLEY and his exploration of the Ruwenzori Mountains in the 1870s. (It is not certain, however, if Ptolemy was actually describing the Ruwenzori Range, or other peaks, such as MOUNT KILIMANJARO and Mount Kenya.) Ptolemy's work included an account of the journey across the Atlas Mountains into the northern SAHARA DESERT undertaken by the Roman officer JULIUS MATERNUS in the first century A.D.

After the decline of Roman rule in Egypt, Ptolemy's *Geographia* was preserved by Arab scholars. Translated into Arabic, it greatly influenced geographic thought in the Muslim world throughout the medieval period. In about 1400, a copy in Greek translation was taken from Constantinople (present-day Istanbul, Turkey) to Florence, along with 27 maps, reported to be copies of originals produced under Ptolemy's direction. The *Geographia,* translated into Latin by 1410, widely circulated in Europe and greatly influenced mapmakers GERARDUS MERCATOR and ABRAHAM ORTELIUS and Italian navigator CHRISTOPHER COLUMBUS. The work detailed the principles of mapmaking, with directions for projecting a spherical image of the world onto a plane, and such now commonly followed practices as orienting a map with north at the top and east to the right, with parallels of latitude and meridians of longitude. In 1477, the first printed atlas of the world, based on Ptolemy's work, was published in Bologna. His writings, and the maps that resulted from them, helped popularize the idea among educated Europeans that the world was round. About the same time that Ptolemy's geographic ideas were being revived in Europe, direct overland contact with Asia was severed by the conquests of the Turks; influenced by his work, geographers and navigators began to turn their attention westward in their search for a new route to the Orient. In addition to his work in geography, Ptolemy's studies in astronomy and his concept of an Earth-centered solar system dominated European thought until the findings of Copernicus in the 16th century.

Pytheas (Pytheas of Marseilles, Pytheas of Massilia, Pytheas of Masilia) (fl. 320s B.C.)

Greek scholar, mariner in the British Isles and the North Sea
Pytheas was born in the Greek colony of Massilia (present-day Marseilles, France) in the early fourth century B.C. Trained in mathematics and astronomy by Plato's student Eudoxus of Cnidus, he went on to become an accomplished navigator, and he is known to have used astronomical observations to determine the latitude of Massilia.

In about 325 B.C., Pytheas set out from Massilia on a voyage to explore westward beyond the STRAIT OF GIBRALTAR and along the west coast of Europe. At that time, Greek mariners had been prevented from venturing from the MEDITERRANEAN SEA into the Atlantic Ocean by the Carthaginians, who dominated the western Mediterranean and maintained a naval blockade of the Strait of Gibraltar. The Greeks had been further discouraged by a belief in sea monsters and other terrible hazards as reported by the Carthaginians HANNO and HIMILCO in their separate Atlantic voyages a century earlier.

Pytheas may have received backing for his expedition from the merchants of Massilia, who were keenly interested in establishing a direct sea route to tin and amber sources in northern Europe. Carthage, then engaged in a war with Rome, had temporarily left the Strait of Gibraltar unguarded, allowing Pytheas to sail along the south coast of Spain to Gades (present-day Cádiz) and into the Atlantic.

Pytheas sailed northward along the coast of Spain to Cape Ortegal, then turned northeast into the Bay of Biscay and reached the coast of Brittany, which he later accurately described as a peninsula, extending westward. From there, he crossed the English Channel and landed on the coast of Cornwall, near Land's End. He established friendly contacts with the natives, who, as tin miners, had frequent contacts with foreign traders, which, Pytheas later noted, had made them civilized and less warlike. In several inland excursions, he noted other aspects of life in southern Britain, including how alcoholic beverages were made: beer from fermented grain and mead from honey.

Pytheas next sailed northward along Britain's west coast, sighted Ireland, and rounded the north coast of Scotland. He heard reports there of an island called Thule, a six-day sail to the north, which he believed to be the northernmost point on Earth. He made an attempt to reach Thule but was forced back by icebergs or dense, chilled fog. Pytheas later reported on the great difference between the length of day and night, indicating he may have approached the high latitudes near the ARCTIC CIRCLE, or, at the very least, reached as far north as the Shetland Islands, or the south coast of Norway near Bergen.

Pytheas completed his exploration of Britain by sailing down its east shore, reportedly completing one of the first circumnavigations of the island. He then sailed across the North Sea in search of principal sources of amber, a commodity highly prized by the Greeks for making jewelry. He entered the Baltic and sailed along its south coast as far as the mouth of the Vistula. After exploring islands in the Baltic as well as Heligoland Island at the mouth of the Elbe River, he followed the Atlantic coast of Europe back to the Mediterranean and Massilia.

Pytheas wrote an account of his voyages called *On the Ocean* (ca. 310 B.C.). Although the work did not survive long after his death, his observations were cited in the works of subsequent ancient geographers, including Polybius, STRABO, and Pliny the Elder. Strabo rejected as outright fabrications much of what Pytheas described on his northern voyage. After Pytheas's expedition, the Carthaginians again closed off the sea route to the Atlantic, and additional seaward exploration of northwestern Europe was not resumed until the Roman expedition to Britain under GAIUS JULIUS CAESAR 200 years later. In terms of trade, Pytheas revealed to the Massilian merchants that the sea route to the tin mines of Cornwall and the amber sources along the Baltic was impractical compared to the much shorter overland route across present-day France and Germany. Yet he demonstrated that the supposed terrors of the Atlantic were imaginary, probably having been invented by the Carthaginians to discourage Greek maritime expansion westward from the Mediterranean.

In addition to being known as the first Arctic explorer, Pytheas is sometimes thought of as the discoverer of Britain, making the first known reference to that island and correctly determining its shape to be triangular. His 8,000-mile voyage, considered to be the longest sea journey undertaken in ancient times, took several years. One result of his expedition was his finding that the NORTH STAR did not lie above true north. Another was his observations on the great effect the moon had on the tides along the North Atlantic coast of Europe, a phenomenon that was much less evident in the Mediterranean basin. Pytheas's report of Thule led to the image of ULTIMA THULE, a literary allusion to the most remote place on Earth. The name was given to the northwestern GREENLAND settlement founded by KNUD JOHAN VICTOR RASMUSSEN in 1910, which after World War II became the site of a major U.S. Air Force base.

Quadra, Juan Francisco de la Bodega y
See BODEGA Y QUADRA, JUAN FRANCISCO DE LA.

Quesada, Gonzolo Jiménez de   See JIMÉNEZ DE
QUESADA, GONZOLO.

Quirós, Pedro Fernández de (Pedro Fernandes de Quirós, Pedro Queiróz, Pero Fernandes de Queiros) (ca. 1565–1615) *Portuguese mariner in South Pacific, in service to Spain*
Born in the Alentejo region of southeastern Portugal (where he was known as Pero Fernandes de Queiros), Pedro Fernández de Quirós settled in Spain as a teenager, becoming a naturalized Spanish citizen and entering the maritime service of the Spanish government as a pilot and navigator.

In 1595, Quirós sailed from Peru with ÁLVARO DE MENDAÑA as second in command and chief pilot on an expedition in search of the Solomon Islands in the South Pacific Ocean, which Mendaña had found on a voyage in 1568. After Mendaña's death, it was Quirós, left in command, who conducted the survivors of the abandoned colony to Manila on the *San Jerónimo* in February 1596. On this voyage, many of the crew died from shortages of food and water, and conditions were compounded by the difficult Doña Isabela, Mendaña's widow, who hoarded supplies for herself and her three brothers. Quirós left the Philippines in August 1597, sailing eastward across the Pacific to Acapulco, Mexico, where he arrived in late 1597. He returned to Spain soon afterward.

In about 1600, Quirós secured a position as tutor of geography to the son of the duke of Sessa, then Spain's ambassador to the Vatican. By that time, Quirós had become convinced that Terra Australis, or the GREAT SOUTHERN CONTINENT—the hypothetical landmass thought to occupy most of the Southern Hemisphere, as depicted on most world maps of the period—lay just south of the islands he had explored with the 1595–96 Mendaña expedition. While serving with Sessa's household in Rome, he was granted an audience with Pope Clement VIII, from whom he sought support for an expedition in search of the continent, where he intended to make Christian converts among its supposedly large population. With a letter of recommendation from the pope, he then approached King Philip III of Spain, who, in 1602, agreed to sponsor a voyage of exploration.

After numerous delays, including a shipwreck in the West Indies in 1604, Quirós arrived in Callao, Peru, from where he planned to set out on his exploration of the South Pacific Ocean. The Spanish government had provided him with provisions and three ships: the *Capitana,* which he commanded; the *Almirante;* and an unnamed launch.

Quirós and his fleet left the Peruvian port on December 21, 1605, carrying 300 men, including Spanish, Portuguese, and Flemish sailors and soldiers, as well as a number of Franciscan missionaries. He followed a more southerly course than had Mendaña, expecting it would lead him to the mainland of Terra Australis. After a month at sea, Quirós had reached as far as 26° south latitude, where rough weather and unfavorable winds forced him to turn to the northwest. He soon came upon the Tuamotu Archipelago, and, on February 10, 1606, he landed on Anaa Island, 200 miles east of Tahiti. From there, he continued westward, and, after landing on numerous small islands in the southwestern Pacific, sighted what appeared to be the mainland of a large continent on May 1, 1606.

A landing was made two days later, in which Quirós proclaimed possession in the name of the king of Spain of all land extending southward from that point to the SOUTH POLE. Believing he had finally located the Great Southern Continent, he named it Australia del Espíritu Santo. Actually he had reached Manicolo, the largest island of the New Hebrides group. Quirós and his expedition held a religious festival on the island but made no attempt to convert the natives. A church was erected, but, after less than six weeks, he was compelled to take leave for reasons that are still not clear. Rough weather may have threatened his ships lying at anchor offshore, or his crew may have threatened mutiny. In any event, he sailed on June 8, 1606, and, although he may have planned to return to Espíritu Santo, contrary winds soon made that impossible.

Meanwhile, the other main ship in Quirós's fleet, the *Almirante,* captained by LUIS VÁEZ DE TORRES, had waited for Quirós off Espíritu Santo. When the *Capitana* failed to return after two weeks, Torres set out on his own to the west and explored the coast of New Guinea.

Quirós and the rest of the expedition headed back eastward across the Pacific along the latitude of Guam, reaching the coast of North America at Acapulco in Mexico in late November 1606. He sailed from Mexico to Madrid the following year, where he published, at his own expense, an account of his voyage. After submitting numerous proposals to the king, he was finally granted support for a new expedition to the South Pacific, but, en route to Peru, he died in Panama in 1614.

Unlike his predecessors, Mendaña and FERDINAND MAGELLAN, Pedro Fernández de Quirós encountered numerous clusters of islands in his explorations of the Pacific, including the islands in what are now known as the Cook Islands and the New Hebrides. These landfalls encouraged subsequent geographers and navigators in their belief that Terra Australis, the Great Southern Continent, still remained to be located, and influenced explorations into the Pacific well into the 18th century, including the voyages of the Frenchman LOUIS-ANTOINE DE BOUGAINVILLE and the Englishman JAMES COOK.

Quoy, Jean-René-Constant (1790–1869)
French naturalist in Australia and the South Pacific

Jean-René-Constant Quoy was born in St. Jean de Liveray, France, near the port city of Rochefort on the Bay of Biscay. Trained as a surgeon at Rochefort, he also studied natural history with Gaspard Vives, a veteran scientist who had sailed the South Pacific Ocean with LOUIS-ANTOINE DE BOUGAINVILLE in 1766–69.

In 1808, Quoy entered the medical service of the French navy, taking part that year in a government expedition to the WEST INDIES, as well as to the island of Reunion in the Indian Ocean. In early 1817, he was selected to serve on the *Uranie* as surgeon and zoologist in LOUIS-CLAUDE DE SAULCES DE FREYCINET's scientific voyage to Australia and the southwestern Pacific.

Quoy was assisted on this voyage by JOSEPH-PAUL GAIMARD. The *Uranie's* scientific team also included botanist CHARLES GAUDICHAUD-BEAUPRÉ and artist JACQUES ARAGO. In the 1817–20 voyage, in which he circumnavigated the world, Quoy collected zoological specimens, which he sent back to the Paris Museum of Natural History, including a type of striped kangaroo from the islands off of Western Australia's Shark Bay and some species of sand lizards that he found near Sydney.

In 1826–29, Quoy served on another French scientific voyage to the South Pacific, sailing as a naturalist aboard the *Astrolabe,* under the command of JULES-SÉBASTIEN-CÉSAR DUMONT D'URVILLE, along with Gaimard. On this expedition, he undertook extensive zoological field research in NEW ZEALAND, where he found species of quail, plover, and dolphin unique to those islands. He also visited New Guinea, where he captured a scrub wallaby, a small kangaroo about the size of a rabbit. In the Fiji Islands, he undertook ethnological studies detailing the life and culture of the native inhabitants.

Jean-René Quoy's reports on the zoology of the South Pacific regions he had visited were first published in 1830–33. He later served as a professor of medicine at the naval school at Rochefort. Upon his return to France from his 1826–29 voyage on the *Astrolabe,* the French Academy of Sciences and the Paris Museum of Natural History credited him with bringing back a larger collection of zoological specimens than had any previous French scientific expedition.

R

Radisson, Pierre-Esprit (ca. 1630—1710)
French fur trader in the Great Lakes, upper Mississippi River region, and Hudson Bay, brother-in-law of Médard Chouart des Groseilliers

A native of France, Pierre-Esprit Radisson arrived in 1651 in French Canada, where he joined his half-sister at Trois-Rivières, Quebec, on the St. Lawrence River. A year later, he was captured and adopted by Mohawk Indians. He learned various Indian dialects while living among them for the next year and a half.

In 1653, Radisson escaped from his captors and made his way to the Dutch settlement of Fort Orange (present-day Albany, New York), where he worked as an interpreter for Dutch fur traders. In 1657, he joined a Jesuit missionary expedition to Onondaga Indian territory near present-day Syracuse, New York.

Radisson's half sister, Marguerite Hayet, was married to fur trader MÉDARD CHOUART DES GROSEILLIERS, who had explored the western Great Lakes in 1654–56. In 1659, Radisson accompanied his brother-in-law on a fur-trading expedition out of Montreal. Traveling by way of a canoe-and-portage route along the Ottawa River and Lake Nipissing to Georgian Bay on Lake Huron, they crossed to Lake Superior and followed the south shore to its western end at Chequamegon Bay, where they established Fort Radisson.

The next year, Radisson took part in further explorations of Lake Superior, reaching as far north as Lake Nipigon. He traveled the entire length of Lake Michigan and explored what is now southern Michigan and northern Illinois. With Groseilliers, he made forays into what is now Wisconsin, as far as Sawyer County, and explored the Fox and Wisconsin Rivers. From the Native Americans, Radisson learned of a possible water route northeast of Lake Superior leading into HUDSON BAY. (He later claimed he had also made an overland journey from Lake Superior to James Bay, but it is thought he made the claim to win over British support for a fur enterprise.)

Radisson and Groseilliers eventually headed back eastward with a valuable cargo of furs. When they reached Montreal, French colonial officials confiscated their goods for unauthorized trading as COUREURS DE BOIS. Radisson and his brother-in-law headed for Boston, where they found employment with New England merchants from 1663 to 1665.

In 1665, Radisson and Groseilliers traveled to England, where, after four years, they succeeded in organizing a syndicate of merchants into the HUDSON'S BAY COMPANY. In 1668–69, Groseilliers made a trip by sea from England to Hudson Bay. Radisson, meanwhile, ran into trouble in Ireland and was forced to turn back. In 1670, Radisson again sailed to Hudson Bay from England and established a post at the mouth of the Nelson River, the first permanent settlement on the west shore of Hudson Bay in what is now northeastern Manitoba, Canada.

During the early 1670s, Radisson served as an interpreter and adviser on Indian affairs for Hudson's Bay

Pierre-Esprit Radisson and the sieur des Groseilliers with some American Indians in the North American wilderness, painting by Frederic Remington *(Library of Congress)*

Company forts. He again worked for French interests for a time, even participating in French naval attacks against the settlement at Fort Nelson as well as English posts on James Bay. By 1684, however, Radisson had returned to the Hudson's Bay Company, and he subsequently retired to England on a company pension.

Radisson's account of his explorations and exploits in North America, *Voyages of Pierre-Esprit Radisson,* was published in 1885. In it he states that he accompanied Groseilliers on a 1654 expedition to the Great Lakes, but this claim has since been discredited.

Pierre-Esprit Radisson took part in the first recorded explorations of Minnesota and Wisconsin and brought back the earliest reports from Indians of the extent of the MISSISSIPPI RIVER and MISSOURI RIVER. His descriptions of the upper Mississippi Valley were the first to cite its great potential as a region for European settlement. His efforts to bring the FUR TRADE to both the western Great Lakes tribes

and those west of Hudson Bay led to increased profits for French and English traders by enabling them to circumvent the Ottawa and Huron Indians who, as middlemen, had dominated the trade on the western St. Lawrence. He was a major force behind the creation of the Hudson's Bay Company, which would play a key role in the exploration of western Canada.

Rae, John (1813–1893) *Scottish physician and explorer in the Canadian Arctic*

John Rae was born near Stromness in northern Scotland's Orkney Islands, the son of an estate manager. At the age of 16, he entered medical school in Edinburgh, graduating four years later. Soon afterward, he obtained an appointment as ship's surgeon aboard the *Prince of Wales,* a HUDSON'S BAY COMPANY supply vessel, and he sailed to Moose Factory on lower James Bay in 1834–35.

Rae stayed on at Moose Factory as a doctor for the Hudson's Bay Company for the next eight years. He accompanied local Cree Indians into the interior on hunting expeditions, during which he became adept at wilderness travel and survival skills. His ability in this regard came to the attention of SIR GEORGE SIMPSON, the Hudson's Bay Company governor, who, in 1843, appointed Rae to survey and chart the region north of Fury and Hecla Strait, above the northernmost end of HUDSON BAY, a part of the eastern Canadian Arctic mainland not yet explored by fur traders.

In July 1846, after studying surveying and map-making in Toronto, Rae led 12 others from Churchill on the southwest shore of Hudson Bay northward aboard two small boats, the *Magnet* and the *North Pole*. At Repulse Bay, just north of Southampton Island, the expedition set up a winter base called Fort Hope, where they survived the winter by hunting and by living in Inuit-style shelters built from snow, thus becoming the first Europeans known to have used igloos.

In spring 1847, Rae undertook a series of explorations northward from Repulse Bay to the Arctic coast, during which he mapped over 600 miles of uncharted shoreline and determined the northern extent of the Boothia Peninsula. He firmly established that it was a peninsula, extending beyond 68° north latitude.

Later in 1847, Rae took part in a British government effort to locate SIR JOHN FRANKLIN and his expedition, which had been missing in the Canadian Arctic since 1845. Along with SIR JOHN RICHARDSON, Rae set out from Great Bear Lake to the Mackenzie River's delta, then followed Canada's Arctic coastline eastward. At Dolphin and Union Strait, ice conditions made it impossible to continue into Coronation Gulf, and Rae and Richardson turned back to Great Bear Lake for the winter. In spring 1849, Rae set out to search again on his own, reaching as far as Cape Krusenstern at the western end of Coronation Gulf. The next year, he crossed over to the Wollaston Peninsula and Prince Albert Sound on Victoria Island, mapping and surveying while continuing his search for Franklin. Rae surveyed Victoria Strait, separating southeastern Victoria Island from King William Island, not realizing at the time that he was less than 100 miles from Franklin's icebound expedition.

In 1852, the ROYAL GEOGRAPHICAL SOCIETY awarded Rae its Founder's Medal for having undertaken extensive explorations on Victoria Island. In 1853, he returned to Repulse Bay in northeastern Hudson Bay, from where he resumed his exploration of the Arctic coastline. On this 1853–54 expedition, he located the strait off the southwest coast of the Boothia Peninsula that now bears his name, and, in so doing, he established that King William Island was not connected to the mainland.

In April 1854, at Pelly Bay on Boothia's east shore, Rae learned from an Inuit man named In-Nook-Poo-Zhee-Jook that whites had been seen several years earlier, marching southward from King William Island toward the estuary of the Back River, and that all of them had eventually died of starvation and exposure. From other Inuit in the region, Rae recovered such relics as silverware inscribed with Franklin's personal crest, as well as Franklin's Order of Merit medal. Rae immediately returned to York Factory, then went on to England with his findings.

In England, Rae was awarded the £10,000 prize that had been offered for conclusive proof of the fate of Franklin and his expedition. Based on Rae's findings, the British Admiralty officially declared that Franklin and his men had perished and ended its search efforts. Yet when Rae's report on the fate of the Franklin expedition revealed that the men had resorted to cannibalism in their final days, the startling news resulted in a storm of controversy directed against Rae, who was publicly criticized for having rushed back to England to claim his monetary reward rather than carry on additional search efforts in the Back River region. Not satisfied with the results, Franklin's widow, Lady JANE FRANKLIN, decided to continue the search at her own expense, culminating in an expedition under SIR FRANCIS LEOPOLD Mc-CLINTOCK in 1857–59.

Rae retired from the Hudson's Bay Company in 1856; soon afterward, he went on a hunting trip to GREENLAND. He married the daughter of a British army officer in 1860. After taking part in a telegraph line survey between Winnipeg and the Pacific coast in 1864, he lived out his life in London and in his hometown on the Orkney Islands.

Underlying Dr. John Rae's great achievements in Arctic exploration was his use of the wilderness skills he had adopted from the native peoples. In his career with the Hudson's Bay Company, he is credited with having walked across 23,000 miles of Canadian wilderness territory and charting 1,500 miles of Arctic coastline. His explorations demonstrated that any NORTHWEST PASSAGE across the top of North America had to pass north of the Boothia Peninsula. From his explorations north of Repulse Bay, he proved the insularity of King William Island, and the strait separating it from the Boothia Peninsula was named Rae Strait in his honor. This channel later proved vital in the first seaward voyage through the Northwest Passage, successfully completed in 1903–06 by Norwegian explorer ROALD ENGELBREGT GRAVNING AMUNDSEN. The Rae River, which empties into western Coronation Gulf, and the Rae Isthmus, north of Repulse Bay, also bear his name. Rae's only book on his Arctic exploits, an account of his first expedition to Repulse Bay, *Narrative of an Expedition to the Shores of the Arctic Sea in 1846 and 1847,* was published in London in 1850.

Raleigh, Sir Walter (Walter Ralegh)

(ca. 1554–1618) *English colonizer in North America, explorer on the Orinoco River in South America, half brother of Sir Humphrey Gilbert*

Walter Raleigh was born at Hayes Barton in Devon, England, into an affluent and landed family. In 1569, he took part in military campaigns in France on behalf of the Huguenots. During the early 1570s, he attended Oxford University, but he did not receive a degree.

In 1578, Raleigh joined his half brother SIR HUMPHREY GILBERT in a voyage to the Americas, during which he took part in raids on Spanish shipping. Two years later, Raleigh won the favor of Queen Elizabeth I after leading English forces in suppressing a rebellion in Ireland. He was rewarded with commercial licenses and trade monopolies, and, in 1584, he was knighted. That same year, he received a royal patent to explore and colonize the region of the eastern seaboard of North America, north of the Spanish settlements in Florida.

In April 1584, Raleigh sent out two ships from Plymouth, England, commanded by Philip Amadas and Arthur Barlowe. They reached the coast of present-day North Carolina and explored the region around Pamlico Sound, naming it "Virginia" in honor of the Virgin Queen, Elizabeth I.

In 1585, Raleigh commissioned SIR RICHARD GRENVILLE to found a colony on the North Carolina coast. A fleet of seven ships carried 600 men, among them the scientist THOMAS HARRIOT and cartographer and painter JOHN WHITE. Yet, the next year, because of trouble with Roanoke Indians, the colonists returned to England with SIR FRANCIS DRAKE after a stopover by him.

In May 1587, Raleigh sent JOHN WHITE to reestablish the Roanoke Colony, this time with 150 men, women, and children. White returned to England for supplies that August, but he was delayed in his return to the settlement by the outbreak of hostilities with Spain in 1588. White finally arrived in 1590 but found no trace of the colony or the settlers. Raleigh's men found the inscription "CROATOAN" on a tree, indicating that the colonists may have moved to a nearby island of that name, but a search turned up no trace.

In 1595, Raleigh won royal authorization for an expedition to search for the fabled kingdom of EL DORADO and its golden city of Manoa, then believed to be somewhere in northern South America. Reports by Spanish explorers DIEGO DE ORDAZ and others led Raleigh to believe that El Dorado would rival the Inca and Aztec civilizations in riches. Raleigh's five ships sailed from Plymouth, England, for South America in February 1595. A stormy Atlantic Ocean crossing scattered the fleet, however. Raleigh arrived in Trinidad, where he soon led an attack on Spanish settlements. From the captured Spanish official ANTONIO DE BERRÍO, he obtained additional reports of El Dorado. While in Trinidad, he visited Pitch Lake, a natural asphalt seepage, which he described in his later published account.

Raleigh's ships regrouped at Port of Spain, Trinidad, from where they embarked on an exploration of the ORINOCO RIVER in the Guiana region. Using small boats, Raleigh led a party of 100 men up the branches of the Orinoco to its confluence with the Caroni. Along the way, they explored Lake Parime and other affluents of the Orinoco in what is now Venezuela. Tropical fever and shortages of supplies soon led Raleigh to abandon the search for El Dorado, and he headed back to the Caribbean coast by way of the Cano Macareo River. His ships then embarked for England, making stops on the Venezuelan coast and in Cuba.

In 1596, Raleigh published an account of his first South American expedition, *The Discoverie of the Beautiful Empire of Guiana, with a Relation of the Great and Golden City of Manoa . . . in the year 1595.*

By the late 1590s, Raleigh had fallen out of favor with Queen Elizabeth. Shortly after King James I came to the English throne in 1603, Raleigh was implicated in a plot against the new monarch and was imprisoned in the Tower of London under sentence of death.

Raleigh remained a prisoner until 1616, when he succeeded in convincing King James to allow him to undertake another expedition to South America in search of El Dorado. In 1617, his ships sailed to Trinidad, where Raleigh

Sir Walter Raleigh *(New York State Library, Albany)*

was stricken with fever. His son Walter and English courtier Lawrence Kemys went ahead to the Orinoco, in search of a gold mine. They entered Spanish-held territory and attempted to take the settlement of São Tomé, but were defeated. Raleigh's son was killed in the conflict, and Kemys committed suicide soon afterward.

Raleigh then returned to England. He had defied the king's orders not to undertake any attacks against the Spanish and had failed to find the fabled El Dorado. For these reasons, the death sentence was reinstated, and, in 1618, Raleigh was beheaded.

Sir Walter Raleigh never visited his short-lived settlement on the coast of what is now North Carolina. The fate of Roanoke, later known as the LOST COLONY, became one of the great mysteries of early colonial American history. Although he failed in his own efforts to found an English colony in North America, Raleigh did indirectly influence the success of the subsequent colony at Jamestown in Virginia, established in 1607. In the 1580s and 1590s, Raleigh was a prominent figure at the court of Queen Elizabeth I, and, as a trend-setter of his day, he popularized tobacco smoking in England. As a result, demand for tobacco soared in England, and after 1612, tobacco became Jamestown's principal export product and the basis for the colony's prosperity and survival as the first permanent English colony in what is now the United States. Raleigh's 1617 Orinoco expedition was the last organized attempt by a European power to find the legendary El Dorado.

Rasmussen, Knud Johan Victor (1879–1933)
Danish-Inuit anthropologist in Greenland and the Canadian Arctic

Knud Rasmussen was born in Jakobshavn, a Danish settlement on the west coast of GREENLAND. The son of a Danish father and an Inuit mother, he was educated in the European tradition, as well as in the ways of the Greenland Inuit.

Rasmussen's interest in the Arctic was focused on the study of the life and culture of the Inuit (Eskimo). In 1902–04, he took part in the Danish Literary Expedition under the leadership of Arctic explorer LUDWIG MYLIUS-ERICHSEN, exploring northwestern Greenland and conducting an ethnological study of the region's Inuit. It was on this expedition that Rasmussen made the first known sledge crossing of Melville Bay on Greenland's northwest coast.

From 1906 to 1908, Rasmussen continued his ethnological studies among the Inuit of northwestern Greenland, reaching native settlements as far north as Smith Sound. In 1910, he founded a permanent settlement on Greenland's northwest coast at North Star Bay, naming it Thule, after the legendary northernmost point on Earth reported by the ancient Greek navigator PYTHEAS (see ULTIMA THULE). In ad-

dition to serving as a base for future expeditions, the settlement asserted Danish sovereignty over the region, thereby ending the exploitation of the Inuit by visiting whalers.

In 1912, Rasmussen began the first of a series of explorations across the northern part of Greenland. He set out from Thule to a point north of 82° north latitude in a west-to-east crossing of Greenland. As a result of this exploration, he determined that Peary Land, the barren stretch of territory north of the Greenland ice cap, was a northern extension of the mainland, and not an island off the north coast as some geographers believed, thus disproving the existence of what was thought to be "Peary Channel."

Rasmussen's greatest Arctic expedition began in 1921. His main goal was to make a comprehensive study of the various Inuit bands living in the Arctic region between Baffin Bay and the BERING STRAIT, and to prove his hypothesis that the Inuit of Greenland and the Canadian Arctic were descended from Asian stock.

Accompanied by an Inuit couple, Knud Rasmussen embarked from Upernavik on September 7, 1921, aboard the ship *King of the Sea*. He first sailed to Denmark Island on the northwest coast of HUDSON BAY, where he established a winter base. During the next two years, he conducted ethnological studies on the life and culture of the nomadic Caribou Inuit.

In spring 1923, Rasmussen and his companions set out on their journey across the entire width of the Canadian Arctic to the Bering Sea, 1,800 miles to the west. After being held captive briefly by the Seal Inuit of the Boothia Peninsula, Rasmussen and his party continued westward to King William Island, where they came upon some skeletal remains of the ill-fated SIR JOHN FRANKLIN expedition of 1845–47. After another Arctic winter, they crossed frozen Viscount Melville Sound to Victoria Island, making the first traverse of the NORTHWEST PASSAGE's 110th meridian by dogsled. In spring 1924, they reached Point Barrow, Alaska, and soon afterward, they passed southward through the Bering Strait, arriving in Nome.

Rasmussen undertook his last Arctic expedition in 1932, traveling from Thule to southeastern Greenland and continuing his study of native peoples.

In addition to exploring much of northernmost North America and Greenland, Knud Rasmussen gathered a great wealth of ethnological data on the Inuit. His books include *The People of the Polar North* (1908), *Myths and Legends from Greenland* (1921–25), *In the Home of the Polar Eskimo* (1923), and *Greenland by the Polar Sea* (1921).

Raynolds, William Franklin (1820–1894)
U.S. Army officer on the northern plains

William F. Raynolds was a native of Canton, Ohio. He graduated from West Point in 1843 as a second lieutenant in the Fifth Infantry. After serving in the U.S.-Mexican War of 1846–48, he was attached to the U.S. Army Corps of Topographical Engineers.

In 1859, Raynolds, now a captain, was given command of a scientific and military expedition to the upper MISSOURI RIVER and Yellowstone River. In addition to 30 soldiers, his command included geologist FERDINAND VANDEVEER HAYDEN, artist Antoine Schoenborn, and an astronomer and meteorologist. Mountain man JAMES BRIDGER was Raynolds's chief guide.

Raynolds was ordered to locate routes for wagon roads between Fort Laramie and Fort Union. He was also to seek a suitable route from Fort Laramie northwestward along the Bighorn Mountains to Fort Benton, in order to provide connections between army posts in the Dakotas and the Platte River. From Fort Benton, he was to find a link by way of the Mullan road and Fort Walla Walla and the Columbia River Basin beyond. In addition, Raynolds was instructed to explore the region between the Yellowstone country and the South Pass.

On June 28, 1859, Raynolds led his expedition westward from Fort Pierre in present-day South Dakota, along the Cheyenne River, and around the northern edge of the Black Hills. He reached the Powder River in what is now north-central Wyoming, then followed its northeastward course into present-day southern Montana. At the Yellowstone River near the mouth of the Bighorn, he divided his group. Part of the expedition explored O'Fallon Fork; Raynolds led the rest of his men southward along the Bighorn River to a trading fort on the Platte, where they rejoined the others and spent the winter.

In May 1860, Raynolds resumed his exploration, heading westward to the Wind River. He attempted to cross into the Yellowstone Park region but was forced back by spring snows and rugged terrain. After exploring the Grand Tetons near Pierre's Hole, he reached the Three Forks of the Missouri and crossed the Continental Divide. On this segment of the trek, Raynolds located and named Union Pass, the same route through the Wind River Mountains used by WILSON PRICE HUNT and the Astorians in 1811.

From the Three Forks of the Missouri, Raynolds and his party headed northward to Fort Benton in what is now north-central Montana. The expedition then traveled by riverboat to Fort Union near the mouth of the Yellowstone, from where they continued overland back to Fort Pierre, arriving on September 7, 1860.

Raynolds went on to serve in the Civil War as chief topographical engineer in the Virginia campaign. After the war, he supervised lighthouse construction and harbor improvements on the Great Lakes.

William F. Raynolds's 14-month expedition through the northern plains and upper Missouri was the final U.S. Army Topographical Survey in the West. Although he failed to find wagon routes connecting the lower Missouri River and the Columbia River Basin, his expedition collected extensive scientific data on the last region of the American West to be explored. Most significantly, Hayden's findings in the Dakotas and Montana completed a total geological profile of the West. Raynolds's official account, *Report on the Exploration of the Yellowstone and the Country Drained by That River,* published in 1868, included extensive information on the disposition of the region's Indian tribes, and the accompanying map was used throughout the Indian wars.

Real, Gaspar Côrte   See CÔRTE-REAL, GASPAR.

Real, Miguel Côrte   See CÔRTE-REAL, MIGUEL.

Rebmann, Johann (Johannes Rebmann)
(1820–1876)   *German missionary in East Africa*
Johann Rebmann was born in Württemberg, Germany, into a peasant family. Educated in Switzerland at the Basel Missionary Institute, he became a missionary in East Africa with the Church Missionary Society, an Anglican organization.

In 1848, Rebmann served as an assistant to JOHANN LUDWIG KRAPF at his Neu-Rabai mission near Mombasa on the Indian Ocean coast of present-day Kenya. Based on reports from native travelers, the German missionaries learned of huge mountains topped with an unknown white substance, as well as a large inland sea, in the interior of East Africa. Krapf, who was then too ill with malaria to venture inland and investigate these accounts himself, sent Rebmann to explore in his place.

Rebmann left Mombasa in April 1848, and, traveling westward in the company of Swahili and Nyika tribesmen, eventually sighted the snow-covered twin peaks of MOUNT KILIMANJARO, which at 19,340 feet is the highest mountain in Africa. Several months later, Krapf himself sighted the snow-covered mountain and also sighted Mount Kenya.

Johann Rebmann and Johann Ludwig Krapf pioneered exploration into the interior of East Africa from the Indian Ocean coast. In 1855, the London Missionary Society published a map of East Africa produced by the missionaries, based on their own explorations and the accounts they had gathered from native travelers. Their depiction of snow-topped mountains lying along the EQUATOR, plus an inland sea as large as the Caspian Sea in the interior of East Africa, was met with skepticism by British geographers and scientists. To SIR RICHARD FRANCIS BURTON and JOHN HANNING SPEKE, however, Rebmann and Krapf's description of East Africa's interior strongly suggested the existence of the fabled MOUNTAINS OF THE MOON, the ultimate source of the NILE RIVER as recounted by ancient Greek geographer PTOLEMY. Encouraged by the missionaries' reports, Burton and Speke embarked on their 1856–59 expedition, which resulted in the European discovery of Lake Tanganyika and Lake Victoria.

Regensburg, Pethahia of   See PETHAHIA OF REGENSBURG.

Ribault, Jean (Jean Ribaut) (ca. 1520–1565)
French naval officer, colonizer in Florida and South Carolina
Jean Ribault, a native of Dieppe, France, was an early Huguenot convert. He went to sea and became a prominent captain in the French navy under Admiral Gaspar de Coligny, a fellow Huguenot.

In 1562, with Coligny's support, Ribault led a colonizing expedition to the southeast coast of North America, which had previously been claimed for France by GIOVANNI DA VERRAZANO. On May 1, 1562, Ribault and his fleet of three ships, carrying 150 colonists, including the Huguenot RENÉ GOULAINE DE LAUDONNIÈRE and artist JACQUES LE MOYNE DE MORGUES, arrived off the coast of northern Florida, near the mouth of the St. Johns River. On landing, Ribault erected a stone monument and claimed the region for France.

From the St. Johns River, Ribault sailed northward into the Sea Islands off the coast of what is now Georgia and South Carolina. He explored and named Port Royal Sound, and, at a point 18 miles up the sound near present-day Parris Island, he established his Huguenot colony, naming it Charlesfort in honor of French king Charles IX. Soon afterward, Ribault returned to France for supplies.

The outbreak of religious war in France prevented Ribault's immediate return. He was forced to flee France to England in October 1562. Queen Elizabeth I proposed that he join Thomas Stukely in an English colonizing venture to Florida. When Ribault declined the offer, he was imprisoned. In the meantime, because Ribault's relief expedition had failed to arrive, the colonists had abandoned Charlesfort. In 1564, Huguenots under Laudonnière made a second attempt to establish a North American colony, founding Fort Caroline on the St. Johns River in Florida, previously explored by Ribault.

In spring 1565, Ribault and a French fleet arrived offshore from the new site. The following August a Spanish naval force under PEDRO MENÉNDEZ DE AVILÉS landed at what is now St. Augustine, Florida, 40 miles to the south. The Spanish attempted a surprise attack on the French, but Ribault and his ships were able to escape. Menéndez then led an attack on the defenseless Fort Caroline, in which he massacred most of the inhabitants. A subsequent French counterattack was foiled by a storm at sea, which all but destroyed Ribault's fleet.

Ribault and his men came ashore near what is now Cape Canaveral, Florida. He attempted to lead his forces northward back to Fort Caroline but was intercepted by the Spanish. Menéndez then tricked Ribault and many of his men into surrendering. Taken captive, most of the French non-Catholics, including Ribault, were put to death on Menéndez's orders.

Jean Ribault's colonizing efforts in 1562 were the first attempt to establish a French settlement on the North American mainland since the expeditions of JACQUES CARTIER. In 1563, while in England, Ribault published an account of his explorations in Florida and South Carolina, entitled *The Whole and True Discovery of Terra Florida*, providing some of the earliest descriptions of the Indian tribes of the region.

Ricci, Matteo (Li Ma-tou, Li Madou) (1552–1610)
Italian missionary in India and China
A native of Italy, Matteo Ricci went to Rome at the age of 17 with plans to study law. Despite his family's protests, he decided instead on a religious career. He attended the Jesuit college, studying astronomy and mathematics under German scholar Christoph Clavicus. In 1577, a chance meeting with a Jesuit priest returning from India inspired Ricci to become a missionary in the Far East.

Later that year, Ricci sailed from Genoa to Portugal, then traveled with the annual trading fleet around the CAPE OF GOOD HOPE to India and the Portuguese colony at Goa, arriving in September 1578. For the next four years, he engaged in theological studies in Goa. During that period, he visited Cochin on southwestern India's Malabar Coast.

In 1582, Ricci sailed to the Portuguese island of Macao near Canton (Guangzhou), China. After a short course of study in Chinese, he crossed over to Canton, where he was soon granted permission to establish a Christian mission in Chao-ch'ing (Zhao-Qing).

Along with a fellow Jesuit, Father Michele Ruggieri, Ricci stayed at his Chao-ch'ing mission for the next seven years, continuing his study of the Chinese language and culture and introducing the Chinese to European scientific and geographic knowledge. In 1584, he produced a translation of ABRAHAM ORTELIUS's 1570 map of the world, which demonstrated to the Chinese the position of their country in relation to continents and oceans of the West. Ricci also introduced the concept of a spherical Earth to Chinese thought.

Driven from Chao-ch'ing by townspeople suspicious of the missionaries' motives, Ricci and Ruggieri headed northward in 1591 toward the capital at Peking (Beijing), hoping to meet with the Chinese emperor Wan-Li (Wanli). Refused time and again, they took up residence in Nanking. In 1601, they were finally invited to meet with the Chinese monarch. Ricci eventually became the official mathematician and astronomer to the court and was allowed to open a mission in Peking. He was also allowed to travel freely and was able to conduct explorations of China's interior. In 1602, Ricci produced a world map, drawing on the work of Chinese scholars, such as CHU SSU-PEN.

In 1607, Ricci sent word to Portuguese missionary BENTO DE GÓES, who was then in western China. Góes had been sent overland from northern India to determine if the Cathay reported by MARCO POLO was the China that the Portuguese were then regularly visiting by sea. Ricci confirmed this fact, which the Portuguese traveler received just days before he died. Ricci lived in China for a total of 28 years, dying in 1610.

Known in China as Li Ma-tou, Father Matteo Ricci traveled widely in the country, sending back to Europe his reports on China. He also wrote several classic religious works in Chinese, which helped introduce Christian theological thought to China. Ricci gave the Chinese a modern geographic perspective, introducing them to the world beyond their borders. In revealing the enormous distance separating China from Europe, he helped allay the concerns the Chinese had about possible encroachment, making the country more open to foreign contacts.

Rice, Alexander Hamilton (Ham Rice)
(1875–1956) *American physician, surveyor in South America*

Born in Boston, Hamilton "Ham" Rice was a Harvard graduate and medical doctor. His interest in tropical diseases led him to embark on a career of exploration in northern South America.

In 1907, Rice traveled over the ANDES MOUNTAINS from Quito, Ecuador, to the Napo River, which he descended to its junction with the AMAZON RIVER in northeastern Peru. From there, he traveled northward across the Amazon Basin to the Uaupes River, which he explored to its confluence with the Rio Negro in northwestern Brazil.

In 1912–13, Rice undertook a survey of the northwestern Amazon Basin. From Cartagena on the Caribbean, he crossed Colombia southward to Bogota, then traversed the Andes to Villavicencio and the Ariari River region. After exploring the Içana and Inírida Rivers, he set out northward in search of the source of the ORINOCO RIVER, but he was forced to withdraw from the area because of hostile Indians.

Rice completed a topographical study of the Rio Negro to its junction with the Amazon at Manaus in 1917. Two years later, he began to explore the Casiquiare River, the natural canal that joins the eastern Rio Negro to the Orinoco and the Amazon. By 1920, he had surveyed the upper reaches of the Rio Negro, from the Uaupes River of southwestern Colombia to the Casiquiare and the Orinoco of southern Venezuela.

Rice's most extensive survey of the northern Amazon Basin was carried out over nine months in 1924–25. He explored the Branco and Uraricoera Rivers, both northern tributaries of the Rio Negro and Amazon system in north-central Brazil. He traced the Uraricoera into the Sierra Parimá, the mountains that skirt the border between southeastern Venezuela and northwestern Brazil, then made his way overland to the upper Orinoco.

Dr. Hamilton Rice initiated 20th-century exploration in South America with his systematic survey of all the rivers draining into the northwestern Amazon Basin. In his 1924–25 expedition, he was the first to employ aircraft and wireless communication to explore large areas of South America. Using a seaplane, members of his expedition flew over 12,000 miles of unexplored territory, taking photographs from the air and communicating by radio their findings to Rice.

Richardson, James (1806–1851) *British minister, antislavery activist in North and West Africa*

James Richardson was born at Lincolnshire in eastern England. Trained as a minister, he became an evangelical preacher and was committed to the spread of Christianity to the peoples of Africa, as well as to the abolition of the African SLAVE TRADE.

Richardson became a leading member of the English Anti-Slavery Society, which sent him to Malta to prepare for his planned journey into Africa. While there, he learned Arabic and studied the geography of the interior of North and West Africa, which at that time was known by Europeans only as far as Lake Chad.

After visiting the Moroccan coast for several months, Richardson undertook his first journey into the interior of North Africa in spring 1845. He landed in Algiers, then traveled to Tripoli, from where he set out into the SAHARA DESERT. Heading southward, he made a stopover at Ghadames, and, in late October 1845, he arrived at the oasis town and former caravan center of Ghat, in present-day southwestern Libya, 600 miles south of the MEDITERRANEAN SEA. During the next several weeks, Richardson recorded his observations of the native people at Ghat and established contacts with Arab sheiks who controlled the desert lands between there and Lake Chad. Soon afterward, he traveled northward through the Fezzan region, arriving in Tripoli on April 8, 1847.

Back in England, Richardson received British foreign minister Lord Palmerston's support for another, more extensive exploration into North and West Africa. Appointed to lead a government-sponsored expedition to investigate the little-known region around Lake Chad, Richardson also planned to establish diplomatic contacts with the Bornu kingdom in what is now northern Nigeria, as a preliminary step in stemming the slave trade in West Africa. The expedition, organized as an international effort, included German scholar and archaeologist HEINRICH BARTH and German geologist ADOLF OVERWEG, both of whom had been recruited through Prussia's ambassador to Great Britain.

Richardson was married just prior to embarking on his second Sahara expedition, and in 1850, he took his new wife to Tripoli, where she would await his return. On March 23, 1850, Richardson, accompanied by Barth and Overweg, set out from Tripoli and undertook a 14-day trek across the waterless Hamada el Homra desert to Murzuk, 500 miles to the south. Along the way, they came upon the ruins of an ancient Roman settlement.

Richardson and his companions made their way southwestward through what is now northern Niger and across the Air Mountains, reaching the southern edge of the Sahara in January 1851. Near Agades, the party decided to separate, with Richardson continuing on his own directly toward Lake Chad, while Overweg went to Maradi and Barth headed for the city of Kano. They planned to join up again at Kuka, the capital of Bornu.

Two months later, Richardson, whose health had begun to suffer as a result of the climate, was stricken with fever at Ungouratona in what is now northern Nigeria, less than two weeks' travel from Lake Chad. He died on March 4, 1851. The native villagers buried him with honors; his journals were later recovered by Barth, who sent them, along with news of his death, back to Tripoli. The year after Richardson's death, Overweg also died, and, over the next three years, Barth carried out extensive explorations of West Africa on his own.

James Richardson's *Travels in Morocco* was edited by his widow Mrs. J. E. Richardson and first published in 1860. His journey to Ghat and Ghadames was recounted in his *Travels in the Desert of Sahara, 1845–6* (1848); and his report on his last expedition, *Mission to Central Africa, 1850–1*, was published posthumously in 1853. He also wrote extensively on the language and culture of the Sahara's Tuareg people. Richardson's explorations encompassed a wide area of the western Sahara and Sudan, and his published accounts described for the first time large areas unknown to Europeans.

Richardson, Sir John (1787–1865) *Scottish physician, naturalist in the Canadian Arctic*

John Richardson was born at Dumfries in southern Scotland, the son of a local magistrate. Scottish poet Robert Burns was a friend of his family, and Richardson attended the local grammar school with Burns's eldest son.

While still in his early teens, Richardson began his medical training with an apprenticeship to his uncle, a surgeon in Dumfries. He continued his education at Edinburgh University in 1801. In 1807, after working several years at a local hospital in Dumfries, Richardson entered the British navy as an assistant surgeon. In the Napoleonic Wars of 1803–15, he saw action in the attack on Copenhagen in 1807, in the Baltic Sea in 1813, and off the southeast coast of the United States in 1815.

Richardson resumed his medical studies at Edinburgh in 1815, where he also undertook the study of botany and mineralogy, receiving his M.D. the following year. After pursuing a private practice, he returned to active naval service in 1819, appointed as surgeon and naturalist for an overland exploration of the Canadian Arctic, under the command of SIR JOHN FRANKLIN, then a naval lieutenant. As part of the British navy's newly revived efforts to find the NORTHWEST PASSAGE, the expedition planned to conduct a survey of the largely unknown Arctic coastline of North America, between HUDSON BAY and the Bering Sea.

Richardson and Franklin, along with midshipmen GEORGE BACK and ROBERT HOOD, sailed from England to York Factory on the southwest shore of Hudson Bay. From there, they traveled northwestward by way of the Nelson and Saskatchewan Rivers, and, after wintering at the fur-trading post Cumberland House in present-day northern Saskatchewan, they reached the north shore of Great Slave Lake and established a base camp. On July 14, 1821, accompanied by VOYAGEURS working for the HUDSON'S BAY COMPANY, Franklin, Richardson, Hood, and Back set out for the Coppermine River, which they descended to the Arctic coast. They then explored eastward along Coronation Gulf as far as Turnagain Point on the Kent Peninsula. On the return trip across the Barren Grounds toward Great Slave Lake, the expedition suffered from a critical shortage of food, and Richardson shot to death a voyageur named Michel who had murdered Hood and resorted to cannibalism.

After a second winter on Great Slave Lake, Richardson returned to England with Franklin and Back in October 1822. They had covered more than 5,500 miles of Canadian territory. Richardson's natural history observations were subsequently incorporated into Franklin's official narrative of the 1819–22 expedition, including studies on the aurora borealis and the fish of the Canadian Arctic.

Richardson was appointed surgeon to a British marine unit in 1824, and the following year, he was named second in command in Franklin's second expedition to the Canadian Arctic. He traveled to Great Bear Lake with Franklin, again accompanied by George Back. After wintering there in 1825–26, they set out in small boats down the Mackenzie River on June 22, 1826, reaching its delta on July 4. They separated there, with Franklin exploring the Arctic coastline westward toward Point Barrow, Alaska, while Richardson and his party made their way eastward in two small boats. Richardson covered 2,000 miles in 10 weeks, reaching as far as the channel between Victoria Island and the mainland, west of Coronation Gulf, which he named Dolphin and Union Strait, after his contingent's two small boats.

Richardson returned to Franklin's base camp at Great Bear Lake on September 1, 1826. He then undertook a geological survey of the lake by CANOE. After another winter in the Canadian Arctic, he returned to England, by way of Cumberland House and New York, in September 1827.

Back in Edinburgh, Richardson wrote an account of his studies of the animal life he had observed in the Canadian Arctic, *Fauna Boreali-Americana*, published from 1829 to 1837. In 1847, after serving as an inspector of hospitals for the British navy, Richardson was appointed to lead the first search efforts for Franklin and his Northwest Passage expedition, which then had been missing in the Canadian Arctic for 18 months. Accompanied by JOHN RAE of the Hudson's Bay Company, he made another descent of the Mackenzie River, then searched for Franklin and his ships along Canada's Arctic coastline eastward, almost as far as the mouth of the Coppermine River. Their efforts were finally halted by impassable ice conditions in Dolphin and Union Strait. After wintering at Great Bear Lake, Richardson returned to England in 1849, while Rae continued the search.

Richardson retired from the British navy in 1855, after 48 years of service. He wrote an account of his 1847–48 expedition, *Arctic Searching Expedition, A Journal of a Boat Voyage Through Rupert's Land* (1851), which included his observations on the region's geology and native inhabitants. He also published *The Polar Regions* (1861). He was elected a member of the ROYAL SOCIETY in 1825 and knighted in 1846.

During his explorations, from the Mackenzie River's delta to the eastern end of Coronation Gulf, Sir John Richardson surveyed a wider area of North America's Arctic coastline than any explorer before him.

Riche, Claude-Antoine-Gaspard (1762–1797)
French physician, naturalist in Australia and the South Pacific

Claude Riche was born in the Beaujolais region of eastern France. While studying medicine, he also pursued an interest in botany and zoology.

In 1791, stricken with tuberculosis, Riche left his medical practice in Montpellier to join a French naval and scientific expedition to the South Pacific Ocean, hoping the long sea voyage might restore his health. He sailed from Brest on September 29, 1791, as a member of the scientific team aboard the *Espérance*, one of the two vessels in ANTOINE-RAYMOND-JOSEPH DE BRUNI, chevalier d'Entrecasteaux's expedition in search of JEAN-FRANÇOIS DE GALAUP, comte de La Pérouse.

In April 1792, Riche, along with the other scientists on the expedition, including JACQUES-JULIEN HOUTOU DE LA BILLARDIÈRE, collected specimens of plant and animal life in the islands that d'Entrecasteaux explored off the southeast coast of TASMANIA. In December 1792, Riche and La Billardière undertook an investigation inland from what came to be known as Esperance Bay on the south coast of present-day Western Australia. It was there that Riche became separated from his companions and was lost for two days before making his way back to La Billardière and the rest of the landing party. He reported that while lost, he had encountered three giant kangaroos. Riche also participated in explorations of the New Hebrides, Friendly, Admiralty, and Santa Cruz island groups.

In February 1794, Riche and the rest of the d'Entrecasteaux expedition were detained as enemies by Dutch authorities in Batavia (present-day Jakarta). The French Revolutionary Wars had erupted the previous year, and the Netherlands had sided with the royalist cause against France. Soon afterward, Riche was permitted to embark for Île de France, where he remained for some time before returning to France, which he finally reached in 1797. His health had deteriorated and, upon his return, he went to the Monts Doré region of central France seeking a cure. He died there in September 1797.

Claude Riche's poor health and early death precluded his preparing a report of his work in the South Pacific. Nonetheless, as a member of the scientific team with the d'Entrecasteaux expedition, he took part in one of the earliest zoological and botanical investigations inland into southwestern Australia and explored a portion of Tasmania that until then had not been visited by Europeans.

Richthofen, Ferdinand Paul Wilhelm von (baron von Richthofen) (1833–1905)
German geologist in China

Born in the southwestern German city of Karlsruhe, Ferdinand von Richthofen became a geologist. His early scientific investigations took him into the Dolomite Alps of northern Italy and the Transylvanian Alps of central Romania.

Richthofen first traveled in the Far East as a member of a Prussian diplomatic and trade mission in 1860–62. He later lived in California for a number of years, working as a geologist.

In 1868, Richthofen arrived in Shanghai, which became his base for a series of expeditions into a wide area of eastern, central, and southern China. That year, he traveled up the YANGTZE RIVER (Chang) to Hankow (part of present-day Wuhan), about 500 miles upstream from Shanghai, then returned downriver as far as Chengchou (Zhengzhou). From there, he headed northward into the Shan-tung (Shandong) Peninsula and continued on into Manchuria. After a visit to Peking (Beijing), he sailed down the Chinese coast back to Shanghai.

In 1869, Richthofen sailed from Shanghai to Canton (Guangzhou) on China's south coast, then set out on a south-to-north crossing of eastern China, as far north as Peking, a distance of more than 1,200 miles.

Back in Shanghai in 1870, Richthofen explored the region south of the Yangtze's mouth, then sailed northward into the Yellow Sea to Tientsin (Tianjin), from where he traveled overland to Peking. He also traveled through southern China's Szechwan (Sichuan) region and visited Shensi (Shaanxi) and Shansi (Shanxi) provinces in east-central China, while tracing the course of the Yangtze River.

Richthofen returned to Germany in 1872, where he wrote his great multivolume work on China. Known by the abbreviated title *China* and published, along with an accompanying *Atlas,* from 1875 to 1883, it included the first comprehensive, modern geographic, geological, and cultural profile of China, including a description of the region's mineral resources.

Baron Ferdinand von Richthofen went on to an academic career, which included professorships at universities in Bonn, Leipzig, and Berlin. In 1911, three more volumes of his work on China were published posthumously. Richthofen's explorations of eastern and southern China, taken together with MARIE-JOSEPH-FRANÇOIS GARNIER's earlier Mekong River explorations, helped give Europeans detailed knowledge of eastern Asia, from the Southeast Asian regions of Thailand and Vietnam as far northward as Manchuria. Richthofen's grandson was the famous World War I air ace, Baron Manfred von Richthofen, the "Red Baron."

Ride, Sally Kristen (1951–   ) *American astronaut, first American woman in space*

Sally Ride was born in Encino, California. She attended Westlake School for Girls in Los Angeles on a tennis scholarship. She enrolled in Swarthmore College in 1968 but dropped out to play professional tennis. She later attended Stanford University, earning a B.S. in physics and a B.A. in English in 1973 and a Ph.D. in physics in 1978. At the age of 27, she was accepted by the NATIONAL AERONAUTICS AND SPACE ADMINISTRATION (NASA) into the training program for ASTRONAUTS aboard the SPACE SHUTTLE. Her training included radio communications, navigation, working in zero gravity, parachute jumping, and water survival.

Ride served as mission control communications officer for the second and third flights of the space shuttle *Columbia* in November 1981 and in March 1982. On June 18, 1983, she became the first American woman in space on the shuttle *Challenger,* orbiting the Earth for six days. (The cosmonaut VALENTINA VLADIMIROVNA TERESHKOVA had become the first woman in space 20 years before in the VOSTOK PROGRAM of the Union of Soviet Socialist Republics.) Ride next served as a mission specialist, participating in SATELLITE launching and retrieval. She again traveled on *Challenger* on an eight-day mission in October 1984.

Ride later formed part of the presidential commission investigating the *Challenger* disaster of 1986 and also became involved in long-range planning of SPACE EXPLORATION. She left NASA in 1987 and has since been affiliated with Stanford University and the University of California at San Diego. She has dedicated herself to promoting science education, especially for girls because of a lack of women scientists and engineers. Some of her activities have been Internet-based. She has written a number of children's books about space.

As the first American woman to walk in space, Sally Ride has a special place in the history of space exploration.

Ritchie, Joseph (ca. 1788–1819) *British physician, writer in North Africa*

Joseph Ritchie was born at Otley in Yorkshire, England. The son of a local doctor, he entered the medical field himself, and, when in his early 20s, he began practicing as a hospital surgeon in York. Then, starting in 1813, he practiced at London's Lock Hospital.

While in London, Ritchie developed contacts among the literary and scientific community, which led to his meeting with the German naturalist and explorer ALEXANDER VON HUMBOLDT in Paris in 1817. Impressed by Ritchie's ability as an observer of natural phenomenon and his talent as a writer, Humboldt recommended him to the British government for its planned expedition to explore the upper NIGER RIVER region of West Africa.

Ritchie was instructed to penetrate the interior of West Africa from the north, with a crossing of the SAHARA DESERT from the Mediterranean coast at Tripoli, Libya. In September 1818, he arrived in Malta, where he was joined by British naval officer GEORGE FRANCIS LYON. They then traveled to Tripoli, where they remained for several months, during which they explored the mountains around nearby Gharyan.

On March 22, 1819, Ritchie and Lyon, disguised as Muslims, began their intended trans-Sahara trek, setting out from Tripoli for Murzuk south of the Fezzan region of southwestern Libya. Short on supplies and funds, their trip from Tripoli was fraught with difficulties, and, by the time they had reached Murzuk, Ritchie had become seriously ill. He died there on November 20, 1819, and, soon afterward,

Lyon was compelled to abandon the expedition and return to Tripoli.

While preparing for the expedition in London in 1817–18, Joseph Ritchie encountered the English Romantic poet John Keats, then 23 years old. Greatly impressed by Keats's recently published poem "Endymion," with its images alluding to the fabled MOUNTAINS OF THE MOON, Ritchie resolved to carry a copy of the work on the expedition and cast it symbolically into the sands of the Sahara. Ritchie was a poet in his own right, and just before he departed for Africa, he wrote a poem in Spenserian stanzas entitled "A Farewell to England." It was published posthumously in 1829. Ironically, Joseph Ritchie had been chosen to lead the expedition partly because of his abilities as a writer, yet he recorded no observations while en route, planning to rely on his memory afterward. Consequently, the history of the journey to Murzuk was written by Lyon, and when published in 1821, it proved to be one of the most popular narratives of African travel of that period.

Rivera y Villalón, Pedro de (ca. 1664–1744)

Spanish soldier, official in Mexico, New Mexico, and Texas

Pedro de Rivera was born in Antequera, Spain. Pursuing a career in the military, he served in the Netherlands in the late 1670s.

It is thought that Rivera had traveled to New Spain (Mexico) in the Americas by the 1690s, where he served as an engineer. He eventually reached the rank of colonel. In 1710, he was appointed governor of Tlaxcala but returned to Spain in 1714–15 to battle the French at Barcelona. Back in New Spain, he campaigned against pirates along the Yucatán Peninsula coast.

In 1724, Rivera was sent to inspect the northern defenses of New Spain. He traveled from the Gulf of California, then northward to Santa Fe in New Mexico and back southward, then east to the Gulf of Mexico in Texas, covering more than 8,000 miles until 1728. Rivera produced a written report of his inspection, and his assistant, Francisco Álvarez Barreiro (or Barreyto), drafted maps.

Rivera became governor of Veracruz in 1731 and then of Guatemala the next year. He retired in 1742 and moved to Mexico City.

Pedro de Rivera's expedition led to the most accurate maps of northern New Spain at that time. His report led to consolidation of the economy and increased defenses against Apache Indians.

Robertson, James (1742–1814) *American frontiersman, colonizer in North Carolina and Tennessee*

Born in Brunswick County, Virginia, James Robertson had, by 1768, moved with his family into North Carolina's Yadkin Valley. Two years later, in fall 1770, he traveled with a hunting expedition to the Holston and Watauga Rivers in northwestern North Carolina and present-day eastern Tennessee.

Robertson took his family from Wake County, North Carolina, to the Watauga region in spring 1771. Other settlers soon followed.

Robertson played a key role in securing the lease on the Watauga region from the Cherokee Indians. Moreover, at the outbreak of Lord Dunmore's War in 1774, his diplomatic efforts ensured Cherokee neutrality.

In February 1779, Robertson left Virginia in command of a small advance party sent by the Transylvania Company to explore and settle the Cumberland River Valley of what is now Tennessee. Soon after this group had planted a crop and laid out a town, the main party of 300 settlers began to arrive, traveling through the APPALACHIAN MOUNTAINS overland through the CUMBERLAND GAP, or by riverboat along the Tennessee River and Cumberland River route. In 1780, Robertson officially organized the settlement as Nashborough, which later became Nashville, the capital of Tennessee. In March of that year, with the colony facing starvation, Robertson undertook an overland trek through the wilderness to obtain supplies at DANIEL BOONE's settlement of Boonesborough, Kentucky.

In 1784, Robertson, with the North Carolinian William Blount, organized a settlement in western Tennessee on the Chickasaw Bluffs of the MISSISSIPPI RIVER, near what is now Memphis.

Throughout the 1780s and 1790s, Robertson was active in the North Carolina legislature. He was one of the organizers of the short-lived state of Franklin, after which he helped establish the state of Tennessee. He was briefly connected with a Spanish plan to annex Tennessee, but he ultimately remained loyal to the United States.

James Robertson's explorations west of the Appalachian Mountains accelerated the rate of non-Indian settlement beyond the mid-Atlantic seaboard in the years immediately before and after the American Revolution. He is known as the "Father of Tennessee."

Roberval, Jean-François de La Roque de (sieur de Roberval) (ca. 1500–1561)

French nobleman, colonizer in North America

Jean-François de La Roque de Roberval was a member of an aristocratic family of northern France's Picardy region, the son of a diplomat and a noblewoman. During the 1520s, he served as an officer with French forces in Italy, and later he was an official in the court of King Francis I of France.

In January 1541, Roberval received a commission from the king to command a colonizing expedition to Canada's St. Lawrence River region. His appointment superceded that of JACQUES CARTIER, who had explored the Gulf of St. Lawrence and the St. Lawrence River in his voyages of 1534 and 1535–36. Cartier remained as Roberval's second in command.

Roberval provided the financing for what was to be Cartier's third voyage to Canada, which sailed from France in spring 1541. Meanwhile, he remained in France for the next 11 months, raising additional funds through privateering raids on Portuguese and English ships in the English Channel. On April 16, 1542, Roberval sailed from La Rochelle to join Cartier, who had by then established a small settlement near what is now the city of Quebec.

On June 7, 1542, Roberval's three ships, the *Marye*, the *Sainte-Anne*, and the *Valletyne*, carrying more than 150 men and women colonists as well as a number of soldiers, arrived at St. John's Harbor on the southeast coast of Newfoundland, a place already known to European fishermen. Less than a week later, Roberval was joined by Cartier and his contingent of colonists, who, after suffering through a severe winter at the St. Lawrence River settlement, had decided to return to France. Cartier was also eager to reach France to learn if the mineral deposits he had discovered in Canada were diamonds and gold.

Despite Roberval's insistence that Cartier accompany him back to the St. Lawrence, Cartier, under cover of darkness, departed the Newfoundland anchorage and sailed for France. Roberval remained at St. John's Harbor for several more weeks, and then, resolving to carry on the colonizing effort on his own, sailed his fleet into the Gulf of St. Lawrence by way of the Strait of Belle Isle. He then ascended the St. Lawrence River to the site of Cartier's colony of Charlesbourg-Royal at the mouth of what is now the Jacques Cartier River. A better-fortified settlement was constructed on the site, which Roberval renamed France-Roy.

In September 1542, two of Roberval's ships returned to France to obtain additional provisions, as well as to find out if Cartier had indeed discovered mineral wealth, which he had not, the minerals brought back to Europe proving to be worthless mica and iron pyrites, the latter known as FOOL'S GOLD. During the next winter, 50 of the colonists died from SCURVY at France-Roy. In spring 1543, Roberval explored southwestward up the St. Lawrence in small boats, in search of a possible westward passage to the Pacific Ocean, as well as the fabled native kingdom SAGUENAY, which, according to what Cartier had learned from the Indians, was rich in gold and precious stones.

Roberval reached the Lachine Rapids near present-day Montreal, where he decided to turn back after losing a boat and eight crewmen. His chief pilot, Jean Alfonce, undertook a similar reconnaissance of the Saguenay River to the northeast, reaching almost as far as its junction with the Chicoutimi River.

By mid-summer 1543, Roberval decided to abandon his settlement, faced with the prospect of another harsh winter on the St. Lawrence and unable to locate either Saguenay or a passage to the Far East. He sailed with the surviving colonists on the one remaining vessel, arriving in France on September 11, 1543. (According to some accounts, Cartier returned to North America that year and picked up the colonists.)

Roberval continued his career as a courtier under Francis's successor, King Henry II, and engaged in several unsuccessful mining ventures. In 1561, he was killed in an outbreak of religious violence in Paris.

After Sieur de Roberval's 1542–43 expedition, France's efforts to explore and settle Canada were suspended for the next 60 years by the outbreak of religious and civil wars. The efforts were not resumed until the voyages of SAMUEL DE CHAMPLAIN in the early 1600s.

Robidoux, Antoine (Antoine Robidou)
(1794–1860) *American fur trader, interpreter in the southern Rocky Mountains*

Antoine Robidoux was born in St. Louis, Missouri, to a family of French-Canadian descent. In 1822, he was one of the first St. Louis traders to embark on the newly opened Santa Fe Trail. In 1824–25, he took part in a fur-trading expedition from Fort Atkinson, near present-day Omaha, to the Green River in what is now northern Utah.

Robidoux then took the FUR TRADE to New Mexico. In 1828, he married into a prominent New Mexico family and settled in Taos, where he became known as the "first fur trader out of Taos." Also in 1828, he established Fort Uncompahgre on the Gunnison River in what is now southwestern Colorado. In 1837, he opened Fort Uinta in northeastern Utah, a post that came to be known as the Robidoux Rendezvous.

Competition from Bent's Fort on the Arkansas River and Fort Laramie to the north, plus Ute Indian uprisings, drove Robidoux out of business by 1844. That year, JOHN CHARLES FRÉMONT and his expedition stopped at Fort Uinta.

After a short stay at St. Joseph, Missouri, which his brother Joseph Robidoux had founded in 1831, Antoine again ventured west in 1846, as an interpreter for General STEPHEN WATTS KEARNY's expedition across the Great Plains and ROCKY MOUNTAINS to New Mexico for engagement in the U.S.-Mexican War. After Kearny's conquest of Santa Fe, Robidoux continued westward into California with the American forces. He was severely wounded at the Battle of San Pascual in December 1846, and he soon retired to St. Joseph, Missouri. Eight years before his death in 1860, he was stricken with blindness.

Antoine Robidoux's five brothers (Joseph, François, Louis, Michel, and Isidore) joined him in trading ventures in the southern Rockies and southern plains. From 1832 to 1844, the Robidoux brothers dominated the trade between northern Utah and what is now southern Arizona, providing north-south supply routes for traders along both the eastern and western slopes of the Rocky Mountains.

Rodríguez, Cermeño   See CERMENHO, SEBASTIÁN MELÉNDEZ RODRÍGUEZ.

Roe, Sir Thomas (Sir Thomas Rowe)
(ca. 1581–1644) *English mariner in South America, traveler, diplomat in India*

Thomas Roe was born at Low Leyton in Essex, England, into a prominent London family, his grandfather having served as that city's lord mayor. After attending Oxford's Magdalen College, Roe studied law in London, and, in about 1601, he became an official in the court of Queen Elizabeth I. After her death in 1603, he gained prominence in service to her successor, King James I, from whom he received a knighthood in 1605.

Roe's closest friend at court was the king's son, Henry, Prince of Wales, through whose influence he gained support for a voyage of exploration to the northeast coast of South America in search of gold. With financial backing from SIR WALTER RALEIGH and the earl of Southampton, Roe sailed from Plymouth in command of two vessels on February 24, 1610.

After reaching the coast of the Guianas, Roe located the mouth of the AMAZON RIVER and sailed his ships 200 miles upriver. He then explored 100 miles farther upstream in small boats, investigating the surrounding Brazilian jungle for signs of gold before returning to the river's mouth. The next year, Roe examined the coastline northward as far as the ORINOCO RIVER delta. Traveling by CANOE, he explored inland along the region's numerous rivers that emptied into the sea, including the Oyapock on the present border between French Guiana and northeastern Brazil.

In July 1611, Roe returned to England without the hoped-for riches. He reportedly made two more voyages to the lower Amazon region the following year, and he may have established a small settlement there.

Soon after Prince Henry's death in 1612, Roe left the royal court to serve as a member of the House of Commons. In 1614, he returned to the king's service, as the royal ambassador to the court of the Mogul Empire in northern India.

Roe's appointment had been instigated by the BRITISH EAST INDIA COMPANY's desire to win from Mogul emperor Jahangir the trade concessions that were vital in an effort to compete effectively with the Portuguese, the chief commer-cial rivals of the English in India. Roe departed England with the British East India Company's fleet in February 1615, sailing aboard the *Lion*. After a voyage around the CAPE OF GOOD HOPE, with stops at the Comoro Islands in the INDIAN OCEAN and Socotra Island, south of the Arabian Peninsula, he arrived at Surat on India's western coast in September 1615. From there, he journeyed inland with a small diplomatic delegation, through Burghanpur and Mandu, and, on Christmas Eve 1615, he reached the Mogul capital, Ajmer.

Roe remained at Jahangir's court for a year. He presented the emperor with such gifts as an English-style coach and two virginals (early-17th-century piano-type instruments), and he traveled with the Mogul ruler on a tour of his domain in northeastern India. Prior British attempts to enter into a commercial treaty with Jahangir had been frustrated by the emperor's general disdain for businessmen and traders, but by demonstrating that the English king was of equal stature to the Mogul emperor, Roe eventually succeeded in obtaining for British merchants the same privileges enjoyed in India by other foreign merchants.

Roe's return route was by way of Persia (present-day Iran), where he discussed matters relating to the silk trade with government officials. He arrived back in England in September 1619. After another year in Parliament, he became British ambassador to the Ottoman Empire, a post he held until 1628. He was made a member of the Order of the Garter in 1636. In the course of his later diplomatic career, he represented England at peace conferences in Europe in connection with the Thirty Years' War.

Sir Thomas Roe was the first Englishman known to have explored the Amazon. In his better-known diplomatic mission to the Mogul emperor, he laid the foundation for Great Britain's subsequent commercial foothold in the Bombay region, which eventually led to British domination of all of India. His journal of his experiences in India was published in 1625 by Samuel Purchas as part of *Hakluytus Posthumas, or Purchas His Pilgrims*. The work introduced Englishmen to the great wealth of India's Moguls, relating how he had witnessed Jahangir receive his weight in gold and jewels as tribute from his subjects. Roe remained an ardent supporter of British voyages of exploration and used his influence to help LUKE FOXE mount his 1631 expedition in search of the NORTHWEST PASSAGE. When Foxe located the stretch of water separating Southampton Island from the northwest shore of HUDSON BAY, he named it Roe's Welcome Sound.

Roerich, Nikolay Konstantinovich (Nicholas Konstantin Roerich) (1874–1947)
Russian painter, writer in central Asia

Nikolay Roerich was born in St. Petersburg; his father, Konstantin Roerich, was a prominent attorney. Showing an early interest in art yet wanting to please his father with a career in law, he simultaneously attended the Academy of Art and St. Petersburg University. After finishing his university thesis, he traveled in Europe for a year, during which he visited museums in Berlin and Paris and began his career as a painter. On his return, he married Helena Blavatsky, a writer interested especially in spiritual themes.

Roerich and Blavatsky lived for a time in New York where they pursued their mutual interests and promoted a cross-fertilization of the arts and world religions. Roerich became secretary of a school associated with the Society for the Encouragement of Art and would later become its director, one of many such positions in the course of his life as a teacher and sponsor of the arts. In addition to working in painting and writing, he designed sets and costumes for theatrical productions. In 1923, the Nicholas Roerich Museum was founded in New York City in his honor.

Also in the 1920s, after the period of unrest during World War I and the Russian Revolution, Roerich and Blavatsky undertook a journey to India and central Asia, along with their son George Roerich, who spoke Chinese, Mongolian, Tibetan, and several Indian languages. They landed in Bombay at the end of 1923 and after meeting prominent scholars and artists, continued to the HIMALAYAS. They traveled in central Asia until 1928, visiting Chinese Turkestan, Altai, Mongolia, and Tibet. Afterward, the family made a home in the Kulu Valley of India's Himalayan foothills and founded the Urusvati Himalayan Research Institute for studies of natural science, archaeology, linguistics, and religion. Roerich wrote about the central Asian expedition in his book *Heart of Asia* and recorded scenes from it in about 500 paintings. Roerich lived in the Himalayas until his death.

Nikolay Roerich, among his many other accomplishments, furthered knowledge among Europeans of Asian culture and history. A central thesis of his work was the common cultural bond of the peoples with whom he came into contact, such as the Tibetans and nomadic people of the Russian steppes. Among Helena Roerich's works is *The Foundations of Buddhism*.

Rogers, Robert (1731–1795) *Colonial American army officer in New York and Great Lakes, seeker of the Northwest Passage*

Robert Rogers was born in Methuen, Massachusetts. As a young child, he moved with his family to the frontier region of New Hampshire, where he learned wilderness skills. While still in his teens, he served as a scout for British troops in King George's War of 1744–48.

Rogers went on to serve in the French and Indian War of 1754–63, reportedly as an alternative to imprisonment on counterfeiting charges. He led a unit of frontiersmen,

known as Rogers' Rangers, in raids against the French-allied Indians of Lake Champlain and the eastern St. Lawrence valley.

In November 1760, following the fall of Quebec and Montreal, Rogers, who had been promoted to major, was sent west to receive the surrender of the French trading posts at Detroit and Mackinac. In 1763, he took part in campaigns against the tribes of the Old Northwest in Pontiac's Rebellion, an uprising led by the Ottawa Indian of that name.

Rogers left Mackinac in 1765, amid charges of illegal trading activities. He went to London to clear his name, and while there wrote and published the book *A Concise Account of North America*. He also had a play produced, *Ponteach*, a sympathetic dramatic portrait of Pontiac.

By 1766, Rogers was back in Mackinac, after winning reappointment as a British administrator of the region's Indian trade. Based on reports by Indians and on old maps, he had long believed a water route, the much sought-after NORTHWEST PASSAGE, led to the Pacific coast from the western Great Lakes. That year, he dispatched JONATHAN CARVER and James Tute from Mackinac on explorations to Lake Superior and northern Minnesota, with instructions to expand the Mackinac trade to outlying Indian tribes and to investigate streams west and north of Lake Superior in hopes of locating the Northwest Passage. Yet, in 1768, Carver and Tute abandoned their search at Grand Portage on the north shore of Lake Superior, because Rogers failed to send the promised supplies.

Rogers was implicated in a Spanish plot to take over the British Great Lakes posts but was acquitted of any wrongdoing. He returned to England in 1769, where he was imprisoned for debt. At the outbreak of the American Revolution in 1775, he returned to America. He served briefly under George Washington but was soon arrested as a Loyalist spy. After escaping to the British, Rogers organized a unit known as the "Loyalist Rangers," but they played no significant role in the war.

Rogers left the United States for England in 1780, where he lived out his remaining years in obscurity.

The heroic exploits of Major Robert Rogers in the French and Indian War are legendary. Nevertheless, his nonmilitary career was checkered with accusations of dishonesty and malfeasance. In terms of exploration, Rogers kept alive the idea of the Northwest Passage in the years between the French and Indian War and the American Revolution. Ironically, the expedition he sponsored, undertaken by Carver and Tute in 1767–68, did reach Grand Portage, where 20 years later NORTH WEST COMPANY fur traders PETER POND and SIR ALEXANDER MACKENZIE would launch their explorations into the Canadian West and ultimately locate a river system that drained into the Pacific Ocean.

Roggeveen, Jakob (Jacob Roggeveen)

(1659–1729) *Dutch mariner in the South Pacific*

Born at Middelburg in the southwestern Netherlands, Jakob Roggeveen was the son of a wine merchant. Trained in theology and law, he also acquired a fair knowledge of navigation, cartography, and the natural sciences.

In 1706, after working as a lawyer in Middelburg for a number of years, Roggeveen sailed to the EAST INDIES (present-day Indonesia), where he had been appointed to a post with the Dutch colonial administration. After nine years, he returned to the Netherlands.

In 1721, the DUTCH WEST INDIA COMPANY appointed Roggeveen commander of an expedition to the South Pacific Ocean in search of Terra Australis, the theoretical GREAT SOUTHERN CONTINENT, which European geographers believed spanned a wide area of the Southern Hemisphere.

From Amsterdam, Roggeveen, in command of a fleet of three ships, sailed to the southern tip of South America and, after passing through Le Maire Strait, continued southward beyond CAPE HORN as far as 60° south latitude. He correctly surmised that the icebergs encountered in those waters indicated a large landmass to the south.

The onset of cold weather conditions compelled Roggeveen to turn back northward before he could investigate further. Sailing west of Cape Horn, he entered the Pacific Ocean along the coast of present-day Chile. After a brief exploration of the Juan Fernandez Islands, Roggeveen and his crew made the first European visit to an island on April 5, 1722, Easter Sunday. In honor of the occasion, he named it Easter Island.

In need of fresh provisions, Roggeveen then headed westward across the Pacific toward the Dutch colonies in the EAST INDIES. Along the way, he made the European discovery of the islands of Samoa and stopped at New Britain.

After sailing along the north coast of New Guinea, Roggeveen arrived at the Dutch port of Batavia (present-day Jakarta, Indonesia). There, his ships were confiscated by officials of the DUTCH EAST INDIA COMPANY, because as an employee of the Dutch West India Company, he was considered to be trespassing in the other company's commercial domain. He was arrested but soon released and sent back to the Netherlands by way of the Cape of Good Hope, thus completing a CIRCUMNAVIGATION OF THE WORLD. He spent his remaining years in his hometown of Middelburg.

Jakob Roggeveen was the first European to report on the giant stone monuments and inscriptions on Easter Island, the origins of which still pose one of the best-known archaeological riddles. His voyage in search of Terra Australis, one of the last major explorations of the South Pacific undertaken by the Dutch, revealed that the missing Southern Continent, if it existed, had to lie even farther south than the cartographers and geographers of his day supposed.

Roggeveen is also credited with the European discovery of Samoa.

Rohlfs, Friedrich Gerhard (1831–1896)

German-born French Foreign Legionnaire in North Africa

Gerhard Rohlfs was born in the German town of Vegesack, near Bremen. He studied medicine at Heidelberg, Würzburg, and Göttingen universities, then briefly served with the Austrian army.

Rohlfs's career as an explorer of West and North Africa began in 1855, when he enlisted in the French Foreign Legion as an assistant pharmacist and took part in French efforts to subdue the Berber tribes of the Great Kabylia region in what is now central Algeria. Over the next several years, while with the Legion in Algeria and Morocco, he became fluent in Arabic and familiar with the teachings of Islam and the culture of the native peoples of the northern SAHARA DESERT.

Rohlfs remained in North Africa after his discharge from the Foreign Legion in 1861. He was appointed physician general for the army of the sultan of Morocco and chief of sanitation for the sultan's harem.

In July 1862, Rohlfs, disguised as a Muslim doctor, set out from Tangier in an attempt to travel southward across the Sahara to TIMBUKTU. From Meknes, he made his way through central Morocco's Atlas Mountains to the Tafilet Oasis, the first European to reach it since RENÉ-AUGUSTE CAILLIÉ, nearly 40 years earlier. Wounded in an attack by bedouin tribesmen, Rohlfs was compelled to turn back, eventually reaching Rabat on the Moroccan coast.

About a year later, Rohlfs undertook a second journey into the Sahara, starting out from Agadir, Morocco. He made his way across the mountains and desert to central Algeria's Touat Oasis, becoming the first European to reach it. From there, he continued eastward to the caravan trade center in In-Salah, then turned northeastward into present-day Libya, stopping at Ghadames before arriving at Tripoli.

In his next expedition, Rohlfs departed Tripoli in 1865, and, after traveling to Murzuk in southern Libya, he crossed the Sahara Desert to Lake Chad and the Bornu Kingdom of what is now northern Nigeria. He examined Lake Chad for a possible connection with the NIGER RIVER, then traveled down the Benue River to its junction with the Niger, which he descended to its outlet in the Gulf of Guinea.

In 1867–68, Rohlfs explored the Abyssinian Highlands of Ethiopia. In 1874, he returned to Tripoli to begin a series of expeditions, at times accompanied by GEORG AUGUST SCHWEINFURTH. He explored eastward toward Alexandria, Egypt, visiting the Siwa Oasis in northwestern Egypt as well as the little-known Kufra Oasis in southeastern Libya, which he reached in 1878. Later that year, Rohlfs led a German government-sponsored expedition into the Wadai region of what is now southeastern Chad.

Rohlfs was back in Ethiopia in 1880–81, where he explored from Massawa on the RED SEA coast inland to the upper reaches of the Blue Nile River. In 1885, he began a brief term as German consul at Zanzibar on the Indian Ocean coast of central Africa. He later retired to Godesberg, Germany.

Gerhard Rohlfs was the first European to complete a north-to-south crossing of the entire bulge of West Africa, from the Mediterranean coast to the Gulf of Guinea. Great Britain's ROYAL GEOGRAPHICAL SOCIETY, in recognition of this accomplishment, awarded him its Patron's Medal in 1868. In the course of his 30 years in Africa, Rohlfs spent more than 16 years engaged in exploration. He covered a vast area of the continent, ranging from Tangier and Tripoli southward to Lagos on the Gulf of Guinea, and from the Niger River eastward to the upper reaches of the Blue Nile in Ethiopia.

Rose, Edward (Nez Coupé, Cut Nose, Five Scalps) (ca. 1775–ca. 1832) *American interpreter, guide in the northern Rocky Mountains*

Details of Edward Rose's life before 1807 are sketchy. He was the son of a non-Indian trader to the Cherokee Indians, and his mother was part African American and part Cherokee. He may have spent some years as a river pirate with Jean Lafitte on the MISSISSIPPI RIVER between southern Illinois and New Orleans.

In 1807, Rose was an interpreter for MANUEL LISA's fur-trading expedition to the Bighorn River region of present-day Montana. While there, he settled among the Crow Indians and became a chief. By that time, Rose was known by the Indians as Nez Coupé or Cut Nose, because a piece of his nose had been bitten off in a brawl. Later in his career, he would be known as Five Scalps, after a reported fight in which he killed five Blackfeet warriors. Two years later, in 1809, Rose was an interpreter for Lisa and his partner ANDREW HENRY in their dealings with the Arikara Indians at their Knife River post in what is now North Dakota.

In 1810, Rose traveled to the Three Forks of the Missouri with Andrew Henry, ANTOINE PIERRE MENARD, JOHN COLTER, and GEORGE DROUILLARD, then explored the Madison River in southeastern Montana and Henrys Fork of the Snake River in eastern Idaho. In 1811, Rose served as an interpreter and guide for WILSON PRICE HUNT and his party of Astorians, heading for Oregon. He was discharged in Crow territory on suspicion of leading the group into an ambush. During the War of 1812, Rose is believed to have assisted Manuel Lisa in keeping the upper Missouri tribes from siding with the British.

In 1823, Rose was an interpreter and negotiator for WILLIAM HENRY ASHLEY's fur-trading expedition to the Arikara and worked with other MOUNTAIN MEN. After warfare erupted between non-Indians and the Arikara, Rose acted as a negotiator on behalf of Colonel HENRY LEAVENWORTH in his punitive military expedition. Rose then joined JEDEDIAH STRONG SMITH in an expedition from Fort Kiowa in present-day South Dakota, overland through the Badlands and Black Hills to the northern ROCKY MOUNTAINS.

In 1825, Rose joined General HENRY ATKINSON's Yellowstone Expedition at Council Bluffs on the Missouri and served as a guide and Indian diplomat to the Crow. Rose is believed to have been killed in an attack by Arikara while hunting with HUGH GLASS on the Yellowstone River, below the mouth of the Bighorn River, during the winter of 1832–33.

Edward Rose's career in the northern plains and Rockies spans the entire period of the early upper Missouri FUR TRADE. His exploits have been confused with those of another part-African mountain man, JAMES PIERSON BECKWOURTH. It is probable that Beckwourth claimed Rose's adventures as his own in a written account of his life.

Ross, Alexander (1783–1856) *Scottish-Canadian fur trader in Pacific Northwest and Montana*

Alexander Ross was a native of Nairnshire, Scotland. When he was about 20 years old, he immigrated to present-day Ontario, Canada, where he worked as a schoolteacher until 1810. That year, he met with WILSON PRICE HUNT in Montreal and soon joined JOHN JACOB ASTOR's fur-trading venture to the Pacific Northwest.

In September 1810, Ross embarked on the *Tonquin* from New York, and sailed around CAPE HORN, to the Oregon Coast. He was one of the founders of the Astoria outpost for Astor's Pacific Fur Company, a subsidiary of the AMERICAN FUR COMPANY, and the first permanent non-Indian settlement in Oregon.

Ross remained at the Astoria post after 1813, when it was purchased by the NORTH WEST COMPANY and renamed Fort George. In 1818, he undertook a trade expedition from the mouth of the COLUMBIA RIVER as far as its confluence with the Snake River. Nearby, he founded Fort Nez Perces, later known as Fort Walla Walla.

In 1823, following the takeover of the North West Company by the HUDSON'S BAY COMPANY, Ross assumed command of the latter company's post at Flathead Lake in what is now western Montana. In February 1824, he led an expedition from the Flathead Lake post into the Snake River country of western Idaho, exploring southward as far as the mouth of the Boise River. Along the way, a group of his Iroquois (Haudenosaunee) trappers were rescued from local Indians by American mountain man and fur trader JEDEDIAH STRONG SMITH. Ross then allowed Smith and his companions to explore the exclusive Hudson's Bay Company trapping grounds in the Oregon Country, a decision that alarmed the company's directors and led to Ross being replaced at Flathead Lake by PETER SKENE OGDEN.

From Flathead Lake, Montana, Ross headed eastward with his Okanagan Indian wife in 1825. He settled at the Red River Colony, near present-day Winnipeg, Manitoba, where, during the next three decades, he played a significant role in the settlement's administration.

Alexander Ross, in the course of his career in the FUR TRADE, explored uncharted territory eastward from the Pacific coast into what is now Idaho, Washington, and Montana. His books, *Adventures of the First Settlers on the Oregon or Columbia River* (1849) and *The Fur Hunters of the Far West* (1853), provide some of the earliest accounts of the first decade and a half of non-Indian settlement in the Pacific Northwest.

Ross, Sir James Clark (1800–1862) *British naval officer in the Canadian Arctic and Antarctic, nephew of Sir John Ross*

Born in London, James Clark Ross was of Scottish descent. At the age of 12, he entered the navy, serving on ships commanded by his uncle SIR JOHN ROSS for the next six years.

In 1818, Ross sailed as a midshipman on the *Isabella* in the elder Ross's expedition to Baffin Bay and Lancaster Sound, undertaken as part of the British navy's newly revived effort to find the NORTHWEST PASSAGE. The next year, he took part in SIR WILLIAM EDWARD PARRY's voyage through Lancaster Sound to Melville Island, and, while wintering there with the expedition, learned survival skills essential to polar exploration.

Ross again accompanied Parry on an 1821–23 exploration of northwestern HUDSON BAY, and, in 1824–25, he took part in Parry's voyage to Lancaster Sound and Prince Regent Inlet, during which he was promoted to lieutenant. In 1827, Ross joined Parry in his unsuccessful attempt to reach the NORTH POLE from Spitsbergen (present-day Svalbard).

Promoted to commander on his return, Ross took a leave from the navy in 1829 to serve as second in command in his uncle John's privately funded Northwest Passage expedition to the Canadian Arctic. While their vessel, the *Victory,* was icebound on the east shore of the Boothia Peninsula, he undertook a series of overland explorations. In spring 1830, he crossed to the west coast of the Boothia Peninsula and reached what he thought was a northward extension of the mainland. He named it King William Land, not realizing that it was actually an island separated from the Boothia Peninsula by a frozen strait. On May 31, 1831, in

Sir James Clark Ross *(Library of Congress)*

the course of another overland expedition, Ross located the NORTH MAGNETIC POLE, then situated at 70°5'17" north latitude and 96°46' west longitude on the west coast of the Boothia Peninsula.

Soon after his return to England in 1833, Ross was promoted to the rank of captain, and, in 1835–38, he conducted an extensive study of terrestrial magnetism throughout the British Isles.

Ross was next given command of a British navy expedition to seek the SOUTH MAGNETIC POLE and explore the seas around Antarctica. In command of the *Erebus,* and accompanied by the *Terror* under FRANCIS RAWDON MOIRA CROZIER, Ross sailed from England in September 1839. The next year, he established a series of magnetic observatories in the Southern Hemisphere on St. Helena Island in the South Atlantic Ocean; at Cape Town, South Africa; in the Kerguelen Islands of the southern Indian Ocean; and in Hobart, Tasmania.

After several months in Hobart, where he was hosted by SIR JOHN FRANKLIN, then Tasmania's governor, and his wife Lady JANE FRANKLIN, Ross and his expedition set out for Antarctica. He sailed due south along the INTERNATIONAL DATE LINE, planning to explore east of those portions of the Antarctic coast already sighted the previous year in the American expedition of CHARLES WILKES and the

French expedition of JULES-SÉBASTIEN-CÉSAR DUMONT D'URVILLE.

On January 1, 1841, Ross and his ships crossed the ANTARCTIC CIRCLE. After forcing a passage through the PACK ICE, they sailed another 500 miles across ice-free seas to the Antarctic mainland at Cape Adare. He then entered what later became known as the Ross Sea, and, on January 11, 1841, he sighted a mountain range on a section of uncharted coastline. He called this Victoria Land in honor of Queen Victoria, and named the mountains the Prince Albert Range after her consort. A landing party sent ashore took possession of the region for Great Britain. An active volcano was soon sighted on the coast, which Ross named Mount Erebus after his ship. He named a nearby, dormant volcanic peak Mount Terror after the expedition's other vessel. A large bay explored in the vicinity was named after Archibald McMurdo, an officer on the *Terror,* and was known afterward as McMurdo Sound.

Ross soon found his efforts to continue southward toward the SOUTH POLE blocked by an immense floating mass of ice, several hundred feet high, extending along the shoreline for more than a thousand miles. Known afterward as the Ross Ice Shelf, it was later determined to cover an area roughly the size of France. Although his southward progress was blocked, Ross nonetheless reached 78°4' south latitude, breaking the record set by navigator JAMES WEDDELL in 1822–23.

After making oceanographic studies in the Ross Sea for the ROYAL SOCIETY, as well as a study of offshore plant, animal, and marine life, Ross and his expedition sailed for Tasmania and Port Jackson (Sydney), Australia, to spend the Antarctic winter.

Ross made his second probe into the Antarctic seas in December 1841. On returning to the Ross Sea, he succeeded in bettering his previous farthest-south record by an additional 11 seconds of latitude. Soon afterward, in early February 1842, his ships were damaged in a collision in the Ross Sea while trying to avoid icebergs. Ross then made for the Falkland Islands for repairs.

In December 1842, after brief explorations of Tierra del Fuego and Hermite Island just west of CAPE HORN, Ross again sailed southward to the Antarctic mainland. This time, he explored along the Antarctic Peninsula (Graham Land), surveying its uncharted Weddell Sea coast, along which he located the island group that now bears his name.

Ross arrived back in England in September 1843 and was knighted soon afterward. Although offered the command of yet another attempt on the Northwest Passage, he resolved to undertake no more long voyages. Sir John Franklin, who had been given command of the expedition in his place, subsequently disappeared in the Canadian Arctic in 1845 with the *Erebus* and the *Terror,* the latter still

commanded by Crozier, along with the expedition's entire complement of 127 officers and men.

In 1848–49, Ross commanded the *Enterprise* and the *Investigator* in the British navy's first seaward search effort for Franklin. Ross managed to navigate through Lancaster Sound as far as Barrow Strait to Somerset Island, wintering on its north shore. Overland expeditions were undertaken to find some trace of Franklin, including one in which Ross, accompanied by SIR FRANCIS LEOPOLD McCLINTOCK, traveled down Peel Sound and reached within 70 miles of where Franklin's ships had become icebound on King William Island. Short of supplies, Ross and McClintock were compelled to return to the ships at the Somerset Island anchorage, without realizing how close they had come to solving the mystery of Franklin's disappearance. Ironically, it may have been Ross's error 18 years earlier, when he had incorrectly charted King William Island as joined to the mainland, that led Franklin to head away from the only navigable strait along that segment of the Northwest Passage, thus dooming his expedition.

After his return to England in 1849, Ross ended his career at sea. Made a rear admiral in 1856, he retired to his home at Aylesbury, near London.

Sir James Clark Ross commanded the first British scientific expedition to Antarctica since the voyages of JAMES COOK in the late 1770s. His two-volume account of the expedition, *A Voyage of Discovery and Research in the Southern and Antarctic Regions During the Years 1839 to 1843,* was published in 1847. In addition to charting the Ross Sea and the Ross Ice Shelf, he also determined that the South Magnetic Pole lay inland from the Antarctic coast. His explorations along the Antarctic mainland ultimately revealed that the geographic South Pole was surrounded by a large landmass. During the first decades of the 20th century, the Ross Sea and the adjoining Ross Ice Shelf, which extend deeper into the continent than any other part of the Antarctic coast, provided an entry way into the continent for the South Polar attempts of ROBERT FALCON SCOTT, ERNEST HENRY SHACKLETON, and ROALD ENGELBREGT GRAVNING AMUNDSEN.

Ross, Sir John (1777–1856) *Scottish-born British naval officer in the Canadian Arctic, uncle of Sir James Clark Ross*

Born near Wigtown, on the southwest coast of Scotland, John Ross entered the British navy when he was only nine years old. He served on British warships in the MEDITERRANEAN SEA and on merchant vessels in the WEST INDIES and the Baltic Sea. In 1799, after several years with the BRITISH EAST INDIA COMPANY, he returned to the navy to serve in the Napoleonic Wars of 1803–15, reaching the rank of commander by 1812.

In 1818, Ross was given command of the navy's effort to explore west of GREENLAND in search of the NORTHWEST PASSAGE. He sailed on the *Isabella,* along with his nephew SIR JAMES CLARK ROSS, then a midshipman. Second in command of the expedition was SIR WILLIAM EDWARD PARRY aboard the *Alexander.*

Ross and his ships rounded the southern tip of Greenland and sailed up Davis Strait into Baffin Bay. In his initial explorations along the west coast of Greenland, he made the European discovery of Melville Bay, where he encountered a theretofore unknown band of Inuit, whom he dubbed the "Arctic Highlanders." He also reported finding meteorites at Cape York. From there, he surveyed the entrances to Smith Sound and Jones Sound, determining that neither one provided a western entrance to a Northwest Passage.

Ross next explored Lancaster Sound, and, after navigating through it for about 50 miles, sighted what he took to be a chain of mountains blocking progress westward, which he named the Croker Mountains. Although a number of his officers, most notably Parry, reported seeing nothing ahead but open water, Ross nonetheless turned back to England, where he informed British naval authorities that all three of the channels he had explored, including Lancaster Sound, were closed-end bays, affording no western outlet from Baffin Bay. A year later, Parry sailed back to Lancaster Sound and navigated westward as far as Melville Island, exploring the islands and channels of the Canadian Arctic and reaching a point that was at least half-way through the Northwest Passage.

Ross's professional reputation suffered after news of Parry's success reached England. As a result, despite his proposal to lead another Arctic expedition, he was offered no new commands. In 1828, however, Felix Booth, a gin distiller who also held the position of sheriff of the City of London, provided Ross with the financial backing to undertake a second Arctic expedition.

In spring 1829, Ross left England for the Canadian Arctic aboard the *Victory,* a paddle-wheel steamer that had formerly served as an English Channel ferry, now rigged with sails and equipped for Arctic navigation. Second in command was his nephew James Clark Ross, who had been promoted to commander after taking part in a series of Arctic explorations with Parry during the 1820s. The elder Ross planned to investigate Prince Regent Inlet, the channel leading southward from Lancaster Sound, which Parry had explored in 1824–25.

After passing through Lancaster Sound, Ross entered Prince Regent Inlet and managed to reach a point 200 miles beyond where Parry's ship, the *Fury,* had been wrecked five years earlier. By October 1829, the *Victory* had become icebound, and the expedition spent the winter aboard the ship at an anchorage Ross called Felix Harbor in honor of his backer. Overland expeditions were undertaken under the command of the younger Ross.

From the reports of the exploring parties and from local Inuit, John Ross determined that they were on the mainland of North America, a region he named the Boothia Peninsula, also in honor of the London gin maker. On an overland expedition in spring 1831, James Clark Ross located the NORTH MAGNETIC POLE.

In 1832, John Ross, concluding that the *Victory* was inextricably entrapped in the ice at Felix Harbor, resolved to abandon the ship and travel northward with his men in sledges and boats to Lancaster Sound, in the hope that they would be picked up there by a passing whaling ship. Unable to progress beyond what remained of the *Fury,* Ross and his men spent the winter of 1832–33 in a shelter made from the wreckage, which Ross called Somerset House. They survived fairly well through the winter, eating the canned and preserved food that had been left on Parry's ship.

In the spring, Ross and his men reached Lancaster Sound, where, on August 26, 1833, they were rescued. The ship that picked them up turned out to be the *Isabella,* the same vessel on which Ross had made his first voyage to Lancaster Sound 15 years before.

Back in England, Ross, who was thought to have perished with his expedition, quickly redeemed himself as one of Great Britain's leading Arctic explorers. He was honored with a knighthood in 1834 for having survived four consecutive Arctic winters and for having brought his men through the ordeal with few losses. In addition, he had made the first European sighting of the Boothia Peninsula, which he determined to be the northernmost point of the North American mainland. The British Parliament awarded Ross and his men £5,000 for having made significant gains in revealing the geography of the Canadian Arctic and the eastern segment of the Northwest Passage. Moreover, the government reimbursed Felix Booth for the costs of mounting his private Arctic expedition.

Ross became a diplomat afterward, serving from 1839 to 1846 as British consul at Stockholm. In 1847, although then entering his seventies, Ross sought to lead a British navy search effort for SIR JOHN FRANKLIN and his expedition, which had been missing in the Canadian Arctic for two years. Although he was turned down by the navy, Ross again won the support of Sir Felix Booth (who had also been knighted for his contribution to British Arctic exploration). Booth provided Ross with the schooner *Felix,* on which Ross wintered at Barrow Strait in 1850–51. Finding no trace of Franklin's expedition, Ross returned to England. He retired to his home, North West Castle, on southern Scotland's Loch Ryan.

Sir John Ross, with his controversial 1818 voyage to Baffin Bay and Lancaster Sound, initiated modern exploration of the Canadian Arctic. In addition, he reaffirmed the findings made by WILLIAM BAFFIN and ROBERT BYLOT in their 1616 voyage, which, after two centuries, had remained largely forgotten. Ross's 1829–33 expedition was the first to employ steam power in polar exploration, even though the *Victory*'s engine proved unreliable and was abandoned in Prince Regent Inlet before the end of the first winter. His landing on the Boothia Peninsula in 1829 marked the first time the North American mainland had been approached from the north. Ross's 1829–33 expedition also indirectly led to the European discovery of one of northern Canada's longest rivers—the Back River—by British naval officer SIR GEORGE BACK, after he had participated in an overland search for Ross in 1833–34.

Rossel, Elisabeth-Paul-Edouard de (chevalier de Rossel) (1765–1829) *French naval officer in the South Pacific*

Elisabeth-Paul-Edouard de Rossel was born in the north-central French town of Sens. He joined the French navy's Marine Guard in 1780 and, after serving in the Caribbean Sea, took part in French efforts in the American Revolution, including the Battle of Yorktown in October 1781.

In 1785, Rossel served with ANTOINE-RAYMOND-JOSEPH DE BRUNI, chevalier d'Entrecasteaux, in the Indian Ocean, becoming his protégé. Promoted to lieutenant in 1789, he went on to sail aboard the *Récherche* as third in command under d'Entrecasteaux in the 1791–94 search for JEAN-FRANÇOIS DE GALAUP, comte de La Pérouse, whose expedition had vanished in the southwestern Pacific Ocean several years earlier.

On the 1791–94 voyage, Rossel made astronomical observations and conducted studies of terrestrial magnetism. In August 1793, while the expedition was off the eastern end of New Guinea, he briefly assumed leadership of the expedition when ALEXANDRE HESMIVY D'AURIBEAU, d'Entrecasteaux's successor, became too ill with SCURVY to carry on his command.

In 1795, Rossel sailed from Surabaja, Java, for France aboard a Dutch vessel. By that time, the expedition had been abandoned, and as a result of the outbreak of the French Revolutionary Wars two years earlier, the ships had been confiscated by pro-royalist Dutch authorities in the EAST INDIES. On the homeward voyage, Rossel's ship was captured by British naval forces, and he was held prisoner in England until 1802, when the Peace of Amiens temporarily ended hostilities. Rossel's account of d'Entrecasteaux's explorations in search of La Pérouse, *Voyage d'Entrecasteaux envoyé à la recherche de La Pérouse* (Journey of d'Entrecasteaux, sent to search for La Pérouse), was published in 1808.

Rossel went on to a distinguished scientific and naval career. After serving as director general of the French navy's department of maps and charts, he reached the rank of rear admiral in 1828. He took part in the planning of JULES-SÉBASTIEN-CÉSAR DUMONT D'URVILLE's expedition of 1826–29, in the course of which the wreckage of one of La Pérouse's ships was finally located. Rossel had been named

to the French Academy of Sciences in 1812, and in 1821, he was founding member of the Geographical Society of Paris.

Rossel Island, one of the islands of the Louisiade Archipelago, which d'Entrecasteaux discovered off the eastern end of New Guinea, was named in honor of the chevalier de Rossel. Captured along with Rossel in 1795 were maps he was carrying of the Australian coastline, which had been prepared by d'Entrecasteaux's hydrographer, CHARLES-FRANÇOIS BEAUTEMPS-BEAUPRÉ. Copies of these French charts were later provided to Captain MATTHEW FLINDERS for his explorations around Australia on the *Investigator* in 1801–03.

Rubrouck, William of   See WILLIAM OF RUBROUCK.

Rumi, Shihab al-Din Abu Abd Allah Yaqut al-
See YAQUT AL-RUMI, SHIHAB AL-DIN ABU ABD ALLAH.

Russell, Osborne (ca. 1814–1892) *American fur trapper in the northern Rocky Mountains and Oregon*

Osborne Russell was born in southern Maine. Little is known of his family background or early life. At the age of 16, he briefly went to sea, then embarked on a career in the FUR TRADE in the frontier regions of present-day Wisconsin and Minnesota.

In 1834, Russell accompanied NATHANIEL JARVIS WYETH and his fur-trading expedition to the Snake River region of what is now southern Idaho, where he took part in the establishment of Fort Hall. Over the next year, he trapped and hunted in the Cache Valley, the Teton Mountains, and the Jackson Hole region of present-day western Wyoming. Soon afterward, Russell joined up with CHRISTOPHER HOUSTON CARSON (Kit Carson), JAMES BRIDGER, and JOSEPH MEEK in trapping forays into the northern ROCKY MOUNTAINS, during which he survived attacks by Blackfeet and Crow Indian war parties.

In 1842, Russell traveled to the Oregon Country with an emigrant wagon train, settling in the upper Willamette Valley. He taught himself law while recovering from an eye injury, and, in 1843, he was appointed to a judgeship by Oregon's provisional government. In 1848, soon after his election to the territorial legislature, he left Oregon for the California goldfields.

After trying his hand at prospecting, Russell operated a general store in Placerville, California, where he also served as a frontier judge. His later business enterprises included a shipping line between Sacramento, California, and Portland, Oregon.

Russell's fortunes sharply declined after a business partner suddenly took off with most of his firm's assets, leaving him seriously in debt for his remaining years in Placerville.

Osborne Russell was one of the few MOUNTAIN MEN known to have kept a written account of his experiences in the Rocky Mountain fur trade. Although he had submitted his journal to a New York City publisher in 1846, it was not printed until 68 years later. His *Journal of a Trapper: or, Nine Years in the Rocky Mountains, 1834–1843,* published in 1914, provides an eyewitness account of the northern Rockies frontier in the decade between the initial exploration of the region and the advent of non-Indian settlement.

Rusta, Abu Ali Ahmad ibn   See IBN RUSTA, ABU ALI AHMAD.

Rut, John   (fl. 1520s) *English mariner in Newfoundland*

John Rut, an English mariner, was given command of an expedition to the Americas in search of a NORTHWEST PASSAGE to the Orient, sailing for King Henry VIII.

In 1527, Rut departed England with two ships, the *Mary Guildford* and the *Samson,* and crossed the Atlantic Ocean to a point off the Labrador coast near the Strait of Belle Isle, which separates Newfoundland from the mainland. He proceeded to the Avalon Peninsula on Newfoundland's east coast and anchored in the harbor opposite present-day St. John's. From there, he sailed southward to Santo Domingo on Hispaniola (the island made up of present-day Haiti and the Dominican Republic) in the WEST INDIES.

John Rut's visit, 30 years after that of JOHN CABOT to the Newfoundland region, held historical importance in that he wrote a letter to King Henry, describing the fishing activity around the island. He reported seeing 14 fishing ships—11 Norman, one Breton, and two Portuguese—in the "Haven of St. John" in the month of August. St. John's, frequented by fishermen from many nations in the 16th century, became a thriving settlement and is represented as "St. Jehan" and "San Joham" on maps of the 1540s.

S

Saavedra Cerón, Álvaro de (unknown–1529)
Spanish mariner in the South Pacific

Born in Spain, Álvaro de Saavedra was a cousin of HERNÁN CORTÉS, serving under him in the conquest of Mexico in 1519–21 and afterward as lieutenant governor of Veracruz.

In 1526, Cortés commissioned Saavedra to undertake a voyage from Mexico, westward across the Pacific Ocean, to rescue the survivors of a previous Spanish expedition stranded in the SPICE ISLANDS (the Moluccas of present-day Indonesia). Three ships were constructed for the expedition—*Santiago, Espíritu Santo,* and *Florida*—and, on October 31, 1527, Saavedra and his fleet sailed from Zihuatanejo on Mexico's Pacific coast, just north of Acapulco.

After a month at sea, two of the vessels were lost in a storm, leaving Saavedra with only his flagship, the *Florida.* On December 29, Guam was sighted. By the end of January, after a stopover on the north coast of New Guinea, he reached the Philippines. He landed on Mindanao on February 2, 1528, where he ransomed some of the crew of the previous Spanish expedition held by natives. He then headed southward for Halmahera and Tidore in the Moluccas.

After picking up more survivors on Tidore and obtaining a valuable cargo of cloves, Saavedra set sail back to Mexico. Although he went northward as far as 14° north latitude, he was forced to return to Tidore on failing to find the westerly winds necessary for an eastward passage across the Pacific. In a second attempt, he sailed even farther to the north, reaching as far as 31° north latitude, making the European discovery of Ponape Island in the Carolines as well as Eniwetok in the Marshalls.

Soon afterward, Saavedra died at sea. The *Florida* returned to the Moluccas in early December 1529, once again unable to locate winds favorable for the homeward voyage. The surviving crew members were taken into custody by Portuguese authorities on Halmahera and held until 1533.

Álvaro de Saavedra was among the first Europeans to sail westward across the Pacific Ocean since the 1519–21 voyage of FERDINAND MAGELLAN. It was not until 1565 that Spanish navigator ANDRÉS DE URDANETA finally succeed in making the first known eastward voyage across the Pacific, sailing from the Philippines to the west coast of Mexico.

Saavedra, Hernandarias   See ARIAS DE SAAVEDRA, HERNANDO.

Sable, Jean Baptist Point (Jean-Baptiste Point du Sable, Jean-Baptiste Pointe du Sable)
(ca. 1745–1818) *Haitian-French fur trader, trapper in the American Midwest, founder of Chicago*

Jean Baptist Point Sable is thought to have been born in Saint Marc in the French colony of Saint Domingue (present-day Haiti), his father a French sailor and his mother a slave of African ancestry. He was raised Catholic.

Many stories of Sable's early life are not confirmed. He may have studied in Paris. He was reportedly shipwrecked off the coast of Louisiana with a friend, Jacques Clemorgan, and after the two were rescued by a passing ship, they were taken to New Orleans, where Sable stayed and worked for French priests. After saving enough money to buy a CANOE and supplies, he possibly traveled up the MISSISSIPPI RIVER to the western Great Lakes. Other accounts indicate Sable reached the Great Lakes by way of French Canada.

Sable came into contact with the Potawatomi Indians, at that time living along the west coast of Lake Michigan. He gained the tribe's permission to hunt and trap on the Eschikagou Plain surrounding present-day Chicago and built his first home in the region, south of Chicago on the Illinois River.

In 1779, during the American Revolution, Sable appears in an official record, a British officer in the Great Lakes region reporting that he was active in the FUR TRADE with sympathies for the French. He was arrested in present-day Indiana and his goods confiscated. He was taken to Fort Michilimackinac in present-day Michigan. The British eventually released him, and he became their liaison to Indians along the Saint Clair River north of present-day Detroit.

In 1784, Sable returned to the Eschikagou Plain, where he built a homestead and trading post at the mouth of the Eschikagou River (now known as the Chicago River) on the site of present-day Chicago. He also built docks on Lake Michigan. At some point, he married a Potawatomi woman, Kittihawa, known to non-Indians as Catherine. On failing to win the tribe's chieftaincy in 1800, he and Kittihawa left the region and lived for a time in Peoria in present-day Illinois and eventually settled at Saint Charles in present-day Missouri.

As the first non-Indian to settle on the site of Chicago, Jean Baptist Point Sable is credited with founding the city; his successor at the trading post, John Kinzie, is also considered a father of Chicago. Sable's house and his role in the city's history are commemorated by a plaque at the corner of Pine and Kinzie Streets.

Sacajawea (Sacagawea, "Bird Woman," Boinaiv, "Grass Maiden," Janey) (ca. 1784–1812 or 1884)

Shoshone Indian interpreter, guide for Lewis and Clark Expedition in the American West, wife of Toussaint Charbonneau, mother of Jean-Baptiste Charbonneau

Sacajawea was born in the Lemhi Mountains region of what is now western Montana, the daughter of a Shoshone Indian chief. When she was about 10 years old, she was taken captive by a band of Hidatsa Indians.

By 1804, Sacajawea had become the wife of French-Canadian fur trapper TOUSSAINT CHARBONNEAU, who re-

Statue of Sacajawea in Portland, Oregon *(Library of Congress)*

portedly had won her and another Indian young woman in a gambling game with the Hidatsa. In the winter of 1804–05, the Corps of Discovery under the command of MERIWETHER LEWIS and WILLIAM CLARK encamped at the Mandan Indian villages at the confluence of the Knife River and MISSOURI RIVER, near present-day Bismarck, North Dakota. There, Toussaint Charbonneau was hired on as the expedition's interpreter, with the understanding that Sacajawea would accompany him on the trek to the Oregon coast.

In February 1805, Sacajawea gave birth to a son, JEAN-BAPTISTE CHARBONNEAU. Two months later, with her newborn infant strapped to her back, she and her husband departed the Mandan Indian villages with Lewis and Clark. Sacajawea served as a guide, as well as interpreter to Indian tribes. The Corps of Discovery reached the Three Forks of the Missouri in August 1805; she guided them along the southwesternmost branch, the Jefferson, then through the Lemhi Pass to her Shoshone homeland. There, she was reunited with her brother Cameahwait, who had by that time become a chief.

Sacajawea convinced her brother to provide the expedition with horses, vital for their continued progress overland to the Clearwater, Snake, and Columbia watershed. She continued westward with Lewis and Clark and their men to the Oregon coast, arriving there in November 1805. On the return journey east in March 1806, she accompanied William Clark and his contingent as they explored the Yellowstone River to its junction with the Missouri. She and her husband left the expedition when it returned to the Mandan villages at the mouth of North Dakota's Knife River in summer 1806.

Details of Sacajawea's life after 1806 are contradictory. According to one account, she accompanied Toussaint Charbonneau to St. Louis in 1809, when he took their young son to William Clark, who had arranged to adopt the boy. She then reportedly returned to the upper Missouri with one of MANUEL LISA's fur-trading expeditions, where she died of fever in 1812.

An alternate, less likely version relates that Sacajawea went on to live with the Comanche Indians, then returned to her homeland and finally settled on the Wind River Indian Reservation in Wyoming, living there until her death at about age 100 in 1884.

Sacajawea was one of the few women to play an active role in the early exploration of North America. Through her skill as an interpreter and diplomat, the Lewis and Clark Expedition had mostly peaceful encounters with the more than 50 Indian tribes they met en route.

Sadlier, George Foster (fl. 1819) *British army officer in Arabia*

In 1819, George Sadlier, a captain with the British army in India, was sent to Arabia on a diplomatic mission to Ibrahim Pasha, the Egyptian military leader who had just defeated the Wahhabis, an Islamic reform movement.

Sadlier landed at Qatif, north of Bahrain on the Persian Gulf coast of Arabia, in June 1819. Accompanied by a small detachment of Egyptian soldiers, he set out westward across the desert of central Arabia, hoping to catch up with Ibrahim Pasha, who was then withdrawing with his army back to Egypt. En route, Sadlier visited Dar'iyah, a city that had never before been seen by Europeans, although by the time of his arrival, it was deserted and mostly destroyed by Ibrahim Pasha's forces.

Halfway across the Arabian Peninsula, near Anaiza, Sadlier learned that Ibrahim Pasha had continued westward to the holy city of Medina. Sadlier continued across the desert and, on reaching the outskirts of Medina, presented Ibrahim Pasha with a ceremonial sword from the British government, as well as an offer of British military aid in support of the continuing campaign against the Wahhabis. Sadlier then headed for the RED SEA port of Yenbo, north of Jidda, arriving on September 20, 1819.

With his trek from the Persian Gulf to the Red Sea, which had taken a little longer than three months, Captain George Sadlier became the first European to cross the Arabian Peninsula, an accomplishment not duplicated until the 1917 journey of HARRY ST. JOHN BRIDGER PHILBY.

St. Denis, Louis Juchereau de (Louis Juchereau de St. Denys) (1676–1744) *French colonizer, trader in Louisiana and Texas*

A native of French Canada, Louis de St. Denis was born in Beauport, near Quebec City, the son of a local seigneur, or titled landowner. In 1698–99, he sailed to Mobile Bay with the brothers PIERRE LE MOYNE, sieur d'Iberville and JEAN-BAPTISTE LE MOYNE, sieur de Bienville, taking part in their colonizing expedition to the lower MISSISSIPPI RIVER.

In 1700, soon after the establishment of the French settlement on Biloxi Bay, St. Denis accompanied Bienville in an exploration up the Red River, ascending it into northwestern Louisiana and eastern Texas, which then was the northeastern frontier of New Spain. Two years later, he took command of a French outpost on the Mississippi Delta, Fort de la Boulaye. During the next three years, he undertook additional explorations westward into the interior.

St. Denis returned to the Red River in 1710, traveling upstream to the land of the Natchitoches Indians, a subgroup of the Caddo, among whom he established trade contacts; he did the same in nearby eastern Texas. In 1713, the French governor of Louisiana, ANTOINE LAUMET DE LA MOTHE, sieur de Cadillac, received word from a Spanish missionary in Mexico, Francisco Hidalgo, informing him that the Spanish had failed to provide enough missionaries to area tribes, and that the presence of French priests might be welcomed. Interpreting this news more as an open invitation for the French to extend their Indian trade into Texas, Cadillac sent St. Denis back up the Red River in 1713, with instructions to cross Texas to the Rio Grande and open up trade contacts with Indians.

St. Denis first traveled back to the Natchitoches village on the Red River, where he established a trading post, then set out across Texas. On July 14, 1714, he arrived at San Juan Bautista, the northernmost Spanish settlement on the Rio Grande, opposite present-day Eagle Pass, Texas, where he was promptly arrested for illegally entering Spanish territory.

St. Denis won the favor of the post commander's grand-daughter, Manuela Sánchez Ramón, but he was later sent to Mexico City and imprisoned. On convincing the viceroy of Mexico that he was sincerely interested in extending Spanish settlement into Texas, he was released. He was so persuasive that the viceroy sent him back to San Juan Bautista, where he married Sánchez Ramón. Several months later, he set out on an expedition with her grandfather, Captain Domingo Ramón, planning to establish additional Spanish settlements to counter the threat of French expansion westward from Louisiana.

Proceeding northeastward from San Juan Bautista, St. Denis and Ramón, jointly in command of a party of 25 soldiers and nine missionaries, crossed from the Rio Grande to the Neches River of eastern Texas, which they reached in July 1716. There, they established the mission of Nuestro Padre San Francisco de los Tejas, as well as Mission San Miguel, not far from the Red River, and Mission Ais, west of the Neches.

St. Denis returned to Mobile soon afterward, where he again entered the service of Cadillac. In 1717, he returned to the Natchitoches trading post on the Red River, from where he recrossed Texas to the Rio Grande. Back at San Juan Bautista, the Spanish confiscated his trading goods. St. Denis traveled to Mexico City to protest this action, but he was again imprisoned. He managed to escape in September 1718, then made his way back to Mobile and on to Natchitoches, where he was soon joined by his wife, Manuela.

St. Denis remained in command of the French Red River post at Fort St. Jean Baptiste de Natchitoches for the next 24 years. In 1731, he succeeded in repelling a siege by Natchez Indians, and the next year, he led a party of soldiers and allied Indians in a counterattack at nearby Sang Pour Sang Hill.

Louis de St. Denis's settlement at Natchitoches became a starting point for a number of French explorations into the Canadian River and Arkansas River regions of Oklahoma and northern Texas; after 1719, it was the first center for the western FUR TRADE. Most significantly, St. Denis's activity on New Spain's northern border with French Louisiana caused the Spanish great concern over the threat of further French incursions and instigated stepped-up Spanish efforts to settle Texas.

St. Vrain, Céran de Hault de Lassus de

(1802–1870) *American fur trader, businessman in the American Southwest*
Céran de St. Vrain was born in Spanish Lake, near St. Louis, Missouri, the son of a former French naval officer. As a youth in the early 1820s, St. Vrain worked as a clerk for one of the fur-trading firms operating out of St. Louis. In fall 1824, he mounted his own fur-trading expedition across the southern plains and into the southern ROCKY MOUNTAINS, arriving in Taos, New Mexico, on March 21, 1825. The next year, St. Vrain, together with mountain man and itinerant preacher WILLIAM SHERLEY WILLIAMS, received permission to trade and trap in the Gila River region of what is now southern Arizona.

St. Vrain entered into partnership with the brothers CHARLES BENT and WILLIAM BENT in 1830, establishing the firm of Bent, St. Vrain & Company, which outfitted fur-trapping and trading expeditions from Taos and Santa Fe. Three years later, the company founded its post on the Arkansas River, near the mouth of the Purgatoire, not far from present-day La Junta in southeastern Colorado. At the same time, St. Vrain and the Bents developed the trail southward from their Arkansas River post to Raton Pass and Taos, widening it to accommodate wagon caravans. Known as the Raton Pass Route, it provided traders from Missouri headed for New Mexico with a safer alternative than the hazardous Cimarron Cutoff, part of the Santa Fe Trail.

In 1847, St. Vrain, who had settled in Taos, led a volunteer force of mountain men in support of U.S. forces in the U.S.-Mexican War of 1846–48. After 1849, he left the FUR TRADE to engage in banking, real estate, and railroad ventures in the newly organized New Mexico Territory, where he also became a leading figure in territorial politics, although he was never elected to public office.

The site of the trading post that Céran de St. Vrain and the Bent brothers established on the Arkansas River was designated as a National Historic Site by the U.S. government in 1960. Known as Bent's Old Fort, it was the focal point of the fur trade in the southern and central Rockies, and, during the 1840s, was the staging area for the exploratory expeditions of CHRISTOPHER HOUSTON CARSON (Kit Carson) and JOHN CHARLES FRÉMONT.

Salle, René-Robert Cavelier de la   See LA SALLE, RENÉ-ROBERT CAVELIER, SIEUR DE.

Sargon (Sargon of Akkad, Sargon the Great, Sargon I, Sharrukin, "the Righteous King")

(fl. 2340s–2300s B.C.) *Mesopotamian ruler in the Persian Gulf and eastern Mediterranean*
Sargon was a ruler of the ancient Mesopotamian kingdom of Akkad, situated at the northern end of the Persian Gulf, comprising much of what is now Iraq. Sargon's reign (from about 2340 to 2305 B.C.) was highlighted by a great campaign of conquest in which he expanded his domain northward, beyond the central Euphrates River Valley, into what is now Syria and southern Turkey, founding the first empire in Mesopotamia. Moreover, he established trade contacts to the east with the peoples of the Indus Valley, to the south

with the peoples of the southeast coast of the Arabian Peninsula, and to the west with the peoples of the eastern MEDITERRANEAN SEA.

According to an ancient account, Sargon mounted several naval campaigns in which he sailed across a great sea west of his kingdom, possibly the Mediterranean, to locate and conquer lands some historians have identified as Crete and Spain. Other scholars have speculated that his maritime exploits were probably limited to the islands and coasts of the Persian Gulf.

Sargon, along with the Egyptian HANNU, is one of the earliest known explorers. The dynasty he founded lasted until about 2180 B.C.

Saris, John (unknown–1646) English trader, mariner in Japan

An English seafarer and merchant, John Saris first visited the Far East in 1604, when he accompanied Sir Henry Middleton of the BRITISH EAST INDIA COMPANY on a voyage to Bantam in the Dutch East Indies.

Saris remained in Bantam as an agent of the British East India Company for the next four years, returning to England in 1609. On April 18, 1612, he sailed from England on the *Clove,* in command of a company fleet bound for Japan. The voyage took him around the CAPE OF GOOD HOPE and along the coast of East Africa to the Ethiopian port of Assab near the mouth of the RED SEA.

After a stopover at Bantam and the SPICE ISLANDS (the Moluccas of present-day Indonesia), Saris landed on Japan's southernmost island of Kyushu in June 1613. There, he was met by his countryman, WILLIAM ADAMS, who had been living in Japan since 1600 as a naval adviser to the emperor. With Adams as his guide and interpreter, Saris made his way northward to the main Japanese island of Honshu. After visiting Osaka, he was received by the emperor at his court in nearby Suruga in early September 1613. Saris presented the emperor with a letter and gifts from King James I of England and, with Adams's help, obtained liberal trading privileges in Japan for the British East India Company.

After founding an English trading establishment on Kyushu and leaving Adams in charge of the company's interests in Japan, Saris sailed for England in November 1613, a journey that took almost a year. It was soon revealed that Saris had carried back a shipment of erotic books and pictures from the Far East, precipitating a minor scandal for the British East India Company that was resolved only when the offending material was destroyed.

John Saris settled near London, remaining as a consultant to the court of King James on matters relating to Far Eastern trade. His published narrative of his experiences was the earliest English account of Japanese life and culture. Although he had commanded the first English ships to land in Japan, his success in opening the country to British trade was short-lived. By the mid-1600s, Japan's rulers had closed the country to all European trade, except for the Dutch, and contact between Japan and the West was not reestablished until 1853, with the arrival of American admiral Matthew Perry and his fleet.

Sarmiento de Gamboa, Pedro

(ca. 1530–ca. 1592) *Spanish mariner, scientist, historian in South America and the Pacific Ocean*

Pedro Sarmiento de Gamboa was born in Galicia, Spain. By 1555, he had reached the Americas, first Mexico, then Peru. An accomplished scientist as well as mariner, in 1564, during the Spanish Inquisition, he had to defend himself against charges of conjuration by the Catholic Church in Lima, but was cleared of wrongdoing, although he would continue to be harassed by religious authorities over the years.

In 1567–69, Sarmiento de Gamboa planned and accompanied an expedition under ÁLVARO DE MENDAÑA that headed westward from Peru in search of the fabled GREAT SOUTHERN CONTINENT, also known as Terra Australis. The excursion made instead the European discovery of the Solomon Islands and the Marshall Islands. Sarmiento de Gamboa also helped suppress Inca Indian resistance to Spanish rule. He wrote a history of the Inca people that was widely read in Europe.

In 1579, following English attacks under SIR FRANCIS DRAKE against Spanish settlements and ships along the coasts of Peru and Mexico, Sarmiento de Gamboa received the naval assignment of intercepting Drake in the STRAIT OF MAGELLAN at the southern tip of South America. Drake, however, returned to the Atlantic Ocean westward by way of the Indian Ocean and the CAPE OF GOOD HOPE. Over the next 16 months, Sarmiento de Gamboa conducted a survey of the strait, returning to Spain in 1580 and reporting his findings to King Philip II. A colonizing expedition of 350 was planned under Sarmiento de Gamboa and Diego Flores de Valdés. Many of the 24 vessels were lost in a storm, and Flores de Valdés led a number of ships back to Spain. Sarmiento de Gamboa continued on to the strait with four ships and 64 colonists, and, in 1584, founded the settlements of Rey Don Felipe and Nombre de Jesús.

On his return voyage to Spain for supplies, Sarmiento de Gamboa was captured by the English. In London, he was interviewed by Queen Elizabeth I in 1588. He borrowed funds to be ransomed but was captured in France and held there until 1590 when he was ransomed by the Spanish Crown. By that time, the colony he had founded had been abandoned, many of the colonists dying of starvation. In 1591, he was assigned the task of organizing another colonizing expedition but died before departure.

Pedro Sarmiento de Gamboa played a part in the Spanish discovery of the Solomon and Marshall Islands and contributed to knowledge of South America through his historical and scientific writings. In addition to his survey of the Strait of Magellan, he is also known for the most accurate calculation of the longitude of Peru up to that time.

Sarychev, Gavriil Andreyevich (1763–1831)
Russian naval officer in Alaska and eastern Siberia

Gavriil Sarychev was a Russian naval officer trained in the art of producing coastal maps from navigational surveys. Starting in 1785, he took part in the Russian government's Northeastern Secret Geographical and Astronomical Expedition, an official exploration of northeasternmost SIBERIA and the Gulf of Alaska, under the leadership of British seafarer JOSEPH BILLINGS.

In 1790–91, as second in command on the ship *Slava Rossy,* Sarychev accompanied Billings in an exploration of the Aleutian Islands and the Gulf of Alaska, during which he charted Alaska's southern coastline eastward as far as Prince William Sound and Cape St. Elias. The next year, he and Billings undertook an examination inland into northeastern Siberia's Chukchi Peninsula.

In 1802, Sarychev continued his hydrographic work with a survey of the west coast of Russia, along the shores of the Gulf of Finland and the Baltic Sea.

In 1806, Gavriil Sarychev's report on his explorations with Billings was published in an English edition as *Account of a Voyage of Discovery to the North-East of Siberia, the Frozen Ocean, and the North-East Sea.* Named as the Russian navy's chief hydrographer in 1808, and made an admiral in 1830, Sarychev was responsible for producing the first accurate charts of the Aleutian Islands, the Gulf of Alaska, and the coast of eastern Siberia's Chukchi Peninsula.

Sauma, Rabban bar   See BAR SAUMA, RABBAN.

Schlagintweit, Adolf von (1829–1857)
German traveler in India and central Asia, brother of Hermann von Schlagintweit and Robert von Schlagintweit

Born in Munich, Adolf von Schlagintweit was the brother of HERMANN VON SCHLAGINTWEIT and ROBERT VON SCHLAGINTWEIT. Starting in 1854, Schlagintweit accompanied his two brothers in their scientific exploration of India, Tibet, and western China. In 1857, he stayed behind in western China after Hermann and Robert had returned to Europe; he was intent on continuing northward into the Pamir region of southern central Asia. Later that year, Schlagintweit followed the Northern Way segment of the ancient SILK ROAD as far as the caravan center of Kashgar, where he was killed by bandits.

Adolf von Schlagintweit's brief career as an explorer in central Asia ended before he was 28 years old. Along with his brothers, he was among the first Europeans to travel from Tibet, northward across the Kun Lun mountain range, into the desert regions of western China's Sinkiang (Xinjiang) province.

Schlagintweit, Hermann von (1822–1882)
German mountain climber in India and central Asia, brother of Adolf von Schlagintweit and Robert von Schlagintweit

Hermann von Schlagintweit was born in Munich, the older brother of ADOLF and ROBERT VON SCHLAGINTWEIT. Schlagintweit, who had become an accomplished mountaineer in his early climbing expedition in the Alps, joined his brothers on an 1854–57 scientific expedition to India, Tibet, and western China.

By the time he had returned to Europe in 1857, Hermann von Schlagintweit had explored the Karakoram mountain range of north-central India, as well as the Kunlun mountain range between northern Tibet and the western Chinese province of Sinkiang (Xinjiang).

Schlagintweit, Robert von (1833–1885)
German mountain climber, geologist in India and central Asia, brother of Adolf von Schlagintweit and Hermann von Schlagintweit

Robert von Schlagintweit was born in Munich, the son of an ophthalmologist. Educated as a geologist, he was also an accomplished mountaineer.

In 1854, on the recommendation of German naturalist ALEXANDER VON HUMBOLDT, Schlagintweit and his older brothers ADOLF VON SCHLAGINTWEIT and HERMANN VON SCHLAGINTWEIT were commissioned by the BRITISH EAST INDIA COMPANY to conduct an extensive scientific survey of India. During the next two years, they traveled throughout the Deccan Plateau of south-central India, as well as the Kashmir and Himalayan regions of northern India, carrying out studies in geology and terrestrial magnetism.

In 1856–57, Schlagintweit and his brothers extended their explorations beyond India's northern border into the Karakoram mountain range, crossed into Tibet, and continued northward across the Kunlun range, entering the desert region of western China's Sinkiang (Xinjiang) province.

Upon his return to Europe in 1857, Schlagintweit accepted a professorship at the University of Giessen and wrote an account of the expedition, *Results of a Scientific Mission to India and High-Asia,* a four-volume work published in 1860–66. In 1867–70, he went on a lecture tour of universities in the United States, during which he undertook additional scientific field work on the Pacific coast.

While in the HIMALAYAS, Robert and Adolf von Schlagintweit set a new MOUNTAIN CLIMBING record by ascending Mount Kamet to a height of 21,000 feet.

Schmidt, Otto Y. (1891–1956) *Soviet scientist in the Russian and Siberian Arctic*

Otto Schmidt, a Russian scientist, became involved with the exploration of the Russian and Siberian Arctic seas in conjunction with his work in geophysics and astronomy.

In 1928, in command of the icebreaker *Sedov,* Schmidt led a scientific expedition to Franz Josef Land, the Arctic archipelago north of Novaya Zemlya, which the Union of Soviet Socialist Republics (USSR, or Soviet Union) had claimed as part of its national territory two years earlier. After establishing a scientific station there, he returned to Leningrad (present-day St. Petersburg), and, two years later, in 1930, he undertook a second voyage to Franz Josef Land.

In 1932, Schmidt, a professor at the Arctic Institute of the USSR in Leningrad, was named as head of the Central Administration of the Northern Sea Route, an agency that had been created to direct the development of the NORTHEAST PASSAGE across northern Europe and Asia as a practical shipping and communications channel, linking European Russia with northern SIBERIA and the Pacific Ocean. That year, he commanded a Soviet expedition aboard the icebreaker *Sibiryakov,* which navigated the entire length of the Northeast Passage on a course through the Severnaya Zemlya Islands and north of Cape Chelyuskin, Asia's northernmost point. Schmidt made the voyage from Murmansk to Vladivostok in two months and four days, demonstrating that the Northeast Passage could be navigated within one season.

Schmidt soon commanded another voyage through the Northeast Passage on the icebreaker *Chelyuskin,* with plans to return westward within the same year. Sailing from Leningrad on July 12, 1933, he was accompanied by a crew of more than 100, including women and children.

In early November 1933, Schmidt and his expedition became icebound in the Chukchi Sea, north of BERING STRAIT. After drifting northward with the PACK ICE, the *Chelyuskin* reached the north coast of Alaska, where it sank on February 13, 1934, crushed by the ice. The expedition was able to abandon the ship with few losses and set up a temporary encampment on the ice, surviving sub-zero temperatures. A makeshift landing strip was soon constructed as well, and in early March, Schmidt and his party were evacuated by a fleet of rescue aircraft.

Schmidt next became involved in scientific research in the Arctic supported by aircraft. On May 21, 1937, he took off from the airfield on Rudolf Island, one of the Franz Josef Land islands, and, with a party of four others, flew to within 13 miles of the NORTH POLE, where he landed. Other aircraft soon followed with additional supplies, and within a few days the first manned scientific station near the North Pole had been set up. Soon afterward, Schmidt flew back to Franz Josef Land. By February 1938, the base had drifted southward with the pack ice to the east coast of GREENLAND, a distance of more than 1,500 miles. Maintaining radio contact with the men at the base, Schmidt determined their position and mounted a rescue mission. In command of two Soviet icebreakers, Schmidt reached the scientific team on February 19, 1938, rescuing them just as the ice floe on which they were drifting was about to break up.

In the course of his explorations in the polar seas of Russia and Siberia, Professor Otto Schmidt undertook extensive studies of Arctic Ocean currents, as well as observations of solar radiation in high latitudes. His 1932 expedition, in which he navigated across northern Europe and Asia within one season, demonstrated that the Northeast Passage could be developed into a practical route for shipping and communication, vital for the development of the Soviet Union's Arctic region. The rescue of his 1933–34 expedition, stranded on the ice of the frozen Chukchi Sea, was the first polar airlift in history. In his 1937 expedition, Schmidt and his party became the first men to reach the vicinity of the North Pole since the 1909 voyage of Admiral ROBERT EDWIN PEARY and MATTHEW ALEXANDER HENSON. In addition, the base Schmidt established near the North Pole that year served as a radio station for a series of Soviet transpolar flights from Moscow to Washington State and California. Schmidt's later scientific work concentrated on developing a theory on the origin of the Earth. In honor of Schmidt's contribution to Soviet exploration in the Arctic, an island he located in Franz Josef Land was named after him.

Schomburgk, Sir Robert Hermann

(1804–1865) *German-born naturalist in South America, in service to Great Britain*

Robert Hermann Schomburgk was born in the eastern German city of Freiburg, the son of a minister. In 1826, after an education in Germany that included training in geology and the natural sciences, he moved to the United States, settling in Richmond, Virginia.

In 1830, after his brief career as a Virginia tobacco merchant ended when a fire destroyed his business, Schomburgk traveled to the WEST INDIES, where he undertook a natural history survey of the coast of Anegada in the British Virgin Islands. His work there came to the attention of Great Britain's ROYAL GEOGRAPHICAL SOCIETY, which, in 1831, commissioned him to explore the interior of British Guiana (present-day Guyana) in northeastern South America.

In 1831–35, Schomburgk traveled to the upper Essequibo River, the longest river in British Guiana, in the course of which he determined its source and discovered a giant water lily, which he named the Victoria Regia. In 1837, he ventured into the Guiana Highlands, exploring the Kanuku Mountains, then undertook an overland journey from Lake Amicu northwestward through difficult terrain to the ORINOCO RIVER. In 1839, he nearly traced the Orinoco River to its source, in a journey that took him through the Casiquiare Canal into the Río Negro.

Back in England in 1840, Schomburgk received a gold medal from the Royal Geographical Society for his work in British Guiana. He was soon appointed to lead a British government survey to establish the colony's boundary with Venezuela. In 1841, he traveled through the Pakaraima Mountains of western British Guiana and also explored the upper Courantyne and Berbice Rivers along British Guiana's border with Brazil. Schomburgk returned to England in 1844. He had become a naturalized British subject, and that year, he was knighted by Queen Victoria.

In 1848, Schomburgk entered the British diplomatic service with an appointment as British consul to Santo Domingo. Starting in 1857, while serving as British consul in Bangkok, he undertook explorations into Southeast Asia, including a survey of the Isthmus of Kra, in connection with a proposed ship canal through the Malay Peninsula. He returned to Europe in 1864 and settled in Berlin, where he died the following year.

In his 1831–35 explorations into the interior of northeastern South America, Sir Robert Schomburgk established a line of astronomically determined points delineating the watershed region between the Essequibo and Orinoco Rivers. Along with an account of his own explorations, *Voyage in Guiana and upon the Shores of the Orinoco during the Years 1835–39* (1840), he also edited a history of the earliest British explorations into the region, *The Discovery of the Empire of Guiana by Sir Walter Raleigh* (1848). His 1841–44 survey along the Venezuela-British Guiana frontier resulted in the establishment of the Schomburgk Line, which became significant in the final resolution of the boundary in the 1890s. In addition to his discovery of the Victoria Regia water lily, he also classified many previously unknown varieties of orchids in South America, one of which has since been named the Schomburgkia orchid in his honor.

Schoolcraft, Henry Rowe (1793–1864)

American geologist, ethnologist on the upper Mississippi River
Henry Rowe Schoolcraft was born in Albany County, New York, where his father was involved in the glassmaking business. He attended Union College, then went on to Middlebury College, studying the natural sciences, especially geology and mineralogy.

Schoolcraft worked as a glassmaker for a time before 1817, then embarked on a trip down the Ohio River to Missouri. In Missouri and Arkansas, he undertook geological

and mineralogical surveys, which served as the basis for his 1819 book, *A View of the Lead Mines of Missouri*.

In 1820, Schoolcraft served as a geologist for Michigan territorial governor Lewis Cass in his expedition in the region of the upper Great Lakes in search of the source of the MISSISSIPPI RIVER. Cass's expedition explored the upper Great Lakes and incorrectly identified the source of the Mississippi River as Upper Red Cedar Lake. Schoolcraft published an account of this expedition in 1821, entitled *A Narrative Journal of Travels from Detroit through the Great Chain of American Lakes to the Sources of the Mississippi*.

In 1822, Schoolcraft undertook further geological surveys of the Lake Superior region. That same year, he was appointed Indian agent for the tribes of northern Michigan Territory and Lake Superior.

Ten years later, in 1832, Schoolcraft again ventured up the Mississippi River in search of its actual source in Minnesota. With a small party of explorers and scientists, he entered the St. Louis River at Fond du Lac in northeastern Minnesota, then portaged westward to Sandy Lake and into the Mississippi. From Cass Lake, a Chippewa (Ojibway) Indian guided him to the lake that was the Mississippi's true source, which he reached on July 13, 1832. Originally known as Elk Lake (Lac la Biche), it was rechristened Lake Itasca by Schoolcraft, from the Latin words *veritas* for "truth" and *caput* for "head." Schoolcraft wrote an account of his second Mississippi exploration, entitled *Narrative of an Expedi-*

Henry Rowe Schoolcraft *(New York State Library, Albany)*

tion through the Upper Mississippi to Itasca Lake, the Actual Source of the Mississippi. It was first published in 1834.

Schoolcraft became superintendent of Indian affairs for Michigan in 1836, serving until 1841. He moved back to New York, where he began a comprehensive study of the Indian tribes of the United States, a project that resulted in a multivolume study published in 1851–57.

Henry Rowe Schoolcraft is credited with locating the source of the Mississippi River. The Schoolcraft River in Minnesota, which joins the Mississippi near its source at Lake Itasca, was named in his honor.

Schouten, Willem Cornelis (Willem Cornelius Schouten, Willem Coreliszoon van Schouten)

(ca. 1580–1625) *Dutch mariner in the South Atlantic and South Pacific*

Willem Schouten was a native of the seaport town of Hoorn in the northern Netherlands. An accomplished seafarer, he served with the DUTCH EAST INDIA COMPANY and visited the WEST INDIES in 1601–03.

Schouten commanded the *Hoorn* in JAKOB LE MAIRE's 1615–16 expedition in search of an alternative to the STRAIT OF MAGELLAN route around the tip of South America.

In addition to the European discovery of Le Maire Strait and CAPE HORN (which he named after his birthplace), Willem Schouten, with Le Maire, explored various island chains in the Pacific. Off the northwest coast of New Guinea, he located an island group that afterward became known as the Schouten Islands. He also located the Bismarck Archipelago.

Schwatka, Frederick (1849–1892) *U.S. Army officer, American lawyer, physician in the Canadian Arctic, Alaska, and northern Mexico*

Born in Galena, Illinois, Frederick Schwatka was 10 years old when he moved with his family to Salem, Oregon. He entered West Point in 1867, graduating in 1871 as a second lieutenant in the U.S. Army, attached to the cavalry. Over the next several years, he served at various posts throughout the United States and also pursued the study of law and medicine. In 1875, he was admitted to the bar in Nebraska, and, in 1876, he was granted a medical degree from New York's Bellevue Hospital Medical College.

Schwatka had in the meantime developed a keen interest in confirming the fate of SIR JOHN FRANKLIN and his expedition, which had been missing in the Canadian Arctic since 1845. After nearly three decades of search efforts, it was known that the ships had become icebound near King William Island and some of the 127 members of the expedition had perished, but remains of many of the crew had never been found.

In 1878, Schwatka secured the support of the AMERICAN GEOGRAPHICAL SOCIETY and a whaling company for a search effort of his own, hoping to finally resolve the mystery of what had happened to Franklin. He sailed from New York on June 19, 1878, accompanied by William H. Gilder, a newspaperman who covered the expedition for the *New York Herald.*

Schwatka planned to establish a base camp at Repulse Bay on the northwest corner of HUDSON BAY, then travel overland to the Back River Estuary and King William Island. Rough weather and ice conditions led to a change of plans, and the camp was set up farther to the south near Chesterfield Inlet. The expedition wintered there, making friendly contacts with Inuit.

In spring 1879, Schwatka, Gilder, and a party of 12 Inuit, including women and children, set out on a sledge journey to the northwest. They reached a river that they named the Hayes River after President Rutherford B. Hayes; they descended it northward, then went overland to the Back River Estuary. From elderly Inuit in the area, Schwatka heard eyewitness accounts of whites dying on the shores of the northern Adelaide Peninsula many years before.

As planned, Schwatka reached King William Island in summer 1879. With the ground then clear of snow and ice, he was able to find several graves and artifacts of the Franklin expedition that previous search expeditions had missed. Moreover, Schwatka learned from Inuit on King William Island that books and papers, probably the expedition's official journals, had been left abandoned on the shore at a site near Starvation Cove by the last of the dying men.

Schwatka's intensive exploration of King William Island also yielded some exposed human remains which, on the basis of personal effects found nearby, were subsequently identified as those of one of Franklin's officers. His men also scoured King William Island as far as Cape Felix, its northernmost point. After covering almost 3,000 miles in nearly a year, the expedition traveled back to the base camp on Hudson Bay. Schwatka and his expedition returned to New York in spring 1880, where his exploits were related in Gilder's stories in the *New York Herald.* Popularly known as "Schwatka's Search," the expedition had the distinction of making the longest sledge journey on record.

Schwatka explored the Yukon River in Alaska in 1883–84, and in 1886, after resigning from the army, he undertook an expedition to Alaska, sponsored by the *New York Times.* In 1890, he went to northern Mexico's Chihuahua state, where he visited the land of the Tarahumari Indians. He wrote about his Arctic experiences in his book *Children of the Cold* (1886) and described his explorations on the Yukon in his *Along Alaska's Great River* (1885). An account of his expedition into northern Mexico was published posthumously in *Land of the Cave and Cliff Dweller* in 1893.

Frederick Schwatka's 1878–80 expedition about what happened to the Franklin expedition, ended 30 years of continuing speculation and confirmed what SIR LEOPOLD FRANCIS McCLINTOCK had determined in 1859. Schwatka also demonstrated that one could survive in the Arctic for extended periods, unaided from the outside world, with the adoption of Inuit survival skills.

Schweinfurth, Georg August (1836–1925)
German naturalist in East Africa

Born in the Latvian city of Riga to a family of German descent, Georg Schweinfurth attended universities in Heidelberg, Munich, and Berlin, where he studied the natural sciences, specializing in geology and botany.

Schweinfurth first traveled to Africa on a specimen-collecting expedition in 1862, in which he ascended the NILE RIVER as far as Khartoum in the Sudan. Based on the results of his botanical research there, he subsequently won the support of a Berlin scientific institute for an extensive exploration into the equatorial region of East Africa.

In 1864, Schweinfurth traveled down the east coast of the RED SEA, then headed inland across northern Ethiopia, returning to Khartoum after a westward trek through the Sudan.

Schweinfurth's most extensive exploration into East Africa began in 1868. He sailed south from Suez, and, after again reaching the Nile from the east, ascended the river to its northern tributaries. He continued southward, then headed westward from the White Nile toward what is now the Central African Republic and Democratic Republic of the Congo. After exploring the watershed region between the While Nile River and the upper CONGO RIVER (Zaire River), he reached the Bahr-el-Jebel River.

On March 19, 1870, Schweinfurth came upon a previously uncharted river, which he believed to be the Chari, flowing northward into Lake Chad. It was later determined that he had actually located the Uele River, a tributary of the Ubangi-Congo river system.

After 1871, Schweinfurth turned his attention to the unknown desert regions of northeastern Africa, accompanying FRIEDRICH GERHARD ROHLFS in his expedition across Libya into western Egypt in the mid-1870s. In 1875, he established a geographical society in Cairo, which served as his base of operations for a number of expeditions into the Arabian Peninsula, including an exploration into Yemen in 1888.

Georg Schweinfurth detailed his explorations in East Africa in his two-volume work *The Heart of Africa*, first published in 1873. His 1868–71 explorations along the White Nile and into the Congo marked the first time both rivers had been reached within the course of a single expedition. In his journey into the watershed region between the upper Congo and White Nile, he made the first European contact with the Mittoo and Loobah tribes, the women members of which practiced the art of lip enlargement to enhance their appearance. He was also the first modern European to encounter the Akka Pygmies of East Africa, whose existence had been mentioned in the ancient Greek writings of Homer and HERODOTUS.

Scoresby, William, Jr. (1789–1857) *British mariner, scientist in the Arctic, son of William Scoresby, Sr.*

Born in the seaport town of Whitby in Yorkshire, England, William Scoresby, Jr., was the son of whaling captain and Arctic navigator WILLIAM SCORESBY, SR. The younger Scoresby developed an early interest in science, studying under the naturalist SIR JOSEPH BANKS of the ROYAL SOCIETY. Starting in 1803, he accompanied his father on annual whaling voyages to the polar seas between Spitsbergen (present-day Svalbard) and the east coast of GREENLAND, in the course of which he undertook field studies in meteorology, oceanography, and the natural history of the Arctic. He joined his father in an Arctic whaling expedition in 1806, during which they reached, east of Greenland, the northernmost point anyone had been until that time.

On a voyage in 1813, Scoresby's ocean-temperature readings revealed the Arctic seas to be warmer at great depths than they were at the surface. In 1817, after returning from an Arctic voyage, Scoresby and his father informed Joseph Banks that the climate in the Arctic was moderating, and that the PACK ICE north of Spitsbergen appeared to be receding. Banks related the news to SIR JOHN BARROW of the British navy, who immediately initiated a campaign of Arctic exploration, including an assault on the NORTH POLE, as well as renewed efforts to locate the NORTHWEST PASSAGE in the Canadian Arctic. In 1818, an expedition commanded by SIR JOHN ROSS, assisted by SIR WILLIAM EDWARD PARRY, set out to search for the Northwest Passage in Baffin Bay and Lancaster Sound, while another expedition, commanded by DAVID BUCHAN and SIR JOHN FRANKLIN, attempted to sail northward from Spitsbergen and cross the Arctic Ocean by way of the North Pole.

Scoresby made his last Arctic voyage in 1822, in which he reached Greenland's east coast as far as 75° north latitude, then explored southward, examining over 400 miles of coastline.

William Scoresby, Jr., pioneered the scientific study of the Arctic. In 1825, he left the whaling business to become an Anglican priest, remaining a strong supporter of British naval efforts to find the Northwest Passage. He continued his scientific work, undertaking a voyage to Australia in 1856 to study terrestrial magnetism. His 1820 book, *Account of the Arctic Regions with a History and Description of the Northern Whale-Fishery*, was the first modern geographic and scientific study of the Arctic, providing details on terrestrial magnetism, Arctic plant and animal life, climate, and ocean temperatures.

Scoresby, William, Sr. (1760–1829) *British whaler in the Arctic, father of William Scoresby, Jr.*

William Scoresby, Sr., was born in Whitby, in Yorkshire, England, the son of a farmer. He first went to sea in his early twenties, and by 1791, he was the captain of his own whaling ship, the *Resolution*.

In his career as a whaler, Scoresby made annual voyages to the Greenland Sea, between eastern GREENLAND and Spitsbergen (present-day Svalbard), accompanied after 1803 by his son, WILLIAM SCORESBY, JR. On one expedition in these waters, he set a farthest-north record, sailing his ship to 81°30' north latitude, which he reached on May 25, 1806—a point within 500 miles of the NORTH POLE.

In 1817, following another voyage to the Arctic, Scoresby and his son reported to SIR JOSEPH BANKS on the moderating ice conditions north of Spitsbergen, information that subsequently inspired renewed interest in Arctic exploration by the British navy.

William Scoresby, Sr., retired from the sea in 1823. In his years in the Arctic, he had pioneered techniques of ice navigation that proved to be essential to Arctic seaward exploration throughout the rest of the 19th century. His report with his son on ice conditions inspired the great land and sea expeditions into the Arctic regions undertaken by the British navy for the next 60 years. In recognition of the geographic and scientific reconnaissance undertaken by Scoresby and his son, the coastal region of that part of eastern Greenland is called Scoresby Land, and an arm of the Greenland Sea, which extends inland into the region for more than 180 miles, is known as Scoresby Sound.

Scott, Robert Falcon (1868–1912) *British naval officer, explorer in Antarctica*

Robert Falcon Scott was born at Davenport in Devonshire, England. At the age of 14, he entered the Royal Navy as a cadet, and later, promoted to lieutenant, served with the British fleet in the Caribbean.

In 1899, with the help of Sir Clements Markham of the ROYAL GEOGRAPHICAL SOCIETY, Scott won an appointment as commander of the British National Antarctic Expedition. Jointly sponsored by the ROYAL SOCIETY and the Royal Geographical Society, and equipped with the Royal Navy vessel the *Discovery*, Scott and the expedition departed England in August 1901.

Scott sailed to Antarctica by way of NEW ZEALAND, landing at Cape Adare on the edge of the Ross Sea in January 1902. He proceeded to Ross Island, where he established a base camp at Hut Point on McMurdo Sound.

From his McMurdo Sound base, Scott undertook several explorations of the Antarctic interior. With expedition members ERNEST HENRY SHACKLETON, EDWARD ADRIAN WILSON, and Frank Wild, he explored the coast of Victoria Land and the Ross Ice Shelf. He reached a peninsula, which he named Edward VII Land. He also proved that Mount Erebus and Mount Terror were not on the mainland but were situated on an island, which he named Ross Island, after SIR JAMES CLARK ROSS. Additionally, his explorations revealed that McMurdo Sound, then thought to be a bay, was actually a strait between Ross Island and the Antarctic mainland.

Scott's chief accomplishment on his first Antarctic expedition was a 200-mile trek southward across the Ross Ice Shelf toward the SOUTH POLE. Accompanied by Shackleton and Wilson, Scott reached a latitude of 82° 17' south, 500 miles from the South Pole, and the farthest point south reached until then. During the Antarctic summer season of 1903, Scott explored westward from McMurdo Sound into the Ferrar Glacier and explored the Polar Plateau region to an altitude of over 9,000 feet.

With the arrival of relief ships in early 1904, Scott and the expedition left the Antarctic, returning to England with a great deal of scientific and topographic data.

Promoted to captain, Scott returned to naval service. In 1909, he began to organize another expedition, this time with plans to reach the South Pole. In June 1910, Scott sailed from England aboard the *Terra Nova*, accompanied by some veteran members of his first expedition, including scientist Edward Wilson. En route, while stopping at Melbourne, Australia, Scott received a telegram from Norwegian polar explorer ROALD ENGELBREGT GRAVNING AMUNDSEN, stating that he also was headed for the Antarctic and, like Scott, intended to make an attempt on the South Pole.

By late January 1911, Scott's second Antarctic expedition reached Ross Island on McMurdo Sound and established its headquarters at Cape Evans. Amundsen had meanwhile set up his base at the Bay of Whales, on the opposite side of the Ross Ice Shelf, 60 miles closer to the South Pole.

Over the next year, Scott and his party established a series of food and fuel depots along their proposed route to the South Pole. In June 1911, Wilson led a party investigating Cape Crozier, where they studied the breeding habits of the emperor penguins.

On November 1, 1911, Scott's team set out from McMurdo Sound, equipped with Manchurian ponies, motorized sledges (tractor-type vehicles), and dogs. He intended to reach the Polar Plateau by way of the Beardmore Glacier, a route Shackleton had pioneered several years earlier. By January 4, Scott's party reached the edge of the Polar Plateau. By then the motorized sledges had broken down. The ponies, weakened by the ordeal, had to be destroyed. The support group returned to McMurdo Sound on sledges pulled by the dogs.

Scott, Wilson, and expedition members Lawrence Oates, Edgar Evans, and Henry Bowers proceeded onward to the South Pole, hauling sledges themselves. On January 12, 1912, they reached the South Pole, only to find a marker and letters from Amundsen, indicating that the Norwegian expedition had been there 33 days earlier. On the return journey, Scott and his party were plagued by severe weather conditions. At the end of March, they were delayed by a nine-day blizzard. Exhausted and suffering from frostbite and starvation, Scott and his men had perished when a search party located their bodies in November, at a point only 11 miles from a supply depot. Diaries and letters left by Scott and his companions revealed what had happened.

Although Amundsen won the race to the South Pole, it was Robert Falcon Scott and his party who first reached this objective solely by manpower, without sled dogs. In addition, Scott's two expeditions brought back a great deal of scientific and topographical data.

Scylax (Scylax of Caria, Scylax of Caryanda)

(fl. late 500s B.C.) *Greek mariner along the Indus River, Arabian Sea, and Red Sea, in service to Persia*

Scylax was a Greek from Caria, an ancient region settled by Greeks and located in present-day southwest Turkey. He became an accomplished mariner.

According to the Greek historian HERODOTUS of the fifth century B.C., Scylax was sent by Darius I, emperor of Persia (present-day Iran), on an exploratory expedition to determine the course of the INDUS RIVER in 510 B.C. After traveling overland through the Near East, he is thought to have entered the Indus from the Kabul River near the present-day town of Attock, Pakistan. He then reportedly followed it to the Arabian Sea, proceeded westward along the coast of what is now southwestern Pakistan and southeastern Iran, continued southwestward along the coast of present-day Oman to the Gulf of Aden, then went up the RED SEA to the Gulf of Suez from where he returned to Persia in 507.

Scylax provided valuable geographic material for Darius's military endeavors. Some of his descriptions were fantastic, such as those of one-eyed men or giant-eared men. He was the first European observer to give an account of India and the first known Greek to sail in the Red Sea.

Selkirk, Alexander (Alexander Sealchriag, Alexander Selcraig) (1676–1721) *Scottish mariner in the eastern Pacific*

Alexander Selkirk was born in Largo on the east coast of Scotland, the seventh son of a shoemaker. At the age of 19, he went to sea to avoid facing criminal charges for an incident in which he allegedly behaved indecently at church.

Selkirk returned to Largo in 1701. He soon found himself in trouble with local authorities again, reportedly for fighting in public along with his brothers. In 1703, he joined an expedition of PRIVATEERS under WILLIAM DAMPIER to the Pacific coast of South America, serving as sailing master on the *Cinque Ports Gallery.*

In September 1704, while off Mas Tierra, one of the Juan Fernandez Islands, about 400 miles west of Valparaíso, Chile, Selkirk became embroiled in a dispute with the ship's captain, which led to his being put ashore at his own request. Although he later changed his mind, he was left behind when the ship sailed.

Selkirk managed to survive fairly well on Mas Tierra over the next four years. He built a shelter and hunted the island's wild goats. In January 1709, he was picked up by another British privateering vessel, commanded by Captain Woodes Rogers and piloted by Dampier. On Dampier's recommendation, Selkirk was made an officer on the ship. After taking part in a series of lucrative raids on Spanish shipping, he returned to England by way of the CAPE OF GOOD HOPE, completing a journey that had taken him around the world.

Selkirk landed in London on October 14, 1711. In spring 1712, he returned to his hometown in Scotland, after an absence of 10 years. His share of the booty taken on his return voyage amounted to £800, which at that time was enough money to make him a man of moderate wealth. He stayed in Largo for only a brief time, reportedly living as a recluse. He took to practicing meditation in a cave-like refuge he built in his father's garden. His behavior at this time may have been a result of his four years of isolation on Mas Tierra Island.

Accounts of Selkirk's experience marooned on an East Pacific island began to appear soon after his return to England. His story was included in Captain Woodes Rogers's *A Cruising Voyage round the World,* published in 1712. The work describes how, in the first days after his rescue, Selkirk had trouble returning to the use of speech and could not immediately get accustomed to eating the food on board the ship. Also in 1712, Selkirk's own account was published as a pamphlet entitled, *Providence Displayed, or a Surprising Account of One Alexander Selkirk . . . written by his own hand.*

By September 1713, Selkirk had left Largo with a young woman named Sophia Bruce. They first went to Bristol, where court records indicate Selkirk was charged with assaulting a shipwright named Richard Nettle. He and Sophia next went to London where they lived together in a common-law marriage for the next several years.

London journalist Sir Richard Steele interviewed Selkirk, publishing an account of the Scottish sailor's adventures in his periodical *The Englishman* in December 1713. Selkirk's story came to the attention of English journalist and novelist Daniel Defoe, who used it as a source for his 1719 novel *Robinson Crusoe.*

In about 1718, Selkirk left Sophia and married a widow named Frances Candis. He then resumed his seafaring career, and in October 1720, he sailed as a lieutenant on a British naval vessel, the *Weymouth*. This proved to be his last ship. He died while on board in December 1721.

The island on which Alexander Selkirk was marooned became known as Isla Robinson Crusoe, and another of the Juan Fernandez islands was renamed Isla Alejandro Selkirk, after him. In 1868, the crew of a visiting British navy vessel left a plaque on Mas Tierra, proclaiming it as the site of his four-year stay. In addition, the town of Largo, Scotland, erected a bronze statue in his honor, commemorating him as the real-life inspiration for the fictional character Robinson Crusoe.

Semyonov, Pyotr Petrovich (Peter Semenov, Pyotr Semyonov-Tianshansky) (1827–1914)
Russian geographer, astronomer in central Asia

Pyotr Semyonov was born in the Russian town of Urusovo. A member of an aristocratic family, he studied geography and natural history in Russia and went on to study astronomy in Berlin, where he became acquainted with German naturalist and explorer ALEXANDER VON HUMBOLDT.

Semyonov was among the first Europeans to venture into the little-known Tian Shan Mountains along Russia's frontier with northwestern China. This range, known as the "Celestial Mountains," comprises a mountain system larger than all the mountain ranges of Europe combined. In his 1857 expedition into the region, Semyonov made an ascent of Khan Tengri, one of the highest peaks in the Tian Shan range.

In 1858, Semyonov extended his explorations into northwestern China, traveling throughout the Dzungaria region and the Altai Mountains. Thirty years later, in 1888, he took part in a scientific survey into Russian Turkestan and the territory east of the Caspian Sea.

Pyotr Semyonov initiated modern Russian exploration of central Asia. In the years when Russia was pushing eastward in its campaign of conquest and expansion in south-central Asia, his explorations provided vital geographic information about the region between the Pamirs and western China. As the first European known to have traversed the Tian Shan Mountains, he was referred to as Pyotr Semyonov-Tianshansky. He also made the first known identification of several mountains and glaciers in the Tian Shan and Altai ranges, and these were later also named in his honor.

Sequira, Diego López de (Diego López de Sequeira) (ca. 1465–ca. 1520) *Portuguese mariner, soldier in India and the East Indies*

Diego López de Sequira was a soldier and seafarer in service to King Manuel I of Portugal. In 1508, he was given command of a naval expedition to reconnoiter the port city of Malacca, an important center for the SPICE TRADE on the southern end of the Malay Peninsula.

Sequira and his fleet sailed from Lisbon in summer 1508, arriving at Calicut on the west coast of India in April 1509. From there, he rounded the tip of India, and, after making an eastward crossing of the Bay of Bengal, he arrived at Malacca in September 1509.

Sequira and his men encountered a variety of kinds of ships from Middle Eastern and Asian ports, including Arab DHOWs, Japanese or Chinese JUNKs—and outrigger CANOEs from the South Pacific islands. At that time, in addition to spices, Malacca was a center for the trade in sandalwood from Indonesia, porcelain from China, precious stones from CEYLON (present-day Sri Lanka), as well as concubines from the Circassian region, east of the Black Sea.

Although Sequira made an attempt to pose as a merchant trader, the local sultan had been warned in advance of his true purpose, based on earlier Portuguese conquests along India's Malabar Coast. A Portuguese delegation ashore was massacred in a surprise attack, and, in the ensuing battle aboard his ships in the harbor, Sequira lost one-third of his crew. Forced to withdraw eastward through the Strait of Malacca, he rounded the southeastern tip of Sumatra and returned to the Portuguese trading settlement at Calicut on India's southwest coast, thus completing the first European circumnavigation of Sumatra.

Diego López de Sequira's expedition brought back to Europe the first news of the riches of the EAST INDIES. Among his officers were FERDINAND MAGELLAN and FRANCISCO SERRANO. Inspired by his experience in Malacca with Sequira, Magellan launched his own expedition to the East Indies, resulting in the first round-the world voyage in history.

Serra, Junípero (Miguel José Serra) (1713–1784)
Spanish missionary in California

Junípero Serra was born on the Spanish Mediterranean island of Majorca. Originally known as Miguel José Serra, he adopted the religious name Junípero on entering the Franciscan order in 1730. He eventually became a professor of theology and philosophy at the university in Palma, Majorca's main city.

In 1749, Serra left the academic life, sailing that year from Cádiz, Spain, for Mexico as a Franciscan missionary. He arrived in Mexico City in early 1750, and during the next 18 years, he worked among the Indians of the Sierra Gordo region and also taught at Mexico City's College of San Fernando. In 1768, following the removal of the Jesuits, Serra was named head of the Franciscan missions in Baja California.

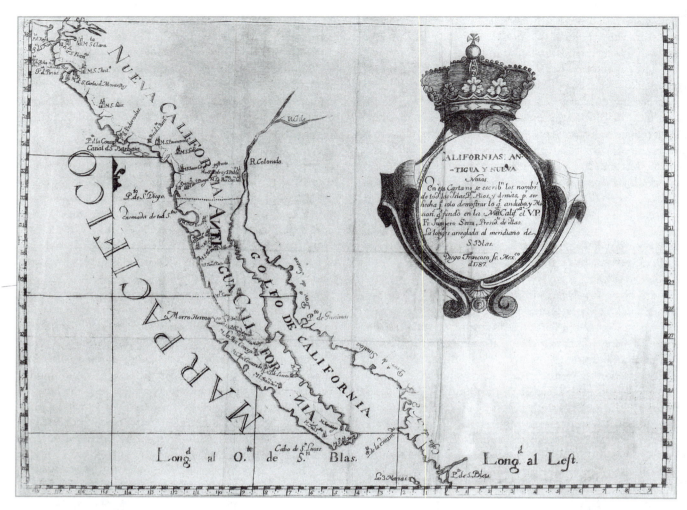

Detail of map showing the California missions of Junípero Serra (1787) *(Library of Congress)*

In 1769, Serra was appointed by Spanish colonial administrator José de Galvez to lead a contingent of missionaries as part of GASPAR DE PORTOLÁ's overland expedition into what is now the state of California. From Loreto, Mexico, on the lower end of the Baja California peninsula, Serra and a small group of priests headed northward. Traveling by land and sea for six weeks, they arrived at San Diego Bay in early July 1769. There, on July 16, 1769, Serra founded San Diego de Alcala, the first mission and church in present-day California.

Serra remained at the San Diego settlement, while Portolá explored northward in search of Monterey Bay, which supposedly had been reached by Spanish explorer SEBASTÍAN VISCAÍNO in 1602. A supply ship, the *San Antonio,* reached San Diego in March 1770. Serra sailed on it northward along the coast, joining Portolá at Monterey. There, on June 3, 1770, Serra founded the second Franciscan mission in California, San Carlos de Borromeo. In December 1771, he moved it several miles to the north near what is now Carmel, California.

In 1772, when Indian attacks led to shortages of food and other supplies at the San Diego colony, Serra walked almost 250 miles into Sonora, Mexico, to obtain aid. He was accompanied on this journey by only one Indian boy. From Sonora, Serra went to Mexico City, where he urged Spanish colonial officials to establish overland supply routes to California from northern Mexico and present-day Arizona.

Serra returned to the Carmel mission to continue his work among the Indians. Over the next decade, he established seven more missions between Monterey and San Diego. Among these were San Gabriel Arcangel, founded in September 1771, which subsequently developed into the city of Los Angeles. Other well-known missions established by Serra were San Luis Obispo in 1772, and San Juan Capistrano and San Francisco de Asis in 1776.

To link the settlements, Serra oversaw the development of a trail along the California coast, which came to be known as El Camino Real (the royal road, or king's highway). Along this route, also known as the Old Mission

Trail, the earliest established north-south road in California, Serra founded additional missions, approximately one day's journey, or 30 miles, apart, between San Diego and San Carlos de Borromeo at Carmel.

Serra died at the Carmel mission in 1784. In 1985, in recognition of his work as a missionary to the Indians, the Catholic Church beatified him, a preliminary step in elevation to sainthood.

Father Junípero Serra's successful colonizing efforts inspired JUAN BAUTISTA DE ANZA's overland expedition from Arizona to the California coast in 1774. The 500-mile-long El Camino Real that he developed became a key transportation and communication link in California and was extended by his successors northward beyond the Golden Gate of San Francisco Bay. The San Gabriel Arcangel mission at present-day Los Angeles became the western terminus for the Old Spanish Trail and for the emigrant route from Salt Lake City.

Serrano, Francisco (Francisco Serrão)

(unknown–1521) *Portuguese mariner, trader in the East Indies*

Francisco Serrano was probably born in Portugal, although there are few details of his origins or early life. Starting in 1505, Serrano, together with his long-time friend FERDINAND MAGELLAN, took part in Portuguese voyages to the Malabar Coast of southwestern India, where he fought in the conquest of the trading centers at Goa, Calicut, and Cochin. In 1508–09, he joined Magellan in DIEGO LÓPEZ DE SEQUIRA's expedition to the Malayan port of Malacca, narrowly escaping with his life when the sultan's forces launched a surprise attack against the visiting Portuguese.

In 1511, Serrano returned to Malacca with a naval force under AFONSO DE ALBUQUERQUE and António de Abreu, which brought that strategically located port under Portuguese domination. Later that year, he commanded the *Sabaia*, one of a fleet of Portuguese vessels sent to investigate the SPICE ISLANDS (the Moluccas) of present-day Indonesia to the east. Another of the expedition's ships was captained by Magellan.

At Amboina in the Spice Islands, Serrano obtained a valuable cargo of nutmeg. On the homeward voyage, his ship was wrecked on a reef and lost, while the other vessels continued back to India. Serrano meanwhile managed to capture a Malay pirate ship with which he explored the north coast of Java, then returned to Amboina. The local sultan on Amboina appointed him as his viceroy to the island of Ternate, where he married a native princess and settled.

In 1513, Serrano established a Portuguese trading fort on Ternate. Over the next several years, he wrote letters to Magellan in Portugal describing the abundance of nutmeg in the Spice Islands and the great commercial potential for European traders.

In early 1521, soon after he had concluded a trade agreement with the nearby island of Tidore, Serrano was poisoned, either on orders of the sultan of Tidore or by rival Portuguese merchants jealous of his influence with the native rulers. Serrano died on Ternate a few days afterward. Eight months later, the remaining ships of Magellan's fleet arrived at Ternate from the Philippines, after the first navigation of the STRAIT OF MAGELLAN. Magellan, who had been killed in the Philippines several months earlier, had planned to meet his old friend on Ternate and, with his help, initiate a lucrative trade in spices.

Francisco Serrano was one of the first Europeans to visit Java, as well as the islands of Ternate and Tidore, since the homeward voyage of MARCO POLO in the early 1290s. Magellan, informed by Serrano of the latitude of Ternate and

Junípero Serra (*Library of Congress*)

Tidore, was inspired to seek a westward route through the Americas, and across the South Pacific Ocean, to the Spice Islands. In this way, Serrano's reports to Magellan helped lead to the first round-the-world voyage.

Shackleton, Sir Ernest Henry (1874–1922)

British mariner, explorer in the Antarctic and South Atlantic

Ernest Henry Shackleton was born in Kilkee, Ireland, the son of a doctor. At the age of 16, after attending Dulwich College in London, he went to sea with the merchant marine.

After 10 years of service on merchant vessels, Shackleton secured an appointment as one of ROBERT FALCON SCOTT's lieutenants in the British National Antarctic Expedition of 1901–04. While at the McMurdo Sound base camp in February 1902, he made a BALLOON ascent in which he took the first aerial photos of the Antarctic.

In November 1902, Shackleton accompanied Scott and the expedition's zoologist, EDWARD ADRIAN WILSON, on an exploration of the Ross Ice Shelf. Using dog sledges, they headed southward, attaining 82°71' south latitude, within 500 miles of the SOUTH POLE and setting a new record for the farthest point south ever reached. They turned back at a location on the Ross Ice Shelf known afterward as Shackleton Inlet, unable to find a pass through the high mountain barrier blocking progress toward the South Pole.

Shackleton, Scott, and Wilson all suffered from SCURVY on the journey back to McMurdo Sound. While Scott and Wilson soon recovered, Shackleton did not and, still in a weakened state, he was compelled to return to England aboard the supply ship *Morning* in March 1903.

On regaining his health, Shackleton tried without success to obtain a commission in the British navy. In 1904, he married and settled in Edinburgh. While serving as secretary to the Scottish Geographical Society, he raised support for his own Antarctic expedition. By 1907, with the financial backing of British industrialist William Beardmore, Shackleton was able to organize what became known as the British Antarctic Expedition.

In July 1907, Shackleton and his team sailed from England on the *Nimrod.* Following a stopover in New Zealand, they reached Antarctica's Ross Sea coast in January 1908, where they established a base at Hut Point, the site of Scott's former encampment. One group, which included SIR DOUGLAS MAWSON, ascended Mount Erebus and reached the SOUTH MAGNETIC POLE; Shackleton and another team set out for the geographic South Pole in fall 1908.

Using sledges pulled by Manchurian ponies, the Shackleton party headed southward across the Ross Ice Shelf. Although their progress was blocked by the 10,000-foot-high Transantarctic Range, they managed to continue southward by ascending a glacier, which Shackleton called the Beard-

more Glacier after his patron. The two-week ascent cost Shackleton and his companies valuable time. Although they continued their trek across the Polar Plateau to within 97 miles of the South Pole, on January 9, 1909, Shackleton decided to turn back, determining that, with the loss of the ponies and their food supplies running low, they would not reach their goal with enough provisions to survive a return trip to base camp.

Upon his return to England in June 1909, Shackleton was heaped with honors, including a knighthood. He had brought back fossils from deep within the interior of the Antarctic and had reported the discovery of seams of coal in the Transantarctic Range. His 1,725-mile trek inland had revealed that the South Pole was located on the 10,000-foot-high Polar Plateau. Moreover, his expedition had taken the first motion pictures in Antarctica and made the first use of an automobile on the continent.

Less than three years after ROALD ENGELBREGT GRAVNING AMUNDSEN had reached the South Pole in 1911, Shackleton set out on the Imperial Trans-Antarctic Expedition, in which he planned to cross the Antarctic continent, from the Weddell Sea to the Ross Sea. With a crew of 27 men, he sailed from England in August 1914, just days after the outbreak of World War I. His ship, the *Endurance*, entered the Weddell Sea, where ice conditions prevented a landing. In January 1915, the ship became icebound off Vahsel Bay and, after 11 months of drifting, it was crushed. Meanwhile, Shackleton and his crew had abandoned the vessel, taking to the surrounding ice floes with small boats and what provisions they could salvage. They drifted for another three months on the ice, and, in April 1915, they managed to land on Elephant Island, off the tip of the Antarctic Peninsula.

Shackleton left 22 of his men on Elephant Island and with five others undertook a hazardous voyage in the *James Caird,* a modified open boat, across almost 1,000 miles of Antarctic seas, to the whaling station on South Georgia Island. They landed on the uninhabited side of South Georgia and had to make an overland crossing of the glaciers and mountains of the island's interior to reach the whaling settlement at Stromness. Using improvised ice-climbing equipment, Shackleton made the trip and sent a ship to pick up the men on the opposite side of the island. After several attempts, he managed to reach the men he had left on Elephant Island, rescuing them with the Chilean tugboat *Yelcho* in August 1916.

Shackleton returned to England to take part in the last phase of World War I, serving with a naval expedition to northern Russia in 1917–18. In 1921, he mounted his last Antarctic expedition, intending to explore Enderby Land on the little-known Indian Ocean coast of the continent. While aboard his ship, the *Quest,* off South Georgia Island, he died of a heart attack in early January 1922.

Sir Ernest Henry Shackleton recounted his 1907–09 expedition in his book *The Heart of the Antarctic* (1909) and told the story of his exploits in the Weddell Sea and South Georgia Island in *South* (1919). The overland crossing of Antarctica, the object of his 1914–16 expedition, was not achieved until the INTERNATIONAL GEOPHYSICAL YEAR of 1957–58, by SIR EDMUND PERCIVAL HILLARY and SIR VIVIAN ERNEST FUCHS. Shackleton pioneered the Beardmore Glacier route in 1908–09, which the ill-fated Scott expedition used to reach the South Pole in 1911–12. In the course of his disastrous 1914–17 expedition, Shackleton carried out one of the most heroic and dangerous rescue missions in the history of Antarctic exploration. He made the first examination of the Atlantic coast of Antarctica since it was explored by JAMES WEDDELL in 1822. Along that section of the Weddell seacoast, he discovered an uncharted section of shoreline, which he named the Caird Coast after the small boat on which he had made his heroic voyage to South Georgia Island. On the final leg of that journey, he made the first crossing of South Georgia Island. The Shackleton Ice Shelf on the Indian Ocean coast of Antarctica was later named for him.

Sheldon, May French (Mary French Sheldon, Bebe Bwana) (1847–1936) *American publisher, writer in central Africa*

May French Sheldon (her original given name was Mary) was born in Beaver, Pennsylvania, near Pittsburgh. Her father, Joseph French, was an engineer; her mother, Dr. Elizabeth Poorman French, was a physician. After her formal education, Sheldon entered the publishing business; by 1876, she was the owner of Saxon & Company, a London publishing house. That year, she married Eli Lemon Sheldon, an American banker and publisher living in London.

In London, Sheldon became a friend of SIR HENRY MORTON STANLEY, and she was inspired by his accounts of his years of exploration and travel in central Africa. Soon after Stanley had returned from his final expedition in 1890, she resolved to undertake an African journey of her own, financed by her husband.

Sheldon's interest in Africa was not limited to exploration. She was also concerned over the impact of colonization on the native population, especially in east-central Africa, where, by 1890, both England and Germany had each established a strong colonial foothold. She hoped her expedition would demonstrate that Europeans could gain the native people's cooperation with friendship instead of force.

In 1891, Sheldon arrived in Mombasa on the coast of what is now Kenya. She planned to travel inland to MOUNT KILIMANJARO in central Africa and, along the way, establish friendly contacts with many of the tribes of the surrounding territory. The expedition that she organized and led inland from Mombasa included 103 porters, guides, and servants, whom Sheldon had hired with the help of the sultan of Zanzibar. He also provided her with a letter of safe conduct to ensure her peaceful passage through his domain in what is now Tanzania.

Near Mount Kilimanjaro, Sheldon visited the village of Taveta, where she found a recently established British trading post. There were also plantations producing corn, tobacco, and sugar cane. She became the first European to witness a native rite known as the "moon dance," performed by men at a funeral ceremony.

While her expedition remained at Taveta, Sheldon explored the surrounding territory with a small group of porters and an official from the British trading post. She came upon Lake Chala, a circular lake formed from the crater of an extinct volcano. In a copper boat left behind by SAMUEL TELEKI's expedition of several years before, she explored the waters, becoming one of the first Europeans to do so. She then rejoined the rest of the expedition and ascended 4,700 feet up the slopes of Kilimanjaro to the native settlement of Kimangelia, where she met with the local sultan. Sheldon became an object of great curiosity for the people from the region, who flocked to the village by the thousands to catch their first glimpse of a white woman. She became known locally as Bebe Bwana for "woman master" in Swahili.

Sheldon had contact with 35 different tribes on her African journey and distributed many gifts among them. She had intended to visit the Masai, a warlike people much feared by the neighboring tribes. Yet she was forced to turn back at the edge of their territory, when her porters and servants threatened to mutiny if she continued. Near the village of Pangani, Sheldon was hurt in a fall down a ravine. Taken to a nearby German trading post, she recovered enough to return to Mombasa, then travel home to England by ship.

Sheldon soon recovered fully from her injuries and began writing an account of her experiences in east-central Africa. Her work, *Sultan to Sultan*, published in 1892, was a great success in both England and the United States. In 1892, she was made a member of the ROYAL GEOGRAPHICAL SOCIETY. That same year, she embarked on a lecture tour in the United States and presented her experiences to the Congress of Women at the Chicago Columbian Exposition. The text of this address was published in 1894 as "An African Expedition."

Sheldon opposed the creation of plantations in the interior of central Africa and the exploitation of its peoples. Instead, she urged that European powers establish industrial training centers, medical facilities, and churches to improve the lives of its indigenous peoples. In 1903, Sheldon traveled to the Belgian Congo (present-day Democratic

Republic of the Congo), where she observed and supported the Belgian government's colonizing efforts.

Sheldon raised money for the Belgian Red Cross during World War I, and after the war, in 1921, she was awarded the Chevalier de l'Ordre de la Couronne by the Belgian government. She continued to lecture on Africa until the age of 78. She died in London in her 90th year.

May French Sheldon was the first European woman to visit many native villages in present-day Kenya and Tanzania. In addition to winning friends among them, she succeeded in gaining the obedience and support of the natives who accompanied her, with equal measures of unwavering authority and concern for their welfare.

Shelikov, Grigory Ivanovich (Grigori Shelekhov, Gregori Shelikof, Gregor Shelikhov) (1747–1795) Russian fur trader in Alaska

Grigory Shelikov was born at Rylsk in European Russia, just north of the Ukraine. In 1773, he headed eastward to Irkutsk, the Siberian center of the FUR TRADE at the southern end of Lake Baikal.

At Irkutsk, Shelikov was employed by Russian fur-trading entrepreneur Ivana L. Golikov, eventually becoming a partner in Golikov's firm. In 1775, Shelikov traveled to Okhotsk on the Pacific coast of SIBERIA, using it as a base to expand his fur-trading enterprise to the Kamchatka Peninsula, the Kuril Islands to the south, and across the Bering Sea to the westernmost Aleutian Islands.

In 1783, Shelikov organized a trading expedition from Siberia to the Gulf of Alaska. Three ships were specially built at Okhotsk for the voyage. On August 27, he left Okhotsk aboard the *Three Saints,* along with Russian mariners GERASIM ALEKSEYEVICH IZMAILOV and DMITRY IVANOVICH BOCHAROV. They reached Bering Island off the west coast of the Kamchatka Peninsula, where they wintered.

The next spring, Shelikov and his expedition sailed across the Bering Sea to Unalaska Island. From there, they reached Kodiak Island in mid-August 1784.

Shelikov had married a successful Irkutsk businesswoman, Natalia Aleksievna, in 1781. His wife joined him on the 1783 voyage, becoming the first known European woman to visit Alaska.

On September 22, 1784, Shelikov established a settlement on Kodiak Island at a harbor he named Three Saints Bay. During the next two years, he initiated additional explorations of the islands and the coastline of the Gulf of Alaska.

In 1786, Shelikov returned to Irkutsk. He sought backing for a royal trade monopoly from Russian empress Catherine the Great. In 1790, he appointed ALEKSANDR ANDREYEVICH BARANOV as director of his fur-trading enterprise in Alaska.

Shelikov died at Irkutsk in 1795. Four years after his death, Czar Paul I granted his widow and son-in-law, Nikolay Petrovich Rezanov, a royal charter for the RUSSIAN-AMERICAN COMPANY.

Grigory Shelikov's fur-trading post on Kodiak Island became the first permanent non-Indian settlement in what is now the state of Alaska. His fur-trading enterprise firmly established Russian sovereignty over Alaska until 1867, when it was purchased by the United States. Shelikov Strait, which separates Kodiak Island from the mainland, is named in his honor. His book, published in London in 1795 as *Journal of the Voyages to the Coast of North America in 1783–87,* provides one of the earliest accounts of Alaska.

Shepard, Alan Bartlett, Jr. (1923–1998)
American astronaut, first American in space

Alan Shepard was born in East Derry, New Hampshire. He pursued his undergraduate studies at the U.S. Naval Academy, graduating in 1944. After service on a destroyer in World War II, he attended the Navy Test Pilot School in Patuxent River, Maryland, and the Naval War College in Newport, Rhode Island.

In 1959, Shepard was selected as one of the original seven ASTRONAUTS in the NATIONAL AERONAUTICS AND SPACE ADMINISTRATION (NASA) and soon afterward, as the pilot of the first manned American space mission, part of the MERCURY PROGRAM. The former Union of Soviet Socialist Republics (USSR, or the Soviet Union) launched the first human in space, YURY ALEKSEYEVICH GAGARIN, on April 12, 1961. Three weeks later, on May 5, 1961, Shepard became the first American in space. In the *Freedom 7* capsule, he reached a suborbital altitude of 115 miles. The flight lasted 15 minutes, 22 seconds, before the capsule's splashdown by parachute in the Atlantic Ocean, where Shepard was retrieved by helicopter. Virgil Grissom also accomplished a suborbital flight in 1961. JOHN HERSCHELL GLENN, JR., became the first American to orbit Earth in February 1962.

Following surgery to correct an ear condition, Shepard was chosen as commander on the *Apollo 14* Moon mission. The APOLLO PROGRAM had successfully put Americans on the Moon: first, NEIL ALDEN ARMSTRONG and Edwin "Buzz" Aldrin in July 1969, then Pete Conrad and Alan La Vern Bean in November 1969 in the *Apollo 11* and *Apollo 12* missions. *Apollo 13* had been discontinued prematurely. *Apollo 14* took off on January 31, 1971. Shepard and Edgar D. Mitchell landed in the *Antares* lunar module near the Moon's Fra Mauro Crater on February 5, 1971, while Stuart A. Roosa orbited in the *Kitty Hawk* command module. Shepard and Mitchell, transporting equipment in a two-wheeled cart, walked 2.1 miles, and reached a distance of some 4,600 feet from the lunar module. They spent a record

Alan Shepard *(Library of Congress)*

33.5 hours on the lunar surface, conducting numerous experiments. Splashdown was accomplished in the Pacific Ocean nine days after takeoff.

Alan Shepard was the first American in space and one of the first men to walk on the Moon. He especially captured the public's imagination during the *Apollo 14* mission when he hit golf balls on the Moon.

Sherley, Sir Anthony (Sir Anthony Shirley)

(ca. 1565–ca. 1635) *English soldier of fortune, diplomat in Persia, Russia, and Morocco*

Anthony Sherley was born at Wiston in Sussex, England, the son of a nobleman. He embarked on a military career, serving with the British army in the Netherlands and France in the late 1580s and early 1590s. In 1596, he commanded an expedition of PRIVATEERS against Spanish shipping and settlements in the Caribbean.

Sherley traveled to Persia (present-day Iran) with his brother Robert Sherley in 1598, where he succeeded in ob-

taining some trade concessions for English merchants. He was then made an ambassador by the Persian ruler, Shah Abbas the Great, who sent him on a diplomatic mission to Europe. In 1600, he traveled from the Persian capital at Esfahan, across the Caspian Sea to Moscow, and on to Prague and Rome. His attempts to raise military support in Europe for a proposed Persian campaign against the Turks met with little success.

In 1605, Sherley entered the service of Holy Roman Emperor Rudolf II, who sent him to Morocco. He stayed until 1606, in an abortive attempt to incite the Arabs against the Turks. In 1609, Sherley commanded a Spanish naval expedition in the MEDITERRANEAN SEA against the Turks, which also met with little success. He later retired in Madrid.

Sir Anthony Sherley (who had been knighted early in his career by Henry IV of France, much to the displeasure of his own sovereign, Elizabeth I) was one of the first Englishmen to travel in Persia. His brother Robert remained in Persia as an ambassador until 1627, when he returned to England with THOMAS HERBERT. Sherley's account of his travels in Persia appeared in London in 1613 as *Sir Anthony Sherley: His Relation of his Travels into Persia, the Dangers and Distresses which Befel him in his Passage.*

Shirase, Nobu (1861–1946) *Japanese explorer of the Antarctic*

Nobu Shirase participated in an exploration of the Kuril Islands to the north of Japan in 1893. As a lieutenant in the army, he presented a plan for the first Japanese expedition to the Antarctic and an attempt to reach the SOUTH POLE. He finally gained the support of Shigenobu Okuma, an influential statesman, and managed to raise the necessary funds.

Shirase departed from Tokyo aboard the tiny *Kainan Maru* in December 1910 and after a brief stopover in Wellington, NEW ZEALAND, headed for Antarctica the following February. The expedition sighted Victoria Land in early March but because of poor weather conditions, did not attempt to land. Continuing on through the Ross Sea, they eventually found their passage blocked by PACK ICE, leading to Shirase's decision to turn back for Australia. They reached Sydney at the beginning of May. The ship's captain and several crew members returned to Japan to raise additional funds, while Shirase and the others waited. Living in poverty, they were ridiculed in the Australian and New Zealand press and distrusted by the Australian public. Professor Edgeworth David of the University of Sydney, a former associate of SIR ERNEST HENRY SHACKLETON, became involved, however, and reassured the public regarding the scientific goals of their expedition. Shirase, meanwhile, abandoned the idea of trying to reach the South Pole and scaled back the expedition to an exploration of King Edward VII Land and the Ross Ice Shelf.

The Japanese expedition set sail for the Antarctic once again in November 1911, reaching the Ross Ice Shelf the following January. At Kainan Bay, so named by the expedition, a party was sent ashore. The expedition then continued westward. Shirase and his men soon encountered another ship, the *Fram*, whose crew awaited ROALD ENGELBREGT GRAVNING AMUNDSEN's return from the South Pole.

While the *Kainan Maru* was moored in the Bay of Whales, Shirase headed the Dash Patrol, as it was called, consisting of seven men, two of whom stayed at a base camp at the edge of the ice shelf, while the others proceeded southward with dog sledges. At the end of January 1912, enduring blizzard conditions, Shirase and his four companions planted a Japanese flag at the top of the ice shelf some 160 miles from their starting point. In the meantime, a second party landed at Biscoe Bay in King Edward VII Land, climbed an ice slope, and reached the foot of the Alexandra Range before returning to the ship. The *Kainan Maru* then returned to the Bay of Whales to pick up the Dash Patrol. After a return stopover at Wellington, the ship reached Japan in June 1912. They were treated as heroes on their return.

Nobu Shirase had the vision to recognize a role for Japan in Antarctic exploration.

Sidi Bombay   See BOMBAY, SIDI.

Silva Porto, Antonio Francisco da   (1817–1890)
Portuguese trader in central Africa
Antonio da Silva Porto was born in Porto, Portugal, the son of an industrialist. He left home in his early teens, immigrating to Brazil. In 1832, he settled in Portuguese West Africa, present-day Angola.

Silva Porto became a trader, venturing into regions seldom visited by Europeans and dealing with the natives of the interior of the colony. In 1853, at the request of the Portuguese colonial governor, he undertook an expedition inland to locate the source of the ZAMBEZI RIVER. Although he penetrated the upper Zambezi country, he was unable to determine the river's source. Yet, in traveling from the Atlantic coast of Angola to the Zambezi's outlet on the Indian Ocean, he completed the first European crossing of Central Africa from west to east.

Soon after his 1853–54 exploration of the Zambezi River and his crossing of Africa, Antonio da Silva Porto provided assistance to Scottish missionary and physician DAVID LIVINGSTONE, who had also just undertaken an examination of the Zambezi.

Simpson, Sir George   (ca. 1792–1860)
Scottish-Canadian director of the Hudson's Bay Company in North America, cousin of Thomas Simpson
George Simpson was born at Loch Broom in western Scotland. In 1809, he went to London, where he worked for his uncle's West Indies Trading Company. In 1820, he joined the HUDSON'S BAY COMPANY, and, that year, he traveled to Canada to take charge of the company's Lake Athabasca posts.

Simpson spent the winter of 1820–21 at Lake Athabasca, and, following the Hudson's Bay Company's merger with the NORTH WEST COMPANY in 1821, he was appointed head of the vast northern department.

In 1824–25, Simpson made his first overland journey across Canada, from York Factory on HUDSON BAY to the company's post on the COLUMBIA RIVER. In 1826, he became governor of all the Hudson's Bay Company operations in North America.

On July 12, 1828, Simpson started out from Hudson Bay on a second cross-continental trip across Canada. Traveling by CANOE with overland portages, he covered 3,260 miles in less than three months, reaching the Pacific coast of British Columbia via the Thompson and Fraser Rivers on October 10, 1828. At that time, it was the longest overland voyage across Canada attempted in one season.

In the mid-1830s, Simpson organized and supported exploring expeditions to the Canadian Arctic, including those of his cousin THOMAS SIMPSON. For his efforts in support of Arctic exploration, Simpson was knighted in 1841. That same year, he undertook a mostly overland trip around the world. Starting out from Liverpool, England, in March 1841, he sailed to Canada by way of Halifax and Boston. He then took the canoe-and-portage route across Canada to Vancouver, from where he went to Sitka, Alaska, and the Aleutian Islands. He crossed the Bering Sea to Okhotsk in SIBERIA, then traveled the length of Asiatic and European Russia to St. Petersburg on the Baltic, and sailed back to England.

After 1833, Simpson lived in Montreal, directing the Hudson's Bay Company operations. During the 1840s and early 1850s, he sponsored additional explorations of the Canadian Arctic, including JOHN RAE's 1846 journey. In his later years, Simpson was prominent in banking and railroad development.

Sir George Simpson's accounts of his overland journeys across Canada were published in 1931. His 1841–42 overland journey around the world was until that time the first such expedition. He published an account of this trip in his 1847 book, *Narrative of a Journey Round the World in 1841 and 1842*. Simpson Falls on western Canada's Peace River and Cape George Simpson in the Canadian Arctic were both named in his honor.

Simpson, James Hervey (1813–1883) *U.S. Army officer, American topographer in the American West*

James H. Simpson, a native of New Brunswick, New Jersey, entered West Point when he was 15. Four years later, in 1832, he graduated as a second lieutenant in the artillery. In 1837, he served in Florida in the campaign against Seminole Indians, and, the following year, he transferred to the U.S. Army Corps of Topographical Engineers.

Throughout the 1840s, Simpson supervised government construction projects in the East and South. In 1849, he accompanied Captain RANDOLPH BARNES MARCY's expedition blazing a wagon route from Fort Smith, Arkansas, to Santa Fe, New Mexico.

In August 1849, Simpson took part in a military expedition against Navajo (Dineh) Indians in the region northwest of Santa Fe. En route, he led a reconnaissance of the upper Chaco River and came upon the ancient Anasazi ruins of Chaco Canyon, New Mexico. He continued westward with the military expedition into present-day northeastern Arizona and accompanied the first known group of Anglo-Americans to penetrate the Navajo stronghold at Canyon de Chelly. He undertook an exploration of the canyon and located more pueblo ruins unknown to non-Indians.

In 1853, Simpson became a captain in the Topographical Corps. In August 1858, he began a series of explorations of Utah's Great Basin. From Camp Floyd, south of Salt Lake City, he led an expedition north and east into Timpanogos Canyon and the Wasatch Mountains, to Fort Bridger.

In October 1858, Simpson explored westward from the Great Salt Lake across northern Nevada and proceeded to Carson City, via Reynolds Pass. Along the way, the expedition blazed a trail along the Walker River, an alternative to the Humboldt River route into the Sierra Nevada.

In May 1859, Simpson led another expedition south and west across the Great Basin to the Mormon settlement at Genoa near Lake Tahoe.

In the Civil War, Simpson was commissioned a colonel of volunteers. Captured by Confederate forces in the Virginia campaign, he was released in a prisoner exchange in 1862. Simpson went on to serve as chief topographical engineer in the Ohio Valley and in Kentucky. After the war, he was appointed chief engineer of the Department of the Interior, and in that capacity he oversaw the construction of the Union Pacific Railroad in 1865–67. He retired from the service in 1880, after a period in which he directed road construction and harbor development in the South and Midwest.

James H. Simpson's explorations of New Mexico, Arizona, Utah, and Nevada spanned more territory in the American West than those of any other army topographer of the time. His exploration of Native American antiquities in New Mexico and Arizona contributed greatly to the archaeological understanding of the Southwest. The first drawings

James H. Simpson *(Library of Congress)*

of the Chaco Canyon and Canyon de Chelly ruins were made by artist-topographer RICHARD HOVENDON KERN, who accompanied Simpson in 1849. Simpson's report of his expeditions between Fort Bridger, the Great Basin, and the Sierra Nevada was published in 1876, and his findings led to the establishment of direct wagon and mail routes between Salt Lake City and California. In 1871, Simpson published *Coronado's March In Search of the Seven Cities of Cibola,* an account of the Spanish CONQUISTADORES' first journey into the region Simpson himself had explored.

Simpson, Thomas (1808–1840) *Scottish fur trader, surveyor in the Canadian Arctic and Alaska, cousin of Sir George Simpson*

Thomas Simpson was born at Dingwall in northern Scotland, a descendant of Scottish statesman Duncan Forbes. He was educated at Aberdeen University, where he earned a master's degree. In 1829, he immigrated to Canada and entered the service of the HUDSON'S BAY COMPANY.

Simpson gained his initial experience in wilderness travel by commanding CANOE convoys between Montreal and the Hudson's Bay Company post at Fort Garry (present-day Winnipeg, Manitoba). From there, he regularly traveled on snowshoes to Fort York on HUDSON BAY, 700 miles to the northeast.

In 1836, to fulfill the Hudson's Bay Company's obligation to continue the search for the NORTHWEST PASSAGE, Simpson's older cousin, Hudson's Bay Company governor SIR GEORGE SIMPSON, sent him and a fellow company employee, PETER WARREN DEASE, to explore the remaining unknown segments of Canada's Arctic coastline.

After undergoing training in surveying techniques at Fort Garry, the younger Simpson joined Dease at Great Bear Lake, where they established a base camp, Fort Confidence. In spring 1837, accompanied by a party of VOYAGEURS, they descended the Mackenzie River to the Arctic coast, then explored westward, reaching the northernmost point of Alaska, Point Barrow, on August 4, 1837. This location was the farthest east FREDERICK WILLIAM BEECHEY had reached in his 1826 seaward exploration of the eastern entrance to the Northwest Passage; it was also the farthest west attained that same year by SIR JOHN FRANKLIN and SIR GEORGE BACK.

After another winter at Great Bear Lake, Simpson and Dease set out again in spring 1838. They descended the Coppermine River, then surveyed the coastline eastward, reaching 100 miles beyond Point Turnagain. The next year, they explored even farther to the east, reaching the south coast of King William Island and the west coast of the Boothia Peninsula. On the return journey, they explored the south shore of Victoria Island.

Although Simpson had planned to extend his explorations eastward as far as Fury and Hecla Strait and into northern Hudson Bay, by the end of 1839 he had still not received authorization for another expedition from his cousin, Sir George. He therefore resolved to return to England and there apply in person to the directors of the Hudson's Bay Company. He began the journey with a 1,500-mile hike southward to the Red River Settlement in present-day Manitoba, which he reached in February 1840. He continued his eastward journey toward Montreal in the spring, accompanied by several mixed-blood Indians. On June 14, 1840, in the lands of the Sioux (Dakota, Lakota, Nakota) Indians, he was found shot to death in his tent. The circumstances of his death are unclear, although the local U.S. territorial authorities declared it a suicide.

Thomas Simpson died without learning that the Hudson's Bay Company board of directors had already assented to his proposed expedition, and that, in recognition of his

exploits, he had been awarded the Queen's Arctic Medal. His explorations of the Canadian Arctic filled in details about the last remaining stretch of unknown coastline between the Mackenzie River delta and Point Barrow, Alaska. In the eastern Canadian Arctic, he surveyed and charted the coastline between Point Turnagain and the west coast of the Boothia Peninsula, providing vital geographic details for the British navy's subsequent attempts to navigate the Northwest Passage during the 1840s.

Sinclair, James (1811–1856) *Canadian pioneer in the Rocky Mountains and Pacific Northwest*

James Sinclair was born at Oxford House, a HUDSON'S BAY COMPANY fur-trading settlement in what is now northeastern Manitoba, Canada. His father, an official with the trading company, was from Scotland, and his mother was a Métis.

After attending school in Edinburgh, Scotland, Sinclair returned to central Canada at the age of 15, eventually becoming a partner in a trading enterprise out of the Red River Settlement. As both merchant and shipper of goods, he traveled widely in central Canada and in what is now the north-central United States, undertaking journeys by CANOE from the Red River Settlement northward to HUDSON BAY and leading wagon caravans southward to settlements in present-day south-central Minnesota.

In 1841, Sinclair was commissioned by the Hudson's Bay Company to lead a group of emigrants from the Red River Settlement westward to the Oregon Country. The project had been instigated by the British government, hoping to reinforce its claim on Oregon with a sudden influx of British settlers from Canada. There were 23 families in the party, which numbered 121 men, women, and children, with 55 wagons and several hundred head of cattle.

Sinclair and the wagon train left the Red River Settlement on June 5, 1841. With the help of the Indian guide Bras Croche, he located White Man Pass, which proved to be a suitable wagon route through the ROCKY MOUNTAINS to the upper COLUMBIA RIVER. They followed the river to Fort Vancouver, opposite present-day Portland, Oregon, arriving on October 13, 1841.

Sinclair soon returned to the Red River Settlement, where he had become a prominent voice in the Métis community. He undertook a second westward expedition in 1850, in which he returned to Oregon, again crossing the Rockies by way of White Man Pass. After two years in Oregon and California, he sailed for Panama, returning to the Red River Settlement by way of New York.

In May 1854, Sinclair set out with another emigrant wagon train, again accompanied by Bras Croche. On this expedition, which reached Walla Walla on December 24, 1854, he pioneered a wagon route through the Kananaskis

Valley and across the Rockies to the Kootenay River Valley and the upper reaches of the Columbia River.

Sinclair stayed in Oregon throughout 1855. Before he could return to the Red River Settlement, from where he planned to lead more emigrant wagon trains into Oregon by way of his newly discovered Rocky Mountain pass, he was killed by Yakama Indians in the Cascade Range in 1856.

The route James Sinclair pioneered through the Canadian Rockies, known afterward as Sinclair's Canyon, was later developed into the highway linking the cities of Banff, Alberta, and Windemere, British Columbia. While the Hudson's Bay Company had developed its network of trails across western Canada primarily as portages for the canoe routes between its various fur-trading forts, Sinclair's explorations led to new overland communication and transportation routes between central Canada and the Pacific Northwest.

Singh, Kishen (Kish Singh, Krishna Singh)

(unknown–1921) *Indian surveyor in western China and Tibet, in service to Great Britain, cousin of Nain Singh*

Kishen Singh was probably a native of northern India's Kashmir region. During the mid-1860s, he entered the service of the British colonial authorities, who trained him as one of their native surveyors, known as the PUNDITS (Hindi for "learned expert").

In 1869, Singh explored westward from the northern Indian city of Dehra Dun into the northern Punjab region of present-day Pakistan. Like other native explorers working for Great Britain at that time, such as KINTUP, he used only basic surveying instruments, measuring the distances he covered by counting his footsteps.

Singh undertook his first exploration of the HIMALAYAS in 1871. Disguised as a Buddhist pilgrim, he started out from Katmandu, Nepal, and investigated a large area of Tibet and southern China extending westward from the Tibetan capital at LHASA and Nam Tso Lake, as far as the eastern edge of Chinese Turkestan. In 1873, he joined his cousin NAIN SINGH in an expedition from the upper Indus city of Leh deep into Chinese Turkestan, to the city of Yarkand in the Taklimakan Desert.

On his own in 1874, Kishen Singh explored the region southwest of Yarkand and Kashgar into the Pamir region of south-central Asia before returning eastward to Leh in northern India. But his most ambitious journey began in 1878, when he set out from Darjeeling in extreme northeastern India to Shigatse and Lhasa in Tibet. Over the next several years, he explored northward as far as the Tsaidam Depression, the swampy region between the branches of western China's Kunlun mountain range. On reaching a point as far north as the southwestern edge of Mongolia's GOBI DESERT, he made his way back to India by

way of Tibet's Tsangpo River, arriving in Darjeeling in 1882.

Kishen Singh's explorations into western China from India provided accurate information about the northern extent of the subcontinent for the British Great Trigonometrical Survey of India, an undertaking that lasted through much of the 19th century.

Singh, Nain (ca. 1826–1882) *Indian surveyor in central Asia, in service to Great Britain, cousin of Kishen Singh*

Nain Singh was a native of the eastern Himalayan kingdom of Bhutan. In 1854–57, he served as a guide in the HIMALAYAS for the German mountaineers, the brothers ADOLF VON SCHLAGINTWEIT, HERMANN VON SCHLAGINTWEIT, and ROBERT VON SCHLAGINTWEIT.

During the early 1860s, Singh entered the British school for native surveyors at the northern Indian city of Dehra Dun. He had been recruited to carry out explorations north of the Himalayas for the ongoing Great Trigonometrical Survey formerly headed by SIR GEORGE SIMPSON. At that time, with the Chinese government forbidding Europeans entry into China and Tibet from India, the British directors of the survey had resorted to employing natives from the mountains of northern India and adjacent lands to carry out a surreptitious reconnaissance of the lands beyond the Himalayas.

In 1864, Singh set out from Bareilly, India, for Tibet, accompanied by his cousin Mani Singh, also a British-trained native surveyor. On being turned back by Chinese border guards, they disguised themselves as merchants from Ladakh and succeeded in penetrating Tibet as far as the Tashilhumpo monastery near Shigatse. Singh met with the 11-year-old Panchen Lama, then continued on to the Tibetan capital at LHASA, which he reached on January 10, 1866. Based on observations of the sun and the stars, he established the city's geographic coordinates. By noting with a thermometer the temperature at which water came to a boil, he also determined its altitude.

After three months, Singh traveled to Lake Mansowar, then traced the upper course of the Brahmaputra River and charted the range of mountains north of the Himalayas, known as the Nyenchentanglhas. He recrossed the Himalayas back to Bareilly, India, having surveyed the trade route into Tibet and having accurately measured 1,200 miles of mountainous territory by counting his footsteps.

In 1867, Singh undertook a survey of the upper Indus Valley, then entered western China by way of the 18,400-foot Mana Pass. He traversed the Tibetan Plateau to Thok-Jalung, where he observed gold-mining operations. In 1873, with his cousin KISHEN SINGH, he traveled from Leh in northern India to Khotan and the edge of western China's

Taklimakan desert. From there, they went to the city of Yarkand.

Nain Singh was the foremost of British India's PUNDITS (Hindi for "learned expert"). In fact, it was his code name, "the Pundit," which came to be used for all the Indian explorers. Along with KINTUP and Kishen Singh, he provided British geographers and cartographers with enough information to produce the first modern maps of the regions north of the Himalayas. His measurements of distances, mostly carried out by counting his footsteps, provided data on more than 3,000 miles of previously uncharted country. The Aling Kangri mountains, which he explored while on the northern edge of the Tibetan Plateau, were formerly known as the Nain Singh range. He received a medal from the ROYAL GEOGRAPHICAL SOCIETY in 1877.

Sitgreaves, Lorenzo (ca. 1811–1888) *U.S. Army officer in the American Southwest*

Lorenzo Sitgreaves was born in Pennsylvania, the son of prominent congressman and lawyer Samuel Sitgreaves. An 1832 graduate of West Point, Lorenzo served as an artillery officer for several years, then left the military to practice engineering. Rejoining the army in 1840, he was appointed a second lieutenant in the U.S. Army Corps of Topographical Engineers.

In the early 1840s, Sitgreaves took part in coastal surveys in the North and South. In September 1846, at the outbreak of the U.S.-Mexican War, he accompanied Captain George W. Hughes and a company of Topographical Engineers into Mexico from Presidio del Rio Grande in western Texas. The expedition blazed a trail south and east for advancing U.S. forces to a point between Chihuahua and Monterrey in Mexico. After participating in the Battle of Buena Vista in February 1847, Sitgreaves was breveted a captain.

In September 1851, Sitgreaves commanded a Topographical Engineers unit accompanying Colonel Edwin V. Sumner's military expedition into the Navajo (Dineh) lands west of the Zuni Indian pueblos of New Mexico. With Sitgreaves was frontier artist and topographer RICHARD HOVENDON KERN; his guide was Antoine Leroux.

Sitgreaves had been ordered to follow up the earlier explorations of Lieutenant JAMES HERVEY SIMPSON and survey a wagon route between Santa Fe, New Mexico, and San Diego, California. Starting out from Santa Fe, he went first to the Zuni pueblos of northwestern New Mexico, then southwestward along the Zuni River as far as its confluence with the Little Colorado River in present-day eastern Arizona.

Near present-day Flagstaff, Arizona, Sitgreaves was advised by Leroux that traveling farther up the Little Colorado would take him into the Grand Canyon. He left the Little

Colorado and led his command westward across a country of high tablelands and lava beds that was totally devoid of water. Suffering repeated Indian attacks along the way, Sitgreaves and his party eventually reached the Colorado River near Mojave Indian villages. With Chief IRATEBA's help they followed the COLORADO RIVER south to Fort Yuma, then crossed overland to San Diego.

In his subsequent report, published by the government in 1853, Sitgreaves provided scientifically charted maps and information on existing Indian settlements and trails in northern Arizona. Sitgreaves went on to serve in the Civil War as an engineering officer, and, by 1864, he had attained the rank of lieutenant colonel. He retired from the army in 1866.

Lorenzo Sitgreaves contributed much in the way of detailed geographic knowledge of the Southwest. His 1849 map of the route taken by U.S. forces on their 1846 drive into Mexico was one of the first to describe the little-known Chihuahua region. His 1851 expedition from Zuni, New Mexico, to San Diego, California, later provided a basis for the Pacific Railroad Surveys along the 35th parallel. Although Sitgreaves did not find a direct route across Arizona to the Pacific coast in 1851, his trail as far as the Colorado River was subsequently adopted by the Santa Fe Railroad.

Smet, Pierre-Jean de   See DE SMET, PIERRE-JEAN.

Smith, James (1737–1812) *American frontiersman, guide, politician in Kentucky*

James Smith was born in Franklin County in south-central Pennsylvania. At the age of 18, he was taken captive by Indians; he lived with them until he managed to escape four years later. In the early 1760s, he served as a guide under Colonel Henry Bouquet in campaigns against the tribes of the Ohio Valley.

In 1766, Smith and four companions undertook a hunting expedition into the region beyond the CUMBERLAND GAP, even though such forays had been expressly forbidden by the British with the imposition of the Proclamation Line of 1763. They were among the few non-Indians to do so since the start of the French and Indian War in 1754.

Smith later settled in eastern Virginia, where he took part in Lord Dunmore's War of 1774 as a captain in the colonial militia. He also served as a colonel with patriot forces in the American Revolution of 1775–83, commanding frontier campaigns against the Indians. In 1788, he moved to Bourbon County in what is now northeastern Kentucky, where he became prominent in state politics, serving for many years in the state legislature. Smith's own account of his explorations beyond the Appalachian frontier,

Remarkable Adventures in the Life and Travels of Colonel James Smith, was first published in 1799.

James Smith's 1766 hunting expedition marked the resumption of exploration west of the APPALACHIAN MOUNTAINS, which had been halted by a decade of warfare between Indians and non-Indians. Soon afterward, inspired by reports brought back by Smith and others, other "long-hunters" ventured into Kentucky, most notably frontiersman DANIEL BOONE.

Smith, Jedediah Strong (Jed Smith) (1799–1831)
American fur trader, trapper in the American West

Jedediah "Jed" Smith was born near what is now Bainbridge, New York. With his family, he migrated to Pennsylvania, where he worked on a Lake Erie trading vessel before moving west to St. Louis to take part in the burgeoning FUR TRADE along the MISSOURI RIVER.

In 1822 and 1823, Smith joined WILLIAM HENRY ASHLEY's fur-trading expeditions to the upper Missouri region of what is now South Dakota. When Ashley's traders were attacked by Arikara Indians on the Missouri, Smith was dispatched upriver to seek help. In summer 1823, he took part in the punitive expedition against the tribe under Colonel HENRY LEAVENWORTH.

With the upper Missouri route to the northern Rocky Mountains cut off by Indian hostility, Smith led a group of MOUNTAIN MEN west from Fort Kiowa in present-day South Dakota, along the White River, into the Badlands and Black Hills. His group included JAMES CLYMAN, THOMAS FITZPATRICK, and WILLIAM LEWIS SUBLETTE. While exploring the Black Hills, Smith was nearly killed in an attack by a wounded grizzly bear. He soon recovered, and, after crossing the Belle Fourche River, he led his party into what is now eastern Wyoming, where they purchased horses from the Cheyenne and Sioux (Dakota, Lakota, Nakota) Indians, then proceeded westward across the Great Plains.

Smith and his men reached Wyoming's Powder River Valley, then crossed the Bighorn Mountains by way of Granite Pass into the Bighorn Basin. Heavy snows prevented further progress through Union Pass, and Smith and the others were forced to encamp for a time near what is now Dubois, Wyoming. From the Indians, Smith learned of a route to the south that led through the ROCKY MOUNTAINS. In February 1824, after following the Wind River, his men reached the Sweetwater River. By following it, they located the SOUTH PASS, which took them west to the abundant beaver hunting grounds of the Green River Valley near the present Wyoming-Utah border.

Smith and his party trapped as far south as the northern end of the Uinta Mountains. From there, they headed north and west to the Snake River, where they met up with a group of Iroquois (Haudenosaunee) Indians trapping for the HUDSON'S BAY COMPANY and rescued them from attack by Paiute Indians. Smith escorted the Iroquois to the Hudson's Bay Company post at Flathead Lake in what is now western Montana. There, ALEXANDER ROSS, director of the Flathead Lake post, hosted Smith and the Americans in the winter of 1824–25. From Flathead Lake, Smith headed northward as far as the Canadian border and explored the upper Snake River region of Idaho. By summer 1825, Smith and his trappers had returned to the Green River, and, at Henrys Fork, attended the first annual fur traders' rendezvous.

Smith returned to St. Louis by way of the Missouri and subsequently became a full partner with Ashley. The next summer, he, DAVID E. JACKSON, and William Sublette bought out Ashley's interests in what was known as the ROCKY MOUNTAIN FUR COMPANY. He set out for the Rockies again in August 1826, from the Cache Lake rendezvous in present-day Utah, and explored south and west to the Great Salt Lake. From the Ute Indians, he heard reports of the fabled Buenaventura River, which supposedly flowed out of the Great Salt Lake to the Pacific Ocean. David E. Jackson and a small party explored for this stream but were unable to locate it. Smith headed south to Utah Lake, then followed the Sevier and Virgin Rivers, eventually reaching the COLORADO RIVER and following it to the Mojave River. Guided by Mission Indians, Smith and his party crossed the Mojave Desert to the San Bernardino Mountains and reached the Mexican settlement of San Gabriel near Los Angeles, California, on November 27, 1826.

Smith ran into difficulties with Mexican authorities, who took a dim view of any American encroachment into their territory. At San Diego, Smith was told by the Mexican governor to leave California over the same route he had come. Instead, he led his men northward into the San Joaquin Valley, as far as the American River near Sacramento. He left some of his party there to trap, then explored for a route east through the Sierra Nevada. On finding Ebbett's Pass, Smith made the first eastward crossing of the Sierra Nevada into what is now Nevada. He traversed central Nevada, and, after nearly dying of thirst in Utah's Great Salt Lake Desert, reached the fur-trading rendezvous at Bear Lake, Utah, on July 3, 1827.

Less than two weeks later, Smith set off again for California. He retraced his earlier route to the Mojave villages on the Colorado River. While crossing the Colorado on rafts, Smith lost 10 of his men in an attack by Mojave warriors. Smith and the survivors made their way through the San Bernardino Mountains to San Gabriel, where the Mexicans jailed the trespassers for almost two months. They were finally released in the custody of an American sea captain in January 1827, who transported them north to Monterey. From there, they headed into the Tehachapi Mountains to the Sacramento Valley, where they rejoined the men left behind the previous year.

Still searching for the Pacific outlet of the Buenaventura River, Smith and his men explored the American, Merced, and Stanislaus Rivers of northern California, then headed northward into the Oregon Country. On the Umpqua River, most of Smith's 18 men were killed in an attack by Indians. Smith and three other survivors made their way to Fort Vancouver on the COLUMBIA RIVER, where JOHN MCLOUGHLIN of the Hudson's Bay Company provided them with assistance and helped recover the furs stolen by the Indians.

Smith trapped in the Wyoming-Montana region in 1828–29, then returned to St. Louis with the intention of farming and entering the mercantile business.

In 1830, Smith conferred with President Andrew Jackson's secretary of war, John Eaton, on the extent of British occupation in the Oregon Country. The following year, he joined David Jackson, William Sublette, and Thomas Fitzpatrick in a trading venture along the Santa Fe Trail to New Mexico. On May 27, 1831, while scouting ahead in the arid region between the Arkansas and Cimarron Rivers of present-day southwestern Kansas, Smith was killed in an attack by Comanche Indians. Smith's journal of his explorations, *The Travels of Jedediah Smith: A Documentary Outline* (edited by Maurice S. Sullivan), was published posthumously in 1934.

Among his contemporaries in the fur trade, Jed Smith was known as the "Knight of the Buckskin." In the course of his explorations of the West, he covered more than 16,000 miles. Smith led the first non-Indians westward through the South Pass and reported on its feasibility as a wagon route for emigrants on the way to Oregon and California. His 1826 expedition across the Southwest from the Great Salt Lake was the first known overland journey to California on that route. His route from the Colorado River to the San Bernardino Mountains developed into the Mormon Cutoff. On his return, Smith undertook the first successful crossing of the Great Salt Lake Desert, the largest desert in North America. Historians also credit Smith with locating the Old Spanish Trail and providing the first precise information about the geography of the American Southwest.

Smith, John (ca. 1580–1631) *English soldier, colonizer in Virginia, explorer of coastal North America*

John Smith was a native of Willoughby in Lincolnshire, England. He spent his early years as a merchant's apprentice in King's Lynn. In 1596, at the age of 16, he left England for the Continent, where he served as a mercenary with the French army in its wars against Spain in the Low Countries. Smith later fought along with Austrian forces against the Crimean Tartars at the Battle of Rotenthurn Pass in the Transylvania region of what is now Hungary. He was taken prisoner and sold as a slave to a Turkish pasha. According to

his own account, an influential Turkish woman saved him by having him sent to the Don River region, from where he was able to escape.

By 1604, Smith was back in England. He soon became a shareholder of the newly chartered VIRGINIA COMPANY of London, a syndicate of merchants licensed to establish a colony in North America. As military captain, he sailed from England with the company's colonizing expedition under CHRISTOPHER NEWPORT in December 1606.

Arriving on the Virginia coast in spring 1607, Smith helped establish the Jamestown colony several miles up the James River. The next year, he explored Chesapeake Bay, as well as the Potomac and Rappahannock Rivers, in search of gold and a route to the Pacific Ocean.

With food supplies dwindling and the colony facing starvation, Smith undertook an expedition up the Chickahominy River, seeking to purchase corn from Indians of the Powhatan Confederacy, headed by Chief Powhatan. He was soon taken prisoner by Indians, however. According to some accounts, he was about to be clubbed to death by Powhatan's warriors when the chief's 13-year-old daughter, Pocahontas, interceded. Smith then returned to the Jamestown settlement, and, under his command, the colony managed to survive.

In 1609, Smith returned to England because of an injury sustained in a gunpowder explosion. Five years later, in

John Smith *(New York State Library, Albany)*

1614, he undertook a second expedition to North America, during which he charted the coast from Cape Cod to the mouth of the Penobscot River, naming the region New England. After establishing trade relations with the Indians, he returned to England with a valuable cargo of furs and salted fish. The next year, Smith attempted to return to the New England coast, but his ship was captured by French pirates. Following a shipwreck on the French coast, Smith reached England.

In 1616, Pocahontas and her husband, Jamestown colonist John Rolfe, visited Smith in England. Smith planned another voyage to North America that year, but poor weather conditions forced him to abandon the project. He subsequently became a writer and promoter of English colonization in the New World.

Jamestown, the colony John Smith helped found and helped to survive in its early years, went on to flourish as the first permanent English settlement in North America. John Smith's 1608 book, *Generall Historie of Virginia,* provides the earliest firsthand account of the Jamestown colony. Smith was a friend of HENRY HUDSON and supplied him with information and maps vital to Hudson's 1609 explorations of the North American coast on behalf of England. Smith's descriptions of the New England coast influenced the later colonizing efforts of the Pilgrims in present-day Massachusetts. Smith also wrote the earliest English handbook for seamen, *A Sea Grammar* (1627).

Solander, Daniel Carl (1733–1782) *Swedish naturalist in South America and the South Pacific*

Daniel Solander was born at Pitea in northern Sweden. At the age of 17, he entered the University of Uppsala, where he had planned to study theology. Instead, as a student of the Swedish botanist Carl Linnaeus, he concentrated on natural history.

Starting in 1753, Solander took part in botanical research expeditions to Lapland, Russia, and the CANARY ISLANDS. In 1760, he went to London, where he introduced Linnaeus's system for naming and classifying plants and animals to British naturalists. Three years later, he was appointed to the staff of the British Museum, and he became assistant curator in 1766. In England, Solander became associated with SIR JOSEPH BANKS, a patron of naturalist studies, who engaged him as principal botanist for his scientific team accompanying JAMES COOK's first voyage of exploration to the South Pacific Ocean in 1768–71.

Solander and Banks collected plant specimens throughout the voyage, beginning on the Atlantic island of Madeira, and also in Brazil around Rio de Janeiro. He later took part in the first scientific examination and systematic classification of plant and animal life in Tierra del Fuego. While in Tahiti, he and Banks extended their studies to include the life and culture of the island's native people. Among the animals they encountered on Tahiti was an unclassified variety of parakeet, which was to become extinct less than 75 years later.

Solander continued his naturalist studies on NEW ZEALAND's North Island, where he and Banks encountered the Kea, the only parrot known to be carnivorous. While the *Endeavor* was in southeastern Australia. Solander and the scientific team found so many unclassified species of plants at a landing site originally known as Stingray Harbor that they renamed it Botany Bay.

On their return to England in July 1771, Solander and Banks received honorary degrees from Oxford University and met with King George III to discuss the scientific results of the voyage. Of the thousands of plant and animal specimens they brought back, almost 1,000 were new to science. They also had collected artifacts of the native culture of the South Pacific islanders, including clothing, weapons, jewelry, and musical instruments, and had undertaken linguistic studies of languages unknown in Europe.

In 1772, Solander accompanied Banks on scientific expeditions to the Hebrides Islands, off western Scotland, and to ICELAND. The next year, he was appointed curator of the British Museum's natural history collection, the holdings of which were largely the result of his efforts on the Cook voyage.

Dr. Daniel Solander's work in the South Pacific set a precedent for all subsequent voyages of exploration, which thereafter regularly included at least one naturalist. The tremendous amount of plant and animal specimens collected on the 1768–71 expedition afforded him an opportunity to apply the classification and nomenclature system developed by Linnaeus. CARL PETER THUNBERG and ANDERS SPARRMAN were also Linnaeus's pupils.

Soleyman (Soleyman the Merchant, Soliman, Sulaimen el Tagir, Suleyman) (fl. 850s) *Arab trader in southern Asia*

Soleyman the Merchant, an Arab trader, was born in the Persian Gulf city of Siraf. In about 850, he undertook a sea voyage to the Far East.

After sailing to India, Soleyman traveled on a Chinese JUNK to the Laccadive and Maldive Islands off the southwest coast of India and then went on to CEYLON (present-day Sri Lanka). He entered the Bay of Bengal, where he made stops in the Andaman Islands, and continued to Malacca and the Chinese port of Khanfu (present-day Guangzhou).

On his return to Siraf in 851, Soleyman related details of his journey to an Arab scholar, who recorded them in a book that came to be known as *Sequence of Historical Events.* It tells of the ruby mines and pearl fisheries he had seen in Ceylon, as well as the sea routes traveled by junk between Khantu and the ports of Basra on the northern end of the

Persian Gulf, and Jidda on the Arabian coast of the RED SEA. In addition to trade information, the work also provides some of the earliest commentary about the society of the Maldives, in which women held political power, and that of the Andaman Islands, in which cannibalism was practiced. Soleyman's description of Khantu includes details on Chinese society, including its sometimes brutal system of justice and the practice of legalized prostitution.

Soleyman the Merchant provided the earliest description by Muslims of India and China. His travel account and the reports of other Arab travelers, together with the works of ancient Greek geographers translated into Arabic, enabled medieval Arab geographers to develop an idea of the world beyond the Middle East. In contrast, Europe remained largely isolated and ignorant of the outside world.

Soto, Hernando de (ca. 1499–1542) *Spanish colonial official, conquistador in the American Southeast, brother-in-law of Vasco Núñez de Balboa*

Hernando de Soto was born into a minor noble family in Badajoz in Spain's west-central Estremadura region. In 1514, he arrived in the Americas and served as an officer under PEDRO ARIAS DE ÁVILA in Panama. In 1516–20, he took part in naval expeditions charting the Central American coastline.

In 1523, de Soto served as a captain under FRANCISCO FERNÁNDEZ DE CORDOBA in the conquest of what is now Nicaragua. He later took part in the conquest of both Guatemala and the Yucatán.

In late 1531, de Soto accompanied FRANCISCO PIZARRO in the conquest of Peru. At his own expense, he took armed men and horses down the coast from Panama and Nicaragua to the island of Puna off the coast of northern Peru. He was with Pizarro's forces when the Inca Empire fell in July 1533. At that time, de Soto, who would later be known for his harsh treatment of the Indians of what is now the southeastern United States, was one of the few Spanish officers who opposed Pizarro's execution of the Inca Indian emperor Atahualpa.

By 1536, de Soto was back in Spain, now wealthy from his exploits in Peru. As a reward for his service, he was appointed governor of Cuba and royal deputy of Florida by Spain's king Charles I. He was given an official license to conquer all of the uncharted lands lying north of Florida.

ÁLVAR NÚÑEZ CABEZA DE VACA had recently returned from his eight years of wandering from Florida to the Gulf of California. On hearing reports of the fabled Seven Cities of CIBOLA, de Soto was inspired to seek gold and silver, as had been found among the Aztec Indians by HERNÁN CORTÉS and among the Inca Indians by Pizarro. Cabeza de Vaca declined de Soto's offer to join a new expedition to Florida.

Hernando de Soto *(Library of Congress)*

In April 1538, de Soto's expedition left the Spanish port of Sanlúcar de Barrameda. His nine ships carried soldiers, colonists, and livestock. The ships stopped at Cuba, where de Soto spent the next year making final preparations for his expedition to Florida and the lands beyond. In early May 1539, the military portion of his expedition—600 soldiers—set sail from Havana, reaching the west coast of Florida on May 28. The exact site of his landing is not known, but it is thought to have been Charlotte Harbor, north of the present-day port of Fort Myers.

De Soto led his men along the same path PÁNFILO DE NARVÁEZ had followed 11 years earlier, heading north and west toward Apalachee Bay on the Florida Panhandle. It was during this march that de Soto encountered one of the survivors of the Narváez expedition, a man named Juan Ortiz, who had been held captive by Indians since 1528. Ortiz had learned several Indian languages and joined the de Soto expedition as an interpreter.

By fall 1539, de Soto and his men had reached the Apalachee Indian village of Apalachen, near present-day Tallahassee. As Narváez had done a decade earlier, de Soto spent the winter there. Although he had been charged by the Spanish Crown to locate suitable sites for colonization and seek a water route to the Pacific Ocean, de Soto's main pre-occupation was locating gold and silver among the Indians. He soon heard reports of a rich domain to the north, ruled by an Indian princess.

Traveling northward into what is now Georgia in spring 1540, de Soto soon reached an Indian village called Cofitachequi. The tribal leader, a woman named Cutifachiqui, whose people probably were part of the Creek Confederacy, welcomed de Soto and his men with gifts of food as well as a quantity of freshwater pearls. Even though these pearls, taken from freshwater mussels, would later prove to be worthless, de Soto interpreted them as proof of riches nearby. De Soto and his soldiers, having the advantage of horses, firearms, and crossbows, managed to take Cutifachiqui hostage, as they would do repeatedly to tribal leaders in order to force the Indians to provide food and slaves.

The CONQUISTADORES proceeded up the Savannah River into the APPALACHIAN MOUNTAINS of what is now western North Carolina. They crossed the Appalachians, probably through the Blue Ridge or Great Smoky Mountains, and entered what is now eastern Tennessee. De Soto soon heard reports of another Indian village and followed the Tennessee River southward, reaching Chiaha at present-day Burns Island, Tennessee, in early June 1540. Finding no gold or other riches among these people, he pushed farther southward into central Alabama and reached the Indian village of Coosa near present-day Childersburg.

In addition to living off the Indians, the Spaniards bred the small herd of swine they had brought with them from Spain into a herd of some 700 during the course of the expedition. It is said that the pigs that escaped from the de Soto expedition were the ancestors of the wild hogs now inhabiting Georgia's Okefenokee Swamp.

In summer 1540, the Spanish encountered resistance among Choctaw, Alabama, and Chickasaw Indian bands as they plundered their way across Alabama. A captured Mobile chief named Tascalusa escaped from de Soto and led an unsuccessful counterattack against the Spaniards at a point north of the head of Mobile Bay.

In fall 1540, de Soto received word that relief ships from Cuba were waiting for him at Mobile Bay. Rather than turn back without any riches, he decided to keep the news of the ships secret. He led his men north and west into what is now the state of Mississippi, spending the winter of

Map based on the explorations of Hernando de Soto (1544) *(Library of Congress)*

Hernando de Soto's discovery of the Mississippi River *(Library of Congress)*

1540–41, at a site near present-day Pontotoc, west of the Tombigbee River.

In the spring, de Soto pushed westward, and on May 8, 1541, he came upon the MISSISSIPPI RIVER at a point south of present-day Memphis, Tennessee, making the first recorded sighting of the river by non-Indians. After constructing barges, the expedition crossed the Mississippi on June 18, 1541.

On the west bank of the Mississippi, the de Soto expedition marched northward, then westward, into what is now Arkansas. Along the way, his men came into contact with the Quapaw, Caddo, Wichita, and other Indians of the lower Mississippi and Arkansas River Valleys. Upon reaching the Arkansas River, the expedition followed it westward.

During this leg of the expedition, de Soto and his men noted the appearance of buffalo goods and heard reports of large herds of these animals to the west. De Soto sent scouting parties westward into the Ozark Mountains to see if a route to the sea could be found. At this time, Europeans knew little about the extent of the North American continent; de Soto and other explorers still believed that much of North America was an appendage of Asia.

De Soto and his men may have reached as far west as the Caddo Mountains of eastern Oklahoma by late 1541. At the same time, FRANCISCO VÁSQUEZ DE CORONADO was several hundred miles away in central Kansas, also searching for Cibola. Although both expeditions knew of each other, no attempt was made to establish contact.

Facing mountain terrain and canebrakes to the west, with supplies low and many weapons damaged, de Soto decided to head southward for the Gulf to obtain additional goods from Cuba. He traveled down the Ouachita River to what is now Camden, Arkansas, where his expedition spent the winter of 1541–42.

De Soto began to lose more and more of his men to fever and Indian attacks, including the interpreter Juan Ortiz. Near the confluence of the Red River and the Mississippi, de Soto himself succumbed to fever on May 21, 1542. To prevent the Indians from learning of the Spanish leader's death and the resulting disarray, the conquistadores weighted his body with rocks and disposed of it in the Mississippi under cover of darkness.

Command of the expedition fell to LUIS DE MOSCOSO, de Soto's chief lieutenant. He decided to lead the survivors westward in the hope of reaching Mexico. The expedition headed into what is now Texas, reaching as far as the upper Brazos River region near the Trinity. Discouraged by the vastness of the land, Moscoso decided to try again for the Gulf of Mexico to the south and returned to the Mississippi.

After wintering on the Mississippi in 1542–43, the Spanish built seven crude barges and, when the river flooded on July 2, 1543, embarked on them, reaching the Gulf of Mexico on July 18. They followed the Texas coastline west and south, until they came to the Spanish settlement of Tampico at the mouth of Mexico's Panuco River. Of the more than 600 members of the de Soto expedition, only 311 returned to Mexico.

Hernando de Soto's failure to find Indian civilizations and riches similar to those in Mexico and Peru plus the expedition's losses halted Spanish exploration of the North American interior for the next century. The Mississippi River would not be visited by non-Indians again until the French voyages of exploration out of Canada a century later. The journals from the de Soto expedition are read for the most part for their ethnological information on Southeast Indians. In 1935–39, the United States government undertook to retrace de Soto's route, publishing its results in the *Final Report of the United States De Soto Commission*.

Spalding, Henry Harmon (1803–1874)
American missionary in the Pacific Northwest
Henry Spalding was born near Bath, New York. He graduated from Western Reserve University in 1833, then attended Lane Theological Seminary until 1836, receiving an appointment by the American Board for Foreign Missions as a Presbyterian missionary to the Indians of the Pacific Northwest.

On March 31, 1836, Spalding and his wife, the former Eliza Hart, set out from St. Louis for the West, traveling with the AMERICAN FUR COMPANY trade caravan to that year's fur-trading rendezvous on the Green River, near the present-day Utah-Wyoming state line. Missionary MARCUS WHITMAN and his wife, the former Narcissa Prentiss, along with a farmer-mechanic named William Gray, were also part of this group. From the Green River, the Spaldings, the Whitmans, and Gray continued westward with a group of HUDSON'S BAY COMPANY traders as far as Fort Boise in what is now southern Idaho.

The Spalding-Whitman party continued into the Oregon Country to Fort Walla Walla, and down the COLUMBIA RIVER to Fort Vancouver, where they were assisted by JOHN McLOUGHLIN of the Hudson's Bay Company. While the Whitmans went on to establish a mission at Waiilatpu, near Walla Walla, among the Cayuse Indians, Spalding and his wife journeyed to Lapwai, near what is now Lewiston, Idaho, where he established a mission to the Nez Perce Indians.

In 1842, Spalding received word of his dismissal by the American Board for Foreign Missions because of critical reports about him from Whitman and other missionary workers. Nevertheless, during his trip to the East that year, Whitman had a change of heart and succeeded in obtaining Spalding's reinstatement.

Shortly after Marcus Whitman, his wife, and others at the Walla Walla mission were killed in a surprise attack by Cayuse Indians in 1847, Spalding and his wife left Idaho and moved to Oregon's Willamette Valley, where he became a school administrator and Indian agent. He returned to Lapwai, Idaho, in 1862 and resumed his missionary work among the Nez Perce, while also serving as superintendent of schools for that tribe. He remained at Lapwai until his death in 1874.

In their 1836 overland journey from St. Louis to the Columbia River, Henry Spalding and Marcus Whitman pioneered the Oregon Trail as an emigrant route, and they were the first party to use wagons in traveling west of Fort Hall. Moreover, Eliza Spalding and Narcissa Whitman were the first non-Indian women to cross the Continental Divide. Spalding's mission at Lapwai was the first permanent non-Indian settlement in what is now Idaho. In 1839, as part of his effort to create a written version of the Nez Perce language, Spalding introduced the first printing press in the Pacific Northwest.

Sparrman, Anders (1747–1820) *Swedish naturalist in South Africa and the South Pacific, in service to Great Britain*
Anders Sparrman was born in Upplands, Sweden. At the age of 17, he served aboard a Swedish merchant ship as an assistant surgeon, returning with a large collection of botanical and zoological specimens from East Asia.

In 1768, Sparrman entered the University of Uppsala, where he studied medicine and became a pupil of the Swedish botanist Carl Linnaeus. He received a medical degree in 1770, and, the following year, he sailed to Cape Town, South Africa, as part of a scientific expedition sponsored by the Swedish government. His work included studies with fellow Swede CARL PETER THUNBERG. While in Cape Town, he met JOHANN REINHOLD FORSTER and his son, JOHANN GEORG ADAM FORSTER, the principal naturalists with JAMES COOK's second expedition, which had stopped there on its way to the South Pacific Ocean. The elder Forster was impressed by Sparrman's abilities as a naturalist, especially his wide knowledge of birds, and soon enlisted him as his assistant aboard the *Resolution*. Over the next two-and-a-half years, Sparrman sailed around the world with the Cook expedition, collecting and identifying hundreds of specimens of flora and fauna throughout the South Pacific. In NEW ZEALAND, he discovered several birds new to science, including the New Zealand parakeet, the spotted cormorant, and the wekas, a type of flightless rail. On the last part of the voyage, at Christmas Channel near CAPE HORN, Sparrman and the Forsters made a study of the region's seals and other marine mammals and discovered two previously unclassified varieties of penguin, the Papua penguin and the Magellan penguin.

Sparrman left the *Resolution* when it returned to Cape Town in March 1775. He resumed his naturalist studies in South Africa and also undertook ethnological research among the region's native Khoikhoi (Hottentot) people.

In 1778, Sparrman was back in Sweden, where he had been appointed president of the natural history collection of Stockholm's Academy of Sciences. In 1787, he traveled to Senegal in West Africa, where he conducted additional natural history and ethnological studies. Sparrman's map of the South African coastline proved that the southernmost tip of Africa was located at Cape Agulhas and not at the CAPE OF GOOD HOPE.

Anders Sparrman's account of Cook's voyage of 1772–75, *A Voyage round the World with Captain James Cook in H.M.S. Resolution,* first published in 1783, includes some of the earliest ethnological studies of the native peoples of South Africa. Like fellow Linnaeus disciple DANIEL CARL SOLANDER, who had sailed with Cook on his 1768–71 voyage, Sparrman helped popularize the newly devised Linnaean system of classification and nomenclature by applying it to the new varieties of plants and animals he had collected.

Speke, John Hanning (1827–1864) *British soldier, sportsman in Africa*

John Hanning Speke was born near Bath in southwestern England, the son of upper-class parents. He embarked on a career as an officer with the British army in India when he was 17, serving in the Punjab region and taking part in the Second Sikh War of 1849. While in northern India, Speke, an avid hunter and sportsman, and fellow officer JAMES AUGUSTUS GRANT undertook hunting and exploring expeditions into the HIMALAYAS in which they crossed into Tibet, later producing some of the first modern maps of the region.

On a visit to Aden in 1854, Speke met SIR RICHARD FRANCIS BURTON and joined his planned expedition into what is now Somalia and Ethiopia. Soon after landing on the Somalian coast, both Speke and Burton were wounded in a native attack at Berbera, and Speke was briefly taken captive.

Speke recovered and went on to serve with a Turkish regiment in the closing months of the Crimean War of 1853–56. In December 1856, he returned to Africa with Burton, as coleader of an expedition in search of the source of the NILE RIVER, sponsored by the ROYAL GEOGRAPHICAL SOCIETY. Starting from Zanzibar on the Indian Ocean coast of present-day Tanzania, they traveled inland. In February 1858, they reached Ujiji and the shores of Africa's second largest lake, Lake Tanganyika, becoming the first Europeans to see it.

Speke explored Lake Tanganyika in a dugout CANOE, while Burton recovered from an infected jaw in Ujiji. Nearly blind from malaria and other ailments himself at this time, Speke was unable to circumnavigate Lake Tanganyika in search of an outlet that might be the Nile. Yet he noted that the lake was scarcely 10 feet higher above sea level than the Nile at Gondokoro in the Sudan, leading him to conclude that it was not the great river's source.

In spring 1858, Speke and Burton began the return journey to Zanzibar. At Tabora, about halfway to the Indian Ocean coast, Speke decided to investigate reports he had heard from Arab slave traders of a larger lake to the north. Burton, too ill with malaria to travel, remained at Tabora, while Speke proceeded about 200 miles northward. On August 3, 1858, he came upon what the natives called Lake Ukerewe, and what he called Lake Victoria after the reigning queen of England. He mapped what he could of the lake, then rejoined Burton at Tabora.

Speke believed that Lake Victoria, by its immensity, was the source of the Nile, but his view was not shared by Burton. As it turned out, Speke arrived back in England two weeks ahead of Burton, who had remained behind for a time in Aden. Although Speke had agreed not to divulge the results of the expedition until they had both reached England, he related his findings to the Royal Geographical Society. As a result, most of the credit for the European discovery of Africa's two greatest lakes went to Speke.

Speke soon raised support for another expedition in which he planned to further examine Lake Victoria and ascertain if it was indeed the long-sought source of the Nile. Joining him was his former partner in India and the Himalayas, James Augustus Grant. In October 1860, he and Grant headed westward into the interior of East Africa from Zanzibar. After a stopover at Tabora, they traveled northward to Lake Victoria. Grant had problems with an old leg injury and remained behind at Karagwe on the west shore of Lake Victoria, while Speke explored northward around the lake.

On July 21, 1862, Speke came upon a river that appeared to flow from Lake Victoria at what he called Ripon Falls, after George Frederick Samuel Robinson, the second earl of Ripon, then president of the Royal Geographical Society. With Grant, he traced the river from the northern end of Lake Victoria, following its course into present-day Uganda. Tribal warfare slowed their progress, and, by the time they had reached Gondokoro in the Sudan, they had already made several detours away from what turned out to be the White Nile.

Near Gondokoro, Speke and Grant met up with SIR SAMUEL WHITE BAKER and his wife, FLORENCE BAKER, who were traveling upriver on their own expedition in search of the source of the Nile. The Bakers provided Speke and Grant with fresh supplies and boats to continue the downriver journey to Khartoum. Before they departed for Europe, Speke and Grant related information to the Bakers, which led the Bakers to reach Lake Albert and Murchison Falls.

Back in England, Speke announced that he had discovered Lake Victoria to be the source of the Nile. Burton, among others, challenged his claim, arguing that Speke had not examined Lake Victoria to see if the Nile flowed into it from a point farther south. Moreover, since Speke had left the Nile at various points on his downstream journey with Grant into the Sudan, there was no certainty that it was actually the same river he had seen flowing out of Lake Victoria. The British Association for the Advancement of Science arranged for Speke and Burton to debate the issue publicly. On September 15, 1864, one day before the debate, Speke was killed in a shooting accident while hunting near his home in Bath. Some speculated his death to be a suicide.

John Hanning Speke's *Journal of the Discovery of the Source of the Nile* was published in 1863. He was the first European to see Lake Victoria, the largest lake in Africa and the second largest freshwater lake in the world. The explorations of SIR HENRY MORTON STANLEY and DAVID LIVINGSTONE in the 1870s confirmed that Lake Victoria was actually one of the principal sources of the White Nile, flowing over Ripon Falls into Lake Albert. With Burton, and later with Grant, Speke pioneered the exploration route from the Indian Ocean westward into central and East Africa.

Speyer, Georg Hohermuth von   See
HOHERMUTH VON SPEYER, GEORG.

Spotswood, Alexander (Alexander Spottswood) (1676–1740) *British colonial governor on the Virginia frontier*

Born in Tangier, Morocco, Alexander Spotswood was the son of a doctor serving there with British troops. At the age of 17, he embarked on a military career and went on to serve in the War of the Spanish Succession, suffering a wound at the Battle of Blenheim in 1704.

In 1710, Spotswood was named lieutenant governor of Virginia. Although under the nominal governorship of George Hamilton, Earl of Orkney, Spotswood was the colony's principal royal administrator. As such, he instituted tighter regulations on the FUR TRADE with the Indians, and, with tax abatements as an incentive, encouraged settlement on Virginia's frontier.

In 1716, Spotswood organized an official expedition to explore the frontier region himself. With a party he called the "Knights of the Golden Horseshoe"—a group of landed gentry, frontiersmen, German indentured servants, and Indian guides—he traveled through the watergap of the James River into the Shenandoah Valley. The party descended the Shenandoah River, which they dubbed the "Euphrates," after the river of ancient Mesopotamia, and sighted a peak in the Blue Ridge they named Mount George, in honor of the British monarch, King George I.

In 1722, his last year in office, Spotswood entered into a peace treaty with the Iroquois (Haudenosaunee) in Albany, under the terms of which the Indians agreed to stay west of the Potomac River and the Blue Ridge. In addition to promoting frontier settlement, Spotswood was a major land speculator of his day, amassing an estate of over 80,000 acres near Spotsylvania, Virginia.

Alexander Spotswood's 1716 expedition with the Knights of the Golden Horseshoe marked one of the first European explorations into the Blue Ridge.

Spruce, Richard (1817–1893) *British botanist in South America*

Born at North Riding in Yorkshire, England, Richard Spruce was the son of a local schoolteacher. He became a teacher himself at a school in York, where he taught mathematics. He also had an interest in collecting and identifying botanical specimens, especially mosses and liverworts, and undertook his first collecting expeditions on the moors near his home.

Starting in 1846, Spruce spent 12 months in the Pyrenees, between France and Spain, having gone there for health reasons. He carried on additional botanical research and collecting. His work soon came to the attention of a group of leading British botanists, and, as a result, in 1849, with the support of London's Kew Gardens, he embarked on a scientific expedition up the lower AMAZON RIVER.

At Santarem, a town at the junction of the Amazon and the Tapajos River, Spruce met naturalists ALFRED RUSSEL WALLACE and HENRY WALTER BATES; at their suggestion, he continued his botanical explorations farther up the Amazon and into the Río Negro at Manaus. Over the next few years, he investigated the Uaupes River, a tributary of the Río Negro, as well as the Casiquiare, the natural canal linking the Orinoco with the Río Negro and the Amazon.

In 1854, Spruce traveled to the upper Amazon Basin by steamer, extending his botanical research to the Marañon and Huallaga Rivers. He then spent two years collecting moss specimens on the eastern slopes of the Peruvian ANDES MOUNTAINS and in the northern Ecuadorian Andes.

In 1859, after 10 years of scientific work in the Amazon Basin, Spruce was commissioned by the British Foreign

Office, on the recommendation of Wallace and CHARLES ROBERT DARWIN, to collect seeds of the cinchona, or red bark tree, the principal natural source of quinine. He was to acquire the seeds from around Chimborazo, the 20,577-foot inactive volcano in central Ecuador, then ship them from the port of Guayaquil to India, where the colonial government hoped to introduce production of the antimalarial drug.

It took Spruce the next two years to fulfill this government mission, during which he risked the hazards of traveling into the Pastaza River region of central Ecuador, a country inhabited by headhunters. An additional danger was posed by the violent revolution then going on in Ecuador. Despite these difficulties, Spruce had managed to collect more than 100,000 cinchona seedlings and send them off to India by ship by 1861. In the course of this work he had explored the little-known Puyu River, a tributary of the Pastaza, and made studies of Indian dialects.

Spruce returned to England in 1864. Although he had been paid a substantial sum by the British government for collecting the cinchona seeds in the Andes, he had lost it all as a result of a bank failure in Guayaquil. With his health weakened from his 15 years in the Amazon Basin and the Andes, he retired to his home in Yorkshire, where he lived on a small government stipend. He had collected more than 30,000 specimens of rare plants. Furthermore, he had explored and mapped three rivers of the upper Amazon Basin previously unknown to Europeans. He was elected a fellow of the ROYAL GEOGRAPHICAL SOCIETY, and, over the next three decades, he produced many scientific papers as well as a major volume on his study of mosses in South America, *The Hepatics of the Amazons and Andes,* published in 1884–85.

Along with his South American botanical and geographic discoveries, Richard Spruce's efforts in the northern Andes of Ecuador directly led to the initiation of quinine production in Asia, especially in India. In recognition of his scientific work, the *Sprucea* moss and the *Sprucella* liverwort were named after him.

Squanto (Tisquantum) (ca. 1580–1622)

Wampanoag traveler to Europe, interpreter, guide for Pilgrims in Massachusetts

Squanto was a member of the Pawtuxet band of Indians, part of the Wampanoag Confederacy, living along coastal New England. According to some sources, he was among the Indians kidnapped from the Maine coast by English navigator GEORGE WEYMOUTH in 1605. Other sources indicate Squanto was one of a group of Indians abducted by Captain Thomas Hunt in 1615, near what is now Plymouth, Massachusetts. According to still another account,

Captain JOHN SMITH captured Squanto during his 1615 expedition along the New England coast.

Squanto is thought to have been sold into slavery in Spain by the English, then to have escaped on his own or to have been ransomed by a sympathetic Englishman. In any case, he made his way back to England in 1617. Squanto reportedly lived in London for the next two years with John Slany, the treasurer of the Newfoundland Company, and then possibly made a voyage to Newfoundland and back to England with Captain Thomas Dermer.

In summer 1619, Squanto sailed to New England with Captain Dermer, serving as a pilot when their ship approached the coast north of Cape Cod. Upon reaching his homeland, he found that his people had been wiped out by an epidemic, possibly smallpox.

Squanto had learned English during his years in England, and, in 1621, he became an interpreter for Wampanoag grand sachem Massasoit in his dealings with the PILGRIMS at their Plymouth colony in present-day Massachusetts. Squanto also provided the Pilgrims with instructions in agriculture, fishing, and wilderness survival skills.

In 1622, Squanto became embroiled in a tribal power struggle. He was held as a prisoner by the Wampanoag for a short time before being released through the efforts of Pilgrim military leader Miles Standish. In the fall of that year, he served as a guide and interpreter for Plymouth colony governor William Bradford's expedition around Cape Cod. At Chatham harbor, on the east shore of Cape Cod, he became ill with fever and died.

Squanto played a vital role in maintaining peaceful relations between the Pilgrims and the Indians. The assistance he provided the settlers contributed to the survival of the Plymouth colony. He was one of the first Native Americans to travel in Europe, survive conditions of slavery and exposure to disease, then return to North America.

Stadukhin, Mikhail (Mikhailo Stadukhin)

(unknown–1666) *Russian Cossack in northeastern Siberia*

Mikhail Stadukhin was a Cossack from the Siberian town of Yakutsk. Starting in 1630, he initiated a series of expeditions of exploration and conquest northward, along the Lena River, toward the Arctic coast of SIBERIA. In 1633, with a party of Cossacks, he traveled westward across north-central Siberia to the Vilyuy River.

In 1641, Stadukhin began expanding his activities into northeastern Siberia. He sailed down the Indigirka River, then pushed eastward along the Siberian Arctic coast. In 1644, he reached the Kolyma River, and, near its mouth on the East Siberian Sea, he established the settlement of Nizhnekolymsk. From there, he returned westward by sea to the Lena, which he ascended on his return to Yakutsk.

Stadukhin next turned his attention to the Gulf of Anadyr, drawn by reports that it was an abundant source of walrus ivory. His unsuccessful attempt to reach Anadyr Island by sea in 1649 was followed by a successful land journey there the following year. In 1659, he returned to Yakutsk, where he later commanded an outlying settlement. In 1666, he died while en route to the Kolyma River.

Nizhnekolymsk, the outpost Mikhail Stadukhin had founded at the mouth of the Kolyma River, served as the starting point for SEMYON IVANOVICH DEZHNEV's 1648 voyage around the northeasternmost tip of Asia, in which he explored Cape Dezhnev and what later came to be known as the BERING STRAIT.

Stanhope, Hester Lucy (Lady Hester Stanhope) (1776–1839) *British traveler in the Middle East*

Born at Chevening in Kent, England, Lady Hester Stanhope was the daughter of British statesman and inventor Charles, third earl of Stanhope.

In 1803, at the age of 27, Stanhope went to live with her maternal uncle, William Pitt, then British prime minister, for whom she worked as official hostess and secretary. Pitt died three years later, leaving her a substantial trust that made her financially independent.

In 1809, Stanhope's brother, a major in the army, and his commanding officer, General Sir John Moore, with whom Stanhope had been romantically linked, were both killed fighting the French at the Battle of La Coruña in the Peninsular War of 1808–14. The double tragedy led her to withdraw first to Wales, then in 1810, to the Middle East. Accompanying her were her physician, Charles Lewis Meryon, and a Welsh woman named Williams.

After surviving a shipwreck in the eastern MEDITERRANEAN SEA off the island of Rhodes, Stanhope and her party arrived in present-day southern Lebanon. Stanhope made a pilgrimage to Jerusalem, then embarked on extensive travel throughout the region, often dressed in native male attire. In January 1813, she crossed the Syrian Desert to the ruins of the ancient city of Palmyra, where she lived among a band of bedouin and, according to her own later account, was proclaimed "Queen of the Desert."

In summer 1814, Stanhope acquired an abandoned convent in the country around Mount Lebanon, upon which she had built a fortress-like residence, surrounded by a garden and a wall. She soon developed a charismatic reputation among the region's Druse people, who came to regard her as a prophetess. Stanhope herself was something of a mystic, an avid adherent of astrology, and a believer in the transmigration of souls. She developed a unique system of religious thought combining elements of local Christian and Muslim sects.

During the next two decades, Stanhope held a commanding position amid the political struggles over Lebanon that periodically erupted between the Ottoman Empire, the rulers of Egypt, and the European powers. She was visited by leading literary figures from Europe, including the French poet Alphonse de Lamartine and English travel writer William Kinglake.

By 1838, Stanhope had fallen severely into debt, and her creditors in Lebanon were awarded what remained of her trust. Left virtually penniless, she walled herself up in her castle-like home, and, after almost a year of self-imposed confinement, she died there in June 1839. Her physician, Charles Lewis Meryon, published two accounts of her life, *Memoirs of Lady Hester Stanhope* (1845) and *Travels of Lady Hester Stanhope* (1846).

Lady Hester Stanhope departed England reportedly to remove herself from the constraints imposed on her by society. Her journeys in the Middle East were made at a time when most private travel into the region was fraught with difficulties and perils. Even more remarkable was her ability to live for an extended time within a culture wary of non-Muslim Europeans and disapproving of females living independently.

Stanley, David Sloan (1828–1902) *U.S. Army officer in American West*

Born in Cedar Valley, Ohio, David S. Stanley was an 1852 West Point graduate. Commissioned a second lieutenant, he began his frontier military career when he was assigned to an exploring expedition westward along the 35th parallel for a proposed transcontinental railroad route.

In 1853, Stanley, accompanying Lieutenant AMIEL WEEKS WHIPPLE and a detachment of the army's Corps of Topographical Engineers, traveled westward from Fort Smith, Arkansas, over the southern plains to Albuquerque, then continued to Fort Yuma on the COLORADO RIVER. They crossed the Mojave Desert and, traversing the Sierra Nevada by way of Cajon Pass, arrived in Los Angeles.

Stanley remained in western military posts throughout the 1850s, serving with a cavalry regiment against the Cheyenne and Comanche Indians on the southern plains. In 1862, during the Civil War, he was breveted a major general; he served with distinction in command of Union forces in Georgia and Missouri and was wounded in an engagement near Nashville.

In 1865, at the war's end, Stanley was assigned to Texas. Soon afterward, he was promoted to the regular rank of lieutenant colonel, in command of frontier garrisons in the Dakota Territory. During this posting, he commanded what was known as the Yellowstone Expedition of 1873, which explored into the unknown parts of Montana and

Wyoming, as he detailed in his *Report on the Yellowstone Expedition,* published in 1874.

Stanley's later military career took him to western Texas in 1879. He was appointed a brigadier general in the regular army in 1884.

David S. Stanley's favorable reports about the country he explored with the Yellowstone Expedition of 1873 inspired a new influx of settlers onto the northern plains.

Stanley, Sir Henry Morton (John Rowlands, Bula Matari) (1841–1904) *Anglo-American journalist, colonizer in central Africa*

Born in Denbigh, Wales, Henry Morton Stanley was the illegitimate son of John Rowlands and Elizabeth Parry. He was given his father's name at birth. He spent his early years at the St. Asaph Union Workhouse, a local charitable institution, where he received some formal education.

Stanley left St. Asaph's when he was 15 and worked briefly for a haberdasher and then a butcher before going to sea as a cabin boy on a vessel bound for the United States. In 1859, he jumped ship in New Orleans, where he found employment with cotton broker Henry Hope Stanley, who became his benefactor and from whom Stanley adopted the name by which he became known.

At the outbreak of the American Civil War in 1861, Stanley enlisted in the Confederate army; he was taken prisoner at the Battle of Shiloh in April 1862. He gained his release by joining a Union artillery unit, but he was discharged on becoming ill with dysentery. After recovering, Stanley went back to Wales, then traveled in Europe before returning to the United States in 1864. He served briefly in the U.S. Navy before deserting.

Stanley embarked on a career as a journalist in 1865. He covered General Winfield Scott Hancock's campaign against the Indians in Kansas in 1867, and, the following year, as a correspondent for the *New York Herald,* he reported on a British military expedition in what is now Ethiopia.

In 1869, while reporting on a revolution in Spain, Stanley received orders from publisher James Gordon Bennett, Jr., of the newspaper the *New York Herald* to undertake a search for the Scottish missionary and explorer, DAVID LIVINGSTONE, who had been missing in East Africa for three years. Stanley did not immediately begin his search for Livingstone, since Bennett hoped a delay might improve Stanley's chances of returning with a great story, rather than merely with the news that Livingstone was still lost.

As instructed, Stanley first traveled to Egypt, where he covered the opening of the Suez Canal and met with SIR SAMUEL WHITE BAKER, who was planning an expedition up the NILE RIVER. Stanley then traveled into the Crimea, where he reported on the battle sites of the Crimean War of 1853–56.

Stanley toured the region around the Caspian Sea before heading southward into Persia (present-day Iran). Continuing to Baghdad, he sent back dispatches on the newly developed railroad through the Euphrates Valley. He later sailed to India, from where he reached the coast of East Africa, arriving in Zanzibar on January 26, 1871, 18 months after Bennett had first commissioned him to look for Livingstone. By then, reports by Arab slave traders indicated that a white fitting Livingstone's description was at Ujiji on the east shore of Lake Tanganyika.

Stanley, who had been provided with almost limitless financial resources by his New York publisher, organized a small army of porters, guides, hunters, and armed escorts, along with pack animals. He departed Bagamoyo on the mainland of present-day Tanzania on March 21, 1871. He followed the Arab slave caravan route inland to Tabora, then continued toward Lake Tanganyika. On November 10, 1871, in Ujiji, he located the missionary, addressing the Scotsman with the now famous greeting, "Dr. Livingstone, I presume?"

Stanley soon learned that Livingstone did not consider himself lost, only temporarily weakened by disease and short on supplies. Moreover, Livingstone was still committed to exploring the great lakes of East Africa, especially in ascertaining their exact connection to the CONGO RIVER (Zaire River) and Nile River. Over the next few months, Stanley accompanied Livingstone in an examination of the northern end of Lake Tanganyika, and, although they found no evidence of a major river flowing out of the lake, they learned that the Ruzizi River flowed into it.

Stanley left Livingstone at Tabora on March 14, 1872, then traveled back to the Indian Ocean coast of present-day Tanzania, arriving there in May. His news of finding Livingstone reached Europe and New York in August 1872. He was greeted with much acclaim when he later arrived in England. His account of the exploit, *How I Found Livingstone* (1872), became an instant best-seller. In 1873, Stanley was awarded a gold medal by the ROYAL GEOGRAPHICAL SOCIETY, and, that same year, he went to what is now Ghana in West Africa to cover Sir Garnet Wolseley's military campaign against the Ashanti.

Stanley had by this time resolved to complete the exploration of central Africa begun by Livingstone. In November 1874, in command of a large expedition jointly sponsored by the *New York Herald* and the *Daily Telegraph* of London, he set out from Bagamoyo for Lake Victoria, planning to confirm whether Lake Victoria was the principal source of the Nile and to establish the exact geographic location of East Africa's other great lakes. Moreover, he planned to find the source of the Congo River and, if possible, follow it to the Atlantic Ocean. Arriving at Lake Victoria in late February 1875, Stanley undertook a circumnavigation of the lake in the *Lady Alice,* a portable steamboat that had been carried in pieces into the interior. He then visited a native kingdom to the north in what is now Uganda, coming upon an uncharted lake, which he named Lake Edward.

Stanley headed southward along Africa's Great Rift Valley and, in spring 1876, he arrived at Lake Tanganyika, which he also circumnavigated in the *Lady Alice.* He then found the lake's principal outlet to be the Lukuga River, which he followed to its confluence with the Lualaba River. Descending the Lualaba northward, he came to Nyangwe, the farthest inland point known to both Arab traders and Europeans. There, he recruited a small armed force, under a local Arab slaver named Tippoo Tib, who guided his expedition to a series of cataracts, later known as Stanley Falls, which they portaged around with considerable difficulty.

Abandoned by Tippoo Tib and his men soon afterward, Stanley and his expedition nevertheless pushed onward, traveling on the river when they could or following its banks. Upon reaching the site of present-day Kisangani in what is now the west-central Democratic Republic of the Congo, Stanley determined that the river could not flow into the Nile, since at that point it was 14 feet lower in elevation than the larger river. He soon found that the river turned sharply west and south and widened to allow relatively easy travel by boat. After a few more months of down-river travel, he discovered a large lake-like expanse, later known as Stanley Pool. On August 9, 1877, Stanley and his party reached the Atlantic at Boma. In his 999-day journey, he had crossed Africa from east to west and had determined that the Congo flowed from the Lualaba River. With this finding, he dispelled Livingstone's theory that the Lualaba was a source of the Nile. Of the original 356 men in the expedition, only 114 remained with him when he reached Boma, the rest having died or deserted. Stanley related his 1874–77 journey across Africa in his book *Through the Dark Continent* (1878).

Stanley's exploration of the Congo in 1874–77 sparked the interest of King Leopold II of Belgium, who commissioned Stanley to direct the development of the Congo Free State. With King Leopold's support, Stanley undertook his next expedition in 1879, retracing his route up the Congo River. During the next five years, he explored the interior of present-day Democratic Republic of the Congo, making the European discovery of Lake Tumba and Lake Leopold II, and directed the construction of overland routes around the Congo River's unnavigable sections.

Stanley's last African expedition began in 1887 as a relief mission to aid MEHMED EMIN PASHA, the German-born governor of southern Sudan's Equatoria province, who had been cut off from Anglo-Egyptian forces to the north since the outbreak of a Muslim revolt six years earlier. Stanley again ascended the Congo, then marched across central Africa toward Emin Pasha's stronghold on Lake Albert. Along the way, he lost nearly half of the 700 members of the expedition, with the survivors trailing behind him over several hundred miles. Ironically, by the time Stanley reached Lake Albert, he was critically low on provisions and had to be resupplied by Emin Pasha, the man he had come to rescue. Stanley and Emin Pasha explored the Semliki River, establishing it as the principal connection between Lake Albert and Lake Edward. In 1889, while in the region, Stanley came upon the Ruwenzori Mountains, thought to be the fabled MOUNTAINS OF THE MOON, which had been described by the second-century geographer PTOLEMY. After a 3,000-mile journey, in which he had traversed Africa from west to east, Stanley and the survivors of his expedition, along with Emin Pasha and the remainder of the Equatoria garrison, reached Zanzibar in late 1889.

Stanley settled in England and married soon after departing Africa. Although he had been naturalized as a U.S. citizen, he again became a British subject, and he served in the House of Commons from 1895 to 1900. He made a brief visit to South Africa in the 1890s, and was knighted in 1899.

Sir Henry Morton Stanley was known by the African natives as Bula Matari (breaker of bones) after the single-minded and often brutal determination with which he conducted his expeditions. In the history of exploration, he is most famous for locating David Livingstone, but he was also the first European to descend the length of the Congo River, and, after VERNEY LOVETT CAMERON, the second European to cross central Africa from east to west. In locating the source of the Congo, he completed the exploration of Africa's last remaining unknown river system, and he later encouraged its development as the main entry route into the interior of Africa. Stanley is also generally credited with having finally resolved the question of the Nile's source, confirming JOHN HANNING SPEKE's contention that the main branch of the world's longest river flowed from Lake Victoria.

Stansbury, Howard (1806–1863) *U.S. Army officer in Utah*

Howard Stansbury was born in New York City. Trained as a civil engineer, he took part in surveying projects for canals and railroads in the Ohio Valley and Lake Erie region from 1828 to 1838.

In 1838, Stansbury joined the U.S. Army Corps of Topographical Engineers as a second lieutenant, and, two years later, he was promoted to captain. During the next nine years, he supervised army topographic and engineering projects from the Great Lakes to the New England coast.

In 1849, Stansbury was directed to lead an exploring expedition across the plains from Fort Leavenworth to Utah's Salt Lake Valley, and there survey the topography as well as make a study of the Mormon settlements.

Stansbury and his 18-man party left Fort Leavenworth on May 31, 1849, heading westward along the Oregon Trail. They reached Fort Bridger in southwestern Wyoming's Green River country on August 11, where Stansbury engaged former mountain man JAMES BRIDGER as a guide.

From Fort Bridger, Stansbury sent half his party southwestward along the known trail to Salt Lake City, under the command of his assistant, Lieutenant JOHN WILLIAMS GUNNISON. Stansbury, Bridger, and the rest of the expedition then headed westward into the northern Wasatch Mountains. Guided by Bridger, Stansbury explored the eastern slopes of the Wasatch Mountains in search of a route to the north shore of the Great Salt Lake. He followed the Bear River to Ogden's Hole and located a pass though the mountains, which led them to the lake's east shore, near what is now Ogden, Utah. Stansbury's group then went northward to Fort Hall and explored the Cache Valley.

The two groups joined up at Salt Lake City. In October 1849, Stansbury undertook a reconnaissance of the Great Salt Lake's west shore. He led his men northward, then circled around into the Lake Bonneville salt flats. From there, they headed westward as far as Pilot Peak near the present-day Utah-Nevada border, then returned eastward across the Great Salt Lake Desert to Salt Lake City, where they wintered.

In spring 1850, Stansbury completed his surveys in Utah with explorations of Utah Lake and the River Jordan. Although he had been instructed to return via the Old Spanish Trail to Santa Fe, Stansbury instead chose to search for a new pass through the ROCKY MOUNTAINS south of the usual route through the SOUTH PASS. At Fort Bridger, he again engaged Jim Bridger as a guide; together they proceeded through the Green River Valley and across south-central Wyoming to Fort Laramie by way of Bridger's Pass and Cheyenne Pass.

Throughout the 1850s, until the outbreak of the Civil War, Stansbury was engaged in government construction projects and topographic surveys in the Great Lakes country and Minnesota. During the Civil War, he directed mustering operations in Ohio and Minnesota.

Howard Stansbury's 1849–50 Utah expedition established a more direct route from Fort Bridger to the Humboldt River by way of Salt Lake City, providing a shorter alternative to the roundabout trail north to Soda Springs and Fort Hall. Stansbury also undertook the first organized exploration of the west shore of the Great Salt Lake. His return trip from Salt Lake to Fort Laramie, through Cheyenne Pass, established a trail 60 miles shorter than the established South Pass route. In the following years, it was adopted by the Overland Stage Line, the Pony Express, and the Union Pacific Railroad. Stansbury's map of the Great Salt Lake and Great Basin region guided topographers in the Pacific Railroad Surveys throughout the 1850s. His account of his Utah expedition, *Exploration and Survey of the Valley of the Great Salt Lake Including a Reconnaissance of a New Route through the Rocky Mountains,* was first issued as a government publication in 1852 and went on to become a literary success in the United States and Great Britain. The work expresses one of the earliest views that the region around the Great Salt Lake was once the site of a great inland sea.

Stark, Freya Madeline (Dame Freya Stark)

(1893–1993) *British traveler, writer, archaeologist in the Middle East and central Asia*

Freya Stark was born in Paris, France, where her parents, Robert and Flora Stark, were pursuing careers as painters. She spent time at both her father's Devon home in England and her mother's Genoa home in Italy. For most of her childhood, she lived in the Italian village of Asolo, near Venice. She attended Bedford College in England, studying English and history. During World War I, she worked as a censor in London and as a nurse in Italy. Proficient in English, Italian, French, and German, she also decided to study Arabic in her late 20s, enrolling at the School of Oriental and African Studies in London.

In 1927, Stark visited countries of the eastern MEDITERRANEAN SEA region. She later traveled to Iraq and worked for a time as a writer for the *Baghdad Times.* She visited Turkey, Syria, Persia (present-day Iran), Kuwait, and Arabia (present-day Saudi Arabia). In 1935, she explored the fertile valley of the Wadi Hadhramaut in present-day Yemen inland from the Gulf of Aden. She frequently stayed on the island of Cyprus between travels. In 1937, she participated, along with Dr. Gertrude Caton-Thompson and Eliner Gardner, in the first archaeological excavations in Yemen, excavating the Moon Temple of Hureidha. During World War II, she worked for British intelligence in the Middle East. After the war, she spent significant time in Turkey. In later life, Stark traveled to central Asia and the Far East, visiting Cambodia, China, Nepal, and Kashmir, and crossed the HIMALAYAS.

Stark's prolific writing included *The Valley of the Assassins* (1934), *Southern Gates of Arabia* (1936), *Baghdad Sketches* (1937), and *Winter in Arabia* (1940). Stark was also known for her photography, her pictures taken with a Leica camera. She worked with and was married for a time to the Arabist and historian Steward Perowne. She lived to the age of 100, dying in Asolo.

Stark's most famous book, *Southern Gates of Arabia,* informed Europeans of the little-known Hadhramaut region. Her work mapping the routes of the Assassins, a society of bandits who traded in hashish and preyed on Europeans during the CRUSADES, as recorded in *The Valley of the Assassins,* led to a medal in 1942 from the ROYAL GEOGRAPHICAL

SOCIETY. She was knighted at the age of 82. In many of the remote places she visited, she was the first European woman to have ventured there.

Stefansson, Vilhjalmur (1879–1962)
Canadian anthropologist, historian in the Canadian Arctic

Vilhjalmur Stefansson was born near Gimli in Manitoba, Canada, the son of Icelandic immigrants. As an infant, he moved with his family to North Dakota, where he was raised.

Stefansson attended the University of North Dakota and the University of Iowa, graduating from the latter in 1903. Two years later, he took part in archaeological studies in ICELAND.

In 1906, Stefansson descended the Mackenzie River to its delta, where he lived for over a year with the region's Inuit, learning their language and Arctic survival skills. In May 1908, he journeyed with HUDSON'S BAY COMPANY supply boats northward from Edmonton, Alberta, to Canada's western Arctic coast, where he made an extensive study of the different Inuit peoples living between Point Barrow and Cape Parry. In 1910–12, he extended his study eastward to Coronation Gulf, where he lived among the Copper Inuit, a people living isolated from non-natives.

Stefansson commanded the Canadian Arctic Expedition of 1913–18, an undertaking sponsored by the Canadian government in which he explored the westernmost regions of the Canadian Arctic Archipelago. With a group of ships, he sailed northward through the BERING STRAIT, then eastward into the Beaufort Sea. He reached as far as 81° north latitude, sighting some uncharted islands to the north of Prince Patrick Island, including Meighen Island, Borden Island, and Brock Island. Some of these sightings were made while adrift on ice floes in the Beaufort Sea. Among the scientific and technical team with Stefansson was SIR GEORGE HUBERT WILKINS, the expedition's photographer, who was later knighted for his polar explorations.

From 1921 to 1925, Stefansson directed expeditions to northeastern SIBERIA's Wrangel Island and Alaska. He later created an international dispute when he attempted to claim Wrangel Island in the Siberian Arctic for Canada. Soon afterward, he settled in New York City, where he continued to lecture and write on polar exploration. The Stefansson Collection, which he established at Dartmouth College, became one of the world's most comprehensive libraries dealing with polar exploration.

Stefansson related his experiences among the native people of the Arctic in his book *My Life with the Eskimos* (1913). In his 1921 book, *The Friendly Arctic,* he made the case that the Arctic was a habitable region with abundant resources waiting to be developed. He later was a consultant

Vilhjalmur Stefansson *(Library of Congress)*

for airlines developing transpolar routes and also advised the U.S. Navy on Arctic survival techniques.

Vilhjalmur Stefansson's 1913–18 expedition set a record for Arctic exploration by spending five consecutive winters above the ARCTIC CIRCLE. The islands Stefansson found in the Canadian Arctic archipelago in the course of that expedition were among the last uncharted landmasses explored on Earth. In 1952, the Canadian government gave his name to Stefansson Island, off the northeastern corner of Victoria Island. Stefansson's approach to Arctic exploration and his ideas on the industrial development of the polar regions had a great impact on Soviet expansion into the Siberian Arctic in the 1920s and 1930s. In addition to being an explorer in his own right, Stefansson was a leading historian of exploration and edited the firsthand accounts of the major voyages in his 1947 book *Great Adventures and Explorations.*

Stein, Sir Marc Aurel (Sir Mark Aurel Stein)
(1852–1943) *Anglo-Hungarian historian, archaeologist in central Asia*

Born in Budapest, Hungary, Aurel Stein immigrated to England, where he became a scholar of ancient Asian history, culture, and art. In 1888, after attending universities in

Hungary, England, and Germany, he traveled to Lahore in what was then northwestern British India (present-day northern Pakistan), where he had been appointed principal of Oriental College.

Stein, an archaeologist as well as a historian, was a member of the Indian Archaeological Survey. In 1900, inspired by SVEN ANDERS HEDIN's reports of ancient ruins in western China, he set out on his first Indian government-sponsored archaeological expedition into central Asia. From Srinagar in northern India's Punjab region, he traveled northward to Gilgit on the edge of the Pamirs, then westward through the Hindu Kush range into northeastern Afghanistan. He turned eastward across the Pamirs into western China's Taklimakan Desert. Accompanying him were surveyors who later produced the first accurate maps of the region. His route back to India took him through Kashgar and Samarkand.

Stein's next archaeological foray into central Asia, in particular western China, began in 1906. Starting out again from the Punjab region, he crossed the Hindu Kush into northeastern Afghanistan, and, by late winter 1907, after traveling around the Taklimakan Desert, he reached Lop Nor, the shifting, shallow lake of western China. Soon afterward, Stein crossed from Russian central Asia along 3,000 miles of the ancient SILK ROAD and reached Tunhuang.

In his archaeological investigations, Stein determined that in ancient times Tunhuang had been the westernmost extent of the Great Wall of China. Outside the town, located in an oasis, he found a series of temples built into caves, known as the Caves of the Thousand Buddhas. Within a walled-up section of one of the caves, he located as many as 9,000 ancient Buddhist texts and paintings, which had been preserved in sealed jars for more than 800 years. Among these was a copy of the Diamond Sutra dating back to A.D. 868; this was later determined to be the oldest existing printed book. With the cooperation of a local official, Stein was able to acquire many of these ancient documents and paintings, which he then sent back to the British Museum in London. He later determined that many of the texts were connected to those brought back from India by the Buddhist monk and pilgrim HSÜAN-TSANG in his travels of 629–645.

From Tunhuang, Stein crossed the southern reaches of the GOBI DESERT, then headed back to India by way of the Taklimakan Desert and the Kunlun mountains. While crossing the Kunluns in 1908, he suffered frostbite and lost all the toes on one foot.

In 1909, in recognition of his discovery at Tunhuang, which has been hailed as one of the greatest archaeological finds in Asia, the ROYAL GEOGRAPHICAL SOCIETY awarded Stein its Founder's Medal. Over the next 20 years, Stein undertook several more expeditions into western China from northern India, exploring the Karakoram Mountains and the region around the Tarim River. In 1913, he explored the Nan Shan Mountains. In 1915, he traveled from Kashgar into the Pamirs and the Hindu Kush. In 1926, he retraced the route that the army of ALEXANDER THE GREAT had followed as it returned from the Indus Valley to Persia (present-day Iran).

Sir Aurel Stein's primary archaeological interest was uncovering the links between the ancient civilizations of the MEDITERRANEAN SEA and those of central Asia. He applied the results of his travels and archaeological inquiries in central Asia to a historical interpretation of the impact that East-West contacts had on the ancient civilizations of the Indus Valley and Mesopotamia. Among his many published works on the subject are *Ruins of Desert Cathay* (1912), *Innermost Asia* (1928), and *On Alexander's Track to the Indus* (1929).

Steller, Georg Wilhelm (1709–1746)
German physician, naturalist in Kamchatka, Alaska, and the islands of the Bering Sea, in service to Russia

Originally from Germany, Georg Wilhelm Steller was a physician and naturalist, who began practicing medicine in St. Petersburg, Russia, in 1734. Three years later, he was appointed to the natural history department of the Academy of Sciences, and before long he was accepted as one of the scientists for the Second Kamchatka Expedition under the command of VITUS JONASSEN BERING.

In 1740, after an overland journey across Russia and Siberia, Steller arrived at the port of Okhotsk. He sailed from there across the Sea of Okhotsk to the Kamchatka Peninsula, where, for the next few months, he collected plant and animal specimens. He was next assigned as ship's surgeon and naturalist for a reconnaissance voyage eastward across what is now known as the Bering Sea. In June 1741, aboard the *St. Peter,* under Bering's command, Steller sailed from Avacha Bay on Kamchatka's Pacific coast.

By late July, the Alaskan mainland was sighted, and soon afterward Steller went ashore on Kayak Island, where he collected specimens of animal and plant life. On the voyage back to Kamchatka, Stellar had the opportunity to make observations of the Aleut people he saw on the Kenai Peninsula. In mid-November 1741, the *St. Peter* was wrecked on an island about 100 miles east of Kamchatka, later known as Bering Island. SCURVY soon became a severe problem, and many of the crew succumbed, including Bering.

Steller kept a journal of his experience on Bering Island in winter 1741–42 and continued to carry out natural history studies. He wrote a study of the marine mammals in which he provided the first description of a type of sea lion later known as Steller's sea lion. Furthermore, he made the earliest report of a giant species of dugong, a sea mammal since identified as Steller's sea cow.

In August 1742, Steller and the survivors of Bering's voyage reached Avacha Bay in a small boat they had managed to construct with wreckage salvaged from the *St. Peter*. Of the 77 men who had set out with Bering, only 45 returned.

Steller remained in Kamchatka for the next two years, during which he undertook studies of the region's birds, identifying species later known as Steller's eagle, Steller's eider, and Steller's white raven. In November 1746, while traveling back to St. Petersburg, he died at the western Siberian town of Tyumen.

Georg Wilhelm Steller was the first scientist to make a study of Alaska's wildlife and provided the earliest ethnological details about the Aleut. His *Description of Kamchatka* was published in 1744, and his study of the animals he had observed on Bering Island, *On Sea Animals*, first appeared in 1751. Steller also wrote the earliest account of the life and habits of the sea otter, the hunting of which became the focal point of Russia's subsequent colonizing efforts in Alaska. The giant sea mammal he had discovered, Steller's sea cow, fell prey to the hunters who soon poured into the region; by 1800, it had become extinct.

Stevens, Thomas (unknown–1619)
English missionary in India

Thomas Stevens was an English Jesuit priest who was compelled to leave his native land in the 1570s. After residing in Italy for a time, he sailed from Lisbon, Portugal, aboard a Portuguese ship bound for India in 1579.

Stevens settled at the Portuguese trading port of Goa on the west coast of India, where he embarked on a career as a missionary. He later mastered the Marathi language, in which he wrote religious poetry for his native converts.

In 1583, Stevens helped gain the release of RALPH FITCH, JOHN NEWBERRY, and other members of an English trade and diplomatic mission to the Mogul emperor, after they had been detained by Portuguese authorities in Goa.

Thomas Stevens was the first Englishman known to have reached India. Soon after his arrival there in 1579, he reportedly sent back to Europe details of Portuguese sailing routes to India, information that the Portuguese government had been keeping as state secrets for almost a century.

Strabo (ca. 63 B.C.–ca. A.D. 21) *Greek traveler in Europe, Africa, and Asia, geographer in ancient Rome*

Strabo, a Greek, was born in Amasia, a city in the region south of the Black Sea in what is now northeastern Turkey and then was part of the ancient Roman province of Pontus. Strabo studied history and philosophy in his native city, as well as in Alexandria and Greece. He also traveled widely in the Middle East, North Africa, and Europe. Eventually he settled in Rome, where he became a noted historian and authority on the geography of the Roman world.

In about A.D. 18, Strabo completed his *Geography*, a work in 17 books encompassing most of what was then known about the lands of the Roman Empire and the world beyond. In addition to his own travel experiences, Strabo drew from the works of earlier geographers, including Eratosthenes, Polybius, and Posidonius, although he rejected most of HERODOTUS. Moreover, he incorporated as fact geographic information gleaned from the epic poetry of Homer and other mythic and traditional sources.

As background for his geographic descriptions, Strabo provided historical accounts of Greeks and Romans, including NEARCHUS's voyage from the Indus River delta to the Persian Gulf. He was highly skeptical of what the Greek navigator PYTHEAS reported concerning his voyage to Britain. Ironically, it was only through the sometimes scathing criticism leveled against him in Strabo's *Geography* that any record of Pytheas's exploits as an explorer of western Europe and the Atlantic Ocean survived.

Strabo's report that the NILE RIVER's main eastern tributary, the Blue Nile, flowed from a lake in Ethiopia was confirmed by JAMES BRUCE's exploration of Lake Tana in 1770.

Strabo's works were translated into Latin in 1469, and copies began to circulate in Europe after 1472. He provided descriptions of the ancient shipping routes between the Roman Empire and India and further suggested that the Indies, the elusive origin of the SPICE TRADE, might be reached by sailing westward from Spain, although he maintained that such a voyage had never been successfully attempted because of the great expanse of open sea that had to be crossed. Nevertheless, Strabo's theories came to the attention of CHRISTOPHER COLUMBUS, and, along with the writings of PTOLEMY, helped inspire him to attempt a westward crossing to the Orient in his 1492 voyage, resulting in the European discovery of the Americas.

Strzelecki, Sir Paul Edmund (Count Paul Edmund de Strzelecki, Paweł Strzelecki)
(1797–1873) *Polish geologist in Australia*

Paul Strzelecki was born in Gluszyna, near Poznań, in western Poland, then under Prussian rule. His aristocratic parents died when he was 10, and he was raised by his mother's family. It is thought that he was educated at Piarists Fathers College in Warsaw. He served for a time in the Prussian cavalry. He traveled in eastern Europe, where he met Prince Francis Sapieha, who hired him to manage his estates in Poland and upon his death, left him a sum of money.

In 1829, Strzelecki departed Poland, traveling first to France, then England and Scotland. Over the years, he pursued an interest in geology and mineralogy. He later visited North and South America, the Marquesas, the HAWAIIAN

ISLANDS (where he studied the volcano of Kilauea), Tahiti, NEW ZEALAND, and, in 1839, Australia.

Strzelecki planned a series of geological surveys of the largely unexplored continent. His first expedition was to the BLUE MOUNTAINS west of Sydney, where he found veins of gold and silver. Although he reported his discovery, the governor of the New South Wales colony, Sir George Gipps, requested he not publicize it because of the difficulty in controlling the colonists, many of them convicts. (Edward Hargraves would receive credit for locating gold in 1851 and starting the Australian gold rush.)

Strzelecki's second Australian expedition, beginning in December 1839, took him to the Snowy Mountains in the southeast. He traveled with James Macarthur and two Aborigine guides. He named one of the peaks he climbed Mount Kosciuszko (the highest peak in Australia) in honor of the Polish patriot Tadeusz Kościuszko. In southeastern Victoria, he named the coastal plain along Bass Strait in what is now southeastern Victoria Gippsland for Governor Gipps. He named Lake King after his friend PHILIP PARKER KING and also the La Trobe River. His work included the creation of topographic and geological maps, based on astronomical observations. The party reached Melbourne in May 1840. In July, Strzelecki traveled by boat across Bass Strait to Van Diemen's Land (present-day TASMANIA).

In Van Diemen's Land, Strzelecki carried out extensive explorations, some of them sponsored by SIR JOHN FRANKLIN, then governor of the colony. One such expedition was to the islands in Bass Strait. He sailed to Sydney in September 1842, where he stayed with King. He continued his geological investigations, exploring the Hunter and Karuah river valleys.

Strzelecki departed Australia in April 1843 and reached Europe by way of the EAST INDIES and China. He settled in England, where he wrote two books about Australia: *Physical Description of New South Wales and Van Diemen's Land* (1845), the first such work on Australian geology, and *Gold and Silver* (1856), arguing his claim to having discovered gold in Australia. He received a commendation from CHARLES ROBERT DARWIN and was awarded the gold Founder's Medal of the ROYAL GEOGRAPHICAL SOCIETY for the 1845 book. In 1853, he was elected a Fellow of the Royal Geographical Society and a Fellow of the ROYAL SOCIETY. Other projects during this period included working on behalf of victims of the Irish famine of 1845–47, traveling to the Crimea on behalf of the British government in 1856, and helping JANE FRANKLIN raise funds to search for her husband, missing in the Arctic.

In addition to his geographic and geological discoveries in Australia and Tasmania, Sir Paul Strzelecki promoted a vision of development of an Australian economy with conservation of resources in mind. He was knighted in 1869 for "five years' explorations in Australia, the discovery of gold, the discovery of new territory accessible to colonization and finally for the construction of topographical and geological maps, based on astronomical observations."

Stuart, John McDouall (John M'Doual Stuart)

(1815–1866) *Scottish surveyor in Australia*

John McDouall Stuart was born at Dysart in eastern Scotland, the son of a British army officer. Educated at a military academy in Edinburgh, he later went into business, then immigrated to South Australia in 1838.

In Adelaide, Stuart went to work for the South Australian Survey Department, serving as a draftsman with CHARLES STURT on an 1844–46 expedition in which they ventured into the interior of the continent north of Lake Eyre, as far as the Simpson Desert.

Stuart went on to become a surveyor and sheep farmer in the bush country west of Lake Torrens. In 1858, in search of new pasture lands, he explored westward to Streaky Bay on the Great Australian Bight. A year later, he undertook an examination into the region west of Lake Eyre, locating the Neales River.

On March 2, 1860, Stuart began the first of a series of attempts to cross the continent from south to north, a feat for which the South Australian government had offered a reward of £2,000. Leaving a sheep ranch at Chambers Creek, about 300 miles north of Adelaide, Stuart and a small party headed northward. Several weeks later, they reached a chain of mountains that Stuart called the Macdonnell Ranges after South Australian governor Sir Richard Macdonnell.

On April 22, 1860, Stuart reached the geographic center of Australia, and, to mark the occasion, he planted a British flag atop a nearby hill, which he had named Central Mount Sturt, after Charles Sturt. (For this achievement, the ROYAL GEOGRAPHICAL SOCIETY awarded Stuart its Patron's Medal in 1861.)

In June 1860, Stuart and his companions arrived at Tennant Creek, a place that he called Attack Creek because of a hostile encounter with Aborigines. At this point, running low on supplies, they were forced to turn back.

Within a month of his return to Adelaide in October 1860, Stuart organized a second attempt to traverse the continent, this time aided by a government grant. He set out on November 29, 1860, and, by the following May, he had reached beyond the farthest point north of his previous expedition, an area now known as Sturt Plain. There, his progress was halted by an impenetrable expanse of thorny scrublands. Although he was then only about 300 miles from Australia's coast, he had run critically short of food and water, and, unable to find a way through the scrublands, he was again compelled to return southward to Adelaide.

Stuart's next attempt to cross Australia began in October 1861, and, after traveling northward from Adelaide, he was back at the edge of the scrublands in early April 1862. This time, he managed to find a route through the scrub to the headwaters of the Roper River. Traveling northwestward to the Daly River on July 24, 1862, he reached the Indian Ocean at Van Diemen Gulf, near the mouth of the Adelaide River and present-day Darwin.

Stuart's health had steadily declined on this last expedition, and, by the time he returned to Adelaide in December 1862, he was practically paralyzed and nearly blind as a result of the combined privations of over three years of continuous explorations in the outback. Just over a week after his return, a search party arrived back in Adelaide with the bodies of ROBERT O'HARA BURKE and WILLIAM JOHN WILLS, who had perished on a similar attempt to cross the continent farther to the east.

Stuart was awarded the South Australian government's prize and a grant of land for making the first south-to-north crossing of the continent. WILLIAM LANDSBOROUGH made the first north-to-south crossing that same year, 1862. Stuart returned to England in 1864 to recover his health, but he died there in 1866.

The trail that John McDouall Stuart had blazed on his trek across the heart of Australia was soon adopted as the route of the Central Overland Telegraph Line, extending northward from Adelaide, through Alice Springs, to Darwin on the Indian Ocean coast. From there, the line continued by way of an undersea cable to the East Asian mainland, providing Australia with its first direct link to British India. The hill he located near the exact geographic center of Australia was later renamed Central Mount Stuart in his honor.

Stuart, Robert (1785–1848) *Scottish fur trader in the Pacific Northwest and northern Rocky Mountains*

A native of Scotland, Robert Stuart arrived in Montreal in 1807, where he entered the FUR TRADE with his uncle, a partner in the NORTH WEST COMPANY. Three years later, he was recruited by JOHN JACOB ASTOR to lead the seaward segment of his Pacific Fur Company (a subsidiary of the AMERICAN FUR COMPANY) venture to the Oregon coast.

On September 8, 1810, Stuart and his party, including GABRIEL FRANCHÈRE, sailed from New York on the *Tonquin*. They arrived at the mouth of the COLUMBIA RIVER in March 1811, after a voyage around CAPE HORN and a stopover in the HAWAIIAN ISLANDS. He supervised the construction of the company's trading fort, Astoria, and directed fur-trading expeditions into the interior. The next year, WILSON PRICE HUNT, in command of the overland contingent of Astorians, arrived in Astoria.

Stuart, accompanied by fur traders Ramsay Crooks and three others, set out on an overland journey to the East with reports for Astor on the progress of the Oregon enterprise. They traveled through the Blue Mountains and the Snake

River Valley of what is now southern Idaho. On October 23, 1812, they located an Indian trail (later known as the SOUTH PASS) that took them eastward through a break in the mountains and around the southern end of the Wind River Range and across the Continental Divide. They spent the winter of 1812–13 in the lands of the Arapaho Indians in what is now west-central Wyoming.

In spring 1813, Stuart and his party resumed their journey eastward, traveling by CANOE down the Sweetwater River to its junction with the North Platte River, then down the MISSOURI RIVER to St. Louis, arriving in late August 1813. In St. Louis, Stuart first learned of the outbreak of the War of 1812, and that Astor's agents, anticipating British seizure of his Oregon enterprise, had sold Astoria to the British-owned North West Company.

Stuart was still with Astor's parent company, the American Fur Company, when the fur trade resumed after the war's end in 1815. Two years later, he and Ramsay Crooks became partners in that firm, directing its operations in the Great Lakes from the company's trading fort on Mackinac Island. He later expanded the American Fur Company's trade contacts to Indian tribes living across a wide area of the upper Mississippi Valley and northern plains, from the Wabash River Valley south of Michigan to the Red River Valley in what is now eastern North Dakota.

Stuart left the fur trade in 1834 when Astor sold his western fur enterprise to St. Louis fur-trading firms. Stuart settled in Detroit, where he entered the real estate business. From 1841 to 1848, he served as the federal superintendent of Indian affairs for Michigan.

By the early 1840s, the route Robert Stuart had pioneered in his 1812–13 overland trip from Oregon to St. Louis had developed into the Oregon Trail, a major wagon route for emigrants bound for the fertile valleys of Oregon and California. He is also credited with being the first non-Indian to travel through the ROCKY MOUNTAINS by way of the South Pass.

Stuck, Hudson (1863–1920) *Anglo-American clergyman, mountain climber on Mount McKinley in Alaska*

Born in London, England, Hudson Stuck immigrated to the United States in 1885. He attended the University of the South in Sewanee, Tennessee, graduating in 1892. In 1894–1904, he served as dean of the Episcopal cathedral in Dallas, Texas. In 1905, he was reassigned to Alaska as an Episcopal archdeacon, where he spent the remainder of his life.

In addition to his church responsibilities, Stuck developed an interest in the geography and native peoples of Alaska and traveled extensively. He also became proficient in MOUNTAIN CLIMBING. In 1913, along with Harry Karstens, Robert Tatum, and Walter Harper, Stuck accomplished the ascent of MOUNT MCKINLEY (named after

President William McKinley in 1897; also known as Denali, "the High One," an Athapascan Indian name), the highest mountain in North America at 20,320 feet above sea level.

Hudson Stuck wrote a number of books about his Alaskan explorations: *The Ascent of Denali (Mount McKinley)* (1914), *Ten Thousand Miles with a Dog Sled* (1914), *Voyages on the Yukon and Its Tributaries* (1917), and *A Winter Circuit of Our Arctic Coast* (1920). Yet it is as one of the first men to reach the summit of Mount McKinley that assured his place in the history of exploration.

Sturt, Charles (1795–1869) *British colonial official in Australia*

Charles Sturt was born in India, the son of an official of the BRITISH EAST INDIA COMPANY. At the age of 18, he joined the British army, serving as an officer in the last years of the Napoleonic Wars in Spain and France, and then in Canada and Ireland.

By 1827, Sturt had reached the rank of captain. That year, he arrived in New South Wales, Australia, attached to a military unit sent to guard convicts in the penal colony. Earlier in his career, he had known the colony's governor, Ralph Darling, who soon appointed Sturt as his military secretary.

Sturt came into contact with ALLAN CUNNINGHAM, HAMILTON HUME, and JOHN JOSEPH WILLIAM MOLESWORTH OXLEY, all of whom had undertaken explorations into the BLUE MOUNTAINS and along the lower reaches of the rivers to the west. Their reports suggested to Sturt that the interior of the continent might contain a network of westward-flowing rivers emptying into a great inland sea.

In his second year in Australia, Sturt led his own exploration in search of the source of the Macquarie River, which had been reached a decade before by Oxley. In November 1828, Sturt left Sydney in command of a small group of soldiers and convicts and, guided by Hume, made his way across the Blue Mountains to the Bogan, Castlereagh, and Macquarie Rivers. That year, the Macquarie had been reduced by severe drought conditions to a series of marshes. He followed the riverbed northwestward, still believing it might lead to an inland sea. Instead, in early January 1829, he came upon the banks of a great river flowing southwestward, which Sturt named the Darling after the colony's governor. They then headed back to Sydney, arriving three months later.

Finding the Darling River reinforced Sturt's belief that the rivers of southeastern Australia drained into an inland sea. In November 1829, he led a second expedition into the interior, this time to the Murrumbidgee River, southwest of Sydney. With boats built on the river's banks, he and some of the men from his first expedition descended the Murrumbidgee to its junction with the Murray River, which he entered in mid-January 1830. A week later, he determined that a river found flowing into the Murray further downstream was actually the outlet of the Darling River.

Sturt and his companions made an easy passage along the Murray to its outlet on a nearly landlocked tidal lagoon on the coast, south of present-day Adelaide, which he named Lake Alexandrina. Although a ship had been sent to meet them at the nearby Gulf of St. Vincent's, Sturt's men were unable to cross an intervening mountain range, and the rough surf made the only entrance to Lake Alexandrina unnavigable for any small craft sent to look for them. As a result, Sturt and his party decided to return the same way they had come, rowing upstream for nearly 900 miles to a supply station in the Hamilton Plains. They returned to Sydney on May 25, 1830.

The trip had weakened Sturt's health, and his eyesight had begun to fail. After serving briefly as commandant at the penal settlement on Norfolk Island, he sailed to England in 1831. Soon afterward, he left the army. In 1834, with his health somewhat recovered, he returned to New South Wales, where he had obtained a land grant, and took up sheep farming.

In 1838, Sturt was appointed to a post with the South Australia Survey Department, directing explorations for new pasture lands north of Adelaide. On August 10, 1844, he left Adelaide in command of an expedition to explore the country west of the Darling River. His 16-man party included the young JOHN MCDOUALL STUART, who served as the expedition's draftsman.

Sturt and his expedition ascended the Murray to the upper Darling region, where they were halted by drought for six months. In July 1845, Sturt and a small group set out westward and traversed the Stony Desert from Cooper's Creek to the Diamantina River. Although he had hoped to make a dash into the center of Australia, territory never before seen by Europeans, he and his men were by then suffering from SCURVY and were unable to find a way around the barren expanse of the Simpson Desert. They were compelled to head back to Adelaide, arriving there on January 19, 1846.

Sturt was nearly blind after this expedition. He served as secretary of South Australia until 1851, then returned to England, settling at the health resort of Cheltenham. He died there in 1869, just before he was to be knighted.

Charles Sturt recounted his first explorations of 1828–30 in his book *Two Expeditions into the Interior of Southern Australia* (1833). The European discovery of the Darling River, the longest river in Australia, revealed that the river system, which originated in the Blue Mountains and Australian Alps and was once thought to flow into an inland sea, actually drained into the Indian Ocean near Adelaide, by way of the Murray River. In his last expedition of 1844–46, detailed in his *Narrative of an Expedition into Central Australia* (1849), Sturt survived 18 months in the desert, explored more than 3,000 miles of territory and came close to reaching the center of the continent. The Sturt Desert, spanning the border between western Queensland and northeastern South Australia, was named in his honor.

Sublette, William Lewis (1799–1845)
American fur trader, merchant in the American West

William ("Bill") Sublette was born in Lincoln County, Kentucky. He was a descendant of Virginia pioneers and a relative of frontiersman and explorer WILLIAM CLARK.

In about 1818, Sublette moved with his family to St. Charles in the Missouri Territory, where his father opened a tavern. William served there for a time as the local constable. Four years later, both his parents now deceased, he joined up with WILLIAM HENRY ASHLEY's fur-trading enterprise to the upper MISSOURI RIVER.

In spring 1823, Sublette survived an attack against Ashley's fur traders by Arikara Indians on the Missouri River in present-day South Dakota. That summer, he took part in Colonel HENRY LEAVENWORTH's punitive military expedition against the tribe. Then, in September 1823, he joined mountain man JEDEDIAH STRONG SMITH's overland expedition westward from Fort Kiowa across the Wyoming plains to the Rocky Mountains, in the course of which the SOUTH PASS was explored.

Sublette, Smith, and DAVID E. JACKSON bought out Ashley's ROCKY MOUNTAIN FUR COMPANY in 1826. Over the next several years, Sublette undertook several fur-trading expeditions into the northern ROCKY MOUNTAINS, financed in part by Ashley.

In 1830, Sublette became a supplier of goods to the fur traders in the northern Rockies. That year, he organized and led the first wagon caravan from St. Louis across the plains and into the Rockies, arriving at that summer's trappers' rendezvous on the Wind River in what is now southwestern Wyoming.

In 1831, Sublette took part in a trading expedition along the Santa Fe Trail from St. Louis, during which Jedediah Smith was killed by Comanche Indians. The next year, Sublette attended the trappers' rendezvous at Pierre's Hole, where he was wounded in an attack by Gros Ventre Indians.

Later, in 1832, Sublette entered into a partnership with fur trader ROBERT CAMPBELL, with whom he established a trading post, Fort William, near the confluence of the Yellowstone and Missouri Rivers in what is now northwestern North Dakota. In 1834, he and Campbell founded another post near the junction of the North Platte and Laramie Rivers in present-day eastern Wyoming. This post, Fort Laramie, was eventually purchased by the AMERICAN FUR COMPANY, as was Fort William.

After 1836, Sublette left the frontier and settled in St. Louis, where he became prominent in business and politics. In 1844, he married Frances Hereford. In 1845, he was stricken with tuberculosis; he was en route to Cape May, New Jersey, to recover his health, when he died in Pittsburgh, Pennsylvania.

William Sublette played an active role in the development of the Rocky Mountain FUR TRADE, taking part in expeditions to the northern Rockies. He helped open up trails that later developed into important overland routes for wagon trains. A stretch of the Oregon Trail was known for a time as Sublette's Cutoff or Sublette's Trace. Fort Laramie, his post on the Platte River, became one of the key stopover points on the Oregon Trail and figured prominently in the settlement of the American West. Sublette's four brothers—Milton, Andrew, Pinckney, and Solomon—also were active in the fur trade during the 1820s and 1830s, operating throughout the West, from Santa Fe to Oregon and California.

Sueur, Pierre-Charles Le   See LE SUEUR, PIERRE-CHARLES.

Sulaiman el Tagir   See SOLEYMAN.

Svarsson, Gardar (Gardar Svavarsson the Swede) (fl. 860s) *Norse mariner in Iceland*

In about 860, Gardar Svarsson, a Swedish Viking, sailed from Norway on a voyage to the Hebrides. While in Pentland Firth, off the north coast of Scotland, he was driven northwestward by a storm to the east shore of ICELAND, where he made a landing.

Svarsson next sailed completely around Iceland, determining that it was an island, and he named it Gardarsholm (Gardar's island). He spent the winter on the north coast at present-day Husavik, where he reportedly constructed the first Viking house on the island. In the spring, Svarsson sailed back to Norway, where he related his adventure.

An account of Gardar Svarsson's voyage appears in traditional Norse literature along with a nearly identical story attributing the Norse discovery of Iceland to the Viking NADDOD. Nonetheless, Svarsson is credited with being the first Viking to winter in Iceland and with making the first circumnavigation of the island. Svarsson's reports may have led to the Norse settlement of Iceland soon afterward.

Sverdrup, Otto Neumann (1855–1930)
Norwegian mariner in Greenland, the Canadian Arctic, and Spitsbergen

A native of Bindalen, Norway, Otto Sverdrup went to sea as a teenager, then returned to work on his family's farm. In 1888, Sverdrup, an expert Nordic skier, began his career in Arctic exploration when he was recruited by FRIDTJOF NANSEN for the first crossing of southern GREENLAND. He again joined Nansen in the 1893–96 voyage of the *Fram*, taking command of the vessel when Nansen undertook his trek over the frozen Arctic Ocean in an unsuccessful attempt on the NORTH POLE. After drifting far to the west, Sverdrup managed to free the icebound *Fram* and return to northern Norway in 1896, where he soon made contact with Nansen, who had by then safely reached Spitsbergen (present-day Svalbard).

In 1898, Sverdrup was commissioned by the Norwegian brewers Amund and Ellef Ringnes, along with the Norwegian government official Axel Heiberg, to lead an expedition to Ellesmere Island and the northwest coast of Greenland. He was again in command of the *Fram;* his 16-man expedition included mariners, scientists, and sportsmen. Sverdrup first attempted to navigate through Kane Basin, hoping to find an ice-free passage leading to Greenland's north coastline. Pushed back by the PACK ICE, he withdrew to winter at Rice Strait. In 1899, he entered Jones Sound and began the first of three summers of methodical exploration along the west coast of Ellesmere Island and the uncharted regions to the west.

Sverdrup and his companions conducted field research in all aspects of Arctic natural history. They also came upon three uncharted islands, which were named Axel Heiberg, Ellef Ringnes, and Amund Ringnes Islands, after the expedition's sponsors. In 1902, Sverdrup returned to Norway with a great number of zoological and botanical specimens, as well as samples of Arctic minerals.

In 1903, Great Britain's ROYAL GEOGRAPHICAL SOCIETY awarded Sverdrup its Patron's Medal in recognition of his achievements in polar exploration. He described his Arctic experiences in his book *New Land* (1904).

Sverdrup operated a plantation in the WEST INDIES f or several years before returning to the Arctic in 1914 to take part in several rescue expeditions. In 1921, he commanded a voyage from England to seaports on the Ob River and Yenisey River deltas, in an attempt to open a commercial sea route to the Kara Sea in the Siberian Arctic. Then, in 1928, he took part in search efforts for the Italian aviator UMBERTO NOBILE after his airship the *Italia* had crashed onto the frozen Arctic Ocean, north of Spitsbergen.

The archipelago in the Canadian Arctic that Otto Sverdrup located west of Ellesmere Island later became known as the Sverdrup Islands in his honor. Together with the Parry Islands, they comprise Arctic Canada's Queen Elizabeth Islands.

Sykes, Sir Percy Molesworth (1867–1945)
British surveyor, diplomat in Persia and southwestern Asia

In 1893, British career diplomat and surveyor Percy Sykes left the port of Baku on the Caspian Sea, and sailed southeastward to Asterabad (present-day Gorgan) in northeastern Persia (present-day Iran). He then traveled eastward along the Atrek River to Meshed.

Sykes next made a north-to-south crossing of Persia's great central desert, the Dashti-e-Lut, to Kerman, in the south-central part of the country. In 1894, he traveled in the southern Persian province of Baluchistan, where he became the first European to climb to the top of 13,261-foot Kuh-i-Taftan, an extinct volcano.

In 1894–96, as diplomatic consul, Sykes covered a wide-ranging area of Persia, extending from Rasht on the Caspian Sea, through central Persia, to Teheran, Yazd, Kerman, and Baluchistan. He was accompanied on this journey by his sister, Ella Constance Sykes, who chronicled her experiences in her book *Through Persia on a Side-Saddle* (1898). In 1896, Sykes took part in a government survey with the Perso-Baluch Boundary Commission, in which he explored much of southeastern Persia, along the border with present-day Pakistan.

Sykes also visited ports along the Persian Gulf, crossing the Strait of Hormuz to Muscat on the Arabian Peninsula. As a surveyor developing a route for the Central Persian Telegraph Line in 1898, he covered a wide area of territory between Kerman, in the interior of what is now southern Iran, and Bandar Abbas at the southern end of the Persian Gulf.

Sykes returned to northeastern Persia in 1906 as British consul at Meshed. During the next four years, he used Meshed as a base for a number of expeditions into the northeastern Persian province of Khorasan. Again Sykes traveled with his sister Ella, who related their journey in her book *Through Deserts and Oases of Central Asia* (1920).

During World War I (1914–18), Sykes organized a Persian military unit in support of British forces and took part in British government surveys throughout a wide area of southwestern Asia, from the Caspian Sea and Baghdad, eastward to the Hindu Kush mountain range.

In 1902, Sir Percy Sykes was awarded a gold medal from the ROYAL GEOGRAPHICAL SOCIETY in recognition of his extensive travels in Persia, which he recounted in his book *Ten Thousand Miles in Persia*, published that same year. In his more than two decades in southwestern Asia, he traveled extensively in nearly every part of Persia, presenting in his published reports geographic observations together with historical and archaeological details.

T

Tasman, Abel Janszoon (Abel Janzoon Tasman) (ca. 1603–1659) *Dutch mariner in Tasmania, New Zealand, Australia, and the southwestern Pacific Ocean*

Abel Tasman was born in Lutjegast, a village near Groningen in the northeastern Netherlands. A seafarer, he entered the service of the DUTCH EAST INDIA COMPANY; by 1634, he had risen to the rank of captain, commanding the trading vessel *Mocha* out of Amboina in the SPICE ISLANDS (the Moluccas) of present-day eastern Indonesia.

In 1639, Tasman served as second in command on a voyage of exploration to the North Pacific Ocean, led by Dutch East India Company sea captain Matthijs Quast. Seeking two fabled islands, Rica de Oro (rich in gold) and Rica de Plata (rich in silver), with which the Dutch East India Company hoped to open trade contacts, they sailed along the coasts of the Philippines, Taiwan, Korea, and Japan, then headed eastward into the Pacific for several thousand miles. Although they located no new lands of any commercial value, the voyage brought Tasman's abilities as a mariner to the attention of Anton van Diemen, governor general of the Dutch East Indies at Batavia (present-day Jakarta, Indonesia).

In 1642, Anton van Diemen commissioned Tasman to explore southward for the legendary GREAT SOUTHERN CONTINENT, or Terra Australis, which was then thought to occupy much of the unexplored Southern Hemisphere.

Van Diemen instructed Tasman to determine if Australia, then known as New Holland, was the northern extent of the Great Southern Continent; to discern whether New Guinea was an island or was joined to Australia; and to seek a shorter sea route from the southern Indian Ocean to the Pacific coast of Chile.

Tasman embarked from Batavia on August 14, 1642, in command of two ships, the *Heemskerck* and the *Zeehaen*, accompanied by Frans Jacobszoon Visscher, a leading Dutch pilot and mapmaker. After sailing westward across the Indian Ocean to the island of Mauritius, he headed southward in early October 1642, hoping to strike the Great Southern Continent somewhere below 54° south latitude, a point farther south than anyone had yet reached. At about 42° south latitude, however, the prevailing winds blew Tasman's ships eastward, well beyond Australia's south coast, until November 24, 1642, when land was sighted. Although rough surf prevented sending a landing party ashore, the ship's carpenter managed to swim to the beach and plant a flag, taking possession of the uncharted land in the name of the Netherlands and the Dutch East India Company.

Tasman named the newly located land Van Diemen's Land (present-day TASMANIA), after the Dutch East Indies governor general. Finding a suitable anchorage on the southeast coast near present-day Hobart, the Dutch explorer and some of his crew briefly went ashore, where they found evidence of human inhabitants, although the natives declined to show themselves.

Continuing eastward, Tasman and his expedition approached the coastline of yet another uncharted land, sighting the peaks of a mountain range later known as the Southern Alps on December 13, 1642. Tasman made a landing at Cape Farewell on the northwestern corner of

NEW ZEALAND's South Island. He came upon what he thought was a large bay, which he named Murderers' Bay (also known as Massacre Bay) after four of his men were killed there by the Maori in the first European encounter with New Zealand's native peoples. Because he could not explore it thoroughly at the time, he was unaware that this was actually a strait (Cook Strait), separating the South Island and the North Island. Tasman continued northward along the west coast of New Zealand's North Island. He named the newly found land Staten Landt, apparently mistaking it for the western side of Staten Island, which had been discovered off the southern tip of South America by JAKOB LE MAIRE and WILLEM CORNELIS SCHOUTEN in their 1615–16 voyage. At the time, Tasman believed he had come upon the western extent of the Great Southern Continent.

Tasman sailed past the northern tip of New Zealand's North Island, which he named Cape Maria van Diemen, after the wife of the Dutch colonial governor, and, on January 6, 1643, he sighted a group of islands he called the Three Kings Islands, because he had reached them on the day of the Epiphany. From there, he sailed northeastward, soon coming upon Tongatapu in the Friendly Islands, where he took on supplies of fresh food and water.

Turning northwestward, Tasman next located the Fiji Islands, although he was unable to land there because of hazardous offshore reefs. After sighting the large atoll of Ontong Java, he made for the coast of northern New Guinea and sighted nearby New Britain and New Ireland, which he erroneously took to be one island.

By the time Tasman had returned to Batavia in June 1643, he had covered more than 5,000 miles of the southern Indian Ocean and southwestern Pacific. He had sailed around Australia without realizing it. By doing so, however, he had demonstrated that it was bounded by water on the south and thus could not be part of the much-sought-after Great Southern Continent.

Governor van Diemen, unsatisfied with these results, sent Tasman out on another voyage in February 1644, hoping he might discover new geographic details of more commercial value to the Dutch. The question of whether New Guinea and Australia were connected was still not resolved, and Tasman was directed to explore New Guinea's south coast, then continue southward into the Gulf of Carpentaria in search of a possible channel through Australia to Van Diemen's Land and the Pacific Ocean.

Accompanied again by the Dutch cartographer Visscher, Tasman sailed from Batavia in February 1644 with three small vessels, the *Limmen,* the *Zeemeeuw,* and the *Bracq.* Heading eastward along New Guinea's south coast, he missed the Torres Strait between New Guinea and Australia, which would have led him into the Coral Sea and the Pacific. Instead, he sailed southward and explored the Gulf of Carpentaria. Determining that it had no southern outlet,

he continued westward along the north coast of the Australian mainland, as far as North West Cape, Shark Bay, and Dirk Hartogs Island, where the coastline of western Australia begins to angle southward. After making the first continuous exploration along Australia's north and northwest coast, he returned northward to Batavia, by way of the Moluccas and the Ceram Sea.

Tasman soon resumed his career with the Dutch East India Company. In about 1649, while in command of an expedition of privateers against a Spanish treasure fleet in the Philippines, he hanged one of his crewmen for deserting his post, an act for which he was admonished by Dutch colonial authorities at Batavia and eventually suspended from the company. Reinstated after several years, he remained in the EAST INDIES, where he acquired great wealth as a trader.

It was not until 1798, more than a century and a half after Tasman had explored Van Diemen's Land, that GEORGE BASS and MATTHEW FLINDERS circumnavigated the island and learned that it was not attached to the Australian mainland. The island, first settled by the British as a penal colony in the early 1800s, became notorious for the cruel treatment of convicts and corrupt administration. It was opened to free settlers in 1853, and the newly organized colonial government changed its name to Tasmania in honor of Tasman, in an attempt to sever its ties with the unsavory past.

Abel Tasman's two voyages in 1642–44 were among the first scientific attempts to explore the Pacific Ocean. Nonetheless, they marked the end of major Dutch exploring efforts in that part of the world for the remainder of the 17th century. Tasman's findings, although at the time not fully appreciated by his superiors in the Dutch East Indies and in the Netherlands, greatly expanded European geographic knowledge of the southwestern Pacific, especially by revealing that the portions of the Australian coastline previously explored by Dutch navigators DIRK HARTOG and FREDERICK HOUTMAN were actually one continuous mainland. In a map of their explorations, Tasman and Visscher delineated for the first time the continental dimensions of western and northern Australia. Tasman's first expedition established the southern limit of Australia, showing that much of the Southern Hemisphere, once thought to contain a great landmass, was actually covered by the southern reaches of the Indian and Pacific Oceans. Further exploration of New Zealand did not occur until the 1769 visit of Captain JAMES COOK. The Tasman Sea, the arm of the Pacific between Australia and New Zealand, was named after the Dutch explorer.

Taylor, Annie Royle (1855–after 1907)
British missionary in India, China, and Tibet

Annie Taylor was born at Egremont in northern England. Her father was the director of a British international steamship line, and a member of the ROYAL GEOGRAPHICAL SO-CIETY. Her mother was a Brazilian-born French Huguenot.

In about 1876, Taylor began doing charity work in London, visiting the sick in poor areas. In 1884, she studied midwifery and basic medicine at London's Queen Charlotte Hospital and later that year she joined the China Inland Mission. In September 1884, she sailed to Shanghai, China; she stayed at a Christian mission on the lower YANGTZE RIVER (Chang) for five months, learning basic Chinese and becoming familiar with native customs. She then traveled up the Yangtze to a more remote mission, where she gave medical advice and taught the Gospel.

In 1887, Taylor took her missionary work to Kansu (Gansu) province in central China. From there, she traveled to the large Tibetan Buddhist monastery of Kum Bum, becoming one of the first Europeans to do so.

After a year in Kansu province, Taylor became ill, probably with tuberculosis. She returned to Shanghai via the Yangtze, surviving the sinking of her boat in the Han Rapids. Taylor sailed from Shanghai to Australia, where she joined her parents, who were vacationing there.

By 1889, Taylor had sufficiently recovered. From Australia, she went to join her sister in the northern Indian city of Darjeeling, remaining there as a missionary for two years and learning the Tibetan language from nomadic Tibetans. In Darjeeling, she acquired the services of a young Tibetan from Lhasa, named Pontso, who became her guide, servant, and traveling companion for the next 20 years.

In March 1891, Taylor left India for China, resolved to make a journey to Tibet, which was then forbidden to foreigners, and to enter LHASA. She returned to western Kansu province in March 1892 and crossed the border into Tibet. She and her small party were soon attacked by bandits and robbed of nearly all their possessions. Nevertheless, disguised in native dress, she pushed onward toward Lhasa for the next four months.

In January 1893, just three weeks from Lhasa, Taylor was arrested by Tibetan officials and sent back to China. She reached Szechwan (Sichuan) province in April 1893 and returned to Great Britain soon afterward. Later in 1893, she lectured on her Tibetan exploits at the Scottish Royal Geographical Society in Edinburgh.

Early in 1894, Taylor took her own missionary group, the Tibetan Pioneer Band, back to India. In Sikkim, a principality of northern India, the Tibetan Pioneer Band was soon reorganized as part of the China Inland Mission, and Taylor set out northward on her own for Tibet. She traveled through the Jelep Pass and reached the Tibetan border city of Yatung. She subsequently served as a nurse in a nearby British army field hospital.

Annie Taylor returned to England in 1907, where she presumably spent the rest of her life. Taylor's diary of her travels, later edited and transcribed by William Carey in his *Adventures in Tibet* (1901), details the everyday life of Tibetans. Her career was also recounted in Isabel Robson's book *Two Lady Missionaries in Tibet* (1909). Although Taylor failed to reach Lhasa, her seven-month, 1,300-mile journey from western China in 1892–93 marked the first visit by a European woman into then-forbidden Tibet.

Teixeira, Pedro de (Pedro Teixeira) (1575–1640)
Portuguese army officer in South America

In 1616, Captain Pedro de Teixeira, a Portuguese army officer in Brazil, helped establish Fort Presepio, a garrison on the southern Amazon delta, which eventually became the site of the city of Belém.

Six years later, Teixeira accompanied Luis Aranha de Vasconcelos in an exploration of the lower Amazon Basin, resulting in the first detailed mapping of the region. Throughout the 1620s, he participated in military actions aimed at evicting French, Dutch, and English trading settlements encroaching upon Portuguese territory on the Xingu River, a southern tributary of the lower AMAZON RIVER, as well as in the northern Amazon delta region, near the Guianas.

In 1637, the local Portuguese colonial governor, Jacome Raimundo Noronha, appointed Teixeira commander of an expedition to explore and map the Amazon from its delta to its upper reaches in the Andes. The project had been instigated by the arrival at Fort Presepio that year of two Spanish Franciscan missionary priests, who had descended the Amazon from their mission on the Napo River in Ecuador, arousing Portuguese concern over possible Spanish designs on the entire Amazon Basin.

Teixeira's party included more than 1,200 Indians and Africans, as well as about 70 Portuguese soldiers, traveling by CANOE, the largest European expedition to embark on an upstream exploration of the Amazon to that time. The group departed Fort Presepio on October 28, 1637, accompanied by Father Domingos Brieva, one of the two Spanish priests who had arrived at the mouth of the Amazon earlier that year, and who would serve as a guide for the upriver expedition back to Quito.

Teixeira and his armada of canoes came upon the mouth of the Rio Negro in early 1638. He claimed it for Portugal, then continued to the Napo River, which he reached in July 1638, encountering another Portuguese expedition led by Pedro de Costa Favela. After ascending the Napo to the Quijos River with an advance party, Teixeira made the last leg of the journey though the ANDES MOUNTAINS to Quito on foot. His arrival in late summer 1638 marked the first time a contingent of Europeans had reached the city from the east. He was received with much acclaim in Quito, the inhabitants celebrating with fireworks, bullfights, and banquets.

Yet, just as the appearance of the two Spanish priests at Fort Presepio the year before had alarmed the Portuguese about Spanish advancement from the west, Teixeira's arrival caused concern for Spanish colonial authorities over possible Portuguese expansion into the upper Amazon from the east. The Spanish soon ordered that he retrace his route down the Amazon, escorted by a group of Spanish observers, headed by Jesuit priest CRISTOBAL DE ACUÑA, brother of Quito's colonial governor.

Teixeira left Quito for Napo and the Amazon on February 16, 1639. He rejoined the bulk of the expedition on the upper Napo, then began his down-river journey to the Amazon. Along the way, he took possession of the region around the mouth of the Rio de Oro in the name of King Philip III of Portugal (who also ruled Spain as King Philip IV). He also marked a site at the mouth of the Aguarico River, a tributary of the upper Napo in what is now northeastern Ecuador, as the point through which passed the north-south demarcation line established by the Treaty of Tordesillas of 1494, dividing Spanish and Portuguese territory in the New World. By October 15, 1639, he was back at the mouth of the Rio Negro, and, although his men wanted to undertake a slave-hunting expedition up that river, he yielded to the wishes of the Jesuit priest Acuña and continued his journey down the Amazon.

About 100 miles farther downstream, Teixeira and his expedition stopped at the large Amazon River island of Tupinambarana, where the natives reported the existence of a tribe of warrior women who lived to the north, echoing the tales of FRANCISCO DE ORELLANA of nearly a century before.

Teixeira returned to the mouth of the Amazon on December 12, 1639. For his efforts, he was rewarded with a promotion to captain major, and, in February 1640, he was appointed governor of the province of Pará. However, he had become too ill to assume the office, possibly suffering from the rigors of his more than two years of travel in the Amazon Basin and the Andes, and he died soon afterward.

Pedro de Teixeira completed the first known continuous ascent of the Amazon, and in so doing undertook the first significant Portuguese exploration into the interior of Brazil since PEDRO ÁLVARS CABRAL landed on the Brazilian coast in 1500. Unlike the earlier downriver voyages of Orellana and LOPE DE AGUIRRE, which were guided by the direction of the river's flow to the sea, Teixeira's upstream expedition had to scout ahead in order to determine whether a particular stretch was a tributary or part of the main stream. As a result of his explorations, much of the upper Amazon Basin came under Portuguese sovereignty when, in 1641, a year after Teixeira's death, Spain and Portugal again became separate kingdoms, with John IV crowned as king of Portugal as well as Brazil.

Teleki, Samuel (Count Teleki) (1845–1916)
Hungarian explorer in East Africa

Samuel Teleki was born to a noble Hungarian family in Szaromberke, located in the Transylvania region of what is now Romania. From 1886 to 1889, Count Teleki explored central East Africa's Great Rift Valley with Baron LUDWIG VON HOEHNEL, traveling from Zanzibar to Nairobi, and climbed MOUNT KILIMANJARO. In northern Kenya in 1888, they located and named Lake Rudolf as well as its major affluent, the Omo River. North and east of Lake Rudolf, the Hungarians came upon another lake in southern Ethiopia, which they named Lake Stefanie.

In locating Lakes Rudolf and Stefanie, Samuel Teleki and Hoehnel made the last major European geographic discoveries in East Africa.

Tenzing Norgay (Tenzing Norkey, Tensing Norkay, Tensing Bhotia, Namgyal Wangdi)
(1919–1986) *Nepalese mountain climber on Mount Everest in the Himalayas*

Tenzing Norgay was born in a village in Nepal; his birth name was Namgyal Wangdi. Like many of his people, the SHERPAS, he became a professional mountain porter and participated in a number of foreign-sponsored climbs in the HIMALAYAS.

In the spring of 1952, Tenzing accompanied Raymond Lambert on a Swiss expedition to within 800 feet of the summit of MOUNT EVEREST, a world record at the time. Based on his earlier climbs, he was invited to be a full-fledged member, rather than a porter, of the British Mount Everest Expedition, sponsored by the Joint Himalayan Committee of the Alpine Club of Great Britain and the ROYAL GEOGRAPHICAL SOCIETY.

The expedition approached from the south side; in 1924, a climb on the north side had cost the life of GEORGE HERBERT LEIGH MALLORY. On May 29, 1953, Tenzing and New Zealander SIR EDMUND PERCIVAL HILLARY reached Mount Everest's summit. Tenzing continued climbing for 20 more years and reached the top of Mount Everest many times, along with other peaks in the Himalayas.

Although much of the international attention went to Hillary, Tenzing Norgay was actually the first man to reach the summit. At the top of the world's highest point, at 29,028 feet above sea level, he buried food as a Buddhist offering.

Tereshkova, Valentina Vladimirovna
(1937–) *Soviet cosmonaut, first woman in space*

Valentina Tereshkova was born near Yaroslavl, north of Moscow, in the former Union of Soviet Socialist Republics (USSR, or Soviet Union); her parents were farmers. She found work in a textile factory at the age of 18. As an ama-

Valentina Tereshkova *(Library of Congress)*

colonel. She went on to graduate from the Zhuykosky Air Force Engineering Academy in 1969. In 1976, Tereshkova also earned a degree in technical science. She later served as the president of the Soviet Women's Committee and became a member of the Supreme Soviet, the Soviet Union's national parliament, and the Presidium, a governmental panel.

Valentina Tereshkova, whose radio call name was *Chaika,* Russian for "seagull," has a place in the history of exploration as the first woman in space. She proved the ability of women to function under difficult conditions by spending more time in orbit than all the astronauts of the United States's Mercury program combined. The second woman in space was Soviet cosmonaut Svetlana Savitskaya on board a Soyuz flight in 1982. SALLY KRISTEN RIDE became the first American woman in space in 1983, aboard the SPACE SHUTTLE *Challenger.*

teur parachutist with a local club, she became interested in aviation.

In 1961, on learning that the Soviet Union was seeking female cosmonauts (*see* ASTRONAUTS), she wrote a letter to the space agency volunteering her services. YURY ALEKSEYE-VICH GAGARIN, the first human in space, oversaw the selection process. In 1963, after extensive interviewing and testing, Tereshkova was one of four women selected for training to be the first woman in space, part of the VOSTOK PROGRAM. All four women were commissioned as second lieutenants in the Soviet air force, which then ran the cosmonaut program. Amidst great secrecy, Tereshkova won the spot for the *Vostok 6* flight, which would be in space at the same time as *Vostok 5.*

Vostok 5, piloted by cosmonaut Valeriy Bykovsky, was launched on June 14, 1963. *Vostok 6,* piloted by Tereshkova, was launched two days later, on June 16, 1963. She orbited the Earth 48 times. *Vostok 5* and *6,* in different orbits, passed within three miles of each other, and Bykovsky and Tereshkova were able to communicate with each other. On June 19, after 70 hours and 50 minutes in space, Tereshkova ejected from the capsule at an altitude of about 20,000 feet and descended by parachute, landing about 380 miles northeast of Karaganda, Kazakhstan.

Tereshkova married fellow cosmonaut Andrian Niko-layev later that year. Their daughter, Elena Andrionovna, was born in 1964, the first child born to parents who had both been in space. Tereshkova was bestowed the title Hero of the Soviet Union and received the Order of Lenin. The United Nations honored her with the Gold Medal of Peace. Staying in the military, she eventually reached the rank of

Thesiger, Wilfred Patrick (1910–) *British traveler in the Middle East*

Wilfred Thesiger was born in Addis Ababa, Ethiopia; his father was an official for the British government and a close friend of the Ethiopian emperor Haile Selassie. Thesiger studied at Eton and Oxford University, then, at the age of 24, he returned to Ethiopia, where he explored the Awash River. He later served as a district commissioner in the Sudan, during which time he made expeditions into the Tibesti Mountains. Thesiger also served in the British army in North Africa and the Middle East.

In 1946–47, Thesiger made his first journey into the Rub' al-Khali, the EMPTY QUARTER—the 250,000-square-mile desert area of the southeastern Arabian Peninsula—dressed in bedouin clothing and with Rashid native guides, making a giant circle from Salahah in present-day Oman on the Arabian Sea. He made a second journey across it in 1947–48, also with Rashid tribesmen, from Mukalla in present-day Yemen on the Gulf of Aden to the Persian Gulf in present-day United Arab Emirates.

In the 1950s, Thesiger worked among the Marsh Arabs of southern Iraq, paddling to their homes by CANOE. With the vice consul of Basra, Iraq, Frank Steele, Thesiger explored Lake Rudolf (Lake Turkana) in Ethiopia and Kenya.

Wilfred Thesiger continued the tradition of his fellow countrymen in the Empty Quarter—BERTRAM SYDNEY THOMAS in 1930–31 and HARRY ST. JOHN BRIDGER PHILBY in 1932. Thesiger wrote about his travels and the nomads he encountered in *Arabian Sands,* published in 1964.

Thomas, Bertram Sydney (1892–1950) *British explorer in Arabia*

Bertram Thomas served as a British political officer in the Persian Gulf region for many years before entering the service of the government of Oman, on the southeast coast of the Arabian Peninsula.

In 1926, Thomas traveled northward from Muscat on the east coast of Oman, to Ash Shariqah in what is now the United Arab Emirates. A year later, he landed at Ras al Hadd on the southeastern tip of the Arabian Peninsula, then traveled along the south coast of Oman to Salalah. From there, he undertook preliminary journeys northward in preparation for an exploration of the Rub' al-Khali, the so-called EMPTY QUARTER, a 250,000-square-mile expanse, nearly devoid of water, encompassing roughly one-quarter of the Arabian Peninsula.

Thomas headed northward from Salalah in October 1930, accompanied by Sheikh Salih Bin Yakut and a party of Rashidi bedouins, and soon began his trek northward across the Rub' al-Khali. Traveling on camels, Thomas and his Arab companions reached the waterhole at Shana, near the desert's center, in early January 1931. Continuing northeastward, they arrived at Doha on the Persian Gulf coast of Qatar a few weeks later.

Bertram Thomas was the first European known to have crossed the Empty Quarter, Arabia's last unexplored region, and he did so without the aid of motorized vehicles or aircraft.

Thompson, David (Koo-Koo-Sint) (1770–1857)
British fur trader, geographer, cartographer in western Canada and northern United States

David Thompson was born in the Westminster section of London, England. He came from a poor family of Welsh descent and was left fatherless at an early age. Despite his family's financial hardship, he managed to receive a good education, attending London's Grey Coat School, where he concentrated in mathematics and geography.

In 1784, at the age of 14, Thompson was apprenticed to the HUDSON'S BAY COMPANY, and in September of that year, he arrived at the company's trading post, Fort Churchill, on the southwest shore of HUDSON BAY. For the next three years, under the command of SAMUEL HEARNE, he worked as a trader in the region west and southwest of Fort Churchill, along the Churchill and Nelson Rivers.

In 1787–88, Thompson journeyed as far west as present-day Calgary, Alberta, where he spent the winter and established the earliest trade contacts with the Blackfeet Indians. Back at Hudson Bay in 1789, he broke his leg in a fall and, while recovering, studied surveying and "practical astronomy" under the Hudson's Bay Company's official surveyor, Philip Turnor.

Skilled as a cartographer and surveyor, Thompson was sent out in 1793 to locate a more direct route from Hudson Bay to Lake Athabasca. Over the next several years, he explored up the Saskatchewan River into the ROCKY MOUN-TAINS and developed a CANOE and portage route to Lake Athabasca from the upper Churchill River by way of the Reindeer River, Reindeer and Wollaston Lakes, and the Black River. During this period, he also surveyed and charted the region between York Factory on Hudson Bay and Cumberland House in what is now eastern Saskatchewan.

Thompson left the Hudson's Bay Company to join the NORTH WEST COMPANY in 1797. Starting that year, he embarked on explorations that took him on an expedition from Lake Superior to Lake Winnipeg and Lake Winnipegosis. He also surveyed the upper Red River and the Assiniboine River. Thompson crossed into what is now North Dakota and explored the upper MISSOURI RIVER, where he made trade contacts with the Mandan Indians. His interpreter to the Mandan was RENÉ JUSSEAUME, who later accompanied the expedition of MERIWETHER LEWIS and WILLIAM CLARK.

In the course of his 1797–98 expedition, Thompson explored what is now northern Minnesota along the headwaters of the MISSISSIPPI RIVER. He may have located the actual source of the Mississippi, but his geographic findings were not revealed until several decades after his death, and he was never credited with the discovery. Before returning to Grand Portage on Lake Superior, Thompson descended downriver as far south as St. Louis.

Thompson set out again in 1798–99. From Île-a-la-Crosse Lake, he followed the Beaver River into what is now north-central Alberta's Lesser Slave Lake region, then explored the Athabasca River. In 1800, Thompson followed the Saskatchewan River into the Rockies, becoming the first non-Indian to find its source.

Soon after becoming a partner in the North West Company in 1804, Thompson began expanding his trade and exploration expeditions west into the Rockies. He had married Charlotte Small, the daughter of a fur trader and an Indian woman, at Île-a-la-Crosse in 1799. In 1807, Thompson, his wife, and their small children made a westward crossing of the Rockies. He was the first non-Indian to locate and use Howse Pass, which led him into the upper COLUMBIA RIVER, where he established the first trading post on the Columbia, Kootenay House.

Thompson was unaware that the Columbia at that point flowed northward before making a hairpin turn around the Selkirk Mountains. Seeking to follow what he thought was the south-flowing Columbia to the Pacific Ocean, he inadvertently explored the Kootenay, Pend Oreille, and the Clark's Fork Rivers into present-day Idaho and Montana. There, he established the earliest non-Indian trading settlements.

In 1810–11, Thompson undertook an exploration of the Columbia River Basin, possibly seeking to assert a British claim to the Pacific Northwest before JOHN JACOB ASTOR's seaward expedition could reach the mouth of the

Columbia. The Howse Pass route through the Rockies was blocked that season by hostile Piegan Indians, part of the Blackfoot Confederacy. Instead, Thompson headed northward along the eastern slopes of the Canadian Rockies until he came upon a route he called Athabasca Pass. He followed it to a south-flowing river, just above the Selkirk Mountains, which he correctly identified as the Columbia. Thompson then descended the Columbia, reaching its junction with the Snake River in what is now southeastern Washington on July 9, 1811. He set up a small marker and claimed the territory for Great Britain and the North West Company. He continued down the Columbia and, several days later, reached the Oregon coast, where he discovered that the American expedition had already established its post at Astoria. He conferred with the AMERICAN FUR COMPANY's ROBERT STUART at Astoria for a short time, then embarked up the Columbia to undertake a survey to its source.

Thompson left the FUR TRADE at the outbreak of the War of 1812. He settled near Montreal, where he drafted the first accurately detailed map of the Canadian West. After the war, in 1816, he began 10 years of service as a surveyor with the British Boundary Commission, during which he charted the U.S.-Canada border from St. Regis on the St. Lawrence to Lake of the Woods in northern Minnesota.

After 1826, Thompson's financial situation declined. He supported himself as a surveyor, but his failing eyesight soon left him without a profession. He died in poverty near Montreal at age 86. His geographic accomplishments were not fully appreciated until the posthumous publication of his personal account, *David Thompson's Narrative,* in 1916. During the 1880s, years after Thompson's death, Canadian researchers revealed that late-18th-century London mapmaker Aaron Arrowsmith had actually based his map of North America on Thompson's charts made in 1787–1800, without crediting Thompson at all. President Thomas Jefferson subsequently used Arrowsmith's map in planning the Lewis and Clark Expedition of 1803–06.

David Thompson was the first non-Indian to travel the entire course of the Columbia River and was the first Englishman to travel southward across the 49th parallel, west of the Continental Divide. His comprehensive map of Canada revealed that although the Columbia did not provide a western outlet for a navigable Northwest Passage, there existed a canoe route through North America that, with short portages, led from the western St. Lawrence, through the Great Lakes and across central Canada into the Pacific via the Columbia. Thompson's explorations in Canada and the United States covered more than 50,000 miles. Based on his surveys, he subsequently mapped a region of North America that encompassed some 1.7 million square miles. The Thompson River in British Columbia was named in his honor by his friend and associate SIMON FRASER. Among the Indians, Thompson was known as Koo-Koo-Sint, "the Man Who Looks at the Stars," because of his extensive use of basic surveying and astronomical instruments to determine his precise position while exploring in the Canadian West.

Thomson, Sir Charles Wyville (1830–1882)
Scottish naturalist, oceanographer on round-the-world scientific voyage

Originally from Scotland, at the age of 24, Charles Wyville Thomson became a university professor of natural history in Belfast, Ireland, specializing in marine animal life.

Thomson was especially interested in life forms existing at great ocean depths and in the deep-sea environment in general. In 1868, with the support of the ROYAL SOCIETY, he obtained the use of a British naval vessel, the *Lightning,* with which he undertook underwater studies of the North Atlantic Ocean. As a result of the deep-sea dredging operations he undertook on this voyage, he determined that life existed at far greater depths than had previously been thought. On a similar expedition in summer 1869 aboard the British navy's *Porcupine,* his dredging operations and deep-sea observations revealed that ocean temperatures were not constant beyond a certain depth, contrary to what most scientists of the time had theorized.

In 1872–76, Thomson sailed around the world as head of the civilian scientific team on the *Challenger,* a steam-driven British warship, again with the support of the Royal Society. Under the command of Captain SIR GEORGE STRONG NARES, the *Challenger* Expedition made three crossings of the Atlantic before sailing to Australia and NEW ZEALAND by way of the CAPE OF GOOD HOPE. Additional research was conducted in the waters of the EAST INDIES, Japan, Tahiti, the HAWAIIAN ISLANDS, and off the southernmost coast of Chile.

In the course of the voyage, Thomson directed depth soundings and temperature studies at more than 350 sites around the globe, undertaking comparative studies in the Atlantic, Pacific, and Indian Oceans. The zoologists aboard retrieved more than 4,000 species of marine life new to science. Thomson also initiated the first comprehensive study of ocean currents, and his deep-sea dredging operations provided a profile of the composition of the ocean floors. One of his most significant findings revealed that the Pacific was much deeper than the Atlantic, and that its bottom was covered with clay containing manganese, quartz, pumice, and mica.

The expedition returned to England by way of the STRAIT OF MAGELLAN having crossed the EQUATOR six times and having covered more than 60,000 miles of the world's oceans. It had also made the first passage across the ANTARCTIC CIRCLE aboard a steam-powered vessel.

Knighted soon after his return, Thomson was appointed director of the government's commission assigned to study and publish the results of the voyage. His two-volume *Voyage of the Challenger* appeared in 1877. From 1870 to 1882, he held a professorship in natural history at the University of Edinburgh.

Sir Charles Wyville Thomson drew upon concepts from geography, geology, physics, marine biology, and meteorology to make the first accurate scientific study of the world's oceans. His work on the *Challenger* Expedition initiated what later became known as the science of oceanography. In pioneering efforts to discover the nature of the ocean depths, he inaugurated the exploration of a region that, although covering most of the Earth's surface, still remains largely unknown.

Thomson, Joseph (1858–1895) *Scottish geologist in Africa*

Born near Thornhill in southern Scotland, Joseph Thomson attended the University of Edinburgh, where he studied under the great Scottish geologist, Sir Archibald Geikie. In 1878, on Geikie's recommendation, the ROYAL GEOGRAPHICAL SOCIETY recruited Thomson as a geologist for an expedition into East Africa, the aim of which was to seek a route from the Indian Ocean coast westward to Lake Nyasa (Lake Malawi). When Alexander Keith Johnston, the group's leader, died six months after they had set out from Dar es Salaam, Thomson assumed command of the project, and in 1879, although only 21 years old, he managed to lead the team across the breadth of what is now southern Tanzania to the north shores of Lake Nyasa.

Thomson next headed northward, making the European discovery of Lake Rukwa before reaching Ujiji on the east shore of Lake Tanganyika. He then traveled to Tanganyika's west shore and its main outlet, the Lukuga River. Although encounters with hostile natives soon led him to cut short his exploration of the Lukuga, he correctly surmised that the river was a tributary of the Lualaba River and Congo River (Zaire River) system. The expedition then returned to the coast at Bagamoyo, traveling by way of Tabora through central Tanzania.

In 1881, while Thomson was still in Africa, the sultan of Zanzibar, impressed by the young Scottish geologist's abilities as a traveler in central Africa as well as by his scientific background, commissioned Thomson to survey the Ruvuma River region of present-day southeastern Tanzania for reported deposits of coal. Although he discovered no mineral resources, he had the opportunity to further augment his understanding of the geological makeup of East Africa.

Soon after his return to England in 1882, Thomson was commissioned by the Royal Geographical Society to seek a route that could be developed into a major transportation link between Mombasa, on the Indian Ocean coast of Kenya, and Lake Victoria.

Accompanied by a seafarer from Malta named James Martin, Thomson started out from Mombasa in March 1883, heading westward to MOUNT KILIMANJARO, which he climbed. From there, he headed northward into the country of the Masai, a nomadic and fiercely territorial people who took a dim view of foreigners traversing their range lands in central Kenya. Despite frequent encounters with openly belligerent natives, Thomson and his companion succeeded in crossing Masai country, traveling by way of Lake Naivasha, the first Europeans to do so. Turning northward, they traveled with a Swahili caravan up the Great Rift Valley, making the European discovery of Lake Baringo along the way, and traversing a group of mountains he named the Abedare Range, after Lord Abedare, a prominent member of the Royal Geographical Society.

In December 1883, Thomson arrived at the northeast shore of Lake Victoria. On the return journey, following a more easterly route, he came upon an extinct volcano, the 14,178-foot Mount Elgon, north of Lake Victoria on the present Uganda-Kenya border, which he climbed and around the base of which he explored a number of prehistoric cave dwellings. Soon afterward, Thomson was seriously injured when a buffalo gored him. After six weeks, he had recuperated enough to resume the journey, arriving back at Mombasa at the end of May 1884.

Back in England in 1885, Thomson received a gold medal from the Royal Geographical Society for being the first European to travel through the lands of the Masai. That same year, he went to West Africa and ascended the NIGER RIVER into the western Sudan, where he negotiated commercial treaties with native rulers at Sokoto and Gando in present-day northern Nigeria on behalf of a British trading firm.

In 1888, Thomson explored the Atlas Mountains in Morocco and Algeria. Two years later, in the service of Cecil Rhodes, he led a trading and diplomatic mission into present-day Zimbabwe in south-central Africa, during which he explored the upper ZAMBEZI RIVER and the southern end of Lake Nyasa, and crossed the Muchinga Mountains to Lake Bangweulu.

Joseph Thomson died when he was just 37, probably from a kidney ailment and complications from pneumonia and tuberculosis. By that time, he had undertaken extensive explorations in all parts of Africa. He detailed his wide-ranging experiences in three books: *To the Central African Lakes and Back* (1880), *Through Masailand* (1885), and *Travels in the Atlas and Southern Morocco* (1889). In his journey of 1878–79, he led the first European expedition to reach Lake Nyasa from the north. In the year after Thomson's death in 1895, construction began on the railroad linking Mombasa and Lake Victoria, which, when completed in 1901, followed portions of the route Thomson had pioneered across

Masai country in his 1883–84 expedition. Based on his geological observations, he was able to formulate one of the earliest scientific explanations for the formation of the Great Rift Valley in central East Africa. The Thomson's gazelle, a type of antelope found in central Africa, was later named in his honor.

Thorvald Ericsson   See ERICSSON, THORVALD.

Thorvaldsson, Eírik   See ERIC THE RED.

Thunberg, Carl Peter (1743–1828) *Swedish naturalist in Japan and South Africa, in service to the Netherlands*
Carl Peter Thunberg was born in the city of Jönköping in southern Sweden. He studied under the Swedish botanist Carl Linnaeus at the University of Uppsala. After obtaining his degree as a doctor of medicine in 1770 (which, at the time, included the fields of botany and zoology), he studied botany in the Netherlands and in France. He received a commission from the DUTCH EAST INDIA COMPANY to collect plant specimens for Dutch botanical gardens in Japan. In order to convince the Japanese that he was Dutch, however, he had to master the language and traveled first to Cape Town in Africa, arriving in 1772.

While studying the Dutch language, Thunberg carried out three expeditions into the South African interior, traveling in a covered wagon drawn by oxen. During his stay in South Africa, he worked in conjunction with fellow Swede ANDERS SPARRMAN, who had also been a student of Linnaeus. He also worked with Francis Masson, and Englishman who was in the employ of the Royal Gardens at Kew in England.

Traveling on one of the Dutch East India Company ships as a surgeon, Thunberg traveled first to Java, then on to Japan in 1775, where he carried out extensive studies of flora and fauna. He returned to Europe by way of Java and CEYLON (present-day Sri Lanka). In 1784, Thunberg was appointed to the chair of medicine and botany at the University of Uppsala, a position he held for 44 years.

Carl Peter Thunberg was a prolific writer, and his *Flora Japonica* (1784) and *Flora Capensis* (1807–13) are considered classics. He has been referred to as the "father of South African botany" for his pioneering work in that country's natural science.

Thyssen, François (fl. 1620s) *Dutch mariner in Australia*
In a 1627 voyage from the Netherlands to the EAST INDIES on the *Gulden Zeepaard*, Dutch navigator François Thyssen

sailed eastward across the southern Indian Ocean along 35° south latitude. Following this bearing, which was somewhat farther south than the usual route used by Dutch trading vessels, Thyssen came upon Cape Leeuwin, Australia's southwesternmost point. After rounding Cape Leeuwin, he sailed eastward into the Great Australian Bight, naming the mainland along the southwest coast Nuyts Land, after a passenger aboard the ship. With no end of the mainland in sight, however, he turned about, completing the journey to the East Indies by sailing northward along the west coast of Australia.

Had François Thyssen continued eastward, he might have determined the true dimensions of Australia. He was, nonetheless, the first European to sail into the Great Australian Bight, providing later Dutch, English, and French navigators with one of the earliest reports of the continent's southern and eastern extent.

Timofeyevich, Yermak   See YERMAK.

Tinné, Alexandrine Petronella Francina (Alexine Tinné, Alexandrina Pieternella Françoise Tinné) (1835–1869) *Dutch explorer in Africa*
Alexandrine, or Alexine, Tinné was born in The Hague into an aristocratic Dutch family. She reportedly was drawn to African exploration after the breakup of a love affair.

In 1862, Tinné went to Egypt, from where she planned to explore the NILE RIVER and take part in the search for its source. At Cairo, she engaged a small fleet of boats and embarked upriver, accompanied by her mother and aunt, a small team of scientists, a staff of European attendants, and about 200 African servants. Her voyage was conducted with some degree of luxury, her own riverboat being equipped with a grand piano.

At Gondokoro, near the head of navigation on the Nile, Tinné hoped to meet with English explorers JOHN HANNING SPEKE and JAMES AUGUSTUS GRANT, who had set out to find the river's source from the East African coast two years earlier. She wanted to bring them assistance, believing they would pass by Gondokoro on their way north from the interior. In the course of the trip, both her mother and aunt, as well as two of the scientists, died of fever in the Nile swamps. With no sign of Speke or Grant, she began to seek the source of the Nile herself, traveling into the Mongalla Mountains of the southern Sudan and southward into the watershed region of the CONGO RIVER (Zaire River) and the Nile in what is now the Democratic Republic of the Congo.

Tinné returned to Gondokoro in September 1862. Learning that Speke and Grant had still not arrived, she headed downriver to Cairo. (The two Englishmen did eventually reach Gondokoro six months later, where they were

Alexandrine Tinné (Library of Congress)

met by SAMUEL WHITE BAKER and his wife, FLORENCE BAKER.)

In the mid-1860s, Tinné turned her attention to North Africa; she traveled to Algeria, planning to cross the SAHARA DESERT southward to the Bornu Kingdom of northern Nigeria. Her first attempt from Algiers was not successful, and, in early 1869, she went on to Tripoli, where she met the German explorer GUSTAV NACHTIGAL, who was then planning a similar journey. Meeting up again several months later in the oasis city of Murzuk in southwestern Libya, Tinne and Nachtigal agreed to travel southward together with the first Arab caravan headed that way. As before, Tinné was accompanied by a large following, this time including servants, Algerian women, and some Dutch sailors.

In the meantime, while Nachtigal went eastward on his own into the Tibesti region, Tinné went to visit with the nomadic Tuareg tribes out on the desert. Although a Tuareg chieftain had provided her with a letter of safe conduct, her camel drivers murdered her en route to the Tuareg encampment for valuables they believed she was carrying.

In her African travels, Alexine Tinné entered regions only recently explored by Europeans. Her voyage up the Nile in 1862 took her to the river's navigable limits, and her later overland journey into the Congo-Nile watershed region was into territory still not mapped. Tinné's sudden

end in the Sahara cut short a career in exploration that may have rivaled that of some of the leading male explorers of her day.

Toll, Eduard von (Baron von Toll) (1858–1902)
Russian geologist in the Siberian Arctic

Baron Eduard von Toll was born in Tallinn, Estonia. He was drawn to exploration in the Siberian Arctic by his interest in geology, especially in the study of fossil remains from earlier geological periods.

Toll took part in a scientific expedition to the New Siberian Islands in 1885–86, sponsored by the St. Petersburg Academy of Sciences. From 1892 to 1894, he undertook geological research around the deltas of eastern SIBERIA's Yana, Indigirka, and Kolyma Rivers. In the course of this expedition, he set up supply depots in the New Siberian Islands in support of FRIDTJOF NANSEN's attempt on the NORTH POLE aboard the *Fram*.

Toll's last expedition embarked in 1900 aboard the Russian research vessel *Zarya*. After two winters, he managed to navigate around Cape Chelyuskin, the northernmost point of the Asian continent. In spring 1902, Toll set out with three others in his party to explore north of the New Siberian Islands in search of "Sannikov Land," a landmass that had been reported in the early 1800s by Russian Arctic explorer Yakov Sannikov. When he did not return, a search party was sent out in spring 1903, led by NIKIFOR ALEKSEYEVICH BEGICHEV. On Bennett Island, letters left by Toll were found at his encampment, indicating that he and his party had died the previous year.

Baron Eduard von Toll made significant fossil discoveries on the Arctic coast of eastern Siberia and in the New Siberian Islands. His search for Sannikov Land was carried on by other Russian explorers for four decades after his death, and it was not determined until 1938 that the supposed Arctic landmass was nonexistent.

Tonti, Henri de (Henri de Tonty) (ca. 1650–1704)
French soldier, fur trader in the Mississippi Valley, cousin of Daniel Greysolon Duluth

Henry de Tonti was the son of Italian banker Lorenzo Tonti, originator of the life insurance annuity plan known as the "tontine." He was born in the Italian city of Gaeta, near Naples, and moved to France as a boy when his family was forced to flee Italy for political reasons.

At the age of 18, Tonti embarked on a military career as a junior officer in the French army. He subsequently was appointed a midshipman in the French navy, taking part in the 1672–78 conflict between France and Spain, the last phase of the Dutch Wars. During an engagement with the Spanish in Sicily, he lost part of his right arm in a grenade explosion and was taken prisoner, later winning release in a prisoner exchange.

In 1678, Tonti became a lieutenant under RENÉ-ROBERT CAVELIER DE LA SALLE and accompanied him from France to Quebec. By December 1678, Tonti was at the mouth of the Niagara River, where, under La Salle's command, he supervised the building of Fort Conti, as well as the construction of the ship the *Griffon*, the first European vessel to sail the western Great Lakes.

Tonti left the Niagara Falls post in summer 1679, and, in search of deserters from La Salle's expedition, explored the north shore of Lake Erie by CANOE. At Lake St. Clair, between Lake Erie and Lake Huron, he rejoined La Salle, and aboard the *Griffon,* they sailed to Green Bay on Lake Michigan's west shore. From there, he scouted ahead to the southern end of Lake Michigan and explored the St. Joseph and upper Illinois Rivers. At what is now Fort Wayne, Indiana, Tonti established Fort Miami, and, on the Illinois River, he founded the settlement of Crèvecoeur near present-day Peoria, Illinois.

While La Salle returned to France for additional support for his proposed expedition to the mouth of the MISSISSIPPI RIVER, Tonti remained in command at the Crèvecoeur post, where he developed fur-trading contacts with the Illinois tribes. In 1681, Iroquois (Haudenosaunee) hostility forced him to leave northern Illinois, and he went to Mackinac Island at the northern end of Lake Michigan, joining up with La Salle at the end of the year. From there, Tonti led an advance party to the Chicago Portage, and, in February 1682, he set out with La Salle on his famous journey from the Illinois post down the Mississippi to the Gulf of Mexico, which they reached in April.

Tonti accompanied La Salle on his return journey up the Mississippi as far as Starved Rock on the Illinois River, where he established Fort St. Louis. The next few years, Tonti operated between this settlement and Mackinac, developing the FUR TRADE with the Illinois tribes.

In February 1686, Tonti set out from his Illinois River post and descended the Mississippi in search of La Salle, who was then stranded at Matagorda Bay on the Texas coast. In early April 1686, he reached the mouth of the Mississippi, but his efforts to locate La Salle were unsuccessful. Tonti planned to follow the Gulf Coast to the Atlantic Ocean and return to Montreal by way of New York, but at the insistence of his men, he returned up the Mississippi to Starved Rock.

In 1687, after taking part in additional campaigns against the Iroquois, he attempted another expedition in search of La Salle, this time reaching the mouth of the Arkansas River, where he established Aux Arcs, also known as Fort Arkansas. (Aux Arcs, which in French signifies "at the Arkansas," was anglicized to denote the Ozarks, the mountain range to the west.) Tonti eventually met up with survivors of La Salle's expedition, among them La Salle's brother and nephew and his assistant HENRI JOUTEL.

In 1689, Tonti, having learned of La Salle's death, led an expedition into Texas in search of other survivors, reaching as far as what is now northern Houston County.

In 1690, back at his post on the Illinois, Tonti received a trade monopoly over the Mississippi River, and, the following year, he established a settlement at Pimitoui near what is now Peoria, Illinois. However, he was unsuccessful in gaining support for the development of the lower Mississippi as a southern outlet for the fur trade, meeting resistance from rival traders in Montreal and the Great Lakes.

In 1695, Tonti went to the Lake Superior region, established trade contacts with the Assiniboine Indians and explored the upper Nelson River, seeking a way to attack the English fur-trading posts on HUDSON BAY.

In the last years of his life, Tonti joined with PIERRE LE MOYNE, sieur d'Iberville, in establishing French colonies along the Gulf coast of what is now Alabama, Mississippi, and Louisiana. In 1704, at Fort Louis-de-la-Louisiane (present-day Mobile, Alabama), he contracted yellow fever and died.

Henri de Tonti carried out many of La Salle's plans to develop French influence in the lower Mississippi Valley. Following La Salle's death in 1687, his efforts led to French dominance over the region between the Great Lakes and the Gulf of Mexico. Among the Indians, Tonti was known as Bras de Fer, or "Iron Arm," because of his artificial right arm. His ability with this artificial limb led the Indians to believe he had supernatural powers and helped gain their loyalty in trade and in military actions against the Iroquois.

Torres, Luis Váez de (unknown–ca. 1615)
Spanish mariner in the South Pacific

Luis Váez de Torres was a leading Spanish sea captain and a friend of PEDRO FERNÁNDEZ DE QUIRÓS. In December 1605, he sailed from Callao, Peru, in command of the *Almirante,* one of the three vessels in Quirós's expedition into the Pacific Ocean in search of Terra Australis, the GREAT SOUTHERN CONTINENT.

In early May 1606, Torres and Quirós landed on the island of Espíritu Santo in the New Hebrides, which Quirós had mistaken for the mainland of the Great Southern Continent. An attempt to establish a settlement there was short-lived; Quirós abandoned the colony in early June 1606. At the start of the return voyage, the ships became separated. Torres waited offshore for 15 days; Quirós headed eastward across the Pacific toward Mexico.

Torres had been provided with sealed instructions from the viceroy of Peru for just such an event. Following these orders, he sailed southwestward as far as 20°30' south latitude, still searching for the Great Southern Continent. He may have sighted the Great Barrier Reef off the coast of

Queensland, Australia, although he reported finding no land.

Torres next turned northwestward and made the European discovery of what later became known as the Louisiade Archipelago off the east coast of New Guinea. Although he had planned to sail northward around New Guinea on his way to the Philippines, strong currents caused him to coast along the south shore of New Guinea, through the Gulf of Papua and into an uncharted passage separating southern New Guinea from northern Australia's Cape York. He then headed for Ternate in the Moluccas, then northward for the Philippines.

When Torres arrived in Manila, his ship was requisitioned by Spanish authorities, and he was compelled to remain there. In July 1607, he sent a letter to King Philip III of Spain relating that he had determined New Guinea to be an island, and that it therefore could not be the northern end of the Great Southern Continent, as had been thought.

Although Luis Váez de Torres had also described the passage he found along New Guinea's south coast, the information was kept secret by Spanish authorities. It was not until after the capture of Manila by British forces in 1762, in which Spanish navigational documents were recovered, that the news of the strait separating New Guinea from Australia became widely known. The first European to confirm the existence of what became known as Torres Strait was JAMES COOK, who passed through it in 1770.

Tovar, Pedro de (Pedro de Tobar) (fl. 1540s)
Spanish army officer in the American Southwest

Pedro de Tovar, a Spanish soldier, was one of FRANCISCO VÁSQUEZ DE CORONADO's lieutenants in his 1540–42 expedition into what is now the southwestern United States. A week after the Spaniards had conquered the Zuni Indian pueblo of Hawikuh in what is now northwestern New Mexico, Coronado detailed Tovar to undertake an exploration to the north and west.

Accompanied by Friar JUAN DE PADILLA, a Franciscan missionary, and a small detachment of soldiers, Tovar set out from Hawikuh on July 15, 1540, and traveled into a region known by the Indians as Tusayan. Within a few weeks, the party came upon the large Hopi Indian pueblo at Awatovi in present-day northeastern Arizona. Although the Hopi at first attacked Tovar and his party, they were quickly subjugated in a brief skirmish. Five nearby Hopi pueblos also surrendered, offering the Spaniards gifts of cloth, animal skins, turquoise, and corn.

When Tovar returned to Hawikuh later that summer, he reported to Coronado that he had learned from the Hopi of a great river to the west, in a region supposedly inhabited by giants. The news prompted Coronado to send out GAR-CÍA LÓPEZ DE CÁRDENAS to investigate, resulting in the Spanish discovery of the Grand Canyon and upper portion of the COLORADO RIVER.

Pedro de Tovar and his party were the first Europeans to make contact with the Hopi. His explorations into northern Arizona were not followed up until ANTONIO ESTEVAN DE ESPEJO visited the region in 1582–83.

Tristão, Nuño (Nuno Tristan) (fl. 1440s)
Portuguese mariner on the coast of West Africa

Nuño Tristão was a member of the royal household of HENRY THE NAVIGATOR, Prince of Portugal.

In 1441, with the support of Prince Henry, Tristão undertook a voyage of exploration along the coast of West Africa. He reached as far south as Cape Blanco. Antão Gonçalves, who was part of the expedition, returned to Portugal with a number of native people.

On a second voyage in 1443, Tristão made the European discovery of Arguin Island, just beyond Cape Blanco. The next year, he landed on the northern delta of the Senegal River, becoming the first modern European to visit West Africa south of the SAHARA DESERT.

Tristão returned in 1448 to Arguin Island, where he established the first Portuguese slaving station on the coast of West Africa.

Nuño Tristão's voyages brought about the first contacts between Europeans and non-Muslim black Africans. The Portuguese SLAVE TRADE, which he had been instrumental in initiating, became a strong incentive for later Portuguese explorations along the African coast. His exploration of Cape Blanco was a significant step in the progression of Portuguese travel along the coast of West Africa, indicating to navigators and geographers that beyond that point, the African mainland began to extend southward.

Truteau, Jean-Baptiste (Jean-Baptiste Trudeau) (1748–1827) *French-Canadian fur trader on the Missouri River, schoolteacher*

Originally from Montreal, Jean-Baptiste Truteau had been an Indian trader in the Des Moines River region of present-day central Iowa before settling in St. Louis in 1774, where he became the town's first schoolmaster.

In 1794, the company of explorers of the upper Missouri (the Missouri Trading Company) commissioned Truteau to lead a trading and exploring expedition up the MISSOURI RIVER. The enterprise had been organized in part by the lieutenant governor of Spanish Louisiana, Zenon Trudeau, a distant relative, who wanted to drive out British fur traders encroaching on Spanish territory in the upper Missouri region. In addition to opening up fur-trading contacts with the upper Missouri tribes, Truteau had been instructed to travel to the source of the Missouri and determine if it led to the Pacific Ocean.

Truteau, accompanied by Jacques Clamorgan of the Missouri Trading Company and a small party, set out from St. Louis on June 7, 1794, traveling up the Missouri by CANOE with trade goods. In what is now southern South Dakota, the expedition encountered Sioux (Dakota, Lakota, Nakota) Indians, with whom they traded for beaver pelts. They continued upstream to the Arikara Indian villages at the mouth of the Grand River near the present South Dakota–North Dakota border.

Truteau and his party spent the winter of 1794–95 at a post they established on the Missouri, south of Sioux country, in what is now south-central South Dakota. In spring 1795, he again visited the Arikara and traveled with a group of them into the Black Hills. He made contact with the Cheyenne and learned of other Plains Indians with whom the French and Spanish could extend their influence in the FUR TRADE on the upper Missouri and the northern plains.

Truteau returned to St. Louis at the end of summer 1795, reporting to Zenon Trudeau that, according to the Indians, large boats could navigate far up the river to its source. He also related what he had learned about the extent of British influence in the fur trade on the upper Missouri.

Jean-Baptiste Truteau resumed his teaching career in St. Louis, serving as the village schoolmaster until the early 1800s. The journal that he had kept of his trip up the Missouri came to the attention of President Thomas Jefferson who in winter 1803–04, sent an English translation of it to MERIWETHER LEWIS at his encampment near St. Louis, where he was preparing for his expedition to the Oregon coast with WILLIAM CLARK. Along with other sources, Truteau's account may have provided the American explorers with information about the Indian tribes they could expect to encounter, as well as geographic details about the little-known country of the upper Missouri River.

Tschudi, Johann Jakob von (1818–1889)
Swiss naturalist, diplomat in South America
Born at Glaurus in northeastern Switzerland, Johann Jakob von Tschudi received his early scientific training as a student of the naturalist Louis Agassiz.

In 1838, at the age of 20, Tschudi traveled to the Pacific coast of South America. In the course of the next four years, he roamed over a wide area of Peru, studying the native culture and visiting sites of archaeological interest. He toured the mining country of the Cerro de Pasco region of central Peru and explored parts of the Peruvian ANDES MOUNTAINS never before visited by Europeans. On his second trip to South America in 1857, Tschudi landed at Buenos Aires, then made a mid-winter crossing of South America to Chile,

during which he traveled through the upper Rio de la Plata region of northern Argentina.

In 1860, Johann von Tschudi became Swiss ambassador to Brazil, and he later went on to a diplomatic post in Austria. Among his works on his experiences in South America are *Travels in Peru* and *Travels in South America* (1847), in which he relates his impressions of Spanish and Indian culture and provides descriptions of exotic animals and plants.

Tsybikov, Gombozhab (1873–1930)
Russian historian, anthropologist in Tibet
Gombozhab Tsybikov was born in Burjatija in southeastern Russia near the Mongolian border. In 1895, he joined the faculty of the Oriental Department of St. Petersburg University. Four years later, he received a commission from the Russian Imperial Geographical Society to travel to Tibet in order to counter British interests. Great Britain had successfully sponsored surveys carried out by the Indian surveyors known as PUNDITS, among them NAIN SINGH, KISHEN SINGH, and KINTUP.

Tsybikov, disguised as a Buddhist pilgrim and traveling with a Mongolian caravan, entered Tibet in 1900. He spent two years based in LHASA and traveled to a number of monasteries, including those at Tashi Lhunpo, Tsetan, and Samye. Returning to Russia, he later taught at universities in Vladivostok and Irkutsk.

Although the Russian government had hoped that Gombozhab Tsybikov's stay in Tibet would lead to political ties, his primary interest was scholarly, and his writings on Tibetan culture and history are a major contribution to the field. A subsequent visit was carried out by another Buddhist scholar, Agran Dorjiev, who proposed a Russian-Tibetan alliance. These activities led to a British military expedition headed by SIR FRANCIS EDWARD YOUNGHUSBAND.

Tudela, Benjamin of   See BENJAMIN OF TUDELA.

Turk (The Turk, El Turco) (unknown–1541) *Plains Indian guide for Spanish under Francisco Vásquez de Coronado*
The American Indian known as the Turk was probably a Pawnee from the Great Plains region of what is now Kansas or Oklahoma.

In 1540, the Turk was living as a slave to Towa Indians at their pueblo on the Pecos River, near present-day Las Vegas, New Mexico. That year, HERNANDO DE ALVARADO, leading a contingent of FRANCISCO VÁSQUEZ DE CORONADO's exploring expedition, arrived at Cicuye Pueblo (Pecos Pueblo) and conquered it.

The Turk, so named by the Spaniards because of his Turkish-style headdress, told Alvarado of QUIVIRA, an Indian land of great wealth far to the north and east.

The Turk led Alvarado and his men eastward along the Pecos and Canadian Rivers onto the Great Plains, then was taken back to Coronado's headquarters at Tiguex on the Rio Grande, near what is now Albuquerque. Coronado's efforts to find the fabled Seven Cities of CIBOLA, with their hoped-for gold and other riches, had so far been fruitless. The Turk's tales rekindled Coronado's hopes of finding an Indian civilization as rich as the Aztec of Mexico or the Inca of Peru.

In spring 1541, the Turk guided Coronado and a large company of soldiers northeastward from Tiguex into the barren Staked Plains region of the Texas Panhandle. Another Plains Indian, named Ysopete, accompanied the expedition.

The Turk led the Spanish northward from Texas, through Oklahoma, to the Arkansas River, which they crossed near what is now Dodge City, Kansas. By that time, Coronado had grown to doubt the truth of Turk's stories and had him placed in chains. The Spaniards continued into Kansas, now led by Ysopete. A small party was sent ahead to what was thought to be Quivira, near present-day Lindsborg, Kansas. The village turned out to be an impoverished settlement probably of the Wichita Indian, on the Kansas plains. Soon afterward, the Spaniards encountered a party of 200 Pawnee warriors. When Coronado learned that the Turk had attempted to incite the Pawnee against his men, he had him executed by the garrote. He then led the expedition back to the Southwest.

The Turk's death at the hands of the Spanish may have stemmed more from their disappointment at not finding gold than from his suspected treachery. Some historians suggest that the Turk may have been sincere about the "riches" of Quivira, intending to take the Spaniards to the Pawnee, whose magic and medicine were highly valued by the Plains Indians. Or he may have been part of a scheme of the Towa Indians to send the Spanish far from their homeland, where they might perish. In any case, the Turk's knowledge of the region's geography was invaluable to the Spaniards in their explorations.

Turner, Samuel (ca. 1749–1802) *British army officer in India and Tibet*

Samuel Turner was born near Gloucester, England. He was a relative of Warren Hastings, governor general of British India and a high-ranking BRITISH EAST INDIA COMPANY official.

Turner himself entered the service of the British East India Company in 1780. In Calcutta, in January 1783, he was put in charge of a diplomatic mission to the "newly reincarnated" Tashi Lama in Tibet. From Calcutta, he followed the route GEORGE BOGLE had taken in his 1774 journey to Tibet. Turner reached Bhutan in June 1783, and, that August, he arrived in the Tibetan city of Shigatse. In December 1783, Turner was granted an audience with the Tashi Lama, who then was only 18 months old. Instructed that the child could understand him, Turner presented the Tibetan leader with greetings from the governor general of India; he then sought to establish diplomatic ties with the Tibetan regency. Turner retraced his route back to India, where he reported the results of his mission to Governor General Hastings at Patna in northeastern India in March 1784.

Throughout the 1790s, Turner took part in military engagements in India under the command of General Charles Cornwallis. In 1800, he retired from the British East India Company at the rank of captain and returned to England, where he was elected a fellow of the ROYAL SOCIETY the following year.

Samuel Turner's *An Account of an Embassy to the Court of the Teshoo Lama in Tibet, containing a Narrative of a Journey through Bootan and part of Tibet* (1800) was the first published description of Tibet written by an Englishman.

Ulloa, Francisco de (unknown–ca. 1540)
Spanish mariner in North America

Francisco de Ulloa was an officer with HERNÁN CORTÉS in the conquest of Mexico in 1519–21, commanding naval forces on Lake Texcoco in the final siege of Mexico City in 1521.

Ulloa went on to accompany Cortés in several voyages of exploration into the lower Gulf of California in the early 1530s, and, in 1535, he was left in charge at Santa Cruz (present-day La Paz), Cortés's settlement on the east shore of southern Baja California.

In 1539, Cortés placed Ulloa in command of a seaward expedition to explore northward along the west coast of Mexico, interest in the region having been sparked by ALVAR NÚÑEZ CABEZA DE VACA's reports describing the supposed riches of the fabled Seven Cities of CIBOLA. Cortés directed Ulloa to conduct a reconnaissance along the Pacific coast of Mexico as far north as possible.

On July 8, 1539, Ulloa embarked from Acapulco in command of three ships, the *Santo Tomás,* the *Santa Águeda,* and the *Trinidad.* In late August, the *Santo Tomas* became separated from the fleet in a storm and sought shelter on the Mexican coast. The vessel was soon seized by government authorities on the order of the viceroy of New Spain, ANTONIO DE MENDOZA, who had forbidden any seaward exploration without his authorization—something Cortés had neglected to obtain. Only a few months earlier, Mendoza himself had sent Fray MARCOS DE NIZA and ESTEVANICO northward on an overland expedition in search of Cibola, and he was concerned that Ulloa might find it first on behalf of Cortés.

Ulloa and his two remaining ships sailed northward to the head of the Gulf of California, making several landings in which he claimed the northern Mexican coast for the king of Spain. Upon reaching the mouth of the COLORADO RIVER, he observed that the outflow of the river made the waters of the gulf appear to be red in color, prompting him to name the area the Vermillion Sea. He explored up the Colorado River for a few miles in one of the ship's boats, reaching far enough upriver to see mountain peaks in the southeasternmost corner of what is now the state of California.

Ulloa then turned southward and surveyed the east coast of Baja. After a stopover at Santa Cruz, he rounded Cape San Lucas, Baja California's southernmost point, and proceeded up the Pacific coast, reaching and naming Cape Santo Lazaro and Punta Santa Eugenia, as well as an island he called Isla de Cedros, after the groves of cedar trees there.

In April 1540, Ulloa sent back one of his ships with a report to Cortés of what he had observed, then continued northward. After this point in the voyage, accounts vary as to what happened next. Some sources suggest Ulloa failed to return from the voyage and nothing was heard of him afterward. Other accounts indicate he sailed up the California coast to a point just south of present-day San Diego, California, and, on encountering unfavorable winds, returned to Acapulco in late May 1540, where he died soon afterward in a fight with another soldier.

Francisco de Ulloa is credited with making the first known European sighting of territory within the present state of California. He was the first to circumnavigate the Gulf of California, and, as a result, made the earliest determination that Baja California, thought to be an island since it was first sighted in 1533, was actually a peninsula. This finding did not become widely known until the 1690s, when Father EUSEBIO KINO mapped the region in his overland travels around the mouth of the Colorado River. A firsthand account of Ulloa's expedition, prepared by his secretary, Francisco Preciado, was translated into English by JAMES BURNEY and published in England in 1803, as *The Voyage of the Right Worshipful Knight Francisco de Ulloa. . . .*

Urdaneta, Andrés de (Andrés Urdaneta, André de Urdaneta, Andrýs de Urdaneta)

(1498–1568) *Spanish mariner in the South Pacific, priest*
Andrés de Urdaneta was born near Guernica in the Basque country of northern Spain. In 1525, he sailed with JUAN SEBASTIÁN DEL CANO as his page on a voyage to the SPICE ISLANDS (the Moluccas in present-day Indonesia). In the course of the expedition, intended as a follow-up to the FERDINAND MAGELLAN voyage of 1519–22, Urdaneta explored the STRAIT OF MAGELLAN in a small boat. Then, beginning in fall 1526, he undertook navigational surveys in the Spice Islands.

Urdaneta remained in the Spice Islands for the next seven years, during which he took part in military campaigns against the Portuguese and also studied mathematics and compiled geographic and navigational information about the region. In 1534, more than four years after Spain had relinquished its claim on the Spice Islands to Portugal, he sailed back to Europe on a Portuguese ship, by way of India and the CAPE OF GOOD HOPE, arriving at Lisbon in June 1536 and thereby completing a round-the-world journey begun more than 10 years earlier.

Urdaneta was detained by Portuguese authorities in Lisbon for seven months before he was permitted to continue to Spain. They also confiscated all the maps and journals he had kept of his travels in the Moluccas and the Philippines. Nevertheless, after he reached the Spanish capital at Valladolid at the end of February 1537, he recreated his work from memory and presented it to Spain's Royal Council. For his exploits in the southwestern Pacific, King Charles I of Spain (also Holy Roman Emperor Charles V) presented him with a substantial cash grant.

Urdaneta soon became known as one of Spain's leading explorers of the southwestern Pacific Ocean, and as a result he was recruited to join with PEDRO DE ALVARADO in a westward voyage to the Philippines from Mexico planned for 1540. He sailed that year to Mexico, where he soon became involved in suppressing an Indian revolt that became

known as the Mixtón War. In 1541, when Alvarado was killed in the course of that campaign, the planned expedition into the Pacific was abandoned.

Urdaneta remained in Mexico, serving in various administrative posts until 1552, when he entered the Augustinian order. He became a priest in 1557. Two years later, King Philip II of Spain called upon him to take part in another expedition to the western Pacific. Although his having become a priest excluded him from command of the voyage, he was instead named as "Prior of the Armada," and, in effect, chief pilot. On Urdaneta's recommendation, his friend and fellow Basque MIGUEL LOPÉZ DE LEGAZPI was placed in charge of the expedition.

Urdaneta and Legazpi embarked from Navidad on Mexico's Pacific coast in November 1564 and, after stopping at Guam, they arrived in the Philippines in February 1565. There, on the island of Cebu, they established the first permanent Spanish settlement.

On June 1, 1565, Urdaneta sailed from the Philippines aboard the *San Pedro,* commanded by Legazpi's grandson Felipe de Salcado, in an attempt to navigate eastward across the Pacific and back to Mexico, a feat that until then had not been possible due to the adverse effect of the northeast trade winds. Urdaneta, as pilot, set a course far to the north of earlier attempts, and, at the latitude of northern Japan, picked up the prevailing easterly winds and the Japan Current, which carried the ship to the California coast, off present-day Santa Barbara. From there the expedition followed the coastline southward, arriving at the port of Acapulco on September 18, 1565.

Although Urdaneta had planned to return to the Philippines to carry on missionary work, his health began to decline. He died in Mexico City in 1568.

Andrés de Urdaneta's voyage on the *San Pedro* was the second eastward crossing of the Pacific Ocean. Another vessel of Legazpi's fleet, the *San Lucas,* under the command of Alonzo de Arellano, had returned to Mexico from the Philippines just several weeks ahead of the *San Pedro.* Only Urdaneta had kept a careful account of the course, however, and his sailing directions enabled the Spanish treasure fleet, the "Manila Galleon," to sail eastward regularly across the Pacific. The sea route he had pioneered across the Pacific, utilized by the Spanish until 1815, made the long, roundabout homeward voyage by way of the Cape of Good Hope unnecessary and completed a practical, two-way link between Spain and the Orient through Mexico.

Ursúa, Pedro de (ca. 1526–1561)
Spanish conquistador in South America
Pedro de Ursúa arrived at Cartagena on the Caribbean coast of present-day Colombia in 1545, where he joined his uncle, Miguel Díaz de Arméndariz, a colonial administrator of

what was then the province of New Granada. Although then only 20 years of age, he was appointed governor of what is now Bogotá by Arméndariz.

In the Bogotá area, Ursúa asserted Spanish authority, leading several successful campaigns against the Musos Indians and establishing several new settlements. He was made mayor of the coastal town of Santa Marta in 1549, where he was less successful in subduing the Tairona.

Ursúa set out for Peru in 1552, drawn there by the prospect of new adventures and possible wealth. Along the way, he stopped in Panama, where he remained for two years, taking part in the suppression of a slave revolt. In Peru, he entered the service of the Spanish viceroy, the Marquis de Cuñete, who, in 1558, commissioned Ursúa to lead an expedition across the ANDES MOUNTAINS and into the Amazon Basin in search of the fabled wealth of the Omagua Indians and the fabled land of EL DORADO.

Ursúa, in command of 300 Spaniards and a number of Indians and slaves, left Lima in February 1559. Traveling with him was his mistress, Doña Inez de Atienza. After a series of delays, caused mainly by difficulties in obtaining sufficient financing and equipment, as well as problems with his lieutenants, he set out down the Huallaga River in October 1560. A contingent of carpenters had been sent ahead to construct boats for the main river journey down the AMAZON RIVER.

From the Huallaga, Ursúa and his expedition made their way into the Marañon and Ucayali Rivers, entering the main course of the Amazon by December 1560. On January 1, 1561, near the Amazon's confluence with the Putumayo River in present-day western Brazil, Ursúa was murdered by mutineers led by LOPE DE AGUIRRE, who soon afterward killed Doña Inez as well. Aguirre then led the expedition down the Amazon and the ORINOCO RIVER to the coast of Venezuela, intent on returning to Peru to stage a full-scale rebellion against the Spanish viceroy.

Pedro de Ursúa led one of the first organized attempts to find the fabled El Dorado, inspired by the earlier tales of FRANCISCO DE ORELLANA. After his murder, the men with whom he had set out from Lima went on to make the second European crossing of South America. Ursúa's death at the hands of Aguirre and his men marked the beginning of one of the bloodiest episodes in the history of Amazon exploration.

Vaca, Álvar Núñez Cabeza de See CABEZA DE
VACA, ÁLVAR NÚÑEZ DE.

Valcavado, Beatus of See BEATUS OF VALCAVADO.

Valdez, Gonzalo Fernández de Oviedo y
See FERNÁNDEZ DE OVIEDO Y VALDEZ, GONZALO.

Valdivia, Pedro de (ca. 1500–1553)
Spanish conquistador in South America
Pedro de Valdivia was born at Villanueva de la Serena in the Estremadura region of west-central Spain. In his early military career, he served with the Spanish army in Italy and Flanders, and, in 1535, he left Spain for the northeast coast of South America, where he took part in the conquest of what is now Venezuela.

In 1537, Valdivia arrived in Peru, becoming an officer under FRANCISCO PIZARRO. The next year, he played a prominent role in the defeat of Pizarro's chief rival, DIEGO DE ALMAGRO. As a reward for Valdivia's support, Pizarro consented to his request to lead an expedition into the lands south of Peru in present-day Chile.

In January 1540, Valdivia set out from Cuzco in command of a party of 24 Spaniards and a contingent of 1,000 Indians. He followed the Inca Road southward along the coast, a route Almagro had previously taken in his unsuc-

cessful probe into Chile five years earlier. After crossing the Atacama Desert, Valdivia founded Copiapó and explored southward into the Coquimbo region, which he named Nueva Estremadura after his homeland. Joined there by another 100 Spaniards, he continued his march southward.

On February 12, 1541, Valdivia established Santiago, the first permanent European settlement in Chile. During the following years, he brought in European settlers to develop the area agriculturally after it had become apparent that the region, unlike Peru, did not contain an abundance of mineral wealth. He also undertook explorations eastward across the ANDES MOUNTAINS into the Pampas of what is now western Argentina and continued to push southward along the coast. In 1544, Valdivia reestablished the seaport at Valparaíso, and, by 1546, he had taken control of the country as far southward as the Bío-bío River.

In 1547, Valdivia returned to Peru to aid in suppressing GONZALO PIZARRO's rebellion against the Spanish viceroy. Named as Chile's first governor general in 1549, in recognition of his loyal service in Peru, Valdivia returned to Santiago and resumed his explorations southward. On October 15, 1550, he established the city of Concepción at the mouth of the Bío-bío, and soon afterward, he initiated coastal explorations by ship, which led to his founding the city of Valdivia in 1552.

Valdivia soon traveled again across the Andes, where he founded the city of Santiago del Estero in 1553, in what is now the Gran Chaco region of Argentina. That same year, he sent out ships to explore southward along the coast, one of which located the western entrance to the STRAIT OF MAGELLAN, making the first west-to-east passage through it. Valdivia himself explored southward along the coast, reaching Reloncavi Bay, and also traversed the Andes again to examine the upper Río Negro in what is now Argentina.

Valdivia's efforts to colonize Chile were continually hampered by Araucanian Indian uprisings. One of his former Araucanian servants, Lautaro, led a rebellion in which the Indians captured Valdivia in an ambush near Concepción in December 1553 and soon executed him.

By the 1550s, Pedro de Valdivia's explorations along the coast and into the interior of Chile had delineated the last remaining geographic details of South America west of the Andes and as far southward as the Strait of Magellan. Valdivia was unique among the other early Spanish CONQUISTADORES in South America in that he established seaports and agricultural settlements rather than just seeking gold. Santiago, Concepción, La Serena, and Valdivia, all founded by him, endured to become the most important cities in Chile. He was later immortalized as the hero of Chilean poet Alonso de Ercilla y Zúñiga's epic work on the Araucanian Indian wars in Chile, *La Araucana,* completed in 1589.

Vambéry, Armin (Arminius Vambéry, Hermann Vambéry) (1832–1913) *Hungarian linguist, traveler in central Asia*

Born in the Hungarian city of Szerdahely, Armin Vambéry was a student of languages. In 1857, Turkish statesman and grammarian Fuad Pasha engaged him as his secretary and French instructor in Constantinople (present-day Istanbul), and while residing there, Vambéry learned several Turkic languages of central Asia.

From 1861 to 1864, Vambéry undertook a series of travels into Armenia, Persia (present-day Iran), Uzbekistan, and Turkistan. Using the alias Rustem Effendi and disguised as a Turkish dervish, he traveled into regions little known to Europeans. Aided by his facility with the local languages, he managed to visit Bukhara and Samarkand, cities that were then forbidden to non-Muslims.

Vambéry had journeyed into central Asia to expand his knowledge of Turkish languages. Yet published accounts of his experiences gained him world-wide renown as a traveler to exotic places. In 1865, he was appointed professor of Oriental languages at the University of Budapest, a position he held until 1905.

Armin Vambéry was one of the first Europeans to travel across Turkistan since the days of MARCO POLO, and one of the last to visit Samarkand and Bukhara before those ancient caravan centers came under Russian domination in the later 1860s.

Vancouver, George (1757–1798) *British naval officer in the Pacific and along the west coast of North America*

Born in King's Lynn on the east coast of England, George Vancouver entered the British navy in 1770. He served as a midshipman with JAMES COOK's second voyage to the South Pacific Ocean in 1772–75, as well as with Cook's third voyage of 1776–80, in the course of which he first sailed along the Pacific coast of North America.

Commissioned a lieutenant in 1780, Vancouver served on naval escorts in the Caribbean Sea and North Sea throughout the 1780s.

Promoted to commander, Vancouver sailed from Falmouth, England, on April 1, 1791, in command of Cook's former ship, the *Discovery,* accompanied by the *Chatham,* under the command of Lieutenant WILLIAM ROBERT BROUGHTON. Vancouver had been directed to survey the west coast of North America in support of British fur-trading interests and continue the search for the western entrance to the NORTHWEST PASSAGE, as well as to carry out a diplomatic mission in the region. He entered the Pacific by way of the CAPE OF GOOD HOPE, and as he sailed northward, he charted the coasts of NEW ZEALAND and Australia and established the exact positions of the HAWAIIAN ISLANDS. By spring 1792, he was off the North American coast at San Francisco Bay. Broughton, meanwhile, had reached North America and explored the mouth of the COLUMBIA RIVER.

Vancouver undertook a detailed coastal survey in which he charted the Strait of Juan de Fuca and the Strait of Georgia on the coast of present-day Washington State. He thoroughly explored a long coastal inlet, naming it Puget Sound in honor of Peter Puget, one of his officers. A glacier-covered mountain on the mainland was sighted, which he named Mount Rainier after another of his officers, Peter Rainier.

At the end of August 1792, Vancouver sailed into Nootka Sound on the coast of present-day British Columbia, where he met with Spanish naval officer JUAN FRANCISCO DE LA BODEGA Y QUADRA and conferred over the Nootka Sound Crisis of 1789, an international dispute between England and Spain concerning territorial rights in those waters.

Vancouver spent the next two summer seasons exploring and charting the coast of North America, from Cook Inlet near present-day Anchorage, Alaska, as far south as San Diego, California. He wintered in the Hawaiian Islands. In charting the coast of what is now British Columbia, Vancouver circumnavigated the largest island on the Pacific coast of North America. It was later named Vancouver Island in his honor.

Vancouver sailed eastward around the tip of South America on the homeward voyage, and, on arriving back in England in September 1795, he had completed a CIRCUM-

NAVIGATION OF THE WORLD. His account of his 1791–95 expedition, *A Voyage of Discovery to the North Pacific Ocean and Round the World,* was first published in 1798, only a few months before his death at the age of 41.

George Vancouver's explorations firmly established that no Northwest Passage linking the Atlantic and Pacific Oceans existed south of the icebound regions of the Bering Sea. The charts he produced of the lower Columbia River based on Broughton's explorations were of help to MERI-WETHER LEWIS and WILLIAM CLARK in 1805, during the final stage of their overland journey to the Oregon coast. England's later claim on the Oregon Country was based partly on Vancouver's extensive survey along the coast of what is now Oregon, Washington, British Columbia, and southeastern Alaska.

Vanderburgh, William Henry (ca. 1798–1832)
American fur trader, trapper on the upper Missouri River and in the northern Rocky Mountains

Born at Vincennes in the Indiana territory, William Vanderburgh was the son of a territorial judge and former Revolutionary War army officer from New York State. He entered West Point in 1813 but left before graduation to embark on a career in the FUR TRADE along the MISSOURI RIVER.

Vanderburgh went to work for WILLIAM HENRY ASHLEY's fur company, taking part in expeditions up the Missouri into the Dakotas. In 1823, he was a captain of volunteers in Colonel HENRY LEAVENWROTH's punitive expedition against the Arikara Indians in what is now north-central South Dakota.

By 1829, Vanderburgh had joined up with JOHN JACOB ASTOR's AMERICAN FUR COMPANY and operated out of Fort Union at the mouth of the Yellowstone River, under the direction of KENNETH MCKENZIE. He was put in charge of the company's activities in the northern ROCKY MOUNTAINS, competing directly with independent fur traders such as JAMES BRIDGER and THOMAS FITZPATRICK. In 1829–30, Vanderburgh penetrated deep into Blackfeet Indian territory in western Montana, where he was involved in a skirmish with the Indians.

In 1832, Vanderburgh followed Bridger and Fitzpatrick into the Rockies, thereby learning the locations of some of the best fur-trapping areas. The two veteran mountain men soon caught on to Vanderburgh's tactic. When they left that year's annual fur traders' rendezvous at Pierre's Hole in what is now western Wyoming, they deliberately led him northward into hostile Blackfeet country. On October 14, 1832, near present-day Three Forks, Montana, Vanderburgh and his party were caught in a Blackfeet ambush. Vanderburgh was killed, along with one of his men; four others with him managed to escape, later returning to recover his remains.

William Vanderburgh's career in the fur trade took him into the upper Missouri and into the northern Rockies at a time when the region was all but unsettled and largely unexplored by non-Indians. His exploits brought him into contact with some well-known frontier figures who played key roles in the exploration of the American West.

Van Noort, Oliver   See NOORT, OLIVER VAN.

Varthema, Ludovico di (Lodovico di Varathema, Lodovico de Barthema)
(ca. 1470–ca. 1517) *Italian traveler in the Middle East, India, and Southeast Asia*

Ludovico di Varthema was born in the northern Italian city of Bologna. Little is known of his life before 1502, when he sailed from Venice into the eastern MEDITERRANEAN SEA, beginning his extensive travels into the Middle East and Asia.

Varthema first visited the Egyptian cities of Cairo and Alexandria, then sailed to the coast of Lebanon, disembarking in Beirut. He headed northward to Tripoli, then entered Syria, arriving in Damascus in April 1503. Having learned enough Arabic to pass himself off as a Muslim, Varthema joined a group of Mameluke soldiers hired as armed escorts for a party of pilgrims heading for the holy cities of Mecca and Medina to the south.

Varthema arrived in Mecca with the pilgrims in late May 1503, the first European non-Muslim known to have reached that sacred city. He remained for almost three weeks. After continuing to Medina, he deserted the Mamelukes and boarded a ship at the RED SEA port of Jidda, with plans to sail to India.

At the port of Aden near the mouth of the Red Sea, Varthema was arrested on orders of the sultan, who suspected that the Italian traveler was a Christian spy. According to his own account, Varthema was at first imprisoned, then managed to gain his release through romantic involvement with one of the sultan's wives. He then traveled extensively in southwestern Arabia and Yemen, heading inland to the city of Sanaa.

After several months in Arabia, Varthema sailed from Aden by way of the Ethiopian coast and the Arabian Sea, landing at the northwestern Indian port of Diu in early 1504. Instead of continuing into India, however, he went up through the Strait of Hormuz and into the Persian Gulf. He then traveled eastward across Persia (present-day Iran) and into Afghanistan, visiting Herat in an unsuccessful attempt to reach the legendary city of Samarkand.

Back at Shiraz in Persia, Varthema befriended a wealthy Persian merchant, with whom he sailed to India, visiting the Malabar Coast city of Calicut before going on to CEYLON (present-day Sri Lanka) and the Madras region on India's southeast coast. From Madras, Varthema and his Persian companion sailed eastward across the Bay of Bengal to Malaya, Burma, and the islands of Java and Sumatra in present-day Indonesia. They traveled into Southeast Asia, touring Siam (present-day Thailand), and probably sailed to the SPICE ISLANDS (the Moluccas) and Celebes Island, also in present-day Indonesia.

Varthema was back in India by 1505, where he entered the service of the Portuguese, taking part in military actions against the local natives at the Malabar Coast city of Cannanore. For his efforts, the Portuguese viceroy of India awarded him a knighthood.

In December 1507, Varthema sailed back to Europe on a Portuguese vessel, making stops at Moçambique and other East African coastal ports, before rounding the CAPE OF GOOD HOPE and reaching Lisbon by way of the AZORES. After a royal reception by King Manuel I of Portugal, Varthema returned to Italy in 1508.

Ludovico di Varthema settled in Rome, where he soon set to work on an account of his exploits. Published in 1510, his *Travels of Ludovico di Varthema in Egypt, Syria, Arabia Deserta and Arabia Felix, in Persia, India, and Ethiopia, A.D. 1503 to 1508* was very well received; the first English edition appeared in 1576–77. Although the Portuguese had perfected a sea route around Africa to India by the time of his visit, Varthema's travels marked the first time a European had reached the Far East by way of the Mediterranean and Red Seas and then had returned to Europe in a sea voyage around Africa. Moreover, Varthema's travel account provided 16th-century European cartographers with a better idea of the geography of Asia.

Vasquez, Louis (1798–1868) *American fur trader, merchant in the Rocky Mountains*

Louis Vasquez, a native of St. Louis, became involved in the FUR TRADE on the nearby MISSOURI RIVER at an early age. In the early 1820s, he worked for WILLIAM HENRY ASHLEY's AMERICAN FUR COMPANY, taking part in trading expeditions up the Missouri River into present-day South and North Dakota and into the northern ROCKY MOUNTAINS in what is now northern Utah and southwestern Wyoming.

Vasquez went into business in the 1830s with ROBERT CAMPBELL, with whom he brought goods and supplies to the annual rendezvous of fur traders on the Green River in 1833. Two years later, together with Andrew Sublette, brother of WILLIAM LEWIS SUBLETTE, Vasquez established a post on the South Platte River, near the site of what later became Denver, Colorado. Known as Fort Vasquez, it soon became a trading hub in the southern Rockies; from there, Vasquez shipped furs and hides down the South Platte and Platte Rivers to the Missouri and on to St. Louis. He also pioneered an overland route southward to Bent's Fort, thereby

linking his post with the Santa Fe Trail and the Arkansas River.

In 1843, Vasquez, in partnership with JAMES BRIDGER, established Fort Bridger on Black's Fork of the Green River in present-day southwest Wyoming. Located near the SOUTH PASS, the settlement served as a key stopping and resupply point along the Oregon and California Trails throughout the 1840s and 1850s. Vasquez sold his interest in Fort Bridger to Mormons in 1855, settling with his family in Westport, Missouri.

Louis Vasquez's frontier business enterprises included the establishment of outposts vital to the development of regular travel and communication in the Rockies. The trail he blazed in the late 1830s between Bent's Fort on the Arkansas River northward and Fort Vasquez on the South Platte became a key route for prospectors in the Pikes Peak (Colorado) gold rush of 1859.

Vásquez de Ayllón, Lucas   See AYLLÓN, LUCAS VÁSQUEZ DE.

Vavasour, Mervin (1819–1866) *British army officer in the Pacific Northwest*

In 1845, Mervin Vavasour, a British army officer in Canada, was directed to undertake a military reconnaissance of the Oregon Country, which was then jointly administered by Great Britain and the United States. On May 5, Vavasour, accompanied by fellow officer HENRY JAMES WARRE, left Montreal, traveling westward along the CANOE-and-portage route to the Great Lakes, the Red River of the North, and Fort Garry (present-day Winnipeg, Manitoba). On this first half of the trip, they were joined by HUDSON'S BAY COMPANY governor SIR GEORGE SIMPSON, who strongly favored establishing a transcontinental military supply route to Oregon. They continued the journey westward from Fort Garry, guided by Hudson's Bay Company officer PETER SKENE OGDEN, with whom they traveled on horseback across the plains. They then traversed the Canadian ROCKY MOUNTAINS by way of White Man Pass and boated down the Columbia River to Fort Vancouver, near present-day Portland, Oregon, arriving there on August 25, 1845.

That winter, Vavasour and Warre visited the American settlement at Oregon City and toured the Pacific coast of Oregon and Washington, including Puget Sound, Vancouver Island, and the area around the mouth of the COLUMBIA RIVER. Vavasour and Warre returned to eastern Canada the following spring, traveling by way of the Athabasca Pass to the Saskatchewan River.

Mervin Vavasour's and Warre's mission had been to determine if British troops could be rapidly deployed to the

Oregon Country in an overland march across the Great Plains and Canadian Rockies, should the need arise. To carry out this assignment without arousing American concerns, they traveled under the guise of being British sportsmen on a hunting trip in the American West. In the report they filed, they concluded that the vast distances involved, the rough terrain, and the lack of abundant food supplies en route made such a plan highly impractical.

Velásquez, Diego (Diego Velázquez de Cuéllar, Diego de Velázquez) (1465–1524)
Spanish conquistador, colonial administrator in the West Indies, uncle of Juan de Grijalva

Diego Velásquez was born into a noble family at Cuéllar in north-central Spain. He embarked on a military career in his early teens, serving in the Spanish army against the Moors in the reconquest of Spain for King Ferdinand and Queen Isabella.

In 1493, Velásquez sailed to the WEST INDIES on CHRISTOPHER COLUMBUS's second voyage of exploration. He settled on Hispaniola (present-day Haiti and the Dominican Republic) and played a leading role in the conquest of the island under Columbus's brother, Bartholomew Columbus. Velásquez prospered as a colonist, establishing the towns of Azua and Jacmel in 1502.

In 1511, Velásquez was commissioned by Hispaniola's governor Diego Columbus (Christopher Columbus's son) to begin the conquest of Cuba. Later that year, in command of a fleet of four ships, he landed on Cuba's eastern end, with a force of 300 men, including HERNÁN CORTÉS, who was one of his chief officers. Velásquez had little difficulty in subduing Cuba's natives. The only significant resistance was overcome when the leader of the uprising, the native cacique (ruler) Hatuey, who had previously fled Hispaniola to escape the Spaniards, was captured and executed by burning at the stake.

In February 1513, Velásquez founded Baracoa, the first permanent European settlement on Cuba. Aided later that year by reinforcements under the command of PÁNFILO DE NARVÁEZ, Velásquez soon completed the conquest of all of Cuba and declared himself governor general of the island—a claim that was upheld by the Spanish government. By the end of 1514, he had established the cities of Bayamo and Santiago de Cuba, which he made his capital.

In 1517, Velásquez sent out a slave-hunting expedition to the Bahamas, commanded by FRANCISCO FERNÁNDEZ DE CÓRDOBA. On that voyage, Fernández de Córdoba's ships were blown far to the south and west, and, on his return to Cuba, he reported to Velasquez the existence of the mainland of Yucatán. Prompted by this news, as well as tales of an advanced Indian civilization possessing quantities of gold and other riches, Velásquez sent out a small

fleet under the command of his nephew JUAN DE GRIJALVA in spring 1518.

When Grijalva sent back word to Cuba that he had indications of wealthy Indian civilizations on the Mexican mainland, Velásquez immediately organized a large force of CONQUISTADORES under the command of Cortés, who sailed for Mexico and the land of the Aztec in fall 1518.

In 1519, Velásquez founded the city of Havana on Cuba. That same year, he sent to the Council of the Indies in Spain one of the earliest detailed maps of the island of Cuba.

In 1520, Velásquez learned that Cortés was seeking the endorsement of King Charles I of Spain (Holy Roman Emperor Charles V) for his claim to the newly explored land of Mexico, territory that Velásquez considered to be rightfully his by virtue of having sponsored the expedition. He soon dispatched Pánfilo de Narváez and a large military force to Veracruz on the Mexican mainland, seeking the arrest of Cortés. Most of Narváez's men, after defeat by Cortés, joined him in the campaign against the Aztec.

Velásquez lost his post as Cuba's governor in 1521, the year of Cortés's great triumph in Mexico. He regained the position two years later and served for one more year, until his death.

Diego Velásquez played a vital role in establishing the initial settlements on both Hispaniola and Cuba, the first permanent European colonies in the Western Hemisphere. The seaward probes he sent out under Fernández de Córdoba, Grijalva, and Cortés helped reveal the extent of Mexico's gulf coast and led to the destruction of the Aztec Empire.

Vérendrye, Louis-Joseph Gaultier de la
See LA VÉRENDRYE, LOUIS-JOSEPH GAULTIER DE.

Vérendrye, Pierre Gaultier de Varennes de la
See LA VÉRENDRYE, PIERRE GAULTIER DE VARENNES DE.

Verrazano, Giovanni da (Giovanni da Verrazzano) (ca. 1485–ca. 1528) *Italian-born mariner in Americas, in service to France*

Born into an upper-class family, Giovanni da Verrazano was a native of Val di Greve in the Tuscany region of northern Italy and was educated in Florence. Embarking on a seafaring career, he undertook several voyages across the MEDITERRANEAN SEA to the Middle East before moving to Dieppe, a seaport on the Normandy coast of France.

In 1522, on an expedition of PRIVATEERS in the service of France, Verrazano captured two of Spanish conquistador HERNÁN CORTÉS's ships, of the GALLEON design, laden with gold and were returning from Mexico. This achievement brought him to the attention of King Francis I of France. At that time, news of FERDINAND MAGELLAN's route around the tip of South America to the Far East had just reached Europe. In 1523, Francis I commissioned Verrazano to undertake a voyage westward across the Atlantic Ocean in the hope of finding a sea passage through the Americas to Asia.

Verrazano sailed from Dieppe in command of a fleet of four ships. A storm soon drove his expedition back to the Brittany coast. In January 1524, he left Dieppe again with one ship, *La Dauphine,* and a crew of 50 men. After a stopover on the Portuguese island of Madeira, he crossed the Atlantic. A storm drove his ship northward from his intended course, causing him to reach the North American coast at Cape Fear in present-day North Carolina in early March 1524.

Verrazano made a landing and had friendly contacts with Indians. He then headed southward in search of a passage to the Pacific Ocean. Fearing an encounter with the Spanish to the south, he turned northward near present-day Charleston, South Carolina. While exploring the coast along Cape Hatteras, he saw Pamlico Sound across a narrow strip of land and took it to be the western ocean.

On April 17, 1524, Verrazano reached the entrance to New York Bay. He anchored at a point in the harbor known as the Narrows, then explored the lower Hudson River in a small boat, making contact with Indians. He and his men remained in New York Bay for two weeks before heading northward along the coast.

Verrazano reached Block Island, and, with the assistance of a local Indian, explored Narragansett Bay, making a landing at the site of present-day Newport, Rhode Island. He then proceeded up the coast of Maine, where he traded with the Abenaki Indians. From there, he sailed to the east shore of Newfoundland, and, from Cape Breton Island, headed back to Europe. After a two-week crossing of the Atlantic, he arrived in Dieppe on July 8, 1524. He claimed all the territory he had explored for France, calling it "Francesca" in honor of French king Francis I.

Verrazano undertook a second voyage across the Atlantic sponsored in part by French admiral Philippe de Chabot, probably in 1526 or 1527. Following a more southerly course, Verrazano reached the coast of Brazil and returned to France with a cargo of tropical lumber, which was highly valued in Europe as a source of dye.

Verrazano made his final voyage to the Americas in spring 1528. He sailed southwest from Dieppe to the Florida coast and the Bahamas, then sailed southward along the Lesser Antilles, still hoping to find a passage to the Orient.

At the island of Guadeloupe, Verrazano went ashore with a small party. They were set upon by Carib Indians; Verrazano was killed and reportedly eaten by the natives. The expedition continued on to Brazil before returning to France.

Verrazano's brother, cartographer Girolamo da Verrazano, who accompanied him on his voyages, produced the first map of North America that identified part of the coast with a Native American name—Oranbega—an Abenaki name for a site in what is now Maine.

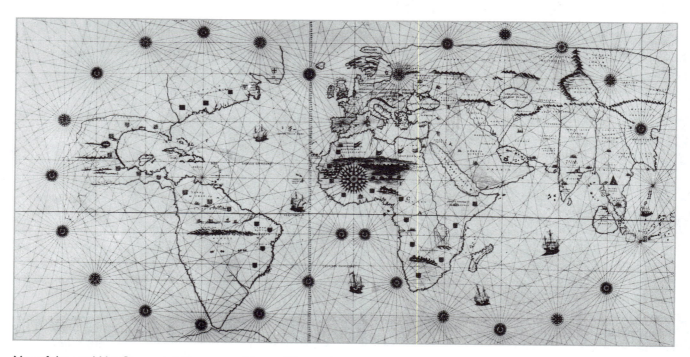

Map of the world by Giovanni da Verrazano *(Library of Congress)*

Giovanni da Verrazano himself was the first to name places in the Americas after locations and people in Europe, although these names did not long endure. Verrazano brought back a description of North America as a large landmass, becoming the first European to base such an interpretation on actual exploration. As a result of his voyages, European geographers learned that the North American coastline was continuous, from the English discoveries in Newfoundland in the north to those of the Spanish in Florida to the south. His report of an inland sea at Pamlico Sound in present-day North Carolina wrongly influenced mapmakers, who, for the next 50 years, indicated the Pacific Ocean as lying not far beyond the east coast of North America. Verrazano, who inspired the explorations of JACQUES CARTIER, was the first European to visit New York Bay, predating HENRY HUDSON's expedition by more than 80 years. The Verrazano-Narrows Bridge, which spans New York Bay at the point where Verrazano anchored in 1524, was named in his honor.

Vespucci, Amerigo (1454–1512) *Italian navigator in the Americas, in service to Spain and Portugal*

Amerigo Vespucci was born in the Italian city-state of Florence, the son of prominent parents with close ties to the ruling Medicis. He was educated in astronomy, geography, and natural philosophy under the supervision of his uncle, a Dominican priest and associate of religious reformer Girolamo Savonarola.

Vespucci was employed by the Medici family's banking firm, serving for more than 20 years in Italy before he was sent to Spain in 1492 to help manage the Medicis' merchant-banking and ship-outfitting operations in Seville. In Spain, he became acquainted with CHRISTOPHER COLUMBUS; Vespucci, as agent for the Medici firm, provided supplies for Columbus's second voyage of exploration in 1493 as well as his third voyage in 1498.

According to his own account (as yet unsubstantiated), Vespucci sailed with Columbus as a commercial observer on the 1493 voyage, after which he embarked on a series of exploring expeditions of his own. He claimed that he sailed from the Spanish port of Cádiz on May 10, 1497, and that, after crossing the Atlantic Ocean by way of the CANARY ISLANDS, he reached the south coast of Mexico at Campeche Bay. After reportedly following the shoreline of the Gulf of Mexico north and east, he rounded Florida, then sailed northward along the coast of what is now the southeastern United States, as far as Cape Hatteras, North Carolina, before returning to Spain later that same year.

Vespucci related that he next took part in a voyage of exploration with Spanish navigator ALONSO DE OJEDA and cartographer JUAN DE LA COSA. On May 16, 1499, the expedition's three vessels sailed from Cádiz. They reached the Americas separately, with Vespucci arriving on the coast of

Amerigo Vespucci *(Library of Congress)*

Brazil near a point known as Cape São Roque, about five degrees of latitude below the EQUATOR. He then supposedly explored the coastline northwestward, locating the mouth of the AMAZON RIVER, which he explored upstream for a short distance before turning back and meeting up with Ojeda and the rest of the expedition in Santo Domingo. He then sailed back to Spain, arriving in Cádiz on September 8, 1500.

In service to King Manuel I of Portugal, Vespucci commanded an expedition aimed at following up PEDRO ÁLVARS CABRAL's European discovery of eastern Brazil in 1500. He sailed from Lisbon on May 10, 1501, reaching his supposed previous landfall at Cape São Roque on August 16, 1501. From there, the northeasternmost point of South America, he headed southward to determine the extent of the mainland. On January 1, 1502, he reached a harbor he named Rio de Janeiro in honor of New Year's Day. He also reported reaching the mouth of the Río de la Plata, and, after following the Patagonian coast due south, reaching as far as 50° south latitude, the southernmost point achieved by Europeans up to that time. If his account is true, the land he reported sighting in those waters may have been South Georgia Island, only a few degrees of latitude north of the ANTARCTIC CIRCLE.

Vespucci arrived back in Portugal on September 7, 1502. He later returned to Spain, where he became a naturalized

Spanish subject and a member of the Casa de Contratación, a government clearinghouse for geographic and navigational knowledge. In 1508, King Ferdinand II appointed him as Spain's first pilot major, a position he held until his death four years later from malaria, which he had contracted in his explorations in South America.

Amerigo Vespucci's fame in the history of exploration is largely due to the work of German geographer MARTIN WALDSEEMÜLLER. In 1507, Vespucci's accounts of his voyages, contained in his letters to Lorenzo di Pier Francesco de Medici, were included in Waldseemüller's *Cosmographia Introductio* (Introduction to cosmography), along with updated maps of the world based on the recent explorations of Columbus and other navigators. Vespucci's descriptions were the first to use the phrase *New World*, as well as the first to suggest that the newly explored lands comprised a new continent, not merely an outlying archipelago of Japan or China. For this reason, Waldseemüller named the foreign lands America, after the Latinized version of Vespucci's first name, Amerigo. When GERARDUS MERCATOR published his world atlas in the 1580s–90s, he applied the name to the northern continent as well, and the two have since become known as South America and North America. While Vespucci's actual contributions as an explorer and navigator are still not clear, he was among the first to comprehend the greater implications of the earliest European discoveries in the Western Hemisphere, and the first to conclude that the new lands were of continental proportions. More so than Columbus, who died convinced he had reached the western fringes of the Orient, Vespucci applied the principals of modern scientific inquiry, then still emerging from the constraints of medieval thought, to ascertain the significance of the geographic findings of his day.

Vial, Pedro (Pierre Vial) (ca. 1746–1814)
French-born guide, interpreter in the American Southwest, in service to Spain

Born in Lyons, France, Pedro Vial immigrated to the Louisiana country sometime before the early 1770s. He settled on the MISSOURI RIVER, where he lived and worked among the Indians as a gunsmith.

In 1786, Vial was commissioned by the Spanish government of Texas to blaze a trail from San Antonio north to Santa Fe, New Mexico; he was chosen for this assignment because of his knowledge of Indian languages and his familiarity with the geography of the Southwest. From San Antonio, Vial went northward to the Red River then headed westward, arriving at Santa Fe on May 26, 1787.

Soon afterward, the governor of New Mexico hired Vial to undertake an expedition eastward from Santa Fe and establish a route to Natchitoches in what is now western Louisiana. The trip took him across the entire width of

Texas. From Natchitoches, Vial headed back to San Antonio, then returned to Santa Fe.

In 1792, New Mexico's governor commissioned Vial to undertake an expedition in search of a route eastward across the southern plains as far as St. Louis on the MISSISSIPPI RIVER. On this trip, Vial was captured by Indians in what is now Kansas, but he managed to escape with the help of some traders, arriving in St. Louis in October 1792.

Vial subsequently settled in Santa Fe, where he served as a guide and interpreter in other explorations of the Southwest and southern plains.

Pedro Vial pioneered the first overland route between the provincial capitals of Texas and New Mexico. His 1792 expedition from Santa Fe to St. Louis was one of the earliest recorded eastward crossings of the southern plains, and it closely followed the route that later became the Santa Fe Trail.

Viale, Agostinho (ca. 1620–1667) *Brazilian colonial official in South America*

Agostinho Viale was born in São Paulo, Brazil, south of Rio de Janeiro. In 1664, King Alfonso VI of Portugal appointed him as Brazil's administrator general of mines and commissioned him to explore the dense forests of the Mato Grosso, to the north and west of São Paulo, in search of emerald mines reported to lie deep in the interior of the little-known region.

Authorized to grant pardons to fugitive outlaws who had fled into the forests of the Mato Grosso, Viale actively sought out desperados to obtain vital geographic information about the west-central Brazilian wilderness, the only other inhabitants of which were the warlike Aymora Indians.

In 1666, Viale led a force of 50 soldiers and about 150 Indians into the Mato Grosso from São Paulo. After 13 months, he managed to penetrate as far as the marshy country near the Serra das Esmeraldas, where he succumbed to malaria, as did a large segment of his expedition. His lieutenant, Barbalho Bezena, then assumed command and led the survivors back to São Paulo.

Agostinho Viale's expedition of 1666–67 was the first European probe into the inland regions of Brazil, south of the AMAZON RIVER. In the years that followed, great mineral wealth was discovered in the Mato Grosso, which led to São Paulo's becoming an important base for subsequent penetrations into the interior.

Viele, Arnaud Cornelius (Cornelissen Arnout Viele) (ca. 1620–ca. 1700) *Dutch trader, interpreter to Indians of Ohio Valley*

Born at Brabant in the Netherlands, Arnaud Cornelius Viele immigrated with his father to the Dutch colony of New Netherland, now New York State, in the early 1630s. They settled at Fort Orange on the site of what became the city of Albany, where the elder Viele operated an Indian trading post.

From his extensive contacts with the Indians who came to trade at his father's post, the younger Viele became proficient in Indian languages and knowledgeable about Indian culture and customs. He went on to become a government interpreter, first for the Dutch, then for the British.

In the early 1680s, Viele served as British colonial governor Thomas Dongan's official envoy to the Iroquois (Haudenosaunee) Indians. Later, under the insurrectionist administration of Jacob Leisler in 1689–91, he was appointed governor of the Iroquois League of Six Nations.

Soon after Leisler's government was overthrown in New York City in 1691, Viele headed westward to the Ohio Valley. The next year, with a party of Indian traders, he traveled down the Ohio River into present-day Kentucky.

Arnaud Cornelius Viele was among the first Europeans to approach the Ohio River from the Hudson Valley, and among the first non-Indians to explore what is now northern Kentucky.

Villalón, Pedro de Rivera y.   See RIVERA Y VILLALÓN, PEDRO DE.

Viscaíno, Sebastián (Sebastien Vizcaino)
(ca. 1550–ca. 1628) *Spanish mariner, merchant on the Pacific coast of Mexico and California*

Sebastián Viscaíno was born in Corcho, Spain, into a family of modest means. When about 17, he served with the Portuguese army. Then, in the mid-1580s, he settled in Mexico.

Viscaíno became a successful merchant, involved in the transpacific trade between Mexico, the Philippines, and China. He sailed from Mexico to the Philippines himself in about 1586; on the return voyage in 1587, his ship, the *Santa Ana,* was captured by one of the English PRIVATEERS, Thomas Cavendish, off the southern end of the Baja California peninsula. Viscaíno was put ashore with the rest of the passengers and crew. After making repairs to the ship, which Cavendish had attempted to burn, Viscaíno sailed back to a port on the west coast of Mexico.

Sebastián Viscaíno's landing at Monterey (painting by Albert Bierstadt) *(Library of Congress)*

In 1594, Viscaíno sent out an expedition under the command of his subordinate Pérez del Castillo to explore the upper Gulf of California and evaluate the region as a source of pearls. Because of dissension among the crew, the attempt was abandoned. Two years later, he led another attempt himself, sailing from Acapulco in June 1596 in command of three ships and 230 men. On this voyage, which had been commissioned by the Spanish viceroy of Mexico, Viscaíno examined the coast of Baja California in search of harbors where Spanish ships returning from the Philippines could find protection from marauding English pirates, who had recently begun to operate in those waters. He reportedly reached as far north along the coast of Baja California as 29°30' north latitude. He found no adequate anchorages and returned southward, reaching Acapulco at the end of 1596.

In 1602, Viscaíno set out again, this time to explore the Pacific coast north of Baja. Instructions from the Spanish viceroy directed him to survey and chart the coast as far northward as Cape Mendocino, as well as to locate safe harbors for Spanish shipping. He was also to carry on the search for the fabled STRAIT OF ANIAN, the mythical passage linking the Atlantic Ocean and the Pacific Ocean, which the Spanish feared had already been located by the English privateer SIR FRANCIS DRAKE, when he sailed the first English vessel into the Pacific in the 1570s.

Viscaíno sailed from the Pacific port of Acapulco on May 5, 1602, in command of a fleet of three ships. Among his crew were missionaries and cosmographers. After an extensive survey of Baja, the expedition began to explore northward; in November 1602, it reached San Diego Bay in present-day California, which Viscaíno charted and named. Soon afterward, he explored the Santa Barbara Islands, which had been visited 60 years earlier by JUAN RODRÍGUEZ CABRILLO; Viscaíno also explored and named Santa Catalina.

On December 15, 1602, Viscaíno came upon a large natural harbor he called Monterey Bay, first spotted seven years before by SEBASTIÁN MELÉNDEZ RODRÍGUEZ CERMENHO. Viscaíno later cited it as the best anchorage for large ships he had ever seen. At this point in the voyage, he sent back one of his ships with those members of the expedition who had become weakened by SCURVY. Heading northward with his two remaining vessels, Viscaíno sailed past San Francisco Bay without seeing it because of bad weather. North of San Francisco Bay, he explored Drakes Bay and sighted and named Punta de los Reyes, now known as Point Reyes.

By January 12, 1603, Viscaíno had reached as far northward as Cape Mendocino. He explored a little beyond that point to the coast of what is now southern Oregon before turning back for Mexico. En route, he charted the Farallon Islands, just west of the Golden Gate, but he again failed to see San Francisco Bay.

Viscaíno arrived at the Mexican port of Mazatlán on February 18, 1603. Soon afterward, he sailed for Spain to report on his exploration of Monterey Bay to the Council of the Indies and propose the establishment there of a permanent colony and port for Spanish ships returning from the Philippines.

Although Viscaíno's proposal to colonize Monterey Bay was approved by 1607, the planned expedition was subsequently canceled by the Spanish viceroy of Mexico, who objected to the project's excessive cost. To make up for the abandoned enterprise, Viscaíno was commissioned in 1611 to explore the Pacific Ocean in search of the fabled islands of Rica de Oro and Rica de Plata (rich in gold and in silver). In the course of the three-year voyage, he failed to find these lands. Moreover, his attempt to open up Spanish trade contacts with Japan was unsuccessful. After 1615, Viscaíno settled in the Mexican province of Avalos.

Sebastían Viscaíno's explorations of 1602–03 resulted in the production of the first reliable maps of the California coast and helped dispel the idea of the Strait of Anian. Despite the fact that he had returned with a slightly favorable description of the lands and climate of what the Spanish came to refer to as Alta California, Spanish interest in the region began to wane soon afterward. With the English maritime menace ended by a treaty between Spain and England, Spain's colonial interests began to focus more on Florida. As a result, no other serious colonization efforts in California were attempted by the Spanish until the expedition of GASPAR DE PORTOLÁ and JUNÍPERO SERRA, more than a century and a half later.

Vivaldi, Ugolino (fl. 1290s) *Italian mariner in the Atlantic*

Ugolino Vivaldi and his brother Guido (or Vadino) were navigators from the Italian city of Genoa. In 1291, they sailed from Genoa in command of two ships, intending to reach India by way of the Atlantic Ocean.

After passing through the STRAIT OF GIBRALTAR, the Vivaldi brothers followed the Moroccan coast southward to Gozara near the CANARY ISLANDS. Nothing was heard from them after that, although later accounts suggest that they may have circumnavigated Africa to Ethiopia, where they were taken prisoner by the legendary PRESTER JOHN, dying while in captivity.

It is not clear whether Ugolino and Guido Vivaldi intended to sail westward across the Atlantic, or around Africa. In any event, their 1291 voyage from Genoa was the first known attempt by Europeans to find a seaward route to India, preceding CHRISTOPHER COLUMBUS and VASCO DA GAMA by two centuries.

W

Waldseemüller, Martin (Martin Waltzemuller, Hylacomylus) (ca. 1470–ca. 1522) *German geographer, cartographer*

Martin Waldseemüller was originally from the city of Freiburg in northern Germany. Educated at the university in Freiburg, he became a clergyman at Saint-Die, a small town in the duchy of Lorraine in what is now northeastern France.

Waldseemüller became associated with a small college (or learned society) known as the Gymnasium Vosagense, and served as a professor of geography. The group acquired a printing press, with plans to produce a new edition of the geographic works of the ancient geographer PTOLEMY.

Waldseemüller had obtained copies of AMERIGO VESPUCCI's letters describing his explorations of the Western Hemisphere, and he included them as part of the text for *Cosmographiae Introductio* (Introduction to geography). Published in 1507, the book, included information on winds, the distances between known places on the Earth, and geographic principles, as well as an account of the "New World," based on the voyages of CHRISTOPHER COLUMBUS, JOHN CABOT, and the brothers GASPAR CÔRTE-REAL and MIGUEL CÔRTE-REAL.

Waldseemüller also included a large map of the world, printed from 12 woodcuts, which measured 36 square feet when put together. On his world map, he cited the great landmass that Vespucci had called the "New World" as *America,* in honor of Vespucci, whom he deemed to be its discoverer. Moreover, he depicted the South American con-tinent as separated from Asia by a great sea to the west. This was a wholly new concept in Europe since most geographers considered the so-called New World to be an eastern exten-sion of Asia.

In 1513, Waldseemüller published another geographic work in which he depicted the newly discovered lands as "Terra Incognita," or "unknown land," apparently having developed doubts about the authenticity of Vespucci's ac-counts. Yet his original designation "America," on more than 1,000 copies of the 1507 map, had become widely accepted throughout Europe. In the 1580s, *America* was also applied by GERARDUS MERCATOR to the landmass to the north, the two continents eventually becoming known as North Amer-ica and South America.

Through his publications, Martin Waldseemüller helped disseminate geographic knowledge of European dis-coveries in the Americas and helped inspire further explo-ration.

Walker, Joseph Reddeford (Joe Walker) (1798–1876) *American fur trader, trapper, guide in the Rocky Mountains and California*

Born in Virginia, Joseph "Joe" Walker was raised in Ten-nessee. By the time he was 20 years old, he had settled at Fort Osage on the Missouri frontier.

In 1820, Walker traveled with a trading caravan across the southern plains to Santa Fe. He was arrested and held for a while by Spanish authorities, but he soon won his release by agreeing to take part in a military campaign against the Pawnee Indians.

In 1824, while operating in the FUR TRADE out of present-day Independence, Missouri, Walker guided a federally sponsored surveying expedition along the Santa Fe Trail. From 1827 to 1832, he served as the sheriff at Independence.

In 1832, Captain BENJAMIN LOUIS EULALIE DE BONNEVILLE hired Walker as a guide for his fur-trading enterprise to what is now northern Utah and southern Wyoming. On July 24, 1833, Walker led an expedition of 50 MOUNTAIN MEN westward from Fort Bonneville in Utah's Green River Valley for the Great Salt Lake, seeking the fabled Buenaventura River, which was believed to flow to the Pacific Ocean. Walker's chief clerk on this trip was ZENAS LEONARD; mountain man WILLIAM SHERLEY WILLIAMS also participated.

From the Great Salt Lake, Walker and his men traveled across Utah's Great Basin into what is now northeastern Nevada. From there, they explored the Humboldt River westward to its sink near the eastern slopes of the Sierra Nevada, where they survived a hostile encounter with Indians, possibly Paiute.

Walker and his party then headed southward in search of a route through the Sierra Nevada. In exploring part of the range, they came upon the lake that now bears his name. The party followed a river through the mountains, also named after Walker, which took them to the watershed between the Merced and Tuolumne Rivers and into the Yosemite Valley.

Walker and his men entered the San Joaquin Valley, and, by November 1833, they had reached Monterey on the Pacific coast. Soon afterward, Walker sought a more southerly route eastward through the Sierra Nevada. Guided by Indians, his party followed the Kern River's South Fork into the mountains through what is now known as Walker Pass. After descending into the Mojave Desert, Walker led his men north and east back to northern Utah, arriving at the annual fur traders' rendezvous on the Bear River on July 3, 1834.

Walker continued as a trapper and trader in the northern and middle Rocky Mountains until the decline in the fur trade in the late 1830s and early 1840s. He then worked as a guide for emigrant wagon trains traveling westward. In spring 1844, he guided JOHN CHARLES FRÉMONT in his explorations into Utah's Great Basin. Walker was again with Frémont in his 1845–46 expedition to California. During this expedition, Walker led a party through the Sierra Nevada by way of Walker Pass.

In 1849, Walker was one of the first to arrive at Sutter's Fort in California following the discovery of gold there, leading to the gold rush. He subsequently led trade caravans through Walker Pass to the goldfields of northern Cal-

ifornia. He settled in California, where he established ranches first near Monterey and then in Contra Costa County. In 1861–62, he returned to the Southwest as guide for a gold-prospecting expedition into Arizona. He spent his remaining years at his ranch near Oakland, California.

Joe Walker was among the first non-Indians to see California's Yosemite Valley and lead the first non-Indian party eastward across the Sierra Nevada. The route he pioneered across Nevada became a significant part of one of the most important emigrant wagon roads in the West, the California Trail. Walker also played a major role in John Charles Frémont's explorations of the American West.

Walker, Thomas (1715–1794) *American physician, surveyor on the Appalachian frontier*

Thomas Walker was born in King and Queen County in eastern Virginia. He attended the College of William and Mary, then studied medicine under his brother-in-law, a physician in Williamsburg, and he later opened his own medical practice in Fredericksburg.

In addition to gaining prominence as a physician and surgeon, Walker operated a general store and import and export business. From his marriage to a landed widow, in 1741, he acquired more than 11,000 acres near present-day Charlottesville, Virginia, an estate known as Castle Hill.

In the late 1740s, Walker became associated with several prominent members of Virginia's House of Burgesses who were involved with obtaining huge tracts of land in western Virginia for speculative purposes. In 1749, he was named as chief agent for the Loyal Land Company, which had received from the colonial government a grant of 800,000 acres in western Virginia.

On March 6, 1750, Walker and a small party set out from Staunton, Virginia, to survey the Loyal Land Company's claim. They crossed the Blue Ridge into the Holston River Valley, then over Powell's Mountain into Powell's Valley. In early April 1750, near the point where the present-day states of Kentucky, Virginia, and Tennessee meet, he located a natural passage through the mountain barrier, which he called the CUMBERLAND GAP in honor of William Augustus, Duke of Cumberand, a prominent British general of that time.

Walker and his expedition passed through the Cumberland Gap and descended the Cumberland River, in the hope of finding the "bluegrass" country, the fertile, level region he had heard of from the Indians, and that Walker hoped to claim as part of the Loyal Land Company's grant. On finding only mountainous, rough country, unsuitable for settlement, he turned back north and east along an ancient Indian trail known as the "Warriors' Path." North of the Cumberland Gap, he constructed what came to be known as "Walker's Cabin," to assert the Loyal Land Company's claim to the region in the Clinch and Holston River Valleys. He returned to Staunton, Virginia, on July 13, 1750.

In 1752, Walker was appointed deputy surveyor for Augusta County, Virginia, a position he held until the outbreak of the French and Indian War. He became commissary-general for George Washington and his Virginia militia forces in 1755, taking part in Braddock's retreat from Fort Duquesne that year. He later became a member of Virginia's colonial legislature.

In the 1760s, Walker took part in negotiations with the Cherokee and Iroquois (Haudenosaunee) Indians to extend the Proclamation Line of 1763 westward, hoping to open up the lands he had surveyed in western Virginia to new settlement. In 1768, he represented Virginia at the Treaty of Fort Stanwix, in New York.

Dr. Thomas Walker's probe into western Virginia and eastern Kentucky, which he recorded in his *Journal of an Exploration in the Spring of the Year 1750, by Dr. Thomas Walker* (1888), resulted in the non-Indian discovery of the Cumberland Gap. This natural passage through the mountains became the principal avenue for westward settlement across the APPALACHIAN MOUNTAINS, as well as a vital segment of DANIEL BOONE's Wilderness Road.

Wallace, Alfred Russel (1823–1913) *British naturalist in South America and Southeast Asia*

Alfred Russel Wallace was born near the town of Monmouth in the south of Wales into a family of limited means. His formal education ended when he was 14, after which he trained himself in the natural sciences and other subjects.

Wallace became a schoolteacher in Leicester, England, where he became acquainted with fellow self-taught naturalist HENRY WALTER BATES. Inspired by the accounts of ALEXANDER VON HUMBOLDT and CHARLES ROBERT DARWIN, they resolved to travel to the Amazon Basin in South America to collect specimens of insects, especially butterflies.

In 1848, Wallace and Bates sailed from England to the mouth of the AMAZON RIVER at Pará (present-day Belem), Brazil. From there, they traveled southward along the Tocantins River for most of that year, collecting specimens of insects. The following year, they ascended the Amazon to Manaus, where they split up. While Bates went farther up the Amazon, Wallace carried out his entomological research along the Río Negro and into the ORINOCO RIVER by way of the Casiquiare, the natural canal linking the two streams. He also traveled on the Uaupes River before returning to Manaus and the seacoast. Herbert Wallace, Alfred's brother, had joined him in 1849 but died of yellow fever at Pará in 1851.

Wallace sailed for England in 1852. He had collected thousands of specimens and made extensive notes detailing his observations on how geography had an impact on the distribution of species throughout the Amazon. In the course of the homeward voyage, the ship caught fire and sank, and although Wallace was rescued after more than two weeks in an open boat, all of his collections and writings were lost. Despite this setback, on his return to England he published an account of his four years of research in South America, *A Narrative of Travels on the Amazon and Rio Negro* (1853).

Wallace next set out for the Malay Archipelago of Southeast Asia. Starting in 1854, he began a scientific survey of life forms, which took him more than 14,000 miles, from Timor and the Moluccas to Malacca on the Malay Peninsula. From his findings on this expedition, during which he collected more than 127,000 specimens, Wallace developed a theory of natural selection, independently of Darwin. His conclusions, jointly published with those of Darwin in 1858, laid the basis for the theory of natural selection and provided the foundation for an understanding of the distribution and evolution of species based on geographic factors.

Wallace returned to England in 1862, where he continued his scientific writings. From his research in Southeast Asia, he had developed an idea of a theoretical boundary, known as Wallace's Line, running through Asia,

Alfred Russel Wallace *(Library of Congress)*

the Malay Archipelago, and Australia, geographically dividing Asian and Australian fauna.

Along with the work of Darwin and Bates, Alfred Russel Wallace's scientific explorations in South America and Southeast Asia had resulted in a new perspective on Earth's life forms and the natural forces determining their development and distribution throughout the world.

Wallis, Samuel (1728–1795) *British naval officer in the South Pacific*

Samuel Wallis was born near Camelford on the northwest coast of Cornwall, England. He joined the British navy in his early teens, and by the age of 20, he had been promoted to the rank of lieutenant. Made a captain in 1756, he served throughout the Seven Years' War of 1756–63 in command of British warships off the coast of Canada and in the English Channel.

In 1766, the British Admiralty appointed Wallis to command a voyage of exploration to the South Pacific Ocean. The expedition had been planned as a follow-up to Commodore JOHN BYRON's 1764–66 voyage in search of the elusive Terra Australis, the GREAT SOUTHERN CONTINENT—the huge, theoretical landmass then thought to occupy much of the largely unexplored Southern Hemisphere.

Wallis sailed from the port of Plymouth on August 22, 1766, in command of Byron's former ship, the *Dolphin*, accompanied by the *Swallow* commanded by PHILIP CARTERET. Three months later, they reached the Atlantic entrance to the STRAIT OF MAGELLAN. During the next four months, Wallis examined the maze of channels of the strait and made landings to study the physical stature of the Patagonian natives. Contrary to reports dating back to FERDINAND MAGELLAN's voyage of 1519–22, Wallis concluded that the Patagonians were not giants, finding most to measure no more than five feet, seven inches tall.

In April 1767, shortly before Wallis and Carteret had entered the Pacific, strong winds and currents separated their ships, and Wallis continued on alone with the *Dolphin*. Instead of following the well-established sea route northward along the coast of Chile, Wallis headed northwestward, traversing a vast, little-known area of the South Pacific. He made landings for fresh provisions in the Tuamotu Islands, then continued northward to the TROPIC OF CAPRICORN, where he turned westward.

On June 23, 1767, Wallis made the first confirmed European sighting of Tahiti, which he named King George the Third's Island to honor his sovereign. After some initial skirmishes caused mainly by misunderstandings, the British established friendly relations with the natives, with Wallis being personally welcomed by Oberea, the queen of Tahiti. The Tahitians provided the expedition with fresh food, trading for nails and other goods made of iron.

Wallis and his men spent five weeks in Tahiti before continuing their voyage westward across the Pacific. Having found a place of such unique beauty and abundance, Wallis decided to return to England to report his findings rather than continue combing the Pacific in search of Terra Australis. They stopped at Tonga and Tinian Islands, then sailed to the Dutch East Indian port of Batavia (present-day Jakarta, Indonesia). Throughout the voyage, Wallis had averted the ravages of SCURVY by introducing sauerkraut and other foods rich in vitamin C into his crew's diet, and it was only in Batavia that he lost any of his men to disease, mainly tropical fever and dysentery incurred in that port.

Wallis and the *Dolphin* completed the round-the-world voyage by way of Cape Town, South Africa, and the island of St. Helena, arriving back in England on May 20, 1768. His report about Tahiti aroused the interest of the Admiralty, which decided that the island was a suitable spot from which to observe the Transit of Venus. It was there that JAMES COOK was sent that same year on the first of his three voyages of exploration.

Wallis remained on active duty with the British navy until 1772. The next year, he saw the publication of his *Account of the Voyage Undertaken for Making Discoveries in the Southern Hemisphere,* detailing his CIRCUMNAVIGATION OF THE WORLD in 1766–68.

Samuel Wallis is credited with the European discovery of Tahiti, even though a French expedition under the command of LOUIS-ANTOINE DE BOUGAINVILLE arrived there only several months afterward and claimed the island for France. Soon after he had left Tahiti, Wallis located a group of islands west of Samoa and north of Fiji, which are known today as the Wallis Archipelago in his honor. Although his voyage provided no conclusive evidence of the existence or nonexistence of Terra Australis, he had nonetheless explored a large and previously unknown portion of the South Pacific, revealing that it contained thousands of square miles of open sea.

Warburton, Peter Egerton (1813–1889)
British army officer in South and Western Australia

Peter Warburton was an officer with the British army in India before settling in South Australia in the early 1850s. In 1857–58, Warburton undertook a series of explorations into the country north of Adelaide and Spencer Gulf, traversing the region between the northern end of Lake Torrens and the southern part of Lake Eyre. From these explorations, he determined that South Australia's central region was open country, dispelling the earlier notion of SIR EDWARD JOHN EYRE who, in examining the region nearly 20 years earlier, had erroneously concluded that an impassable barrier of salt lakes and marshes lay to the north of Spencer Gulf.

Warburton extended his probes deeper into the interior of South Australia. In 1866, he explored the region northeast of Lake Eyre, locating a river flowing between Lake Eyre and Goyders Lagoon, afterward known as the Warburton River.

Warburton's most ambitious undertaking began in mid-April 1873, when he set out westward from the newly established telegraph relay station at Alice Springs, near the center of the Australian continent, in an attempt to reach the Indian Ocean coast at Perth in Western Australia. In addition to his son, two other European companions, and a young Aborigine boy, the expedition included two Afghani camel-drivers and 17 camels.

After skirting the northern edge of the Macdonnell Ranges, Warburton and his companions proceeded past Mount Wedge, then northwestward to Lake Mackay. They crossed into barren country, nearly devoid of usable water, and entered the Great Sandy Desert.

Although Warburton had planned to cross southwestward to Perth, he pushed northwestward because of the lack of water. In December 1873, after 10 months of traveling across 2,000 miles of some of the most inhospitable desert country in the world, the expedition arrived at Roebourne, about 750 miles north of Perth, on Western Australia's Indian Ocean coast.

Peter Warburton made the first successful east-to-west crossing of Western Australia, from the center of the continent at Alice Springs to the west coast. Moreover, he was the first to make extensive use of camels to explore the vast arid expanses of the plains and deserts of the Northern Territory and Western Australia.

Warre, Henry James (1819–1898) *British soldier, artist in the Pacific Northwest*

Henry James Warre, a lieutenant in the British army, served in Canada starting in the late 1830s. A sportsman, he took part in a hunting expedition to the northern plains, west of the upper reaches of the MISSOURI RIVER, in 1840.

In 1845, Warre served as aide de camp to his uncle, the commander in chief of British forces in Canada. That year, he was detailed, along with Lieutenant MERVIN VAVASOUR, on a military reconnaissance into the Oregon Country. Throughout the expedition, they pretended to be civilians on a hunting trip, hoping to avoid arousing the suspicions of U.S. officials in the region, which was then jointly governed by Great Britain and the United States.

Henry James Warre was an artist as well as a soldier, and, in the course of his 1845–46 travels through the Pacific Northwest, he produced a series of sketches of the region. Made into engravings, they were published in book form in London, as *Sketches in North America and the Oregon Territory* (1848). They provide a pictorial record of the

Oregon Country on the eve of the region's acquisition by the United States.

Watkins, Henry George (Gino Watkins)
(1907–1932) *British scientist, surveyor in Labrador and Greenland*

In 1928, Henry George "Gino" Watkins, a 21-year-old undergraduate at Cambridge University of England, began his explorations into the subarctic regions by examining the interior of Labrador, inland from Hamilton Inlet on the east coast, along the Churchill River.

In 1930, Watkins organized the British Arctic Air Route Expedition in order to survey a proposed airline link between London and Canada by way of ICELAND, GREENLAND, Baffin Bay, and HUDSON BAY. With 13 others, he landed at Angmagssalik, on Greenland's largely uncharted southeast coast, and, over the next year and a half, he directed meteorological studies and coastal surveys.

Watkins himself led a group that penetrated the Greenland ice cap 250 miles inland from Angmagssalik, while another party trekked across Greenland's southern region to Ivigtut on the southwest coast. A weather observation station was established high on the ice cap, which expedition member AUGUSTINE COURTAULD manned throughout one winter season.

Watkins's coastal explorations made use of aircraft, motorboats, and kayaks. In one survey, he traveled along 600 miles of the south coast, rounding Cape Farewell on Greenland's southern tip, to arrive at Julianehab on the southwest coast.

Gino Watkins was drowned in 1932, while hunting seals from a kayak off Angmagssalik. In his brief career as an explorer, he made extensive use of Inuit survival techniques to carry out some of the first modern meteorological studies in southern Greenland.

Webber, John (Johann Waber) (1751–1793)
British artist in the South Pacific and on the northwest coast of North America

Born in London, John Webber was the son of a Swiss sculptor who had settled in England. While very young, he was sent to Berne, Switzerland, to be raised by his aunt. He showed an early talent for art, studying under the Swiss landscape and portrait painter Johann Ludwig Aberli. In 1769–70, he was in Paris, where he continued his art training under Johann Georg Wille.

In 1771, Webber returned to London to attend the Royal Academy of Arts, and he later found work creating interior decorations for a house builder. His first show of landscapes and portraits at the Royal Academy of Arts in 1776 caught the attention of naturalists SIR JOSEPH BANKS and

DANIEL CARL SOLANDER, and, on their recommendation, he was recruited as an artist for Captain JAMES COOK's third voyage of exploration to the Pacific Ocean.

From July 1776 to August 1780, Webber sailed on the *Resolution,* sketching scenes and native people in the Tongatapu Islands, Tahiti, and the HAWAIIAN ISLANDS. On the Pacific coast of what is now British Columbia, he made extensive pictorial studies of the Nootka Indians of Nootka Sound.

Back in England in 1780, Webber's work was very well received, and many of his original drawings were engraved and published as illustrations in the official journals of Cook's voyage. He was made an associate of the Royal Academy of Arts in 1785; soon afterward, he undertook sketching trips in the English countryside and in Switzerland.

John Webber's career as an artist was cut short at the age of 41, when he died in London of a kidney ailment. His works on Cook's third voyage contained some of the first depictions of the life and culture of the Nootka, including studies of the interiors of their dwellings and ceremonial items such as masks and rattles. He produced one of the first illustrations of the sea otters of the Pacific Northwest, creatures whose fur later provided the main impetus for subsequent exploration and settlement in the region. Among his most dramatic renderings of the voyage was his "Death of Cook," later published by Florentine engraver Francesco Bartolozzi.

Weber, John H. (1799–1859) *Danish fur trader in the northern Rocky Mountains*

John Weber left his native Denmark at an early age to go to sea. In about 1822, soon after he had arrived in the United States, he joined with ANDREW HENRY and WILLIAM HENRY ASHLEY in the FUR TRADE on the upper MISSOURI RIVER.

In 1824–25, Weber commanded one of Ashley's expeditions into the northern ROCKY MOUNTAINS, which included among its members frontiersman JAMES BRIDGER. While exploring south of the Green River in what is now northern Utah, Weber and his party may have been the first non-Indians to come upon the Great Salt Lake.

John Weber was among the first fur traders to work the western slopes of the Rockies and visit the Great Salt Lake region, helping open the region to further non-Indian development.

Weddell, James (1787–1834) *Scottish mariner, sealer in the South Atlantic and Antarctic*

James Weddell was born in the Netherlands to Scottish parents. At an early age, he went to sea with the British sealing fleet; by the time he was in his early 30s, he had made two

voyages to the South Atlantic Ocean and was commander and part-owner of his own vessel.

In 1821, Weddell sailed his ship, the *Jane,* from England. After a stopover at South Georgia Island, he ventured southward into the subantarctic region of the South Atlantic, in search of richer sealing grounds. Before he returned to England at the end of the Southern Hemisphere's summer season of 1821–22, he had located and named the South Orkney Islands.

Weddell was back in South Georgia in 1822–23. Accompanied by the escort vessel *Beaufoy,* under the command of Captain Matthew Brisbane, he sailed the *Jane* farther south than any other mariner had in that longitude. In February 1823, he found the sea to be ice-free as far southward as 74°15'. He named this arm of the South Atlantic, east of the Antarctic Peninsula, King George IV Sea in honor of the reigning king of England. Weddell returned to England later in 1823, having broken the farthest-south record set by JAMES COOK in the late 1770s.

In addition to having made some of the most accurate navigational studies in the Antarctic to that time, James Weddell took back to England one of the first specimens of the leopard seal. His voyage also demonstrated that the ocean extended much farther southward than had previously been thought, greatly reducing the size of the supposed Antarctic landmass. In the early 1840s, British naval commander SIR JAMES CLARK ROSS made use of Weddell's records for his own voyages into the Antarctic. In 1900, the large, ice-free expanse of ocean that Weddell had reached was renamed the Weddell Sea. The adjoining Antarctic mainland was not explored until SIR ERNEST HENRY SHACKLETON's expedition of 1914–17.

Wegener, Alfred Lothar (1880–1930) *German geologist, meteorologist in Greenland*

Born in Berlin, Germany, Alfred Wegener was educated at the University of Marburg, where he studied meteorology, astronomy, and geology. Wegener made his first trip to Greenland as a meteorologist with LUDWIG MYLIUS-ERICHSEN's expedition of 1906–08. In 1912–13, he took part in a Danish government-sponsored exploration of GREENLAND's inland ice with Johann Peter Koch. Together, they traversed the width of central Greenland, traveling 700 miles from Upernavik to the east coast. In the course of this trek, Wegener made weather observations and undertook studies of ice conditions.

In 1924, Wegener was appointed professor of meteorology at the University of Graz in Austria. Five years later, having been named leader of the German Greenland Expedition, he went to western Greenland and established two permanent weather stations. One of them, Weststation, was located on the west coast near Godhavn, north of the ARC-

TIC CIRCLE. The other base, Eismitte, was located 250 miles inland near the geographic center of the Greenland ice cap. From these stations, in 1929–30, Wegener conducted the first year-round climate and weather studies made in Greenland.

In November 1930, Wegener, along with an Inuit companion named Rasmus Willemsen, died of exposure while attempting to return to the west coast of Greenland from Eismitte.

By the time of his death, Alfred Wegener had become famous for his geological theories on continental drift, postulating that the world's oceans and continents had been created by displacements in the Earth's crust. Some of his geological ideas had been developed from his explorations in Greenland, during which he studied the thickness of the ice cap and calculated Greenland's rate of drift. His account of his last expedition, published posthumously, appeared in an English edition entitled *Greenland Journey* (1939).

Weiser, Conrad (Johann Conrad Weiser)
(1696–1760) *German-American interpreter, guide in colonial New York and Pennsylvania*

Conrad Weiser was born in the village of Astaedt in Wurttemberg, Germany, where his father was prominent as a local judge. In 1710, he immigrated with his family to North America, settling in Livingston Manor, New York. After being befriended by the Mohawk Indian chief Quagnant, Weiser went to live with the Indians in 1713. He became proficient in the Iroquoian language, and the next year he settled at an Indian village near Schoharie, New York.

From 1719 to 1729, Weiser aided colonists on the New York frontier as an interpreter to the Indians. In 1729, he traveled down the Susquehanna River into Pennsylvania, settling at Tulpehocken. Two years later, the Pennsylvania colonial government appointed him as its official interpreter to the Indians, and throughout the 1730s, he took part in many diplomatic conferences with the tribes of central and western Pennsylvania. In 1737, on a diplomatic trip to the Iroquois (Haudenosaunee) Indian council at Onondaga, near present-day Syracuse, New York, he located ancient Indian mounds, similar to those later found in southern Ohio.

Weiser accompanied Lutheran and Moravian missionaries to the Indians of Pennsylvania and New York, including the evangelical expeditions of Count Zinzendorf and David Zeissberger in the early 1740s. He was associated for a time with the religious community of Ephrata on the Pennsylvania frontier. In 1741, Weiser became Pennsylvania's principal Indian agent, and in that capacity he helped negotiate various treaties with the Iroquois against the French.

In 1755, Weiser was commissioned a colonel in the colonial militia, but deteriorating health prevented him from taking an active part in the French and Indian War of 1754–63. He helped establish the settlement of Reading, Pennsylvania, where he died in 1760, the victim of a cholera outbreak.

In his time, Conrad Weiser was known as the foremost expert on the Indians of colonial New York and Pennsylvania. His diplomatic ability, his facility with Native American languages, and his knowledge of Indian trails helped open the frontier of western Pennsylvania to non-Indian settlement in the years immediately before the French and Indian War.

Wellsted, James (unknown–1836) *British naval officer in southern Arabia*

In 1834, James Wellsted, a lieutenant with the Bombay Marine, the naval branch of the British East India Company, began an extended survey along the little-known south coast of the Arabian Peninsula. The expedition had been undertaken at the behest of the BRITISH EAST INDIA COMPANY, which was then interested in establishing coaling stations along the shipping route between Suez and Bombay. To this end, it was necessary to learn the extent of the political influence that the sultan of Muscat had over the region known as the Hadhramaut.

Aboard the ship *Palinurus,* Wellsted coasted along the shore of Yemen. He landed at Bir Ali to study some ancient ruins, where he recorded inscriptions written in Himyaritic, the Arabic language of southern Arabia. He later visited Oman, where he undertook excursions deep into the interior.

Wellsted later returned to Yemen, where he made additional archaeological investigations of the ruins at Nakab-al-Hayar. He committed suicide in 1836 while on the Hadhramaut coast.

In his journeys in Oman, James Wellsted traveled inland as far as the edge of the Rub' al-Khali, or EMPTY QUARTER, becoming the first European to see that vast desert region of southeastern Arabia. He left two accounts of his experiences, both published posthumously, *Travels in Arabia* (1838) and *Travels to the City of Caliphs* (1840).

Wen-chi (Lady Wen-chi, Wenji) (ca. 178–unknown) *Chinese poet in Mongolia*

Wen-chi was born into a noble family of the Han dynasty, her father a well-respected scholar and statesman among the Chinese. She grew up in the village of Honan (present-day Luoyang) in east-central China.

In about A.D. 190, when Wen-chi was 12, she was taken captive by the Hsiung-nu, a branch of the Huns living to the northwest beyond the Great Wall on the steppes of Mongolia. There, she became the wife of the chieftain and lived as a nomad. She bore him two children. About 15 years after her abduction, Chinese officials arranged for her ransom, forcing her to choose between her homeland and her family. She chose the latter and henceforth wrote a series of poems about her experiences and travels. In the 12th century, her writings were transferred to a painted scroll. The work has survived as *Eighteen Songs of the Nomad Flute.*

Because of her poems, which provide details of nomadic life on the Mongolian steppes, Wen-chi is one of the earliest women known for travel writing.

Wentworth, William Charles (1790–1872)
Australian colonist in the Blue Mountains, statesman

William Charles Wentworth, among the first generation of Australian-born English, was probably born on Norfolk Island, east of Australia, the location of a British colony where his Irish father, D'Arcy Wentworth, served as an assistant surgeon. Some sources indicate he was born in Port Jackson (present-day Sydney). His mother, Catherine Crowley, had arrived in Australia as a convict. Wentworth traveled to England for studies, including the University of Cambridge. On returning to Australia at the age of 20, he worked on his father's estates on the Cumberland Plain west of Sydney.

The governor of New South Wales, Lachlan Macquarie, encouraged exploration of the BLUE MOUNTAINS, part of the GREAT DIVIDING RANGE west of Port Jackson, in order to locate new grazing lands. In 1813, Wentworth, GREGORY BLAXLAND, a surveyor by the name of William Lawson, an Aborigine guide known as James Burnes, and British convicts acting as servants and bearers departed Blaxland's farm at South Creek with packhorses. The party followed ridges, managing to make their way westward without having to descend into the valleys. Finally, from one peak (now known as Mount Blaxland), they were able to see Bathurst Plain, virgin grazing lands naturally irrigated by the Lett River.

In 1816, Wentworth traveled again to England to study law. Back in Australia in 1824, in addition to practicing as an attorney, he founded the newspaper the *Australian.* He used the newspaper and his legal skills to campaign on behalf of emancipists, as former convicts were called, as well as Australian-born colonists. His efforts helped lead to New South Wales having a representative government. As a member of the Legislative Council, he also helped create a formal constitution in 1854. In 1862, Wentworth retired to England. After his death 10 years later, his body was returned to Australia for burial.

William Charles Wentworth was part of the first significant inland exploration of Australia, one that led to expansion westward of colonists hoping to claim a homestead. His work in journalism and politics has led to his being known as the "Australian Patriot."

Westall, William (1781–1850) *British landscape artist in Australia*

William Westall was born in Hertford, England, near London. He studied art under his older brother, Richard Westall, a painter of historical scenes, and, at the age of 19, he was engaged as a landscape painter under Captain MATTHEW FLINDERS for his voyage of exploration to Australia.

In July 1801, Westall sailed from England aboard the *Investigator.* In February 1802, he joined Flinders, along with the expedition's naturalist ROBERT BROWN, and natural history artist FERDINAND LUCAS BAUER, in an expedition to the upper reaches of Spencer Gulf on the coast of what is now South Australia, north of present-day Adelaide. Near present-day Port Augusta at the gulf's northernmost end, they landed and scaled a peak Flinders had named Mount Brown.

Westall was among those shipwrecked on the Great Barrier Reef for two months; he was sent back to Sydney on a rescue vessel in October 1803, while Flinders continued on to Île de France (Mauritius). From Australia, the young artist went to China, then to India, returning to England from Bombay in 1805. Back in London, Westall went on to a long career as a landscape artist, regularly exhibiting his work until his death in 1850.

From drawings he made on Flinders's expedition, William Westall produced oil paintings of scenes of the Australian coastline. Some of the best-known of these are "Wreck Reef Bank," depicting the temporary encampment on the Great Barrier Reef, where the crew awaited rescue; "Site of Port Jackson in 1802"; and "View of Port Lincoln," one of the first artistic renderings of the area around the mouth of South Australia's Spencer Gulf.

Weymouth, George (George Waymouth)
(fl. early 1600s) *English mariner, trader on the New England coast*

English navigator George Weymouth made his first expedition to North America in 1602, during which he explored Hudson Strait in search of the NORTHWEST PASSAGE. Then, in 1605, he was commissioned by a group of merchants in Bristol, England, to explore the coast of Maine and establish trading contacts with the region's Indians.

In command of the ship the *Archangel,* Weymouth sailed from Dartmouth, England, in March 1605 and reached Nantucket Island, off the New England coast, in early May. On May 12, he landed on Monhegan Island off the Maine coast, which he explored. He then made a reconnaissance of some other islands off the south coast of Maine and explored parts of the mainland, including the mouth of the Penobscot River. He traded with the Indians, dispensing sugar candy and raisins, items that were very well received.

Weymouth and his men captured five of the Maine Indians and took them back to England in mid-July 1605. One of them is thought to have been SQUANTO, who later returned to New England and aided the PILGRIMS in their 1620 colonizing expedition in Massachusetts.

George Weymouth was one of the earliest British navigators to explore the Atlantic coast of New England, helping open up the region to European settlement in the following decades.

Weyprecht, Karl (1838–1881)
German-born Austrian army officer in the Arctic

A native of the German city of Koenig, Karl Weyprecht embarked on a military career as an officer with the army of Austria-Hungary. In 1871, Weyprecht and fellow army officer JULIUS VON PAYER became the coleaders of the Austro-Hungarian Arctic Expedition, the aim of which was to navigate the NORTHEAST PASSAGE, and, if possible, determine whether there were an ice-free polar sea between Europe and North America. After a preliminary journey to Spitsbergen (present-day Svalbard) and Novaya Zemlya in 1871, they embarked on the main expedition in 1872. Their vessel became icebound and they drifted northward for more than a year. In summer 1873, they reached an uncharted Arctic archipelago, which they called Franz Josef Land in honor of the emperor of Austria-Hungary.

After spending the winter aboard the icebound ship off Franz Josef Land, Weyprecht and Payer had the expedition abandon the ship and head southward over the ice, hauling sledges and small boats. When they reached open water, they took to the boats. After continuing southward to the coast of Novaya Zemlya, they were picked up by a passing Russian whaling vessel, which carried them to safety on the north coast of Lapland.

Throughout the 1870s, Karl Weyprecht became a leading advocate for international cooperation in Arctic exploration and was instrumental in promoting the first International Polar Year of 1882–83. The Arctic islands he explored with Payer served as a base for LUIGI AMEDEO DI SAVOIA D'ABRUZZI's expedition in 1899–1900.

Wheeler, George Montague (1842–1905)
U.S. Army engineer, American topographer in the American West

Originally from Hopkinton, Massachusetts, George M. Wheeler graduated from West Point in 1866 as a second lieutenant in the U.S. Army Corps of Engineers. From 1866 to 1871, he took part in military surveys and engineering projects near California's San Francisco Bay.

In 1871, Wheeler, now a first lieutenant, was given command of an army project to map the entire West, known as the U.S. Geographic Surveys West of the One-Hundredth Meridian. That year, and continuing over the next eight years, Wheeler directed comprehensive surveys of the West, gathering topographic data as well as zoological, geological, and ethnological information.

In May 1871, Wheeler led one of his surveying expeditions up the COLORADO RIVER into the Grand Canyon, as far as Diamond Creek, retracing Lieutenant JOSEPH CHRISTMAS IVES's route of 1858. On subsequent explorations, Wheeler traversed Death Valley and surveyed the area of the Comstock Lode in Nevada.

Wheeler was promoted to captain in 1879, and his project was consolidated under the U.S. Geological Survey. He spent the rest of his military career involved in the preparation and publication of his official report. He retired from the army in 1888, at the rank of major.

In all, Wheeler undertook 14 expeditions covering much of California, Arizona, Nevada, Colorado, and Utah. He led his men across territory that ranged in altitude from 200 feet below sea level in Death Valley to 15,000 feet above sea level in the Sierra Nevada and Cascade Range. His subsequent maps detailed the topography of one-third of the continental United States west of the 100th meridian of longitude and south of the 40th parallel of latitude; these are the earliest contour maps of the American West. His official account, *Report upon United States Geographical Surveys West of the One-Hundredth Meridian,* included pictures derived from the earliest photographs of Death Valley and the Grand Canyon, taken by frontier photographers Timothy O'Sullivan and William Bell.

Whipple, Amiel Weeks (1816–1863) *U.S. Army officer in the American Southwest*

Amiel Weeks Whipple was born in Greenwich, Massachusetts. He attended Amherst College, then went on to West Point. Graduating in 1841 as a second lieutenant in the artillery, he was soon transferred to the United States Army Corps of Topographical Engineers.

In 1844–49, Whipple took part in a survey of the northeastern portion of the U.S.-Canada international border. In 1849–53, he served under Lieutenant WILLIAM HEMSLEY EMORY in the Mexican Boundary Commission Survey from the Rio Grande to what is now western Arizona. While engaged in this project, he led an expedition that succeeded in locating the confluence of the Gila River and COLORADO RIVER.

In 1853–56, Whipple commanded one of the Pacific Railroad Surveys. In the course of this project, he led a party of soldiers, topographers, and scientists westward from Fort Smith, Arkansas, along the Canadian River route across the southern plains to Albuquerque. He was joined there by a detachment under the command of Lieutenant JOSEPH

CHRISTMAS IVES. The Mojave Indian chief IRATEBA served as guide.

Whipple had been instructed to evaluate the feasibility of a railroad west to the Pacific Ocean along the 35th parallel. From Albuquerque, he led his command to the Zuni pueblos in what is now northwestern New Mexico, then traveled across present-day Arizona to the San Francisco Mountains and the Bill Williams Fork of the Colorado. He located a pass through the mountains and found his way to the Colorado River. Heading northward, Whipple and his party crossed the Colorado at Needles, then followed the Mojave River through the desert. For the final leg, they traveled the Old Spanish Trail and the Mormon wagon road to San Bernardino. Whipple was able to confirm an earlier report that the Cajon Pass through the southern Sierra Nevada was unsuitable for railroads.

From 1856 until the outbreak of the Civil War in 1861, Whipple participated in government engineering projects in the Great Lakes. In 1861, he was chief topographical engineer for Union forces at the Battle of Bull Run. Promoted to major and breveted a brigadier general of volunteers, he took part in balloon reconnaissances over Confederate lines. In May 1863, Whipple was wounded in the Battle of Chancellorsville; he died soon afterward in Washington, D.C.

Amiel Weeks Whipple led one of the principal military expeditions of the American West preceding extensive non-Indian settlement and development. In his official report of his 35th Parallel Survey, he provided detailed information on Indian tribes along the proposed route, describing them as distinct and diverse cultures. Moreover, he reported that the region of the Southwest he surveyed was far more suitable to agricultural development than had previously been reported.

White, Edward Higgins, II (1930–1967)

American astronaut, first American to walk in space

Edward White was born in San Antonio, Texas. He attended the U.S. Military Academy at West Point, graduating in 1952, and later earned a master's degree in aeronautical engineering from the University of Michigan. In 1959, he attended the Air Force Test Pilot School at Edwards Air Force Base in California and later served at Wright-Patterson Air Force Base in Ohio, as an experimental test pilot with the Aeronautical Systems Division. In 1962, he was selected for the team of ASTRONAUTS in the NATIONAL AERONAUTICS AND SPACE ADMINISTRATION (NASA).

White first traveled into space on June 3, 1965, as pilot of the *Gemini 4* capsule, part of the GEMINI PROGRAM. On day one of the mission, he became the first American to perform extravehicular activity (EVA), that is, floating freely in space, popularly known as a "space-

walk." Although the first human to walk in space was the cosmonaut ALEXEI ARKHIPOVICH LEONOV, on March 18, 1965, as part of the VOSKHOD PROGRAM of the Union of Soviet Socialist Republics (USSR, or the Soviet Union), White was the first human to control himself in space outside a capsule, tethered to the capsule by a lifeline that supplied him with oxygen. To move he used a handheld maneuvering unit that fired bursts of compressed oxygen. The EVA lasted about 22 minutes while *Gemini 4* was over the Pacific Ocean. *Gemini 4* orbited Earth 62 times before landing on June 7.

White's next assignment was as backup commander for *Gemini 7* the following December. He was also selected as command module pilot on the first manned orbital test of the APOLLO PROGRAM, scheduled for launch in February 1967. It would have been the first three-man U.S. flight; White's fellow astronauts on this mission were to be Virgil "Gus" Grissom and Roger Chaffee. On January 26, 1967, however, during a training simulation on the launch pad at the Kennedy Space Center in Florida, a spark led to a flash fire, which killed all three men. After the *Apollo 1* disaster, Apollo capsules were redesigned; materials were made more flame resistant, the atmosphere was under lower pressure, and the escape system was more efficient.

As the first American to walk in space, Edward White has a special place in the history of SPACE EXPLORATION. SALLY KRISTEN RIDE became the first American woman to carry out EVA in 1983.

White, John (fl. 1580s–1590s) *English artist, colonist in eastern North America*

Little is known of John White's origins and early life. By 1577, he had become an accomplished artist and cartographer, and that year, he accompanied SIR MARTIN FROBISHER on his voyage to GREENLAND and Baffin Island. On this expedition, White produced some of the earliest paintings of Inuit (Eskimos).

In 1585, White sailed with SIR RICHARD GRENVILLE as part of SIR WALTER RALEIGH's first colonizing venture to the coast of present-day North Carolina. The colonists stayed on Roanoke Island for a year, but because of conflicts with Roanoke Indians, they returned to England the following summer with SIR FRANCIS DRAKE.

Raleigh selected White as leader of a second colonizing attempt in North America. White's expedition left Plymouth, England, on May 8, 1587. His fleet of three ships sailed first to the Caribbean Sea, stopping briefly at Dominica and St. Croix, then headed through the Bahamas and along the Florida coast. White had planned to establish the new colony on Chesapeake Bay, near the mouth of the James River. But, on July 22, 1587, the pilot of the fleet, Simon Fernandes, refused to take the colonists any farther to the north and left them at Roanoke Island in the Outer Banks of North Carolina, the site of Raleigh's earlier and unsuccessful colony.

White helped organize a plantation on Roanoke, founding a settlement known as the City of Raleigh. White's married daughter Eleanor, along with her husband, Ananias Dare, were part of the colonizing expedition. On August 18, 1587, she gave birth to a daughter, Virginia Dare, the first English child born in North America.

Chosen by the colonists to return to England and seek additional supplies from Raleigh, White sailed in late August 1587. The interceding naval war with Spain, including the battle with the Spanish Armada in 1588, delayed his return for three years.

Finally, in March 1590, White sailed from Plymouth, England, aboard the ship *Hopewell* and crossed the Atlantic Ocean by way of the CANARY ISLANDS. The relief expedition first cruised the Caribbean, pillaging Spanish settlements and capturing some Spanish ships. On August 17, 1590, White and his party reached Roanoke, but they found the colony abandoned. The only trace of the colonists was the inscription "CROATOAN"—the name of an Indian village near Cape Hatteras, North Carolina—carved on a tree. With a storm approaching and the ship in need of repairs, the captain of White's ship, John Watts, declined to investigate Croatoan and sailed for the Caribbean. Although he intended to return the following spring, no subsequent relief expeditions were made. The fate of the LOST COLONY, as it came to be known, remains unknown. It is speculated that the colonists intermarried with Native Americans and settled somewhere along the Outer Banks or inland, or were wiped out in a raid. Some may have built a boat in an attempt to reach Chesapeake Bay.

White returned to England, and in 1593, he settled in Ireland. Few details are known about his later life.

John White produced an early map of the North American coast, detailing the region between Florida and Chesapeake Bay. He also painted watercolors of the native peoples, animals, and plant life that he saw on his voyages to the Caribbean and the Virginia coast. Published by German engraver Theodore de Bry in the 1590s, they provided Europeans with some of the first pictorial renderings of the Americas.

Whitman, Marcus (1802–1847) *American physician, missionary, guide on the Oregon Trail, pioneer in the Pacific Northwest*

Marcus Whitman was born in the central New York State town of Rushville, near Ithaca. He attended the College of Physicians and Surgeons of the Western District of New York at Fairfield, receiving the degree of doctor of medicine in 1832.

Whitman practiced medicine in Canada for several years, then returned to Rushville, New York, where he operated a sawmill with his brother. He was active in the Presbyterian Church, and, by 1835, he had been appointed a deacon and authorized as a missionary. That year, he became associated with fellow missionary Samuel Parker, who arranged to have Whitman accompany him on an expedition to the Pacific Northwest to investigate sites for proposed missions to the Indians.

In April 1835, Whitman and Parker left St. Louis and traveled up the MISSOURI RIVER with that year's AMERICAN FUR COMPANY trading expedition. After reaching what is now Omaha, Nebraska, on June 22, 1835, they headed overland westward to Fort Laramie. They crossed through the SOUTH PASS of the Wind River range of the ROCKY MOUNTAINS and arrived for that summer's fur traders rendezvous at Ham's Fork of the Green River in what is now southwestern Wyoming. While there, Whitman removed the arrowhead that had been lodged in mountain man JAMES BRIDGER's back since his fight with Indians at Pierre's Hole three years earlier.

While Parker remained in the Northwest, Whitman returned to New York, where he married Narcissa Prentiss, also a missionary. In spring 1836, Whitman, his wife, and another missionary couple, HENRY HARMON SPALDING and his wife Eliza, set out from St. Louis to establish missions to the Indians of the Oregon Country. They traveled with the American Fur Company's trade caravan along the Oregon Trail to the Green River rendezvous, where they then joined HUDSON'S BAY COMPANY traders on their way to the COLUMBIA RIVER. They were guided along the Oregon Trail by THOMAS FITZPATRICK.

Following a stopover at Fort Vancouver, the Whitmans headed to the junction of the Columbia and Walla Walla Rivers in present-day southeastern Washington State, where he established his mission to the Cayuse Indians at Waiilatpu. Spalding and his wife meanwhile opened a missionary settlement to the Nez Perce Indians near present-day Lewiston, Idaho.

By 1842, Whitman's main sponsors, the American Board of Commissioners for Foreign Missions in Boston, had decided to close the Pacific Northwest missions. To regain their support, Whitman undertook a midwinter journey to the East. Traveling on horseback, he left Waiilatpu on October 3, 1842, and traveled as far as Fort Hall, Idaho. At that point, Indian hostility forced him to go south to Taos. From there, he reached Bent's Fort on the Arkansas River, then proceeded to St. Louis and Boston. Making his case in person, he succeeded in regaining support for the Oregon Country missions.

Before returning west, Whitman visited Washington, D.C., where he conferred with War Department officials on the necessity of establishing forts and supply posts for future emigrants on the Oregon Trail. In spring 1843, at Elm Grove, Missouri, he joined the first large overland party of settlers bound for Oregon, known as the Great Migration, for whom he served as a guide along the Oregon Trail. Pioneer trailblazer JESSE APPLEGATE was one of the group's leaders.

Following his return to the mission on the Walla Walla, Whitman faced increasing difficulties with the Cayuse. Blaming Whitman for an outbreak of measles among their people, warriors under Chief Tiloukaikt killed Whitman, his wife, and a number of other settlers on November 29, 1847. Frontiersman JOSEPH L. MEEK subsequently made an overland journey to Washington, D.C., to summon military aid.

Marcus Whitman was one of the few non-Indians not involved in the fur trade to play a significant role in the opening of the Oregon Country to further settlement. His 1836 expedition brought the first wagons along the Oregon Trail. His wife, Narcissa Whitman, and Eliza Spalding were the first non-Indian women to cross the Rockies and the Continental Divide.

Whymper, Edward (1840–1911) *British mountain climber in the Alps and Andes Mountains*

Edward Whymper was born in London. He pursued a career as an illustrator, and in 1860, he was commissioned by a British publisher to sketch scenes in the French Alps for the book *Peaks, Passes and Glaciers.* This experience sparked an interest in MOUNTAIN CLIMBING.

In 1861–64, Whymper scaled Mont Pelvoux and Barre des Écrins, as well as numerous other peaks in the Dauphiné Alps. He then decided to attempt the as-yet-unscaled Matterhorn (14,780 feet above sea level) in Switzerland's Western Alps, near the Swiss-Italian border. He failed to do so in six tries on the southwestern face. Attempting the eastern face, considered more difficult, he and his party finally succeeded in 1865. During the descent, however, four of his six companions died in a fall, among them Lord Francis Douglas. Whymper was heavily criticized for the Matterhorn incident, one of the most famous disasters in mountain-climbing history.

In 1880, Whymper became the first climber to reach the summit of Chimborazo, at 20,702 feet above sea level, the highest peak in the Ecuadorean ANDES MOUNTAINS. Whymper climbed other major Andean peaks, including ACONCAGUA, in Argentina, the highest mountain in South America; Tupungato, located on the Chilean-Argentine border; and Cotopaxi, in Ecuador, the world's highest active volcano. He wrote about his expeditions in *Scrambles Amongst the Alps in the Years 1860–69* (1871), with his own illustrations; and *Travels Amongst the Great Andes of the Equator* (1892). Whymper also visited GREENLAND and the Canadian ROCKY MOUNTAINS.

During his time in Ecuador, Edward Whymper made a study of mountain sickness and determined that the reason it affected humans more in the Andes than at comparable heights in the Alps was related to barometric pressure. He made recommendations for acclimatization that helped future climbers deal with this condition and for improvements in the aneroid barometer, a device for measuring air pressure. His pioneering work helped in Arctic exploration as well as mountain climbing. He also contributed to natural science with his detailed notes on flora and fauna.

Wickham, Sir Henry Alexander (1846–1928) *British traveler in South America*

Born in England, Henry Wickham first traveled to the WEST INDIES and South America in 1866, at the age of 20. In South America, he explored the Orinoco River and its tributaries, the Atabapo River and Río Negro. By 1869, he was operating a rubber plantation on the AMAZON RIVER near Santarém, Brazil.

Wickham made a return visit to England in 1871, where he published an account of his travels, entitled *Rough Notes of a Journey Through the Wilderness from Trinidad to Para, Brazil, by way of the Great Cataracts of the Orinoco, Atabapo, and Rio Negro* (1872). The work contained illustrations by Wickham himself, one of which, that of a sprouting rubber tree seedling, came to the attention of SIR JOSEPH DALTON HOOKER, director of London's Kew Gardens. Hooker contacted Wickham and commissioned him to ship back a quantity of living rubber tree seedlings to England.

Wickham was back in the lower Amazon region in 1873. After a year spent organizing the project, he managed to load as many as 7,000 rubber tree seedlings aboard the British steamer *Amazonas,* at a site near the junction of the Tapajos and Amazon Rivers. Despite prohibitions by the Brazilian government against such exports, Wickham slipped his illegal cargo by customs authorities at Pará (Belém), and, several months later, he arrived in Liverpool, from where the trees were hurried to London's Kew Gardens.

Three years later, the seedlings Wickham had taken back to England had developed into trees, and, in 1876, the first group was transported to CEYLON (present-day Sri Lanka), thus initiating the rubber industry in the Far East. Wickham himself, amply rewarded for the achievement, settled in Queensland, Australia, for several years, where he had little success as a tobacco and coffee grower. He later went to Ceylon and served in the colonial government.

Henry Wickham, whose travels in the Amazon Basin had resulted in the introduction of the rubber industry to Ceylon and Malaya, was knighted for his efforts in 1920.

Wilkes, Charles (1798–1877) *U.S. Navy officer in the Antarctic, the Pacific, and South and North America*

Charles Wilkes was born in New York City, the son of a prominent businessman. After receiving an education in mathematics, modern languages, and navigation from his father, he went to sea at the age of 17. Three years later, in 1818, he was appointed a midshipman in the U.S. Navy. After attending a naval school in Boston, Wilkes took part in cruises in the MEDITERRANEAN SEA and the Pacific Ocean. In 1826, he was promoted to lieutenant.

In 1832–33, Wilkes undertook a navigational survey of Narragansett Bay and was named director of the U.S. Navy's Depot of Charts and Instruments, the precursor to the U.S. Naval Observatory.

In 1838, Wilkes took command of the United States South Sea Surveying and Exploring Expedition. The goals of this project, first proposed 10 years earlier, included the charting of Antarctic waters for U.S. merchant ships and whalers and the exploration of the islands of the Pacific and the northwest coast of North America.

Wilkes left Norfolk, Virginia, in August 1838, in command of a fleet of six ships: his flagship the *Vincennes,* the *Peacock,* the *Relief,* the *Porpoise,* the *Sea Gulf,* and the *Flying Fish.* After stops in the AZORES off Portugal and in the Cape Verde Islands off Africa's west coast, Wilkes and his expedition headed southward along the east coast of South America to CAPE HORN, where they established a base camp. From there, he undertook a survey of the islands in the waters bordering the Antarctic, including the South Orkney and South Shetland Islands. He then explored and charted part of the coast of Antarctica.

After more than a month of exploring in Antarctic waters, without sighting land beyond the PACK ICE, Wilkes headed northward along the west coast of South America. At Valparaíso, Chile, Wilkes sent a scientific party inland to explore the ANDES MOUNTAINS. During another stopover at Lima, Peru, scientists with the expedition examined the ruins of the Inca Indian civilization.

Wilkes then headed westward across the Pacific to Australia and NEW ZEALAND. He made stops at Tahiti, Samoa, and other island groups, where teams of scientists went ashore for observations. The expedition then headed southward once again and undertook a second exploration of Antarctica. In January 1840, after traveling 1,600 miles along the icebound and fog-shrouded coastline, the expedition sighted land jutting out of what appeared to be a continental landmass.

After returning to Sydney, Australia, Wilkes visited the Fiji Islands and the Sandwich Islands (Hawaii), then sailed for the northwest coast of North America. In April 1841, he reached the mouth of the COLUMBIA RIVER, where one of the ships, the *Peacock,* was wrecked.

Wilkes sent parties inland to explore the Oregon Country between the Columbia and Sacramento Rivers. One of the parties, led by Lieutenant GEORGE FOSTER EMMONS, explored the Willamette and Sacramento River Valleys, as far south as Sutter's Fort near present-day Sacramento, California. The Wilkes expedition also undertook an exploration and survey of the Columbia River to the mouth of the Snake River in what is now southeastern Washington State. Ethnologists and anthropologists attached to the Wilkes expedition obtained some of the earliest scientific data on the life and culture of the Northwest Coast Indians. Naturalists and painters also made observations; among the artists with the Wilkes expedition was Titian Ramsey Peale.

Wilkes charted 800 miles of the coastline, from San Francisco to the Strait of Juan de Fuca and Puget Sound. The remaining ships then headed westward across the Pacific, and, accomplishing a CIRCUMNAVIGATION OF THE WORLD, arrived at New York City in June 1842. Only two of the original ships completed the entire voyage, the *Vincennes* and the *Porpoise.* The others had either been wrecked or suffered so much damage that they were sold en route.

The Wilkes expedition covered more than 80,000 miles in less than four years. Wilkes was promoted to the rank of commodore upon his return, and, over the next 17 years, he helped write the 20-volume government report of his round-the-world voyage. His account, *Narrative of the United States Exploring Expedition,* was published in 1844.

At the outbreak of the Civil War in 1861, Wilkes, in command of the U.S. warship the *San Jacinto,* stopped the British commercial vessel *Trent* in international waters and arrested two Confederate government officials. The incident, which became known as the "*Trent* Affair," raised international tensions and nearly led to war with Great Britain.

Wilkes was then assigned to command U.S. naval forces in the Caribbean Sea and provide protection for U.S. shipping. On this assignment, he also overstepped his authority and infringed upon the rights of neutral ships. He was later court-martialed and demoted. He retired from the navy as a rear admiral in 1866.

The expedition of 1838–42 led by Charles Wilkes succeeded in making the first U.S. government-sponsored circumnavigation of the world. Scientists with the expedition brought back more than 5,000 species of plants and made extensive meteorological, geological, and ethnological studies of the Pacific islanders and the Indians of the American Northwest. Among the major scientific results of the expedition were the findings of JAMES DWIGHT DANA, whose studies of marine biology confirmed CHARLES ROBERT DARWIN's theories on the formation of coral islands. Although Wilkes's reported discovery of an Antarctic landmass was disputed by both JULES-SÉBASTIEN-CÉSAR DUMONT D'URVILLE and SIR JAMES CLARK ROSS, his findings were later confirmed by SIR ERNEST HENRY SHACKLETON. In 1848, Wilkes was awarded the Founder's Medal by Great Britain's ROYAL GEOGRAPHICAL SOCIETY. Wilkes's charts of the South Pacific island groups he visited were so accurate that they were used 100 years after his expedition to guide U.S. military operations in World War II. Wilkes's explorations also inspired the 1843–44 expedition of JOHN CHARLES FRÉMONT. The part of the Antarctic coast that Wilkes explored in 1840 was named Wilkes Land in his honor.

Wilkins, Sir George Hubert (1888–1958)
Australian photographer, aviator in the Arctic and Antarctic
Hubert Wilkins was born at Mount Bryan East, a sheep ranching settlement in South Australia. Trained in engineering and photography, he left Australia in 1908 for a career as a photojournalist.

In 1913, after service as a war correspondent in the Balkans, Wilkins was attached to the Canadian Arctic Expedition, under the leadership of VILHJALMUR STEFANSSON, as a photographer and reporter for the London *Times*. During the next five years, under Stefansson's direction, he learned polar survival skills while taking both still photos and motion pictures in the Canadian Arctic Archipelago.

A trained aviator, Wilkins was a captain in the Royal Australian Flying Corps in World War I, serving in the final months of the war as an aerial photographer in France. In 1919, he competed in an air race between England and Australia, in which his aircraft was forced down on Crete in the eastern MEDITERRANEAN SEA.

Wilkins's first venture in the Antarctic was as second in command with the British Imperial Antarctic Expedition of 1919–20. He then served as a naturalist with SIR ERNEST HENRY SHACKLETON's last Antarctic expedition of 1921–22.

Back in Australia in 1923, Wilkins undertook a study of the tropical region along the continent's north coast for the British Museum, an experience he detailed in his 1928 book *Undiscovered Australia.*

Starting in 1926, Wilkins became involved with aerial exploration of the Arctic, and, on April 15, 1928, he flew from Point Barrow, Alaska, to Spitsbergen (present-day Svalbard), north of Norway, making the first trans-Arctic flight from North America to Europe.

Later in 1928, after being knighted for his contributions to polar exploration, Wilkins returned to the Antarctic. In November of that year, he made the first airplane flight in Antarctica, flying over Palmer Land and the Antarctic Peninsula, in the course of which he sighted several uncharted islands off the Antarctic Peninsula and determined that Graham Land was actually two distinct islands.

Inspired by Jules Verne's *Twenty Thousand Leagues Under the Sea,* Wilkins next turned his attention to undersea polar exploration. He acquired a former U.S. Navy submarine he renamed the *Nautilus,* after the undersea vessel in

Sir George Hubert Wilkins *(Library of Congress)*

Verne's novel, and in June 1931, he embarked from Spitsbergen in an attempt to reach the NORTH POLE by sailing under the ice of the Arctic Ocean. Mechanical problems with the craft forced him to turn back from beyond 82° north latitude, the farthest north a vessel had reached under its own power until that time. He detailed the experience in his book *Under the North Pole* (1931).

From 1933 to 1936, Wilkins assisted American aviator LINCOLN ELLSWORTH in planning for aerial exploration of Antarctica. In 1938, he was in the Siberian and North American Arctic, taking part in search efforts for a downed Soviet aviator. Although no trace of the missing pilot was found, Wilkins's flights resulted in the mapping of large areas of the previously unknown Arctic Ocean. He had experimented with mental telepathy in the search, an experience he related in *Thoughts Through Space* (1942), which he coauthored with H. M. Sherman.

During World War II, Wilkins served as an adviser on arctic survival techniques for the U.S. Navy and as an intelligence officer in the Middle East and Far East.

Sir Hubert Wilkins died in November 1958. Six months later, the U.S. nuclear submarine *Skate* surfaced at the North Pole, where, according to his wishes, Wilkins's ashes were scattered. His wideranging exploits in the Arctic and Antarctic included his pioneer flight over the Arctic

Ocean and the first aerial sighting of uncharted islands off the Antarctic Peninsula.

William of Rubrouck (William of Rubruck, William of Rubruk, William of Rubrouc, William of Ruysbroeck, William de Rubrick, Willem van Rujsbroek, Willem van Rusbroeck, Wilhelmus Rubruquis, Guillaume de Rubruquis)

(ca. 1215–ca. 1270) *Flemish missionary in central Asia*
William of Rubrouck was originally from Flanders in what is now northern France. Little is known about his early life except that he entered the Franciscan Order sometime before 1250.

In 1252, William was summoned to Acre on the coast of present-day Israel to meet with King Louis IX of France (Saint Louis), then engaged in a crusade in the Holy Land. The French monarch directed William to undertake a missionary expedition to the Mongols, hoping to dissuade the central Asian nomads from continuing their eastward campaign of conquest toward Europe and to win their allegiance against the Muslim Turks.

William sailed from Constantinople (present-day Istanbul) in May 1253, accompanied by a small party that included another Franciscan friar Bartholomew of Cremona, an interpreter, and several servants. After a voyage across the Black Sea to the Crimea, he and his party traveled in carts along the Don and Volga Rivers to the Ural River, which they followed to its mouth on the Caspian Sea. In his later account of the trip, William made the first confirmed report that the Caspian was an enclosed sea and not an arm of the northern ocean, as was thought in Europe.

William and his party then made a crossing of the steppes of Kazakhstan and into the Pamir region of central Asia, where they became the first Europeans to see such creatures as the wild ass and wild long-horned mountain sheep. At the end of December 1253, after traversing the Tara Tau Range in what is now Kirghizia, he reached the encampment of the Mongol leader Mangu Khan, and soon afterward he was received by Mangu, the latest in a long line of Great Khans, at his capital at Karakorum. William later observed that the Mongol ruler, well aware of the proselytizing efforts of both Christians and MUSLIMS, was mainly interested in these religions for the purpose of political advantage.

William made an extensive study of the life and society of the Mongols, before setting out on his return journey in early July 1254. Friar Bartholomew had decided to remain behind to preach among the Mongols.

Upon reaching the city of Serai on the Volga River near present-day Volgograd, William traveled into Armenia and crossed what is now northeastern Turkey to the eastern MEDITERRANEAN SEA, hoping to meet with Louis in the Holy Land. The French king, however, had since returned to Paris, where William eventually went after spending time at a monastery in Acre.

In Paris, William wrote an account of his travels, entitled *Journey to the Eastern Parts of the World.* One of the earliest medieval travel accounts, it includes the first suggestions that silk originated from a land to the east of Mongolia, which he identified as Cathay.

William of Rubrouck, as well as GIOVANNI DA PIAN DEL CARPINI and MARCO POLO and his father and uncle, were among the first Europeans to travel overland into central Asia, and William was one of the first Europeans to see the Mongol capital at Karakorum.

Williams, William (fl. 1830s–1840s) *British settler in New Zealand*

In 1839, William Williams, one of the earliest European settlers on NEW ZEALAND's North Island, undertook an exploration of the island's interior. From the site of the settlement of Wellington on the island's southern tip, Williams followed the Rangitikei River northward to Lake Taupo, then continued northeastward to the Bay of Plenty.

In addition to locating the Hot Springs District around Lake Taupo, William Williams was the first European known to have made a south-to-north crossing of the North Island of New Zealand.

Williams, William Sherley (Old Bill Williams)

(1787–1849) *Fur trader, trapper, interpreter, guide in the Rocky Mountains*
William "Bill" Williams may have been born in Rutherford County, North Carolina, although some sources indicate he was a native of Kentucky. He became an itinerant Baptist preacher, and, by 1813, he had settled in the then-frontier region of what is now western Missouri and eastern Kansas. He lived among that region's Osage Indians and reportedly married an Indian woman.

In 1825–26, Williams acted as an interpreter to the Osage for a U.S. government surveying expedition of the Santa Fe Trail led by Joseph C. Brown. Williams then embarked on a career as a fur trader and trapper in the ROCKY MOUNTAINS, ranging across a wide area of the West, from the Gila River in what is now southern Arizona to the Yellowstone River in what is now Wyoming.

Williams was part of JOSEPH REDDEFORD WALKER's 1833–34 expedition across Utah's Great Basin and the Sierra Nevada into California. Upon his return from the Pacific coast, Williams settled among the Ute Indians of western Colorado.

Williams returned to Missouri for a brief visit in 1841, but he set out the next year from Bent's Fort on the Arkansas

River in Colorado, accompanied by WILLIAM THOMAS HAMILTON. During the next three years, Williams and Hamilton traveled throughout the North Platte River region and Green River Valley in present-day Wyoming and Utah, before returning to Colorado and Santa Fe.

In 1846, Williams was a guide in the Rockies for JOHN CHARLES FRÉMONT's third expedition, but he did not travel to California with him. He again settled for a time with the Ute Indians, then went into the FUR TRADE out of Taos, New Mexico.

Williams's last expedition into the Rockies began in fall 1848. Again acting as a guide for Frémont, he set out from Bent's Fort and made an extremely hazardous crossing of the Sangre de Cristo Range, in search of an all-weather railroad pass through the mountains. The expedition crossed the Continental Divide and reached the headwaters of the Rio Grande, but it then became lost in a blizzard. Short of adequate clothing and supplies, 11 members of the party died of starvation or exposure. Forced to abandon the enterprise, Frémont and the other survivors retreated to Taos. Frémont reportedly blamed the disaster on Williams, who had claimed to know of a route through the San Juan Mountains.

In March 1849, Williams accompanied one of the survivors, BENJAMIN JORDAN KERN, back into the mountains to retrieve papers and equipment that had been left behind. Along the way, they were killed in an attack by a band of Ute warriors in retaliation for a recent raid on a Ute village by a U.S. Army detachment.

Bill Williams covered a wide area of the American West in his years as a trapper and guide. With Walker in 1833–34, he was among the first non-Indians to visit California's Yosemite Valley, and he took part in the first eastward crossing of the Sierra Nevada. Southern Arizona's Bill Williams River, a tributary of the COLORADO RIVER, is named in his honor.

Willoughby, Sir Hugh (ca. 1516–1554)
English mariner in the European Arctic

Hugh Willoughby was born near Nottingham, England, the son of a soldier and baronet. He became a soldier himself, serving as an officer with English forces in Scotland, for which he was knighted in 1544. After commanding a garrison on the Scottish border in 1548–49, he became associated with SEBASTIAN CABOT and the MUSCOVY COMPANY of merchants in London.

In 1553, Willoughby was named as captain-general of the company's first expedition, a voyage that was intended to navigate the NORTHEAST PASSAGE across the top of Europe and Asia to the Orient and thereby open English trade contacts with China and India. Three ships were assembled for the voyage: the *Edward Bonaventure*, captained by STEPHEN BOROUGH and with the expedition's chief pilot, RICHARD CHANCELLOR; the *Bona Confidentia*, captained by Cornelius Durforth; and the flagship, the *Bona Esperanza*, commanded by Willoughby.

Willoughby and his fleet sailed from London on May 10, 1553, although they did not leave the English coast until more than a month later. Off northern Norway's Lofoten Islands, the ships became separated in a storm. While Willoughby's ship and the *Bona Confidentia* remained together, the *Edward Bonaventure* continued on alone into the White Sea. Willoughby then proceeded eastward. Although he made the first known sighting of what turned out to be the southwest coast of Novaya Zemlya, he was unable to land there because of ice and shallow waters along the shore. Instead, he turned back westward across the Barents Sea to the northern end of the Kola Peninsula, part of Russian Lapland. He found a harbor where he planned to winter, near the mouth of the Arzina River, east of the present-day Russian port of Murmansk.

The two ships soon became icebound, and, during the winter of 1553–54, Willoughby and all the men on both vessels died. Although the likely causes of the disaster were the extreme cold and SCURVY, some sources suggest that carbon monoxide fumes emitted from stoves used to heat the interior of the ships may have killed the crew. Meanwhile, Chancellor and Borough had landed near what is now Archangel and succeeded in reaching Moscow, where they established commercial ties with the Russian monarch, Czar Ivan IV (Ivan the Terrible).

In spring 1554, Willoughby's fate became known when Russian fishermen found his ships, containing the frozen corpses of Willoughby and the more than 60 men with him. His journal, which was recovered and sent back to England, revealed the eastward extent of his explorations in the Barents Sea, indicating that he had survived until at least January 1554.

Sir Hugh Willoughby commanded the first English expedition to sail northward across the ARCTIC CIRCLE in the first attempt to find the Northeast Passage. Although he did not survive to report his finding, he is considered the first European known to have sighted the islands of Novaya Zemlya.

Wills, William John (1834–1861) *British surveyor in Australia*

A native of Devonshire, England, William Wills immigrated to Victoria, Australia, at the age of 18. He settled in Melbourne, where he studied medicine and worked as a surveyor, eventually finding employ for the government's meteorological office.

In 1860, Wills was commissioned as second in command to ROBERT O'HARA BURKE in an expedition, sponsored by the government of Victoria, aimed at making the first south-to-north crossing of Australia. The group left Melbourne in August 1860, arriving two months later at Menindee on the Darling River in west-central New South Wales. From there, they pressed on to Cooper's Creek in central Queensland, from where Burke, Wills, and two others, John King and Charles Gray, headed for the north coast, reaching the estuary of the Flinders River, near the coast of the Gulf of Carpentaria, in February 1861.

Wills returned to Cooper's Creek with Burke and King in April 1861. Gray had died on the trip back from the gulf. The relief party that was supposed to have waited for them had departed only hours before their arrival. Short on food and supplies, they made a desperate attempt to reach a settlement to the south. By the end of June 1861, both Wills and Burke had died of starvation; only one member of the expedition, the camel driver John King, survived, having been kept alive by Aborigines until he was rescued by a search party from Melbourne. The search party also found the bodies of Burke and Wills and recovered Wills's extensive journal, detailing the outbound journey and the expedition's last desperate days.

Along with Robert O'Hara Burke, William Wills is credited with taking part in a south-to-north crossing of Australia.

Wilson, Edward Adrian (1872–1912)
British physician, zoologist in Antarctica
Edward Wilson was a British medical doctor who accompanied ROBERT FALCON SCOTT on his first explorations of Antarctica in 1901–04.

In addition to serving as the expedition's surgeon, Wilson, a zoologist, was part of the group's scientific team. In 1902, on the coast of Antarctica's Ross Sea, he made the first known discovery of an emperor penguin rookery.

Later in 1902, Wilson accompanied Scott and another of the expedition's members, SIR ERNEST HENRY SHACKLETON, on the first exploration into Antarctica, setting a farthest-south record in a trek across the Ross Ice Shelf.

In 1910, Wilson returned to Antarctica as the chief of the scientific team with Scott's second expedition. In June 1911, he and a small party traveled to Cape Crozier, where he obtained the first samples of emperor penguin eggs.

Wilson accompanied Scott to the SOUTH POLE in January 1912. On the return trek, he was among the last of the five-man party to perish in a blizzard two months later.

When the group's remains were found by a search party in November 1912, it was learned that just prior to his death, Wilson had continued his scientific studies, making notes on the fossils and geological specimens he had collected near the South Pole.

Winslow, Edward (1595–1655) *English colonial leader in Massachusetts, explorer in Connecticut*
Edward Winslow was born in Droitwich in Worcestershire, England, the son of affluent parents. In 1617, he moved to Leyden in the Netherlands to attend that city's university. He soon joined the English Protestant group known as the PILGRIMS, who were then living in voluntary exile in Leyden.

Winslow sailed to New England with the Pilgrims aboard the *Mayflower,* landing at present-day Plymouth, Massachusetts, on December 21, 1620. He was elected as one of the ruling council of the Plymouth colony, and in 1621, aided by SQUANTO, he negotiated an important treaty with Massasoit, grand sachem of the Wampanoag Confederacy.

Winslow returned to England in 1623, where he acted as an agent for the Plymouth colony and also wrote and published an account of the colony's progress, entitled *Good News From New England or a True Relation of Things very remarkable at the Plantation of Plimoth in New England* (1624).

Winslow returned to the Plymouth colony in 1624. Over the next 20 years, he served a number of terms as the colony's governor and made several return trips to England to obtain additional support. He also explored and traded along the New England coast.

In 1632, Winslow headed south and west from the Plymouth colony into what is now Connecticut. Although Dutch navigator ADRIAEN BLOCK had explored the Connecticut River from Long Island Sound in 1614, no steps had been taken to assert Dutch sovereignty there. The next year, 1633, Winslow sent William Holmes to establish a trading post on the Connecticut River near present-day Windsor, Connecticut.

Winslow was imprisoned in England for a short time in 1635, accused of having performed marriage ceremonies in New England without clerical authority. He won his release based on the argument that he acted in a civil capacity as a magistrate.

Winslow left the Plymouth colony for the last time in 1646. Back in England, he became prominent in the government of Oliver Cromwell after 1649 and continued to serve as the principal agent for the Plymouth colony in New England.

In 1655, Cromwell appointed Winslow one of the commissioners in a naval expedition against the Spanish in the Caribbean Sea. While en route with the fleet to attack Jamaica, Winslow contracted a fever and died.

Edward Winslow, unlike most of the Pilgrim founders, came from an upper-class background. He was the first Englishman to visit the upper Connecticut River Valley, and his explorations led to the establishment of the first European settlement in Connecticut.

Wissmann, Hermann von (1853–1905)

German army officer, colonial administrator in central Africa
Born in Frankfurt, Germany, Hermann von Wissmann was an officer in the German army. He undertook explorations in central Africa on behalf of the German Africa Society. In 1880, Wissmann set out from Luanda on the Atlantic coast of Angola, along the Lulua and Kasai Rivers, to Nyangwe in present-day Republic of the Congo. From there, he continued eastward by way of Lake Tanganyika and the region of Tabora, and reached Zanzibar (part of present-day Tanzania) on the Indian Ocean coast in 1882, completing a west-to-east crossing of central Africa.

Wissmann returned to the Congo region in 1883. During the next two years, in the service of King Leopold II of Belgium, he explored the Kasai River system. In addition to determining that the river was mostly navigable, he also came upon an uncharted branch of the Kasai, known as the Sankuru.

Wissmann made an unsuccessful attempt to reach the Lomami River in 1886–87. Soon afterward, he was appointed as a colonial commissioner in German East Africa. In this role, he succeeded in suppressing an Arab revolt in present-day Tanzania in 1889–92; during the same period, he brought the Masai people of what is now Kenya under German colonial rule.

Largely as a result of Wissmann's efforts, the region between Lake Nyasa and Lake Tanganyika was brought under German colonial administration. He also founded several settlements in the interior, including Moshi at the base of MOUNT KILIMANJARO and Langenburg on Lake Nyasa. Wissmann served as governor of German East Africa in 1895–96, before he was compelled by illness to return to Europe.

Hermann von Wissmann's exploits were recounted in his book *My Second Journey Through Equatorial Africa* (1891). His explorations resulted in the expansion of European colonial influence over a wide area of central Africa, including much of what is now the Democratic Republic of the Congo, Tanzania, and Kenya.

Wolfskill, William (1798–1866) *American fur trader, frontiersman in the American Southwest*

William Wolfskill was born in Richmond, Kentucky, which was then a settlement on the Appalachian frontier. When about 10 years old, he moved with his family to what is now north-central Missouri. As a teenager, he returned to Kentucky to attend school for several years, then was back on the Missouri frontier in the early 1820s.

In 1822, Wolfskill first visited the Southwest with WILLIAM BECKNELL's second trading expedition from Franklin, Missouri, along the Santa Fe Trail to the newly opened markets in New Mexico. He later settled in Taos, where he trapped the Rio Grande and other rivers of north-eastern New Mexico with EWING YOUNG. In an 1824 trapping expedition north and west of Taos, Wolfskill worked alongside the first party of Americans to explore what is now southern Utah.

In 1830–31, Wolfskill, in partnership with GEORGE CONCEPCION YOUNT, led a caravan of packhorses along the Old Spanish Trail, from Taos to California along a route meandering north and west into Utah, across northern Arizona, and through the San Bernardino Mountains to San Gabriel Mission and Los Angeles. Wolfskill eventually settled in California, where he helped develop California's citrus and winemaking industries.

Although far longer and less direct than the westward route across the deserts of southern Arizona, the Old Spanish Trail route pioneered by Wolfskill and Young had abundant sources of water along the way, making it practical as a route for both caravans of goods-laden packhorses and for cattle herds being driven between New Mexico and California. Moreover, travelers along the Old Spanish Trail were less subject to Indian attacks.

Wood, Abraham (1608–ca. 1680) *English colonial military leader in Virginia, sponsor of trading expeditions*

There are few details of Abraham Wood's origins or early life. In 1646, as a captain in the Virginia colonial militia, he was commissioned by the Virginia Assembly to establish Fort Henry, a military outpost at the falls of the Appomattox River near present-day Petersburg, Virginia. This was one of a series of forts erected along the fall line of the rivers leading into the Piedmont region. Wood was granted a large tract of land near the fort, where he established a lucrative farming and trading business.

In 1650, Wood, along with James Bland and a number of other English colonists, set out from Fort Henry and explored the region between the upper James and Roanoke Rivers. They were in search of a river that, according to Indian reports, might lead them to a great "South Sea"—the Pacific Ocean—and the Spanish silver mines in Mexico. They penetrated the Piedmont for a distance of about 100 miles, then returned to Fort Henry after five days. Civil strife in England during the 1650s halted Wood's further explorations in Virginia.

It was not until 1671 that Wood, by then a major general, was able to sponsor subsequent expeditions into the APPALACHIANS. That year, he sent THOMAS BATTS and ROBERT FALLAM to explore south from Fort Henry to the Blue Ridge of what is now North Carolina. They crossed the Appalachians and returned to Fort Henry with reports of rivers flowing into the Ohio Valley.

In 1673, Wood sent out two more Englishmen, GABRIEL ARTHUR and JAMES NEEDHAM, to explore beyond the Allegheny Mountains in an attempt to expand the FUR TRADE to the Indians west of the Piedmont. They penetrated the interior as far as what is now western North Carolina and eastern Tennessee. Although Needham was killed by his Indian guide on this expedition, Arthur survived Indian captivity and traveled from Florida to the Ohio River before returning to Fort Henry in 1674.

Bacon's Rebellion of 1676–77 halted further efforts by Wood to send expeditions into the Appalachian frontier. Of his later life little is known.

Abraham Wood was one of the earliest settlers on the Virginia frontier. The expeditions he undertook himself, as well as those he sponsored, increased geographic knowledge of the interior of Virginia beyond the coastal plain and into the Piedmont. Two of his men, Batts and Fallam, were the first Englishmen to cross the Appalachians into the Ohio Valley from the Atlantic seaboard.

Woodward, Henry (unknown–ca. 1686)
British surgeon, colonist in South Carolina and Georgia

Little is known of the early life of Dr. Henry Woodward before 1664, when he arrived in North America at the Carolina colony near Cape Fear in what is now North Carolina. Two years later, he landed in what is present-day South Carolina, near the Georgia border, with an expedition that had originated in Barbados at Port Royal. Having a grant as a "tenant at will" of the Lord Proprietors of Carolina, he settled among the Yamasee Indians in Santa Elena, a town established by Spanish missionaries.

In 1667, the Yamasee turned Woodward over to the Spanish, who, after he professed being Catholic, let him work as a surgeon at their settlement of St. Augustine in Florida. He managed to escape the next year, however, during an attack by English pirates and returned to the north.

In 1670, Charles Town (now Charleston, South Carolina) was founded as the capital of the Carolina colony. That year, Woodward carried out an exploratory expedition from Charles Town into the interior, traveling up the Wateree River. In 1674, he cut southwestward to the site of present-day Augusta, Georgia, on the Savannah River and negotiated trade relations with Westo Indians. He returned to England three years later, where he received a commission from the Lord Proprietors to explore beyond the Savannah. In 1680, he led colonists and Westo and other Indian allies in their attacks on Spanish missions and their Indian converts in Georgia. In 1685–86, he led Charles Town traders southwestward and negotiated trade relations with the Creek (Muskogee) Indians living in the Lower Villages on the Chattahoochee River in Georgia. It is thought he died soon after his return to Charles Town.

Henry Woodward was the individual most responsible for opening up trade routes westward from Charles Town. In the ensuing years, English traders spread throughout the Southeast. JOHN LAWSON would explore the territory northwest of Charles Town, starting in 1701.

Wootton, Richens Lacy (Uncle Dick)
(1816–1893) *American trader, fur trapper, entrepreneur in the West*

Richens Lacy Wootton was born in Mecklenburg County in southern Virginia. While still a child, he moved west with his family to Kentucky and spent part of his teens on a cotton plantation operated by a relative in Mississippi.

In 1836, at the age of 20, Wootton set out for the western frontier, traveling by way of Independence, Missouri, to Bent's Fort on the Arkansas River, near present-day La Junta, Colorado. There, he became a trapper for the fur-trading firm of Bent, St. Vrain & Company, owned by CHARLES BENT and CÉRAN DE HAULT DE LASSUS ST. VRAIN.

After a year of trapping in the Colorado ROCKY MOUNTAINS, Wootton and a party of mountain men undertook an extensive trapping expedition into every major river region of the American West. Starting in 1838, they traveled from Bent's Fort to the upper reaches of the Arkansas River, then crossed the Rockies to the Green River region of what is now northern Utah and southwestern Wyoming. From there, they went on to trap in the Big Horn River region of what is now southern Montana. They hunted beaver in the upper Yellowstone River, before turning westward for the Snake River and COLUMBIA RIVER in present-day Idaho, Washington, and Oregon.

After a stopover at the HUDSON'S BAY COMPANY's Fort Vancouver, near present-day Portland, Oregon, Wootton and his party made their way southward through central California to Los Angeles. They then returned eastward, trapping along the Colorado and Gila Rivers in southern Arizona, before traversing Utah's Great Basin and arriving at Bent's Fort on the Arkansas River in 1840.

In the early 1840s, Wootton became a rancher near present-day Pueblo, Colorado, raising buffalo cows and calves and trading in buffalo skins with the Comanche Indians. In the U.S.-Mexican War of 1846–48, he took part in Alexander Doniphan's campaign into Chihuahua in 1847, serving as a scout. At the war's end, he settled for a time in Taos, New Mexico, and, in 1852, he undertook a highly profitable cattle drive to California.

Wootton returned to Pueblo in the early 1850s, where he operated a ranch as well as several other business enterprises. During the Pikes Peak (Colorado) gold rush of 1859, he had a hotel and saloon business in Denver. Beginning in 1866, he operated a toll road that traversed 27 miles of rough terrain in Raton Pass to link the Santa Fe Trail and the Canadian River, an enterprise that lasted until he was bought out in 1879 by the Atchison, Topeka, & Santa Fe Railroad, which constructed a rail line along his right-of-way.

Richens Lacy Wootton's career as a mountain man and fur trapper was highlighted by his spectacular 1838–40 expedition, in which he traversed the entire American West, taking in much of the Rockies, the Pacific Northwest, and

California, as well as the Southwest. He was a veritable legend in his own time; his life spanned most of the major periods of the history of the American West, from the height of the FUR TRADE in the 1830s to just after the official end of the frontier period in 1890. Known familiarly as "Uncle Dick," he related his western experiences in interviews included in *Uncle Dick Wootton* (1890), a biography by H. L. Conrad.

Work, John (ca. 1792–1861) *Irish fur trader in the Pacific Northwest*

Born in County Donegal, Ireland, where his family was known as Wark, John Work entered the FUR TRADE in 1814, as an employee of the HUDSON'S BAY COMPANY in the HUDSON BAY region. In 1823, soon after the Hudson's Bay Company had merged with the NORTH WEST COMPANY, Work was sent west to the COLUMBIA RIVER region. Over the next seven years, under the direction of PETER SKENE OGDEN, he trapped and explored from the Oregon coast to the Fraser River in British Columbia.

In 1830, Work took charge of the Hudson's Bay Company's operations in the Snake River region of what is now eastern Washington and western Idaho. That year, he led an expedition eastward from Walla Walla into the Salmon River region of central Idaho, then southward to trap in the Humboldt River valley of present-day northern Nevada. He later returned to his base at Fort Spokane by way of central Oregon's John Day River.

Work led a party of trappers into western Montana in 1831, reaching the upper reaches of the MISSOURI RIVER before being forced to withdraw because of repeated attacks by Blackfeet Indian war parties. The next year, he went southward into Oregon and northern California's Sacramento Valley. He stopped at San Francisco Bay and the Russian settlement at Fort Ross before returning northward in 1833.

In 1846, Work succeeded JOHN MCLOUGHLIN as the Hudson's Bay Company's chief factor in the Pacific Northwest. He later settled in Victoria, British Columbia, where he became prominent in provincial politics.

In his career as a fur trader, John Work covered a wide area of the Pacific Northwest and northern plains. His personal account of his experiences was published in 1923 as *The Journal of John Work*, which includes a detailed account of his travels from 1830 to 1833.

Workman, Fanny Bullock (1859–1925)
American traveler, mountain climber, writer in Europe, North Africa, and central Asia

Fanny Workman, née Bullock, came from a wealthy Worcester, Massachusetts, family that was involved in trade and the manufacture of gunpowder. In 1866, her father was elected governor of the state.

Workman was educated in New York, Paris, and Dresden and became fluent in both French and German. She returned to the United States in 1879; two years later, she married Dr. William Hunter Workman, a prominent physician.

In the 1880s, Workman was introduced by her husband to mountain climbing in New Hampshire's White Mountains. She climbed 6,293-foot Mount Washington several times. In 1888, she and her husband went to Europe and together embarked on a 20-year career of travel and mountaineering.

In the 1890s, the Workmans undertook a series of mountain-climbing expeditions in the Alps, during which Fanny climbed such peaks as Zinal Rothorn, the Matterhorn, and MONT BLANC. In 1895–96, the Workmans bicycled through Spain and also toured the Atlas Mountains of Morocco and Algeria. In 1897, they went to India and bi-

Fanny Workman *(Library of Congress)*

cycled through the Indian subcontinent to Burma, then traveled to Java. They returned to India the next year and undertook mountaineering expeditions into the HIMALAYAS, including the Karakoram Range.

From 1899 to 1912, Workman participated with her husband in six more expeditions in central Asia, during which she set mountain-climbing altitude records for women. The Swiss mountaineer MATTHIAS ZURBRIGGEN served as her guide. The Workmans contributed geographic data on these uncharted mountainous regions to Britain's Great Trigonometrical Survey of India.

In 1905, Workman became the second woman, after IS-ABELLA LUCY BIRD BISHOP, to address the ROYAL GEO-GRAPHICAL SOCIETY on her travels. At the outbreak of World War I, Workman and her husband settled in the south of France, where she died in 1925.

With her husband, Fanny Workman authored a number of books detailing their travels, including *Algerian Memories: A Bicycle Tour Over the Atlas Mountains to the Sahara* (1895), *Sketches Awheel in Modern Iberia* (1897), *In the Ice World of the Himalaya* (1900), and *Through Town and Jungle: 14,000 Miles A-wheel among the Temples and Peoples of the Indian Plain* (1904). The Workmans took portable Kodak cameras on their expeditions, and their travel books were among the first to be illustrated with photographs taken en route.

Wyeth, Nathaniel Jarvis (1802–1856)

American entrepreneur, fur trader in the Pacific Northwest
Nathaniel Wyeth was born in Cambridge, Massachusetts, into a family prominent in the hotel business in nearby Boston. As a young man, he became a partner in a business that supplied ice from New England to the WEST INDIES.

In 1831, inspired by earlier efforts to promote American settlement in the Oregon Country, Wyeth organized a colonizing and trading expedition of his own to the Pacific Northwest. He sent a ship, the *Sultana*, around CAPE HORN to the Pacific Ocean; he intended to meet the vessel at the mouth of the COLUMBIA RIVER, where he planned to sell its cargo of trade goods and send it back loaded with furs.

In May 1832, Wyeth and a party of trappers and artisans left Independence, Missouri, for the Oregon Country, accompanying a supply wagon led by WILLIAM LEWIS SUB-LETTE of the ROCKY MOUNTAIN FUR COMPANY. They followed the North Platte River northwestward to the Sweetwater, then traveled through the SOUTH PASS to the Teton Mountains. At the fur traders' rendezvous at Pierre's

Hole, a number of Wyeth's party decided to abandon the venture. Soon afterward, he took part in a skirmish with the Gros Ventre Indians that became known as the Battle of Pierre's Hole.

Wyeth and the remaining 18 members of his expedition continued to the Snake River without Sublette, reaching Fort Vancouver on the Columbia River, opposite the future site of Portland, Oregon, in October 1833. Wyeth learned that the *Sultana* had been wrecked in the South Pacific, causing him to curtail the enterprise for that year.

On his overland journey back to Boston in spring and summer 1833, Wyeth met with fur trader THOMAS FITZ-PATRICK on the Green River and entered into an agreement to supply trade goods for the summer 1834 rendezvous.

Wyeth was in Boston in winter 1833–34, where he organized the Columbia River Fishing and Trading Company. Another ship, the *May Dacre,* was sent to the Pacific Northwest in order to bring back a cargo of pickled Columbia River salmon. On his second overland journey to Oregon, which left from Boston in spring 1834, Wyeth was accompanied by naturalist THOMAS NUTTALL, as well as a group of settlers headed by Methodist missionary Jason Lee.

When Wyeth reached the summer 1834 rendezvous at Ham's Fork of the Green River, Fitzpatrick reneged on his promise to buy his goods. In response, planning to sell his merchandise to other fur traders, Wyeth, along with OS-BORNE RUSSELL, established Fort Hall on the Snake River in what is now southern Idaho. He then resumed the westward journey to the Columbia River's mouth, which he reached in September 1834. Another setback occurred when Wyeth's ship arrived on the Oregon coast too late for that year's salmon fishing season, having stopped in Chile for repairs. Wyeth remained in the Pacific Northwest for another year, returning to Boston in spring 1836 to resume his career as an ice dealer. Soon afterward, he sold Fort Hall to the HUD-SON'S BAY COMPANY.

Although Nathaniel Wyeth's enterprises in the Pacific Northwest were less than commercially successful, the route he blazed in his two expeditions west of the South Pass soon became well established as the Oregon Trail. Starting in the early 1840s, Fort Hall, his trading settlement on the Snake River near what is now Pocatello, Idaho, became an important stopping point for pioneers heading to California and Oregon. Jason Lee and the migrants who traveled to the West with Wyeth in 1834 went on to establish the first permanent American settlement in Oregon. Wyeth left an account of his transcontinental journeys, published in 1899 as *The Correspondence and Journals of Captain Nathaniel J. Wyeth.*

Xavier, Francis (Saint Francis Xavier, Francisco Javier, Francisco de Yasu y Javier) (1506–1552)

Spanish missionary in India, Indonesia, and Japan

Francis Xavier was born into a noble Basque family in Spain's province of Navarre. In 1525, he began studying in Paris, eventually becoming an associate of Spanish churchman Ignatius of Loyola. In 1534, with Loyola, he was one of the seven founding members of the Society of Jesus, the Jesuit order.

Ordained as a priest in Venice in 1537, Xavier spent several years in service to his order in Rome. In 1540, he was named papal nuncio to the Indies, and the following year, under the sponsorship of King John III of Portugal, he set out on a missionary expedition to India from Lisbon.

After a voyage around the CAPE OF GOOD HOPE, Xavier arrived at the Portuguese colony of Goa on the west coast of India in 1542. For the next three years, he traveled along the south coast of India, winning many converts and establishing missions. He also undertook missionary work on the island of CEYLON (present-day Sri Lanka).

In 1545, Xavier sailed for Malacca at the southern end of the Malay Peninsula, where he carried on missionary work. He continued eastward into the Indonesian archipelago, visiting Ternate in the Moluccas, then known as the SPICE ISLANDS, in 1546.

Returning to India, Xavier supervised the assignment of additional Jesuit missionaries to posts in India. In 1549, he led a group of missionaries to Japan, landing at Kagoshima on southernmost Kyushu Island, where he met up with the Portuguese traveler FERNÃO MENDES PINTO. After two years in Japan, during which he was permitted to open a number of missions and Christian settlements, Xavier returned to India.

In 1552, Xavier was named as superior of the Jesuit Province of the Indies. With plans to take his missionary work to China, he set out from Goa. He contracted fever en route and died on Shangchuan Island near the Chinese port of Canton (Guangzhou).

Canonized in 1622, Saint Francis Xavier became known as the Apostle to the Indies. After Pinto, he was one of the first Europeans to visit Japan, providing an early description of that land and its people in his letters to his fellow Jesuits in Europe.

Xenophon (ca. 430–355 B.C.) *Greek soldier, historian in the Middle East*

Xenophon was born in ancient Athens, a son of one of that city-state's prominent families. In his youth, he studied under the Athenian Greek philosopher Socrates.

In 401 B.C., Xenophon embarked on a military career as a young officer with a Greek mercenary force in service to the Persian prince Cyrus the Younger. He was among the so-called Ten Thousand Greeks who took part in a military expedition that marched eastward across present-day Syria and Iraq in an attempt to defeat the ruler of Persia (present-day Iran), Artaxerxes II, Cyrus's older brother.

Xenophon traveled with the Greek army from Anatolia through the Cilician Gates, the pass in the Taurus Mountains of what is now southern Turkey. They followed the Euphrates River southward toward the Persian capital at Babylon. In the ensuing Battle of Cunaxa, near what is now Fallujah, northeast of present-day Baghdad, Iraq, Cyrus was killed by Persian forces. Afterward, although the Persians agreed to escort the Greeks back to the MEDITERRANEAN SEA, they instead murdered most of the remaining officers.

Command of the Greek forces then went to Xenophon. He led the army northward up the Tigris River, through the ruins of the ancient Assyrian capital at Nineveh, across the Kurdistan region of northern Iraq and southern Turkey, and into the mountains of present-day Armenia and Georgia. Eventually, the forces reached Trabzon on the central Black Sea coast of what is now northern Turkey. From there, they sailed back to Greece, arriving at Lake Scutari on the northern border of Albania. The five-month journey had taken them through more than 2,000 miles of territory unknown to the Greeks.

Xenophon continued his military career in the service of Sparta before returning to Athens, where he settled in 365 B.C. Thereafter, he devoted himself to historical writing. Among his work was his *Anabasis* (Upmarch), chronicling his experiences leading the Ten Thousand Greeks back from the Persian campaign.

As a result of Xenophon's report on the retreat across Persia, Greek geographic knowledge was extended eastward to include much of present-day Turkey and large portions of southeastern Europe and the Middle East. His east-to-west march back to Greece was followed some 70 years later by the west-to-east campaign of conquest by ALEXANDER THE GREAT.

Y

Yaqut al-Rumi, Shihab al-Din Abu Abd Allah (Yaqut al-Hamawi) (1179–1229) *Greek-born traveler in the Middle East*

Yaqut al-Rumi was born a Christian to a Greek family in what is now western Turkey, at that time a province of the Byzantine Empire. As a child, he was taken captive by Muslim maidens and sold into slavery.

Purchased by a Baghdad merchant named al-Hamawi (whose name he apparently adopted), Yaqut was raised and educated as a Muslim. He later undertook commercial journeys on behalf of his owner, traveling widely into the regions of Persia (present-day Iran) and Arabia adjoining the Persian Gulf.

Granted his freedom in 1196, Yaqut continued to travel in the Middle East for his former owner, operating out of Baghdad until al-Hamawi's death in 1213. By that time, he had developed an interest in geography, and, over the next 20 years, he extended his travels in the Middle East to include visits to cities and small villages in Egypt and Mesopotamia (present-day Iraq and Syria).

Yaqut al-Rumi eventually settled in Aleppo, where, in 1228–29, he completed his great geographic work *Mu'jam al-Buldan* (Dictionary of countries). In it, he provided an index of place names he had compiled in his travels, along with topographic, historical, and economic details. One of the most comprehensive geographic works of the Islamic medieval period, it was also the first gazetteer-type geographic study ever produced.

Yermak (Timofeyevich, Timofeevich, Timofeiev, Ermak) (unknown–ca. 1584) *Russian Cossack in western Siberia*

Details of Yermak's origins and early life are obscure. By the 1570s, he was a leading commander among the Cossack bands of the Volga and Don Rivers. His name sometimes appears as Yermak Timofeyevich in historical writings.

In about 1579, Yermak and some 1,000 of his followers, who had been raiding merchant vessels along the Volga River, withdrew up the Volga, pursued by a Russian government military expedition. They reached the region of the upper Kama and Chusovaya Rivers, where the Stroganov family had established a series of trading settlements on the extensive land grants they had received from Czar Ivan IV (Ivan the Terrible).

Yermak and his Cossack army were soon engaged by the Stroganovs to defend their lands against the Tatar tribes from the east. In 1581, Yermak led as many as 1,600 Cossacks eastward across the Ural Mountains in a campaign of conquest against the Khanate of Sibir. With superior military force, he soon succeeded in overthrowing the Tatar ruler, Kuchum Khan, and, in 1582, occupying his capital on the Irtysh River, known then as the Tatar city of Sibir. The Stroganovs sent news of Yermak's victory to Ivan in Moscow, along with furs from the newly conquered lands. Accepting the territory as part of his domain, the Russian monarch dispatched an army to occupy the region.

Probably in 1584 or 1585, before Russian reinforcements reached Yermak at Sibir, he was killed in a native uprising. Nonetheless, within two years, the region had come under Russian control, and Sibir was replaced by nearby Tobolsk, the new capital city that the Russians established in 1587.

The conquests of Yermak marked the beginning of Russian eastward expansion across central Asia to the Pacific Ocean. The Sibir region, which he had brought under Russian rule, gave its name to the vast land stretching eastward to the Pacific, known thereafter as SIBERIA. Yermak's route eastward from the Stroganov settlements at present-day Perm, through the Urals to present-day Tobolsk, was adopted by the Trans-Siberian Railroad in the 1890s.

Young, Brigham (1801–1877) *American religious leader, territorial governor of Utah*

Brigham Young was born to a farming family in Whittingham, Vermont. He had little formal education, and by the time he was 16, he was self-employed as a painter, carpenter, and glazier. By 1824, he had moved into western New York, settling at Mendon, near Rochester. In 1832, Young became a member of the Church of Jesus Christ of Latter Day Saints—the Mormons—which had been established in nearby Palmyra, New York, two years earlier by Joseph Smith.

Throughout the 1830s, Young rose to prominence as a leader in the Mormon movement, organizing a settlement at Kirtland in northeastern Ohio and taking part in evangelical expeditions to England. He was instrumental in the establishment of the large Mormon settlement at Nauvoo, Illinois, and, in 1844, following the murder of Joseph Smith, he became the church's principal leader.

Facing persecution by civil authorities and resentful non-Mormon settlers in Illinois, Young evacuated the 16,000 Mormons from Nauvoo, crossed the MISSISSIPPI RIVER into Missouri, then set up temporary settlements at Council Bluffs, Iowa, as well as at Winter Quarters, Nebraska, on the MISSOURI RIVER not far from present-day Omaha.

In April 1847, Young led an advance party of 148 Mormon men and women, known as the "Pioneer Band," westward from Winter Quarters to the Platte River. Influenced by the recently published reports by JOHN CHARLES FRÉMONT, Young had decided to establish a homeland for the Mormons in the remote and arid Great Salt Lake Valley. They traveled in 72 wagons and drove a large cattle herd with them across the Nebraska plains.

Young followed the north bank of the Platte, a departure from the south bank route usually taken by emigrants heading for the Oregon and California Trails. They proceeded along the Platte and North Platte Rivers north and

Brigham Young *(New York State Library, Albany)*

west into what is now Wyoming. Near present-day Casper, Wyoming, they crossed the North Platte in a boat they had carried with them, the *Revenue Cutter*. A small group from the Pioneer Band party remained at this point, where they established a profitable ferry service that charged non-Mormon emigrants a fee to cross the river, an enterprise that would continue for the next 20 years.

Young and the Pioneer Band arrived at Fort Laramie in June 1847 and from there followed the Oregon Trail to Fort Bridger. Mountain man JAMES BRIDGER warned Young that the route he planned to take to the Great Salt Lake led into mountains and deserts that would be difficult to cross with wagons. Nevertheless, Young led his party southwestward from Fort Bridger into the Uinta and Wasatch Mountains, making a perilous crossing of 120 miles of desert. In early July 1847, the first Mormons reached the tablelands southeast of the Great Salt Lake. Young, stricken with mountain fever, did not arrive until July 24, 1847, at which time he reportedly declared, "This is the place."

Young oversaw the establishment of the Mormon settlement at Great Salt Lake, and soon afterward, he headed back East to organize the subsequent migration of the bulk of the Mormons who had begun to follow his route westward from the Missouri River. As a result of Young's efforts, thousands of Mormons poured into the Great Salt Lake settlement during the next several years. In 1851, he was named governor of the newly organized territory of Utah.

Seeking to provide the Mormon settlement with an outlet to the Pacific Ocean, he organized parties of Mormon emigrants that established communities south and southwest of the Great Salt Lake—from Utah Lake, across northern Nevada, to Cajon Pass into the Sierra Nevada, where the Mormons established San Bernardino. By that time, the rest of the route westward to San Diego and the Pacific coast was well known, having been blazed in 1826 by JEDEDIAH STRONG SMITH.

Although conflicts with federal authorities led to Young's removal as Utah governor in 1858, he remained a dominant force in the Mormon community until his death in 1877.

The route along the north bank of the Platte established by Brigham Young in 1847 became known as the Mormon Trail. It provided expanded access to the Oregon and California Trails for westbound emigrants until the advent of the transcontinental railroad in 1869. The route across the Great Basin established in the 1850s became known as the Mormon Corridor.

Young, Charles Denton (1864–1922) *U.S. Army officer, American cartographer in Haiti and Liberia*

Charles Young was born in Mays Lick, Kentucky; both his parents were African-American slaves. They gained their freedom at the end of the Civil War, in which his father, Gabriel Young, served in the Fifth U.S. Colored Artillery. After the war, the family moved to Ripley, Ohio, where Young graduated from high school with honors, then taught at his grammar school. He later applied to the U.S. Military Academy at West Point and was admitted in 1884. He graduated in 1889, despite the hostility of some of his peers, becoming the ninth African American to be enrolled and the third to graduate.

Young's first assignment was as a second lieutenant with the Buffalo Soldiers in the Ninth Cavalry in Nebraska, then in Utah. In 1894, he was assigned as a teacher of tactics and military science at Wilberforce University in Ohio. In 1898, with the outbreak of the Spanish-American War, he was given training duty at Camp Algers in Virginia. In 1901–02, he saw active duty in the Philippines. In 1903, he was acting superintendent of Sequoia and General Grant National Parks in California, then a troop commander at the Presidio of San Francisco.

In 1904–07, Young, at the rank of captain, served in Port-au-Prince, Haiti, as one of the army's first military attachés for the newly founded Military Information Division, observing the training of Haitian troops and writing reports on the political situation and geography as well as producing maps. He also traveled to the Dominican Republic. During his time there, he wrote his book *Military Morale of Nations and Races*, published in 1912.

Subsequent postings included Washington, D.C., the Philippines, Wyoming, and Texas. In 1912–15, Young was sent to Liberia in West Africa as a military attaché and helped reorganize the Liberian Frontier Force and Constabulary. He traveled throughout the country, again drafting maps. For his work there he was given the Spingarn Medal by the National Association for the Advancement of Colored People (NAACP), awarded annually to an African American for distinguished achievement.

In 1916–17, Young served in Mexico, commanding a cavalry squadron in pursuit of the bandit Pancho Villa, whose forces had crossed the border and murdered American citizens. His successes in battle led to a promotion to lieutenant colonel, the first African American to reach that rank.

Although Young was the highest-ranking African-American officer in the army, he was denied a leadership role in World War I on grounds of high blood pressure. Despite his protests and those of others who believed the decision to be racially motivated, he was retired in 1917. He was returned to active duty the next year, and, in 1919, he went again to Liberia as a military attaché. In 1921, he reported to the U.S. government on mistreatment of Liberians by non-natives. He died in Lagos, Nigeria, three years later, while on an inspection visit. He was buried at Arlington National Cemetery.

In addition to his many academic and military accomplishments, as well as his firsts as an African American, Charles Young became accomplished in mapmaking and helped chart wilderness areas in Haiti, the Dominican Republic, and Liberia.

Young, Ewing (ca. 1792–1841) *American fur trader, pioneer in the Southwest, California, and Oregon*

Ewing Young was born in eastern Tennessee; his parents were among the original frontier settlers of the region. When about 18, he moved westward himself, settling for a time in north-central Missouri, where he took up farming.

In 1822, Young became a trader, traveling westward with WILLIAM BECKNELL's wagon caravan along the Santa Fe Trail to New Mexico. He remained in Taos, where, in the 1820s, he became associated with GEORGE CONCEPCION YOUNT and WILLIAM WOLFSKILL, with whom he trapped beaver along the rivers of northeastern New Mexico.

By 1826, Young had become a seasoned fur trapper as well as a veteran trader, plying the Santa Fe Trail between St. Louis and the settlements of northern New Mexico. That year, he embarked with a large brigade of trappers southwestward from Taos into the Gila River and Salt River region of what is now south-central Arizona. On this expedition, he rescued JAMES OHIO PATTIE and Michel

Robidoux, a brother of ANTOINE ROBIDOUX, survivors of an Indian attack.

After trapping along the Gila to the lower COLORADO RIVER, Young turned northward to the Green River region of what is now northern Utah. He returned to Taos in 1827, by way of the Old Spanish Trail, where local New Mexican authorities confiscated his furs, charging him with having operated in the Gila River region without proper authorization.

Young's next major fur-trapping expedition left Taos in August 1829. The young CHRISTOPHER HOUSTON CARSON (Kit Carson) was among the party of MOUNTAIN MEN he led across Arizona by way of the Mojave River, and through Cajon Pass to San Gabriel Mission, near Los Angeles, California. He spent the next year leading his trappers into central California's San Joaquin River region. In 1831, he drove the first herds of mules and horses from California back to New Mexico along the Old Spanish Trail.

In 1832, Young duplicated this expedition, this time in partnership with DAVID E. JACKSON. He remained in California to hunt sea otters in the islands off the southern California coast, then undertook additional beaver-trapping expeditions into northern California as well as eastward along the lower Colorado River.

In San Diego, in summer 1834, Young met Oregon settlement promoter Hall Jackson Kelley, who induced Young to head northward with him to Oregon. When he and Kelley arrived at Fort Vancouver in October 1834, they had with them a small herd of horses they had brought from California. JOHN McLOUGHLIN, the HUDSON'S BAY COMPANY factor there, having been incorrectly informed that the livestock had been stolen in California, refused to allow Young to stay at the post, making him one of the few travelers ever to have been refused his assistance and hospitality at Fort Vancouver. Undaunted, Young established a ranch in the Oregon Country, which soon developed into a small community of American settlers, complete with a gristmill and a sawmill.

In 1837, Young returned to California to drive the first large cattle herd back to Oregon. At the time of his death in 1841, he had considerable holdings in both land and cattle. Because Young had died without a will, the American community was prompted to organize an ad hoc probate court to administer his estate, an event that marked the first official action of what was to become Oregon's provisional government.

In his westward journeys from St. Louis to New Mexico and California, Ewing Young was instrumental in developing several central routes. He revived the Old Spanish Trail as a cattle trail to California and developed the trail along the Gila River, in effect extending the Santa Fe Trail westward to Los Angeles.

Younghusband, Sir Francis Edward

(1863–1942) *British army officer and diplomat in central and Southeast Asia*

Born to a British colonial family at Murree in what is now northern Pakistan, Francis Younghusband attended schools in England before entering the British army as a commissioned officer in 1882.

In 1886, Younghusband began his travels in Asia with a journey to Peking (Beijing). From there, he went northward into Manchuria, and, the next year, he made an east-to-west crossing of China and Mongolia, traversing the GOBI DESERT and skirting the Altai Mountains to the Tarim Basin and the ancient SILK ROAD cities of Kashgar and Yarkand. He then headed southward into the Karakoram range, where he made the European discovery of the Mustagh Pass, which he followed into northern India's Kashmir region.

In 1888, while serving with British forces in Burma, Younghusband traveled the length of the country, from Moulmein, up the Salween River and across to the upper reaches of the Mekong River, into southeastern China.

Back in India in 1889, Younghusband repeated his earlier journey across the Karakoram range in reverse, traveling from Rawalpindi northward to Yarkand in western China. He then undertook a topographic survey in the Pamir region.

Younghusband was awarded a gold medal by the ROYAL GEOGRAPHICAL SOCIETY in 1890, and transferred that same year to the political department of the army. He continued to travel and explore, extending the Great Trigonometrical Survey of India into the Hindu Kush, Karakoram, and Pamir mountain ranges. In 1892–94, he undertook a two-year exploration and survey expedition along the Amu Darya River in northern Afghanistan.

In 1902, Younghusband was sent on a diplomatic mission to Tibet, the British foreign office having become concerned over Russian designs on the remote Himalayan principality. When Russian expansion into Tibet seemed imminent, Younghusband was placed in command of a large military force that occupied the country. On August 2, 1904, he led his command into Tibet's capital at LHASA, a city forbidden to outsiders.

While in Lhasa, Younghusband directed the first scientific survey of the area, making the first accurate determination of the city's precise geographic position. Other surveying teams under his command explored the Tsangpo and Brahmaputra Rivers, upstream from Shigatse.

Younghusband retired from the army after 1908, at the rank of lieutenant colonel. He had recounted his explorations in Asia in his books *Heart of a Continent* (1898) and *India and Tibet* (1912). He served as president of the Royal Geographical Society in 1919–22. During the 1920s, he turned his attention to the ascent of MOUNT EVEREST, making three unsuccessful attempts.

In his 1904 expedition into Tibet, Sir Francis Younghusband became the first European to enter Lhasa since the visit of ÉVARISTE-RÉGIS HUC in 1846.

Yount, George Concepcion (1794–1865)

American fur trader, trailblazer in the American Southwest

George Yount was born in western North Carolina's Burke County, the son of an American Revolutionary War veteran. At the age of 10, he moved west with his family to the newly acquired Louisiana Territory and settled in Cape Girardeau on the MISSISSIPPI RIVER in what is now southeastern Missouri.

During the War of 1812, Yount and his father and brothers served with a local militia unit, defending the surrounding region against attacks by British-allied Indians. Married in 1818, Yount moved with his new wife to Howard County in north-central Missouri, where he became a cattle rancher.

As a result of a severe financial setback in 1825, Yount was compelled to leave his family and seek his fortune in New Mexico. He traveled with a trading caravan along the Santa Fe Trail into the Southwest, and, after establishing himself in Taos, became a trapper with EWING YOUNG.

In 1827, Yount accompanied JAMES OHIO PATTIE and his father, Sylvester Pattie, in a fur-trapping expedition to the Gila River, which they followed to its mouth on the COLORADO RIVER in western Arizona. The next year, he trapped in the northern ROCKY MOUNTAINS, attending the 1828 fur traders' rendezvous near Bear Lake on the present Utah-Wyoming border. He trapped for beaver around the upper reaches of the Yellowstone River in northwestern Wyoming, where a mountain in the region was named Younts Peak in his honor.

While in the northern Rockies, Yount met JEDEDIAH STRONG SMITH, from whom he heard accounts of his 1826–29 explorations across the Great Basin and the Sierra Nevada into California and Oregon.

Back in Taos in 1830, Yount joined with mountain man WILLIAM WOLFSKILL in a packhorse expedition along the Old Spanish Trail to California. In September 1830, they left Taos and traveled northwestward to the Green River, then turned southwestward across Utah and into Arizona. After crossing the San Bernardino Mountains by way of Cajon Pass, they arrived at the San Gabriel Mission, near Los Angeles, in February 1831.

Yount decided to remain in California, where he worked in the early 1830s as a carpenter in the settlements along the south coast. In 1834, he moved to northern California, where he obtained a land grant from the Mexican government in the Napa Valley region. In honor of his converting to Catholicism, he adopted the middle name Concepcion. In 1844, he was joined in northern California by his two daughters from Missouri, although his wife, believing that he had died, had since remarried.

In his 1830–31 expedition with William Wolfskill, George Yount made the first known journey along the entire length of the Old Spanish Trail. More than 50 years after it had first been explored by Spanish missionaries FRANCISCO SILVESTRE VÉLEZ DE ESCALANTE, FRANCISCO ATANASIO DOMÍNGUEZ, and FRANCISCO TOMÁS HERMENEGILDO GARCÉS in the 1770s, Yount and Wolfskill demonstrated that the trail was suitable for packhorses carrying trade goods from New Mexico to California. Their efforts led to the development of the first direct overland link between the settlements of northern New Mexico and southern California.

Z

Zagoskin, Lavrenty Alekseyevich
(Lavrenti Alekseev Zagoskin) (1807–1890)
Russian naval officer in Alaska

Lavrenty Alekseyevich Zagoskin grew up to become a lieutenant in the Russian navy. In 1838, he joined the RUSSIAN-AMERICAN COMPANY. After an overland journey from European Russia to the Pacific coast of SIBERIA, he sailed to Alaska in command of the company's vessel the *Okhotsk,* arriving in Sitka in summer 1839.

During the next three years, Zagoskin commanded company ships in voyages between the fur-trading settlements in the eastern Gulf of Alaska and in northern California, and back to Siberia. In 1842, he won approval for a plan to explore the two great rivers of Alaska's interior, the largely unknown Yukon and Kuskokwim.

In summer 1842, Zagoskin sailed to St. Michael on the south shore of Norton Sound, where he explored the Unalakleet River. The next winter, he traveled inland by dogsled to Nulato, near the confluence of the Yukon and the Koyukuk Rivers. In spring 1843, he examined the Koyukuk, the Yukon's main northern tributary, and that summer, he undertook the first of a series of extensive explorations by kayak along the middle and lower reaches of the Yukon River, exploring its course from the mouth of the Tanana River to its great bend westward near Anvik. In summer 1844, he turned his attention to the Kuskokwim and the lower Yukon Rivers. The next year, he left the Russian-American Company, returning to European Russia by way of Okhotsk and Siberia.

Lavrenty Alekseyevich Zagoskin's account of his inland journeys, published in 1847–48, provides a contemporary view of the later period of Russian settlement in Alaska. He is credited with making the most extensive explorations into the interior of Alaska until that time, and, by his own account, he made the European discovery of the Yukon River in 1842.

Zheng He   See CHENG HO.

Zhu Siben   See CHU SSU-PEN.

Zurbriggen, Matthias (1856–1917) *Swiss mountain climber and guide in the Alps, Himalayas, Southern Alps, and Andes Mountains*

Born in the village of Macugnaga in northern Italy, Matthias Zurbriggen was a Swiss citizen. He developed skills as a mountain climber in the Alps and found work as a guide to expeditions.

In 1892, Zurbriggen and the British mountaineer Sir William Martin Conway set the record for altitude by reaching the summit of Pioneer Peak in the Karakoram Range of the HIMALAYAS. In 1894, Zurbriggen, as part of British climber Edward Fitzgerald's expedition, made climbs in NEW ZEALAND's Southern Alps. He made a solo ascent of Mount Cook, the highest peak in New Zealand, only three months after the New Zealanders T. C. Fyfe, Peter Graham, and J. Clark first conquered it. Zurbriggen and Fitzgerald made the first ascents of Mount Tasman and Mount Haidinger that same year.

In 1897, Zurbriggen, once again as part of a Fitzgerald expedition, completed a solo ascent of ACONCAGUA, the highest peak in the ANDES MOUNTAINS and the entire Western Hemisphere, at 22,834 feet above sea level. He later worked for the American FANNY BULLOCK WORKMAN in the Himalayas and helped her set an altitude record for women.

Matthias Zurbriggen became legendary as a mountain climber and guide for completing ascents that his employers and companions could not. He was also the first mountaineering guide to publish his autobiography, *From the Alps to the Andes: Being the Autobiography of a Mountain Guide* (1899).

Appendix A
EXPLORERS BY
MOST RELEVANT OCCUPATION

Some of the "occupations" listed below might be better described as "activities," nor are they exclusive since many individuals had more than one occupation. Those indicated are most relevant to exploration. Some individuals are listed under "explorers" because they considered exploration as their only or primary calling. Since many of the individuals wrote about their explorations, there is no separate entry for writers other than "travelers and travel writers."

ARTISTS

Arago, Jacques
Atkinson, Thomas Wittlam
Baines, Thomas
Bauer, Ferdinand Lucas
Bodmer, Karl
Catlin, George
Choris, Louis
Kane, Paul
Kern, Richard Hovendon
Kurz, Rudolph Friederich
Le Moyne de Morgues, Jacques
Mee, Margaret Ursula
Miller, Alfred Jacob
Roerich, Nikolay Konstantinovich
Warre, Henry James
Webber, John
Westall, William
White, John

AVIATORS, ASTRONAUTS, AND COSMONAUTS

Andrée, Salomon August
Armstrong, Neil Alden

Byrd, Richard Evelyn
Ellsworth, Lincoln
Gagarin, Yury Alekseyevich
Glenn, John Herschell, Jr.
Leonov, Alexei Arkhipovich
Nobile, Umberto
Piccard, Auguste
Ride, Sally Kristen
Shepard, Alan Bartlett, Jr.
Tereshkova, Valentina Vladimirovna
White, Edward Higgens, II
Wilkins, Sir George Hubert

COLONISTS AND PIONEERS

Alfinger, Ambrosius
Applegate, Jesse
Arthur, Gabriel
Ayllón, Lucas Vásquez de
Batts, Thomas
Beutler, August
Blaxland, Gregory
Bozeman, John Merin
Burke, Robert O'Hara

Cabral, Gonçalo Velho
Colenso, William
Eiríksdottir, Freydis
Escandón, José de
Eyre, Sir Edward John
Fallam, Robert
Federmann, Nikolaus
Hohermuth von Speyer, Georg
Landsborough, William
Laudonnière, René Goulaine de
Le Moyne, Jean-Baptiste
Needham, James
Oñate, Juan de
Portolá, Gaspar de
Raleigh, Sir Walter
Robertson, James
Roberval, Jean-François de La Roque de
Sinclair, James
Smith, John
Wentworth, William Charles
Williams, William
Winslow, Edward
Woodward, Henry

EXPLORERS
(ONLY OR PRIMARY OCCUPATION)

Amundsen, Roald Engelbregt Gravning
Baker, Florence
Baker, Sir Samuel White
Baumann, Oskar
Binger, Louis-Gustave
Borchgrevink, Carsten Egeberg
Boyd, Louise Arner
Bruce, James
Bruce, William Spiers
Burton, Sir Richard Francis
Caillié, René-Auguste
Charcot, Jean-Baptiste-Étienne-Auguste
Cook, Frederick Albert
Courtauld, Augustine
Crevaux, Jules-Nicolas
Drygalski, Erich Dagobert von
Duveyrier, Henri
Espejo, Antonio Estevan de
Forrest, Alexander
Forrest, John
Fuchs, Sir Vivian Ernest
García, Alejo
Giles, Ernest
Gordon, Robert
Hall, Charles Francis
Hayes, Isaac Israel
Hedin, Sven Anders

Henson, Matthew Alexander
Hoehnel, Ludwig von
Hornemann, Friedrich Conrad
Hovell, William Hilton
Hume, Hamilton
Jackson, Frederick George
Junker, Wilhelm Johann
Kennedy, Edmund
Koldewey, Karl Christian
Lander, Richard Lemon
Lederer, John
Lenz, Oskar
Mylius-Erichsen, Ludwig
Nansen, Fridtjof
Nordenskjöld, Nils Adolf Erik
Park, Mungo
Penha, Joseph de la
Rae, John
Schwatka, Frederick
Shackleton, Sir Ernest Henry
Shirase, Nobu
Speke, John Hanning
Stanley, Sir Henry Morton
Teleki, Samuel
Tinné, Alexandrine Petronella Francina

GUIDES AND INTERPRETERS

Black Beaver
Boone, Daniel
Bombay, Sidi
Carson, Christopher Houston
Charbonneau, Jean-Baptiste
Charbonneau, Toussaint
Donnaconna
Dorion, Marie
Dorion, Pierre, Jr.
Dorion, Pierre, Sr.
Drouillard, George
Estevanico
Guancanagari
Irateba
Jusseaume, René
Kenton, Simon
Malinche
Matonabbee
Pascoe, William
Rose, Edward
Sacajawea
Smith, James
Squanto
Turk
Vial, Pedro
Weiser, Conrad

MARINERS

(see also MILITARY—NAVAL)

Adams, William
Álvarez de Pineda, Alonso
Baffin, William
Bakhov, Ivan
Baldaya, Afonso Gonçalves
Barents, Willem
Batakov, Anton
Begichev, Nikifor Alekseyevich
Bekovich-Cherkassky, Aleksandr
Bering, Vitus Jonassen
Bernier, Joseph Elzéar
Berrío, Antonio de
Billings, Joseph
Biscoe, John
Block, Adriaen
Bocharov, Dmitry Ivanovich
Borough, Stephen
Borough, William
Brunel, Olivier
Bylot, Robert
Cabot, John
Cabot, Sebastian
Cabral, Pedro Álvars
Cabrillo, Juan Rodríguez
Cadamosto, Alvise da
Cano, Juan Sebastián del
Cão, Diogo
Cartier, Jacques
Cermenho, Sebastián Meléndez Rodríguez
Chancellor, Richard
Chelyuskin, Simeon
Columbus, Christopher
Côrte-Real, Gaspar
Côrte-Real, Miguel
Cosa, Juan de la
Dallman, Eduard
Dampier, William
Davis, John
Dias, Bartolomeu
Dias, Dinís
Díaz de Solís, Juan de
Diogenes
Drake, Sir Francis
Eannes, Gil
Ericsson, Leif
Ericsson, Thorvald
Eric the Red
Etholen, Arvid Adolf
Eudoxus
Fanning, Edmund
Fernandes, Álvaro

Fernandes, João
Ferrelo, Bartolomé
Foxe, Luke
Frobisher, Sir Martin
Fuca, Juan de
Gama, Vasco da
Gomes, Diogo
Gomes, Estevão
Gosnold, Bartholomew
Gray, Robert
Hall, James
Hannu
Hartog, Dirk
Hawkins, Sir John
Herjulfsson, Bjarni
Himilco
Hippalus
Houtman, Cornelius
Houtman, Frederik
Hudson, Henry
Izmailov, Gerasim Alekseyevich
James, Thomas
Jansz, Willem
Jörgenson, Jörgen
Jourdain, John
Jourdain, Silvester
Karlsefni, Thorfinn
Kashevarov, Aleksandr Filippovich
Kerguélen-Trémarec, Yves-Joseph de
Knight, John
Krenitsyn, Pyotr Kuzmich
Kupe
Lancaster, Sir James
Ledyard, John
Legazpi, Miguel López de
Le Maire, Jakob
Magellan, Ferdinand
Mendaña, Álvaro de
Middleton, Christopher
Moor, William
Munk, Jens Eriksen
Naddod
Nearchus
Newport, Christopher
Niebuhr, Sigismund
Niño, Andrés
Noort, Oliver van
Pacheco, Duarte
Palmer, Nathaniel Brown
Pinzón, Arias Martín
Pinzón, Francisco Martín
Pinzón, Martín Alonso
Pinzón, Vicente Yáñez

Popham, George
Pribylov, Gavrilo Loginovich
Pring, Martin
Quirós, Pedro Fernández de
Roe, Sir Thomas
Roggeveen, Jakob
Rut, John
Saavedra Cerón, Álvaro de
Schouten, Willem Cornelis
Scoresby, William, Jr.
Scoresby, William, Sr.
Scylax
Selkirk, Alexander
Sequira, Diego López de
Serrano, Francisco
Svarsson, Gardar
Sverdrup, Otto Neumann
Tasman, Abel Janszoon
Thyssen, François
Torres, Luis Váez de
Tristão, Nuño
Ulloa, Francisco de
Urdaneta, Andrés de
Verrazano, Giovanni da
Vespucci, Amerigo
Viscaíno, Sebastián
Vivaldi, Ugolino
Weddell, James
Weymouth, George
Willoughby, Sir Hugh

MERCHANTS AND TRADERS

General

Aco, Michel
Adair, James
Anabara, Semyon
Ashley, William Henry
Astor, John Jacob
Baranov, Aleksandr Andreyevich
Bashmakov, Pyotr
Basov, Emelyan
Bent, Charles
Bent, William
Boller, Henry A.
Bourgmont, Étienne-Veniard de
Campbell, Robert (Scottish)
Chisholm, Jesse
Chouart des Groseilliers, Médard
Chouteau, Auguste Pierre
Chouteau, Jean Pierre
Chouteau, Pierre
Chouteau, René Auguste
Conti, Niccolò di

Cooper, Thomas Thornville
Cresap, Thomas
Croghan, George
Dease, Peter Warren
Dubuque, Julien
Duluth, Daniel Greysolon
Dupuis, Jean
Finley, John
Fitch, Ralph
Franchère, Gabriel
Fraser, Simon
Gist, Christopher
Glazunov, Andrey
Gomes, Fernão
Hearne, Samuel
Henday, Anthony
Henry, Alexander (the elder)
Henry, Alexander (the younger)
Hunt, Wilson Price
Ibn Rusta, Abu Ali Ahmad
Jolliet, Louis
Kelsey, Henry
Khabarov, Yerofey Pavlovich
Kittson, Norman Wolfred
Knight, James
Laclede, Pierre Ligueste
La Harpe, Jean-Baptiste Bénard de
La Salle, René-Robert Cavelier de
La Vérendrye, Louis-Joseph Gaultier de
La Vérendrye, Pierre Gaultier de Varennes de
Le Sueur, Pierre-Charles
Lisa, Manuel
Mackenzie, Sir Alexander
Mackenzie, Donald
Mallet, Pierre-Antoine
McKenzie, Kenneth
McLoughlin, John
Menard, Antoine Pierre
Newberry, John
Nicolet, Jean
Ogden, Peter Skene
Perrot, Nicolas
Polo, Maffeo
Polo, Marco
Polo, Niccolò
Pond, Peter
Popov, Fyodot Alekseyev
Radisson, Pierre-Esprit
Ross, Alexander
Sable, Jean Baptist Point
St. Denis, Louis Juchereau de
St. Vrain, Céran de Hault de Lassus de
Saris, John
Shelikov, Grigory Ivanovich

Silva Porto, Antonio Francisco da
Simpson, Sir George
Simpson, Thomas
Soleyman
Stuart, Robert
Thompson, David
Tonti, Henri de
Truteau, Jean-Baptiste
Viele, Arnaud Cornelius
Work, John
Wyeth, Nathaniel Jarvis

Mountain Men
(Fur Traders and Trappers in Rocky Mountains and American West)

Álvarez, Manuel
Baker, James
Becknell, William
Beckwourth, James Pierson
Bridger, James
Campbell, Robert (American)
Chatillon, Henri
Clyman, James
Colter, John
Ferris, Warren Angus
Fitzpatrick, Thomas
Fontenelle, Lucien
Fowler, Jacob
Fraeb, Henry
Glass, Hugh
Greenwood, Caleb
Hamilton, William Thomas
Henry, Andrew
Jackson, David E.
Larpenteur, Charles
Leonard, Zenas
Meek, Joseph L.
Newell, Robert
Pattie, James Ohio
Pilcher, Joshua
Provost, Étienne
Robidoux, Antoine
Russell, Osborne
Smith, Jedediah Strong
Sublette, William Lewis
Vanderburgh, William Henry
Vasquez, Louis
Walker, Joseph Reddeford
Weber, John H.
Williams, William Sherley
Wolfskill, William
Wootton, Richens Lacy
Young, Ewing
Yount, George Concepcion

MILITARY

General
AMERICAN
Abbott, Henry Larcom
Abert, James William
Allen, Henry Tureman
Atkinson, Henry
Beckwith, Edward Griffin
Bonneville, Benjamin Louis Eulalie de
Clark, William
Dodge, Henry
Emory, William Hemsley
Frémont, John Charles
Greely, Adolphus Washington
Gunnison, John Williams
Ives, Joseph Christmas
Kearny, Stephen Watts
Leavenworth, Henry
Lewis, Meriwether
Long, Stephen Harriman
Macomb, John N.
Marcy, Randolph Barnes
Parke, John Grubb
Pike, Zebulon Montgomery
Pope, John B.
Raynolds, William Franklin
Rogers, Robert
Simpson, James Hervey
Sitgreaves, Lorenzo
Stanley, David Sloan
Stansbury, Howard
Wheeler, George Montague
Whipple, Amiel Weeks
Young, Charles Denton

AUSTRIAN
Payer, Julius von
Weyprecht, Karl

BRITISH
Carver, Jonathan
Chaillé-Long, Charles
Denham, Dixon
Fawcett, Percy Harrison
Grant, James Augustus
Hearsey, Hyder Jung
Houghton, Daniel
Laing, Alexander Gordon
Lawrence, Thomas Edward
McLeod, William C.
Pottinger, Sir Henry
Sadlier, George Foster
Turner, Samuel
Vavasour, Mervin

Warburton, Peter Egerton
Younghusband, Sir Francis Edward

FRENCH

Brûlé, Étienne
Champlain, Samuel de
Flatters, Paul-Xavier
Joutel, Henri
Lahontan, Louis-Armand de Lom d'Arce de
Marchand, Jean-Baptiste
Rohlfs, Friedrich Gerhard

GERMAN

Filchner, Wilhelm
Hutten, Philip von
Wissmann, Hermann von

GREEK AND MACEDONIAN

Alexander the Great
Xenophon

MONGOL

Genghis Khan

PORTUGUESE

Teixeira, Pedro de

ROMAN

Agricola, Gnaeus Julius
Caesar, Gaius Julius
Gallus, Gaius Aeilius
Maternus, Julius
Paulinus, Suetonius

RUSSIAN

Andreyev, Stepan
Atlasov, Vladimir Vasilyevich
Beketov, Pyotr
Bukhgolts, Ivan Dmitryevich
Daurkin, Nikolay
Dezhnev, Semyon Ivanovich
Morozko, Luka
Poyarkov, Vasily Danilovich
Stadukhin, Mikhail
Yermak

SPANISH

Aguirre, Lope de
Alarcón, Hernando de
Almagro, Diego de
Alvarado, Hernando de
Alvarado, Pedro de
Anza, Juan Bautista de
Ávila, Pedro Arias de
Ayolas, Juan de
Bastidas, Rodrigo de
Benalcázar, Sebastián Moyano de
Cabeza de Vaca, Álvar Núñez
Coronado, Francisco Vásquez de
Cortés, Hernán

Díaz, Melchor
Díaz del Castillo, Bernal
Erauso, Catalina de
Fernández de Córdoba, Francisco (in Yúcatan)
Fernández de Córdoba, Francisco (in Panama/Nicaragua)
Garay, Juan de
Grijalva, Juan de
Guzmán, Nuño Beltrán de
Ibarra, Francisco de
Jiménez de Quesada, Gonzalo
León, Alonso de
López de Cárdenas, García
Martínez de Irala, Domingo
Mendoza, Pedro de
Montejo, Francisco de
Montejo y León, Francisco de
Moscoso, Luis de
Narváez, Pánfilo de
Nicuesa, Diego de
Núñez de Balboa, Vasco
Ojeda, Alonso de
Ordaz, Diego de
Orellana, Francisco de
Pizarro, Francisco
Pizarro, Gonzalo
Pizarro, Hernando
Ponce de León, Juan
Rivera y Villalón, Pedro de
Soto, Hernando de
Tovar, Pedro de
Ursúa, Pedro de
Valdivia, Pedro de
Velásquez, Diego

Naval

AMERICAN

De Haven, Edwin Jesse
De Long, George Washington
Emmons, George Foster
Kane, Elisha Kent
Peary, Robert Edwin
Wilkes, Charles

BELGIAN

Gerlache de Gomery, Adrien-Victor-Joseph de

BRITISH

Anson, George
Back, Sir George
Bass, George
Beechey, Frederick William
Belcher, Sir Edward
Bligh, William
Bransfield, Edward

Broughton, William Robert
Buchan, David
Burney, James
Button, Sir Thomas
Byron, John
Cameron, Verney Lovett
Carteret, Philip
Clapperton, Hugh
Clerke, Charles
Collinson, Sir Richard
Cook, James
Crozier, Francis Rawdon Moira
Fitzroy, Robert
Flinders, Matthew
Franklin, Sir John
Furneaux, Tobias
Gore, John
Grenville, Sir Richard
Hood, Robert
King, James
King, Philip Parker
Lyon, George Francis
McClintock, Sir Francis Leopold
McClure, Sir Robert John le Mesurier
Musters, George Chaworth
Nares, Sir George Strong
Parry, Sir William Edward
Phillip, Arthur
Phipps, Constantine John
Ross, Sir James Clark
Ross, Sir John
Scott, Robert Falcon
Vancouver, George
Wallis, Samuel
Wellsted, James

CARTHAGINIAN
Hanno

CHINESE
Cheng Ho

FRENCH
Auribeau, Alexandre Hesmivy d'
Baudin, Thomas-Nicolas
Bougainville, Hyacinthe-Yves-Philippe Potentien de
Bougainville, Louis-Antoine de
Bouvet de Lozier, Jean-Baptiste-Charles
Bruni, Antoine-Raymond-Joseph de
Chesnard de la Giraudais, François
Doudart de Lagrée, Ernest-Marc-Louis de Gonzague
Duclos-Guyot, Pierre-Nicolas
Dumont d'Urville, Jules-Sébastien-César
Duperrey, Louis-Isadore
Dupetit-Thouars, Abel-Aubert
Fleuriot de Langlé, Paul-Antoine-Marie

Freycinet, Louis-Claude de Saulces de
Galaup, Jean-François de
Huon de Kermadec, Jean-Michel
Jacquinot, Charles-Hector
Le Moyne, Pierre
Ribault, Jean
Rossel, Elisabeth-Paul-Edouard de

PORTUGUESE
Albuquerque, Afonso de
Almeida, Francisco de
Almeida, Lourenço de

RUSSIAN
Basargin, Grigory Gavrilovich
Bellingshausen, Fabian Gottlieb Benjamin von
Chirikov, Aleksey Ilyich
Davydov, Gavriil Ivanovich
Golovnin, Vasily Mikhailovich
Kotzebue, Otto von
Krusenstern, Adam Ivan Ritter von
Lazarev, Mikhail Petrovich
Lisiansky, Yury Fyodorovich
Litke, Fyodor Petrovich
Nevelskoy, Gennady Ivanovich
Sarychev, Gavriil Andreyevich
Zagoskin, Lavrenty Alekseyevich

SPANISH
Andagoya, Pascual de
Bodega y Quadra, Juan Francisco de la
Heceta, Bruno
Malaspina, Alessandro
Menéndez de Avilés, Pedro
Pérez Hernández, Juan Josef

MISSIONARIES AND RELIGIOUS LEADERS
(see also SCHOLARS—RELIGIOUS SCHOLARS)
Acosta, José de
Acuña, Cristóbal de
Albanel, Charles
Allouez, Claude-Jean
Álvares, Francisco
Andrade, Antonio de
Arculf
Azevado, Francisco de
Bar Sauma, Rabban
Benavides, Alonzo de
Benjamin of Tudela
Brébeuf, Jean de
Bréhant de Galinée, René de
Brendan, Saint
Bressani, Francesco-Gioseppe
Bruyas, Jacques
Cabral, João
Cacella, Estevão

Campbell, John
Carpini, Giovanni da Pian del
Davion, Albert
Desideri, Ippolito
De Smet, Pierre-Jean
Dollier de Casson, François
Domínguez, Francisco Atanasio
Egede, Hans
Escalante, Francisco Silvestre Vélez de
Fritz, Samuel
Garcés, Francisco Tomás Hermenegildo
Gibault, Pierre
Góes, Bento de
Grenfell, George
Grueber, Johann
Hennepin, Louis
Huc, Évariste-Régis
Jogues, Isaac
John of Montecorvino
Kino, Eusebio Francisco
Krapf, Johann Ludwig
Lalemant, Gabriel
Le Moyne, Simon
Livingstone, David
Lobo, Jerónimo
Marignolli, Giovanni de
Marquette, Jacques
Marsden, Samuel
Ménard, René
Moffat, Mary
Moffat, Robert
Niza, Marcos de
Noué, Charles-Edouard de la
Odoric of Pordenone
Orville, Albert d'
Padilla, Juan de
Páez, Pedro
Palgrave, William Gifford
Rebmann, Johann
Ricci, Matteo
Richardson, James
Serra, Junípero
Spalding, Henry Harmon
Stevens, Thomas
Taylor, Annie Royle
Whitman, Marcus
William of Rubrouck
Xavier, Francis
Young, Brigham

MOUNTAIN CLIMBERS

Abruzzi, Luigi Amedeo di Savoia
Balmat, Jacques

Hillary, Sir Edmund Percival
Mallory, George Herbert Leigh
Meyer, Hans
Peck, Annie Smith
Schlagintweit, Adolf von
Schlagintweit, Hermann von
Schlagintweit, Robert von
Stuck, Hudson
Tenzing Norgay
Whymper, Edward
Workman, Fanny Bullock
Zurbriggen, Matthias

POLITICAL LEADERS, OFFICIALS, AND DIPLOMATS

Arias de Saavedra, Hernando
Baptista, Pedro João
Barrow, Sir John
Bogle, George
Brazza, Pierre-Paul-François-Camille Savorgnan de
Brydges, Harford Jones
Burnes, Sir Alexander
Chang Ch'ien
Clavijo, Ruy González de
Covilhã, Pero da
Elias, Ney
Emin Pasha, Mehmed
Fernández de Oviedo y Valdez, Gonzalo
Garnier, Marie-Joseph-François
Grey, Sir George
Hatshepsut
Henry the Navigator
Herkhuf
Jenkinson, Anthony
Johnston, Sir Harry Hamilton
Kaempfer, Engelbrecht
Kan Ying
Lacerda, Francisco de
La Mothe, Antoine Laumet de
Langford, Nathaniel Pitt
Leo Africanus
Lesseps, Jean-Baptiste-Barthélemy de
Megasthenes
Mendoza, Antonio de
Mitchell, Sir Thomas Livingstone
Nachtigal, Gustav
Necho II
Oxley, John Joseph William Molesworth
Pavie, Auguste-Jean-Marie
Perrin du Lac, François-Marie
Philby, Harry St. John Bridger
Pires, Tomé
Sargon

Sherley, Sir Anthony
Spotswood, Alexander
Sturt, Charles
Sykes, Sir Percy Molesworth
Thomas, Bertram Sydney
Viale, Agostinho
Wood, Abraham

SCHOLARS

Archaeologists
Bell, Gertrude Margaret Lowthian
Bent, James Theodore
Stein, Sir Marc Aurel

Anthropologists
Heyerdahl, Thor
Rasmussen, Knud Johan Victor
Stefansson, Vilhjalmur

Astronomers
Hipparchus
Holywood, John
Nicollet, Joseph Nicolas
Schmidt, Otto Y.

Geographers and Cartographers
Anville, Jean-Baptiste Bourguignon d'
Barth, Heinrich
Beatus of Valcavado
Beautemps-Beaupré, Charles-François
Behaim, Martin
Biruni, Abu ar-Rayhan Muhammad ibn Ahmad al-
Blaeu, Willem Janszoon
Brosses, Charles de
Chu Ssu-pen
Cresques, Abraham
Eratosthenes
Galton, Sir Francis
Gilbert, Sir Humphrey
Gutiérrez, Diego
Hakluyt, Richard
Idrisi, Abu Abd Allah Muhammad ash-Sharif al-
Indicopleustes, Cosmas
Kropotkin, Peter
Linschoten, Jan Huyghen van
Llewellyn, Martin
Mercator, Gerardus
Ortelius, Abraham
Petermann, August Heinrich
Pliny the Elder
Ptolemy
Pytheas
Semyonov, Pyotr Petrovich

Strabo
Waldseemüller, Martin
Yaqut al-Rumi, Shihab al-Din Abu Abd Allah

Geologists
Hind, Henry Youle
Mawson, Sir Douglas
Newberry, John Strong
Nordenskjöld, Nils Otto Gustaf
Overweg, Adolf
Powell, John Wesley
Richthofen, Ferdinand Paul Wilhelm von
Schoolcraft, Henry Rowe
Strzelecki, Sir Paul Edmund
Thomson, Joseph
Toll, Eduard von
Wegener, Alfred Lothar

Historians
Bingham, Hiram
Burckhardt, Johann Ludwig
Charlevoix, Pierre-François-Xavier de
Hecataeus of Miletus
Herodotus
Masudi, Abu al-Hasan Ali al-
Tsybikov, Gombozhab

Linguists
Vambéry, Armin

Naturalists (including Botanists and Zoologists)
Akeley, Carl Ethan
Akeley, Delia Denning
Akeley, Mary Leonore Jobe
Audubon, John James
Azara, Félix de
Baikie, William Balfour
Banks, Sir Joseph
Bartram, John
Bartram, William
Bates, Henry Walter
Berlandier, Jean-Louis
Bradbury, John
Brown, Robert
Burchell, William John
Catesby, Mark
Chamisso de Boncourt, Louis-Charles-Adélaïde
Commerson, Joseph-Philibert
Cunningham, Allan
Dana, James Dwight
Darwin, Charles Robert
Dietrich, Koncordie Amalie Nelle
Eschscholtz, Johann Friedrich
Fedchenko, Aleksey Pavlovich

Fedchenko, Olga
Ferreira, Alexandre Rodrigues
Forbes, Edward
Forster, Johann Georg Adam
Forster, Johann Reinhold
Gaimard, Joseph-Paul
Gaudichaud-Beaupré, Charles
Gmelin, Johann Georg
Harriot, Thomas
Hooker, Sir Joseph Dalton
Humboldt, Alexander von
Kern, Benjamin Jordan
Krasheninnikov, Stepan Petrovich
La Billardière, Jacques-Julien Houtou de
La Condamine, Charles-Marie de
Langsdorff, Georg Heinrich Ritter von
Leichhardt, Friedrich Wilhelm Ludwig
Lesson, René-Primevère
Lesueur, Charles-Alexandre
Martius, Carl Friedrich Phillipp von
Maximilian, Alexander Philipp
Mertens, Karl Heinrich
Messerschmidt, Daniel Gottlieb
Moorcroft, William
Moreno, Francisco
Mouhot, Henri
Muir, John
Nuttall, Thomas
Orbigny, Alcide-Charles-Victor Dessalines d'
Oudney, Walter
Pavy, Octave
Péron, François
Porte, François de la
Przhevalsky, Nikolay Mikhailovich
Quoy, Jean-René-Constant
Richardson, Sir John
Riche, Claude-Antoine-Gaspard
Schomburgk, Sir Robert Hermann
Schweinfurth, Georg August
Solander, Daniel Carl
Sparrman, Anders
Spruce, Richard
Steller, Georg Wilhelm
Thomson, Sir Charles Wyville
Thunberg, Carl Peter
Tschudi, Johann Jakob von
Wallace, Alfred Russel
Wilson, Edward Adrian

Oceanographers
Beebe, Charles William
Cousteau, Jacques-Yves
Marsili, Luigi Ferdinando

Maury, Matthew Fontaine
Piccard, Jacques Ernest-Jean

Religious Scholars
Ch'ang-ch'un
Fa-hsien
Hsüan-tsang
Ibn Battutah, Abu Abd Allah Muhammad
Ibn Fadlan, Ahmad
Ibn Hawqal, Abu al-Qasim ibn Ali al-Nasibi
Ibn Jubayr, Abu al-Hasan Muhammad
I-ching

Surveyors and Topographers
Beale, Edward Fitzgerald
Brunner, Thomas
Christie, Charles
Dunbar, Sir William
Everest, Sir George
Foureau, Fernand
Freeman, Thomas
Gosse, William Christie
Gregory, Sir Augustus Charles
Gregory, Francis Thomas
Hayden, Ferdinand Vandeveer
Kern, Edward Meyer
King, Clarence
Kintup
Lawson, John
Niebuhr, Carsten
Palliser, John
Rice, Alexander Hamilton
Sarmiento de Gamboa, Pedro
Singh, Kishen
Singh, Nain
Stuart, John McDouall
Walker, Thomas
Watkins, Henry George
Wills, William John

TRAVELERS AND TRAVEL WRITERS
Adams, Harriet Chalmers
Atkinson, Lucy
Baret, Jeanne
Beltrami, Giacomo Costantino
Bishop, Isabella Lucy Bird
Blunt, Anne Isabella
Blunt, Wilfrid Scawen
Bonin, Charles
Brackenridge, Henry Marie
Cheadle, Walter Butler
Ctesias of Cnidus
David-Néel, Alexandra

Doughty, Charles Montagu
Du Chaillu, Paul Belloni
Eberhardt, Isabelle
Evliya, Çelebi
Fiennes, Celia
Franklin, Jane
Godin des Odanais, Isabela
Herbert, Thomas
Irving, John Treat
Kingsley, Mary Henrietta
Livingstone, Mary Moffat
Manning, Thomas
Mazuchelli, Elizabeth Sarah

Milton, William-Wentworth Fitzwilliam
Pethahia of Regensburg
Pfeiffer, Ida Reyer
Pigafetta, Francesco Antonio
Pinto, Fernão Mendes
Ritchie, Joseph
Sheldon, May French
Stanhope, Hester Lucy
Stark, Freya Madeline
Thesiger, Wilfred Patrick
Varthema, Ludovico di
Wen-chi
Wickham, Sir Henry Alexander

Appendix B
EXPLORERS BY REGION OF ACTIVITY

Note: Certain individuals appear on more than one list.

EUROPE, ICELAND, AND EASTERN ATLANTIC ISLANDS

Agricola, Gnaeus Julius
Balmat, Jacques
Banks, Sir Joseph
Bar Sauma, Rabban
Behaim, Martin
Brendan, Saint
Brunel, Olivier
Cabral, Gonçalo Velho
Caesar, Gaius Julius
Eric the Red
Evliya, Çelebi
Fiennes, Celia
Forbes, Edward
Gore, John
Hecataeus of Miletus
Herodotus
Himilco
Ibn Battutah, Abu Abd Allah Muhammad
Ibn Fadlan, Ahmad
Ibn Hawqal, Abu al-Qasim ibn Ali al-Nasibi
Ibn Jubayr, Abu al-Hasan Muhammad
Ibn Rusta, Abu Ali Ahmad
Idrisi, Abu Abd Allah Muhammad ash-Sharif al-
Jenkinson, Anthony
Jörgenson, Jörgen

Kropotkin, Peter
Masudi, Abu al-Hasan Ali al-Naddod
Paulinus, Suetonius
Peck, Annie Smith
Pethahia of Regensburg
Pfeiffer, Ida Reyer
Pytheas
Sargon
Squanto
Stefansson, Vilhjalmur
Strabo
Svarsson, Gardar
Whymper, Edward
Zurbriggen, Matthias

NORTH AFRICA

Alexander the Great
Arculf
Barth, Heinrich
Blunt, Anne Isabella
Blunt, Wilfrid Scawen
Burckhardt, Johann Ludwig
Clapperton, Hugh
Covilhã, Pero da
Denham, Dixon
Duveyrier, Henri

Eberhardt, Isabelle
Evliya, Çelebi
Flatters, Paul-Xavier
Foureau, Fernand
Gallus, Gaius Aelius
Hecataeus of Miletus
Herodotus
Hornemann, Friedrich Conrad
Ibn Battutah, Abu Abd Allah Muhammad
Ibn Hawqal, Abu al-Qasim ibn Ali al-Nasibi
Ibn Jubayr, Abu al-Hasan Muhammad
Idrisi, Abu Abd Allah Muhammad ash-Sharif al-
Indicopleustes, Cosmas
Leo Africanus
Lyon, George Francis
Masudi, Abu al-Hasan Ali al-
Maternus, Julius
Nachtigal, Gustav
Oudney, Walter
Overweg, Adolf
Paulinus, Suetonius
Richardson, James
Ritchie, Joseph
Rohlfs, Friedrich Gerhard
Sherley, Sir Anthony
Stark, Freya Madeline
Strabo
Tinné, Alexandrine Petronella Francina
Workman, Fanny Bullock

COASTAL AFRICA

Albuquerque, Afonso de
Almeida, Francisco de
Baldaya, Afonso Gonçalves
Beechey, Frederick William
Belcher, Sir Edward
Cadamosto, Alvise da
Cão, Diogo
Cheng Ho
Covilhã, Pero da
Dias, Bartolomeu
Dias, Dinís
Eannes, Gil
Eudoxus
Fernandes, Álvaro
Gama, Vasco da
Gomes, Diogo
Gomes, Fernão
Hanno
Hannu
Indicopleustes, Cosmas
Masudi, Abu al-Hasan Ali al-
Pacheco, Duarte

Tristão, Nuño
Vivaldi, Ugolino

SUB-SAHARAN AFRICA

Abruzzi, Luigi Amedeo di Savoia d'
Akeley, Carl Ethan
Akeley, Delia Denning
Akeley, Mary Leonore Jobe
Álvares, Francisco
Baikie, William Balfour
Baines, Thomas
Baker, Florence
Baker, Sir Samuel White
Baptista, Pedro João
Barth, Heinrich
Baumann, Oskar
Bent, James Theodore
Beutler, August
Binger, Louis-Gustave
Bombay, Sidi
Brazza, Pierre-Paul-François-Camille Savorgnan de
Bruce, James
Burchell, William John
Burton, Sir Richard Francis
Cadamosto, Alvise da
Caillié, René-Auguste
Cameron, Verney Lovett
Campbell, John
Chaillé-Long, Charles
Clapperton, Hugh
Denham, Dixon
Diogenes
Du Chaillu, Paul Belloni
Emin Pasha, Mehmed
Foureau, Fernand
Fuchs, Sir Vivian Ernest
Galton, Sir Francis
Gordon, Robert
Grant, James Augustus
Grenfell, George
Herkhuf
Hoehnel, Ludwig von
Hornemann, Friedrich Conrad
Houghton, Daniel
Ibn Battutah, Abu Abd Allah Muhammad
Ibn Hawqal, Abu al-Qasim ibn Ali al-Nasibi
Johnston, Sir Harry Hamilton
Junker, Wilhelm Johann
Kingsley, Mary Henrietta
Krapf, Johann Ludwig
Lacerda, Francisco de
Laing, Alexander Gordon
Lander, Richard Lemon

Lenz, Oskar
Leo Africanus
Livingstone, David
Livingstone, Mary Moffat
Lobo, Jerónimo
Marchand, Jean-Baptiste
Meyer, Hans
Moffat, Mary
Moffat, Robert
Nachtigal, Gustav
Oudney, Walter
Overweg, Adolf
Páez, Pedro
Park, Mungo
Pascoe, William
Rebmann, Johann
Richardson, James
Schweinfurth, Georg August
Sheldon, May French
Silva Porto, Antonio Francisco da
Sparrman, Anders
Speke, John Hanning
Stanley, Sir Henry Morton
Teleki, Samuel
Thomson, Joseph
Tinné, Alexandrine Petronella Francina
Thunberg, Carl Peter
Wissmann, Hermann von
Young, Charles Denton

Near East

Alexander the Great
Arculf
Bar Sauma, Rabban
Bell, Gertrude Margaret Lowthian
Benjamin of Tudela
Bent, James Theodore
Bishop, Isabella Lucy Bird
Blunt, Anne Isabella
Blunt, Wilfrid Scawen
Brydges, Harford Jones
Burckhardt, Johann Ludwig
Burton, Sir Richard Francis
Cabot, John
Cheng Ho
Christie, Charles
Conti, Niccolò di
Covilhã, Pero da
Ctesias of Cnidus
Doughty, Charles Montagu
Evliya, Çelebi
Franklin, Jane
Gallus, Gaius Aelius

Grueber, Johann
Hannu
Hecataeus of Miletus
Herbert, Thomas
Herodotus
Ibn Battutah, Abu Abd Allah Muhammad
Ibn Hawqal, Abu al-Qasim ibn Ali al-Nasibi
Ibn Jubayr, Abu al-Hasan Muhammad
Ibn Rusta, Abu Ali Ahmad
Idrisi, Abu Abd Allah Muhammad ash-Sharif al-
John of Montecorvino
Kan Ying
Lawrence, Thomas Edward
Leo Africanus
Nearchus
Newberry, John
Niebuhr, Carsten
Palgrave, William Gifford
Pethahia of Regensburg
Pfeiffer, Ida Reyer
Philby, Harry St. John Bridger
Pottinger, Sir Henry
Sadlier, George Foster
Sargon
Scylax
Sherley, Sir Anthony
Stanhope, Hester Lucy
Stark, Freya Madeline
Strabo
Sykes, Sir Percy Molesworth
Thesiger, Wilfred Patrick
Thomas, Bertram Sydney
Varthema, Ludovico di
Wellsted, James
Xenophon
Yaqut al-Rumi, Shihab al-Din Abu Abd Allah

Central Asia and the Indian Subcontinent

Abruzzi, Luigi Amedeo di Savoia d'
Albuquerque, Afonso d'
Alexander the Great
Almeida, Francisco de
Almeida, Lourenço de
Andrade, Antonio de
Atkinson, Lucy
Atkinson, Thomas Wittlam
Azevado, Francisco de
Basargin, Grigory Gavrilovich
Bekovich-Cherkassky, Aleksandr
Benjamin of Tudela
Biruni, Abu ar-Rayhan Muhammad ibn Ahmad al-
Bishop, Isabella Lucy Bird

Bogle, George
Bonin, Charles
Brydges, Harford Jones
Bukhgolts, Ivan Dmitryevich
Burnes, Sir Alexander
Burton, Sir Richard Francis
Cabral, João
Cabral, Pedro Álvars
Cacella, Estavão
Carpini, Giovanni da Pian del
Chang Ch'ien
Ch'ang-ch'un
Cheng Ho
Christie, Charles
Clavijo, Ruy González de
Conti, Niccolò di
Cooper, Thomas Thornville
Covilhã, Pero da
Ctesias of Cnidus
David-Néel, Alexandra
Desideri, Ippolito
Elias, Ney
Eudoxus
Everest, Sir George
Fa-hsien
Fedchenko, Aleksey Pavlovich
Fedchenko, Olga
Filchner, Wilhelm
Fitch, Ralph
Gama, Vasco da
Genghis Khan
Gmelin, Johann Georg
Góes, Bento de
Grueber, Johann
Hearsey, Hyder Jung
Hedin, Sven Anders
Hippalus
Hillary, Sir Edmund Percival
Hooker, Sir Joseph Dalton
Hsüan-tsang
Huc, Évariste-Régis
Humboldt, Alexander von
Ibn Battutah, Abu Abd Allah Muhammad
I-ching
Indicopleustes, Cosmas
Jenkinson, Anthony
John of Montecorvino
Jourdain, John
Kan Ying
Kintup
Krasheninnikov, Stepan Petrovich
Leo Africanus
Linschoten, Jan Huyghen van

Mallory, George Herbert Leigh
Manning, Thomas
Marignolli, Giovanni de
Masudi, Abu al-Hasan Ali al-
Mazuchelli, Elizabeth Sarah
Megasthenes
Messerschmidt, Daniel Gottlieb
Moorcroft, William
Nearchus
Newberry, John
Odoric of Pordenone
Orville, Albert d'
Pacheco, Duarte
Pfeiffer, Ida Reyer
Polo, Maffeo
Polo, Marco
Polo, Niccolò
Pottinger, Sir Henry
Przhevalsky, Nikolay Mikhailovich
Ricci, Matteo
Roe, Sir Thomas
Roerich, Nikolay Konstantinovich
Schlagintweit, Adolf von
Schlagintweit, Hermann von
Schlagintweit, Robert von
Scylax
Semyonov, Pyotr Petrovich
Sequira, Diego López de
Singh, Kishen
Singh, Nain
Soleyman
Stark, Freya Madeline
Stein, Sir Marc Aurel
Stevens, Thomas
Strabo
Taylor, Annie Royle
Tenzing Norgay
Tsybikov, Gombozhab
Turner, Samuel
Vambéry, Armin
Varthema, Ludovico di
William of Rubrouck
Workman, Fanny Bullock
Xavier, Francis
Yermak
Younghusband, Sir Francis Edward
Zurbriggen, Matthias

FAR EAST AND SIBERIA

Adams, William
Albuquerque, Afonso d'
Anabara, Semyon
Anson, George

Atlasov, Vladimir Vasilyevich
Auribeau, Alexandre Hesmivy d'
Baranov, Aleksandr Andreyevich
Basov, Emelyan
Batakov, Anton
Baudin, Thomas-Nicolas
Beechey, Frederick William
Beketov, Pyotr
Bering, Vitus Jonassen
Billings, Joseph
Bishop, Isabella Lucy Bird
Bonin, Charles
Broughton, William Robert
Cano, Juan Sebastián del
Chaillé-Long, Charles
Chamisso de Boncourt, Louis-Charles-Adélaïde
Chirikov, Aleksey Ilyich
Choris, Louis
Clerke, Charles
Conti, Niccolò di
Cook, James
Daurkin, Nikolay
David-Néel, Alexandra
Davydov, Gavriil Ivanovich
Dezhnev, Semyon Ivanovich
Doudart de Lagrée, Ernest-Marc-Louis de Gonzague
Dupuis, Jean
Etholen, Arvid Adolf
Fitch, Ralph
Galaup, Jean-François de
Garnier, Marie-Joseph-François
Gmelin, Johann Georg
Góes, Bento de
Golovnin, Vasily Mikhailovich
Grueber, Johann
Houtman, Cornelius
Houtman, Frederik
Ibn Battutah, Abu Abd Allah Muhammad
Ibn Rusta, Abu Ali Ahmad
I-ching
Izmailov, Gerasim Alekseyevich
John of Montecorvino
Jourdain, John
Kaempfer, Engelbrecht
Khabarov, Yerofey Pavlovich
Krasheninnikov, Stepan Petrovich
Kropotkin, Peter
Krusenstern, Adam Ivan Ritter von
Lancaster, Sir James
Langsdorff, Georg Heinrich Ritter von
Ledyard, John
Lesseps, Jean-Baptiste-Barthélemy de
Linschoten, Jan Huyghen van

Magellan, Ferdinand
Marignolli, Giovanni de
Masudi, Abu al-Hasan Ali al-
McLeod, William C.
Mertens, Karl Heinrich
Messerschmidt, Daniel Gottlieb
Morozko, Luka
Mouhot, Henri
Nevelskoy, Gennady Ivanovich
Newport, Christopher
Odoric of Pordenone
Orville, Albert d'
Pavie, Auguste-Jean-Marie
Pfeiffer, Ida Reyer
Pinto, Fernão Mendes
Pires, Tomé
Polo, Maffeo
Polo, Marco
Polo, Niccolò
Popov, Fyodot Alekseyev
Poyarkov, Vasily Danilovich
Ricci, Matteo
Richthofen, Ferdinand Paul Wilhelm von
Saris, John
Sarychev, Gavriil Andreyevich
Sequira, Diego López de
Serrano, Francisco
Shelikov, Grigory Ivanovich
Simpson, Sir George
Soleyman
Stadukhin, Mikhail
Stark, Freya Madeline
Steller, Georg Wilhelm
Taylor, Annie Royle
Thunberg, Carl Peter
Varthema, Ludovico di
Wallace, Alfred Russel
Wen-chi
William of Rubrouck
Workman, Fanny Bullock
Xavier, Francis
Younghusband, Sir Francis Edward

WEST INDIES, CENTRAL AMERICA, AND MEXICO

Acosta, José de
Alvarado, Pedro de
Álvarez de Pineda, Alonso
Ávila, Pedro Arias de
Baldaya, Afonso Gonçalves
Bastidas, Rodrigo de
Baudin, Thomas-Nicolas
Belcher, Sir Edward

Benalcázar, Sebastián Moyano de
Cabrillo, Juan Rodríguez
Cacella, Estevão
Catesby, Mark
Catlin, George
Columbus, Christopher
Cortés, Hernán
Cosa, Juan de la
Desideri, Ippolito
Díaz, Melchor
Díaz del Castillo, Bernal
Díaz de Solís, Juan
Drake, Sir Francis
Fernández de Córdoba, Francisco (in Yucatán)
Fernández de Córdoba, Francisco (in Panama, Nicaragua)
Fernández de Oviedo y Valdez, Gonzalo
Ferrelo, Bartolomé
Grijalva, Juan de
Guancanagari
Guzmán, Nuño Beltrán de
Hawkins, Sir John
Humboldt, Alexander von
Ibarra, Francisco de
Kino, Eusebio Francisco
Malinche
Montejo, Francisco de
Montejo y León, Francisco de
Narváez, Pánfilo de
Nicuesa, Diego de
Niño, Andrés
Núñez de Balboa, Vasco
Ojeda, Alonso de
Ordaz, Diego de
Padilla, Juan de
Pinzón, Arias Martín
Pinzón, Francisco Martín
Pinzón, Martín Alonso
Pinzón, Vicente Yáñez
Ponce de León, Juan
Popham, George
Porte, François de la
Schwatka, Frederick
Soto, Hernando de
Velásquez, Diego
Young, Charles Denton

SOUTH AMERICA, SOUTH ATLANTIC, AND EAST PACIFIC ISLANDS

Acosta, José de
Acuña, Cristóbal de
Adams, Harriet Chalmers
Aguirre, Lope de

Alfinger, Ambrosius
Almagro, Diego de
Alvarado, Pedro de
Andagoya, Pascual de
Anson, George
Arias de Saavedra, Hernando
Ayolas, Juan de
Azara, Félix de
Banks, Sir Joseph
Baret, Jeanne
Bastidas, Rodrigo de
Bates, Henry Walter
Baudin, Thomas-Nicolas
Beechey, Frederick William
Belcher, Sir Edward
Benalcázar, Sebastián Moyano de
Berrío, Antonio de
Bingham, Hiram
Bougainville, Louis-Antoine de
Bouvet de Lozier, Jean-Baptiste-Charles
Burchell, William John
Burton, Sir Richard Francis
Byron, John
Cabeza de Vaca, Álvar Núñez
Cabot, Sebastian
Cabral, Pedro Álvars
Cano, Juan Sebastián del
Castelnau, François de la Porte de
Catlin, George
Chamisso de Boncourt, Louis-Charles-Adélaïde
Chesnard de la Giraudais, François
Choris, Louis
Clerke, Charles
Columbus, Christopher
Commerson, Joseph-Philibert
Cook, James
Cosa, Juan de la
Crevaux, Jules-Nicolas
Darwin, Charles
Davis, John
Dias, Bartolomeu
Díaz de Solís, Juan
Drake, Sir Francis
Duclos-Guyot, Pierre-Nicolas
Dumont d'Urville, Jules-Sébastien-César
Duperrey, Louis-Isadore
Dupetit-Thouars, Abel-Aubert
Erauso, Catalina de
Fawcett, Percy Harrison
Federmann, Nikolaus
Ferreira, Alexandre Rodrigues
Fitzroy, Robert
Fritz, Samuel

Garay, Juan de
García, Alejo
Gaudichaud-Beaupré, Charles
Godin des Odanais, Isabela
Gomes, Estevão
Hawkins, Sir John
Heyerdahl, Thor
Hohermuth von Speyer, Georg
Humboldt, Alexander von
Hutten, Phillip von
Jiménez de Quesada, Gonzalo
King, Philip Parker
La Condamine, Charles-Marie de
Lancaster, Sir James
Langsdorff, Georg Heinrich Ritter von
Le Maire, Jakob
Lesson, René-Primevère
Magellan, Ferdinand
Malaspina, Alessandro
Martínez de Irala, Domingo
Martius, Carl Friedrich Phillipp von
Maximilian, Alexander Philipp
Mee, Margaret Ursula
Mendoza, Pedro de
Mertens, Karl Heinrich
Meyer, Hans
Moreno, Francisco
Musters, George Chaworth
Niebuhr, Sigismund
Niza, Marcos de
Noort, Oliver van
Noué, Charles-Edouard de la
Ojeda, Alonso de
Orbigny, Alcide-Charles-Victor Dessalines d'
Ordaz, Diego de
Orellana, Francisco de
Peck, Annie Smith
Pfeiffer, Ida Reyer
Pigafetta, Francesco Antonio
Pinzón, Arias Martín
Pinzón, Francisco Martín
Pinzón, Vicente Yáñez
Pizarro, Francisco
Pizarro, Gonzalo
Pizarro, Hernando
Popham, George
Raleigh, Sir Walter
Rice, Alexander Hamilton
Roe, Sir Thomas
Sarmiento de Gamboa, Pedro
Schomburgk, Sir Robert Hermann
Schouten, Willem Cornelis
Selkirk, Alexander

Solander, Daniel Carl
Soto, Hernando de
Spruce, Richard
Teixeira, Pedro de
Tschudi, Johann Jakob von
Ursúa, Pedro de
Valdivia, Pedro de
Vespucci, Amerigo
Viale, Agostinho
Wallace, Alfred Russel
Weddell, James
Wickham, Sir Henry Alexander
Wilkes, Charles
Whymper, Edward
Zurbriggen, Matthias

NORTH AMERICA, EAST OF THE MISSISSIPPI RIVER

Aco, Michel
Adair, James
Albanel, Charles
Allouez, Claude-Jean
Álvarez de Pineda, Alonso
Arthur, Gabriel
Audubon, John James
Ayllón, Lucas Vásquez de
Banks, Sir Joseph
Bartram, John
Bartram, William
Batts, Thomas
Beltrami, Giacomo Costantino
Block, Adriaen
Boone, Daniel
Brébeuf, Jean de
Bréhant de Galinée, René de
Bressani, Francesco-Gioseppe
Brûlé, Étienne
Bruyas, Jacques
Cabeza de Vaca, Álvar Núñez
Cabot, John
Cabot, Sebastian
Cartier, Jacques
Carver, Jonathan
Castelnau, François de la Porte de
Catesby, Mark
Catlin, George
Champlain, Samuel de
Charlevoix, Pierre-François-Xavier de
Chouart des Groseilliers, Médard
Cook, James
Côrte-Real, Gaspar
Côrte-Real, Miguel
Cresap, Thomas

Croghan, George
Davion, Albert
Dollier de Casson, François
Donnaconna
Drake, Sir Francis
Duluth, Daniel Greysolon
Eiríksdottir, Freydis
Ericsson, Leif
Ericsson, Thorvald
Estevanico
Fallam, Robert
Finley, John
Gibault, Pierre
Gilbert, Sir Humphrey
Gist, Christopher
Gomes, Estevão
Gosnold, Bartholomew
Grenville, Sir Richard
Harriot, Thomas
Hawkins, Sir John
Hennepin, Louis
Henry, Alexander (the elder)
Herjulfsson, Bjarni
Hind, Henry Youle
Hudson, Henry
James, Thomas
Jogues, Isaac
Jolliet, Louis
Jourdain, Silvester
Karlsefni, Thorfinn
Kenton, Simon
Knight, John
Lahontan, Louis-Armand de Lom d'Arce de
Lalemant, Gabriel
La Mothe, Antoine Laumet de
La Salle, René-Robert Cavelier de
Laudonnière, René Goulaine de
Lawson, John
Lederer, John
Le Moyne, Jean-Baptiste
Le Moyne, Pierre
Le Moyne, Simon
Le Moyne de Morgues, Jacques
Lesueur, Charles-Alexandre
Le Sueur, Pierre-Charles
Marquette, Jacques
Ménard, René
Menéndez de Avilés, Pedro
Middleton, Christopher
Moor, William
Moscoso, Luis de
Munk, Jens Eriksen
Narváez, Pánfilo de

Needham, James
Newport, Christopher
Nicolet, Jean
Nuttall, Thomas
Penha, Joseph de la
Perrot, Nicolas
Ponce de León, Juan
Popham, George
Pring, Martin
Radisson, Pierre-Esprit
Ribault, Jean
Rivera y Villalón, Pedro de
Robertson, James
Roberval, Jean-François de la Roque de
Rogers, Robert
Rut, John
Sable, Jean Baptist Point
St. Denis, Louis Juchereau de
Schoolcraft, Henry Rowe
Smith, James
Smith, John
Soto, Hernando de
Spotswood, Alexander
Squanto
Tonti, Henri de
Verrazano, Giovanni da
Vespucci, Amerigo
Viele, Arnaud Cornelius
Walker, Thomas
Weiser, Conrad
Weymouth, George
White, John
Winslow, Edward
Wood, Abraham
Woodward, Henry

NORTH AMERICA, WEST OF MISSISSIPPI RIVER

Abbott, Henry Larcom
Abert, James William
Akeley, Mary Leonore Jobe
Alarcón, Hernando de
Allen, Henry Tureman
Alvarado, Hernando de
Álvarez, Manuel
Álvarez de Pineda, Alonso
Anza, Juan Bautista de
Applegate, Jesse
Ashley, William Henry
Astor, John Jacob
Atkinson, Henry
Audubon, John James
Baker, James

Baranov, Aleksandr Andreyevich
Bashmakov, Pyotr
Beale, Edward Fitzgerald
Becknell, William
Beckwith, Edward Griffin
Beckwourth, James Pierson
Beechey, Frederick William
Belcher, Sir Edward
Benavides, Alonzo de
Bent, Charles
Bent, William
Bering, Vitus Jonassen
Berlandier, Jean-Louis
Billings, Joseph
Bishop, Isabella Lucy Bird
Black Beaver
Bligh, William
Bocharov, Dmitry Ivanovich
Bodega y Quadra, Juan Francisco de la
Bodmer, Karl
Boller, Henry A.
Bonneville, Benjamin Louis Eulalie de
Bourgmont, Étienne-Veniard de
Bozeman, John Merin
Brackenridge, Henry Marie
Bradbury, John
Bridger, James
Broughton, William Robert
Cabeza de Vaca, Álvar Núñez
Cabrillo, Juan Rodríguez
Campbell, Robert (American)
Campbell, Robert (Scottish)
Carson, Christopher Houston
Castelnau, François de la Porte de
Catlin, George
Cermenho, Sebastián Meléndez Rodríguez
Chamisso de Boncourt, Louis-Charles-Adélaïde
Charbonneau, Jean-Baptiste
Charbonneau, Toussaint
Chatillon, Henri
Cheadle, Walter Butler
Chirikov, Aleksey Ilyich
Chisholm, Jesse
Chouteau, Auguste Pierre
Chouteau, Jean Pierre
Chouteau, Pierre
Chouteau, René Auguste
Clark, William
Clerke, Charles
Clyman, James
Cocking, Matthew
Colter, John
Cook, James

Coronado, Francisco Vásquez de
Dana, James Dwight
Daurkin, Nikolay
Davydov, Gavriil Ivanovich
De Haven, Edwin Jesse
De Smet, Pierre-Jean
Díaz, Melchor
Dodge, Henry
Domínguez, Francisco Atanasio
Dorion, Marie
Dorion, Pierre, Jr.
Dorion, Pierre, Sr.
Drake, Sir Francis
Drouillard, George
Dubuque, Julien
Dunbar, Sir William
Emmons, George Foster
Emory, William Hemsley
Escalante, Francisco Silvestre Vélez de
Escandón, José de
Eschscholtz, Johann Friedrich
Espejo, Antonio Estevan de
Estevanico
Etholen, Arvid Adolf
Ferrelo, Bartolomé
Ferris, Warren Angus
Fitzpatrick, Thomas
Fontenelle, Lucien
Fowler, Jacob
Fraeb, Henry
Franchère, Gabriel
Fraser, Simon
Freeman, Thomas
Frémont, John Charles
Fuca, Juan de
Galaup, Jean-François de
Garcés, Francisco Tomas Hermenegildo
Glass, Hugh
Glazunov, Andrey
Golovnin, Vasily Mikhailovich
Gore, John
Gray, Robert
Greenwood, Caleb
Gunnison, John Williams
Hamilton, William Thomas
Hayden, Ferdinand Vandeveer
Hearne, Samuel
Heceta, Bruno
Henry, Alexander (the elder)
Henry, Alexander (the younger)
Henday, Anthony
Henry, Andrew
Hind, Henry Youle

Hooker, Sir Joseph Dalton
Hunt, Wilson Price
Irateba
Irving, John Treat
Ives, Joseph Christmas
Jackson, David E.
Kane, Elisha Kent
Joutel, Henri
Jusseaume, René
Kane, Paul
Kashevarov, Aleksandr Filippovich
Kearny, Stephen Watts
Kelsey, Henry
Kern, Benjamin Jordan
Kern, Edward Meyer
Kern, Richard Hovendon
King, Clarence
Kino, Eusebio Francisco
Kittson, Norman Wolfred
Knight, James
Kotzebue, Otto von
Krenitsyn, Pyotr Kuzmich
Krusenstern, Adam Ivan Ritter von
Kurz, Rudolph Friederich
Laclede, Pierre Ligueste
La Harpe, Jean-Baptiste Bénard de
Langford, Nathaniel Pitt
Langsdorff, Georg Heinrich Ritter von
Larpenteur, Charles
La Vérendrye, Louis-Joseph Gaultier de
La Vérendrye, Pierre Gaultier de Varennes de
Leavenworth, Henry
León, Alonso de
Leonard, Zenas
Lewis, Meriwether
Lisa, Manuel
Lisiansky, Yury Fyodorovich
Litke, Fyodor Petrovich
Long, Stephen Harriman
López de Cárdenas, García
Mackenzie, Sir Alexander
Mackenzie, Donald
Macomb, John N.
Malaspina, Alessandro
Mallet, Pierre Antoine
Marcy, Randolph Barnes
Matonabbee
Maximilian, Alexander Philipp
McKenzie, Kenneth
McLoughlin, John
Meek, Joseph L.
Menard, Antoine Pierre
Mertens, Karl Heinrich

Miller, Alfred Jacob
Milton, William-Wentworth Fitzwilliam
Moscoso, Luis de
Muir, John
Nárvaez, Pánfilo de
Newberry, John Strong
Newell, Robert
Nicollet, Joseph Nicolas
Niza, Marcos de
Nuttall, Thomas
Ogden, Peter Skene
Oñate, Juan de
Padilla, Juan de
Palliser, John
Parke, John Grubb
Pattie, James Ohio
Pérez Hernández, Juan Josef
Perrin du Lac, François Marie
Pike, Zebulon Montgomery
Pilcher, Joshua
Pond, Peter
Pope, John B.
Portolá, Gaspar de
Powell, John Wesley
Pribylov, Gavrilo Loginovich
Provost, Étienne
Raynolds, William Franklin
Robidoux, Antoine
Rose, Edward
Ross, Alexander
Russell, Osborne
Sacajawea
St. Denis, Louis Juchereau de
St. Vrain, Céran de Hault de Lassus
Sarychev, Gavriil Andreyevich
Serra, Junípero
Shelikov, Grigory Ivanovich
Simpson, Sir George
Simpson, James Hervey
Simpson, Thomas
Sinclair, James
Sitgreaves, Lorenzo
Smith, Jedediah Strong
Soto, Hernando de
Spalding, Henry Harmon
Stanley, David Sloan
Stansbury, Howard
Steller, Georg Wilhelm
Stevens, Thomas
Stuart, Robert
Stuck, Hudson
Sublette, William Lewis
Thompson, David

Tovar, Pedro de
Truteau, Jean Baptiste
Turk
Ulloa, Francisco de
Vancouver, George
Vanderburgh, William Henry
Vasquez, Louis
Vavasour, Mervin
Vial, Pedro
Viscaíno, Sebastián
Walker, Joseph Reddeford
Warre, Henry James
Webber, John
Weber, John H.
Wheeler, George Montague
Whipple, Amiel Weeks
Whitman, Marcus
Wilkes, Charles
Williams, William Sherley
Wolfskill, William
Wootton, Richens Lacy
Work, John
Wyeth, Nathaniel Jarvis
Young, Brigham
Young, Ewing
Yount, George Concepcion
Zagoskin, Lavrenty Alekseyevich

COASTAL AUSTRALIA, SOUTH AND WEST PACIFIC ISLANDS

Arago, Jacques
Auribeau, Alexandre Hesmivy d'
Banks, Sir Joseph
Baret, Jeanne
Barrow, Sir John
Bass, George
Baudin, Thomas-Nicolas
Bauer, Ferdinand Lucas
Beautemps-Beaupré, Charles François
Beechey, Frederick William
Belcher, Sir Edward
Bellingshausen, Fabian Gottlieb Benjamin von
Bishop, Isabella Lucy Bird
Bligh, William
Bougainville, Hyacinthe-Yves-Philippe Potentien de
Bougainville, Louis-Antoine de
Broughton, William Robert
Brown, Robert
Bruni, Antoine-Raymond-Joseph de
Burney, James
Byron, John
Cano, Juan Sebastián del
Carteret, Philip

Chamisso de Boncourt, Louis-Charles-Adélaïde
Chesnard de la Giraudais, François
Choris, Louis
Clerke, Charles
Commerson, Joseph-Philibert
Cook, James
Dallman, Eduard
Dampier, William
Dana, James Dwight
Darwin, Charles Robert
De Haven, Edwin Jesse
Drake, Sir Francis
Duclos-Guyot, Pierre-Nicolas
Dumont d'Urville, Jules-Sébastien-César
Duperrey, Louis-Isadore
Dupetit-Thouars, Abel-Aubert
Emmons, George Foster
Eschscholtz, Johann Friedrich
Eyre, Sir Edward John
Fanning, Edmund
Fitzroy, Robert
Fleuriot de Langlé, Paul-Antoine-Marie
Flinders, Matthew
Forster, Johann Georg Adam
Forster, Johann Reinhold
Franklin, Sir John
Freycinet, Louis-Claude de Saulces de
Furneaux, Tobias
Gaimard, Joseph-Paul
Galaup, Jean-François de
Gaudichaud-Beaupré, Charles
Gore, John
Hartog, Dirk
Hooker, Sir Joseph Dalton
Houtman, Frederik
Huon de Kermadec, Jean-Michel
Jacquinot, Charles-Hector
Jansz, Willem
Jörgenson, Jörgen
King, James
King, Philip Parker
Kotzebue, Otto von
Krusenstern, Adam Ivan Ritter von
Kupe
La Billardière, Jacques-Julien Houtou de
Lazarev, Mikhail Petrovich
Ledyard, John
Legazpi, Miguel López de
Le Maire, Jakob
Lesseps, Jean-Baptiste-Barthélemy de
Lesson, René-Primevère
Lesueur, Charles-Alexandre
Lisiansky, Yury Fyodorovich

Litke, Fyodor Petrovich
Magellan, Ferdinand
Malaspina, Alessandro
Mendaña, Álvaro de
Mertens, Karl Heinrich
Noort, Oliver van
Péron, François
Pfeiffer, Ida Reyer
Phillip, Arthur
Pigafetta, Francesco Antonio
Quirós, Pedro Fernández de
Quoy, Jean-René-Constant
Riche, Claude-Antoine-Gaspard
Roggeveen, Jakob
Rossel, Elisabeth-Paul-Edouard de
Saavedra Cerón, Álvaro de
Sarmiento de Gamboa, Pedro
Schouten, Willem Cornelis
Solander, Daniel Carl
Sparrman, Anders
Tasman, Abel Janszoon
Thyssen, François
Torres, Luis Váez de
Urdaneta, Andrés de
Vancouver, George
Wallis, Samuel
Webber, John
Westall, William
Wilkes, Charles

CONTINENTAL AUSTRALIA AND NEW ZEALAND

Baines, Thomas
Bass, George
Bauer, Ferdinand Lucas
Bishop, Isabella Lucy Bird
Blaxland, Gregory
Brown, Robert
Brunner, Thomas
Burke, Robert O'Hara
Colenso, William
Cunningham, Allan
Dietrich, Koncordie Amalie Nelle
Eyre, Sir Edward John
Flinders, Matthew
Forrest, Alexander
Forrest, John
Franklin, Jane
Franklin, Sir John
Giles, Ernest
Gosse, William Christie
Gregory, Sir Augustus Charles
Gregory, Francis Thomas

Grey, Sir George
Hovell, William Hilton
Hume, Hamilton
Kennedy, Edmund
Kupe
Landsborough, William
Leichhardt, Friedrich Wilhelm Ludwig
Marsden, Samuel
Mitchell, Sir Thomas Livingstone
Oxley, John Joseph William Molesworth
Strzelecki, Sir Paul Edmund
Stuart, John McDouall
Sturt, Charles
Warburton, Peter Egerton
Wentworth, William Charles
Williams, William
Wills, William John
Zurbriggen, Matthias

CANADIAN, EUROPEAN, AND SIBERIAN ARCTIC, GREENLAND, AND THE NORTH POLE

Abruzzi, Luigi Amedeo di Savoia d'
Amundsen, Roald Engelbregt Gravning
Andrée, Salomon August
Andreyev, Stepan
Back, Sir George
Baffin, William
Bakhov, Ivan
Barents, Willem
Batakov, Anton
Beechey, Frederick William
Begichev, Nikifor Alekseyevich
Belcher, Sir Edward
Bering, Vitus Jonassen
Bernier, Joseph Elzéar
Billings, Joseph
Borough, Stephen
Borough, William
Boyd, Louise Arner
Bruce, William Spiers
Brunel, Olivier
Buchan, David
Button, Sir Thomas
Bylot, Robert
Byrd, Richard Evelyn
Cabot, Sebastian
Campbell, Robert (Scottish)
Chancellor, Richard
Chelyuskin, Simeon
Chirikov, Aleksey Ilyich
Clerke, Charles
Collinson, Sir Richard
Cook, Frederick Albert

Cook, James
Côrte-Real, Gaspar
Courtauld, Augustine
Crozier, Francis Rawdon Moira
Davis, John
Dease, Peter Warren
De Haven, Edwin Jesse
De Long, George Washington
Dezhnev, Semyon Ivanovich
Drygalski, Erich von
Egede, Hans
Ellsworth, Lincoln
Eiríksdottir, Freydis
Ericsson, Leif
Ericsson, Thorvald
Eric the Red
Fernandes, João
Foxe, Luke
Franklin, Sir John
Frobisher, Sir Martin
Fuchs, Sir Vivian Ernest
Gerlache de Gomery, Adrien-Victor-Joseph de
Greely, Adolphus Washington
Hall, Charles Francis
Hall, James
Hayes, Isaac Israel
Hearne, Samuel
Henson, Matthew Alexander
Herjulfsson, Bjarni
Hood, Robert
Hudson, Henry
Jackson, Frederick George
James, Thomas
Kane, Elisha Kent
Karlsefni, Thorfinn
Knight, John
Koldewey, Karl Christian
Kropotkin, Peter
Linschoten, Jan Huyghen van
Litke, Fyodor Petrovich
Mackenzie, Sir Alexander
McClintock, Sir Francis Leopold
McClure, Sir Robert John le Mesurier
Messerschmidt, Daniel Gottlieb
Middleton, Christopher
Moor, William
Munk, Jens Eriksen
Mylius-Erichsen, Ludwig
Nansen, Fridtjof
Nares, Sir George Strong
Nobile, Umberto
Nordenskjöld, Nils Adolf Erik
Nordenskjöld, Nils Otto Gustaf

Parry, Sir William Edward
Pavy, Octave
Payer, Julius von
Peary, Robert Edwin
Phipps, Constantine John
Popov, Fyodot Alekseyev
Rae, John
Rasmussen, Knud Johan Victor
Richardson, Sir John
Ross, Sir James Clark
Ross, Sir John
Sarychev, Gavriil Andreyevich
Schmidt, Otto Y.
Schwatka, Frederick
Scoresby, William, Jr.
Scoresby, William, Sr.
Simpson, Thomas
Stadukhin, Mikhail
Stefansson, Vilhjalmur
Sverdrup, Otto Neumann
Toll, Eduard von
Watkins, Henry George
Wegener, Alfred Lothar
Weyprecht, Karl
White, John
Wilkins, Sir George Hubert
Willoughby, Sir Hugh

ANTARCTIC AND SOUTH POLE

Amundsen, Roald Engelbregt Gravning
Bellingshausen, Fabian Gottlieb Benjamin von
Biscoe, John
Borchgrevink, Carsten Egeberg
Bransfield, Edward
Bruce, William Spiers
Byrd, Richard Evelyn
Charcot, Jean-Baptiste-Étienne-Auguste
Cook, Frederick Albert
Cook, James
Crozier, Francis Rawdon Moira
Dallman, Eduard
De Haven, Edwin Jesse
Drygalski, Erich von
Dumont d'Urville, Jules-Sébastien-César
Ellsworth, Lincoln
Filchner, Wilhelm
Fuchs, Sir Vivian Ernest
Furneaux, Tobias
Gerlache de Gomery, Adrien-Victor-Joseph de
Hillary, Sir Edmund Percival
Hooker, Sir Joseph Dalton
Jacquinot, Charles-Hector
Kerguélen-Trémarec, Yves-Joseph de

Lazarev, Mikhail Petrovich
Mawson, Sir Douglas
Nordenskjöld, Nils Otto Gustaf
Palmer, Nathaniel Brown
Ross, Sir James Clark
Scott, Robert Falcon
Shackleton, Sir Ernest Henry
Shirase, Nobu
Weddell, James
Wilkes, Charles
Wilkins, Sir George Hubert
Wilson, Edward Adrian

UNDERSEA

Beebe, Charles William
Cousteau, Jacques-Yves
Marsili, Luigi Ferdinando
Maury, Matthew Fontaine
Piccard, Jacques Ernest-Jean

SPACE

Armstrong, Neil Alden
Gagarin, Yury Alekseyevich
Glenn, John Herschell, Jr.
Leonov, Alexei Arkhipovich
Piccard, Auguste
Ride, Sally Kristen
Shepard, Alan Bartlett, Jr.
Tereshkova, Valentina Vladimirovna
White, Edward Higgens, II

CARTOGRAPHY, GEOGRAPHY, AND SPONSORSHIP

Anville, Jean-Baptiste Bourguignon d'
Astor, John Jacob

Banks, Sir Joseph
Barrow, Sir John
Beatus of Valcavado
Behaim, Martin
Blaeu, Willem Janzoon
Brosses, Charles de
Cabot, Sebastian
Chu Ssu-pen
Cresques, Abraham
Eratosthenes
Franklin, Jane
Gilbert, Sir Humphrey
Gutiérrez, Diego
Hakluyt, Richard
Hatshepsut
Henry the Navigator
Herodotus
Hipparchus
Holywood, John
Idrisi, Abu Abd Allah Muhammad ash-Sharif al-
Indicopleustes, Cosmas
Lancaster, Sir James
Llewellyn, Martin
Mendoza, Antonio de
Mercator, Gerardus
Necho II
Ortelius, Abraham
Petermann, August Heinrich
Pliny the Elder
Ptolemy
Raleigh, Sir Walter
Strabo
Waldseemüller, Martin
Wood, Abraham

Appendix C
EXPLORERS BY SPONSORING COUNTRY OR BY NATIONALITY/NATIVE LAND

Explorers are listed by countries sponsoring their most important expeditions or activities relating to exploration, or they are listed by their ancestry when their expeditions or activities relating to exploration were not government-backed. (Government sponsorship in some instances means official sanctioning or partial support.)

**SPONSORING COUNTRIES
(GOVERNMENT-BACKED EXPLORATION)**

Australia (Colonial)
Burke, Robert O'Hara
Cunningham, Allan
Eyre, Sir Edward John
Forrest, Alexander
Forrest, John
Gosse, William Christie
Gregory, Sir Augustus Charles
Gregory, Francis Thomas
Grey, Sir George
Kennedy, Edmund
Landsborough, William
Leichhardt, Friedrich Wilhelm Ludwig
Mawson, Sir Douglas
Mitchell, Sir Thomas Livingstone
Oxley, John Joseph William Molesworth
Stuart, John McDouall
Sturt, Charles
Wills, William John

Austria
Martius, Carl Friedrich Phillipp von
Payer, Julius von
Weyprecht, Karl

Belgium
Gerlache de Gomery, Adrien-Victor-Joseph de
Grenfell, George

Canada
Bernier, Joseph Elzéar
Hind, Henry Youle
Stefansson, Vilhjalmur

Carthage
Hanno
Himilco

China
Chang Ch'ien
Cheng Ho
Chu Ssu-pen
Kan Ying

Denmark

Hall, James
Munk, Jens Eriksen
Mylius-Erichsen, Ludwig
Niebuhr, Carsten
Rasmussen, Knud Johan Victor

Egypt

Eudoxus
Hannu
Hatshepsut
Herkhuf
Hippalus
Necho II

France

Aco, Michel
Albanel, Charles
Arago, Jacques
Auribeau, Alexandre Hesmivy d'
Baudin, Thomas-Nicolas
Beautemps-Beaupré, Charles François
Binger, Louis-Gustave
Bougainville, Hyacinthe-Yves-Philippe Potentien de
Bougainville, Louis-Antoine de
Bourgmont, Étienne-Veniard de
Bouvet de Lozier, Jean-Baptiste-Charles
Brazza, Pierre-Paul-François-Camille Savorgnan de
Brosses, Charles de
Brûlé, Étienne
Bruni, Antoine-Raymond-Joseph de
Caillié, René-Auguste
Cartier, Jacques
Champlain, Samuel de
Charcot, Jean-Baptiste-Étienne-Auguste
Chesnard de la Giraudais, François
Commerson, Joseph-Philibert
Donnaconna
Doudart de Lagrée, Ernest-Marc-Louis de Gonzague
Duclos-Guyot, Pierre-Nicolas
Duluth, Daniel Greysolon
Dumont d'Urville, Jules-Sébastien-César
Duperrey, Louis-Isadore
Dupetit-Thouars, Abel-Aubert
Duveyrier, Henri
Flatters, Paul-Xavier
Fleuriot de Langlé, Paul-Antoine-Marie
Foureau, Fernand
Freycinet, Louis-Claude de Saulces de
Gaimard, Joseph-Paul
Galaup, Jean-François de
Garnier, Marie-Joseph-François
Gaudichaud-Beaupré, Charles

Hennepin, Louis
Huon de Kermadec, Jean-Michel
Jacquinot, Charles-Hector
Jolliet, Louis
Joutel, Henri
Kerguélen-Trémarec, Yves-Joseph de
La Billardière, Jacques-Julien Houtou de
La Condamine, Charles-Marie de
La Harpe, Jean-Baptiste Bénard de
Lahontan, Louis-Armand de Lom d'Arce de
La Mothe, Antoine Laumet de
La Salle, René-Robert Cavelier de
Laudonnière, René Goulaine de
Le Moyne, Jean-Baptiste
Le Moyne, Pierre
Le Moyne de Morgues, Jacques
Lesseps, Jean-Baptiste-Barthélemy de
Lesson, René-Primevère
Lesueur, Charles-Alexandre
Marchand, Jean-Baptiste
Marquette, Jacques
Nicolet, Jean
Noué, Charles-Edouard de la
Palgrave, William Gifford
Pavie, Auguste-Jean-Marie
Péron, François
Perrin du Lac, François-Marie
Perrot, Nicolas
Porte, François de la
Quoy, Jean-René-Constant
Ribault, Jean
Riche, Claude-Antoine-Gaspard
Roberval, Jean-François de la Roque de
Rossel, Elisabeth-Paul-Edouard de
St. Denis, Louis Juchereau de
Tonti, Henri de
Verrazano, Giovanni da

Germany

Baumann, Oskar
Drygalski, Erich Dagobert von
Filchner, Wilhelm
Koldewey, Karl Christian
Wegener, Alfred Lothar
Wissmann, Hermann von

Great Britain

Anson, George
Back, Sir George
Baffin, William
Baikie, William Balfour
Baines, Thomas
Banks, Sir Joseph

Barrow, Sir John
Barth, Heinrich
Bass, George
Bauer, Ferdinand Lucas
Beechey, Frederick William
Belcher, Sir Edward
Bent, James Theodore
Biscoe, John
Bligh, William
Bogle, George
Bombay, Sidi
Borough, Stephen
Borough, William
Bransfield, Edward
Broughton, William Robert
Brown, Robert
Bruce, James
Bruce, William Spiers
Brydges, Harford Jones
Buchan, David
Burchell, William John
Burnes, Sir Alexander
Burney, James
Burton, Sir Richard Francis
Button, Sir Thomas
Bylot, Robert
Byron, John
Cabot, John
Cabot, Sebastian
Cameron, Verney Lovett
Carteret, Philip
Chaillé-Long, Charles
Chancellor, Richard
Christie, Charles
Clapperton, Hugh
Clerke, Charles
Collinson, Sir Richard
Cook, James
Courtauld, Augustine
Crozier, Francis Rawdon Moira
Dampier, William
Darwin, Charles Robert
Davis, John
Denham, Dixon
Drake, Sir Francis
Emin Pasha, Mehmed
Everest, Sir George
Fawcett, Percy Harrison
Fitch, Ralph
Fitzroy, Robert
Flinders, Matthew
Forster, Johann Georg Adam
Forster, Johann Reinhold

Foxe, Luke
Franklin, Sir John
Frobisher, Sir Martin
Fuchs, Sir Vivian Ernest
Furneaux, Tobias
Gilbert, Sir Humphrey
Gore, John
Gosnold, Bartholomew
Grant, James Augustus
Grenville, Sir Richard
Hakluyt, Richard
Harriot, Thomas
Hawkins, Sir John
Hearne, Samuel
Hearsey, Hyder Jung
Hillary, Sir Edmund Percival
Hood, Robert
Hooker, Sir Joseph Dalton
Hornemann, Friedrich Conrad
Houghton, Daniel
James, Thomas
Jenkinson, Anthony
Johnston, Sir Harry Hamilton
Jourdain, John
Jourdain, Silvester
King, James
King, Philip Parker
Kintup
Knight, John
Laing, Alexander Gordon
Lancaster, Sir James
Lander, Richard Lemon
Lawrence, Thomas Edward
Lederer, John
Livingstone, David
Lyon, George Francis
Matonabbee
McClintock, Sir Francis Leopold
McClure, Sir Robert John le Mesurier
McLeod, William C.
Middleton, Christopher
Moor, William
Moorcroft, William
Musters, George Chaworth
Nares, Sir George Strong
Newberry, John
Newport, Christopher
Nuttall, Thomas
Oudney, Walter
Overweg, Adolf
Palliser, John
Park, Mungo
Parry, Sir William Edward

Pascoe, William
Penha, Joseph de la
Philby, Harry St. John Bridger
Phillip, Arthur
Phipps, Constantine John
Popham, George
Pottinger, Sir Henry
Pring, Martin
Rae, John
Raleigh, Sir Walter
Richardson, James
Richardson, Sir John
Ritchie, Joseph
Roe, Sir Thomas
Ross, Sir James Clark
Ross, Sir John
Rut, John
Sadlier, George Foster
Saris, John
Schlagintweit, Adolf von
Schlagintweit, Hermann von
Schlagintweit, Robert von
Schomburgk, Sir Robert Hermann
Scoresby, William, Jr.
Scoresby, William, Sr.
Scott, Robert Falcon
Shackleton, Sir Ernest Henry
Sherley, Sir Anthony
Singh, Kishen
Singh, Nain
Smith, John
Solander, Daniel Carl
Sparrman, Anders
Speke, John Hanning
Spotswood, Alexander
Spruce, Richard
Stein, Sir Marc Aurel
Sykes, Sir Percy Molesworth
Tenzing Norgay
Thomson, Sir Charles Wyville
Thomson, Joseph
Turner, Samuel
Vancouver, George
Vavasour, Mervin
Wallis, Samuel
Warre, Henry James
Watkins, Henry George
Webber, John
Weddell, James
Wellsted, James
Westall, William
Weymouth, George
White, John
Wilkins, Sir George Hubert

Willoughby, Sir Hugh
Wilson, Edward Adrian
Younghusband, Sir Francis Edward

Greece
Alexander the Great
Megasthenes
Nearchus
Pytheas
Xenophon

Italy
Abruzzi, Luigi Amedeo di Savoia d'
Nobile, Umberto

Japan
Shirase, Nobu

Mesopotamia
Sargon

Mexico
Berlandier, Jean-Louis

Mongolia
Ch'ang-ch'un
Genghis Khan

Morocco
Leo Africanus

Netherlands
Adams, William
Barents, Willem
Block, Adriaen
Brunel, Olivier
Hartog, Dirk
Houtman, Cornelius
Houtman, Frederik
Hudson, Henry
Jansz, Willem
Le Maire, Jakob
Niebuhr, Sigismund
Noort, Oliver van
Roggeveen, Jakob
Schouten, Willem Cornelis
Tasman, Abel Janszoon
Thunberg, Carl Peter
Thyssen, François

New Zealand (Colonial)
Brunner, Thomas

Norway
Amundsen, Roald Engelbregt Gravning
Nansen, Fridtjof
Sverdrup, Otto Neumann

Oman

Thomas, Bertram Sydney

Persia

Scylax

Portugal

Albuquerque, Afonso de
Almeida, Francisco de
Almeida, Lourenço de
Álvares, Francisco
Baldaya, Afonso Gonçalves
Baptista, Pedro João
Behaim, Martin
Cabral, Gonçalo Velho
Cabral, Pedro Álvars
Cadamosto, Alvise da
Cão, Diogo
Côrte-Real, Gaspar
Côrte-Real, Miguel
Covilhã, Pedro da
Dias, Bartolomeu
Dias, Dinís
Eannes, Gil
Fernandes, Álvaro
Fernandes, João
Gama, Vasco da
Góes, Bento de
Gomes, Diogo
Gomes, Estevão
Gomes, Fernão
Henry the Navigator
Lacerda, Francisco de
Pacheco, Duarte
Pires, Tomé
Sequira, Diego López de
Serrano, Francisco
Silva Porto, Antonio Francisco da
Teixeira, Pedro de
Tristão, Nuño
Vespucci, Amerigo
Viale, Agostinho

Prussia

Nachtigal, Gustav

Rome

Agricola, Gnaeus Julius
Caesar, Gaius Julius
Gallus, Gaius Aelius
Maternus, Julius
Paulinus, Suetonius
Pliny the Elder

Russia

Andreyev, Stepan
Atlasov, Vladimir Vasilyevich
Bakhov, Ivan
Baranov, Aleksandr Andreevich
Basargin, Grigory Gavrilovich
Basov, Emelyan
Batakov, Anton
Begichev, Nikifor Alekseyevich
Beketov, Pyotr
Bekovich-Cherkassky, Aleksandr
Bellingshausen, Fabian Gottlieb Benjamin von
Bering, Vitus Jonassen
Billings, Joseph
Bocharov, Dmitr Ivanovich
Bukhgolts, Ivan Dmitryevich
Chamisso de Boncourt, Louis-Charles-Adélaïde
Chelyuskin, Simeon
Chirikov, Aleksey Ilyich
Choris, Louis
Daurkin, Nikolay
Davydov, Gavriil Ivanovich
Dezhnev, Semyon Ivanovich
Eschscholtz, Johann Friedrich
Etholen, Arvid Adolf
Fedchenko, Aleksey Pavlovich
Fedchenko, Olga
Glazunov, Andrey
Gmelin, Johann Georg
Golovnin, Vasily Mikhailovich
Izmailov, Gerasim Alekseyevich
Kashevarov, Aleksandr Filippovich
Khabarov, Yerofey Pavlovich
Kotzebue, Otto von
Krasheninnikov, Stepan Petrovich
Krenitsyn, Pyotr Kuzmich
Kropotkin, Peter
Krusenstern, Adam Ivan Ritter von
Langsdorff, Georg Heinrich Ritter von
Lazarev, Mikhail Petrovich
Lisiansky, Yury Fyodorovich
Litke, Fyodor Petrovich
Mertens, Karl Heinrich
Messerschmidt, Daniel Gottlieb
Morozko, Luka
Nevelskoy, Gennady Ivanovich
Popov, Fyodot Alekseyev
Poyarkov, Vasily Danilovich
Pribylov, Gavrilo Loginovich
Przhevalsky, Nikolay Mikhailovich
Sarychev, Gavriil Andreyevich
Shelikov, Grigory Ivanovich
Stadukhin, Mikhail
Steller, Georg Wilhelm

Tsybikov, Gombozhab
Yermak
Zagoskin, Lavrenty Alekseyevich

Sicily

Idrisi, Abu Abd Allah Muhammad ash-Sharif al-

Union of Soviet Socialist Republics

Gagarin, Yury Alekseyevich
Leonov, Alexei Arkhipovich
Schmidt, Otto Y.
Tereshkova, Valentina Vladimirovna

Spain

Acuña, Cristóbal de
Aguirre, Lope de
Alarcón, Hernando de
Almagro, Diego de
Alvarado, Hernando de
Alvarado, Pedro de
Álvarez de Pineda, Alonso
Andagoya, Pascual de
Anza, Juan Bautista de
Arias de Saavedra, Hernando
Ávila, Pedro Arias de
Ayllón, Lucas Vásquez de
Ayolas, Juan de
Bastidas, Rodrigo de
Benalcázar, Sebastián Moyano de
Berrío, Antonio de
Bodega y Quadra, Juan Francisco de la
Cabeza de Vaca, Álvar Núñez
Cabrillo, Juan Rodríguez
Cano, Juan Sebastián del
Cermenho, Sebastián Meléndez Rodríguez
Clavijo, Ruy González de
Columbus, Christopher
Coronado, Francisco Vásquez de
Cortés, Hernán
Cosa, Juan de la
Cresques, Abraham
Díaz, Melchor
Díaz del Castillo, Bernal
Díaz de Solis, Juan
Domínguez, Francisco Atanasio
Escalante, Francisco Silvestre Vélez de
Escandón, José de
Estevanico
Fernández de Córdoba, Francisco (in Yucatán)
Fernández de Córdoba, Francisco (in Panama, Nicaragua)
Fernández de Oviedo y Valdez, Gonzalo
Ferrelo, Bartolomé

Fritz, Samuel
Fuca, Juan de
Garay, Juan de
Garcés, Francisco Tomás Hermenegildo
Grijalva, Juan de
Guancanagari
Gutiérrez, Diego
Guzmán, Nuño Beltrán de
Heceta, Bruno
Ibarra, Francisco de
Jiménez de Quesada, Gonzalo
Kino, Eusebio Francisco
Legazpi, Miguel López de
León, Alonso de
López de Cárdenas, García
Magellan, Ferdinand
Malaspina, Alessandro
Malinche
Martínez de Irala, Domingo
Mendaña, Álvaro de
Mendoza, Antonio de
Mendoza, Pedro de
Menéndez de Avilés, Pedro
Montejo, Francisco de
Montejo y León, Francisco de
Moscoso, Luis de
Narváez, Pánfilo de
Nicuesa, Diego de
Niño, Andrés
Niza, Marcos de
Núñez de Balboa, Vasco
Ojeda, Alonso de
Oñate, Juan de
Ordaz, Diego de
Orellana, Francisco de
Padilla, Juan de
Pérez Hernández, Juan Josef
Pigafetta, Francesco Antonio
Pinzón, Arias Martín
Pinzón, Francisco Martín
Pinzón, Martín Alonso
Pinzón, Vicente Yáñez
Pizarro, Francisco
Pizarro, Gonzalo
Pizarro, Hernando
Ponce de León, Juan
Portolá, Gaspar de
Quirós, Pedro Fernández de
Rivera y Villalón, Pedro de
Saavedra Cerón, Álvaro de
Sarmiento de Gamboa, Pedro
Serra, Junípero
Soto, Hernando de

Torres, Luis Váez de
Tovar, Pedro de
Turk
Ulloa, Francisco de
Urdaneta, Andrés de
Ursúa, Pedro de
Valdivia, Pedro de
Velásquez, Diego
Viscaíno, Sebastían

Sweden

Andrée, Salomon August
Kaempfer, Engelbrecht
Nordenskjöld, Nils Adolf Erik
Nordenskjöld, Nils Otto Gustaf

United States (Colonial)

Adair, James
Arthur, Gabriel
Batts, Thomas
Carver, Jonathan
Croghan, George
Fallam, Robert
Lawson, John
Needham, James
Rogers, Robert
Squanto
Walker, Thomas
Weiser, Conrad
Wood, Abraham
Woodward, Henry

United States (Post Colonial)

Abbott, Henry Larcom
Abert, James William
Allen, Henry Tureman
Armstrong, Neil Alden
Atkinson, Henry
Beale, Edward Fitzgerald
Beckwith, Edward Griffin
Black Beaver
Bonneville, Benjamin Louis Eulalie de
Boyd, Louise Arner
Byrd, Richard Evelyn
Carson, Christopher Houston
Charbonneau, Toussaint
Clark, William
Dana, James Dwight
De Haven, Edwin Jesse
De Long, George Washington
Dodge, Henry
Dorion, Pierre, Jr.
Dorion, Pierre, Sr.

Drouillard, George
Ellsworth, Lincoln
Emmons, George Foster
Emory, William Hemsley
Freeman, Thomas
Frémont, John Charles
Glenn, John Herschell, Jr.
Gray, Robert
Greely, Adolphus Washington
Gunnison, John Williams
Hall, Charles Francis
Hayden, Ferdinand Vandeveer
Henson, Matthew Alexander
Irving, John Treat
Ives, Joseph Christmas
Jusseaume, René
Kane, Elisha Kent
Kearny, Stephen Watts
Kern, Benjamin Jordan
Kern, Edward Meyer
Kern, Richard Hovendon
King, Clarence
Langford, Nathaniel Pitt
Leavenworth, Henry
Lewis, Meriwether
Long, Stephen Harriman
Macomb, John N.
Marcy, Randolph Barnes
Maury, Matthew Fontaine
Newberry, John Strong
Nicollet, Joseph Nicolas
Palmer, Nathaniel Brown
Parke, John Grubb
Pavy, Octave
Peary, Robert Edwin
Piccard, Jacques Ernest-Jean
Pike, Zebulon Montgomery
Pope, John B.
Powell, John Wesley
Raynolds, William Franklin
Ride, Sally Kristen
Schoolcraft, Henry Rowe
Schwatka, Frederick
Shepard, Alan Bartlett, Jr.
Simpson, James Hervey
Sitgreaves, Lorenzo
Stanley, David Sloan
Stansbury, Howard
Wheeler, George Montague
Whipple, Amiel Weeks
White, Edward Higgens, II
Wilkes, Charles
Young, Charles Denton

NATIONALITY/NATIVE LAND (INDEPENDENT EXPLORATION)

American (Colonial)
Boone, Daniel
Gist, Christopher
Kenton, Simon

American (Post Colonial)
Adams, Harriet Chalmers
Akeley, Carl Ethan
Akeley, Delia Denning
Akeley, Mary Leonore Jobe
Álvarez, Manuel
Applegate, Jesse
Ashley, William Henry
Astor, John Jacob
Audubon, John James
Baker, James
Bartram, John
Bartram, William
Becknell, William
Beckwourth, James Pierson
Beebe, Charles William
Bent, Charles
Bent, William
Bingham, Hiram
Boller, Henry A.
Bozeman, John Merin
Brackenridge, Henry Marie
Bridger, James
Campbell, Robert (American)
Catlin, George
Charbonneau, Jean-Baptiste
Chatillon, Henri
Chisholm, Jesse
Chouteau, Auguste Pierre
Chouteau, Jean Pierre
Chouteau, Pierre
Chouteau, René Auguste
Clyman, James
Colter, John
Cook, Frederick Albert
Dorion, Marie
Fanning, Edmund
Ferris, Warren Angus
Fitzpatrick, Thomas
Fontenelle, Lucien
Fowler, Jacob
Fraeb, Henry
Fraser, Simon
Glass, Hugh
Greenwood, Caleb
Hamilton, William Thomas

Hayes, Isaac Israel
Henry, Alexander (the elder)
Henry, Alexander (the younger)
Henry, Andrew
Hunt, Wilson Price
Irateba
Jackson, David E.
Larpenteur, Charles
Ledyard, John
Leonard, Zenas
Lisa, Manuel
Meek, Joseph L.
Miller, Alfred Jacob
Muir, John
Newell, Robert
Pattie, James Ohio
Peck, Annie Smith
Pilcher, Joshua
Pond, Peter
Provost, Étienne
Rice, Alexander Hamilton
Robertson, James
Robidoux, Antoine
Rose, Edward
Russell, Osborne
Sacajawea
St. Vrain, Céran de Hault de Lassus de
Sheldon, May French
Smith, James
Smith, Jedediah Strong
Spalding, Henry Harmon
Stanley, Sir Henry Morton
Stuck, Hudson
Sublette, William Lewis
Vanderburgh, William Henry
Vasquez, Louis
Walker, Joseph Reddeford
Weber, John H.
Whitman, Marcus
Williams, William Sherley
Wolfskill, William
Wootton, Richens Lacy
Workman, Fanny Bullock
Wyeth, Nathaniel Jarvis
Young, Brigham
Young, Ewing
Yount, George Concepcion

Argentine
Moreno, Francisco

Australian (Colonial)
Blaxland, Gregory
Grueber, Johann

Hume, Hamilton
Wentworth, William Charles

Austrian
Pfeiffer, Ida Reyer

Belgian
De Smet, Pierre-Jean

Brazilian
Ferreira, Alexandre Rodrigues

British
Atkinson, Lucy
Atkinson, Thomas Wittlam
Baker, Sir Samuel White
Bates, Henry Walter
Bell, Gertrude Margaret Lowthian
Bishop, Isabella Lucy Bird
Blunt, Anne Isabella
Blunt, Wilfrid Scawen
Bradbury, John
Campbell, John
Campbell, Robert (Scottish)
Catesby, Mark
Cheadle, Walter Butler
Colenso, William
Cooper, Thomas Thornville
Cresap, Thomas
Doughty, Charles Montagu
Dunbar, Sir William
Elias, Ney
Fiennes, Celia
Forbes, Edward
Franklin, Jane
Galton, Sir Francis
Giles, Ernest
Gordon, Robert
Henday, Anthony
Herbert, Thomas
Holywood, John
Hovell, William Hilton
Jackson, Frederick George
Kelsey, Henry
Kingsley, Mary Henrietta
Knight, James
Livingstone, Mary Moffat
Llewellyn, Martin
Mackenzie, Sir Alexander
Mackenzie, Donald
Mallory, George Herbert Leigh
Manning, Thomas
Marsden, Samuel
Mazuchelli, Elizabeth Sarah
McKenzie, Kenneth

Mee, Margaret Ursula
Milton, William-Wentworth Fitzwilliam
Moffat, Mary
Moffat, Robert
Ross, Alexander
Selkirk, Alexander
Simpson, Sir George
Simpson, Thomas
Stanhope, Hester Lucy
Stark, Freya Madeline
Stevens, Thomas
Stuart, Robert
Taylor, Annie Royle
Thesiger, Wilfred Patrick
Thompson, David
Wallace, Alfred Russel
Warburton, Peter Egerton
Whymper, Edward
Wickham, Sir Henry Alexander
Williams, William
Winslow, Edward

Canadian (Colonial)
Dease, Peter Warren
Dubuque, Julien
Franchère, Gabriel
Gibault, Pierre
Kittson, Norman Wolfred
La Vérendrye, Louis-Joseph Gaultier de
La Vérendrye, Pierre Gaultier de Varennes et de
Mallet, Pierre-Antoine
McLoughlin, John
Menard, Antoine Pierre
Ogden, Peter Skene
Sinclair, James
Truteau, Jean-Baptiste

Chinese
Fa-hsien
Hsüan-tsang
I-ching
Wen-chi

Danish
Jörgenson, Jörgen

Dutch
Beutler, August
Blaeu, Willem Janzoon
Linschoten, Jan Huyghen van
Tinné, Alexandrine Petronella Francina
Viele, Arnaud Cornelius

Egyptian
Indicopleustes, Cosmas

Flemish
Mercator, Gerardus
Orville, Albert d'
Ortelius, Abraham
William of Rubrouck

Frankish
Arculf

French
Allouez, Claude-Jean
Anville, Jean-Baptiste Bourguignon d'
Balmat, Jacques
Baret, Jeanne
Bonin, Charles
Brébeuf, Jean de
Bréhant de Galinée, René de
Bruyas, Jacques
Charlevoix, Pierre-François-Xavier de
Chouart des Groseilliers, Médard
Crevaux, Jules-Nicolas
Cousteau, Jacques-Yves
David-Néel, Alexandra
Davion, Albert
Dollier de Casson, François
Du Chaillu, Paul Belloni
Dupuis, Jean
Huc, Évariste-Régis
Jogues, Isaac
Laclede, Pierre Ligueste
Lalemant, Gabriel
Le Moyne, Simon
Le Sueur, Pierre-Charles
Ménard, René
Mouhot, Henri
Orbigny, Alcide-Charles-Victor Dessalines d'
Radisson, Pierre-Esprit
Vial, Pedro

German
Alfinger, Ambrosius
Dallman, Eduard
Dietrich, Koncordie Amalie Nelle
Federmann, Nikolaus
Hohermuth von Speyer, Georg
Humboldt, Alexander von
Hutten, Philip von
Junker, Wilhelm Johann
Krapf, Johann Ludwig
Lenz, Oskar
Maximilian, Alexander Philipp
Meyer, Hans
Petermann, August Heinrich
Pethahia of Regensburg

Rebmann, Johann
Richthofen, Ferdinand Paul Wilhelm von
Rohlfs, Friedrich Gerhard
Schweinfurth, Georg August
Waldseemüller, Martin

Greek
Ctesias of Cnidus
Diogenes
Eratosthenes
Hecataeus of Miletus
Herodotus
Hipparchus
Ptolemy
Strabo
Yaqut al-Rumi, Shihab al-Din Abu Abd Allah

Haitian
Sable, Jean Baptist Point

Hungarian
Baker, Florence
Hoehnel, Ludwig von
Teleki, Samuel
Vambéry, Armin

Irish
Brendan, Saint
Finley, John
Kane, Paul
Work, John

Italian
Beltrami, Giacomo Costantino
Bressani, Francesco-Gioseppe
Carpini, Giovanni da Pian del
Conti, Niccolò di
Desideri, Ippolito
Marignolli, Giovanni de
Marsili, Luigi Ferdinando
John of Montecorvino
Odoric of Pordenone
Polo, Maffeo
Polo, Marco
Polo, Niccolò
Ricci, Matteo
Varthema, Ludovico di
Vivaldi, Ugolino

Middle Eastern/North African (Muslim)
Biruni, Abu Ar-Rayhan Muhammad ibn Ahmad al-
  (Arabic) (Persian Empire)
Ibn Battutah, Abu Abd Allah Muhammad (Arabic)
  (Morocco)

Ibn Fadlan, Ahmad (Baghdad)
Ibn Hawqal, Abu al-Qasim ibn Ali al-Nasibi (Arabic)
     (Mesopotamia)
Ibn Jubayr, Abu al-Hasan Muhammad (Valencia)
Ibn Rusta, Abu Ali Ahmad (Arabic)
Masudi, Abu al-Hasan Ali al- (Arabic) (Baghdad)
Soleyman (Arabic) (Persian Gulf)

Norwegian
Borchgrevink, Carsten Egeberg
Egede, Hans
Heyerdahl, Thor

Peruvian
Godin des Odanais, Isabela

Polish
Strzelecki, Sir Paul Edmund

Polynesian
Kupe

Portuguese
Andrade, Antonio de (Portuguese or Spanish)
Azevado, Francisco de (Portuguese or Spanish)
Cabral, João
Cacella, Estevão
García, Alejo
Lobo, Jerónimo
Pinto, Fernão Mendes

Russian
Anabara, Semyon
Bashmakov, Pyotr
Roerich, Nikolay Konstantinovich
Semyonov, Pyotr Petrovich
Toll, Eduard von

Scandinavian (Viking)
Eiríksdottir, Freydis
Ericsson, Leif
Ericsson, Thorvald
Eric the Red
Herjulfsson, Bjarni
Karlsefni, Thorfinn
Naddod
Svarsson, Gardar

Spanish
Acosta, José de
Andrade, Antonio de (Portuguese or Spanish)
Azara, Félix de
Azevado, Francisco de (Portuguese or Spanish)
Beatus of Valcavado
Benavides, Alonzo de
Benjamin of Tudela
Erauso, Catalina de
Espejo, Antonio Estevan de
Páez, Pedro
Xavier, Francis

Swedish
Hedin, Sven Anders

Swiss
Bodmer, Karl
Burckhardt, Johann Ludwig
Eberhardt, Isabelle
Kurz, Rudolph Friederich
Piccard, Auguste
Tschudi, Johann Jakob von
Zurbriggen, Matthias

Turkish
Bar Sauma, Rabban
Evliya, Çelebi

Appendix D
EXPLORERS IN CHRONOLOGICAL ORDER BY BIRTH DATE

Names are listed under century or, later, decade of birth, unless information is incomplete; incomplete dates, marked by asterisks, are listed at end of centuries, except B.C.

B.C.

Hatshepsut (1501–1479)
Hannu (fl. 2750s)*
Sargon (fl. 2340s–2300s)
Herkhuf (fl. 2270s)*
Necho II (unknown–593)*
Hecataeus of Miletus (fl. 520s–490s)*
Scylax (fl. late 500s)*
Herodotus (490–420)
Himilco (fl. 480s)*
Hanno (fl. 470s)*
Xenophon (ca. 430–355)
Ctesias of Cnidus (fl. 420s–410s)*
Nearchus (ca. 360–312)
Alexander the Great (356–323)
Pytheas (fl. 320s)*
Megasthenes (fl. 290s)*
Eratosthenes (ca. 276–ca. 195)
Hipparchus (ca. 190–ca. 120)
Eudoxus (fl. 120s–110s)*
Chang Ch'ien (unknown–ca. 107)*
Caesar, Gaius Julius (100–44)

Strabo (ca. 63 B.C.–ca. A.D. 21)
Gallus, Gaius Aelius (fl. 20s)*

A.D. 1–99

Pliny the Elder (ca. 23–79)
Agricola, Gnaeus Julius (ca. 37–93)
Ptolemy (ca. 90–ca. 150)
Paulinus, Suetonius (unknown–ca. 70)*
Hippalus (fl. 40s)*
Diogenes (fl. 40s–50s)*
Maternus, Julius (fl. 50s)*
Kan Ying (fl. 90s)*

100–199

Wen-chi (fl. 190s)

300–399

Fa-hsien (319–414)

400–499

Brendan, Saint (ca. 484–ca. 578)

500–599

Indicopleustes, Cosmas (fl. 540s)*

600–699

Hsüan-tsang (ca. 600–664)
I-ching (634–ca. 700)
Arculf (fl. ca. 680s)*

700–799

Beatus of Valcavado (fl. 770s)*
Izmailov, Gerasim Alekseyevich (fl. 770s–790s)*

800–899

Soleyman (fl. 850s)*
Svarsson, Gardar (fl. 860s)*
Naddod (fl. 860s–870s)*

900–999

Eric the Red (ca. 950–1010)
Biruni, Abu ar-Rayhan Muhammad ibn Ahmad al- (973–1048)
Ericsson, Leif (ca. 975–ca. 1020)
Ibn Rusta, Abu Ali Ahmad (fl. 900s–920s)*
Ibn Fadlan, Ahmad (fl. 920s)*
Ibn Hawqal, Abu al-Qasim ibn Ali al-Nasibi (fl. 940s–970s)*
Masudi, Abu al-Hasan Ali al- (unknown–ca. 956)*
Kupe (fl. ca. 950)*
Herjulfsson, Bjarni (fl. 980s)*

1000–1099

Idrisi, Abu Abd Allah Muhammad ash-Sharif al- (ca. 1099–ca. 1165)
Ericsson, Thorvald (unknown–ca. 1007)*
Eiríksdottir, Freydis (fl. 1010s)*
Karlsefni, Thorfinn (fl. 1010s)*

1100–1199

Ibn Jubayr, Abu al-Hasan Muhammad (1145–1217)
Ch'ang-ch'un (1148–1227)
Genghis Khan (ca. 1162–1227)
Yaqut al-Rumi, Shihab al-Din Abu Abd Allah (1179–1229)
Carpini, Giovanni da Pian del (1182–1252)
Benjamin of Tudela (unknown–1173)*
Pethahia of Regensburg (fl. 1180s–1190s)*

1200–1299

Holywood, John (ca. 1200–ca. 1250)
William of Rubrouck (ca. 1215–ca. 1270)
Bar Sauma, Rabban (1220–1294)

John of Montecorvino (1247–1328)
Polo, Marco (1254–1324)
Odoric of Pordenone (ca. 1265–1331)
Chu Ssu-pen (1273–1337)
Marignolli, Giovanni de (ca. 1290–unknown)*
Polo, Maffeo (fl. 1260s–1290s)*
Polo, Niccolò (fl. 1260s–1290s)*
Vivaldi, Ugolino (fl. 1290s)*

1300–1399

Ibn Battutah, Abu Abd Allah Muhammad (1304–1378)
Cheng Ho (1371–1435)
Cabral, Gonçalo Velho (ca. 1386–ca. 1447)
Henry the Navigator (1394–1460)
Eannes, Gil (ca. 1395–ca. 1445)
Conti, Niccolò di (ca. 1395–1469)
Cresques, Abraham (fl. 1370s)*

1430–1439

Cadamosto, Alvise da (1432–1488)
Behaim, Martin (ca. 1436–ca. 1506)

1440–1449

Gomes, Diogo (ca. 1440–ca. 1482)
Pinzón, Martín Alonso (ca. 1441–1493)
Ávila, Pedro Arias de (ca. 1442–1531)

1450–1459

Cão, Diogo (ca. 1450–1486)
Cabot, John (ca. 1450–ca. 1499)
Dias, Bartolomeu (ca. 1450–1500)
Côrte-Real, Gaspar (ca. 1450–ca. 1501)
Almeida, Francisco de (1450–1510)
Columbus, Christopher (1451–1506)
Albuquerque, Afonso de (1453–1515)
Vespucci, Amerigo (1454–1512)

1460–1469

Côrte-Real, Miguel (ca. 1460–ca. 1502)
Cosa, Juan de la (ca. 1460–1510)
Ponce de León, Juan (ca. 1460–1521)
Gama, Vasco da (ca. 1460–1524)
Bastidas, Rodrigo de (1460–1526)
Covilhã, Pero da (ca. 1460–ca. 1530)
Pinzón, Francisco Martín (1462–1500)
Pinzón, Vicente Yáñez (1463–ca. 1523)
Pinzón, Arias Martín (1465–1510)
Ojeda, Alonso de (ca. 1465–ca. 1515)
Sequira, Diego López de (ca. 1465–ca. 1520)
Velásquez, Diego (1465–1524)
Cabral, Pedro Álvarez (ca. 1467–ca. 1520)
Pires, Tomé (ca. 1468–ca. 1540)

1470–1479

Díaz de Solís, Juan (ca. 1470–1516)
Varthema, Ludovico di (ca. 1470–ca. 1517)
Waldseemüller, Martin (ca. 1470–ca. 1522)
Núñez de Balboa, Vasco (ca. 1475–1519)
Ayllón, Lucas Vásquez de (ca. 1475–1526)
Fernández de Córdoba, Francisco (ca. 1475–ca. 1526)
Niño, Andrés (1475–ca. 1530)
Pizarro, Francisco (ca. 1475–1541)
Cabot, Sebastian (ca. 1475–1557)
Cano, Juan Sebastían del (ca. 1476–1526)
Almagro, Diego de (ca. 1478–1538)
Fernández de Oviedo y Valdez, Gonzalo (1478–1557)
Pizarro, Hernando (ca. 1478–1578)
Montejo y León, Francisco de (ca. 1479–ca. 1549)
Benalcázar, Sebastían Moyano de (ca. 1479–1551)

1480–1489

Magellan, Ferdinand (ca. 1480–1521)
Narváez, Pánfilo de (ca. 1480–ca. 1528)
Ordaz, Diego de (1480–1535)
Gomes, Estevão (ca. 1484–ca. 1538)
Verrazano, Giovanni da (ca. 1485–ca. 1528)
Alvarado, Pedro de (ca. 1485–1541)
Cortés, Hernán (1485–1547)
Leo Africanus (ca. 1485–ca. 1554)
Mendoza, Pedro de (ca. 1487–1537)
Grijalva, Juan de (ca. 1489–1527)

1490–1499

Donnaconna (ca. 1490–ca. 1539)
Álvares, Francisco (ca. 1490–1540)
Orellana, Francisco de (ca. 1490–ca. 1546)
Mendoza, Antonio de (ca. 1490–1552)
Cabeza de Vaca, Álvar Núñez (ca. 1490–ca. 1560)
Pigafetta, Francesco Antonio (ca. 1491–ca. 1535)
Cartier, Jacques (1491–1557)
Díaz del Castillo, Bernal (ca. 1492–ca. 1584)
Andagoya, Pascual de (ca. 1495–1548)
Niza, Marcos de (ca. 1495–1558)
Urdaneta, Andrés de (1498–1568)
Soto, Hernando de (ca. 1499–1542)
Ferrelo, Bartolomé (1499–1548)

1400–1499, INCOMPLETE

Clavijo, Ruy González de (unknown–1412)*
Baldaya, Afonso Gonçalves (fl. 1430s)*
Dias, Dinís (fl. 1440s)*
Fernandes, Álvaro (fl. 1440s)*
Tristão, Nuño (fl. 1440s)*
Gomes, Fernão (fl. 1470s)*
Guancanagari (fl. 1490s)*

1500–1509

Estevanico (ca. 1500–1539)
Padilla, Juan de (ca. 1500–1542)
Cabrillo, Juan Rodríguez (ca. 1500–1543)
Valdivia, Pedro de (ca. 1500–1553)
Roberval, Jean-François de la Roque de (ca. 1500–1561)
Federmann, Nikolaus (1501–1542)
Pizarro, Gonzalo (ca. 1506–1548)
Xavier, Francis (1506–1552)
Malinche (ca. 1508–1528)
Montejo, Francisco de (1508–1565)
Martínez de Irala, Domingo (ca. 1509–1557)
Jiménez de Quesada, Gonzalo (ca. 1509–1579)
Pinto, Fernão Mendes (1509–1583)

1510–1519

Coronado, Francisco Vásquez de (1510–1554)
Aguirre, Lope de (ca. 1510–1561)
Legazpi, Miguel López de (1510–1572)
Hutten, Philip von (1511–1546)
Mercator, Gerardus (1512–1594)
Willoughby, Sir Hugh (ca. 1516–1554)
Menéndez de Avilés, Pedro (1519–1574)

1520–1529

Chancellor, Richard (ca. 1520–1556)
Ribault, Jean (ca. 1520–1565)
Berrío, Antonio de (ca. 1520–1598)
Borough, Stephen (1525–1584)
Ursúa, Pedro de (ca. 1526–1561)
Garay, Juan de (ca. 1528–1583)

1530–1539

Ibarra, Francisco de (ca. 1530–1575)
Sarmiento de Gamboa, Pedro (ca. 1530–ca. 1592)
Hawkins, Sir John (1532–1595)
Frobisher, Sir Martin (ca. 1535–1594)
Borough, William (1536–1599)
Fuca, Juan de (1536–1602)
Gilbert, Sir Humphrey (ca. 1537–1583)
Acosta, José de (1539–1600)

1540–1549

Brunel, Olivier (ca. 1540–1585)
Grenville, Sir Richard (1540–1591)
Drake, Sir Francis (ca. 1540–1596)
Houtman, Cornelius (ca. 1540–1599)
Mendaña, Álvaro de (ca. 1541–1595)

1550–1559

Davis, John (ca. 1550–1605)
Popham, George (ca. 1550–1608)

Fitch, Ralph (ca. 1550–1611)
Hudson, Henry (ca. 1550–ca. 1611)
Viscaíno, Sebastián (ca. 1550–ca. 1628)
Oñate, Juan de (ca. 1550–ca. 1630)
Ricci, Matteo (1552–1610)
Hakluyt, Richard (ca. 1552–1616)
Lancaster, Sir James (ca. 1554–1618)
Raleigh, Sir Walter (ca. 1554–1618)

1560–1569

Harriot, Thomas (1560–1621)
Arias de Saavedra, Hernando (1561–1634)
Góes, Bento de (1562–1607)
Linschoten, Jan Huyghen van (1563–1611)
Adams, William (ca. 1564–1620)
Páez, Pedro (1564–1622)
Quirós, Pedro Fernández de (ca. 1565–1615)
Le Maire, Jakob (ca. 1565–1616)
Newport, Christopher (ca. 1565–1617)
Sherley, Sir Anthony (ca. 1565–ca. 1635)
Champlain, Samuel de (1567–1635)
Noort, Oliver van (1568–ca. 1622)

1570–1579

Houtman, Frederik (1571–1627)
Blaeu, Willem Janzoon (1571–1638)
Gosnold, Bartholomew (ca. 1572–1607)
Teixeira, Pedro de (1575–1640)
Azevado, Francisco de (1578–1660)
Munk, Jens Eriksen (1579–1628)

1580–1589

Squanto (ca. 1580–1622)
Schouten, Willem Cornelis (ca. 1580–1625)
Smith, John (ca. 1580–1631)
Andrade, Antonio de (ca. 1580–1634)
Roe, Sir Thomas (ca. 1581–1644)
Baffin, William (ca. 1584–1622)
Cacella, Estevão (1585–1630)
Erauso, Catalina de (1585–1650)
Foxe, Luke (1586–1635)

1590–1599

Brûlé, Étienne (ca. 1592–1633)
James, Thomas (ca. 1593–ca. 1635)
Brébeuf, Jean de (1593–1649)
Lobo, Jerónimo (1593–1678)
Winslow, Edward (1595–1655)
Acuña, Cristóbal de (1597–ca. 1676)
Nicolet, Jean (ca. 1598–1642)
Cabral, João (ca. 1599–1669)

1500–1599, INCOMPLETE

Alarcón, Hernando de (1500–unknown)*
João Fernandes (unknown–ca. 1501)*
Almeida, Lourenço de (unknown–1508)*
Nicuesa, Diego de (unknown–1511)*
Fernández de Córdoba, Francisco (unknown–1518)*
Álvarez de Pineda, Alonso (unknown–ca. 1519)*
Serrano, Francisco (unknown–1521)*
García, Alejo (unknown–ca. 1526)*
Saavedra Cerón, Álvaro de (unknown–1529)*
Pacheco, Duarte (unknown–ca. 1530)*
Alfinger, Ambrosius (unknown–1533)*
Ayolas, Juan de (unknown–ca. 1538)*
Díaz, Melchor (unknown–1540)*
Hohermuth von Speyer, Georg (unknown–1540)*
Ulloa, Francisco de (unknown–ca. 1540)*
Turk (unknown–1541)*
Guzmán, Nuño Beltrán de (unknown–1544)*
Gutierrez, Diego (unknown–1554)*
Yermak (unknown–ca. 1584)*
Newberry, John (unknown–ca. 1585)*
Le Moyne de Morgues, Jacques (unknown–1588)*
Barents, Willem (unknown–1597)*
Rut, John (fl. 1520s)*
Moscoso, Luis de (fl. 1530s–1540s)*
López de Cárdenas, García (fl. 1540s)*
Tovar, Pedro de (fl. 1540s)*
Laudonnière, René Goulaine de (fl. 1560s)*
Espejo, Antonio Estevan de (fl. 1580s)*
White, John (fl. 1580s–1590s)*
Cermenho, Sebastián Meléndez Rodríguez (fl. 1590s)*

1600–1609

Tasman, Abel Janszoon (ca. 1603–1659)
Ménard, René (1604–1661)
Le Moyne, Simon (1604–1665)
Dezhnev, Semyon Ivanovich (ca. 1605–1672)
Jogues, Isaac (1607–1646)
Wood, Abraham (1608–ca. 1680)

1610–1619

Lalemant, Gabriel (1610–1649)
Evliya, Çelebi (1611–1684)
Bressani, Francesco-Gioseppe (1612–1672)
Albanel, Charles (ca. 1613–1696)
Chouart des Groseilliers, Médard
    (ca. 1618–ca. 1697)

1620–1629

Viale, Agostinho (ca. 1620–1667)
Viele, Arnaud Cornelius (ca. 1620–1700)
Orville, Albert d' (1621–1662)

Allouez, Claude-Jean (1622–1689)
Grueber, Johann (1623–1680)
Noué, Charles-Edouard de la (1624–1691)
Hennepin, Louis (1626–ca. 1705)

1630–1639

Radisson, Pierre-Esprit (ca. 1630–1710)
Niebuhr, Sigismund (1631–1699)
Bruyas, Jacques (1635–1712)
Dollier de Casson, François (1636–1701)
Duluth, Daniel Greysolon (1636–1710)
Marquette, Jacques (1637–1675)

1640–1649

León, Alonso de (ca. 1640–1691)
Knight, James (ca. 1640–ca. 1721)
La Salle, René-Robert Cavelier de (1643–1687)
Perrot, Nicolas (ca. 1644–1717)
Bréhant de Galinée, René de (ca. 1645–1678)
Jolliet, Louis (1645–1700)
Kino, Eusebio Francisco (ca. 1645–1711)
Joutel, Henri (ca. 1645–ca. 1730)

1650–1659

Tonti, Henri de (ca. 1650–1704)
Dampier, William (ca. 1651–1715)
Kaempfer, Engelbrecht (1651–1716)
Le Sueur, Pierre-Charles (ca. 1657–ca. 1705)
La Mothe, Antoine Laumet de (1658–1730)
Marsili, Luigi Ferdinando (1658–1730)
Fritz, Samuel (ca. 1659–1725)
Roggeveen, Jakob (1659–1729)

1660–1669

Le Moyne, Pierre (1661–1706)
Fiennes, Celia (1662–1741)
Rivera y Villalón, Pedro de (ca. 1664–1744)
Lahontan, Louis-Armand de Lom d'Arce de (ca. 1666–1716)

1670–1679

Kelsey, Henry (ca. 1670–1729)
Selkirk, Alexander (1676–1721)
Spotswood, Alexander (1676–1740)
St. Denis, Louis Juchereau de (1676–1744)
Catesby, Mark (ca. 1679–1749)

1680–1689

Bourgmont, Étienne-Veniard de (1680–ca. 1730)
Le Moyne, Jean-Baptiste (1680–1768)
Bering, Vitus Jonassen (1681–1741)
Charlevoix, Pierre-François-Xavier de (1682–1761)

Desideri, Ippolito (1684–1733)
Messerschmidt, Daniel Gottlieb (1685–1735)
La Vérendrye, Pierre Gaultier de Varennes de (1685–1749)
Egede, Hans (1686–1758)

1690–1699

Weiser, Conrad (1696–1760)
Anson, George (1697–1762)
Anville, Jean-Baptiste Bourguigon d' (1697–1782)
Bartram, John (1699–1777)

1600–1699, INCOMPLETE

Knight, John (unknown–ca. 1606)*
Jenkinson, Anthony (unknown–1611)*
Hall, James (unknown–1612)*
Torres, Luis Váez de (unknown–ca. 1615)*
Jourdain, John (unknown–1619)*
Stevens, Thomas (unknown–1619)*
Button, Sir Thomas (unknown–1634)*
Llewellyn, Martin (unknown–1634)*
Saris, John (unknown–1646)*
Jourdain, Silvester (unknown–1650)*
Stadukhin, Mikhail (unknown–1666)*
Needham, James (unknown–1673)*
Woodward, Henry (unknown–ca. 1686)*
Batts, Thomas (unknown–1698)*
Morozko, Luka (unknown–ca. 1699)*
Jansz, Willem (fl. early 1600s)*
Pring, Martin (fl. early 1600s)*
Weymouth, George (fl. early 1600s)*
Block, Adriaen (fl. 1610s)*
Bylot, Robert (fl. 1610s)*
Hartog, Dirk (fl. 1610s)*
Benavides, Alonzo de (fl. 1620s)*
Herbert, Thomas (fl. 1620s)*
Thyssen, François (fl. 1620s)*
Beketov, Pyotr (fl. 1620–1660s)*
Popov, Fyodot Alekseyev (fl. 1640s)*
Poyarkov, Vasily Danilovich (fl. 1640s)*
Khabarov, Yerofey Pavlovich (fl. 1650s)*
Lederer, John (fl. 1660s–1670s)*
Arthur, Gabriel (fl. 1670s)*
Fallam, Robert (fl. 1670s)*
Aco, Michel (fl. 1680s–1690s)*
Penha, Joseph de la (fl. 1680s–1690s)*

1700–1799

Mallet, Pierre-Antoine (1700–ca. 1751)
Escandón, José de (1700–1770)
Middleton, Christopher (ca. 1700–1770)
La Condamine, Charles-Marie de (1701–1774)

Cresap, Thomas (ca. 1702–ca. 1790)
Chirikov, Aleksey Ilyich (1703–1748)
Bouvet de Lozier, Jean-Baptiste-Charles
    (1704–1786)
Basov, Emelyan (ca. 1705–ca. 1765)
Gist, Christopher (ca. 1706–1759)
Steller, Georg Wilhelm (1709–1746)
Gmelin, Johann Georg (1709–1755)
Brosses, Charles de (1709–1777)

1710–1719

Carver, Jonathan (1710–1780)
Krasheninnikov, Stepan Petrovich (1711–1755)
Serra, Junípero (1713–1784)
Walker, Thomas (1715–1794)
La Vérendrye, Louis-Joseph Gaultier de (1717–1761)

1720–1729

Adair, James (ca. 1720–1783)
Finley, John (1722–ca. 1769)
Portolá, Gaspar de (ca. 1722–ca. 1784)
Duclos-Guyot, Pierre-Nicolas (1722–1794)
Byron, John (1723–1786)
Laclede, Pierre Ligueste (1724–1778)
Pérez Hernández, Juan Josef (ca. 1725–1775)
Commerson, Joseph-Philibert (1727–1773)
Cook, James (1728–1779)
Wallis, Samuel (1728–1795)
Godin des Odanais, Isabela (1729–1792)
Forster, Johann Reinhold (1729–1798)
Bougainville, Louis-Antoine de (1729–1811)

1730–1739

Gore, John (1730–1790)
Bruce, James (1730–1794)
Rogers, Robert (1731–1795)
Solander, Daniel Carl (1733–1782)
Carteret, Philip (ca. 1733–1796)
Niebuhr, Carsten (1733–1815)
Kerguélen-Trémarec, Yves-Joseph de (1734–1797)
Boone, Daniel (1734–1820)
Furneaux, Tobias (1735–1781)
Anza, Juan Bautista de (1735–1788)
Matonabbee (ca. 1736–1782)
Gibault, Pierre (1737–1804)
Smith, James (1737–1812)
Garcés, Francisco Tomás Hermenegildo
    (1738–1781)
Phillip, Arthur (1738–1814)
Bruni, Antoine-Raymond-Joseph de (1739–1793)
Bartram, William (1739–1823)
Henry, Alexander (the elder) (1739–1824)

1740–1749

Houghton, Daniel (ca. 1740–1791)
Baret, Jeanne (ca. 1740–ca. 1803)
Domínguez, Francisco Atanasio (ca. 1740–1805)
Pond, Peter (1740–1807)
Clerke, Charles (1741–1779)
Galaup, Jean-François de (1741–ca. 1788)
Robertson, James (1742–1814)
Cocking, Matthew (1743–1799)
Banks, Sir Joseph (1743–1820)
Thunberg, Carl Peter (1743–1828)
Fleuriot de Langlé, Paul-Antoine-Marie (1744–1787)
Bodega y Quadra, Juan Francisco de la
    (ca. 1744–1794)
Escalante, Francisco Silvestre Vélez de (ca. 1745–1780)
Hearne, Samuel (1745–1792)
Sable, Jean Baptist Point (ca. 1745–1818)
Bogle, George (1746–1781)
Azara, Felix de (1746–1811)
Vial, Pedro (ca. 1746–1814)
Shelikov, Grigory Ivanovich (1747–1795)
Baranov, Aleksandr Andreyevich (1747–1819)
Sparrman, Anders (1747–1820)
Huon de Kermadec, Jean-Michel (1748–1793)
Truteau, Jean-Baptiste (1748–1827)
Turner, Samuel (ca. 1749–1802)
Dunbar, Sir William (1749–1810)
Chouteau, René Auguste (1749–1829)

1750–1759

King, James (1750–1784)
Dorion, Pierre, Sr. (ca. 1750–ca. 1820)
Burney, James (1750–1821)
Ledyard, John (1751–1789)
Webber, John (1751–1793)
Heceta, Bruno (1751–1807)
Lacerda, Francisco de (1753–1798)
Forster, Johann Georg Adam (1754–1794)
Baudin, Thomas-Nicolas (1754–1803)
Bligh, William (1754–1817)
Gray, Robert (1755–1806)
Malaspina, Alessandro (ca. 1755–1810)
La Billardière, Jacques-Julien Houtou de (1755–1834)
Kenton, Simon (1755–1836)
Ferreira, Alexandre Rodrigues (1756–1815)
Vancouver, George (1757–1798)
Billings, Joseph (ca. 1758–1806)
Charbonneau, Toussaint (ca. 1758–ca. 1840)
Chouteau, Jean Pierre (1758–1849)

1760–1769

Bauer, Ferdinand Lucas (1760–1826)
Scoresby, William, Sr. (1760–1829)

Riche, Claude-Antoine-Gaspard (1762–1797)
Dubuque, Julien (1762–1810)
Broughton, William Robert (1762–1821)
Balmat, Jacques (1762–1834)
Sarychev, Gavriil Andreyevich (1763–1831)
Astor, John Jacob (1763–1848)
Greenwood, Caleb (1763–1850)
Mackenzie, Sir Alexander (1764–1820)
Marsden, Samuel (1764–1838)
Barrow, Sir John (1764–1848)
Moorcroft, William (1765–1825)
Rossel, Elisabeth-Paul-Edouard de (1765–1829)
Fowler, Jacob (1765–1850)
Perrin du Lac, François-Marie (1766–1824)
Lesseps, Jean-Baptiste-Barthélemy de (1766–1834)
Campbell, John (1766–ca. 1840)
Menard, Antoine Pierre (1766–1844)
Beautemps-Beaupré, Charles-François (1766–1854)
Bradbury, John (1768–1823)
Fanning, Edmund (1769–1841)
Humboldt, Alexander von (1769–1859)

1770–1779

Drouillard, George (ca. 1770–1810)
Clark, William (1770–1838)
Krusenstern, Adam Ivan Ritter von (1770–1846)
Thompson, David (1770–1857)
Bass, George (1771–ca. 1803)
Park, Mungo (1771–1806)
Hornemann, Friedrich Conrad (1772–1801)
Lisa, Manuel (1772–1820)
Manning, Thomas (1772–1840)
Lisiansky, Yury Fyodorovich (1773–1839)
Brown, Robert (1773–1858)
Lewis, Meriwether (1774–1809)
Flinders, Matthew (1774–1814)
Brydges, Harford Jones (1774–1829)
Langsdorff, Georg Heinrich Ritter von (1774–1852)
Péron, François (1775–1810)
Colter, John (ca. 1775–1813)
Rose, Edward (ca. 1775–ca. 1832)
Henry, Andrew (ca. 1775–1833)
Golovnin, Vasily Mikhailovich (1776–1831)
Stanhope, Hester Lucy (1776–1839)
Fraser, Simon (1776–1862)
Ross, Sir John (1777–1856)
Ashley, William Henry (ca. 1778–1838)
Lesueur, Charles-Alexandre (1778–1846)
Bellingshausen, Fabian Gottlieb Benjamin von (1778–1852)
Blaxland, Gregory (1778–1853)
Pike, Zebulon Montgomery (1779–1813)

Freycinet, Louis-Claude de Saulces de (1779–1842)
Beltrami, Giacomo Costantino (1779–1855)

1780–1789

Glass, Hugh (ca. 1780–1833)
Jörgenson, Jörgen (1780–1841)
Chamisso de Boncourt, Louis-Charles-Adélaïde (1781–1836)
Westall, William (1781–1850)
Hearsey, Hyder Jung (1782–1840)
Atkinson, Henry (1782–1842)
Hunt, Wilson Price (ca. 1782–1842)
Bougainville, Hyacinthe-Yves-Philippe Potentien de (1782–1846)
Provost, Étienne (1782–1850)
Burchell, William John (ca. 1782–1863)
Dodge, Henry (1782–1867)
Maximilian, Alexander Philipp (1782–1887)
Oxley, John Joseph William Molesworth (ca. 1783–1828)
Leavenworth, Henry (1783–1834)
Mackenzie, Donald (1783–1851)
Ross, Alexander (1783–1856)
Davydov, Gavriil Ivanovich (1784–1809)
Sacajawea (ca. 1784–1812)
Burckhardt, Johann Ludwig (1784–1817)
McLoughlin, John (1784–1857)
Long, Stephen Harriman (1784–1864)
Stuart, Robert (1785–1848)
Audubon, John James (1785–1851)
Bransfield, Edward (ca. 1785–1851)
Denham, Dixon (1786–1828)
Chouteau, Auguste Pierre (1786–1838)
Nicollet, Joseph Nicolas (1786–1843)
Franklin, Sir John (1786–1847)
Dorion, Marie (1786–ca. 1853)
Nuttall, Thomas (1786–1859)
Franchère, Gabriel (1786–1863)
Duperrey, Louis-Isadore (1786–1865)
Brackenridge, Henry Marie (1786–1871)
Hovell, William Hilton (1786–1875)
Weddell, James (1787–1834)
Kotzebue, Otto von (1787–1846)
Williams, William Sherley (1787–1849)
Richardson, Sir John (1787–1865)
Ritchie, Joseph (ca. 1788–1819)
Clapperton, Hugh (1788–1827)
Lazarev, Mikhail Petrovich (1788–1851)
Dease, Peter Warren (1788–1863)
Jusseaume, René (ca. 1789–ca. 1830)
Gaudichaud-Beaupré, Charles (1789–1854)
Pottinger, Sir Henry (1789–1856)

Scoresby, William, Jr. (1789–1857)
Chouteau, Pierre (1789–1865)

1790–1799

Oudney, Walter (1790–1824)
Dumont d'Urville, Jules-Sébastien-César (1790–1842)
Pilcher, Joshua (1790–1843)
Buchan, David (1790–1845)
Arago, Jacques (1790–1855)
Parry, Sir William Edward (1790–1855)
Becknell, William (ca. 1790–1865)
Everest, Sir George (1790–1866)
Quoy, Jean-René-Constant (1790–1869)
Wentworth, William Charles (1790–1872)
Cunningham, Allan (1791–1839)
Young, Ewing (ca. 1792–1841)
Mitchell, Sir Thomas Livingstone (1792–1855)
Simpson, Sir George (ca. 1792–1860)
Work, John (ca. 1792–1861)
Franklin, Jane (1792–1875)
Clyman, James (1792–1881)
Laing, Alexander Gordon (1793–1826)
Eschscholtz, Johann Friedrich (1793–1831)
King, Philip Parker (1793–1856)
Dupetit-Thouars, Abel-Aubert (1793–1864)
Schoolcraft, Henry Rowe (1793–1864)
Biscoe, John (1794–1843)
Kearny, Stephen Watts (1794–1848)
Lesson, René-Primevère (1794–1849)
Ogden, Peter Skene (1794–1854)
Álvarez, Manuel (1794–1856)
Robidoux, Antoine (1794–1860)
Yount, George Concepcion (1794–1865)
Martius, Carl Friedrich Phillipp von (1794–1869)
Choris, Louis (1795–1828)
Lyon, George Francis (1795–1832)
Sturt, Charles (1795–1869)
Moffat, Mary (1795–1871)
Moffat, Robert (1795–1883)
Mertens, Karl Heinrich (1796–1830)
Crozier, Francis Rawdon Moira (1796–1848)
Beechey, Frederick William (1796–1856)
Gaimard, Joseph-Paul (1796–1858)
Catlin, George (1796–1872)
Back, Sir George (1796–1878)
Bonneville, Benjamin Louis Eulalie de (1796–1878)
Jacquinot, Charles-Hector (1796–1879)
Pfeiffer, Ida Reyer (1797–1858)
Hume, Hamilton (1797–1873)
Strzelecki, Sir Paul Edmund (1797–1873)
Litke, Fyodor Petrovich (1797–1882)
Vanderburgh, William Henry (ca. 1798–1832)
Wolfskill, William (1798–1866)

Vasquez, Louis (1798–1868)
Walker, Joseph Reddeford (1798–1876)
Wilkes, Charles (1798–1877)
Smith, Jedediah Strong (1799–1831)
Caillié, René-Auguste (1799–1838)
Sublette, William Lewis (1799–1845)
Bent, Charles (1799–1847)
Fitzpatrick, Thomas (ca. 1799–1854)
Weber, John H. (1799–1859)
Atkinson, Thomas Wittlam (1799–1861)
Etholen, Arvid Adolf (1799–1876)
Belcher, Sir Edward (1799–1877)
Palmer, Nathaniel Brown (1799–1877)

1700–1799, INCOMPLETE

Atlasov, Vladimir Vasilyevich (unknown–1711)*
Lawson, John (unknown–1711)*
Bekovich-Cherkassky, Aleksandr (unknown–ca. 1717)*
Davion, Albert (unknown–1726)*
Bakhov, Ivan (unknown–1762)*
Moor, William (unknown–1765)*
Krenitsyn, Pyotr Kuzmich (unknown–1770)*
Croghan, George (unknown–1782)*
Auribeau, Alexandre Hesmivy d' (unknown–1794)*
Anabara, Semyon (fl. 1710s)*
Bukhgolts, Ivan Dmitryevich (fl. 1710s)*
La Harpe, Jean-Baptiste Bénard de (fl. 1710s)*
Chelyuskin, Simeon (fl. 1740s)*
Bashmakov, Pyotr (fl. 1750s)*
Beutler, August (fl. 1750s)*
Henday, Anthony (fl. 1750s–1760s)*
Andreyev, Stepan (fl. 1760s)*
Chesnard de la Giraudais, François (fl. 1760s)*
Daurkin, Nikolay (fl. 1760s–1790s)*
Phipps, Constantine John (fl. 1770s)*
Gordon, Robert (fl. 1770s)*
Bocharov, Dmitry Ivanovich (fl. 1770s–1790s)*
Pribylov, Gavrilo Loginovich (fl. 1780s)*
Batakov, Anton (fl. 1780s–1790s)*

1800–1809

Hood, Robert (ca. 1800–1821)
Fontenelle, Lucien (ca. 1800–ca. 1840)
McKenzie, Kenneth (ca. 1800–1861)
Ross, Sir James Clark (1800–1862)
Beckwourth, James Pierson (ca. 1800–ca. 1866)
De Smet, Pierre-Jean (1801–1873)
Young, Brigham (1801–1877)
Whitman, Marcus (1802–1847)
Wyeth, Nathaniel Jarvis (1802–1856)
Orbigny, Alcide-Charles-Victor Dessalines d'
    (1802–1857)
St. Vrain, Céran de Hault de Lassus de (1802–1870)

Spalding, Henry Harmon (1803–1874)
Lander, Richard Lemon (1804–1834)
Pattie, James Ohio (ca. 1804–ca. 1851)
Schomburgk, Sir Robert Hermann (1804–1865)
Campbell, Robert (American) (1804–1879)
Bridger, James (1804–1881)
Burnes, Sir Alexander (1805–1841)
Berlandier, Jean-Louis (ca. 1805–1851)
Fitzroy, Robert (1805–1865)
Charbonneau, Jean-Baptiste (1805–1866)
Chisholm, Jesse (ca. 1805–1868)
Richardson, James (1806–1851)
Stansbury, Howard (1806–1863)
Maury, Matthew Fontaine (1806–1873)
Black Beaver (1806–1880)
Newell, Robert (1807–1869)
Larpenteur, Charles (1807–1872)
McClure, Sir Robert John le Mesurier (1807–1873)
Palliser, John (1807–1887)
Zagoskin, Lavrenty Alekseyevich (1807–1890)
Simpson, Thomas (1808–1840)
Kashevarov, Aleksandr Filippovich (1808–1866)
Campbell, Robert (Scottish) (1808–1894)
Leonard, Zenas (1809–1857)
Carson, Christopher Houston (1809–1868)
Bent, William (1809–1869)
Darwin, Charles Robert (1809–1882)
Bodmer, Karl (1809–1893)

1810–1819

Kane, Paul (1810–1871)
Ferris, Warren Angus (1810–1873)
Miller, Alfred Jacob (1810–1874)
Meek, Joseph L. (1810–1875)
Krapf, Johann Ludwig (1810–1881)
Sinclair, James (1811–1856)
Collinson, Sir Richard (1811–1883)
Emmons, George Foster (1811–1884)
Emory, William Hemsley (1811–1887)
Applegate, Jesse (1811–1888)
Sitgreaves, Lorenzo (ca. 1811–1888)
Macomb, John N. (1811–1889)
Colenso, William (1811–1899)
Gunnison, John Williams (1812–1853)
Marcy, Randolph Barnes (1812–1887)
Porte, François de la (1812–1880)
Grey, Sir George (1812–1898)
Irving, John Treat (1812–1906)
Leichhardt, Friedrich Wilhelm Ludwig (1813–ca. 1848)
Huc, Évariste-Régis (1813–1860)
Livingstone, David (1813–1873)
Simpson, James Hervey (1813–1883)
Warburton, Peter Egerton (1813–1889)

Frémont, John Charles (1813–1890)
Rae, John (1813–1893)
Dana, James Dwight (1813–1895)
Nevelskoy, Gennady Ivanovich (1814–1876)
Irateba (ca. 1814–1878)
Kittson, Norman Wolfred (1814–1888)
Russell, Osborne (ca. 1814–1892)
Forbes, Edward (1815–1854)
Stuart, John McDouall (1815–1866)
Eyre, Sir Edward John (1815–1901)
Whipple, Amiel Weeks (1816–1863)
De Haven, Edwin Jesse (1816–1865)
Chatillon, Henri (1816–1875)
Wootton, Richens Lacy (1816–1893)
Silva Porto, Antonio Francisco da (1817–1890)
Spruce, Richard (1817–1893)
Hooker, Sir Joseph Dalton (1817–1911)
Kennedy, Edmund (1818–1848)
Kern, Benjamin Jordan (1818–1849)
Kurz, Rudolph Friederich (1818–1871)
Beckwith, Edward Griffin (1818–1881)
Tschudi, Johann Jakob von (1818–1889)
Baker, James (1818–1898)
Vavasour, Mervin (1819–1866)
Warre, Henry James (1819–1898)
Gregory, Sir Augustus Charles (1819–1905)
McClintock, Sir Francis Leopold (1819–1907)

1820–1829

Kane, Elisha Kent (1820–1857)
Abert, James William (1820–1871)
Rebmann, Johann (1820–1876)
Raynolds, William Franklin (1820–1894)
Kern, Richard Hovendon (1821–1853)
Burke, Robert O'Hara (ca. 1821–1861)
Livingstone, Mary Moffat (1821–1862)
Barth, Heinrich (1821–1865)
Hall, Charles Francis (1821–1871)
Gregory, Francis Thomas (1821–1888)
Burton, Sir Richard Francis (1821–1890)
Dietrich, Koncordie Amalie Nelle (1821–1891)
Baker, Sir Samuel White (1821–1893)
Overweg, Adolf (1822–1852)
Brunner, Thomas (1822–1874)
Baines, Thomas (1822–1875)
Petermann, August Heinrich (1822–1878)
Schlagintweit, Hermann von (1822–1882)
Newberry, John Strong (1822–1892)
Pope, John B. (1822–1892)
Beale, Edward Fitzgerald (1822–1893)
Hamilton, William Thomas (1822–1908)
Galton, Sir Francis (1822–1911)
Kern, Edward Meyer (1823–1863)

Doudart de Lagrée, Ernest-Marc-Louis de Gonzague
(1823–1868)
Hind, Henry Youle (1823–1908)
Wallace, Alfred Russel (1823–1913)
Baikie, William Balfour (1825–1864)
Landsborough, William (1825–1886)
Bates, Henry Walter (1825–1892)
Mouhot, Henri (1826–1861)
Singh, Nain (ca. 1826–1882)
Palgrave, William Gifford (1826–1888)
Speke, John Hanning (1827–1864)
Grant, James Augustus (1827–1892)
Parke, John Grubb (1827–1900)
Moreno, Francisco (1827–ca. 1905)
Semyonov, Pyotr Petrovich (1827–1914)
Ives, Joseph Christmas (1828–1868)
Stanley, David Sloan (1828–1902)
Schlagintweit, Adolf von (1829–1857)
Hayden, Ferdinand Vandeveer (1829–1887)
Dupuis, Jean (1829–1912)

1830–1839

Thomson, Sir Charles Wyville (1830–1882)
Dallman, Eduard (1830–1896)
Rohlfs, Friedrich Gerhard (1831–1896)
Du Chaillu, Paul Belloni (ca. 1831–1903)
Bishop, Isabella Lucy Bird (1831–1904)
Nares, Sir George Strong (1831–1915)
Abbott, Henry Larcom (1831–1927)
Flatters, Paul-Xavier (1832–1881)
Hayes, Isaac Israel (1832–1881)
Nordenskjöld, Nils Adolf Erik (1832–1901)
Langford, Nathaniel Pitt (1832–1911)
Vambéry, Armin (1832–1913)
Mazuchelli, Elizabeth Sarah (1832–1914)
Schlagintweit, Robert von (1833–1885)
Richthofen, Ferdinand Paul Wilhelm von
(1833–1905)
Wills, William John (1834–1861)
Nachtigal, Gustav (1834–1885)
Powell, John Wesley (1834–1902)
Bozeman, John Merin (1835–1867)
Giles, Ernest (1835–1897)
Cheadle, Walter Butler (1835–1919)
Schweinfurth, Georg August (1836–1925)
Koldewey, Karl Christian (1837–1908)
Blunt, Anne Isabella (1837–1917)
Weyprecht, Karl (1838–1881)
Muir, John (1838–1914)
Tinné, Alexandrine Petronella Francina (1839–1869)
Garnier, Marie-Joseph-François (1839–1873)
Milton, William-Wentworth Fitzwilliam
(1839–1877)

Cooper, Thomas Thornville (1839–1878)
Przhevalsky, Nikolay Mikhailovich (1839–1888)

1840–1849

Duveyrier, Henri (1840–1892)
Emin Pasha, Mehmed (1840–1892)
Junker, Wilhelm Johann (1840–1892)
Whymper, Edward (1840–1911)
Blunt, Wilfrid Scawen (1840–1922)
Musters, George Chaworth (1841–1879)
Stanley, Sir Henry Morton (1841–1904)
Baker, Florence (ca. 1841–1918)
Gosse, William Christie (1842–1881)
King, Clarence (1842–1901)
Wheeler, George Montague (1842–1905)
Payer, Julius von (1842–1915)
Chaillé-Long, Charles (1842–1917)
Kropotkin, Peter (1842–1921)
Doughty, Charles Montagu (1843–1926)
Fedchenko, Aleksey Pavlovich (1844–1873)
De Long, George Washington (1844–1881)
Pavy, Octave (1844–1884)
Cameron, Verney Lovett (1844–1894)
Elias, Ney (1844–1897)
Greely, Adolphus Washington (1844–1935)
Teleki, Samuel (1845–1916)
Fedchenko, Olga (1845–1921)
Wickham, Sir Henry Alexander (1846–1928)
Crevaux, Jules-Nicolas (1847–1882)
Forrest, John (1847–1918)
Pavie, Auguste-Jean-Marie (1847–1925)
Sheldon, May French (1847–1936)
Lenz, Oskar (1848–1925)
Schwatka, Frederick (1849–1892)
Forrest, Alexander (1849–1901)
Grenfell, George (1849–1906)

1850–1859

Foureau, Fernand (1850–1914)
Peck, Annie Smith (1850–1935)
Bent, James Theodore (1852–1897)
Brazza, Pierre-Paul-François-Camille Savorgnan de
(1852–1905)
Bernier, Joseph Elzéar (1852–1934)
Stein, Sir Marc Aurel (1852–1943)
Wissmann, Hermann von (1853–1905)
Andrée, Salomon August (1854–1897)
Taylor, Annie Royle (1855–ca. 1909)
Sverdrup, Otto Neumann (1855–1930)
Zurbriggen, Matthias (1856–1917)
Peary, Robert Edwin (1856–1920)
Binger, Louis-Gustave (1856–1936)
Hoehnel, Ludwig von (1857–ca. 1910)

Thomson, Joseph (1858–1895)
Toll, Eduard von (1858–1902)
Johnston, Sir Harry Hamilton (1858–1927)
Meyer, Hans (1858–1929)
Workman, Fanny Bullock (1859–1925)
Allen, Henry Tureman (1859–1930)

1860–1869

Jackson, Frederick George (1860–1938)
Nansen, Fridtjof (1861–1930)
Shirase, Nobu (1861–1946)
Kingsley, Mary Henrietta (1862–1900)
Stuck, Hudson (1863–1920)
Marchand, Jean-Baptiste (1863–1934)
Younghusband, Sir Francis Edward (1863–1942)
Baumann, Oskar (1864–1899)
Young, Charles Denton (1864–1922)
Akeley, Carl Ethan (1864–1926)
Borchgrevink, Carsten Egeberg (1864–1934)
Bonin, Charles (1865–1929)
Cook, Frederick Albert (1865–1940)
Drygalski, Erich Dagobert von (1865–1949)
Hedin, Sven Anders (1865–1952)
Gerlache de Gomery, Adrien-Victor-Joseph de (1866–1934)
Henson, Matthew Alexander (1866–1955)
Bruce, William Spiers (1867–1921)
Fawcett, Percy Harrison (1867–ca. 1925)
Charcot, Jean-Baptiste-Étienne-Auguste (1867–1936)
Sykes, Sir Percy Molesworth (1867–1945)
Scott, Robert Falcon (1868–1912)
Bell, Gertrude Margaret Lowthian (1868–1926)
David-Néel, Alexandra (1868–1969)
Nordenskjöld, Nils Otto Gustaf (1869–1928)

1870–1879

Mylius-Erichsen, Ludwig (1872–1907)
Wilson, Edward Adrian (1872–1912)
Amundsen, Roald Engelbregt Gravning (1872–1928)
Tsybikov, Gombozhab (1873–1930)
Abruzzi, Luigi Amedeo di Savoia d' (1873–1933)
Shackleton, Sir Ernest Henry (1874–1922)
Begichev, Nikifor Alekseyevich (1874–1927)
Roerich, Nikolay Konstantinovich (1874–1947)
Adams, Harriet Chalmers (1875–1937)
Bingham, Hiram (1875–1956)
Rice, Alexander Hamilton (1875–1956)
Akeley, Delia Denning (1875–1970)
Eberhardt, Isabelle (1877–1904)
Filchner, Wilhelm (1877–1957)
Beebe, Charles William (1877–1962)

Rasmussen, Knud Johan Victor (1879–1933)
Stefansson, Vilhjalmur (1879–1962)

1880–1889

Wegener, Alfred Lothar (1880–1930)
Ellsworth, Lincoln (1880–1951)
Mawson, Sir Douglas (1882–1958)
Piccard, Auguste (1884–1962)
Philby, Harry St. John Bridger (1885–1960)
Nobile, Umberto (1885–1980)
Mallory, George Herbert Leigh (1886–1924)
Akeley, Mary Leonore Jobe (1886–1966)
Boyd, Louise Arner (1887–1972)
Lawrence, Thomas Edward (1888–1935)
Byrd, Richard Evelyn (1888–1957)
Wilkins, Sir George Hubert (1888–1958)

1890–1899

Schmidt, Otto Y. (1891–1956)
Thomas, Bertram Sydney (1892–1950)
Stark, Freya Madeline (1893–1993)

1800–1899, INCOMPLETE

Christie, Charles (unknown–1812)*
Dorion, Pierre, Jr. (unknown–1814)*
Henry, Alexander (the younger) (unknown–1814)*
Freeman, Thomas (unknown–1821)*
Pascoe, William (unknown–1833)*
Wellsted, James (unknown–1836)*
Jackson, David E. (unknown–1837)*
Fraeb, Henry (unknown–1841)*
Basargin, Grigory Gavrilovich (unknown–1853)*
McLeod, William C. (unknown–1880)*
Bombay, Sidi (unknown–1885)*
Baptista, Pedro João (fl. early 1800s)*
Sadlier, George Foster (fl. 1810s)*
Atkinson, Lucy (fl. 1820s–1860s)*
Glazunov, Andrey (fl. 1830s–1840s)*
Williams, William (fl. 1830s–1840s)*
Kintup (fl. 1880s)*

1900–1909

Courtauld, Augustine (1904–1959)
Watkins, Henry George (1907–1932)
Fuchs, Sir Vivian Ernest (1908–1999)
Mee, Margaret Ursula (1909–1988)

1910–1919

Cousteau, Jacques-Yves (1910–1997)
Thesiger, Wilfred Patrick (1910–   )
Heyerdahl, Thor (1914–2002)
Hillary, Sir Edmund Percival (1919–   )
Tenzing Norgay (1919–1986)

1920–1929

Glenn, John Herschell, Jr. (1921–   )
Piccard, Jacques Ernest-Jean (1922–   )
Shepard, Alan Bartlett, Jr. (1923–1998)
Singh, Kishen (unknown–1921)

1930–1939

Armstrong, Neil Alden (1930–   )
White, Edward Higgens, II (1930–1967)

Gagarin, Yury Alekseyevich (1934–1968)
Leonov, Alexei Arkhipovich (1934–   )
Tereshkova, Valentina Vladimirovna (1937–   )

1950–1959

Ride, Sally Kristen (1951–   )

Index for Volume I

Page numbers in **boldface** indicate main entries. Page numbers in *italics* indicate photographs.